THE
DOW JONES
AVERAGES
1885-1980

Edited by Phyllis S. Pierce

Dow Jones-Irwin   Homewood, Illinois   60430

ISBN 0-87094-353-7

Library of Congress Catalog Card No. 82-72368
Printed in the United States of America.

3 4 5 6 7 8 9 F 9 8 7 6 5 4 3

Introduction

The Wall Street Journal on October 7, 1981, completed 85 years of continuous publication of the Dow Jones industrial and railroad (now transportation) averages.

Dow Jones & Co. pioneered in the United States stock averages field. On July 3, 1884, the Customer's Afternoon Letter—a two-page financial news bulletin and forerunner of The Wall Street Journal—listed the average closing prices of 11 active "representative" stocks:

Chicago & North Western	Union Pacific
D. L. & W.	Missouri Pacific
Lake Shore	Louisville & Nashville
New York Central	Pacific Mail
St. Paul	Western Union
Northern Pacific pfd.	

But this average and subsequent Dow Jones & Co. averages were published irregularly.

Business historians argue whether the Dow Jones 1884 average was the first true index of American stocks, but it is undisputed that the 1884 list was the first published index of American stocks. Further, Charles Henry Dow, first editor of The Wall Street Journal and co-founder (in 1882) of Dow Jones & Co., is generally assigned credit for the compilation.

Dow did not use a weighted mean or make adjustments of any nature. He simply added the closing price of stocks in his average and divided the total by the number of companies included in the list. A historian as well as a journalist, Dow found charts and statistics useful and in his editorials advised traders to keep various records on individual stocks as well as the full list. There is no evidence Dow looked upon the averages as containing anything more than an indication of the statistical nature of the trend of the stock market as a whole.

The first average compiled in 1884 was a mixed bag. It contained nine railroads, reflecting the importance of railroads to the market of those days, and two industrials. Dow found it desirable to include "active" stocks in his compilation, but it wasn't easy to find them. A quarter-million shares traded was the average day's activity on the Big Board, mostly in railroads.

Industrials were new and speculative. They had no past for comparative purposes. Despite this, Dow clearly foresaw the role industrial companies would play in the economic life of the nation, and he continued to work toward compilation of an industrial average. It took 12 years of additions, deletions and substitutions before Dow, on May 26, 1896, came up with a list consisting entirely of industrial stocks. The list included:

American Cotton Oil	Laclede Gas
American Sugar	National Lead
American Tobacco	North American
Chicago Gas	Tenn. Coal & Iron
Distilling & Cattle Feeding	U.S. Leather pfd.
General Electric	U.S. Rubber

The list was published irregularly until October 7, 1896, at which time continuous publication began. It is generally reckoned that the present Dow Jones industrial and railroad averages had their inception on this date.

In 85 years, industrial stocks have come a long way, and the industrial average came right along with them. The industrial list is venerable. It's popular—one hears or sees it mentioned by all type of media every day; it was the theme of a Broadway musical years ago. It's the most widely used stock market indicator, and this in itself is an advantage because it forms a common basis for much stock market discussion, some of which is critical.

The industrials have been accused of many things: misleading the public, distorting the market, creating near-panic with large point fluctuations, causing an unfavorable public attitude toward the financial community, containing too few stocks to fairly represent the market. A newspaper business editor years ago suggested the industrials were "old enough to retire."

Complaints like these come regularly during a "down" market. They taper off during a "high" market when occasionally brokers or mutual fund operators receive complaints from customers that the industrial average is rising faster than the customers' holdings.

The industrials are nothing more than a statistical compilation called an "average" and, like any average, do not reflect individual—only combined—performances. The two great advantages of the industrials are simplicity and continuity. The present "high" level of the average is a byproduct of its continuity. Its base has never changed; to do so would, in effect, start a new average.

On the other hand, the average does exaggerate market movements since it runs—in points—about ten times the straight average price of industrial stocks. Stocks have been split over the years and the industrial average has not. It is hoped that this fact is so widely and generally understood no harm really comes of it.

There have been suggestions that the publisher split the industrials one-for-ten or move the decimal one point to the left. If the information is more useful to an individual on a one-to-ten basis, the decimal can be moved one place to the left. There is no guarantee, however, that if the publisher moved the decimal the reader would not move it back. The feeling is that the average has gone to its lofty figures and moves up and down strictly according to the arithmetic. If the arithmetic should be changed, continuity would be destroyed and continuity is the greatest advantage the average has.

Dow Jones supplies the averages, if indirectly, to newspapers, television and radio stations, but it has no control over the manner in which the averages, in turn, are presented by those media. Dow Jones has made available to any interested party considerable material concerning the averages, basis for calculation and other pertinent information.

The Wall Street Journal, on December 26, 1950, began daily publication of changes from the previous close in the Dow Jones stock averages tabulated and expressed on a percentage basis as well as on a net change basis. The policy is aimed at making movements of the industrial, transportation and utility averages more directly comparable to each other. This data is published by the Dow Jones News Service every 30 minutes. However, there's no question that the Dow Jones averages can be confusing in this era of growing stock market interest.

The confusion springs from the fact that the "averages" really aren't averages any more. They were in the beginning, and usage still so labels them. But, though they are useful measures of the stock market's over-all movement, the numbers themselves should not be mistaken for dollars-per-share prices of stocks.

This applies to all stock averages (or indexes, as some are called). Here's a sample of well-known ones, compared with a simple averaging of prices of all stocks on the New York Stock Exchange, as of December 31, 1980:

Dow Jones Industrials	963.99
Associated Press Industrials	567.80
Standard and Poor's Industrials	154.45
Average Price, NYSE shares	77.86

With the so-called averages expressed in figures so much higher than the dollars-per-share prices of individual stocks, misunderstanding sometimes arises. A 10-point fall in the D-J from the 800 level is about 1.2%, comparable to a decline of 60 cents on a $50 stock.

The reason for this disparity? Stock splits.

A split occurs when a company, feeling the per-share price of its stock has risen too high for broad investor appeal, arbitrarily splits the high-priced shares into more, lower-priced shares. Say, for example, a stock is selling for $100 a share and the company splits it two-for-one. Other things being equal, the new price will be $50. But, of course, each owner of the old $100 stock must be given two shares of the new $50 stock so the value of his holding won't be reduced.

The stock splitting—which goes on all the time, year after year—would distort the averages, were it not for a statistical adjustment. An extremely simplified example illustrates the point. Say we have three different stocks selling at $30, $20 and $10. Adding the share prices and dividing by three gives us an average of $20.

Then the $30 stock is split two-for-one. The man who had one share worth $30 now has two shares worth $15 each. If we computed the average with no adjustment—adding $15, $20 and $10—for a total of $45—we would have a new average of $15, down 25% from the former average. Obviously, that wouldn't be right. The dollar value of all outstanding shares of the three companies hasn't gone down at all; it's unchanged.

An adjustment must be made so that the "average" will remain at 20. This can be done in different ways; the method used to compute the Dow Jones averages is to change the divisor—the number divided into the total of the stock prices. In this case, the statisticians would come up with a new divisor of 2.25, instead of 3. Divided into the total of $45, this gives an unchanged "average" of 20.

Over the years, each component-stock split has dropped the industrial divisor lower. While today's industrial list includes 30 component stocks, the divisor for obtaining the Dow Jones average of the 30 industrials has been adjusted steadily downward from 30 to give effect to component-stock splits. By 1939 the divisor had been adjusted downward to 15.1. By 1950 the industrial divisor stood at 8.92. At the end of 1980 it was 1.465.

Thus, Dow Jones averages are not dollar averages of current market prices, but market movement indicators, kept essentially undistorted by stock splits for over three-quarters of a century.

The Dow Jones industrial average, first computed on May 26, 1896, was based on 12 stocks. In 1916 the list was expanded to 20 and in 1928 to 30. Whenever any particular component stock for any reason becomes unrepresentative of the American industrial sector, a substitution is made and the divisor is adjusted, just as when a split occurs.

The criticism is sometimes made that the Dow Jones industrial average covers only 30 companies, big ones at that, and so fails to reflect the movement of hundreds of other stock prices. But these aren't just 30 randomly picked securities. They are chosen as representatives of the broad market and of American industry. The companies are major factors in their industries and their stocks are widely held by individuals and institutional investors. The total market value of these 30 issues accounts for about one-fourth of the value of stocks listed on the New York Stock Exchange. Changes in the components are made entirely by the editors of The Wall Street Journal without consultation with the companies, the stock exchange or any official agency. For the sake of continuity, such changes are made rarely. Most substitutions have been the result of mergers, but from time to time changes may be made to achieve a better representation.

Besides the 30-stock industrial average, Dow Jones publishes an average of 20 transportation common stocks (called the railroad average through December 31, 1969), one for 15 utility common stocks and a "composite" average of all 65 stocks. Also computed are six bond averages and one composed of yields on a group of bonds.

The function of all these averages is the same—to give a general rather than precise idea of fluctuations in the securities markets and to reflect the historical continuity of security price movements.

And there is only one purpose for publishing the averages: To serve the business community. It's the same reason which motivated Dow, some 100 years ago, to put on the handwritten news-sheets his study of market movements. It is not a rainbow leading to a pot of gold. Our editors long ago wrote:

> It cannot too often be said that the road to ruin lies in dogmatizing on charts, systems and generalizations. Trading on any such basis is gambling as distinguished from legitimate speculation. It is no more defensible than an attempt to break the bank at Monte Carlo with one of the innumerable systems which have tempted weak human beings since the prehistoric ages when man first learned to count beyond the number of his fingers and toes.

This warning is as true now as it was in the 1880s.

Charles Henry Dow hardly could have imagined that the occasional stock average he computed with paper and pencil one day would become part of the language of American finance.

—WILLIAM McSHERRY

History of the Dow Jones Averages

July 3, 1884   Published first average of American stocks in Customer's Afternoon Letter. List included:

Chicago & North Western	Union Pacific
D. L. & W.	Missouri Pacific
Lake Shore	Louisville & Nashville
New York Central	Pacific Mail
St. Paul	Western Union
Northern Pacific pfd.	

Feb. 16, 1885   List of 12 railroads and two industrials published:

Central Pacific	Louisville & Nashville
Central RR of New Jersey	Missouri Pacific
Chic. Milwaukee & St. Paul	New York Central
Chicago North Western	Northern Pacific pfd.
Delaware & Hudson Canal	Union Pacific
Del., Lackawanna & Western	Pacific Mail Steamship
Lake Shore Railroad	Western Union

Jan. 2, 1886   The above list replaced by average of 12 stocks, 10 of which were railroads and two industrials:

Chic. Milwaukee & St. Paul	Missouri Pacific
Chicago North Western	Northern Pacific pfd.
Delaware & Hudson Canal	New York Central
Del., Lackawanna & Western	Union Pacific
Lake Shore Railroad	Pacific Mail Steamship
Louisville & Nashville	Western Union

Apr. 9, 1894   Following substitutions were made:

Delete from average:	Add to average:
Lake Shore Railroad	Chic., Burlington & Quincy
New York Central	Chic., Rock Island & Pacific
Pacific Mail Steamship	American Sugar

May 26, 1896   Average consisting entirely of industrial stocks published for first time. The list contained:

American Cotton Oil	Laclede Gas
America Sugar	National Lead
American Tobacco	North American
Chicago Gas	Tenn. Coal & Iron
Distilling & Cattle Feeding	U.S. Leather pfd.
General Electric	U.S. Rubber

(The first average computed from this list of stocks was 40.94. It declined gradually during June and July and on August 8, 1896, stood at 28.48 which is the lowest point on record for the industrial average.)

Aug. 26, 1896   Distilling & Cattle Feeding became American Spirits Manufacturing and U.S. Cordage pfd. was substituted for North American.

Oct. 7, 1896   Daily publication in The Wall Street Journal began with following news comment:

"DAILY MOVEMENT OF AVERAGES"

"Following is the daily average price of 20 railroad stocks and 12 industrials for 30 days last passed:

	12 Indus.	20 Railroads
Tuesday, Sept. 8	$35.50	$48.55
Wednesday, Sept. 9	35.39	48.56
Thursday, Sept. 10	35.58	47.71
Friday, Sept. 11	35.30	48.27
Saturday, Sept. 12	35.02	47.86
Monday, Sept. 14	34.86	47.66
Tuesday, Sept. 15	34.13	47.22
Wednesday, Sept.16	33.32	46.68
Thursday, Sept. 17	34.33	47.77
Friday, Sept. 18	34.81	47.82
Saturday, Sept. 19	35.03	47.91
Monday, Sept. 21	35.53	48.65
Tuesday, Sept. 22	35.59	48.43
Wednesday, Sept. 23	35.78	48.67
Thursday, Sept.24	36.23	49.16
Friday, Sept. 25	36.61	49.81
Saturday, Sept. 26	36.75	50.21
Monday, Sept. 28	36.35	49.80
Tuesday, Sept. 29	36.33	50.21
Wednesday, Sept. 30	36.05	50.21
Thursday, Oct. 1	36.01	50.17
Friday, Oct. 2	35.88	50.00
Saturday, Oct. 3	35.82	49.86
Monday, Oct. 5	35.92	50.10
Tuesday, Oct. 6	35.91	49.71

"Twelve industrial stocks used are: Sugar, Tobacco, Leather pfd., Cotton Oil, Cordage pfd., Rubber com., Chicago Gas, Tennessee Coal & Iron, General Electric, Lead, American Spirits and Laclede Gas.

"The 20 active stocks used are: Erie, Kansas & Texas pfd., Chesapeake & Ohio, Minneapolis & St. Louis 2d pfd., Susquehanna & Western pfd., New York Central, Atchinson, CCC & St. Louis, Southern Railway pfd., Missouri Pacific, Jersey Central, Pacific Mail, Northwest, Louisville & Nashville, Western Union, Rock Island, Burlington, St. Paul, Texas & Pacific and Lake Shore."

(Persons interested in extending the present Dow Jones averages backward as far as possible can consider this the beginning of the railroad average (now transportation) provided they bear in mind that there are two industrial stocks included in the list. It should also be kept in mind that, originally, market quotations were all in percentages. On October 13, 1915, the Stock Exchange ruled that all stocks should sell on a dollar-share basis. For the sake of continuity, the average of Pennsylvania, Reading and Lehigh Valley, all having $50 par values, was computed on a percentage basis which was obtained by doubling their market quotations.)

Oct. 19, 1896   Philadelphia & Reading and No. Pacific pfd. substituted for Minneapolis & St. Louis 2nd pfd. and Texas Pacific in the rail list.

Oct. 26, 1896   Manhattan Elevated and Wabash pfd. were substituted for Pacific Mail and Western Union in the 20 railroads.

(This marked the first time the average was computed entirely of railroad stocks.)

Nov. 10, 1896   Pacific Mail Steamship substituted for U.S. Rubber in the industrials.

Dec. 23, 1896   Standard Rope & Twine substituted for U.S. Cordage pfd. in the industrials.

Jan. 4, 1897	N.Y. Ontario & Western substituted for Susquehanna & Western pfd. in the rail list which included:

Atchison	Missouri Kansas & Texas pfd.
Burlington	Missouri Pacific
C.C.C. & St. Louis	New York Central
Chesapeake & Ohio	Northern Pacific pfd.
Chicago & North Western	New York, Ontario & Western
Erie	Phila. & Reading
Jersey Central	Rock Island
Lake Shore	St. Paul
Louisville & Nashville	Southern Railway pfd.
Manhattan Elevated	Wabash pfd.

March 24, 1898   Peoples Gas substituted for Chicago Gas in the industrials.

May 6, 1898   Metropolitan Traction & Union Pacific pfd. substituted for Ontario & Western and Lake Shore.

Sept. 1898   U.S. Rubber substituted for General Electric in the industrials.

April 21, 1899   Continental Tobacco, Federal Steel, General Electric, American Steel & Wire substituted for American Spirits Mfg., American Tobacco, Laclede Gas and Standard Rope & Twine in the industrials.

May 22, 1899   Brooklyn Rapid Transit, Denver & Rio Grande pfd. and Norfolk & Western pfd. substituted for Metropolitan Street Railway, Reading and Erie in the railroads.

April 1, 1900   Southern Pacific common substituted for Wabash pfd. in the railroads.

April 7, 1900   Union Pacific common substituted for Norfolk & Western pfd. in the railroads.

May 27, 1901   Baltimore & Ohio and Illinois Central substituted for Burlington and So. Pacific common in the railroads.

June 24, 1901   Southern Railway common substituted for Southern Railway pfd. in the railroads.

June 29, 1901   Pennsylvania substituted for Northern Pacific pfd. in the railroads.

April 1, 1901   Amalgamated Copper, American Smelting & Refining, International Paper pfd., U.S. Steel common and U.S. Steel pfd. were substituted for American Cotton Oil, Federal Steel, General Electric, Pacific Mail and American Steel & Wire in the industrials.

July 1, 1901   American Car Foundry and Colorado Fuel & Iron substituted for Continental Tobacco and International Paper pfd. in the industrials.

Sept. 20, 1902   Reading, Canadian Pacific, Delaware & Hudson and Minneapolis & St. Louis were substituted for Missouri, Kansas & Texas pfd., Rock Island, Chesapeake & Ohio and Jersey Central in the railroads.

May 17, 1904   Southern Pacific common substituted for Minneapolis & St. Louis in the railroads.

June 25, 1904	Wabash pfd. and Metropolitan Street Railway substituted for C.C.C. & St. Louis and Denver pfd. in the railroads.

April 11, 1905	Erie substituted for Wabash pfd. in the railroads.

April 1, 1905	U.S. Rubber 1st pfd. substituted for U.S. Leather pfd. in the industrials.

May 19, 1905	Northern Pacific common and Norfolk & Western substituted for Manhattan and Union Pacific pfd. in the railroads.

The rail list, now entirely composed of common stocks, had these issues:

Atchison	Missouri Pacific
Baltimore & Ohio	New York Central
Brooklyn Rapid Transit	No. Pacific common
Canadian Pacific	Norfolk & Western
Chicago & North Western	Pennsylvania
Delaware & Hudson	Reading
Erie	St. Paul
Illinois Central	Southern Pacific common
Louisville & Nashville	Southern Railways common
Metropolitan Street Railway	Union Pacific common

May 4, 1906	Twin City Rapid Transit substituted for Metropolitan Street Railway in the railroads.

Nov. 7, 1907	General Electric substituted for Tennessee Coal & Iron in the industrials.

Aug. 25, 1912	Rock Island and Lehigh Valley substituted for Brooklyn Rapid Transit and Twin City Rapid Transit in the railroads.

May 12, 1912	Central Leather common substituted for Colorado Fuel & Iron in the industrials.

Dec. 12, 1914	Chesapeake & Ohio, Kansas City Southern and N.Y.N.H. & Hartford substituted for Chicago & North Western, Missouri Pacific and Rock Island in the railroads.

March 16, 1915	General Motors substituted for U.S. Rubber 1st pfd. in the industrials.

July 29, 1915	Anaconda substituted for Amalgamated Copper.

Oct. 4, 1916	A list of 20 industrials, all common, substituted for the old list of 12. National Lead, Peoples Gas, General Motors and U.S. Steel pfd. were dropped and 12 new companies added. The list became:

American Beet Sugar	General Electric
American Can	Goodrich
American Car & Foundry	Republic Iron & Steel
American Locomotive	Studebaker
American Smelting	Texas Co.
American Sugar	U.S. Rubber
American Tel & Tel	U.S. Steel
Anaconda Copper	Utah Copper
Baldwin Locomotive	Westinghouse
Central Leather	Western Union

(At this time (1916) Stock Exchange quotations were all in dollars instead of percentages, so the fact that Utah had a par of $10 and Westinghouse a par of $50 caused no immediate confusion in the new averages. However, in order to make continuity for the industrial averages, the records of the 20 new stocks were figured backward to the reopening of the Stock Exchange on December 12, 1914, after the war closing, so that the published record of averages is as if the 20 stocks mentioned above had been quoted on the dollar basis from that date.)

March 1, 1920 Corn Products substituted for American Beet Sugar in the industrials.

Jan. 22, 1924 American Tobacco, Du Pont, Mack Trucks and Sears, Roebuck substituted for Corn Products, Central Leather, Goodrich and Texas Co. in the industrials.

Feb. 6, 1924 Standard Oil of California substituted for Utah in the industrials.

April 10, 1924 D.L. & W. and St. Louis Southwestern substituted for Kansas City Southern and Lehigh Valley in the railroads.

May 12, 1924 Studebaker non-par and Woolworth $25 par substituted for old Studebaker and Republic Iron & Steel in the industrials.

(After the change from 12 to 20 industrials in 1916, Texas Co. reduced its par from $100 to $25. Then, American Locomotive changed from $100 par to non-par, issuing two new shares for one old share. Studebaker changed from $100 par to non-par, issuing two and a half shares of new for one of old. The compilation arising from the Texas, American Locomotive and Studebaker changes brought about new adjustment.

Texas Co. and Corn Products were dropped. American Locomotive was retained at the actual new quotation. These changes, made January 22, 1924, were so fitted into the scheme of quotations that, while the closing prices on a Tuesday averaged 97.41 on the old stocks, the average on the new stocks was 97.23, all being figured on the dollar basis.)

The railroad list as of August 31, 1925, was:

Atchinson	Illinois Central	Reading
Baltimore & Ohio	Louisville & Nashville	St. L. Southwestern
Canadian Pacific	New York Central	St. Paul
Chesapeake & Ohio	New Haven	Southern Pacific
Delaware & Hudson	Norfolk & Western	Southern Railway
Del., Lack. & W.	Northern Pacific	Union Pacific
Erie	Pennsylvania	

Aug. 31, 1925 General Motors, International Harvester, Kennecott, Texas Co. and U.S. Realty were substituted for Anaconda, Baldwin, Du Pont, Standard Oil of Calif. and Studebaker in the industrial list. These changes made no appreciable difference in the averages.

Dec. 7, 1925 Allied Chemical and Paramount Famous Lasky substituted for U.S. Realty and Westinghouse Electric in the industrials.

Dec. 31, 1925 Remington Typewriter and Mack Trucks, ex-stock dividend, were substituted for Kennecott and Mack Trucks stock dividend attached in the industrials.

March 16, 1927 United Drug substituted for Remington Typewriter in the industrials.
The industrial list on December 31, 1927, was:

Allied Chemical	American Locomotive
American Can	American Smelting

American Car & Foundry   American Sugar
American Tel & Tel   Sears, Roebuck
American Tobacco   Texas Corp.
General Electric   United Drug
General Motors   U.S. Rubber
International Harvester   U.S. Steel
Mack Trucks   Western Union
Paramount Famous Lasky   Woolworth

All stocks used in both the railroad and industrial lists are common stocks. The averages of these stocks are compiled from closing prices. In case there is no sale of a particular stock the last closing is used.

As of December 31, 1927, to obtain the average daily price of the 20 railroad stocks, take the total sum of their closing quotations (with Pennsylvania and Reading doubled) and divide by 20. The industrial average is computed in the same manner except that in certain cases in the past (prior to 1927) attempt was made to compensate or average the averages to make allowances for stock split-ups. Therefore, in order to get the total to be divided by 20, the closing price of American Can is multiplied by 6, that of General Electric by 4, Sears, Roebuck by 4, American Car & Foundry by 2 and American Tobacco by 2.

The present Dow Jones industrial average of 30 stocks began October 1, 1928, when the list was expanded to 30 from 20 and several substitutions were made. On October 1, 1928, the stocks making up the industrial average were:

Allied Chemical   General Railway Signal   Sears, Roebuck
American Can   Goodrich   Standard Oil (N.J.)
American Smelting   International Harvester   Texas Corp.
American Sugar   International Nickel   Texas Gulf Sulphur
American Tobacco B   Mack Trucks   Union Carbide
Atlantic Refining   Nash Motors   U.S. Steel
Bethlehem Steel   North American   Victor Talking Machine
Chrysler   Paramount Publix   Westinghouse Electric
General Electric   Postum, Inc.   Woolworth
General Motors   Radio Corp.   Wright Aeronautical

The divisor on October 1, 1928, was 16.67.

Subsequent changes in stocks making up the industrial average and changes in the divisor, together with the dates, were:

Date		Divisor	Explanation
1928 November	5	16.02	Atlantic Refining split 4 for 1
December	13	14.65	General Motors split 2½ for 1
			International Harvester split 4 for 1
December	26	13.92	International Nickel reorganization
1929 January	8	12.11	American Smelting split 3 for 1
			Radio Corp. split 5 for 1
			National Cash Register replaced Victor Talking Machine
May	1	11.7	Wright-Aeronautical split 2 for 1
May	20	11.18	Union Carbide split 3 for 1
June	25	10.77	Woolworth split 2½ for 1
July	25	10.77	Postum name changed to General Foods
September	14	10.47	Curtiss-Wright replaced Wright Aeronautical
1930 January	29	9.85	General Electric split 4 for 1
			Johns-Manville replaced North American
July	18	10.38	Borden replaced American Sugar
			Eastman Kodak replaced American Tobacco B
			Goodyear replaced Atlantic Refining
			Liggett & Myers replaced General Railway Signal
			Standard Oil of California replaced Goodrich
			United Air Transport replaced Nash Motors
			Hudson Motor replaced Curtiss-Wright

Date			Divisor	Explanation
1932	May	26	15.46	American Tobacco B replaced Liggett & Myers
				Drug Inc. replaced Mack Trucks
				Procter & Gamble replaced United Air Transport
				Loew's replaced Paramount Publix
				Nash Motors replaced Radio Corp.
				International Shoe replaced Texas Gulf Sulphur
1932	May	26	15.46	International Business Machines replaced National Cash Register
				Coca Cola replaced Hudson Motor
1933	August	15	15.71	Corn Products Refining replaced Drug, Inc.
				United Aircraft replaced International Shoe
1934	August	13	15.74	National Distillers replaced United Aircraft
1935	November	20	15.1	Du Pont replaced Borden
				National Steel replaced Coca Cola
1937	January	8	15.1	Nash Motors name changed to Nash Kelvinator
1939	March	14	15.1	United Aircraft replaced Nash Kelvinator
				American Tel & Tel replaced International Business Machines
1945	May	10	14.8	Loew's Inc. split 3 for 1
	May	11	14.2	Westinghouse Mfg. split 4 for 1
	October	23	13.6	Sears, Roebuck split 4 for 1
1946	August	1	13.3	National Distillers split 3 for 1
1947	May	16	12.2	Eastman Kodak split 5 for 1
	June	2	11.76	Johns-Manville split 3 for 1
	July	14	11.44	Chrysler Corp. split 2 for 1
	December	3	11.36	American Smelting 20% stock dividend
1948	January	19	10.98	Bethlehem Steel split 3 for 1
	May	17	10.55	Union Carbide split 3 for 1
	June	7	10.20	International Harvester split 3 for 1
	November	26	10.14	National Steel 10% stock dividend
1949	June	3	9.88	U.S. Steel split 3 for 1
	June	16	9.06	Du Pont split 4 for 1
1950	March	22	8.92	Procter & Gamble split 1½ for 1
	March	31	8.57	National Steel split 3 for 1
	September	5	7.76	Allied Chemical split 4 for 1
	October	3	7.54	General Motors split 2 for 1
1951	March	12	7.36	Standard Oil of California split 2 for 1
	May	2	7.33	United Aircraft 20% stock dividend
	June	12	7.14	Texas Corp. split 2 for 1
	June	13	6.90	Standard Oil (N.J.) split 2 for 1
	September	11	6.72	Goodyear split 2 for 1
	December	3	6.53	American Smelting split 2 for 1
1952	May	2	6.16	American Can split 2 for 1 and 100% stock dividend
1954	June	14	5.92	General Electric split 3 for 1
	July	1	5.89	United Aircraft distributed 1 share of Chance-Vought for every 3 United Aircraft held
1955	January	24	5.76	Goodyear split 2 for 1
	May	23	5.62	Corn Products Refining split 3 for 1
	June	3	5.52	U.S. Steel split 2 for 1
	September	26	5.46	United Aircraft 50% stock dividend (3 for 2)
	November	10	5.26	General Motors split 3 for 1
	December	19	5.11	Sears, Roebuck split 3 for 1
1956	March	19	4.89	Standard Oil (N.J.) split 3 for 1
	March	26	4.79	Johns-Manville split 2 for 1
	June	8	4.69	General Foods split 2 for 1
1956	June	11	4.56	Texas Co. split 2 for 1
	June	18	4.452	Standard Oil of California split 2 for 1
	June	25	4.351	Procter & Gamble split 2 for 1
	July	3	4.581	International Paper replaced Loew's Inc.
	September	11	4.566	American Tel & Tel rights offering (1 share for each 10 held)
1957	February	7	4.283	Bethlehem Steel split 4 for 1
	November	18	4.257	United Aircraft 20% stock dividend (6 for 5)
1959	April	14	4.13	Eastman Kodak split 2 for 1
	June	1	3.964	American Tel & Tel split 3 for 1
				Anaconda replaced American Smelting
				Swift & Co. replaced Corn Products

Date			Divisor	Explanation
1959	June	1	3.964	Aluminum Co. of America replaced National Steel
				Owens-Illinois Glass replaced National Distillers
	December	29	3.824	Goodyear split 3 for 1
1960	January	25	3.739	Allied Chemical split 2 for 1
	February	2	3.659	Westinghouse Electric split 2 for 1
	May	3	3.569	American Tobacco split 2 for 1
	May	31	3.48	International Nickel split 2 for 1
	August	24	3.38	General Foods split 2 for 1
	December	30	3.28	International Paper Co. split 3 for 1
1961	April	10	3.165	Procter & Gamble split 2 for 1
	August	11	3.09	Texaco split 2 for 1
1962	May	1	3.03	American Tobacco split 2 for 1
	June	5	2.988	Du Pont distributed ½ share General Motors stock for each share of Du Pont common held
1963	May	13	2.914	Chrysler Corp. split 2 for 1
	November	21	2.876	Du Pont distributed 36-100 share General Motors stock for each share of Du Pont common held
1964	January	13	2.822	Chrysler Corp. split 2 for 1
	June	18	2.754	F. W. Woolworth split 3 for 1
	June	23	2.670	American Tel & Tel split 2 for 1
	November	19	2.615	Du Pont distributed ½ share of General Motors for each share of Du Pont common held
1965	March	23	2.543	Sears, Roebuck split 2 for 1
	April	12	2.499	International Harvester split 2 for 1
	May	24	2.410	Eastman Kodak split 2 for 1
	June	1	2.348	Owens-Illinois Glass split 2 for 1
	June	16	2.278	Union Carbide split 2 for 1
	November	1	2.245	United Aircraft split 3 for 2
1967	June	6	2.217	Swift split 2 for 1
	June	12	2.163	Anaconda split 2 for 1
1968	May	27	2.078	Eastman Kodak split 2 for 1
	August	19	2.011	International Nickel split 2½ for 1
1969	April	1	1.967	Johns-Manville split 2 for 1
	May	7	1.934	Goodyear split 2 for 1
	August	11	1.894	Texaco split 2 for 1
1970	May	19	1.826	Procter & Gamble split 2 for 1

For many years prior to 1970, editors of The Wall Street Journal tried to devise a new average to replace the railroads. On January 2, 1970, the transportation average was introduced. A Wall Street Journal staff reporter, on January 5, 1970, reported the change:

Starting with the market prices of last Friday (January 2, 1970) the Dow Jones average of 20 railroad stocks was modified to include other forms of transportation.

The transportation average, as it will be known henceforth, is a continuation of the railroad average, except that nine railroad stocks have been deleted and replaced by nine other transportation securities.

Thus the number of stocks in the average remains at 20, and the total in the Dow Jones composite average continues unchanged at 65.

Transition to the revised average has been effected smoothly through adjustment of divisors for the transportation average and the average of 65 stocks.

Continued in the transportation average from the railroad average are the stocks of the following 11 railroads: Canadian Pacific Railway, Great Northern Railway, Louisville & Nashville Railroad, Norfolk & Western Railway, Penn-Central, St. Louis-San Francisco Railway, Santa Fe Industries, Inc., Seaboard Coast Line Industries Inc., Southern Pacific Co., Southern Railway and Union Pacific Corp.

To these have been added the stocks of the following nine companies: American Airlines, Consolidated Freightways Inc., Eastern Air Lines, Northwest Airlines, Pacific Intermountain Express Co., Pan American World Airways, Trans World Airlines, UAL Inc. (holding company for United Air Lines) and U.S. Freight Co.

Stocks of the following nine concerns, which were in the railroad average, have been deleted from the transportation average: Cheasapeake & Ohio Railway, Florida East Coast Ry., Gulf, Mobile & Ohio Railroad, Illinois Central Industries Inc., Kansas City Southern Industries Inc., Missouri Pacific Railroad, Northwest Industries Inc., Rio Grande Industries Inc. and Western Pacific Railroad.

The additions and deletions created a divisor for the Dow Jones transportation average of 4.084, compared with the old rail average divisor of 4.721, and changed the divisor for the 65 stocks to 10.141 from 10.568.

Dictating the change in the average is the drastically altered pattern of commercial transportation itself. When the railroad average was begun toward the end of the 19th Century, the rails were the giant movers of both freight and people. Automobiles, trucks, buses and airplanes hadn't even arrived on the scene.

As recently as 20 years ago, the rails still carried 62% of all intercity freight on a ton-mileage basis. By 1969, though, that share had shrunk to 41%. And, over the same 20 years, the share carried by commercial truckers nearly doubled, rising from 11% to 21%. The rest of the load is moved by pipelines, water transport and airplanes.

By 1969 the railroad movement of intercity passengers had shrunk to a thin 1.2% of the total, on a passenger-mile basis, from nearly 10% two decades earlier. Private autos carried a huge 86% of the intercity passenger load last year, airlines had 9.4% of the traffic and buses 2.5%.

Also considered in revision of the average was the contraction through merger of the number of leading railroads and the diversification of some railroad companies into non-transportation business.

Date			Divisor	Explanation
1971	March	30	1.779	General Foods split 2 for 1
	June	8	1.712	General Electric split 2 for 1
	December	16	1.661	Westinghouse Electric split 2 for 1
1972	November	1	1.661	Standard Oil (N.J.) name changed to Exxon
1973	May	30	1.661	Swift name changed to Esmark
	December	11	1.626	Standard Oil (Calif.) split 2 for 1
1974	February	4	1.598	Aluminum Co. of America split 3 for 2
1975	May	1	1.598	United Aircraft name changed to United Technologies
	October	1	1.588	Esmark split 5 for 4
1976	April	21	1.588	International Nickel named changed to Inco
	May	19	1.554	United Technologies split 2 for 1
	June	2	1.527	U.S. Steel split 3 for 2
	July	26	1.473	Exxon split 2 for 1
	August	9	1.504	Minnesota Mining & Manufacturing replaced Anaconda
1977	April	11	1.474	Owens-Illinois split 2 for 1
	July	18	1.443	Sears, Roebuck split 2 for 1
1979	June	29	1.465	International Business Machines replaced Chrysler
				Merck replaced Esmark
				Du Pont split 3 for 1

THE DOW JONES STOCK AVERAGES
1931-1980

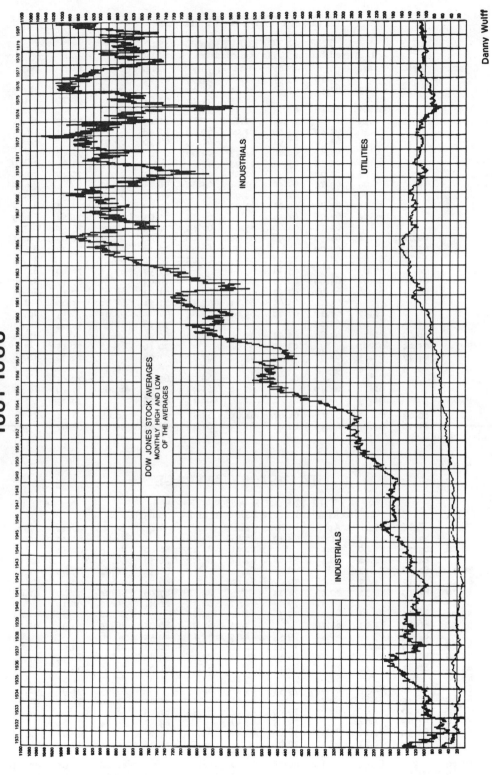

DOW JONES STOCK AVERAGES
MONTHLY HIGH AND LOW
OF THE AVERAGES

INDUSTRIALS

INDUSTRIALS

UTILITIES

Danny Wulff

THE 14-STOCK AVERAGE

THE 14-STOCK AVERAGE—1885
14 Mixed Stocks....12 Railroads and 2 Industrials

Date	Jan.	Feb.	Mar.	Apr.	May	June	July	Aug.	Sept.	Oct.	Nov.	Dec.
1				62.40	63.97	61.98	61.95	67.89	69.09	69.54	*	79.59
2			64.83	62.51	63.80	62.34	61.49	*	69.59	68.92	78.24	79.84
3			64.60		*	62.73	62.16	67.61	69.30	70.22	†	79.94
4			64.07	62.46	62.23	62.33	†	67.81	69.07	*	77.64	80.27
5			64.50	*	61.92	61.84	*	67.65	68.44	70.93	78.71	81.12
6			64.36	62.40	62.56	62.00	62.16	67.98	*	71.04	78.01	*
7			65.35	61.59	61.91	*	61.94	68.56	66.92	72.40	78.84	80.00
8			*	61.81	62.76	61.73	62.98	†	67.46	72.43	*	80.22
9			65.53	63.35	63.21	61.93	63.11	*	67.75	72.68	78.40	80.01
10			65.54	62.68	*	62.08	63.11	68.84	67.11	73.47	79.04	78.81
11			65.99	63.74	62.50	62.64	64.34	68.71	67.32	*	80.25	78.92
12			65.39	*	62.22	62.96	*	69.55	67.60	73.55	80.17	77.67
13			64.91	63.70	62.22	63.02	65.23	69.09	*	74.01	80.81	*
14			65.21	63.97	62.22	*	65.51	69.91	68.38	74.31	80.13	76.95
15			*	65.12	62.66	63.51	66.44	70.73	68.08	73.58	*	78.38
16		62.76	64.92	64.52	62.98	63.29	66.09	*	68.75	74.67	80.61	79.71
17		63.60	64.24	64.09	*	63.29	66.97	72.10	68.52	75.72	81.63	79.08
18		63.88	63.87	63.70	63.11	63.67	67.85	70.50	69.07	*	81.87	79.55
19		64.29	63.07	*	63.12	64.13	*	71.54	69.54	76.46	82.75	70.01
20		63.78	62.92	64.09	62.80	64.65	66.78	70.93	*	77.31	82.07	*
21		64.73	62.08	63.93	63.17	*	66.81	71.03	68.79	77.33	80.93	78.44
22		†	*	64.12	63.65	63.81	67.85	71.31	68.89	75.90	*	77.04
23			62.57	64.20	63.90	63.68	68.85	*	68.95	76.33	79.75	77.22
24		65.62	61.87	63.90	*	64.38	67.95	70.58	68.58	76.64	82.01	78.12
25		66.67	62.39	63.86	63.05	63.98	66.93	69.92	68.26	*	81.61	†
26		65.62	62.91	*	63.31	63.54	*	70.19	68.28	75.43	†	79.70
27		64.47	62.93	63.97	62.97	63.12	67.21	71.08	*	76.39	80.38	*
28		64.74	62.84	64.12	62.75	*	67.36	70.60	69.33	76.90	80.75	78.97
29			*	64.20	62.28	62.50	68.04	69.50	69.21	76.44	*	80.25
30			62.11	64.40	†	62.36	67.95	*	69.68	77.40	80.31	80.29
31			62.33		*		68.15	69.55		78.25		80.14
High		66.67	65.99	65.12	63.97	64.65	68.85	72.10	69.68	78.25	82.75	81.12
Low		62.76	61.87	61.59	61.91	61.73	61.49	67.61	66.92	68.92	77.64	76.95

*Sunday †Holiday

THE 12-STOCK AVERAGE

THE 12-STOCK AVERAGE—1886
12 Stocks mixed....10 Railroads and 2 Industrials

Date	Jan.	Feb.	Mar.	Apr.	May	June	July	Aug.	Sept.	Oct.	Nov.	Dec.
1		83.62	83.47	81.75	78.49	82.81	84.19	*	84.86	89.20	92.11	93.33
2	86.26	83.79	84.90	80.42	*	82.31	84.27	86.80	85.28	89.42	†	93.60
3	*	84.28	84.92	80.43	77.28	81.81	85.37	86.34	86.13	*	92.38	94.25
4	86.33	84.36	84.12	*	78.07	82.54	*	86.44	86.04	89.92	91.71	93.89
5	85.54	85.13	84.23	80.58	79.07	82.02	†	86.84	*	90.71	91.60	*
6	85.76	84.19	84.32	80.56	78.14	*	84.12	87.08	86.54	90.60	91.92	93.67
7	85.57	*	*	81.31	79.04	82.32	84.55	86.54	86.27	90.19	*	92.32
8	85.04	85.85	84.01	81.21	79.36	82.11	84.02	*	86.88	90.25	91.64	92.95
9	85.41	86.69	83.81	81.29	*	83.14	83.92	86.05	86.45	89.91	91.70	93.31
10	*	85.60	83.79	81.42	79.53	82.35	84.13	86.56	86.86	*	92.23	92.07
11	84.68	85.89	84.05	*	79.44	82.88	*	86.04	87.28	89.50	91.63	91.56
12	84.48	86.04	82.57	82.71	80.40	82.94	83.03	85.90	*	88.94	91.93	*
13	83.32	86.83	82.40	82.05	80.11	*	83.40	85.66	87.66	90.48	92.03	90.55
14	83.90	*	*	82.02	79.15	83.20	83.50	85.80	87.55	91.01	*	89.28
15	82.27	86.24	82.87	80.94	79.33	83.28	84.33	*	87.63	91.02	92.23	87.31
16	81.60	86.45	82.87	80.39	*	84.08	84.31	85.21	88.09	91.11	92.61	88.48
17	*	86.00	81.60	80.63	79.69	84.44	84.41	84.03	88.37	*	92.44	88.25
18	80.86	84.83	81.74	*	79.03	84.81	*	83.52	89.14	90.64	92.76	88.56
19	81.65	84.52	82.26	80.37	78.88	85.59	83.91	84.28	*	90.98	92.85	*
20	81.43	83.79	82.21	80.82	79.60	*	84.51	85.31	89.85	90.45	92.47	86.46
21	82.17	*	*	81.29	80.09	84.81	84.76	85.36	90.13	91.01	*	87.46
22	81.59	†	81.94	81.19	80.78	84.62	84.71	*	90.08	90.61	92.49	87.73
23	80.47	84.25	80.12	†	*	85.31	84.54	85.01	89.93	90.73	92.17	87.88
24	*	84.26	79.75	81.11	80.53	84.00	84.66	85.31	90.18	*	92.24	87.75
25	80.28	84.00	80.46	*	80.61	84.78	*	84.59	90.25	90.20	†	†
26	81.05	83.94	80.24	81.09	81.51	84.76	85.04	84.69	*	90.85	92.55	*
27	81.06	83.66	80.61	80.85	82.24	*	85.16	85.17	89.37	90.74	92.68	86.87
28	81.55	*	*	79.95	81.44	84.52	85.76	85.25	90.42	91.20	*	87.82
29	81.52		80.16	79.61	82.51	83.86	85.29	*	90.68	91.25	93.34	88.88
30	82.60		80.91	78.93	*	83.84	85.61	85.13	89.80	91.86	92.50	89.73
31	*		81.38		†		86.20	84.57		*		90.09
High	86.33	86.83	84.92	82.71	82.51	85.59	86.20	87.08	90.68	91.86	93.34	94.25
Low	80.28	83.62	79.75	78.93	77.28	81.81	83.03	83.52	84.86	88.94	91.60	86.46

*Sunday †Holiday

THE 12-STOCK AVERAGE—1887
12 Mixed Stocks....10 Railroads and 2 Industrials

Date	Jan.	Feb.	Mar.	Apr.	May	June	July	Aug.	Sept.	Oct.	Nov.	Dec.
1		86.11	88.45	90.50	*	92.49	88.50	83.48	84.38	83.15	80.29	82.17
2		86.82	89.30	90.83	91.02	91.64	†	82.26	84.74	*	80.28	82.80
3	89.85	86.34	89.62	*	90.98	91.95	†	83.82	86.30	82.03	80.13	82.94
4	88.25	86.96	88.92	91.08	91.16	92.08	†	84.65		82.30	81.42	*
5	88.50	87.98	89.10	91.33	91.58	*	87.75	85.57	†	81.91	81.03	83.66
6	89.03	*		91.19	91.34	92.12	87.32	85.25	86.03	82.37	*	82.85
7	88.08	87.97	89.73	91.62	90.87	91.91	87.46	*	84.89	81.50	80.94	82.52
8	88.21	88.46	89.81	†		91.45	*	86.66	84.58	80.99	†	81.69
9	*	89.30	89.30	91.77	90.90	91.45	86.90	84.59	85.41		81.38	82.20
10	88.48	89.57	89.02	*	91.14	91.67		84.59	84.85	80.08	80.56	81.79
11	88.38	89.03	89.09	91.43	91.72	91.35	86.98	84.54		80.27	81.50	*
12	88.91	89.36	88.82	91.57	92.23	*	86.89	84.94	84.26	78.43	81.66	80.71
13	88.21	*	*	91.05	92.32	90.71	85.33	85.55	84.56	79.20	*	80.38
14	88.78	88.76	88.34	91.22	92.19	90.17	86.15	*	83.52	77.54	82.63	81.41
15	89.17	86.61	89.08	90.97	*	90.42	86.33	85.59	83.02	77.44	82.98	81.19
16	*	88.78	89.19	91.38	92.42	90.92	86.84	85.63	83.10		84.00	81.35
17	88.85	88.19	88.87	*	92.52	90.50	*	85.46	83.05	77.89	84.24	81.48
18	89.10	88.56	89.05	91.40	93.27	90.77	86.95	84.94		78.56	84.26	*
19	89.55	88.92	89.39	91.16	92.83	*	86.11	84.75	81.19	78.31	83.83	81.08
20	89.15	*		91.66	92.85	90.79	86.60	84.50	81.28	80.13	*	80.90
21	88.55	88.66	89.02	91.18	92.90	90.77	87.15	*	81.78	80.12	83.47	81.12
22	88.68	†	89.07	91.29	*	90.06	86.95	83.84	82.37	79.68	83.71	81.41
23	*	89.42	89.08	91.43	92.19	89.06	86.83	84.00	82.15	*	84.42	82.03
24	86.55	89.93	89.79	*	92.13	88.02	*	82.94	81.70	78.18	†	†
25	88.00	90.03	89.50	91.53	92.33	88.13	86.40	82.26	*	79.12	84.29	*
26	87.20	89.30	90.07	90.74	92.53	*	85.75	82.31	81.81	79.65	84.03	†
27	86.90	*	*	91.09	91.94	86.69	84.75	82.76	82.52	79.82	*	82.51
28	87.53	88.90	90.52	90.93	92.17	87.47	85.43	*	83.11	79.17	82.83	82.10
29	87.09		90.60	91.55	*	89.25	83.84	82.83	83.09	79.36	82.91	82.67
30	*		90.36	91.48	†	88.45	82.51	81.21	83.28	*	82.51	82.51
31	86.62		90.80		92.44		*	82.98		78.79		
High	89.85	90.03	90.80	91.77	93.27	92.49	88.50	85.63	86.30	83.15	84.42	83.66
Low	86.55	86.11	88.34	90.50	90.87	86.69	82.51	81.21	81.19	77.44	80.13	80.38

*Sunday. †Holiday.

THE 12-STOCK AVERAGE—1888
12 Mixed Stocks....10 Railroads and 2 Industrials

Date	Jan.	Feb.	Mar.	Apr.	May	June	July	Aug.	Sept.	Oct.	Nov.	Dec.
1	*	82.66	81.47		83.54	78.69	*	84.46	†	88.10	86.30	83.56
2	†	82.19	80.97	75.28	82.36	78.50	78.35	84.39		87.39	86.02	*
3	82.25	81.97	80.78	76.24	82.35	*	78.44	84.25	†	87.23	85.98	82.65
4	81.90	81.58	*	77.50	81.95	78.94	†	84.41	87.23	87.44	*	82.28
5	82.26	*	80.12	77.54	81.88	78.52	78.76	*	87.49	86.92	86.52	81.88
6	82.68	81.73	80.48	78.72	*	78.65	79.84	85.39	87.02	86.23	†	82.92
7	82.73	81.66	79.85	78.33	81.28	79.22	79.92	85.67	87.51	*	86.86	83.11
8	*	81.17	79.84	*	80.63	79.03		85.95	87.52	86.10	86.32	82.57
9	83.38	81.53	80.00	77.81	81.11	78.44	79.53	85.54	*	86.90	86.41	*
10	83.33	81.75	80.01	77.09	80.25	*	80.60	85.91	87.08	86.41	86.32	82.32
11	82.81	81.51	*	77.19	80.69	77.38	81.16	85.85	87.48	86.69	*	82.90
12	82.96	*	†	77.55	80.56	77.57	80.79	*	87.25	86.91	85.49	83.73
13	82.59	81.40	†	78.00	*	77.12	81.78	85.89	85.91	86.73	84.82	83.28
14	82.92	81.33	80.12	77.86	80.58	77.60	82.69	84.74	85.34	*	85.16	82.82
15	*	81.75	80.20	*	80.37	77.92	*	85.37	84.51	85.95	84.84	83.02
16	82.84	81.92	79.48	78.14	80.73	78.50	82.01	84.88	*	86.28	85.13	*
17	82.72	82.62	79.06	78.66	80.23	*	82.78	83.81	84.85	86.20	85.47	84.13
18	82.71	82.53		78.41	80.59	78.83	82.92	83.76	85.71	86.74	*	83.63
19	81.76	*	80.05	79.03	80.71	78.42	82.30	*	86.69	86.21	84.62	84.31
20	81.70	82.07	79.13	79.42	*	78.46	82.28	84.69	86.68	86.51	85.12	84.33
21	82.00	82.07	77.76	79.81	80.66	78.88	82.56	85.28	85.89	*	83.95	85.04
22	*	†	78.42	*	80.18	79.18	*	85.34	85.58	85.90	83.89	85.13
23	81.51	82.37	77.98	80.10	79.82	79.08	83.12	85.34	*	86.03	84.28	*
24	81.38	82.32	78.05	80.89	79.24	*	83.81	85.22	85.16	85.78	84.49	86.68
25	81.85	81.92	*	81.17	79.98	78.26	82.23	85.47	85.36	85.93	*	†
26	82.38	*	77.81	81.58	79.06	78.31	83.70	*	86.03	86.28	83.62	86.61
27	82.66	81.19	77.53	81.51	*	78.43	83.83	86.09	87.03	86.05	84.54	86.04
28	83.20	81.48	77.14	82.40	78.50	78.65	83.22	86.51	87.61	*	84.39	86.06
29	*	80.98	77.02	*	78.99	78.92	*	86.33	87.80	85.24	†	86.04
30	83.24		†	83.09	†	78.51	83.72	86.31	85.60		*	*
31	82.66		75.85		78.57		84.37	86.19		85.81		86.48
High	83.38	82.66	81.47	83.09	83.54	79.22	84.37	86.51	87.80	88.10	86.86	86.68
Low	81.38	80.98	75.85	75.28	78.50	77.12	78.35	83.76	84.51	85.24	83.62	81.88

*Sunday. †Holiday.

THE 12-STOCK AVERAGE—1889
12 Mixed Stocks....10 Railroads and 2 Industrials

Date	Jan.	Feb.	Mar.	Apr.	May	June	July	Aug.	Sept.	Oct.	Nov.	Dec.
1	†	87.77	87.17	84.17		90.12	89.67	87.80		92.66	91.04	*
2	86.03	87.55	87.23	84.70	87.16	*	89.06	88.02	†	92.75	90.89	90.48
3	85.54	*	*	84.39	87.48	90.20	88.17	88.11	92.21	91.82		90.44
4	85.59	87.22	87.54	84.98	87.32	90.10	†	88.83	92.03		91.19	90.25
5	85.55	87.05	87.07	85.52	*	90.60	88.04		93.00		91.67	90.47
6		87.41	86.74	85.72	87.52	90.71	87.71	89.15	93.26		91.64	91.56
7	85.80	87.71	86.82		87.22	90.72	*	89.10	93.30	91.04	91.90	91.78
8	85.38	87.05	86.60	85.06	87.50	90.54	87.12	89.46		91.33	91.30	
9	85.79	87.03	85.63	85.43	87.15	*	87.23	89.81	93.40	91.90	91.25	91.63
10	85.77	*	*	85.93	86.80	90.88	87.74	89.76	92.92	91.91		91.76
11	86.23	87.54	86.06	86.30	86.99	91.22	88.53		93.67	91.57	90.86	91.58
12	86.58	87.29	86.03	86.42	*	91.38	87.36	90.19	93.44	91.90	91.40	91.14
13	*	87.30	85.77	86.36	87.41	91.34	87.92	89.95	93.42		91.20	91.29
14	87.13	87.57	85.29	*	87.31	90.81	*	89.93	93.17	91.90	91.86	91.62
15	86.51	87.77	84.50	85.99	87.59	90.81	87.94	90.01		91.44	92.50	*
16	86.05	87.69	84.69	85.88	87.75	*	87.96	90.17	92.50	91.66	92.68	91.73
17	86.55			85.89	87.77	90.75	87.69	90.16	92.86	90.70		91.95
18	86.02	87.77	83.59	85.92	88.16	91.28	87.26		92.67	91.15	92.70	91.80
19	85.93	87.23	84.53	†	*	90.68	86.84	89.77	92.83	91.04	92.01	92.09
20		87.21	84.76	86.09	88.46	90.76	86.36	89.89	92.50	*	92.62	92.10
21	86.38	86.70	85.05	*	88.54	90.51	*	90.01	92.75	89.86	92.29	92.21
22	86.08	†	84.82	86.20	88.76	90.46	86.28	88.85		90.61	92.23	*
23	85.77	87.01	84.69	85.78	89.57	*	87.10	88.82	92.78	91.10	92.23	92.03
24	85.88	*		86.10	89.41	90.13	86.91	89.08	92.45	90.93	*	91.98
25	86.02	86.63	84.51	86.83	89.86	90.16	87.39		92.75	91.70	92.41	†
26	85.92	86.96	84.38	86.61	*	90.17	87.19	90.01	93.21	91.79	92.32	91.92
27	*	86.59	84.84	86.78	89.98	89.82	87.25	90.50	93.03		91.76	91.67
28	86.16	86.69	84.50		90.44	89.40	*	90.87	93.11	91.19	†	90.97
29	86.46		83.82		89.96	89.38	87.20	90.85	*	91.22	90.90	*
30	86.46		84.06	†	89.96		87.61	91.15	92.95	91.31	90.30	90.55
31	86.97				90.31		87.76	91.57		91.04		91.26
High	87.13	87.77	87.54	86.83	90.44	91.38	89.67	91.57	93.67	92.75	92.70	92.21
Low	85.38	86.59	83.59	84.17	86.80	89.38	86.28	87.80	92.03	89.86	90.30	90.25

*Sunday †Holiday

THE 12-STOCK AVERAGE—1890
12 Mixed Stocks....10 Railroads and 2 Industrials

Date	Jan.	Feb.	Mar.	Apr.	May	June	July	Aug.	Sept.	Oct.	Nov.	Dec.
1	†	92.90	90.15	91.16	97.05	*	96.64	95.30	†	91.47	86.84	80.53
2	91.19	*		91.24	96.83	97.38	96.45	94.45	94.60	91.09	*	81.68
3	91.85	92.40	90.29	91.58	96.53	98.30	96.45		94.70	90.35	87.06	81.33
4	92.14	92.65	90.33	†		98.24		95.02	94.14	89.52	†	80.81
5	*	92.50	90.11	91.31	97.30	98.66	†	94.77	93.98		86.22	80.08
6	92.12	92.58	90.35	*	97.28	98.57	*	94.24	93.57	89.32	85.15	77.16
7	91.52	92.77	90.88	91.23	96.82	98.46	96.03	94.40		89.73	84.10	*
8	91.74	92.68	90.77	91.37	97.00		96.29	94.39	93.42	88.43	83.50	76.77
9	92.01	*		91.11	97.77	98.51	95.58	93.30	93.98	88.73		79.19
10	92.26	92.30	90.57	91.00	97.67	98.29	95.80	*	93.85	89.36	80.67	77.87
11	92.13	91.82	91.30	90.67	*	97.62	96.40	92.42	92.97	89.22	80.51	78.56
12	*	91.91	91.71	90.83	97.63	97.92	96.35	93.56	92.87		82.91	80.22
13	91.55	92.01	91.42	*	98.25	97.33		93.51	92.26	89.30	82.03	80.05
14	91.24	91.94	91.29	91.34	99.00	97.30	96.63	94.17	*	87.87	80.65	
15	91.37	91.48	91.30	91.72	98.47	*	96.88	94.73	91.51	87.38	79.33	80.53
16	91.13			91.74	98.73	97.26	96.76	95.04	92.13	86.88		79.25
17	91.42	91.10	91.28	92.08	99.14	96.95	96.60		92.19	88.18	80.07	80.54
18	91.34	91.43	90.72	92.08	*	96.29	96.62	94.29	92.66	88.30	78.86	80.63
19	*	91.27	90.67	92.53	99.02	96.12	96.70	93.66	93.28		79.89	80.32
20	91.57	91.19	90.71	*	98.57	96.44	*	93.73	92.89	87.67	80.26	80.40
21	91.87	90.63	91.04	92.96	98.13	96.12		91.78	*	88.17	82.25	
22	92.20	†	91.05	92.96	98.69	*	96.44	92.86	91.94	88.80	83.35	79.91
23	92.06	*		93.36	98.70	96.28	96.57	92.76	92.15	88.10		79.77
24	92.36	90.84	91.33	94.30	99.00	96.42	96.73		92.37	87.90	84.71	79.55
25	92.57	90.74	90.99	94.92	*	96.81	96.27	93.13	91.98	87.27	83.45	†
26	*	90.51	91.30	95.23	98.87	96.20	96.27	94.54	91.65		84.16	79.33
27	92.81	90.32	91.20		98.39	95.84	*	93.76	91.43	87.35	†	79.78
28	93.16	90.10	90.85	95.69	98.68	96.11	95.57	94.39	*	86.98	84.30	*
29	92.85		90.90	96.30	98.11		95.91	94.40	91.38	86.56	83.27	81.30
30	92.84		*	96.07	†	96.77	96.28	94.44	91.65	86.60	80.77	80.77
31	92.88		90.93		98.16		95.40	95.40		86.91		81.59
High	93.16	92.90	91.71	96.30	99.14	98.66	96.88	95.30	94.70	91.47	87.06	81.68
Low	91.13	90.10	90.11	90.67	96.53	95.84	95.40	91.78	91.38	86.56	78.86	76.77

*Sunday †Holiday

THE 12-STOCK AVERAGES—1891
12 Mixed Stocks....10 Railroads and 2 Industrials

Date	Jan.	Feb.	Mar.	Apr.	May	June	July	Aug.	Sept.	Oct.	Nov.	Dec.
1	†	*	*	84.70	88.71	84.43	83.29	81.78	88.89	88.08	*	88.23
2	82.21	85.43	85.14	84.56	88.67	84.80	83.02	*	88.59	89.71	88.98	88.64
3	82.57	85.16	85.66	84.98	*	84.51	83.73	82.19	87.82	90.75	†	88.76
4	*	*	86.47	84.81	85.16	84.41	†	81.33	89.75	*	88.58	88.40
5	83.12	86.22	84.78	*	87.71	84.68	*	81.56	90.22	90.56	87.81	88.71
6	83.05	86.58	83.60	85.69	88.16	84.79	84.07	81.54	*	90.48	87.09	*
7	83.38	86.61	83.13	85.46	87.32	*	84.22	81.85	†	89.90	87.36	88.15
8	83.90	*	*	86.09	86.44	84.65	84.48	81.94	90.21	90.07	*	88.56
9	84.70	86.89	83.60	86.71	85.84	83.90	83.96	*	90.20	90.12	86.19	88.75
10	85.14	86.86	83.56	86.62	*	84.15	84.50	81.40	89.83	89.96	87.84	88.98
11	*	86.42	84.06	86.41	86.31	84.28	84.55	81.01	89.80	*	87.87	88.75
12	84.71	85.63	84.01	*	85.14	84.62	*	81.73	89.80	89.12	87.18	88.21
13	85.82	85.44	84.05	86.21	85.93	85.25	84.39	81.92	*	89.31	87.94	*
14	85.81	85.72	84.54	85.97	85.79	*	84.07	82.44	90.00	88.59	87.87	88.41
15	84.88	*	*	85.83	85.38	85.28	84.03	83.40	90.76	89.22	*	88.61
16	84.52	86.22	85.21	86.21	85.10	85.13	84.12	*	90.73	90.05	87.41	88.90
17	84.92	85.64	84.82	86.42	*	84.69	83.62	84.45	91.45	89.95	87.52	89.54
18	*	85.52	84.48	86.57	83.98	84.91	83.29	84.71	91.89	*	87.69	89.47
19	84.79	85.81	84.11	*	83.79	84.73	*	84.61	92.51	89.52	87.75	89.68
20	84.85	85.85	83.85	87.52	85.15	84.90	82.94	84.37	*	89.83	88.77	*
21	84.61	85.90	83.92	87.25	84.50	*	82.76	84.58	92.95	90.63	88.84	89.44
22	84.43	*	*	87.81	86.19	84.20	83.06	84.69	92.23	90.11	*	90.10
23	83.53	†	84.47	88.04	86.44	84.32	82.79	*	92.17	90.03	88.51	90.67
24	83.08	85.38	84.29	88.48	*	83.93	82.65	85.29	89.96	90.35	88.93	91.16
25	*	85.33	84.45	88.72	86.16	83.91	82.32	86.38	91.15	*	89.03	†
26	82.58	85.96	84.39	*	86.02	83.25	*	86.51	91.22	89.97	†	*
27	83.73	85.67	†	88.05	85.88	82.51	81.65	86.20	*	89.63	88.89	*
28	84.03	85.44	84.37	88.59	86.00	*	81.92	87.47	90.94	88.97	88.79	91.47
29	84.25		*	88.35	85.45	82.20	81.52	88.47	90.05	89.72	*	90.75
30	84.37		85.32	89.15	*	83.13	80.82	*	89.63	89.10	88.95	90.55
31	84.25		84.90		*		81.00	89.23		89.19		90.65
High	85.82	86.89	85.66	89.15	88 71	85.28	84.55	89.23	92.95	90.75	89.03	91.47
Low	82.21	85.16	83.13	84.56	83.79	82.20	80.82	81.01	87.82	88.08	86.19	88.15

*Sunday   †Holiday

THE 12-STOCK AVERAGE—1892
12 Mixed Stocks....10 Railroads and 2 Industrials

Date	Jan.	Feb.	Mar.	Apr.	May	June	July	Aug.	Sept.	Oct.	Nov.	Dec.
1	†	89.69	93.68	90.95	*	90.88	91.12	92.42	88.50	88.05	90.12	86.06
2	91.19	90.02	93.70	90.81	93.06	91.13	†	92.31	88.40	*	89.73	86.56
3	*	89.64	93.33	*	92.69	90.92	†	92.21	88.68	88.82	89.92	86.89
4	91.21	89.67	94.65	91.68	93.40	90.66	*	92.04	*	89.18	89.85	*
5	90.75	90.29	93.46	91.81	92.92	*	89.36	92.28	†	89.51	89.84	87.29
6	90.76	90.70	*	93.00	93.10	90.06	89.21	92.09	88.82	89.37	*	86.87
7	90.32	*	93.64	93.32	92.95	89.60	89.73	*	89.33	89.19	90.01	87.05
8	90.44	91.65	92.92	92.79	*	89.90	90.07	91.62	89.28	89.03	†	86.89
9	90.25	91.12	93.61	92.93	93.47	90.36	90.10	91.64	89.21	*	89.80	87.67
10	*	91.09	93.58	*	93.23	90.15	*	91.89	88.93	89.07	90.30	88.31
11	90.18	91.95	94.12	93.58	92.98	90.62	89.41	91.28	*	89.44	90.04	*
12	90.86	91.87	93.47	93.39	92.58	*	89.91	91.42	87.92	†	89.96	87.98
13	90.46	91.89	*	93.84	92.13	91.54	90.30	91.09	87.87	90.26	*	87.98
14	90.04	*	93.54	94.22	91.80	91.80	90.02	*	87.22	90.31	89.29	88.13
15	89.93	93.17	93.66	†	*	91.61	89.79	91.23	86.19	90.50	89.66	87.01
16	90.01	92.67	93.57	94.45	92.40	90.87	90.03	91.67	87.12	*	89.40	86.48
17	*	92.19	93.64	*	91.83	91.05	*	91.05	87.27	90.01	89.00	85.96
18	89.08	92.44	93.12	94.58	91.85	90.96	89.90	91.14	*	89.70	89.25	*
19	88.11	91.72	93.42	93.89	91.27	*	90.08	91.04	87.92	89.70	88.82	85.76
20	89.64	91.44	*	94.10	90.93	90.80	90.42	90.95	87.42	89.73	*	86.57
21	89.82	*	92.82	93.50	91.15	91.64	90.66	*	87.53	†	88.32	86.29
22	89.52	†	93.52	93.47	*	91.50	90.77	91.94	87.81	†	88.41	86.18
23	89.40	91.95	92.64	92.91	91.65	91.24	90.69	91.84	88.28	*	88.10	85.87
24	*	91.01	92.84	*	91.05	91.13	*	91.98	87.95	90.11	†	86.04
25	88.80	91.61	92.71	92.67	91.55	91.20	90.54	91.76	*	90.06	87.16	*
26	90.13	91.36	92.17	92.52	91.65	*	90.70	91.23	88.69	89.86	87.08	†
27	90.18	92.05	*	92.36	91.55	91.28	91.25	91.33	88.50	89.58	*	86.33
28	90.91	*	92.12	92.71	91.70	91.27	92.03	*	88.34	89.62	87.15	86.57
29	90.45	93.71	91.73	93.10	*	91.46	92.48	90.81	88.22	89.69	86.55	87.63
30	90.10		91.87	93.01	†	91.11	92.22	90.98	88.14	*	86.06	87.30
31	*		91.62		91.33		*	89.89		90.21		87.61
High	91.21	93.71	94.65	94.58	93.47	91.80	92.48	92.42	89.33	90.50	90.30	88.31
Low	88.11	89.64	91.62	90.81	90.93	89.60	89.21	89.89	86.19	88.05	86.06	85.76

*Sunday   †Holiday

THE 12-STOCK AVERAGE—1893
12 Mixed Stocks....10 Railroads and 2 Industrials

Date	Jan.	Feb.	Mar.	Apr.	May	June	July	Aug.	Sept.	Oct.	Nov.	Dec.
1	†	89.69	85.71	86.07	81.79	76.90	76.47	64.82	70.02	*	77.72	78.75
2	†	89.37	85.92	*	81.84	76.21	*	68.46	70.91	71.25	76.75	78.41
3	87.07	89.30	85.27	86.05	80.44	76.34	76.11	67.14	*	71.63	76.86	*
4	86.92	89.48	85.08	85.44	79.29	*	†	69.28	†	71.57	76.77	78.03
5	86.56	*	*	86.66	80.62	76.61	75.12	68.87	72.54	71.29	*	76.97
6	86.68	88.88	84.31	86.47	80.55	76.36	75.50	*	72.08	72.26	76.38	76.90
7	86.90	88.96	84.96	86.76	*	76.32	75.87	67.46	71.39	72.34	†	77.16
8	*	88.40	84.91	86.62	80.82	76.83	75.44	66.80	72.68	*	77.20	76.90
9	87.19	88.08	84.77	*	79.43	78.17	*	67.00	72.97	72.51	76.40	76.65
10	87.27	87.88	84.49	86.23	77.70	78.80	74.61	68.06	*	71.55	76.38	*
11	87.14	88.00	84.37	85.82	78.16	*	72.13	68.44	73.59	71.64	76.15	75.72
12	87.95	*	*	85.95	77.97	77.93	71.65	67.76	72.32	72.13	*	76.00
13	88.87	88.25	84.30	84.55	76.37	77.71	72.53	*	72.80	70.43	75.79	76.13
14	88.81	87.67	84.03	84.77	*	77.62	72.88	66.59	72.72	70.42	75.25	75.93
15	*	87.78	82.75	84.47	76.47	77.35	72.48	66.22	72.26	*	75.25	75.59
16	89.46	87.66	82.86	*	77.41	77.80	*	66.34	72.28	70.76	75.70	75.28
17	88.95	87.79	83.52	83.75	78.62	77.90	70.96	65.95	*	70.39	75.28	*
18	89.60	87.84	84.18	84.31	78.44	*	68.17	65.63	72.17	71.55	76.04	74.21
19	89.47	*	*	83.27	79.93	77.66	68.42	66.09	72.50	71.82	*	74.07
20	89.98	86.69	83.58	82.70	79.41	77.00	69.51	*	72.38	72.62	75.87	73.81
21	90.38	86.61	83.45	83.26	*	77.83	69.06	67.05	72.47	73.29	77.00	72.69
22	*	†	83.81	82.75	79.17	77.95	68.39	66.62	72.48	*	77.41	72.34
23	89.81	84.65	84.15	*	78.43	77.38	*	66.66	72.05	75.14	67.91	72.42
24	90.04	85.39	84.77	83.43	78.10	77.02	67.88	66.82	*	75.61	78.05	*
25	89.69	84.87	85.18	84.01	78.80	*	66.12	67.28	70.82	76.75	78.46	†
26	90.12	*	*	84.10	78.64	76.14	61.94	67.94	70.27	76.35	*	71.91
27	90.05	84.47	84.94	†	78.12	77.27	65.15	*	70.01	77.29	77.43	72.05
28	89.93	85.52	84.84	83.87	*	75.40	65.02	68.37	71.44	78.63	78.10	71.41
29	*		84.90	83.10	77.81	75.46	63.72	69.43	72.00	*	78.12	71.39
30	89.05		85.61	*	†	76.07	*	69.59	71.96	77.33	*	71.87
31	89.33		†		77.88		64.14	68.85		76.67		
High	90.38	89.69	85.92	86.76	81.84	78.80	76.47	69.59	73.59	78.63	78.46	78.75
Low	86.56	84.47	82.75	82.70	76.37	75.40	61.94	64.82	70.01	70.39	75.25	71.39

*Sunday   †Holiday

THE 12-STOCK AVERAGE—1894
12 Mixed Stocks....10 Railroads and 2 Industrials

Date	Jan.	Feb.	Mar.	Apr.	May	June	July	Aug.	Sept.	Oct.	Nov.	Dec.
1	†	75.40	75.59	*	77.58	74.02	*	72.31	77.76	73.61	71.38	71.51
2	71.11	75.11	74.89	77.75	77.38	74.36	72.73	72.33	*	73.42	71.83	*
3	71.91	75.19	75.16	77.90	76.75	*	73.08	73.34	†	73.22	71.91	71.82
4	72.63	*	*	77.70	77.18	74.76	†	73.66	78.56	73.52	*	71.69
5	72.33	75.07	75.69	78.01	76.94	74.73	72.82	*	78.14	74.03	72.38	71.76
6	73.96	74.94	75.28	78.77	*	75.64	72.44	73.30	77.90	74.21	†	71.71
7	*	74.58	75.76	78.46	76.73	75.52	71.78	74.05	77.23	*	73.44	72.79
8	72.44	74.59	75.35	*	76.67	75.51	*	74.54	77.46	73.59	73.50	72.26
9	72.86	74.68	75.48	78.27	76.32	75.02	72.01	74.93	*	73.30	74.63	*
10	72.43	74.55	75.80	77.79	76.71	*	71.60	74.81	77.95	73.09	75.05	71.78
11	71.60	*	*	77.89	76.63	74.76	72.69	74.43	78.09	73.27	*	72.22
12	72.04	73.85	76.04	77.57	76.79	74.85	72.46	*	78.34	73.51	74.36	72.69
13	72.37	73.64	76.58	77.85	*	75.04	73.03	76.03	78.04	73.44	74.38	73.59
14	*	73.92	76.37	77.88	76.70	74.05	73.36	76.10	77.86	*	73.43	73.14
15	73.94	73.87	75.93	*	75.90	73.87	*	75.75	77.50	72.73	73.01	72.70
16	73.64	74.35	76.66	77.75	75.41	73.96	73.88	76.56	*	72.76	72.55	*
17	73.43	74.26	76.46	77.44	75.42	*	73.63	77.10	76.41	73.10	72.02	72.77
18	73.29	*	*	77.20	74.61	74.03	73.90	77.88	76.26	73.15	*	72.33
19	74.19	74.00	76.75	77.23	74.03	73.59	73.52	*	76.63	73.68	72.10	71.75
20	74.68	74.05	77.06	77.62	*	73.46	73.38	78.01	76.91	73.42	71.91	71.94
21	*	74.38	76.95	77.46	73.39	73.23	73.54	77.17	76.02	*	71.38	71.86
22	74.56	†	76.66	*	73.72	72.71	*	77.49	76.33	73.21	71.56	71.76
23	74.25	74.14	†	76.65	74.82	72.44	73.15	78.51	*	73.04	71.30	*
24	74.29	74.13	76.70	76.97	74.34	*	73.10	78.65	75.52	73.19	71.80	71.79
25	74.08	*	*	77.16	75.30	72.41	72.60	78.35	75.63	72.78	*	†
26	74.37	74.26	77.14	76.73	75.19	72.94	72.89	*	75.35	72.45	71.63	71.26
27	74.83	74.58	76.98	76.45	*	73.80	72.76	78.93	75.01	71.56	72.10	71.23
28	*	74.94	77.72	76.67	74.60	73.15	72.70	78.21	74.79	*	71.21	71.31
29	74.71		77.20	*	74.89	73.15	*	77.64	74.44	70.65	†	71.58
30	75.06		77.92	77.12	†	73.06	72.35	77.73	*	71.00	70.66	*
31	75.38		78.22		74.28		72.53	77.44		70.95		71.52
High	75.38	75.40	78.22	78.77	77.58	75.64	73.90	78.93	78.56	74.21	75.05	73.59
Low	71.11	73.64	74.89	76.45	73.39	72.41	71.60	72.31	74.44	70.65	70.66	71.23

*Sunday   †Holiday

THE 12-STOCK AVERAGE—1895
12 Mixed Stocks....10 Railroads and 2 Industrials

Date	Jan.	Feb.	Mar.	Apr.	May	June	July	Aug.	Sept.	Oct.	Nov.	Dec.
1	†	71.65	69.09	72.62	75.45	77.75	78.00	81.45	†	81.91	78.83	*
2	70.80	71.70	68.77	72.79	75.97	*	77.66	80.55	82.60	82.60	78.49	77.89
3	70.93	*		72.00	75.54	78.30	77.75	80.82	83.57	82.60	*	77.77
4	70.60	71.81	69.05	71.92	75.58	77.93	†	*	84.23	81.65	77.63	77.42
5	70.50	71.45	69.40	72.04	*		77.40	78.39	80.82	83.02	81.37	†	77.21
6	*	71.78	68.96	71.95	76.53	77.62	78.51	80.56	83.51	*	77.21	77.77
7	70.66	71.72	69.39	*	77.60	77.61	*	80.67	83.69	81.34	78.07	77.68
8	70.93	70.84	69.08	72.03	77.17	77.71	78.86	80.67	*	80.73	77.34	*
9	71.62	70.64	69.12	71.82	78.15	*	78.58	81.18	82.64	81.59	77.10	77.46
10	71.30	*		71.97	78.56	78.05	79.16	81.27	82.60	81.14	*	77.32
11	71.81	70.15	69.82	72.07	79.05	78.82	78.46	*	81.98	81.22	77.36	77.21
12	72.04	70.22	69.83	†	*	78.84	78.43	80.95	81.71	81.56	78.56	77.06
13	*	70.32	69.91	72.50	78.48	79.17	78.15	81.22	80.43	*	78.69	77.03
14	72.30	70.05	69.89	*	78.39	79.02	*	80.73	79.53	81.45	78.79	77.04
15	72.05	69.78	69.79	72.96	77.56	78.97	78.10	80.92	*	82.38	78.39	*
16	72.19	70.10	69.88	73.04	79.08	*	78.01	81.00	80.05	81.80	78.38	77.75
17	72.52			73.36	79.17	79.34	78.39	81.21	80.63	81.56	*	76.81
18	72.53	69.96	70.51	74.26	78.80	79.22	78.41	*	81.06	81.50	78.12	76.01
19	71.94	69.95	71.37	74.12	*	79.37	78.35	81.12	81.74	81.28	77.50	75.06
20	*	70.32	71.27	74.41	78.03	79.21	78.66	81.34	81.68	*	77.64	70.10
21	71.36	70.17	71.58	*	78.57	78.68	*	81.09	81.97	81.39	77.32	67.93
22	71.13	†	71.36	74.55	77.90	78.23	79.46	81.29	*	81.09	77.00	*
23	70.78	70.02	72.26	75.46	78.21	*	79.63	81.18	82.82	80.57	77.04	70.90
24	70.90	*	*	74.71	78.65	78.86	79.38	81.42	81.98	80.25	*	72.70
25	70.94	69.56	72.79	75.19	78.64	78.98	79.56	*	82.08	80.40	77.31	†
26	70.81	69.18	72.43	75.09	*	78.46	80.10	81.83	82.01	80.07	77.51	73.03
27	*	69.33	71.78	75.04	78.67	77.82	80.46	82.73	82.09	*	77.88	71.43
28	70.13	68.68	71.96	*	77.75	77.71	*	82.75	82.16	79.82	†	71.86
29	69.83		72.27	75.34	77.94	77.64	81.14	82.65	*	79.27	77.64	*
30	70.22		72.97	74.81	†	*	81.12	82.59	81.47	78.66	77.56	71.47
31	70.78				77.88		81.60	82.81		78.59		72.70
High	72.53	71.81	72.97	75.46	79.17	79.37	81.60	82.81	84.23	82.60	78.83	77.89
Low	69.83	68.68	68.77	71.82	75.45	77.40	77.66	80.55	79.53	78.59	77.00	67.93

*Sunday   †Holiday

THE 12-STOCK AVERAGE—1896
12 Mixed Stocks....10 Railroads and 2 Industrials

Date	Jan.	Feb.	Mar.	Apr.	May	June	July	Aug.	Sept.	Oct.	Nov.	Dec.
1	†	74.68	*	75.73	77.79							
2	72.34	*	76.05	75.92	77.94							
3	72.15	74.30	76.42	†	*							
4	71.29	74.91	77.18	76.27	78.20							
5	*	75.77	76.70	*	77.82							
6	69.54	75.81	76.46	75.64	77.67							
7	69.45	76.12	76.50	75.98	76.79							
8	70.23	76.41	*	75.68	76.94							
9	70.89	*	76.66	75.48	77.22							
10	71.56	77.03	76.54	75.66	*							
11	71.45	75.96	76.45	75.80	76.43							
12	*		76.83	*	76.21							
13	72.47	76.79	76.51	76.33	76.69							
14	72.33	76.36	76.28	76.40	76.89							
15	72.34	76.23	*	76.70	76.30							
16	72.39	*	75.95	76.91	76.32							
17	71.77	76.57	76.33	76.52	*							
18	70.86	76.72	75.59	76.93	76.39							
19	*	76.86	75.48	*	76.15							
20	71.19	77.57	75.23	77.89	76.48							
21	71.56	77.58	75.40	77.88	76.86							
22	72.08	†	*	78.69	77.03							
23	71.76	*	74.58	78.40	77.50							
24	72.65	78.11	74.48	78.20	*							
25	73.09	77.84	74.70	78.00	76.70							
26	*	77.42	74.53	*								
27	73.41	77.38	74.47	78.52								
28	74.13	76.20	74.98	78.08								
29	74.29	76.04	*	77.71								
30	74.59		75.23	77.75								
31	74.82		75.69									
High	74.82	78.11	77.18	78.69	78.20							
Low	69.45	74.30	74.47	75.48	76.15							

*Sunday   †Holiday

12 Mixed Stock Average
was compiled for the last time
at the close May 25, 1896.

THE 12 INDUSTRIAL STOCK AVERAGE

THE 12 INDUSTRIAL STOCK AVERAGE—1896

Date	May	June	July	Aug.	Sept.	Oct.	Nov.	Dec.
1		40.60	34.59	31.74	32.02	36.01	*	41.98
2		40.04	34.91	*	33.49	35.88	40.93	41.95
3		39.77	34.74	31.49	33.80	35.82	†	42.22
4		39.94	†	30.99	34.70	*	42.79	42.07
5		40.32		30.93	35.07	35.92	41.86	41.97
6		40.34	34.87	29.99	*	35.91	43.33	*
7		*	35.15	28.66	†	35.30	44.08	41.58
8		39.81	35.19	28.48	35.50	35.42	*	41.60
9		39.34	34.68	*	35.39	34.96	44.44	41.78
10		38.41	34.84	28.96	34.58	35.09	44.56	41.48
11		39.40	35.60	30.30	35.30	*	44.33	41.42
12		39.31	*	29.37	35.02	34.74	44.90	41.40
13		39.55	34.69	30.37	*	36.18	44.50	*
14		*	33.43	30.73	34.86	36.15	44.54	40.42
15		39.93	32.28	30.61	34.13	36.20	*	39.50
16		40.45	31.95	*	33.32	36.26	43.59	39.96
17		40.54	31.94	31.06	34.33	35.57	43.59	40.80
18		39.76	31.50	30.99	34.81	*	43.63	38.59
19		40.03	*	31.31	35.03	36.50	43.44	39.37
20		39.89	30.50	30.72	*	37.42	43.24	*
21		*	30.68	30.55	35.53	37.32	42.91	39.80
22		38.73	31.99	30.91	35.59	37.86	*	39.53
23		38.14	32.29	*	35.78	38.49	42.95	39.76
24		38.27	31.54	30.67	36.23	38.87	42.71	40.02
25		37.97	31.68	30.61	36.61	†	42.47	†
26	40.94	37.89	*	30.29	36.75	38.71	*	*
27	40.58	37.04	31.46	30.31	*	38.88	41.90	*
28	40.20	*	30.82	30.88	36.35	38.39	41.78	40.14
29	40.63	35.53	30.97	31.24	36.33	37.75	*	40.52
30	†	36.15	31.48	*	36.05	39.40	41.00	40.62
31	*		32.02	31.97		39.53		40.45
High		40.60	35.60	31.97	36.75	39.53	44.90	42.22
Low		35.53	30.50	28.48	32.02	34.74	40.93	38.59

*Sunday   †Holiday

THE 20-STOCK AVERAGE

THE 20-STOCK AVERAGE—1889
20 Mixed Stocks....18 Railroads and 2 Industrials

Date	Jan.	Feb.	Mar.	Apr.	May	June	July	Aug.	Sept.	Oct.	Nov.	Dec.
1										73.05	71.49	*
2										73.18	71.60	70.84
3										72.44	*	70.99
4										72.48	71.57	70.80
5										72.31	†	70.76
6										*	72.08	72.05
7										71.75	72.21	72.16
8										71.91	71.54	*
9										72.43	71.68	72.08
10										72.41	*	72.25
11										72.00	71.29	72.13
12										72.31	71.87	71.78
13										*	71.29	71.83
14										72.55	72.35	72.17
15										72.08	72.48	*
16										72.12	72.91	72.25
17										71.41	*	72.38
18										71.74	72.81	72.15
19										71.41	72.81	72.39
20											72.77	72.52
21										70.72	72.46	72.60
22										71.29	72.52	
23									72.91	71.76	72.70	72.42
24									72.56	71.55		72.43
25									72.89	72.24	72.64	†
26									73.19	72.22	72.64	72.38
27									73.20	*	72.21	72.13
28									73.20	71.79	†	71.51
29										71.81	71.45	
30									73.26	71.85	70.96	71.21
31										71.93		72.17
High									73.26	73.18	72.91	72.60
Low									72.56	70.72	70.96	70.76

*Sunday   †Holiday

THE 20-STOCK AVERAGE—1890
20 Mixed Stocks....18 Railroads and 2 Industrials

Date	Jan.	Feb.	Mar.	Apr.	May	June	July	Aug.	Sept.	Oct.	Nov.	Dec.
1	†	73.13	70.81	71.46	75.86	*	75.62	74.58	†	70.86	67.38	61.25
2	72.06	*	*	71.50	75.80	76.54	75.55	74.68	74.01	70.45	*	62.21
3	72.68	72.65	70.93	71.83	75.65	77.40	75.62	*	73.85	69.64	67.78	61.86
4	72.91	72.70	70.95	†	*	78.38	†	74.29	73.04	68.97	†	61.21
5	*	72.60	70.65	71.66	76.48	77.82		74.06	73.25	*	67.13	60.62
6	72.89	72.78	70.81	*	76.49	77.70	*	73.66	72.88	69.09	65.91	58.48
7	72.42	72.99	71.32	71.55	76.08	77.54	75.20	73.77	*	67.60	64.82	*
8	72.50	72.90	71.18	71.62	76.26	*	75.60	73.71	72.93	68.03	64.28	58.10
9	72.77	*	*	71.41	76.98	77.78	74.93	72.93	73.33	68.66	*	60.15
10	72.90	72.54	71.03	71.25	77.01	77.60	75.06	*	73.16	68.70	61.06	59.23
11	72.81	72.15	71.41	70.95	*	76.96	75.63	72.20	72.18	68.70		59.79
12	*	72.23	71.89	71.04	76.71	77.33	75.52	73.44	72.05	*	63.29	61.21
13	72.20	72.28	71.73	*	77.13	76.97	*	73.47	73.47	68.58	62.54	61.10
14	71.99	72.22	71.63	71.48	77.71	76.88	75.75	73.92	*		61.28	*
15	72.08	71.85	71.72	71.68	77.32	*	75.93	74.21	71.53	67.72	59.60	60.40
16	71.86	*	*	71.73	77.63	76.66	75.91	74.50		67.72	*	61.22
17	72.09	71.53	71.79	72.03	78.01	76.36	75.62	*	71.58	68.85	60.65	61.33
18	71.97	71.78	71.31	72.07	*		75.58	73.80	72.65	69.03	59.25	60.97
19	*	71.72	71.20	72.44	78.03		75.61	73.29	72.23	*	60.03	61.11
20	72.12	71.67	71.16	*	77.95		*	73.54	72.23	68.45	60.14	
21	72.35	71.25	71.47	72.85	77.33	75.41	75.40	71.78	*	68.78	63.07	*
22	72.56	†	71.55	72.84	77.88	*	75.52	72.70	71.22	69.23	63.07	60.80
23	72.60	*	*	73.06	77.83	75.55	75.69	72.49	71.38	68.56	*	60.67
24	72.90	71.31	71.72	73.73	78.04	75.56	75.84	*	71.68	68.32	64.03	60.51
25	72.96	71.30	71.52	74.25	*	75.80	75.54	72.85	71.16	67.76	63.03	†
26	*	70.98	71.70	74.53	78.03	75.19	75.47	74.04	70.85	*	63.75	60.19
27	73.16	70.86	71.55	*	77.52	74.93	*	73.37	70.70	68.00	†	60.58
28	73.35	70.76	71.33	74.98	77.86	75.21	74.85	73.88	*	67.65	64.09	*
29	73.16		71.26	75.31	77.25	*	75.08	73.89	70.71	67.19	63.26	61.75
30	73.06		*	75.16	†	75.70	75.31	73.94	70.97	67.09	*	61.40
31	73.06		71.23		77.31		74.64	*		67.44		61.96
High	73.35	73.13	71.89	75.31	78.04	78.38	75.93	74.68	74.01	70.86	67.78	62.21
Low	71.86	70.76	70.65	70.95	75.65	74.93	74.64	71.78	70.70	67.09	59.25	58.10

*Sunday †Holiday

THE 20-STOCK AVERAGE—1891
20 Mixed Stocks....18 Railroads and 2 Industrials

Date	Jan.	Feb.	Mar.	Apr.	May	June	July	Aug.	Sept.	Oct.	Nov.	Dec.
1	†	*	*	64.98	68.68	64.99	63.77	62.52	69.76	69.41	*	69.88
2	62.75	65.18	65.15	64.76	68.68	65.31	63.58	*	69.43	70.63	70.24	70.16
3	62.98	65.03	65.56	65.05	*	64.98	64.18	62.81	68.71	71.63	†	70.28
4	*	65.94	64.68	65.26	68.30	64.78	†	62.16	70.21	*	69.87	69.86
5	63.35	65.88	64.70	*	67.79	65.03	*	62.40	70.50	71.60	69.31	70.18
6	63.33	66.10	63.83	65.93	68.22	65.15	65.03	62.48	*	71.50	68.61	*
7	63.73	66.15	63.49	65.75	67.44	*	64.88	62.76	†	70.98	68.69	69.96
8	64.08	*	*	66.23	66.83	64.84		62.87	70.75	71.03	*	70.28
9	64.82	66.48	63.88	66.79	66.29	64.38	64.63	*	70.50	71.21	69.10	70.48
10	65.35	66.35	63.70	66.74	*	64.58	65.11	62.55	70.40	71.09	69.16	70.78
11	*	65.99	64.15	66.57	66.55	64.72		62.37	70.40	*	68.76	70.63
12	65.06	65.41	64.11	*	65.55	65.01	*	62.90		70.31	69.43	70.16
13	66.25	65.25	64.12	66.44	66.18	65.55	65.00	63.24	*	70.43	69.60	*
14	66.11	65.47	64.67	66.19	66.13	*	64.72	63.64	71.16	69.88		70.42
15	65.20	*	*	66.19	65.73	65.61	64.75	64.32	71.11	70.24	*	70.49
16	64.92	65.98	65.10	66.48	65.43	65.46	64.75	*	71.66	70.96	69.23	70.77
17	65.38	65.53	64.76	66.60	*	65.17	64.29	65.59	70.85	70.85	69.14	71.31
18	*	65.30	64.53	66.80	64.63	65.32	64.03	65.84	72.20	*	69.21	71.36
19	65.20	65.41	64.15	*	64.47	65.02	*	65.86	72.68	70.55	69.29	71.58
20	65.18	65.49	63.92	67.70	65.53	65.08	63.71	65.72	*	70.78	70.15	*
21	64.93	65.56	63.98	67.43	64.95	*	63.55	65.81	73.21	71.41	70.38	71.55
22	64.78	*	*	68.89	66.45	64.49	63.77	65.88	72.53	71.10	*	72.06
23	64.19	†	64.51	68.21	66.71	64.43	63.54	*	72.60	71.34	70.12	72.44
24	63.85	65.38	64.31	68.57	*	64.18	63.37	66.43	70.80	70.80	70.41	72.93
25	*	65.26	64.55	68.82	66.45	64.03	62.99	67.31	71.96	*	70.45	†
26	63.11	65.75	64.51	*	66.33	63.38	*	67.56	72.06	71.13	†	
27	64.20	65.63	†	68.28	66.26	62.94	62.40	67.34	*	70.85	70.39	*
28	64.21	65.38	64.44	68.75	66.40	*	62.67	68.51	71.75	70.05	70.33	73.25
29	64.31		*	68.43	65.86	62.67	62.33	69.26	70.79	70.83	*	72.84
30	64.41		65.28	69.05	†	63.64	61.50	*	70.67	70.42	70.49	72.60
31	64.20		65.15		*		61.85	69.89		70.45		72.88
High	66.25	66.48	65.56	69.05	68.68	65.61	65.11	69.89	73.21	71.63	70.49	73.25
Low	62.75	65.03	63.49	64.76	64.47	62.67	61.50	62.16	68.71	69.41	68.61	69.86

*Sunday †Holiday

THE 20-STOCK AVERAGE—1892
20 Mixed Stocks....18 Railroads and 2 Industrials

Date	Jan.	Feb.	Mar.	Apr.	May	June	July	Aug.	Sept.	Oct.	Nov.	Dec.
1	†	72.20	74.95	72.21	*	71.30	71.76	73.08	69.53	69.54	71.75	67.52
2	73.45	72.43	74.98	72.02	73.33	71.62	†	72.93	69.53	*	70.84	67.96
3	*	72.01	74.63	*	73.05	71.62	*	72.83	69.73	70.24	70.97	68.11
4	73.51	72.16	75.68	72.60	73.55	71.26	†	72.45	*	70.58	70.97	*
5	73.23	72.61	74.90	72.61	73.26	*	70.27	73.08	†	70.76	71.01	68.54
6	73.43	73.08	*	73.75	73.41	70.76	70.06	72.56	69.74	70.72	*	68.10
7	72.95	*	74.66	73.68	73.49	70.29	70.59	*	70.24	70.48	71.14	68.30
8	73.21	74.00	74.22	73.46	*	70.61	70.96	72.31	70.30	70.41	*	68.13
9	72.98	73.37	74.91	73.40	73.84	70.95	70.99	72.41	70.36	*	70.78	68.67
10	*	73.37	74.88	*	73.45	70.72	*	72.55	69.91	70.51	71.21	69.11
11	72.81	74.31	75.41	73.86	73.58	71.41	70.55	72.08	*	70.85	70.84	*
12	73.37	74.17	75.08	73.65	72.98	*	70.73	72.15	69.07	†	70.80	68.69
13	73.11	74.20	*	74.03	72.56	72.03	71.10	71.93	69.08	71.35	*	68.80
14	72.73	*	75.00	74.41	72.13	72.38	70.70	*	68.59	71.40	70.10	68.90
15	72.65	75.34	75.02	†	*	72.15	70.68	72.00	67.97	71.43	70.48	68.01
16	72.61	74.83	74.92	74.62	72.73	71.50	70.86	72.45	68.48	*	70.18	67.64
17	*	74.37	74.92	*	72.22	71.70	*	71.80	68.68	71.00	69.81	67.21
18	71.78	74.59	74.35	74.85	72.30	71.63	70.76	71.95	*	70.79	70.04	*
19	70.78	73.92	74.57	74.31	71.73	*	70.91	71.63	69.30	70.76	69.88	66.88
20	72.20	73.58	*	74.41	71.28	71.54	71.28	71.56	68.95	70.91	*	67.71
21	72.40	*	74.01	74.00	71.59	72.31	71.55	*	69.03	*	69.35	67.45
22	72.53	†	74.56	73.85	*	72.18	71.61	72.70	69.37	†	69.51	67.25
23	72.31	74.11	73.86	73.40	72.03	72.08	71.52	72.58	69.84	*	69.09	66.86
24	*	73.36	73.92	*	71.54	71.94	*	72.73	69.56	71.33	†	66.98
25	71.55	73.48	73.71	73.21	72.20	71.99	71.45	72.50	*	71.31	68.34	*
26	72.68	73.63	73.40	73.17	72.20	*	71.55	72.07	70.08	70.97	68.26	†
27	72.58	73.96	*	72.85	72.05	72.09	72.02	72.09	69.99	70.81	*	67.29
28	73.29	*	73.26	73.22	72.21	72.02	72.60	*	69.85	70.85	68.30	67.38
29	73.01	74.98	73.83	73.49	*	72.09	72.99	71.54	69.66	70.90	67.90	68.11
30	72.56		72.96	73.37	†	71.76	72.81	71.73	69.54	*	67.58	67.74
31	*		72.78		71.86		70.78			71.26		68.10
High	73.51	75.34	75.68	74.85	73.84	72.38	72.99	73.08	70.36	71.43	71.75	69.11
Low	70.78	72.01	72.78	72.02	71.28	70.29	70.06	70.78	67.97	69.54	67.58	66.86

*Sunday †Holiday

THE 20-STOCK AVERAGE—1893
20 Mixed Stocks....18 Railroads and 2 Industrials

Date	Jan.	Feb.	Mar.	Apr.	May	June	July	Aug.	Sept.	Oct.	Nov.	Dec.
1	*	70.09	65.43	65.74	61.85	56.77	55.91	45.90	51.04	*	56.88	57.35
2	†	69.76	65.59	*	61.72	56.08	*	48.90	52.08	51.96	55.93	57.26
3	67.65	69.83	64.93	65.73	60.22	56.22	55.73	47.68	52.00	52.00	55.86	*
4	67.43	70.04	64.81	65.12	59.06	*	†	49.51	†	52.01	55.86	56.94
5	67.14	*		66.31	60.38	56.47	54.71	49.26	53.19	51.81	*	56.11
6	67.33	69.36	63.90	66.06	60.01	56.38	55.04	*	52.74	52.58	55.54	56.07
7	67.63	69.51	64.58	66.25	*	56.16	55.40	48.25	52.14	52.63	†	56.26
8		69.13	64.38	65.96	60.78	56.65	55.08	47.43	53.26	*	56.10	56.07
9	67.86	68.62	64.15	*	59.44	57.76	*	47.73	53.58	52.73	55.40	55.08
10	67.95	68.47	63.94	65.66	57.65	58.33	54.33	48.53	*	52.12	55.30	*
11	67.83	68.67	63.92	65.29	58.21	*	52.46	48.76	54.08	52.20	55.23	55.18
12	68.57	*	*	65.48	58.08	57.56	52.14	48.22	53.18	52.39	*	55.31
13	69.33	68.80	63.98	64.28	56.52	57.33	52.55	*	53.73	50.86	54.90	55.55
14	69.37	68.22	63.75	64.46	*	57.12	52.96	47.34	53.41	50.89	54.74	55.30
15	*	68.26	62.80	64.14	56.68	56.98	52.78	47.15	53.00	*	54.65	54.98
16	70.00	68.04	62.83	*	57.53	57.26	*	47.23	52.96	51.11	54.91	54.76
17	69.58	67.84	63.33	63.58	58.61	57.32	51.58	46.71	*	50.75	54.48	*
18	70.15	67.61	63.81	64.06	58.47	*	48.96	46.56	52.68	51.82	54.96	54.05
19	70.01	*	*	63.13	59.84	57.23	49.24	46.98	52.98	52.08	*	53.76
20	70.60	66.31	63.33	62.66	59.60	56.67	50.25	*	52.93	52.67	54.73	53.63
21	70.87	66.33	63.30	63.11	*	57.37	49.71	47.84	52.86	53.15	55.73	52.70
22	*	†	63.60	62.75	59.18	57.15	49.15	47.45	52.80	*	55.81	52.30
23	70.46	64.80	63.91	*	58.41	56.58	*	47.48	52.41	54.85	55.49	52.40
24	70.48	65.38	64.57	63.26	58.09	56.36	48.46	47.81	*	55.46	56.57	*
25	70.16	64.89	65.01	63.73	58.76	*	46.94	48.30	51.31	56.38	56.90	†
26	70.37	*	*	63.90	58.45	55.50	43.47	48.71	50.68	56.08	*	51.75
27	70.34	64.25	64.81	†	57.95	56.38	46.35	*	50.27	56.73	56.08	51.88
28	70.28	65.18	64.59	63.68	*	54.78	46.03	49.16	51.81	57.82	56.71	51.15
29	*		64.55	63.16	57.35	54.83	45.00	50.13	52.49	*	56.90	51.15
30	69.33		65.30	*	†	55.50	*	50.60	52.38	56.60	†	51.35
31	69.65		†		57.52		45.28	50.00		55.93		*
High	70.87	70.09	65.59	66.31	61.85	58.33	55.91	50.60	54.08	57.82	56.90	57.35
Low	67.14	64.25	62.80	62.66	56.52	54.78	43.47	45.90	50.27	50.75	54.48	51.15

*Sunday †Holiday

THE 20-STOCK AVERAGE—1894
20 Mixed Stocks....18 Railroads and 2 Industrials

Date	Jan.	Feb.	Mar.	Apr.	May	June	July	Aug.	Sept.	Oct.	Nov.	Dec.
1	†	54.36	54.79	*	56.18	53.20	*	51.45	56.52	52.91	51.63	51.65
2	50.73	54.06	54.21	56.40	56.01	53.41	52.19	51.51	*	53.00	52.00	*
3	51.43	54.16	54.45	56.44	55.24	*	52.40	52.20	†	52.90	52.19	51.83
4	52.05	*	*	56.17	55.48	53.81	52.56	*	57.13	53.16	*	51.78
5	51.83	54.12	54.97	56.78	55.31	53.68	52.45	*	56.77	53.60	52.61	51.75
6	53.17	53.99	54.60	57.27	*	54.45	52.20	52.26	56.48	53.90	†	51.75
7	*	53.69	55.08	56.98	55.21	54.55	51.59	52.75	56.23	*	53.37	52.62
8	52.11	53.70	54.77	*	55.14	54.55	*	53.06	56.20	53.36	53.19	52.18
9	52.24	53.76	54.88	56.91	54.89	54.23	51.83	53.41	*	52.99	54.20	*
10	51.90	53.66	55.08	56.74	55.24	*	51.65	53.45	56.65	52.88	54.78	51.75
11	51.28	*	*	56.77	55.10	53.98	52.22	53.20	56.78	53.01	*	52.03
12	51.65	53.10	55.35	56.44	55.18	54.03	52.17	*	56.68	53.18	54.06	52.45
13	51.81	52.95	55.90	56.62	*	54.19	52.45	54.41	56.32	53.20	54.18	53.22
14	*	53.22	55.68	56.62	55.06	53.45	52.80	54.86	56.10	*	53.53	52.66
15	53.22	53.20	55.28	*	54.39	53.25	*	54.52	55.80	52.65	53.34	52.35
16	52.83	53.68	55.88	56.23	53.95	53.30	52.98	55.15	*	52.73	53.14	*
17	52.72	53.54	55.71	56.08	53.87	*	52.92	55.57	54.86	52.96	52.54	52.51
18	52.62	*	*	55.95	53.17	53.26	52.96	56.11	54.90	53.01	*	52.18
19	53.46	53.33	55.86	55.88	52.84	52.98	52.66	*	55.36	53.51	52.65	51.76
20	53.71	53.32	56.17	56.25	*	52.89	52.57	56.48	55.50	53.28	52.55	52.00
21	*	53.55	56.03	56.16	52.45	52.80	52.60	55.75	54.92	*	51.95	52.10
22	53.79	†	55.85	*	52.71	52.27	*	56.16	55.22	53.18	52.04	51.79
23	53.48	53.38	†	55.41	53.58	52.03	52.20	57.15	*	53.04	51.87	*
24	53.61	53.41	55.89	55.48	53.19	*	52.30	57.39	54.57	53.13	52.32	51.76
25	53.43	*	*	55.65	53.93	51.97	52.00	57.01	54.54	52.84	*	†
26	53.67	53.46	56.25	55.40	53.87	52.45	52.14	*	54.13	52.66	51.87	51.24
27	53.91	53.82	56.03	55.25	*	53.11	52.05	57.60	54.10	52.12	52.06	51.17
28	*	54.26	56.52	55.43	53.23	52.58	51.85	56.76	53.83	*	51.36	50.99
29	53.82		56.06	*	53.55	52.41	*	56.33	53.60	51.24	†	51.16
30	54.24		56.65	55.71	†	52.30	51.61	56.58	*	51.49	50.99	*
31	54.31		56.82		53.25		51.70	56.23		51.25		51.06
High	54.31	54.36	56.82	57.27	56.18	54.55	52.98	57.60	57.13	53.90	54.78	53.22
Low	50.73	52.95	54.21	55.25	52.45	51.97	51.59	51.45	53.60	51.24	50.99	50.99

*Sunday   †Holiday

THE 20-STOCK AVERAGE—1895
20 Mixed Stocks....18 Railroads and 2 Industrials

Date	Jan.	Feb.	Mar.	Apr.	May	June	July	Aug.	Sept.	Oct.	Nov.	Dec.
1	†	51.11	49.08	52.23	54.91	57.51	58.09	60.82	*	61.79	58.65	*
2	50.52	51.07	48.75	52.35	55.31	*	57.89	60.20	†	62.24	58.23	57.45
3	50.72	*	*	51.83	54.96	58.07	58.03	60.42	63.43	62.15	*	57.88
4	50.40	51.21	48.98	51.70	55.01	57.71	†	*	63.77	61.46	57.08	57.25
5	50.38	50.88	49.35	51.77	*	57.07	58.34	60.18	62.88	61.23	†	57.03
6	*	51.18	48.87	51.63	55.75	57.13	58.30	60.04	63.02	*	56.91	57.31
7	50.72	51.17	49.04	*	56.66	57.13	*	60.06	63.26	61.22	57.58	57.22
8	50.93	50.45	48.76	51.79	56.45	57.36	58.67	60.02	*	60.82	56.78	*
9	51.28	50.15	48.88	51.66	57.41	*	58.28	60.45	63.58	61.30	56.77	56.98
10	51.03	*	*	51.93	58.00	57.55	58.82	60.61	62.47	61.00	*	57.03
11	51.43	49.73	49.29	52.08	58.56	58.33	58.13	*	61.96	61.05	57.28	56.83
12	51.38	49.81	49.42	†	*	58.54	58.18	60.45	61.70	61.32	58.31	56.82
13	*	49.93	49.46	52.64	58.00	58.71	57.96	60.53	60.48	*	58.28	57.05
14	51.60	49.78	49.48	*	57.84	58.55	*	60.24	59.66	61.20	58.38	57.00
15	51.40	49.52	49.34	52.84	56.90	58.55	58.05	60.35	*	61.87	57.99	*
16	51.66	49.76	49.48	52.91	58.47	*	57.80	60.39	60.20	61.38	58.00	57.75
17	51.90	*	*	53.20	58.59	58.93	58.26	60.51	60.83	61.10	*	56.90
18	51.95	49.71	50.08	53.96	58.15	58.97	58.24	*	60.91	60.94	57.72	56.22
19	51.62	49.68	50.95	53.90	*	59.05	58.29	60.55	61.61	60.84	57.31	55.21
20	*	49.90	50.74	54.10	57.38	59.00	58.50	60.79	61.70	*	57.41	50.51
21	51.15	49.83	51.14	*	58.01	58.51	*	60.66	61.99	60.85	57.23	48.56
22	50.94	†	50.90	54.13	57.43	58.17	59.25	60.81	*	60.74	56.96	*
23	50.45	49.66	51.66	54.84	57.77	*	59.48	60.76	62.50	60.32	56.98	51.11
24	50.59	*	*	54.41	58.14	58.78	59.41	60.93	61.80	60.00	*	52.62
25	50.57	49.38	52.12	54.76	58.25	58.91	59.51	*	62.01	60.35	57.55	†
26	50.41	49.00	52.03	54.88	*	58.45	59.93	61.36	61.84	60.08	57.45	52.76
27	*	49.21	51.28	54.78	58.42	57.99	60.23	62.25	62.00	*	57.90	51.50
28	49.96	48.77	51.63	*	57.51	57.78	*	62.54	62.08	59.87	†	51.75
29	49.70		51.86	54.85	57.66	57.72	60.65	62.52	*	59.27	57.65	*
30	49.83		52.46	54.53	†	*	60.64	62.41	61.50	58.80	57.38	51.30
31	50.37		*		57.73		60.93	62.71		58.62		52.23
High	51.95	51.21	52.46	54.88	58.59	59.05	60.93	62.71	63.77	62.24	58.65	57.88
Low	49.70	48.77	48.75	51.63	54.91	57.07	57.80	60.02	59.66	58.62	56.77	48.56

*Sunday   †Holiday

THE 20-STOCK AVERAGE—1896
20 Mixed Stocks....18 Railroads and 2 Industrials

Date	Jan.	Feb.	Mar.	Apr.	May	June	July	Aug.	Sept.	Oct.	Nov.	Dec.
1	†	54.17	*	53.85	55.35	54.03	50.17	46.51	45.97	50.17	*	53.64
2	51.83	*	54.88	53.95	55.50	53.36	50.83	*	47.40	50.00	53.12	53.83
3	51.76	53.68	54.97	†	*	53.38	50.65	46.26	47.17	49.86	†	54.23
4	50.80	54.40	55.65	54.15	55.63	53.58	*	45.51	48.24	*	54.58	54.35
5	*	55.15	55.23	*	55.27	53.88	*	45.31	48.32	50.10	53.72	54.13
6	49.34	55.07	54.96	53.89	55.06	53.80	50.72	44.26	*	49.71	55.07	*
7	49.10	55.26	54.98	54.06	54.32	*	50.89	42.92	†	49.05	55.94	53.70
8	49.80	55.57	*	53.84	54.52	53.31	50.71	41.82	48.55	48.91	*	53.74
9	50.21	*	54.99	53.67	54.70	53.12	50.09	*	48.56	48.44	56.52	53.62
10	50.80	56.06	54.96	53.85	*	51.89	50.50	44.27	47.71	47.97	56.68	53.28
11	50.93	55.12	54.88	53.91	53.89	53.08	51.69	44.34	48.27	*	56.10	53.30
12	*	†	55.01	*	53.86	53.29	*	43.65	47.86	47.51	56.38	53.24
13	52.06	55.91	54.90	54.35	54.28	53.86	50.30	44.91	*	48.54	55.67	*
14	51.96	55.36	54.68	54.43	54.37	*	49.31	45.29	47.66	48.85	55.75	52.24
15	52.11	55.17	*	54.68	53.85	54.70	47.84	45.21	47.22	48.42	*	51.95
16	52.06	*	54.51	54.65	53.88	55.07	47.34	*	46.68	48.46	55.09	52.32
17	51.46	55.41	54.74	54.44	*	55.26	47.18	45.71	47.77	48.46	54.99	52.75
18	50.62	55.28	54.08	54.64	54.03	54.38	46.77	45.64	47.82	*	55.03	49.98
19	*	55.58	53.81	*	53.85	54.46	*	45.91	47.91	49.14	55.04	50.68
20	50.83	56.16	54.76	55.51	54.13	54.16	45.64	45.24	*	49.98	54.62	*
21	51.18	56.31	53.80	55.70	54.29	*	45.84	44.50	48.65	50.32	54.23	51.57
22	51.88	†	*	56.18	54.42	53.11	47.30	44.72	48.43	50.54	*	50.78
23	51.36	*	52.96	56.01	54.71	52.99	47.15	*	48.67	50.99	54.21	50.84
24	52.33	56.79	52.97	55.94	*	53.43	46.53	44.33	49.16	51.15	54.35	51.19
25	52.66	56.43	53.20	55.75	54.30	53.36	47.36	44.06	49.81	*	54.03	†
26	*	56.13	53.13	*	54.22	53.42	*	43.94	50.21	51.72	†	†
27	52.96	56.10	53.06	56.05	53.98	52.47	46.70	44.17	*	51.22	53.76	*
28	53.28	55.15	53.33	55.77	53.45	*	45.76	45.30	49.80	50.80	53.50	51.00
29	53.46	54.84	*	55.67	53.99	50.96	45.93	45.62	50.21	49.59	*	51.61
30	53.66		53.58	55.44	†	51.57	46.23	*	50.21	51.42	52.76	51.51
31	54.11		54.01		*		46.81	46.06		51.98		51.33
High	54.11	56.79	55.65	56.18	55.63	55.26	51.69	46.51	50.21	51.98	56.68	54.35
Low	49.10	53.68	52.96	53.67	53.45	50.96	45.64	41.82	45.97	47.51	52.76	49.98

*Sunday †Holiday

20 Mixed Stocks compiled for the last time Oct. 24, 1896. From Oct. 26, 1896 figures represent average price of 20 railroad stocks.

THE
DOW JONES
AVERAGES

THE DOW-JONES DAILY INDUSTRIAL AVERAGES

1897—INDUSTRIALS

Date:	Jan.	Feb.	Mar.	Apr.	May	June	July	Aug.	Sept.	Oct.	Nov.	Dec.
1	†	42.38	41.69	39.77	38.73	40.01	44.21	*	55.44	51.54	49.11	48.41
2	40.74	42.02	41.88	39.81	*	40.22	44.18	48.84	55.77	52.59	†	48.31
3	*	41.93	42.13	39.89	38.78	40.28	43.88	50.10	55.64	*	47.67	48.31
4	40.37	41.30	41.34	*	39.48	40.52	*	50.74	55.65	52.66	47.31	48.23
5	40.87	41.23	41.45	39.74	39.18	41.04	†	51.25	*	52.26	45.73	*
6	40.95	41.42	41.31	39.57	39.54	*	43.60	51.72	†	51.79	46.32	48.79
7	40.87	*	*	39.73	39.59	41.32	44.07	51.80	55.75	51.37	*	49.46
8	40.97	41.11	41.90	40.37	39.62	41.74	43.92	*	55.60	51.64	45.65	49.39
9	40.90	40.57	41.62	40.21	*	42.21	44.16	51.32	55.81	50.88	46.53	49.60
10	*	40.57	41.79	40.29	39.95	42.38	44.37	51.73	55.82	*	47.12	49.18
11	40.75	40.27	41.94	*	39.90	42.54	*	51.80	55.71	50.64	46.19	49.48
12	41.40	†	42.05	39.95	39.69	42.57	45.05	51.97	*	48.64	46.44	*
13	41.45	39.72	42.29	40.43	39.27	*	45.61	51.50	54.61	49.25	47.12	49.81
14	41.79	*	*	39.76	38.94	41.96	45.71	51.97	55.35	48.79	*	49.67
15	42.27	39.74	42.08	39.41	38.67	42.80	45.27	*	55.62	48.42	46.47	49.02
16	42.82	40.30	41.93	†	*	42.39	45.48	52.19	55.27	48.59	47.05	48.54
17	*	40.30	41.50	39.07	38.67	42.69	45.52	51.55	55.46	*	46.83	48.11
18	42.76	40.32	41.60	*	39.20	43.07	*	51.79	55.35	49.20	46.99	48.84
19	43.25	40.28	41.12	38.49	38.80	42.89	46.45	51.80	*	49.84	47.27	*
20	42.78	40.59	41.25	38.69	38.67	*	46.76	51.65	54.66	50.39	47.23	48.45
21	42.52	*	*	38.91	38.83	42.62	46.95	51.84	52.53	49.82	*	48.25
22	42.42	†	41.39	38.57	38.98	42.80	47.73	*	53.45	50.00	46.89	48.54
23	42.02	40.69	40.86	38.49	*	43.18	47.88	52.39	53.60	49.66	46.63	48.84
24	*	40.76	40.60	38.54	39.33	43.39	47.92	52.53	52.48	*	46.21	49.39
25	41.91	40.21	40.58	*	39.20	43.28	*	52.13	52.30	48.76	†	†
26	42.22	41.29	40.07	39.22	39.55	43.70	47.71	52.56	*	49.10	46.70	*
27	42.21	41.71	39.52	†	39.21	*	47.11	52.92	52.93	48.60	47.19	49.29
28	41.88	*	*	39.02	39.64	44.61	47.86	53.10	52.31	48.46	*	49.34
29	42.06		39.13	39.01	39.91	44.27	47.70	*	51.90	48.81	46.80	49.33
30	42.56		39.86	38.96	*	44.10	47.95	53.23	50.98	49.03	47.46	49.21
31	*		39.47		†		47.88	54.81		*		49.41
High	43.25	42.38	42.29	40.43	39.95	44.61	47.95	54.81	55.82	52.66	49.11	49.81
Low	40.37	39.72	39.13	38.49	38.67	40.01	43.60	48.84	50.98	48.42	45.65	48.14

*Sunday
†Holiday

THE DOW-JONES DAILY RAILROAD AVERAGES

1897—RAILROADS

Date:	Jan.	Feb.	Mar.	Apr.	May	June	July	Aug.	Sept.	Oct.	Nov.	Dec.
1	†	53.46	53.15	50.21	49.05	51.22	55.04	*	63.91	62.70	60.94	61.11
2	51.71	53.09	53.40	50.58	*	51.55	55.01	58.44	64.33	63.91	†	60.78
3	*	53.22	54.07	50.46	49.44	51.35	54.68	59.21	64.83	*	59.63	60.88
4	51.24	52.92	53.32	*	49.95	51.86	*	59.46	65.04	63.94	59.20	60.76
5	51.77	52.81	53.38	49.87	49.35	52.35	†	59.73	*	63.61	57.90	*
6	51.85	52.77	53.19	50.10	49.79	*	54.30	60.34	†	63.00	58.14	60.96
7	52.16	*	*	50.12	49.75	52.46	54.68	61.40	65.30	62.90	*	61.64
8	51.94	52.53	53.36	50.71	49.78	52.16	54.33	*	65.32	63.13	57.45	61.96
9	52.07	52.61	53.07	50.34	*	52.39	54.51	60.79	65.60	62.15	58.55	62.28
10	*	52.66	53.11	50.15	50.07	51.73	54.50	61.26	66.17	*	59.50	61.68
11	51.67	52.40	53.51	*	50.16	53.06	*	61.94	66.18	62.06	58.57	61.90
12	52.13	†	53.82	49.78	50.20	53.10	54.45	62.08	*	60.37	59.25	*
13	52.08	52.06	53.96	50.52	49.77	*	54.83	61.69	65.88	61.23	59.59	62.50
14	52.39	*	*	50.18	49.49	53.64	55.18	62.16	66.30	60.38	*	62.35
15	52.99	51.93	54.00	49.62	49.22	53.50	55.02	*	66.83	60.30	59.15	62.26
16	53.72	52.62	54.21	†	*	53.17	55.35	62.20	66.65	60.43	59.56	62.00
17	*	52.38	53.99	49.28	49.51	53.53	55.55	61.53	67.23	*	59.06	61.68
18	53.57	52.06	53.95	*	49.96	53.60	*	61.67	67.03	61.41	59.25	62.58
19	53.91	52.13	53.44	48.12	49.80	53.51	56.06	61.53	*	62.01	59.40	*
20	53.46	52.25	53.40	49.15	49.35	*	55.92	61.13	66.10	62.38	59.15	62.33
21	53.01	*	*	49.81	49.57	53.58	56.07	61.20	64.15	62.00	*	61.93
22	52.80	†	53.16	49.59	49.60	54.21	56.78	*	65.51	61.83	59.03	62.04
23	52.48	52.38	52.25	49.64	*	54.57	57.15	62.45	65.68	61.53	59.30	62.40
24	*	52.18	51.88	49.38	50.11	54.82	57.28	62.35	64.31	*	59.08	62.75
25	52.22	51.97	51.40	*	50.08	54.61	*	62.32	63.93	60.11	†	†
26	52.81	52.83	51.21	50.10	50.47	55.12	57.12	62.68	*	60.73	59.42	*
27	52.67	53.18	50.58	†	50.46	*	57.15	63.24	64.61	60.13	60.06	62.64
28	52.63	*	*	49.78	50.74	55.58	57.71	63.71	63.87	60.11	*	62.49
29	52.77		49.75	49.62	50.79	55.02	57.89	*	63.38	60.71	59.61	62.20
30	53.57		50.58	49.21	*	54.61	57.92	63.78	62.30	60.84	60.22	62.23
31	*		49.77		†		58.05	63.81		*		62.29
High	53.91	53.46	54.21	50.71	50.79	55.58	58.05	63.81	67.23	63.94	60.94	62.75
Low	51.24	51.93	49.75	48.12	49.05	51.22	54.30	58.44	62.30	60.11	57.45	60.76

*Sunday
†Holiday

DAILY STOCK SALES ON NEW YORK STOCK EXCHANGE

1897—DAILY STOCK SALES ON N. Y. STOCK EXCHANGE
(000 Omitted)

Date	Jan.	Feb.	Mar.	Apr.	May	June	July	Aug.	Sept.	Oct.	Nov.	Dec.
1	†	186	178	212	36	243	278	*	544	488	160	389
2	56	116	147	190	*	236	191	398	598	227	†	476
3	*	132	202	80	105	197	108	478	686	*	334	312
4	102	141	227	*	210	209	*	544	301	456	352	92
5	110	167	158	139	155	158	†	554	*	337	588	*
6	148	52	73	126	159	*	154	535	†	343	197	317
7	158	*	*	119	140	245	178	329	591	308	*	421
8	149	187	152	186	73	269	190	*	567	245	431	431
9	41	133	146	188	*	270	149	753	604	170	371	379
10	*	138	91	85	34	344	58	510	651	*	394	343
11	127	124	102	*	173	302	*	637	235	385	285	127
12	116	†	139	158	125	112	262	743	*	483	247	*
13	116	110	111	198	145	*	312	557	596	561	123	354
14	105	*	*	230	136	264	310	265	514	384	*	307
15	214	189	234	153	79	263	247	*	630	419	174	450
16	204	177	239	†	*	233	158	423	622	123	195	334
17	*	154	193	76	137	248	121	429	588	*	176	355
18	302	118	277	*	134	235	*	335	240	228	148	172
19	221	106	178	265	159	89	454	334	*	282	196	*
20	155	39	103	224	150	*	369	422	504	411	62	268
21	153	*	*	187	111	166	313	169	878	293	*	163
22	151	†	165	118	55	178	450	*	603	264	180	175
23	84	98	196	104	*	262	396	440	561	83	160	206
24	*	120	336	45	153	245	205	421	516	*	156	279
25	124	88	236	*	209	473	*	284	240	379	†	†
26	83	154	203	150	185	155	453	226	*	244	181	*
27	100	86	113	†	135	*	466	367	370	266	131	284
28	87	*	*	131	120	422	420	231	381	254	*	320
29	122		328	90	115	500	452	*	473	179	324	175
30	114		231	96	*	292	281	455	387	101	231	164
31	*		266		†		172	585		*		157
Total	3,342	2,813	5,026	3,549	3,331	6,609	7,146	11,424	12,882	7,914	5,793	7,349

*Sunday. †Holiday.

1898—INDUSTRIALS

Date:	Jan.	Feb.	Mar.	Apr.	May	June	July	Aug.	Sept.	Oct.	Nov.	Dec.
1	†	49.76	47.47	44.14	*	52.87	53.00	54.60	60.50	52.52	54.94	58.16
2	*	49.54	46.58	44.60	48.60	53.36	†	55.26	60.38	*	54.51	58.14
3	49.31	49.54	46.55	*	48.30	52.77	†	55.46	†	53.62	54.95	58.45
4	48.91	49.82	46.16	45.58	†	53.13	†	55.26	†	53.80	54.75	*
5	49.53	50.23	45.73	45.06	49.43	*	52.99	55.85	†	53.76	54.93	58.30
6	50.18	*	*	46.02	49.16	53.33	52.78	55.93	60.16	53.36	*	58.30
7	50.67	50.11	44.86	45.98	50.40	53.30	53.09	*	58.92	53.08	55.57	58.52
8	50.62	49.62	45.30	45.48	*	53.15	53.25	56.31	58.54	53.27	†	59.04
9	*	49.86	45.51	45.54	51.05	53.12	53.48	56.30	57.77	*	55.30	59.75
10	50.53	50.16	45.38	*	50.46	53.71	*	56.61	58.38	52.51	56.02	60.11
11	50.33	50.14	44.44	45.95	51.63	53.26	53.35	56.55	*	51.85	56.40	*
12	50.19	†	43.29	46.32	51.09	*	53.16	56.21	58.08	51.81	57.14	60.28
13	49.85	*	*	45.19	50.82	52.61	52.61	56.83	57.55	52.87	*	59.53
14	49.63	49.49	44.73	46.06	50.68	52.20	53.15	*	57.42	52.28	57.08	59.38
15	49.15	50.04	44.41	45.37	*	50.87	52.53	57.50	58.38	51.90	56.90	58.97
16	*	48.97	45.53	44.53	50.33	51.77	52.37	58.45	58.04	*	56.77	58.81
17	49.36	49.23	44.55	*	51.26	52.13	*	58.89	58.16	52.18	56.79	58.74
18	48.81	48.59	44.86	44.92	50.55	51.53	52.27	58.08	*	51.76	56.58	*
19	49.28	47.79	44.84	44.48	51.04	*	52.32	59.09	57.61	51.56	56.82	58.78
20	49.06	*	*	44.56	50.74	51.90	52.64	†	57.23	51.80	*	59.11
21	48.92	47.11	44.50	43.27	51.40	51.73	53.13	*	58.33	52.21	56.75	59.19
22	48.88	†	43.45	43.87	*	51.38	53.01	59.39	57.73	53.01	56.97	59.43
23	*	46.16	43.22	44.55	51.73	51.74	53.21	59.63	57.63	*	56.71	60.09
24	48.00	44.67	42.73	*	52.29	52.01	*	59.72	57.53	52.85	†	†
25	48.66	45.31	42.00	44.02	51.87	52.36	53.67	60.52	*	53.64	56.27	*
26	49.53	45.17	42.95	44.36	51.90	*	54.17	60.97	56.55	54.23	56.50	†
27	49.78	*	*	44.40	52.08	52.66	53.78	60.68	55.22	54.24	*	60.42
28	49.32	46.17	45.34	45.01	52.14	52.44	53.85	*	54.52	54.89	56.79	59.00
29	49.56		44.49	45.75	*	52.79	54.02	59.57	54.88	54.75	56.89	60.16
30	*		46.15	46.00	†	52.62	54.20	59.92	53.44	*	57.20	60.52
31	50.01		45.42		52.74		54.20	60.35		55.43		†
High	50.67	50.23	47.47	46.32	52.74	53.71	54.20	60.97	60.50	55.43	57.20	60.52
Low	48.00	44.67	42.00	43.27	48.30	50.87	52.27	54.60	53.44	51.56	54.51	58.14

*Sunday
†Holiday

1898—RAILROADS

Date:	Jan.	Feb.	Mar.	Apr.	May	June	July	Aug.	Sept.	Oct.	Nov.	Dec.
1	†	66.00	63.01	57.90	*	66.53	65.47	66.00	68.59	65.95	66.58	71.59
2	*	65.76	62.05	58.34	60.61	66.56	†	66.29	68.65	*	66.26	71.42
3	61.86	65.70	62.24	*	60.54	65.97	†	66.60	†	66.30	66.71	71.53
4	61.24	66.15	61.51	59.16	†	66.95	†	66.85	†	66.80	66.90	*
5	62.15	66.32	60.97	58.66	62.27	*	65.55	67.35	†	67.11	67.05	71.21
6	63.03	*	*	59.49	61.90	67.23	65.31	67.88	68.78	66.91	*	71.80
7	63.53	66.08	59.36	59.19	63.22	66.93	65.71	*	68.20	66.57	67.63	71.97
8	63.73	65.65	59.98	58.91	*	66.52	65.93	68.19	67.98	66.60	†	72.05
9	*	65.64	60.09	59.00	63.65	66.40	66.31	68.00	67.58	*	67.83	72.70
10	63.51	66.32	59.36	*	63.13	66.90	*	68.60	67.73	66.12	68.87	73.16
11	63.82	65.94	58.46	59.62	64.40	66.48	66.46	68.43	*	65.98	68.86	*
12	64.00	†	56.46	59.32	63.73	*	66.15	67.89	67.04	66.27	69.26	73.85
13	64.26	*	*	57.94	63.82	66.10	65.34	68.14	66.50	66.76	*	73.70
14	63.74	65.06	58.51	58.31	63.48	66.75	65.96	*	67.14	67.14	69.60	73.96
15	63.01	65.86	58.47	58.38	*	65.13	64.93	68.81	67.83	66.25	69.10	74.15
16	*	64.68	59.75	57.97	62.81	66.11	64.68	69.10	67.61	*	69.78	73.78
17	63.78	65.11	58.70	*	63.52	65.85	*	69.51	68.06	66.14	69.96	73.46
18	63.07	64.74	58.99	58.00	63.26	65.52	64.61	68.77	*	66.11	69.60	*
19	63.58	64.10	59.15	57.38	63.76	*	64.30	69.61	67.38	65.85	69.83	73.40
20	63.28	*	*	57.46	63.70	65.87	64.73	†	67.03	66.01	*	73.73
21	62.98	62.99	58.80	55.89	63.95	65.68	64.83	*	67.65	66.35	70.10	73.85
22	62.98	†	57.45	56.63	*	65.56	64.78	69.84	67.03	66.47	70.66	73.96
23	*	62.03	57.27	57.12	64.50	66.10	65.12	69.60	67.23	*	70.94	74.01
24	62.38	60.46	56.76	*	65.71	66.18	*	69.26	67.19	65.66	†	†
25	63.53	61.18	56.08	56.35	65.43	66.24	65.12	69.64	*	66.29	70.83	*
26	64.65	61.20	56.90	56.84	65.49	*	65.90	70.16	67.01	66.65	71.08	†
27	65.13	*	*	56.89	65.57	65.98	65.71	69.95	66.52	67.01	*	74.65
28	65.18	61.93	59.99	57.30	65.73	65.60	65.55	*	66.27	67.24	71.59	74.13
29	65.90		58.69	58.26	*	65.21	65.73	69.16	66.60	66.68	71.20	74.76
30	*		60.61	58.56	†	65.14	65.98	69.30	66.20	*	71.20	74.99
31	66.17		59.67		66.33		65.98	68.59		66.74		†
High	66.17	66.32	63.01	59.62	66.33	67.23	66.46	70.16	68.78	67.24	71.59	74.99
Low	61.24	60.46	56.08	55.89	60.54	65.13	64.30	66.00	66.20	65.85	66.26	71.21

*Sunday
†Holiday

1898—DAILY STOCK SALES ON N. Y. STOCK EXCHANGE
(000 Omitted)

Date	Jan.	Feb.	Mar.	Apr.	May	June	July	Aug.	Sept.	Oct.	Nov.	Dec.
1	†	399	438	514	*	465	142	97	402	223	345	471
2	*	411	399	285	611	466	†	236	319	*	251	528
3	249	305	283	*	363	547	†	277	†	434	208	194
4	213	521	300	353	†	251	†	324	*	499	256	*
5	243	251	227	267	538	*	638	322	†	403	122	398
6	401	*	*	354	524	498	527	374	302	391	*	365
7	465	417	592	252	341	424	576	*	411	275	290	320
8	288	404	377	166	*	461	282	250	592	128	†	540
9	*	365	247	103	635	510	546	513	578	*	517	551
10	346	408	279	*	402	649	*	429	234	302	748	405
11	379	406	386	267	614	280	398	452	*	302	792	*
12	494	†	300	210	467	*	646	585	388	387	381	890
13	511	†	*	351	348	546	417	392	365	316	*	921
14	509	402	431	208	147	414	344	*	499	295	699	819
15	283	330	428	215	*	381	127	178	470	120	590	729
16	*	539	351	142	338	390	340	554	501	*	585	703
17	447	416	280	*	431	310	*	686	198	250	689	280
18	345	350	289	140	351	150	264	887	*	168	521	*
19	301	267	119	193	270	*	263	697	405	131	241	635
20	311	*	*	272	284	284	234	†	490	178	*	603
21	302	578	190	303	111	192	316	†	397	214	619	834
22	128	†	269	250	*	241	116	475	366	153	513	866
23	*	505	284	126	297	297	173	636	260	*	444	872
24	412	728	338	*	422	296	*	546	163	382	†	†
25	365	480	341	147	385	126	230	522	*	342	463	†
26	515	177	260	124	280	*	257	466	348	318	226	†
27	493	*	*	86	349	287	229	676	494	367	*	931
28	482	375	844	180	134	272	466	*	428	381	508	854
29	203		436	297	*	207	216	289	396	210	574	721
30	*		644	174	†	228	566	494	383	*	423	853
31	564		507		549		*	455		343		
Total	9,251	9,031	9,840	5,979	9,192	9,173	8,312	11,810	9,389	7,513	11,004	15,285

*Sunday. †Holiday.

1899—INDUSTRIALS

Date:	Jan.	Feb.	Mar.	Apr.	May	June	July	Aug.	Sept.	Oct.	Nov.	Dec.
1	*	64.44	66.64	75.15	74.59	68.40	70.67	73.89	75.57	*	75.17	75.47
2	†	63.93	65.90	*	76.04	70.11		74.29	75.76	70.95	75.72	75.68
3	60.41	63.61	67.02	76.02	76.00	70.13	†	74.61	*	70.97	75.34	*
4	60.69	63.39	66.73	76.04	75.39	*	†	74.68	†	71.73	74.93	74.26
5	60.91	*	*	75.87	74.48	69.73	71.48	74.08	77.61	72.03	*	73.57
6	60.86	63.05	65.95	74.17	73.83	70.09	71.92	*	76.97	72.30	75.13	73.53
7	61.35	61.95	66.40	73.08	*	70.71	72.15	73.68	76.61	72.68	†	73.03
8	*	62.23	67.29	73.14	72.18	71.03	71.69	74.23	76.56	*	75.13	70.27
9	61.98	62.10	67.66	*	69.98	72.29	*	74.59	77.01	72.67	74.38	69.25
10	61.45	62.11	68.14	72.63	72.47	72.42	70.55	75.37	*	73.47	73.67	*
11	61.31	†	68.16	74.49	71.88	*	71.35	75.19	75.59	73.00	73.06	67.43
12	61.23	*	*	75.10	72.18	73.08	71.55	75.79	74.68	72.45	*	67.54
13	61.71	†	68.89	75.33	69.36	71.88	71.67	*	76.11	71.81	74.08	64.03
14	61.43	62.55	68.98	76.04	*	71.92	71.02	76.23	75.65	71.85	74.16	65.26
15	*	62.50	68.90	76.30	69.77	71.71	71.14	75.63	74.55	*	74.67	66.21
16	61.28	62.70	70.71	*	70.96	71.62	*	75.15	73.54	72.47	75.48	63.84
17	61.41	63.13	71.26	75.96	72.75	71.30	70.90	75.62	*	72.22	75.80	*
18	61.93	64.76	72.02	76.36	71.84	*	71.37	75.64	72.39	72.93	75.93	58.27
19	62.30	*	*	76.29	71.81	70.43	71.07	76.06	73.10	72.86	*	61.02
20	62.40	66.76	71.19	76.05	71.77	70.30	71.57	*	72.55	73.11	75.63	61.19
21	62.18	66.89	71.28	76.71	*	69.39	72.08	75.73	73.10	73.39	75.05	59.97
22	*	†	71.83	77.01	71.71	68.84	71.69	75.10	74.22	*	75.20	58.69
23	62.37	67.32	71.56	*	71.01	69.82	*	76.00	73.86	74.61	75.50	60.57
24	61.80	67.35	71.98	76.53	70.27	69.96	71.75	75.61	*	74.31	75.80	*
25	63.05	67.52	72.40	77.28	70.76	*	72.19	75.59	72.76	74.41	†	†
26	63.83	*	*	77.14	70.29	69.85	71.99	75.61	72.40	74.52	*	62.00
27	64.64	66.98	73.73	77.03	69.51	70.44	72.48	75.61	72.64	74.42	75.69	64.47
28	64.87	66.78	74.70	77.10	*	70.54	72.95	75.64	72.87	74.83	75.48	64.39
29	*		74.17	76.71	†	70.18	73.00	75.26	†	*	75.55	65.73
30	65.02		74.33	*	*	70.38	*	76.04	†	74.37	†	66.08
31	64.35		†		67.51		73.73	75.66		74.97		*
High	65.02	67.52	74.70	77.28	76.04	73.08	73.73	76.23	77.61	74.07	75.93	75.68
Low	60.41	61.95	65.90	72.60	67.51	68.40	70.55	73.68	72.39	70.95	73.06	58.27

*Sunday
†Holiday

1899—RAILROADS

Date:	Jan.	Feb.	Mar.	Apr.	May	June	July	Aug.	Sept.	Oct.	Nov.	Dec.
1	*	82.01	82.78	87.01	83.18	77.38	83.83	84.52	84.73	*	83.68	82.93
2	†	81.65	81.60	*	84.30	79.00		84.35	84.89	79.48	84.49	83.07
3	75.08	82.00	82.44	87.04	84.01	78.74	†	84.17	*	79.38	83.92	*
4	74.96	82.03	82.46	86.52	83.61	*	†	83.90	†	80.13	83.53	82.15
5	75.18	*	*	86.66	82.27	78.45	83.96	83.51	85.55	80.15	*	81.58
6	74.70	82.08	81.55	85.13	81.59	79.17	83.41	*	85.37	80.68	83.60	81.85
7	75.13	80.98	81.91	84.56	*	79.97	84.05	83.56	84.49	80.76	†	81.87
8	*	81.31	82.74	84.63	80.38	80.04	83.55	83.91	84.22	*	83.25	80.68
9	75.64	81.53	82.78	*	78.88	81.13	*	83.98	84.26	80.50	82.31	80.33
10	76.10	81.94	82.96	84.63	80.88	81.16	82.38	84.18	*	81.05	81.75	*
11	76.55	†	82.85	86.01	80.37	*	83.35	83.95	83.08	80.85	81.19	79.89
12	76.64	*	*	86.01	80.53	81.26	83.88	84.18	82.63	80.18	*	79.61
13	77.43	†	82.83	86.00	78.65	80.48	83.77	*	83.71	79.68	82.37	77.70
14	77.83	82.52	82.41	86.11	*	80.25	83.05	84.21	82.90	79.75	81.75	78.47
15	*	82.46	82.31	86.53	79.06	79.95	83.23	83.53	81.99	*	82.16	79.23
16	77.46	83.43	83.07	*	79.65	80.02	*	83.66	81.07	80.31	83.22	76.90
17	77.28	84.12	82.63	85.89	80.79	79.87	82.85	84.36	*	80.75	82.73	*
18	77.98	84.24	82.60	86.38	80.47	*	83.01	84.63	80.13	81.54	83.33	73.60
19	79.00	*	*	86.27	80.21	79.50	82.62	85.05	80.67	81.10	*	74.98
20	79.70	84.92	83.13	86.15	80.00	80.00	83.24	*	80.48	81.70	82.55	74.57
21	80.90	84.81	83.11	86.23	*	79.83	83.66	84.72	81.40	81.80	82.57	73.28
22	*	†	83.49	86.38	79.28	79.85	83.57	84.31	82.17	*	82.81	72.48
23	81.31	84.25	83.61	*	78.97	80.39	*	84.79	81.69	82.73	82.86	73.87
24	79.60	84.00	84.14	85.66	78.52	80.89	83.70	84.95	*	82.38	83.02	*
25	81.96	83.56	84.87	86.03	79.22	*	83.62	84.81	80.83	83.15	†	†
26	82.10	*	*	86.16	79.16	80.54	83.39	84.85	80.48	83.03	*	74.65
27	82.23	83.88	85.60	85.87	79.23	82.42	83.74	*	81.11	83.11	82.93	76.40
28	82.36	82.90	86.41	85.68	*	82.92	84.37	85.06	80.93	83.66	83.13	76.63
29	*		86.31	85.06	†	82.76	84.51	84.48	†	*	83.35	77.36
30	82.01		86.26	*	*	83.27	*	84.96	†	83.49	†	77.73
31	81.63		†		77.51		84.83	84.93		83.38		*
High	82.36	84.92	86.41	87.04	84.30	83.27	84.83	85.06	85.55	83.66	84.48	83.07
Low	74.70	80.98	81.55	84.56	77.51	77.38	82.38	83.51	80.13	79.38	81.19	72.48

*Sunday
†Holiday

1899—DAILY STOCK SALES ON N. Y. STOCK EXCHANGE
(000 Omitted)

Date	Jan.	Feb.	Mar.	Apr.	May	June	July	Aug.	Sept.	Oct.	Nov.	Dec.
1	*	872	670	641	851	652	279	605	438	*	626	498
2	†	790	708	*	718	524	*	492	126	406	939	299
3	741	940	640	1273	545	288	†	399	*	402	637	*
4	731	453	409	1070	714	*	†	473	†	296	320	585
5	915	*	*	875	447	393	632	183	426	283	*	507
6	767	722	583	970	451	291	527	*	620	413	617	656
7	469	727	431	1294	*	381	577	382	493	189	†	470
8	*	874	643	383	1010	623	281	293	439	*	686	721
9	1089	585	619	*	1031	656	*	338	239	335	747	540
10	1023	460	317	556	1030	309	548	512	*	436	725	*
11	948	†	323	723	632	*	398	396	636	271	349	1111
12	1026	*	*	751	631	599	537	202	782	353	*	669
13	1034	†	583	795	755	567	415	*	572	366	660	1071
14	696	379	475	598	*	491	335	464	485	227	498	1036
15	*	618	540	513	595	377	126	616	711	*	471	593
16	1069	843	948	*	450	316	*	588	387	397	749	504
17	760	946	767	815	653	130	340	608	*	385	621	*
18	839	675	352	630	748	*	267	632	1100	444	360	1549
19	1097	*	*	575	458	333	265	291	748	415	*	892
20	1242	1238	908	550	184	376	234	*	930	446	544	902
21	761	957	629	493	*	340	318	709	703	194	447	720
22	*	†	653	308	424	382	116	688	781	*	404	797
23	1603	975	722	*	411	317	*	759	318	692	463	356
24	1371	899	692	565	393	191	169	654	*	612	828	*
25	1136	516	548	547	436	*	225	436	453	709	†	†
26	1528	*	*	745	395	516	257	211	466	606	*	424
27	1033	836	1213	540	244	519	294	*	365	522	823	663
28	563	800	1083	497	*	565	467	533	232	294	577	676
29	*		1142	264	†	441	215	606	†	*	589	583
30	1037		954	*	†	359	*	428	†	688	†	311
31	784		†		670		266	487		516		*
Total	24,252	16,106	19,727	17,080	14,876	10,936	8,388	12,985	12,451	10,899	13,682	17,132

*Sunday. †Holiday.

1900—INDUSTRIALS

Date:	Jan.	Feb.	Mar.	Apr.	May	June	July	Aug.	Sept.	Oct.	Nov.	Dec.
1	†	67.34	63.59	*	61.32	59.38	*	57.06	†	54.96	59.18	66.35
2	68.13	67.86	61.95	65.55	61.05	58.80	55.48	57.21	*	54.52	59.39	*
3	66.61	67.88	62.76	65.17	61.02	*	55.67	57.29	†	54.74	59.80	66.43
4	67.15	*	*	65.11	61.18	57.97	†	57.70	58.55	55.29	*	65.42
5	66.71	68.36	62.12	65.47	61.36	57.48	56.51	*	58.58	55.70	60.87	66.05
6	66.02	68.03	61.87	66.15	*	56.98	56.13	57.57	58.50	55.51	†	65.07
7	*	67.94	61.83	66.15	60.62	57.56	56.03	57.71	58.32	*	62.90	64.17
8	66.41	67.46	61.39	*	59.26	56.62	*	57.88	57.88	55.38	63.76	63.98
9	64.99	66.86	61.11	65.46	59.94	56.41	55.76	57.74	*	55.51	65.15	*
10	64.14	66.66	61.68	64.55	60.10	*	56.91	58.00	58.07	54.90	66.48	64.65
11	63.27	*	*	64.78	58.62	56.03	56.77	58.09	58.10	55.34	*	65.54
12	64.93	†	63.31	64.40	58.12	56.15	56.71	*	58.25	56.09	67.33	65.45
13	64.80	67.39	62.88	†	*	57.12	55.98	58.50	58.20	56.58	65.73	64.89
14	*	66.90	62.03	†	57.55	56.51	55.88	58.77	57.47	*	66.23	65.54
15	64.22	67.08	61.81	*	56.62	56.17	*	58.90	56.56	57.90	66.81	65.91
16	64.29	66.40	61.91	61.55	57.12	55.42	56.22	58.86	*	57.82	68.19	*
17	64.56	65.81	62.50	61.80	56.76	*	56.75	58.84	56.67	57.89	68.70	65.70
18	64.28	*	*	61.82	57.76	54.96	56.61	58.69	55.63	58.46	*	66.52
19	65.29	66.25	62.91	62.38	58.18	55.08	57.27	*	55.63	58.73	68.88	67.19
20	64.83	66.16	63.45	62.20	*	54.39	58.35	58.80	54.37	59.54	69.07	67.38
21	*	65.59	64.08	60.47	57.40	54.65	58.41	58.55	54.37	*	68.97	68.63
22	65.37	†	64.06	*	58.10	54.11	*	58.65	53.43	60.63	68.41	70.03
23	64.38	64.52	63.67	61.19	58.35	53.68	59.02	58.42	*	60.79	66.92	*
24	64.72	64.12	64.26	61.69	57.51	*	58.35	58.30	52.96	60.79	66.75	†
25	65.05	*	*	61.89	57.26	53.68	58.18	58.17	53.13	60.64	*	†
26	64.23	63.56	64.06	63.05	57.55	54.00	57.93	*	53.25	60.50	67.23	70.85
27	64.27	63.35	64.71	62.25	*	54.11	58.03	58.22	54.53	60.08	67.01	71.04
28	*	63.96	65.12	61.79	57.67	54.75	57.70	57.79	54.14	*	66.59	69.79
29	64.45		64.07	*	58.01	54.83	*	58.43	54.27	59.31	†	70.20
30	66.06		65.39	61.33	†	54.93	57.13	58.39	*	59.53	66.59	*
31	66.13		66.02		59.10		56.80	57.81		59.04		70.71
High	68.13	68.36	66.02	66.15	61.36	59.38	59.02	58.90	58.58	60.79	69.07	71.04
Low	63.27	63.35	61.11	60.47	56.62	53.68	55.48	57.06	52.96	54.52	59.18	63.98

*Sunday

†Holiday

1900—RAILROADS

Date:	Jan.	Feb.	Mar.	Apr.	May	June	July	Aug.	Sept.	Oct.	Nov.	Dec.
1	†	78.17	78.58	*	79.77	79.98	*	76.33	†	76.00	79.73	88.63
2	78.86	78.84	77.86	82.19	79.17	79.71	75.28	76.45	*	75.85	79.71	*
3	77.43	78.86	78.05	82.35	79.51	*	75.23	76.76	†	76.84	80.01	88.59
4	77.95	*	*	82.65	79.68	78.76	†	76.83	77.03	76.79	*	87.58
5	77.94	79.83	78.11	82.23	79.68	78.65	75.77	*	77.33	77.00	81.16	87.87
6	77.51	80.51	78.02	82.30	*	77.99	75.14	76.66	77.45	76.71	†	87.90
7	*	80.11	77.97	82.91	79.21	78.03	74.93	76.51	77.34	*	82.83	87.26
8	77.06	79.61	77.69	*	77.71	77.34	*	76.41	77.13	76.11	83.64	87.21
9	76.17	79.28	77.70	82.59	77.55	77.12	74.96	76.56	*	76.33	84.27	*
10	76.42	78.84	78.32	81.88	78.09	*	75.91	76.77	77.38	76.16	84.34	87.63
11	75.95	*	*	81.96	76.95	76.85	76.50	76.82	77.38	76.04	*	88.53
12	77.10	†	79.05	82.47	76.56	77.06	76.36	*	77.48	76.68	84.64	88.65
13	77.03	79.60	79.14	†	*	77.58	75.47	77.43	77.08	76.88	84.10	88.31
14	*	79.63	78.69	†	76.91	76.98	75.45	77.81	76.45	*	84.69	89.40
15	76.50	79.58	78.63	*	77.30	76.66	*	78.06	75.38	78.25	85.53	90.15
16	76.83	79.16	78.48	81.45	78.13	75.36	75.60	77.65	*	78.38	86.88	*
17	77.06	78.72	78.69	80.99	77.91	*	76.24	77.74	75.65	78.31	87.35	90.78
18	77.08	*	*	80.97	78.63	75.03	75.95	77.51	75.89	78.61	*	90.47
19	77.89	79.28	78.82	80.98	79.12	74.87	76.01	*	75.00	79.32	86.76	91.10
20	77.79	79.22	79.58	81.58	*	74.36	76.51	77.31	74.23	79.96	87.80	91.51
21	*	79.10	80.03	80.40	78.15	74.61	76.63	77.35	74.45	*	88.23	92.38
22	78.00	†	80.71	*	78.18	73.90	*	77.48	73.91	80.21	88.42	93.01
23	77.03	78.60	80.17	80.08	78.30	72.99	77.55	77.38	*	80.10	86.84	*
24	77.41	78.13	81.00	79.89	77.90	*	76.75	77.21	73.77	80.40	87.39	†
25	77.85	*	*	80.02	77.77	73.28	76.61	76.94	74.35	80.22	*	†
26	77.13	78.23	81.50	80.88	77.80	73.89	76.25	*	74.42	80.50	88.26	93.72
27	76.95	78.08	81.65	80.38	*	73.55	76.65	76.80	75.70	80.08	88.28	93.83
28	*	78.78	82.20	80.11	77.70	74.60	76.49	76.60	74.83	*	88.18	94.02
29	76.96		81.99	*	78.30	74.36	*	77.18	75.35	79.46	†	94.55
30	77.86		82.08	79.51	†	74.49	75.75	77.18	*	79.85	88.88	*
31	78.08		82.40		79.15		75.95	77.13		79.55		94.99
High	78.86	80.51	82.40	82.91	79.77	79.98	77.55	78.06	77.48	80.50	88.88	94.99
Low	75.95	78.08	77.69	79.51	76.56	72.99	74.93	76.33	73.77	75.85	79.71	87.21

*Sunday

†Holiday

1900—DAILY STOCK SALES ON N. Y. STOCK EXCHANGE
(000 Omitted)

Date	Jan.	Feb.	Mar.	Apr.	May	June	July	Aug.	Sept.	Oct.	Nov.	Dec.
1	†	443	532	*	337	431	*	197	†	334	248	393
2	657	597	592	816	445	162	295	172	*	186	242	*
3	811	333	271	925	313	*	209	189	†	385	176	667
4	718	*	*	851	228	281	†	92	208	433	*	650
5	599	717	517	732	107	287	361	*	254	328	451	717
6	234	908	437	718	*	244	347	176	147	138	†	761
7	*	857	303	394	259	197	86	135	187	*	1425	604
8	460	566	262	*	626	289	*	115	72	274	1038	307
9	385	412	250	756	694	180	245	91	*	198	1452	*
10	546	168	184	720	457	*	307	112	120	175	868	554
11	576	*	*	675	591	260	390	64	146	173	*	808
12	488	†	521	652	313	205	307	*	105	248	1668	830
13	244	382	436	†	*	219	193	193	114	172	1156	715
14	*	421	476	†	505	153	76	298	177	*	945	1237
15	336	420	503	*	469	141	*	340	245	601	861	818
16	197	318	331	882	470	266	313	214	*	536	1221	*
17	280	181	151	934	436	*	291	148	252	440	824	1491
18	273	*	*	551	432	509	203	72	115	454	*	1258
19	346	338	494	544	233	313	204	*	261	623	1229	1429
20	161	343	752	471	*	356	387	195	437	358	1314	1563
21	*	426	755	415	345	397	144	116	313	*	1535	1216
22	260	†	983	*	404	392	*	86	197	853	1192	1006
23	312	410	688	741	298	246	388	99	*	543	1073	*
24	191	300	471	592	418	*	338	117	369	852	426	†
25	300	*	*	570	271	518	225	60	268	688	*	†
26	232	572	971	537	83	377	183	*	332	612	912	1436
27	93	626	898	644	*	247	177	202	433	233	1009	1458
28	*	536	949	215	214	319	90	120	283	*	622	1451
29	243		932	*	252	250	*	143	135	446	†	669
30	513		702	637	307	69	260	144	*	381	676	*
31	707		408		†		211	131		233		1373
Total	9,964	10,265	14,447	14,973	9,509	7,309	6,230	4,021	5,170	10,895	22,565	23,412

*Sunday. †Holiday.

1901—INDUSTRIALS

Date:	Jan.	Feb.	Mar.	Apr.	May	June	July	Aug.	Sept.	Oct.	Nov.	Dec.
1	†	67.71	67.76	70.91	75.93	76.59	77.08	71.71	*	66.07	64.67	*
2	70.44	†	67.67	71.02	75.19		77.07	71.28	†	65.94	64.83	64.02
3	67.97	*	*	71.35	74.37	77.73	76.60	71.22	72.65	64.48		64.44
4	69.33	68.46	67.58	72.01	74.90	77.07	†	*	73.27	64.57	64.48	64.87
5	67.68	69.27	67.35	†		76.37	†	69.21	73.06	63.48	†	64.84
6	*	69.89	67.39		75.55	76.45		69.05	72.23		64.56	63.82
7	67.12	69.33	67.72	*	75.02	76.31		69.53	69.03	63.72	64.78	62.96
8	67.65	69.80	67.55	71.47	71.72	76.07	74.04	70.42		63.84	65.10	*
9	67.53	70.16	67.30	72.51	67.38		74.66	69.66	70.69	64.13	65.66	63.68
10	67.89	*	*	73.11	71.67	76.27	72.78	69.36	71.45	65.36		63.27
11	67.85	70.48	67.48	72.62	†	76.11	72.22	*	71.01	65.91	66.52	62.75
12	67.36	†	67.28	72.88		76.55	70.77	69.91	70.25	65.52	66.35	61.61
13	*	69.45	67.18	73.65	71.92	77.31	71.05	70.33	67.25		66.03	61.84
14	67.26	70.62	67.54	*	69.59	77.07	*	70.71	†	65.79	65.36	62.22
15	66.50	70.78	67.33	75.35	70.06	77.43	69.46	71.71		65.30	66.10	
16	65.71	70.18	67.47	75.42	70.84	*	69.67	71.58	70.01	64.91	66.12	61.95
17	65.30			74.88	73.09	78.26	71.55	71.01	69.87	65.23		62.27
18	65.21	68.92	68.42	75.10	73.86	77.82	71.91	*	70.25	65.48	65.87	62.79
19	64.77	68.37	68.73	75.89	*	77.56	71.97	71.01	†	65.81	65.62	62.86
20	*	67.96	68.82	75.66	72.76	77.22	71.32	71.08	70.47	*	65.15	63.17
21	64.92	68.55	68.93	*	73.44	77.94	*	71.40	69.73	65.42	65.45	63.12
22	65.53	68.92	68.92	74.56	73.51	77.71	70.43	72.10		65.66	65.88	*
23	66.37	†	68.82	73.80	72.83		71.39	73.03	67.57	65.66	65.68	62.11
24	65.65	*	*	73.21	73.73	77.71	70.91	73.70	67.43	65.44	*	61.52
25	66.16	68.27	68.59	73.63	73.62	76.93	71.69	*	66.22	65.29	65.15	†
26	66.68	67.36	68.52	74.35	*	76.87	72.13	73.83	66.89	65.09	65.18	62.62
27	*	68.11	69.27	†	73.67	76.82	72.70	72.81	67.69	67.69	65.78	63.31
28	66.29	67.00	69.39	*	74.01	76.47		72.71	67.40	64.01	†	63.76
29	66.56		69.43	75.23	74.51	77.94	72.94	72.82	*	64.46	65.68	*
30	66.72		69.92	75.80	†	*	72.65	73.47	66.66	64.86	65.01	63.33
31	66.81		*		75.77		71.63	*		64.45		64.56
High	70.44	70.78	69.92	75.89	75.93	78.26	77.08	73.83	73.27	66.07	66.52	64.87
Low	64.77	67.00	67.18	70.91	67.38	76.07	69.46	69.05	66.22	63.48	64.48	61.52

*Sunday
†Holiday

1901—RAILROADS

Date:	Jan.	Feb.	Mar.	Apr.	May	June	July	Aug.	Sept.	Oct.	Nov.	Dec.
1	†	97.61	97.80	105.48	117.86	114.58	115.35	107.74	*	108.18	111.65	*
2	94.79	†	97.90	106.20	117.73	*	115.16	107.08	†	107.69	111.76	113.08
3	92.66	*	*	107.69	116.25	115.69	114.76	106.78	110.12	107.19	*	113.53
4	95.70	98.90	98.58	107.75	116.60	115.69	†		110.92	107.19	111.38	114.52
5	95.50	99.48	99.01	†	*	115.43	†	104.86	110.56	106.63	†	114.56
6	*	99.77	99.37	†	117.68	115.23		105.36	110.56	*	113.05	112.91
7	96.48	99.11	99.30	*	117.05	115.24		105.80	106.17	106.20	113.34	112.00
8	95.45	99.28	99.34	105.65	111.62	111.53	110.61	106.68		106.77	113.74	*
9	96.84	99.02	99.55	107.13	103.37		112.16	106.38	108.36	106.96	114.23	112.23
10	96.24	*	*	108.39	110.06	114.45	109.64	106.05	109.58	108.38	*	111.91
11	97.18	99.06	99.55	107.68	†	114.39	108.23	*	108.52	109.48	114.56	111.00
12	97.85	†	99.78	108.43		114.91	106.43	106.42	108.60	108.62	113.90	110.08
13	*	97.98	100.09	109.25	109.63	116.52	106.80	107.73	105.30	*	113.93	110.58
14	96.86	93.29	100.25	*	104.54	116.73	*	108.13	†	108.93	112.35	110.75
15	96.45	99.33	100.61	109.02	106.74	117.55	106.35	109.15		108.63	113.47	
16	96.03	98.86	101.50	109.49	107.85	*	107.11	108.61	109.01	108.59	113.55	110.96
17	95.52			109.36	110.25	117.65	110.13	107.83	108.92	108.87		111.82
18	94.65	97.95	102.53	110.35	110.09	116.73	111.50		110.10	109.05	113.01	112.18
19	93.56	97.64	102.88	111.83	*	116.46	109.68	108.40	†	109.15	112.86	111.96
20	*	97.11	102.66	112.68	108.79	116.30	108.08	109.13	110.30	*	113.00	112.81
21	94.16	97.39	102.95	*	109.54	117.18	*	109.19	110.82	108.98	114.38	112.93
22	94.90	†	103.00	111.71	109.36	116.83	105.81	109.86	*	110.00	115.21	
23	95.00	†	103.25	111.05	108.65	*	107.65	110.52	109.90	110.83	114.94	112.45
24	93.90	*	*	111.89	108.99	117.08	106.68	111.35	109.86	110.70		112.27
25	94.83	97.36	102.58	112.89	108.71	116.20	107.15	*	107.96	110.67	114.70	†
26	95.79	97.71	102.85	113.70	*	115.78	107.68	111.69	108.48	110.88	114.83	113.28
27	*	97.76	103.45	†	108.53	115.46	107.93	110.66	109.29	*	114.98	113.97
28	95.75	97.34	103.70	*	109.31	116.39	*	110.68	109.22	109.60	†	114.28
29	95.75		104.54	115.66	110.16	117.21	108.33	111.00	*	110.61	114.57	*
30	96.08		105.03	116.35	*	†	107.76	111.54	108.21	111.03	114.20	114.21
31	97.16		*		112.15		107.39		†	110.79		114.85
High	97.85	99.77	105.03	116.35	117.86	117.65	115.35	111.69	110.92	111.03	115.21	114.85
Low	92.66	97.11	97.80	105.48	103.37	114.39	105.81	104.86	105.30	106.20	111.38	110.08

*Sunday
†Holiday

1901—DAILY STOCK SALES ON N. Y. STOCK EXCHANGE
(000 Omitted)

Date	Jan.	Feb.	Mar.	Apr.	May	June	July	Aug.	Sept.	Oct.	Nov.	Dec.
1	†	1565	790	1717	2823	936	399	447	*	338	457	*
2	1606	†	384	1622	2855	*	188	363	†	489	353	841
3	1588	*	*	1843	2945	1788	332	160	504	411	*	709
4	1808	1401	875	1864	983	1488	*	*	484	593	442	733
5	1182	1472	1002	†	*	1442	†	659	497	246	†	653
6	*	1884	1116	†	2255	975	†	423	310	*	1024	754
7	3138	1737	862	*	2040	740	*	313	900	728	1208	699
8	1453	1414	906	1748	2464	506	1095	413	*	517	925	*
9	1671	583	492	1385	3123	*	858	310	813	378	500	1034
10	1270	*	*	1904	1892	829	895	143	778	656	*	723
11	1085	1014	780	1682	*	688	1196	*	497	974	1087	688
12	1037	†	778	1398	*	627	1088	288	409	499	936	963
13	*	1114	902	765	1135	950	495	428	1081	*	749	613
14	1189	853	880	*	1207	1098	*	464	†	514	998	344
15	1128	911	1209	1627	1437	438	957	467	*	716	663	*
16	1248	537	741	1766	921	*	622	472	991	466	429	505
17	1046			1644	966	1077	1035	144	769	433	*	540
18	1241	1169	1629	1659	607	965	1013	*	709	521	649	706
19	635	805	1637	2174	*	730	1071	275	†	201	785	481
20	*	779	1265	1134	971	485	374	445	646	*	650	680
21	1150	694	1222	*	653	634	*	398	345	300	710	299
22	920	†	1335	2355	770	241	793	377	*	378	1179	*
23	1067	†	601	1765	860	*	666	650	819	788	593	509
24	770	*	*	1992	732	492	500	434	739	820	*	642
25	632	1068	1324	2067	285	754	462	*	81	655	1207	†
26	549	1109	1162	1658	*	529	432	785	631	337	758	741
27	*	960	1437	†	523	659	247	752	528	*	746	900
28	1010	843	1476	*	632	426	*	462	285	665	†	421
29	802		1475	2620	850	298	573	295	*	525	788	*
30	1065		781	3281	†	*	329	405	474	551	474	834
31	1067		*		1396		431	†		338		740
Total	30,285	21,903	27,061	41,719	35,292	19,796	16,052	10,772	13,290	14,036	18,310	16,751

*Sunday. †Holiday.

1902—INDUSTRIALS

Date:	Jan.	Feb.	Mar.	Apr.	May	June	July	Aug.	Sept.	Oct.	Nov.	Dec.
1	†	65.04	65.13	67.20	67.11	*	64.25	65.91	†	66.45	65.80	62.53
2	64.32	*	*	67.17	65.89	66.26	64.76	65.83	66.55	66.44	*	62.22
3	64.25	64.77	65.30	67.01	66.25	66.17	64.89	*	66.64	66.58	65.55	62.06
4	64.59	64.62	64.77	66.82	*	65.96	†	65.96	66.60	66.60	†	61.90
5	*	64.96	64.97	66.84	66.06	65.32		66.12	66.80	*	64.55	61.76
6	64.90	64.92	66.16	*	67.01	65.46	*	66.47	66.56	64.21	64.37	61.73
7	64.22	65.31	65.56	66.60	66.36	65.49	65.09	66.52	*	63.84	64.19	*
8	64.87	64.94	65.60	66.60	66.66	*	64.51	66.53	67.12	64.28	62.90	62.14
9	64.08	*	*	66.76	66.40	65.68	64.27	†	67.03	65.06	*	62.19
10	63.85	64.82	65.11	65.95	65.95	66.11	64.65	*	66.89	64.76	62.35	60.71
11	64.02	65.16	65.32	66.18	*	66.20	64.50	66.19	66.67	63.84	60.96	59.97
12	*	†	64.88	66.33	65.51	65.94	64.45	66.07	66.05	*	61.61	60.19
13	63.31	64.58	65.26	*	65.90	65.94	*	66.48	66.30	64.17	61.81	59.85
14	62.57	64.61	65.38	66.03	65.95	66.05	64.64	66.78	*	65.02	60.62	*
15	63.16	64.65	65.59	66.46	66.06	*	64.79	66.59	66.11	65.37	61.60	59.57
16	63.59	*	*	66.86	65.35	65.90	65.55	66.50	66.40	66.10	*	59.71
17	64.02	65.30	65.59	67.44	64.85	65.89	65.90	*	66.89	66.57	62.19	60.10
18	63.54	64.81	65.92	67.75	*	65.43	66.03	66.38	67.25	66.50	61.61	61.18
19	*	65.53	66.50	67.61	64.73	64.91	66.04	66.46	67.77	66.10	61.69	61.36
20	63.45	64.68	67.25	*	65.33	64.76	*	66.28	67.40	66.58	62.04	61.87
21	63.44	64.98	67.52	67.10	65.86	64.78	66.01	65.33	*	65.81	62.94	*
22	63.54	†	67.31	66.20	65.88	*	66.44	65.80	66.91	65.89	62.87	62.67
23	64.01	*	*	66.84	66.44	64.20	66.50	65.80	65.45	65.78	*	62.00
24	64.13	65.30	67.30	68.44	66.82	63.67	66.37	*	65.42	66.37	62.79	62.61
25	63.90	65.53	67.01	67.62	*	63.82	66.59	65.87	65.81	66.44	62.15	†
26	*	65.20	67.25	67.63	66.46	64.04	66.59	65.79	66.34	*	61.41	63.21
27	64.17	65.27	67.21	*	66.25	63.73	*	66.19	66.28	66.06	†	63.69
28	65.17	64.81	†	67.31	66.21	63.87	67.28	66.28	*	65.92	62.14	*
29	64.76		†	67.37	66.42	*	66.51	66.28	64.07	65.13	62.05	63.30
30	64.87		*	67.01	†	64.31	66.56	†	66.15	65.43	*	63.96
31	64.95		67.19				65.82	*		66.05		64.29
High	65.17	65.58	67.52	68.44	67.11	66.26	67.28	66.78	67.77	66.58	65.80	64.29
Low	62.57	64.58	64.77	65.95	64.73	63.67	64.25	65.33	64.07	63.84	60.62	59.57

*Sunday
†Holiday

1902—RAILROADS

Date:	Jan.	Feb.	Mar.	Apr.	May	June	July	Aug.	Sept.	Oct.	Nov.	Dec.
1	†	114.06	113.65	115.78	121.86	*	120.67	125.78	†	124.61	121.29	118.51
2	115.85	*	*	115.84	119.75	119.19	120.90	125.33	127.96	124.19	*	117.57
3	115.08	113.69	114.25	117.13	120.32	119.00	121.66	*	128.55	123.93	120.75	117.47
4	114.95	114.03	113.69	117.56	*	118.99	†	125.43	127.87	122.51	†	116.76
5	*	114.78	114.23	117.48	119.52	118.35		125.73	128.28	*	119.13	116.59
6	115.40	115.73	114.98	*	121.28	118.38	*	126.04	127.93	120.99	119.39	116.45
7	114.34	115.72	114.55	116.58	120.66	118.47	122.21	126.60	*	119.98	119.41	*
8	114.58	115.60	114.45	117.18	120.86	*	122.53	126.51	128.68	120.58	117.26	116.94
9	114.06	*	*	117.65	120.36	118.53	122.39	†	129.36	121.88	*	116.59
10	113.63	115.88	113.71	116.95	119.51	119.31	122.52	*	129.07	120.98	116.79	114.60
11	113.89	115.80	113.70	117.03	*	119.56	122.98	125.38	128.82	119.33	115.25	113.08
12	*	†	114.07	117.36	118.31	119.46	123.17	125.42	127.50	*	115.86	114.01
13	112.92	115.13	114.19	*	119.23	120.21	*	125.73	127.91	118.97	115.76	113.08
14	111.73	115.35	114.65	118.12	119.53	120.40	123.98	126.29	*	120.56	113.70	*
15	112.41	115.21	115.07	118.80	119.94	*	124.06	125.75	127.49	120.95	115.21	113.21
16	112.40	*	*	118.93	118.28	120.61	124.78	125.59	127.77	122.70	*	113.59
17	113.51	115.55	115.44	119.74	117.76	120.76	125.02	*	128.16	123.93	115.68	114.03
18	113.18	115.27	115.64	120.18	*	121.45	125.59	125.31	128.80	123.43	114.81	116.13
19	*	115.50	115.66	120.38	117.46	120.58	125.91	125.93	128.68	*	116.00	115.91
20	112.68	113.63	115.71	*	118.46	120.71	*	126.48	128.31	123.38	116.65	116.06
21	112.68	113.96	116.41	119.67	119.00	120.60	125.06	125.53	*	122.21	118.39	*
22	112.71	†	116.32	118.96	119.25	*	125.52	126.22	127.68	122.33	118.32	117.33
23	113.18	*	*	118.85	119.57	120.31	126.17	126.31	125.23	121.94	*	116.47
24	112.93	113.99	116.48	119.80	119.58	119.63	126.33	*	124.70	122.25	118.50	117.19
25	112.45	114.43	115.98	120.17	*	119.72	127.08	127.10	125.01	122.28	117.30	†
26	*	113.97	115.87	120.24	118.88	120.11	127.16	126.98	125.78	*	116.45	117.92
27	112.60	114.05	115.66	*	118.91	120.22	*	126.91	124.98	121.10	†	118.05
28	113.82	113.65	†	120.80	118.91	120.58	126.45	126.70	*	121.13	117.78	*
29	113.38		†	121.63	119.32	*	125.56	127.23	120.41	120.10	117.48	117.12
30	113.99		*	121.26	†	120.38	126.03	†	124.78	120.68	*	118.42
31	114.19		116.08		†		125.85	*		121.68		118.98
High	115.85	115.88	116.48	121.63	121.86	121.45	127.16	127.23	129.36	124.61	121.29	118.98
Low	111.73	113.63	113.65	115.78	117.46	118.35	120.67	125.31	120.41	118.97	113.70	113.08

*Sunday
†Holiday

1902—DAILY STOCK SALES ON N. Y. STOCK EXCHANGE
(000 Omitted)

Date	Jan.	Feb.	Mar.	Apr.	May	June	July	Aug.	Sept.	Oct.	Nov.	Dec.
1	†	228	196	437	801	*	279	357	†	974	160	673
2	1026	*	*	411	984	273	288	135	1186	490	*	704
3	1034	713	361	669	599	184	367	*	1473	880	390	461
4	426	457	383	1069	*	188	†	340	1106	398	†	379
5	*	592	530	399	765	389	†	311	878	*	583	370
6	878	774	576	*	889	233	*	447	405	962	649	167
7	903	701	609	638	1156	56	390	652	*	897	441	*
8	869	343	203	712	630	*	575	626	899	610	673	282
9	695	*	*	990	446	178	489	†	1131	731	*	245
10	575	732	597	1195	289	276	629	*	1222	369	1391	570
11	245	862	561	781	*	382	504	620	1027	316	998	1180
12	*	†	678	448	651	266	194	414	725	*	1252	1092
13	598	883	573	*	497	330	*	491	297	1023	709	402
14	692	653	478	1022	366	149	670	677	637	821	1369	*
15	614	271	268	1767	304	*	750	623	637	605	661	854
16	395	*	*	1321	445	399	823	219	423	1017	*	645
17	541	471	601	1387	339	401	1138	*	454	1098	722	628
18	312	605	626	1573	*	741	1072	381	472	510	645	949
19	*	532	594	890	599	592	457	568	842	*	905	789
20	546	1041	589	*	517	362	*	900	441	636	768	279
21	418	571	632	1995	551	161	908	864	*	615	1085	*
22	308	†	371	1580	594	*	804	617	650	446	527	746
23	394	*	*	1187	361	479	927	418	1076	393	*	592
24	460	630	650	1248	232	504	946	*	1358	302	867	365
25	249	470	553	1400	*	272	936	957	806	205	871	†
26	*	617	422	475	512	296	389	1300	708	*	684	690
27	436	416	489	*	314	268	*	991	520	440	†	371
28	581	425	†	1013	361	139	806	650	*	314	540	*
29	615		†	888	321	*	745	758	1039	545	237	569
30	488		*	1042		315	664	†	1197	359	*	708
31	483		418		†		577			406		1008
Total	14,779	2,987	11,957	26,538	13,522	7,835	16,327	14,315	20,972	16,361	17,126	15,719

*Sunday. †Holiday.

1903—INDUSTRIALS

Date:	Jan.	Feb.	Mar.	Apr.	May	June	July	Aug.	Sept.	Oct.	Nov.	Dec.
1	†	*	*	63.47	63.84	59.59	58.81	50.75	52.75	47.06	*	44.35
2	64.60	65.53	66.01	62.63	63.86	59.87	58.08	*	52.60	47.62	45.46	45.50
3	64.65	66.06	65.68	62.55	*	59.90	58.21	50.57	51.85	47.53	†	46.23
4	*	66.40	65.81	62.28	64.06	58.86	†	49.22	51.93	*	44.90	46.50
5	65.38	66.55	64.70	*	64.01	58.53	*	47.98	†	47.05	43.60	46.06
6	65.88	66.38	64.82	62.40	63.89	58.50	58.08	49.36	*	47.23	43.94	*
7	65.73	66.47	64.13	62.09	63.55	*	57.84	48.64	†	46.96	43.71	47.40
8	66.33	*	*	62.28	63.70	57.97	57.95	47.38	51.53	45.51	*	47.34
9	66.21	67.10	64.42	62.32	63.55	57.37	56.97	*	51.39	45.34	42.15	47.34
10	65.85	67.22	63.90	†	*	56.78	56.61	48.06	51.00	44.71	43.34	46.35
11	*	67.19	64.28	†	63.76	58.28	55.89	48.67	50.93	*	42.83	46.12
12	65.65	†	63.92	*	63.50	59.38	*	50.31	50.80	43.67	42.93	46.03
13	64.98	66.93	64.11	60.79	63.63	58.94	56.12	51.36	*	43.20	43.41	*
14	64.89	67.05	64.31	62.12	63.15	*	54.92	52.80	50.16	42.42	43.13	46.70
15	64.50	*	*	62.14	63.01	57.75	54.37	52.97	50.30	42.25	*	46.83
16	64.80	67.70	64.19	62.87	62.69	57.84	54.10	*	49.82	44.41	43.36	46.86
17	65.07	67.69	64.51	63.84	*	57.55	54.73	53.88	49.44	45.07	43.50	46.70
18	*	67.32	64.86	64.14	62.12	56.89	54.10	53.61	48.73	*	44.20	47.16
19	64.52	66.69	65.40	*	62.28	57.48	*	51.43	48.50	43.19	44.53	47.33
20	64.19	67.26	65.75	64.43	61.25	57.12	52.76	51.76	*	44.75	44.19	*
21	65.00	†	65.69	64.56	61.95	*	51.45	51.45	48.45	45.10	44.15	46.95
22	64.83	*	*		62.56	56.65	52.01	51.63	48.43	44.77	*	46.63
23	64.30	†	65.39	64.21	61.40	57.61	50.83	*	47.75	44.59	44.55	47.55
24	64.31	67.43	64.43	64.07	*	57.60	49.84	51.36	46.62	44.48	43.64	47.75
25	*	67.09	63.96	63.79	60.67	57.31	49.08	52.27	46.64	*	43.91	†
26	64.90	66.52	64.15	*	61.53	57.27	*	52.32	46.19	45.33	†	†
27	65.36	66.16	63.45	63.48	61.16	57.64	50.11	52.38	*	45.41	44.25	*
28	65.37	66.19	63.44	63.77	60.52	*	51.52	53.02	45.09	45.46	44.14	48.64
29	65.55		*	64.09	60.27	58.77	51.02	53.17	46.67	45.21	*	49.35
30	64.96		62.86	63.78	†	59.08	52.72	*	45.80	44.82	44.33	49.06
31	65.18		63.64		*		50.76	53.19		45.13		49.11
High	66.33	67.70	66.01	64.56	64.06	59.90	58.81	53.88	52.75	47.62	45.46	49.35
Low	64.19	65.53	62.86	60.79	60.27	56.65	49.08	47.38	45.09	42.25	42.15	44.35

*Sunday
†Holiday

1903—RAILROADS

Date:	Jan.	Feb.	Mar.	Apr.	May	June	July	Aug.	Sept.	Oct.	Nov.	Dec.
1	†	*	*	110.01	109.56	103.35	104.01	96.37	97.46	91.45	*	94.41
2	119.17	119.33	114.58	109.15	109.55	104.20	102.91	*	97.67	92.77	93.23	94.36
3	119.05	119.26	113.91	109.60	*	104.23	103.05	95.90	96.99	91.99	†	95.60
4	*	119.86	114.34	109.16	110.82	102.69	†	93.84	97.90	*	92.68	95.79
5	119.56	120.00	112.22	*	110.62	102.45	*	91.93	†	91.19	91.41	95.42
6	121.02	119.55	113.20	109.42	110.73	102.44	103.06	93.32	*	91.01	91.75	*
7	120.20	119.58	111.38	109.14	110.03	*	103.07	92.89	†	91.31	92.18	96.28
8	121.00	*	*	109.34	109.93	101.41	103.20	90.70	97.20	90.13	*	96.10
9	121.28	120.19	111.82	108.91	109.23	100.46	101.83	*	97.41	90.21	92.15	96.56
10	121.00	120.03	110.51	†	*	99.40	100.53	91.79	97.05	89.90	91.76	95.60
11	*	119.89	111.82	†	109.61	102.18	99.56	92.54	97.37	*	90.98	95.48
12	120.43	†	111.54	*	109.47	103.88	*	94.66	96.83	89.63	90.10	95.20
13	120.44	119.92	111.60	105.75	109.24	103.58	99.58	96.13	*	89.65	91.05	*
14	120.33	119.50	111.77	107.36	108.55	*	97.89	98.26	95.20	89.36	90.71	96.23
15	119.89	*	*	107.20	107.98	101.91	97.10	97.96	95.50	89.76	*	96.41
16	120.30	119.80	110.93	108.36	107.75	102.48	97.77	*	95.09	91.85	91.26	96.40
17	120.45	119.35	111.26	108.86	*	102.26	99.20	98.60	94.81	91.88	91.45	95.90
18	*	117.81	112.06	109.11	106.68	101.81	98.50	98.84	94.33	*	92.54	96.55
19	119.63	117.04	112.86	*	107.05	102.45	*	96.88	93.91	89.81	93.43	96.57
20	119.12	117.80	113.62	109.84	105.68	102.25	97.28	96.88	*	91.45	93.00	*
21	120.10	†	113.48	110.42	106.59	*	96.99	95.86	94.01	91.96	92.53	96.58
22	119.77	*	*		106.93	101.70	97.81	96.53	93.80	92.01	*	96.59
23	118.83	†	112.58	109.98	105.12	102.18	95.92	*	92.80	91.52	93.12	97.58
24	118.81	117.26	111.23	110.06	*	101.83	95.40	96.52	91.26	91.58	92.61	97.78
25	*	116.82	110.48	109.68	103.77	101.63	95.00	97.41	91.95	*	92.91	†
26	119.78	115.86	110.59	108.77	105.10	101.43	*	97.28	90.51	92.84	†	†
27	119.43	115.19	109.11	108.77	104.96	102.03	97.00	96.93	*	93.25	93.07	*
28	119.29	115.19	109.38	108.65	104.20	*	97.08	97.41	88.80	93.10	93.06	98.88
29	119.53		*	109.53	103.78	103.63	97.01	97.56	91.27	92.63	*	98.94
30	118.86		108.76	108.86	†	103.67	96.72	*		92.65	92.80	98.36
31	119.06		109.98		*		96.48	98.05		92.81		98.33
High	121.28	120.19	114.58	110.42	110.82	104.23	104.01	98.84	97.90	93.25	93.80	98.94
Low	118.81	115.19	108.76	105.75	103.77	99.40	95.00	90.70	88.80	89.36	90.10	94.36

*Sunday
†Holiday

1903—DAILY STOCK SALES ON N. Y. STOCK EXCHANGE
(000 Omitted)

Date	Jan.	Feb.	Mar.	Apr.	May	June	July	Aug.	Sept.	Oct.	Nov.	Dec.
1	†	*	*	418	224	510	370	140	223	732	*	522
2	818	529	500	293	135	738	264	*	314	751	185	600
3	275	521	877	746	*	750	160	190	260	239	†	930
4	*	598	426	253	409	760	†	651	217	*	398	1126
5	790	745	912	*	502	878	*	984	†	438	555	345
6	1056	438	788	472	342	307	179	973	*	300	589	*
7	996	303	408	390	464	*	233	545	†	530	213	719
8	1168	*	*	321	316	841	151	426	279	673	*	1052
9	1521	383	967	717	185	879	437	*	183	566	435	878
10	569	772	783	†	*	325	803	793	283	244	844	926
11	*	500	691	†	344	926	410	524	315	*	759	812
12	718	†	471	*	353	928	*	777	131	764	764	346
13	899	666	416	1259	493	473	917	1119	*	529	565	*
14	787	114	218	882	399	*	733	934	500	459	245	573
15	513	*	*	664	441	679	1233	394	609	428	*	546
16	452	473	597	510	221	771	811	*	311	926	505	318
17	235	473	411	738	*	656	681	729	461	424	404	407
18	*	395	519	280	648	499	238	1131	321	*	425	446
19	529	529	580	*	551	489	*	849	274	685	558	287
20	457	394	527	679	801	204	731	640	*	565	637	*
21	504	†	246	681	766	*	816	575	414	657	194	432
22	424	*	*	†	604	333	721	132	279	459	*	229
23	428	†	316	484	388	341	658	*	468	383	450	381
24	199	441	444	404	*	353	1319	278	794	103	494	363
25	*	496	490	238	1106	212	474	253	898	*	345	†
26	319	458	540	*	641	188	*	204	349	367	†	†
27	432	656	867	378	587	146	660	161	*	775	447	*
28	297	338	450	515	883	*	642	283	946	392	135	680
29	398		*	396	476	646	490	115	922	280	*	868
30	414		616	340	†	636	471	*	731	152	428	674
31	144		710		*		271	470		72		380
Total	15,344	10,223	14,772	12,057	12,279	15,471	14,875	14,272	10,482	12,897	10,575	14,841

*Sunday. †Holiday.

1904—INDUSTRIALS

Date:	Jan.	Feb.	Mar.	Apr.	May	June	July	Aug.	Sept.	Oct.	Nov.	Dec.
1	†	49.03	47.86	†	*	48.26	49.31	52.73	54.94	58.05	63.72	72.05
2	47.38	48.69	47.87	49.08	48.42	48.10	†	52.68	55.15	*	64.76	72.46
3	*	48.40	48.00	*	48.33	48.17	*	52.75	†	58.65	64.87	72.86
4	47.77	48.35	47.90	48.68	48.60		†	52.70	*	58.27	65.31	*
5	48.09	47.87	47.28	48.89	48.56	*	49.62	52.85	†	58.18	65.25	73.23
6	47.07	47.65	*	49.30	48.71	48.08	50.09	52.90	55.38	57.59	*	72.57
7	47.16	*	47.18	49.98	48.59	48.27	49.96	*	55.68	57.96	66.21	68.97
8	47.92	48.10	47.72	49.59	*	48.60	50.44	52.73	55.94	58.22	†	68.00
9	48.02	46.98	47.04	49.65	48.71	48.66	50.84	53.03	56.54	*	67.07	69.22
10	*	47.76	46.93	*	48.42	49.06	*	53.13	57.43	58.75	67.58	70.01
11	47.82	48.16	46.46	49.98	48.30	49.12	50.67	53.28	*	59.03	68.03	*
12	47.63	†	46.41	49.58	47.93	*	51.37	53.39	56.46	59.23	68.19	65.77
13	47.77	48.11	*	49.73	47.72	48.88	51.73	54.03	56.32	60.16	*	66.42
14	47.85	*	46.50	49.41	47.72	49.05	51.87	*	57.10	61.42	68.78	66.17
15	47.97	48.86	47.73	49.35	*	48.86	52.06	53.98	56.66	62.07	69.17	66.62
16	48.08	48.39	47.77	49.38	47.56	48.83	52.50	53.54	57.19	*	69.11	68.73
17	*	48.16	48.30	*	47.67	48.73	*	54.08	56.58	62.06	70.08	68.47
18	48.82	47.90	47.91	49.33	47.43	48.89	52.50	54.25	*	62.16	69.69	*
19	48.65	47.51	48.76	48.92	47.45	*	52.96	53.76	56.55	61.72	70.01	68.48
20	48.58	47.31	*	48.62	47.53	48.97	52.80	53.35	55.67	62.12	*	69.09
21	49.38	*	48.26	49.10	48.06	49.03	52.47	*	56.00	62.35	70.62	68.38
22	49.94	†	48.50	49.09	*	49.46	52.65	53.13	55.72	62.97	69.80	67.87
23	49.91	46.86	48.62	49.12	48.53	49.47	53.14	53.91	56.31	*	69.89	68.47
24	*	46.71	48.16	*	48.01	49.32	*	54.13	56.50	63.17	†	†
25	49.61	47.47	48.15	48.65	48.14	49.12	52.98	54.41	*	62.68	70.83	*
26	50.18	47.14	48.21	48.81	48.23	*	52.27	54.44	56.91	62.63	71.56	†
27	50.50	47.08	*	48.95	48.26	49.29	52.43	54.47	57.14	61.97	*	69.13
28	49.42	*	48.68	48.86	†	49.12	52.39	*	57.44	63.39	72.36	70.20
29	49.11	47.53	48.60	48.90	*	49.08	52.12	54.61	57.11	64.54	72.35	71.07
30	48.91		48.77	48.80	†	49.25	52.13	54.44	57.59	*	72.02	70.05
31	*		49.12		48.18		*	54.57		63.03		69.61
High	50.50	49.03	49.12	49.98	48.71	49.47	53.14	54.61	57.59	64.54	72.36	73.23
Low	47.07	46.71	46.41	48.62	47.43	48.08	49.31	52.68	54.94	57.59	63.72	65.77

*Sunday
†Holiday

1904—RAILROADS

Date·	Jan.	Feb.	Mar.	Apr.	May	June	July	Aug.	Sept.	Oct.	Nov.	Dec.
1	†	97.70	92.61	†	*	94.33	97.53	101.20	105.31	109.11	113.30	118.68
2	96.30	97.55	92.80	95.96	95.22	94.15	†	100.85	106.31	*	114.06	119.33
3	*	96.96	92.90	*	95.37	94.41	*	101.29	†	109.19	113.95	119.46
4	96.55	96.61	93.09	96.04	95.60	94.41	†	101.30	*	109.56	113.78	*
5	97.08	95.50	92.40	96.25	95.17	*	98.63	101.51	†	110.00	113.47	119.36
6	95.61	95.50	*	96.93	95.36	94.54	99.55	101.60	107.12	109.23	*	118.67
7	95.88	*	92.77	97.15	95.23	94.80	98.72	*	106.81	109.68	114.37	116.82
8	96.65	93.90	92.36	96.81	*	95.13	99.47	101.50	107.28	110.31	†	116.26
9	97.23	94.75	92.33	96.98	95.23	95.43	99.63	101.98	107.83	*	115.28	116.94
10	*	94.05	92.31	*	94.87	95.77	*	102.25	108.12	110.32	115.32	117.31
11	97.33	94.06	91.66	97.58	94.93	96.04	99.26	102.99	*	110.85	116.72	*
12	96.39	†	91.53	96.75	94.45	*	100.40	103.13	106.91	110.92	116.92	113.53
13	96.67	94.11	*	97.13	94.10	95.66	100.79	103.56	106.81	110.95	*	114.00
14	96.85	*	91.31	96.57	93.83	96.48	100.50	*	107.86	112.31	116.31	113.78
15	96.81	94.54	93.10	96.57	*	96.04	100.89	104.02	107.67	113.06	117.21	114.60
16	96.80	94.61	93.33	96.35	93.55	96.26	101.11	103.83	107.89	*	116.82	116.07
17	*	94.23	94.35	*	93.90	95.86	*	104.15	107.38	113.22	117.46	116.15
18	97.73	93.76	93.81	96.22	93.88	96.16	101.62	104.48	*	113.58	116.85	*
19	98.21	93.51	95.08	95.96	93.75	*	102.24	103.98	106.90	113.40	117.00	116.16
20	98.45	93.18	*	95.96	94.11	96.45	102.21	103.31	106.30	113.69	*	116.91
21	99.43	*	94.51	96.65	94.74	96.85	101.85	*	107.05	114.60	117.27	115.94
22	99.76	†	95.86	96.85	*	97.17	102.01	104.50	106.43	114.78	116.41	115.30
23	99.78	92.17	95.88	96.90	95.20	97.23	102.06	104.40	106.96	*	116.54	115.92
24	*	91.83	94.90	*	94.90	97.25	*	104.71	107.01	114.72	†	†
25	98.73	92.65	94.65	96.37	94.39	97.17	101.60	105.30	*	114.63	117.01	*
26	99.26	92.18	94.80	96.45	94.43	*	100.80	105.32	107.53	114.04	117.54	†
27	99.50	92.13	*	96.68	94.41	97.05	99.75	105.50	107.97	113.01	*	116.85
28	98.21	*	95.92	96.57	†	97.00	101.21	*	108.32	114.42	118.22	117.68
29	98.06	92.28	96.50	96.14	*	97.30	100.81	106.10	108.00	115.20	118.27	118.55
30	97.90		96.35	96.04	†	97.32	100.52	105.83	108.78	*	118.93	117.90
31	*		96.49		94.36		*	105.22		113.36		117.43
High	99.78	97.70	96.50	97.58	95.60	97.32	102.24	106.10	108.78	115.20	118.93	119.46
Low	95.61	91.83	91.31	95.96	93.55	94.15	97.53	100.85	105.31	109.11	113.30	113.53

*Sunday
†Holiday

1904—DAILY STOCK SALES ON N. Y. STOCK EXCHANGE

(000 Omitted)

Date	Jan.	Feb.	Mar.	Apr.	May	June	July	Aug.	Sept.	Oct.	Nov.	Dec.
1	†	1292	171	†	*	157	194	249	574	411	1380	1314
2	435	391	126	107	294	133	†	323	561	*	1398	1747
3	*	436	128		287	128	*	250	†	1009	1102	869
4	622	485	192	573	208	51	†	299	*	1350	1185	*
5	467	493	137	627	178	*	348	242	†	1332	436	1659
6	727	358	*	597	127	210	810	88	847	1000	*	1493
7	414	*	288	711	39	178	547	*	906	758	1181	2310
8	402	945	292	529	*	252	452	340	951	282	†	2881
9	266	581	180	162	109	123	239	339	979	*	2328	1646
10	*	665	70	*	143	325	*	498	561	818	1633	852
11	477	271	147	461	130	128	458	750	*	862	1755	*
12	311	†	170	474	410	*	534	600	1274	912	824	2053
13	208	95	*	378	388	279	831	314	1070	820	*	1597
14	331	*	440	359	176	277	689	*	1101	1495	1537	1185
15	384	173	475	283	*	457	848	849	1128	882	1562	733
16	102	250	577	101	465	296	324	606	942	*	1389	919
17	*	308	559	*	484	217	*	584	360	1835	1678	656
18	446	220	603	264	159	77	796	683	*	1510	1534	*
19	505	234	333	430	171	*	663	496	543	1749	584	615
20	563	180	*	352	141	240	883	266	998	1300	*	559
21	928	*	606	310	146	197	739	*	643	1893	1153	859
22	952	†	1033	254	*	209	418	475	578	989	1369	422
23	377	447	1319	71	337	213	141	503	450	*	1181	289
24	*	488	603	*	241	225	*	488	291	1890	†	†
25	755	362	633	262	210	87	413	567	*	1981	1351	*
26	478	296	95	190	128	*	545	493	764	1742	869	†
27	584	97	*	152	122	147	606	222	770	1750	*	494
28	677	*	293	165	†	87	524	*	885	1391	1592	829
29	394	168	569	181	*	105	382	706	805	1050	1492	1113
30	245		692	67	†	168	79	701	827	*	1466	1104
31	*		385		137		*	552		1569		494
Total	12,052	9,240	11,121	8,059	5,231	4,966	12,462	12,485	18,807	32,574	31,981	28,693

*Sunday.   †Holiday.

1905—INDUSTRIALS

Date:	Jan.	Feb.	Mar.	Apr.	May	June	July	Aug.	Sept.	Oct.	Nov.	Dec.
1	*	70.91	76.06	80.67	76.90	73.17	77.48	81.35	79.66	*	84.14	89.62
2	†	71.19	76.81	*	77.77	73.31	*	81.31	79.71	82.17	83.92	89.50
3	70.39	71.47	75.92	81.13	76.51	73.43	78.70	81.63	*	82.62	83.78	*
4	70.22	71.53	76.14	81.31	74.68	*	†	81.90	†	82.38	82.93	89.56
5	70.23	*	*	82.17	76.82	73.51	78.65	81.75	80.73	82.78	*	90.82
6	69.46	71.80	76.33	82.76	76.17	72.53	79.33	*	78.92	82.55	83.32	90.91
7	69.23	72.63	76.02	83.12	*	72.94	79.54	82.20	78.60	82.02	†	92.37
8	*	72.54	76.29	82.45	74.52	73.05	79.47	81.90	79.78	*	82.17	93.20
9	69.52	72.26	77.36	*	75.78	73.27	*	81.83	79.02	81.65	81.56	92.84
10	70.10	73.27	77.88	82.20	76.34	74.68	79.47	82.03	*	82.02	82.57	*
11	70.03	73.34	77.72	81.93	77.15	*	78.02	82.20	79.06	80.83	82.25	93.59
12	69.61	*	*	82.64	78.05	74.61	79.09	82.01	80.13	80.96	*	95.13
13	70.31	†	78.22	83.23	77.45	73.95	78.93	*	79.43	81.54	80.83	95.68
14	70.70	73.48	78.17	83.75	*	74.11	78.56	82.12	80.11	81.47	81.67	95.47
15	*	73.57	77.89	83.12	77.46	73.76	78.68	82.35	80.52	*	82.77	96.05
16	70.94	73.63	77.81	*	76.89	73.96	*	82.45	81.11	81.48	82.47	96.09
17	70.67	73.92	77.18	83.41	76.65	73.36	79.10	82.73	*	81.43	84.19	*
18	70.98	74.23	77.27	82.60	74.63	*	79.10	82.03	81.38	80.96	84.53	95.71
19	70.67	*	*	83.44	73.87	73.68	79.26	82.14	80.77	81.41	*	95.64
20	70.63	74.94	78.02	80.95	73.22	74.43	79.60	*	81.45	82.27	85.22	94.61
21	70.14	75.51	77.51	†	*	75.19	79.30	82.26	81.77	82.83	85.84	94.20
22	*	†	76.44	†	71.37	75.70	78.05	82.10	81.91	*	86.11	94.43
23	69.45	75.34	77.42	*	71.57	75.78	*	82.82	81.78	82.86	85.93	95.05
24	69.39	76.11	79.27	79.97	73.75	75.69	78.69	82.61	*	82.84	85.81	*
25	68.76	76.16	78.89	80.85	72.91	*	78.36	82.37	81.05	82.66	86.94	†
26	70.07	*	*	81.26	73.01	77.45	78.66	82.61	81.30	82.08	*	95.84
27	70.43	75.75	78.58	78.53	72.91	77.45	79.27	*	81.13	81.97	89.43	94.04
28	70.82	75.15	78.13	77.87	*	77.78	80.46	82.22	80.92	81.51	89.77	95.37
29	*		78.70	76.08	74.12	77.19	80.64	82.79	81.39	*	89.89	96.56
30	70.77		79.23	*	†	76.87	*	82.05	81.90	82.33	†	96.20
31	71.33		80.02		74.32		81.70	80.63		83.77		*
High	71.33	76.16	80.02	83.75	78.05	77.78	81.70	82.82	81.91	83.77	89.89	96.56
Low	68.76	70.91	75.92	76.08	71.37	72.53	77.48	80.63	78.60	80.83	80.83	89.50

*Sunday
†Holiday

1905—RAILROADS

Date:	Jan.	Feb.	Mar.	Apr.	May	June	July	Aug.	Sept.	Oct.	Nov.	Dec.
1	*	120.70	124.95	124.98	119.81	117.00	123.38	125.63	127.91	*	132.37	130.00
2	†	121.30	125.20	*	120.63	117.19	*	125.58	129.08	131.99	132.23	129.93
3	118.50	122.03	124.51	125.43	119.44	117.16	124.65	126.35	*	132.42	132.47	*
4	118.16	121.63	125.05	125.03	117.35	*	†	126.84	†	131.47	131.45	129.65
5	118.12	*	*	125.43	118.96	117.58	124.05	126.80	130.32	131.40	*	130.81
6	117.38	121.30	125.25	126.21	118.35	116.59	124.58	*	128.19	131.53	131.99	130.64
7	117.03	121.95	124.65	125.88	*	117.30	124.93	127.78	127.37	130.92	†	130.98
8	*	122.36	125.19	125.41	117.61	117.42	124.90	127.88	128.92	*	130.51	131.04
9	117.35	122.20	125.90	*	118.47	117.55	*	127.83	128.33	130.35	129.00	131.33
10	117.55	122.40	126.46	125.62	118.23	119.42	124.58	127.47	*	131.26	129.83	*
11	117.74	122.25	126.70	125.41	119.36	*	123.17	130.11	128.76	130.04	128.91	131.95
12	117.21	*	*	125.90	120.02	119.13	125.17	130.07	129.83	130.10	*	132.03
13	117.96	†	127.16	126.24	119.42	118.35	124.82	*	129.45	131.01	127.91	132.81
14	118.49	122.42	126.78	127.01	*	118.93	124.92	130.83	130.50	130.73	129.34	132.23
15	*	122.75	126.75	126.28	119.85	118.56	125.19	130.36	130.00	130.08	*	132.08
16	118.31	122.36	126.45	*	119.33	118.78	*	131.10	130.93	130.80	129.37	131.90
17	118.16	122.23	125.21	126.39	119.24	118.35	125.25	131.28	*	130.49	130.69	*
18	118.63	122.43	124.87	124.70	117.44	*	125.01	130.25	131.43	130.13	130.95	131.28
19	118.60	*	*	125.66	116.91	118.86	125.38	130.53	130.54	130.51	*	131.71
20	119.40	122.86	126.00	123.40	115.88	119.69	125.04	*	131.60	131.82	131.97	131.93
21	119.24	123.50	125.14	†	*	120.67	124.16	131.54	131.91	132.62	132.13	132.26
22	*	†	123.91	†	114.52	121.27	122.95	131.58	132.33	*	131.98	133.05
23	118.18	122.94	124.65	*	114.76	121.50	*	132.17	132.19	132.65	132.00	133.14
24	117.59	124.63	125.26	122.57	117.36	120.91	123.73	132.06	*	132.61	131.26	*
25	117.26	125.48	125.51	123.80	116.47	*	123.79	131.75	130.97	132.49	131.65	†
26	118.97	*	*	124.04	116.70	122.07	123.95	131.83	131.27	131.95	*	133.17
27	119.14	125.08	124.48	120.88	116.90	122.01	124.92	*	131.38	131.36	132.26	131.08
28	120.30	123.78	123.46	120.48	*	123.37	126.03	131.31	130.93	130.70	131.63	132.30
29	*		124.69	117.81	118.57	122.46	126.06	132.19		*	131.34	133.54
30	120.58		124.45	*	†	122.57	*	131.30	131.86	131.25	†	133.26
31	121.05		124.89		119.30		126.28	129.57		132.33		*
High	121.05	125.48	127.16	127.01	120.63	123.37	126.28	132.19	132.33	132.65	132.47	133.54
Low	117.03	120.70	123.46	117.81	114.52	116.59	122.95	125.58	127.37	130.04	127.91	129.65

*Sunday
†Holiday

1905—DAILY STOCK SALES ON N. Y. STOCK EXCHANGE
(000 Omitted)

Date	Jan.	Feb.	Mar.	Apr.	May	June	July	Aug.	Sept.	Oct.	Nov.	Dec.
1	*	936	1075	407	1683	522	327	589	857	*	1059	986
2	†	1096	1537	*	1019	777	*	469	319	675	1288	389
3	848	1349	1060	1155	950	249	851	451	*	689	1271	*
4	780	511	352	1095	1317	*	†	552	†	853	680	937
5	683	*	*	1094	950	563	1053	141	765	550	*	1159
6	858	954	1104	1550	317	446	817	*	1192	569	897	1195
7	334	964	753	1524	*	308	840	573	902	336	†	1174
8	*	1249	986	739	843	263	291	577	629	*	1125	1284
9	592	967	1299	*	555	182	*	533	314	716	1300	808
10	418	976	1555	1357	530	472	685	758	*	472	875	*
11	519	497	915	1115	622	*	786	1016	641	873	467	1926
12	486	*	*	1137	1045	622	611	430	934	702	*	1410
13	703	†	1643	1501	306	489	733	*	684	395	1072	1709
14	717	780	1378	1548	*	265	516	936	794	162	903	1806
15	*	1066	1088	675	584	134	161	759	506	*	955	1382
16	1261	952	1509	*	413	137	*	969	317	371	1284	724
17	823	834	1134	1158	634	86	435	1184	*	546	1080	*
18	1401	501	641	1442	1107	*	274	909	776	598	537	1646
19	938	*	*	1223	1115	196	352	256	548	728	*	1264
20	954	1535	1091	1885	622	406	496	*	753	930	1266	1374
21	489	1724	913	†	*	897	389	639	745	647	1320	1060
22	*	†	1260	†	1411	854	410	1043	857	*	1525	1315
23	932	1687	1399	*	952	866	*	1167	407	1067	1689	661
24	662	1266	1318	1712	910	286	413	1122	*	839	1340	*
25	1048	1258	636	1124	790	*	336	904	702	1184	557	†
26	776	*	1204	456		756	320	317	582	758	*	1600
27	921	1912	1027	1605	102	715	474	*	485	785	1718	1264
28	692	1672	1083	1625	*	733	728	820	421	548	1477	1520
29	*		886	1222	494	611	317	967	543	*	1137	1952
30	1292		650	*	†	476	*	897	339	668	†	983
31	1218		788		757		656	1229		1011		*
Total	20,343	24,688	29,079	29,098	20,484	12,313	13,274	20,206	16,012	17,675	26,824	31,528

*Sunday.   †Holiday.

1906—INDUSTRIALS

Date:	Jan.	Feb.	Mar.	Apr.	May	June	July	Aug.	Sept.	Oct.	Nov.	Dec.
1	†	101.55	93.83	*	88.03	94.01	*	93.72	94.42	95.77	93.80	95.16
2	95.00	101.71	93.86	97.84	87.16	94.38	86.12	93.37	*	95.42	94.28	*
3	95.63	99.77	93.85	98.19	86.45	*	86.64	92.44	†	95.22	94.17	95.35
4	94.44	*	*	97.48	89.08	95.19	†	91.67	93.31	94.66	*	95.23
5	96.09	100.05	92.90	97.00	89.75	95.04	86.58	*	93.77	95.48	94.60	95.27
6	97.09	100.39	94.00	97.09	*	95.21	87.79	92.85	94.63	95.88	†	94.82
7	*	99.60	94.09	96.56	90.78	95.12	87.97	92.97	94.22	*	93.93	95.30
8	98.03	99.50	94.69	*	92.08	94.50	*	92.10	94.50	96.53	93.58	95.19
9	97.85	99.93	96.43	95.93	92.86	93.99	87.87	91.70	*	96.75	93.37	*
10	98.09	99.76	96.33	95.05	93.21	*	87.26	91.92	94.55	96.51	93.32	95.58
11	99.06	*	*	96.44	93.41	94.38	86.37	92.03	93.53	96.65	*	95.89
12	100.25	†	96.40	96.02	93.13	94.10	85.70	*	92.53	95.38	92.38	95.36
13	99.79	100.08	96.96	96.51	*	93.63	85.18	92.53	95.27	96.04	93.06	94.10
14	*	99.27	96.44	97.02	92.80	92.91	85.40	92.70	95.89	*	94.01	94.82
15	100.80	97.88	95.79	*	93.06	92.25	*	92.94	95.53	95.78	94.25	95.46
16	100.81	97.31	95.33	97.01	93.77	91.02	86.45	92.59	*	96.14	94.76	*
17	101.67	96.51	95.10	96.84	93.05	*	86.91	93.38	95.63	95.78	95.20	94.50
18	102.26	*	*	95.67	92.75	90.66	86.54	95.34	95.84	95.65	*	93.54
19	103.00	97.31	93.05	94.23	92.68	91.43	87.21	*	95.47	94.77	94.92	93.11
20	102.72	97.07	94.35	95.29	*	92.00	88.12	95.96	96.07	92.76	95.04	93.81
21	*	96.25	94.38	95.25	92.20	90.55	88.51	95.60	96.00	*	95.32	94.59
22	102.37	†	94.96	*	92.15	90.95	*	95.09	95.50	94.58	95.25	93.45
23	102.50	96.76	95.06	93.46	92.16	89.85	88.59	95.35	*	94.47	95.33	*
24	102.53	96.87	94.77	93.60	92.76	*	88.12	96.07	95.92	93.85	94.57	92.94
25	102.66	*	*	93.02	93.42	89.02	89.59	96.08	94.68	93.12	*	†
26	102.90	97.38	96.25	92.44	93.15	89.38	90.03	*	94.82	93.16	94.77	93.13
27	101.86	96.44	95.82	89.92	*	87.71	91.41	95.19	94.77	93.47	95.05	94.34
28	*	93.94	96.64	88.70	93.29	88.70	91.80	94.01	94.98	*	95.27	94.28
29	99.32		96.43	*	93.69	87.29	*	94.89	94.84	93.85	†	93.63
30	98.31		96.60	90.53	†	87.01	91.72	94.31	*	93.68	95.12	
31	100.69		96.95		93.75		92.41	94.01		92.91		94.35
High	103.00	101.71	96.96	98.19	93.77	95.21	92.41	96.08	96.07	96.75	95.33	95.89
Low	94.44	93.94	92.90	88.70	86.45	87.01	85.18	91.67	93.31	92.76	92.38	92.94

*Sunday
†Holiday

1906—RAILROADS

Date:	Jan.	Feb.	Mar.	Apr.	May	June	July	Aug.	Sept.	Oct.	Nov.	Dec.
1	†	135.93	129.98	*	120.70	128.82	*	130.45	136.10	136.86	132.93	136.30
2	133.12	135.70	130.13	133.13	120.61	129.35	121.76	131.11	*	136.57	133.49	*
3	133.23	133.89	130.00	132.60	120.30	*	122.41	130.40	†	136.24	133.70	136.86
4	132.36	*	*	132.68	123.29	129.98	†	129.70	136.09	135.98	*	136.60
5	133.73	133.73	128.54	132.05	124.01	129.44	122.88	*	136.41	136.87	133.91	136.11
6	134.48	134.50	129.48	132.34	*	129.93	124.73	130.99	137.16	136.53	†	135.37
7	*	133.73	129.22	131.76	124.25	130.55	124.96	131.21	136.62	*	133.55	136.65
8	134.76	133.83	130.46	*	126.10	130.56	*	131.08	137.05	136.68	132.88	136.28
9	134.73	135.34	131.40	130.45	126.14	129.71	124.81	130.18	*	136.78	132.67	*
10	134.65	134.87	130.88	130.07	126.91	*	124.24	130.62	137.09	137.65	132.24	136.61
11	135.58	*	*	131.85	128.16	131.05	123.54	131.07	135.77	137.68	*	137.56
12	136.65	†	130.53	131.45	127.60	130.82	122.43	*	137.72	137.60	131.45	136.63
13	136.80	135.23	131.46	132.13	*	129.96	122.45	131.71	136.61	136.78	132.28	134.93
14	*	134.66	130.85	132.56	127.23	129.25	122.71	131.93	137.68	*	134.08	136.73
15	136.86	133.55	130.40	*	127.05	128.40	*	132.10	137.82	136.84	134.35	136.78
16	137.12	132.28	130.59	132.66	127.83	127.21	124.03	131.39	*	136.76	135.42	*
17	137.06	131.10	130.41	132.66	127.46	*	124.33	133.63	137.84	135.98	136.13	135.36
18	137.07	*	*	131.14	126.90	126.77	123.55	135.41	137.75	135.86	*	133.14
19	138.29	132.60	128.96	128.36	126.91	128.48	124.47	*	137.03	134.12	136.44	130.84
20	138.25	132.41	130.16	129.01	*	129.53	125.46	136.98	137.83	131.62	136.06	131.23
21	*	131.47	129.63	128.96	126.93	128.23	125.82	135.60	137.70	*	136.83	131.31
22	138.36	†	130.50	*	126.75	128.76	*	134.83	136.92	133.87	136.68	129.65
23	138.11	132.06	130.87	126.56	126.29	127.64	126.01	135.15	*	133.43	136.31	*
24	137.20	131.79	130.75	126.76	127.78	*	125.27	136.95	137.26	133.27	135.01	128.37
25	137.45	*	*	126.18	128.31	126.72	126.83	137.06	135.71	132.05	*	†
26	137.79	132.58	132.03	125.73	128.03	127.10	127.71	*	135.69	132.17	134.90	128.51
27	136.36	131.24	131.32	122.95	*	124.89	128.08	136.04	135.25	132.34	135.96	130.34
28	*	129.56	132.53	121.89	127.89	125.93	129.02	135.04	135.89	*	135.90	130.02
29	133.98		132.17	*	128.41	123.91	*	135.96	135.92	132.70	†	128.95
30	133.55		132.70	124.06	†	123.31	128.31	135.34	*	132.60	136.01	*
31	135.34		132.73		128.61		129.11	135.20		131.37		129.80
High	138.36	135.93	132.73	133.13	128.61	131.05	129.11	137.06	137.84	137.68	136.83	137.56
Low	132.36	129.56	128.54	121.89	120.30	123.31	121.76	129.70	135.25	131.37	131.45	128.37

*Sunday
†Holiday

1906—DAILY STOCK SALES ON N. Y. STOCK EXCHANGE
(000 Omitted)

Date	Jan.	Feb.	Mar.	Apr.	May	June	July	Aug.	Sept.	Oct.	Nov.	Dec.
1	†	1684	889	*	1427	364	*	1338	430	1291	873	197
2	1576	1428	824	1261	2464	227	1119	1293	*	1346	1096	*
3	1340	846	443	1124	1358	*	832	985	†	1243	386	736
4	1364	*	*	916	1539	804	†	347	1340	700	*	775
5	1324	998	1479	739	712	834	823	*	1155	932	685	856
6	1071	956	991	904	*	618	692	646	1245	471	†	666
7	*	756	672	307	1179	856	415	764	1081	*	957	785
8	1613	933	866	*	1334	581	*	641	485	900	507	292
9	1322	942	1173	721	1312	305	500	810	*	768	667	*
10	1318	464	480	1010	1039	*	303	474	931	1069	288	751
11	1537	*	*	934	1217	514	502	398	1056	1275	*	1216
12	1990	†	731	666	441	632	931	*	1122	887	972	850
13	977	1101	863	411	*	547	607	698	1093	434	696	1358
14	*	925	611	435	1055	1207	201	613	1415	*	968	1282
15	1535	1152	505	*	1122	982	*	978	854	673	1193	490
16	1276	1161	541	852	854	450	680	1224	*	491	1253	*
17	1724	569	131	823	1026	*	414	2525	1671	618	717	947
18	1479	*	*	1246	584	1069	410	1603	1499	616	*	1621
19	1825	1076	749	1542	148	1013	342	*	1408	1349	1379	1702
20	889	1192	623	1194	*	984	888	2732	1115	1037	877	774
21	*	1048	663	399	358	1027	326	1940	830	*	939	684
22	1686	†	689	*	451	906	*	1575	395	1154	1087	542
23	1967	623	729	1185	779	392	964	1343	*	827	769	*
24	1975	309	207	1237	765	*	607	1407	1136	532	491	882
25	1602	*	*	915	1091	995	753	1058	1129	707	*	†
26	1336	834	763	1381	252	1178	898	*	1111	891	811	602
27	734	857	882	1791	*	1120	1077	1305	1438	247	781	783
28	*	1420	840	1006	475	1221	470	1597	1500	*	551	607
29	1655		704	*	425	977	*	1570	610	510	†	428
30	2024		775	1838	†	545	885	1346	*	304	498	
31	1514		445		518		691	584		479		555
Total	38,653	21,276	19,269	24,837	23,926	20,349	16,333	31,794	26,051	21,750	19,442	20,384

*Sunday. †Holiday.

1907—INDUSTRIALS

Date:	Jan.	Feb.	Mar.	Apr.	May	June	July	Aug.	Sept.	Oct.	Nov.	Dec.
1	†	90.59	90.12	82.30	83.87	77.93	81.27	78.36	*	67.95	57.56	*
2	94.25	90.48	89.62	81.84	84.57	*	80.90	78.87	†	67.62	57.39	60.14
3	94.35	*	*	81.94	85.02	77.40	81.38	78.48	73.51	67.94	*	59.47
4	95.98	90.50	88.00	83.13	84.50	79.11	†	*	72.74	67.76	58.48	60.11
5	96.17	91.60	86.44	83.96	*	78.62	81.85	77.41	73.59	67.31	†	61.16
6	*	91.45	87.28	84.22	84.31	78.83	82.52	76.55	73.89	*	57.75	61.77
7	96.37	92.35	86.52	*	83.54	79.35	*	74.91	73.56	67.56	56.39	61.01
8	95.65	92.46	85.21	84.36	83.48	79.92	82.52	75.29	*	67.05	56.68	*
9	96.07	92.13	84.89	84.70	83.28	*	81.57	74.72	73.44	65.51	56.48	59.72
10	95.89	*	*	84.78	83.06	79.95	80.64	73.31	71.68	65.50	*	58.51
11	95.53	92.94	85.70	84.19	82.85	79.15	80.61	*	70.96	63.51	56.88	58.22
12	95.78	†	86.53	83.85	*	79.07	80.71	71.18	69.86	62.34	55.87	58.17
13	*	93.39	83.12	82.23	83.56	78.62	81.46	72.37	69.69	*	55.37	57.29
14	95.58	92.73	76.23	*	83.42	78.01	*	69.63	68.30	62.14	54.36	57.33
15	95.36	93.07	81.33	81.40	83.84	77.66	81.20	70.32	*	62.09	53.00	*
16	94.41	93.19	83.69	82.84	83.42	*	81.51	69.29	68.14	60.46	53.89	57.03
17	94.34	*	*	82.89	83.10	77.90	80.40	69.36	69.17	60.53	*	56.85
18	92.62	92.81	82.13	83.07	82.71	78.11	80.77	*	69.05	59.13	55.05	57.71
19	92.58	92.28	81.55	83.11	*	78.09	81.16	69.50	69.80	58.65	53.45	58.08
20	*	92.11	80.94	83.10	80.79	77.86	81.33	70.01	70.10	*	53.18	58.98
21	93.28	91.87	81.97	*	78.77	77.43	*	69.25	70.45	60.81	53.27	59.46
22	93.66	†	80.40	84.80	79.33	77.44	81.11	70.37	*	59.11	53.08	*
23	93.90	†	78.76	84.63	79.04	*	80.98	69.27	69.53	58.21	55.02	58.21
24	94.03	*	*	83.94	79.45	77.93	81.32	69.25	69.82	58.18	*	58.00
25	93.00	90.33	75.39	83.88	79.00	79.53	81.11	*	69.43	58.30	53.63	†
26	92.72	90.61	77.78	83.51	*	79.44	81.25	70.43	69.01	58.31	55.05	57.60
27	*	89.75	77.39	83.95	77.30	80.22	81.21	70.27	67.72	*	55.55	58.65
28	91.89	90.54	78.21	*	77.32	80.00	*	70.97	67.16	58.13	†	58.83
29	91.76		80.15	84.37	78.27	80.36	80.10	71.18	*	57.23	57.51	*
30	90.77		†	84.30	†		79.86	72.28	67.72	58.42	58.41	59.47
31	91.70				78.10		78.87	†		57.70		58.75
High	96.37	93.39	90.12	84.80	85.02	80.36	82.52	78.87	73.89	67.95	58.48	61.77
Low	90.77	89.75	75.39	81.40	77.30	77.40	78.87	69.25	67.16	57.23	53.00	56.85

*Sunday
†Holiday

1907—RAILROADS

Date:	Jan.	Feb.	Mar.	Apr.	May	June	July	Aug.	Sept.	Oct.	Nov.	Dec.
1	†	120.28	117.98	107.70	109.28	100.42	105.72	104.96	*	98.73	84.36	*
2	129.90	120.20	116.96	107.16	110.41	*	104.78	105.37	†	98.08	84.14	88.28
3	129.71	*	*	106.88	110.36	99.50	105.70	105.27	99.44	97.81	*	87.32
4	131.60	119.58	114.77	109.05	109.64	100.78	†	*	98.68	97.81	85.05	89.11
5	131.95	120.76	112.56	110.48	*	100.45	106.34	103.71	100.11	97.56	†	90.30
6	*	120.67	114.31	109.83	108.87	101.03	107.23	102.34	100.45	*	85.72	90.56
7	131.63	122.00	112.51	*	108.14	102.06	·	100.90	100.26	98.11	84.27	90.56
8	130.38	121.59	110.86	109.77	108.23	102.96	106.84	101.35	*	97.31	85.09	*
9	129.74	120.82	111.09	109.30	107.58	*	105.48	100.36	100.38	95.56	85.07	89.19
10	129.65	*	*	109.32	106.76	102.81	103.90	98.51	98.91	95.77	*	87.88
11	128.78	121.70	111.83	108.69	107.08	101.76	103.99	*	99.02	94.50	85.91	87.85
12	129.56	†	112.53	108.36	*	101.95	104.48	95.87	98.30	93.34	85.41	87.85
13	*	122.81	107.52	106.72	108.04	101.65	105.66	97.66	99.10	*	84.80	86.94
14	128.53	121.90	99.71	*	107.25	100.73	*	95.25	98.44	92.83	84.15	87.76
15	128.53	122.13	105.95	105.56	106.52	100.36	105.68	96.16	*	93.18	82.50	*
16	127.18	122.94	108.71	107.29	106.06	*	106.38	95.31	98.88	92.03	82.97	86.73
17	126.80	*	*	106.57	105.72	100.90	105.60	95.22	99.91	92.48	*	86.61
18	124.55	122.14	106.71	107.16	105.16	100.75	106.00	*	99.78	90.88	84.60	87.23
19	124.25	121.25	105.51	107.20	*	100.96	106.94	95.52	100.36	90.30	82.93	87.39
20	*	120.78	105.73	107.51	103.57	100.83	107.20	96.49	100.36	*	82.38	88.78
21	125.22	120.30	106.21	*	102.45	100.44	*	95.88	101.03	92.23	81.41	89.35
22	125.25	†	103.15	109.65	103.38	100.42	106.91	96.63	*	88.73	81.49	*
23	125.75	†	100.77	109.70	102.70	*	106.68	95.14	100.19	86.69	83.40	88.11
24	125.68	*	*	108.65	103.40	101.18	107.68	94.93	100.38	84.82	*	87.61
25	124.08	117.71	98.27	108.83	102.50	103.11	107.37	*	100.01	85.90	81.72	†
26	123.68	118.26	101.94	108.45	*	102.86	107.36	96.39	99.28	85.88	83.51	87.01
27	*	117.15	102.56	108.93	99.98	103.75	107.51	96.41	98.27	*	84.09	88.41
28	122.34	118.68	103.23	*	99.95	103.77	*	97.41	97.21	86.13	†	88.35
29	122.18		105.85	109.73	101.33	105.06	106.23	97.11	*	83.49	85.80	*
30	121.52		†	109.97	†		106.41	97.83	98.35	84.85	87.13	89.50
31	122.25				100.92		105.26	†		84.02		88.77
High	131.95	122.94	117.98	110.48	110.41	105.06	107.68	105.37	101.03	98.73	87.13	90.56
Low	121.52	117.15	98.27	105.56	99.95	99.50	103.90	94.93	97.21	83.49	81.41	86.61

*Sunday
†Holiday

1907—DAILY STOCK SALES ON N. Y. STOCK EXCHANGE
(000 Omitted)

Date	Jan.	Feb.	Mar.	Apr.	May	June	July	Aug.	Sept.	Oct.	Nov.	Dec.
1	†	1266	1130	1032	553	226	522	524	*	498	334	*
2	531	427	403	1045	768	*	468	294	†	450	187	851
3	586	*	*	948	811	716	515	74	553	532	*	836
4	906	673	1495	1221	358	597	†	*	447	264	484	777
5	811	586	1751	1354	*	500	437	406	691	152	†	993
6	*	586	2357	591	598	494	378	901	765	*	439	685
7	1056	803	1403	*	645	520	*	1076	232	315	382	447
8	952	326	1892	837	374	376	650	915	*	395	437	*
9	562	378	839	1107	752	*	572	592	312	706	990	671
10	702	*	*	890	719	541	936	533	819	675	*	654
11	1123	751	1186	886	261	634	462	*	597	838	326	608
12	492	†	811	770	*	390	239	1170	936	635	373	449
13	*	997	2165	650	515	176	245	1106	813	*	337	430
14	786	868	2522	*	512	502	*	965	357	772	478	186
15	597	761	1744	1070	612	150	561	921	*	618	583	*
16	1271	353	904	649	342	*	483	761	672	1028	267	501
17	873	*	*	731	480	244	572	353	500	873	*	515
18	1537	751	1122	312	230	276	430	*	492	1075	499	597
19	1058	1085	1361	327	*	259	544	476	548	455	428	439
20	*	447	910	126	754	176	245	704	458	*	489	426
21	1417	596	639	*	1355	211	*	343	155	816	574	219
22	788	†	913	872	1009	550	476	532	*	1361	289	*
23	697	†	840	776	556	*	372	442	396	913	309	236
24	501	*	*	751	580	139	670	322	376	996	*	169
25	646	915	1701	455	224	459	776	*	290	654	417	†
26	562	993	1254	371	*	560	562	530	410	234	445	244
27	*	1277	1289	155	1023	490	212	402	575	*	421	460
28	1057	1122	830	*	690	756	*	523	372	363	†	270
29	1087		887	525	561	294	458	315	*	631	668	*
30	1349		†	764	†	*	416	416	579	525	373	373
31	1120		*		532		622	†		597		420
Total	23,068	15,901	32,347	19,216	15,818	10,233	12,823	15,596	12,346	17,372	10,529	12,505

*Sunday. †Holiday.

1908—INDUSTRIALS

Date:	Jan.	Feb.	Mar.	Apr.	May	June	July	Aug.	Sept.	Oct.	Nov.	Dec.
1	†	61.83	*	67.84	69.92	74.38	72.76	80.57	84.55	79.50	*	87.63
2	59.61	*	61.09	67.82	70.05	74.03	72.87	*	83.76	80.53	82.90	87.67
3	60.62	61.82	60.97	67.22	*	73.89	73.12	81.07	82.57	81.20	†	86.58
4	60.87	62.14	61.19	67.15	69.78	72.66	†	82.13	83.55	*	84.87	87.26
5	*	61.02	61.29	*	70.62	73.16	*	82.07	†	80.56	85.81	86.68
6	61.75	61.15	61.68	67.04	71.09	73.67	74.50	83.80	*	80.93	87.28	*
7	61.42	60.77	63.23	67.48	70.91	*	74.84	84.46	†	81.33	87.77	86.38
8	61.75	59.90	*	67.81	71.26	73.38	75.83	84.89	83.67	80.68	*	87.02
9	63.50	*	63.66	68.64	71.78	72.91	76.37	*	83.61	80.64	87.47	87.42
10	63.01	58.80	63.50	68.76	*	73.40	75.63	85.40	82.95	80.75	87.54	87.35
11	64.27	59.11	63.87	68.47	72.47	73.42	75.34	84.43	82.00	*	87.09	86.61
12	*	†	64.13	*	72.30	72.82	*	84.69	82.43	81.49	87.62	86.47
13	64.98	58.62	65.15	68.17	73.09	72.90	76.06	83.71	*	81.21	88.38	*
14	65.84	59.73	66.11	68.52	73.95	*	76.87	82.08	82.48	81.54	88.09	85.31
15	65.44	59.17	*	68.01	74.38	72.93	76.72	81.61	81.42	81.65	*	85.15
16	64.19	*	65.23	68.44	74.56	73.48	76.81	*	80.21	81.81	87.68	85.88
17	64.53	58.88	65.78	†	*	73.12	77.08	82.61	79.00	81.35	87.69	83.99
18	64.45	58.84	65.07	†	75.12	73.55	78.28	83.00	79.85	*	86.87	83.91
19	*	59.08	65.77	*	73.78	72.65	*	82.51	78.66	81.26	86.70	83.71
20	63.19	59.68	66.41	67.94	73.83	72.71	78.75	82.57	*	82.21	86.69	
21	63.21	60.20	67.26	68.32	74.21	*	78.62	82.15	77.68	82.82	86.19	83.46
22	62.10	†	*	68.38	73.73	71.71	79.13	82.29	77.07	82.83		84.57
23	61.44	*	68.32	69.10	72.43	71.70	79.56		78.87	82.44	86.17	85.48
24	61.31	60.00	69.08	70.01	*	71.90	78.55	81.91	79.59	82.48	87.61	85.68
25	61.76	59.92	69.92	69.93	73.04	72.33	79.64	82.03	80.19	*	87.15	†
26	*	59.98	69.43	*	72.40	72.34	*	82.65	79.25	82.22	*	†
27	62.06	60.16	69.78	69.80	72.64	72.22	79.10	83.84	*	83.55	87.61	*
28	62.53	61.07	68.69	70.23	72.15	*	79.36	84.10	79.58	82.72	87.63	86.97
29	62.08	60.54	*	70.29	72.76	72.91	79.46	84.56	79.23	83.15	*	86.22
30	62.32		68.64	69.55	†	72.59	79.61	*	79.93	82.92	87.30	85.91
31	62.70		67.51		*		80.34	84.66		82.53		86.15
High	65.84	62.14	69.92	70.29	75.12	74.38	80.34	85.40	84.55	83.55	88.38	87.67
Low	59.61	58.62	60.97	67.04	69.78	71.70	72.76	80.57	77.07	79.50	82.90	83.46

*Sunday
†Holiday

1908—RAILROADS

Date:	Jan.	Feb.	Mar.	Apr.	May	June	July	Aug.	Sept.	Oct.	Nov.	Dec.
1	†	91.26	*	92.38	98.35	102.05	99.92	106.90	109.13	105.91	*	117.13
2	89.81	*	86.87	92.45	98.72	102.35	99.74	*	109.19	107.26	110.46	116.21
3	90.38	90.90	86.80	91.78	*	101.90	99.96	106.41	108.03	108.05	†	116.35
4	90.37	91.49	87.15	92.43	98.11	100.30	†	106.99	109.13	*	112.48	117.20
5	*	90.52	87.26	*	98.65	100.65	*	106.78	†	107.45	111.93	116.70
6	91.12	90.45	87.79	92.23	99.42	101.34	101.24	107.45	*	107.69	113.63	*
7	91.15	89.60	89.45	92.20	99.02	*	101.58	107.58	†	107.90	114.53	116.54
8	90.82	88.34	*	93.51	99.90	101.21	102.73	108.01	109.50	106.52	*	117.39
9	92.86	*	90.71	94.30	100.58	100.70	102.95	*	110.33	106.35	114.45	117.80
10	92.03	86.21	90.03	94.18	*	101.03	101.91	109.12	110.14	106.28	115.47	118.05
11	93.75	86.46	91.10	93.77	101.37	100.95	101.65	107.97	109.14	*	115.08	117.81
12	*	†	91.18	*	100.55	99.65	*	108.71	109.50	107.79	115.46	118.18
13	94.27	86.18	91.88	93.53	101.54	99.85	102.36	107.73	*	108.00	116.73	*
14	95.06	87.53	92.84	93.94	102.24	*	103.15	106.05	110.14	107.96	116.53	118.00
15	95.10	86.55	*	93.69	102.56	99.90	103.23	106.17	108.87	108.46	*	117.36
16	94.68	*	91.93	94.06	103.10	100.76	103.12	*	107.55	108.19	116.94	117.98
17	95.27	86.04	92.60	†	*	100.44	103.13	106.76	106.00	107.54	117.51	116.43
18	95.75	86.60	91.11	†	104.45	100.65	104.17	106.77	107.41	*	116.80	116.58
19	*	86.95	91.50	*	103.16	99.08	*	106.09	105.77	107.92	115.78	116.03
20	94.67	87.43	91.98	93.51	102.71	99.25	105.25	106.41	*	109.03	115.95	
21	93.09	87.61	92.25	93.93	103.42	*	104.23	106.20	103.78	109.73	114.77	115.20
22	92.76	†	*	93.88	102.50	97.96	105.68	106.22	103.43	109.78		117.19
23	92.46	*	93.10	94.96	100.26	97.97	106.74		104.18	109.26	114.94	118.14
24	91.66	87.29	93.83	96.41	*	98.19	105.09	106.21	105.97	109.40	116.58	118.15
25	92.22	86.79	94.06	96.22	101.32	98.89	106.15	106.08	106.38	*	116.01	†
26	*	86.66	93.16	*	99.65	99.47	*	107.31	105.68	109.88	*	†
27	92.73	86.77	94.40	96.95	99.15	99.16	105.25	108.83	*	110.15	117.23	*
28	93.40	87.36	93.46	97.68	98.53	*	105.80	108.67	105.45	109.51	117.01	119.80
29	92.40	86.52	*	97.86	99.14	100.06	105.63	109.11	105.43	109.95	*	119.28
30	92.44		93.21	96.95	†	99.88	105.77	*	105.95	110.16	117.10	119.43
31	92.19		92.00		*		106.76	109.10		109.57		120.05
High	95.75	91.49	94.40	97.86	104.45	102.35	106.76	109.12	110.33	110.16	117.51	120.05
Low	89.81	86.04	86.80	91.78	98.11	97.96	99.74	106.05	103.43	105.91	110.46	115.20

*Sunday
†Holiday

1908—DAILY STOCK SALES ON N. Y. STOCK EXCHANGE

(000 Omitted)

Date	Jan.	Feb.	Mar.	Apr.	May	June	July	Aug.	Sept.	Oct.	Nov.	Dec.
1	†	323	*	555	644	989	148	472	580	253	*	999
2	508	*	299	461	409	968	100		676	629	546	1136
3	636	452	386	389	*	864	71	576	714	471	†	885
4	256	264	319	220	625	700	†	829	463	*	1367	1065
5	*	451	298	*	440	366	*	774	†	904	1143	696
6	627	407	287	288	751	201	495	811	*	745	1544	*
7	539	316	451	259	673	*	508	1358	†	789	955	707
8	469	432	*	455	919	412	623	540	693	727	*	661
9	801	*	677	557	497	182	644	*	798	815	1641	1067
10	1030	953	564	614	*	186	543	920	1021	232	1638	945
11	386	569	956	228	1061	149	243	870	725	*	1640	1001
12	*	†	607	*	860	483	*	802	335	581	1275	553
13	911	654	662	354	814	180	384	702	*	483	1667	*
14	920	589	662	273	1219	*	446	1195	692	428	663	1041
15	733	424	*	241	1218	175	640	510	781	423	*	1020
16	944	*	792	294	577	307	506	*	888	560	1111	706
17	839	510	674	†	*	326	361	653	995	193	1102	1002
18	527	395	888	†	1123	294	356	893	790	*	1144	1048
19	*	522	613	*	1254	450	*	654	515	313	1051	556
20	832	632	559	304	1404	110	994	738	*	523	1281	*
21	983	416	446	328	1118	*	873	660	1086	912	455	1327
22	731	†	*	336	968	422	834	1117	1435	727	*	1234
23	579	*	701	591	749	384	969	*	807	608	727	1246
24	510	308	949	876	*	202	772	385	998	190	989	860
25	239	297	779	399	836	234	422	608	907	*	962	†
26	*	216	983	*	707	203	*	277	351	342	†	†
27	635	257	751	732	893	120	708	898	*	518	779	*
28	544	305	400	1117	682	*	625	869	448	522	471	1029
29	584	208	*	1085	457	345	435	407	420	486	*	907
30	378		617	577	†	179	419	*	367	608	975	829
31	351		695		*		688	609		287		565
Total	16,492	9,900	16,018	11,532	20,896	9,432	13,807	19,127	17,486	14,269	25,126	23,083

*Sunday. †Holiday.

1909—INDUSTRIALS

Date:	Jan.	Feb.	Mar.	Apr.	May	June	July	Aug.	Sept.	Oct.	Nov.	Dec.
1	†	84.44	82.72	85.37	88.32	92.38	92.95	*	97.50	100.36	99.44	96.88
2	86.27	85.03	83.28	85.37	*	92.64	93.14	97.52	98.12	100.50	†	96.66
3	*	84.67	82.58	85.94	88.76	94.06	†	98.14	98.47	*	100.23	97.46
4	85.26	84.69	81.79	*	89.22	94.16	*	98.00	†	100.19	100.44	98.08
5	84.85	84.86	82.10	86.92	89.32	94.46	*	97.07	*	99.02	99.80	*
6	85.14	84.64	82.21	86.81	90.13	*	93.13	98.30	98.73	*	99.33	97.52
7	86.95	*	*	86.90	91.40	93.97	93.16	98.48	97.41	98.88	*	98.28
8	86.22	85.61	82.20	87.78	91.56	93.98	93.04	*	97.05	98.07	99.41	98.13
9	85.36	85.60	81.64	†	*	93.78	92.90	98.37	95.86	98.00	98.67	98.69
10	*	85.76	81.78	†	90.94	*	92.98	98.37	97.22	*	98.78	98.41
11	85.28	86.22	81.90	*	91.25	93.98	*	99.02	96.19	96.95	98.77	98.47
12	85.05	†	82.03	88.11	91.08	94.05	93.40	99.11	*	†	98.77	*
13	84.60	†	82.03	87.56	90.79	*	92.82	98.85	96.17	96.79	99.16	99.00
14	84.77	*	*	87.43	90.93	94.19	93.06	99.26	96.93	98.06	*	98.58
15	84.48	86.72	81.88	87.16	90.82	92.62	93.45	*	98.29	98.57	99.31	98.67
16	85.31	86.42	82.65	86.56	*	92.32	94.09	98.35	99.06	98.64	99.21	98.61
17	*	85.93	83.06	87.65	90.84	91.16	94.19	98.91	99.16	*	99.53	98.86
18	84.79	84.76	82.81	*	91.36	91.34	*	98.14	99.08	98.78	100.34	99.04
19	85.11	84.33	82.40	87.81	91.41	91.18	94.33	97.71	*	98.15	100.53	*
20	84.76	82.82	82.33	87.86	90.88	*	94.68	97.50	99.73	98.02	100.02	98.84
21	85.72	*	*	87.65	91.15	89.66	94.03	98.23	99.92	98.11	*	98.87
22	85.72	†	83.28	88.10	91.51	90.03	94.19	*	99.13	96.82	98.98	98.85
23	85.83	79.91	82.94	87.66	*	91.29	93.39	98.89	99.08	95.70	98.35	98.56
24	*	81.44	83.32	88.12	91.76	91.86	94.32	99.06	99.17	*	98.03	98.61
25	85.86	80.57	83.22	*	91.58	91.51	*	98.51	†	96.83	†	†
26	85.69	81.34	83.60	87.63	91.18	91.38	94.02	96.30	*	96.21	98.73	*
27	85.77	81.85	84.73	87.44	91.65	*	94.51	97.18	99.32	97.04	97.81	98.28
28	85.10	*	*	88.13	92.18	91.59	94.90	96.78	100.12	98.03	*	98.63
29	84.62		85.31	88.03	†	92.82	95.31	*	99.94	98.97	95.89	99.28
30	84.09		85.29	88.29	*	92.28	96.17	98.32	99.55	99.07	96.02	99.18
31	*		86.12		†		96.79	97.90		*		99.05
High	86.95	86.72	86.12	88.29	92.18	94.46	96.79	99.26	100.12	100.50	100.53	99.28
Low	84.09	79.91	81.64	85.37	88.32	89.66	92.82	96.30	95.86	95.70	95.89	96.66

*Sunday
†Holiday

1909—RAILROADS

Date:	Jan.	Feb.	Mar.	Apr.	May	June	July	Aug.	Sept.	Oct.	Nov.	Dec.
1	†	117.00	116.90	122.22	123.57	126.11	127.56	*	130.16	132.55	129.91	126.51
2	120.93	117.87	117.18	121.11	*	125.96	127.93	131.55	130.94	132.61	†	125.92
3	*	117.91	116.51	121.70	124.18	127.14	†	131.58	131.10	*	129.96	127.05
4	119.76	117.94	115.96	*	124.44	128.23	*	131.54	†	132.64	129.79	127.78
5	118.76	117.94	116.26	122.80	123.90	128.21	*	131.08	*	131.58	129.56	*
6	118.67	117.65	116.06	121.94	123.88	*	128.08	132.35	*	131.45	128.98	127.43
7	119.95	*	*	122.29	124.66	127.79	128.20	132.48	129.35	131.69	*	128.10
8	119.59	118.03	116.44	122.68	124.76	128.21	127.67	*	128.99	130.60	128.69	128.08
9	118.50	117.88	115.99	†	*	127.95	127.53	132.61	127.48	130.48	128.08	128.88
10	*	118.10	116.19	†	124.35	128.15	127.66	132.60	130.30	*	128.36	128.38
11	118.16	118.61	115.86	*	125.40	128.28	*	133.61	129.68	129.20	127.86	128.58
12	117.63	†	116.35	122.96	125.68	128.23	128.15	134.08	*	†	128.20	*
13	117.67	†	116.16	122.17	126.13	*	127.78	133.76	129.10	129.64	128.44	129.13
14	118.26	*	*	122.66	125.78	128.11	128.00	134.46	130.10	130.48	*	128.78
15	118.28	119.90	115.95	122.46	125.70	126.97	128.08	*	131.25	131.05	128.03	129.08
16	119.38	119.78	116.68	121.21	*	127.28	128.21	133.87	131.96	130.83	127.76	129.28
17	*	119.33	117.41	122.00	125.18	126.18	128.90	134.31	132.73	*	128.10	129.71
18	119.05	118.08	117.33	*	125.61	126.50	*	133.03	132.76	130.83	128.67	130.03
19	119.72	117.98	116.99	123.00	125.75	126.50	128.93	131.41	*	130.40	128.93	*
20	119.35	117.15	116.93	123.25	125.09	*	129.36	131.36	132.88	129.93	128.08	129.58
21	119.97	*	*	122.75	125.23	124.92	128.59	132.56	132.58	130.20	*	129.34
22	119.32	†	118.15	123.48	125.80	125.03	128.65	*	131.16	128.71	127.61	129.30
23	119.32	113.90	117.66	122.85	*	126.30	128.85	132.72	130.97	127.29	127.46	129.18
24	*	115.56	118.40	123.05	125.79	127.05	128.95	132.70	130.77	*	127.35	129.41
25	119.25	114.92	118.55	*	125.43	126.93	*	131.28	†	128.23	†	†
26	119.15	116.21	118.56	122.39	124.93	126.75	128.78	128.71	*	127.46	128.38	*
27	119.30	116.36	119.51	122.33	125.37	*	129.35	129.66	131.09	128.36	127.73	129.06
28	118.33	*	*	123.25	125.51	127.15	129.60	128.85	132.48	128.63	*	129.18
29	117.81		120.72	123.13	†	127.60	130.35	*	132.69	129.84	126.30	129.99
30	116.93		120.55	123.45	*	127.15	130.95	130.79	132.31	129.61	126.05	130.04
31	*		121.64		†		131.24	130.70		*		130.41
High	120.93	119.90	121.64	123.48	126.13	128.28	131.24	134.46	132.88	132.64	129.96	130.41
Low	116.93	113.90	115.86	121.11	123.57	124.92	127.53	128.71	127.48	127.29	126.05	125.92

*Sunday
†Holiday

1909—DAILY STOCK SALES ON N. Y. STOCK EXCHANGE
(000 Omitted)

Date	Jan.	Feb.	Mar.	Apr.	May	June	July	Aug.	Sept.	Oct.	Nov.	Dec.
1	†	441	836	1125	256	707	396	*	551	939	632	858
2	391	418	541	958	*	800	437	982	547	447	†	570
3	*	441	435	435	1038	1485	†	1060	678	*	694	801
4	1557	471	468	*	1155	1640	*	824	†	914	1035	569
5	1200	636	503	955	923	778	†	814	*	1118	905	*
6	1066	197	261	876	753	*	401	799	†	1115	403	751
7	946	*	*	720	959	1135	511	539	754	1024	*	624
8	981	419	343	869	661	1054	478	*	778	1017	582	826
9	643	346	437	†	*	1048	452	880	933	362	515	764
10	*	355	478	†	790	887	162	703	1543	*	665	841
11	886	394	390	*	732	766	*	966	588	1135	515	347
12	678	†	338	979	1102	371	456	1455	*	†	554	*
13	741	†	128	870	856	*	422	1206	844	875	356	837
14	577	*	*	811	1018	756	395	694	707	952	*	812
15	587	580	317	913	205	1050	563	*	1072	1195	916	626
16	555	472	377	759	*	930	555	1138	1136	579	787	571
17	*	344	673	451	519	1258	444	1113	1096	*	557	466
18	686	832	592	*	506	619	*	1074	458	1058	741	396
19	597	715	480	967	820	194	731	1200	*	841	876	*
20	506	515	215	975	830	*	581	1451	847	792	692	748
21	570	*	*	821	517	864	734	520	1258	813	*	479
22	666	†	514	909	347	715	622	*	1019	899	1293	484
23	334	1570	615	843	*	527	452	898	763	652	1265	716
24	*	1206	573	395	506	708	287	799	637	*	1003	503
25	412	977	494	*	477	594	*	1029	†	831	*	†
26	525	591	436	715	532	252	323	1293	*	827	775	*
27	542	449	528	607	433	*	411	1177	716	970	638	877
28	693	*	*	748	687	334	652	571	1113	885	*	609
29	622		993	703	†	659	600	*	1421	1050	1002	666
30	423		806	569	*	440	1062	789	820	340	1037	686
31	*		986		†		600	628		*		879
Total	17,381	12,372	13,668	18,962	16,620	20,553	12,726	24,596	20,369	21,758	18,437	17,308

*Sunday. †Holiday.

1910—INDUSTRIALS

Date:	Jan.	Feb.	Mar.	Apr.	May	June	July	Aug.	Sept.	Oct.	Nov.	Dec.
1	†	91.33	91.77	89.71	*	85.69	81.64	76.14	78.58	79.95	85.10	81.43
2	*	90.40	92.62	89.71	85.51	85.25	†	77.69	78.68	*	85.45	80.60
3	98.34	87.50	92.61	*	84.72	82.70	*	77.14	†	80.68	85.85	80.77
4	98.30	87.77	92.83	89.75	86.41	83.06	†	77.04	*	81.34	85.64	*
5	97.06	88.39	92.98	90.96	87.32	*	80.23	77.58	†	80.76	85.82	81.00
6	97.62	*	*	91.16	86.51	82.05	80.27	78.19	78.35	81.46	*	79.68
7	97.67	85.35	94.35	90.89	86.72	84.50	80.66	*	78.43	81.48	85.70	80.46
8	97.87	85.03	94.56	89.53	*	84.55	80.83	78.13	78.39	81.51	†	80.50
9	*	87.32	94.30	89.36	88.03	84.89	81.19	79.30	78.44	*	84.29	81.00
10	97.10	87.85	93.92	*	88.63	83.46	*	79.20	78.57	81.91	83.50	81.54
11	96.64	89.07	92.63	91.10	88.73	83.39	81.07	78.78	*	82.38	83.53	*
12	95.85	†	92.78	90.92	88.52	*	80.14	79.65	79.13	*	83.55	80.96
13	96.16	*	*	92.10	88.72	83.88	80.79	80.05	79.71	84.06	*	80.77
14	93.69	89.65	93.10	92.36	89.13	84.28	81.41	*	79.40	84.63	84.40	81.47
15	94.45	89.23	91.92	92.04	*	83.84	81.29	79.77	78.38	85.27	84.88	81.28
16	*	90.09	91.35	92.62	88.78	84.12	81.08	81.04	78.55	*	85.21	81.20
17	93.75	90.65	92.14	*	88.62	84.26	*	81.41	78.65	85.63	84.57	81.43
18	93.92	90.92	92.71	91.67	88.26	84.43	80.89	80.85	*	86.02	85.12	*
19	92.35	91.14	92.14	91.78	88.71	*	81.22	80.31	78.48	85.11	85.40	82.16
20	93.29	*	*	90.37	89.34	85.08	81.53	80.44	78.37	86.00	*	81.80
21	94.41	90.70	92.33	90.52	89.66	85.29	79.21	*	79.17	85.35	84.90	81.94
22	94.52	†	92.36	89.97	*	86.28	77.78	79.47	79.08	85.94	84.84	81.42
23	*	90.62	91.30	90.09	88.77	86.01	77.16	79.68	78.65	*	85.05	81.33
24	93.08	91.22	91.31	*	89.06	84.93	*	78.96	78.51	85.01	†	†
25	90.66	91.31	†	88.73	88.67	85.25	75.87	78.59	78.59	84.61	85.32	*
26	92.69	90.64	†	88.83	88.14	*	73.62	79.28	79.19	84.59	85.30	†
27	91.62	*	*	88.18	87.86	83.14	75.81	79.19	79.01	85.51	*	80.45
28	91.91	91.34	89.72	86.29	†	83.14	78.09	*	78.96	85.45	83.28	80.65
29	92.42		90.21	87.17	*	81.60	77.57	79.67	79.07	84.96	83.62	81.76
30	*		89.47	86.20	†	81.18	76.48	79.59	79.72	*	82.52	81.41
31	91.91		89.71		86.32		*	79.68		84.77		81.36
High	98.34	91.34	94.56	92.62	89.66	86.28	81.64	81.41	79.72	86.02	85.85	82.16
Low	90.66	85.03	89.47	86.20	84.72	81.18	73.62	76.14	78.35	79.95	82.52	79.68

*Sunday
†Holiday

1910—RAILROADS

Date:	Jan.	Feb.	Mar.	Apr.	May	June	July	Aug.	Sept.	Oct.	Nov.	Dec.
1	†	122.11	123.62	121.73	*	118.32	112.09	108.38	111.08	114.69	117.06	112.59
2	*	121.36	124.40	121.80	117.47	118.01	†	110.43	111.01	*	117.21	112.01
3	129.48	119.80	124.22	*	117.25	115.64	*	110.04	†	115.21	117.69	112.30
4	129.90	120.33	124.09	121.69	119.18	115.68	†	109.96	*	115.18	117.13	*
5	128.53	121.11	124.22	122.87	120.28	*	110.63	110.33	†	114.33	117.31	112.62
6	128.85	*	*	123.17	119.20	114.59	111.22	110.83	110.57	115.01	*	111.33
7	129.05	119.06	125.41	122.71	119.66	117.38	111.75	*	111.11	115.66	117.43	111.95
8	129.19	118.95	125.64	121.43	*	117.10	111.54	110.94	110.92	115.06	†	112.30
9	*	121.10	125.59	121.22	120.73	117.73	112.33	112.50	111.27	*	115.76	112.97
10	127.47	121.11	125.43	*	121.59	116.85	*	112.01	111.29	115.60	115.19	113.20
11	126.85	121.85	124.48	123.23	121.55	116.28	112.66	112.13	*	115.81	115.09	*
12	125.98	†	124.75	122.73	121.51	*	111.69	113.38	111.71	†	115.02	112.65
13	126.57	*	*	124.00	121.73	117.08	112.70	113.75	112.88	116.68	*	112.63
14	123.90	122.56	124.79	124.36	121.66	117.44	113.65	*	112.63	117.36	115.82	113.07
15	124.74	122.06	123.54	124.14	*	117.30	113.02	113.27	111.41	117.66	116.35	113.18
16	*	122.98	122.96	124.35	121.82	117.46	112.66	114.83	111.65	*	116.56	113.36
17	123.53	123.28	123.50	*	121.50	117.67	*	115.47	111.90	118.00	115.73	113.63
18	123.35	124.06	124.16	123.61	121.33	118.15	112.48	113.96	*	118.44	116.45	*
19	122.51	123.43	123.33	123.81	122.01	*	112.64	113.74	111.96	117.67	116.79	114.46
20	123.71	*	*	122.59	123.10	118.78	112.33	113.51	112.08	118.43	*	114.10
21	124.46	123.33	123.66	122.67	123.32	118.38	111.73	*	113.45	117.83	116.11	113.91
22	124.27	†	123.88	122.06	*	119.40	110.51	112.20	112.99	118.11	116.11	113.45
23	*	123.27	123.33	122.06	122.43	118.83	109.57	112.46	112.60	*	116.28	113.34
24	122.78	124.41	123.34	*	122.79	117.73	*	111.49	112.59	117.07	†	†
25	120.91	123.80	†	120.49	121.50	117.73	108.24	110.88	*	116.80	116.48	*
26	122.70	123.10	†	120.58	122.30	*	105.59	111.83	113.59	116.50	116.50	†
27	121.85	*	*	119.66	121.96	115.49	108.02	111.71	113.61	117.32	*	112.98
28	122.38	123.55	121.98	118.16	†	115.17	110.70	*	113.58	117.13	114.25	113.08
29	122.98		122.45	119.61	*	112.96	110.18	112.28	113.95	116.70	114.68	114.04
30	*		121.63	118.29	†	111.63	109.19	112.26	114.45	*	113.19	114.11
31	122.73		121.83		119.62		*	112.10		116.76		114.06
High	129.90	124.41	125.64	124.36	123.32	119.40	113.65	115.47	114.45	118.44	117.69	114.46
Low	120.91	118.95	121.63	118.16	117.25	111.63	105.59	108.38	110.57	114.33	113.19	111.33

*Sunday
†Holiday

1910—DAILY STOCK SALES ON N. Y. STOCK EXCHANGE
(000 Omitted)

Date	Jan.,	Feb.	Mar.	Apr.	May	June	July	Aug.	Sept.	Oct.	Nov.	Dec.
1	†	564	503	244	*	1305	833	321	401	145	279	881
2	*	651	814	137	1083	772	†	627	187	*	291	894
3	948	1663	718	*	792	1493	*	512	†	568	504	266
4	1117	986	399	344	792	645	†	315	*	434	666	*
5	1246	443	189	430	828	*	799	402	†	495	273	359
6	951	*	*	463	727	993	916	108	278	336	*	724
7	877	1278	930	280	261	1055	573	*	314	275	405	782
8	333	1046	567	*	*	779	683	380	258	90	†	769
9	*	906	1079	304	637	460	323	558	165	*	829	638
10	570	808	737	*	628	530	*	461	57	197	1158	263
11	806	727	853	810	672	285	498	315	*	396	447	*
12	839	†	225	594	484	*	656	490	218	†	164	446
13	1116	*	*	856	238	350	524	223	440	680	*	356
14	1268	731	447	744	210	324	489	*	407	972	485	248
15	859	591	663	512	*	358	309	325	458	462	460	286
16	*	727	751	257	352	303	134	542	391	*	489	311
17	1145	801	542	*	292	177	*	622	185	988	456	116
18	1129	883	586	569	229	158	571	553	*	745	377	*
19	1633	413	248	506	222	*	228	481	243	645	191	422
20	1144	*	*	678	299	340	305	122	362	885	*	355
21	993	511	422	369	295	313	534	*	475	926	308	321
22	859	†	514	612	*	463	739	422	357	388	337	223
23	*	392	600	143	477	344	387	331	376	*	247	111
24	1009	433	322	*	251	601	*	548	113	629	†	†
25	1626	540	†	577	663	213	834	484	*	584	177	*
26	900	257	†	699	345	*	1284	336	477	679	65	†
27	1111	*	†	918	299	781	945	100	491	740	*	265
28	813	503	648	1300	†	772	923	*	304	555	808	243
29	429		674	760	†	1039	545	346	333	130	593	287
30	*		685	426	†	1533	234	297	453	*	744	302
31	508		545		762		*	160		460		94
Total	24,202	15,854	14,992	14,100	11,937	16,374	14,266	10,415	7,745	13,465	10,734	9,960

*Sunday. †Holiday.

1911—INDUSTRIALS

Date:	Jan.	Feb.	Mar.	Apr.	May	June	July	Aug.	Sept.	Oct.	Nov.	Dec.
1	*	85.33	84.53	83.40	84.14	85.79	85.93	85.47	79.17	*	77.69	80.31
2	†	85.97	82.66	*	83.69	86.17	*	84.80	†	76.75	78.07	80.68
3	82.11	85.60	82.32	83.33	83.87	86.18	85.64	84.40	*	76.52	78.19	*
4	82.26	86.02	81.80	83.32	83.16	*	†	82.95	†	76.15	78.38	80.54
5	82.09	*	*	83.02	83.15	86.35	85.28	82.65	79.77	76.70	*	80.31
6	82.44	85.84	82.47	82.93	83.04	86.25	85.80	*	80.28	76.50	79.00	79.82
7	82.75	85.87	82.81	82.89	*	86.50	86.22	83.15	79.63	76.53	†	79.34
8	*	85.48	82.46	83.06	82.88	86.31	86.26	82.53	79.09	*	78.14	79.19
9	82.51	85.67	82.37	*	82.85	86.02	*	81.85	78.67	76.52	80.42	79.41
10	81.88	85.42	82.54	83.08	82.60	86.35	86.28	81.43	*	76.85	81.01	*
11	81.70	85.57	82.39	82.82	83.04	*	86.38	80.71	78.79	77.15	80.55	80.33
12	82.05	*	*	82.89	82.92	86.70	86.17	80.40	79.07	†	*	80.43
13	82.96	†	83.00	82.81	82.68	86.94	86.22	*	78.21	77.94	79.98	81.51
14	83.07	85.47	83.98	†	*	87.02	85.98	81.31	78.13	78.66	79.92	81.61
15	*	85.41	84.09	†	82.71	86.63	86.03	81.28	77.88	*	79.71	81.97
16	82.46	84.51	83.73	*	84.63	86.61	*	80.18	78.87	78.34	79.91	82.48
17	83.38	85.09	83.15	82.56	85.41	86.68	85.72	80.05	*	78.11	81.08	*
18	83.32	85.30	83.35	81.56	86.17	*	86.37	80.86	78.66	77.77	81.12	81.89
19	83.52	*	*	81.91	85.78	87.06	86.44	81.38	77.75	77.64	*	82.27
20	83.80	85.59	84.13	81.86	86.08	86.62	86.33	*	77.01	78.11	80.59	82.30
21	83.53	85.58	84.03	81.84	*	86.61	86.47	80.51	75.53	77.75	81.56	82.22
22	*	†	83.72	81.32	86.32	86.14	86.45	80.64	74.15	*	81.47	82.11
23	83.37	85.70	83.71	*	86.25	86.33	*	80.55	73.62	77.77	81.86	†
24	83.78	84.33	83.40	82.12	85.78	86.76	86.22	79.73	*	77.68	81.47	*
25	83.44	84.33	83.43	82.20	85.62	*	86.19	79.13	72.94	77.72	81.53	†
26	83.67	*	*	82.32	85.94	86.38	86.26	78.93	73.33	77.14	*	82.08
27	84.02	84.51	83.69	82.45	86.01	86.36	85.92	*	73.51	74.82	81.35	81.84
28	83.89	85.02	84.00	83.31	*	86.06	85.73	79.31	75.05	75.36	81.50	81.30
29	*		83.58	83.65	86.40	86.32	85.90	79.13	75.15	*	80.97	81.58
30	84.93		83.86	*	†	85.98	*	79.00	76.31	75.06	†	81.68
31	84.93		83.27		85.55		86.02	79.25		75.79		*
High	84.93	86.02	84.53	83.65	86.40	87.06	86.47	85.47	80.28	78.66	81.86	82.48
Low	81.70	84.33	81.80	81.32	82.60	85.79	85.28	78.93	72.94	74.82	77.69	79.19

*Sunday
†Holiday

1911—RAILROADS

Date:	Jan.	Feb.	Mar.	Apr.	May	June	July	Aug.	Sept.	Oct.	Nov.	Dec.
1	*	119.40	117.14	117.80	119.23	121.65	122.76	121.92	113.10	*	115.81	116.54
2	†	119.65	115.75	*	119.00	122.28	*	120.71	†	111.24	115.72	117.28
3	115.13	119.14	115.78	117.84	119.45	122.36	122.00	120.30	*	111.35	115.96	*
4	114.89	119.76	115.87	118.20	118.30	*	†	118.81	†	111.41	116.60	117.25
5	115.21	*	*	118.13	118.28	122.43	121.09	118.44	113.78	111.75	*	116.79
6	115.38	119.51	116.27	118.11	118.31	122.33	121.98	*	114.11	111.55	117.11	116.12
7	115.93	119.97	116.63	117.72	*	123.01	122.06	119.07	112.83	111.55	†	115.68
8	*	119.66	116.07	117.72	118.24	122.96	122.05	118.43	111.89	*	116.48	115.47
9	115.59	119.70	116.16	*	118.23	123.10	*	116.92	111.06	111.79	117.79	115.74
10	115.45	119.56	116.34	117.57	118.06	123.23	122.24	116.41	*	112.08	118.53	*
11	114.96	119.67	116.25	117.37	118.55	*	122.81	115.19	111.18	112.49	118.15	116.79
12	115.23	*	*	117.51	118.23	123.21	122.70	114.76	111.28	†	*	116.86
13	116.55	†	116.61	117.56	118.15	123.10	122.90	*	110.26	113.23	117.44	117.41
14	116.34	119.62	117.73	†	*	123.08	122.81	116.09	110.59	114.06	117.13	117.24
15	*	119.60	117.77	†	118.23	122.59	122.62	115.74	110.64	*	116.75	117.35
16	116.34	118.15	117.38	*	119.96	122.36	*	114.11	111.95	113.75	117.28	117.62
17	117.80	118.68	116.83	117.28	120.70	122.28	122.29	114.48	*	113.80	117.92	*
18	117.51	119.26	117.25	116.05	120.91	*	123.51	115.44	111.77	113.41	117.61	117.16
19	117.68	*	*	116.63	120.71	122.65	123.75	115.88	110.75	113.79	*	117.51
20	117.43	119.45	117.86	116.58	121.00	122.30	123.31	*	110.68	114.13	117.08	117.18
21	117.23	119.23	117.77	116.38	*	122.11	123.86	114.76	110.46	113.66	117.74	116.98
22	*	†	117.63	116.12	121.09	121.61	123.83	114.70	110.91	*	118.03	117.12
23	116.88	119.36	117.63	*	121.07	122.25	*	114.61	111.00	113.79	119.21	†
24	117.13	117.20	117.50	116.48	120.43	123.31	123.42	113.64	*	113.98	118.43	*
25	116.68	117.07	117.43	116.73	120.20	*	123.15	113.05	110.32	114.03	118.36	†
26	117.10	*	*	117.11	120.25	123.09	123.15	112.92	110.70	113.87	*	117.11
27	117.85	116.90	118.06	117.15	120.43	123.31	122.40	*	109.80	112.97	118.03	116.79
28	117.98	117.34	118.73	117.66	*	122.71	122.71	113.09	110.90	113.56	118.06	116.15
29	*		118.33	118.25	120.71	123.06	122.62	112.66	110.51	*	117.24	116.57
30	118.36		118.53	*	†	122.77	*	112.60	111.28	113.85	†	116.83
31	118.82		117.71		120.55		123.00	112.91		114.46		*
High	118.82	119.97	118.73	118.25	121.09	123.31	123.86	121.92	114.11	114.46	119.21	117.62
Low	114.89	116.90	115.75	116.05	118.06	121.61	121.09	112.60	109.80	111.24	115.72	115.47

*Sunday
†Holiday

1911—DAILY STOCK SALES ON N. Y. STOCK EXCHANGE
(000 Omitted)

Date	Jan.	Feb.	Mar.	Apr.	May	June	July	Aug.	Sept.	Oct.	Nov.	Dec.
1	*	873	271	77	530	623	94	176	249	*	926	265
2	†	811	678	*	386	800	*	443	†	431	776	208
3	406	562	503	179	495	384	216	408	*	444	594	*
4	528	339	265	190	450	*	†	748	†	518	344	231
5	414	*	*	277	328	533	320	560	316	413	*	266
6	300	536	267	134	97	408	270	*	340	464	672	325
7	312	563	217	130	*	468	207	528	415	284	†	449
8	*	504	271	77	248	603	63	706	612	*	579	475
9	525	455	169	*	187	331	*	598	401	468	1259	189
10	378	341	169	169	170	202	330	1051	*	254	1146	*
11	381	149	66	196	247	*	233	729	744	334	484	545
12	365	*	*	115	167	523	184	638	520	†	*	383
13	564	†	212	113	67	523	113	*	653	371	814	595
14	365	306	413	†	*	523	86	789	887	326	739	865
15	*	366	375	†	147	475	52	435	514	*	656	503
16	407	705	204	*	1003	328	*	971	309	491	640	407
17	585	474	196	113	930	174	137	807	*	368	753	*
18	678	332	161	506	845	*	252	465	500	487	265	583
19	540	*	*	423	526	279	454	211	436	554	*	398
20	382	394	368	258	208	244	247	*	446	684	466	378
21	165	252	262	157	*	193	199	560	1268	222	382	397
22	*	†	200	213	576	476	162	590	1409	*	480	260
23	545	267	169	*	555	208	*	274	467	330	597	†
24	308	1001	163	453	597	375	215	688	*	195	616	‡
25	452	405	54	273	413	*	420	695	1441	228	158	†
26	233	*	*	272	212	634	371	316	1103	345	*	205
27	405	292	150	262	115	417	431	*	1742	365	507	302
28	246	334	337	250	*	375	225	545	1390	396	603	376
29	*		281	241	268	242	62	474	811	*	599	407
30	442		250	*	†	231	*	425	289	621	†	160
31	506		251		876		120	301		400		*
Total	10,434	10,259	6,921	5,077	10,744	10,572	5,462	15,130	17,560	10,992	15,053	9,170

*Sunday. †Holiday.

1912—INDUSTRIALS

Date:	Jan.	Feb.	Mar.	Apr.	May	June	July	Aug.	Sept.	Oct.	Nov.	Dec.
1	†	80.50	82.07	89.05	90.33	88.32	91.35	90.47	*	93.90	90.51	*
2	82.36	80.51	81.96	88.82	90.40	*	91.69	90.16	†	93.50	†	90.85
3	82.02	80.40	*	88.78	88.96	88.59	91.61	89.93	90.62	94.12	*	90.36
4	82.04	*	82.60	89.52	88.77	89.29	†	*	90.76	93.70	90.29	89.00
5	81.95	80.33	82.83	†	*	90.42	89.60	90.03	91.33	93.94	†	87.88
6	82.14	80.46	82.65	90.01	87.59	90.67	90.33	89.84	91.18	*	91.94	87.80
7	*	80.62	83.38	*	87.68	90.37	*	90.12	91.45	93.93	91.67	87.84
8	82.12	80.80	83.50	90.21	87.86	90.45	89.14	90.00	*	94.12	91.31	*
9	81.28	80.67	83.44	90.70	88.41	*	89.07	90.19	91.21	93.68	90.37	86.03
10	81.88	80.15	*	90.27	88.97	90.55	88.18	90.53	91.13	93.94	*	86.02
11	81.64	*	83.13	89.90	89.58	89.85	88.06	*	90.38	92.62	89.58	85.25
12	82.00	†	83.47	89.18	*	89.94	87.97	90.72	90.53	*	90.10	86.05
13	81.76	80.64	83.96	89.12	89.53	89.95	88.06	91.33	90.52	*	89.96	86.18
14	*	80.83	85.12	*	89.83	89.40	*	91.78	90.62	92.40	90.40	85.78
15	81.48	81.06	85.15	89.71	89.58	89.53	88.29	91.30	*	92.73	90.09	*
16	81.63	80.75	84.51	89.22	89.23	*	88.71	91.40	90.67	93.70	90.16	86.22
17	81.68	80.85	*	89.31	89.35	89.79	89.18	91.19	91.55	93.52	*	86.21
18	81.59	*	85.35	89.22	90.32	89.70	89.45	*	91.65	93.61	89.97	85.66
19	81.96	81.05	85.52	89.16	*	90.07	89.77	91.23	91.66	93.46	90.05	86.78
20	82.32	81.15	86.57	89.19	90.34	90.87	89.70	91.70	92.27	*	90.30	87.85
21	*	80.78	86.92	*	90.48	90.76	*	91.62	92.79	92.31	91.43	87.72
22	81.98	†	87.60	88.72	89.97	90.65	89.75	91.11	*	92.41	91.01	*
23	81.88	81.27	88.39	89.58	89.77	*	89.38	91.34	93.08	91.60	90.52	87.22
24	81.73	81.17	*	89.37	90.25	90.06	89.45	91.40	93.43	91.58	*	87.36
25	81.84	*	88.54	90.43	90.37	89.86	90.00	*	93.38	90.91	89.87	†
26	81.80	80.98	88.62	90.93	*	91.00	89.50	91.54	93.42	91.14	90.34	87.33
27	81.27	81.04	88.48	90.81	90.01	90.67	89.45	92.06	93.61	*	90.62	87.25
28	*	81.57	88.09	*	90.15	91.09	*	91.66	94.00	91.44	†	87.14
29	81.27	81.40	88.23	90.46	89.53	90.92	88.97	91.63	*	90.35	91.26	*
30	81.27		88.27	90.30	†	*	89.18	91.57	94.15	90.41	91.40	87.26
31	80.19		*		88.01		89.71	†		90.71		87.87
High	82.36	81.57	88.62	90.93	90.48	91.09	91.69	92.06	94.15	94.12	91.94	90.85
Low	80.19	80.15	81.96	88.72	87.59	88.32	87.97	89.84	90.38	90.35	89.58	85.25

*Sunday
†Holiday

1912—RAILROADS

Date:	Jan.	Feb.	Mar.	Apr.	May	June	July	Aug.	Sept.	Oct.	Nov.	Dec.
1	†	115.07	115.98	119.43	121.40	118.71	119.93	121.71	*	124.03	120.45	*
2	117.05	115.06	115.90	119.26	121.74	*	120.14	121.57	†	123.53	†	120.09
3	116.80	115.07	*	119.42	119.92	118.75	120.24	121.63	121.03	124.10	*	119.75
4	116.71	*	116.25	120.11	120.04	119.40	†	*	121.02	123.87	120.76	119.21
5	116.53	114.92	116.32	†	*	120.48	119.75	121.90	121.86	124.35	†	118.65
6	116.74	115.21	116.13	120.66	119.34	120.66	119.90	121.65	121.37	*	122.79	118.55
7	*	115.53	116.80	*	119.93	120.19	*	122.26	121.47	123.98	122.28	118.36
8	116.51	115.61	116.86	120.51	119.80	119.81	119.18	122.06	*	123.95	121.68	*
9	115.22	115.69	116.76	121.21	119.78	*	118.85	122.61	121.08	123.47	120.50	116.65
10	115.85	115.22	*	120.58	120.41	119.78	118.18	123.42	120.87	123.60	*	116.80
11	115.58	*	116.38	120.76	120.97	118.93	119.20	*	120.44	121.91	119.83	115.63
12	115.81	†	116.49	119.93	*	119.11	117.68	123.57	120.50	*	120.85	116.15
13	115.51	115.61	116.56	119.96	121.06	119.30	117.89	123.65	120.77	*	120.67	116.16
14	*	115.53	117.16	*	121.56	118.65	*	124.16	120.63	121.68	121.11	115.61
15	115.53	115.80	117.28	120.93	121.68	118.70	118.35	123.67	*	122.24	120.77	*
16	116.10	115.41	116.44	120.18	120.87	*	118.74	123.68	120.95	122.92	121.01	116.62
17	116.00	115.62	*	120.53	121.15	118.94	119.51	123.15	122.13	122.56	*	116.15
18	115.72	*	116.96	120.37	121.47	118.86	119.50	*	121.89	122.66	120.79	115.86
19	116.73	115.69	117.13	120.24	*	119.05	119.86	123.23	121.84	122.56	120.43	116.58
20	117.03	115.75	118.19	120.09	121.08	119.76	119.68	123.32	123.09	*	120.68	117.55
21	*	115.26	117.91	*	121.03	119.73	*	123.09	123.21	121.36	121.36	117.06
22	116.83	†	118.02	119.87	120.43	119.58	119.75	122.14	*	121.43	121.03	*
23	116.72	115.62	118.41	121.00	120.43	*	119.27	122.11	123.33	120.54	120.70	116.69
24	116.39	115.52	*	120.70	120.61	119.24	119.12	122.16	123.70	120.51	*	116.83
25	116.60	*	118.56	121.80	120.80	119.32	119.79	*	123.56	120.28	119.91	†
26	116.54	115.16	118.76	122.12	*	120.33	120.02	121.98	123.37	120.68	120.36	116.85
27	115.56	115.16	118.49	121.98	120.48	120.15	119.88	122.88	124.13	*	120.10	116.48
28	*	115.83	118.74	*	120.31	119.91	*	122.53	124.16	120.96	†	116.25
29	115.50	115.73	119.15	122.09	120.10	119.77	119.56	122.46	*	119.57	120.44	*
30	116.07		119.26	121.58	†	*	119.74	122.24	123.95	120.01	120.75	116.07
31	115.06		*		118.37		120.67	†		120.38		116.84
High	117.05	115.83	119.26	122.12	121.74	120.66	120.67	124.16	124.16	124.35	122.79	120.09
Low	115.06	114.92	115.90	119.26	118.37	118.65	117.68	121.57	120.44	119.57	119.83	115.62

*Sunday
†Holiday

1912—DAILY STOCK SALES ON N. Y. STOCK EXCHANGE
(000 Omitted)

Date	Jan.	Feb.	Mar.	Apr.	May	June	July	Aug.	Sept.	Oct.	Nov.	Dec.
1	†	928	415	684	817	331	253	559	*	636	233	*
2	509	538	191	657	540	*	423	429	†	651	†	364
3	427	200	*	509	834	283	538	197	354	669	*	576
4	492	*	431	827	436	309	†		235	779	336	637
5	377	282	617	†	*	548	312	345	286	342	†	970
6	172	482	335	510	897	610	123	222	254	*	1019	771
7	*	330	618		741	394	*	339	133	445	764	209
8	430	316	506	948	520	138	555	438		393	540	*
9	453	248	217	984	522	*	357	333	285	569	395	1021
10	435	245	*	852	534	285	515	263	282	620	*	1036
11	449	*	408	880	471	519	437	*	394	749	475	1279
12	468	†	257	848	*	154	304	505	381	†	724	922
13	237	399	365	310	570	183	165	477	213		340	550
14	*	308	545	*	613	449	*	611	57	607	413	170
15	416	294	745	906	691	113	198	491	*	520	270	*
16	394	309	364	768	916	*	237	377	236	510	343	912
17	329	84	*	494	492	147	302	241	604	500	*	466
18	252	*	531	457	334	150	244	*	444	479	231	423
19	402	172	518	327	*	197	301	324	371	265	265	437
20	381	129	830	234	480	397	80	367	708	*	289	556
21	*	294	780	*	354	289	*	367	346	625	490	406
22	470	†	718	475	615	82	209	504	*	499	280	*
23	344	242	466	672	373	*	183	293	620	856	128	264
24	377	158	*	571	306	234	189	114	627	578	*	119
25	249	*	1144	643	134	222	314	*	769	699	435	†
26	446	207	937	909	*	351	242	293	708	249	263	98
27	411	172	978	344	223	346	58	354	626	*	152	126
28	*	424	822	*	145	278	*	315	377	317	†	116
29	608	357	635	604	559	159	212	241	*	626	202	*
30	477		328	606	†	*	129	148	805	660	107	173
31	924		*		615		304	†		365		182
Total	10,930	7,119	14,703	16,078	13,733	7,106	7,185	9,147	10,114	14,209	8,691	12,783

*Sunday. †Holiday.

1913—INDUSTRIALS

Date:	Jan.	Feb.	Mar.	Apr.	May	June	July	Aug.	Sept.	Oct.	Nov.	Dec.
1	†	83.64	80.62	81.92	79.62	*	75.43	78.21	†	80.79	78.42	75.77
2	88.42	*	*	81.76	79.34	77.27	75.84	78.26	80.94	81.43	*	76.23
3	87.45	83.26	81.33	82.16	79.31	76.68	75.83	*	80.30	80.79	77.76	76.83
4	87.76	83.38	80.71	83.19	*	75.67	†	78.75	80.27	80.59	†	77.01
5	*	83.05	81.69	82.68	79.95	75.07	†	79.52	81.13	*	78.11	76.89
6	87.20	82.94	81.33	*	79.21	75.21	*	79.16	81.40	79.82	77.33	76.37
7	88.02	83.46	80.60	82.35	79.52	74.98	75.67	79.51	*	79.89	77.04	*
8	88.01	83.54	79.68	82.92	79.40	*	75.52	79.32	81.39	79.17	76.71	76.87
9	88.57	*	*	82.59	79.23	73.90	75.23	79.16	81.50	79.27	*	75.97
10	88.25	82.93	79.27	82.64	78.97	72.34	75.51	*	82.12	79.07	75.94	76.17
11	87.68	82.17	79.95	82.14	*	72.11	75.40	79.73	82.17	78.29	76.36	76.26
12	*	†	79.46	82.16	78.58	74.28	75.62	80.68	82.95	*	76.96	75.59
13	85.96	81.34	79.93	*	79.04	74.58	*	80.93	83.43	†	76.86	75.89
14	84.96	81.79	79.81	82.11	78.72	75.52	75.23	80.46	*	77.64	77.25	*
15	85.47	81.42	79.73	81.09	78.51	*	75.41	79.50	82.81	77.85	77.21	75.27
16	85.75	*	*	81.08	78.83	74.58	76.51	79.85	83.04	77.09	*	75.69
17	85.61	80.57	79.26	81.28	78.71	74.91	76.18	*	82.38	77.37	77.07	75.78
18	85.75	79.82	78.68	81.05	*	75.85	77.10	79.85	82.53	78.00	77.25	75.78
19	*	80.44	78.27	81.00	78.73	75.41	76.94	79.96	82.58	*	76.94	76.71
20	81.55	80.20	78.25	*	79.06	74.91	*	80.37	82.57	78.06	76.48	77.61
21	82.57	79.93	†	81.73	79.01	74.03	78.16	80.14	*	79.60	76.18	*
22	83.34	†	†	81.46	79.50	*	78.09	80.07	83.01	79.02	76.14	78.06
23	82.94	*	*	81.25	79.50	74.33	77.84	80.09	82.72	78.40	*	78.11
24	82.22	79.26	78.91	80.76	79.88	75.21	78.65	*	82.13	78.61	76.11	78.34
25	82.37	78.72	80.20	79.72	*	75.58	78.36	80.30	82.19	78.58	76.86	†
26	*	80.05	80.31	79.41	79.72	74.93	78.47	80.29	81.96	*	76.68	78.85
27	82.53	80.56	79.78	*	79.22	74.70	*	80.15	81.95	79.38	†	78.70
28	83.13	80.32	80.51	79.32	78.48	75.28	79.06	81.33	*	78.94	76.21	78.70
29	82.92		81.11	78.39	78.38	*	78.93	81.81	81.23	79.13	75.94	78.48
30	83.80		*	78.54	†	74.89	78.59		80.37	78.60	*	78.26
31	83.72		80.92		†		78.48	*		78.30		78.78
High	88.57	83.64	81.69	83.19	79.95	77.27	79.06	81.81	83.43	81.43	78.42	78.85
Low	81.55	78.72	78.25	78.39	78.38	72.11	75.23	78.21	80.27	77.09	75.94	75.27

*Sunday
†Holiday

1913—RAILROADS

Date:	Jan.	Feb.	Mar.	Apr.	May	June	July	Aug.	Sept.	Oct.	Nov.	Dec.
1	†	115.36	110.95	112.85	108.83	*	104.40	105.29	†	107.42	104.11	102.84
2	117.61	*	*	112.57	108.52	105.55	104.09	105.29	106.43	107.83	*	103.05
3	117.08	115.13	111.83	113.16	108.37	104.96	104.10	*	105.73	107.33	103.59	104.10
4	117.54	114.93	111.18	113.65	*	103.96	†	106.02	105.60	107.23	†	104.19
5	*	114.51	111.59	113.22	109.40	103.56	†	106.51	106.15	*	103.83	104.11
6	116.76	114.46	111.21	*	108.42	104.43	*	106.19	106.25	106.66	103.12	104.15
7	117.40	114.63	110.59	112.43	108.78	103.97	103.58	106.72	*	106.78	103.35	*
8	117.66	114.75	109.83	113.08	108.65	*	103.42	106.70	105.87	105.96	102.78	104.56
9	118.10	*	*	112.58	108.58	102.98	103.11	106.30	106.13	106.01	*	103.63
10	117.90	113.75	109.04	112.23	108.26	101.18	103.31	*	107.16	105.50	101.87	103.70
11	117.66	113.08	109.70	111.53	*	100.50	103.16	107.10	107.01	104.80	102.29	103.59
12	*	†	109.80	111.87	108.01	103.18	103.52	107.71	108.27	*	103.11	102.71
13	116.25	112.08	110.25	*	108.43	103.30	*	107.76	109.17	†	103.01	102.90
14	115.01	112.30	110.03	111.63	107.93	104.75	103.41	107.28	*	104.19	103.38	*
15	114.57	111.98	109.88	111.29	107.70	*	103.96	106.28	108.57	103.99	103.26	102.11
16	114.89	*	*	111.58	108.13	103.85	104.86	106.60	109.00	102.90	*	102.20
17	114.60	110.95	109.35	111.78	107.90	104.25	104.61	*	108.34	102.95	103.10	102.25
18	114.77	110.30	108.94	111.36	*	105.05	105.25	107.03	108.93	103.62	103.27	102.15
19	*	111.15	109.13	111.26	108.04	104.65	104.98	106.73	108.62	*	103.08	103.56
20	114.20	110.92	109.01	*	108.41	104.15	*	107.03	108.65	103.46	102.80	104.21
21	115.21	110.56	†	111.91	108.36	102.84	105.83	106.59	*	105.42	102.87	*
22	115.93	†	†	111.66	108.90	*	105.98	106.74	108.78	104.58	102.84	104.45
23	115.43	*	*	111.46	108.88	103.40	105.66	106.91	108.63	104.08	*	103.80
24	114.61	110.11	109.65	110.41	109.51	104.48	106.21	*	108.10	104.71	102.93	104.41
25	114.90	109.45	110.65	109.81	*	104.35	106.45	106.90	107.72	104.62	103.77	†
26	*	110.65	110.79	109.40	109.03	104.13	106.45	106.85	108.05	*	103.32	104.23
27	114.71	111.35	110.26	*	108.71	103.65	*	106.50	108.02	105.26	†	103.94
28	115.27	110.94	111.09	109.14	107.83	104.38	106.99	107.40	*	104.63	103.18	*
29	115.34		111.81	108.14	107.41	*	106.86	107.14	107.46	104.90	103.03	103.48
30	115.56		*	107.75	†	103.61	106.11		107.01	104.43	*	103.41
31	115.49		111.69		†		105.77	*		104.05		103.72
High	118.10	115.36	111.83	113.65	109.51	105.55	106.99	107.76	109.17	107.83	104.11	104.56
Low	114.20	109.45	108.94	107.75	107.41	100.50	103.11	105.29	105.60	102.90	101.87	102.11

*Sunday
†Holiday

1913—DAILY STOCK SALES ON N. Y. STOCK EXCHANGE

(000 Omitted)

Date	Jan.	Feb.	Mar.	Apr.	May	June	July	Aug.	Sept.	Oct.	Nov.	Dec.
1	†	163	131	504	530	*	212	168	†	315	44	104
2	316	*	*	309	240	515	161	63	271	277	*	213
3	297	305	394	416	87	339	101	*	310	222	193	297
s	130	254	273	694	*	794	*	160	221	163	†	342
5	*	226	321	221	266	509	†	358	283	*	229	202
6	337	170	219	*	338	593	*	259	106	369	350	116
7	215	171	299	251	294	142	163	262	*	175	210	*
8	214	83	288	456	193	*	128	277	198	377	127	248
9	301	*	*	506	190	455	232	78	168	440	*	258
10	215	184	456	368	69	871	164	*	360	318	379	229
11	181	369	346	377	*	575	67	285	262	224	223	273
12	*	†	355	135	168	832	44	538	531	*	234	295
13	493	477	299	*	189	533	*	509	396	†	224	165
14	804	316	279	177	178	238	79	306	*	468	240	*
15	522	127	81	422	193	*	94	287	496	315	72	284
16	314	*	*	210	146	331	299	173	465	384	*	205
17	457	431	207	243	94	354	203	*	434	339	119	152
18	130	417	203	238	*	253	322	216	418	178	117	283
19	*	450	439	80	165	186	121	237	403	*	112	362
20	316	223	241	*	214	207	*	189	81	280	122	309
21	341	256	†	223	171	279	340	208	*	580	109	*
22	323	†	†	217	299	*	299	191	175	267	50	482
23	400			150	151	268	192	81	304	304	*	369
24	266	468	234	266	219	279	310	*	307	278	57	410
25	80	528	323	358	*	254	392	162	363	79	200	†
26	*	405	444	313	246	223	94	216	275	*	88	482
27	146	383	249	*	276	135	*	199	133	224	†	181
28	447	240	380	385	356	134	294	390	*	280	102	*
29	375		292	551	195	*	231	293	313	212	74	346
30	685		*	428	†	190	333	†	434	173	*	333
31	459		393		†		261	*		191		199
Total	8,766	6,646	7,143	8,457	5,467	9,581	5,139	6,107	7,706	7,434	3,777	7,138

*Sunday. †Holiday.

1914 INDUSTRIALS

Date	Jan.	Feb.	Mar.	Apr.	May	June	July	Aug.	Sept.	Oct.	Nov.	Dec.
1	†	*	*	82.46	80.11	80.98	80.33					
2	78.59	82.55	81.66	82.47	79.83	80.50	80.64					
3	78.43	83.19	81.72	82.11	*	80.82	81.27					
4	*	82.90	82.19	82.07	79.89	81.17	†					
5	79.00	82.85	81.75	*	79.89	81.19	*					
6	79.26	82.34	81.12	82.18	79.78	81.48	81.40					
7	79.17	82.51	81.28	82.18	79.85	*	81.60					
8	78.81	*	*	81.92	79.16	81.64	81.79					
9	79.06	82.44	81.36	81.56	79.56	81.81	81.61					
10	79.15	82.36	81.94	†	*	81.84	81.30					
11	*	82.50	81.57	81.30	80.03	81.61	81.25					
12	79.29	†	81.20	*	80.10	81.76	*					54.62
13	79.62	82.84	81.64	81.05	80.05	81.57	80.86					*
14	80.64	83.09	81.94	80.55	81.05	*	81.11					56.76
15	80.95	*	*	80.00	81.11	81.46	80.34					55.07
16	80.81	82.60	81.68	79.90	80.82	81.28	80.43					55.35
17	80.77	82.48	82.32	79.72	*	81.03	80.41					55.36
18	*	82.69	82.32	79.86	81.36	81.25	80.57					55.09
19	81.21	82.65	82.54	*	81.66	81.33	*					55.20
20	81.01	82.78	83.43	78.88	81.46	81.52	80.41					*
21	81.92	82.52	83.02	79.35	80.89	*	80.76					54.46
22	82.66	*	*	79.52	80.85	81.58	80.83					54.42
23	82.70	†	83.19	78.73	81.40	81.19	80.52					53.46
24	82.18	82.34	83.10	77.52	*	80.23	79.71					53.17
25	*	81.31	82.57	76.97	81.23	79.30	79.67					†
26	82.88	81.47	82.31	*	81.25	80.06	*					53.34
27	82.68	82.00	81.83	77.82	81.56	80.11	79.07					*
28	82.12	82.26	81.65	78.79	81.55	*	76.28					54.55
29	81.72		*	78.61	81.57	80.00	76.72					54.58
30	82.80		81.64	79.12	†	80.66	71.42					54.55
31	82.85		82.39		*		†					54.58
High	82.88	83.19	83.43	82.47	81.66	81.84	81.79					56.76
Low	78.43	81.31	81.12	76.97	79.16	79.30	71.42					53.17

†Holiday
*Sunday

new average ↓ (Dec.)

Change in the Industrial Average

When the Stock Exchange closed in July, 1914 because of the war, there were 12 stocks in the industrial average. In September, 1916, a new list of 20 stocks was adopted and computed back to the reopening of the Exchange on December 12, 1914. For those students of the averages who wish to trace the price movement as computed on the basis of 12 stocks from the reopening of the Exchange on December 12, 1914 to September 30, 1916 when the old average was discontinued, the figures for the old averages are given on opposite page.

1914—RAILROADS

Date:	Jan.	Feb.	Mar.	Apr.	May	June	July	Aug.	Sept.	Oct	Nov.	Dec.
1	†	*	*	104.97	102.45	102.53	102.05					
2	103.72	108.59	104.73	104.98	102.08	101.80	102.24					
3	103.51	109.07	104.80	104.43	*	102.12	102.68					
4	*	108.70	105.51	104.39	102.66	102.37	†					
5	104.08	108.39	105.13	*	102.43	102.35	*					
6	104.23	107.70	103.70	104.51	102.31	102.91	102.70					
7	104.25	107.48	103.26	104.65	102.03	*	103.05					
8	104.15	*	*	104.16	101.36	103.01	102.76					
9	104.11	106.84	103.40	103.78	101.50	103.38	102.75					
10	104.35	106.88	103.95	†	*	103.30	101.85					
11	*	106.93	103.58	103.40	102.01	103.02	101.80					
12	104.48	†	103.17	*	102.18	103.23	*					90.21
13	104.60	107.26	103.65	103.13	101.96	103.20	101.06					*
14	105.92	107.18	103.79	102.82	102.90	*	101.34					92.29
15	106.65	*	*	102.48	103.05	103.14	100.70					90.95
16	106.52	106.36	103.82	102.41	102.91	102.86	100.63					90.89
17	106.55	106.03	104.25	101.69	*	102.60	100.01					90.88
18	*	106.65	103.94	101.73	103.41	102.78	100.49					90.78
19	107.25	106.69	104.13	*	103.49	102.94	*					91.01
20	107.25	106.76	104.96	100.63	103.37	103.06	98.30					*
21	108.13	106.38	104.87	101.45	102.68	*	98.77					90.13
22	108.75	*	*	101.26	102.68	103.54	98.49					89.73
23	109.31	†	105.76	100.53	103.24	102.91	97.95					87.91
24	108.77	106.10	105.60	99.48	*	101.73	97.05					87.40
25	*	105.04	104.91	99.24	103.08	100.63	97.16					†
26	108.87	105.17	104.75	*	103.01	101.31	*					87.75
27	108.80	105.67	104.00	99.65	103.64	101.39	96.58					*
28	108.33	105.48	103.85	100.96	103.48	*	93.14					88.80
29	107.75		*	100.38	103.11	101.28	94.12					88.50
30	109.29		104.02	101.23	†	102.41	89.41					88.19
31	109.43		104.75		*		†					88.53
High	109.43	109.07	105.76	104.98	103.64	103.54	103.05					92.29
Low	103.51	105.04	103.17	99.24	101.36	100.63	89.41					87.40

Exchange closed on account of War

*Sunday
†Holiday

1914—DAILY STOCK SALES ON N. Y. STOCK EXCHANGE
(000 Omitted)

Date	Jan.	Feb.	Mar.	Apr.	May	June	July	Aug.	Sept.	Oct.	Nov.	Dec.
1	†	*	*	180	456	106	135					
2	187	483	99	210	147	200	89					
3	198	417	124	195	*	156	152					
4	*	511	200	64	317	185	†					
5	231	345	330	*	272	92	*					
6	482	321	408	106	179	131	93					
7	347	167	318	111	215	*	205					
8	310	*	*	222	299	160	209					
9	290	281	336	270	150	146	198					
10	139	314	299	†	*	107	264					
11	*	221	269	121	202	111	108					
12	303	†	199	*	117	119	*					112
13	268	240	219	249	157	37	275					*
14	384	156	123	536	300	*	239					231
15	561	*	*	309	251	91	358	Exchange closed				269
16	504	343	160	420	70	151	298					105
17	147	232	254	402	*	114	312					84
18	*	439	211	200	262	82	120					215
19	351	204	144	*	188	78	*					50
20	359	158	322	386	139	61	207					*
21	628	115	149	354	210	*	266					106
22	783	*	*	281	93	185	182					123
23	614	†	333	303	103	195	195					157
24	311	136	221	516	*	349	300					109
25	*	396	234	347	111	457	212					†
26	474	317	215	*	76	284	*					23
27	412	276	144	392	165	59	492					*
28	460	163	109	413	132	*	1027					130
29	464		*	267	115	68	809					58
30	555		198	288	†	260	1307					50
31	377		244		*		†					73
Total	10,136	6,235	5,860	7,141	4,728	3,985	8,051					1,895

*Sunday. †Holiday.

CHANGE IN THE INDUSTRIAL AVERAGE—OLD 12 INDUSTRIAL STOCKS

Date	1914 Dec.	Jan.	Feb.	March	April	May	June	July	Aug.	Sept.	Oct.
					1915						
1	....	†	76.54	74.76	82.51	90.78	84.16	89.84	*	100.85	112.76
2	....	74.65	76.40	74.87	†	*	85.36	89.52	92.92	100.35	114.32
3	....	*	75.94	75.78	82.80	88.79	88.42	89.11	93.20	100.12	*
4	....	75.53	75.59	75.75	*	89.22	89.50	*	94.27	100.41	115.26
5	....	75.87	74.98	76.69	83.41	87.52	89.37	†	95.08	*	112.09
6	....	75.69	75.50	76.47	83.48	88.18	*	89.52	95.51	†	111.91
7	....	76.33	*	*	84.13	84.41	90.16	88.62	95.97	100.88	112.78
8	....	76.79	76.08	76.83	84.56	84.42	89.81	88.34	*	101.38	113.77
9	....	76.87	76.16	76.40	87.32	*	88.50	87.27	97.78	102.16	113.83
10	....	*	76.58	76.39	86.81	81.44	90.30	88.02	97.89	101.76	*
11		77.30	77.51	76.46	*	84.55	91.77	*	97.20	100.68	114.67
12	74.56	77.51	†	75.91	86.73	83.87	92.38	90.05	97.96	*	†
13	*	77.54	76.90	76.05	87.56	82.41	*	c90.73	97.72	101.68	114.00
14	76.86	77.83	*	*	88.27	79.83	91.54	91.29	97.62	101.97	113.25
15	75.83	77.43	76.56	76.42	88.67	81.87	91.45	92.14	*	101.93	112.54
16	76.02	77.17	76.09	75.92	89.25	*	91.84	92.86	98.72	101.83	113.27
17	75.89	*	75.32	76.08	90.43	83.23	91.67	93.12	98.64	104.08	*
18	75.60	77.75	75.04	75.97	*	82.46	91.27	*	99.26	105.18	115.28
19	75.95	78.05	74.85	76.60	88.80	82.64	91.31	92.04	98.06	*	115.29
20	*	78.03	74.73	77.12	90.01	83.00	*	91.77	97.02	106.25	115.51
21	75.31	78.41	*	*	89.54	84.21	91.93	92.45	94.37	109.21	117.22
22	74.90	78.01	†	78.03	89.26	84.89	91.94	92.27	*	110.78	118.05
23	73.57	78.00	74.19	a79.38	89.39	*	91.36	92.12	94.64	110.19	118.14
24	73.48	*	73.18	80.03	89.84	84.66	89.50	91.91	96.80	110.84	*
25	†	77.73	74.31	80.13	*	83.92	89.62	*	97.76	111.82	117.76
26	73.77	78.09	74.62	80.31	89.44	83.48	90.27	92.21	98.58	*	117.66
27	*	76.57	74.86	81.18	89.13	83.93	*	92.59	99.50	114.05	117.27
28	74.50	76.60	*	*	89.78	83.84	90.48	93.10	99.51	113.59	116.08
29	74.42	75.50		81.96	90.58	83.94	89.64	93.08	*	113.17	118.59
30	74.36	76.09		82.14	90.91	*	89.98	b92.29	98.90	110.22	121.29
31	74.73	*		81.95		†		92.18	98.64		*

Date	1915 Nov.	Dec.	Jan.	Feb.	March	April	May	June	July	Aug.	Sept.
						1916					
1	117.63	126.47	†	121.68	119.03	122.48	118.52	122.96	120.96	123.68	129.62
2	†	125.42	*	122.46	118.15	*	116.61	124.32	*	121.53	126.21
3	117.18	126.54	127.77	123.68	121.29	122.19	116.94	128.12	121.36	121.69	*
4	119.91	129.33	128.19	121.75	121.27	121.77	112.91	*	†	123.86	*
5	119.15	*	127.02	121.75	*	122.04	115.57	129.42	123.54	123.61	128.36
6	118.69	132.90	120.62	*	123.04	122.84	117.11	127.97	123.95	*	128.95
7	*	131.96	125.34	123.01	122.07	121.60	*	125.05	125.28	123.62	129.07
8	118.20	134.00	125.71	124.06	121.26	121.79	117.78	122.72	122.12	123.98	132.05
9	116.79	131.98	*	124.76	122.67	*	118.02	123.35	*	124.60	133.18
10	118.56	130.55	124.38	124.75	123.38	122.73	117.64	123.32	120.44	125.81	*
11	121.15	131.42	122.50	126.02	123.03	121.92	118.09	123.10	123.10	130.18	133.93
12	121.01	*	125.09	†	*	121.72	118.64	124.07	120.05	130.02	140.12
13	121.31	131.34	125.29	*	123.45	120.32	121.03	124.16	121.20	*	146.36
14	*	132.43	126.34	125.00	125.17	118.41	*	123.90	121.17	131.21	149.56
15	121.42	131.13	126.12	124.88	125.29	119.31	121.15	125.02	119.55	130.64	149.55
16	121.43	128.56	*	122.96	125.50	*	118.66	123.30	*	131.48	149.39
17	122.32	128.13	125.89	124.57	125.64	118.06	118.47	123.00	121.30	131.25	*
18	124.06	128.09	126.93	124.70	125.61	116.89	121.15	*	116.72	131.30	146.22
19	123.07	*	126.82	125.01	*	115.05	120.10	121.66	122.01	131.20	147.21
20	122.71	127.42	125.53	*	123.40	115.45	120.12	122.06	120.02	*	145.88
21	*	128.89	126.53	125.10	122.04	*	120.26	121.05	122.04	132.09	146.19
22	122.83	128.59	126.27	†	122.54	109.92	120.77	120.77	122.37	132.60	142.21
23	123.13	125.28		123.25	122.18		127.27	120.56	*	129.94	152.10
24	123.70	126.82	126.21	121.72	121.85	111.22	127.77	121.20	122.33	131.84	*
25	†	†	126.55	122.29	124.18	114.14	125.38		123.03	131.29	150.88
26	126.15	*	122.82	121.31		114.06	124.17	119.84	122.68	131.86	152.34
27	126.51	128.65	123.95	*	122.93	115.92	124.58	120.48	122.98	*	155.77
28	*	127.94	123.59	120.15	121.31	117.16		122.13	123.40	128.80	155.12
29	127.04	125.95	121.65	120.45	121.89	115.77	124.57	121.20	123.51	131.21	156.67
30	126.98	126.58	*		121.62		121.23		123.50	131.77	155.13
31		129.94	120.23		122.27		123.41			126.48	

a—General Motors was substituted for U. S. Rubber 1st preferred.
b—In twelve industrials average Anaconda Copper was substituted for Amalgamated Copper.
c—The twelve industrials average crossed the twenty railroads for the first time in history. †Holiday *Sunday

1915—INDUSTRIALS

Date:	Jan.	Feb.	Mar.	Apr.	May	June	July	Aug.	Sept.	Oct.	Nov.	Dec.
1	†	55.59	55.29	61.05	71.51	64.86	69.85	*	81.79	90.88	95.16	95.90
2	54.63	57.26	55.66	†	*	65.72	69.98	76.46	81.03	91.98	†	94.78
3	*	56.90	55.88	61.49	69.54	67.75	69.56	76.71	80.70	*	94.76	95.91
4	55.44	56.83	56.00	*	69.58	67.71	*	77.33	80.90	90.98	96.06	96.78
5	55.50	56.16	56.51	62.29	67.53	68.56	†	77.21	*	89.16	94.81	*
6	55.40	56.33	56.41	62.78	68.23	*	69.87	77.21	†	88.23	94.18	97.86
7	56.08	*	*	62.55	65.13	69.21	68.85	76.71	81.02	90.20	*	97.71
8	56.55	56.31	56.98	63.15	62.77	68.92	68.65	*	81.16	90.50	92.80	98.45
9	56.54	56.85	56.88	65.02	*	67.27	67.88	77.70	81.88	90.63	91.08	97.18
10	*	57.05	56.66	65.15	62.06	69.02	68.38	77.86	80.96	*	92.18	96.13
11	57.37	57.83	56.86	*	64.64	70.55	*	77.45	80.40	92.37	93.64	96.51
12	57.44	†	56.66	64.66	64.46	71.12	70.05	78.14	*	†	94.71	*
13	57.35	57.20	56.35	65.54	63.01	*	70.26	78.38	81.40	93.63	95.33	95.96
14	57.51	*	*	66.14	60.38	70.93	70.80	78.82	81.91	92.76	*	98.30
15	57.90	57.02	56.70	67.42	61.93	71.05	71.50	*	81.71	92.56	95.05	98.18
16	57.19	56.64	56.59	69.36	*	71.30	71.78	81.28	82.54	93.34	96.33	96.57
17	*	55.70	56.67	69.60	63.41	71.16	71.85	81.78	83.27	*	96.18	97.40
18	58.12	55.53	56.57	*	62.70	70.98	*	81.86	84.26	94.61	95.48	97.57
19	58.11	55.38	56.98	67.86	63.08	71.16	70.84	80.31	*	93.38	95.27	*
20	58.42	55.20	57.40	68.64	63.68	*	71.00	79.31	84.83	94.61	95.02	97.70
21	58.51	*	*	68.43	64.88	71.83	72.05	76.76	85.88	95.35	*	97.66
22	58.21	†	58.10	68.20	65.50	71.90	73.82	*	85.55	96.46	95.45	97.98
23	58.52	54.40	59.10	68.65	*	71.28	74.10	76.88	86.48	96.11	95.87	98.25
24	*	54.22	59.26	69.64	65.46	69.78	74.18	79.07	86.81	*	97.18	98.36
25	58.06	54.61	59.25	*	64.79	70.23	*	80.65		95.88	†	†
26	58.24	55.02	59.51	68.97	64.42	70.71	74.60	81.12	*	95.81	97.28	*
27	57.07	55.18	59.60	68.90	64.95	*	74.83	81.88	89.20	94.72	97.07	99.21
28	57.25	*	*	70.22	65.01	70.74	75.53	81.95	89.73	93.34	*	99.16
29	56.54		60.13	70.95	64.67	70.08	75.79	*	89.90	95.34	97.56	97.96
30	57.16		61.30	71.78	*	70.06	75.53	81.70	90.58	96.02	96.71	98.20
31	*		60.83		†		75.34	81.20		*		99.15
High	58.52	57.83	61.30	71.78	71.51	71.90	75.79	81.95	90.58	96.46	97.56	99.21
Low	54.63	54.22	55.29	61.05	60.38	64.86	67.88	76.46	80.40	88.23	91.08	94.78

*Sunday
†Holiday

1915—RAILROADS

Date:	Jan.	Feb.	Mar.	Apr.	May	June	July	Aug.	Sept.	Oct.	Nov.	Dec.
1	†	91.91	87.94	92.84	96.94	91.68	92.55	*	93.91	97.68	107.89	105.87
2	88.46	91.52	88.18	†	*	92.46	92.03	92.61	93.49	97.55	†	105.22
3	*	91.21	88.98	93.39	95.97	93.85	91.88	92.88	94.10	*	107.90	105.79
4	89.63	90.89	88.80	*	96.16	93.87	*	92.91	94.95	97.85	108.28	106.09
5	89.95	90.09	89.98	93.91	94.80	93.49	†	93.13	*	97.70	107.05	*
6	89.43	90.11	89.71	94.05	95.33	*	91.81	93.66	†	98.87	106.56	107.20
7	89.94	*	*	93.93	93.53	93.06	90.51	93.42	95.01	99.54	*	106.55
8	89.85	90.38	90.47	93.64	93.09	92.87	89.48	*	94.89	101.80	105.91	106.40
9	89.95	89.81	90.02	95.78	*	92.54	88.66	93.53	95.33	103.20	105.26	105.91
10	*	90.22	89.97	96.44	91.75	93.38	89.51	95.70	95.00	*	106.79	105.21
11	90.83	90.92	90.18	*	93.60	94.10	*	95.69	94.61	103.53	106.53	105.58
12	90.78	†	89.61	95.67	93.26	94.17	90.64	94.93	*	†	106.82	*
13	90.58	90.23	89.71	95.89	92.55	*	90.50	94.00	95.01	102.55	106.80	104.97
14	90.91	*	*	95.16	90.75	93.95	90.43	94.07	94.87	101.40	*	105.90
15	91.22	89.91	89.95	96.26	92.06	93.26	90.86	*	94.82	101.06	106.55	105.71
16	91.28	89.65	89.59	96.47	*	93.69	90.48	94.20	94.60	101.33	107.20	104.88
17	*	89.14	89.56	97.10	92.79	93.36	90.26	94.24	94.82	*	106.91	105.13
18	92.00	89.26	89.45	*	92.16	93.07	*	94.10	95.73	102.48	107.57	105.30
19	92.91	88.96	89.83	97.72	92.16	93.11	90.68	93.48	*	102.15	107.06	*
20	93.18	88.88	89.90	98.75	92.47	*	90.93	93.00	95.95	101.79	106.81	105.50
21	94.05	*	*	98.45	92.75	93.40	90.87	91.95	95.68	101.54	*	105.45
22	93.51	†	90.09	97.91	93.13	94.01	90.29	*	95.94	102.29	106.55	105.38
23	93.46	87.90	91.30	97.58	*	93.80	90.16	92.28	96.27	102.51	106.76	106.54
24	*	87.85	92.01	98.09	92.98	93.08	90.16	92.76	97.91	*	107.15	106.43
25	93.23	87.91	92.56	*	92.56	93.26	*	93.62	98.94	103.06	†	†
26	93.70	88.08	92.88	97.69	92.31	93.77		93.63	*	103.45	106.80	*
27	92.21	88.21	92.95	97.33	92.50	*	92.50	93.78	98.96	103.35	106.75	107.35
28	92.52	*	*	97.73	92.14	93.47	92.25	93.93	98.31	105.00	*	106.63
29	90.80		93.37	97.96	92.06	92.55	92.17	*	98.15	106.26	106.40	106.53
30	91.60		92.98	97.35	*	92.96	92.05	94.03	97.93	107.04	106.36	106.88
31	*		92.82		†		92.02	94.08		*		108.05
High	94.05	91.91	93.37	98.75	96.94	94.17	92.55	95.70	98.96	107.04	108.28	108.05
Low	88.46	87.85	87.94	92.84	90.75	91.68	88.66	91.95	93.49	97.55	105.26	104.88

*Sunday
†Holiday

1915—DAILY STOCK SALES ON N. Y. STOCK EXCHANGE
(000 Omitted)

Date	Jan.	Feb.	Mar.	Apr.	May	June	July	Aug.	Sept.	Oct.	Nov.	Dec.
1	†	285	158	540	513	207	252	*	661	1497	1132	458
2	23	201	135	†	*	279	334	597	654	710	†	678
3	*	155	228	278	1025	731	191	718	495	*	1112	470
4	127	204	175	*	623	971	*	671	155	1417	1040	222
5	148	316	257	681	895	291	†	913	*	1166	1006	*
6	130	109	92	626	611	*	222	775	†	1497	457	553
7	154	*	*	523	1158	472	530	324	372	1419	*	715
8	203	213	270	647	562	470	346	*	437	1345	809	550
9	65	252	210	1282	*	544	379	692	585	633	1079	653
10	*	256	176	838	1179	478	220	1094	542	*	1249	585
11	210	352	166	*	589	849	*	948	231	1274	948	296
12	170	†	227	874	711	394	499	888	*	†	934	*
13	131	139	78	1069	452	*	613	828	352	1203	330	379
14	119	*	*	1046	685	665	471	360	452	1032	*	466
15	174	225	129	1224	241	475	534	*	516	849	793	625
16	100	160	169	1119	*	307	668	948	464	401	978	675
17	*	189	117	665	288	331	425	1053	731	*	1060	519
18	256	188	217	*	208	329	*	1001	399	917	785	194
19	376	148	262	1480	196	122	716	1090	*	1058	593	*
20	302	130	166	1255	274	*	436	988	890	911	327	412
21	381	*	*	1003	394	410	752	541	887	1067	*	339
22	345	†	370	697	365	457	665	*	1107	1057	399	548
23	129	222	609	624	*	385	470	879	977	520	316	597
24	*	232	590	455	535	436	281	798	956	*	485	582
25	167	145	430	*	263	291	*	1063	577	1149	†	†
26	144	171	376	770	393	202	877	713	*	1171	641	*
27	350	90	267	689	268	*	866	917	1451	1116	234	861
28	275	*	*	894	164	264	1128	343	1662	1330	*	621
29	437		547	960	132	309	1361	*	1474	1371	471	400
30	120		682	982	*	229	839	737	1495	719	433	446
31	*		737		†		252	592		*		965
Total	5,038	4,382	7,841	21,221	12,722	10,900	14,329	20,469	18,523	26,828	17,614	13,808

*Sunday. †Holiday.

THE DOW-JONES DAILY AVERAGES OF 40 BONDS

1915—BOND AVERAGES

Date:	Jan.	Feb.	Mar.	Apr.	May	June	July	Aug.	Sept.	Oct.	Nov.	Dec.
1				90.86	91.77	90.53	90.52	*	89.90	90.74	92.70	94.30
2				†	*	90.64	90.44	90.15	89.75	90.61	†	94.19
3				90.83	91.73	90.76	90.38	90.21	89.79	*	92.85	94.19
4				*	91.77	90.99	*	90.25	89.81	90.68	93.10	94.25
5				90.88	91.65	91.01	†	90.26	*	90.62	93.19	*
6				90.90	91.67	*	90.29	90.34	†	90.63	93.20	94.18
7				90.99	91.43	91.09	90.13	90.32	89.71	90.70	*	94.32
8				91.00	91.43	91.08	90.09	*	89.70	90.84	93.24	94.31
9				91.13	*	91.07	90.09	90.42	89.69	90.94	93.22	94.29
10				91.17	91.19	91.06	90.11	90.56	89.64	*	93.30	94.19
11				*	91.23	91.16	*	90.56	89.67	91.09	93.54	94.21
12				91.19	91.25	91.11	90.07	90.55	*	†	93.76	*
13				91.24	91.27	*	90.22	90.56	89.75	91.19	93.83	94.13
14				91.21	91.04	91.20	90.19	90.61	89.72	91.28	*	94.12
15				91.21	91.06	91.20	90.14	*	89.70	91.29	94.04	94.16
16				91.30	*	91.28	90.19	90.56	89.64	91.33	94.11	94.16
17				91.33	91.01	91.34	90.20	90.53	89.67	*	94.16	94.11
18				*	91.02	91.34	*	90.40	89.70	91.55	94.33	94.10
19				91.43	90.90	91.41	90.11	90.42	*	91.74	94.42	*
20				91.34	90.78	*	90.07	90.25	89.86	91.89	94.42	94.02
21				91.36	90.73	91.44	90.13	90.24	89.82	92.16	*	94.00
22				91.33	90.81	91.39	90.12	*	90.02	92.22	94.56	94.04
23				91.40	*	91.35	90.16	90.06	90.12	92.22	94.63	94.02
24				91.41	90.89	91.24	90.08	90.21	90.32	*	94.64	93.95
25				*	90.90	91.00	*	90.21	90.43	92.30	†	†
26				91.47	90.76	91.00	90.10	89.96	*	92.42	94.47	*
27				91.53	90.76	*	90.17	90.06	90.63	92.51	94.47	94.03
28				91.60	90.71	90.92	90.25	90.00	90.79	92.54	*	94.08
29				91.65	90.69	90.74	90.28	*	90.76	92.66	94.39	94.13
30				91.70	*	90.55	90.25	90.00	90.63	92.78	94.34	94.07
31					†		90.19	90.00		*		94.08
High				91.70	91.77	91.44	90.52	90.61	90.79	92.78	94.64	94.32
Low				90.83	90.69	90.53	90.07	89.96	89.64	90.61	92.70	93.95

*Sunday
†Holiday

1916—INDUSTRIALS

Date:	Jan.	Feb.	Mar.	Apr.	May	June	July	Aug.	Sept.	Oct.	Nov.	Dec.
1	†	91.93	90.69	93.69	90.30	91.87	88.93	89.05	91.19	*	105.90	106.17
2	*	93.69	90.52	*	89.02	91.22	*	88.34	92.29	103.01	105.70	106.81
3	98.81	94.40	91.71	94.13	88.61	91.53	89.37	88.83	*	103.45	106.28	*
4	97.72	93.19	91.48	93.97	87.71	*	†	88.41	†	103.41	105.93	106.20
5	97.41	93.39	*	94.12	88.51	92.19	90.53	88.55	93.36	104.15	*	106.43
6	96.44	*	92.93	94.46	90.51	91.73	90.40	*	94.51	102.85	107.21	106.76
7	97.34	94.96	92.58	93.38	*	91.84	89.71	88.88	94.59	103.40	†	106.43
8	97.52	94.91	92.58	93.31	90.36	92.01	89.51	88.15	94.63	*	106.83	106.51
9	*	95.86	93.50	*	89.71	92.78	*	90.26	95.53	100.23	107.68	105.68
10	95.69	96.10	93.11	94.22	89.78	92.70	88.60	90.05	*	101.35	107.65	*
11	94.07	96.15	92.90	93.77	90.08	*	87.63	90.32	95.74	99.98	106.72	104.67
12	95.31	†	*	93.28	90.94	93.61	87.63	90.50	96.65	†	*	100.35
13	94.71	*	94.75	91.28	91.71	93.19	86.42	*	97.71	98.94	105.63	102.61
14	96.47	95.28	95.40	91.63	*	93.33	86.95	90.75	98.84	98.98	107.04	98.23
15	96.55	95.26	95.76	91.48	92.43	93.33	87.36	91.48	98.39	*	107.72	97.93
16	*	94.50	96.08	*	92.01	92.49	*	91.91	98.00	101.42	108.48	99.11
17	96.63	94.11	96.00	91.08	91.51	91.90	87.15	92.08	*	102.42	109.62	*
18	96.16	94.35	95.76	90.65	92.05	*	87.25	92.08	98.51	102.35	110.13	98.07
19	95.25	94.77	*	88.46	91.76	90.00	88.10	91.93	98.57	102.55	*	97.76
20	93.60	*	93.60	88.11	91.81	90.57	89.00	*	98.47	103.68	110.10	95.26
21	94.78	94.36	93.58	†	*	90.03	89.03	93.25	99.55	103.88	110.15	90.16
22	94.65	†	93.97	84.96	92.06	89.54	89.75	93.83	100.77	*	108.65	95.09
23	*	94.35	93.76	*	92.10	88.88	*	93.61	101.30	105.17	107.43	94.60
24	93.87	93.37	93.65	87.00	92.37	89.26	89.10	93.66	*	105.15	109.07	*
25	94.24	93.85	93.23	88.12	92.62	*	88.83	92.90	100.89	104.57	109.95	†
26	93.49	92.78	*	87.23	92.29	87.68	88.13	92.91	101.39	104.56	*	96.10
27	92.99	*	93.57	88.78	91.62	88.43	88.00	*	101.85	105.28	108.23	95.63
28	93.25	90.89	93.81	89.65	*	88.29	88.35	92.49	103.11	104.83	107.01	94.01
29	91.93	91.03	93.36	89.78	91.95	89.51	88.79	91.63	103.73	*	105.97	95.00
30	*		92.73	*	†	89.58	*	91.32	102.90	104.30	†	†
31	90.58		93.25		91.80		89.25	92.25		104.61		†
High	98.81	96.15	96.08	94.46	92.62	93.61	90.53	93.83	103.73	105.28	110.15	106.81
Low	90.58	90.89	90.52	84.96	87.71	87.68	86.42	88.15	91.19	98.94	105.63	90.16

*Sunday
†Holiday

1916—RAILROADS

Date:	Jan.	Feb.	Mar.	Apr.	May	June	July	Aug.	Sept.	Oct.	Nov.	Dec.
1	†	102.05	100.65	101.61	102.46	107.06	105.78	103.89	104.01	*	110.07	108.69
2	*	102.56	100.69	*	101.66	106.63	*	103.43	104.62	109.96	110.42	109.10
3	107.76	102.88	101.14	101.96	101.24	106.87	106.62	103.28	*	110.83	110.23	*
4	107.50	101.68	100.86	102.10	100.68	*	†	103.34	†	112.28	110.28	108.65
5	107.32	101.84	*	102.73	101.40	106.91	106.91	103.31	104.75	108.88	*	108.92
6	106.75	*	101.35	102.88	102.03	107.29	107.11	*	104.83	111.00	110.96	108.77
7	107.13	102.26	101.31	102.21	*	108.23	106.60	103.21	105.41	111.30	†	108.56
8	107.36	102.16	101.41	102.10	102.69	108.43	106.62	103.59	105.70	*	110.34	108.33
9	*	102.62	101.74	*	103.08	108.80	*	105.51	105.86	109.40	110.00	107.79
10	106.54	103.00	101.72	102.13	102.58	108.53	106.08	104.75	*	110.47	109.61	*
11	106.18	103.32	101.66	101.85	102.75	*	105.41	105.16	105.69	109.26	109.11	106.91
12	106.69	†	*	101.79	103.70	109.08	105.45	104.93	105.61	†	*	105.09
13	106.48	*	102.20	100.96	103.97	108.63	104.99	*	106.21	108.89	108.17	106.73
14	106.79	102.41	103.37	101.00	*	108.51	105.10	105.28	106.68	109.14	107.76	106.22
15	106.73	102.34	103.73	101.12	104.68	108.26	105.17	105.76	107.59	*	107.23	106.22
16	*	101.45	103.44	*	104.43	107.47	*	106.25	109.16	110.24	108.15	107.53
17	106.56	101.50	103.63	101.08	104.28	107.15	105.21	105.80	*	110.03	108.25	*
18	106.22	101.86	103.70	101.28	106.15	*	105.11	105.44	108.76	110.38	108.26	107.41
19	105.90	101.73	*	100.06	106.97	105.60	105.38	105.27	108.39	110.23	*	107.31
20	105.02	*	102.94	100.17	107.35	106.31	104.96	*	107.59	110.52	109.21	106.53
21	105.55	101.59	102.98	†	*	105.85	104.73	105.63	108.13	110.34	108.42	103.53
22	105.41	†	103.03	99.11	108.76	105.71	104.89	107.14	108.43	*	108.03	105.91
23	*	101.46	103.20	*	108.38	105.30	*	106.99	108.43	111.03	107.59	106.08
24	104.07	101.03	103.08	99.78	107.18	105.45	104.43	106.68	*	110.40	108.03	*
25	103.98	101.69	102.96	100.02	106.76	*	104.15	106.00	108.53	110.02	108.02	†
26	102.74	101.36	*	99.98	106.58	104.04	103.81	106.03	109.33	109.89	*	106.17
27	102.42	*	102.81	101.95	106.26	104.53	103.40	*	110.26	110.18	107.81	106.27
28	102.37	101.00	102.71	101.78	*	104.55	103.54	105.89	109.76	109.96	107.71	105.42
29	101.83	101.13	102.20	101.73	106.89	105.52	103.73	105.13	110.03	*	107.85	105.15
30	*		101.72	*	†	105.95	*	104.44	110.05	109.95	†	†
31	100.75		101.63		106.68		103.65	105.05		109.95		†
High	107.76	103.32	103.73	102.88	108.76	109.08	107.11	107.14	110.26	112.28	110.96	109.10
Low	100.75	101.00	100.65	99.11	100.68	104.04	103.40	103.21	104.01	108.88	107.23	103.53

*Sunday
†Holiday

1916—DAILY STOCK SALES ON NEW YORK STOCK EXCHANGE
(000 Omitted)

Date	Jan.	Feb.	Mar.	Apr.	May	June	July	Aug.	Sept.	Oct.	Nov.	Dec.
1	†	721	752	202	908	365	166	329	709	*	1233	1099
2	†	645	393	*	617	732	*	380	274	992	1710	792
3	1018	645	348	513	585	271	264	344	*	1124	1120	*
4	878	900	165	594	526	*	†	212	†	1135	527	1382
5	889	360	*	464	895	531	479	49	1007	1280	*	968
6	801	*	484	537	578	632	561	*	1368	1416	1430	1079
7	808	593	548	587	*	455	491	123	1033	684	†	1406
8	378	435	535	244	848	582	154	254	1050	*	2100	1061
9	*	543	702	*	731	531	*	572	677	2017	1530	672
10	677	720	600	461	426	185	458	563	*	1206	2029	*
11	826	565	233	316	477	*	665	337	1218	1373	938	1014
12	710	†	*	325	682	697	567	261	1279	†	*	2460
13	508	*	910	719	317	581	676	*	1318	980	1529	1759
14	683	650	1105	630	*	607	685	421	1751	458	1651	2498
15	407	591	902	179	912	422	160	557	1297	*	1384	2435
16	*	595	980	*	659	367	*	834	784	1018	2089	837
17	574	468	702	511	723	236	362	868	*	1387	2074	*
18	545	424	314	414	780	*	348	716	1199	1117	1038	1250
19	576	264	*	718	1290	761	452	208	1065	1366	*	1748
20	619	*	810	598	1208	475	437	*	1159	1294	2176	1586
21	563	279	613	†	*	596	367	867	1366	742	1745	3177
22	178	†	503	588	930	601	170	1325	1524	*	1753	1780
23	*	293	465	*	872	724	*	1058	1024	1422	1617	528
24	657	578	476	791	818	189	419	762	*	1239	1360	*
25	462	340	238	905	711	*	361	761	2393	1276	799	†
26	746	370	*	549	401	685	462	250	1565	1290	*	792
27	735	*	503	734	215	522	256	*	1504	1222	1351	897
28	538	805	507	719	*	352	244	605	1536	657	1234	988
29	292	526	468	279	261	583	101	523	1876	*	1296	734
30	*		498	*	†	445	*	696	832	1101	†	†
31	948		454		338		219	845		975		†
Total	16,015	12,311	15,210	12,718	16,707	13,125	9,523	13,874	30,810	27,543	35,713	32,940

*Sunday. †Holiday.

1916—BOND AVERAGES

Date:	Jan.	Feb.	Mar.	Apr.	May	June	July	Aug.	Sept.	Oct.	Nov.	Dec.
1	†	94.42	94.46	94.47	94.10	94.49	93.97	93.74	93.68	*	95.16	95.55
2		94.51	94.40	*	94.09	94.56	*	93.74	93.70	94.50	95.27	95.54
3	94.19	94.62	94.38	94.43	94.09	94.49	93.99	93.77	*	94.51	95.30	*
4	94.21	94.67	94.44	94.47	94.04	*	†	93.69	†	94.59	95.29	95.35
5	94.21	94.71	*	94.31	94.05	94.56	93.99	93.67	93.73	94.84	*	95.24
6	94.18	*	94.42	94.51	94.11	94.49	93.98	*	93.70	94.90	95.32	95.16
7	94.15	94.74	94.43	94.49	*	94.45	93.95	93.73	93.72	94.90	†	95.18
8	94.20	94.74	94.44	94.46	94.07	94.44	93.98	93.73	93.71	*	95.42	95.15
9	*	94.80	94.47	*	94.05	94.46	*	93.72	93.73	94.87	95.38	95.18
10	94.24	94.79	94.47	94.48	94.05	94.40	94.02	93.77	*	94.94	95.38	95.18
11	94.20	94.79	94.45	94.47	94.07	*	93.96	93.71	93.71	94.97	95.42	95.18
12	94.19	†	*	94.46	94.13	94.40	93.93	93.73	93.70	†	*	95.00
13	94.30	*	94.44	94.44	94.13	94.37	93.94	*	93.71	94.93	95.38	94.92
14	94.32	94.80	94.44	94.38	*	94.38	93.83	93.69	93.84	94.92	95.42	94.81
15	94.31	94.79	94.42	94.35	94.14	94.36	93.84	93.69	93.87	*	95.45	94.77
16		94.82	94.44	*	94.23	94.34		93.79	93.84	94.95	95.47	94.80
17	94.33	94.77	94.48	94.33	94.19	94.38	93.79	93.75	*	95.03	95.49	
18	94.40	94.80	94.54	94.33	94.24		93.77	93.79	93.91	95.02	95.49	94.82
19	94.39	94.77	*	94.20	94.31	94.32	93.78	93.77	93.98	95.10	*	94.89
20	94.40		94.47	94.11	94.35	94.23	93.78	*	93.99	95.20	95.54	94.97
21	94.47	94.74	94.50	†	*	94.10	93.78	93.81	94.01	95.18	95.55	94.89
22	94.49	†	94.48	94.03	94.45	94.13	93.81	93.90	94.16	*	95.55	94.84
23		94.72	94.46		94.46	94.02		93.93	93.93	94.17	95.18	95.56	94.86
24	94.43	94.61	94.51	93.96	94.53	94.06	93.80	93.86	*	95.15	95.58	
25	94.51	94.58	94.51	93.97	94.52	*	93.79	93.90	94.21	95.16	95.65	†
26	94.51	94.50	*	93.97	94.61	93.90	93.77	93.88	94.24	95.12	*	94.97
27	94.50	*	94.47	94.04	94.54	93.93	93.77	*	94.25	95.11	95.67	94.92
28	94.48	94.48	94.48	94.09	*	93.88	93.77	93.86	94.38	95.11	95.59	95.08
29	94.49	94.50	94.48	94.12	94.51	93.94	93.77	93.81	94.48	*	95.58	95.16
30	*		94.42	*	†	93.96	*	93.72	94.52	95.13	†	†
31	94.45		94.48		94.49		93.75	93.66		95.15		*
High	94.51	94.82	94.54	94.51	94.61	94.56	94.02	93.93	94.52	95.20	95.67	95.55
Low	94.15	94.42	94.38	93.96	94.04	93.88	93.75	93.66	93.68	94.50	95.16	94.77

*Sunday
†Holiday

1917—INDUSTRIALS

Date:	Jan.	Feb.	Mar.	Apr.	May	June	July	Aug.	Sept.	Oct.	Nov.	Dec.
1	†	88.52	91.10	*	93.42	97.89	*	92.26	†	83.58	71.41	72.86
2	96.15	87.01	92.82	97.06	92.48	97.59	95.23	92.87	*	83.49	72.52	*
3	99.18	89.97	93.63	96.34	90.98	*	95.31	92.96	*	82.45	72.32	72.55
4	97.15	*	*	95.83	90.45	97.00	†	†	*	81.20	80.62	70.72
5	96.16	92.03	95.04	94.61	90.20	†	93.57	*	83.66	81.75	69.93	71.68
6	96.75	92.81	95.30	†	*	98.43	93.90	93.85	83.42	81.35	†	71.01
7	*	92.19	95.30	93.10	91.20	98.16	94.28	93.30	83.49	*	71.54	70.29
8	96.40	90.94	95.28	*	90.22	98.58	*	91.47	83.18	80.48	68.58	70.31
9	97.64	90.20	96.46	92.41	89.08	99.08	93.64	92.23	*	79.26	69.36	*
10	95.70	91.56	96.78	91.20	90.41	*	93.10	91.90	83.88	77.32	70.30	70.49
11	96.02	*	*	92.82	89.77	97.86	94.14	91.81	83.51	77.83	*	68.78
12	95.75	†	95.03	93.10	89.62	97.52	93.64	*	82.19	†	70.65	67.30
13	95.13	92.37	95.05	93.18	*	98.31	92.33	92.65	83.14	†	70.35	66.96
14	*	91.86	95.16	93.76	90.78	97.95	92.57	91.69	83.44	*	69.15	68.65
15	95.59	91.65	95.63	*	90.19	97.22	*	92.10	83.04	75.13	69.10	67.53
16	97.55	91.81	95.65	92.21	92.26	96.95	91.38	91.44	*	77.08	69.75	*
17	96.60	92.70	96.22	91.87	92.75	*	91.95	91.61	81.55	76.11	70.41	67.08
18	97.50	*	*	91.63	91.96	94.89	91.05	91.42	81.63	77.85	*	67.31
19	97.35	93.66	96.97	91.83	92.37	95.36	90.48	*	84.01	78.21	71.51	65.95
20	97.97	94.91	98.20	90.84	*	94.78	91.59	91.27	84.82	79.80	72.80	67.13
21	*	93.97	97.61	90.98	93.47	95.77	92.61	90.75	85.23	*	73.57	68.25
22	96.60	†	96.78	*	94.09	96.63	*	89.16	84.53	79.06	72.95	68.23
23	96.26	92.56	97.27	90.96	94.26	97.60	91.61	88.15	*	78.50	74.23	*
24	96.66	92.22	97.73	90.66	95.20	*	91.26	88.91	85.70	78.30	73.51	69.29
25	97.41	*	*	92.98	96.76	97.57	91.24	89.06	86.02	77.68	*	†
26	97.36	93.35	96.32	93.06	97.58	96.81	91.42	*	84.61	77.35	74.03	68.33
27	96.71	92.68	96.46	93.10	*	95.98	91.75	88.40	84.60	78.91	73.80	70.49
28	*	91.56	97.01	92.65	97.20	95.41	92.11	86.12	83.46	*	73.25	72.13
29	95.78		96.75	*	97.41	95.38	*	85.95	83.81	76.28	†	72.45
30	95.83		96.72	93.23	*	95.87	92.13	84.51	*	75.53	72.65	*
31	95.43		95.41		97.38		91.75	83.40		74.50		74.38
High	99.18	94.91	98.20	97.06	97.58	99.08	95.31	93.85	86.02	83.58	74.23	74.38
Low	95.13	87.01	91.10	90.66	89.08	94.78	90.48	83.40	81.20	74.50	68.58	65.95

*Sunday
†Holiday

1917—RAILROADS

Date:	Jan.	Feb.	Mar.	Apr.	May	June	July	Aug.	Sept.	Oct.	Nov.	Dec.
1	†	99.31	96.53		96.17	94.84	*	93.63	†	85.66	77.21	76.21
2	105.41	97.50	97.00	100.72	95.35	93.78	92.45	93.84	*	85.20	78.00	*
3	105.76	98.16	97.63	99.25	93.39	*	92.93	93.95	†	85.03	77.37	75.55
4	105.02	*	*	99.25	92.13	93.56	†	†	87.06	84.46	*	74.90
5	104.75	98.59	97.76	98.16	91.74	†	92.16	*	87.93	85.81	75.35	77.23
6	104.74	97.93	97.36	†	*	94.20	92.46	93.91	87.88	85.88	†	76.40
7	*	96.97	97.06	97.11	92.41	94.57	93.08	94.16	87.91	*	76.69	75.86
8	104.88	96.75	96.83	*	91.79	95.06	*	93.28	87.84	85.07	74.54	75.74
9	104.56	96.81	97.40	96.15	90.63	95.27	92.80	93.90	*	84.70	75.88	*
10	103.33	96.11	97.30	96.05	91.88	*	93.55	93.20	87.88	83.51	76.58	75.91
11	103.11	*	*	96.88	91.02	94.79	93.94	93.26	87.60	83.38	*	73.43
12	103.41	†	97.75	96.96	91.04	95.27	94.12	*	86.05	*	76.72	72.17
13	103.47	98.08	97.28	97.83	*	95.72	94.02	93.49	86.17	†	76.48	72.43
14	*	97.15	96.95	97.81	91.35	95.51	95.09	93.46	86.88	*	75.60	73.98
15	103.65	96.90	97.27	*	90.73	95.27	*	93.45	87.10	81.50	75.70	73.18
16	105.01	97.13	97.67	96.71	92.06	95.32	94.96	92.96	*	83.07	75.01	*
17	104.36	97.61	97.85	96.97	92.89	*	95.05	92.06	85.95	82.51	75.34	72.93
18	105.10	*	*	97.03	92.76	94.66	94.05	92.08	85.58	83.66	*	72.96
19	104.84	98.03	99.55	96.91	92.95	94.68	93.72	*	87.01	83.82	77.05	70.75
20	104.76	98.68	100.18	97.10	*	94.49	93.75	91.41	86.71	84.34	77.58	71.50
21	*	99.05	99.48	96.88	93.21	94.90	94.08	90.96	87.04	*	78.32	72.03
22	104.55	†	99.48	*	94.18	95.26	*	90.20	87.41	83.57	78.26	71.84
23	104.02	98.60	101.98	96.58	94.11	95.46	93.66	90.31	*	83.17	78.46	*
24	104.87	98.52	102.30	96.27	94.30	*	93.40	91.35	88.03	82.65	78.16	72.80
25	104.47	*	*	97.40	93.88	96.28	93.43	91.38	89.08	81.73	*	†
26	104.40	98.70	100.54	97.90	94.01	96.53	93.36	*	88.23	81.96	78.13	71.61
27	104.16	98.08	100.36	97.61	*	96.01	93.49	91.13	88.12	82.61	77.13	78.02
28	*	97.37	101.27	96.75	95.15	95.60	93.65	90.26	86.30	*	76.42	79.86
29	103.68		100.73	*	95.20	95.09		90.53	86.55	81.08	†	79.63
30	103.66		100.96	96.80	*	94.20	93.48	89.87	*	80.50	75.80	*
31	102.71		100.33		95.20		93.57	89.45		79.61		79.73
High	105.76	99.31	102.30	100.72	96.17	96.53	95.09	94.16	89.08	85.88	78.46	79.86
Low	102.71	96.11	96.53	96.05	90.63	93.56	92.16	89.45	85.58	79.61	74.54	70.75

*Sunday
†Holiday

1917—DAILY STOCK SALES ON N. Y. STOCK EXCHANGE
(000 Omitted)

Date	Jan.	Feb.	Mar.	Apr.	May	June	July	Aug.	Sept.	Oct.	Nov.	Dec.
1	†	2058	449	*	525	1248	*	251	†	613	1444	136
2	969	1332	440	695	457	513	634	356	*	740	927	*
3	1165	1035	380	948	925	*	541	411	†	549	354	272
4	1461	*	*	781	600	645	†	†	1105	918	*	553
5	887	1222	864	931	317	†	629	*	1180	807	1134	881
6	411	999	952	†	*	1055	596	430	667	243	†	466
7	*	965	902	658	464	1313	217	427	618	*	981	334
8	605	697	559	*	445	1005	*	660	281	442	1307	106
9	624	456	793	687	908	445	508	547	*	757	823	*
10	853	183	594	770	564	*	661	484	443	1143	349	280
11	1031	*	*	635	438	971	686	168	465	979	*	494
12	642	†	848	653	222	749	856	*	811	†	605	790
13	236	415	524	507	*	1143	910	373	694	†	514	791
14	*	306	383	318	465	862	399	502	416	*	641	558
15	406	313	460	*	438	880	*	538	188	1043	364	266
16	826	334	381	702	753	278	866	514	*	1030	281	*
17	785	253	384	634	1057	*	676	358	687	836	157	468
18	613	*	*	499	860	794	655	93	670	821	*	322
19	598	445	1314	516	251	889	540	*	827	974	419	464
20	280	647	1355	647	*	936	447	265	825	522	777	594
21	*	595	1337	254	942	582	309	513	660	*	828	610
22	848	†	1010	*	1020	634	*	794	412	726	583	173
23	390	549	1035	409	1307	320	499	840	*	584	513	*
24	386	153	634	422	1112	*	561	435	637	252	350	423
25	435	*	*	938	1712	857	366	113	866	670	*	†
26	459	427	873	1013	834	795	314	*	593	484	448	420
27	238	463	620	610	*	1015	335	313	398	343	536	1199
28	*	456	571	245	1353	760	226	571	542	*	417	1192
29	469		579	*	1045	675	*	580	220	846	†	493
30	598		589	332	†	397	350	406	*	972	362	*
31	708		288		1028		503	913		1172		929
Total	16,978	14,358	19,117	14,801	20,042	19,761	12,598	11,856	14,203	18,463	15,111	13,213

*Sunday. †Holiday.

1917—BOND AVERAGES

Date:	Jan.	Feb.	Mar.	Apr.	May	June	July	Aug.	Sept.	Oct.	Nov.	Dec.
1	†	95.72	94.09	*	91.89	90.55	*	90.02	†	88.08	86.43	84.52
2	95.14	95.53	94.12	93.94	91.87	90.57	90.03	90.06	*	87.98	86.04	*
3	95.23	95.48	94.13	93.87	91.63	*	90.09	90.12	†	87.97	86.04	84.56
4	95.34	*	*	93.85	91.63	90.60	†	†	88.94	87.88	*	84.26
5	95.40	94.99	94.20	93.87	91.61	†	89.99	*	88.74	87.70	85.81	84.05
6	95.50	94.71	94.14	†	*	90.62	89.95	90.14	88.74	87.69	†	84.10
7	*	94.74	94.22	93.73	91.30	90.56	90.03	90.11	88.64		85.65	83.94
8	95.56	94.57	94.17	*	91.15	90.60	*	90.12	88.68	87.68	85.34	83.88
9	95.65	94.37	94.31	93.51	90.99	90.59	89.99	90.06	*	87.64	85.24	*
10	95.78	94.27	94.35	93.30	91.03	*	90.02	90.06	88.61	87.47	85.10	83.72
11	95.85	*	*	93.14	90.80	90.50	90.12	90.07	88.57	87.40	*	83.50
12	95.89	†	94.30	92.17	90.74	90.35	90.16	*	88.37	†	85.03	83.35
13	95.97	94.11	94.29	92.52	*	90.34	90.19	89.98	88.49	†	84.88	82.96
14	*	94.22	94.29	92.43	90.69	90.33	90.18	89.93	88.42	*	84.69	82.87
15	96.12	94.30	94.22	*	90.61	90.34	*	89.89	88.41	87.23	84.57	82.84
16	96.20	94.22	94.31	92.28	90.50	90.32	90.21	89.83	*	87.18	84.26	*
17	96.21	94.30	94.28	92.04	90.52	*	90.23	89.74	88.47	87.21	84.22	82.68
18	96.25	*	*	91.98	90.53	90.29	90.37	89.71	88.14	87.25	*	82.56
19	96.15	94.32	94.27	91.93	90.46	90.29	90.21	*	88.06	87.16	84.12	82.26
20	96.16	94.40	94.28	92.02	*	90.24	90.24	89.64	87.98	87.11	84.23	82.21
21	*	94.46	94.36	92.02	90.52	90.21	90.23	89.42	87.89	*	84.40	82.27
22	96.11	†	94.31	*	90.60	90.32	*	89.37	87.88	87.08	84.47	82.27
23	96.06	94.28	94.28	91.89	90.62	90.29	90.22	89.36	*	86.90	84.49	*
24	96.05	94.21	94.30	91.94	90.68	*	90.24	89.26	88.09	86.86	84.64	82.26
25	96.08	*	*	91.98	90.67	90.23	90.21	89.25	88.12	86.82	*	†
26	96.11	94.14	94.24	91.96	90.62	90.19	90.20	*	88.12	86.75	84.78	82.19
27	96.08	94.18	94.21	92.00	*	90.17	90.19	89.19	88.15	86.73	84.78	82.31
28	*	94.19	94.12	92.02	90.52	90.11	90.17	89.08	88.07	*	84.79	82.52
29	96.05		94.13	*	90.65	90.12	*	89.02	88.05	86.87	†	82.84
30	96.09		93.99	92.05	†	90.11	90.12	89.02	*	86.72	84.53	*
31	96.13		93.91		90.59		90.00	88.95		86.54		83.15
High	96.25	95.72	94.36	93.94	91.89	90.62	90.37	90.14	88.94	88.08	86.43	84.56
Low	95.14	94.11	93.91	91.89	90.46	90.11	89.95	88.95	87.88	86.54	84.12	82.19

*Sunday. †Holiday

1918—INDUSTRIALS

Date:	Jan.	Feb.	Mar.	Apr.	May	June	July	Aug.	Sept.	Oct.	Nov.	Dec.
1	†	79.28	79.93	77.16	78.16	77.93	81.81	80.71	*	83.95	85.53	*
2	76.68	79.77	78.98	76.69	78.90	*	81.98	80.76	†	84.45	85.23	81.13
3	76.18	*	*	77.01	78.64	78.55	82.49	80.90	83.84	84.95	*	82.46
4	75.56	†	79.01	77.42	78.59	79.60	†	81.57	83.61	85.31	85.74	82.45
5	73.75	79.28	79.50	77.03	*	79.54	82.96	81.57	83.63	84.87	†	82.89
6	*	78.93	79.20	77.95	79.36	78.95	83.20	81.13	82.56	*	86.62	82.45
7	74.86	77.78	79.53	*	80.51	78.53	*	80.97	82.91	84.35	87.61	82.71
8	74.63	78.44	79.50	77.69	80.32	79.16	82.60	81.13	*	84.30	87.66	*
9	75.61	78.98	79.71	77.40	81.30	*	82.76	81.65	81.80	83.36	88.06	83.41
10	76.33	*	*	76.85	81.29	78.93	82.09	82.04	81.33	84.15	*	84.50
11	75.00	†	79.78	75.58	81.82	79.10	81.09	*	80.46	84.83	†	84.27
12	74.48	†	78.67	76.25	*	79.76	81.23	81.58	†	†	86.56	83.53
13	*	78.73	78.68	76.01	82.16	80.53	81.15	81.68	80.29	*	86.12	82.65
14	73.48	78.71	79.13	*	82.21	80.61	*	81.70	81.49	86.35	85.53	82.96
15	73.38	79.96	79.06	77.51	84.04	81.21	80.58	81.58	*	86.21	86.15	*
16	74.60	80.08	78.98	77.21	84.03	*	81.71	81.77	81.48	86.63	85.35	83.23
17	74.48	*	*	76.89	83.50	80.61	81.45	81.51	81.80	88.27	*	83.41
18	74.55	81.53	77.93	78.11	83.35	80.98	82.92	*	81.92	89.07	85.01	83.01
19	74.89	82.08	78.13	78.60	*	80.93	82.31	81.63	81.64	88.88	84.68	82.40
20	*	81.28	78.14	79.73	82.47	81.83	82.29	81.92	81.96	*	84.33	81.72
21	76.11	80.53	78.71	*	82.87	81.65	*	81.91	82.33	88.15	83.84	81.87
22	75.75	†	77.71	79.42	82.22	81.95	81.22	81.61	*	87.79	82.60	*
23	75.43	79.88	76.24	78.30	82.21	*	*	82.15	82.44	87.10	81.83	81.51
24	75.92	*	*	78.01	81.58	82.50	80.93	82.83	82.80	87.10	*	80.59
25	76.50	79.17	76.45	77.88	81.16	82.40	81.28	*	82.64	86.52	79.87	†
26	76.44	80.65	76.49	78.23	*	83.02	81.51	82.93	82.84	87.70	81.43	80.44
27	*	80.50	76.72	77.86	78.65	82.78	81.49	83.01	84.03	*	80.16	81.17
28	†	80.39	76.41	*	78.42	82.58	*	83.18	83.85	87.28	†	81.55
29	77.13		†	77.79	78.44	82.68	81.10	82.73		86.39	80.93	*
30	76.98		76.72	77.51	†		80.79	82.46	84.68	84.08	81.13	80.78
31	79.80		*		78.08		81.23	82.84		85.51		82.20
High	79.80	82.08	79.93	79.73	84.04	83.02	83.20	83.18	84.68	89.07	88.06	84.50
Low	73.38	77.78	76.24	75.58	78.08	77.93	80.51	80.71	80.29	83.36	79.87	80.44

*Sunday
†Holiday

1918—RAILROADS

Date:	Jan.	Feb.	Mar.	Apr.	May	June	July	Aug.	Sept.	Oct.	Nov.	Dec.
1	†	80.92	81.00	80.20	79.24	82.65	82.67	82.46	*	85.17	88.63	*
2	79.46	81.03	80.40	79.53	79.75	*	82.57	82.51	†	85.25	88.53	87.75
3	80.02	*	*	79.67	79.48	82.26	82.75	82.56	86.93	85.11	*	87.86
4	80.28	†	80.13	79.81	79.30	83.43	†	82.69	86.47	84.87	89.71	87.63
5	79.19	80.59	80.20	79.51	*	83.08	83.16	82.56	86.54	84.95	†	87.77
6	*	79.98	80.60	80.08	80.11	82.93	83.10	82.56	85.55	*	90.57	87.60
7	79.12	79.33	80.61	*	80.63	82.46	*	82.76	85.67	85.39	92.73	87.66
8	79.33	79.34	82.40	79.53	81.81	82.68	82.83	82.84	*	85.04	92.45	*
9	79.76	79.38	81.71	79.21	82.45	*	83.31	83.08	85.11	85.16	92.91	87.72
10	79.53	*	*	78.90	82.36	82.53	83.31	83.33	84.50	85.33	*	88.25
11	78.96	†	82.56	78.00	82.31	82.48	82.76	*	83.68	86.17	†	87.90
12	78.53	†	81.91	78.45	*	82.95	82.75	84.12	†	†	92.14	87.07
13	*	79.06	81.76	78.26	82.75	83.23	82.81	85.00	83.32	*	91.25	86.50
14	77.50	79.87	82.70	*	84.08	83.27	*	84.57	83.70	87.87	90.77	86.45
15	77.21	80.86	82.06	79.15	84.39	83.38	82.19	84.43	*	87.20	90.88	*
16	77.70	80.70	82.23	78.98	84.32	*	82.46	84.65	83.59	87.28	90.39	86.54
17	77.90	*	*	78.60	84.20	83.25	82.30	84.32	83.81	88.18	*	86.58
18	77.91	81.41	81.24	79.28	83.81	83.31	82.99	*	84.13	89.45	89.91	85.88
19	78.14	81.31	81.21	79.38	*	83.26	82.81	84.48	83.76	89.68	89.56	84.79
20	*	80.98	81.25	79.52	83.59	83.50	82.97	84.83	84.20	*	89.45	84.25
21	78.14	80.50	81.55	*	84.00	83.24	*	84.81	84.21	90.34	89.28	84.30
22	77.90	†	80.70	79.55	83.09	83.31	82.80	84.55	*	91.80	88.45	*
23	77.63	80.90	78.73	79.45	82.51	*	82.36	85.45	84.36	90.26	87.51	83.75
24	77.71	*	*	79.26	82.40	83.42	82.58	86.38	84.42	89.58	*	83.63
25	78.68	80.23	79.16	78.99	83.20	83.36	82.80	*	84.21	88.78	85.10	†
26	79.11	80.95	79.42	79.05	*	83.69	82.82	86.05	84.13	89.55	86.06	83.05
27	*	81.13	79.82	78.84	82.27	83.37	82.86	86.09	84.55	*	85.56	83.10
28	†	81.13	79.72	*	82.97	83.20	*	85.93	84.43	89.21	†	83.76
29	79.63		†	78.84	83.50	83.11	83.13	85.90		88.85	87.16	*
30	79.36		79.98	78.68	†		82.90	85.88	85.50	87.46	87.08	83.10
31	81.03		*		82.88		82.86	86.36		88.11		84.32
High	81.03	81.41	82.70	80.20	84.39	83.69	83.31	86.38	86.93	91.80	92.91	88.25
Low	77.21	79.06	78.73	78.00	79.24	82.26	82.19	82.46	83.32	84.87	85.10	83.05

*Sunday
†Holiday

1918—DAILY STOCK SALES ON N. Y. STOCK EXCHANGE
(000 Omitted)

Date	Jan.	Feb.	Mar.	Apr.	May	June	July	Aug.	Sept.	Oct.	Nov.	Dec.
1	†	958	342	185	357	312	459	247	*	862	827	*
2	1183	359	266	149	470	*	367	137	†	641	404	479
3	1401	*	*	179	338	742	358	69	503	556	*	571
4	951	†	341	226	158	744	†	*	556	592	698	423
5	530	511	289	143	*	599	290	267	393	214	†	439
6	*	540	364	210	498	531	191	244	821	*	660	268
7	566	633	238	*	921	407	*	154	174	638	1197	183
8	796	468	610	248	976	193	411	161	*	435	871	*
9	474	220	269	176	1095	*	265	321	351	620	465	365
10	531	*	*	194	1223	267	303	232	560	638	*	640
11	495	†	376	347	512	376	618	*	386	838	†	542
12	358	*	346	216	*	427	236	424	†	†	1111	411
13	*	460	256	122	1252	506	103	387	394	*	759	415
14	519	397	382	*	1183	620	*	366	147	983	616	215
15	507	696	318	309	1200	329	464	281	*	742	850	*
16	384	364	185	359	1794	*	327	176	226	945	326	346
17	702	*	*	341	1136	560	272	102	231	1216	*	456
18	475	799	501	540	500	391	616	*	251	1639	562	346
19	215	1011	299	544	*	410	489	172	166	879	456	405
20	*	762	216	301	1034.	432	143	187	215	*	541	520
21	296	633	260	*	585	589	*	211	146	1129	565	236
22	467	†	319	582	790	277	336	180	*	1100	674	*
23	396	361	477	463	884	*	356	251	233	1113	335	357
24	313	*	*	400	891	653	282	323	298	713	*	411
25	408	633	648	280	448	565	294	*	303	581	985	†
26	234	502	381	155	*	637	316	439	246	347	648	674
27	*	761	328	156	934	651	111	420	532	*	728	741
28	†	613	344	*	919	434	*	401	236	978	†	588
29	499		†	184	732	193	184	384	*	568	661	*
30	459		104	568	†	*	340	226	752	972	278	1195
31	955		*		583		362	161		820		945
Total	14,112	11,680	8,458	7,576	21,412	11,843	8,490	6,922	8,122	20,756	15,214	12 174

*Sunday.   †Holiday.

1918—BOND AVERAGES

Date:	Jan.	Feb.	Mar.	Apr.	May	June	July	Aug.	Sept.	Oct.	Nov.	Dec.
1	†	84.34	84.27	83.31	83.66	84.33	83.41	83.10	*	82.06	85.14	*
2	83.45	84.40	84.39	83.30	83.84	*	83.42	83.04	†	82.10	85.29	87.95
3	83.51	*	*	83.38	83.84	84.33	83.45	82.99	82.86	82.18	*	87.95
4	83.52	†	84.28	83.40	83.90	84.29	†	83.02	82.85	82.25	85.64	87.96
5	83.49	84.43	84.03	83 36	*	84.20	83.42	83.02	82.85	82.34	†	87.88
6	*	84.50	84.01	83.47	83.96	84.15	83.45	82.97	82.70	*	86.02	87.87
7	83.44	84.44	83.97	*	84.12	84.14	*	83.01	82.67	82.50	86.47	87.83
8	83.61	84.47	83.87	83.46	84.09	84.11	83.47	83.03	*	82.56	87.44	*
9	83.63	84.54	83.83	83.39	84.25	*	83.46	82.97	82.57	82.83	87.68	87.83
10	83.71	*	*	83.44	84.42	84.03	83.31	82.96	82.61	83.01	*	87.85
11	83.80	†	83.76	83.42	84.46	83.92	83.33	*	82.50	83.32	‡	87 77
12	83.85	*	83.73	83.46	*	83.87	83.34	82.92	†	†	88.14	87.71
13	*	84.58	83.76	83.45	84.41	83.75	83.32	82.94	82.44	*	88.47	87.73
14	83.79	84.53	83.73	*	84.42	83.58	*	82.96	82.50	83.74	88.58	87.76
15	83.61	84.54	83.62	83.47	84.49	83.58	83.22	83.01	*	83.96	88.51	*
16	83.64	84.55	83.63	83.55	84.67	*	83.21	83.02	82.48	83.97	88.51	87.84
17	83.49	*	*	83.51	84.77	83.56	83.25	82.99	82.35	84.15	*	87.66
18	83.54	84.55	83.57	83.51	84.73	83.65	83.25	*	82.24	84.40	88.47	87.56
19	83.57	84.58	83.41	83.61	*	83.56	83.28	82.95	82.16	84.52	88.48	87.40
20	*	84.49	83.45	83.72	84.79	83.54	83.25	82.96	81.99	*	88.38	87.14
21	83.66	84.47	83.63	*	84.80	83.49	*	82.95	81.95	84.85	88.09	87.11
22	83.74	†	83.59	83.72	84.72	83.48	83.24	82.93	*	85.09	88.02	*
23	83.83	84.46	83.59	83.78	84.73	*	83.25	82.83	81.96	85.07	88.01	86.86
24	83.89	*	*	83.76	84.66	83.58	83.19	82.86	81.94	85.02	*	86.65
25	83.96	84.45	83.46	83.59	84.57	83.43	83.19	*	81.95	84.89	87.87	†
26	84.03	84.39	83.38	83.60	*	83.38	83.24	82.80	81.99	84.86	87.64	86.62
27	*	84.37	83.25	83.61	84.48	83.36	83.19	82.93	81.94	*	87.68	86.39
28	†	84.33	83.29	*	84.46	83.35	*	82.85	81.94	84.93	†	86.38
29	84.14		†	83.62	84.36	83.37	83.19	82.79	*	85.10	87.72	*
30	84.27		83.28	83.63	†	*	83.24	82.79	81.97	85.01	87.83	86.23
31	84.42		*		84.35		83.20	82.80		84.99		86.19
High	84.42	84.58	84.39	83.78	84.80	84.33	83.47	83.10	82.86	85.10	88.58	87.96
Low	83.44	84.33	83.25	83.66	83.35	83.35	83.19	82.79	81.94	82.06	85.14	86.19

*Sunday
†Holiday

1919—INDUSTRIALS

Date:	Jan.	Feb.	Mar.	Apr.	May	June	July	Aug.	Sept.	Oct.	Nov.	Dec.
1	†	80.55	84.04	88.84	93.26	*	108.13	107.99	†	111.12	118.63	104.03
2	82.60	*	*	89.30	94.30	106.92	108.56	†	106.26	111.19	*	104.41
3	83.35	80.91	85.58	88.91	94.78	103.83	109.90	*	108.55	108.90	119.62	105.75
4	83.05	81.08	85.10	89.59	*	105.66	†	102.82	108.27	110.26	†	107.97
5	*	80.70	84.24	89.65	94.92	107.55	†	102.40	106.96	*	118.48	107.42
6	82.45	79.68	85.64	*	†	107.46	*	105.78	106.33	112.04	117.78	107.39
7	82.44	79.35	86.23	90.18	96.16	107.55	109.41	100.80	*	112.55	117.18	*
8	82.60	79.15	87.27	90.59	97.65	*	109.97	101.88	106.51	113.55	115.54	107.83
9	82.76	*	*	91.01	98.61	107.35	110.46	104.33	108.30	113.40	*	106.85
10	82.30	79.65	87.43	90.11	98.19	105.43	110.00	*	†	114.42	112.93	107.01
11	81.66	80.25	88.10	90.11	*	105.16	109.92	103.94	107.68	114.39	110.75	105.01
12	*	†	88.30	89.61	98.53	105.05	110.71	105.10	107.10	*	107.15	103.73
13	81.79	81.07	88.18	*	99.23	102.85	*	104.28	108.30	†	110.69	105.61
14	82.00	81.20	87.87	90.48	100.37	102.78	112.23	102.86	*	112.41	110.49	*
15	82.40	81.96	87.68	91.47	99.45	*	111.66	102.25	108.39	112.88	109.81	105.06
16	82.20	*	*	91.07	99.92	99.56	111.47	†	108.81	112.51	*	106.61
17	81.35	82.55	88.41	90.88	100.10	103.28	110.65	*	107.55	112.98	109.09	107.26
18	80.93	81.92	87.87	†	*	105.08	110.69	99.70	106.78	113.20	107.45	103.78
19	*	82.58	88.26	91.67	99.16	104.49	†	100.58	105.84	*	106.15	104.63
20	80.14	82.93	87.81	*	99.88	106.13	*	98.46	104.99	115.43	108.19	104.55
21	79.88	84.21	89.05	92.21	99.65	106.45	107.24	99.47	*	115.62	107.73	*
22	80.00	†	88.66	92.24	99.88	*	109.34	100.84	106.30	117.62	108.42	103.55
23	80.20	*	*	92.36	100.47	106.09	110.73	101.44	106.89	114.88	*	103.79
24	81.75	84.62	87.97	91.65	101.60	104.58	109.98	*	106.83	115.57	108.86	103.95
25	81.33	84.61	†	92.09	*	104.91	110.03	101.63	107.30	112.73	109.02	†
26	*	85.60	86.83	92.48	103.80	105.63	111.10	103.29	108.66	*	107.50	105.63
27	81.47	85.68	87.65	*	103.58	106.66	*	101.91	110.06	114.88	†	106.08
28	81.60	84.81	88.86	93.17	104.00	107.14	110.94	103.01	*	116.30	103.72	*
29	80.56		88.88	93.51	105.50	*	109.72	104.75	110.32	117.43	103.60	105.18
30	80.94		*	92.88	†	106.98	108.91	†	111.42	117.33	*	105.46
31	80.61		88.85		†		107.16	*		118.92		107.23
High	83.35	85.68	89.05	93.51	105.50	107.55	112.23	107.99	111.42	118.92	119.62	107.97
Low	79.88	79.15	84.04	88.84	93.26	99.56	107.16	98.46	104.99	108.90	103.60	103.55

*Sunday
†Holiday

1919—RAILROADS

Date:	Jan.	Feb.	Mar.	Apr.	May	June	July	Aug.	Sept.	Oct.	Nov.	Dec.
1	†	81.76	84.71	83.73	85.63	*	86.28	86.63	†	81.97	80.01	74.93
2	84.31	*	*	83.80	85.98	90.78	86.56	†	81.30	81.51	*	75.27
3	84.84	81.68	84.88	83.71	86.15	89.41	86.89	*	81.48	80.95	79.90	75.65
4	84.48	82.54	83.65	84.79	*	89.63	†	83.22	81.35	82.06	†	75.97
5	*	82.70	82.78	84.62	87.28	90.53	†	81.93	80.60	*	80.23	76.61
6	83.93	82.18	83.33	*	†	90.05	*	82.41	80.36	82.48	80.66	76.99
7	84.08	81.85	84.13	84.78	87.48	90.19	87.66	80.66	*	82.23	81.18	*
8	84.43	81.61	84.66	84.50	87.48	*	87.76	79.96	80.27	82.04	80.90	76.85
9	84.33	*	*	84.55	87.01	89.91	88.59	81.31	80.43	81.70	*	76.44
10	84.01	81.65	84.96	84.25	86.78	88.68	87.87	*	†	82.31	79.98	76.02
11	84.06	81.89	85.81	83.76	*	88.35	88.10	81.28	80.15	82.38	79.80	74.29
12	*	†	85.47	83.66	86.75	88.23	88.22	81.46	79.89	*	78.57	73.63
13	83.90	81.80	85.26	*	87.27	86.92	*	81.01	80.63	†	79.32	74.21
14	83.97	82.08	85.00	83.88	88.53	86.76	88.13	80.16	*	81.61	81.65	*
15	83.85	82.31	84.73	83.79	88.43	*	88.71	80.33	81.08	81.50	81.58	73.96
16	83.31	*	*	83.62	89.72	85.85	90.24	†	80.63	81.28	*	74.75
17	82.99	82.80	84.73	83.36	90.50	87.08	89.48	*	80.32	81.36	81.86	74.88
18	82.62	83.00	84.61	†	*	87.33	89.40	78.89	79.53	81.15	80.34	74.53
19	*	83.16	84.61	83.50	90.10	87.08	†	79.11	79.43	*	79.36	75.56
20	81.69	83.19	84.03	*	90.35	87.79	*	78.60	78.98	81.14	79.65	75.86
21	80.86	83.64	84.26	83.53	89.53	87.90	88.33	78.60	*	80.85	79.40	*
22	81.40	†	84.21	84.51	89.41	*	88.73	79.63	79.40	80.88	79.39	75.35
23	82.08	*	*	84.46	89.87	87.65	88.58	80.05	79.53	81.09	*	74.86
24	82.68	84.18	83.93	84.24	90.33	87.95	88.12	*	79.60	82.15	79.40	74.93
25	82.70	83.69	†	84.58	*	87.29	88.25	81.29	79.25	80.99	78.87	†
26	*	84.36	83.00	85.81	91.13	86.83	88.40	81.16	79.69	*	77.97	75.48
27	82.51	84.60	83.10	*	91.13	86.78	*	79.78	80.11	81.07	†	74.98
28	82.66	84.22	83.53	85.57	90.82	86.76	88.20	80.33	*	80.60	75.33	*
29	82.11		83.41	85.38	91.08	*	87.85	81.21	80.22	80.63	75.86	74.23
30	82.13		*	85.03	†	86.56	87.26	†	80.25	80.62	*	73.85
31	81.97		83.59		†		86.50	*		80.28		75.30
High	84.84	84.60	85.81	85.81	91.13	90.78	90.24	86.63	81.48	82.48	81.86	76.99
Low	80.86	81.61	82.78	83.36	85.63	85.85	86.28	78.60	78.98	80.25	75.33	73.63

*Sunday
†Holiday

1919—DAILY STOCK SALES ON NEW YORK STOCK EXCHANGE
(000 Omitted)

Date	Jan.	Feb.	Mar.	Apr.	May	June	July	Aug.	Sept.	Oct.	Nov.	Dec.
1	†	181	396	897	1380	*	1204	997	†	1566	763	1047
2	491	*	*	889	1658	1776	1512	†	1119	1417	*	857
3	754	290	768	825	754	2220	1771	*	1516	1242	1767	823
4	284	352	840	820	*	1567	†	1944	1584	499	†	1176
5	*	381	799	551	1384	1861	†	1934	1414	*	1577	1032
6	503	457	791	*	†	1780	*	1376	383	1318	1615	496
7	377	348	1045	1041	1525	786	2095	1750	*	1429	1237	*
8	305	154	754	1326	1768	*	1717	2072	660	1566	652	1005
9	596	*	*	1255	1824	1616	1701	620	1178	1466	*	988
10	466	308	1231	1414	1017	1893	1648	*	†	1696	1441	676
11	223	356	978	1311	*	1401	1605	947	1164	789	1906	936
12	*	†	1239	533	1550	1377	842	781	794	*	2504	1388
13	438	643	1170	*	1494	1627	*	953	504	†	2220	562
14	372	407	1026	1117	1928	707	1869	1007	*	1692	1490	*
15	415	446	547	1222	1534	*	1905	743	1148	1389	493	880
16	490	*	*	1319	1625	1519	1862	†	1048	1412	*	1018
17	601	785	1163	1022	744	1434	1740	*	1235	1331	1123	978
18	316	628	1015	†	*	1500	1496	1215	868	801	1109	684
19	*	584	932	700	1601	1288	†	1042	777	*	1711	1126
20	546	896	867	*	1351	1328	*	969	498	1858	1198	445
21	680	870	1255	1601	1510	800	1490	1272	*	1719	1074	*
22	464	†	595	1545	1250	*	1398	774	848	1755	393	951
23	415	*	*	1728	1378	1292	1520	326	1013	2235	*	765
24	605	930	752	1296	882	1314	1609	*	1068	1577	831	608
25	414	671	†	1088	*	939	1039	703	833	1015	1093	†
26	*	944	796	835	2024	880	487	994	939	*	1199	1251
27	387	933	681	*	1839	1213	*	831	737	1317	†	742
28	392	804	932	1551	1612	640	834	757	*	1587	1389	*
29	589		579	1592	1538	*	1181	914	1407	1449	809	1218
30	433		*	1744	†	1141	1273	†	1489	1531	*	1349
31	353		769		†		1203	*		1973		1381
Total	11,911	12,366	21,911	29,220	35,168	33,447	35,313	24,920	24,222	37,630	29,593	24,371

*Sunday. †Holiday.

1919—BOND AVERAGES

Date:	Jan.	Feb.	Mar.	Apr.	May	June	July	Aug.	Sept.	Oct.	Nov.	Dec.
1	†	85.45	85.44	84.90	84.48	*	85.25	83.99	†	82.09	81.46	79.02
2	86.33	*	*	84.89	84.61	86.08	85.11	†	82.39	82.10	*	78.97
3	86.33	85.48	85.37	84.81	84.65	86.10	85.08	*	82.37	82.16	81.59	78.91
4	86.34	85.60	85.36	84.65	*	85.97	†	83.81	82.21	82.29	†	79.08
5	*	85.61	85.34	84.69	84.73	85.97	†	83.60	82.33	*	81.47	79.08
6	86.43	85.70	85.31	*	†	85.94	*	83.50	82.32	82.42	81.33	79.21
7	86.52	85.55	85.21	84.69	84.80	85.96	85.13	83.49	*	82.80	81.35	*
8	86.53	85.56	85.31	84.70	85.10	*	85.03	83.39	82.25	83.09	81.26	79.17
9	86.47	*	*	84.69	85.10	85.70	84.90	83.43	82.21	83.11	*	79.17
10	86.47	85.57	85.36	84.60	85.22	85.59	84.87	*	†	83.08	81.26	79.04
11	86.33	85.54	85.43	84.55	*	85.62	84.91	83.23	82.18	83.16	81.08	78.95
12	*	†	85.37	84.55	85.31	85.62	84.92	83.08	81.94	*	80.93	78.68
13	86.35	85.55	85.38	*	85.33	85.54	*	82.82	81.98	†	80.79	78.54
14	86.30	85.53	85.46	84.44	85.51	85.51	84.91	82.78	*	83.10	80.94	*
15	86.28	85.60	85.47	84.55	85.67	*	84.94	82.62	81.87	83.13	80.99	78.45
16	86.14	*	*	84.59	85.63	85.46	84.85	†	81.92	82.95	*	78.39
17	86.04	85.67	85.53	84.56	85.69	85.48	84.79	*	81.87	82.86	81.02	78.47
18	86.06	85.74	85.46	†	*	85.49	84.66	82.60	81.86	82.84	80.92	78.46
19	*	85.77	85.30	84.59	85.85	85.41	†	82.48	81.83	*	80.74	78.46
20	85.77	85.73	85.21	*	85.85	85.31	*	82.27	81.71	82.85	80.42	78.52
21	85.64	85.71	85.21	84.53	85.89	85.32	84.53	82.18	*	82.77	80.37	*
22	85.47	†	85.21	84.54	85.87	*	84.54	82.21	81.55	82.61	80.30	78.70
23	85.41	*	*	84.49	85.84	85.40	84.49	82.25	81.56	82.49	*	78.66
24	85.38	85.63	85.09	84.41	85.86	85.40	84.45	*	82.17	82.46	79.97	78.89
25	85.52	85.51	†	84.41	*	85.42	84.44	82.17	82.21	82.43	79.90	†
26	*	85.56	85.11	84.39	85.84	85.27	84.40	82.21	81.71	*	79.60	79.09
27	85.47	85.55	85.07	*	85.95	85.30	*	82.20	81.78	82.22	†	79.18
28	85.70	85.43	85.04	84.43	85.88	85.30	84.33	82.29	*	82.06	79.18	*
29	85.62		85.04	84.52	86.04	*	84.22	82.34	82.03	81.88	79.08	79.49
30	85.47		*	84.48	†	85.22	84.03	†	82.03	81.64	*	79.44
31	85.50		85.01		†		84.00	*		81.44		79.81
High	86.53	85.77	85.53	84.90	86.04	86.10	85.25	83.99	82.39	83.16	81.59	79.81
Low	85.38	85.43	85.01	84.39	84.48	85.22	84.00	82.17	81.53	81.44	79.08	78.39

*Sunday
†Holiday

1920—INDUSTRIALS

Date:	Jan.	Feb.	Mar.	Apr.	May	June	July	Aug.	Sept.	Oct.	Nov.	Dec.
1	†	*	92.40	102.66	†	90.20	91.26	*	86.34	84.00	85.48	76.50
2	108.76	103.01	91.68			90.65	92.20	84.95	87.22	84.50	†	77.30
3	109.88	99.96	91.95	†	94.03	90.90	†	85.54	88.05		84.99	77.08
4	*	97.23	94.22	*	94.27	91.90	*	85.58		85.25	84.45	77.63
5	108.85	95.50	94.58	102.98	94.41	92.25	†	84.06	*	85.56	83.48	*
6	107.36	95.75	94.55	104.32	94.17	*	93.00	84.56	†	85.60	82.86	76.73
7	107.55	96.13	*	105.45	93.45	91.13	94.04	84.10	88.21	85.23	*	76.73
8	107.24	*	97.38	105.65	94.75	91.46	94.51	*	87.13	84.40	81.51	75.49
9	106.59	95.73	97.11	105.38	*	92.20	94.43	83.24	88.33	84.42	79.94	74.22
10	106.33	92.12	99.46	105.23	93.33	91.92	94.20	83.20	87.98	*	80.62	73.29
11	*	90.66	99.80	*	92.52	93.06	*	84.83	86.98	84.00	79.95	72.06
12	104.22	†	98.55	103.94	91.29	93.20	92.08	84.75	*	†	77.56	*
13	104.53	92.66	99.31	104.61	90.80	*	91.58	85.89	86.96	84.39	76.90	70.48
14	102.00	94.21	*	105.18	91.35	91.75	91.20	85.57	87.64	85.22	*	72.29
15	103.62	*	100.55	104.41	91.90	91.68	90.26	*	87.82	85.40	76.63	71.28
16	101.94	92.60	100.39	104.73	*	91.75	89.95	85.07	88.63	84.96	76.65	70.60
17	102.43	93.56	102.11	104.45	91.24	91.37	90.24	83.90	89.95	*	75.21	70.26
18	*	94.44	103.98	*	91.21	92.00	*	84.01	89.81	84.31	74.36	69.55
19	102.72	94.15	103.66	101.87	87.36	91.92	90.21	85.31	*	84.60	73.12	*
20	103.48	95.57	103.56	99.48	88.16	*	90.68	86.22	88.88	85.26	74.03	68.52
21	102.62	95.63	*	95.93	88.20	91.32	90.45	86.86	87.96	84.65	*	66.75
22	102.36	*	104.17	97.15	88.40	90.16	90.74	*	87.45	85.06	77.15	67.02
23	101.90	†	103.55	95.46	*	90.83	89.63	85.78	86.47	85.57	77.20	69.63
24	102.65	92.98	100.33	95.76	87.57	90.88	89.85	87.29	85.90	*	76.65	68.91
25	*	89.98	101.54	*	90.24	90.95	*	86.93	86.35	85.73	†	†
26	103.74	91.37	103.63	97.20	90.01	90.88	87.66	87.22	*	85.61	75.53	*
27	104.15	91.18	103.40	96.41	91.01	*	87.68	86.81	83.82	84.92	75.46	68.01
28	103.96	91.31	*	94.75	91.81	90.45	86.96	86.60	84.53	84.61	*	67.96
29	103.60	*	102.23	93.16	92.06	90.36	87.89	*	83.83	85.08	76.18	69.20
30	104.21		102.45	93.54	*	90.76	86.86	86.43	82.95	84.95	76.04	70.03
31	103.82		102.81		†		86.85	86.16		*		71.95
High	109.88	103.01	104.17	105.65	94.75	93.20	94.51	87.29	89.95	85.73	85.48	77.63
Low	101.90	89.98	91.68	93.16	87.36	90.16	86.85	83.20	82.95	84.00	73.12	66.75

*Sunday
†Holiday

1920—RAILROADS

Date:	Jan.	Feb.	Mar.	Apr.	May	June	July	Aug.	Sept.	Oct.	Nov.	Dec.
1	†	*	75.04	75.98	†	72.28	70.97	*	78.22	82.76	83.31	77.45
2	75.62	74.68	74.83			72.14	71.33	73.07	78.74	84.28	†	77.47
3	76.48	73.56	74.25	†	71.80	71.98	†	74.36	78.88		85.37	77.55
4	*	71.97	74.65	*	72.68	72.01	*	74.91		84.30	85.09	77.50
5	76.41	71.51	74.51	75.78	73.33	71.95	†	74.03	*	83.81	84.98	*
6	75.89	70.83	74.42	76.28	73.54	*	71.77	73.90	†	84.26	84.08	76.28
7	75.90	71.40	*	76.53	73.11	71.68	72.42	73.90	78.79	84.61	*	76.68
8	75.59	*	76.20	76.35	73.76	71.70	73.06	*	78.05	83.84	83.21	76.75
9	75.56	71.09	76.88	75.90	*	71.14	74.06	72.95	78.07	83.50	81.42	75.78
10	75.62	69.00	78.55	75.64	73.53	70.88	74.43	73.10	77.90	*	82.10	74.73
11	*	67.83	78.46	*	72.80	71.15	*	73.70	77.28	83.31	81.99	73.32
12	74.91	†	77.46	74.76	72.36	70.71	74.30	73.40	*	†	78.75	*
13	75.06	69.38	78.73	74.86	71.73	*	73.81	74.05	77.40	84.11	78.10	71.70
14	74.46	70.14	*	75.40	72.29	70.19	73.84	73.93	78.35	84.18	*	73.63
15	74.68	*	78.33	74.86	72.25	70.17	73.20	*	78.31	84.65	78.95	73.10
16	74.61	69.53	77.82	75.16	*	70.78	72.65	73.89	79.01	84.05	79.64	72.89
17	74.96	72.68	77.57	75.30	72.31	70.56	72.84	73.55	79.61	*	77.72	72.53
18	*	73.02	78.51	*	71.70	71.03	*	73.53	80.25	83.44	77.20	71.73
19	74.71	75.46	78.40	74.56	69.99	70.99	72.61	73.90	*	83.85	75.97	*
20	74.68	74.98	78.13	73.26	70.23	*	72.88	74.66	80.19	83.90	77.46	71.36
21	74.46	75.55	*	71.64	70.69	70.87	73.08	74.94	80.11	83.27	*	69.80
22	74.28	*	77.75	72.39	70.62	70.31	73.45	*	80.15	83.43	79.73	70.74
23	74.22	†	77.39	71.65	*	70.36	73.03	75.63	80.14	83.64	78.58	72.63
24	74.29	75.25	76.75	72.01	69.95	70.49	73.00	75.81	79.97	*	78.43	72.33
25	*	73.14	76.36	*	71.28	70.86	*	75.66	80.30	83.22	*	†
26	74.29	74.34	77.30	74.98	71.37	71.08	72.10	76.55	*	83.36	78.83	*
27	74.35	74.67	77.11	73.71	71.72	*	71.98	76.45	79.70	82.83	78.53	72.66
28	74.25	74.77	*	73.38	72.89	70.72	71.80	76.59	80.23	82.10	*	73.05
29	73.90	*	76.61	72.71	73.24	70.85	72.88	*	80.62	82.57	78.52	75.50
30	74.18		76.46	72.21	*	70.91	72.56	77.12	81.33	82.62	77.55	75.56
31	74.68		76.11		†		73.03	77.50		*		75.96
High	76.48	75.55	78.73	76.53	73.76	72.28	74.43	77.50	81.33	84.65	85.37	77.55
Low	73.90	67.83	74.25	71.64	69.95	70.17	70.97	72.95	77.28	82.10	75.97	69.80

*Sunday
†Holiday

1920—DAILY STOCK SALES ON NEW YORK STOCK EXCHANGE
(000 Omitted)

Date	Jan.	Feb.	Mar.	Apr.	May	June	July	Aug.	Sept.	Oct.	Nov.	Dec.
1	†	*	831	608	†	516	272	*	659	969	575	1100
2	1125	487	452	†		443	469	972	758	553	†	1020
3	861	1088	492	†	1096	420	†	1158	654	*	996	750
4	*	1759	867	*	871	390	*	817	†	950	1204	444
5	1321	1279	842	896	811	317	†	1158	*	940	1058	*
6	1257	1486	223	1204	920	*	590	1073	†	862	634	749
7	786	469	*	1696	594	418	851	252	630	813	*	766
8	853	*	1750	1641	452	385	790	*	576	712	1241	882
9	943	780	1429	1224	*	351	920	1036	462	289	1466	1027
10	466	1052	1487	502	842	408	337	516	429	*	1355	1208
11	*	1435	1439	*	832	549	*	486	244	511	826	528
12	1076	†	1072	1175	743	336	792	426	*	†	1291	*
13	916	1388	491	1033	762	*	668	396	356	548	777	1453
14	1190	607	*	1285	492	507	530	130	476	562	*	1342
15	1022	*	1051	1348	249	335	392	*	593	813	1148	895
16	1068	832	1247	997	*	336	593	288	468	244	847	731
17	527	922	1049	437	538	317	136	440	1005	*	1178	708
18	*	977	1921	*	350	539	*	405	435	504	1193	517
19	764	949	1389	1360	1264	195	320	316	*	394	1549	*
20	491	1061	689	1670	1334	*	321	533	1064	487	658	984
21	482	440	*	2060	693	540	305	219	772	569	*	1713
22	490	*	1572	1927	345	407	323	*	765	411	1157	1493
23	563	†	1259	1439	*	319	495	407	966	205	1170	1164
24	369	1098	1751	481	697	333	173	637	644	*	734	635
25	*	1242	1284	*	825	285	*	633	303	486	†	†
26	759	962	1406	1030	765	131	664	440	*	417	752	*
27	681	1093	736	1250	625	*	1066	541	1090	474	306	722
28	704	495	*	1329	577	261	611	164	797	850	*	894
29	551	*	837	1118	310	266	594	*	986	516	595	1252
30	545		678	914	*	330	401	319	971	224	834	1155
31	346		815		†		174	558		*		1217
Total	19,954	21,899	29,057	28,624	16,985	9,635	12,486	14,319	16,105	14,364	23,542	24,134

*Sunday. †Holiday.

1920—BOND AVERAGES

Date:	Jan.	Feb.	Mar.	Apr.	May	June	July	Aug.	Sept.	Oct.	Nov.	Dec.
1	†	*	77.46	77.30	†	73.30	72.77	*	75.00	77.65	78.63	76.22
2	80.01	78.66	77.53	†	*	73.22	72.94	74.11	75.19	77.86	†	76.17
3	80.12	78.45	77.53	†	73.64	73.26	†	74.08	75.43	*	78.55	76.18
4	*	78.35	77.63	*	73.52	73.26	*	74.18	†	78.06	78.72	76.23
5	80.15	78.14	77.74	77.32	73.52	73.25	†	74.27	*	78.25	78.82	*
6	80.12	77.95	77.81	77.30	73.53	*	73.02	74.20	†	78.39	78.80	76.11
7	80.16	77.93	*	77.19	73.40	73.29	73.14	74.29	75.41	78.42	*	75.90
8	80.13	*	77.81	77.00	73.34	73.25	73.26	*	75.23	78.55	78.61	75.65
9	80.21	77.95	77.84	76.66	*	73.19	73.56	74.07	75.31	78.59	78.44	75.36
10	80.37	77.75	77.94	76.58	73.33	73.11	73.61	74.09	75.36	*	78.10	75.06
11	*	77.39	78.02		73.19	73.07		74.13	75.45	78.53	77.89	74.89
12	80.40	†	78.02	76.13	73.23	73.18	73.67	74.03	*	†	77.73	*
13	80.23	77.07	77.91	75.87	73.04	*	73.80	73.98	75.42	78.62	77.62	74.58
14	80.03	77.07	*	75.41	72.91	73.08	73.74	74.07	75.32	78.53	*	74.42
15	80.03	*	77.93	75.17	72.92	72.86	73.85	*	75.52	78.63	77.31	74.82
16	79.92	77.10	77.94	75.20	*	72.89	73.90	73.94	75.61	78.71	77.05	74.83
17	79.90	76.90	77.92	75.15	72.84	72.91	73.93	73.82	75.65	*	76.90	74.84
18	*	77.31	77.94		72.49	72.94		73.80	75.70	78.89	76.81	74.66
19	79.82	77.32	77.96	74.94	72.14	73.01	73.76	73.82	*	78.86	76.67	*
20	79.72	77.73	78.01	74.76	72.04	*	73.66	73.92	75.74	78.99	76.57	74.32
21	79.67	77.71	*	74.43	71.96	73.05	73.71	73.96	75.88	79.16	*	73.92
22	79.54	†	77.95	74.15	72.04	72.99	73.68	*	76.01	79.19	76.45	73.40
23	79.37	†	77.91	74.00	*	72.87	73.88	73.97	76.09	79.13	76.58	73.24
24	79.30	77.86	77.74	74.04	72.00	72.87	73.94	73.88	76.04	*	76.54	73.77
25	*	77.66	77.65		72.14	72.92		74.00	76.14	79.13	†	†
26	79.15	77.20	77.68	74.09	72.42	72.94	73.83	74.21	*	79.00	76.59	*
27	79.03	77.24	77.63	74.20	72.85	*	73.71	74.46	76.66	78.91	76.55	73.92
28	78.92	77.34	*	74.03	73.38	72.89	73.68	74.62	76.77	78.67	*	73.85
29	78.89	*	77.64	73.79	73.55	72.65	73.65	*	77.02	78.67	76.57	74.02
30	78.70		77.55	73.75	*	72.69	73.78	74.62	77.27	78.71	76.39	74.34
31	78.65		77.48		†		73.77	74.76				75.17
High	80.40	78.66	78.02	77.32	73.64	73.30	73.94	74.76	77.27	79.19	78.82	76.23
Low	78.65	76.90	77.46	73.75	71.96	72.65	72.77	73.80	75.00	77.65	76.39	73.24

*Sunday
†Holiday

1921—INDUSTRIALS

Date:	Jan.	Feb.	Mar.	Apr.	May	June	July	Aug.	Sept.	Oct.	Nov.	Dec.
1	†	75.48	74.71	75.72	*	73.51	68.35	69.68	66.83	71.68	73.44	78.12
2	*	74.98	75.19	75.27	79.65	73.06	†	69.95	68.00	*	73.52	78.73
3	72.67	74.34	75.23	*	79.23	72.37	*	69.71	*	71.61	73.98	79.00
4	72.76	74.74	75.11	75.16	79.61	72.55	†	69.50	†	*	73.94	*
5	73.13	75.05	75.25	76.16	80.03	*	67.71	68.61	*	70.46	73.91	78.93
6	74.31	*	*	76.58	79.68	71.18	69.86	68.56	69.12	70.42	*	79.36
7	75.21	74.80	75.26	76.16	79.48	71.56	69.72	*	69.49	70.66	74.20	79.19
8	74.80	75.54	74.91	75.61	*	71.03	68.35	68.63	69.15	71.17	†	78.80
9	*	75.48	74.60	75.73	78.81	69.85	68.54	68.00	70.58	*	75.75	79.60
10	76.00	75.59	73.60	*	78.61	69.92	68.69	66.71	71.92	70.95	75.61	80.16
11	76.14	75.59	72.25	76.15	77.98	69.70	68.69	66.42	*	71.06	†	80.63
12	75.88	†	72.76	76.28	77.60	*	68.70	66.88	70.68	†	76.46	80.69
13	74.43	*	*	75.93	77.57	70.03	68.65	66.75	71.72	70.90	*	80.69
14	74.48	76.41	72.99	75.06	77.19	70.05	67.85	*	71.68	70.15	75.50	81.04
15	75.14	76.90	73.87	76.18	*	69.00	67.25	66.02	70.68	70.09	75.80	81.50
16	*	77.14	75.20	76.33	77.23	68.16	67.44	65.27	70.95	*	77.13	80.95
17	75.21	76.40	75.44	*	77.65	67.57	*	66.09	70.83	69.46	77.07	80.57
18	75.40	76.28	76.30	76.15	77.51	67.25	67.87	65.96	*	69.81	76.94	*
19	76.76	75.93	76.56	76.10	76.96	*	68.24	65.34	70.06	70.21	77.06	80.31
20	76.08	*	*	76.08	76.07	64.90	68.21	65.09	69.43	70.77	*	80.30
21	74.65	75.10	76.03	76.54	75.65	66.25	68.11	*	69.45	71.00	76.69	79.02
22	74.91	†	76.60	77.63	*	66.23	68.27	64.50	70.25	71.11	76.21	78.76
23	*	75.66	77.78	78.15	75.86	65.36	69.23	64.38	70.90	*	76.34	79.31
24	74.77	74.66	77.39	*	74.43	66.20	*	63.90	70.81	71.81	†	79.61
25	74.98	75.23	†	78.55	74.26	67.85	69.80	63.91	*	72.22	77.31	*
26	75.19	75.46	77.13	78.86	74.81	*	69.20	65.54	70.65	72.27	77.85	†
27	75.71	*	*	78.11	74.31	67.03	69.18	65.56	70.30	72.78	*	80.69
28	76.23	74.98	76.19	78.77	†	67.63	68.18	*	70.14	73.80	78.01	80.80
29	76.34		77.13	78.57	*	68.73	68.37	66.18	71.19	73.93	77.76	80.34
30	*		76.26	78.84	†	68.45	68.86	67.80	71.08	*	77.30	80.80
31	76.13		75.76		73.44		*	67.11		73.21		81.10
High	76.76	77.14	77.78	78.86	80.03	73.51	69.86	69.95	71.92	73.93	78.01	81.50
Low	72.67	74.34	72.25	75.06	73.44	64.90	67.25	63.90	66.83	69.46	73.44	78.12

*Sunday
†Holiday

1921—RAILROADS

Date:	Jan.	Feb.	Mar.	Apr.	May	June	July	Aug.	Sept.	Oct.	Nov.	Dec.
1	†	75.38	72.41	70.41	*	71.89	70.58	74.03	71.31	74.58	72.53	76.22
2	*	75.21	72.83	70.18	71.63	71.75	†	75.21	71.84	*	72.58	75.50
3	75.98	74.41	72.96	*	71.68	71.87	*	74.42	*	74.38	72.70	75.50
4	76.21	74.56	73.23	70.05	72.51	72.38	†	73.97	†	74.06	72.49	*
5	75.91	74.90	73.42	70.46	73.99	*	70.33	72.85	*	73.76	72.43	75.01
6	76.49	*	*	70.56	74.11	71.31	72.26	72.66	72.19	73.55	*	75.24
7	77.03	74.58	72.87	69.98	74.31	70.13	72.49	*	72.92	73.67	72.70	74.60
8	77.21	74.92	72.54	69.59	*	70.57	71.35	72.64	72.62	73.90	†	74.22
9	*	74.66	71.61	69.53	75.38	69.92	71.90	72.61	73.00	*	73.58	74.35
10	77.33	74.42	70.20	*	74.68	69.20	72.02	72.02	73.41	73.47	73.51	74.48
11	76.99	73.60	69.10	69.36	73.90	68.99	71.65	71.30	*	73.10	†	*
12	77.30	†	69.56	69.79	72.90	*	71.70	71.93	73.28	†	73.51	74.38
13	76.65	*	*	68.88	73.10	68.91	71.10	71.87	74.30	72.46	*	74.21
14	77.15	74.19	69.18	67.86	72.89	69.69	70.96	*	73.92	71.84	72.92	74.08
15	77.56	73.66	70.16	70.28	*	69.64	70.32	71.97	73.28	71.11	73.25	74.20
16	*	74.08	71.62	70.31	73.36	69.31	70.33	71.61	73.39	*	74.20	74.38
17	76.71	73.95	70.76	*	73.26	68.88	*	71.75	73.26	70.00	74.20	74.83
18	76.40	74.15	70.75	69.88	74.16	67.85	70.70	72.28	*	70.60	74.48	*
19	76.45	74.25	70.99	69.33	73.53	*	71.45	72.30	72.78	71.14	74.58	74.95
20	76.22	*	*	69.27	72.02	65.52	71.59	72.16	72.54	71.73	*	74.57
21	75.47	73.87	70.07	69.54	71.36	66.79	71.90	*	72.67	71.53	74.36	73.95
22	75.45	†	70.31	70.10	*	67.00	72.48	71.17	73.75	71.63	74.20	73.47
23	*	74.11	71.04	71.30	71.83	66.45	73.02	70.73	74.69	*	74.10	73.30
24	75.68	73.75	70.90	*	71.26	67.13	*	69.87	74.66	72.40	†	73.67
25	75.70	74.08	†	71.33	71.45	68.80	73.09	70.21	*	71.88	75.17	*
26	76.00	73.75	71.06	71.45	72.38	*	72.93	71.21	74.30	71.46	75.60	†
27	76.19	*	*	70.54	71.98	68.00	73.08	71.16	73.61	72.20	*	73.71
28	76.67	73.32	70.18	71.26	†	68.70	73.58	*	73.45	72.94	76.06	73.88
29	76.60		71.71	71.27	*	69.27	73.33	71.43	74.10	72.80	76.66	73.71
30	*		71.10	71.25	†	71.04	73.68	72.46	74.17	*	76.33	73.86
31	76.17		70.78		71.83		*	72.15		72.56		74.27
High	77.56	75.38	73.42	71.45	75.38	72.38	73.68	75.21	74.69	74.58	76.66	76.22
Low	75.45	73.32	69.10	67.86	71.26	65.52	70.32	69.87	71.31	70.00	72.43	73.30

*Sunday
†Holiday

1921—DAILY STOCK SALES ON N. Y. STOCK EXCHANGE
(000 Omitted)

Date	Jan.	Feb.	Mar.	Apr.	May	June	July	Aug.	Sept.	Oct.	Nov.	Dec.
1	†	448	607	577	*	595	439	400	377	280	640	658
2	*	527	493	272	1190	586	†	307	532	*	591	836
3	812	579	432	*	873	658	*	517	†	556	574	397
4	908	533	484	541	854	354	†	330	*	528	595	*
5	757	209	143	593	1286	*	327	417	†	579	226	821
6	967	*	*	507	1175	745	937	130	752	430	*	768
7	1233	355	490	468	429	1163	873	*	636	553	517	956
8	512	486	456	365	*	598	731	275	489	290	†	699
9	*	470	401	189	985	835	236	300	709	*	885	608
10	1194	392	800	*	832	775	*	489	548	429	850	510
11	1168	373	1112	352	939	417	429	549	*	454	†	*
12	926	†	504	616	854	*	361	423	741	†	386	729
13	885	*	*	494	848	1089	423	125	675	529	*	937
14	517	514	625	591	382	787	361	*	891	657	977	857
15	286	667	652	701	*	752	391	396	612	395	711	1048
16	*	589	850	312	700	908	117	465	522	*	960	875
17	478	622	827	*	592	782	*	479	241	681	924	447
18	472	568	811	424	666	402	352	414	*	434	923	*
19	785	369	414	471	453	*	336	421	594	540	447	754
20	908	*	*	411	658	1254	352	146	528	450	*	571
21	744	632	688	718	296	1058	293	*	612	514	781	700
22	368	†	596	1139	*	949	314	463	582	391	712	750
23	*	447	1305	575	658	855	208	536	643	*	687	547
24	526	543	645	*	845	532	*	639	235	584	†	342
25	466	510	†	1108	846	466	418	623	*	797	760	*
26	505	326	348	898	569	*	361	687	491	668	481	†
27	506	*	*	870	547	483	455	231	435	711	*	632
28	522	437	698	894	†	608	497	*	474	1050	913	882
29	271		681	1155	*	619	444	400	493	412	872	806
30	*		645	579	†	747	351	624	451	*	882	787
31	516		566		482		*	544		732		473
Total	17,232	10,596	16,272	15,819	17,958	19,017	9,845	11,328	13,261	13,643	16,293	18,401

*Sunday. †Holiday.

1921—BOND AVERAGES

Date:	Jan.	Feb.	Mar.	Apr.	May	June	July	Aug.	Sept.	Oct.	Nov.	Dec.
1	†	77.67	76.82	76.87	*	76.21	75.60	78.10	77.96	79.40	79.65	84.06
2	*	77.55	76.72	76.94	76.95	76.21	†	78.09	78.14	*	79.91	84.11
3	75.51	77.51	76.71	*	76.93	76.06	*	78.17	†	79.34	80.42	84.00
4	75.71	77.47	76.87	76.84	76.97	76.01	†	78.27	*	79.34	80.62	*
5	75.94	77.54	76.91	76.87	77.32	*	76.05	78.17	†	79.32	80.71	84.09
6	76.19	*	*	76.88	77.39	75.89	76.20	78.21	78.22	79.31	*	84.11
7	76.49	77.55	76.82	77.12	77.47	75.63	76.30	*	78.34	79.37	80.84	84.13
8	76.68	77.56	76.63	77.08	*	75.57	76.54	77.96	78.53	79.36	†	83.99
9	*	77.48	76.62	77.02	77.57	75.56	76.49	77.79	78.52	*	81.03	83.88
10	76.81	77.40	76.56	*	77.53	75.36	*	77.82	78.73	79.49	81.13	83.87
11	77.10	77.39	76.41	76.92	77.51	75.30	76.47	77.66	*	79.49	†	*
12	77.22	†	76.32	76.92	77.40	*	76.50	77.65	78.85	†	81.21	83.81
13	77.46	*	*	76.90	77.21	75.21	76.62	77.64	78.98	79.45	*	83.90
14	77.54	77.37	76.30	76.79	77.13	75.31	76.73	*	79.04	79.40	81.29	83.82
15	77.69	77.31	76.37	76.79	*	75.41	76.76	77.64	79.10	79.05	81.45	83.87
16	*	77.18	76.49	76.92	77.01	75.37	76.62	77.55	79.06	*	81.64	83.95
17	77.80	77.25	76.58	*	76.98	75.21	*	77.55	79.17	78.79	81.80	83.95
18	78.00	77.40	76.52	76.90	76.96	75.27	76.56	77.62	*	78.77	82.08	*
19	78.13	77.31	76.65	76.86	76.96	*	76.60	77.80	79.16	78.83	82.15	84.00
20	78.26	*	*	76.94	76.88	75.20	76.68	77.80	79.09	78.92	*	83.95
21	78.42	77.28	76.76	76.93	76.85	75.11	76.76	*	79.12	78.98	82.56	83.63
22	78.44	†	76.79	76.88	*	75.15	76.99	77.77	79.30	78.99	82.86	83.58
23	78.42	77.24	76.78	76.84	76.69	75.12	77.21	77.67	79.39	*	83.29	83.39
24	78.42	77.12	76.76	*	76.49	75.15	*	77.63	79.47	78.99	†	83.39
25	78.44	76.93	†	76.96	76.38	75.17	77.29	77.62	*	78.99	83.45	*
26	78.36	77.02	76.73	76.85	76.38	*	77.43	77.69	79.52	78.99	83.55	†
27	78.05	*	*	76.73	76.29	75.25	77.56	77.74	79.25	79.03	*	83.44
28	77.96	76.92	76.80	76.64	†	75.29	77.76	*	79.22	79.35	83.86	83.50
29	78.08		76.77	76.61	*	75.40	78.08	77.61	79.39	79.40	84.04	83.46
30	*		76.81	76.92	†	75.51	78.07	77.66	79.42	*	84.11	83.61
31	77.93		76.88		76.25		*	77.81		79.46		83.76
High	78.44	77.67	76.91	77.12	77.57	76.21	78.08	78.27	79.52	79.49	84.11	84.13
Low	75.51	76.92	76.30	76.61	76.25	75.11	75.60	77.55	77.96	78.77	79.65	83.39

*Sunday. † Holiday.

1922—INDUSTRIALS

Date:	Jan.	Feb.	Mar.	Apr.	May	June	July	Aug.	Sept.	Oct.	Nov.	Dec.
1	*	81.68	85.33	89.08	93.35	96.03	92.90	96.25	101.28	*	96.23	95.73
2	†	82.86	86.03	*	93.64	96.36	*	96.51	101.29	97.67	98.50	95.91
3	78.91	82.93	86.46	90.05	93.81	96.31	92.92	96.81	*	98.90	99.29	95.10
4	79.61	83.61	85.91	89.30	93.18	*	†	97.11	†	99.93	99.06	*
5	78.68	*	*	90.67	93.18	95.98	92.97	97.03	101.67	100.34	*	95.03
6	78.96	83.70	86.30	90.80	93.59	95.59	93.97	*	100.60	100.81	98.45	96.75
7	79.12	83.38	86.90	90.80	*	95.15	94.63	97.37	101.05	100.50	†	96.91
8	*	82.74	86.73	90.63	92.84	95.11	93.53	97.07	101.22	*	99.53	97.88
9	78.87	83.60	86.95	*	92.57	93.60	*	96.93	101.68	102.26	98.98	97.72
10	78.59	83.05	87.18	91.11	91.58	93.20	93.90	96.51	*	101.55	97.50	*
11	80.03	82.96	87.93	91.91	91.50	*	94.17	96.82	102.05	101.72	95.88	97.85
12	79.96	*	*	91.77	92.50	90.73	94.88	97.04	101.88	*	*	97.75
13	80.82	†	87.56	92.48	92.93	92.04	94.65	*	101.10	102.60	95.37	98.28
14	81.23	83.81	87.92	†	*	93.08	94.96	96.21	100.79	103.43	93.61	98.19
15	*	84.09	87.30	93.06	92.08	91.25	95.35	96.90	100.99	*	95.11	98.03
16	81.36	83.98	88.11	*	92.63	91.11	*	97.41	*	102.76	94.72	98.13
17	81.90	83.88	88.46	92.75	93.71	91.45	95.26	97.93	*	102.60	95.09	*
18	82.33	84.28	88.47	91.15	93.91	*	96.53	98.60	98.88	102.00	95.36	97.64
19	81.91	*	*	92.52	94.80	91.95	96.69	99.01	99.93	101.21	*	98.23
20	82.95	84.85	88.28	92.43	94.65	93.51	96.76	*	100.14	102.01	95.82	97.52
21	82.53	85.81	88.11	93.21	*	93.02	96.13	99.71	98.37	101.95	95.59	97.88
22	*	†	87.26	93.46	94.86	93.15	95.78	100.75	98.55	*	94.29	98.62
23	82.29	85.36	86.90	*	94.66	93.07	*	100.32	99.10	100.11	94.08	†
24	82.43	85.18	87.40	93.00	94.70	93.16	94.64	99.71	*	100.10	94.10	†
25	82.57	83.33	87.08	92.72	94.36	*	95.69	99.82	98.90	99.55	92.78	*
26	81.54	*	*	91.96	95.05	93.48	94.84	100.05	98.45	98.00	*	99.04
27	81.34	84.58	86.60	91.10	95.47	92.47	96.36	*	96.81	98.76	92.03	99.22
28	81.75	85.46	87.20	91.93	*	92.24	96.69	99.21	96.58	98.68	93.85	98.14
29	*		87.90	92.74	96.41	92.06	96.83	100.70	97.12	*	94.65	98.17
30	81.33		88.87	*	†	92.93		100.75	96.30	96.90	†	98.73
31	81.30		89.05		95.63		97.05	100.78		96.11		
High	82.95	85.81	89.05	93.46	96.41	96.36	97.05	100.78	102.05	103.43	99.53	99.22
Low	78.59	81.68	85.33	89.08	91.50	90.73	92.90	96.21	96.30	96.11	92.03	95.03

* *Sunday*
† *Holiday*

1922—RAILROADS

Date:	Jan.	Feb.	Mar.	Apr.	May	June	July	Aug.	Sept.	Oct.	Nov.	Dec.
1	*	74.68	77.99	80.68	84.45	85.23	84.45	88.35	92.41	*	89.28	85.56
2	†	75.19	78.31	*	84.34	85.14	*	88.46	92.10	90.76	90.86	85.86
3	73.48	75.88	78.10	81.26	84.44	85.01	84.52	88.65	*	91.96	91.11	*
4	73.91	76.23	77.79	80.86	84.40	*	†	88.55	†	92.15	90.87	85.16
5	73.56	*	*	81.55	84.68	84.94	84.66	89.18	92.16	92.10	*	84.31
6	73.65	76.70	77.21	82.78	84.65	84.78	87.58	*	91.20	91.93	90.16	84.51
7	73.85	76.38	77.87	83.20	*	84.48	87.16	89.79	92.19	91.90	†	84.39
8	*	76.60	77.99	83.91	84.30	84.43	86.11	89.43	93.51	*	90.48	84.56
9	73.43	76.81	78.53	*	83.98	83.37	*	89.43	93.88	92.05	90.43	84.60
10	73.53	76.77	78.68	84.01	83.13	83.25	86.14	89.60	*	91.81	89.50	*
11	74.01	76.81	78.83	83.61	83.12	*	86.45	89.58	93.99	92.50	88.20	84.35
12	74.65	*	*	83.44	83.44	81.81	86.95	89.32	93.42	*	*	84.54
13	74.98	†	78.71	83.46	83.90	82.76	86.47	*	92.55	92.79	87.53	84.83
14	75.36	77.46	79.56	†	*	83.09	86.24	88.06	93.67	93.26	85.85	84.88
15	*	77.49	79.26	84.32	83.58	82.28	86.56	89.01	93.70	*	86.07	84.58
16	75.76	77.50	79.21	*	83.34	81.91	*	89.84	93.38	93.70	85.59	84.59
17	76.56	77.28	79.28	84.77	84.00	81.95	86.55	90.31	*	93.55	86.15	*
18	76.58	77.33	79.53	83.85	84.41	*	86.50	90.55	91.97	92.85	86.10	83.75
19	76.18	*	*	84.32	85.28	81.88	86.82	91.51	92.70	92.59	*	83.98
20	75.85	77.61	79.92	84.74	86.13	82.85	86.60	*	92.70	93.28	86.11	84.31
21	75.68	78.08	80.07	84.80	*	82.62	86.49	93.05	91.36	93.45	85.83	85.24
22	*	*	79.61	84.84	86.17	83.60	86.41	92.54	91.36	*	84.33	85.87
23	75.50	78.38	79.13	*	86.12	83.73	*	92.03	91.88	92.56	83.70	†
24	75.58	78.73	79.08	84.84	85.94	84.46	85.63	92.32	*	92.72	83.46	†
25	75.30	79.16	79.19	85.09	85.66	*	86.14	91.76	91.82	93.06	82.58	*
26	74.83	*	*	84.36	86.33	84.73	85.59	91.54	91.41	91.43	*	85.98
27	74.84	78.52	78.79	83.60	86.66	83.63	87.63	*	89.96	91.90	82.17	85.55
28	74.94	78.66	79.15	84.20	*	83.49	87.70	90.59	89.93	91.71	83.50	84.86
29	*		80.16	84.43	86.83	83.73	88.21	91.92	90.08	*	84.56	85.79
30	74.98		80.86	*	†	84.45		92.68	89.60	89.84	†	86.11
31	74.73		80.66		85.53		88.98	92.48		89.25		
High	76.58	79.16	80.86	85.09	86.83	85.23	88.98	93.05	93.99	93.70	91.11	86.11
Low	73.43	74.68	77.21	80.68	83.12	81.81	84.45	88.06	89.60	89.25	82.17	83.75

* *Sunday*
† *Holiday*

1922—DAILY STOCK SALES ON N. Y. STOCK EXCHANGE
(000 Omitted)

Date	Jan.	Feb.	Mar.	Apr.	May	June	July	Aug.	Sept.	Oct.	Nov.	Dec.
1	*	438	978	432	1179	1297	236	727	1101	*	1264	925
2	†	794	834	*	1189	1658	*	571	351	767	1138	505
3	996	846	988	1358	1471	883	237	628	*	1047	1093	*
4	838	504	455	1412	1497	*	†	566	†	1329	477	793
5	890	*	*	1214	1173	1244	627	287	927	1389	*	708
6	620	903	868	1639	650	1135	917	*	1006	1360	682	807
7	291	820	717	1704	*	1133	1016	619	963	541	†	1026
8	*	784	877	895	1043	805	417	829	1003	*	882	900
9	558	742	888	*	1083	1259	*	611	546	1362	1100	457
10	518	760	844	1556	922	643	634	606	*	1513	925	*
11	463	296	604	1479	1232	*	*	590	1059	1292	612	748
12	512	*	*	1693	1314	1806	883	317	1056	*	†	783
13	646	†	1064	1552	734	1354	855	*	1262	1129	1081	895
14	457	673	938	†	*	1055	837	637	1196	691	1474	911
15	*	840	1264	997	1224	1452	325	563	1059	*	1190	914
16	829	819	1216	*	1052	1152	*	740	483	1253	1137	516
17	802	736	1270	2129	1707	496	536	699	*	1133	995	*
18	959	343	595	1801	1475	*	707	721	1332	1337	289	1181
19	871	*	*	1571	1807	750	842	439	945	1369	*	834
20	1201	844	1213	1503	937	1151	755	*	978	1203	620	867
21	573	1025	972	1291	*	1162	768	1009	1194	510	684	899
22	*	†	1000	836	1668	922	324	1041	1139	*	1006	880
23	655	1183	897	*	1378	713	*	1018	386	1286	994	†
24	552	1025	916	1329	1045	356	898	945	*	965	762	†
25	725	565	435	1412	1134	*	753	994	739	1052	549	†
26	866	*	*	1395	1340	829	779	361	891	1234	*	939
27	543	1064	775	1537	714	881	819	*	2000	1016	1159	1075
28	273	819	663	1177	*	676	813	834	1201	376	1076	1305
29	*		794	790	1282	734	303	810	1202	*	924	991
30	489		1001	†	*	582	*	1018	430	1181	†	595
31	429		1140		1282		784	922		1195		*
Total	16,555	16,823	24,204	32,799	31,530	26,127	16,653	19,094	23,505	27,529	22,114	20,453

*Sunday. †Holiday.

1922—BOND AVERAGES

Date:	Jan.	Feb.	Mar.	Apr.	May	June	July	Aug.	Sept.	Oct.	Nov.	Dec.
1	*	85.78	86.23	87.60	89.30	88.96	89.21	90.55	91.58	*	89.41	88.68
2	†	85.76	86.32	*	89.43	89.05	*	90.61	91.71	91.10	89.61	88.83
3	84.58	85.76	86.35	87.62	89.43	89.07	89.25	90.73	*	91.24	89.76	
4	84.34	85.85	86.31	87.53	89.43	*	†	90.85	†	91.30	89.80	88.90
5	84.42	*	*	87.51	89.36	88.97	89.39	90.93	91.67	91.45	*	88.92
6	84.56	85.96	86.20	87.37	89.42	88.93	89.75	*	91.69	91.36	89.64	88.99
7	84.64	86.07	86.16	87.63	*	88.86	89.86	90.93	91.71	91.31	†	89.08
8	*	86.09	86.22	87.68	89.36	88.86	89.92	90.96	91.77	*	89.54	89.06
9	84.60	86.15	86.22	*	89.11	88.82	*	90.99	91.81	91.21	89.48	89.03
10	84.86	86.06	86.23	87.82	89.15	88.89	89.91	91.02	*	91.14	89.30	*
11	85.16	86.05	86.26	87.82	88.98	*	89.81	91.04	91.82	90.77	89.23	88.99
12	85.26	*	*	87.93	88.99	88.79	90.00	91.19	91.90	†	*	89.08
13	85.66	†	86.33	88.13	89.05	88.77	90.20	*	92.05	90.63	88.88	89.16
14	85.90	86.03	86.53	†	*	88.71	90.18	91.05	92.12	90.63	88.56	89.08
15	*	86.05	86.61	88.26	89.09	88.69	90.32	91.00	92.11	*	88.35	89.13
16	86.15	85.99	86.61	*	88.99	88.70	*	91.10	92.10	90.44	88.57	89.04
17	86.06	86.15	86.81	88.47	88.98	88.72	90.25	91.19	*	90.19	88.46	
18	86.14	86.10	86.89	88.57	89.00	*	90.30	91.37	91.92	90.23	88.42	88.91
19	86.03	*	*	88.53	89.11	88.60	90.35	91.50	91.93	90.05	*	88.80
20	86.12	86.14	87.03	88.71	89.11	88.66	90.45	*	91.96	90.03	88.41	88.90
21	86.21	86.09	87.12	88.86	*	88.79	90.48	91.54	91.95	90.04	88.43	88.82
22	*	†	87.27	88.94	89.28	88.90	90.47	91.53	91.87	*	88.47	88.75
23	86.20	86.07	87.25	*	89.25	89.00	*	91.76	91.94	90.00	88.33	†
24	86.27	86.13	87.09	89.17	89.19	89.08	90.35	91.76	*	89.70	88.39	*
25	86.22	86.12	87.14	89.13	89.08	*	90.30	91.83	91.84	89.63	88.38	†
26	86.20	*	*	89.18	89.10	89.21	90.35	91.77	91.79	89.50	*	88.85
27	85.99	86.01	87.18	89.17	89.12	89.24	90.33	*	91.49	89.55	88.28	88.72
28	85.98	86.01	87.25	89.12	*	89.20	90.47	91.69	91.27	89.78	88.36	88.76
29	*		87.36	89.14	89.10	89.18	90.50	91.66	91.11	*	88.42	88.84
30	85.94		87.45	*	*	89.18	*	91.65	91.03	89.74	†	89.06
31	85.83		87.48		89.02		90.57	91.63		89.63		*
High	86.27	86.15	87.48	89.18	89.43	89.24	90.57	91.83	92.12	91.45	89.80	89.16
Low	84.34	85.76	86.16	87.37	88.98	88.60	89.21	90.55	91.03	89.50	88.28	88.68

*Sunday.
† Holiday.

1923—INDUSTRIALS

Date:	Jan.	Feb.	Mar.	Apr.	May	June	July	Aug.	Sept.	Oct.	Nov.	Dec.
1	†	97.71	104.23	*	97.40	95 36	*	87.96	93.22	88.06	88.41	93.15
2	98.77	98.70	104.65	101.51	98.05	95 75	88.95	88.20	*	88.09	88.91	*
3	99.42	99.33	104.51	101.60	96.30	*	87.87	†	†	90.45	89.63	92.64
4	98.57	*	*	101.40	96.60	96.14	*	87.20	92.25	89.93	*	92.68
5	98.88	100.03	104.77	102.36	96.73	96.29	87.90	*	92.98	89.41	89.36	92.81
6	97.77	101.01	104.79	102.70	*	97.24	88.65	88.51	93.00	89.29	†	92.94
7	*	101.05	105.23	102.56	95.41	97.17	89.41	89.55	92.84	*	89.48	93.80
8	98.06	101.05	104.70	*	96.54	96.66	*	88.63	92.93	88.56	90.75	93.85
9	97.23	100.82	104.48	102.11	98.19	97.10	89 26	88.67	*	88.06	91.14	*
10	97.29	101.70	103.82	101.86	97.61	*	88.44	†	93.31	87.54	91.39	93.86
11	98.12	*	*	101.08	96.45	97.22	87.80	89.11	93.61	87.16	*	93.65
12	98.63	†	104.22	101.71	95.40	95.97	87.64	*	92.05	†	91.08	94.11
13	99.09	102.16	104.79	101.81	*	95.79	89.07	88.95	89.93	87.13	90.75	94.70
14	*	101.85	105.28	102.09	96.91	95.44	89.40	89.60	89.63	*	90.44	94.93
15	98.04	102.57	104.74	*	95.95	94.86	*	90.23	89.05	88.06	90.87	95.23
16	96.96	103.23	103.93	101.76	95.53	94.73	89.22	90.86	*	86.91	90.33	*
17	97.05	103.21	104.89	102.14	95.41	*	89.50	91.64	89.41	87.56	89.65	95.26
18	98.09	*	*	102.24	95.07	92.64	90.01	92.32	88.49	87.46	*	93.66
19	97.85	102.96	105.36	102.58	94.70	92 76	91.35	†	89.17	87.51	91.35	93.63
20	97.61	103.56	105.38	101.38	*	90.81	91.72	91.71	88.16	87.83	91.26	94.00
21	*	103.59	105.23	101.10	92.77	92 26	91.39	92.18	88.07	*	92.17	93.51
22	97.25	†	105.09	*	93.58	93.55	*	92.13	88.54	87.48	91.83	93.63
23	97.43	103 27	103.98	100.73	93.90	93.30	91.58	92.04	*	87.37	92.13	*
24	97.16	102.85	103.28	101.08	96.03	*	90.16	91.92	89.21	87.13	92.60	94.42
25	97.79	*	*	101.36	96.65	91.48	90.87	91.59	87.94	86.43	*	†
26	98.15	102.40	102.36	101.37	97.48	90.11	91.06	*	88.53	86.01	92.88	95.61
27	98.00	102.79	103.03	101.16	*	88.66	88.37	92.48	88.53	85.76	92.61	94.98
28	*	103.90	103.45	100.63	97.25	89.38	87.33	93.20	87.97	*	92.41	95.12
29	98.26		102.77	*	97.66	88.40	*	93.70	87.89	86.20	†	95.23
30	97.75		†	98.38	†	87.85	88.11	93.40	*	85.91	92.34	
31	97.43		102.75		97.53		86.91	93.46		88.53		95.52
High	99.42	103.90	105.38	102.70	98.19	97.24	91.72	93.70	93.61	90.45	92.88	95.61
Low	96.96	97.71	102.36	98.38	92.77	87.85	86.91	87.20	87.89	85.76	88.41	92.64

* Sunday
† Holiday

1923—RAILROADS

Date:	Jan.	Feb.	Mar.	Apr.	May	June	July	Aug.	Sept.	Oct.	Nov.	Dec.
1	†	86.08	89.37	*	84.91	81.42	*	77.91	79.88	78.83	80.01	81.18
2	86.10	86.63	89.66	85.84	85.29	81.59	78.40	77.28	*	78.96	79.95	*
3	86.07	87.34	90.63	86.17	84.22	*	77.15	†	†	80.13	79.93	80.96
4	85.68	*	*	86.30	83.87	82.15	†	76.78	78.96	80.00	*	81.28
5	85.96	88.08	90.51	86.08	84.01	82.41	77.64	*	79.66	79.96	80.03	81.80
6	85.46	88.93	90.25	86.55	*	82.71	77.99	78.02	79.55	80.81	†	82.40
7	*	88.80	89.75	86.53	80.37	83.01	78.70	78.36	79.93	*	79.73	82.43
8	85.41	88.91	89.36	*	81.55	83.31	*	77.86	80.10	80.72	79.92	82.10
9	84.96	89.17	89.19	86.58	82.31	84.92	78.72	77.90	*	80.33	80.28	*
10	84.85	89.56	88.98	86.48	82.15	*	78.38	†	80.31	79.76	80.58	81.64
11	84.59	*	*	86.28	82.20	84.51	77.73	78.11	80.53	79.23	*	80.81
12	85.09	†	89.06	86.29	81.68	83.71	78.11	*	79.30	†	80.50	81.17
13	85.29	89.49	89.66	86.34	*	83.75	79.08	78.10	78.53	79.19	81.20	81.15
14	*	89.05	89.73	87.23	82.71	83.46	79.20	78.31	78.42	*	81.00	80.40
15	85.35	89.14	89.33	*	81.87	83.65	*	78.74	78.03	79.66	80.70	80.65
16	84.60	89.24	88.67	87.09	81.70	83.48	79.16	78.91	*	78.28	80.28	*
17	84.53	89.29	89.11	87.41	81.58	*	79.33	79.17	78.39	78.41	79.80	80.18
18	84.90	*	*	88.56	81.33	82.14	79.25	79.66	78.07	78.42	*	79.42
19	85.33	89.80	89.36	88.00	81.00	81.74	80.05	*	78.48	78.67	80.56	79.34
20	85.36	90.17	89.60	87.35	*	80.60	80.51	79.53	78.36	78.95	80.77	79.80
21	*	90.43	89.67	86.75	80.13	81.24	80.75	79.31	78.37	*	81.45	79.74
22	85.10	†	89.40	*	80.66	82.40	*	78.76	78.76	78.38	81.59	79.67
23	85.77	90.12	88.80	86.47	80.91	82.43	79.98	78.85	*	78.33	81.25	*
24	86.11	90.20	88.78	86.67	82.70	*	79.45	78.92	78.86	78.41	81.20	79.84
25	86.46	*	*	86.76	82.35	81.46	79.64	78.65	78.36	77.78	*	80.12
26	86.43	89.76	87.69	86.79	82.58	80.23	80.00	*	78.86	77.65	81.52	80.12
27	86.47	89.53	87.71	86.52	*	78.48	78.12	79.04	79.05	77.65	81.48	79.81
28	*	89.56	87.93	86.60	83.16	78.94	77.40	79.57	78.48	*	81.61	80.10
29	87.20		87.26	*	83.09	77.97	*	79.97	78.33	77.86	†	80.62
30	86.58		†	84.86	†	76.85	78.13	80.01	*	77.67	81.09	
31	86.26		87.15		83.04		77.14	80.30		78.82		80.86
High	87.20	90.43	90.63	88.56	85.29	84.92	80.75	80.30	80.53	80.81	81.61	82.43
Low	84.53	86.08	87.15	84.86	80.13	76.85	77.14	76.78	78.03	77.65	79.73	79.34

* Sunday
† Holiday

1923—DAILY STOCK SALES ON N. Y. STOCK EXCHANGE
(000 Omitted)

Date	Jan.	Feb.	Mar.	Apr.	May	June	July	Aug.	Sept.	Oct.	Nov.	Dec.
1	†	644	1372	*	1549	1043	*	626	241	628	1218	558
2	890	808	1391	1303	996	430	934	592	*	521	1080	*
3	940	638	752	1232	1221	*	753	†	†	1120	548	1099
4	1377	*	*	917	1566	559	†	420	587	792	*	835
5	961	1031	1251	1069	440	492	739	*	552	612	798	1010
6	533	1431	1328	1416	*	650	617	468	626	330	†	1268
7	*	1248	1278	445	1436	608	339	498	516	*	745	1344
8	691	1243	1274	*	987	666	*	421	212	723	1188	742
9	770	1283	931	702	1048	435	538	379	*	764	1206	*
10	738	753	499	882	1241	*	385	†	598	609	392	987
11	816	*	*	1243	940	650	384	159	631	672	*	1147
12	1050	†	724	887	625	797	366	*	893	†	981	973
13	632	1456	986	865	*	1093	416	322	1119	228	970	1277
14	*	1430	1091	425	874	804	167	553	896	*	974	1375
15	1191	1415	1065	*	682	790	*	658	437	536	856	532
16	971	1554	949	695	744	221	298	629	*	733	846	*
17	684	719	489	897	611	*	388	616	569	580	691	1187
18	874	*	*	995	551	995	433	399	744	445	*	1181
19	961	1318	1180	1797	407	1118	687	*	852	579	910	1074
20	342	1088	1254	1007	*	1201	750	585	586	274	914	924
21	*	1087	1391	639	1292	1292	299	591	739	*	1374	777
22	602	*	1177	*	1369	761	*	722	282	496	1534	392
23	624	1092	1232	1045	902	275	508	607	*	552	1037	*
24	729	530	588	685	1201	*	533	518	626	547	571	767
25	680	*	*	735	1178	701	445	285	733	584	*	†
26	726	1075	1290	701	596	1090	394	*	600	724	1198	1326
27	348	899	1108	691	*	1120	855	534	688	306	1189	1262
28	*	1119	1082	359	1089	1186	368	692	670	*	963	1163
29	782		186	*	754	825	*	814	326	635	†	741
30	770		†	1209	†	514	820	884	*	602	681	*
31	776		367		689		833	582		1360		1035
Total	20,457	23,860	26,741	22,838	24,987	20,317	13,498	13,562	15,418	15,964	22,862	24,988

*Sunday. †Holiday.

1923—BOND AVERAGES

Date:	Jan.	Feb.	Mar.	Apr.	May	June	July	Aug.	Sept.	Oct.	Nov.	Dec.
1	†	88.11	87.59	*	86.63	87.54	*	86.95	87.23	85.98	86.82	86.63
2	89.26	88.40	87.63	85.78	86.55	87.53	86.23	86.91	*	86.09	86.87	*
3	89.36	88.47	87.67	85.79	86.50	*	86.30	†	†	86.00	86.82	86.66
4	89.39	*	*	86.14	86.43	87.58	†	86.83	87.19	86.13	*	86.65
5	89.38	88.62	87.70	86.14	86.44	87.55	86.29	*	87.07	86.11	86.78	86.67
6	89.34	88.75	87.55	86.30	*	87.51	86.47	86.81	87.13	86.21	†	86.78
7	*	88.71	87.42	86.34	86.42	87.61	86.60	87.03	87.11	*	86.82	86.80
8	89.21	88.76	87.28	*	86.47	87.58	*	87.19	87.14	86.36	86.81	86.93
9	89.18	88.74	87.09	86.62	86.63	87.60	86.65	87.24	*	86.37	86.79	*
10	89.06	88.78	87.06	86.66	86.73	*	86.82	†	87.07	86.35	86.84	86.99
11	89.00	*	*	86.57	86.76	87.60	86.82	87.21	87.05	86.31	*	86.87
12	89.01	†	86.99	86.55	86.79	87.58	86.73	*	87.10	†	87.00	86.85
13	89.00	88.81	87.04	86.40	*	87.55	86.76	87.28	87.04	86.36	87.07	86.83
14	*	88.73	86.79	86.44	86.78	87.55	86.74	87.29	86.83	*	86.94	86.77
15	88.86	88.56	86.80	*	86.93	87.46	*	87.34	86.75	86.30	86.95	86.81
16	88.80	88.48	86.75	86.45	86.94	87.45	86.78	87.35	*	86.26	86.81	*
17	88.50	88.45	86.77	86.58	87.98	*	86.81	87.27	86.77	86.25	86.69	86.77
18	88.32	*	*	86.76	87.17	87.27	86.91	87.33	86.67	86.27	*	86.71
19	88.39	88.56	86.56	86.83	87.23	87.00	86.96	*	86.52	86.33	86.69	86.75
20	88.35	88.54	86.48	86.85	*	86.80	87.10	87.35	86.46	86.40	86.73	86.61
21	*	88.47	86.51	86.78	87.21	86.55	87.18	87.27	86.41	*	86.73	86.53
22	88.26	†	86.30	*	87.14	86.70	*	87.26	86.43	86.48	86.70	86.65
23	88.20	88.15	86.31	86.77	87.25	86.79	87.29	87.34	*	86.48	86.63	*
24	88.20	87.95	86.21	86.70	87.54	*	87.18	87.38	86.32	86.50	86.56	86.75
25	88.18	*	*	86.63	87.66	86.79	87.11	87.33	86.37	86.56	*	†
26	88.12	87.78	86.05	86.63	87.71	86.65	87.16	*	86.38	86.47	86.56	86.66
27	88.01	87.69	85.78	86.63	*	86.56	87.01	87.24	86.13	86.50	86.56	86.62
28	*	87.59	85.78	86.72	87.81	86.30	86.91	87.31	86.09	*	86.56	86.60
29	88.11		85.77	*	87.67	86.22	*	87.32	86.01	86.53	†	86.61
30	88.08		†	86.73	†	86.22	86.85	87.30	*	86.58	86.58	*
31	88.06		85.78		87.66		86.83	87.18		86.63		86.66
High	89.39	88.81	87.70	86.85	87.81	87.61	87.29	87.38	87.23	86.63	87.07	86.99
Low	88.01	87.59	85.77	85.78	86.42	86.22	86.23	86.81	86.01	85.98	86.56	86.53

*Sunday
†Holiday

1924—INDUSTRIALS

Date	Jan.	Feb.	Mar.	Apr.	May	June	July	Aug.	Sept.	Oct.	Nov.	Dec.
1	†	100.70	97.49	93.50	92.12	*	96.45	102.12	†	104.08	104.17	110.44
2	95.65	100.84	*	94.50	91.68	90.15	96.38	102.89	104.95	103.63	*	110.71
3	94.88	*	97.10	94.33	91.93	91.23	96.48	*	104.02	102.64	103.89	110.83
4	95.40	101.08	97.50	94.69	*	90.72	†	103.28	102.77	102.85	†	111.56
5	96.26	101.08	97.55	94.05	92.23	90.41	96.43	102.52	101.07	*	105.11	111.26
6	*	101.31	98.45	*	92.24	89.18	*	102.57	100.76	102.58	104.06	111.10
7	96.54	100.99	98.61	93.03	92.47	89.52	96.91	102.30	*	102.38	104.86	*
8	96.77	100.20	98.25	92.85	92.04	*	97.56	101.79	101.26	102.06	105.53	111.30
9	97.04	100.88	*	92.24	91.40	90.15	97.40	102.08	101.98	102.60	*	112.11
10	97.23	*	97.21	90.86	90.55	90.53	96.65	*	101.13	101.38	105.91	111.07
11	97.46	100.91	97.81	91.71	*	92.00	97.38	102.20	101.79	101.33	107.58	110.84
12	97.25	†	97.58	90.78	89.48	92.19	97.60	101.51	101.91	*	108.14	111.96
13	*	99.81	98.25	*	89.69	92.68	*	101.60	101.97	†	108.58	112.76
14	95.68	100.05	98.86	89.91	88.77	92.85	97.50	102.86	*	99.18	108.96	*
15	96.09	96.63	98.02	90.52	89.18	*	97.40	104.01	101.38	100.11	108.68	113.40
16	96.65	98.06	*	90.78	89.78	93.80	96.85	104.62	101.75	100.16	*	113.73
17	96.42	*	96.60	91.34	89.33	93.57	96.85	*	103.49	100.86	109.51	114.35
18	96.28	96.33	96.69	†	*	93.52	97.40	104.99	103.42	101.76	110.73	115.17
19	96.60	96.07	96.89	91.13	89.81	93.79	98.09	105.38	103.63	*	110.24	116.13
20	*	96.58	95.88	*	88.33	93.48	*	105.57	103.85	101.14	110.50	116.41
21	97.28	97.40	95.87	89.18	89.35	93.53	99.02	104.83	*	101.85	109.63	*
22	97.23	†	95.72	89.22	90.10	*	99.36	103.89	103.25	101.96	109.55	116.84
23	97.73	97.88	*	90.43	90.04	92.65	99.40	103.51	104.16	102.18	*	115.78
24	98.59	*	95.58	90.44	90.66	93.13	99.36	*	104.68	102.53	109.81	116.74
25	99.81	97.16	94.12	91.51	*	93.67	99.60	103.53	104.13	102.04	110.08	†
26	100.00	96.45	93.67	92.02	90.60	94.71	100.36	103.58	103.98	*	110.15	118.59
27	*	96.75	92.90	*	90.15	95.33	*	103.23	103.93	101.73	†	119.18
28	99.35	97.69	92.54	90.99	89.90	95.55	101.09	102.67	*	102.45	111.10	*
29	99.16	97.22	92.28	90.65	89.90	*	100.87	104.14	102.96	102.41	111.38	118.63
30	99.40		*	90.63	†	96.37	101.16	105.16	103.16	103.00	*	118.02
31	100.66		93.01		†		102.14	*		104.06		120.51
High	100.66	101.31	98.86	94.69	92.47	96.37	102.14	105.57	104.95	104.08	111.38	120.51
Low	94.88	96.33	92.54	89.18	88.33	89.19	96.38	101.51	100.76	99.18	103.89	110.44

*Sunday
†Holiday

1924—RAILROADS

Date	Jan.	Feb.	Mar.	Apr.	May	June	July	Aug.	Sept.	Oct.	Nov.	Dec.
1	†	82.15	81.32	81.48	81.63	*	85.83	89.87	†	90.28	89.36	96.28
2	80.79	82.35	*	82.04	81.48	82.15	85.78	90.02	90.58	90.11	*	96.60
3	80.76	*	80.51	82.83	81.51	82.58	86.00	*	90.13	88.97	89.53	97.21
4	81.01	82.61	80.75	83.43	*	82.78	†	89.79	89.45	88.90	†	98.03
5	81.33	82.50	80.90	83.23	81.58	83.22	86.16	89.78	88.90	*	90.80	97.40
6	*	82.48	81.21	*	81.71	82.58	*	89.73	88.76	88.43	91.23	97.25
7	81.78	81.76	81.10	82.80	81.88	82.76	86.66	90.18	*	88.31	93.40	*
8	81.93	81.40	81.09	82.17	81.94	*	87.27	90.20	89.07	88.26	94.10	96.99
9	83.06	81.74	*	81.76	81.83	83.16	87.32	90.74	89.89	88.48	*	96.75
10	82.80	*	80.61	81.00	81.71	83.44	86.83	*	88.92	87.66	93.55	95.78
11	82.59	82.21	80.93	81.51	*	84.30	87.09	92.20	89.06	87.65	94.32	95.76
12	82.63	†	81.03	81.38	81.58	84.60	87.15	91.50	89.45	*	93.63	96.93
13	*	81.62	81.31	*	81.63	85.13	*	91.23	89.56	†	93.04	97.30
14	81.75	81.65	81.47	80.55	81.59	85.21	87.51	91.38	*	86.12	93.93	*
15	79.98	80.39	81.39	80.74	81.77	*	87.68	91.91	89.34	86.66	93.88	97.93
16	80.81	81.00	*	81.10	82.07	85.01	88.08	92.10	89.40	86.40	*	98.06
17	80.76	*	81.05	81.64	81.85	84.68	88.00	*	89.97	87.20	94.76	99.31
18	80.80	80.23	81.00	†	*	84.75	88.60	92.65	89.69	88.04	95.60	99.50
19	80.79	80.68	81.50	81.55	81.88	85.13	88.69	92.10	89.60	*	95.26	99.30
20	*	80.63	81.45	*	81.37	85.32	*	91.44	89.81	87.70	96.19	99.24
21	80.85	81.08	81.46	81.13	82.38	85.23	89.15	90.93	*	88.12	95.77	*
22	80.76	†	81.99	81.20	82.58	*	89.37	90.10	89.50	88.72	95.96	98.71
23	80.67	81.33	*	81.41	82.88	84.66	89.60	89.82	90.03	88.91	*	97.88
24	80.80	*	82.01	81.13	82.96	84.94	90.10	*	90.71	89.33	95.80	98.25
25	81.56	80.96	81.38	81.30	*	86.05	90.40	89.88	90.51	89.23	96.53	†
26	81.89	80.78	81.40	81.25	83.34	86.41	90.41	89.81	90.35	*	96.48	98.89
27	*	80.68	81.29	*	83.02	86.22	*	89.85	90.55	88.71	†	98.90
28	82.16	81.58	81.05	80.95	82.67	86.11	90.36	89.48	*	89.03	96.25	*
29	81.93	81.00	80.95	80.90	82.29	*	90.04	89.83	89.99	88.86	96.35	98.46
30	81.81		*	81.06	†	85.80	89.80	90.60	90.20	88.90	*	97.67
31	82.09		81.26		†		90.08	*		89.28		98.33
High	83.06	82.61	82.01	83.43	83.34	86.41	90.41	92.65	90.71	90.28	96.53	99.50
Low	80.67	80.23	80.51	80.55	81.37	82.15	85.78	89.48	88.76	86.12	89.36	95.76

*Sunday
†Holiday

1924—DAILY STOCK SALES ON N. Y. STOCK EXCHANGE
(000 Omitted)

Date	Jan.	Feb.	Mar.	Apr.	May	June	July	Aug.	Sept.	Oct.	Nov.	Dec.
1	†	1257	441	535	847	*	944	1194	†	913	460	2229
2	848	580	*	735	632	306	856	596	756	821	*	1653
3	1011	*	801	881	273	655	707	*	735	985	909	2031
4	881	1272	656	924	*	758	†	1284	814	323	†	2360
5	622	1192	699	533	632	589	212	1054	1132	*	1746	2610
6	*	677	812	*	550	665	*	921	516	699	1697	951
7	1330	1128	538	782	642	304	679	817	*	639	2332	*
8	1253	991	430	609	476	*	889	928	822	502	1466	1620
9	1416	491	*	645	472	492	973	371	848	562	*	1817
10	1329	*	676	947	453	547	957	*	952	814	2289	2060
11	1170	744	496	967	*	989	836	906	672	382	2472	1848
12	596	†	610	422	742	986	466	1187	564	*	2411	1661
13	*	935	708	*	536	933	*	996	214	†	2233	881
14	1250	1059	841	955	715	388	960	858	*	1131	1917	*
15	963	1848	482	919	563	*	1021	999	529	949	754	1774
16	942	725	*	676	539	877	1023	537	482	629	*	1984
17	1145	*	1131	610	236	807	1133	*	849	734	1783	1920
18	851	1346	998	†	*	712	1238	1171	924	463	2302	2047
19	460	1084	1042	317	406	773	541	1178	777	*	2453	2089
20	*	842	1032	*	834	874	*	1368	363	765	2616	941
21	900	768	818	1092	643	363	1064	1180	*	859	2248	*
22	995	†	500	869	724	*	1258	1124	747	1055	989	1806
23	1053	444	*	676	516	651	1212	459	845	902	*	1135
24	1112	*	819	665	350	659	1161	*	1084	957	2021	1090
25	1273	675	1161	859	*	919	1047	872	995	382	1908	†
26	711	836	813	415	608	1118	520	693	870	*	2134	1464
27	*	638	728	*	572	993	*	721	482	607	†	1049
28	1290	913	962	633	416	509	1192	596	*	720	2478	*
29	1183	887	318	717	419	*	1276	720	899	575	1186	1951
30	1273		*	713	†	852	1204	500	789	738	*	1750
31	1325		712		†		1165	*		1037		1652
Total	27,180	21,332	19,243	17,128	13,795	17,718	24,535	23,329	18,660	19,144	42,802	44,371

*Sunday. †Holiday.

1924—BOND AVERAGES

Date:	Jan.	Feb.	Mar.	Apr.	May	June	July	Aug.	Sept.	Oct.	Nov.	Dec.
1	†	88.10	87.41	87.97	88.41	*	90.35	91.18	†	90.89	90.98	90.80
2	86.73	88.10	*	88.03	88.43	88.70	90.28	91.15	89.30	90.86	*	90.82
3	86.79	*	87.41	88.07	88.40	88.76	90.29	*	90.23	90.81	91.00	90.88
4	86.74	88.11	87.38	88.27	*	88.82	†	91.23	90.21	90.76	†	90.87
5	86.77	88.10	87.45	88.27	88.39	88.86	90.30	91.15	90.35	*	91.09	90.89
6	*	88.03	87.40	*	88.42	88.93	*	91.06	90.36	90.80	91.12	90.83
7	87.03	88.01	87.34	88.27	88.47	89.00	90.38	91.04	*	90.74	91.23	*
8	87.08	87.78	87.31	88.25	88.54	*	90.50	91.17	90.40	90.78	91.33	90.87
9	87.32	87.78	*	88.22	88.53	89.06	90.50	91.10	90.45	90.81	*	90.86
10	87.39	*	87.40	88.19	88.49	89.29	90.57	*	90.38	90.81	91.30	90.78
11	87.53	87.79	87.38	88.07	*	89.51	90.52	91.02	90.34	90.85	91.37	90.66
12	87.67	†	87.41	88.12	88.49	89.89	90.48	91.00	90.28	*	91.23	90.66
13	*	87.66	87.38	*	88.48	89.98	*	91.10	90.32	†	91.19	90.68
14	87.90	87.57	87.51	88.01	88.51	90.17	90.45	91.08	*	90.79	91.12	*
15	88.04	87.59	87.57	87.92	88.49	*	90.55	91.03	90.29	90.69	91.10	90.61
16	88.04	87.51	*	87.90	88.57	90.28	90.64	91.01	90.20	90.64	*	90.70
17	88.06	*	87.59	87.97	88.61	90.18	90.69	*	90.26	90.70	91.08	90.65
18	87.94	87.46	87.64		*	90.18	90.79	91.03	90.43	90.70	91.02	90.62
19	87.96	87.40	87.77	87.98	88.62	90.18	90.81	90.95	90.48	*	90.90	90.61
20	*	87.37	87.86	88.00	88.61	90.16	*	90.90	90.54	90.71	90.84	90.61
21	87.88	87.42	88.01	88.00	88.56	90.16	90.80	90.69	*	90.77	90.84	*
22	88.00	†	88.10	87.94	88.72	*	90.94	90.46	90.62	90.77	90.76	90.61
23	88.03	87.45	*	87.93	88.88	90.16	91.06	90.39	90.76	90.82	*	90.62
24	88.10	*	88.22	88.02	88.89	90.19	91.06	*	90.77	90.84	90.76	90.63
25	88.13	87.46	88.13	88.14	*	90.14	91.11	90.19	90.84	90.88	90.72	†
26	88.29	87.47	88.07	88.17	89.06	90.21	91.17	90.19	90.92	*	90.82	90.60
27	*	87.35	88.05	*	88.98	90.33	*	90.15	91.01	90.87	†	90.63
28	88.25	87.25	88.05	88.27	88.81	90.32	91.32	90.11	*	90.76	90.79	*
29	88.11	87.44	88.01	88.26	88.74	*	91.20	90.14	90.93	90.77	90.78	90.60
30	88.10		*	88.23	†	90.29	91.22	90.26	90.88	90.95	*	90.60
31	88.05		87.96				91.17	*		91.00		90.59
High	88.29	88.11	88.22	88.27	89.06	90.33	91.32	91.23	91.01	91.00	91.37	90.89
Low	86.73	87.25	87.31	87.90	88.39	88.70	90.28	90.11	90.20	90.64	90.72	90.59

*Sunday
†Holiday

1925—INDUSTRIALS

Date	Jan.	Feb.	Mar.	Apr.	May	June	July	Aug.	Sept.	Oct.	Nov.	Dec.
1	†	*	*	118.07	121.10	129.69	131.76	134.55	139.78	144.77	*	152.11
2	121.25	120.46	123.93	117.61	121.96	130.42	131.53	*	137.22	146.13	157.88	152.88
3	122.20	120.08	125.25	117.40	*	130.41	131.52	135.81	139.91	146.65	†	153.80
4	*	120.56	123.26	118.25	122.86	128.89	†	136.38	140.88	*	158.05	154.60
5	119.46	120.83	124.81	*	123.63	128.98	*	135.73	141.30	146.81	157.67	154.63
6	121.13	121.48	125.68	119.43	124.32	128.85	132.31	135.71	*	145.11	159.39	*
7	121.18	121.50	124.98	118.78	125.16	*	132.70	137.40	†	145.60	158.48	154.21
8	121.61	*	*	118.90	124.74	127.12	133.07	137.98	140.86	146.75	*	153.84
9	122.32	122.37	124.33	119.06	124.64	127.21	131.83	*	142.40	147.20	157.43	152.57
10	122.16	121.73	122.62	†	*	126.75	131.33	137.41	143.83	147.43	151.60	153.71
11	*	121.23	123.26	119.33	124.14	127.85	131.43	137.80	145.38	*	154.18	154.21
12	123.21	†	124.60	*	124.45	128.38	*	137.48	145.95	†	155.47	154.65
13	123.56	121.73	123.25	120.18	124.21	129.38	131.71	138.60	*	147.40	157.76	*
14	122.97	120.86	124.16	121.54	124.16	*	132.95	139.51	146.63	148.96	156.36	154.70
15	121.38	*	*	121.11	126.00	128.43	133.40	140.20	143.89	149.18	*	154.07
16	121.71	117.96	120.76	120.67	126.50	129.66	133.50	*	145.87	149.56	153.11	152.88
17	123.13	118.48	118.53	121.41	*	129.80	134.00	141.56	146.46	147.89	153.48	152.78
18	*	120.07	118.25	122.02	127.09	128.88	134.68	142.60	147.16	*	150.35	152.67
19	122.35	119.71	119.38	*	128.38	129.26	*	141.82	147.73	148.53	152.27	153.21
20	121.74	121.64	120.91	121.23	128.68	129.16	135.00	141.66	*	150.29	152.45	*
21	122.11	121.85	119.60	119.53	128.70	*	134.93	142.63	146.11	151.61	151.08	152.35
22	123.60	*	*	120.52	128.95	128.25	133.87	142.87	145.74	152.13	*	153.91
23	123.09	†	116.82	120.82	128.85	127.17	135.33	*	146.02	153.29	148.60	155.98
24	122.98	121.48	116.78	119.74	*	127.80	135.58	142.76	143.98	153.47	148.18	157.01
25	*	122.15	118.71	119.75	127.78	128.28	135.63	143.18	145.56	*	151.04	†
26	121.90	122.86	116.78	*	128.43	129.17	*	141.88	144.26	153.60	†	*
27	121.53	122.24	117.48	119.46	129.13	129.73	136.50	141.54	*	152.92	152.70	*
28	121.98	122.71	116.30	120.00	129.60	*	135.62	141.13	144.15	155.25	151.78	156.87
29	122.44		*	120.40	129.95	129.23	134.48	141.26	145.06	154.88	*	155.83
30	123.49		115.00	120.01	†	131.01	134.16	*	143.46	155.65	151.08	155.81
31	123.22		116.75		*		133.81	141.18		156.52		156.66
High	123.60	122.86	125.68	122.02	129.95	131.01	136.50	143.18	147.73	156.52	159.39	157.01
Low	119.46	117.96	115.00	117.40	121.10	126.75	131.33	134.45	137.22	144.77	148.18	152.11

*Sunday
†Holiday

1925—RAILROADS

Date	Jan.	Feb.	Mar.	Apr.	May	June	July	Aug.	Sept.	Oct.	Nov.	Dec.
1	†	*	*	94.29	96.56	99.10	98.85	99.02	100.90	102.60	*	107.37
2	99.22	99.63	100.76	94.03	97.08	98.81	99.08	*	99.93	102.59	105.19	107.30
3	99.33	99.41	100.96	93.84	*	98.80	98.95	99.32	100.67	102.54	†	107.30
4	*	100.46	100.12	94.71	97.75	98.41	†	99.56	101.36	*	105.13	107.82
5	99.14	100.49	100.56	*	97.66	98.41	*	100.02	101.63	102.33	104.37	108.66
6	100.27	100.46	100.72	95.81	97.65	98.60	99.02	99.78	*	101.46	103.90	*
7	100.35	100.29	100.24	95.67	97.68	*	99.38	100.63	†	101.36	103.87	109.27
8	100.19	*	*	94.88	97.36	97.22	98.89	100.63	101.58	101.64	*	108.96
9	100.78	100.10	99.50	94.79	97.09	97.15	98.60	*	102.75	101.73	104.05	108.26
10	100.40	100.15	98.58	†	*	96.98	98.48	100.58	102.40	101.66	103.23	108.80
11	*	99.69	98.87	94.97	96.43	97.38	98.43	100.58	102.22	*	105.10	109.80
12	100.47	†	99.65	*	97.11	97.67	*	100.83	102.22	†	105.46	109.68
13	100.53	99.44	98.96	94.96	97.13	98.26	98.71	101.23	*	101.73	107.81	*
14	99.59	98.88	99.17	95.46	96.85	*	99.15	101.88	102.78	102.14	108.10	110.29
15	98.36	*	*	95.91	97.20	97.80	99.16	101.99	102.37	101.93	*	111.52
16	98.41	97.83	97.63	96.13	97.25	98.09	99.42	*	102.94	102.26	106.62	112.38
17	99.30	98.33	96.96	96.59	*	98.14	99.23	103.28	102.78	102.08	106.63	111.53
18	*	99.55	96.46	96.64	97.50	97.58	99.19	103.30	103.66	*	105.70	110.91
19	99.05	99.18	96.68	*	97.93	98.27	*	102.96	103.68	103.86	107.39	110.87
20	98.46	99.97	97.81	96.31	98.03	98.33	99.28	102.93	*	104.65	107.13	*
21	98.49	99.89	97.35	95.09	98.27	*	98.91	103.00	103.18	104.75	106.86	110.10
22	98.77	*	*	95.61	99.05	97.77	98.61	103.28	103.41	104.78	*	110.34
23	98.93	†	95.66	95.52	99.01	97.50	99.19	*	103.78	104.51	105.78	111.11
24	98.86	100.15	94.32	95.26	*	98.06	98.90	103.53	103.56	104.62	105.88	111.58
25	*	100.30	95.31	95.75	99.15	98.04	99.03	103.38	103.65	*	106.73	†
26	98.35	100.86	94.51	*	98.83	98.41	*	103.08	103.31	105.10	†	*
27	98.45	99.72	94.70	95.68	99.53	98.57	99.22	102.88	*	104.56	107.21	*
28	99.18	99.88	93.73	96.18	99.26	*	99.75	102.80	102.88	104.51	107.16	112.25
29	98.58		*	95.98	99.98	97.80	99.31	102.36	103.04	104.51	*	112.32
30	98.96		92.98	96.15	†	98.41	99.08	*	102.88	104.79	107.52	112.62
31	99.26		93.94		*		98.74	101.95		105.03		112.93
High	100.78	100.86	100.96	96.64	99.98	99.10	99.75	103.53	103.78	105.03	108.10	112.93
Low	98.35	97.83	92.98	93.84	96.43	96.98	98.43	99.02	99.93	101.36	103.23	107.30

*Sunday
†Holiday

1925—DAILY STOCK SALES ON NEW YORK STOCK EXCHANGE
(000 Omitted)

Date	Jan.	Feb.	Mar.	Apr.	May	June	July	Aug.	Sept.	Oct.	Nov.	Dec.
1	†	*	*	1143	1276	1469	1553	510	1206	1945	*	1883
2	2042	1643	1681	1078	700	1372	1482	*	1685	2403	2697	1771
3	1504	1550	1957	819	*	1376	1379	1237	1122	1274	†	2130
4	*	1697	1815	539	1360	1198	†	1526	1115	*	2905	2289
5	2375	2049	1647	*	1537	1130	*	1694	617	2102	2791	1047
6	1796	1797	1590	1238	2005	648	1096	1534	*	2315	2732	*
7	1822	816	671	1227	1822	*	1440	1701	†	1818	1373	2183
8	1739	*	*	929	1655	1287	1496	772	1293	1863	*	2123
9	2092	1441	1339	804	908	1282	1485	*	1570	2117	2506	1805
10	1132	1680	1585	†	*	1803	1278	1259	1778	1074	3427	1303
11	*	1890	1776	423	1696	1219	440	1532	1735	*	2638	1808
12	2108	†	1729	*	1674	1499	*	1557	914	†	2397	754
13	2161	1157	1392	802	1479	708	885	1410	*	2146	3086	*
14	2031	814	579	1185	1241	*	1082	1372	2032	2139	1542	1651
15	1714	*	*	1214	1333	1202	1422	593	2086	2664	*	2065
16	1557	2307	1693	1426	645	1085	1608	*	1733	2823	2596	2342
17	1709	2199	2313	1193	*	1165	1370	1529	1737	1730	2122	1965
18	*	1683	2230	790	1408	1565	663	1717	1607	*	2641	1745
19	1472	1457	1680	*	1690	1408	*	1558	978	2676	2075	757
20	1183	1737	1347	1224	2163	656	1323	1458	*	2287	2043	*
21	1179	931	759	1395	2031	*	1547	1372	1900	2623	1039	1548
22	1468	*	*	1264	1899	1068	1347	644	1863	2581	*	1609
23	1776	†	1609	1071	910	1080	1378	*	1661	2523	1814	1617
24	540	1294	1688	1018	*	1066	1418	1491	1956	1398	2015	1770
25	*	1204	1491	433	1694	1065	692	1570	1676	*	1606	†
26	1475	1574	1354	*	1491	1289	*	1621	829	2329	†	*
27	1374	1575	1208	867	1581	638	1645	1429	*	2638	1668	*
28	1642	828	505	801	1505	*	2079	1309	1587	2306	962	2137
29	1961		*	1002	1384	1397	1554	552	2077	2552	*	2105
30	1686		1671	1210	†	1271	1427	*	1754	2392	1630	2031
31	931		1253		*		1514	1089		1393		2079
Total	43,468	33,325	38,561	25,093	37,086	30,944	34,603	34,084	38,522	56,110	50,304	44,515

*Sunday. †Holiday.

1925—BOND AVERAGES

Date:	Jan.	Feb.	Mar.	Apr.	May	June	July	Aug.	Sept.	Oct.	Nov.	Dec.
1	†		*	91.20	92.18	93.16	92.79	91.69	92.00	92.19	*	92.57
2	90.60	91.23	91.56	91.24	92.26	93.20	92.93		91.98	92.15	92.18	92.59
3	90.63	91.30	91.64	91.26	*	93.20	92.90	91.65	91.99	92.20	†	92.54
4	*	91.33	91.67	91.30	92.34	93.21	†	91.65	92.04	*	92.33	92.60
5	90.68	91.40	91.62	*	92.37	93.15	*	91.60	92.03	92.14	92.37	92.57
6	90.74	91.42	91.56	91.32	92.56	93.16	92.92	91.54	*	92.20	92.25	*
7	90.69	91.45	91.57	91.35	92.62	*	92.95	91.47	†	92.15	92.41	92.61
8	90.78	*	*	91.31	92.63	93.14	92.95	91.49	92.10	92.14	*	92.58
9	90.81	91.62	91.57	91.34	92.67	93.11	92.94	*	92.06	92.10	92.41	92.65
10	90.89	91.56	91.46	†	*	93.15	92.85	91.47	92.09	92.06	92.34	92.65
11	*	91.62	91.34	91.39	92.63	93.17	92.74	91.50	92.17	*	92.40	92.68
12	91.10	†	91.38	*	92.67	93.14	*	91.48	92.28	†	92.48	92.69
13	91.11	91.61	91.42	91.40	92.74	93.15	92.73	91.54	*	92.10	92.62	*
14	91.06	91.58	91.41	91.48	92.73	*	92.52	91.49	92.27	92.14	92.64	92.67
15	91.05	*	*	91.45	92.88	93.15	92.54	91.50	92.25	92.05	*	92.77
16	91.01	91.54	91.47	91.59	92.91	93.20	92.45	*	92.31	92.11	92.62	92.88
17	91.06	91.48	91.39	91.64	*	93.17	92.43	91.50	92.39	92.17	92.57	92.93
18	*	91.49	91.36	91.67	92.89	93.13	92.43	91.60	92.35	*	92.44	92.94
19	91.03	91.70	91.26	*	92.94	93.17	*	91.61	92.33	92.15	92.43	92.95
20	91.04	91.68	91.30	91.70	93.02	93.17	92.39	91.71	*	92.21	92.45	*
21	90.99	91.73	91.24	91.72	93.04	*	92.35	91.83	92.33	92.23	92.48	93.00
22	90.97	*	*	91.94	93.11	93.19	92.27	91.86	92.25	92.25	*	92.93
23	91.03	†	91.14	91.96	93.10	93.24	92.34	*	92.24	92.29	92.41	92.95
24	91.00	91.68	91.28	92.16	*	93.19	92.32	91.93	92.18	92.26	92.42	92.95
25	*	91.66	91.33	92.12	93.11	93.08	92.29	91.97	92.24	*	92.48	†
26	91.08	91.65	91.30	*	93.10	92.97	*	92.07	92.32	92.24	†	†
27	91.10	91.57	91.23	92.07	93.06	93.00	92.16	92.01	*	92.26	92.45	*
28	91.09	91.60	91.25	92.03	93.12	*	92.15	91.95	92.31	92.17	92.48	92.97
29	91.05		*	92.10	93.08	92.90	91.99	92.05	92.28	92.15	*	92.94
30	91.10		91.20	92.08	†	92.92	91.86	*	92.22	92.13	92.53	92.98
31	91.21		91.18				91.77	92.02		92.14		93.04
High	91.21	91.73	91.67	92.16	93.12	93.24	92.95	92.07	92.39	92.29	92.64	93.04
Low	90.60	91.23	91.14	91.20	92.18	92.90	91.77	91.47	91.98	92.05	92.18	92.54

*Sunday
†Holiday

1926—INDUSTRIALS

Date:	Jan.	Feb.	March	April	May	June	July	Aug.	Sept.	Oct.	Nov.	Dec.
1	†	156.83	150.90	140.35	143.40	142.30	153.01	*	163.93	159.69	150.51	157.31
2	158.54	157.95	147.06	†	*	143.55	154.15	161.84	163.23	159.64	†	158.00
3	*	159.40	144.44	140.39	140.53	145.03	†	163.40	163.75	*	151.23	158.50
4	158.75	160.53	150.76	*	141.38	145.28	*	163.23		156.78	152.76	159.05
5	157.60	159.98	150.40	141.08	141.49	145.36	†	163.34	*	154.86	152.88	*
6	158.00	159.99	149.86	142.43	142.13	*	154.37	164.16	†	153.99	153.03	159.30
7	158.93	*	*	141.97	140.10	145.56	155.05	165.21	166.10	152.50	*	158.86
8	158.76	159.10	150.10	140.67	140.23	145.40	155.66	*	165.05	153.39	154.78	158.35
9	159.10	160.31	151.27	140.95	*	145.56	153.74	166.14	164.94	151.18	154.82	158.94
10	*	161.58	153.13	139.93	138.87	145.95	155.06	162.89	163.35	*	153.41	159.61
11	157.58	162.31	153.00	*	139.05	147.21	*	161.68	162.16	149.35	154.66	159.89
12	157.39	†	153.03	136.53	139.78	148.61	155.58	163.28	*		155.00	*
13	158.31	162.08	150.07	138.90	139.45	*	156.83	164.85	158.97	150.78	154.58	160.01
14	156.90	*		136.36	138.84	150.13	157.12	166.64	160.57	152.10	*	160.65
15	155.10	158.30	150.65	137.08	138.02	149.37	155.84	*	159.35	147.95	155.00	160.63
16	155.23	158.88	149.88	136.27	*	151.31	157.81	166.10	158.71	146.85	156.53	159.32
17	*	160.05	149.28	136.83	137.97	153.44	158.81	164.14	156.74	*	155.15	160.66
18	155.98	161.09	146.32	*	137.53	151.92	*	164.41	157.86	148.20	154.51	161.86
19	153.81	160.92	145.11	136.91	137.16	153.33	158.94	162.43	*	145.66	152.86	*
20	155.04	160.93	144.80	137.47	138.66	*	157.63	162.06	156.26	146.73	153.95	160.75
21	153.20	*	*	139.91	140.27	154.03	156.41	162.78	157.56	149.38	*	160.46
22	154.26	†	146.32	141.11	140.41	153.54	155.58	*	156.65	148.51	155.01	160.29
23	155.16	158.83	143.86	142.55	*	151.45	155.43	163.41	156.96	149.56	155.83	160.22
24	*	158.55	140.31	144.83	141.16	151.87	154.59	161.46	158.65	*	155.73	160.46
25	155.28	156.54	140.81	*	141.20	150.80	*	160.41	159.27	148.78	†	†
26	154.63	154.68	141.76	142.93	141.64	150.68	155.71	161.18	*	149.35	157.37	*
27	156.46	154.45	139.02	143.15	142.43	*	156.73	161.36	158.42	151.87	156.43	159.32
28	157.20	*	*	144.55	143.43	151.08	159.33	161.88	158.01	151.45	*	157.19
29	157.35		135.49	144.43	†	152.61	160.58	*	157.71	150.76	155.93	157.50
30	157.44		135.20	143.71	*	153.04	160.18	161.83	158.19	150.38	156.55	156.65
31			140.46		†		160.47	162.51		*		157.20
High	159.10	162.31	153.13	144.83	143.43	154.03	160.58	166.64	166.10	159.69	157.37	161.86
Low	153.20	154.45	135.20	136.27	137.16	142.30	153.01	160.41	156.26	145.66	150.51	156.65

* Sunday
† Holiday

1926—RAILROADS

Date:	Jan.	Feb.	March	April	May	June	July	Aug.	Sept.	Oct.	Nov.	Dec.
1	†	110.42	107.15	105.42	107.89	109.46	114.80	*	122.05	121.83	117.88	117.51
2	113.10	111.25	105.42	†	*	109.48	115.01	116.66	122.12	121.53	†	117.80
3	*	111.03	103.20	105.41	106.41	109.74	†	116.31	123.33		118.01	118.22
4	112.40	110.93	106.34	*	107.05	110.53	*	115.60		119.82	119.25	117.85
5	112.36	111.15	108.25	106.04	107.16	110.84	†	115.43	*	117.67	118.95	*
6	112.45	111.05	107.93	107.01	107.22	*	114.71	116.66	†	116.74	118.96	117.50
7	113.12	*	*	106.56	106.48	110.91	114.86	116.84	123.02	115.96	*	117.73
8	112.45	110.56	107.00	106.79	106.27	110.63	115.70	*	121.79	116.68	119.53	117.71
9	112.31	110.88	107.81	106.76	*	111.20	115.21	117.41	121.76	115.57	119.09	118.81
10	*	111.11	108.69	106.89	106.00	111.57	115.69	116.10	120.49		118.43	119.91
11	112.48	111.33	110.41	*	106.29	112.62	*	115.48	120.10	114.95	118.69	119.76
12	111.92	†	111.21	105.11	106.75	112.68	116.03	117.55	*		118.86	*
13	112.42	111.46	109.06	105.88	106.45	*	116.29	118.41	119.98	115.95	118.80	119.60
14	111.26	*	*	105.30	106.45	112.41	116.04	118.43	120.96	117.68	*	119.76
15	109.80	109.58	109.03	105.01	106.25	112.05	115.47	*	120.58	115.62	118.80	120.48
16	109.70	110.23	108.85	105.18	*	112.03	115.34	118.85	120.56	115.05	118.81	119.90
17	*	110.76	107.91	105.28	106.25	112.70	115.44	117.89	119.21	*	118.81	121.91
18	110.34	110.60	106.78	*	106.45	112.37	*	118.56	120.99	115.76	118.53	122.48
19	108.93	111.20	106.39	105.23	106.42	113.31	115.08	117.95	*	115.28	117.45	*
20	109.22	111.22	106.73	105.70	107.51	*	114.51	118.21	120.48	114.70	117.66	122.45
21	108.26	*	*	107.98	108.10	113.68	113.90	118.16	120.71	116.95		122.38
22	109.30	†	107.83	108.20	108.91	113.63	112.78	*	120.28	116.36	117.70	121.52
23	109.00	109.90	107.67	109.08	*	113.56	112.75	118.57	120.97	116.51	118.07	121.95
24	*	109.91	106.32	108.93	108.84	114.21	112.89	117.78	121.46	*	118.53	121.58
25	109.83	109.23	106.88	*	109.23	114.13	*	117.80	121.88	116.76	†	†
26	109.53	107.68	107.24	109.13	109.57	114.05	113.81	118.67	*	117.23	118.35	*
27	109.78	107.96	107.26	109.01	109.89	*	113.90	118.79	121.75	118.77	117.98	121.37
28	110.21	*	*	108.83	110.23	114.43	114.45	118.60	121.52	118.15	*	120.02
29	111.32		105.15	108.94	†	114.55	114.20	*	120.89	117.83	117.80	120.33
30	111.36		102.41	108.29	*	114.70	114.99	119.79	121.23	117.57	117.66	120.15
31	*		105.53		†		116.52	121.56		*		120.86
High	113.12	111.46	111.21	109.13	110.23	114.70	116.52	121.56	123.33	121.83	119.53	122.48
Low	108.26	107.68	102.41	105.01	106.00	109.46	112.75	115.43	119.21	114.70	117.45	117.50

* Sunday
† Holiday

1926—DAILY STOCK SALES ON NEW YORK STOCK EXCHANGE
(000 Omitted)

Date	Jan.	Feb.	Mar.	Apr.	May	June	July	Aug.	Sept.	Oct.	Nov.	Dec.
1	†	1556	2538	1874	478	878	1764	*	2341	1981	1001	1513
2	1071	1353	3182	†	*	1297	1405	1973	1701	920	†	1725
3	*	1880	3874	678	1556	1694	†	2843	1546	*	1151	1830
4	2284	1972	2663	*	1100	1644	*	2544	†	1808	1485	911
5	2055	2022	2178	1044	682	652	†	1818	*	2534	1591	*
6	1731	1009	869	1244	613	*	1253	1967	†	2670	696	1285
7	1832	*	*	1256	810	1179	1454	979	1946	2474	*	1555
8	2235	2168	1676	1065	359	1803	1672	*	1774	1774	1462	1373
9	1128	2063	1291	909	*	1564	1679	2337	1381	865	1559	1582
10	*	2041	1678	547	1211	1398	578	2310	2090	*	1366	1676
11	2362	1930	1899	*	753	1623	*	1908	831	2078	1223	884
12	1789	†	1580	1683	1009	859	1482	1700	*	†	1895	*
13	1652	1212	1054	1416	926	*	1614	2068	1466	1406	691	1858
14	1619	*	*	1342	850	2086	1891	1163	1564	1710	*	2112
15	2315	2373	1513	1420	572	1981	1441	*	1773	2329	1336	1924
16	982	1533	1425	1055	*	2029	1645	1827	1589	1103	1491	2374
17	*	1344	1533	361	1073	2447	1074	2289	2346	*	1479	2633
18	1363	1397	2264	*	974	2358	*	1920	881	1749	1525	1273
19	1821	1485	2122	1050	914	921	1746	1748	*	1852	1579	*
20	2082	714	897	943	1257	*	2068	1684	1950	2186	597	2015
21	1474	*	*	1495	1333	1904	1763	643	1822	1875	*	1349
22	1461	†	1437	1731	613	1843	1894	*	1623	1782	1345	1411
23	765	1530	1315	2329	*	1724	1211	1525	1374	746	1510	1530
24	*	1957	2776	973	1121	1364	449	1526	1461	*	1706	1475
25	1285	1622	2371	*	1316	1329	*	1661	918	991	†	†
26	1254	2410	1703	1568	1406	437	806	1556	*	1167	1549	*
27	1612	965	1067	1079	1399	*	1121	1371	1418	1538	827	1726
28	1853	*	*	1261	1576	954	1711	799	1429	1810	*	2036
29	1097		2761	†	1462	1462	2452	*	1517	1131	1549	1697
30	809		3356	1213	*	1711	2458	1686	1465	531	1248	1509
31	*		2609		†		962	1964		*		1383
Total	39,929	37,538	53,672	31,049	24,100	39,139	37,593	45,807	38,382	41,007	31,859	42,647

*Sunday. †Holiday.

1926—BOND AVERAGES

Date:	Jan.	Feb.	Mar.	Apr.	May	June	July	Aug.	Sept.	Oct.	Nov.	Dec.
1	†	94.20	94.12	93.88	95.26	95.29	95.17	*	95.15	94.73	95.34	95.87
2	93.07	94.21	93.99	†	*	95.26	95.17	94.91	95.09	94.69	†	95.91
3	*	94.25	93.84	93.98	95.17	95.26	†	94.99	95.11	*	95.35	96.00
4	93.14	94.32	93.76	*	94.98	95.31	*	95.06	†	94.69	95.40	95.98
5	93.20	94.28	93.85	93.99	95.08	95.30	†	95.17	*	94.75	95.50	*
6	93.20	94.28	93.82	94.15	95.13	*	95.19	95.17	†	94.75	95.55	95.98
7	93.25	*	*	94.34	95.19	95.28	95.21	95.18	95.14	94.81	*	95.99
8	93.30	94.30	93.84	94.38	95.18	95.35	95.22	*	95.14	94.82	95.54	96.03
9	93.32	94.34	93.88	94.50	*	95.33	95.27	95.21	95.15	94.88	95.54	96.06
10	*	94.25	93.98	94.64	95.16	95.37	95.27	95.19	95.12	*	95.59	96.04
11	93.35	94.31	94.04	*	95.15	95.43	*	95.17	95.13	94.88	95.62	96.04
12	93.40	†	94.10	94.83	95.33	95.52	95.27	95.20	*	†	95.60	*
13	93.48	94.34	94.14	94.74	95.42	*	95.25	95.07	95.10	94.85	95.61	96.03
14	93.47	*	*	94.76	95.31	95.46	95.19	94.98	95.00	94.93	*	96.12
15	93.47	94.36	94.11	94.82	95.32	95.42	95.03	*	94.99	94.95	95.71	96.12
16	93.42	94.33	94.13	94.79	*	95.41	95.04	94.98	95.02	94.97	95.68	96.12
17	*	94.33	94.24	94.76	95.26	95.40	95.07	94.99	94.97	*	95.73	96.13
18	93.44	94.46	94.23	*	95.26	95.38	*	94.92	95.02	94.90	95.76	96.16
19	93.43	94.49	94.07	94.87	95.26	95.33	95.07	94.92	*	94.92	95.82	*
20	93.53	94.43	94.07	94.91	95.29	*	95.05	94.93	95.02	94.89	95.82	96.19
21	93.76	*	*	95.05	95.38	95.33	94.95	94.91	95.01	94.93	*	96.17
22	93.83	†	94.07	95.14	95.35	95.38	94.85	*	94.86	94.97	95.83	96.16
23	93.89	94.40	94.10	95.09	*	95.35	94.79	94.92	94.88	95.08	95.82	96.15
24	*	94.37	94.06	95.09	95.36	95.30	94.83	94.89	94.83	*	95.85	96.08
25	93.82	94.33	94.03	*	95.36	95.22	*	94.92	94.89	95.08	†	†
26	93.90	94.29	94.00	95.17	95.33	95.22	94.87	94.95	*	95.17	95.97	*
27	93.96	94.28	94.07	95.13	95.35	*	94.83	94.95	94.84	95.15	95.91	96.09
28	94.02	*	*	95.14	95.34	95.22	94.93	94.97	94.81	95.22	*	96.09
29	94.09		94.03	95.16	*	95.18	94.87	*	94.77	95.27	95.91	96.08
30	94.16		93.92	95.27	95.15	*	94.93	95.00	94.76	95.28	95.84	96.12
31	*		93.81		†		94.90	95.01		*		96.15
High	94.16	94.49	94.24	95.27	95.42	95.52	95.27	95.21	95.15	95.28	95.97	96.19
Low	93.07	94.20	93.76	93.88	94.98	95.15	94.79	94.89	94.76	94.69	95.34	95.87

*Sunday
†Holiday

1927—INDUSTRIALS

Date:	Jan.	Feb.	March	April	May	June	July	Aug.	Sept.	Oct.	Nov.	Dec.
1	†	156.26	161.42	160.71	*	171.98	168.06	184.21	191.56	198.36	181.65	196.58
2	*	154.80	159.07	160.66	164.55	171.88	169.29	185.55	192.83	*	184.61	196.75
3	155.16	154.94	160.89	*	165.85	169.65	*	183.56	191.26	199.78	187.49	197.34
4	155.53	154.51	159.68	161.70	168.05	170.16	†	184.64	*	198.88	186.50	*
5	155.54	154.33	159.23	162.68	167.75	*	170.95	182.87	†	199.22	188.47	196.96
6	155.16	*	*	162.69	167.85	171.13	172.27	182.51	196.91	199.22	*	196.44
7	155.53	154.31	158.62	162.50	167.94	170.18	171.96	*	197.75	197.50	190.57	195.43
8	155.85	154.86	158.84	162.52	*	170.22	171.50	180.27	196.92	190.29	†	193.58
9	*	155.29	159.86	162.69	168.15	170.85	171.98	182.05	194.60	*	189.31	196.19
10	156.56	155.53	160.87	*	168.25	170.21	*	182.20	195.86	189.03	190.70	196.38
11	155.68	156.05	160.18	163.61	167.58	170.63	172.65		*	189.29	193.34	*
12	155.50	†	160.73	163.38	167.06	*	173.11	177.13	194.00	†	194.11	197.35
13	155.45	*	*	164.17	168.15	†	173.19	179.34	196.81	190.45	*	198.05
14	154.91	157.56	161.43	164.78	168.46	167.63	174.38	*	198.00	190.02	195.91	196.74
15	154.99	157.61	160.03	†	*	168.78	174.87	181.93	198.97	190.18	195.37	197.09
16	*	157.41	161.61	165.59	166.68	170.26	174.93	183.36	198.85	*	194.53	198.93
17	153.91	157.97	161.78	*	168.09	170.15	*	184.30	197.70	186.81	195.47	199.95
18	154.11	158.56	160.68	165.48	168.98	169.85	175.40	184.15	*	187.32	196.68	*
19	155.53	158.71	160.56	165.93	170.29	*	177.02	185.10	196.38	184.48	196.83	200.93
20	155.16	*	160.10	166.10	171.75	169.50	177.83	185.80	196.97	183.00	*	200.93
21	155.51	158.80	160.81	166.66	172.06	169.87	177.75	*	196.26	181.43	194.90	200.63
22	155.17	†	158.41	167.36	*	169.50	177.83	187.32	194.65	179.78	196.20	200.62
23	*	160.43	158.85	166.80	171.67	167.82	178.11	187.49	195.42	*	197.10	200.81
24	154.43	160.11	160.30	*	171.06	168.04	*	188.07	196.83	181.43	†	200.30
25	152.73	160.68	160.21	163.73	171.51	168.04	179.28	187.50	195.38	185.31	196.88	*
26	153.36	160.83	160.55	165.12	171.31	*	179.72	188.81	194.64	184.78	196.97	†
27	153.13	*	*	165.23	172.15	165.73	180.09	189.30	195.38	183.96	*	200.32
28	153.86	161.96	161.01	163.53	172.56	166.40	180.73	*	194.11	181.68	194.80	198.60
29	155.18		160.62	164.64	*	166.53	181.40	190.00	194.80	180.32	196.95	199.96
30	*		159.66	164.21	†	166.23	182.61	190.63	197.59	*	198.21	200.70
31	156.41		160.08		172.96		*	189.79		181.73		202.40
High	156.56	161.96	161.78	167.36	172.96	171.98	182.61	190.63	198.97	199.78	198.21	202.40
Low	152.73	154.31	158.41	160.66	164.55	165.73	168.06	177.13	191.56	179.78	181.65	193.58

* Sunday
† Holiday

1927—RAILROADS

Date:	Jan.	Feb.	March	April	May	June	July	Aug.	Sept.	Oct.	Nov.	Dec.
1	†	120.76	127.33	129.95	*	137.85	134.06	142.47	139.38	143.03	134.22	140.10
2	*	122.65	125.48	130.07	131.01	137.70	134.77	142.97	140.41	*	135.24	142.95
3	120.09	123.03	126.57	*	132.11	136.02	*	140.86	140.63	144.82	136.41	143.44
4	119.87	123.30	125.78	131.16	132.30	136.95	†	141.70	*	143.10	136.12	*
5	119.77	123.21	125.21	131.59	132.40	*	136.08	140.12	†	142.24	138.00	142.63
6	119.69	*	*	131.28	133.08	138.18	136.48	139.83	140.28	143.53	*	142.02
7	120.40	123.29	124.65	131.88	133.55	137.18	136.08	*	140.46	142.16	139.21	141.09
8	120.73	124.48	124.53	132.55	*	137.41	135.98	138.16	139.98	141.56	†	140.05
9	*	124.17	125.51	132.65	134.08	137.15	135.93	139.23	139.18	*	137.73	141.40
10	120.73	124.29	126.24	*	133.76	136.46	*	139.17	139.12	140.02	138.03	140.72
11	120.90	124.80	127.52	132.67	133.38	136.29	136.57	138.05	*	139.40	138.77	*
12	121.01	†	127.39	132.01	132.91	*	137.19	136.10	138.65	†	139.41	140.51
13	120.57	*	*	131.83	133.76	†	138.54	136.87	140.33	140.83	*	141.38
14	120.63	124.85	127.14	131.80	133.78	133.70	138.46	*	140.25	141.03	139.86	140.56
15	121.33	125.71	126.01	†	*	135.36	138.41	139.03	140.08	140.54	139.53	140.90
16	*	126.71	127.26	132.24	133.13	136.39	138.76	140.16	139.69	*	139.46	141.46
17	122.32	128.47	128.07	*	133.78	137.04	*	139.68	139.26	139.06	139.71	141.16
18	122.18	129.16	126.63	132.04	134.36	136.91	138.93	139.94	*	139.36	140.00	
19	122.53	128.47	127.07	131.81	134.87	*	138.76	139.65	138.58	138.70	140.04	140.40
20	122.51	*	132.30		135.65	136.65	138.90	139.81	140.19	137.51	*	141.03
21	122.56	127.01	128.11	132.80	135.60	136.12	138.73	*	139.93	135.81	139.20	141.04
22	122.20	†	126.93	133.72	*	136.13	138.39	140.32	138.51	135.12	139.88	141.19
23	*	127.93	127.68	133.83	135.91	134.86	138.27	140.89	138.79	*	140.40	141.21
24	121.95	127.51	128.28	*	135.63	135.01	*	141.21	139.21	135.38	†	141.52
25	119.88	127.00	127.84	132.33	135.60	135.04	138.87	141.17	*	137.01	140.85	*
26	120.41	127.24	128.32	132.47	136.88	*	139.20	141.05	138.48	137.78	140.65	†
27	119.61	*	*	132.17	137.16	133.36	139.16	140.00	138.73	137.23	*	141.11
28	119.29	127.76	130.01	130.28	137.35	133.36	138.98	*	139.68	134.55	139.72	139.71
29	120.23		129.53	130.84	*	133.48	139.96	140.03	140.05	133.61	139.83	139.29
30	*		129.71	131.05	†	133.72	141.26	139.30	142.05	*	140.45	139.93
31	120.83		130.31		137.26		*	138.56		134.27		140.30
High	122.56	129.16	130.31	133.83	137.35	138.18	141.26	142.97	142.05	144.82	140.85	143.44
Low	119.29	120.76	124.53	129.95	131.01	133.36	134.06	136.10	138.48	133.61	134.22	139.29

* Sunday
† Holiday

1927—DAILY STOCK SALES ON NEW YORK STOCK EXCHANGE
(000 Omitted)

Date	Jan.	Feb.	Mar.	Apr.	May	June	July	Aug.	Sept.	Oct.	Nov.	Dec.
1	†	1503	2107	2154	*	2272	1344	1981	1737	1149	1668	2837
2	*	1836	2402	1116	1507	2618	537	2196	1957	*	1627	3006
3	1371	1771	1811	*	1929	2652		2688	900	2607	2369	1468
4	1525	2072	2257	1936	2192	987	†	2394	*	3147	2064	*
5	1445	1087	973	2584	2105	*	1411	2886	†	2336	1016	2314
6	1421	*		2623	2019	2204	1822	943	2238	2051	*	2374
7	1322	2152	1603	2385	948	2453	1704		2642	2014	2002	2617
8	819	2455	1751	2113	*	2691	1494	1801	2599	1077	†	2451
9	*	2813	1857	1240	1950	2362	636	1618	2488	*	2098	2425
10	1427	1939	1945	*	1648	2033	*	1851	884	2524	1733	1344
11	1321	2010	2128	2530	1962	1022	1567	1967	*	1832	1876	*
12	1401	†	931	2193	1907	*	1697	2914	2093	†	925	2483
13	1394	*		2043	1670		1758	989	1888	1708	*	2740
14	1336	2028	1888	2108	891	2452	1565	*	2696	1958	2064	2546
15	798	2154	2013	†	*	2045	1785	1670	2428	812	2376	2612
16	*	2527	2009	1058	1654	2155	789	2069	2450	*	2213	3106
17	1809	2415	2015	*	1532	2056	*	1905	1301	2032	2482	1512
18	1656	2326	2226	2099	2050	990	1378	1534	*	2015	2619	*
19	1596	958	939	2092	2355	*	1849	1602	2497	2522	1279	2846
20	1317	*	*	2149	2478	1867	1771	793	2332	2440	*	2905
21	1590	2132	1854	2313	1279	1754	2085	*	2083	2559	2472	2880
22	1098	†	1991	2446	*	1753	1916	1956	2276	1527	2504	2543
23	*	2217	2306	1286	2145	2018	745	2014	1602	*	2949	2269
24	1574	2134	1917	*	2060	1481	*	2027	854	2174	†	1257
25	2114	2023	1735	2442	2226	690	1617	2306	*	1996	2538	*
26	1461	1147	840	1965	2511	*	1866	2160	1922	2171	1203	†
27	1248	*	2054	2441	2119		1922	934	1911	1869	*	2148
28	1232	2587	1892	2562	1070	1386	2034	*	2080	2284	2658	2473
29	740		1927	1904	*	1398	2064	1907	2101	1084	2654	2396
30	*		2278	925	†	1374	1126	1795	2335	*	2909	2237
31	1534		2262		2144		1750			1606		1152
Total	34,689	44,286	49,856	50,319	46,670	46,832	38,480	50,649	50,292	49,493	50,293	60,949

*Sunday. †Holiday.

1927—BOND AVERAGES

Date:	Jan.	Feb.	Mar.	Apr.	May	June	July	Aug.	Sept.	Oct.	Nov.	Dec.
1	†	96.64	96.31	97.33	*	97.31	96.84	97.32	97.92	98.41	98.71	99.23
2	*	96.61	96.30	97.37	97.24	97.32	96.88	97.28	97.93	*	98.71	99.30
3	96.14	96.58	96.33	*	97.22	97.31		97.35	†	98.48	98.70	99.25
4	96.22	96.46	96.30	97.38	97.41	97.29	†	97.56	*	98.52	98.76	*
5	96.26	96.44	96.28	97.47	97.45	*	96.93	97.67	†	98.59	98.81	99.26
6	96.28	*	*	97.49	97.58	97.27	96.98	97.68	97.94	98.63	*	99.27
7	96.35	96.39	96.30	97.45	97.69	97.21	96.99	*	97.90	98.67	98.77	99.26
8	96.37	96.40	96.32	97.40	*	97.10	97.06	97.78	97.99	98.74	†	99.26
9	*	96.41	96.35	97.39	97.77	96.95	97.11	97.68	98.00	*	98.80	99.25
10	96.40	96.37	96.47	*	97.78	96.92	*	97.68	98.00	98.69	98.87	99.24
11	96.44	96.36	96.57	97.33	97.78	96.91	97.12	97.78	*	98.74	98.97	
12	96.49	†	96.64	97.31	97.60	*	97.01	97.79	97.99	†	98.96	99.28
13	96.55	*	*	97.38	97.58	†	96.97	97.78	97.93	98.65	*	99.29
14	96.52	96.41	96.59	97.29	97.61	96.92	97.02	*	97.95	98.67	99.01	99.29
15	96.54	96.40	96.61	†	*	96.86	97.02	97.75	98.00	98.66	99.06	99.28
16	*	96.39	96.69	97.35	97.59	96.96	97.05	97.80	97.99	*	99.13	99.29
17	96.62	96.44	96.81	*	97.56	96.99	*	97.86	97.95	98.63	99.17	99.21
18	96.68	96.38	96.89	97.34	97.65	96.99	97.10	97.97	*	98.68	99.19	*
19	96.67	96.42	96.94	97.28	97.59	*	97.08	97.99	98.01	98.63	99.23	99.22
20	96.68	*	*	97.32	97.56	97.00	97.10	98.02	98.02	98.70	*	99.23
21	96.72	96.38	97.02	97.32	97.56	96.91	97.10	*	98.05	98.76	99.23	99.22
22	96.81	†	97.04	97.34	*	96.85	97.11	97.98	98.13	98.74	99.21	99.22
23	*	96.39	97.00	97.31	97.55	96.88	97.12	98.01	98.18	*	99.16	99.18
24	96.82	96.43	97.05	*	97.56	96.89	*	97.97	98.22	98.71	†	99.21
25	96.67	96.40	97.16	97.33	97.42	96.86	97.06	97.98	*	98.67	99.13	*
26	96.66	96.40	97.19	97.24	97.42	*	97.11	97.99	98.30	98.67	99.16	†
27	96.62	*	*	97.24	97.47	96.88	97.20	98.01	98.30	98.72	*	99.18
28	96.62	96.34	97.15	97.23	97.45	96.80	97.17	*	98.41	98.72	99.12	99.24
29	96.62		97.20	97.21		96.80	97.20	97.99	98.47	98.68	99.16	99.27
30	*		97.19	97.22	†	96.82	97.24	97.97	98.40		99.20	99.29
31	96.60		97.29		97.36			97.94		98.67		99.36
High	96.82	96.64	97.29	97.49	97.78	97.32	97.24	98.02	98.47	98.76	99.23	99.36
Low	96.14	96.34	96.28	97.21	97.22	96.80	96.84	97.28	97.90	98.41	98.70	99.18

*Sunday
†Holiday

1928—INDUSTRIALS

Date	Jan.	Feb.	Mar.	Apr.	May	June	July	Aug.	Sept.	Oct.	Nov.	Dec.
1	*	197.98	194.81	*	213.48	220.27	*	216.78	240.38	‡240.01	255.23	290.80
2	†	199.20	194.53	209.33	213.88	220.96	208.21	214.90	*	238.14	254.38	*
3	203.35	196.30	195.43	209.95	214.62	*	211.90	216.15	†	237.75	254.16	289.23
4	202.24	196.53	*	209.82	217.66	216.62	†	216.67	240.25	240.00	*	291.30
5	199.61	*	197.80	212.12	†	217.80	214.43		240.02	240.44	257.58	290.68
6	201.45	196.63	199.51	†	*	215.51	212.49	218.04	239.06	240.17	†	279.79
7	201.97	196.85	197.48	†	219.51	215.08	213.55	218.06	241.72	*	260.68	271.05
8	*	197.86	198.26	*	220.09	211.51	*	215.19	241.11	239.55	261.11	257.33
9	199.63	199.35	201.32	211.53	218.71	209.01	213.86	215.10	*	241.73	263.05	*
10	197.52	199.02	200.24	209.23	218.43	*	212.71	214.91	238.82	246.53	265.58	263.95
11	197.43	199.16	*	212.46	220.74	205.74	206.43	215.29	241.05	247.69	*	269.34
12	198.35	*	203.33	212.13	*	202.65	206.71	*	241.48	*	269.67	266.82
13	199.51	†	202.31	216.93	*	209.01	207.83	215.53	*	249.13	269.89	266.88
14	197.96	197.93	201.04	215.15	220.88	210.76	207.77	214.08	239.62	*	268.60	272.26
15		197.59	202.91	*	219.52	205.96	*	219.40	240.02	249.85	269.42	270.72
16	195.41	196.30	204.70	215.79	216.65	205.75	205.10	221.34	*	249.43	276.66	*
17	195.35	192.48	204.03	213.02	218.76	*	206.42	222.41	241.25	250.87	277.48	270.23
18	194.50	191.80	*	213.36	217.64	201.96	209.30	223.61	240.11	251.88	*	275.42
19	196.24	*	203.66	214.07	†	202.01	208.73	*	239.61	256.59	278.78	280.50
20	198.06	191.33	205.23	210.90	*	204.49	209.95	225.77	239.08	253.75	283.90	282.01
21	198.46	192.81	206.78	†	214.33	204.15	208.79	228.79	239.37	*	280.53	286.53
22	*	†	206.67	*	211.73	204.25	*	229.71	238.84	253.60	290.34	285.94
23	199.72	193.09	208.56	207.94	215.45	203.30	210.84	229.24	*	256.04	288.22	*
24	201.01	193.15	209.10	208.85	217.53	*	212.00	233.68	240.13	257.03	†	287.89
25	198.58	193.08	*	208.96	217.74	203.95	213.04	234.98	240.41	256.48	*	†
26	199.60	*	210.36	210.18	†	206.08	212.65	*	239.40	251.44	291.16	286.13
27	200.31	192.12	210.38	212.25	*	208.42	215.66	234.83	236.86	255.51	292.39	290.95
28	198.87	193.94	210.03	212.55	214.05	209.63	215.89	236.55	237.38	*	295.62	296.52
29	*	194.78	210.76	*	217.28	210.37	*	238.28	239.43	257.13	†	297.28
30	197.57		214.45	211.63	*	210.55	216.62	238.85	*	253.70	293.38	*
31	198.59		213.35		219.81		216.00	240.41		252.16		300.00
High	203.35	199.35	214.45	216.93	220.88	220.96	216.62	240.41	241.72	257.13	295.62	300.00
Low	194.50	191.33	194.53	207.94	211.73	201.96	205.10	214.08	236.86	237.75	254.16	257.33

*Sunday. †Holiday. ‡Beginning Oct. 1, 1928, the Dow-Jones Industrial Average was revised to include 30 stocks. Closing averages for years following 1928 are given in daily range tables.

1928—RAILROADS

Date	Jan.	Feb.	Mar.	Apr.	May	June	July	Aug.	Sept.	Oct.	Nov.	Dec.
1	*	136.10	134.19		144.85	144.20		138.30	143.47	142.02	142.74	151.40
2	†	136.44	134.66	140.43	145.16	144.33	136.80	137.55	*	141.12	142.22	*
3	140.61	135.26	134.61	142.19	145.68	*	138.45	137.24	†	140.75	142.20	151.08
4	140.39	134.89	*	141.81	145.86	142.78	†	137.39	144.34	140.47	*	150.49
5	140.08	*	135.26	142.91	†	142.40	139.48		143.75	139.70	142.99	149.07
6	141.02	134.38	135.37		*	141.51	139.31	137.71	143.01	139.75	†	145.78
7	140.81	133.35	135.30	†	146.35	140.93	139.83	138.08	143.08	*	143.65	144.56
8	*	133.33	135.27	*	146.63	139.26	*	137.58	142.67	139.52	143.94	143.25
9	139.48	133.88	135.75	142.98	147.65	138.06	139.66	136.98	*	138.86	146.08	*
10	138.48	134.03	135.78	142.14	147.41	*	138.65	136.90	142.41	140.15	148.29	144.33
11	138.80	134.91	*	143.56	147.36	135.86	136.77	136.90	142.52	139.97	*	145.66
12	138.75	*	136.56	142.37	†	134.78	136.13	*	142.60	†	148.80	145.26
13	139.65	†	136.69	142.74	*	137.63	136.56	136.76	142.56	140.45	148.19	144.66
14	139.06	134.46	137.34	142.26	147.12	138.16	136.48	136.34	142.81	*	147.94	145.74
15	*	134.01	138.23	*	146.41	136.33	*	136.73	143.90	141.16	148.10	145.78
16	137.58	134.55	139.95	141.91	145.11	136.27	135.31	138.18	*	141.48	149.30	*
17	137.96	132.93	140.92	141.25	144.48	*	135.39	138.40	144.15	142.38	149.40	145.38
18	136.98	132.75	*	141.26	145.34	133.15	135.86	139.80	143.03	142.61	*	146.21
19	137.40	*	140.30	142.09	†	133.51	136.13	*	143.19	142.45	149.43	147.33
20	138.17	132.60	140.07	140.53	*	134.88	135.90	139.85	142.51	142.08	150.75	146.95
21	138.12	133.80	140.41	†	143.22	136.16	136.03	141.38	142.26	*	149.03	148.18
22	*	†	140.30	*	142.02	136.43	*	141.01	141.99	141.87	150.03	148.06
23	138.99	134.03	140.37	140.08	143.70	135.38	136.65	141.21	*	141.76	150.46	*
24	139.06	134.93	140.11	140.77	143.90		137.25	141.70	142.40	142.72	†	148.64
25	137.90	135.82	*	143.61	143.52	135.99	137.50	142.00	142.05	142.80	*	†
26	138.68	*	140.66	144.80	†	136.47	137.58	*	141.88	141.35	152.35	148.70
27	138.05	134.66	140.95	145.16	*	137.24	137.84	141.63	141.97	141.91	152.70	148.66
28	137.33	134.77	141.23	144.96	142.57	137.55	137.89	142.21	141.53	*	152.29	149.51
29	*	134.35	141.35	*	143.01	138.20	*	142.70	142.61	142.94	†	150.26
30	137.12		141.96	144.55	†	138.21	138.53	142.73	*	142.09	151.78	*
31	137.18		141.25		144.10		138.53	143.15		141.66		151.14
High	141.02	136.44	141.96	145.16	147.65	144.33	139.83	143.15	144.34	142.94	152.70	151.40
Low	136.98	132.60	134.19	140.03	142.02	133.51	135.31	136.34	141.53	138.86	142.20	143.25

*Sunday. †Holiday.
Closing averages for years following 1928 are given in daily range tables.

1928—DAILY STOCK SALES ON NEW YORK STOCK EXCHANGE
(000 Omitted)

Date	Jan.	Feb.	Mar.	Apr.	May	June	July	Aug.	Sept.	Oct.	Nov.	Dec.
1	*	2065	1811	*	3898	3433	*	2277	2236	3501	3446	2654
2	†	2151	1777	3491	3852	1756	1710	1781	*	3851	3488	*
3	2408	2640	1281	3029	3498	*	1847	2344	†	4057	1407	4487
4	3355	1313	*	3270	4441	4090	†	968	3733	4332	*	4920
5	3428	*	3134	3844	†	3264	2383	*	4326	4363	3740	4379
6	2866	2095	2779	†	*	3475	1974	2162	4476	2286	†	5408
7	1544	2901	2698	†	4542	3173	792	2382	4722	*	4827	6185
8	*	2820	2077	*	4287	3152	*	1991	2048	3943	4852	3750
9	2800	2976	3678	4235	4060	1778	1853	1677	*	3822	4947	*
10	3328	2165	2095	4111	3620	*	1972	2111	3833	4169	3278	5222
11	2370	1233	*	4303	4033	3690	2589	785	4211	3969	*	3916
12	2050	*	3811	4382	†	5110	2532	*	4592	†	5681	3999
13	2159	†	4058	4569	*	3623	1875	1633	4130	1952	5239	3268
14	1056	2037	3306	2383	4409	2907	525	2107	4562	*	5414	3009
15	*	2001	3594	*	4658	2724	*	2647	1824	4038	4733	1291
16	2370	2022	3907	4309	4886	1056	1288	2802	*	4532	6734	*
17	1522	2874	2140	4263	3830	*	1347	2900	4172	3960	3163	2231
18	1782	1632	*	3515	4162	2145	1661	921	4400	4403	*	2273
19	1477	*	3092	3572	†	3243	1364	*	3809	4559	5100	3401
20	1847	2603	3313	3744	*	2257	1290	2372	3922	2229	6441	3813
21	1057	1826	3796	†	2927	1714	536	2981	4758	*	6165	3464
22	*	†	4013	*	3079	1459	*	3160	2142	3857	5838	1907
23	2647	1745	3586	3528	2965	678	1380	3056	*	4157	6943	*
24	2658	1837	2042	2814	3105	*	1778	3851	4281	4552	†	3698
25	2801	868	*	3235	3113	1097	1763	2067	4453	4210	*	†
26	2417	*	4249	4030	†	1499	1558	*	4162	4516	5316	3622
27	2797	1787	4656	4323	*	2172	1841	3537	4022	1741	5278	3567
28	1353	1536	4140	2434	3508	1842	845	3376	3707	*	6367	4798
29	*	1982	3694	*	3537	2426	*	3729	1811	3693	†	2687
30	2195		4759	4017	†	838	1825	3408	*	3452	6405	*
31	2133		2491		3774		1477	4135		3489		4888
Total	56,399	47,109	85,773	81,398	84,187	64,600	39,994	67,160	90,332	97,632	114,811	92,837

*Sunday. †Holiday.

1928—BOND AVERAGES

Date:	Jan.	Feb.	Mar.	Apr.	May	June	July	Aug.	Sept.	Oct.	Nov.	Dec.
1	*	99.31	99.08	*	98.88	98.12	*	95.76	96.21	96.65	96.85	96.59
2	†	99.36	99.05	99.33	98.99	98.03	97.19	95.75	*	96.54	96.95	*
3	99.27	99.32	99.04	99.29	98.98	*	97.19	95.80	†	96.62	96.94	96.56
4	99.37	99.33	*	99.32	99.07	97.98	†	95.78	96.33	96.55	*	96.56
5	99.32	*	98.99	99.39	†	97.69	97.28	*	96.44	96.48	96.89	96.45
6	99.29	99.31	99.01	†	*	97.52	97.36	95.75	96.48	96.50	†	96.34
7	99.33	99.27	99.02	†	99.02	97.49	97.24	95.73	96.45	*	97.02	96.16
8	*	99.36	99.11	*	98.97	97.29	*	95.85	96.59	96.47	97.09	96.14
9	99.37	99.32	99.16	99.35	98.93	97.23	97.26	95.71	*	96.53	97.03	*
10	99.38	99.35	99.18	99.32	98.91	*	97.18	95.65	96.60	96.52	97.00	95.99
11	99.42	99.40	*	99.23	98.94	97.17	96.89	95.61	96.45	96.49	*	96.01
12	99.46	*	99.19	99.19	†	97.08	96.65	*	96.47	†	97.02	96.13
13	99.48	†	99.26	99.23	*	96.91	96.59	95.66	96.45	96.56	96.96	96.06
14	99.47	99.45	99.20	99.21	98.95	97.11	96.47	95.68	96.52	96.54	96.94	96.09
15	*	99.40	99.25	*	98.93	97.13	*	95.69	96.65	96.55	96.89	96.07
16	99.37	99.42	99.29	99.23	98.92	97.15	96.35	95.74	*	96.55	96.92	*
17	99.31	99.41	99.32	99.15	98.76	*	96.22	95.89	96.61	96.63	96.94	95.97
18	99.35	99.35	*	99.15	98.76	97.14	96.15	95.87	96.68	96.56	*	96.00
19	99.30	*	99.33	99.16	†	97.01	96.22	*	96.62	96.58	96.90	96.06
20	99.30	99.24	99.36	99.10	*	97.06	96.20	95.80	96.59	96.64	96.87	96.07
21	99.34	99.21	99.33	†	98.59	96.96	96.14	95.87	96.61	*	96.83	96.07
22	*	†	99.33	*	98.43	97.09	*	95.95	96.61	96.63	96.79	96.04
23	99.38	99.15	99.28	99.08	98.28	97.17	96.11	96.00	*	96.55	96.78	*
24	99.42	99.09	99.28	98.98	98.29	*	96.09	96.13	96.62	96.61	†	96.10
25	99.34	99.06	*	99.00	98.22	97.18	96.04	96.13	96.65	96.61	*	†
26	99.34	*	99.32	98.92	†	97.09	95.82	*	96.65	96.77	96.72	96.07
27	99.34	99.07	99.27	98.95	*	97.06	95.80	96.11	96.62	96.82	96.72	95.97
28	99.33	99.06	99.23	98.94	98.20	97.02	95.82	96.07	96.67	*	96.69	95.97
29	*	99.13	99.26	*	98.10	97.08	*	96.08	96.64	96.72	†	96.01
30	99.31		99.31	99.02	†	97.10	95.89	96.12	*	96.73	96.62	*
31	99.34		99.35		98.19		95.80	96.18		96.75		95.99
High	99.48	99.45	99.36	99.39	99.07	98.12	97.36	96.18	96.68	96.82	97.09	96.59
Low	99.27	99.06	98.99	98.92	98.10	96.91	95.80	95.61	96.21	96.49	96.69	95.97

*Sunday
†Holiday

OCTOBER, 1928

Date	Industrials High	Low	Close	Railroads High	Low	Close	Daily Sales	40 Bonds
1	242.46	238.24	240.01	143.10	140.52	142.02	3,501	96.65
2	241.54	235.42	238.14	142.04	140.35	141.12	3,851	96.54
3	239.14	233.60	237.75	141.05	139.75	140.75	4,057	96.62
4	242.53	237.72	240.00	141.16	139.96	140.47	4,332	96.55
5	243.08	238.22	240.44	140.53	139.35	139.70	4,363	96.48
6	241.66	239.23	240.17	139.95	139.41	139.75	2,286	96.50
7	*	*	*					
8	243.33	237.72	239.55	140.13	139.19	139.52	3,943	96.47
9	242.86	236.79	241.73	139.15	138.50	138.86	3,822	96.53
10	249.06	241.57	246.53	140.68	139.49	140.15	4,169	96.52
11	250.14	245.57	247.69	140.62	139.78	139.97	3,969	96.49
12	†	†	†	†		†		†
13	250.43	247.35	249.13	140.70	140.23	140.45	1,952	96.56
14	*		*				*	
15	252.70	247.33	249.85	141.77	140.58	141.16	4,038	96.54
16	255.27	247.92	249.43	142.07	141.05	141.48	4,532	96.55
17	253.60	247.74	250.87	142.96	141.41	142.38	3,960	96.63
18	255.24	249.65	251.88	143.55	142.05	142.61	4,403	96.56
19	259.19	250.35	256.59	143.05	142.14	142.45	4,559	96.58
20	257.75	252.58	253.75	142.52	141.88	142.08	2,229	96.64
21	*	*	*	*		*	*	*
22	257.32	250.08	253.6c	142.46	141.71	141.87	3,857	96.63
23	258.60	252.73	256.04	142.35	141.29	141.76	4,157	96.55
24	260.39	249.09	257.03	143.10	141.93	142.72	4,552	96.61
25	260.03	254.93	256.48	143.46	142.44	142.80	4,210	96.61
26	259.16	250.00	251.44	142.31	141.28	141.35	4,516	96.77
27	257.20	252.24	255.51	142.10	141.29	141.91	1,741	96.82
28	*	*	*	*			*	
29	259.76	255.03	257.13	143.66	142.40	142.94	3,693	96.72
30	259.00	252.39	253.70	143.26	141.95	142.09	3,452	96.73
31	256.16	248.76	252.16	142.63	140.95	141.66	3,489	96.75
High			257.13			142.94	97,632	96.82
Low			237.75			138.86		96.47

*Sunday. †Holiday.

The computation of the daily high, low and close figures on the industrial and railroad averages was begun on October 1, 1928. Daily range figures previous to that date are not available. On daily volume of sales on the New York Stock Exchange and on monthly total three ciphers (000) are omitted.

NOVEMBER, 1928

Date	Industrials High	Low	Close	Railroads High	Low	Close	Daily Sales	40 Bonds
1	256.59	251.56	255.23	143.21	141.35	142.74	3,446	96.85
2	256.99	252.46	254.38	142.84	141.98	142.22	3,488	96.95
3	255.33	253.29	254.16	142.43	141.96	142.20	1,407	96.94
4	*	*	*	*	*	*	*	*
5	259.68	253.89	257.58	143.44	142.30	142.99	3,740	96.89
6	†	†	†	†		†		†
7	263.97	258.48	260.68	144.35	143.27	143.65	4,827	97.02
8	265.26	258.96	261.11	144.60	143.54	143.94	4,852	97.09
9	266.24	259.37	263.05	146.66	144.11	146.08	4,947	97.03
10	266.74	262.90	265. 8	148.55	146.66	148.29	3,278	97.00
11	*	*	*	*				*
12	272.47	264.42	269.67	150.11	147.92	148.80	5,681	97.02
13	272.03	264.88	269.89	148.88	146.75	148.19	5,239	96.96
14	272.94	266.80	268.60	148.23	147.35	147.94	5,414	96.94
15	271.63	266.48	269.42	148.71	147.24	148.10	4,733	96.89
16	278.65	271.48	276.66	149.88	148.38	149.30	6,734	96.92
17	279.50	274.43	277.48	149.95	148.90	149.40	3,163	96.94
18	*	*	*	*			*	
19	280.68	272.98	278.78	149.78	148.28	149.43	5,100	96.90
20	288.13	278.05	283.90	151.30	149.63	150.75	6,441	96.87
21	288.71	276.91	280.53	151.08	148.51	149.03	6,165	96.83
22	292.12	281.28	290.34	150.36	148.67	150.03	5,838	96.79
23	295.17	284.40	288.22	151.22	149.04	150.46	6,943	96.78
24	†	†	†	†		†	†	†
25	*	*	*	*				*
26	296.10	288.14	291.16	152.81	150.10	152.35	5,316	96.78
27	294.75	289.28	292.39	153.93	152.02	152.70	5,278	96.72
28	299.35	290.68	295.62	153.38	151.71	152.29	6,367	96.69
29	†	†	†	†		†		†
30	299.07	288.82	293.38	153.46	150.78	151.78	6,414	96.62
High			295.62			152.70	114,811	97.09
Low			254.16			142.20		96.62

*Sunday †Holiday

DECEMBER, 1928

Date	Industrials			Railroads			Daily Sales	40 Bonds
	High	Low	Close	High	Low	Close		
1	295.22	289.76	290.80	152.23	150.96	151.40	2,654	96.59
2	*	*	*				*	*
3	291.05	283.89	289.23	151.56	149.66	151.08	4,487	96.56
4	295.61	287.61	291.30	151.87	150.18	150.49	4,920	96.56
5	294.20	289.91	290.68	150.25	148.32	149.07	4,379	96.45
6	292.56	278.66	279.79	149.13	145.41	145.78	5,408	96.34
7	284.44	269.58	271.05	146.76	143.91	144.56	6,185	96.16
8	270.32	255.02	257.33	144.61	142.82	143.25	3,750	96.14
9	*	*	*				*	*
10	266.22	254.36	263.95	144.90	142.78	144.33	5,222	95.99
11	270.41	263.71	269.34	146.20	144.86	145.66	3,916	96.01
12	272.74	264.95	266.82	146.44	144.93	145.26	3,999	96.13
13	269.53	260.51	266.88	145.67	144.31	144.66	3,268	96.06
14	275.45	266.99	272.26	146.15	144.50	145.74	3,009	96.09
15	274.26	269.01	270.72	146.24	145.33	145.78	1,291	96.07
16	*	*	*				*	*
17	272.27	266.21	270.23	146.00	144.58	145.38	2,231	96.08
18	276.41	269.61	275.42	146.63	145.68	146.21	2,273	95.97
19	282.84	275.09	280.50	148.36	146.46	147.33	3,401	96.00
20	285.60	277.91	282.01	147.66	146.02	146.95	3,813	96.06
21	288.39	281.31	286.53	149.00	146.28	148.18	3,464	96.07
22	288.17	284.64	285.94	148.39	147.85	148.06	1,907	96.04
23	*	*	*				*	*
24	291.17	284.30	287.89	149.08	147.95	148.64	3,698	96.10
25	†	†	†	†	†	†	†	†
26	292.53	283.94	286.13	149.56	148.32	148.70	3,622	96.11
27	291.39	281.55	290.95	149.01	147.55	148.66	3,567	96.07
28	297.79	283.68	296.52	150.25	148.83	149.51	4,798	95.97
29	300.61	294.43	297.28	150.84	149.68	150.26	2,687	96.01
30	*	*	*				*	*
31	301.61	291.99	300.00	151.56	150.28	151.14	4,888	95.99
High			300.00			151.40	92,837	96.59
Low			257.33			143.25		95.97

*Sunday †Holiday

JANUARY, 1929

Date	Industrials			Railroads			Utilities Close	Daily Sales	40 Bonds
	High	Low	Close	High	Low	Close			
1	†	†	†	†	†	†	†	†	†
2	308.66	300.31	307.01	153.00	151.00	152.75	85.64	5,413	96.10
3	311.46	302.90	305.72	154.20	152.03	152.63	85.85	5,095	96.20
4	307.51	299.92	304.75	154.90	151.63	154.10	86.44	5,532	96.19
5	308.91	300.48	302.43	154.80	153.25	153.53	85.54	2,840	96.19
6	*	*	*	*				*	*
7	301.85	293.35	297.70	153.50	151.35	151.79	84.33	4,795	96.32
8	300.87	292.89	296.98	152.25	150.88	151.78	84.42	3,850	96.18
9	303.04	296.37	300.83	153.10	151.14	152.30	85.49	4,053	96.21
10	305.20	299.60	301.58	153.35	152.22	152.82	86.14	4,022	96.20
11	305.85	298.68	301.66	154.16	152.38	153.09	86.81	4,242	96.17
12	303.63	298.43	301.25	153.28	152.58	152.91	86.73	1,724	96.23
13	*	*	*	*	*			*	*
14	306.26	299.06	304.06	153.61	152.45	153.37	87.10	3,921	96.18
15	306.09	295.78	297.66	153.71	151.85	152.05	86.37	4,181	96.14
16	304.36	297.00	302.66	152.75	151.68	152.45	87.83	3,670	96.04
17	306.96	301.09	303.95	153.83	152.33	152.95	87.81	4,255	96.05
18	308.05	301.05	304.14	154.65	152.83	153.61	88.04	4,936	96.04
19	307.81	303.57	305.96	154.78	153.47	154.41	88.15	2,603	96.05
20	*	*	*	*				*	*
21	308.22	302.36	304.64	155.50	153.76	154.41	88.02	4,897	96.05
22	310.08	303.05	307.06	155.10	154.02	154.60	89.00	5,124	96.09
23	315.49	306.46	310.33	155.81	154.25	154.86	90.45	4,920	96.07
24	314.01	305.94	309.39	155.39	153.69	154.00	90.69	4,497	96.05
25	319.36	311.28	315.13	155.45	153.58	154.10	91.64	5,505	96.02
26	316.20	311.58	314.56	154.83	153.57	154.16	92.83	2,403	96.03
27	*	*	*	*	*	*		*	*
28	319.58	310.44	314.04	155.72	154.34	154.83	93.84	4,979	95.85
29	316.33	309.23	312.60	155.28	153.81	154.55	95.75	4,291	95.89
30	316.15	308.47	312.60	155.63	154.05	155.26	98.45	4,130	95.92
31	319.96	311.34	317.51	159.22	155.95	158.54	97.92	4,680	95.93
High			317.51			158.54	98.45	110,804	96.32
Low........			296.98			151.78	84.33		95.85

*Sunday †Holiday

FEBRUARY, 1929

Date	Industrials High	Industrials Low	Industrials Close	Railroads High	Railroads Low	Railroads Close	Utilities Close	Daily Sales	40 Bonds
1	324.16	315.64	319.68	162.29	158.96	161.18	97.82	4,971	95.86
2	322.49	317.88	319.76	162.56	160.81	161.32	97.28	2,333	95.69
3			*	*	*	*	*		*
4	323.74	316.91	319.05	162.78	159.99	160.52	95.52	4,051	95.75
5	324.51	317.28	322.06	160.36	159.35	159.71	95.86	4,068	95.73
6	323.31	313.32	317.18	159.86	157.31	158.19	95.16	4,681	95.68
7	312.56	302.40	305.75	156.56	154.13	154.79	92.26	5,212	95.63
8	309.26	298.03	301.53	155.53	153.13	154.23	91.20	4,553	95.65
9	†	†	†	†	†	†	†	†	†
10									
11	311.24	299.58	310.35	156.02	154.13	156.00	94.10	3,889	95.65
12	†	†	†	†	†	†	†	†	†
13	316.06	307.15	308.07	157.28	155.28	155.50	94.64	4,528	95.54
14	308.29	300.60	306.49	154.92	153.40	154.31	94.51	3,726	95.49
15	309.79	299.38	300.41	155.19	152.75	152.86	93.04	3,902	95.46
16	299.83	295.85	295.85	152.04	151.13	151.58	91.34	2,492	95.41
17			*	*	*	*	*		*
18	301.68	293.40	300.74	152.94	151.30	152.78	94.17	3,476	95.34
19	305.58	299.00	301.10	153.55	152.70	152.99	94.56	3,205	95.31
20	307.55	301.05	305.99	154.45	153.53	154.01	94.98	2,907	95.31
21	311.31	303.45	310.06	155.31	153.88	154.94	94.79	3,395	95.36
22	†	†	†	†	†	†	†	†	†
23	†	†	†	†	†	†	†	†	†
24			*	*	*	*	*		*
25	315.08	308.10	311.24	156.11	154.63	155.11	93.72	3,506	95.26
26	313.49	307.04	311.25	155.55	154.46	154.97	93.53	3,736	95.27
27	317.03	309.71	314.53	156.00	154.90	155.62	94.47	4,366	95.30
28	319.69	312.91	317.41	156.48	155.00	155.49	96.12	4,971	95.32
High			322.06			161.32	97.82	77,972	95.86
Low			295.85			151.58	91.20		95.26

*Sunday   †Holiday

MARCH, 1929

Date	Industrials High	Industrials Low	Industrials Close	Railroads High	Railroads Low	Railroads Close	Utilities Close	Daily Sales	40 Bonds
1	324.40	317.79	321.18	159.03	155.88	158.62	97.13	6,021	95.36
2	321.66	316.51	319.12	158.76	157.71	158.46	96.89	2,473	95.32
3	*	*	*	*	*	*	*		*
4	320.22	312.85	313.86	158.64	156.56	157.20	96.02	4,557	95.28
5	316.17	308.22	310.20	159.45	156.55	157.03	94.97	4,430	95.25
6	313.45	302.93	305.20	157.63	154.88	155.22	93.26	4,487	95.18
7	310.39	303.05	308.99	156.06	154.78	155.80	94.13	3,633	95.32
8	313.25	304.78	311.59	155.87	154.04	155.37	94.11	3,945	95.14
9	314.37	309.66	311.61	155.51	154.13	154.82	94.49	1,948	95.02
10			*	*	*	*	*		*
11	312.96	305.20	305.75	154.88	152.73	153.85	93.40	3,627	94.95
12	312.76	305.20	306.14	154.04	153.08	153.46	93.31	3,062	94.71
13	312.30	306.79	310.29	154.07	153.19	153.55	94.24	3,330	94.58
14	317.98	311.02	316.26	154.36	153.38	154.18	95.24	4,625	94.60
15	322.75	315.92	319.70	154.71	153.86	154.08	95.05	5,885	94.65
16	321.55	317.24	320.00	154.35	153.82	153.97	95.31	2,718	94.67
17			*	*	*	*	*		*
18	321.70	315.49	317.59	153.91	153.05	153.31	94.95	5,021	94.70
19	321.28	315.23	317.53	154.64	152.86	154.00	94.95	4,450	94.75
20	320.06	313.27	316.44	153.85	152.85	153.18	95.18	5,191	94.61
21	319.31	313.12	314.63	153.46	152.47	152.64	95.29	4,459	94.63
22	316.94	307.50	310.26	152.14	150.98	151.34	94.25	4,831	94.57
23	311.45	305.07	306.21	151.31	150.45	150.63	93.67	2,145	94.60
24			*	*	*	*	*		*
25	311.55	294.34	297.50	150.38	148.05	148.43	91.06	5,860	94.47
26	300.60	281.51	296.51	148.75	145.75	147.41	89.66	8,247	94.26
27	305.87	293.70	303.22	150.37	148.36	149.75	92.71	5,619	94.05
28	311.13	302.93	308.85	151.03	149.68	150.90	95.24	5,096	94.12
29	†	†	†	†	†	†	†	†	†
30	†	†	†	†	†	†	†	†	†
31									
High			321.18			158.62	97.13	105,635	95.36
Low			296.51			147.41	89.66		94.05

*Sunday   †Holiday

APRIL, 1929

Date	Industrials High	Industrials Low	Industrials Close	Railroads High	Railroads Low	Railroads Close	Utilities Close	Daily Sales	40 Bonds
1	304.21	294.11	300.40	149.31	148.06	148.52	92.53	4,163	94.13
2	305.20	298.07	303.49	149.50	148.70	149.26	93.24	3,777	94.15
3	307.70	298.58	300.35	149.86	148.60	148.77	92.40	3,703	94.21
4	306.99	295.79	305.37	151.31	148.53	151.10	93.00	3,330	94.23
5	307.97	301.39	303.04	151.90	150.25	150.75	92.26	3,406	94.28
6	302.81	299.18	302.81	152.28	149.90	152.16	92.20	1,615	94.31
7	*	*	*	*	*	*	*	*	*
8	305.70	299.52	301.49	153.06	150.40	150.76	91.36	2,720	94.28
9	306.29	297.17	299.13	150.65	148.87	149.40	89.83	3,629	94.14
10	304.60	295.71	300.67	149.97	149.15	149.38	90.24	3,282	94.21
11	307.90	299.40	304.09	151 35	149.38	150.95	91.73	3,102	94.19
12	309.79	303.61	305.43	150.98	150.10	150.29	91.96	3,405	94.34
13	306.21	303.36	304.41	151.42	148.89	150.13	91.71	1,363	94.37
14	*	*	*	*	*	*	*	*	*
15	305.55	301.54	302.43	150.63	149.98	150.13	91.06	2,643	94.39
16	305.51	299.30	304.19	150.46	149.58	150.02	90.60	2,369	94.61
17	311.19	304.16	309.91	150.75	149.78	150.25	91.96	3,503	94.63
18	315.22	309.63	311.87	151.16	150.33	150.79	92.67	3,769	94.90
19	313.81	308.67	310.58	151.03	150.06	150.35	93.23	3,055	95.06
20	312.34	308.71	311.07	150.94	150.58	150.66	93.30	1,292	95.04
21	*	*	*	*	*	*	*	*	*
22	318.26	311.98	315.33	151.75	150.71	151.33	95.66	3,569	95.03
23	320.10	314.20	316.62	152.11	151.13	151.73	95.92	4,132	95.07
24	320.00	313.56	315.66	152.78	151.36	151.75	95.29	4,068	95.13
25	317.23	312.37	314.28	152.51	151.00	151.78	94.61	3,338	95.06
26	319.31	311.00	314.15	153.00	151.34	151.83	94.71	4,012	95.12
27	317.50	313.21	315.68	152.38	151.75	152.06	95.20	1,741	95.07
28	*	*	*	*	*	*	*	*	*
29	315.55	309.62	313.84	152.07	151.21	151.68	95.43	3,273	95.07
30	321.09	314.02	319.29	152.59	151.30	152.03	97.53	4,315	94.94
High			319.29			152.16	97.53	82,595	95.13
Low			299.13			148.52	89.83		94.13

*Sunday   †Holiday

MAY, 1929

Date	Industrials High	Industrials Low	Industrials Close	Railroads High	Railroads Low	Railroads Close	Utilities Close	Daily Sales	40 Bonds
1	323.99	317.90	320.13	152.81	151.75	152.33	96.84	4,689	94.86
2	324.60	317.73	321.52	152.61	151.59	152.00	97.43	4,180	94.90
3	329.11	322.33	325.56	152.70	151.95	152.12	98.65	4,527	94.89
4	328.08	323.39	327.08	153.15	152.43	152.87	98.69	1,992	94.85
5	*	*	*	*	*	*	*	*	*
6	331.01	323.01	326.16	153.49	152.39	152.60	98.05	3,813	94.78
7	327.57	320.60	321.91	152.90	151.95	152.13	98.37	3,493	94.78
8	325.90	318.87	323.51	152.14	151.30	151.65	98.30	3,468	94.65
9	324.87	317.09	321.17	151.31	150.25	150.85	98.10	3,657	94.58
10	328.00	321.49	325.70	152.13	150.73	151.80	99.24	3,920	94.58
11	328.01	323.09	324.59	152.21	151.56	151.81	99.56	1,978	94.48
12	*	*	*	*	*	*	*	*	*
13	324.49	313.56	316.49	152.37	150.44	150.63	97.13	4,626	94.55
14	322.33	315.17	320.79	149.86	148.83	149.53	98.25	3,634	94.50
15	324.38	317.93	319.35	150.18	148.97	149.34	98.25	3,352	94.43
16	321.89	314.51	320.09	149.53	148.50	149.08	99.21	3,443	94.14
17	325.64	318.81	321.38	150.20	149.03	149.26	99.15	3,334	94.16
18	323.33	318.90	321.48	149.92	148.96	149.15	98.86	1,250	94.22
19	*	*	*	*	*	*	*	*	*
20	322.65	312.18	312.70	155.29	148.68	151.49	96.47	3,812	94.19
21	316.41	308.32	314.09	153.88	151.36	153.06	95.19	4,410	94.13
22	311.89	300.54	300.83	151.88	148.99	149.26	93.84	4,844	93.92
23	309.51	300.42	308.09	150.28	148.84	149.98	95.89	3,814	93.88
24	313.30	304.32	305.64	151.38	149.87	149.96	94.74	3,272	93.79
25	306.28	302.02	304.33	150.22	149.08	149.73	94.33	1,210	93.64
26	*	*	*	*	*	*	*	*	*
27	304.19	291.82	293.42	148.96	147.00	147.18	92.06	4,354	93.66
28	300.08	291.80	298.87	150.13	147.06	149.82	93.38	3,937	93.50
29	302.32	295.18	296.76	153.80	150.04	152.08	93.73	2,977	93.29
30	†	†	†	†	†	†	†	†	†
31	300.27	290.02	297.41	154.43	151.27	153.95	96.95	3,296	93.28
High			327.08			153.95	99.56	91,306	94.90
Low			293.42			147.18	92.06		93.28

*Sunday   †Holiday

JUNE, 1929

Date	Industrials High	Low	Close	Railroads High	Low	Close	Utilities Close	Daily Sales	40 Bonds
1	301.58	296.46	299.12	155.43	153.96	154.88	98.82	1,534	93.36
2	*								
3	307.07	298.53	304.20	156.79	154.66	155.83	98.76	3,018	93.36
4	311.44	304.33	310.57	156.60	155.02	155.48	99.12	3,414	93.48
5	311.97	305.42	307.68	155.71	153.92	154.58	99.51	3,340	93.52
6	310.50	305.33	307.72	155.81	154.07	155.10	100.37	2,928	93.60
7	312.00	304.75	307.46	155.72	153.99	154.19	100.50	3,078	93.68
8	307.44	303.79	305.12	154.67	154.01	154.31	100.19	1,202	93.71
9	*								
10	307.60	301.86	303.27	154.30	153.33	153.36	99.68	2,201	93.67
11	307.60	301.22	306.64	154.02	152.75	153.55	100.28	2,144	93.58
12	309.29	304.25	306.68	153.95	152.91	153.23	101.05	2,131	93.69
13	314.21	306.80	313.05	154.36	152.71	153.46	104.37	3,156	93.56
14	317.39	311.76	313.68	155.10	153.37	154.18	103.67	3,235	93.44
15	314.57	312.58	314.26	156.18	155.10	155.88	103.54	1,264	93.44
16	*								
17	322.43	313.58	319.33	157.85	156.05	156.80	105.05	3,208	93.46
18	323.30	317.64	319.67	157.65	156.43	156.85	107.63	3,344	93.56
19	321.26	314.62	316.41	157.39	156.13	156.63	108.94	3,057	93.60
20	320.43	314.32	317.73	156.90	156.01	156.43	109.39	2,762	93.66
21	323.46	316.32	320.68	158.57	156.70	158.38	109.39	3,194	93.55
22	324.09	320.57	322.23	159.88	158.88	158.95	109.99	1,480	93.45
23	*								
24	325.73	319.91	321.15	160.40	158.63	159.16	108.98	3,033	93.36
25	327.95	319.27	326.16	160.70	158.43	160.15	109.99	2,928	93.28
26	332.75	325.13	328.60	161.91	160.03	161.02	111.54	4,030	93.28
27	333.66	325.68	328.91	162.05	160.39	161.15	113.55	3,912	93.33
28	335.25	328.15	331.65	161.81	160.38	161.01	116.07	3,950	93.41
29	334.57	331.08	333.79	162.00	160.48	161.68	118.50	1,996	93.35
30	*								
High			333.79			161.68	118.50	69,548	93.71
Low			299.12			153.23	98.76		93.28

*Sunday †Holiday

JULY, 1929

Date	Industrials High	Low	Close	Railroads High	Low	Close	Utilities Close	Daily Sales	40 Bonds
1	339.09	332.23	335.22	164.20	161.41	163.63	116.95	4,087	93.23
2	343.07	333.48	340.28	167.61	163.94	167.04	116.05	4,594	93.27
3	345.84	337.50	341.99	169.51	166.28	167.00	116.01	4,690	93.30
4	†	†	†	†	†	†	†		†
5	348.67	340.84	344.27	169.01	166.94	167.42	115.25	3,748	93.37
6	345.75	341.31	344.66	168.36	167.17	168.00	115.96	1,586	93.32
7	*								
8	350.09	342.45	346.55	170.43	167.87	169.48	115.85	3,522	93.25
9	349.29	342.00	345.57	170.41	167.81	168.85	116.58	4,247	93.35
10	347.64	340.19	343.30	169.75	168.13	168.80	117.67	4,210	93.25
11	347.12	340.12	343.04	170.00	167.61	168.74	119.87	4,211	93.48
12	350.26	343.34	346.37	170.67	168.90	169.95	122.60	4,759	93.38
13	348.28	344.70	345.94	175.00	170.33	174.78	122.65	2,023	93.29
14	*								
15	347.04	340.05	341.93	179.13	174.26	178.07	121.84	4,286	93.28
16	347.98	339.98	344.24	179.50	176.48	177.46	123.28	4,502	93.31
17	349.79	341.41	345.63	178.47	176.31	177.52	123.04	4,358	93.33
18	347.69	343.40	344.59	177.71	175.31	176.33	123.18	3,728	93.33
19	349.19	343.15	345.20	178.89	177.85	178.56	124.87	4,201	93.36
20	347.82	343.46	345.87	179.96	178.02	179.13	125.20	1,996	93.31
21	*								
22	347.85	339.32	341.37	180.26	176.73	177.13	124.45	3,679	93.23
23	347.85	339.65	345.48	179.51	177.91	178.37	125.55	3,784	93.18
24	349.30	341.95	343.04	178.89	176.46	176.95	125.74	3,779	93.31
25	348.15	340.09	344.67	177.32	174.75	175.50	126.17	3,479	93.25
26	349.45	341.95	345.47	176.17	173.21	174.00	125.83	3,552	93.22
27	347.50	341.85	343.73	174.25	172.00	172.53	125.04	1,371	93.17
28	*								
29	344.93	336.36	339.21	173.30	169.71	170.85	122.08	2,760	93.09
30	346.04	339.10	343.12	172.85	170.55	172.53	123.98	2,686	93.10
31	349.79	342.65	347.70	174.22	172.41	173.43	126.12	3,407	93.15
High			347.70			179.13	126.17	93,379	93.48
Low			335.22			163.63	115.25		93.09

*Sunday †Holiday

AUGUST, 1929

Date	Industrials			Railroads			Utilities	Daily	40
	High	Low	Close	High	Low	Close	Close	Sales	Bonds
1	353.30	346.39	350.56	174.51	172.69	173.43	127.64	3,323	92.75
2	358.31	349.77	353.08	176.68	173.02	174.80	130.15	4,032	92.80
3	357.31	351.86	355.62	175.63	174.32	175.40	131.66	1,824	92.86
4	*			*			*		
5	358.66	350.68	352.50	175.93	173.46	174.67	132.58	3,861	92.73
6	354.52	346.98	351.39	174.62	172.25	173.41	131.15	3,796	92.72
7	353.27	344.67	348.44	175.84	172.56	173.15	128.35	3,161	92.76
8	354.17	347.79	352.10	175.77	173.15	174.41	129.91	2,831	92.72
9	344.89	336.13	337.99	171.63	168.85	169.68	122.84	5,022	92.54
10	346.63	339.06	344.84	172.88	169.93	172.58	125.51	1,478	92.58
11	*			*			*		
12	354.36	345.71	351.13	175.20	173.06	174.14	127.28	3,610	92.55
13	357.88	348.24	354.03	175.56	173.36	174.81	128.28	4,097	92.40
14	361.55	352.05	354.86	176.47	174.05	174.63	128.69	4,199	92.37
15	358.65	351.68	354.42	176.77	174.20	175.63	128.60	3,414	92.36
16	364.39	356.84	361.49	179.31	176.61	178.21	131.01	4,796	92.30
17	363.56	354.34	360.70	179.94	178.13	178.90	131.90	2,227	92.32
18	*			*			*		
19	367.78	355.68	365.20	180.57	178.59	179.97	134.44	3,976	92.39
20	372.59	366.31	367.67	181.60	179.10	180.45	135.15	4,638	92.30
21	374.67	363.41	365.55	181.93	179.06	179.42	132.81	4,717	92.34
22	373.45	365.39	369.95	181.34	179.28	180.14	133.38	3,436	92.25
23	378.66	369.96	374.61	181.31	179.16	180.05	134.80	4,795	92.17
24	378.12	374.55	375.44	180.23	179.13	179.71	135.74	2,127	92.17
25	*			*			*		
26	380.18	372.09	374.46	182.69	179.14	181.34	136.23	4,425	92.10
27	378.16	371.76	373.79	183.78	181.18	182.62	135.90	3,896	92.23
28	377.56	370.34	372.06	186.85	183.26	184.87	134.31	3,956	92.40
29	378.76	370.79	376.18	189.40	185.40	187.36	136.26	3,476	92.30
30	383.96	376.16	380.33	189.81	186.67	188.76	140.41	4,572	92.25
31	†	†	†	†	†	†	†	†	†
High			380.33			188.76	140.41	95,603	92.86
Low			337.99			169.68	122.84		92.10

*Sunday   †Holiday

SEPTEMBER, 1929

Date	Industrials			Railroads			Utilities	Daily	40
	High	Low	Close	High	Low	Close	Close	Sales	Bonds
1	*			*			*	*	*
2	†	†	†	†	†	†	†	†	†
3	386.10	378.23	381.17	190.50	188.13	189.11	142.40	4,439	92.29
4	380.12	376.33	379.61	189.64	186.55	187.52	140.29	4,692	92.25
5	382.01	367.35	369.77	188.74	183.70	184.51	138.11	5,564	92.42
6	378.71	369.46	376.29	187.11	185.68	186.44	142.67	5,122	92.39
7	381.44	374.94	377.56	187.50	186.06	186.61	143.58	2,592	92.33
8	*			*			*	*	*
9	380.57	373.49	374.93	187.19	184.39	185.32	142.65	4,860	92.33
10	379.16	364.46	367.29	185.76	182.68	182.93	139.40	4,521	92.37
11	375.05	366.22	370.91	184.39	181.56	183.18	141.18	4,793	92.31
12	375.52	363.11	366.35	184.31	180.78	181.18	139.81	5,017	92.28
13	369.67	359.70	366.85	182.18	179.95	181.66	140.39	5,067	92.10
14	369.68	365.28	367.01	182.79	181.26	182.48	140.26	2,141	92.25
15	*			*			*	*	*
16	373.63	364.80	372.39	183.67	182.06	182.72	142.15	4,184	92.34
17	374.96	366.89	368.52	183.78	181.65	182.39	142.95	4,288	92.33
18	374.03	365.65	370.90	183.43	181.94	182.61	144.10	4,044	92.34
19	375.20	367.70	369.97	184.19	182.31	183.09	144.20	4,134	92.35
20	371.10	360.44	362.05	183.89	181.73	182.38	144.40	4,882	92.24
21	364.67	359.65	361.16	182.27	181.41	181.63	144.61	2,063	92.32
22	*			*			*	*	*
23	365.03	355.63	359.00	182.33	179.84	181.04	143.80	4,391	92.18
24	363.67	350.84	352.61	182.41	179.11	179.44	141.25	4,409	92.18
25	355.42	344.85	352.57	179.18	176.18	177.93	140.76	4,957	92.18
26	358.16	349.73	355.95	178.82	177.36	178.16	143.53	4,004	92.20
27	354.63	343.26	344.87	177.22	174.81	175.35	141.34	4,591	92.14
28	348.26	341.03	347.17	176.24	174.56	175.88	141.71	2,205	92.18
29	*			*			*	*	*
30	349.37	341.06	343.45	175.63	172.69	173.78	139.61	3,212	92.11
High			381.17			189.11	144.61	100,056	92.42
Low			343.45			173.78	138.11		92.10

*Sunday   †Holiday

OCTOBER, 1929

Date	Industrials			Railroads			Utilities Close	Daily Sales	40 Bonds
	High	Low	Close	High	Low	Close			
1	345.67	335.99	342.57	173.83	170.15	172.96	136.39	4,525	92.07
2	350.19	339.45	344.50	174.80	172.22	173.99	137.54	3,368	92.23
3	345.30	327.71	329.95	173.68	169.96	170.26	128.79	4,747	92.27
4	333.28	320.45	325.17	171.21	167.82	168.26	127.14	5,624	91.76
5	342.59	329.44	341.36	171.85	169.23	171.21	133.43	2,452	91.78
6	*	*	*	*	*	*			
7	348.54	338.86	345.72	176.42	171.97	175.84	135.40	4,262	91.95
8	349.67	340.86	345.00	177.02	175.01	175.74	136.75	3,758	92.11
9	349.03	338.86	346.66	176.13	174.21	175.49	136.21	3,157	92.17
10	355.63	345.63	352.86	178.08	175.57	177.76	139.32	4,000	92.17
11	358.77	349.64	352.69	179.59	177.29	178.53	138.88	3,964	92.39
12	↕	↕	↕	↕	↕	↕		↕	
13									
14	358.20	348.94	350.97	179.33	177.68	177.91	136.64	2,756	92.50
15	354.09	345.58	347.24	179.24	176.64	177.94	134.48	3,107	92.68
16	346.99	335.12	336.13	178.91	175.39	175.74	126.25	4,088	92.88
17	343.24	332.11	341.86	176.95	174.76	176.12	127.51	3,864	93.00
18	343.12	332.16	333.29	176.46	174.41	174.91	122.87	3,508	93.13
19	332.72	321.71	323.87	173.74	171.50	171.72	117.13	3,942	93.16
20	*	*	*	*	*	*	*	*	*
21	328.28	314.55	320.91	172.27	169.17	170.03	114.38	6,092	93.41
22	333.01	322.03	326.51	173.99	171.31	172.38	119.45	4,130	93.61
23	329.94	303.84	305.85	173.23	167.06	167.28	110.20	6,369	93.83
24	312.76	272.32	299.47	168.46	160.18	165.50	105.33	12,895	93.58
25	306.02	295.59	301.22	168.07	165.07	166.51	106.24	5,923	93.52
26	303.60	295.98	298.97	167.23	166.01	166.32	104.75	2,088	93.71
27	*	*	*	*	*	*	*	*	*
28	295.18	256.75	260.64	165.39	155.07	155.41	86.96	9,213	93.68
29	252.38	212.33	230.07	152.38	142.66	147.06	74.31	16,410	93.13
30	260.93	230.98	258.47	154.25	145.70	152.66	87.75	10,727	93.52
31	281.54	264.97	273.51	162.35	156.91	159.82	95.34	7,149	92.71
High			352.86			178.53	139.32	141,668	93.83
Low........			230.07			147.06	74.31		91.76

*Sunday   †Holiday

NOVEMBER, 1929

Date	Industrials			Railroads			Utilities Close	Daily Sales	40 Bonds
	High	Low	Close	High	Low	Close			
1	↕	↕	↕	↕	↕	↕	↕	↕	↕
2	•	•	•	•	•	•	•	•	•
3									
4	269.75	255.43	257.68	158.58	154.87	156.22	89.39	6,203	93.16
5	†	†	†	†	†	†	†	†	†
6	252.20	228.35	232.13	153.85	145.25	145.49	78.47	5,915	93.36
7	242.10	217.84	238.19	147.77	140.39	147.05	81.41	7,184	93.26
8	245.28	234.63	236.53	149.24	146.31	147.52	80.46	3,215	93.22
9	↕	↕	↕	↕	↕	↕	↕	↕	↕
10									
11	235.13	219.34	220.39	147.56	142.80	142.88	73.91	3,637	93.11
12	222.56	208.09	209.74	139.53	133.68	134.34	67.55	6,453	92.81
13	211.92	195.35	198.69	133.85	127.37	128.07	64.72	7,761	92.44
14	219.49	205.61	217.28	136.16	129.98	135.75	73.57	5,569	91.93
15	232.77	222.50	228.73	142.23	137.80	141.25	76.88	4,340	92.03
16	↕	↕	↕	↕	↕	↕	↕	↕	↕
17									
18	233.36	224.71	227.56	142.25	139.78	140.23	74.91	2,747	92.23
19	234.56	222.93	234.02	142.71	139.11	142.23	78.48	2,718	92.26
20	243.48	235.18	241.23	145.98	143.52	145.08	81.42	2,829	92.90
21	249.57	238.61	248.49	148.28	145.23	147.84	85.00	3,139	93.38
22	250.75	243.36	245.74	149.48	147.42	148.36	85.25	2,929	93.64
23	↕	↕	↕	↕	↕	↕	↕	↕	↕
24									
25	246.06	237.41	243.44	148.69	146.67	147.53	84.33	3,020	93.84
26	243.97	234.51	235.35	147.25	145.33	145.60	80.46	3,634	93.89
27	240.66	233.59	238.95	146.54	144.72	145.89	82.63	2,432	94.05
28	†	†	†	†	†	†	†	†	†
29	↕	↕	↕	↕	↕	↕	↕	↕	↕
30	†	†	†	†	†	†	†	†	†
High			257.68			156.22	89.39	72,460	94.05
Low........			198.69			128.07	64.72		91.93

*Sunday   †Holiday

DECEMBER, 1929

Date	Industrials High	Low	Close	Railroads High	Low	Close	Utilities Close	Daily Sales	40 Bonds
1 .... *									
2	243.39	236.13	241.70	146.03	144.13	144.61	83.50	2,513	94.13
3	251.13	241.38	249.61	147.30	145.01	146.81	87.62	3,809	94.39
4	256.63	248.05	254.64	150.03	147.58	149.50	90.83	4,437	94.39
5	256.45	249.55	251.51	150.40	148.55	149.41	90.95	4,377	94.46
6	261.52	250.27	260.12	152.31	148.44	151.48	92.55	4,715	94.58
7	265.65	258.40	263.46	152.16	151.29	151.84	93.96	3,003	94.57
8 .... *									
9	267.56	257.41	259.18	153.45	150.44	151.95	91.11	5,018	94.51
10	263.98	255.52	262.20	153.19	150.32	151.88	92.08	3,647	94.38
11	264.23	256.45	258.44	152.50	150.87	151.08	91.95	3,897	94.35
12	258.56	241.40	243.14	150.38	146.93	147.21	84.77	4,505	94.23
13	251.79	239.58	249.60	149.61	146.22	149.05	87.53	4,387	94.16
14	254.41	248.60	253.02	152.21	149.61	151.68	87.97	1,654	94.12
15 .... *									
16	253.17	244.34	245.88	151.25	149.10	149.55	84.33	2,592	94.06
17	250.23	243.63	249.58	149.98	148.98	149.61	86.03	2,438	93.87
18	250.51	245.03	246.84	149.70	148.75	148.95	85.98	2,285	93.91
19	247.14	238.80	240.42	148.65	147.05	147.21	83.28	3,412	94.00
20	241.92	227.20	230.89	146.62	142.56	143.02	79.58	5,546	93.80
21	237.26	231.04	235.42	145.79	144.46	145.42	80.88	1,734	93.73
22 .... *									
23	236.37	226.39	232.65	144.74	142.63	143.37	79.90	3,492	93.77
24	237.94	231.96	234.07	144.76	143.25	143.91	80.70	996	93.81
25 .... †									
26	242.62	233.89	240.96	144.90	143.96	144.70	82.93	2,577	93.76
27	246.35	239.13	240.66	145.26	143.58	143.80	83.62	3,354	93.71
28	240.89	236.52	238.43	143.80	143.06	143.30	82.90	1,635	93.76
29 .... *									
30	242.95	235.95	241.06	144.13	142.95	143.29	84.15	4,160	93.76
31	249.24	241.90	248.48	145.03	143.25	144.72	88.27	2,678	93.77
High			263.46			151.95	93.96	83,584	94.58
Low			230.89			143.02	79.58		93.71

*Sunday †Holiday

JANUARY, 1930

Date	Industrials High	Low	Close	Railroads High	Low	Close	Utilities High	Low	Close	Daily Sales	40 Bonds
1 .... †											
2	252.29	241.78	244.20	146.03	144.40	144.68	89.75	84.80	86.38	2,933	93.85
3	248.71	243.00	247.19	144.89	144.46	144.76	87.75	85.98	86.97	2,072	93.96
4	250.25	246.48	248.85	145.09	144.66	144.85	88.71	87.08	88.09	1,315	94.00
5 .... *											
6	250.37	245.49	248.10	144.85	144.26	144.68	88.43	86.48	87.27	2,172	93.96
7	249.40	243.80	246.50	144.55	144.00	144.07	87.38	85.55	86.17	2,029	94.07
8	248.04	243.80	245.70	145.40	144.30	144.96	87.18	85.89	86.51	1,639	94.24
9	250.52	245.67	249.68	145.57	144.69	145.25	89.66	87.00	89.43	2,397	94.34
10	252.91	248.80	250.03	145.85	145.38	145.55	90.33	88.27	88.64	2,386	94.34
11	249.49	247.38	248.71	145.64	145.05	145.41	88.65	87.78	88.31	874	94.31
12 .... *											
13	250.83	246.82	249.62	146.65	145.21	146.31	89.03	87.77	88.64	1,460	94.24
14	252.39	248.98	250.44	147.14	145.92	146.58	89.61	88.17	88.61	1,883	94.24
15	252.57	247.76	251.54	147.35	146.40	147.12	90.13	88.10	89.66	2,630	94.16
16	253.49	248.16	248.99	147.80	146.98	147.15	91.09	89.24	89.75	3,044	94.01
17	249.88	244.50	246.33	147.27	146.47	146.55	89.74	87.20	87.82	2,679	94.05
18	247.33	243.37	246.84	146.60	146.30	146.54	87.32	85.95	87.06	1,331	94.07
19 .... *											
20	248.92	244.86	247.31	146.71	146.05	146.43	88.02	86.77	87.55	1,693	93.98
21	250.62	246.25	249.58	147.36	146.50	146.91	88.59	87.23	88.28	2,233	93.84
22	251.85	248.60	250.19	147.59	146.91	147.42	89.17	87.81	88.25	2,306	93.78
23	254.39	249.62	253.52	148.41	147.16	148.16	89.15	87.58	88.65	3,229	93.69
24	258.98	252.98	256.31	148.90	147.91	148.25	90.50	88.56	89.37	3,481	93.72
25	259.40	256.00	259.06	148.84	148.16	148.70	90.72	89.32	90.64	1,527	93.80
26 .... *											
27	262.57	257.24	260.93	149.17	148.35	148.63	92.13	90.03	90.91	3,458	93.70
28	261.89	256.70	257.90	148.76	147.93	148.28	91.15	89.37	89.75	2,913	93.76
29	263.73	257.38	262.18	148.97	147.87	148.71	91.32	89.30	90.53	3,246	93.74
30	266.30	260.48	263.28	149.31	147.82	148.43	91.63	89.52	89.93	3,643	93.76
31	268.71	262.81	267.14	149.18	148.32	148.86	92.20	89.73	92.09	3,739	93.77
High			267.14			148.86			92.09	62,308	94.34
Low			244.20			144.07			86.17		93.69

*Sunday †Holiday

FEBRUARY, 1930

Date	Industrials High	Low	Close	Railroads High	Low	Close	Utilities High	Low	Close	Daily Sales	40 Bonds
1	269.20	265.67	268.41	149.49	148.75	149.40	93.75	91.92	93.27	1,925	93.75
2	*										
3	271.54	264.84	266.54	151.00	149.59	150.08	93.79	91.20	91.49	3,798	93.78
4	270.00	264.41	268.48	151.15	149.64	150.30	93.61	90.86	93.42	3,225	93.72
5	274.01	268.85	272.06	151.66	150.33	151.20	96.25	93.73	94.70	4,362	93.82
6	273.59	266.96	268.56	152.00	150.45	151.07	96.11	93.31	93.82	3,709	93.92
7	271.62	265.36	267.82	154.12	151.03	153.10	95.71	92.86	93.78	3,391	94.01
8	270.50	266.52	269.78	156.28	153.20	156.07	94.99	93.41	94.31	1,658	94.08
9	*										
10	271.78	266.37	268.56	157.39	155.13	156.15	96.22	94.00	95.32	3,166	94.05
11	272.67	267.00	271.05	156.30	154.37	155.23	97.81	95.14	97.02	3,322	94.02
12	†	†	†	†	†	†	†	†	†	†	†
13	275.00	268.97	272.27	156.22	154.95	155.24	99.22	96.75	97.78	3,669	93.82
14	274.20	268.60	271.52	156.84	154.44	156.26	99.38	96.96	98.28	3,514	93.84
15	272.23	267.91	269.25	155.98	155.16	155.25	98.07	97.00	97.38	1,697	93.81
16	*										
17	271.62	265.29	270.54	155.48	154.51	155.09	98.99	96.31	98.66	3,289	93.80
18	274.41	268.98	270.73	156.18	154.65	155.44	100.63	98.28	99.24	3,795	93.80
19	273.35	267.09	268.46	155.89	154.78	154.95	101.28	98.45	99.02	3,485	93.83
20	269.72	262.43	263.41	154.25	152.27	152.49	99.75	96.03	96.58	3,661	93.88
21	266.68	262.01	265.81	154.53	151.91	154.11	98.52	96.44	98.11	2,567	93.96
22	†	†	†	†	†	†	†	†	†	†	†
23	*										
24	266.33	261.40	262.47	153.60	152.73	152.97	98.47	96.20	96.70	2,320	93.98
25	264.64	259.78	262.80	153.02	151.57	152.17	97.95	95.65	97.09	2,633	93.95
26	269.92	262.94	269.06	153.11	152.04	152.90	98.91	96.85	98.18	3,018	93.97
27	272.13	267.43	269.39	153.30	152.20	152.66	100.21	98.44	99.36	3,310	94.00
28	272.55	267.41	271.11	152.78	151.64	152.34	100.97	97.97	100.50	3,210	94.12
High			272.27			156.26			100.50	68,723	94.12
Low			262.47			150.08			91.49		93.72

*Sunday †Holiday

MARCH, 1930

Date	Industrials High	Low	Close	Railroads High	Low	Close	Utilities High	Low	Close	Daily Sales	40 Bonds
1	274.16	270.38	273.24	152.65	152.28	152.52	102.03	100.35	101.64	1,807	94.02
2	*										
3	274.47	269.59	271.11	153.66	152.35	153.05	102.48	100.09	100.90	3,634	94.04
4	275.19	269.16	273.51	152.92	152.00	152.28	102.36	100.17	101.48	3,456	94.04
5	276.10	269.03	270.59	153.61	152.15	152.61	102.30	99.21	100.01	3,715	94.17
6	276.05	269.01	274.51	153.36	152.18	152.98	101.55	99.81	100.86	3,350	94.31
7	278.48	272.84	275.57	153.23	152.43	152.60	101.50	99.98	100.38	3,635	94.45
8	276.94	274.03	275.46	152.79	152.12	152.43	101.17	100.26	100.71	1,691	94.47
9	*										
10	279.40	273.71	276.85	152.82	152.01	152.50	101.26	99.43	100.42	3,994	94.46
11	278.76	274.25	276.25	152.78	152.21	152.54	101.01	99.69	100.38	2,636	94.51
12	277.06	270.01	272.13	152.91	151.33	152.16	101.00	98.41	98.86	4,470	94.59
13	274.77	269.60	273.47	152.30	151.46	151.84	100.43	98.19	99.99	3,853	94.94
14	275.82	270.38	271.34	152.56	151.60	152.08	101.21	98.91	99.50	3,951	95.02
15	271.89	268.97	270.25	151.91	151.21	151.36	99.17	98.09	98.36	1,531	95.21
16	*										
17	274.84	268.94	274.26	151.75	150.94	151.63	99.63	97.63	99.36	3,640	95.51
18	279.79	273.90	277.27	154.73	152.16	154.26	101.13	99.24	100.76	4,248	95.69
19	281.05	274.91	277.88	155.51	154.00	155.27	102.27	100.29	101.03	4,336	95.78
20	282.23	275.25	279.41	156.32	155.24	155.78	102.63	100.76	101.75	3,263	96.16
21	284.08	276.78	280.55	156.28	155.38	155.68	103.29	101.08	102.07	4,629	95.92
22	281.66	274.63	276.43	155.55	154.99	155.11	102.56	99.96	100.22	2,315	95.96
23	*										
24	280.92	275.03	279.11	155.82	155.00	155.61	101.86	99.81	101.05	4,126	95.96
25	284.01	278.21	280.50	156.14	155.38	155.47	102.07	99.58	99.81	4,526	95.80
26	285.38	279.31	283.22	156.49	155.23	155.83	104.17	99.92	104.01	5,029	95.76
27	286.10	279.98	281.63	156.35	155.16	155.41	105.33	102.13	102.85	4,707	95.58
28	287.06	280.83	283.85	157.40	155.27	157.01	105.34	103.22	104.83	5,065	95.64
29	287.88	283.00	286.19	158.38	157.26	157.94	105.88	104.43	105.41	2,791	95.51
30	*										
31	289.13	282.85	286.10	158.24	156.98	157.28	107.11	104.50	106.13	5,161	95.41
High			286.19			157.94			106.13	96,559	96.16
Low			270.25			151.36			98.36		94.02

*Sunday †Holiday

APRIL, 1930

Date	Industrials High	Industrials Low	Industrials Close	Railroads High	Railroads Low	Railroads Close	Utilities High	Utilities Low	Utilities Close	Daily Sales	40 Bonds
1	290.15	283.64	287.11	157.69	156.71	157.02	107.38	104.09	106.63	5,395	95.35
2	290.15	283.59	285.27	156.69	155.65	155.86	107.67	104.39	104.75	5,304	95.44
3	288.17	282.29	285.77	156.34	155.35	155.78	106.26	103.81	105.50	4,634	95.49
4	291.44	284.92	288.35	157.07	155.58	156.68	107.66	105.08	106.50	5,932	95.43
5	291.06	286.21	289.96	156.74	156.25	156.39	107.43	105.39	107.10	2,524	95.33
6	*	*	*	*	*	*	*	*	*		
7	293.43	287.03	290.19	156.22	155.56	155.73	108.30	105.58	106.50	5,490	95.30
8	291.89	285.96	288.36	156.29	154.70	155.32	107.08	105.03	105.28	4,689	95.28
9	293.36	287.37	291.15	155.71	154.70	155.15	108.36	105.03	107.83	5,189	95.23
10	295.98	289.18	292.19	155.43	154.54	154.88	109.76	107.68	107.92	5,681	95.25
11	296.35	288.42	292.65	155.15	153.97	154.33	110.11	107.04	108.41	5,627	95.20
12	294.54	290.17	293.43	154.21	153.93	154.04	109.02	107.20	108.62	2,119	95.23
13	*	*	*	*	*	*	*	*	*		
14	295.81	289.72	293.18	153.94	153.00	153.43	110.00	107.65	108.53	4,150	95.13
15	295.69	289.34	293.26	153.21	152.35	152.65	109.38	107.01	108.61	4,219	95.08
16	297.25	290.27	292.20	152.83	151.66	151.93	110.17	107.23	107.73	4,398	94.91
17	296.05	290.38	294.07	152.19	151.28	152.08	109.11	107.02	108.28	3,943	94.83
18	†	†	†	†	†	†	†	†	†		†
19											
20											
21	295.88	287.24	288.23	152.28	150.81	150.96	108.93	105.87	106.22	4,492	94.86
22	291.39	284.28	290.01	151.08	149.90	150.61	107.44	104.65	107.10	4,589	94.83
23	293.27	286.25	288.78	150.84	150.21	150.38	109.16	106.86	107.95	5,569	94.87
24	290.58	283.74	286.18	150.82	149.83	150.30	108.75	106.30	107.07	5,233	94.78
25	289.28	283.68	285.76	150.18	149.54	149.85	108.78	106.23	107.19	4,726	94.95
26	287.70	283.26	285.46	149.76	149.18	149.43	108.30	106.45	107.16	2,316	94.95
27	*	*	*	*	*	*	*	*	*		
28	286.12	275.71	276.94	148.88	146.64	146.72	107.21	103.73	103.96	4,852	94.85
29	280.71	272.24	278.43	146.35	144.23	144.98	104.96	102.18	104.05	5,410	94.77
30	283.51	275.97	279.23	145.78	144.21	145.08	105.96	104.06	105.15	4,553	94.87
High			294.07			157.02			108.62	111,041	95.49
Low			276.94			144.98			103.96		94.77

*Sunday †Holiday

MAY, 1930

Date	Industrials High	Industrials Low	Industrials Close	Railroads High	Railroads Low	Railroads Close	Utilities High	Utilities Low	Utilities Close	Daily Sales	40 Bonds
1	281.95	273.00	274.59	144.97	140.10	140.68	106.18	102.35	102.86	4,640	94.87
2	276.81	264.93	266.56	141.68	139.56	140.33	103.90	98.40	98.57	5,986	95.23
3	266.80	256.99	258.31	141.35	139.71	140.24	98.26	94.35	94.61	4,868	95.07
4	*	*	*	*	*	*	*	*	*		*
5	262.84	249.82	259.68	140.66	137.61	139.16	95.81	90.23	94.20	8,279	94.85
6	270.34	259.04	268.81	143.18	139.95	143.03	99.20	94.78	98.41	4,756	94.91
7	272.15	262.20	263.69	143.78	141.82	142.16	99.74	96.45	96.95	4,295	95.05
8	266.11	257.74	263.93	142.25	140.74	141.82	98.13	95.25	97.61	3,756	95.13
9	269.08	261.64	267.29	143.21	141.81	143.03	99.41	96.93	98.72	3,009	95.14
10	272.20	266.70	272.01	143.25	142.93	143.12	101.27	99.03	101.04	1,880	95.22
11	*	*	*	*	*	*	*	*	*		*
12	275.11	268.56	270.16	143.55	142.86	143.26	102.20	99.71	100.54	3,027	95.25
13	276.09	269.51	274.17	143.46	142.93	143.17	101.90	100.11	101.50	2,697	95.17
14	277.22	272.22	274.40	145.38	143.38	144.61	103.60	101.33	103.40	3,180	95.11
15	274.35	268.45	269.91	144.48	143.56	143.69	104.10	101.63	102.28	2,675	95.16
16	272.96	268.54	271.52	144.58	143.75	144.52	102.99	101.72	102.28	2,087	95.12
17	273.43	270.72	272.41	145.01	144.66	144.93	102.38	101.73	102.08	791	95.20
18	*	*	*	*	*	*	*	*	*		
19	272.36	264.63	265.87	144.90	143.76	143.80	101.71	99.00	99.43	2,414	95.11
20	268.40	260.76	267.10	144.11	143.16	143.86	99.78	96.90	99.23	3,527	95.17
21	268.94	262.67	265.52	145.38	143.98	144.80	99.94	97.90	98.81	2,078	95.16
22	268.65	262.53	266.89	144.83	144.40	144.55	99.53	97.83	99.10	1,860	95.21
23	272.14	267.01	270.01	144.62	144.07	144.45	99.86	97.96	99.16	2,158	95.25
24	272.15	268.79	271.33	145.21	144.30	145.11	100.10	99.05	99.92	961	95.21
25	*	*	*	*	*	*	*	*	*		
26	276.18	270.64	272.14	145.90	145.19	145.31	101.41	99.64	100.13	2,247	95.21
27	274.72	270.54	272.43	145.20	144.67	144.77	102.46	100.20	101.61	2,258	95.28
28	275.17	270.64	273.84	145.21	143.73	144.31	103.16	101.43	101.99	2,405	95.34
29	276.66	273.05	275.07	144.30	143.20	143.86	103.28	101.74	102.95	2,204	95.25
30	†	†	†	†	†	†	†	†	†		†
31	†										
High			275.07			145.31			103.40	78,040	95.34
Low			258.31			139.16			94.20		94.85

*Sunday †Holiday

JUNE, 1930

Date	Industrials High	Low	Close	Railroads High	Low	Close	Utilities High	Low	Close	Daily Sales	40 Bonds
1											
2	276.86	273.03	274.45	144.13	143.20	143.73	103.61	102.43	103.03	1,711	95.30
3	274.69	270.01	271.18	143.95	143.10	143.49	103.00	101.46	102.05	1,750	95.28
4	274.03	269.54	272.44	142.95	142.48	142.66	102.65	101.48	102.30	1,694	95.26
5	272.65	266.90	268.59	142.89	141.92	142.06	102.17	99.68	100.37	2,393	95.28
6	268.69	263.29	263.93	141.75	140.88	141.13	100.05	97.88	98.01	2,155	95.31
7	262.33	256.87	257.82	140.96	139.77	139.86	97.48	95.53	96.03	2,246	95.36
8											
9	259.60	249.51	250.78	139.65	137.86	138.01	96.58	91.75	92.19	4,646	95.29
10	257.72	247.62	257.29	138.81	136.73	138.40	95.78	91.11	95.41	4,773	95.22
11	257.24	243.90	249.08	137.36	135.66	135.88	95.75	90.20	91.65	4,477	95.27
12	250.90	241.00	247.18	135.96	134.31	135.13	93.40	89.03	91.22	3,901	95.26
13	251.63	243.27	249.69	135.75	134.52	135.30	92.71	89.61	91.84	2,225	95.30
14	250.25	243.48	244.25	135.25	134.44	134.46	91.91	88.85	88.91	1,256	95.38
15											
16	242.18	228.94	230.05	133.60	130.70	130.85	88.28	82.60	83.21	5,657	95.35
17	234.94	224.37	228.57	132.16	129.58	131.33	85.33	81.35	83.10	5,019	95.26
18	226.29	212.27	218.84	131.36	128.18	128.97	82.03	76.94	79.50	6,426	95.16
19	229.83	219.83	228.97	131.39	129.13	131.21	84.68	79.81	83.80	3,763	95.15
20	232.69	219.70	221.92	132.00	129.88	130.05	85.41	80.21	81.08	5,656	95.36
21	219.78	212.32	215.30	129.55	128.41	128.60	80.55	78.23	78.54	1,967	95.30
22											
23	221.26	209.16	219.58	129.45	127.36	128.88	81.60	76.52	80.96	3,836	95.16
24	222.89	211.07	211.84	129.99	125.71	126.00	82.01	77.35	77.66	2,866	95.15
25	216.80	207.74	215.58	125.98	123.71	125.03	79.10	75.80	78.00	3,396	94.88
26	222.11	214.25	220.58	128.46	125.43	128.13	81.18	77.93	80.47	2,272	94.89
27	222.84	213.97	218.78	128.80	126.24	126.98	81.40	78.33	79.95	2,081	94.97
28	220.05	216.19	219.12	127.02	126.31	126.63	80.16	79.07	80.06	587	94.99
29											
30	226.85	219.06	226.34	128.20	126.58	128.00	82.91	80.35	82.79	1,843	94.91
High			274.45			143.73			103.03	78,593	95.38
Low			211.84			125.03			77.66		94.88

*Sunday   †Holiday

JULY, 1930

Date	Industrials High	Low	Close	Railroads High	Low	Close	Utilities High	Low	Close	Daily Sales	40 Bonds
1	229.53	221.92	223.03	129.94	128.01	128.97	83.83	81.10	81.20	2,279	95.07
2	227.24	222.14	225.25	129.76	128.63	129.23	82.90	80.95	82.33	1,231	95.16
3	226.26	219.94	222.46	129.50	127.66	128.36	82.33	80.35	80.85	1,384	95.21
4											
5											
6											
7	221.31	216.33	218.33	128.40	127.30	127.53	80.34	78.72	79.07	1,481	95.33
8	220.22	214.64	219.08	127.79	126.55	127.65	79.67	77.75	79.33	1,555	95.28
9	223.52	219.11	222.04	129.71	128.28	129.51	81.02	79.80	80.40	1,358	95.28
10	228.35	219.18	227.39	132.50	129.56	132.28	82.78	79.96	82.45	2,167	95.40
11	228.65	223.97	224.86	132.42	131.58	131.86	83.20	81.42	81.94	1,526	95.39
12	229.51	223.80	229.23	132.43	131.82	132.39	83.61	81.85	83.58	906	95.41
13											
14	234.54	229.02	234.21	134.70	133.06	134.51	85.65	83.21	85.45	2,738	95.48
15	237.19	231.73	233.79	134.98	133.71	134.18	87.13	84.80	85.91	3,092	95.54
16	236.47	230.59	235.63	134.44	133.39	134.18	86.58	84.91	86.16	2,585	95.55
17	240.27	234.03	239.07	134.79	133.68	134.67	86.95	85.42	86.55	2,498	95.56
18	242.01	236.47	240.57	135.71	134.66	135.46	88.09	86.09	87.67	2,751	95.59
19	240.64	236.01	236.65	135.48	135.18	135.25	87.68	86.31	86.55	872	95.64
20											
21	236.58	228.72	229.29	134.81	133.45	133.61	86.28	83.72	83.86	1,947	95.55
22	235.29	228.81	234.30	134.20	132.83	133.92	85.43	83.25	84.95	2,081	95.59
23	241.76	234.94	239.33	134.73	134.08	134.58	87.37	85.36	86.63	2,527	95.72
24	239.51	234.65	235.51	134.58	134.15	134.15	86.84	85.02	85.49	1,475	95.82
25	238.58	233.77	237.48	134.32	133.83	133.95	86.09	84.77	85.91	1,356	95.86
26	241.14	237.43	240.31	134.09	133.82	134.06	87.55	86.15	87.24	994	95.88
27											
28	243.65	239.04	240.81	134.83	134.11	134.38	89.75	87.60	88.65	2,425	95.89
29	241.53	237.00	238.40	133.98	132.00	132.49	89.67	87.63	88.80	1,856	95.97
30	239.93	230.53	231.08	132.41	131.45	131.55	88.95	85.64	85.78	2,507	95.98
31	235.19	229.09	233.99	131.48	130.33	130.95	86.86	84.55	86.46	2,163	95.99
High			240.81			135.43			88.80	47,746	95.99
Low			218.33			127.53			79.07		95.07

*Sunday   †Holiday

AUGUST, 1930

Date	Industrials High	Low	Close	Railroads High	Low	Close	Utilities High	Low	Close	Daily Sales	40 Bonds
1	235.78	231.86	233.57	130.93	130.62	130.77	86.21	84.34	84.79	1,090	96.02
2	234.99	232.80	234.50	131.01	130.95	131.01	85.40	84.56	85.32	366	96.03
3	*	*	*	*	*	*	*	*	*	*	*
4	238.57	233.26	238.16	131.56	130.93	131.48	86.96	84.66	86.73	1,202	96.19
5	240.95	237.22	238.47	132.63	131.48	132.06	86.94	85.88	86.40	1,221	96.25
6	237.99	233.67	234.38	131.68	130.56	130.62	85.81	84.35	84.58	1,317	96.28
7	234.39	230.50	232.69	130.43	129.19	129.35	84.37	82.93	83.70	1,451	96.33
8	231.73	222.24	222.82	129.07	127.13	127.48	83.43	80.03	80.19	3,308	96.29
9	224.32	218.82	222.59	127.79	126.64	127.40	80.76	79.20	80.25	1,508	96.25
10	*	*	*	*	*	*	*	*	*	*	*
11	226.05	220.09	224.13	128.70	126.83	128.26	81.59	79.38	80.83	1,745	96.26
12	223.74	216.48	217.24	127.96	126.55	126.74	81.20	78.98	79.36	2,085	96.28
13	221.35	214.49	220.35	127.31	126.05	126.92	80.55	78.01	80.27	2,289	96.37
14	224.38	219.24	221.08	127.65	126.23	126.56	81.30	79.68	80.38	1,525	96.46
15	229.44	219.82	228.55	128.26	126.18	128.20	82.80	80.25	82.77	2,106	96.47
16	229.91	224.61	228.02	129.31	128.31	129.03	83.28	81.98	82.85	975	96.48
17	*	*	*	*	*	*	*	*	*	*	*
18	229.08	224.42	227.79	129.10	128.12	128.59	82.96	81.09	82.35	1,414	96.56
19	233.46	227.43	230.68	129.49	128.51	129.10	84.11	82.18	83.05	1,862	96.61
20	235.26	229.84	232.98	129.16	128.74	128.91	85.15	83.30	84.41	1,818	96.64
21	234.91	229.21	231.27	128.34	127.51	127.77	84.63	83.08	83.65	1,713	96.67
22	234.04	229.64	232.63	127.73	126.81	127.46	84.53	83.18	84.07	1,336	96.73
23	234.74	232.35	234.42	127.67	127.21	127.62	84.60	84.06	84.46	690	96.87
24	*	*	*	*	*	*	*	*	*	*	*
25	236.46	230.68	231.52	128.73	127.81	127.95	85.26	83.71	83.98	1,600	96.79
26	236.30	230.73	235.47	129.16	127.86	129.08	85.28	83.51	85.10	1,747	97.10
27	239.54	235.38	237.93	130.33	129.33	129.83	86.54	85.02	85.79	2,200	97.09
28	239.33	235.19	237.79	130.21	129.55	129.96	86.19	85.09	85.64	1,437	97.02
29	241.35	236.75	240.42	131.55	130.12	131.28	87.01	85.45	86.76	1,859	97.08
30	†	†	†	†	†	†	†	†	†	†	†
31											
High			240.42			132.06			86.76	39,870	97.10
Low			217.24			126.56			79.36		96.02

*Sunday   †Holiday

SEPTEMBER, 1930

Date	Industrials High	Low	Close	Railroads High	Low	Close	Utilities High	Low	Close	Daily Sales	40 Bonds
1	†	†	†	†	†	†	†	†	†	†	†
2	242.77	238.51	240.42	131.91	131.16	131.60	87.34	86.02	86.66	1,774	97.09
3	242.40	236.71	237.54	131.59	131.03	131.26	86.58	85.22	85.48	1,745	97.15
4	239.65	234.35	236.04	131.40	130.64	130.97	85.73	84.13	84.66	1,519	97.27
5	240.93	236.09	240.37	131.44	130.73	131.32	86.18	84.64	86.10	1,652	97.29
6	244.48	239.90	243.64	132.20	131.54	132.16	87.44	85.90	87.19	1,409	97.31
7	*	*	*	*	*	*	*	*	*	*	*
8	246.08	241.78	242.84	132.48	131.69	132.03	88.22	86.79	87.07	2,241	97.31
9	245.48	241.55	244.29	132.57	131.89	132.38	88.38	86.73	88.34	1,942	97.24
10	247.21	243.30	245.09	133.20	132.21	132.73	89.60	88.12	88.77	2,481	97.21
11	245.23	241.67	242.88	132.94	132.34	132.66	88.95	87.72	88.24	1,739	97.14
12	244.42	239.49	241.17	132.72	131.78	131.87	89.20	87.16	87.47	1,906	97.18
13	241.34	237.22	240.34	131.97	131.50	131.89	87.85	86.41	87.58	1,022	97.16
14	*	*	*	*	*	*	*	*	*	*	*
15	239.96	234.95	236.62	131.81	130.83	131.29	87.59	86.03	86.40	1,563	97.18
16	237.75	232.85	237.22	131.36	130.62	130.94	86.98	85.43	86.81	1,765	97.27
17	239.31	236.51	237.74	131.10	130.70	130.86	87.90	86.71	87.51	1,189	97.36
18	237.45	233.47	234.18	130.69	130.17	130.33	87.31	85.89	86.18	1,377	97.39
19	233.52	226.39	229.02	130.22	129.25	129.71	85.63	83.68	84.33	2,948	97.50
20	231.03	226.99	229.85	129.84	129.45	129.75	84.65	83.24	84.13	832	97.50
21	*	*	*	*	*	*	*	*	*	*	*
22	229.29	222.00	222.78	129.62	128.24	128.55	83.97	81.13	81.39	2,333	97.48
23	227.30	221.82	226.75	128.98	127.71	128.43	82.95	81.35	82.70	1,923	97.53
24	228.87	218.08	222.10	128.38	127.02	127.64	83.71	80.36	81.57	3,442	97.58
25	223.89	215.31	217.75	127.80	126.50	126.67	81.80	78.60	79.60	3,068	97.64
26	220.21	211.31	213.27	126.68	125.16	125.42	80.66	78.38	78.80	3,705	97.66
27	214.88	210.17	212.52	125.00	123.68	124.19	79.50	78.30	78.80	1,710	97.61
28	*	*	*	*	*	*	*	*	*	*	*
29	216.96	207.30	208.14	124.47	122.22	122.50	80.24	76.85	77.15	3,762	97.68
30	209.95	201.95	204.90	123.04	120.87	121.67	77.21	75.21	75.91	4,497	97.53
High			245.09			132.73			88.77	53,545	97.68
Low			204.90			121.67			75.91		97.09

*Sunday   †Holiday

OCTOBER, 1930

Date	Industrials High	Low	Close	Railroads High	Low	Close	Utilities High	Low	Close	Daily Sales	40 Bonds
1	215.32	205.92	214.14	124.21	121.53	124.06	79.95	76.51	79.30	3,155	97.70
2	214.76	206.25	211.04	124.11	122.35	122.89	79.80	76.95	78.46	2,316	97.66
3	216.89	211.13	214.18	124.22	122.90	123.57	80.13	78.55	79.38	2,053	97.57
4	215.83	210.34	211.10	123.52	122.45	122.57	79.70	77.90	78.29	898	97.57
5	*			*			*			*	*
6	209.01	201.90	202.76	121.62	119.58	119.90	77.44	74.57	75.09	2,365	97.40
7	207.04	198.51	203.62	120.67	119.13	120.20	75.83	72.80	74.53	3,568	97.10
8	205.21	198.61	200.56	120.60	119.23	119.70	75.01	73.20	73.93	2,067	97.04
9	199.96	190.17	192.00	119.29	116.50	117.34	73.46	69.28	69.91	5,051	96.71
10	198.86	186.70	198.50	118.18	115.14	117.83	71.69	67.35	71.38	6,297	96.43
11	199.80	192.00	193.05	117.67	116.23	116.54	72.23	69.32	69.48	1,728	96.57
12	*			*			*			*	*
13	†			†			†			†	†
14	198.01	186.99	196.70	116.88	115.00	116.67	71.43	67.68	71.00	3,389	96.41
15	201.64	193.40	200.26	117.87	116.58	117.64	72.96	70.51	72.55	2,378	96.56
16	200.13	194.78	196.62	117.96	117.15	117.31	72.50	70.68	71.18	1,855	96.52
17	195.30	186.74	187.37	117.13	114.92	114.94	70.71	68.02	68.16	2,656	96.46
18	187.84	183.63	185.29	114.64	113.53	113.67	67.90	66.19	66.76	2,162	96.41
19	*			*			*			*	*
20	194.44	187.07	193.32	115.17	113.47	115.00	69.64	66.90	69.18	2,139	96.41
21	193.95	184.22	186.40	114.92	113.33	113.60	69.58	66.55	67.33	2,432	96.24
22	188.34	181.53	184.98	113.77	112.07	112.90	67.82	65.60	66.88	2,742	96.01
23	190.95	184.75	188.10	113.91	110.82	111.10	69.02	66.86	67.98	2,665	95.84
24	195.79	189.07	195.09	113.86	110.77	113.75	70.55	68.42	70.44	2,763	95.76
25	196.94	192.32	193.34	114.19	113.30	113.51	71.60	70.23	70.47	1,152	95.87
26	*			*			*			*	*
27	195.73	189.17	195.09	114.21	112.94	114.07	71.31	69.46	71.01	1,812	95.92
28	198.59	193.28	194.95	115.72	114.76	115.23	72.34	70.92	71.47	2,016	96.01
29	194.35	189.33	190.73	115.15	114.40	114.74	71.24	70.05	70.23	1,673	96.01
30	190.55	185.99	188.07	114.44	113.64	113.88	70.19	68.61	69.38	1,914	96.03
31	188.00	181.64	183.35	113.47	112.19	112.50	69.17	67.30	67.73	2,249	96.00
High			214.18			124.06			79.38	65,497	97.70
Low			183.35			111.10			66.76		95.76

*Sunday †Holiday

NOVEMBER, 1930

Date	Industrials High	Low	Close	Railroads High	Low	Close	Utilities High	Low	Close	Daily Sales	40 Bonds
1	185.65	181.26	184.89	112.84	112.10	112.66	68.14	66.70	67.60	1,001	95.99
2	*			*			*			*	*
3	187.23	183.12	185.39	113.46	112.74	113.19	68.63	67.51	68.00	1,264	96.04
4	†			†			†			†	†
5	185.47	178.78	179.81	113.23	111.59	111.66	67.91	64.98	65.20	2,146	95.89
6	182.40	177.80	180.72	111.58	110.44	110.87	65.80	63.79	65.06	2,447	95.82
7	181.00	172.85	174.38	110.41	106.62	106.91	65.00	61.94	62.36	3,368	95.76
8	176.51	171.54	173.14	107.07	105.60	105.70	63.11	60.67	60.96	2,071	95.63
9	*			*			*			*	*
10	177.07	168.32	171.60	106.43	103.04	103.94	62.39	58.82	59.68	4,423	95.38
11	176.93	169.38	173.30	104.90	102.94	104.21	62.17	59.21	60.81	3,334	95.36
12	177.50	168.58	177.33	104.96	102.01	104.33	62.50	59.08	62.34	3,420	95.30
13	183.08	174.96	180.38	107.01	104.48	106.43	64.91	61.64	64.11	3,451	95.40
14	184.64	177.69	184.03	108.40	106.56	107.80	66.35	63.76	65.75	2,641	95.51
15	187.59	182.39	186.68	108.98	108.03	108.67	66.86	65.34	66.46	1,710	95.53
16	*			*			*			*	*
17	185.13	178.86	180.50	108.32	106.78	106.91	65.89	63.38	64.18	2,138	95.54
18	184.16	177.63	183.42	107.16	105.40	106.62	65.13	63.10	64.93	2,023	95.44
19	188.61	182.21	187.57	108.51	107.00	108.31	67.21	64.61	66.95	2,481	95.60
20	191.04	185.76	187.09	109.70	108.70	109.12	67.46	65.76	66.16	2,627	95.63
21	191.28	185.32	190.30	112.65	109.19	112.17	67.46	65.50	67.11	2,245	95.57
22	190.12	186.92	188.04	111.69	110.87	110.91	67.20	66.13	66.65	988	95.58
23	*			*			*			*	*
24	189.08	184.32	188.27	110.47	109.48	109.86	66.91	65.41	66.62	1,631	95.59
25	191.28	185.17	185.47	110.82	109.19	109.47	67.80	65.91	66.07	2,153	95.57
26	186.98	181.93	183.11	108.99	107.34	107.55	65.78	64.15	64.46	1,950	95.51
27	†			†			†			†	†
28	183.06	178.88	180.91	106.43	104.20	105.04	64.41	62.95	63.56	1,744	95.27
29	183.82	179.96	183.39	105.73	104.46	105.54	64.22	63.26	64.10	697	95.07
30	*			*			*			*	*
High			190.30			113.19			68.00	51,946	96.04
Low			171.60			103.94			59.68		95.07

*Sunday †Holiday

DECEMBER, 1930

Date	Industrials			Railroads			Utilities			Daily Sales	40 Bonds
	High	Low	Close	High	Low	Close	High	Low	Close		
1	186.33	182.32	185.48	107.28	105.59	106.93	65.11	63.68	64.85	1,100	94.87
2	187.96	183.36	186.82	107.54	106.31	107.16	65.72	64.32	65.30	1,580	94.98
3	187.07	183.30	184.11	106.60	105.30	105.44	65.38	64.15	64.43	1,217	95.02
4	184.06	179.75	180.99	105.12	103.96	104.32	64.23	62.58	62.91	1,591	94.91
5	181.70	177.26	181.11	104.23	102.80	103.84	63.08	61.62	62.75	1,589	94.87
6	180.58	177.58	178.37	103.82	102.81	103.11	62.73	61.78	61.94	720	94.85
7	*			*			*			*	*
8	177.98	174.27	176.09	102.40	99.90	100.46	61.89	60.70	61.08	1,984	94.65
9	178.21	173.88	176.50	100.87	98.60	99.94	61.87	60.07	61.40	2,116	94.15
10	178.10	170.21	173.98	100.30	97.93	98.80	61.75	59.14	59.86	3,147	93.73
11	173.02	166.97	170.31	98.67	96.30	97.68	59.98	57.81	59.18	2,889	93.28
12	173.08	167.99	168.68	98.27	96.88	97.16	60.19	58.50	58.69	2,025	93.04
13	167.48	162.88	163.34	96.72	95.21	95.42	58.33	56.88	56.93	1,957	93.02
14	*			*			*			*	*
15	166.13	160.66	163.34	95.40	92.97	93.58	57.68	56.15	56.89	3,440	93.17
16	166.04	156.44	157.51	94.53	91.12	91.65	58.18	54.90	55.14	4,156	92.88
17	166.83	154.45	165.60	94.64	89.49	93.77	58.05	54.13	57.81	5,006	92.83
18	171.64	164.99	166.71	97.34	94.36	95.86	60.10	57.85	58.66	3,290	93.27
19	170.43	164.96	168.99	100.12	95.96	99.74	59.28	57.88	58.52	2,270	93.64
20	170.91	168.01	169.42	100.17	98.67	98.96	59.58	58.59	59.03	1,028	94.15
21	*	*		*	*		*	*		*	*
22	170.02	162.15	162.42	98.49	95.78	95.91	59.10	56.89	57.10	2,104	94.23
23	165.93	160.22	162.93	96.76	94.48	96.14	57.71	55.94	56.94	2,453	94.04
24	168.00	163.57	165.20	97.42	96.10	96.78	58.71	57.22	57.98	1,582	94.22
25	†	†	†	†	†	†	†	†	†	†	†
26	166.96	160.63	161.18	96.61	94.69	94.79	58.15	56.43	56.78	1,801	94.38
27	161.33	158.70	160.30	95.02	94.15	94.62	56.96	56.15	56.57	1,395	94.29
28	*			*			*			*	*
29	162.60	158.41	160.16	94.76	92.78	93.44	57.31	55.91	56.41	2,789	94.59
30	165.34	159.68	163.09	98.22	93.44	96.05	58.68	56.36	58.23	3,431	94.72
31	167.99	162.48	164.58	97.87	96.25	96.58	61.23	58.32	60.80	1,935	95.20
High			186.82			107.16			65.30	58,764	95.20
Low			157.51			91.65			55.14		92.83

*Sunday †Holiday

JANUARY, 1931

Date	Industrials			Railroads			Utilities			Daily Sales	40 Bonds
	High	Low	Close	High	Low	Close	High	Low	Close		
1	†	†	†	†	†	†	†	†	†	†	†
2	170.09	161.46	169.84	98.89	96.07	98.63	61.99	58.63	61.81	2,031	95.54
3	173.03	169.76	172.12	101.01	99.58	100.87	63.19	61.80	63.01	1,548	95.99
4	*			*			*			*	*
5	173.30	167.77	170.71	101.02	99.50	100.28	62.25	60.72	61.33	2,087	96.06
6	173.48	168.43	172.66	102.72	100.53	102.27	62.46	60.85	62.15	1,907	96.38
7	175.32	171.07	171.86	104.66	103.20	103.91	63.10	61.92	62.24	2,140	96.54
8	173.62	170.02	173.04	104.79	102.67	104.61	63.25	61.56	63.08	1,706	96.54
9	175.66	169.68	170.18	107.13	104.52	105.04	64.26	62.28	62.40	2,795	96.45
10	172.32	168.99	171.71	105.51	104.74	105.42	62.75	61.81	62.43	779	96.40
11	*			*			*			*	*
12	172.12	167.23	167.99	104.86	103.06	103.51	62.70	61.18	61.43	1,501	96.36
13	168.42	164.76	165.95	103.41	102.20	103.15	61.88	60.51	60.99	1,713	96.10
14	168.20	164.90	167.46	104.24	103.08	103.97	61.60	60.48	61.42	1,276	96.02
15	167.72	161.95	162.82	104.57	102.88	103.06	61.39	59.14	59.32	1,933	96.22
16	165.55	161.52	164.94	103.75	102.41	103.73	60.33	59.13	60.21	1,321	96.25
17	166.10	162.74	162.89	103.93	103.27	103.41	60.83	60.04	60.17	642	96.39
18	*			*			*			*	*
19	163.18	160.09	161.45	103.80	103.30	103.63	60.21	59.24	59.71	1,115	96.39
20	166.42	162.06	165.82	104.83	103.86	104.71	60.95	59.83	60.90	1,329	96.60
21	167.18	163.29	164.76	106.46	105.16	105.86	61.56	60.70	60.99	1,408	96.64
22	168.78	164.25	168.46	107.22	105.99	107.17	62.47	61.00	62.38	1,861	96.63
23	172.97	168.87	171.84	108.90	107.25	108.43	64.16	62.55	63.93	2,868	96.74
24	172.54	168.73	169.80	108.82	108.30	108.53	64.16	62.99	63.48	1,127	96.68
25	*	*		*	*		*	*		*	*
26	172.12	168.03	171.19	109.74	108.39	109.55	64.24	62.85	64.10	1,535	96.76
27	172.33	168.91	170.82	109.76	108.95	109.26	64.34	63.18	63.53	1,602	96.63
28	170.44	165.69	166.84	109.18	107.59	107.71	63.32	61.88	62.13	1,624	96.44
29	169.82	164.81	168.87	108.08	107.02	107.95	63.21	61.21	63.07	1,646	96.04
30	172.42	168.15	169.34	108.80	107.99	108.51	63.76	62.52	62.77	2,214	95.85
31	169.88	166.69	167.55	108.60	108.07	108.18	62.91	62.01	62.41	797	95.68
High			173.04			109.55			64.10	42,503	96.76
Low			161.45			98.63			59.32		95.54

*Sunday †Holiday

FEBRUARY, 1931

Date	Industrials High	Low	Close	Railroads High	Low	Close	Utilities High	Low	Close	Daily Sales	40 Bonds
1	*										
2	169.32	165.60	168.71	108.58	107.49	108.26	62.74	61.73	62.41	1,160	95.59
3	170.77	167.59	169.71	108.62	108.01	108.57	63.18	62.38	63.11	1,188	95.60
4	172.13	168.89	171.13	108.70	108.08	108.45	63.85	62.98	63.54	1,518	95.85
5	171.31	167.16	169.38	108.07	107.28	107.83	63.38	62.15	62.63	1,489	95.92
6	171.84	168.55	169.88	108.37	107.38	107.59	63.37	62.55	63.07	1,661	96.00
7	173.38	169.62	172.90	108.06	107.52	107.99	64.07	62.81	63.91	1,167	96.04
8	*										
9	178.58	173.24	177.72	109.24	108.25	109.08	65.91	64.23	65.65	4,126	96.26
10	184.12	176.83	181.20	111.92	109.22	111.07	67.11	65.42	66.16	4,760	96.27
11	185.89	179.14	181.88	111.63	110.38	110.71	68.75	65.80	67.13	4,699	96.33
12	†	†	†	†	†	†	†	†	†	†	†
13	184.50	179.14	180.99	110.37	109.63	109.83	67.72	66.36	66.67	2,747	96 27
14	181.40	178.20	180.41	109.64	108.73	109.19	66.80	65.86	66.55	1,093	96.29
15	*										
16	184.77	180.68	182.88	110.68	109.01	110.15	68.53	66.51	67.86	3,170	96.20
17	186.29	178.70	179.55	110.79	109.38	109.42	68.97	66.41	66.86	3,986	96.20
18	184.69	179.22	181.10	110.09	109.38	109.52	68.94	66.97	67.80	2,843	96.30
19	185.35	181.51	184.46	110.42	109.34	110.33	68.89	67.64	68.43	2,477	96.26
20	189.55	184.86	188.22	110.54	110.04	110.24	69.91	68.49	69.16	3,834	96.27
21	192.06	187.72	191.32	111.65	110.37	111.53	70.77	69.36	70.65	2,435	96.31
22	*										
23	†	†	†	†	†	†	†	†	†	†	†
24	196.96	190.19	194.35	112.24	110.96	111.58	73.28	70.76	72.89	5,346	96.35
25	195.17	188.75	190.72	111.81	110.66	110.83	73.31	70.93	71.74	4,388	96.48
26	195.95	189.81	192.23	111.28	110.38	110.97	74.52	71.59	73.19	4,623	96.43
27	194.53	183.92	193.34	111.17	110.41	110.79	73.97	71.93	72.10	3,725	95 36
28	190.87	187.22	189.66	109.92	108.79	109.49	72.26	70.91	71.61	1,748	96.31
High			194.36			111.58			73.19	64,182	96.48
Low			168.71			107.59			62.41		95.59

*Sunday   †Holiday

MARCH, 1931

Date	Industrials High	Low	Close	Railroads High	Low	Close	Utilities High	Low	Close	Daily Sales	40 Bonds
1	*										
2	191.93	183.53	184.38	109.98	106.83	106.95	72.19	69.39	69.65	3,318	96.34
3	186.56	182.00	183.76	107.51	106.53	107.13	70.72	68.84	69.80	2,936	96.44
4	184.65	179.39	180.96	105.86	103.60	104.40	71.07	68.61	70.18	3,088	96.45
5	185.18	179.41	184.69	105.54	103.75	105.16	72.04	69.47	71.66	2,731	96.58
6	186.62	178.49	179.73	105.50	104.12	104.18	72.57	69.05	70.05	3,861	96.69
7	184.20	179.96	183.85	105.40	104.45	105.29	71.54	69.43	71.44	1,567	96.68
8	*										
9	186.51	181.80	185.38	105.94	105.17	105.36	72.40	70.70	72.12	2,851	96.67
10	188.10	182.49	183.63	105.76	105.04	105.37	73.83	71.55	72.18	3,241	96.63
11	185.01	180.51	181.91	105.40	103.29	103.47	72.81	71.21	71.62	2,294	96.54
12	182.96	178.57	180.14	102.57	101.39	101.97	72.49	70.50	71.34	2,490	96.43
13	180.47	175.89	178.91	101.97	100.96	101.48	71.53	69.30	70.26	2,378	96.47
14	181.63	178.67	180.76	101.94	101.48	101.83	71.36	70.32	71.08	1,109	96.49
15	*										
16	184.11	180.32	183.61	102.51	101.90	102.19	72.85	71.15	72.73	2,132	96.56
17	185.82	179.94	180.61	102.24	100.54	100.61	73.54	71.63	71.79	2,801	96.36
18	184.53	179.62	183.95	100.65	98.88	100.18	73.10	71.38	72.83	2,097	96.32
19	188.42	184.06	186.56	100.69	99.72	100.05	74.11	72.83	73.40	3,525	96.40
20	189.31	185.15	187.72	101.16	100.00	100.80	73.78	72.70	73.28	2,742	96.40
21	187.66	184.57	185.24	100.96	100.61	100.65	73.16	72.45	72.61	1,313	96.43
22	*										
23	186.38	182.05	184.32	100.65	99.90	100.24	72.55	71.23	71.86	1,994	96.29
24	186.86	181.65	186.00	101.79	99.95	101.53	72.63	71.01	72.37	1,878	96.34
25	187.18	183.20	184.28	101.60	100.51	100.68	72.80	71.78	72.04	2,097	96.33
26	185.56	180.85	181.70	100.58	99.71	100.00	72.61	71.20	71.49	2,554	96.27
27	182.02	176.63	177.30	99.56	98.53	98.67	71.45	69.79	70.03	2,948	96.30
28	177.22	173.12	174.06	98.47	97.79	97.86	69.83	68.04	68.24	2,119	96.22
29	*										
30	175.42	170.64	172.56	97.83	96.92	97.54	68.41	66.70	67.14	3,188	96.13
31	176.50	171.09	172.36	98.01	96.74	96.88	68.93	66.89	67.54	2,406	95.95
High			187.72			107.13			73.40	65,658	96.69
Low			172.36			96.88			67.14		95.95

*Sunday   †Holiday

APRIL, 1931

Date	Industrials			Railroads			Utilities			Daily Sales	40 Bonds
	High	Low	Close	High	Low	Close	High	Low	Close		
1	173.72	169.18	170.82	96.53	94.99	95.34	67.71	66.10	66.46	2,265	96.04
2	173.15	168.30	169.89	95.70	94.88	95.38	67.23	64.95	65.63	2,506	95.96
3	†	†	†	†	†	†	†	†	†		
4	173.36 *	170.01 *	172.43 *	95.84	95.42	95.76	67.01 *	65.85 *	66.54 *	874	96.04
5											
6	174.69	169.44	169.72	96.32	95.63	96.82	67.67	65.85	66.00	1,464	95.96
7	170.44	166.10	167.03	95.68	94.46	94.65	66.17	64.70	65.03	2,193	95.81
8	171.49	166.34	169.54	95.07	94.08	94.72	66.67	65.01	66.20	2,048	95.72
9	171.43	167.66	168.77	94.72	91.84	92.02	66.65	65.60	65.82	1,944	95.69
10	171.06	166.96	168.72	92.83	90.83	92.26	66.50	65.41	66.05	1,566	95.60
11	170.21	167.65	168.03 *	92.66	92.27	92.34 *	66.39 *	65.95 *	66.14 *	616	95.68
12											
13	171.61	167.11	171.07	92.61	91.88	92.54	67.68	65.78	67.53	1,630	95.71
14	173.24	167.11	168.43	93.18	92.08	92.28	68.17	66.13	66.53	1,938	95.74
15	167.64	163.89	164.66	92.21	90.45	90.68	66.23	64.86	65.20	2,046	95.68
16	165.64	161.63	162.59	91.03	90.27	90.52	65.23	64.00	64.35	2,331	95.66
17	164.34	158.50	160.23	90.86	89.83	90.25	64.86	62.43	62.70	2,545	95.71
18	162.93 *	159.26 *	162.37 *	90.79	90.00	90.49 *	63.60	62.20	63.15 *	1,293	95.74
19											
20	164.42	159.45	163.41	91.07	90.23	90.84	63.55	62.01	63.18	1,564	95.65
21	164.06	157.82	158.83	91.14	88.51	88.89	63.49	61.23	61.54	1,993	95.52
22	160.06	155.61	156.37	88.86	87.40	87.64	61.93	60.28	60.60	2,671	95.45
23	159.53	153.13	157.43	88.53	86.55	87.28	61.60	59.34	60.61	3,816	95.42
24	159.45	153.55	155.76	88.90	86.67	88.36	61.81	60.10	61.05	2,603	95.40
25	156.20	151.58	151.98 *	87.52	86.76	86.83 *	61.05	59.66	59.74 *	1,418	95.43
26											
27	152.98	146.31	149.78	86.93	85.11	85.75	59.85	57.81	58.92	3,650	95.18
28	151.09	144.52	147.95	86.40	84.77	85.51	59.53	57.76	58.85	2,857	95.09
29	147.59	141.78	143.61	86.41	84.89	85.94	58.80	57.05	57.46	3,182	95.01
30	152.50	142.12	151.19	88.37	85.37	88.14	60.42	57.18	60.20	3,335	95.34
High			172.43			95.82			67.53	54,347	96.04
Low			143.61			85.51			57.46		95.01

*Sunday   †Holiday

MAY, 1931

Date	Industrials			Railroads			Utilities			Daily Sales	40 Bonds
	High	Low	Close	High	Low	Close	High	Low	Close		
1	153.82	144.91	145.58	88.51	86.39	86.54	61.19	58.75	58.85	2,872	95.29
2	148.44	143.17 *	147.49 *	86.55	85.91	86.31	59.83	58.31	59.52 *	1,267	95.20
3											
4	151.26	146.80	150.50	87.19	86.19	87.01	60.49	59.09	60.28	1,361	95.25
5	153.19	147.88	148.99	87.39	86.25	86.40	61.36	59.87	60.13	1,575	95.33
6	150.54	145.65	149.73	86.71	85.83	86.43	60.66	59.16	60.37	1,499	95.43
7	152.57	146.77	148.88	86.88	85.89	86.03	60.98	59.14	59.61	1,693	95.57
8	155.65	147.43	154.41	86.97	85.49	86.86	62.00	59.18	61.66	2,658	95.95
9	156.17 *	150.75 *	151.31 *	87.01 *	86.48 *	86.60 *	61.83 *	60.33 *	60.46 *	1,157	96.10
10											
11	153.37	148.19	151.56	86.77	85.93	86.35	61.55	59.75	60.76	1,651	96.05
12	152.10	148.28	150.24	85.87	84.24	84.68	61.06	59.93	60.43	1,310	96.05
13	152.63	147.55	149.63	83.81	82.52	83.31	60.97	59.55	60.23	1,667	95.99
14	150.61	146.02	146.64	82.70	80.44	80.68	60.28	58.94	59.13	1,770	95.87
15	147.23	141.84	144.49	80.56	78.89	79.63	59.14	57.80	58.44	2,380	95.72
16	145.56 *	142.55 *	142.95 *	79.93	79.24 *	79.40 *	58.74	58.11 *	58.29 *	763	95.73
17											
18	143.09	138.54	139.52	78.34	75.35	75.58	58.02	56.11	56.24	2,536	95.64
19	141.93	136.05	138.86	76.87	75.05	75.85	56.97	54.97	55.77	2,778	95.50
20	142.49	136.18	137.74	78.04	76.20	76.69	57.08	54.73	55.23	2,315	95.58
21	141.07	135.19	139.54	80.03	76.70	79.05	56.21	54.17	55.58	2,352	95.40
22	141.37	136.93	139.49	80.38	78.86	79.74	56.53	55.35	56.01	1,560	95.51
23	140.16	137.50 *	137.90 *	79.79	78.67	78.81 *	56.30	55.56 *	55.67 *	550	95.55
24											
25	137.43	132.15	132.87	77.96	76.37	76.58	55.35	53.45	53.66	1,875	95.54
26	136.38	130.75	133.11	77.09	75.52	76.12	54.47	52.91	53.63	2,414	95.56
27	134.59	127.95	130.76	75.89	74.08	74.74	54.29	52.28	52.82	2,512	95.17
28	134.16	128.72	131.81	75.16	73.64	74.55	54.13	52.44	53.40	2,090	95.03
29	134.60	127.30	128.46	74.71	71.42	72.06	54.26	51.98	52.35	2,053	94.67
30	†	†	†	†	†	†	†	†	†		†
31											
High			154.41			87.01			61.66	46,660	96.10
Low			128.46			72.06			52.35		94.67

*Sunday   †Holiday

JUNE, 1931

Date	Industrials High	Low	Close	Railroads High	Low	Close	Utilities High	Low	Close	Daily Sales	40 Bonds
1	128.40	121.76	122.77	70.56	67.73	67.94	52.30	49.96	50.08	3,102	94.12
2	126.20	119.89	121.70	68.99	66.24	66.85	51.16	48.94	49.63	3,317	93.74
3	130.64	120.79	130.37	71.01	66.91	70.98	53.08	48.90	52.90	3,306	93.82
4	136.10	128.35	134.73	75.37	70.58	74.57	55.15	52.39	54.65	3,170	94.24
5	138.89	131.69	133.33	78.18	74.31	76.17	55.45	53.53	53.83	2,846	94.36
6	133.24	129.39	129.91	75.56	73.57	73.72	53.70	52.15	52.33	833	94.24
7	*			*			*				
8	136.40	127.96	135.92	74.31	71.92	74.11	54.30	51.75	54.19	1,708	94.51
9	138.88	132.08	132.97	75.37	73.61	73.98	55.15	52.95	53.38	1,889	94.52
10	137.30	132.04	136.82	75.52	73.76	75.16	55.45	53.08	55.15	1,804	94.68
11	138.47	134.24	136.57	77.57	74.26	77.45	55.53	54.37	55.20	1,745	94.74
12	138.16	133.98	136.98	80.04	76.19	79.60	55.78	54.39	55.42	1,587	94.89
13	137.71	135.30	137.03	79.79	78.46	79.65	55.52	54.96	55.37	543	94.87
14	*			*			*				
15	138.58	134.82	135.26	80.22	78.53	78.79	56.08	54.90	55.10	1,267	94.98
16	136.39	132.93	135.47	79.37	77.61	79.02	55.47	54.46	55.23	1,115	94.87
17	135.93	132.91	133.68	78.24	76.87	77.16	55.63	54.76	54.95	917	94.95
18	133.58	130.09	130.56	76.66	76.03	76.16	54.99	53.75	53.85	1,149	95.13
19	131.86	128.64	130.31	75.71	74.31	74.71	53.95	52.93	53.68	1,147	95.00
20	139.84	131.94	138.96	78.90	75.96	78.83	57.03	54.23	56.86	1,508	95.23
21	*			*			*				*
22	147.97	140.08	145.82	82.38	79.79	81.76	60.48	57.41	59.84	4,588	95.31
23	146.71	141.41	143.89	81.53	80.19	80.70	60.05	58.31	58.90	2,600	95.28
24	153.42	144.56	151.60	84.95	80.62	84.20	61.53	59.09	60.63	5,066	95.35
25	156.33	148.79	150.36	86.13	83.18	83.65	62.08	59.89	60.15	4,317	95.30
26	155.50	150.75	154.04	88.41	84.15	88.03	62.40	60.52	61.91	3,117	95.44
27	157.93	152.67	156.93	88.57	87.45	88.31	62.81	61.30	62.58	1,919	95.42
28	*			*			*				*
29	156.59	151.30	152.67	87.38	86.05	86.28	62.45	60.69	60.94	2,138	95.40
30	153.67	148.63	150.18	85.80	84.15	84.36	61.56	59.74	60.37	1,945	95.31
High			156.93			88.31			62.58	58,644	95.44
Low			121.70			66.85			49.63		93.74

*Sunday   †Holiday

JULY, 1931

Date	Industrials High	Low	Close	Railroads High	Low	Close	Utilities High	Low	Close	Daily Sales	40 Bonds
1	153.86	147.44	152.66	85.92	83.49	85.48	61.62	59.65	61.27	1,711	95.42
2	154.84	150.72	151.48	85.65	84.83	85.02	62.03	60.61	60.81	1,333	95.46
3	156.74	152.21	155.26	86.51	85.04	86.13	62.73	61.25	62.24	2,052	95.78
4	†	†	†	†	†	†	†	†	†	†	†
5	*			*			*				
6	154.08	151.20	152.80	85.81	85.03	85.22	62.07	61.17	61.65	1,045	95.88
7	155.39	144.65	145.92	85.20	81.13	81.39	62.33	58.79	59.21	3,010	95.88
8	147.24	141.36	143.83	81.79	80.24	81.21	59.60	57.69	58.37	2,357	95.95
9	145.97	142.24	144.91	82.35	80.99	81.65	59.20	57.90	58.69	1,514	95.79
10	148.50	143.46	146.97	82.66	81.60	82.35	59.73	58.51	59.38	1,285	95.98
11	145.94	143.05	143.88	82.19	81.88	81.98	58.88	58.15	58.38	592	96.02
12	*			*			*				
13	143.44	139.59	142.43	80.93	79.85	80.33	58.08	56.86	57.70	1,283	95.93
14	143.19	139.67	140.85	80.59	79.76	80.18	57.92	56.78	57.15	1,105	95.91
15	140.13	134.39	137.86	79.28	76.76	77.33	56.74	54.70	55.92	2,605	95.63
16	142.30	137.30	141.99	78.26	76.43	77.47	57.45	55.70	57.36	1,517	95.60
17	144.84	141.44	142.61	79.38	78.37	79.15	58.62	57.58	57.93	1,272	95.74
18	142.82	141.00	142.42	79.06	78.87	79.03	57.88	57.31	57.75	380	95.81
19	*			*			*				
20	145.00	142.75	144.48	79.71	79.19	79.59	58.68	58.01	58.57	705	95.87
21	147.69	144.21	146.70	81.22	80.25	80.99	59.70	58.65	59.28	1,149	95.75
22	145.88	142.11	142.52	80.63	79.61	79.85	58.96	57.91	58.03	993	95.75
23	143.77	140.81	142.63	79.57	78.94	79.47	58.21	57.41	57.94	786	95.69
24	142.41	138.20	139.01	79.27	77.83	77.90	57.84	56.60	56.76	1,065	95.63
25	138.98	137.69	138.24	77.83	77.77	77.79	56.68	56.23	56.44	413	95.59
26	*			*			*				
27	140.16	137.72	139.64	77.35	76.68	76.92	57.05	56.36	56.90	572	95.55
28	142.12	139.65	141.53	77.66	76.93	77.55	57.65	56.92	57.60	651	95.37
29	139.26	134.99	136.19	75.99	74.58	75.01	56.78	55.54	55.98	1,577	95.34
30	138.05	134.33	136.93	74.98	73.41	74.69	56.47	55.21	56.23	1,354	95.22
31	138.12	133.70	135.39	74.12	73.10	73.44	56.46	55.46	55.86	1,220	95.11
High			155.26			86.13			62.24	33,546	96.02
Low			135.39			73.44			55.86		95.11

*Sunday   †Holiday

AUGUST, 1931

Date	Industrials High	Low	Close	Railroads High	Low	Close	Utilities High	Low	Close	Daily Sales	40 Bonds
1	137.82	135.28	136.65	73.62	73.39	73.50	56.48	55.83	56.38	398	95.06
2	*										
3	139.35	136.36	137.50	74.70	73.59	74.19	57.26	56.52	56.85	879	94.78
4	137.77	134.85	136.50	73.94	72.66	72.82	56.88	56.20	56.57	724	94.91
5	135.83	133.59	134.10	72.79	72.05	72.16	56.34	55.64	55.77	818	94.72
6	134.93	132.55	133.77	72.16	71.41	71.58	55.64	54.61	55.10	910	94.54
7	135.72	132.96	135.13	71.72	70.63	71.25	55.55	54.61	55.31	736	94.19
8	135.87	134.47	134.94	71.27	70.19	70.29	55.56	55.28	55.40	295	94.19
9	*										
10	134.85	132.79	134.26	70.04	67.92	68.78	55.41	54.75	55.20	707	94.04
11	141.42	133.80	140.16	71.60	68.00	70.77	57.34	55.18	56.96	1,603	93.95
12	140.99	137.03	137.63	71.48	69.90	70.05	57.26	56.23	56.36	1,259	93.96
13	141.30	137.03	140.22	70.22	69.18	70.11	57.20	56.26	56.96	1,379	93.84
14	145.05	140.82	144.15	71.43	70.15	70.82	58.55	57.33	58.21	1,830	93.59
15	146.41	143.82	145.80	71.79	71.05	71.67	59.28	58.51	59.05	902	93.41
16	*										
17	144.27	140.34	140.98	71.27	69.81	69.99	58.83	57.50	57.68	1,315	93.43
18	144.43	139.36	141.26	70.42	68.83	69.26	58.65	57.31	57.70	1,706	93.20
19	142.61	140.04	141.72	69.96	69.11	69.64	58.03	57.31	57.71	1,077	93.04
20	143.93	140.96	141.93	70.32	69.82	70.04	58.68	57.95	58.21	1,065	92.96
21	142.49	137.35	138.60	69.93	68.88	69.00	58.23	56.61	56.95	1,308	92.92
22	138.57	136.88	137.76	68.58	68.17	68.33	56.92	56.57	56.78	424	92.86
23	*										
24	137.99	135.62	137.62	68.10	67.24	67.75	56.71	55.93	56.62	823	92.65
25	139.22	135.69	136.65	68.16	67.24	67.54	57.00	56.22	56.50	861	92.57
26	140.32	135.98	139.93	68.41	67.05	68.16	57.33	56.36	57.25	839	92.58
27	140.75	137.88	138.66	68.25	67.63	67.90	57.53	56.74	56.98	829	92.83
28	142.11	138.82	140.78	68.65	67.53	68.35	57.95	57.11	57.64	930	93.06
29	142.58	140.92	142.08	69.06	68.76	69.02	58.10	57.71	58.01	473	93.17
30	*										
31	142.07	138.96	139.41	68.79	68.03	68.18	57.94	57.22	57.33	739	93.34
High			145.80			74.19			59.05	24,829	95.06
Low			133.77			67.54			55.10		92.57

*Sunday   †Holiday

SEPTEMBER, 1931

Date	Industrials High	Low	Close	Railroads High	Low	Close	Utilities High	Low	Close	Daily Sales	40 Bonds
1	140.54	138.51	140.13	68.55	67.75	68.52	57.55	57.06	57.43	536	93.55
2	140.08	136.62	137.31	67.87	65.70	65.83	57.46	56.41	56.52	962	93.39
3	136.54	132.21	133.14	65.62	64.41	64.68	56.31	55.07	55.21	2,130	93.10
4	133.82	131.44	132.62	64.96	64.32	64.66	55.43	54.26	54.47	1,195	92.97
5	†	†	†	†	†	†	†	†	†	†	†
6	†										
7	†										
8	131.57	127.91	129.19	63.67	61.80	62.14	54.18	52.28	52.92	2,044	92.94
9	130.67	126.36	128.43	62.40	60.76	61.73	53.36	52.16	52.75	2,024	92.69
10	130.45	126.04	127.30	62.34	59.62	60.19	53.22	51.55	51.87	1,505	92.44
11	129.47	124.50	128.23	61.60	59.30	60.91	52.62	50.93	52.41	1,974	92.31
12	128.17	123.56	123.85	60.66	59.22	59.44	52.37	50.70	50.76	761	92.09
13	*										
14	123.00	119.12	121.30	59.09	57.10	57.91	50.48	48.84	49.49	2,449	91.27
15	123.03	118.70	120.59	58.25	56.10	56.92	50.29	48.45	48.99	2,165	91.07
16	123.10	118.41	119.26	57.78	56.03	56.73	49.73	47.70	47.83	1,978	90.93
17	123.28	117.29	121.76	58.05	55.08	57.40	49.40	47.05	48.72	2,420	90.95
18	121.27	114.47	115.08	56.74	53.79	53.97	48.29	46.20	46.38	2,897	90.51
19	115.39	111.00	111.74	53.95	52.47	53.08	46.20	44.55	44.70	2,438	90.07
20	*										
21	114.59	104.79	110.83	57.08	50.62	54.55	45.08	41.80	43.49	4,396	88.80
22	112.65	108.12	109.40	55.30	53.17	54.27	44.61	42.51	42.86	2,052	88.56
23	117.75	110.77	115.99	62.40	55.45	61.86	46.05	43.08	45.34	2,933	89.85
24	116.95	106.64	107.79	60.72	55.06	55.58	45.56	41.76	41.98	3,051	89.25
25	112.64	104.73	109.86	58.14	54.26	56.91	43.84	41.15	42.88	2,849	88.93
26	110.89	106.88	107.36	57.26	55.73	55.85	43.36	42.05	42.33	686	88.90
27	*										
28	108.80	103.58	104.39	56.32	54.69	54.88	42.61	41.31	41.51	1,486	88.73
29	104.64	99.02	99.80	55.71	53.30	53.59	41.43	39.53	39.76	2,902	87.91
30	102.39	95.76	96.61	55.68	53.33	53.59	40.52	37.80	37.91	3,207	87.01
High			140.13			68.52			57.43	51,040	93.55
Low			96.61			53.08			37.91		87.01

*Sunday   †Holiday

OCTOBER, 1931

Date	Industrials High	Industrials Low	Industrials Close	Railroads High	Railroads Low	Railroads Close	Utilities High	Utilities Low	Utilities Close	Daily Sales	40 Bonds
1	98.51	92.88	95.66	55.15	52.35	53.32	38.65	36.44	37.50	3,638	86.05
2	100.03	93.64	96.88	54.64	51.19	51.93	39.63	37.15	38.31	2,534	86.05
3	96.53	92.30	92.77	51.92	49.44	49.71	38.48	37.17	37.36	1,029	85.88
4	*										
5	92.14	85.51	86.48	48.86	45.44	45.68	37.04	34.64	34.88	3,191	84.99
6	100.49	87.51	99.34	51.64	46.22	50.68	40.21	35.31	39.48	4,305	85.18
7	103.84	96.79	97.32	52.87	49.71	50.12	41.36	38.33	38.56	2,823	86.08
8	106.43	98.19	105.79	54.95	50.15	54.69	41.93	38.61	41.62	2,874	86.59
9	108.98	102.79	104.46	59.26	53.97	57.40	42.86	41.06	41.60	3,216	87.21
10	106.51	103.33	105.61	57.90	56.51	57.43	42.37	41.23	42.02	826	87.35
11	*										
12	†	†	†	†	†	†	†	†	†	†	†
13	105.37	99.74	100.24	56.38	54.05	54.24	41.73	39.84	39.91	1,249	86.40
14	102.50	96.01	97.27	55.08	52.24	52.66	40.41	38.26	38.71	1,636	85.38
15	102.67	97.45	98.71	55.38	52.79	53.70	40.82	39.11	39.55	1,376	85.18
16	103.19	98.24	102.49	56.89	53.95	56.64	40.89	39.30	40.78	1,421	84.86
17	104.10	101.68	102.28	57.14	55.82	55.94	41.10	40.41	40.56	628	85.19
18	*										
19	104.19	100.87	103.45	56.29	55.19	55.85	41.02	40.14	40.95	859	84.80
20	109.59	104.69	108.65	58.89	56.48	58.18	43.24	41.36	42.89	2,513	85.12
21	109.69	103.86	108.39	55.95	53.81	54.97	43.97	41.30	43.38	2,242	84.93
22	108.58	104.09	105.02	54.74	52.95	53.08	43.29	41.53	41.71	1,393	84.75
23	109.17	104.58	108.88	54.69	52.90	54.41	42.93	41.58	42.75	1,329	84.76
24	110.53	108.05	109.70	54.54	54.03	54.33	43.27	42.69	43.13	758	84.75
25	*										
26	109.36	105.69	106.37	53.70	52.35	52.52	42.79	41.61	41.78	1,186	84.59
27	106.31	102.43	104.25	52.57	50.40	51.15	41.75	40.49	41.19	1,392	84.51
28	104.50	99.20	100.52	50.96	48.99	49.76	41.16	39.28	39.49	1,774	84.10
29	101.66	98.19	100.66	50.59	48.72	49.86	39.81	38.68	39.50	1,343	83.92
30	104.51	100.75	103.97	52.71	49.50	52.40	40.68	39.05	40.43	1,556	84.04
31	106.41	104.26	105.43	53.07	51.99	52.19	40.98	40.28	40.51	805	84.23
High			109.70			58.18			43.38	47,897	87.35
Low			86.48			45.68			34.88		83.92

*Sunday   †Holiday

NOVEMBER, 1931

Date	Industrials High	Industrials Low	Industrials Close	Railroads High	Railroads Low	Railroads Close	Utilities High	Utilities Low	Utilities Close	Daily Sales	40 Bonds
1	*										
2	107.76	103.94	104.50	52.56	51.46	51.60	41.73	40.57	40.74	1,458	84.24
3	†	†	†	†	†	†	†	†	†	†	†
4	108.85	103.19	108.33	52.33	50.73	52.09	41.80	40.31	41.62	1,476	84.60
5	110.68	107.45	108.58	52.58	51.60	51.74	42.28	41.16	41.44	1,524	85.02
6	113.28	106.43	112.72	53.42	51.61	53.17	42.93	40.80	42.75	2,276	85.28
7	117.30	112.42	115.60	54.78	53.34	54.43	44.16	42.84	43.77	2,041	85.80
8	*										
9	119.15	114.47	116.79	56.83	53.56	55.37	45.07	43.47	44.39	3,047	86.39
10	116.58	112.24	113.98	56.29	54.37	55.60	44.27	42.91	43.50	1,750	86.45
11	114.63	110.38	112.01	56.61	54.81	55.20	43.66	42.35	42.91	1,491	86.40
12	114.61	110.86	111.95	55.76	53.89	53.93	43.34	42.40	42.65	1,442	86.32
13	112.39	106.71	107.33	53.69	51.49	51.62	42.78	41.12	41.23	1,794	86.04
14	107.69	104.63	106.35	50.89	49.83	50.10	41.26	40.20	40.63	1,134	85.82
15	*										
16	107.86	103.43	104.76	50.63	48.86	49.08	41.01	39.74	40.01	1,512	85.82
17	108.02	103.76	106.16	49.76	48.23	49.21	40.92	39.53	40.36	1,461	85.55
18	105.86	101.21	101.69	49.26	47.32	47.53	40.30	39.00	39.13	1,673	85.22
19	103.81	99.83	101.25	48.62	46.25	47.50	39.83	38.69	39.15	1,509	84.87
20	100.99	96.45	97.96	46.98	44.71	45.09	38.95	37.52	38.02	2,043	84.42
21	100.38	96.35	97.42	46.50	44.92	45.33	38.47	37.23	37.60	874	84.39
22	*										
23	98.83	95.00	96.60	44.74	43.17	43.62	37.96	36.96	37.46	1,349	83.65
24	100.10	96.53	98.61	44.60	43.32	43.92	38.37	37.23	37.96	1,247	83.48
25	98.54	93.67	94.15	43.95	41.78	42.04	37.85	36.66	36.84	1,495	83.36
26	†	†	†	†	†	†	†	†	†	†	†
27	93.79	90.65	91.55	41.54	39.80	40.11	36.59	35.67	36.01	1,824	82.70
28	92.10	89.31	90.02	40.31	38.65	38.96	35.93	35.27	35.47	932	82.20
29	*										
30	95.77	89.35	93.87	41.62	38.65	40.84	37.53	35.30	37.06	2,003	81.94
High			116.79			55.60			44.39	37,355	86.45
Low			90.02			38.96			35.47		81.94

*Sunday   †Holiday

DECEMBER, 1931

Date	Industrials High	Low	Close	Railroads High	Low	Close	Utilities High	Low	Close	Daily Sales	40 Bonds
1	93.38	87.78	91.17	41.99	38.20	40.89	37.32	35.54	36.99	2,032	81.87
2	93.06	87.39	87.90	41.93	37.90	38.25	37.60	35.66	35.81	1,887	80.74
3	90.59	86.28	89.70	40.09	37.86	39.65	36.63	35.30	36.50	1,801	80.02
4	91.97	85.75	86.76	40.80	38.13	38.58	37.15	35.06	35.46	1,921	79.67
5	90.29	87.22	90.14	40.43	38.93	40.37	36.68	35.78	36.66	872	79.52
6	*			*			*				*
7	92.60	89.16	90.11	41.01	39.55	39.95	37.57	36.46	36.76	1,457	79.82
8	90.98	85.81	86.50	41.00	37.61	37.94	37.04	35.52	35.89	1,597	79.77
9	86.52	82.49	84.14	37.63	35.95	36.59	35.75	34.36	34.73	2,263	79.25
10	84.15	80.75	82.46	36.43	34.50	35.81	34.69	33.16	33.81	2,664	78.53
11	83.11	79.26	79.63	36.47	34.63	35.09	34.05	32.72	32.91	2,354	77.73
12	80.05	77.22	78.93	35.41	34.22	34.85	33.02	31.95	32.43	1,540	77.03
13	*			*			*				*
14	82.57	76.15	77.22	35.51	33.06	33.87	33.46	31.30	31.75	2,885	75.99
15	79.44	75.50	78.60	34.19	32.81	33.77	32.51	31.08	32.16	2,632	74.53
16	80.00	75.93	76.49	34.22	32.36	32.70	32.69	31.28	31.48	1,956	74.28
17	76.33	71.79	73.79	32.52	30.94	31.42	31.33	30.06	30.71	2,943	73.36
18	81.10	72.62	80.69	36.22	31.47	35.91	33.03	29.71	32.80	3,622	74.71
19	83.09	79.88	80.75	37.76	35.78	36.72	33.73	32.57	32.71	1,627	75.88
20	*			*			*				*
21	81.76	77.55	78.08	37.27	35.40	35.74	33.16	31.78	31.96	1,925	76.46
22	80.32	77.26	79.55	36.62	35.70	36.24	32.79	32.12	32.48	1,397	77.14
23	80.17	75.42	76.02	36.15	33.66	33.78	32.57	31.31	31.47	1,560	76.71
24	77.45	75.14	75.84	34.22	33.48	33.72	31.86	31.12	31.41	1,106	76.90
25	†			†			†				†
26	†			†			†				†
27	*			*			*				*
28	76.27	72.41	73.84	34.29	32.31	32.78	31.47	30.18	30.55	2,003	76.04
29	77.81	73.54	75.84	34.46	32.45	33.50	32.09	30.41	31.31	2,440	76.21
30	77.86	75.12	77.14	34.19	32.67	33.53	32.16	31.08	31.90	2,112	76.32
31	79.92	76.92	77.90	34.43	33.42	33.63	32.96	31.35	31.41	1,509	77.77
High			91.77			40.89			36.99	50,106	81.87
Low			73.79			31.42			30.55		73.36

*Sunday †Holiday

JANUARY, 1932

Date	Industrials High	Low	Close	Railroads High	Low	Close	Utilities High	Low	Close	Daily Sales	40 Bonds
1	†	†	†	†	†	†	†	†	†	†	†
2	78.09	74.25	74.62	33.84	33.07	33.11	31.73	30.53	30.60	722	77.78
3	*			*			*			*	
4	74.06	70.91	71.59	32.94	31.55	31.63	30.36	29.48	29.66	1,513	77.06
5	72.78	69.85	71.24	31.94	30.77	31.36	30.18	29.12	29.64	1,419	77.16
6	77.16	73.02	76.31	33.97	32.37	33.87	31.69	30.34	31.63	1,838	77.47
7	80.17	76.11	78.03	36.62	34.08	35.63	32.80	31.67	32.11	2,179	78.40
8	82.11	76.74	81.80	37.05	35.14	36.83	33.45	31.61	33.40	1,970	79.21
9	82.65	79.38	79.98	37.47	36.58	36.70	33.62	32.50	32.68	1,152	79.70
10	*			*			*				*
11	82.20	77.23	80.44	39.94	36.13	39.00	33.31	31.86	32.70	1,797	80.09
12	82.08	78.84	79.39	40.02	38.45	38.65	33.34	32.26	32.52	1,364	80.00
13	84.67	79.96	84.36	41.00	38.82	40.70	34.13	32.63	33.93	2,068	80.79
14	87.78	84.70	85.35	42.11	40.58	41.28	34.92	33.96	34.16	2,648	81.22
15	86.59	83.24	85.88	41.76	40.00	41.30	34.56	33.69	34.27	1,635	81.22
16	85.52	83.11	84.44	40.94	40.07	40.42	34.35	33.48	33.78	733	80.94
17	*			*			*				*
18	85.32	81.29	81.45	40.35	38.53	38.59	33.91	32.92	32.98	1,383	80.69
19	82.79	80.35	81.10	40.05	38.29	39.29	33.29	32.58	32.79	1,090	80.56
20	83.79	80.45	83.57	40.25	38.72	40.16	33.40	32.42	33.31	1,212	80.67
21	85.03	82.70	83.42	41.62	40.24	40.92	33.81	33.20	33.37	1,240	81.04
22	83.51	78.56	78.81	41.60	38.96	39.12	33.39	32.19	32.24	1,561	80.83
23	79.76	77.09	77.98	39.17	38.06	38.60	32.27	31.59	31.85	835	80.58
24	*			*			*				*
25	79.94	77.42	78.66	39.60	38.44	39.15	32.14	31.51	31.75	829	80.40
26	80.79	78.92	79.76	40.12	39.07	39.22	32.29	31.81	32.03	764	80.37
27	79.20	76.66	77.82	39.62	38.39	39.31	31.84	31.21	31.51	1,279	80.25
28	78.03	75.85	76.73	39.35	38.16	38.71	31.70	30.95	31.26	1,116	79.72
29	77.14	74.19	76.55	38.21	36.58	37.30	31.13	30.15	30.76	1,528	79.97
30	77.14	75.71	76.19	37.34	36.81	37.02	30.96	30.48	30.61	489	78.93
31	*			*			*				*
High			85.88			41.30			34.27	34,362	81.22
Low			71.24			31.36			29.64		77.06

*Sunday †Holiday

FEBRUARY, 1932

Date	Industrials High	Low	Close	Railroads High	Low	Close	Utilities High	Low	Close	Daily Sales	40 Bonds
1	80.62	76.32	79.63	39.00	37.84	38.37	32.24	30.71	31.98	1,516	79.41
2	80.74	77.61	77.82	39.07	37.25	37.38	32.46	31.25	31.34	1,118	79.49
3	78.96	76.77	78.26	37.68	36.90	37.31	31.58	30.93	31.49	808	79.08
4	78.88	77.15	77.66	37.23	36.58	36.65	31.65	31.19	31.32	675	79.00
5	77.50	74.71	75.00	36.22	34.11	34.30	31.21	30.46	30.56	1,083	78.98
6	75.02	73.78	74.45	34.15	33.42	33.65	30.51	30.21	30.39	660	78.82
7	*	*	*	*	*	*	*	*	*	*	*
8	75.15	72.31	73.45	34.06	32.73	33.01	30.63	30.00	30.33	1,151	78.59
9	74.50	71.85	72.38	33.43	32.54	32.76	30.54	29.80	29.94	1,156	78.24
10	73.98	70.64	71.80	33.61	32.27	33.01	30.43	29.46	29.85	1,303	78.01
11	79.62	74.27	78.60	36.00	33.81	35.57	31.97	30.48	31.80	2,563	78.10
12	†	†	†	†	†	†	†	†	†		
13	86.46	80.90	85.82	40.63	36.56	39.70	35.13	32.86	34.87	2,626	78.50
14	*	*	*	*	*	*	*	*	*	*	
15	85.36	80.88	82.18	39.92	38.20	38.58	34.99	33.68	33.96	1,976	78.90
16	86.51	80.49	85.75	40.66	38.11	40.45	35.76	33.61	35.48	2,502	79.11
17	87.18	81.67	82.24	40.90	38.63	38.81	35.76	33.91	34.01	2,186	79.17
18	85.74	81.45	85.13	39.07	37.75	38.83	35.09	33.88	34.96	1,682	79.39
19	89.84	85.26	85.98	40.43	38.97	39.21	36.31	34.95	35.13	2,431	79.51
20	85.68	82.93	83.59	38.75	38.04	38.16	34.89	34.15	34.28	705	79.56
21	*	*	*	*	*	*	*	*	*		
22	†	†	†	†	†	†	†	†	†	†	†
23	84.03	79.85	80.26	38.13	36.50	36.67	34.35	33.23	33.33	1,281	79.65
24	83.32	79.57	82.73	37.38	36.20	37.26	34.21	33.06	33.93	1,083	79.73
25	82.92	80.13	82.05	36.90	36.28	36.71	33.97	33.26	33.65	1,035	79.74
26	83.53	81.37	82.09	36.79	36.32	36.52	33.93	33.36	33.49	894	79.96
27	82.55	81.28	82.02	36.57	36.25	36.45	33.72	33.38	33.53	401	79.92
28	*	*	*	*	*	*	*	*	*		
29	83.89	80.84	81.44	36.86	36.23	36.29	33.96	33.15	33.25	881	79.96
High			85.98			40.45			35.48	31,716	79.96
Low			71.80			32.76			29.85		78.01

*Sunday †Holiday

MARCH, 1932

Date	Industrials High	Low	Close	Railroads High	Low	Close	Utilities High	Low	Close	Daily Sales	40 Bonds
1	82.20	80.50	81.87	36.34	35.71	35.95	33.51	33.07	33.35	733	80.05
2	86.50	82.10	86.28	37.50	36.10	37.34	35.01	33.59	34.91	1,763	80.26
3	88.35	85.47	86.13	38.31	37.26	37.46	35.56	34.65	34.85	1,720	80.51
4	87.87	84.54	86.11	37.91	37.01	37.26	35.72	34.56	34.98	1,513	80.98
5	88.84	86.25	88.49	38.82	37.38	38.65	35.93	35.25	35.85	1,163	81.27
6	*	*	*	*	*	*	*	*	*	*	*
7	89.78	86.80	87.16	38.85	37.68	37.74	36.17	35.11	35.25	1,583	81.40
8	89.87	86.90	88.78	38.61	37.62	38.23	36.39	35.18	35.92	1,638	81.65
9	89.87	86.57	86.94	38.62	37.60	37.75	36.20	35.30	35.45	1,331	82.00
10	87.47	85.44	86.25	37.75	37.14	37.28	35.54	34.93	35.21	1,049	82.30
11	85.70	83.26	83.61	37.09	35.99	36.10	34.95	34.08	34.16	1,258	82.24
12	85.00	83.24	84.52	36.46	36.02	36.21	34.56	34.08	34.40	648	82.09
13	*	*	*	*	*	*	*	*	*	*	*
14	84.30	80.44	81.12	35.84	34.12	34.37	34.34	33.36	33.56	2,034	81.77
15	82.44	79.66	81.02	34.64	33.16	33.77	33.94	33.11	33.41	1,469	81.28
16	81.84	78.76	79.11	33.85	32.56	32.66	33.60	32.77	32.86	1,464	81.07
17	81.55	77.57	80.87	34.26	31.86	34.05	33.60	32.53	33.44	1,772	80.93
18	80.59	77.63	78.82	34.03	32.57	33.09	33.03	31.59	32.11	1,407	80.58
19	78.92	77.72	78.09	33.28	32.84	32.97	32.30	31.85	31.94	827	80.52
20	*	*	*	*	*	*	*	*	*		
21	80.19	77.32	79.90	34.00	33.16	33.74	32.54	31.66	32.43	890	80.42
22	80.59	77.79	79.55	34.00	33.06	33.54	32.66	31.79	32.28	1,080	80.62
23	80.08	78.23	78.64	33.68	32.91	32.96	32.36	31.84	31.93	841	80.40
24	79.58	77.49	77.99	32.99	32.26	32.49	32.05	31.50	31.70	838	80.17
25	†	†	†	†	†	†	†	†	†		†
26	77.28	75.00	75.69	32.02	31.17	31.37	31.45	30.61	30.75	1,056	79.94
27	*	*	*	*	*	*	*	*	*	*	*
28	75.79	73.55	75.09	31.08	30.31	30.78	30.72	29.85	30.39	1,353	79.32
29	76.98	74.68	75.50	31.43	30.70	30.91	30.92	29.99	30.40	1,114	79.08
30	77.64	75.08	77.15	31.66	30.95	31.39	30.91	30.15	30.67	1,007	79.13
31	77.80	72.49	73.28	31.78	29.39	29.57	30.51	28.40	28.60	1,482	78.33
High			88.78			38.65			35.92	33,031	82.30
Low			73.28			29.57			28.60		78.33

*Sunday †Holiday

APRIL, 1932

Date	Industrials			Railroads			Utilities			Daily Sales	40 Bonds
	High	Low	Close	High	Low	Close	High	Low	Close		
1	74.38	71.21	72.18	29.66	28.07	28.53	28.95	27.91	28.16	1,530	77.69
2	72.09	69.85	71.30	28.26	26.99	27.53	28.15	27.37	27.68	1,046	77.26
3	*										*
4	71.84	68.32	71.19	27.78	26.07	27.43	27.75	26.52	27.42	1,614	75.96
5	70.67	67.29	68.07	26.87	25.25	25.77	25.11	25.83	26.10	1,483	75.90
6	68.93	65.85	66.46	25.65	24.53	24.90	26.40	24.91	25.12	2,995	75.28
7	68.29	65.23	66.20	25.26	24.42	24.69	25.80	24.49	25.05	1,795	75.07
8	65.73	61.98	62.90	24.51	23.17	23.44	25.13	23.88	24.40	2,126	74.45
9	66.82	63.92	64.48	24.44	23.58	23.79	25.72	24.76	25.01	1,148	74.10
10	*										*
11	64.54	60.76	62.04	23.60	22.37	22.45	25.03	23.80	24.49	1,695	73.86
12	64.13	60.62	62.33	22.87	21.18	21.73	25.12	23.88	24.59	1,553	73.42
13	63.74	60.66	61.18	22.21	20.75	20.94	25.23	24.29	24.44	1,097	73.34
14	63.84	59.10	63.27	22.39	20.05	22.15	25.56	23.73	25.36	1,724	73.45
15	66.51	62.21	64.49	23.69	21.84	22.95	27.05	25.30	26.30	1,542	74.69
16	65.58	62.87	63.39	23.30	22.31	22.36	26.58	25.63	25.78	579	76.16
17	*										*
18	63.21	60.57	60.85	23.14	22.04	22.29	25.76	24.66	24.72	848	76.09
19	61.45	58.91	59.75	22.58	21.90	22.26	24.91	24.11	24.45	1,033	75.79
20	60.81	58.70	59.46	23.45	22.42	23.02	24.78	24.07	24.40	991	75.82
21	62.71	59.04	62.01	24.74	23.00	24.45	25.59	24.34	25.35	1,106	76.13
22	61.39	58.26	58.88	23.91	22.46	22.64	25.06	24.15	24.31	915	76.31
23	59.70	58.20	59.22	22.98	22.40	22.90	24.66	24.10	24.56	471	76.23
24	*										*
25	60.51	58.06	58.92	23.23	22.54	22.80	25.03	24.32	24.68	640	76.19
26	61.01	58.51	59.71	24.00	23.06	23.58	25.56	24.81	25.11	790	76.11
27	62.15	59.40	61.28	24.57	23.52	23.95	26.12	25.11	25.80	1,120	75.99
28	61.36	57.98	58.24	23.84	22.80	22.85	25.77	24.67	24.72	925	75.63
29	57.81	55.37	55.93	22.32	21.46	21.84	24.58	23.93	24.21	1,164	75.24
30	56.74	55.29	56.11	21.75	21.24	21.44	24.36	23.93	24.22	439	74.98
High			72.18			28.53			28.16	31,471	77.69
Low			55.93			20.94			24.21		73.34

*Sunday †Holiday

MAY, 1932

Date	Industrials			Railroads			Utilities			Daily Sales	40 Bonds
	High	Low	Close	High	Low	Close	High	Low	Close		
1	*									*	
2	56.28	54.20	55.37	21.13	20.40	20.66	24.26	23.64	23.92	776	74.68
3	56.12	53.80	54.15	20.83	20.19	20.33	24.16	23.46	23.58	901	74.52
4	55.21	52.33	54.88	20.58	19.72	20.48	24.03	23.10	23.90	1,319	73.61
5	55.74	52.73	54.10	20.54	19.42	20.02	24.05	23.28	23.68	1,003	73.59
6	59.76	54.58	59.01	21.57	20.08	21.39	25.29	23.83	25.10	1,630	73.65
7	60.01	57.55	58.04	22.14	21.39	21.65	25.32	24.63	24.70	639	73.89
8	*										*
9	58.74	56.29	57.04	21.53	20.75	20.92	24.97	24.31	24.54	638	73.94
10	58.94	56.68	57.68	21.27	20.68	20.90	24.96	24.38	24.62	738	73.89
11	59.52	57.47	57.83	21.21	20.50	20.58	24.93	24.40	24.50	687	73.95
12	57.71	54.91	55.62	20.25	19.03	19.27	24.38	23.58	23.78	919	73.45
13	55.33	53.23	53.46	18.98	18.11	18.17	23.61	22.86	22.92	867	72.81
14	53.20	51.81	52.48	18.10	17.74	17.83	22.77	22.33	22.60	600	72.41
15	*										*
16	54.63	50.21	53.96	18.62	16.76	18.25	23.11	21.79	22.92	1,307	71.83
17	55.65	52.16	54.04	18.51	17.38	18.05	23.16	22.25	22.71	933	71.62
18	54.68	52.28	52.81	18.08	17.42	17.57	22.78	21.95	22.08	684	71.39
19	53.88	51.79	53.14	17.64	17.05	17.40	22.16	21.51	21.92	675	70.82
20	55.50	52.97	53.31	18.32	17.54	17.67	22.60	21.63	21.73	767	70.91
21	53.45	52.34	53.04	17.45	17.22	17.40	21.81	21.48	21.76	305	70.64
22	*										*
23	54.34	52.61	52.98	17.56	17.17	17.26	21.97	21.36	21.56	558	70.25
24	53.20	50.59	50.85	17.13	16.25	16.29	21.50	20.53	20.61	983	69.59
25	50.79	48.65	49.10	16.17	15.41	15.63	20.54	19.84	20.03	1,302	69.15
26	50.72	47.02	49.99	16.15	14.96	15.94	20.36	18.92	20.01	1,853	68.49
27	49.94	47.17	47.47	15.95	15.30	15.37	20.07	18.98	19.04	902	67.95
28	47.97	46.31	47.70	15.44	14.97	15.27	19.23	18.46	19.12	675	67.75
29	*										*
30	†	†	†	†	†	†	†	†	†	†	†
31	46.93	44.27	44.74	15.11	14.24	14.30	18.75	17.68	17.74	1,476	66.30
High			59.01			21.65			25.10	23,137	74.68
Low			44.74			14.30			17.74		66.30

*Sunday †Holiday

Date	Industrials			Railroads			Utilities			Daily Sales	40 Bonds
	High	Low	Close	High	Low	Close	High	Low	Close		
1	48.60	44.13	44.93	15.69	13.86	14.10	19.08	16.61	16.73	1,842	65.78
2	47.74	43.49	47.25	15.18	13.68	15.02	17.60	15.78	17.40	1,867	66.18
3	50.29	47.35	48.40	16.46	15.52	15.87	19.54	17.80	18.73	1,887	68.56
4	51.21	49.20	50.88	17.79	16.46	17.64	20.26	19.23	19.83	999	70.95
5	*										
6	50.63	48.54	49.32	17.61	16.67	17.07	19.80	18.90	19.31	962	71.21
7	49.74	47.18	47.47	17.16	16.22	16.25	19.59	18.38	18.47	833	71.43
8	47.21	45.01	45.20	15.90	15.09	15.14	18.36	17.23	17.31	986	70.85
9	47.55	44.45	45.32	15.95	15.06	15.25	18.00	16.82	17.06	1,187	70.31
10	49.52	45.22	48.94	16.44	15.43	16.38	18.58	17.10	18.48	1,270	70.49
11	51.09	48.01	48.26	17.56	16.39	16.62	19.28	18.29	18.37	809	70.64
12	*										
13	48.97	47.12	48.11	16.72	16.30	16.43	18.45	17.84	18.12	568	70.52
14	49.70	47.59	49.00	17.10	16.27	16.83	18.95	17.98	18.59	756	70.59
15	51.43	49.37	50.62	17.62	16.89	17.37	19.67	18.88	19.26	1,155	70.66
16	51.43	49.73	50.34	18.34	17.14	17.71	19.61	19.02	19.25	851	70.94
17	50.36	47.44	47.56	17.45	16.27	16.32	19.05	18.07	18.11	786	70.92
18	48.01	46.85	47.55	16.43	16.18	16.32	18.35	17.99	18.25	341	71.03
19	*										
20	48.66	47.41	47.80	16.86	16.30	16.43	18.53	18.05	18.26	388	71.05
21	48.42	46.47	46.58	16.73	16.09	16.10	18.41	17.68	17.83	497	71.01
22	46.66	45.43	46.27	16.06	15.69	15.91	17.96	17.48	17.83	607	70.85
23	47.47	46.15	46.83	16.07	15.77	15.90	18.24	17.74	18.15	472	70.62
24	47.57	44.55	44.84	16.06	14.91	14.92	18.16	17.25	17.32	773	70.22
25	45.08	44.31	44.76	14.94	14.66	14.74	17.80	17.46	17.66	310	70.13
26	*										
27	44.82	42.52	42.93	14.36	13.64	13.76	17.85	17.02	17.13	767	69.88
28	44.30	42.31	43.18	14.14	13.26	13.45	17.53	16.80	17.09	830	69.85
29	44.21	42.54	43.66	13.75	13.28	13.56	17.38	16.88	17.27	631	69.76
30	44.44	42.41	42.84	13.95	13.25	13.43	17.45	16.90	17.08	627	69.62
High			50.88			17.71			19.83	23,001	71.43
Low			42.84			13.43			16.73		65.78

*Sunday †Holiday

Date	Industrials			Railroads			Utilities			Daily Sales	40 Bonds
	High	Low	Close	High	Low	Close	High	Low	Close		
1	44.63	42.64	44.39	13.91	13.48	13.84	17.96	17.15	17.91	605	69.69
2	†										
3	*										
4	†										
5	44.43	42.53	43.47	13.85	13.50	13.75	17.78	17.05	17.33	613	69.66
6	44.50	42.31	44.08	14.08	13.53	14.00	17.66	16.98	17.56	728	69.72
7	44.26	41.63	41.81	14.41	13.78	13.82	17.65	16.83	16.88	784	69.90
8	42.61	40.56	41.22	13.61	13.16	13.23	17.00	16.41	16.53	720	70.09
9	41.89	41.08	41.63	13.42	13.23	13.32	16.60	16.42	16.56	235	70.23
10	*										
11	43.03	40.92	42.99	14.10	13.60	14.10	17.05	16.35	17.00	597	70.31
12	43.65	42.36	42.68	14.43	13.94	14.20	17.41	16.85	17.08	700	70.52
13	45.05	42.35	44.88	14.74	14.11	14.70	18.00	17.06	17.98	980	70.93
14	45.85	43.91	44.34	15.25	14.68	14.81	18.44	17.63	17.75	999	71.10
15	45.82	43.74	45.47	15.76	14.74	15.66	18.38	17.50	18.31	807	71.24
16	45.98	45.02	45.29	15.99	15.65	15.73	18.46	18.18	18.33	350	71.45
17	*										
18	45.61	43.83	44.07	15.95	15.16	15.19	18.29	17.70	17.76	612	71.37
19	44.51	43.53	43.79	15.18	14.89	15.05	17.77	17.43	17.65	465	71.51
20	45.56	44.22	45.43	16.11	15.61	16.01	18.26	17.80	18.20	627	71.96
21	46.86	45.12	46.50	16.81	16.02	16.76	18.56	18.16	18.46	925	72.46
22	48.31	46.35	47.69	17.78	16.97	17.49	19.20	18.45	18.98	1,448	72.97
23	47.98	47.05	47.84	17.57	17.21	17.42	19.05	18.79	18.99	369	73.19
24	*										
25	50.23	48.01	49.78	18.51	17.68	18.39	20.00	19.08	19.91	1,546	73.49
26	50.41	48.49	49.04	18.60	17.71	17.78	20.18	19.46	19.58	1,498	73.61
27	51.71	48.18	51.34	18.92	17.43	18.82	21.10	19.29	20.98	1,701	73.56
28	53.84	50.67	52.61	20.64	18.73	19.74	22.26	20.86	21.74	2,734	74.24
29	54.68	51.52	53.89	21.88	19.42	21.59	23.05	21.30	22.79	2,102	74.90
30	54.74	53.02	54.26	22.07	21.41	21.74	23.00	22.30	22.79	911	74.97
31	*										
High			54.26			21.74			22.79	23,057	74.97
Low			41.22			13.23			16.53		69.66

*Sunday †Holiday

AUGUST, 1932

Date	Industrials High	Low	Close	Railroads High	Low	Close	Utilities High	Low	Close	Daily Sales	40 Bonds
1	56.92	53.59	54.94	22.24	21.16	21.34	23.73	22.38	22.79	2,107	75.52
2	55.57	52.40	53.16	21.17	19.81	20.00	22.73	21.43	21.68	1,439	75.40
3	58.69	52.99	58.22	22.15	19.95	22.00	24.04	21.60	23.87	2,399	75.39
4	62.13	57.90	59.63	23.22	21.76	21.95	25.25	23.68	24.20	3,521	75.80
5	63.42	59.73	62.60	22.87	21.83	22.48	25.56	24.30	25.21	2,684	75.82
6	67.57	63.36	66.56	25.63	22.47	24.72	26.92	25.37	26.48	2,728	76.30
7	*		*	*		*	*		*		*
8	71.49	64.86	67.71	28.60	24.18	26.79	28.63	25.96	27.30	5,461	77.24
9	69.53	65.36	67.08	27.90	25.87	26.77	29.60	26.56	28.25	3,838	77.23
10	71.34	65.65	69.39	29.51	26.52	28.62	29.82	27.89	29.29	4,430	78.24
11	71.62	66.95	68.90	30.00	27.66	28.63	30.24	28.26	29.15	4,402	78.62
12	69.06	62.45	63.11	28.86	25.90	26.28	29.89	26.93	27.07	3,706	79.12
13	64.32	60.89	63.19	26.19	24.56	25.54	27.71	25.97	27.05	1,757	78.80
14	*		*	*		*	*		*		*
15	66.72	62.93	66.51	28.34	25.87	28.30	28.84	26.93	28.74	1,906	79.27
16	70.54	67.16	68.91	30.83	28.77	30.11	30.40	29.06	29.70	3,612	79.80
17	70.56	65.62	67.50	30.31	27.98	28.76	30.83	28.58	29.35	2,874	79.93
18	68.52	65.65	67.93	30.38	28.38	30.32	30.20	28.86	29.95	1,785	80.64
19	69.47	66.10	66.84	31.32	29.39	29.89	30.67	29.18	29.75	2,168	81.37
20	67.58	65.99	67.18	30.28	29.50	30.14	29.86	29.08	29.70	661	81.85
21	*		*	*		*	*		*		*
22	71.11	67.50	70.87	33.29	30.37	33.20	31.85	29.90	31.71	3,175	82.98
23	73.80	70.69	72.13	34.46	32.76	33.45	33.03	31.68	32.26	4,572	83.26
24	74.01	70.82	73.55	36.62	32.65	36.32	32.97	31.56	32.69	3,692	82.59
25	75.88	72.54	73.31	37.94	35.91	36.36	33.43	32.11	32.28	4,170	82.24
26	75.41	71.28	74.43	37.00	34.38	36.36	33.20	31.25	32.86	3,117	81.88
27	76.48	74.76	75.61	36.85	35.92	36.25	34.75	32.93	34.21	2,202	82.10
28	*		*	*		*	*		*		*
29	77.01	74.25	75.22	36.79	35.25	35.68	35.16	33.88	34.41	3,926	82.29
30	76.73	73.59	74.30	37.03	34.90	35.87	34.74	33.53	33.65	3,295	82.11
31	74.44	71.11	73.16	36.99	34.38	36.53	33.73	32.08	33.10	2,998	81.53
High			75.61			36.53			34.41	82,626	83.26
Low			53.16			20.00			21.68		75.39

*Sunday †Holiday

SEPTEMBER, 1932

Date	Industrials High	Low	Close	Railroads High	Low	Close	Utilities High	Low	Close	Daily Sales	40 Bonds
1	74.55	71.92	73.67	37.78	35.81	37.52	33.91	32.80	33.59	2,419	81.74
2	77.12	74.00	76.77	39.22	37.56	38.52	34.86	33.77	34.73	3,487	82.03
3	79.22	77.24	78.33	39.64	38.49	39.27	35.91	35.00	35.58	2,440	82.07
4	*		*	*		*	*		*		*
5	†		†	†		†	†		†		†
6	80.36	76.66	77.28	39.81	37.75	37.99	36.16	34.28	34.46	4,363	82.05
7	80.28	76.78	79.93	39.17	37.40	39.06	36.28	34.12	36.11	4,153	82.09
8	81.39	76.92	77.49	40.85	38.12	38.35	36.67	34.53	34.71	5,370	81.94
9	79.91	75.69	76.19	39.77	37.59	37.80	35.43	33.78	34.05	4,036	82.12
10	77.36	74.96	76.54	38.37	36.95	37.94	34.60	33.40	34.29	1,498	82.10
11	*		*	*		*	*		*		*
12	76.68	70.81	72.33	37.26	33.09	34.22	34.16	31.53	32.24	4,050	81.62
13	71.54	66.38	69.85	33.58	29.72	32.57	31.41	28.53	30.73	5,102	81.05
14	72.41	65.54	65.88	33.58	29.55	29.71	32.06	28.68	28.80	3,248	80.89
15	68.58	64.27	67.94	31.54	28.99	31.28	30.35	28.39	30.12	3,142	80.86
16	69.84	66.11	67.10	33.16	30.81	32.08	30.71	29.13	29.38	1,914	80.78
17	68.03	65.92	66.44	33.08	31.64	32.04	29.96	28.98	29.11	725	80.93
18	*		*	*		*	*		*		*
19	67.40	64.82	65.06	32.62	31.17	31.43	29.67	28.46	28.70	1,260	80.89
20	67.65	64.68	67.49	32.54	31.13	32.48	29.51	28.42	29.42	1,251	81.00
21	75.53	69.46	75.16	36.42	33.53	36.22	33.10	30.61	33.01	4,346	81.51
22	76.01	72.14	72.71	37.64	35.11	35.68	33.48	31.88	32.08	3,685	81.35
23	75.16	72.42	73.92	37.16	35.52	36.22	33.28	32.10	32.74	2,195	81.46
24	75.68	73.88	74.83	37.52	36.47	36.95	33.68	32.81	33.43	1,336	81.51
25	*		*	*		*	*		*		*
26	75.67	70.41	71.06	36.96	34.43	34.71	33.58	31.19	31.42	2,083	81.63
27	73.42	69.98	71.49	35.73	34.25	34.82	32.32	31.18	31.72	1,399	81.61
28	74.07	71.40	73.52	35.91	34.55	35.62	32.83	31.58	32.58	1,382	81.66
29	74.36	71.24	71.53	35.94	34.54	34.70	32.92	31.85	31.90	1,336	81.81
30	72.00	69.75	71.56	35.01	33.81	34.61	31.87	30.99	31.61	1,159	81.69
High			79.93			39.27			36.11	67,381	82.12
Low			65.06			29.71			28.70		80.78

*Sunday †Holiday

OCTOBER, 1932

Date	Industrials High	Low	Close	Railroads High	Low	Close	Utilities High	Low	Close	Daily Sales	40 Bonds
1	72.31	71.18	72.09	34.92	34.41	34.80	31.93	31.55	31.88	338	81.81
2	*	*	*	*	*	*	*	*	*	*	*
3	72.32	69.88	71.21	34.41	33.08	33.67	32.05	31.11	31.71	1,003	81.63
4	72.63	70.45	71.16	34.15	33.26	33.46	32.45	31.55	31.92	1,240	81.50
5	70.92	65.90	66.07	33.29	29.38	29.52	31.95	29.45	29.59	2,953	80.92
6	67.08	64.67	66.28	30.06	28.48	29.31	29.96	29.02	29.62	1,944	80.73
7	66.89	62.16	62.67	29.38	26.81	27.05	29.68	27.83	28.25	2,303	80.45
8	62.71	60.39	61.17	27.14	25.44	25.96	28.16	27.02	27.30	1,533	80.14
9	*	*	*	*	*	*	*	*	*	*	*
10	62.57	57.67	58.47	26.53	23.38	23.65	27.48	25.25	25.51	2,282	79.42
11	62.52	59.07	61.66	26.18	24.40	25.77	27.46	25.90	27.28	1,745	79.40
12	†	†	†	†	†	†	†	†	†	†	†
13	62.54	58.84	59.76	26.59	24.68	25.07	27.34	25.63	26.03	1,228	79.32
14	65.45	60.27	63.84	28.42	25.71	27.71	28.40	26.16	27.68	2,029	79.67
15	65.18	63.59	64.22	28.77	27.61	27.95	28.40	27.74	27.96	594	79.75
16	*	*	*	*	*	*	*	*	*	*	*
17	64.07	62.21	62.69	28.02	26.97	27.30	28.11	27.30	27.57	770	79.74
18	64.82	62.06	63.49	28.49	27.40	28.08	28.53	27.59	28.04	1,021	79.65
19	66.06	63.35	65.74	29.76	28.09	29.45	29.28	28.08	29.15	1,303	79.79
20	66.13	63.92	64.40	30.54	29.10	29.76	29.30	28.43	28.58	1,056	80.08
21	63.64	60.71	61.01	29.09	26.99	27.28	28.21	26.90	27.01	1,242	79.81
22	61.82	60.32	60.85	28.10	27.02	27.26	27.31	26.80	26.94	448	79.69
23	*	*	*	*	*	*	*	*	*	*	*
24	61.58	60.07	61.03	27.47	26.83	27.33	27.18	26.52	27.07	551	79.52
25	61.69	59.70	60.32	27.50	26.84	27.12	27.24	26.57	26.81	604	79.20
26	61.73	59.03	61.36	27.75	26.47	27.64	27.29	26.41	27.18	861	78.87
27	62.83	60.77	61.86	28.46	27.46	27.86	27.79	27.03	27.42	717	79.06
28	63.51	61.81	63.09	28.89	28.05	28.67	28.25	27.50	28.01	693	79.18
29	63.67	61.85	62.09	29.12	28.05	28.22	28.25	27.67	27.71	360	79.22
30	*	*	*	*	*	*	*	*	*	*	*
31	62.19	61.06	61.90	28.21	27.39	28.01	27.58	27.20	27.45	385	78.96
High			72.09			34.80			31.92	29,202	81.81
Low			58.47			23.65			25.51		78.87

*Sunday   †Holiday

NOVEMBER, 1932

Date	Industrials High	Low	Close	Railroads High	Low	Close	Utilities High	Low	Close	Daily Sales	40 Bonds
1	61.57	59.86	60.22	27.52	26.74	26.88	27.42	26.48	26.64	522	78.73
2	61.13	57.96	58.53	26.94	24.90	25.33	26.86	25.63	25.83	1,101	78.39
3	59.06	57.21	58.28	25.32	24.17	24.70	25.96	25.27	25.63	1,020	78.01
4	62.07	58.99	61.53	26.77	25.21	26.45	27.15	25.95	26.90	969	78.17
5	62.77	61.48	62.41	27.20	26.54	26.91	27.29	26.82	27.08	463	78.30
6	*	*	*	*	*	*	*	*	*	*	*
7	65.43	63.22	64.58	28.66	27.34	28.04	28.20	27.28	27.67	1,610	78.37
8	†	†	†	†	†	†	†	†	†	†	†
9	65.42	61.02	61.67	28.65	26.57	26.94	28.03	26.39	26.72	1,268	78.34
10	65.61	61.44	65.54	28.98	26.94	28.93	28.70	26.61	28.65	1,567	78.45
11	68.27	65.41	68.03	30.80	29.23	30.58	29.95	28.81	29.88	2,632	78.96
12	68.87	67.07	68.04	30.98	29.93	30.61	30.21	29.56	29.90	889	79.04
13	*	*	*	*	*	*	*	*	*	*	*
14	67.88	64.87	65.57	30.35	29.12	29.31	29.93	28.86	29.03	1,307	78.75
15	66.17	63.54	65.26	29.62	28.70	29.39	29.28	28.11	28.93	1,049	78.83
16	65.26	62.56	63.24	29.10	28.08	28.26	29.10	27.95	28.25	947	78.75
17	63.83	62.18	62.99	28.35	27.52	27.79	28.45	27.80	28.09	709	78.59
18	64.73	62.66	62.96	28.17	27.35	27.41	28.61	27.82	27.92	728	78.55
19	64.35	62.81	64.14	27.94	27.21	27.87	28.39	27.81	28.30	386	78.33
20	*	*	*	*	*	*	*	*	*	*	*
21	64.68	63.23	63.65	28.28	27.69	27.90	28.78	28.16	28.38	612	78.20
22	64.40	62.86	63.16	28.25	27.80	27.89	28.68	28.22	28.35	535	78.11
23	62.60	59.10	59.47	27.73	26.58	26.73	28.13	27.01	27.22	1,201	77.92
24	†	†	†	†	†	†	†	†	†	†	†
25	59.54	57.47	58.78	26.78	25.77	26.55	27.14	26.44	26.90	1,003	77.76
26	59.99	58.67	58.89	27.11	26.42	26.47	27.36	26.83	27.00	376	77.71
27	*	*	*	*	*	*	*	*	*	*	*
28	59.71	58.10	59.17	26.65	25.99	26.41	27.01	26.43	26.76	540	77.68
29	59.74	58.31	58.77	26.73	26.13	26.27	27.03	26.53	26.71	526	77.53
30	59.33	55.94	56.35	26.36	24.59	25.04	26.94	25.84	26.08	1,093	77.29
High			68.04			30.61			29.90	23,054	79.04
Low			56.35			24.70			25.63		77.29

*Sunday   †Holiday

DECEMBER, 1932

Date	Industrials High	Low	Close	Railroads High	Low	Close	Utilities High	Low	Close	Daily Sales	40 Bonds
1	58.40	56.02	58.02	26.01	24.82	25.75	26.71	25.84	26.60	756	77.25
2	57.50	55.70	55.91	25.23	24.44	24.57	26.31	25.42	25.48	686	77.06
3	56.12	55.04	55.83	24.52	24.12	24.33	25.51	25.09	25.40	400	76.82
4	*									*	
5	58.06	55.58	56.53	25.30	24.29	24.59	26.19	25.26	25.59	725	76.74
6	59.96	56.95	59.58	26.93	25.21	26.81	26.84	25.72	26.70	1,109	76.83
7	60.97	59.12	59.77	27.67	26.74	26.98	27.24	26.42	26.61	1,194	76.91
8	60.51	58.97	60.05	27.23	26.67	27.00	26.92	26.39	26.81	705	77.01
9	61.90	59.28	61.58	27.87	26.66	27.73	27.96	26.79	27.80	1,180	77.19
10	61.98	60.81	61.25	27.91	27.45	27.57	27.91	27.51	27.61	483	77.20
11	*	*	*	*	*	*	*	*	*	*	*
12	62.50	60.68	61.48	28.27	27.40	27.87	28.28	27.55	27.93	923	77.57
13	61.38	59.98	60.35	27.85	27.23	27.47	28.06	27.41	27.70	734	77.45
14	62.11	59.19	61.93	28.21	27.14	28.16	28.40	27.27	28.33	1,018	77.45
15	62.89	60.98	61.16	28.61	27.69	27.84	28.85	28.05	28.14	1,177	77.57
16	61.40	59.75	60.52	27.94	27.09	27.70	28.24	27.66	28.00	916	77.37
17	60.74	59.82	60.11	27.78	27.49	27.59	28.26	27.90	28.10	414	77.52
18	*	*	*	*	*	*	*	*	*		
19	61.51	59.82	60.08	27.88	27.31	27.35	28.50	27.94	28.01	917	77.55
20	60.19	58.28	58.78	27.20	26.16	26.39	27.85	27.14	27.37	1,000	77.25
21	59.65	58.27	58.97	26.60	25.77	25.88	27.56	27.09	27.27	730	76.99
22	59.29	56.24	56.55	25.82	24.17	24.30	27.46	26.35	26.39	1,298	76.79
23	57.30	56.07	56.80	24.60	23.87	24.05	26.74	26.05	26.35	926	76.62
24	58.27	57.05	57.98	24.59	24.18	24.48	26.78	26.40	26.65	330	76.61
25							*			*	*
26	†	†	†	†	†	†	†	†	†	†	†
27	58.57	56.95	57.60	24.62	23.89	24.24	26.82	26.41	26.59	800	76.65
28	59.49	57.10	57.85	25.53	23.96	24.69	27.20	26.31	26.66	1,600	76.85
29	59.38	57.39	59.12	25.59	24.45	25.40	27.29	26.43	27.16	1,610	77.01
30	60.84	58.82	60.26	26.39	25.28	26.06	27.85	27.10	27.71	1,050	77.51
31	60.72	59.59	59.93	26.25	25.74	25.90	27.91	27.40	27.50	540	77.74
High			61.93			28.16			28.33	23,195	77.74
Low			55.83			24.05			25.40		76.61

*Sunday   †Holiday

JANUARY, 1933

Date	Industrials High	Low	Close	Railroads High	Low	Close	Utilities High	Low	Close	Daily Sales	40 Bonds
1	*						*			*	*
2	†	†	†	†	†	†	†	†	†	†	†
3	60.17	58.87	59.29	26.02	25.40	25.59	27.67	27.10	27.30	489	77.73
4	62.62	59.54	62.35	27.08	25.70	26.99	28.58	27.39	28.49	1,093	78.35
5	63.39	61.58	62.25	27.45	26.76	26.95	28.79	28.14	28.31	1,144	79.11
6	63.85	62.07	62.96	28.58	27.12	28.24	29.03	28.30	28.78	1,142	79.27
7	†	†	†	†	†	†	†	†	†	†	†
8											
9	63.64	61.90	62.31	29.10	28.09	28.32	28.96	28.28	28.35	933	79.72
10	64.57	61.83	64.35	29.53	28.13	29.44	29.03	28.09	29.00	1,149	80.06
11	65.28	63.62	63.81	30.35	29.18	29.52	29.75	28.81	29.05	1,617	80.47
12	64.80	62.84	63.09	29.83	28.98	29.08	29.33	28.72	28.82	916	80.63
13	63.94	62.12	63.18	29.24	28.57	28.86	28.98	28.41	28.70	834	80.52
14	63.47	62.35	63.09	28.60	28.26	28.47	28.74	28.37	28.65	361	80.48
15	*		*	*	*	*	*	*	*		
16	63.87	61.38	61.62	28.81	27.33	27.47	28.85	27.76	27.81	868	80.34
17	62.09	60.93	61.75	27.72	27.02	27.59	28.08	27.60	27.95	664	79.97
18	62.03	60.07	60.36	27.84	26.79	26.98	28.10	27.35	27.51	687	79.67
19	61.99	60.37	61.02	27.83	27.09	27.38	28.00	27.34	27.59	624	79.62
20	62.68	60.90	61.63	28.53	27.61	28.06	28.08	27.43	27.69	707	79.90
21	62.37	61.49	61.79	28.79	28.27	28.38	27.97	27.64	27.75	366	80.12
22	*		*	*	*	*	*	*	*		
23	62.10	60.55	61.46	28.17	27.54	27.81	27.77	27.33	27.55	664	80.06
24	61.99	60.67	61.30	28.08	27.56	27.78	27.68	27.13	27.36	493	80.09
25	62.66	60.84	62.33	28.34	27.19	27.99	27.93	27.24	27.79	752	80.17
26	62.79	61.61	61.73	28.62	27.80	27.97	27.96	27.56	27.65	809	80.49
27	61.98	60.03	61.43	28.74	27.30	28.48	27.73	27.03	27.45	972	80.49
28	61.04	60.42	60.71	28.44	27.91	28.13	27.41	27.22	27.31	300	80.50
29	*		*	*	*	*	*	*	*		
30	61.05	60.09	60.77	28.81	28.01	28.69	27.28	27.03	27.16	477	80.62
31	61.34	60.48	60.90	29.39	28.72	28.92	27.18	26.49	26.69	657	80.54
High			64.35			29.52			29.05	18,718	80.63
Low			59.29			25.59			26.69		77.73

*Sunday   †Holiday

FEBRUARY, 1933

Date	Industrials			Railroads			Utilities			Daily Sales	40 Bonds
	High	Low	Close	High	Low	Close	High	Low	Close		
1	60.89	58.63	59.08	29.55	28.11	28.39	26.68	25.66	25.81	1,191	80.54
2	58.90	57.45	58.03	28.34	27.26	27.67	25.71	24.90	25.26	1,252	80.24
3	58.46	57.11	58.11	28.27	27.38	28.16	25.35	24.56	24.91	907	79.91
4	58.15	57.29	57.55	28.15	27.72	27.84	25.01	24.69	24.76	420	79.98
5	*			*			*				
6	58.27	56.65	58.07	28.08	27.36	27.90	24.90	24.48	24.76	671	79.80
7	58.67	57.50	58.38	28.34	27.82	28.05	25.21	24.65	25.04	585	79.97
8	59.21	57.85	58.87	28.75	28.11	28.56	25.50	24.96	25.38	724	80.13
9	60.85	59.17	60.09	29.85	28.93	29.47	26.15	25.55	25.88	1,080	80.54
10	60.06	58.81	59.11	29.97	29.16	29.49	25.93	25.35	25.45	723	80.53
11	59.67	58.80	59.43	29.66	29.23	29.40	25.56	25.33	25.50	345	80.60
12	*			*			*				*
13	†	†	†	†	†	†	†	†	†	†	†
14	58.19	56.04	56.57	28.76	26.94	27.45	25.19	24.06	24.36	1,541	79.74
15	57.59	56.08	56.71	27.84	27.05	27.38	24.61	23.80	23.97	746	79.69
16	56.63	54.69	55.49	27.16	25.87	26.33	23.92	23.16	23.50	1,080	79.12
17	56.78	55.15	56.37	27.34	26.46	27.05	23.94	23.46	23.84	654	78.51
18	56.60	55.85	56.04	27.26	26.79	26.81	23.98	23.64	23.69	305	78.51
19	*			*			*				*
20	55.61	53.82	54.26	26.63	25.83	25.99	23.60	22.91	23.03	859	77.89
21	54.84	53.52	53.99	26.34	25.48	25.61	23.19	22.65	22.75	692	77.18
22	†	†	†	†	†	†	†	†	†		†
23	53.60	51.65	51.94	25.22	23.84	24.03	22.56	21.57	21.74	1,325	76.13
24	54.13	51.13	53.84	25.25	23.80	25.09	22.47	21.35	22.38	1,069	76.78
25	52.70	50.26	50.93	24.61	23.13	23.43	21.93	20.88	21.14	988	76.14
26	*		*				*				
27	52.13	49.68	50.16	24.42	23.32	23.49	21.65	20.75	20.90	1,253	75.47
28	52.12	49.83	51.39	24.50	23.30	24.08	21.82	20.80	21.68	906	75.00
High			60.09			29.49			25.88	19,314	80.60
Low			50.16			23.43			20.90		75.00

*Sunday †Holiday

MARCH, 1933

Date	Industrials			Railroads			Utilities			Daily Sales	40 Bonds
	High	Low	Close	High	Low	Close	High	Low	Close		
1	52.97	50.81	52.54	24.70	23.63	24.57	21.97	21.07	21.83	788	74.72
2	53.01	50.25	52.54	24.18	23.03	23.94	21.75	20.59	21.30	1,004	74.02
3	55.44	51.54	53.84	25.45	23.63	24.76	22.65	20.89	21.95	1,413	73.21
4											
5 .... *											
6											
7											
8	Stock Exchange closed			Stock Exchange closed			Stock Exchange closed				
9	Banking Moratorium			Banking Moratorium			Banking Moratorium				
10											
11											
12 .... *											
13											
14											
15	62.55	57.11	62.10	29.41	26.25	29.19	24.75	23.08	24.58	3,070	75.14
16	64.56	62.05	62.95	30.02	28.77	29.19	25.38	24.42	24.62	3,300	76.45
17	62.54	60.32	60.73	29.61	28.15	28.58	24.61	23.50	23.60	1,730	76.35
18	61.24	59.93	60.56	29.30	28.61	29.09	23.74	23.25	23.40	580	76.28
19	*		*			*			*		*
20	61.33	59.72	59.90	29.88	28.97	29.12	23.58	22.71	22.78	779	76.48
21	59.85	57.23	57.58	29.14	27.51	27.65	22.51	21.36	21.50	1,209	75.97
22	58.48	56.35	56.86	28.09	26.85	27.07	21.75	20.91	21.05	991	75.84
23	59.91	57.69	58.06	29.08	28.01	28.34	22.24	21.14	21.37	980	76.13
24	58.41	56.90	57.93	28.83	27.99	28.41	21.54	20.93	21.30	643	76.13
25	58.02	56.97	57.71	28.17	27.65	27.98	21.31	20.96	21.23	376	75.64
26	*		*			*			*		
27	57.62	56.31	56.53	28.03	27.21	27.33	21.18	20.55	20.60	501	76.48
28	58.02	56.12	57.92	27.87	26.95	27.83	21.07	20.37	20.98	601	75.17
29	57.90	56.57	56.81	27.89	27.00	27.14	20.96	20.35	20.41	640	74.93
30	57.17	56.10	56.49	27.05	26.51	26.74	20.60	20.17	20.40	624	74.75
31	57.05	54.94	55.40	26.98	25.16	25.54	20.34	19.15	19.33	881	74.41
High			62.95			29.19			24.62	20,097	76.48
Low			52.54			23.94			19.33		73.21

*Sunday †Holiday

APRIL, 1933

Date	Industrials High	Industrials Low	Industrials Close	Railroads High	Railroads Low	Railroads Close	Utilities High	Utilities Low	Utilities Close	Daily Sales	40 Bonds
1	56.12	55.03	55.66	25.63	24.57	25.06	19.56	19.08	19.38	447	74.36
2	*			*			*				*
3	56.62	55.26	55.69	25.54	24.56	24.99	19.63	19.10	19.33	600	74.14
4	56.61	55.00	56.09	25.16	24.19	24.55	19.53	19.02	19.33	721	73.78
5	58.69	56.53	57.50	25.57	23.60	23.64	20.11	19.23	19.52	1,145	73.55
6	59.56	57.73	58.80	25.02	24.00	24.41	20.18	19.38	19.58	1,227	73.55
7	60.06	58.18	58.78	24.97	24.38	24.52	19.93	19.35	19.49	954	73.62
8	59.38	58.15	59.30	25.05	24.44	25.00	19.86	19.47	19.83	439	73.60
9	*			*			*				*
10	62.23	59.98	62.11	26.54	25.58	26.46	21.17	20.18	21.11	1,760	74.03
11	62.65	60.71	61.15	26.81	26.05	26.17	21.91	21.13	21.22	1,435	74.36
12	61.08	59.68	60.26	26.23	25.63	25.80	21.14	20.51	20.68	748	74.27
13	63.31	60.35	62.69	25.94	26.01	26.60	21.66	20.78	21.35	1,660	74.73
14	†	†	†	†	†	†	†	†	†	†	†
15	63.90	62.37	62.88	27.09	26.45	26.60	21.56	20.88	20.97	959	74.72
16	*			*			*				*
17	62.75	60.93	61.59	26.32	25.53	25.70	21.10	20.26	20.75	1,005	74.41
18	63.31	60.74	62.65	26.50	25.52	26.12	21.17	20.41	20.99	1,435	74.76
19	68.70	63.56	68.31	27.90	26.02	27.59	21.70	20.00	21.24	5,088	73.76
20	75.20	69.78	72.27	29.35	27.78	28.75	25.03	21.36	24.62	7,128	73.53
21	72.80	68.64	69.78	31.88	29.16	29.51	24.56	22.36	22.64	5,215	74.10
22	72.44	68.79	72.24	30.76	29.08	30.66	23.29	21.84	23.17	2,276	74.35
23	*			*			*				*
24	74.84	72.32	73.69	31.77	30.50	31.08	24.60	23.11	23.70	4,805	75.05
25	73.70	70.77	72.45	30.77	29.68	30.11	23.82	22.78	23.28	3,504	75.20
26	73.58	70.86	72.64	31.85	30.02	31.17	24.40	22.98	23.77	2,915	75.67
27	73.06	70.72	71.71	31.15	30.09	30.44	24.25	23.25	23.58	1,880	76.20
28	73.34	69.78	73.10	31.08	29.71	30.87	23.93	22.79	23.71	2,164	76.45
29	78.15	74.55	77.66	32.57	31.32	32.37	25.21	24.01	25.09	3,389	76.56
30	*			*			*				*
High			77.66			32.37			25.09	52,897	76.56
Low			55.66			23.64			19.33		73.53

*Sunday †Holiday

MAY, 1933

Date	Industrials High	Industrials Low	Industrials Close	Railroads High	Railroads Low	Railroads Close	Utilities High	Utilities Low	Utilities Close	Daily Sales	40 Bonds
1	79.98	76.91	77.79	34.69	32.58	33.46	26.45	25.15	25.73	6,052	76.76
2	78.37	75.66	77.29	35.82	32.99	35.68	26.56	25.08	26.03	3,896	77.03
3	78.92	75.69	77.37	35.73	34.07	34.34	27.12	25.80	26.10	4,644	77.23
4	79.80	76.19	79.16	36.22	34.31	35.52	26.83	25.78	26.47	4,590	77.84
5	81.27	78.81	79.78	36.70	35.61	35.78	27.78	26.60	27.05	4,997	78.72
6	80.33	77.31	77.61	36.20	34.71	34.87	27.39	26.12	26.23	2,094	78.73
7	*			*			*				*
8	79.67	76.01	76.63	35.79	33.84	33.97	26.99	25.55	25.65	3,200	78.65
9	78.03	75.61	77.23	34.73	33.49	34.24	26.21	25.33	25.75	2,229	78.86
10	81.01	77.95	80.78	36.10	34.61	36.03	27.16	26.34	27.02	3,818	79.60
11	83.61	81.18	82.48	37.92	36.41	37.43	28.75	27.39	28.48	6,164	80.69
12	82.75	80.13	82.14	37.73	36.56	37.31	29.09	27.94	28.67	4,557	81.00
13	82.44	80.41	80.85	38.09	36.52	36.88	28.85	27.71	27.90	2,274	81.00
14	*			*			*				*
15	81.23	79.06	79.70	37.10	35.96	36.39	28.14	27.37	27.70	3,152	80.99
16	82.25	79.54	81.29	37.68	36.42	37.28	29.00	27.47	28.56	3,292	81.63
17	84.18	81.33	82.64	38.84	37.52	37.92	29.90	28.41	28.67	4,794	81.54
18	84.13	80.70	82.57	39.33	37.54	38.62	29.21	27.61	28.60	4,113	81.65
19	83.20	80.65	81.75	39.26	37.84	38.46	28.51	27.64	27.88	3,275	82.00
20	81.67	79.81	80.21	38.62	37.14	37.47	27.85	27.27	27.40	1,300	81.99
21	*			*			*				*
22	81.08	78.61	79.94	37.99	36.70	37.27	27.76	26.82	27.31	2,223	81.86
23	83.49	80.56	83.06	39.42	37.97	39.23	28.51	27.34	28.22	3,144	82.00
24	85.47	83.53	84.29	40.85	39.66	40.28	29.17	28.28	28.70	4,707	82.39
25	85.48	82.70	83.73	41.42	39.78	40.23	29.43	28.11	28.52	4,008	82.82
26	86.98	83.47	86.42	41.29	40.25	40.99	29.19	28.29	28.86	4,346	83.07
27	90.44	87.87	89.61	42.80	41.48	42.28	30.06	29.03	29.51	4,311	83.30
28	*			*			*				*
29	91.33	87.87	90.02	43.37	41.37	42.94	30.45	29.03	29.92	6,954	83.31
30	†	†	†	†	†	†	†	†	†	†	†
31	91.05	87.72	88.11	43.93	42.26	42.42	30.81	29.35	29.50	6,076	83.11
High			90.02			42.94			29.92	104,214	83.31
Low			76.63			33.46			25.65		76.76

*Sunday †Holiday

JUNE, 1933

Date	Industrials High	Low	Close	Railroads High	Low	Close	Utilities High	Low	Close	Daily Sales	40 Bonds
1	90.57	87.37	89.10	44.06	41.77	43.40	30.21	29.18	29.58	4,754	83.62
2	92.66	88.97	92.21	44.45	43.11	44.16	32.15	29.31	32.01	6,878	84.18
3	92.81	89.28	90.02	44.92	43.06	43.27	32.80	31.32	31.51	3,588	84.34
4	*										
5	92.37	89.14	91.89	45.07	42.75	44.41	33.00	31.10	32.83	5,008	84.37
6	93.83	90.66	91.90	45.06	42.82	43.33	34.29	32.41	33.49	6,216	84.34
7	94.38	91.04	92.98	44.41	42.96	43.53	35.15	33.60	34.22	6,641	84.62
8	95.15	91.59	93.52	44.68	41.91	43.04	35.20	33.60	34.26	6,357	84.77
9	95.03	91.64	94.29	43.39	41.80	43.00	34.82	33.05	34.52	5,310	84.64
10	95.56	93.63	94.42	43.82	42.80	42.98	35.83	34.50	35.36	2,786	84.48
11	*										
12	97.10	94.16	96.75	44.83	43.03	44.43	37.65	35.51	37.50	5,812	84.62
13	97.92	94.21	94.79	46.14	43.80	44.30	38.10	35.84	36.06	6,304	84.55
14	96.29	91.41	94.06	44.71	42.64	43.77	37.10	34.91	35.88	5,548	84.56
15	93.94	88.17	88.87	44.33	41.25	41.41	36.12	32.71	32.94	4,893	84.34
16	91.11	86.48	89.22	42.52	39.85	41.17	34.22	31.60	33.03	5,710	84.07
17	91.02	89.10	90.23	42.21	41.23	41.67	33.75	32.93	33.39	1,568	84.18
18	*										
19	96.36	92.86	95.99	44.88	42.90	44.73	36.35	34.73	36.26	5,482	84.55
20	98.34	94.57	95.23	45.86	44.00	44.22	36.79	34.80	34.98	5,543	84.76
21	97.34	94.41	95.91	45.39	43.92	44.39	35.70	34.51	34.95	3,892	84.78
22	97.79	91.69	92.93	45.49	42.54	43.19	35.80	33.10	33.61	4,374	84.98
23	95.59	91.93	95.53	44.66	42.75	44.56	34.88	32.91	34.72	3,314	84.99
24	96.42	94.46	95.67	45.02	44.01	44.48	34.86	34.01	34.56	1,696	85.28
25	*										
26	99.10	95.93	98.49	45.81	44.72	45.46	35.58	34.38	35.20	4,530	85.51
27	100.27	98.01	98.74	47.87	46.12	47.07	36.10	35.21	35.46	5,640	85.84
28	100.48	96.69	97.74	48.64	46.32	47.19	36.08	34.55	34.89	5,510	85.94
29	99.23	95.90	96.99	48.11	46.44	46.95	35.72	33.88	34.25	4,590	86.08
30	98.69	95.50	98.14	48.86	46.62	48.60	34.54	33.63	34.35	3,630	86.20
High			98.74			48.60			37.50	125,620	86.20
Low			88.87			41.17			29.58		83.62

*Sunday   †Holiday

JULY, 1933

Date	Industrials High	Low	Close	Railroads High	Low	Close	Utilities High	Low	Close	Daily Sales	40 Bonds
1	101.61	99.15	100.92	50.14	49.12	49.78	35.16	34.50	34.93	2,791	86.40
2	*			*			*			*	*
3	104.99	101.64	103.77	53.58	50.54	53.38	36.95	35.15	36.45	6,715	86.74
4	†	†	†	†	†	†				†	†
5	104.70	101.02	102.73	54.66	51.74	54.36	36.74	35.00	35.66	5,802	86.73
6	105.56	101.21	104.98	56.82	53.80	56.38	37.00	35.41	36.52	6,542	87.31
7	107.51	103.23	105.35	58.09	55.48	56.53	37.54	35.91	36.71	6,973	87.47
8	106.25	103.88	105.15	56.60	55.23	55.67	36.90	36.03	36.53	3,008	87.86
9	*										
10	105.87	103.12	104.08	55.47	54.10	54.73	37.86	35.89	36.88	4,837	87.55
11	105.10	101.97	103.08	55.70	53.39	54.24	37.25	35.96	36.25	5,237	87.59
12	105.46	101.87	104.55	54.71	53.08	54.30	37.35	35.82	36.86	5,185	87.73
13	107.77	104.54	105.51	56.94	54.59	55.52	38.98	37.10	37.73	7,451	88.41
14	107.63	103.94	105.04	55.80	54.22	54.81	38.26	36.95	37.18	5,226	88.51
15	106.75	104.50	106.10	55.01	53.89	54.69	37.64	36.95	37.19	2,242	88.67
16	*										
17	110.30	106.22	108.27	56.15	54.61	55.10	38.53	37.24	37.56	6,381	88.84
18	110.53	106.98	108.67	56.68	55.13	55.63	38.43	37.32	37.51	6,586	89.07
19	109.23	102.32	103.58	56.85	53.08	54.01	38.65	35.88	36.20	7,450	89.04
20	105.65	94.76	96.26	55.27	49.02	49.56	36.91	32.52	32.92	8,117	88.67
21	98.69	84.45	88.71	50.69	43.05	44.82	33.73	28.44	30.30	9,572	87.87
22	91.27	85.51	88.42	45.63	42.55	44.32	30.73	28.53	29.58	4,224	87.46
23	*			*			*			*	*
24	94.75	90.63	94.28	47.66	45.16	47.37	32.25	30.50	32.13	3,415	87.59
25	96.27	91.77	92.83	49.03	46.49	46.98	33.36	31.36	31.60	3,538	87.78
26	95.50	92.23	95.05	47.87	46.34	47.25	32.46	31.43	32.25	2,040	88.07
27	97.28	94.12	96.03	49.36	47.51	48.31	32.90	31.69	32.21	2,462	88.24
28	95.90	93.75	94.54	48.67	47.31	47.81	32.25	31.45	31.56	..1,391	88.23
29	†	†	†	†	†	†	†	†	†		†
30											
31	94.18	87.75	90.77	47.50	44.06	45.46	31.40	29.26	29.99	3,085	88.02
High			108.67			56.53			37.73	120,271	89.07
Low			88.42			44.32			29.58		86.40

*Sunday. †Holiday.

AUGUST, 1933

Date	Industrials			Railroads			Utilities			Daily Sales	40 Bonds
	High	Low	Close	High	Low	Close	High	Low	Close		
1	93.23	89.61	92.70	47.04	44.90	46.81	31.09	29.83	31.01	1,784	88.09
2	95.27	91.97	94.84	47.82	46.29	47.64	31.94	30.75	31.78	1,727	88.05
3	95.86	93.21	94.10	48.06	46.89	47.23	32.06	31.03	31.34	1,509	87.97
4	93.45	92.03	92.62	47.04	46.62	46.77	31.03	30.55	30.73	500	87.91
5	‡	‡	‡	‡	‡	‡	‡	‡	‡	‡	‡
6											
7	93.32	91.63	92.55	47.09	46.36	46.69	30.53	29.76	30.04	765	87.93
8	96.10	93.16	95.84	48.02	46.53	47.91	30.97	30.18	30.70	1,232	88.03
9	99.39	96.17	99.06	49.96	47.97	49.67	32.03	30.87	31.82	2,502	88.12
10	100.14	96.48	97.58	50.54	48.87	49.29	32.46	31.11	31.48	2,822	88.19
11	98.68	96.28	97.47	50.14	48.66	49.27	31.75	31.03	31.34	1,343	88.15
12	‡	‡	‡	‡	‡	‡	‡	‡	‡	‡	‡
13											
14	97.40	94.63	96.53	48.96	47.94	48.58	31.07	30.25	30.78	1,222	87.98
15	97.53	95.72	96.63	49.03	48.40	48.58	31.06	30.41	30.59	907	87.92
16	96.28	92.95	94.44	47.79	46.25	46.89	30.42	29.13	29.57	1,804	87.97
17	99.49	93.59	99.30	49.09	46.46	49.08	31.03	29.13	30.92	2,474	87.99
18	100.77	96.81	98.32	49.81	48.15	48.55	31.21	29.98	30.21	2,087	87.91
19	‡	‡	‡	‡	‡	‡	‡	‡	‡	‡	‡
20											
21	100.86	98.57	100.17	49.91	48.79	49.67	30.94	30.15	30.58	1,562	87.90
22	101.71	99.02	101.34	50.87	49.38	50.79	30.81	30.10	30.61	1,964	88.01
23	102.75	99.58	100.38	51.67	50.04	50.51	30.83	29.89	30.05	2,583	87.78
24	102.77	99.52	101.41	51.62	50.35	51.09	30.39	29.71	30.23	1,727	87.68
25	105.60	102.84	105.07	53.65	51.80	53.37	31.61	30.41	31.18	3,328	87.58
26	‡	‡	‡	‡	‡	‡	‡	‡	‡	‡	‡
27											
28	105.53	103.02	104.72	53.88	52.59	53.60	31.35	30.65	31.05	2,122	87.52
29	105.39	100.23	103.59	54.81	52.21	53.81	32.00	30.32	31.11	3,118	87.57
30	104.13	100.38	102.35	53.82	51.84	52.80	31.53	30.38	31.03	2,171	87.33
31	103.31	101.48	102.41	52.75	52.13	52.46	31.38	30.68	30.86	1,142	87.17
High			105.07			53.81			31.82	42,457	88.19
Low			92.55			46.69			29.57		87.17

*Sunday †Holiday

SEPTEMBER, 1933

Date	Industrials			Railroads			Utilities			Daily Sales	40 Bonds
	High	Low	Close	High	Low	Close	High	Low	Close		
1	103.89	101.86	103.66	52.68	51.67	52.56	31.05	30.51	30.86	1,219	87.17
2	‡	‡	‡	‡	‡	‡	‡	‡	‡	‡	‡
3											
4	†	†	†	†	†	†	†	†	†	†	†
5	103.34	99.80	100.22	52.11	50.26	50.42	30.81	29.83	29.88	1,253	87.16
6	100.90	97.74	100.33	50.47	48.49	49.85	29.98	29.05	29.80	1,885	86.87
7	101.12	98.82	99.20	50.43	49.27	49.46	29.78	29.17	29.31	1,072	86.61
8	100.41	98.16	99.58	49.55	48.25	48.96	29.67	28.95	29.26	1,295	86.49
9	99.76	99.11	99.42	49.24	48.91	49.11	29.40	29.10	29.20	279	86.61
10											
11	103.74	99.26	103.59	51.47	49.21	51.37	30.36	29.11	30.30	1,917	86.79
12	104.90	102.33	102.84	51.77	50.75	50.83	30.68	29.83	30.00	2,243	86.92
13	104.13	102.90	103.65	50.75	50.42	50.68	30.06	29.68	29.82	735	86.93
14	106.53	103.81	104.66	52.39	50.85	51.17	30.30	29.10	29.23	2,896	87.06
15	106.14	102.14	102.63	51.65	49.17	49.28	29.15	27.63	27.85	2,453	86.97
16	105.56	102.76	105.32	50.41	49.43	50.38	28.45	27.51	28.38	1,001	86.85
17											
18	107.68	104.36	105.30	51.26	49.01	49.25	28.91	27.39	27.85	2,722	85.68
19	106.25	102.44	105.74	49.51	47.45	49.28	27.86	26.74	27.56	2,818	85.02
20	105.71	102.26	103.99	48.58	46.57	46.86	27.25	26.33	26.58	2,417	84.47
21	102.29	97.15	97.56	45.84	42.73	42.85	26.41	25.31	25.48	3,652	83.68
22	99.93	95.73	99.06	44.35	41.83	43.95	26.79	25.18	26.46	3,315	84.31
23	101.02	99.16	99.78	44.91	44.13	44.59	27.38	26.65	26.86	1,005	84.69
24											
25	99.34	96.46	98.03	44.05	42.86	43.51	26.83	25.95	26.25	1,309	84.55
26	100.23	96.84	97.41	44.08	42.75	43.11	26.78	25.87	25.98	1,432	84.44
27	96.91	92.44	93.18	43.07	41.01	41.19	26.11	25.13	25.25	2,320	84.24
28	95.30	92.89	94.66	41.86	41.02	41.60	25.81	25.13	25.65	1,444	83.84
29	97.21	93.94	94.24	42.64	40.97	41.07	26.22	25.07	25.11	1,644	83.94
30	95.32	94.82	94.82	41.03	39.88	40.95	25.81	24.70	25.61	1,010	83.96
High			105.74			52.56			30.86	43,334	87.17
Low			93.18			40.95			25.11		83.68

*Sunday †Holiday

OCTOBER, 1933

Date	Industrials High	Low	Close	Railroads High	Low	Close	Utilities High	Low	Close	Daily Sales	40 Bonds
1	*	*	*							*	*
2	95.32	92.69	92.99	41.01	40.02	40.16	25.60	24.82	24.87	960	83.81
3	94.43	91.93	93.55	40.36	39.42	40.06	25.22	24.59	24.81	932	83.81
4	99.21	94.89	98.60	42.99	40.49	42.83	26.56	25.12	26.34	2,137	83.86
5	99.34	96.95	98.05	42.76	41.95	42.11	26.82	25.93	26.18	1,659	84.06
6	99.18	95.92	97.54	42.31	41.20	41.59	26.35	25.32	25.65	1,461	84.08
7	98.79	97.28	98.20	42.05	41.60	41.84	26.06	25.58	25.77	602	84.15
8	*			*			*				
9	100.58	98.14	99.72	43.39	41.82	42.98	26.56	25.80	26.48	1,246	84.21
10	100.20	98.05	98.77	42.97	42.26	42.57	27.32	26.42	26.78	1,135	84.52
11	99.94	97.54	98.85	43.01	42.14	42.52	27.17	26.45	26.73	1,028	84.77
12	†	†	†	†	†	†	†	†	†		
13	98.77	95.14	95.36	42.33	40.83	40.85	26.94	25.95	25.98	1,265	85.18
14	95.98	93.79	95.59	40.81	40.13	40.62	26.25	25.61	26.15	802	84.88
15	*			*			*				
16	94.93	89.35	90.49	40.21	37.21	37.84	25.93	24.38	24.76	2,667	84.61
17	93.47	88.69	92.67	39.10	37.08	38.77	25.78	24.17	25.39	2,483	84.58
18	92.72	88.47	88.95	38.62	36.15	36.39	25.43	24.10	24.15	1,734	84.41
19	88.62	84.26	84.38	35.98	33.84	33.96	24.10	23.13	23.24	2,896	84.11
20	88.41	83.57	86.63	36.14	33.63	35.37	24.27	22.89	23.76	2,695	84.21
21	87.69	82.20	83.64	36.15	33.70	34.10	24.00	22.89	23.14	1,260	84.17
22	*			*			*				
23	90.54	86.25	88.13	37.16	35.48	36.10	24.63	23.68	23.85	2,127	83.90
24	91.67	87.10	91.35	38.29	35.70	37.98	24.62	23.46	24.48	2,113	83.88
25	95.23	91.23	93.54	39.58	37.64	38.72	25.58	24.24	24.90	2,878	83.87
26	93.95	91.29	92.02	38.77	37.62	37.87	25.10	24.08	24.30	1,223	83.59
27	94.11	90.83	93.22	38.67	37.44	38.27	24.90	24.01	24.60	1,107	83.40
28	93.29	91.63	92.01	38.18	37.74	37.84	24.55	24.24	24.36	377	83.42
29	*			*			*				
30	93.99	88.05	88.43	38.44	35.99	36.09	24.67	23.15	23.36	1,466	82.90
31	89.44	86.50	88.16	36.53	35.43	35.94	23.38	22.75	23.08	1,129	82.59
High			99.72			42.98			26.78	39,372	85.18
Low			83.64			33.90			23.08		82.59

*Sunday †Holiday

NOVEMBER, 1933

Date	Industrials High	Low	Close	Railroads High	Low	Close	Utilities High	Low	Close	Daily Sales	40 Bonds
1	89.92	86.83	89.62	36.36	35.27	36.16	23.30	22.38	22.91	1,142	82.44
2	91.38	89.17	90.54	37.09	36.23	36.91	23.35	22.68	23.20	1,123	82.51
3	93.92	89.96	93.60	38.52	36.68	38.37	24.00	23.03	23.94	1,500	82.24
4	93.92	92.06	93.09	38.96	38.27	38.82	23.93	23.56	23.76	704	82.15
5	*			*			*				
6	93.14	91.67	92.50	38.60	38.06	38.27	23.75	23.25	23.52	685	81.95
7	†	†	†	†	†	†	†	†	†	†	†
8	96.05	91.82	95.54	39.57	38.14	39.43	24.73	23.41	24.53	1,803	81.74
9	98.34	95.46	96.40	40.77	39.46	39.85	25.41	24.33	24.62	2,903	81.54
10	97.21	94.60	95.06	40.30	38.94	39.26	24.74	23.95	24.08	1,366	80.65
11	96.19	94.32	96.10	39.74	39.24	39.71	24.46	23.93	24.38	472	80.56
12	*			*			*				
13	97.15	95.25	95.98	39.54	38.69	38.89	24.65	24.00	24.21	1,091	80.39
14	98.26	94.73	95.50	39.78	38.01	38.23	24.60	23.50	23.66	2,169	80.16
15	96.35	93.27	94.36	38.28	37.01	37.34	23.72	23.02	23.31	1,354	79.75
16	99.34	94.12	99.01	39.10	37.26	38.98	24.05	23.17	23.80	2,577	78.92
17	100.59	97.54	98.09	39.76	38.46	38.61	24.13	23.11	23.21	2,324	78.80
18	99.49	98.31	98.67	38.63	38.19	38.29	23.39	22.88	23.03	578	79.04
19	*			*			*				
20	101.83	98.52	101.28	39.70	38.22	39.45	23.82	22.87	23.62	1,895	79.03
21	101.94	99.67	100.29	40.65	39.51	39.98	23.85	23.28	23.40	1,801	79.36
22	101.61	98.80	100.07	40.29	39.23	39.62	23.64	22.99	23.26	1,574	78.62
23	100.29	97.20	98.59	39.43	38.51	38.89	23.35	22.83	23.07	1,371	78.69
24	100.81	98.09	99.52	40.00	38.96	39.55	24.55	23.20	24.09	1,420	79.48
25	100.11	98.84	99.28	39.66	39.41	39.54	24.73	24.10	24.60	478	79.90
26	*			*			*				
27	99.45	95.32	95.77	39.18	37.75	37.92	24.70	23.61	23.73	1,557	80.25
28	97.79	95.59	96.23	38.29	37.39	37.65	24.12	23.44	23.58	1,007	80.04
29	98.51	96.57	98.14	38.36	37.63	38.18	23.83	23.65	23.45	752	80.18
30	†	†	†	†	†	†	†	†	†	†	†
High			101.28			39.98			24.62	33,647	82.51
Low			89.62			36.16			22.91		78.62

*Sunday †Holiday

DECEMBER, 1933

Date	Industrials			Railroads			Utilities			Daily Sales	40 Bonds
	High	Low	Close	High	Low	Close	High	Low	Close		
1	100.08	98.41	98.89	38.85	38.26	38.43	23.96	23.42	23.45	813	80.33
2	99.33	98.29	99.07	38.16	37.90	38.11	23.53	23.16	23.38	336	80.66
3	*			*			*				
4	99.41	98.19	98.89	38.79	38.11	38.54	23.40	22.98	23.20	671	81.12
5	102.44	99.20	101.99	40.15	38.67	39.83	24.11	23.21	23.88	2,022	81.61
6	102.72	100.70	101.28	40.94	39.97	40.53	24.21	23.60	23.63	1,442	81.97
7	103.01	101.07	102.04	41.91	40.34	41.53	23.86	23.35	23.50	1,684	82.39
8	102.47	100.30	101.04	41.73	40.78	41.19	23.75	23.23	23.48	1,325	82.51
9	103.04	100.81	102.92	42.12	41.04	42.07	23.82	23.30	23.67	1,070	82.69
10	*			*			*				
11	103.97	101.63	101.94	43.73	42.63	43.09	24.80	23.69	24.33	2,453	82.98
12	103.03	101.06	101.64	43.30	42.09	42.47	24.74	24.10	24.37	1,650	83.12
13	101.98	99.94	100.69	42.82	41.72	41.99	24.93	24.15	24.45	1,333	83.11
14	102.92	100.58	101.44	42.91	41.85	42.19	24.81	24.03	24.13	1,556	83.34
15	101.67	99.44	99.95	42.37	41.29	41.45	24.15	23.45	23.70	1,173	83.14
16	99.77	97.39	98.06	41.36	40.35	40.54	23.66	23.01	23.23	896	83.03
17	*			*			*				
18	98.42	95.77	97.20	40.51	39.61	40.15	23.36	22.69	23.01	1,343	82.94
19	97.99	96.30	97.25	40.49	39.68	39.96	23.19	22.64	22.72	1,025	82.79
20	97.96	93.70	95.28	40.47	38.39	39.33	22.88	21.89	22.15	2,163	82.78
21	96.16	94.78	95.50	39.59	38.77	39.13	22.34	21.78	21.86	1,021	82.82
22	99.90	95.93	98.87	40.60	39.21	40.37	22.82	21.33	22.02	2,420	83.01
23	98.94	97.38	98.04	40.70	39.74	40.23	22.24	21.75	22.03	738	83.11
24	*			*			*				
25	†	†	†	†	†	†	†	†	†	†	†
26	97.76	95.56	96.30	40.15	39.08	39.26	21.95	21.21	21.40	1,303	83.25
27	98.21	95.16	96.80	40.09	38.78	39.42	22.51	21.18	21.98	3,076	83.54
28	100.04	97.16	99.29	40.68	39.59	40.48	23.30	22.19	23.06	1,477	83.97
29	99.73	97.85	98.67	41.03	40.18	40.42	23.45	22.68	23.09	1,133	84.34
30	100.47	98.86	99.90	40.93	40.44	40.80	23.48	23.00	23.29	752	84.60
31											
High			102.92			43.09			24.45	34,876	84.60
Low			95.28			38.11			21.40		80.33

*Sunday †Holiday

JANUARY, 1934

Date	Industrials			Railroads			Utilities			Daily Sales	40 Bonds
	High	Low	Close	High	Low	Close	High	Low	Close		
1	†	†	†	†	†	†	†	†	†	†	†
2	101.94	99.61	100.36	41.46	40.75	40.97	23.75	23.10	23.19	1,267	84.66
3	100.83	97.75	99.09	41.52	40.16	40.54	23.43	22.28	22.68	1,383	84.97
4	99.13	96.48	98.78	40.60	39.73	40.40	22.77	22.01	22.58	1,188	84.75
5	99.39	96.97	97.23	40.56	39.75	39.85	22.99	22.29	22.48	1,055	84.73
6	97.58	96.52	96.94	40.09	39.70	39.97	22.60	22.35	22.45	462	84.73
7	*			*			*				
8	97.93	96.26	96.73	40.41	39.93	40.12	22.80	22.31	22.42	715	84.80
9	98.53	97.09	97.57	40.97	40.18	40.60	23.11	22.55	22.80	869	85.08
10	99.99	97.78	99.77	41.65	40.84	41.58	24.05	23.08	23.99	1,415	85.44
11	100.49	98.77	99.38	42.22	41.48	42.01	24.96	23.78	24.83	1,695	86.07
12	99.98	98.24	98.73	42.16	41.55	41.71	25.01	24.23	24.33	1,601	86.45
13	99.12	97.80	98.66	41.79	41.31	41.62	24.56	24.12	24.36	750	86.52
14	*			*			*				
15	103.48	99.50	103.19	44.45	42.38	44.26	26.43	24.70	26.17	3,743	86.99
16	104.60	102.66	103.40	46.75	44.98	46.25	26.78	25.97	26.23	3,444	87.71
17	104.87	102.38	103.50	46.99	45.73	46.29	26.66	25.91	26.13	2,848	87.88
18	104.48	102.50	103.30	47.01	45.94	46.34	26.42	25.70	25.88	2,127	88.14
19	106.19	103.46	105.60	48.39	46.57	48.23	27.05	26.06	26.78	3,542	88.55
20	106.58	104.99	105.52	48.67	47.86	48.02	27.33	26.82	26.95	1,954	88.73
21	*			*			*				
22	106.92	104.34	105.09	48.41	47.22	47.54	27.51	26.63	26.85	2,660	88.82
23	107.00	104.47	106.62	48.19	47.02	48.11	27.08	26.48	26.96	2,380	88.60
24	108.20	106.26	107.02	49.55	48.28	48.82	27.61	26.96	27.23	3,360	88.90
25	107.52	105.44	106.85	49.00	47.94	48.57	27.27	26.63	26.89	2,270	88.91
26	107.93	105.85	106.38	49.00	48.01	48.47	26.95	26.48	26.55	2,510	89.00
27	106.82	105.45	106.03	48.56	47.90	48.20	26.66	26.38	26.45	1,200	88.98
28	*			*			*				
29	108.42	106.11	107.90	49.24	48.16	49.03	27.10	26.40	26.87	2,784	89.15
30	110.06	107.91	108.99	50.84	49.46	50.55	27.18	26.84	27.10	4,237	89.62
31	109.17	106.81	107.22	50.79	49.62	49.77	27.71	26.90	27.05	3,105	89.75
High			108.99			50.55			27.23	54,565	89.75
Low			96.73			39.85			22.42		84.66

*Sunday †Holiday

FEBRUARY, 1934

Date	Industrials High	Low	Close	Railroads High	Low	Close	Utilities High	Low	Close	Daily Sales	40 Bonds
1	110.35	107.94	108.95	51.65	50.41	50.94	28.55	27.30	28.11	4,712	90.21
2	109.69	107.67	108.31	51.60	50.48	51.04	28.60	27.90	28.15	2,873	90.66
3	109.96	108.18	109.41	52.04	50.95	51.85	28.51	28.00	28.40	2,081	90.85
4	*										
5	111.93	109.50	110.74	53.37	52.30	52.97	30.08	28.75	29.60	4,940	91.48
6	111.25	108.88	110.24	53.07	51.95	52.60	31.12	29.53	31.03	4,331	91.22
7	110.20	106.53	107.95	52.35	50.33	50.94	31.08	29.18	29.71	4,499	90.73
8	109.09	106.05	108.45	51.53	49.88	51.20	29.90	28.50	29.61	3,200	90.70
9	108.76	104.29	106.09	51.39	49.38	50.30	29.76	28.31	28.90	3,337	90.88
10	106.07	103.08	105.47	49.81	48.51	49.66	28.73	27.75	28.55	2,187	90.73
11	*										
12	†	†	†	†	†	†	†	†	†	†	†
13	107.35	104.78	106.10	51.00	49.86	50.37	28.88	28.16	28.43	2,060	91.16
14	107.21	104.64	106.78	50.81	49.86	50.70	28.75	27.95	28.66	1,939	91.49
15	109.04	106.92	108.30	52.14	51.01	51.84	29.41	28.70	29.16	2,976	91.99
16	109.96	107.60	108.61	52.60	51.69	52.01	29.55	29.81	29.03	2,770	92.39
17	109.61	107.90	109.07	52.21	51.58	52.02	29.10	28.76	28.92	1,165	92.45
18	*										
19	109.57	107.04	107.53	52.40	51.42	51.62	28.96	28.08	28.27	2,346	92.45
20	108.68	107.24	108.14	52.19	51.51	51.79	28.37	27.93	28.20	1,220	92.36
21	109.39	107.55	108.50	52.16	51.31	51.81	28.60	28.10	28.31	1,900	92.29
22	†	†	†	†	†	†	†	†	†	†	†
23	109.36	105.72	106.14	52.12	49.86	50.02	28.45	27.44	27.60	2,290	92.03
24	106.17	104.56	104.77	49.99	49.00	49.08	27.57	27.08	27.13	1,223	91.89
25	*										
26	104.49	102.21	103.12	48.70	47.33	47.90	26.85	26.13	26.47	2,188	91.45
27	104.55	102.63	103.67	48.33	47.31	47.94	26.85	26.31	26.64	1,271	91.47
28	105.37	103.09	103.46	48.65	47.57	47.80	27.11	26.34	26.45	1,322	91.61
High			110.74			52.97			31.03	56,830	92.45
Low			103.12			47.80			26.45		90.21

*Sunday †Holiday

MARCH, 1934

Date	Industrials High	Low	Close	Railroads High	Low	Close	Utilities High	Low	Close	Daily Sales	40 Bonds
1	103.81	101.93	103.18	47.79	46.86	47.57	26.59	25.88	26.32	1,242	91.52
2	105.99	103.74	105.79	49.24	47.94	49.19	27.15	26.35	27.08	1,481	91.55
3	106.37	105.10	105.56	49.48	49.10	49.22	27.25	26.84	26.92	799	91.67
4	*										
5	105.89	103.79	105.02	49.11	48.45	48.89	26.93	26.45	26.72	952	91.78
6	104.94	103.40	103.84	48.98	48.53	48.69	26.80	26.40	26.54	806	91.83
7	104.59	101.12	101.59	48.94	47.42	47.60	26.73	25.83	25.90	1,734	91.95
8	103.44	100.78	103.21	48.42	47.07	48.32	26.48	25.72	26.36	1,696	92.02
9	103.91	102.13	102.44	48.86	47.95	48.12	26.61	26.06	26.16	1,370	92.46
10	102.99	101.71	102.77	48.11	47.67	48.02	26.31	25.98	26.21	572	92.59
11	*										
12	104.61	102.66	104.23	48.84	48.01	48.65	27.10	26.22	27.00	1,259	93.00
13	104.89	103.54	104.00	49.54	48.64	49.30	27.57	26.85	27.13	1,275	93.29
14	104.69	103.31	103.54	50.44	49.48	49.81	27.54	26.90	27.04	1,359	93.57
15	103.73	101.43	102.21	49.52	48.47	48.86	27.00	26.32	26.55	1,341	93.54
16	103.26	101.46	102.72	48.84	48.29	48.77	26.75	26.28	26.57	1,169	93.38
17	102.76	101.24	101.65	48.89	48.27	48.40	26.67	26.28	26.33	725	93.40
18	*										
19	101.04	98.99	99.68	48.07	46.94	47.21	26.15	25.53	25.68	1,513	93.12
20	101.82	98.75	101.01	48.19	46.81	47.94	26.21	25.56	26.12	1,542	92.77
21	100.73	98.45	99.33	47.80	46.52	46.94	26.04	25.46	25.71	1,069	92.58
22	100.94	98.87	100.54	47.74	46.79	47.69	26.33	25.68	26.26	1,025	92.49
23	100.53	99.47	99.80	47.86	47.38	47.59	26.40	26.00	26.05	759	92.46
24	101.29	100.34	100.92	48.25	47.78	47.92	26.45	26.17	26.37	682	92.55
25	*										
26	102.67	100.70	100.95	48.71	47.73	47.84	26.79	26.30	26.36	1,275	92.86
27	99.32	97.41	98.76	46.84	46.03	46.62	25.98	25.43	25.72	1,587	92.66
28	99.84	98.60	99.02	47.50	46.41	46.90	26.02	25.65	25.79	843	92.51
29	100.83	99.18	100.31	47.52	47.12	47.31	26.28	25.88	26.19	1,021	92.53
30	†	†	†	†	†	†	†	†	†	†	†
31	102.06	99.99	101.85	47.98	47.45	47.92	26.15	25.80	26.02	814	92.62
High			105.79			49.81			27.13	29,910	93.57
Low			98.76			46.62			25.68		91.52

*Sunday †Holiday

APRIL, 1934

Date	Industrials High	Low	Close	Railroads High	Low	Close	Utilities High	Low	Close	Daily Sales	40 Bonds
1	*			*			*				
2	102.82	101.41	101.96	48.37	47.92	48.11	26.34	25.85	25.96	1,368	92.67
3	103.00	101.18	102.74	48.72	47.94	48.58	26.08	25.64	25.96	1,335	92.81
4	103.91	102.21	103.19	49.06	48.56	48.81	26.15	25.68	25.83	1,564	93.34
5	104.09	102.47	103.37	49.08	48.40	48.79	26.83	25.56	26.23	1,419	93.75
6	104.30	102.86	103.97	49.34	48.47	49.20	26.40	25.91	26.14	1,014	93.91
7	103.91	103.20	103.60	49.34	49.04	49.22	26.10	25.91	26.00	549	94.06
8	*			*			*				
9	104.07	102.92	103.54	49.22	48.92	49.00	25.98	25.67	25.72	850	94.21
10	105.51	103.95	105.05	49.93	49.08	49.81	26.01	25.60	25.85	1,406	94.34
11	106.23	104.64	105.16	50.68	49.83	50.28	26.05	25.68	25.85	1,553	94.46
12	105.82	104.30	104.80	50.48	49.81	49.96	26.52	25.75	26.15	1,332	94.66
13	105.72	104.42	104.98	49.83	49.49	49.55	26.51	25.99	26.22	1,183	94.70
14	105.37	104.67	105.04	49.61	49.43	49.57	26.35	26.05	26.21	501	94.79
15	*			*			*				
16	105.31	102.88	103.57	49.79	48.75	49.03	26.24	25.58	25.71	1,291	94.61
17	104.82	103.34	104.46	49.36	48.83	49.31	26.08	25.54	25.90	944	94.60
18	106.26	104.58	105.45	50.14	49.53	49.93	26.67	25.95	26.41	1,540	94.89
19	106.18	104.34	105.52	50.79	49.89	50.35	26.61	26.13	26.40	1,325	95.08
20	107.00	105.08	106.55	51.23	50.07	51.01	27.03	26.33	26.90	1,887	95.21
21	106.94	106.05	106.34	51.05	50.47	50.68	26.93	26.62	26.71	903	95.20
22	*			*			*				
23	106.73	105.31	105.92	50.91	50.12	50.56	26.77	26.36	26.54	1,113	95.18
24	106.19	104.70	105.31	50.64	49.95	50.18	26.55	26.19	26.32	1,274	95.03
25	105.55	104.53	105.05	50.11	49.69	49.92	26.27	25.92	26.08	961	94.99
26	105.51	102.95	103.56	50.69	49.12	49.32	26.21	25.52	25.63	1,639	94.82
27	104.30	103.12	103.65	49.56	49.14	49.28	25.77	25.47	25.60	842	94.93
28	104.04	102.75	102.90	49.11	48.75	48.78	25.70	25.48	25.50	564	94.97
29	*			*			*				
30	102.72	100.31	100.49	48.30	47.30	47.39	25.51	24.98	25.05	1,490	94.83
High			106.55			51.01			26.90	29,845	95.21
Low			100.49			47.39			25.05		92.76

*Sunday †Holiday

MAY, 1934

Date	Industrials High	Low	Close	Railroads High	Low	Close	Utilities High	Low	Close	Daily Sales	40 Bonds
1	101.20	99.55	100.62	47.40	46.64	47.06	25.17	24.70	24.97	1,339	94.82
2	101.36	98.47	98.82	47.24	46.14	46.29	24.91	23.98	24.10	1,338	94.72
3	100.06	98.36	98.94	47.09	46.30	46.54	24.29	23.85	23.95	1,110	94.74
4	100.66	99.02	99.29	47.32	46.65	46.74	24.28	23.56	23.64	840	94.82
5	100.09	97.69	98.20	46.65	45.49	45.68	23.70	22.91	23.16	873	94.78
6	*			*			*				
7	98.71	94.30	95.51	45.56	43.20	43.70	23.20	21.93	22.29	2,364	94.43
8	97.73	94.47	97.16	44.86	43.20	44.57	23.13	22.03	22.91	1,859	94.21
9	97.81	95.38	95.71	44.80	43.42	43.64	23.30	22.50	22.67	1,028	94.30
10	95.59	92.16	93.91	43.24	41.65	42.52	22.91	21.93	22.47	2,126	94.09
11	95.19	92.99	93.18	42.85	41.63	41.70	22.81	22.13	22.20	996	93.82
12	93.19	91.23	92.22	41.65	40.60	41.11	22.40	21.90	22.11	1,110	93.58
13	*			*			*				
14	92.95	89.10	91.81	41.83	40.35	41.40	22.58	21.72	22.30	1,681	93.23
15	93.65	91.47	92.84	42.40	41.47	42.07	23.08	22.48	22.73	894	93.52
16	93.83	91.95	92.73	42.56	41.70	42.24	22.96	22.50	22.66	717	93.69
17	96.17	92.63	95.98	43.72	42.21	43.63	23.59	22.80	23.53	1,287	93.94
18	96.57	94.62	95.17	44.44	43.49	43.64	23.74	23.16	23.30	911	94.08
19	95.35	94.68	91.13	43.72	43.39	43.70	23.26	23.06	23.18	249	94.05
20	*			*			*				
21	95.96	94.81	95.76	43.80	43.53	43.77	23.40	23.18	23.31	382	94.08
22	96.29	93.26	93.61	43.79	42.62	42.84	23.66	22.91	23.00	831	94.12
23	93.74	92.23	92.86	42.69	42.07	42.37	22.98	22.54	22.69	657	93.99
24	94.08	92.57	93.37	42.92	42.40	42.75	23.01	22.71	22.88	496	93.96
25	94.96	93.25	94.50	43.17	42.59	43.01	23.27	22.90	23.24	535	93.97
26	95.51	94.64	95.05	43.57	43.22	43.44	23.39	23.20	23.30	279	94.03
27	*			*			*				
28	96.33	95.32	95.56	44.26	43.79	43.96	23.75	23.38	23.49	615	94.10
29	95.85	94.85	95.32	43.78	43.34	43.51	23.47	23.31	23.38	379	94.17
30	†	†	†	†	†	†	†	†	†		†
31	94.78	93.71	94.00	43.05	42.59	42.70	23.16	22.81	22.86	438	94.07
High			100.62			47.06			24.97	25,336	94.82
Low			91.81			41.11			22.11		93.23

*Sunday †Holiday

JUNE, 1934

Date	Industrials High	Low	Close	Railroads High	Low	Close	Utilities High	Low	Close	Daily Sales	40 Bonds
1	93.71	91.70	91.79	42.29	41.70	41.77	22.80	22.43	22.48	627	93.87
2	91.74	90.85	91.41	41.72	41.45	41.68	22.57	22.24	22.48	410	93.89
3	*			*			*			*	
4	93.04	91.84	92.73	42.28	41.86	42.24	22.82	22.51	22.70	358	93.89
5	94.94	92.74	94.66	43.30	42.35	43.14	23.32	22.78	23.22	741	93.99
6	95.68	94.27	94.77	44.08	43.64	43.78	23.31	22.97	23.05	665	94.06
7	95.24	94.04	94.72	43.46	43.13	43.29	23.08	22.85	22.91	467	94.15
8	98.55	94.82	98.44	45.16	43.33	45.09	24.10	23.00	24.04	1,608	94.38
9	99.40	98.41	98.90	45.47	45.13	45.31	24.21	23.96	24.05	703	94.65
10	*			*			*			*	
11	98.70	97.40	97.82	45.18	44.52	44.69	24.21	23.77	23.90	749	94.58
12	99.60	97.77	98.78	45.58	44.62	45.23	24.46	23.88	24.20	946	94.64
13	99.92	98.32	98.75	45.97	45.35	45.55	24.85	24.25	24.43	883	94.83
14	98.49	96.92	97.15	45.24	44.06	44.69	24.46	23.88	23.98	633	94.83
15	99.29	97.23	98.70	45.54	44.54	45.25	24.63	23.98	24.46	731	94.90
16	100.27	99.33	99.85	46.29	45.80	46.25	25.13	24.59	25.08	576	95.04
17	*			*			*			*	
18	100.70	99.32	100.42	46.34	45.87	46.15	25.24	24.78	25.11	605	95.12
19	101.11	98.75	99.02	46.55	45.52	45.58	25.32	24.65	24.65	851	95.17
20	99.10	97.94	98.25	45.39	45.02	45.17	24.73	24.32	24.40	549	95.01
21	98.62	97.39	97.50	45.25	44.46	44.68	24.48	24.01	24.05	530	94.94
22	97.87	95.48	95.93	44.71	43.67	44.04	24.08	23.32	23.48	932	94.74
23	96.78	95.99	96.59	44.20	43.93	44.13	23.84	23.56	23.76	233	94.72
24	*			*			*			*	
25	97.03	95.49	95.79	44.12	43.50	43.65	23.91	23.51	23.61	483	94.73
26	97.53	95.46	97.33	44.66	43.70	44.57	24.16	23.70	24.10	613	94.65
27	98.31	96.74	96.94	44.89	44.43	44.47	24.48	24.06	24.11	629	94.71
28	97.88	96.18	97.14	44.78	44.08	44.59	24.36	23.98	24.21	640	94.85
29	96.84	95.59	95.75	44.45	43.89	43.93	24.13	23.75	23.77	436	94.83
30	95.94	95.38	95.72	44.03	43.90	43.98	23.84	23.69	23.76	189	94.74
High			100.42			46.25			25.11	16,800	95.17
Low			91.41			41.68			22.48		93.87

*Sunday †Holiday

JULY, 1934

Date	Industrials High	Low	Close	Railroads High	Low	Close	Utilities High	Low	Close	Daily Sales	40 Bonds
1	*			*			*			*	*
2	95.71	94.59	94.80	43.27	42.64	42.79	23.70	23.35	23.50	412	94.58
3	95.13	94.25	94.77	43.01	42.56	42.83	23.50	23.20	23.35	401	94.53
4	†			†			†			†	†
5	96.92	95.19	96.44	43.45	42.93	43.30	23.78	23.32	23.56	441	94.58
6	97.80	96.56	97.32	43.72	43.35	43.55	23.94	23.65	23.86	458	94.54
7	97.46	96.97	97.15	43.79	43.51	43.57	23.85	23.74	23.77	182	94.62
8	*			*			*			*	
9	97.54	96.54	97.04	43.77	43.53	43.60	23.85	23.63	23.73	316	94.78
10	98.63	97.02	98.07	44.43	43.65	44.18	24.13	23.56	23.79	649	94.94
11	99.35	98.12	98.67	44.67	44.00	44.19	24.01	23.66	23.72	649	95.09
12	99.01	97.93	98.32	43.89	43.38	43.51	23.63	23.33	23.38	466	95.38
13	99.08	97.66	98.82	43.54	42.08	43.27	23.42	23.08	23.31	533	95.42
14	99.20	98.77	99.02	43.27	43.09	43.11	23.28	23.20	23.24	194	95.48
15	*			*			*			*	
16	98.51	96.91	97.04	43.07	42.19	42.23	23.04	22.54	22.59	590	95.43
17	97.75	96.50	96.79	42.33	41.82	41.95	22.75	22.45	22.53	617	95.26
18	98.45	97.18	98.26	42.66	42.23	42.57	22.82	22.56	22.76	490	95.23
19	98.70	96.92	97.24	42.78	42.02	42.11	22.83	22.46	22.51	614	95.37
20	97.20	94.43	94.74	42.05	40.50	40.64	22.61	21.93	21.96	1,243	95.44
21	94.89	94.31	94.62	40.48	40.10	40.27	21.99	21.73	21.83	620	95.38
22	*			*			*			*	
23	95.17	91.96	91.98	40.30	38.17	38.41	21.87	20.80	21.03	1,878	95.12
24	92.91	90.63	91.01	38.79	37.74	37.90	21.32	20.73	20.80	1,595	94.91
25	92.08	90.09	91.57	37.97	36.71	37.59	21.11	20.60	20.90	1,348	94.51
26	91.32	84.58	85.51	37.05	33.91	34.29	20.85	19.39	19.60	3,338	93.25
27	88.86	86.64	87.84	35.82	34.51	34.99	20.35	19.18	19.58	2,213	93.59
28	89.28	88.30	88.72	35.76	35.18	35.47	20.01	19.71	19.86	469	93.63
29	*			*			*			*	
30	88.96	86.90	88.17	35.54	34.55	35.16	20.21	19.45	19.88	806	93.76
31	88.51	87.17	88.05	35.18	34.12	34.68	20.06	19.65	19.90	359	93.42
High			99.02			44.19			23.86	21,113	95.48
Low			85.51			34.29			19.58		93.25

*Sunday †Holiday

AUGUST, 1934

Date	Industrials High	Low	Close	Railroads High	Low	Close	Utilities High	Low	Close	Daily Sales	40 Bonds
1	90.96	88.55	90.57	35.85	35.00	35.75	20.63	19.98	20.53	779	93.65
2	91.12	89.75	90.87	35.80	35.23	35.71	20.80	20.26	20.72	564	93.80
3	91.08	89.82	90.14	35.73	35.30	35.33	20.84	20.42	20.46	465	93.98
4	89.74	88.30	88.43	35.06	34.17	34.22	20.28	20.02	20.07	304	93.88
5	*			*			*				
6	88.51	86.32	88.11	34.15	33.18	33.91	20.06	19.51	19.94	783	93.72
7	89.10	86.70	87.47	34.16	33.23	33.46	20.21	19.72	19.85	609	93.46
8	89.28	87.16	88.97	34.13	32.85	33.93	20.21	19.78	20.10	692	93.17
9	91.80	87.19	91.34	34.97	33.19	34.65	20.76	19.84	20.69	1,417	92.81
10	91.47	89.39	89.66	34.51	33.70	33.77	20.88	20.28	20.36	773	92.64
11	90.21	88.69	89.79	33.71	33.16	33.60	20.33	20.12	20.21	310	91.83
12	*			*			*				
13	92.56	89.69	91.80	34.90	33.77	34.66	20.74	20.14	20.58	809	91.67
14	91.98	90.82	91.12	34.64	34.23	34.38	20.57	20.23	20.23	531	92.20
15	91.70	90.66	91.00	35.21	34.21	34.62	20.37	20.06	20.16	575	92.54
16	92.51	91.08	91.69	35.40	34.74	34.97	20.70	20.22	20.45	610	92.78
17	92.25	91.00	91.12	35.16	34.60	34.64	20.55	20.18	20.20	477	93.04
18	91.15	90.70	90.86	34.56	34.31	34.36	20.17	20.06	20.13	164	93.12
19	*			*			*				
20	91.02	90.08	90.44	34.83	34.48	34.54	20.21	20.03	20.10	275	93.11
21	92.70	90.87	92.57	35.77	34.95	35.68	20.55	20.20	20.48	579	93.17
22	94.95	92.68	94.32	37.56	35.93	37.24	21.15	20.65	21.04	1,296	93.15
23	94.97	93.64	94.05	37.58	36.92	37.14	21.22	20.87	21.08	748	93.18
24	95.55	93.85	95.48	38.24	37.09	38.20	21.69	20.96	21.60	747	93.37
25	96.00	95.11	95.71	38.50	38.02	38.42	21.78	21.55	21.72	437	93.49
26	*			*			*				
27	95.31	94.25	94.46	38.17	37.54	37.64	21.53	21.11	21.16	534	93.42
28	94.48	93.55	94.19	37.53	37.16	37.31	21.21	20.89	21.06	404	93.11
29	95.59	93.64	93.69	37.90	37.00	37.01	21.11	20.68	20.71	762	93.05
30	93.59	92.01	92.76	36.60	35.80	36.12	20.71	20.43	20.55	650	92.92
31	93.05	92.05	92.86	36.25	35.79	36.17	20.56	20.30	20.46	401	92.78
High			95.71			38.42			21.72	16,691	93.98
Low			87.47			33.46			19.85		91.67

*Sunday †Holiday

SEPTEMBER, 1934

Date	Industrials High	Low	Close	Railroads High	Low	Close	Utilities High	Low	Close	Daily Sales	40 Bonds
1	92.86	92.52	92.64	36.13	35.93	36.07	20.49	20.41	20.48	113	92.78
2	†	†	†	†	†	†	†	†	†	†	†
3	†			†			†			†	
4	92.59	91.74	92.30	36.00	35.53	35.87	20.45	20.22	20.30	310	92.63
5	93.96	92.64	93.65	36.74	35.98	36.53	20.61	20.30	20.53	476	92.55
6	94.05	91.67	91.82	36.76	35.71	35.72	20.73	20.26	20.33	603	92.46
7	92.52	90.50	90.99	35.66	34.99	35.11	20.32	19.96	20.03	690	92.28
8	91.13	90.51	90.83	35.18	35.02	35.14	20.07	19.91	19.96	211	92.20
9	*			*			*				
10	91.32	89.04	89.27	35.10	33.96	34.10	20.08	19.55	19.61	696	91.95
11	89.75	88.42	89.25	34.35	33.83	34.21	19.72	19.39	19.58	631	91.71
12	90.14	89.14	89.62	34.93	34.35	34.57	19.71	19.43	19.50	401	91.30
13	90.45	89.12	89.44	34.85	34.45	34.52	19.51	19.28	19.31	416	91.12
14	89.25	86.64	86.83	34.15	33.29	33.43	19.27	18.68	18.81	835	90.65
15	87.58	86.59	87.34	33.49	33.03	33.42	18.81	18.53	18.75	345	90.54
16	*			*			*				
17	87.41	85.72	86.69	33.56	32.83	33.19	18.87	18.45	18.73	648	90.27
18	87.84	86.57	87.37	33.43	33.02	33.23	18.91	18.63	18.80	534	90.31
19	89.58	87.91	89.34	34.36	33.57	34.27	19.34	18.90	19.26	557	90.82
20	89.93	88.76	89.35	34.94	34.27	34.71	19.43	19.11	19.21	487	91.16
21	91.34	89.65	91.10	35.53	34.74	35.39	19.76	19.21	19.65	712	91.48
22	91.55	90.84	91.08	35.61	35.29	35.41	20.10	19.66	19.80	284	91.61
23	*			*			*				
24	91.50	89.97	90.45	35.67	34.99	35.06	20.15	19.71	19.80	514	91.76
25	92.79	89.91	92.72	36.31	34.85	36.27	20.68	19.75	20.64	842	91.72
26	93.12	92.05	92.44	36.53	35.98	36.01	21.10	20.54	20.65	796	92.00
27	94.02	92.23	93.40	36.91	35.96	36.62	20.95	20.50	20.80	799	92.26
28	93.52	92.24	92.49	36.65	36.13	36.22	20.69	20.35	20.38	512	92.20
29	92.78	92.08	92.63	36.34	36.03	36.33	20.42	20.22	20.40	222	92.04
30	*			*			*				
High			93.65			36.62			20.80	12,636	92.78
Low			86.69			33.19			18.73		90.27

*Sunday †Holiday

OCTOBER, 1934

Date	Industrials High	Low	Close	Railroads High	Low	Close	Utilities High	Low	Close	Daily Sales	40 Bonds
1	92.17	90.14	90.41	35.76	34.74	34.95	20.28	19.63	19.73	620	91.81
2	91.44	90.30	90.88	35.33	34.95	35.12	19.90	19.60	19.71	370	91.99
3	91.82	90.66	91.04	35.53	35.08	35.20	19.91	19.66	19.68	410	92.25
4	91.44	89.84	91.01	35.28	34.74	35.11	19.80	19.37	19.70	608	92.38
5	93.58	91.74	92.96	36.32	35.72	36.08	20.38	19.90	20.25	872	92.52
6	93.16	92.56	92.85	36.06	35.90	35.97	20.20	20.05	20.13	231	92.65
7	*			*			*				
8	93.21	92.16	92.50	35.84	35.56	35.61	20.16	19.92	19.96	451	92.69
9	93.03	91.31	91.71	35.67	35.02	35.11	19.94	19.51	19.61	773	92.68
10	94.01	91.78	93.75	36.17	35.07	36.15	20.11	19.56	19.99	987	92.73
11	96.04	93.94	95.50	37.07	36.32	36.81	20.50	20.05	20.38	1,395	93.03
12	†	†	†	†	†	†	†	†	†	†	
13	95.42	94.42	94.90	36.67	36.25	36.39	20.38	20.10	20.21	412	93.09
14	*			*			*				
15	95.37	94.01	94.16	36.32	35.91	35.98	20.28	20.00	20.05	511	93.17
16	95.81	94.15	95.25	36.65	36.06	36.36	20.28	20.05	20.12	678	93.42
17	96.36	94.83	95.29	37.09	36.42	36.57	20.28	19.98	20.00	662	93.43
18	96.03	94.63	95.34	36.68	36.13	36.28	20.19	19.77	19.88	655	93.35
19	95.33	94.39	94.90	36.32	35.91	36.08	19.93	19.68	19.86	527	93.43
20	95.22	94.62	95.02	36.08	35.95	36.03	19.92	19.79	19.88	229	93.41
21	*			*			*				
22	95.79	94.65	94.78	36.19	35.65	35.71	20.06	19.70	19.73	573	93.59
23	95.17	94.19	94.65	35.59	35.33	35.49	19.78	19.55	19.66	543	93.74
24	95.71	93.96	95.60	37.77	35.47	37.69	19.95	19.50	19.90	772	93.86
25	96.15	94.05	94.19	37.48	35.77	35.79	20.21	19.40	19.44	1,028	93.93
26	93.86	92.20	93.01	35.44	34.80	34.98	19.43	19.06	19.21	870	93.44
27	93.38	92.70	92.86	35.11	34.90	34.98	19.29	19.13	19.19	204	93.46
28	*			*			*				
29	93.60	92.37	92.53	35.04	34.60	34.69	19.35	19.05	19.13	428	93.49
30	93.46	92.59	93.05	35.06	34.64	34.79	19.21	19.01	19.13	432	93.47
31	94.04	92.90	93.36	35.04	34.71	34.78	19.27	19.02	19.17	417	93.26
High			95.60			37.69			20.38	15,660	93.93
Low			90.41			34.69			19.13		91.81

*Sunday †Holiday

NOVEMBER, 1934

Date	Industrials High	Low	Close	Railroads High	Low	Close	Utilities High	Low	Close	Daily Sales	40 Bonds
1	93.98	92.79	93.46	34.79	34.00	34.26	19.23	18.86	19.04	541	93.16
2	94.94	93.83	94.42	35.02	34.43	34.73	19.44	19.07	19.26	651	93.20
3	95.15	94.44	94.95	34.83	34.69	34.76	19.43	19.20	19.36	311	93.25
4	*			*			*				
5	96.17	94.83	96.06	34.99	34.59	34.92	19.52	19.26	19.40	758	93.18
6	†		†	†		†	†		†	†	†
7	97.81	95.31	97.55	35.96	34.90	35.84	19.91	19.37	19.79	1.112	93.29
8	98.31	96.83	97.26	36.06	35.33	35.43	19.82	19.47	19.53	843	93.47
9	99.34	96.97	99.02	36.43	35.40	36.33	19.82	19.40	19.76	1,228	93.56
10	99.60	98.65	99.21	36.52	36.16	36.35	19.78	19.56	19.70	688	93.68
11	*			*			*			*	*
12	†	†	†	†	†	†	†	†	†	†	†
13	99.98	98.49	99.19	36.46	35.77	36.09	19.61	18.82	18.94	1,132	93.62
14	99.81	98.49	99.42	36.39	35.72	36.27	18.94	18.40	18.63	958	93.59
15	100.80	99.34	99.72	36.88	36.20	36.36	18.86	18.47	18.56	1,544	93.68
16	100.08	98.70	99.39	36.33	35.67	35.87	18.46	17.79	17.96	1,032	93.72
17	99.75	98.93	99.45	35.91	35.51	35.80	17.85	17.45	17.68	453	93.75
18	*			*			*				
19	100.68	99.24	99.89	36.43	35.82	35.94	17.78	17.15	17.50	984	93.73
20	100.14	98.96	99.90	35.76	35.12	35.36	17.73	17.21	17.68	869	93.74
21	100.43	98.95	99.47	35.33	34.42	34.94	18.00	17.55	17.85	805	93.78
22	100.48	98.93	99.93	35.37	34.62	35.25	18.18	17.86	17.96	770	93.83
23	101.99	100.17	101.62	35.99	35.25	35.84	18.36	17.92	18.19	1,130	93.92
24	102.50	101.72	102.40	36.54	36.11	36.44	18.46	18.16	18.35	672	94.04
25	*			*			*			*	*
26	103.51	102.16	103.08	37.12	36.48	36.67	19.42	18.47	19.32	1,410	94.25
27	103.12	101.80	102.38	37.36	36.46	37.19	19.17	18.72	18.86	1,013	94.46
28	103.47	101.90	102.75	37.38	36.62	36.88	19.46	18.56	19.20	1,164	94.55
29	†		†	†		†	†		†	†	†
30	103.36	101.94	102.94	36.88	36.48	36.69	19.16	18.76	19.00	802	94.48
High			103.08			37.19			19.79	20,871	94.55
Low			93.46			34.26			17.50		93.16

*Sunday †Holiday

DECEMBER, 1934

Date	Industrials High	Low	Close	Railroads High	Low	Close	Utilities High	Low	Close	Daily Sales	40 Bonds
1	103.27	102.68	102.93	37.14	36.74	36.93	19.15	18.91	18.98	469	94.54
2	*	*	*	*	*	*	*	*	*		*
3	102.77	101.74	101.92	37.23	36.58	36.67	19.01	18.78	18.82	753	94.42
4	102.93	101.59	102.57	37.99	36.84	37.72	19.14	18.70	19.00	952	94.63
5	104.08	102.69	103.42	38.37	37.81	37.96	19.39	18.85	19.05	1,637	94.96
6	104.23	102.91	103.47	38.20	37.69	37.75	19.13	18.73	18.81	1,422	95.14
7	103.90	102.75	103.16	37.71	37.05	37.14	18.92	18.63	18.65	1,023	95.26
8	103.16	102.49	102.83	37.09	36.74	36.93	18.64	18.47	18.50	459	95.28
9	*	*	*	*	*	*	*	*	*		*
10	103.52	102.18	102.76	37.24	36.58	37.05	18.73	18.43	18.60	851	95.13
11	103.58	100.50	100.81	37.64	36.36	36.40	18.76	18.23	18.28	1,282	95.14
12	101.62	100.52	100.97	36.80	36.25	36.50	18.48	18.16	18.26	787	95.10
13	102.02	100.39	100.68	37.15	36.29	36.41	18.31	17.90	17.96	997	95.24
14	101.30	100.34	100.69	36.77	36.25	36.35	18.11	17.82	17.94	939	95.27
15	101.11	100.23	100.84	36.46	36.22	36.36	18.08	17.90	18.01	464	95.21
16	*	*	*	*	*	*	*	*	*		*
17	101.66	100.45	100.92	36.58	36.16	36.34	18.49	18.00	18.18	900	95.32
18	101.37	100.41	101.00	36.65	36.22	36.40	18.31	17.90	18.11	822	95.32
19	100.88	99.40	99.78	36.33	35.75	35.81	17.98	17.37	17.51	983	95.35
20	100.01	98.93	99.59	35.96	35.57	35.77	17.38	16.94	17.12	877	95.23
21	100.38	98.99	99.90	36.12	35.42	35.69	17.28	16.82	17.05	917	95.11
22	100.27	99.44	99.73	35.76	35.38	35.41	17.15	16.89	17.00	503	95.10
23	*	*	*	*	*	*	*	*	*		*
24	101.00	99.52	100.69	35.70	35.09	35.57	17.42	17.01	17.28	810	95.14
25	†	†	†	†	†	†	†	†	†		†
26	101.32	100.05	100.35	35.94	35.23	35.30	17.26	16.67	16.83	1,050	95.09
27	101.41	99.58	100.26	35.68	35.10	35.34	17.25	16.60	17.00	1,630	95.12
28	103.29	100.57	103.15	36.41	35.63	36.35	17.53	16.91	17.44	1,280	95.27
29	104.32	103.17	103.90	36.88	36.46	36.66	17.84	17.42	17.63	760	95.44
30	*	*	*	*	*	*	*	*	*		*
31	104.46	103.36	104.04	36.89	36.29	36.44	18.10	17.55	17.80	1,016	95.82
High			104.04			37.96			19.05	23,589	95.82
Low			99.59			35.30			16.83		94.42

*Sunday. †Holiday.

JANUARY, 1935

Date	Industrials High	Low	Close	Railroads High	Low	Close	Utilities High	Low	Close	Daily Sales	40 Bonds
1	†	†	†	†	†	†	†	†	†		†
2	104.93	103.05	104.51	36.65	36.00	36.32	18.00	17.62	17.80	879	95.90
3	105.63	104.12	105.14	36.55	36.24	36.47	17.94	17.57	17.74	1,066	96.11
4	105.43	104.18	104.69	37.35	36.52	36.73	17.95	17.50	17.60	965	96.29
5	105.67	104.53	105.56	36.84	36.61	36.82	17.74	17.50	17.68	494	96.40
6	*	*	*	*	*	*	*	*	*		*
7	106.71	105.24	105.88	37.59	36.83	37.26	17.90	17.53	17.64	1,286	96.49
8	106.22	104.56	105.03	37.54	36.97	37.15	17.80	17.41	17.54	1,194	96.62
9	105.68	104.28	105.05	37.25	36.62	36.88	17.81	17.37	17.75	897	96.66
10	105.65	104.41	104.87	37.21	36.67	37.01	18.28	17.61	18.03	779	96.77
11	105.49	102.50	103.35	36.83	35.65	35.86	18.20	17.51	17.66	1,378	96.62
12	103.17	101.70	102.30	35.65	34.89	35.27	17.57	17.28	17.41	666	96.33
13	*	*	*	*	*	*	*	*	*		*
14	103.37	102.39	102.76	35.55	35.17	35.44	17.65	17.34	17.44	554	96.39
15	103.20	99.54	100.49	35.80	33.71	34.14	17.50	16.96	17.11	1,370	96.09
16	101.95	100.40	101.54	34.95	34.45	34.77	17.42	17.21	17.33	667	96.09
17	102.30	101.04	101.92	35.03	34.54	34.74	17.50	17.20	17.36	736	96.25
18	102.63	101.58	102.36	34.73	34.39	34.58	17.45	17.26	17.36	685	96.37
19	103.12	102.44	102.96	35.26	34.83	35.14	17.38	17.28	17.35	392	96.50
20	*	*	*	*	*	*	*	*	*		*
21	103.93	102.57	103.35	35.34	34.92	35.06	17.63	17.29	17.51	689	96.62
22	103.64	102.60	102.77	34.97	34.72	34.84	17.61	17.31	17.41	593	96.66
23	103.43	102.43	102.88	34.78	34.38	34.59	17.49	17.26	17.41	620	96.61
24	102.85	102.01	102.44	34.64	34.42	34.52	17.47	17.18	17.35	437	96.72
25	103.12	102.32	102.86	34.78	34.55	34.62	17.75	17.26	17.65	517	96.77
26	103.01	102.39	102.50	34.66	34.19	34.30	17.70	17.53	17.58	323	96.79
27	*	*	*	*	*	*	*	*	*		*
28	102.31	101.03	101.51	34.18	33.52	33.71	17.54	17.17	17.26	692	96.62
29	101.58	100.24	100.69	33.93	33.25	33.37	17.32	17.05	17.16	575	96.36
30	101.39	100.38	101.00	33.63	33.29	33.42	17.30	17.11	17.25	426	96.29
31	102.12	101.05	101.69	33.99	33.43	33.75	17.46	17.17	17.25	525	96.27
High			105.88			37.26			18.03	19,409	96.79
Low			100.49			33.37			17.11		95.90

*Sunday †Holiday

FEBRUARY, 1935

Date	—Industrials—			—Railroads—			—Utilities—			Daily Sales	40 Bonds
	High	Low	Close	High	Low	Close	High	Low	Close		
1	102.05	101.10	101.53	33.60	33.20	33.42	17.32	17.08	17.23	494	96.27
2	102.36	101.44	102.20	33.65	33.18	33.49	17.20	17.03	17.13	399	96.41
3 *											
4	102.17	101.35	101.56	33.38	33.05	33.13	17.16	16.98	17.05	345	96.37
5	101.40	100.46	100.74	32.94	32.36	32.47	17.01	16.81	16.85	559	96.08
6	100.90	99.95	100.23	32.19	31.67	31.79	16.84	16.55	16.64	557	95.90
7	101.34	100.02	101.00	32.33	31.64	32.25	16.75	16.48	16.69	524	96.18
8	102.58	101.16	102.35	33.27	32.67	33.20	16.85	16.53	16.73	587	96.44
9	102.90	102.35	102.66	33.31	33.01	33.18	16.91	16.68	16.80	293	96.57
10 *											
11	102.67	101.65	102.42	32.87	32.53	32.74	16.86	16.63	16.82	359	96.59
12 †	†	†	†	†	†	†	†	†	†	†	†
13	103.06	102.18	102.69	32.82	32.51	32.61	16.85	16.61	16.70	386	96.59
14	103.31	102.56	103.05	32.73	32.45	32.61	16.72	16.54	16.64	405	96.85
15	105.07	103.43	104.67	33.01	32.64	32.73	16.80	16.39	16.51	726	97.06
16	105.01	104.28	104.54	32.74	32.52	32.55	16.46	16.28	16.35	353	96.99
17 *											
18	108.29	103.64	107.17	36.08	32.31	34.43	17.03	16.18	16.71	1,911	97.22
19	107.36	105.59	105.89	34.90	33.65	33.68	16.79	16.21	16.25	1,104	97.38
20	106.25	104.60	104.97	33.53	32.61	32.77	16.21	15.63	15.80	966	97.47
21	105.47	104.28	104.86	32.95	32.48	32.57	16.05	15.68	15.86	701	97.46
22 †	†	†	†	†	†	†	†	†	†	†	†
23	104.58	103.09	103.25	32.33	31.45	31.51	16.26	15.75	15.80	536	97.40
24 *											
25	103.57	102.33	103.14	31.55	30.99	31.26	16.11	15.70	16.02	744	96.99
26	103.60	102.08	102.24	31.46	29.97	30.14	16.15	15.70	15.83	946	96.48
27	102.86	101.27	102.55	30.70	29.81	30.63	16.07	15.59	16.01	933	96.55
28	103.27	102.14	102.38	30.89	30.33	30.37	16.10	15.80	15.88	574	96.76
High			107.17			34.43			17.23	14,405	97.47
Low			100.23			30.14			15.80		95.90

*Sunday †Holiday

MARCH, 1935

Date	—Industrials—			—Railroads—			—Utilities—			Daily Sales	40 Bonds
	High	Low	Close	High	Low	Close	High	Low	Close		
1	103.59	102.03	103.27	31.16	30.55	31.10	16.00	15.75	15.92	637	96.57
2	103.67	102.92	103.22	31.11	30.86	30.91	15.98	15.86	15.88	279	96.67
3 *											
4	103.16	102.24	102.58	30.81	30.48	30.52	15.87	15.68	15.79	420	96.52
5	102.29	100.00	100.09	30.10	29.12	29.24	15.68	15.28	15.35	900	96.26
6	101.94	98.77	100.22	29.80	28.46	28.91	15.58	15.10	15.26	1,290	96.08
7	101.37	100.13	101.17	29.41	28.51	29.07	15.56	15.22	15.50	540	95.84
8	102.37	101.27	101.58	29.20	28.82	28.95	15.83	15.53	15.61	440	95.72
9	101.49	100.91	101.18	28.76	28.34	28.56	15.61	15.48	15.56	288	95.65
10 *											
11	101.60	99.24	99.39	28.75	27.85	27.92	15.68	15.26	15.33	800	95.40
12	99.62	97.60	97.66	28.04	27.20	27.31	15.42	15.03	15.03	1,050	94.99
13	98.52	96.81	98.02	27.71	27.11	27.60	15.08	14.63	14.88	1,080	94.62
14	98.50	96.49	96.71	28.01	27.40	27.45	14.86	14.39	14.46	810	94.81
15	98.51	96.47	98.21	28.13	27.42	28.05	14.86	14.43	14.79	770	94.51
16	98.63	97.72	97.79	28.10	27.84	27.88	14.90	14.65	14.69	301	94.55
17 *											
18	97.62	95.95	97.01	27.75	27.29	27.64	14.73	14.39	14.57	594	94.47
19	98.61	97.05	98.31	28.17	27.74	28.00	15.02	14.55	14.97	510	94.46
20	99.11	97.75	98.29	28.08	27.68	27.72	15.15	14.90	14.97	488	94.53
21	100.55	98.03	99.72	28.96	27.74	28.51	16.35	14.96	15.98	890	94.64
22	100.88	99.10	100.68	29.19	28.13	29.10	16.45	15.68	16.38	781	94.84
23	100.67	99.73	99.84	29.12	28.67	28.69	16.48	16.06	16.25	299	94.86
24 *											
25	99.99	98.63	99.50	28.51	27.71	28.14	16.36	15.98	16.26	460	94.64
26	99.80	98.61	98.97	28.11	27.59	27.66	16.36	16.09	16.14	140	94.44
27	100.72	98.87	100.35	28.03	27.53	27.91	16.58	16.13	16.42	460	94.10
28	101.54	99.69	100.59	28.21	27.32	27.50	16.74	16.26	16.61	610	93.84
29	101.33	100.26	100.78	27.96	27.61	27.80	16.68	16.41	16.51	460	93.57
30	101.19	100.58	100.81	28.01	27.77	27.97	16.68	16.46	16.60	247	93.43
31 *											
High			103.27			31.10			16.61	15,850	96.67
Low			96.71			27.31			14.46		93.43

*Sunday †Holiday

APRIL, 1935

Date	Industrials			Railroads			Utilities			Daily Sales	40 Bonds
	High	Low	Close	High	Low	Close	High	Low	Close		
1	101.59	100.67	101.23	29.12	28.32	28.70	16.73	16.48	16.60	440	93.53
2	101.86	100.84	101.00	28.68	28.09	28.11	16.96	16.55	16.70	530	93.52
3	101.11	99.75	100.39	27.90	27.65	27.85	16.72	16.43	16.68	530	93.57
4	101.38	100.34	101.13	28.71	28.13	28.66	17.20	16.69	17.10	560	93.65
5	102.87	101.35	102.53	29.76	28.75	29.49	17.90	17.20	17.66	1,210	94.09
6	103.24	102.55	103.04	29.83	29.40	29.76	17.81	17.56	17.70	464	94.33
7	*			*			*				
8	103.40	102.31	102.65	30.16	28.93	29.12	17.91	17.53	17.61	706	94.43
9	104.46	102.58	104.32	30.11	29.11	30.06	17.92	17.45	17.84	857	94.46
10	105.06	103.74	104.06	30.53	29.90	30.00	17.91	17.45	17.50	990	94.72
11	104.59	103.57	104.03	30.07	29.76	29.81	17.48	17.11	17.15	734	94.71
12	104.69	103.59	104.45	30.72	29.92	30.49	17.61	17.17	17.56	840	94.79
13	105.63	104.65	105.42	30.86	30.54	30.80	18.05	17.69	17.94	702	94.80
14	*			*			*				
15	106.44	105.05	105.93	31.17	29.90	30.13	18.13	17.76	17.95	1,107	94.94
16	106.67	105.44	106.33	30.36	29.90	30.04	17.93	17.69	17.83	743	94.79
17	106.67	105.24	105.43	29.99	29.25	29.44	17.94	17.50	17.61	854	94.86
18	108.33	105.68	107.97	30.11	29.41	30.01	17.80	17.49	17.73	816	94.80
19	†	†	†	†	†	†	†	†	†	†	†
20	109.95	108.21	109.76	30.73	30.16	30.56	18.16	17.82	18.08	881	94.92
21	*			*			*				
22	110.91	109.42	110.27	31.00	30.44	30.54	18.95	18.19	18.63	1,380	95.06
23	110.70	109.56	110.06	31.43	30.64	31.27	19.10	18.55	18.93	1,227	95.17
24	110.75	109.08	109.45	31.65	30.83	31.01	19.38	18.83	19.06	1,279	95.17
25	111.52	108.94	110.47	31.67	31.06	31.34	19.45	18.78	19.03	1,639	95.28
26	111.33	109.23	110.37	31.84	31.10	31.61	19.06	18.54	18.66	1,522	95.27
27	110.38	109.51	109.68	31.72	31.22	31.30	18.56	18.20	18.29	585	95.18
28	*			*			*				
29	110.40	108.65	109.91	31.50	30.22	30.90	18.63	17.99	18.50	886	95.17
30	110.61	108.75	109.45	30.54	30.09	30.23	18.49	18.10	18.17	861	95.14
High			110.47			31.61			19.06	22,409	95.28
Low			100.39			27.85			16.60		93.52

†Holiday   *Sunday

MAY, 1935

Date	Industrials			Railroads			Utilities			Daily Sales	40 Bonds
	High	Low	Close	High	Low	Close	High	Low	Close		
1	110.26	108.52	108.71	30.52	30.11	30.21	18.38	18.12	18.21	821	95.10
2	109.47	107.82	108.84	30.74	29.93	30.62	18.52	18.07	18.36	883	95.11
3	110.93	109.04	110.49	30.91	30.54	30.64	18.78	18.35	18.61	953	95.21
4	111.17	110.50	110.83	31.08	30.76	30.82	18.83	18.64	18.80	474	95.22
5	*			*			*				
6	111.60	110.22	110.53	31.62	30.30	30.42	18.86	18.56	18.59	1,028	95.41
7	110.68	109.23	109.79	30.40	29.66	29.83	18.66	18.35	18.45	814	95.24
8	112.74	110.18	112.63	30.44	29.94	30.28	19.20	18.53	19.17	1,395	95.21
9	113.92	112.11	113.10	31.01	30.33	30.65	19.50	19.04	19.18	1,655	95.22
10	114.50	112.84	113.67	30.98	30.38	30.47	19.85	19.18	19.50	1,583	95.27
11	114.39	113.37	114.08	30.76	30.40	30.71	19.74	19.45	19.65	635	95.31
12	*			*			*				
13	114.93	113.36	114.23	31.53	30.82	31.22	19.67	19.21	19.39	1,125	95.27
14	115.03	113.71	114.18	31.61	31.12	31.23	19.39	18.94	19.06	1,208	95.28
15	115.11	113.87	114.61	32.05	31.26	31.67	19.38	18.95	19.18	1,053	95.15
16	117.30	114.67	116.58	32.45	31.81	32.09	19.60	19.12	19.36	2,422	95.38
17	117.09	115.28	115.81	32.36	31.54	31.60	19.84	19.28	19.64	1,822	95.26
18	115.63	114.13	114.58	31.48	31.22	31.38	19.58	19.30	19.44	600	95.19
19	*			*			*				
20	115.27	114.18	114.67	31.57	31.22	31.32	19.66	19.26	19.44	972	95.11
21	116.31	114.57	115.56	31.55	31.19	31.22	19.58	19.25	19.38	1,139	95.16
22	116.69	115.07	116.24	31.40	30.94	31.16	19.52	19.10	19.30	1,147	95.13
23	117.51	116.20	116.81	31.41	31.05	31.20	19.44	19.11	19.19	1,286	95.17
24	117.43	115.91	116.17	32.23	31.31	31.67	19.53	19.16	19.28	1,181	95.24
25	116.31	115.53	115.90	31.74	31.50	31.65	19.30	19.01	19.15	493	95.40
26	*			*			*				
27	117.12	115.32	116.74	32.15	31.67	32.00	19.41	19.01	19.32	823	95.43
28	117.62	112.99	113.76	32.50	31.22	31.44	20.25	19.30	19.56	2,308	95.28
29	113.67	111.37	111.85	31.44	30.90	30.96	20.63	19.50	20.26	1,495	95.15
30	†	†	†	†	†	†	†	†	†	†	†
31	112.62	110.40	110.64	31.26	30.66	30.68	21.04	20.10	20.24	1,124	95.12
High			116.81			32.09			20.26	30,440	95.43
Low			108.71			29.83			18.21		95.10

*Sunday   †Holiday

JUNE, 1935

Date	Industrials High	Low	Close	Railroads High	Low	Close	Utilities High	Low	Close	Daily Sales	40 Bonds
1	110.18	108.64	109.74	30.56	30.27	30.48	20.15	19.77	20.04	676	94.92
2	*	*	*	*	*	*	*	*	*	*	*
3	111.84	110.15	111.45	30.93	30.54	30.77	20.53	20.01	20.41	600	94.91
4	113.73	111.95	113.58	31.36	30.98	31.22	20.79	20.34	20.71	868	94.93
5	115.08	112.96	113.92	31.63	31.11	31.25	21.41	20.56	21.00	1,104	94.95
6	114.89	113.27	113.54	31.44	31.04	31.10	21.12	20.63	20.71	680	95.16
7	114.27	113.15	114.01	31.46	31.13	31.33	21.13	20.68	20.98	590	95.24
8	114.86	114.12	114.72	31.65	31.41	31.50	21.05	20.89	20.98	342	95.29
9	*	*	*	*	*	*	*	*	*	*	*
10	116.12	114.04	115.89	31.43	31.08	31.42	21.20	20.56	21.01	632	95.44
11	117.53	115.77	117.08	32.52	31.49	32.34	21.50	20.98	21.25	1,147	95.65
12	118.53	116.27	117.14	32.94	32.12	32.41	21.02	20.30	20.65	1,290	95.87
13	118.40	116.49	117.89	32.73	32.36	32.45	20.82	20.46	20.65	861	95.90
14	119.67	117.64	119.00	33.37	32.52	33.16	21.21	20.66	21.00	1,276	96.18
15	119.67	118.63	119.17	33.62	33.25	33.54	21.19	21.03	21.14	580	96.38
16	*	*	*	*	*	*	*	*	*	*	*
17	119.33	118.21	118.67	33.89	33.27	33.37	21.70	21.09	21.48	914	96.47
18	119.71	118.67	119.32	34.04	33.28	33.93	21.65	21.38	21.46	886	96.54
19	119.76	117.47	118.12	34.20	33.04	33.36	22.41	21.25	21.84	1,626	96.53
20	117.47	115.85	117.24	33.13	32.47	33.02	21.82	21.31	21.72	996	96.51
21	120.04	117.80	119.48	33.89	33.16	33.56	22.50	21.81	22.30	1,517	96.79
22	120.84	119.56	120.75	33.70	33.46	33.54	22.86	22.26	22.74	787	96.87
23	*	*	*	*	*	*	*	*	*	*	*
24	121.30	119.67	120.04	33.86	33.41	33.45	23.06	22.52	22.66	1,117	97.01
25	119.64	117.85	118.73	33.53	32.88	33.14	22.41	21.81	21.95	1,144	96.99
26	119.49	117.51	117.64	33.26	32.68	32.76	22.11	21.59	21.68	957	96.92
27	118.50	116.91	117.56	32.82	32.30	32.63	21.80	21.34	21.56	737	96.69
28	118.83	117.69	118.36	33.04	32.61	32.83	22.32	21.67	22.08	757	96.73
29	118.52	117.93	118.21	32.94	32.81	32.87	22.09	21.85	21.89	253	96.72
30	*		*			*	*	*	*		*
High			120.75			33.93			22.74	22,336	97.01
Low			109.74			30.48			20.04		94.91

*Sunday †Holiday

JULY, 1935

Date	Industrials High	Low	Close	Railroads High	Low	Close	Utilities High	Low	Close	Daily Sales	40 Bonds
1	119.30	117.97	118.82	33.10	32.81	32.92	22.31	21.80	22.04	684	96.90
2	119.70	118.32	118.69	33.17	32.19	32.36	22.90	22.17	22.30	1,199	96.96
3	118.98	117.80	118.81	32.41	32.06	32.37	22.61	22.23	22.58	720	97.01
4	†	†	†	†	†	†	†	†	†	†	†
5	120.75	119.02	120.61	32.70	32.38	32.62	22.98	22.56	22.78	881	97.18
6	121.16	120.48	121.02	32.72	32.41	32.48	23.01	22.67	22.81	516	97.27
7	*	*	*	*	*	*	*	*	*	*	*
8	122.68	120.69	122.55	32.76	32.28	32.68	22.98	22.63	22.86	1,310	97.15
9	123.34	121.74	122.15	33.43	32.87	33.00	22.99	22.61	22.86	1,346	97.17
10	123.14	121.97	122.69	33.58	32.92	33.24	23.15	22.66	22.76	1,150	97.10
11	122.90	121.14	121.93	33.11	32.73	32.89	22.65	22.04	22.21	996	96.92
12	122.63	121.29	122.20	33.31	32.82	33.21	22.42	21.99	22.28	1,098	96.79
13	122.47	121.68	121.88	33.51	33.20	33.39	22.35	22.16	22.21	443	96.88
14	*	*	*	*	*	*	*	*	*	*	*
15	122.74	121.40	121.72	34.00	33.51	33.63	22.30	21.91	22.06	950	96.95
16	122.56	121.00	122.34	33.77	33.34	33.59	22.16	21.87	22.09	900	96.98
17	123.49	122.25	122.91	34.00	33.49	33.81	22.46	22.11	22.28	1,360	97.01
18	124.24	122.60	123.41	34.07	33.56	33.64	22.50	21.99	22.21	1,500	97.04
19	123.88	121.94	122.33	33.77	33.29	33.35	22.38	22.02	22.10	1,150	97.08
20	122.91	121.99	122.69	33.44	33.22	33.41	22.14	21.97	22.04	430	96.99
21	*	*	*	*	*	*	*	*	*	*	*
22	124.34	122.67	124.10	34.12	33.43	34.09	22.18	21.83	22.03	1,369	96.83
23	125.36	123.58	124.14	34.90	34.11	34.43	22.33	21.75	22.00	1,734	96.85
24	124.93	123.83	124.60	34.58	34.18	34.31	22.42	21.93	22.22	1,305	96.98
25	125.27	123.19	123.80	34.37	33.58	33.77	22.57	22.07	22.15	1,334	96.92
26	124.45	123.37	124.02	34.12	33.72	34.01	22.78	22.24	22.70	986	96.89
27	125.43	124.04	125.27	34.36	34.09	34.22	23.04	22.74	22.95	734	96.86
28	*	*	*	*	*	*	*	*	*	*	*
29	126.89	125.10	126.56	35.40	34.52	35.25	23.34	22.81	23.28	1,750	96.98
30	126.78	125.03	125.57	35.50	34.81	34.86	23.23	22.83	22.90	1,680	96.85
31	127.04	125.00	126.23	35.56	34.88	35.25	23.98	22.90	23.85	1,910	96.96
High			126.56			35.25			23.85	29,428	97.27
Low			118.69			32.36			22.00		96.79

*Sunday †Holiday

AUGUST, 1935

Date	Industrials			Railroads			Utilities			Daily Sales	40 Bonds
	High	Low	Close	High	Low	Close	High	Low	Close		
1	126.88	125.19	125.85	35.75	34.85	35.04	24.13	23.53	23.76	1,890	96.88
2	126.13	124.28	124.93	35.50	34.45	34.73	24.44	23.75	23.92	1,520	96.77
3	126.11	124.95	125.90	34.98	34.66	34.89	25.15	24.05	25.03	1,001	96.81
4	*	*	*	*		*			*		*
5	126.62	125.31	126.07	35.18	34.60	34.87	25.63	25.06	25.39	1,736	96.85
6	126.96	125.00	125.64	35.27	34.24	34.63	25.62	24.77	25.11	1,773	96.65
7	126.54	125.18	125.61	34.48	33.91	34.10	25.33	24.75	24.96	1,389	96.69
8	126.59	125.16	125.98	34.67	33.90	34.31	25.17	24.78	25.00	1,433	96.65
9	127.80	125.72	127.27	35.29	34.36	35.23	26.25	25.09	26.00	2,188	96.75
10	128.52	127.27	127.94	35.66	35.29	35.46	26.86	26.21	26.80	1,211	96.78
11	*	*	*	*		*			*		*
12	128.84	127.44	128.00	36.36	35.44	36.00	27.35	26.55	26.91	2,430	96.69
13	128.85	127.15	128.09	36.74	35.63	36.39	27.86	26.53	27.46	2,630	96.62
14	128.94	127.35	128.27	36.85	36.31	36.49	27.66	27.15	27.29	1,950	96.66
15	128.72	127.07	127.47	36.41	35.85	35.96	27.31	26.80	26.89	1,580	96.49
16	128.03	126.51	127.63	36.91	35.73	36.87	27.75	26.49	27.69	1,710	96.53
17	128.33	127.66	127.96	37.27	36.77	36.98	28.37	27.76	28.18	1,076	96.60
18	*	*	*	*		*			*		*
19	128.39	126.07	126.33	36.97	35.44	35.51	28.06	26.80	27.01	2,070	96.43
20	126.68	124.97	126.31	35.69	34.63	35.56	27.24	25.71	27.01	1,980	96.30
21	128.25	126.59	127.66	36.17	35.48	35.86	27.45	26.71	27.07	1,750	96.35
22	129.49	127.33	128.52	36.24	35.71	35.80	27.74	26.73	27.01	1,670	96.40
23	129.59	127.82	128.93	36.67	35.63	36.08	26.78	25.88	26.40	1,890	96.34
24	129.16	127.79	127.93	36.10	35.23	35.30	26.10	24.91	25.07	1,125	96.23
25	*	*	*	*		*			*		*
26	129.53	127.61	128.99	35.96	35.38	35.72	25.69	24.61	25.46	1,430	96.19
27	129.97	126.27	126.81	35.94	35.54	34.73	25.65	24.06	24.18	2,160	96.05
28	127.32	125.65	126.61	34.96	34.36	34.68	24.59	23.83	24.36	1,390	95.91
29	127.62	126.57	126.95	35.16	34.78	34.83	25.11	24.60	24.88	900	95.80
30	127.70	126.76	127.35	35.14	34.76	34.92	25.31	24.84	25.21	830	95.96
31	128.03	127.36	127.89	35.28	34.99	35.20	25.79	25.32	25.70	491	95.91
High			128.99			36.98			28.18	42,925	96.88
Low			124.93			34.10			23.76		95.80

*Sunday †Holiday

SEPTEMBER, 1935

Date	Industrials			Railroads			Utilities			Daily Sales	40 Bonds
	High	Low	Close	High	Low	Close	High	Low	Close		
1	*	*	*	*	*	*	*	*	*	*	*
2	†	†	†	†	†	†	†	†	†	†	†
3	128.47	126.81	127.27	35.29	34.76	35.07	25.71	24.91	25.16	904	95.98
4	128.70	126.43	128.46	35.62	34.84	35.62	25.70	24.93	25.63	1,001	96.04
5	130.34	128.29	129.34	36.30	35.74	36.01	26.21	25.57	25.98	1,892	96.20
6	131.34	128.94	130.75	37.00	36.30	36.72	26.54	25.92	26.36	2,154	96.46
7	132.33	131.15	131.86	37.24	36.77	36.94	26.96	26.50	26.71	1,290	96.62
8	*	*	*	*		*			*		*
9	133.36	131.13	132.48	37.31	36.59	36.95	26.96	26.37	26.58	2,000	96.61
10	134.06	131.50	133.22	37.07	36.48	37.02	26.80	26.14	26.56	1,978	96.68
11	135.05	132.90	134.01	37.83	37.04	37.25	27.10	26.45	26.71	2,591	96.72
12	134.72	132.63	133.33	37.35	36.57	36.75	27.13	26.39	26.48	1,880	96.66
13	134.67	132.88	133.52	37.20	36.43	36.52	26.72	26.20	26.25	1,731	96.58
14	134.05	133.04	133.40	36.68	36.24	36.45	26.33	25.96	26.11	632	96.72
15	*	*	*	*		*			*		*
16	133.86	131.91	132.91	36.65	36.01	36.19	26.15	25.63	25.85	1,491	96.65
17	133.78	131.86	133.11	36.57	35.98	36.16	25.98	25.53	25.85	1,334	96.52
18	135.34	133.07	134.11	37.26	36.39	36.74	26.15	25.61	25.84	1,939	96.57
19	134.49	131.10	131.44	37.28	36.26	36.36	25.90	25.20	25.26	1,923	96.54
20	130.38	127.98	128.42	35.85	34.95	35.00	25.08	24.43	24.51	2,218	96.21
21	129.24	128.16	128.78	35.25	34.92	35.07	24.68	24.34	24.51	674	96.15
22	*	*	*	*		*			*		*
23	130.66	128.97	129.55	35.70	35.13	35.23	25.18	24.70	24.86	1,008	96.25
24	131.68	130.26	131.02	35.63	35.15	35.17	25.46	24.96	25.25	1,009	96.47
25	132.45	130.99	131.52	35.91	35.37	35.45	25.70	25.28	25.35	1,083	96.53
26	131.67	129.95	131.06	35.52	34.97	35.30	25.53	25.08	25.41	1,091	96.38
27	132.12	130.74	131.48	35.46	35.16	35.28	25.69	25.06	25.19	1,123	96.36
28	132.08	131.47	131.75	35.35	35.23	35.32	25.31	25.12	25.18	519	96.47
29	*	*	*	*		*			*		*
30	132.60	131.17	131.92	35.43	34.62	34.93	25.64	25.08	25.21	1,257	96.44
High			134.11			37.25			26.71	34,727	96.72
Low			127.27			34.93			24.51		95.98

*Sunday †Holiday

OCTOBER, 1935

Date	Industrials			Railroads			Utilities			Daily Sales	40 Bonds
	High	Low	Close	High	Low	Close	High	Low	Close		
1	133.19	131.18	131.51	35.09	34.08	34.16	25.40	24.78	24.83	1,422	96.36
2	130.43	127.56	128.06	33.83	32.33	32.61	24.80	23.80	23.92	2,190	95.87
3	129.41	126.95	129.05	32.93	32.19	32.78	24.45	23.71	24.40	1,485	95.67
4	130.59	128.82	129.76	33.20	32.16	32.54	25.00	24.40	24.61	1,420	95.72
5	130.62	129.79	130.35	32.90	32.59	32.73	24.80	24.55	24.70	697	95.84
6	*	*	*	*	*	*	*	*	*		*
7	131.35	130.24	130.77	33.34	32.76	33.28	25.03	24.58	24.86	954	95.88
8	131.30	129.85	130.06	33.25	32.77	32.80	25.33	24.74	25.03	1,182	95.89
9	130.81	129.51	130.59	32.93	32.33	32.83	25.36	24.93	25.15	883	95.78
10	133.09	131.14	132.99	33.37	32.90	33.17	25.83	25.21	25.78	1,864	95.70
11	134.56	133.03	133.56	33.46	32.71	32.80	26.16	25.56	25.81	2,055	95.71
12	†	†	†	†	†	†	†	†	†	†	†
13	*	*	*	*	*	*	*	*	*		*
14	135.25	133.17	135.03	33.27	32.42	33.18	26.18	25.51	25.94	1,588	95.56
15	137.11	134.85	136.26	34.08	33.08	33.99	26.41	25.71	26.03	2,573	95.62
16	137.15	134.83	135.68	34.60	33.67	33.93	26.32	25.66	25.90	2,243	95.71
17	136.76	135.10	135.57	34.21	33.49	33.54	26.40	25.73	25.85	1,613	95.79
18	136.11	134.54	135.13	33.76	33.28	33.37	26.01	25.53	25.70	1,450	95.60
19	137.22	135.71	137.09	33.77	33.47	33.73	26.21	25.77	26.11	992	95.73
20	*	*	*	*	*	*	*	*	*		*
21	139.50	137.11	138.96	34.14	33.54	33.82	26.46	26.00	26.25	2,872	95.72
22	140.08	137.84	138.77	34.71	34.01	34.50	27.17	26.13	27.06	2,836	95.90
23	140.46	138.32	139.58	35.03	34.03	34.72	27.44	26.60	26.82	2,757	96.06
24	140.84	138.41	139.42	34.97	34.16	34.25	27.26	26.53	26.66	2,156	96.16
25	141.89	139.58	140.68	35.14	34.62	34.82	27.58	26.66	27.18	2,471	96.26
26	141.74	140.77	141.47	35.23	34.92	35.04	27.60	27.28	27.47	1,183	96.25
27	*	*	*	*	*	*	*	*	*		*
28	142.08	139.86	140.78	35.44	34.76	34.90	27.87	27.23	27.45	2,112	96.24
29	141.23	139.49	140.49	35.35	34.67	34.83	27.91	27.18	27.77	1,708	96.29
30	140.56	138.40	139.35	34.93	34.35	34.44	28.40	27.39	27.60	2,147	96.13
31	140.52	138.85	139.74	34.90	34.41	34.61	28.00	27.46	27.71	1,814	96.14
High			141.47			35.04			27.77	46,658	96.36
Low			128.06			32.54			23.92		95.56

*Sunday †Holiday

NOVEMBER, 1935

Date	Industrials			Railroads			Utilities			Daily Sales	40 Bonds
	High	Low	Close	High	Low	Close	High	Low	Close		
1	141.77	140.07	141.31	35.06	34.48	34.74	28.21	27.76	28.03	2,038	96.26
2	141.97	140.78	141.20	35.01	34.57	34.87	28.22	27.63	27.78	1,265	96.26
3	*	*	*	*	*	*	*	*	*	*	*
4	141.78	139.99	141.07	35.34	34.68	35.06	28.13	27.60	28.00	1,748	96.35
5	†	†	†	†	†	†	†	†	†	†	†
6	143.48	141.19	142.90	35.84	34.97	35.60	28.44	27.92	28.15	3,075	96.49
7	145.28	142.15	143.40	35.89	35.32	35.46	28.65	27.90	28.30	2,785	96.44
8	145.40	142.80	144.25	35.66	34.97	35.09	29.88	28.84	29.30	3,351	96.34
9	144.83	143.56	144.36	35.72	35.09	35.54	29.30	28.66	28.98	1,167	96.28
10	*	*	*	*	*	*	*	*	*	*	*
11	†	†	†	†	†	†	†	†	†	†	†
12	144.60	142.20	142.56	36.12	34.90	35.04	29.25	28.35	28.45	2,140	96.17
13	143.97	141.60	143.59	36.17	35.01	36.13	28.82	28.20	28.75	2,048	96.07
14	146.39	143.85	145.59	37.46	36.41	36.93	29.48	28.76	29.07	3,948	96.39
15	147.40	145.10	146.32	37.67	37.00	37.34	29.27	28.85	28.96	2,938	96.56
16	147.64	146.30	147.31	37.68	37.29	37.59	29.40	28.86	29.35	1,639	96.63
17	*	*	*	*	*	*	*	*	*	*	*
18	148.94	146.35	147.06	37.87	37.12	37.18	29.90	29.21	29.40	3,198	96.70
19	148.81	146.93	148.44	37.71	37.02	37.59	29.96	29.35	29.72	2,883	96.92
20	149.42	145.98	146.65	37.78	36.80	36.97	30.10	29.20	29.48	3,815	96.82
21	147.83	145.96	147.37	38.43	37.16	38.20	29.89	29.34	29.67	3,280	97.05
22	148.10	143.48	144.61	38.86	37.14	37.59	30.01	28.76	29.05	3,919	97.03
23	146.60	145.08	146.12	39.22	37.94	39.17	29.80	29.20	29.60	1,919	97.17
24	*	*	*	*	*	*	*	*	*	*	*
25	147.50	143.89	144.72	39.91	38.53	38.84	29.98	29.11	29.37	3,372	97.21
26	145.25	141.80	142.59	39.33	37.97	38.40	29.56	28.82	28.97	2,332	97.24
27	144.30	141.94	143.38	39.52	38.57	39.38	29.26	28.77	29.15	1,859	97.47
28	†	†	†	†	†	†	†	†	†	†	†
29	144.27	141.15	142.34	39.98	38.54	38.96	29.27	28.40	28.63	2,171	97.53
30	142.70	141.82	142.35	39.36	38.91	39.20	28.74	28.40	28.62	670	97.53
High			148.44			39.38			29.72	57,460	97.53
Low			141.07			34.74			27.78		96.07

*Sunday †Holiday

DECEMBER 1935

Date	Industrials High	Low	Close	Railroads High	Low	Close	Utilities High	Low	Close	Daily Sales	40 Bonds
1			*								
2	142.95	140.38	140.72	39.67	38.61	39.10	28.79	28.05	28.22	1,519	97.51
3	143.71	140.60	143.58	40.50	39.04	40.46	29.03	28.18	28.92	1,927	97.66
4	145.13	143.29	144.04	41.91	40.39	41.74	29.38	28.80	29.11	2,964	97.84
5	145.09	143.12	143.72	41.90	41.06	41.39	29.61	28.99	29.20	2,260	98.02
6	144.78	143.09	143.48	41.75	41.00	41.21	29.66	29.15	29.33	2,370	98.20
7	144.84	143.44	144.47	41.82	41.17	41.69	29.90	29.33	29.78	1,319	98.27
8			*								
9	145.07	143.06	144.10	42.21	41.43	41.84	29.98	29.38	29.60	2,508	98.31
10	144.32	141.61	142.31	41.88	41.04	41.23	29.50	28.88	29.06	2,341	98.21
11	143.90	141.63	142.84	41.57	40.93	41.28	29.44	28.76	29.23	2,126	98.22
12	143.46	140.86	141.34	41.66	40.58	40.74	29.38	28.78	28.87	2,136	98.10
13	142.12	139.56	140.16	41.03	39.98	40.23	28.90	28.20	28.34	1,894	98.00
14	140.85	139.81	140.38	40.25	39.90	40.05	28.48	28.23	28.37	667	97.81
15			*								
16	141.28	138.91	139.11	40.28	39.48	39.55	28.66	28.09	28.16	1,402	97.68
17	140.89	138.90	140.60	40.17	39.58	40.08	28.43	27.91	28.30	1,391	97.69
18	141.73	139.71	140.10	40.49	39.92	40.00	28.63	28.14	28.20	1,692	97.83
19	139.95	138.33	138.94	39.98	39.44	39.50	28.29	27.81	28.04	1,264	97.84
20	140.00	138.46	139.50	39.98	39.43	39.77	28.25	27.83	28.13	1,412	97.85
21	140.87	139.35	140.19	39.87	39.59	39.76	28.41	28.13	28.33	1,098	97.97
22			*								
23	141.42	139.75	140.58	39.81	39.33	39.47	28.56	28.08	28.35	1,919	98.08
24	141.88	140.04	141.53	39.72	39.28	39.59	28.66	28.18	28.52	1,706	98.15
25	†	†	†	†	†	†	†	†	†	†	†
26	142.64	140.87	141.54	40.06	39.45	39.72	29.35	28.55	29.11	2,336	98.21
27	142.83	140.67	141.58	39.95	39.31	39.43	29.32	28.67	28.82	2,134	98.27
28	142.16	140.34	140.76	39.63	39.19	39.39	28.90	28.45	28.69	1,140	98.31
29			*								
30	143.37	141.35	143.00	40.22	39.56	40.02	29.48	28.81	29.35	1,627	98.42
31	145.02	142.93	144.13	40.68	39.98	40.48	29.80	29.26	29.55	2,440	98.74
High			144.47			41.84			29.78	45,589	98.74
Low			138.94			39.10			28.04		97.51

*Sunday †Holiday

JANUARY, 1936

Date	Industrials High	Low	Close	Railroads High	Low	Close	Utilities High	Low	Close	Daily Sales	40 Bonds
1	†	†	†	†	†	†	†	†	†	†	†
2	145.22	143.34	144.13	41.00	40.27	40.66	29.93	29.31	29.73	2,241	98.92
3	145.28	143.49	144.69	41.71	40.65	41.48	30.20	29.60	30.08	2,831	99.41
4	144.98	143.84	144.08	42.62	41.33	42.14	30.24	29.91	30.03	1,592	99.62
5			*								
6	145.35	141.55	143.11	42.50	40.87	41.43	30.74	29.56	30.05	3,732	99.47
7	145.22	142.05	144.92	42.65	41.16	42.44	31.11	30.14	30.97	3,084	99.66
8	147.29	144.62	146.16	43.36	42.36	42.55	31.60	30.89	31.05	2,525	99.99
9	146.83	144.63	145.66	43.03	42.08	42.55	31.20	30.30	30.48	2,996	99.98
10	148.02	145.68	147.08	43.36	42.53	42.70	30.91	30.36	30.56	3,271	100.16
11	147.89	146.37	146.73	42.95	42.59	42.68	30.71	30.28	30.36	1,641	100.26
12			*								
13	147.45	145.67	146.52	43.53	42.49	43.27	30.88	30.20	30.48	2,601	100.56
14	146.89	145.41	146.32	43.73	43.01	43.55	31.11	30.50	30.97	2,786	100.78
15	147.13	145.02	145.66	43.91	42.99	43.16	31.30	30.62	30.83	4,634	100.65
16	146.73	145.03	145.92	43.54	42.53	43.24	31.63	30.87	31.35	3,111	100.72
17	146.58	144.64	145.81	43.32	42.83	43.08	31.54	31.00	31.18	2,352	100.90
18	145.69	144.53	144.93	42.99	42.58	42.64	31.21	30.83	30.93	1,073	100.81
19			*								
20	145.23	143.60	144.06	42.58	42.22	42.33	31.10	30.40	30.63	1,805	100.74
21	144.29	142.77	143.50	42.74	41.91	42.45	30.71	30.23	30.38	1,329	100.79
22	146.36	143.79	145.99	43.69	42.75	43.57	31.05	30.53	30.95	2,146	101.06
23	147.70	145.80	146.97	44.50	43.64	44.34	31.40	30.80	31.21	2,938	101.41
24	147.91	146.15	146.59	44.53	43.83	43.95	31.40	30.88	31.08	2,542	101.23
25	147.16	145.24	147.01	44.18	43.48	44.06	31.50	30.68	31.43	1,657	101.17
26			*								
27	148.30	146.73	147.30	45.14	44.14	44.61	32.03	31.47	31.64	3,100	101.29
28	147.84	146.38	146.94	45.49	44.68	45.16	32.18	31.51	31.76	2,288	101.24
29	148.50	146.33	147.71	45.93	45.01	45.82	32.11	31.63	31.93	2,680	101.39
30	148.50	146.25	146.98	46.26	45.35	45.54	32.25	31.52	31.71	3,012	101.36
31	150.00	146.79	149.49	46.42	45.29	46.20	32.46	31.56	32.24	3,225	101.26
High			149.49			46.20			32.24	67,202	101.41
Low			143.11			40.66			29.73		98.92

*Sunday. †Holiday.

Daily and Monthly sales (000) omitted.

FEBRUARY, 1936

Date	Industrials High	Low	Close	Railroads High	Low	Close	Utilities High	Low	Close	Daily Sales	40 Bonds
1	150.86	149.18	149.58	46.52	45.70	46.10	32.48	31.43	31.83	1,759	101.34
2											
3	151.05	148.32	150.62	46.39	45.70	46.21	32.15	31.77	32.00	2,324	101.28
4	151.77	149.92	150.94	47.08	46.07	46.88	32.46	31.81	32.13	3,009	101.40
5	151.94	150.07	150.60	47.24	46.41	46.55	32.52	32.03	32.20	2,922	101.61
6	151.97	150.14	150.86	47.30	46.63	46.93	33.01	32.10	32.61	2,754	101.67
7	151.67	149.50	150.17	47.28	46.55	46.76	32.98	32.36	32.61	2,571	101.80
8	150.73	149.72	150.40	46.80	46.51	46.65	32.73	32.46	32.62	1,252	101.92
9											
10	151.88	149.72	151.15	47.30	46.57	47.19	33.09	32.50	32.86	2,459	102.07
11	153.16	150.80	152.25	48.38	47.37	48.01	33.71	32.80	33.48	3,354	102.37
12	†	†	†	†	†	†	†	†	†		†
13	153.67	151.48	152.53	48.88	48.02	48.75	34.08	33.44	33.64	2,924	102.36
14	153.01	150.86	151.97	48.88	48.16	48.40	33.98	33.27	33.59	2,604	102.62
15	152.78	151.53	152.40	48.86	48.24	48.76	33.88	33.48	33.76	1,374	102.59
16											
17	153.57	150.43	151.40	49.38	47.74	48.37	35.36	32.30	32.75	4,718	102.61
18	153.76	151.23	153.36	49.26	48.20	49.18	33.04	32.00	32.55	3,527	102.66
19	155.69	152.54	153.09	50.56	49.30	49.63	32.80	31.34	31.49	4,578	102.84
20	155.14	152.30	154.43	51.37	49.65	51.27	32.49	31.37	32.30	3,457	103.02
21	155.14	153.05	153.74	51.73	50.78	51.07	32.81	32.30	32.50	3,021	103.24
22	†	†	†	†	†	†	†	†	†		†
23											
24	153.75	152.00	152.74	50.95	50.00	50.31	32.54	31.94	32.25	2,198	103.03
25	153.25	149.99	150.78	50.63	49.03	49.27	32.30	31.53	31.68	2,390	102.74
26	151.10	149.08	149.81	49.49	48.56	48.87	32.10	31.33	31.76	2,036	102.56
27	153.02	150.59	152.64	50.26	49.24	50.16	32.55	31.92	32.45	2,315	102.74
28	153.94	151.61	152.53	50.55	49.22	49.48	32.76	31.99	32.20	2,459	102.78
29	152.74	151.65	152.15	49.11	48.30	48.58	32.29	32.00	32.11	881	102.61
High			154.43			51.27			33.76	60,884	103.24
Low			149.58			46.10			31.49		101.28

*Sunday †Holiday

MARCH, 1936

Date	Industrials High	Low	Close	Railroads High	Low	Close	Utilities High	Low	Close	Daily Sales	40 Bonds
1											
2	154.54	151.65	154.08	49.31	48.49	49.22	32.59	31.96	32.50	1,983	102.67
3	156.61	154.08	156.19	49.90	49.14	49.57	33.01	32.52	32.81	2,697	102.84
4	158.24	155.45	156.70	49.94	49.26	49.56	33.38	32.66	33.07	2,979	103.00
5	158.56	156.03	157.52	50.86	49.62	50.33	33.35	32.81	33.07	2,590	103.06
6	159.87	157.27	158.75	50.56	49.96	50.15	33.41	32.86	32.98	2,889	103.15
7	159.77	156.93	157.86	49.93	49.28	49.61	32.96	32.48	32.59	1,472	103.16
8											
9	156.86	153.33	153.50	49.02	47.83	47.86	32.41	31.66	31.77	2,753	102.63
10	155.87	153.35	155.37	48.70	47.82	48.54	32.25	31.60	31.98	2,322	102.44
11	157.95	155.37	156.85	49.19	48.16	48.82	32.66	32.00	32.31	2,193	102.52
12	156.63	152.35	153.13	48.43	46.86	47.06	32.08	31.23	31.41	2,918	102.15
13	153.46	149.65	150.42	47.02	45.65	45.96	31.50	30.55	30.71	2,660	101.65
14	154.75	152.19	154.07	47.23	46.55	47.13	31.98	31.24	31.84	1,426	101.81
15											
16	154.73	152.14	153.25	47.31	46.57	46.72	32.31	31.52	32.01	1,835	101.85
17	156.73	153.85	156.34	48.30	47.14	47.92	32.84	32.16	32.54	2,241	102.08
18	157.30	155.04	155.82	48.13	47.36	47.46	32.80	32.03	32.21	1,747	102.23
19	158.22	155.85	157.40	48.14	47.53	47.88	32.60	31.97	32.11	2,016	102.28
20	158.81	156.69	157.42	47.94	47.23	47.33	32.26	31.61	31.83	1,888	102.17
21	157.28	156.20	156.42	47.29	47.00	47.10	31.98	31.62	31.76	840	102.24
22											
23	158.22	156.20	157.62	47.71	47.09	47.53	32.42	31.77	32.24	1,679	102.23
24	158.76	156.23	156.56	48.06	47.40	47.53	32.52	31.95	32.08	1,903	102.24
25	158.74	155.81	157.88	47.81	47.23	47.56	32.56	32.01	32.38	1,908	102.08
26	159.53	157.08	157.73	48.39	47.50	47.85	32.78	32.31	32.33	1,872	102.08
27	157.82	155.01	155.52	47.95	47.04	47.17	32.48	31.66	31.81	1,553	101.96
28	155.91	154.66	155.54	47.31	46.98	47.16	31.98	31.66	31.87	657	101.81
29											
30	156.73	155.16	155.37	47.35	46.77	46.81	32.20	31.76	31.81	946	101.74
31	157.01	155.06	156.34	47.12	46.64	46.93	32.15	31.71	31.93	1,041	101.61
High			158.75			50.33			33.07	51,017	103.16
Low			150.42			45.96			30.71		101.61

*Sunday †Holiday

Daily and Monthly sales (000) omitted.

APRIL, 1936

Date	Industrials High	Low	Close	Railroads High	Low	Close	Utilities High	Low	Close	Daily Sales	40 Bonds
1	159.42	157.04	158.96	47.89	47.33	47.70	32.66	31.96	32.44	1,687	101.85
2	161.55	159.12	160.43	49.23	48.21	49.04	33.00	32.38	32.54	2,193	102.04
3	161.84	159.80	160.09	49.30	48.55	48.58	32.78	32.34	32.45	1,563	102.17
4	161.89	160.15	161.50	49.23	48.46	49.10	32.78	32.35	32.66	1,011	102.25
5 •											
6	163.07	161.18	161.99	49.80	49.19	49.35	33.40	32.64	33.06	2,032	102.33
7	162.33	160.42	160.94	49.40	48.66	48.85	33.53	32.91	33.15	1,575	102.32
8	162.54	160.34	160.97	49.62	48.84	49.23	33.70	33.06	33.27	1,653	102.38
9	161.44	159.46	160.25	49.95	48.93	49.70	33.56	32.95	33.13	1,654	102.42
10 †											
11	161.14	159.64	160.48	50.08	49.43	50.05	33.28	32.93	33.15	798	102.42
12 •											
13	161.26	159.71	160.76	50.53	49.78	50.41	33.23	32.80	32.90	1,448	102.43
14	161.10	157.51	158.41	50.25	48.78	49.01	32.99	32.07	32.37	1,937	102.27
15	160.27	157.92	159.61	49.43	48.85	49.08	32.79	32.31	32.60	1,318	102.15
16	160.33	157.93	158.49	49.18	48.60	48.71	32.96	32.33	32.51	1,147	102.15
17	159.22	157.32	157.78	48.83	48.20	48.32	32.61	32.07	32.11	1,164	102.02
18	157.57	155.57	156.07	48.32	47.73	47.90	32.20	31.78	31.90	810	101.95
19 •											
20	156.73	152.10	152.40	47.66	46.36	46.41	32.04	31.20	31.25	1,656	101.85
21	154.09	151.29	153.36	46.61	45.73	46.15	31.70	31.00	31.30	1,882	101.75
22	155.59	153.60	154.92	46.97	46.18	46.62	31.89	31.39	31.65	1,204	101.79
23	155.16	149.63	151.08	46.47	44.30	44.79	31.63	30.25	30.69	2,063	101.57
24	152.51	149.63	151.54	45.06	44.01	44.68	30.94	30.28	30.59	1,656	101.50
25	152.66	151.44	151.93	45.12	44.70	44.93	30.95	30.58	30.80	536	101.54
26 •											
27	151.81	145.96	147.05	44.76	42.48	43.01	30.76	29.33	29.61	2,296	101.26
28	147.79	144.80	146.75	43.63	42.43	43.40	30.00	29.06	29.58	2,232	101.08
29	147.23	143.20	143.65	43.50	42.23	42.30	29.62	28.48	28.63	1,787	100.93
30	146.20	141.53	145.67	43.50	41.71	43.28	29.27	28.06	29.19	2,309	100.91
Low			161.99			50.41			33.27	39,610	102.43
High			143.65			42.30			28.63		100.91

•Sunday. †Holiday.

MAY, 1936

Date	Industrials High	Low	Close	Railroads High	Low	Close	Utilities High	Low	Close	Daily Sales	40 Bonds
1	147.86	145.67	147.07	43.95	43.26	43.51	29.45	28.85	29.05	1,160	101.09
2	147.09	145.54	146.41	43.54	43.20	43.39	29.15	28.76	28.96	402	101.15
3 •											
4	147.63	144.18	146.96	43.70	42.65	43.52	29.10	28.32	28.95	1,071	101.22
5	149.97	147.69	148.56	44.48	43.67	43.86	29.83	29.13	29.44	1,175	101.46
6	150.52	148.52	149.73	44.88	43.96	44.58	29.85	29.35	29.70	1,131	101.70
7	149.96	146.29	147.14	44.63	43.57	43.75	29.77	28.88	29.03	1,006	101.59
8	147.33	145.68	146.87	43.73	43.27	43.47	29.25	28.70	29.05	780	101.48
9	148.44	147.11	147.85	43.85	43.59	43.75	29.31	29.06	29.19	342	101.46
10 •											
11	148.85	146.44	146.85	43.96	43.32	43.38	29.38	28.91	28.93	678	101.44
12	148.16	146.10	146.70	43.66	43.23	43.29	29.25	28.85	29.01	599	101.43
13	148.38	146.92	147.90	43.88	43.65	43.72	29.31	28.99	29.18	586	101.59
14	151.97	149.00	151.49	45.10	44.30	44.99	30.26	29.47	30.18	1,391	101.87
15	152.43	150.56	151.60	45.47	44.83	45.21	30.46	29.93	30.19	985	101.94
16	151.74	150.96	151.42	45.20	45.00	45.11	30.55	30.11	30.53	371	101.95
17 •											
18	152.44	150.09	150.35	45.79	44.88	44.94	30.96	30.29	30.41	993	101.95
19	149.56	147.21	147.49	44.68	43.97	44.06	30.19	29.68	29.76	910	101.87
20	149.28	147.30	148.94	44.56	44.14	44.41	30.15	29.64	30.01	686	102.00
21	150.21	148.46	148.80	44.62	44.13	44.19	30.61	29.89	30.03	668	101.98
22	150.26	148.61	149.58	44.63	44.22	44.50	30.76	30.01	30.62	679	102.04
23	150.92	149.82	150.65	44.88	44.59	44.81	31.00	30.70	30.90	439	102.15
24 •											
25	151.62	150.31	150.83	45.32	44.94	45.06	31.13	30.65	30.81	694	102.15
26	152.48	150.48	152.26	46.34	45.12	46.21	31.74	30.80	31.65	1,143	102.19
27	153.57	151.44	152.57	46.87	45.97	46.33	31.90	31.30	31.51	1,220	102.31
28	152.91	151.49	151.77	46.32	45.91	45.99	31.65	31.13	31.23	763	102.26
29	152.92	151.53	152.64	46.55	46.01	46.28	31.54	31.10	31.40	740	102.37
30 †											
31 •											
High			152.64			46.33			31.65	20,614	102.37
Low			146.41			43.29			28.93		101.09

†Holiday •Sunday

Daily and Monthly sales (ooo) omitted.

JUNE, 1936

Date	Industrials			Railroads			Utilities			Daily Sales	40 Bonds
	High	Low	Close	High	Low	Close	High	Low	Close		
1	154.02	152.62	152.84	47.03	46.43	46.49	31.73	31.34	31.39	786	102.43
2	153.22	151.30	151.97	46.66	46.15	46.39	31.54	31.06	31.30	756	102.41
3	152.38	151.20	151.53	46.49	45.99	46.08	31.47	31.00	31.11	635	102.38
4	151.10	149.22	149.39	46.00	45.41	45.43	31.30	30.69	30.76	767	102.37
5	149.95	148.52	149.26	45.55	45.00	45.28	30.87	30.55	30.73	635	102.27
6	150.01	149.43	149.84	45.47	45.27	45.40	30.99	30.78	30.96	254	102.29
7 .... *											
8	152.01	150.40	151.39	45.99	45.64	45.75	31.51	31.06	31.32	694	102.31
9	153.12	151.44	152.90	46.28	45.78	46.16	32.25	31.36	32.21	876	102.47
10	153.87	152.44	153.02	46.90	46.37	46.60	32.58	32.11	32.26	1,035	102.52
11	155.38	152.65	155.16	47.11	46.49	47.07	32.64	32.11	32.50	1,086	102.53
12	155.91	153.55	153.71	47.28	46.61	46.64	32.63	32.05	32.13	998	102.58
13	154.71	153.98	154.64	46.81	46.46	46.73	32.71	32.11	32.65	375	102.61
14 .... *											
15	155.81	154.57	155.09	46.88	46.41	46.50	33.09	32.57	32.73	723	102.62
16	156.94	154.88	156.70	47.41	46.61	47.30	33.43	32.77	33.38	1,115	102.79
17	157.96	156.47	156.97	47.92	47.35	47.46	33.68	33.09	33.23	1,221	102.86
18	158.05	156.54	157.38	48.31	47.56	47.96	33.50	33.04	33.20	943	102.88
19	157.46	156.11	156.53	48.01	47.42	47.52	33.16	32.58	32.69	828	102.84
20	157.46	156.44	157.21	47.63	47.42	47.56	32.90	32.66	32.83	317	102.76
21 .... *											
22	159.66	157.40	159.13	48.39	47.77	48.18	33.46	32.88	33.29	985	102.83
23	160.25	158.24	158.94	48.13	47.47	47.60	33.50	32.93	33.11	972	102.73
24	161.15	158.56	160.66	48.10	47.55	47.89	33.38	32.97	33.20	1,237	102.71
25	161.00	158.27	158.64	48.23	47.56	47.64	33.31	32.63	32.73	1,341	102.65
26	159.54	157.86	158.21	48.77	47.44	47.88	32.86	32.41	32.46	890	102.60
27	158.84	157.55	158.46	48.15	47.73	48.11	32.58	32.22	32.48	366	102.56
28 .... *											
29	159.66	157.58	158.01	48.43	47.87	47.90	32.80	32.27	32.38	770	102.61
30	158.76	157.11	157.69	48.16	47.62	47.84	32.83	32.31	32.48	822	102.61
High			160.66			48.18			33.38	21,429	102.88
Low			149.26			45.28			30.73		102.27

*Sunday †Holiday

JULY, 1936

Date	Industrials			Railroads			Utilities			Daily Sales	40 Bonds
	High	Low	Close	High	Low	Close	High	Low	Close		
1	159.16	156.82	158.38	48.10	47.59	47.85	33.01	32.31	32.91	966	102.56
2	159.55	156.87	157.51	48.50	47.70	47.84	33.35	32.76	32.99	1,073	102.55
3	159.13	156.93	158.11	48.25	47.80	48.05	33.60	32.88	33.41	1,020	102.69
4 .... †											
5 .... *											
6	158.86	156.73	157.11	48.27	47.63	47.71	33.60	33.03	33.20	845	102.70
7	156.87	154.86	155.60	47.86	46.73	47.41	33.32	32.80	33.00	970	102.64
8	156.76	154.85	156.20	48.45	47.67	48.31	33.62	32.86	33.50	869	102.70
9	158.17	156.05	157.71	49.40	48.72	49.18	34.03	33.45	33.75	1,292	102.89
10	160.67	158.07	160.07	50.08	49.56	49.86	34.51	33.83	34.38	1,692	103.14
11	161.06	160.14	160.72	50.40	49.91	50.34	34.78	34.31	34.71	867	103.25
12 .... *											
13	162.14	160.33	161.35	51.32	50.30	51.01	34.90	34.39	34.55	1,435	103.33
14	163.22	160.99	162.80	52.79	51.70	52.67	35.28	34.46	35.16	1,660	103.44
15	164.42	162.28	163.24	52.81	52.01	52.46	35.40	34.75	34.87	1,978	103.35
16	164.38	162.27	163.64	53.07	51.78	52.71	35.15	34.58	34.86	1,481	103.37
17	165.07	163.02	163.55	53.42	52.50	52.91	35.13	34.65	34.81	1,555	103.21
18	164.67	163.49	164.42	53.05	52.70	52.87	35.14	34.79	35.01	557	103.27
19 .... *											
20	165.48	163.84	164.43	53.51	52.78	53.01	35.58	34.98	35.23	1,424	103.35
21	165.81	163.75	165.23	53.73	52.96	53.44	35.50	34.98	35.22	1,587	103.45
22	166.06	163.99	164.49	53.44	52.66	52.90	35.45	34.85	35.03	1,453	103.56
23	165.06	163.46	164.61	53.38	52.54	53.23	35.22	34.76	35.13	1,336	103.56
24	165.31	164.00	164.37	53.66	53.01	53.21	35.33	34.86	35.04	1,321	103.60
25	165.91	164.38	165.56	53.45	53.20	53.31	35.43	35.02	35.37	612	103.54
26 .... *											
27	167.63	165.51	166.92	54.24	53.35	54.04	36.05	35.46	35.79	1,826	103.61
28	168.23	165.98	167.01	54.72	53.77	54.19	36.01	35.40	35.59	1,904	103.70
29	167.83	165.13	165.67	54.41	53.40	53.51	35.57	35.07	35.14	1,948	103.66
30	167.05	165.13	165.98	54.08	53.34	53.89	35.50	34.96	35.13	1,513	103.67
31	167.27	164.32	164.86	54.28	53.36	53.50	35.35	34.76	34.89	1,160	103.71
High			167.01			54.19			35.79	34,793	103.71
Low			155.60			47.41			32.91		102.55

*Sunday †Holiday

Daily and Monthly sales (000) omitted.

AUGUST, 1936

Date	Industrials			Railroads			Utilities			Daily Sales	40 Bonds
	High	Low	Close	High	Low	Close	High	Low	Close		
1	165.81	164.61	165.42	53.65	53.38	53.55	34.94	34.70	34.86	491	103.68
2											
3	166.53	164.63	165.32	53.78	53.20	53.25	35.35	34.80	34.99	1,005	103.53
4	165.91	164.41	165.41	53.72	53.14	53.51	35.16	34.68	34.98	1,049	103.62
5	166.57	163.91	165.07	53.99	53.21	53.49	35.33	34.76	35.02	1,284	103.44
6	166.24	164.17	165.71	54.27	53.12	54.18	35.15	34.72	34.98	1,172	103.58
7	168.63	165.34	168.01	55.54	54.40	55.27	35.37	34.96	35.24	1,672	103.81
8	169.66	167.88	169.10	55.96	55.50	55.74	35.93	35.32	35.83	865	103.90
9											
10	170.15	168.15	168.80	56.02	55.18	55.38	36.05	35.38	35.56	1,335	103.89
11	169.08	167.20	167.86	55.43	54.85	54.91	35.74	35.18	35.35	1,100	103.87
12	169.63	167.50	169.05	55.67	54.94	55.36	35.65	35.15	35.45	1,261	103.92
13	169.59	167.30	167.64	55.83	55.03	55.10	35.73	35.06	35.16	1,398	103.91
14	167.80	165.40	165.75	55.12	54.06	54.23	35.29	34.63	34.73	1,072	103.87
15	166.44	165.51	165.86	54.24	53.87	53.98	34.92	34.63	34.76	366	103.88
16											
17	167.01	164.66	165.38	54.11	53.41	53.61	34.86	34.42	34.53	833	103.82
18	166.37	164.89	165.42	53.91	53.43	53.53	34.83	34.47	34.61	791	103.79
19	166.87	165.26	166.04	54.25	53.40	54.07	34.96	34.52	34.77	1,006	103.84
20	166.70	165.23	165.59	54.26	53.44	53.63	34.84	34.38	34.54	962	103.83
21	164.69	160.52	160.80	52.99	51.74	51.84	34.47	33.44	33.51	1,480	103.59
22	162.35	161.05	162.14	52.52	51.95	52.44	33.85	33.47	33.78	432	103.54
23											
24	164.64	162.90	163.78	53.31	52.70	53.06	34.26	33.76	33.86	803	103.71
25	165.23	163.60	164.34	53.31	52.67	52.70	34.26	33.90	33.98	800	103.85
26	165.00	162.98	163.32	53.08	52.35	52.45	34.20	33.66	33.80	907	103.82
27	166.94	163.21	166.77	53.85	52.63	53.81	34.25	33.57	34.16	1,336	103.94
28	168.02	166.31	166.78	54.41	53.81	54.10	34.88	34.18	34.62	1,377	104.02
29	167.22	166.34	166.91	55.17	54.19	55.01	34.78	34.51	34.70	618	104.11
30											
31	167.25	165.84	166.29	55.31	54.59	54.78	34.98	34.53	34.77	1,149	104.17
High			169.10			55.74			35.83	26,564	104.17
Low			160.80			51.84			33.51		103.44

*Sunday †Holiday

SEPTEMBER, 1936

Date	Industrials			Railroads			Utilities			Daily Sales	40 Bonds
	High	Low	Close	High	Low	Close	High	Low	Close		
1	167.21	165.24	166.35	54.98	54.30	54.62	34.90	34.46	34.64	1,144	104.20
2	167.89	166.15	166.65	55.35	54.53	54.96	35.16	34.61	34.88	1,352	104.35
3	167.25	165.64	166.24	55.28	54.60	54.88	35.11	34.67	34.83	1,048	104.44
4	167.62	166.01	167.04	55.36	54.75	55.18	35.27	34.71	35.01	1,175	104.46
5	167.97	167.21	167.80	55.74	55.28	55.68	35.22	35.00	35.11	716	104.49
6											
7	†	†	†	†	†	†	†	†	†	†	†
8	170.02	168.32	169.55	56.27	55.69	56.11	35.51	35.03	35.15	1,716	104.50
9	169.73	168.07	168.50	56.34	55.68	55.95	35.33	34.85	35.04	1,572	104.56
10	169.59	168.05	169.00	56.70	56.03	56.15	35.33	34.88	35.01	1,547	104.60
11	169.38	167.59	168.59	56.34	55.60	55.91	35.34	34.68	35.06	1,404	104.58
12	168.76	167.94	168.02	56.07	55.73	55.83	35.14	34.86	34.95	495	104.65
13											
14	167.98	166.11	166.86	55.77	55.15	55.46	34.80	34.29	34.54	1,005	104.67
15	167.14	165.41	166.44	55.62	54.75	55.26	34.78	34.16	34.41	1,128	104.61
16	166.75	164.97	165.16	55.31	54.60	54.65	34.40	33.63	33.67	1,038	104.59
17	166.51	164.82	166.25	55.27	54.52	55.20	33.96	33.52	33.82	774	104.58
18	168.36	166.10	167.76	55.91	55.34	55.68	34.28	33.70	34.11	1,274	104.65
19	169.16	168.01	168.93	56.56	55.96	56.36	34.60	34.11	34.50	897	104.72
20											
21	170.25	168.34	168.90	56.89	56.27	56.36	35.03	34.19	34.33	1,766	104.75
22	170.47	168.37	169.47	56.82	56.21	56.47	34.66	34.05	34.25	1,548	104.96
23	170.72	168.68	169.01	56.94	56.21	56.30	34.43	33.95	34.05	1,484	105.01
24	169.79	168.10	169.14	56.75	55.98	56.55	34.32	33.76	34.14	1,193	105.09
25	169.03	165.91	166.36	56.60	55.23	55.44	34.14	33.50	33.63	1,155	104.92
26	169.55	167.33	168.07	56.79	55.99	56.50	34.06	33.63	33.83	901	105.02
27											
28	169.62	167.72	168.79	56.73	55.96	56.26	34.43	33.76	34.18	1,450	105.03
29	169.85	168.01	168.48	56.76	56.05	56.33	34.48	34.02	34.24	1,381	104.90
30	169.55	167.47	167.82	56.43	55.76	55.88	34.62	33.93	34.09	1,353	105.01
High			169.55			56.55			35.15	30,873	105.09
Low			165.16			54.62			33.63		104.20

*Sunday †Holiday

Daily and Monthly sales (000) omitted.

OCTOBER, 1936

Date	Industrials			Railroads			Utilities			Daily Sales	40 Bonds
	High	Low	Close	High	Low	Close	High	Low	Close		
1	168.83	167.54	168.26	56.11	55.68	55.76	34.29	33.86	33.93	1,099	105.02
2	170.94	168.63	170.76	57.21	55.96	57.18	34.63	34.09	34.52	1,929	105.29
3	172.89	171.34	172.44	58.11	57.49	57.85	34.99	34.54	34.81	1,632	105.40
4											
5	174.04	172.04	172.81	58.65	57.63	58.20	35.03	34.46	34.53	2,082	105.34
6	174.82	172.93	174.42	58.66	58.00	58.54	34.77	34.36	34.45	2,258	105.48
7	175.92	173.94	174.59	59.06	58.13	58.41	35.50	34.46	35.16	3,027	105.43
8	175.49	173.41	174.93	59.06	58.11	58.75	35.57	35.02	35.32	2,227	105.48
9	176.45	174.23	175.19	59.53	58.65	59.03	35.66	35.10	35.20	2,235	105.52
10	176.21	175.14	176.05	59.62	58.98	59.55	35.38	35.13	35.30	971	105.49
11											
12	†	†	†	†	†	†	†	†	†	†	†
13	177.68	175.87	176.29	60.48	59.54	59.85	35.53	34.76	34.81	2,066	105.53
14	176.79	175.03	175.57	60.30	59.40	59.89	35.17	34.58	34.73	1,642	105.49
15	176.32	174.13	175.22	59.84	58.92	59.19	35.03	34.50	34.62	1,786	105.42
16	177.31	175.33	176.66	60.20	59.22	59.85	35.27	34.58	35.03	2,049	105.49
17	178.06	177.01	177.63	60.18	59.67	59.85	35.33	34.93	35.09	1,153	105.57
18											
19	178.44	176.66	177.42	60.21	59.53	59.65	35.43	34.91	35.04	1,888	105.50
20	177.82	175.98	176.78	59.57	58.80	58.89	35.61	34.92	35.31	1,669	105.39
21	177.63	175.81	176.70	59.53	58.96	59.27	35.63	34.92	35.28	1,632	105.26
22	177.01	174.50	174.90	59.45	58.35	58.54	35.80	35.06	35.37	1,975	105.14
23	176.23	174.64	175.60	58.79	58.27	58.51	35.82	35.16	35.51	1,514	105.06
24	176.19	175.44	175.91	58.76	58.46	58.61	35.59	35.33	35.43	619	105.11
25											
26	174.74	172.16	172.30	58.40	57.23	57.35	35.29	34.55	34.61	1,478	104.90
27	174.90	172.89	174.36	58.23	57.49	58.03	35.20	34.75	34.98	1,312	104.92
28	176.61	174.47	174.84	58.81	58.02	58.22	35.35	34.82	34.90	1,630	104.99
29	176.60	174.61	176.31	59.10	58.19	58.98	35.83	35.01	35.83	1,709	105.14
30	178.09	176.20	177.15	59.38	58.67	58.92	36.30	35.70	36.03	1,678	105.17
31	177.83	176.73	177.19	58.97	58.42	58.66	36.32	35.84	36.08	733	105.17
High			177.63			59.89			36.08	43,995	105.57
Low			168.26			55.76			33.93		104.90

*Sunday   †Holiday

NOVEMBER, 1936

Date	Industrials			Railroads			Utilities			Daily Sales	40 Bonds
	High	Low	Close	High	Low	Close	High	Low	Close		
1											
2	177.74	175.35	176.67	58.51	57.78	58.15	36.00	35.00	35.20	1,600	105.11
3	†	†	†	†	†	†	†	†	†	†	†
4	181.15	177.00	180.66	58.64	57.66	58.27	34.95	33.71	34.05	3,290	105.03
5	183.31	180.57	182.25	59.15	58.41	58.74	35.35	34.21	35.04	3,620	105.18
6	183.53	180.68	181.60	58.90	58.03	58.08	35.55	34.76	34.95	2,720	105.40
7	183.76	181.76	183.38	58.05	57.58	57.92	35.41	34.93	35.33	1,750	105.46
8											
9	184.77	182.39	183.65	59.15	57.77	58.60	35.51	34.93	35.09	3,139	105.55
10	185.24	182.82	184.01	58.90	57.97	58.30	35.18	34.57	34.66	2,704	105.60
11	†	†	†	†	†	†	†	†	†	†	†
12	185.52	182.26	183.15	58.53	57.21	57.46	34.87	34.18	34.26	2,582	105.55
13	184.28	181.39	182.24	57.62	56.28	56.43	34.46	33.83	34.01	2,482	105.53
14	181.82	180.21	181.45	56.20	55.66	56.02	33.98	33.68	33.93	1,154	105.41
15											
16	183.39	181.00	182.65	56.70	56.01	56.30	34.87	34.04	34.80	2,375	105.49
17	185.55	182.94	184.90	57.60	56.55	57.32	35.35	34.70	35.14	3,273	105.62
18	186.39	183.73	184.44	57.78	56.75	56.85	35.52	34.80	34.94	2,922	105.57
19	184.26	181.63	182.21	56.76	55.95	56.10	35.32	34.50	34.84	2,442	105.57
20	182.35	180.24	180.74	55.92	55.18	55.40	35.18	34.53	34.75	1,822	105.51
21	182.44	181.15	182.01	56.11	55.67	56.05	35.26	34.79	35.10	802	105.43
22											
23	181.78	177.91	178.62	55.85	54.62	54.73	35.20	34.18	34.33	2,160	105.26
24	181.51	178.84	181.11	55.43	54.58	55.28	35.03	34.37	34.84	1,924	105.38
25	181.49	179.68	180.78	55.50	54.88	55.08	35.00	34.51	34.69	1,856	105.43
26	†	†	†	†	†	†	†	†	†	†	†
27	183.27	180.91	182.81	56.10	54.93	55.94	35.83	34.78	35.65	2,276	105.59
28	183.85	182.83	183.32	56.13	55.61	55.73	36.16	35.59	35.88	1,434	105.67
29											
30	184.03	181.87	183.22	55.76	55.09	55.40	36.13	35.43	35.75	2,140	105.61
High			184.90			58.74			35.88	50,467	105.67
Low			176.67			54.73			33.93		105.03

*Sunday   †Holiday

Daily and Monthly sales (ooo) omitted.

DECEMBER, 1936

Date	Industrials			Railroads			Utilities			Daily Sales	40 Bonds
	High	Low	Close	High	Low	Close	High	Low	Close		
1	183.59	181.56	182.05	55.63	54.91	55.03	36.09	35.40	35.51	2,234	105.72
2	181.89	179.66	180.25	55.26	54.18	54.33	35.78	35.14	35.36	2,320	105.72
3	181.92	179.90	181.29	54.93	54.28	54.57	35.70	35.16	35.33	2,042	105.69
4	182.34	180.36	180.97	55.34	54.33	54.47	35.70	35.08	35.15	2,155	105.83
5	181.77	180.75	181.05	54.70	54.41	54.56	35.45	35.10	35.28	1,001	105.80
6	•			•			•				
7	181.49	179.74	180.13	54.55	53.99	54.10	35.35	34.80	34.93	1,677	105.78
8	181.29	179.95	180.57	54.85	54.05	54.45	35.30	34.85	35.07	1,619	105.79
9	181.77	179.93	181.16	55.46	54.29	55.11	35.35	34.75	35.23	1,856	105.81
10	182.77	180.67	182.18	55.94	55.14	55.50	35.62	34.99	35.16	2,440	105.90
11	182.33	180.76	181.10	55.77	54.87	54.97	35.43	34.79	35.12	2,612	105.94
12	181.73	180.30	180.92	55.18	54.80	54.93	35.43	34.90	35.26	1,236	106.01
13	•			•			•				
14	182.67	180.74	181.87	55.18	54.63	54.82	36.12	35.09	35.61	2,876	105.90
15	183.30	181.30	181.97	55.65	54.88	55.00	35.93	35.11	35.29	2,478	105.91
16	182.57	180.87	181.58	55.26	54.81	54.96	35.55	34.88	35.28	1,945	105.88
17	182.18	180.35	180.78	55.31	54.60	54.74	35.60	34.88	35.09	1,953	105.80
18	181.10	179.03	179.42	54.95	54.08	54.23	35.41	34.58	34.74	1,906	105.59
19	179.08	177.07	177.61	53.96	51.90	52.70	34.88	34.30	34.44	1,215	105.35
20	•			•			•				
21	178.28	175.31	175.85	52.96	51.83	51.96	34.68	33.80	33.83	1,762	105.15
22	178.20	176.14	177.30	52.26	51.50	51.68	34.70	33.94	34.42	1,667	105.14
23	179.00	176.70	178.36	52.41	51.50	52.01	34.87	34.28	34.55	1,868	105.23
24	179.54	177.75	178.60	53.02	52.20	52.58	34.96	34.54	34.65	1,607	105.35
25	†			†			†			†	†
26	†			†			†			†	†
27	•			•			•				
28	179.52	176.71	177.12	53.36	52.15	52.20	34.82	34.18	34.25	1,787	105.24
29	178.48	176.26	177.60	52.56	51.75	52.26	34.57	34.01	34.40	2,280	105.23
30	181.13	178.02	180.57	53.74	52.50	53.61	35.18	34.38	34.92	2,305	105.43
31	181.77	179.34	179.90	54.23	53.51	53.63	35.19	34.63	34.83	1,760	105.58
High			182.18			55.50			35.61	48,600	106.01
Low			175.85			51.68			33.83		105.14

•Sunday †Holiday

JANUARY, 1937

Date	Industrials			Railroads			Utilities			Daily Sales	40 Bonds
	High	Low	Close	High	Low	Close	High	Low	Close		
1	†			†			†			†	†
2	179.87	178.01	178.52	53.58	53.13	53.28	34.93	34.53	34.66	691	105.50
3	•			•			•				
4	178.39	176.96	177.72	53.38	52.80	53.15	34.86	34.41	34.70	1,508	105.54
5	179.66	177.64	179.07	53.85	53.17	53.63	35.22	34.65	34.96	1,869	105.60
6	179.90	178.17	178.92	54.15	53.45	53.84	35.71	34.86	35.42	1,921	105.63
7	182.11	179.32	181.77	54.86	54.06	54.66	36.52	35.51	36.40	3,056	105.59
8	183.58	181.36	182.95	55.65	54.36	55.31	36.83	36.16	36.52	3,217	105.73
9	183.48	182.20	182.75	55.41	55.00	55.13	36.58	36.23	36.38	1,449	105.77
10	•			•			•				
11	183.82	181.77	183.26	55.76	55.13	55.46	36.86	36.09	36.59	3,076	105.79
12	184.49	182.08	183.30	55.73	54.90	55.37	37.28	36.32	37.14	3,565	105.69
13	184.01	182.25	183.01	55.82	55.16	55.65	37.66	36.76	37.54	3,683	105.69
14	184.66	182.53	183.71	55.94	55.32	55.43	37.72	36.83	37.06	3,259	105.74
15	185.40	183.55	184.53	56.32	55.16	55.66	37.41	36.88	37.05	2,897	105.77
16	186.04	184.47	185.73	56.35	55.75	56.31	37.53	36.96	37.26	1,705	105.89
17	•			•			•				
18	185.93	183.74	184.95	56.33	55.71	55.86	37.61	36.96	37.31	2,861	105.89
19	185.16	183.22	184.02	56.51	55.54	56.00	37.18	36.30	36.64	2,619	105.78
20	186.88	184.10	185.96	56.86	55.96	56.44	37.03	36.42	36.71	3,271	105.73
21	187.49	184.98	186.90	57.03	56.16	56.69	37.35	36.54	37.06	2,992	105.74
22	187.80	185.01	186.53	56.68	55.70	56.08	37.44	36.70	36.94	2,684	105.65
23	187.28	185.85	186.69	56.31	55.78	56.06	37.18	36.83	37.02	1,116	105.56
24	•			•			•				
25	186.97	185.02	185.62	55.93	55.07	55.25	36.96	36.30	36.48	2,219	105.21
26	185.68	182.64	183.19	54.98	54.08	54.22	36.53	35.84	35.88	2,175	104.70
27	184.32	182.15	183.97	54.91	54.10	54.77	36.44	35.59	36.25	1,937	104.84
28	185.59	182.77	183.41	55.11	54.29	54.45	36.51	35.83	35.87	2,343	104.92
29	185.41	182.34	184.74	55.04	54.59	54.77	36.02	35.47	35.71	1,965	104.84
30	186.10	184.37	185.74	55.05	54.58	55.00	35.90	35.36	35.83	1,965	104.86
31	•			•			•				
High			186.90			56.69			37.54	58,671	105.89
Low			177.72			53.15			34.66		104.70

•Sunday †Holiday

Daily and Monthly sales (000) omitted.

FEBRUARY, 1937

Date	Industrials High	Low	Close	Railroads High	Low	Close	Utilities High	Low	Close	Daily Sales	40 Bonds
1	187.77	185.10	186.61	55.28	54.68	54.86	36.16	35.63	35.73	2,357	104.86
2	189.13	186.13	188.20	55.65	54.89	55.25	36.33	35.61	35.96	2,429	104.85
3	189.94	187.48	188.69	56.38	55.53	56.13	36.33	35.75	35.93	2,452	104.83
4	189.64	187.65	188.39	56.91	56.30	56.48	36.11	35.62	35.71	2,388	104.92
5	189.07	184.85	186.01	57.03	55.58	55.93	35.83	34.86	35.08	3,321	104.79
6	187.35	185.57	187.11	57.35	55.97	57.29	35.33	34.86	35.11	1,453	104.78
7											
8	188.66	186.68	187.82	58.35	57.47	57.80	35.41	34.85	35.08	2,987	104.84
9	188.79	186.74	187.68	58.23	57.53	57.66	35.25	34.54	34.88	2,593	104.82
10	189.83	187.58	189.35	58.31	57.45	57.92	35.90	35.16	35.44	2,920	104.80
11	191.39	188.69	190.29	58.50	57.57	58.01	35.70	35.10	35.30	2,917	104.56
12	†	†	†								
13	190.70	188.94	190.03	58.25	57.75	58.00	35.21	34.91	35.12	1,371	104.37
14											
15	189.58	187.45	188.39	57.96	57.11	57.37	35.26	34.75	35.09	1,960	104.23
16	189.20	187.05	188.18	57.80	57.06	57.44	35.46	34.73	35.24	2,221	103.94
17	189.39	187.30	187.98	58.62	57.53	58.00	35.53	34.96	35.15	2,579	104.00
18	188.90	186.82	188.07	58.63	58.00	58.23	35.26	34.68	34.75	2,131	104.08
19	190.42	187.71	189.37	58.98	58.15	58.59	35.28	34.48	35.04	2,725	104.22
20	190.35	188.70	189.37	58.96	58.37	58.73	35.12	34.63	34.76	1,485	104.26
21											
22	†	†	†	†	†	†	†	†	†	†	†
23	189.36	185.96	186.50	58.91	57.20	57.45	34.81	33.96	34.02	2,869	104.22
24	187.88	185.15	187.35	57.91	57.10	57.73	34.41	33.82	34.20	2,084	104.02
25	188.31	186.19	186.68	58.48	57.33	57.43	34.36	33.95	34.06	2,227	103.96
26	187.93	185.82	187.17	58.06	57.20	57.81	34.26	33.81	34.02	1,776	104.00
27	187.69	186.79	187.30	58.15	57.78	58.01	34.24	33.85	34.08	1,004	104.02
28											
High			190.29			58.73			35.96	50,248	104.92
Low			186.01			54.86			34.02		103.94

*Sunday. †Holiday.

MARCH, 1937

Date	Industrials High	Low	Close	Railroads High	Low	Close	Utilities High	Low	Close	Daily Sales	40 Bonds
1	188.48	186.00	187.68	58.53	57.60	58.21	34.42	33.85	34.10	1,662	104.04
2	190.41	187.64	189.91	59.05	58.12	58.90	34.45	33.91	34.20	2,295	103.95
3	193.86	190.29	192.91	60.65	59.03	60.52	34.48	33.95	34.11	3,568	103.93
4	193.95	190.98	191.63	61.26	60.11	60.28	34.97	34.15	34.33	2,726	103.89
5	195.17	192.17	194.14	61.92	60.61	61.61	34.65	34.05	34.18	2,828	103.88
6	195.04	193.29	194.15	62.81	61.91	62.69	34.52	34.06	34.23	1,767	103.97
7											
8	195.20	191.53	192.69	63.22	61.62	62.10	35.00	34.11	34.37	3,175	103.91
9	194.89	191.65	193.29	62.73	61.73	62.20	34.76	34.01	34.37	2,388	103.73
10	195.59	192.77	194.40	63.28	61.85	63.06	34.75	33.93	34.00	2,824	103.72
11	195.33	191.77	192.22	63.72	62.33	62.61	34.03	33.15	33.22	2,739	103.38
12	192.27	189.39	191.24	62.66	61.30	62.27	33.29	32.55	33.00	2,290	103.19
13	191.62	189.85	190.58	62.64	61.95	62.06	33.06	32.70	32.88	1,129	103.10
14											
15	190.81	188.59	189.41	62.52	61.43	62.03	33.13	32.56	32.85	1,767	102.88
16	191.29	188.88	189.95	63.53	62.06	63.06	33.20	32.65	32.84	1,750	102.61
17	190.52	188.15	188.50	65.08	63.81	64.46	33.36	32.74	32.97	2,117	102.38
18	187.52	183.72	184.73	63.76	62.04	62.44	33.19	32.60	32.14	2,276	101.88
19	185.94	183.72	184.56	63.53	62.03	62.58	33.19	32.59	32.73	1,741	102.05
20	185.14	183.19	184.04	62.88	62.36	62.58	32.94	32.65	32.79	713	101.95
21											
22	182.83	179.28	179.82	61.69	59.86	60.18	32.69	31.88	31.92	2,026	101.65
23	182.96	179.93	181.87	61.43	60.35	61.13	32.55	31.96	32.31	1,596	101.60
24	184.97	181.63	184.32	61.63	60.76	61.34	32.52	32.05	32.24	1,430	101.83
25	186.11	183.73	184.08	61.92	60.72	60.79	32.45	31.88	32.00	1,250	102.08
26	†	†	†	†	†	†	†	†	†		
27	185.29	183.99	184.95	61.09	60.71	61.05	32.13	31.88	32.02	532	102.07
28											
29	185.75	183.79	184.09	61.38	60.78	60.94	32.20	31.73	31.80	871	102.24
30	186.93	183.64	186.77	62.33	60.80	62.30	32.18	31.65	32.06	1,225	102.18
31	187.99	185.77	186.41	62.47	61.59	61.73	32.43	31.88	32.08	1,663	102.13
High			194.40			64.46			34.37	50,346	104.04
Low			179.82			58.21			31.80		101.60

*Sunday †Holiday

Daily and Monthly sales (000) omitted.

APRIL, 1937

Date	Industrials			Railroads			Utilities			Daily Sales	40 Bonds
	High	Low	Close	High	Low	Close	High	Low	Close		
1	186.63	184.37	185.19	61.66	60.86	61.09	32.16	31.66	31.74	1,208	101.64
2	184.43	180.89	182.75	60.66	59.20	60.13	31.72	31.25	31.49	1,635	101.23
3	184.13	182.76	183.54	60.81	60.08	60.46	31.69	31.40	31.56	643	101.31
4	*	*	*	*			*	*	*		*
5	185.09	183.39	184.19	60.98	60.36	60.56	31.91	31.60	31.75	976	101.33
6	184.66	182.06	182.98	60.60	59.77	60.08	31.91	31.47	31.61	1,251	101.12
7	182.13	177.68	178.07	60.07	58.00	58.26	31.71	30.85	30.98	2,290	100.94
8	179.94	176.72	178.18	59.05	57.55	58.50	31.45	30.63	31.01	1,920	100.57
9	180.38	175.86	178.94	59.08	57.62	58.65	31.38	30.59	31.16	1,733	100.57
10	179.89	178.02	178.26	58.88	58.58	58.72	31.23	31.01	31.03	480	100.55
11	*	*	*	*			*	*	*		*
12	180.12	176.39	179.74	59.38	58.10	59.33	31.23	30.73	31.11	1,134	100.47
13	183.43	180.59	182.10	60.77	59.58	60.20	31.59	31.01	31.42	1,585	100.86
14	183.34	181.27	181.93	60.93	59.92	60.31	31.99	31.41	31.52	1,479	101.19
15	182.25	180.69	181.19	60.56	59.93	60.18	31.72	31.31	31.38	941	101.43
16	182.27	179.70	180.75	60.45	59.73	60.26	31.60	31.13	31.21	1,068	101.47
17	181.08	179.94	180.51	60.20	59.95	60.02	31.26	31.07	31.13	444	101.60
18	*	*	*	*			*	*	*		*
19	181.38	179.76	180.82	60.63	59.88	60.52	31.30	30.90	31.07	818	101.65
20	182.63	180.28	181.44	61.49	60.46	60.95	31.34	30.90	31.03	1,126	101.81
21	184.05	181.39	183.60	61.72	61.06	61.53	31.36	30.95	31.14	1,248	101.76
22	184.33	181.28	181.70	61.75	60.87	60.95	31.33	30.46	30.53	1,180	101.55
23	182.60	178.00	178.54	61.50	60.10	60.24	30.65	29.99	30.17	1,203	101.49
24	177.81	176.01	176.98	59.88	59.30	59.54	30.11	29.77	29.94	808	101.35
25	*	*	*	*			*	*	*		*
26	175.33	171.20	171.97	58.63	56.85	57.26	29.68	28.92	29.02	2,023	100.89
27	175.18	172.36	174.52	58.16	57.26	57.96	29.58	28.97	29.40	1,412	100.83
28	173.78	168.77	170.13	57.61	55.96	56.61	29.36	28.15	28.36	2,526	100.79
29	172.88	169.37	170.52	58.11	56.23	56.90	29.00	28.31	28.46	2,026	100.97
30	174.66	171.51	174.27	58.93	57.62	58.63	29.29	28.43	29.01	1,450	101.12
High			185.19			61.53			31.75	34,607	101.81
Low			170.13			56.61			28.36		100.47

*Sunday   †Holiday

MAY, 1937

Date	Industrials			Railroads			Utilities			Daily Sales	40 Bonds
	High	Low	Close	High	Low	Close	High	Low	Close		
1	175.45	174.02	174.42	58.83	58.21	58.26	29.33	29.03	29.16	551	101.13
2	*	*	*	*			*	*	*		*
3	175.58	174.16	174.59	58.75	58.16	58.25	29.52	29.12	29.29	638	101.16
4	176.69	175.20	176.30	59.50	58.94	59.41	30.02	29.45	29.81	870	101.35
5	176.81	174.41	174.67	59.70	59.00	59.05	30.08	29.49	29.57	766	101.60
6	176.05	174.06	175.81	60.42	58.69	60.32	29.65	29.19	29.50	755	101.60
7	176.91	175.50	175.89	61.10	60.33	60.63	29.65	29.21	29.28	817	101.79
8	176.05	175.22	175.54	60.33	60.03	60.14	29.34	29.13	29.23	285	101.72
9	*	*	*	*			*	*	*		*
10	175.19	172.78	173.04	59.58	58.51	58.61	29.23	28.68	28.73	780	101.55
11	173.28	171.59	172.55	59.15	58.38	58.95	28.73	28.25	28.38	746	101.51
12	173.72	171.81	172.24	59.81	58.79	58.89	28.60	27.96	28.03	674	101.56
13	171.43	166.88	167.46	58.86	56.99	57.27	27.98	26.95	27.17	1,772	101.26
14	169.89	166.58	169.15	58.13	56.96	57.76	27.80	27.09	27.56	1,226	101.18
15	170.13	169.08	169.60	58.13	57.81	57.90	27.67	27.45	27.53	344	101.23
16	*	*	*	*			*	*	*		*
17	169.98	167.64	167.84	58.10	57.06	57.13	27.71	27.07	27.10	597	101.15
18	170.55	166.20	169.97	58.14	56.35	57.92	27.48	26.55	27.28	1,195	101.20
19	170.85	169.11	169.75	58.41	57.68	57.88	27.36	26.85	27.04	790	101.29
20	173.99	170.00	173.59	59.19	57.96	58.89	27.75	27.01	27.56	1,227	101.40
21	174.59	173.12	173.83	58.98	58.48	58.60	28.07	27.63	27.91	768	101.54
22	175.37	173.95	175.00	59.07	58.65	58.96	28.38	28.00	28.34	481	101.55
23	*	*	*	*			*	*	*		*
24	176.25	174.51	175.59	59.00	58.43	58.75	28.70	28.16	28.48	684	101.60
25	176.11	173.30	173.79	58.25	57.10	57.21	28.50	28.06	28.13	842	101.59
26	174.47	172.62	173.70	57.51	56.87	57.13	28.30	27.88	28.01	584	101.50
27	175.03	173.22	174.19	57.25	56.62	56.76	28.29	27.88	28.03	597	101.35
28	175.22	174.04	174.71	57.14	56.55	56.82	28.22	27.88	27.95	559	101.26
29	†	†	†	†	†	†	†	†	†	†	†
30	*	*	*	*	*	*	*	*	*	*	*
31	†	†	†	†	†	†	†	†	†	†	†
High			176.30			60.63			29.81	18,549	101.79
Low			167.46			56.76			27.04		101.13

*Sunday   †Holiday

JUNE, 1937

Date	Industrials			Railroads			Utilities			Daily Sales	40 Bonds
	High	Low	Close	High	Low	Close	High	Low	Close		
1	172.69	170.72	171.59	56.61	55.40	56.09	27.88	27.28	27.56	746	101.25
2	173.73	172.25	172.63	56.61	56.13	56.26	27.95	27.48	27.61	535	101.29
3	173.09	171.56	172.82	56.53	55.73	56.32	27.79	27.41	27.69	552	101.31
4	175.39	172.19	175.14	57.03	56.14	56.97	27.80	27.36	27.65	778	101.55
5	175.66	174.67	175.00	57.37	57.05	57.13	27.86	27.68	27.75	342	101.67
6	*			*			*			*	
7	175.40	173.56	173.88	57.23	56.72	56.77	27.83	27.40	27.41	585	101.70
8	174.91	173.25	174.33	57.20	56.74	57.00	27.77	27.34	27.62	598	101.72
9	175.00	173.12	173.47	57.40	56.78	56.90	27.70	27.33	27.37	624	101.74
10	174.06	172.53	172.82	57.28	56.78	56.83	27.55	27.11	27.18	567	101.64
11	172.59	170.33	170.77	56.45	55.41	55.60	27.25	26.74	26.78	722	101.54
12	170.57	169.00	169.51	55.51	55.03	55.26	26.71	26.46	26.55	387	101.50
13	*			*			*			*	
14	168.45	163.73	165.51	54.70	52.96	53.75	26.41	25.66	25.98	1,310	101.26
15	168.10	164.69	167.40	54.55	53.38	54.18	26.41	25.81	26.23	928	101.19
16	167.59	165.49	165.86	54.19	53.51	53.57	26.41	25.96	26.06	699	101.18
17	167.95	163.31	167.74	54.01	52.31	53.88	26.28	25.49	26.13	1,259	101.07
18	169.37	167.05	168.79	54.26	53.45	53.65	26.96	26.10	26.56	694	101.05
19	169.26	168.36	168.60	53.68	53.35	53.38	26.62	26.44	26.51	221	101.01
20	*			*			*			*	
21	168.79	167.28	167.98	53.23	52.53	52.75	26.53	26.13	26.21	424	101.91
22	169.42	167.59	168.20	53.16	52.51	52.86	26.59	26.18	26.37	534	100.80
23	169.72	168.22	169.01	53.33	52.76	53.05	26.65	26.07	26.26	551	100.70
24	170.46	168.79	170.08	53.29	52.77	53.15	26.40	26.06	26.18	553	100.69
25	170.98	169.10	169.59	53.30	52.32	52.37	26.55	26.09	26.29	575	100.34
26	169.23	168.08	168.45	51.76	50.91	51.06	26.30	26.02	26.06	288	100.13
27	*			*			*			*	
28	168.99	166.26	166.71	51.23	49.78	50.17	26.05	25.36	25.45	730	99.71
29	168.10	166.11	167.11	50.95	50.21	50.55	25.80	25.35	25.56	550	99.54
30	170.02	167.00	169.32	51.48	50.60	51.35	26.37	25.61	26.31	690	99.94
High			175.14			57.13			27.75	16,449	101.91
Low			165.51			50.17			25.45		99.54

*Sunday †Holiday

JULY, 1937

Date	Industrials			Railroads			Utilities			Daily Sales	40 Bonds
	High	Low	Close	High	Low	Close	High	Low	Close		
1	171.28	169.13	170.13	51.92	51.25	51.48	26.71	26.25	26.50	670	100.51
2	172.49	169.58	172.22	52.17	51.28	52.06	27.08	26.57	27.03	839	100.84
3	†	†	†	†	†	†	†	†	†	†	†
4											
5	†	†	†	†	†	†	†	†	†	†	†
6	177.08	173.18	176.80	53.80	52.40	53.72	27.94	27.23	27.87	1,412	101.06
7	178.88	176.25	177.74	54.59	53.74	54.26	28.70	27.91	28.33	1,409	101.43
8	178.38	176.49	177.70	54.85	54.11	54.71	28.56	28.03	28.26	1,032	101.47
9	178.36	176.65	177.40	54.85	54.25	54.30	28.48	28.06	28.18	845	101.55
10	177.46	176.37	176.72	54.28	53.85	54.00	28.15	28.00	28.06	298	101.60
11	*			*			*			*	
12	179.16	176.69	178.70	54.76	54.24	54.67	28.48	27.82	28.21	1,023	101.58
13	179.53	177.50	178.24	54.84	54.12	54.21	28.26	27.76	27.88	849	101.63
14	180.17	177.83	178.57	54.49	53.53	53.70	28.40	27.85	28.11	1,037	101.58
15	180.09	177.78	179.71	53.96	53.31	53.82	28.31	27.87	28.18	737	101.63
16	180.45	178.65	179.53	53.63	53.05	53.34	28.45	28.03	28.18	704	101.50
17	179.88	178.93	179.72	53.36	53.13	53.28	28.23	28.08	28.17	248	101.57
18	*			*			*			*	
19	182.39	180.11	182.06	54.03	53.33	53.83	28.98	28.25	28.85	950	101.58
20	183.90	182.01	183.32	55.20	54.18	55.03	29.56	28.96	29.32	1,196	101.58
21	183.94	181.87	182.35	55.46	54.61	54.70	29.65	29.05	29.13	981	101.59
22	184.13	182.14	182.96	55.06	54.61	54.71	29.70	29.13	29.40	956	101.66
23	184.75	182.70	183.78	55.38	54.68	54.80	30.08	29.55	29.85	914	101.66
24	184.93	183.60	184.85	55.11	54.76	55.05	30.67	29.90	30.65	506	101.77
25	*			*			*			*	
26	185.15	183.72	184.42	55.25	54.71	54.83	30.98	30.41	30.65	896	101.79
27	184.73	183.43	184.24	54.56	54.20	54.40	30.61	30.18	30.32	736	101.69
28	184.54	182.17	182.57	54.18	53.50	53.52	30.44	29.86	29.93	867	101.52
29	183.61	182.07	183.01	53.35	52.79	52.95	29.97	29.67	29.96	611	101.51
30	184.66	182.92	184.01	53.30	52.77	52.85	30.14	29.71	29.96	617	101.31
31	185.85	184.29	185.61	52.98	52.68	52.95	30.17	29.94	30.09	390	101.32
High			185.61			55.05			30.65	20,722	101.79
Low			170.13			51.48			26.50		100.51

*Sunday †Holiday

AUGUST, 1937

Date	Industrials High	Low	Close	Railroads High	Low	Close	Utilities High	Low	Close	Daily Sales	40 Bonds
1	*	*	*	*	*	*	*	*	*	*	*
2	187.28	185.35	186.91	53.08	52.58	52.83	30.02	29.66	29.76	791	101.19
3	187.14	185.43	185.91	52.91	52.08	52.20	29.88	29.37	29.41	897	101.17
4	187.31	185.38	186.80	53.55	52.20	53.38	29.56	29.15	29.38	903	101.26
5	187.22	185.76	186.09	53.71	53.03	53.13	29.49	28.98	29.06	795	101.34
6	186.56	185.16	185.43	53.13	52.52	52.64	29.08	28.68	28.81	679	101.27
7	186.60	185.57	186.41	53.02	52.61	52.95	29.01	28.70	28.92	315	101.26
8	*		*			*			*		
9	187.33	186.06	186.75	53.62	53.09	53.28	29.19	28.90	29.03	751	101.26
10	187.67	186.23	186.98	53 35	53.01	53.08	29.33	29.00	29.13	692	101.24
11	187.31	185.93	186.72	53.17	52.86	53 00	29.14	28.86	28.96	572	101.26
12	188.30	186.39	187.62	53.60	53.03	53.57	29.20	28.90	29.03	793	101.30
13	189.76	187.35	189.29	54.02	53 45	53.89	29.33	28.92	29.11	1,036	101.32
14	190.38	189.38	190.02	54.23	53.90	54.13	29.38	29.08	29.23	467	101.34
15	*		*			*			*		
16	189.94	188.60	189.34	53.96	53.56	53.62	29.25	28.86	28.92	618	101.26
17	189.18	188.12	188.68	53 56	53.11	53.21	28.98	28.69	28.77	657	101.09
18	189.10	187.30	187.39	53.30	52.47	52.55	28.83	28.31	28.36	702	101.01
19	186.97	184.75	185.28	52.75	52.25	52.38	28.33	27.93	27.99	762	100.66
20	185.28	182 30	182.95	52.38	51.75	51.87	28.10	27.60	27.65	802	100.40
21	183.94	182.55	183.74	52.15	51.85	52.10	27.88	27.66	27.83	281	100.36
22	*		*			*			*		
23	184.20	181.31	181.88	52.30	51.76	51.77	28.09	27.70	27.77	575	100.49
24	182.87	180.80	182.39	52.19	51.51	52.01	27.93	27.51	27.78	560	100.46
25	183.00	181.39	181.70	52.12	51.48	51.60	28.15	27.74	27.83	498	100.44
26	180.71	177.57	178.52	51.22	50.22	50.37	27.82	27.31	27.45	966	100.19
27	179.23	175.09	175.91	50.18	49.28	49.40	27.65	27.12	27.23	886	100.02
28	176.44	175.53	175.93	49.71	49.41	49.46	27.36	27.20	27.26	254	99.99
29	*		*			*			*		
30	178.26	176.10	177.88	49.83	49.31	49.73	27.58	27.20	27.45	455	100.03
31	179.10	177.29	177.41	50.22	49.55	49.60	27.66	27.35	27.38	504	100.07
High			190.02			54.13			29.76	17,213	101.34
Low			175.91			49.40			27.23		99.99

*Sunday. †Holiday.

SEPTEMBER, 1937

Date	Industrials High	Low	Close	Railroads High	Low	Close	Utilities High	Low	Close	Daily Sales	40 Bonds
1	176.11	172.89	173.08	49.11	48.18	48.21	27.28	26.71	26.73	820	99.93
2	172.71	169.75	170.84	48.00	46.89	47.13	26.92	26.40	26.54	1,202	99.79
3	174.03	171.82	172.17	47.73	47.06	47.21	26.99	26.62	26.80	691	99.78
4	172.81	171.77	172.55	47.43	47.16	47.43	26.96	26.81	26.86	230	99.81
5	*		*			*			*		*
6	†	†	†	†	†	†	†	†	†	†	†
7	170.29	163.18	164.39	46.58	44.06	44.37	26.70	25.21	25.37	1,871	99.33
8	166.06	162.17	163.37	44.56	43.16	43.53	25.80	25.01	25.28	2,256	98.86
9	168.06	164.88	166.36	45.27	44.05	44.66	26.26	25.55	25.94	1,412	98.95
10	166.87	157.35	157.98	44.71	41.44	41.67	26.08	24.70	24.83	2,322	98.85
11	161.25	157.98	159.96	42.46	41.53	42.34	25.19	24.60	24.97	1,404	98.62
12	*		*			*			*		*
13	163.12	154.94	158.00	43.01	39.69	40.77	25.57	23.96	24.39	2,562	98.30
14	164.37	160.00	162.90	42.40	41.06	41.25	25.50	24.41	25.25	1,510	98.34
15	165.16	161.26	162.85	42.40	41.20	41.45	25.94	24.86	25.36	1,143	98.41
16	165.37	162.29	164.75	43.95	41.83	43.87	25.76	25.10	25.65	886	98.66
17	164.19	161.59	162.15	43.53	42.34	42.72	25.61	24.91	25.05	814	98.70
18	160.59	157.40	157.83	42.20	41.52	41.80	24.97	24.40	24.50	703	98.45
19	*		*			*			*		*
20	156.92	152.36	155.56	41.98	40.80	41.80	24.67	23.95	24.43	1,550	98.17
21	159.26	155.96	156.56	43.05	42.00	42.31	25.01	24.46	24.63	981	98.37
22	158.89	156.55	157.45	43.00	42.12	42.33	25.02	24.46	24.58	739	98.33
23	157.51	153.79	153.98	42.36	41 18	41.25	24.66	23.95	23.96	888	98.06
24	151.58	146.22	147.38	40 81	39.41	39.67	23.87	22.83	22.95	2,482	97.43
25	150.08	146.94	147.47	39.68	38.79	38.93	23.30	22.73	22.77	1,470	97.12
26	*		*			*			*		*
27	152.49	146.25	152.03	40.56	38.98	40.40	23.89	22.90	23 73	2,209	97.04
28	155.22	151.41	153.16	41.32	40.27	40.83	24.30	23 70	24.08	1,308	97.15
29	155.24	150.09	154.70	41.51	40.00	41.31	24.32	23.48	24.18	1,354	97.31
30	157.12	153.97	154.57	42.08	41.12	41.25	24.58	24.06	24.15	1,046	97.62
High			173.08			48.21			26.86	33,853	99.93
Low			147.38			38.93			22.77		97.04

*Sunday. †Holiday.

OCTOBER, 1937

Date	Industrials High	Low	Close	Railroads High	Low	Close	Utilities High	Low	Close	Daily Sales	40 Bonds
1	155.11	152.50	153.89	41.11	40.15	40.69	24.31	23.81	24.03	675	97.94
2	154.37	153.43	154.08	41.18	40.43	41.06	24.13	23.96	24.06	285	98.09
3	*			*			*				
4	154.63	151.84	152.19	41.36	40.31	40.43	24.16	23.76	23.82	632	98.04
5	149.97	143.01	144.08	40.03	38.30	38.68	23.63	22.66	22.80	1,683	97.76
6	147.62	141.63	147.18	39.24	37.74	38.99	23.32	22.49	23.21	1,785	97.31
7	150.47	145.76	146.59	39.63	38.56	38.67	23.65	22.94	23.07	1,191	97.33
8	148.26	143.00	144.03	38.95	37.15	37.26	23.19	22.41	22.48	1,153	96.92
9	144.49	143.17	143.93	37.56	37.06	37.39	22.67	22.46	22.61	489	96.88
10	*			*			*				
11	143.66	137.71	138.79	36.90	35.33	35.40	22.69	21.71	21.80	1,748	96.45
12	†	†	†	†	†	†	†	†	†	†	†
13	140.94	134.79	138.20	36.07	34.48	35.26	22.24	20.98	21.59	2,567	96.07
14	140.88	136.09	136.54	35.66	34.16	34.29	22.08	21.28	21.37	1,681	95.84
15	138.14	133.95	135.48	34.28	33.07	33.64	21.75	20.88	21.07	2,538	95.07
16	137.39	134.75	136.30	33.78	33.05	33.33	21.36	20.83	20.96	1,320	94.94
17	*			*			*				
18	137.00	125.14	125.73	33.40	30.44	30.55	21.41	19.71	19.84	3,230	94.26
19	127.61	115.84	126.85	30.51	27.76	30.09	19.90	17.77	19.65	7,290	93.15
20	135.48	126.87	134.56	32.83	30.35	32.65	21.80	19.89	21.65	4,340	94.39
21	137.82	132.09	135.48	35.26	32.78	35.03	22.75	21.57	22.43	3,640	95.29
22	135.66	131.74	132.26	36.89	34.38	35.28	22.45	21.76	21.88	2,113	95.53
23	131.50	126.87	127.15	34.18	32.03	32.32	21.71	20.75	20.84	1,565	94.95
24	*			*			*				
25	135.12	124.56	134.43	34.40	31.61	34.04	22.33	20.65	22.11	2,344	95.41
26	136.79	131.77	132.78	34.49	33.10	33.33	22.29	21.25	21.39	1,823	95.06
27	134.01	130.48	132.26	33.55	32.55	32.90	21.74	20.97	21.33	1,064	94.39
28	138.31	132.58	135.22	34.33	33.09	33.74	22.67	21.64	22.11	2,460	94.32
29	141.22	136.46	138.48	35.39	33.81	34.68	23.43	22.22	22.93	2,800	94.74
30	139.08	137.07	138.17	35.02	34.40	34.63	23.13	22.62	22.83	714	94.77
31											
High			154.08			41.06			24.06	51,130	98.09
Low			125.73			30.09			19.65		93.15

*Sunday †Holiday

NOVEMBER, 1937

Date	Industrials High	Low	Close	Railroads High	Low	Close	Utilities High	Low	Close	Daily Sales	40 Bonds
1	137.01	135.00	135.94	34.28	33.56	33.89	22.64	22.20	22.36	1,029	94.79
2	†	†	†	†	†	†	†	†	†	†	†
3	135.49	129.56	130.14	33.69	32.17	32.38	22.29	21.36	21.48	1,736	94.42
4	130.17	126.67	128.84	32.65	31.65	32.27	21.76	21.13	21.56	1,471	94.17
5	132.31	128.35	128.92	33.27	32.20	32.56	22.33	21.51	21.65	1,245	93.76
6	127.94	124.80	125.25	32.30	31.57	31.67	21.58	21.14	21.21	766	93.47
7	*			*			*				
8	124.93	121.61	123.98	31.90	30.86	31.70	21.40	20.79	21.31	1,378	93.07
9	127.11	124.07	126.16	32.29	31.60	32.08	22.35	21.34	21.96	1,049	93.12
10	132.59	128.63	132.16	34.11	32.86	34.03	23.52	22.60	23.48	1,924	93.38
11	†	†	†	†	†	†	†	†	†	†	†
12	135.70	131.64	133.09	34.78	33.70	33.97	23.89	23.00	23.28	1,883	93.57
13	133.24	131.73	133.05	34.29	33.93	34.26	23.49	23.04	23.43	510	93.54
14	*			*			*				
15	134.36	129.08	129.22	34.68	33.20	33.23	24.01	22.76	22.80	1,445	93.44
16	129.63	125.34	127.98	33.28	32.41	32.98	23.03	22.15	22.88	1,269	93.21
17	129.94	127.02	127.54	33.17	32.62	32.73	23.12	22.54	22.61	758	93.19
18	127.73	124.35	125.48	32.55	31.84	32.01	22.62	22.05	22.31	903	92.88
19	124.32	117.98	118.13	31.53	30.03	30.07	22.11	20.84	20.91	1,887	92.38
20	120.88	116.68	120.45	31.10	29.71	31.06	21.92	20.74	21.85	1,232	92.13
21	*			*			*				
22	119.28	113.77	114.19	30.57	29.43	29.55	22.02	20.99	21.16	1,517	92.03
23	117.08	112.54	115.78	29.73	28.78	29.35	21.71	20.65	21.53	1,641	91.60
24	116.17	112.72	113.64	29.85	29.03	29.15	21.62	20.85	21.10	987	91.54
25	†	†	†	†	†	†	†	†	†	†	†
26	118.78	114.37	118.26	30.57	29.63	30.48	22.45	21.39	22.23	1,184	91.97
27	124.36	120.57	123.71	31.92	31.00	31.71	23.06	22.50	22.96	1,141	92.40
28	*			*			*				
29	123.39	120.37	121.58	31.75	31.04	31.54	22.91	22.31	22.48	1,150	92.42
30	125.43	121.49	123.48	32.87	31.90	32.25	22.95	22.40	22.60	1,150	92.64
High			135.94			34.26			23.48	29,255	94.79
Low			113.64			29.15			20.91		91.54

*Sunday †Holiday

DECEMBER, 1937

Date	Industrials			Railroads			Utilities			Daily Sales	40 Bonds
	High	Low	Close	High	Low	Close	High	Low	Close		
1	124.09	121.41	122.11	32.14	31.44	31.56	22.63	22.10	22.17	697	92.65
2	125.38	120.21	125.14	31.77	30.71	31.75	22.55	21.86	22.50	938	92.63
3	129.40	125.52	127.55	32.67	31.65	32.35	22.98	22.39	22.51	1,557	93.24
4	128.72	126.63	127.79	32.81	32.44	32.62	22.63	22.29	22.41	567	93.44
5	*			*			*				
6	128.36	125.76	126.21	32.49	31.83	31.91	22.63	22.16	22.28	836	93.43
7	128.56	124.85	128.31	32.11	31.46	32.01	22.35	21.93	22.30	965	93.38
8	131.15	128.22	129.80	33.18	32.30	32.64	22.76	22.16	22.52	1,520	93.72
9	130.37	127.62	128.15	32.93	32.20	32.35	22.57	22.09	22.15	1,082	93.75
10	128.27	125.49	126.72	32.85	31.83	32.17	22.26	21.79	21.98	1,075	93.58
11	127.21	126.08	126.83	32.40	32.06	32.36	22.05	21.86	21.97	390	93.67
12	*	*	*	*			*	*	*		
13	125.86	122.18	122.83	32.01	31.27	31.30	21.89	21.41	21.50	1,017	93.63
14	124.25	121.85	123.50	31.58	31.10	31.30	21.53	21.15	21.35	896	93.58
15	125.63	123.33	124.19	31.71	31.14	31.38	21.70	21.33	21.46	929	93.43
16	126.92	124.52	125.75	31.96	31.33	31.68	21.85	21.45	21.57	1,034	93.42
17	126.29	124.44	124.98	31.81	31.38	31.43	21.65	21.31	21.42	793	93.44
18	126.92	125.16	126.63	31.94	31.58	31.91	21.64	21.38	21.56	501	93.55
19	*			*			*				
20	130.38	127.29	129.08	32.80	32.23	32.58	22.04	21.60	21.80	1,399	93.79
21	130.76	128.60	129.98	32.98	32.43	32.65	22.08	21.61	21.81	1,284	93.82
22	130.52	127.99	128.55	32.72	32.20	32.28	21.85	21.33	21.42	1,155	93.73
23	128.53	126.50	127.63	32.16	31.44	31.76	21.47	21.01	21.31	1,057	93.61
24	128.60	126.85	127.36	31.71	31.35	31.49	21.46	21.09	21.17	835	93.56
25	†	†	†	†	†	†	†	†	†	†	†
26											
27	126.59	122.96	123.45	31.31	30.42	30.49	21.22	20.48	20.56	1,360	93.29
28	122.51	118.31	118.93	30.00	28.82	28.91	20.63	19.77	19.97	2,382	92.94
29	121.00	117.71	120.15	29.45	28.53	29.15	20.10	19.48	19.88	2,460	92.67
30	122.63	120.71	121.56	29.72	29.25	29.38	20.56	20.13	20.35	913	92.91
31	121.49	119.65	120.85	29.66	29.29	29.46	20.46	20.18	20.35	780	93.00
High			129.98			32.65			22.52	28,422	93.82
Low			118.93			28.91			19.88		92.63

*Sunday †Holiday

JANUARY, 1938

Date	Industrials			Railroads			Utilities			Daily Sales	40 Bonds
	High	Low	Close	High	Low	Close	High	Low	Close		
1	†	†	†	†	†	†	†	†	†	†	†
2											
3	123.07	119.60	120.57	30.26	29.18	29.35	20.91	20.31	20.46	915	92.50
4	124.96	121.69	124.61	29.86	29.30	29.80	21.00	20.43	20.91	942	92.31
5	127.27	124.17	124.66	30.17	29.02	29.17	21.28	20.80	20.93	1,151	92.19
6	129.23	125.38	128.97	30.59	29.54	30.58	21.48	20.78	21.43	1,205	92.57
7	129.51	127.30	128.21	30.86	30.30	30.47	21.68	21.13	21.38	1,054	92.61
8	131.06	128.84	130.84	31.31	30.62	31.21	21.85	21.38	21.80	779	92.70
9	*	*	*	*	*	*	*			*	
10	134.27	130.81	133.55	32.46	31.31	32.33	21.88	21.36	21.64	1,827	92.59
11	134.63	132.36	134.35	32.56	31.96	32.25	22.02	21.44	21.78	1,506	92.44
12	134.95	132.94	133.22	32.77	32.10	32.21	22.20	21.80	21.86	1,210	92.33
13	133.40	131.27	131.60	32.40	31.74	31.81	22.08	21.61	21.73	971	92.32
14	132.37	130.29	131.84	32.03	31.48	31.96	22.05	21.45	21.80	848	92.08
15	134.95	132.05	134.31	32.43	31.91	32.33	21.91	21.57	21.75	738	92.01
16	*	*	*	*	*	*	*	*	*	*	
17	134.70	132.19	132.49	32.36	31.74	31.81	21.60	20.85	20.95	933	91.65
18	132.98	130.88	131.53	31.58	30.98	31.06	21.05	20.65	20.78	779	90.91
19	131.68	128.68	130.09	30.68	29.46	29.97	20.91	20.45	20.71	1,002	90.56
20	132.54	130.39	132.33	30.58	30.06	30.45	21.23	20.79	21.04	818	90.55
21	133.23	130.56	130.69	30.58	29.74	29.80	21.16	20.68	20.78	791	90.10
22	130.35	129.37	130.00	29.83	29.53	29.79	20.65	20.43	20.58	405	89.74
23	*	*	*	*	*	*	*	*	*	*	
24	130.52	129.13	129.89	29.89	29.48	29.70	20.86	20.56	20.73	537	89.57
25	129.47	127.97	128.33	29.61	29.24	29.34	20.72	20.38	20.46	535	89.17
26	126.10	121.86	123.23	28.74	28.05	28.31	20.19	19.58	19.80	1,616	89.10
27	124.54	120.44	121.57	28.63	27.63	27.87	20.03	19.13	19.32	1,208	88.79
28	122.32	118.94	120.66	27.76	27.13	27.35	19.52	18.97	19.15	1,190	88.74
29	121.41	119.71	120.14	27.64	27.36	27.45	19.21	18.92	19.05	434	89.14
30	*		*	*	*		*				
31	122.28	120.09	121.87	28.11	27.38	27.96	19.43	18.90	19.21	760	89.59
High			134.35			32.33			21.86	24,154	92.70
Low			120.14			27.35			19.05		88.74

*Sunday †Holiday

FEBRUARY, 1938

Date	Industrials			Railroads			Utilities			Daily Sales	40 Bonds
	High	Low	Close	High	Low	Close	High	Low	Close		
1	124.71	122.69	123.97	28.50	28.14	28.36	19.70	19.22	19.53	692	90.23
2	125.00	122.74	123.06	28.42	27.96	27.97	19.46	19.10	19.16	584	90.28
3	121.49	117.78	118.49	27.55	26.90	27.08	18.85	18.10	18.25	1,088	89.70
4	120.91	117.13	120.52	27.54	26.81	27.42	18.52	17.95	18.44	806	89.75
5	123.42	120.76	122.88	27.65	27.33	27.56	18.95	18.49	18.83	446	90.04
6	*	*	*	*	*	*	*	*	*	*	*
7	123.15	120.88	121.39	27.46	27.08	27.10	18.81	18.51	18.58	513	89.92
8	125.76	122.39	125.52	27.94	27.29	27.88	19.01	18.52	18.98	773	90.24
9	126.98	124.65	125.00	28.61	28.08	28.13	19.25	18.81	18.86	748	90.41
10	127.23	124.56	125.54	29.40	28.39	29.11	19.03	18.66	18.85	632	90.97
11	126.53	124.45	124.94	29.34	28.90	28.96	18.93	18.70	18.74	387	91.14
12	†	†	†	†	†	†	†	†	†	†	†
13	*	*	*	*	*	*	*	*	*	*	*
14	126.44	125.04	125.97	29.23	28.97	29.16	19.02	18.76	19.00	401	91.11
15	127.00	124.60	124.93	29.50	28.95	29.04	19.18	18.80	18.90	523	91.19
16	125.35	123.39	124.90	28.91	28.48	28.71	18.98	18.75	18.92	472	91.10
17	128.35	125.03	127.59	29.42	28.77	29.30	19.44	18.86	19.32	857	91.22
18	128.74	125.61	126.29	29.33	28.53	28.66	19.55	19.15	19.23	769	91.21
19	127.64	126.36	127.50	28.78	28.63	28.76	19.37	19.16	19.33	296	91.18
20	*	*	*	*	*	*	*	*	*	*	*
21	130.19	127.60	129.49	29.47	28.95	29.35	19.86	19.35	19.75	758	91.08
22	†	†	†	†	†	†	†	†	†	†	†
23	132.86	130.69	132.41	30.60	29.72	30.52	20.30	19.82	20.20	1,299	91.43
24	132.05	130.47	130.85	30.37	29.96	30.05	20.27	19.88	20.07	720	91.49
25	132.66	129.85	131.58	30.81	29.90	30.50	20.41	19.88	20.20	898	91.79
26	131.81	130.99	131.26	30.56	30.22	30.29	20.28	20.13	20.18	303	91.59
27	*	*	*	*	*	*	*	*	*	*	*
28	130.89	128.63	129.64	30.13	29.75	29.90	20.10	19.61	19.82	560	91.28
High			132.41			30.52			20.20	14,525	91.79
Low			118.49			27.08			18.25		89.70

*Sunday †Holiday

MARCH, 1938

Date	Industrials			Railroads			Utilities			Daily Sales	40 Bonds
	High	Low	Close	High	Low	Close	High	Low	Close		
1	131.03	128.84	130.47	30.11	29.70	30.02	19.95	19.66	19.91	534	91.21
2	130.68	129.19	129.38	29.90	29.65	29.71	19.88	19.59	19.70	407	91.08
3	128.75	127.39	128.22	29.51	29.14	29.36	19.61	19.40	19.50	467	90.86
4	129.57	127.37	127.78	29.40	28.95	28.97	19.75	19.37	19.43	489	90.67
5	127.99	127.25	127.67	28.82	28.66	28.75	19.42	19.30	19.35	222	90.45
6	*	*	*	*	*	*	*	*	*	*	*
7	127.63	125.19	125.38	28.66	28.01	28.05	19.43	19.06	19.11	620	90.06
8	125.85	122.81	125.33	27.81	26.82	27.55	19.11	18.76	19.00	738	89.53
9	126.83	124.57	125.67	27.92	27.08	27.21	19.18	18.90	18.98	562	89.04
10	126.35	124.52	124.71	27.00	26.36	26.36	19.10	18.81	18.83	455	88.37
11	123.89	121.93	122.44	26.19	25.61	25.66	18.74	18.48	18.54	770	87.89
12	123.00	121.77	122.58	25.97	25.61	25.85	18.64	18.49	18.59	300	87.87
13	*	*	*	*	*	*	*	*	*	*	*
14	124.53	122.85	123.68	26.61	26.22	26.35	18.83	18.58	18.68	428	88.06
15	127.44	124.52	127.24	26.75	26.20	26.58	19.06	18.53	19.01	760	88.13
16	126.10	121.84	122.87	26.22	24.90	25.11	18.91	18.22	18.37	1,024	87.61
17	124.60	121.90	122.03	25.43	24.49	24.54	18.68	18.09	18.15	642	87.18
18	121.92	117.20	118.41	24.61	23.40	23.71	18.02	17.54	17.68	1,578	86.52
19	121.00	119.74	120.43	23.85	23.43	23.68	18.03	17.79	17.96	442	86.79
20	*	*	*	*	*	*	*	*	*	*	*
21	122.48	120.09	120.29	24.20	23.55	23.61	18.35	17.79	17.86	542	87.14
22	120.35	116.47	117.11	23.40	22.58	22.62	17.94	17.49	17.56	693	86.89
23	115.95	112.78	114.38	22.03	21.40	21.75	17.57	17.03	17.30	1,468	86.15
24	115.97	112.73	114.64	22.23	21.55	21.99	17.54	17.07	17.31	885	85.92
25	114.37	108.12	108.57	21.07	19.83	19.95	17.25	16.35	16.38	1,678	85.54
26	109.44	106.05	106.63	20.11	19.58	19.68	16.63	15.97	16.09	1,383	85.14
27	*	*	*	*	*	*	*	*	*	*	*
28	108.55	105.68	107.25	20.66	19.83	20.46	16.41	15.85	16.11	1,250	84.89
29	105.87	101.56	101.92	20.11	19.18	19.23	16.08	15.29	15.33	1,722	84.31
30	103.89	100.17	100.97	19.66	19.06	19.23	15.71	15.03	15.18	1,666	83.89
31	102.86	97.46	98.95	19.65	18.85	19.00	15.54	14.98	15.14	1,272	83.39
High			130.47			30.02			19.91	22,997	91.21
Low			98.95			19.00			15.14		83.39

*Sunday †Holiday

APRIL, 1938

Date	Industrials			Railroads			Utilities			Daily Sales	40 Bonds
	High	Low	Close	High	Low	Close	High	Low	Close		
1	103.37	100.95	103.02	19.93	19.35	19.81	16.00	15.40	15.86	859	83.46
2	106.98	104.55	106.11	20.60	20.13	20.46	16.71	16.07	16.58	604	83.99
3	*		*	*			*				
4	106.79	104.47	105.58	21.50	20.78	21.24	17.14	16.55	16.97	687	84.63
5	108.67	104.85	108.36	21.65	21.07	21.45	17.50	16.75	17.42	693	85.15
6	107.90	105.72	106.29	21.15	20.64	20.80	17.25	16.87	17.05	476	84.87
7	106.93	104.78	105.43	21.00	20.70	20.80	17.11	16.84	16.88	331	84.86
8	110.23	106.89	109.57	21.88	21.25	21.71	17.59	17.08	17 51	828	85.21
9	115.71	112.92	115.32	22.91	22.21	22.75	18.55	17.93	18.44	1,414	85.76
10	*			*			*				
11	115.71	112.43	112.93	23.24	22.36	22.48	18.41	17.75	17.83	1,099	85.58
12	114.15	111.60	113.88	22.63	22.02	22.40	17.90	17.50	17.82	600	85.31
13	116.29	113.79	114.85	21.89	21.51	21.65	17.91	17.55	17.64	638	84.96
14	117.57	113.56	116.82	21.71	20.99	21.39	17.95	17.53	17.85	1,010	84.56
15	†	†	†	†	†	†	†	†	†	†	†
16	121.42	118.46	121.00	22.06	21.53	22.00	18.43	18.03	18.33	1,058	85.04
17	*		*	*			*				*
18	121.54	118.45	118.99	21.98	21.53	21.65	18.45	17.89	18.01	857	84.96
19	118.46	116.00	116.34	21.69	21.31	21.35	17.76	17.41	17.47	572	84.79
20	115.50	112.47	114.90	21.36	20.93	21.26	17.61	17.21	17.52	776	84.70
21	115.98	114.05	115.40	21.41	21.21	21.33	18.15	17.67	18.03	595	84.96
22	119.67	115.74	118.52	22.39	21.63	22.23	18.88	18.22	18.75	1,116	86.10
23	119.21	117.50	117.64	22.36	22.03	22.07	19.08	18.65	18.81	411	86.63
24	*		*	*			*				*
25	116.86	115.40	116.23	22.14	21.96	22.09	18.80	18.40	18.61	396	86.49
26	115.70	113.51	113.94	21.98	21.77	21.83	18.75	18.31	18.43	445	86.39
27	116.22	114.75	115.25	22.10	21.70	21.73	18.67	18.33	18.45	425	86.59
28	114.83	111.73	111.98	21.59	21.20	21.21	18.36	17.83	17.88	538	86.49
29	111.88	109.83	111.66	21.32	20.98	21.21	18.01	17.60	17.98	543	86.24
30	111.97	111.05	111.28	21.40	21.21	21.26	17.94	17.90	17.90	148	86.23
High			121.00			22.75			18.81	17,119	86.63
Low			103.02			19.81			15.86		83.46

*Sunday †Holiday

MAY, 1938

Date	Industrials			Railroads			Utilities			Daily Sales	40 Bonds
	High	Low	Close	High	Low	Close	High	Low	Close		
1	*		*	*			*				*
2	110.55	109.40	110.09	21.07	20.85	20.95	17.85	17.67	17.80	353	86.26
3	113.12	110.75	112.71	21.48	21.15	21.45	18.29	17.77	18.21	472	86.27
4	114.32	111.69	113.88	21.55	21.30	21.51	18.51	18.05	18.45	551	86.58
5	115.42	112.86	113.46	21.80	21.50	21.57	18.91	18.39	18.58	687	86.80
6	117.44	113.27	117.16	22.94	21.66	22.90	19.99	18.57	19.91	1,022	87.46
7	118.00	116.53	117.21	22.88	22.60	22.64	20.08	19.73	19.85	556	87.78
8	*		*	*		*	*		*	*	*
9	119.81	116.36	119.43	23.55	22.46	23.50	20.56	19.44	20.46	1,018	88.06
10	120.28	117.75	117.93	23.78	23.13	23.19	20.65	19.95	20.08	1,044	88.11
11	119.70	117.78	118.52	23.93	23.17	23.48	20.77	19.98	20.45	978	88.56
12	119.67	117.88	118.55	23.83	23.43	23.48	20.49	20.10	20.24	597	88.37
13	118.41	116.30	116.87	23.41	22.89	23.15	20.18	19.62	19.93	605	88.27
14	117.36	116.39	117.21	22.98	22.84	22.96	19.88	19.61	19.77	233	88.01
15	*		*	*			*				*
16	117.11	115.19	115.38	22.80	22.56	22.57	19.73	19.26	19.30	395	87.84
17	116.65	114.75	116.36	22.58	22.35	22.54	19.60	19.10	19.50	414	87.55
18	117.49	116.31	117.02	22.64	22.50	22.54	19.65	19.30	19.45	398	87.58
19	117.08	114.92	115.28	22.54	22.20	22.26	19.50	19.11	19.17	491	87.46
20	115.48	114.08	114.99	22.03	21.83	21.90	19.27	18.97	19.15	440	87.19
21	114.40	113.07	113.25	21.84	21.72	21.73	19.41	18.95	19.04	286	86.96
22	*		*	*		*	*		*	*	*
23	114.27	112.88	113.97	21.90	21.65	21.81	19.17	18.90	19.09	328	86.94
24	114.66	112.26	112.35	21.86	21.41	21.43	19.21	18.78	18.78	417	86.79
25	112.24	110.43	110.60	21.25	20.95	20.98	18.70	18.33	18.41	555	86.45
26	111.30	108.14	108.28	20.98	20.33	20.35	18.38	17.69	17.76	781	86.20
27	108.55	106.44	107.98	20.36	19.98	20.26	18.00	17.55	17.91	761	85.96
28	109.47	108.36	108.90	20.67	20.51	20.58	18.25	18.01	18.12	217	85.99
29	*		*	*		*	*		*	*	*
30	†			†	†	†	†	†	†	†	†
31	108.50	106.94	107.74	20.45	20.20	20.31	18.08	17.70	17.88	400	85.70
High			119 43			23.50			20.46	13,999	88.56
Low			107.74			20.26			17.76		85.70

*Sunday †Holiday

JUNE, 1938

Date	Industrials High	Low	Close	Railroads High	Low	Close	Utilities High	Low	Close	Daily Sales	40 Bonds
1	110.87	107.58	110.61	20.70	20.30	20.60	18.58	17.99	18.53	538	85.84
2	111.94	110.35	110.68	20.74	20.45	20.52	**19.17	18.45	18.76	475	85.95
3	110.52	109.35	109.71	20.38	20.15	20.22	18.60	18.35	18.45	285	85.82
4	112.30	110.04	111.82	20.63	20.42	20.57	18.92	18.55	18.77	307	85.93
5	*										
6	114.27	112.01	113.19	20.77	20.56	20.58	19.20	18.86	18.98	467	86.05
7	114.51	112.84	113.12	20.75	20.51	20.55	19.22	18.78	18.88	372	86.08
8	114.04	112.78	113.75	20.56	20.37	20.48	18.94	18.65	18.82	278	85.85
9	116.03	113.79	115.74	20.88	20.43	20.81	19.28	18.84	19.25	591	85.59
10	116.08	114.29	114.47	20.75	20.51	20.53	19.36	19.11	19.13	406	85.57
11	114.71	114.13	114.23	20.56	20.45	20.53	19.06	19.00	19.04	107	85.30
12	*										
13	113.37	111.75	111.87	20.41	20.14	20.16	18.90	18.53	18.54	327	84.91
14	113.06	111.54	112.78	20.51	20.01	20.40	18.70	18.27	18.45	346	84.83
15	114.18	112.88	113.24	20.38	20.21	20.23	18.66	18.46	18.56	345	84.36
16	114.30	112.93	113.97	20.22	19.99	20.05	18.70	18.48	18.65	342	83.96
17	114.51	112.82	113.06	19.98	19.54	19.68	18.67	18.42	18.49	328	83.56
18	113.41	113.05	113.23	19.76	19.69	19.73	18.55	18.47	18.54	105	83.59
19	*										
20	118.92	115.31	118.61	20.76	20.06	20.70	19.45	18.80	19.36	1,087	84.49
21	122.36	119.01	121.34	21.68	21.05	21.51	19.84	19.35	19.60	1,457	84.84
22	124.74	120.65	123.99	22.63	21.50	22.46	20.52	19.51	20.36	1,712	85.63
23	128.49	123.71	127.40	24.96	23.06	24.60	20.91	20.15	20.51	2,403	86.30
24	130.71	127.54	129.06	25.61	24.90	25.06	20.79	19.95	20.13	2,291	86.51
25	132.12	127.97	131.94	25.54	24.91	25.45	20.68	20.17	20.58	1,162	86.68
26	*										
27	132.98	129.79	130.48	25.70	24.95	25.00	21.20	20.38	20.65	2,106	86.62
28	132.28	129.44	130.38	25.13	24.46	24.57	21.05	20.38	20.60	1,290	86.33
29	136.13	130.36	135.87	26.27	24.71	26.18	21.54	20.54	21.21	2,659	86.90
30	138.19	133.24	133.88	26.82	25.85	26.02	21.75	20.85	21.06	2,581	87.11
High			135.87			26.18			21.21	24,368	87.11
Low			109.71			19.68			18.45		83.56

*Sunday †Holiday **Number of issues used in computing utilities average changed to 15 from 20.

JULY, 1938

Date	Industrials High	Low	Close	Railroads High	Low	Close	Utilities High	Low	Close	Daily Sales	40 Bonds
1	137.13	133.53	136.53	26.83	25.81	26.69	22.35	20.98	22.05	2,025	87.55
2	139.12	136.83	138.53	27.68	27.03	27.57	22.42	22.15	22.27	1,472	87.99
3	*										
4	†	†	†	†	†	†	†	†	†	†	†
5	138.50	135.19	136.52	27.72	26.83	27.21	22.30	21.58	21.83	1,696	87.96
6	138.20	134.57	137.78	27.68	26.62	27.59	22.23	21.57	22.19	1,817	88.88
7	140.05	136.44	137.45	28.92	27.76	27.93	22.84	21.98	22.15	2,774	88.67
8	136.76	134.51	135.66	27.63	26.81	27.20	21.87	21.25	21.58	1,567	88.50
9	136.66	135.19	136.20	27.42	27.00	27.31	21.80	21.47	21.70	592	88.64
10	*										
11	136.72	133.97	134.56	27.28	26.56	26.61	21.70	21.13	21.23	1,087	88.48
12	138.22	133.84	137.49	27.57	26.26	27.32	21.88	21.10	21.68	1,620	88.68
13	140.52	136.46	136.90	28.05	27.06	27.12	22.16	21.51	21.55	2,619	88.92
14	137.85	135.22	135.81	27.45	26.70	26.81	21.40	21.01	21.05	1,161	88.69
15	138.17	135.52	137.30	27.25	26.77	27.13	21.68	21.02	21.35	933	88.97
16	139.14	137.69	138.53	27.29	27.11	27.18	21.50	21.26	21.39	627	89.06
17	*										
18	140.78	137.70	140.39	27.99	27.23	27.96	21.70	21.25	21.64	1,556	89.33
19	144.12	141.27	143.67	29.26	28.38	29.13	22.25	21.55	22.06	2,942	89.52
20	143.97	141.09	141.84	30.38	29.23	29.60	22.73	21.70	22.07	2,511	89.81
21	143.51	140.52	141.92	30.53	29.38	29.78	22.56	21.89	22.07	1,812	90.21
22	143.13	141.20	142.25	30.25	29.59	29.88	22.05	21.72	21.85	1,222	90.37
23	144.39	142.31	144.24	30.40	30.01	30.38	22.00	21.75	21.99	776	90.51
24	*										
25	146.31	144.23	144.91	30.77	30.06	30.14	22.51	21.89	22.08	2,107	90.83
26	144.18	142.48	143.33	29.98	29.53	29.67	22.01	21.55	21.72	1,252	90.61
27	144.03	139.39	140.24	29.67	28.01	28.28	21.68	20.47	20.72	1,974	90.14
28	142.50	139.51	142.20	28.73	27.90	28.54	21.02	20.65	20.88	1,066	90.36
29	143.57	140.93	141.20	29.10	28.39	28.44	21.22	20.60	20.69	1,204	90.43
30	142.01	140.73	141.25	28.58	28.33	28.45	20.72	20.60	20.63	359	90.37
31	*										
High			144.91			30.38			22.55	38,771	90.83
Low			134.56			26.61			20.63		87.55

*Sunday †Holiday

AUGUST, 1938

Date	Industrials High	Low	Close	Railroads High	Low	Close	Utilities High	Low	Close	Daily Sales	40 Bonds
1	140.96	139.83	140 37	28.40	28.07	28.15	20.66	20.40	20.50	587	90.19
2	142.50	139.90	141.97	28.48	27.98	28.33	20.75	20.42	20.63	818	90.30
3	143.40	141.10	141.73	28.60	28.01	28.05	20.71	20.36	20.38	817	90.09
4	142.76	141.04	142.13	28.28	28.01	28.16	20.58	20.34	20.48	610	89.87
5	144.76	142.34	144.47	29.33	28.35	29.28	20.98	20.50	20.80	1,170	90.00
6	146.28	144.73	145.67	30.00	29.58	29.77	21.08	20.80	20.93	829	90.21
7										*	
8	145.89	143.75	144.33	30.06	29.40	29.60	21.20	20.67	20.77	914	90.01
9	143.87	141.59	143.21	29.81	29.03	29.80	20.65	20.27	20.48	830	89.90
10	143.67	141.80	142.40	30.14	29.45	29.56	20.50	20.26	20.30	810	89.65
11	142.75	139.13	139.32	29.49	28.56	28.57	20.40	19.80	19.83	1,101	89.34
12	138.31	135.38	136.51	28.15	27.27	27.68	19.80	19.38	19.62	1,479	89.16
13	136.91	135.75	136.21	27.70	27.40	27.57	19.59	19.40	19.43	396	89.07
14										*	
15	138.20	136.45	136.98	28.10	27.56	27.76	19.69	19.31	19.41	594	88.94
16	139.38	137.09	138.44	28.29	27.56	27.96	19.90	19.57	19.80	614	88.95
17	140.89	138.58	139.03	28.35	27.93	27.94	20.05	19.71	19.77	596	89.05
18	139.76	138.38	139.33	27.90	27.58	27.70	19.79	19.53	19.64	447	88.95
19	142.05	139.18	141.13	28.86	27.86	28.31	19.85	19.59	19.75	826	88.98
20	141.66	140.95	141.20	28.55	28.38	28.45	19.80	19.72	19.79	246	88.91
21										*	
22	141.61	140.12	140.92	28.39	28.10	28.25	19.76	19.62	19.69	397	88.83
23	144.00	141.03	143.70	29.01	28.30	28.96	20.20	19.85	20.11	1,077	89.07
24	145.30	143.28	143.53	29 71	29.08	29.25	20.35	20.05	20.08	1,236	89.32
25	144.36	142.57	144.07	29.73	29.16	29.61	20.37	19.99	20.25	827	89 36
26	144.61	142.69	142.94	29.88	29.26	29.31	20.50	20.05	20.12	820	89.38
27	142.40	141.29	141.95	28.96	28.58	28.71	19.98	19.81	19.89	351	89.27
28										*	
29	139.56	136.64	137.06	28.00	27.36	27.48	19.60	19.02	19.13	1,249	88.87
30	138.89	137.08	138.26	27.75	27.35	27.69	19.43	19.19	19.31	631	88.56
31	139.80	138.30	139.27	27.78	27.32	27.41	19.49	19.12	19.28	461	88.47
High			145.67			29.80			20.93	20,733	90.30
Low			136.21			27.41			19.13		88.47

*Sunday   †Holiday

SEPTEMBER, 1938

Date	Industrials High	Low	Close	Railroads High	Low	Close	Utilities High	Low	Close	Daily Sales	40 Bonds
1	139.45	137.65	138.36	27.15	26.37	26.63	19.40	19.11	19.25	509	88.07
2	141.48	138.52	141.38	27.35	26.82	27.33	19.49	19.15	19.44	554	88.24
3	142.87	141.76	142.48	27.88	27.66	27.78	19.65	19.51	19.59	357	88.27
4										*	
5	†	†	†	†	†	†	†	†	†	†	†
6	142.80	141.10	141.47	27.65	27.33	27.48	19.60	19.31	19.42	415	88.17
7	143.42	141.05	143.08	28.06	27.42	27.88	19.52	19.10	19.46	893	88.21
8	142.90	141.63	142.19	27.71	27.40	27.56	19.34	19.08	19.19	570	88.23
9	141.39	139.20	139.90	27.18	26.70	26.85	19.07	18.78	18.85	703	87.81
10	139.61	137.97	138.29	26.77	26.60	26.63	18.85	18.56	18.60	416	87.76
11										*	
12	140.67	138.16	140.19	26.70	26.25	26.65	18.82	18.52	18.73	602	87.58
13	141.95	133.90	134.19	27.03	24.86	24.91	19.19	18.02	18.05	1,701	87.33
14	136.91	130.38	132.93	25.71	23.45	24.22	18.34	17.06	17.50	2,819	86.68
15	136.97	134.47	136.22	25.42	24.79	25.19	18.41	17.87	18.23	1,142	86.95
16	135.53	134.06	134.85	25.05	24.39	24.67	18.17	17.79	17.94	672	86.69
17	133.87	131.03	131.82	24.42	23.71	24.01	17.65	17.28	17.34	744	86.42
18										*	
19	135.24	133.49	134.10	25.03	24.65	24.75	18.12	17.71	17.96	825	86.36
20	139.49	137.11	138.41	25.89	25.31	25.57	18.89	18.50	18.70	1,198	86.90
21	140.20	137.57	139.29	26.11	25.41	25.86	18.96	18.57	18.88	1,025	87.11
22	138.17	136.81	137.35	25.47	25.16	25.34	18.69	18.45	18.50	467	87.10
23	136.07	133.71	134.08	24.79	24.28	24.45	18.27	17.84	17.93	721	86.83
24	134.23	130.34	133.02	24.42	23.55	24.35	17.87	17.33	17.83	797	86.34
25										*	
26	131.82	127.88	129.91	23.36	22.39	23.03	17.60	16.93	17.49	1,226	86.04
27	132.49	129.62	130.19	23.58	22.71	23.08	17.60	17.10	17.25	771	85.81
28	134.54	127.85	133.68	24.36	22.68	24.08	18.07	16.95	18.00	1,573	85.95
29	137.45	134.58	137.16	25.65	24.79	25.62	18.72	18.08	18.62	1,229	86.49
30	142.05	139.61	141.45	27.10	26.35	26.61	19.75	19.05	19.44	1,896	87.18
High			143.08			27.88			19.59	23,825	88.27
Low			129.91			23.03			17.25		85.81

*Sunday   †Holiday

OCTOBER, 1938

Date	Industrials			Railroads			Utilities			Daily Sales	40 Bonds
	High	Low	Close	High	Low	Close	High	Low	Close		
1	143.29	141.56	143.13	27.48	26.87	27.43	19.95	19.57	19.93	946	87.63
2	*			*			*			*	
3	145.21	142.64	144.29	27.88	27.31	27.54	20.49	19.85	20.20	1,462	88.46
4	144.83	143.26	144.23	27.78	27.19	27.63	20.31	19.89	20.08	948	88.67
5	148.51	144.59	148.32	29.51	27.90	29.49	20.76	20.15	20.74	2,236	89.51
6	150.48	147.70	148.10	30.71	29.70	29.88	21.16	20.55	20.71	2,451	89.55
7	149.43	147.29	148.41	30.61	29.91	30.14	21.03	20.59	20.80	1,465	89.52
8	150.09	148.46	149.75	31.00	30.37	30.91	21.18	20.87	21.12	1,113	89.73
9	*			*			*			*	
10	150.57	148.70	149.55	31.06	30.46	30.53	21.94	21.07	21.70	1,664	89.87
11	150.40	148.21	149.41	30.91	30.23	30.44	22.07	21.45	21.80	1,534	89.56
12	†	†	†	†	†	†	†	†	†	†	†
13	152.93	150.05	152.46	31.74	30.83	31.50	22.80	21.98	22.57	2,361	89.94
14	153.19	150.96	151.45	31.63	30.95	31.13	23.63	22.68	23.50	1,954	89.72
15	152.56	151.16	151.96	31.15	30.80	30.86	24.80	23.65	24.63	1,469	89.76
16	*			*			*			*	
17	153.15	150.46	150.81	31.01	30.17	30.33	25.42	24.15	24.35	2,521	89.42
18	152.36	148.68	152.10	30.74	29.76	30.63	24.50	23.70	24.36	2,408	89.45
19	153.02	149.41	150.02	31.61	30.59	30.71	24.44	23.36	23.45	2,434	89.58
20	151.90	149.46	151.52	31.03	30.38	30.99	23.92	23.21	23.84	1,616	89.59
21	153.01	151.36	152.15	31.68	31.05	31.13	24.04	23.46	25.53	1,715	89.76
22	154.53	152.27	154.11	31.78	31.31	31.59	23.84	23.48	23.69	1,127	89.90
23	*			*			*			*	
24	155.38	153.52	154.12	32.06	31.59	31.73	24.57	23.83	24.20	1,678	89.99
25	155.22	153.46	154.17	32.32	31.72	32.00	24.72	24.27	24.41	1,488	90.01
26	153.52	151.28	152.40	31.90	31.30	31.58	24.71	23.85	24.67	1,702	90.12
27	153.93	151.46	152.69	32.45	31.58	31.94	25.37	24.46	25.19	1,996	90.23
28	152.82	150.75	151.07	32.53	31.83	32.13	25.46	24.60	24.67	1,563	90.27
29	151.56	150.48	151.07	32.21	31.77	31.89	24.65	24.32	24.44	614	90.24
30	*			*			*			*	
31	152.17	150.28	151.73	31.68	30.91	31.49	24.56	23.92	24.35	1,090	90.12
High			154.17			32.13			25.19	41,555	90.27
Low			143.13			27.43			19.93		87.63

*Sunday † Holiday

NOVEMBER, 1938

Date	Industrials			Railroads			Utilities			Daily Sales	40 Bonds
	High	Low	Close	High	Low	Close	High	Low	Close		
1	152.83	150.93	151.39	31.93	31.43	31.50	24.57	23.87	23.94	1,284	90.10
2	152.64	150.68	152.21	31.80	31.35	31.66	24.10	23.66	23.90	784	90.05
3	153.13	151.72	152.31	32.64	31.73	32.56	24.15	23.80	23.95	1,065	89.96
4	153.08	151.44	152.10	32.43	31.59	31.76	24.13	23.48	23.60	1,196	90.07
5	152.46	151.73	152.12	31.91	31.65	31.78	23.65	23.43	23.59	434	90.05
6	*	*	*	*	*	*	*	*	*	*	
7	155.56	152.02	154.91	32.21	31.75	32.04	24.11	23.54	24.01	1,762	90.25
8	†	†	†	†	†	†	†	†	†	†	†
9	158.39	155.62	158.08	33.28	32.34	33.18	25.07	24.35	24.97	3,100	90.68
10	158.90	156.79	157.47	33.71	33.01	33.17	25.25	24.58	24.72	2,176	90.88
11	†	†	†	†	†	†	†	†	†	†	†
12	158.81	157.72	158.41	33.41	32.97	33.17	24.93	24.55	24.69	1,006	90.96
13	*	*	*	*	*	*	*	*	*	*	
14	157.57	155.16	155.61	32.88	32.28	32.36	24.59	23.97	24.05	1,651	90.83
15	155.33	153.17	154.66	32.11	31.63	31.95	24.15	23.61	23.87	1,466	90.51
16	155.60	151.41	151.54	32.46	31.23	31.28	23.95	23.10	23.17	1,795	90.20
17	153.18	151.34	152.78	31.88	31.34	31.75	23.65	23.14	23.60	995	90.24
18	153.19	149.16	149.93	31.83	30.53	30.80	23.68	22.63	22.95	1,416	90.00
19	150.80	149.98	150.38	31.10	30.77	30.94	23.02	22.85	22.94	437	90.01
20	*	*	*	*	*	*	*	*	*	*	
21	151.03	149.15	150.26	31.00	30.41	30.77	23.27	22.83	23.13	943	89.86
22	150.14	148.90	149.56	30.76	30.32	30.53	23.09	22.63	22.74	880	89.76
23	151.00	149.27	149.88	30.78	29.90	30.42	23.03	22.60	22.76	1,002	89.85
24	†	†	†	†	†	†	†	†	†	†	†
25	151.13	149.79	150.10	30.73	30.28	30.43	22.86	22.60	22.63	809	89.82
26	149.89	148.20	148.45	30.35	29.86	29.89	22.61	22.30	22.34	687	89.72
27	*	*	*	*	*	*	*	*	*	*	
28	147.93	145.21	146.14	29.33	28.68	28.95	22.02	21.44	21.60	1,238	89.30
29	147.85	146.38	147.07	29.36	28.91	29.06	21.95	21.54	21.64	817	89.32
30	149.97	147.68	149.82	29.80	29.10	29.76	22.20	21.65	22.15	983	89.41
High			158.41			33.18			24.97	27,926	90.96
Low			146.14			28.95			21.60		89.30

*Sunday †Holiday

DECEMBER, 1938

Date	Industrials			Railroads			Utilities			Daily Sales	40 Bonds
	High	Low	Close	High	Low	Close	High	Low	Close		
1	150.20	148.17	148.63	30.20	29.60	29.78	22.53	21.95	22.10	863	89.46
2	148.50	146.68	147.57	29.61	29.21	29.33	22.05	21.69	21.93	817	89.26
3	147.78	147.16	147.50	29.32	29.09	29.23	21.91	21.77	21.83	322	89.32
4	*	*	*	*	*	*	*	*	*	*	*
5	147.88	146.44	147.47	29.13	28.75	29.01	21.91	21.52	21.75	680	89.12
6	149.27	147.01	148.33	29.36	28.76	29.13	22.06	21.64	21.77	986	89.09
7	149.98	148.30	148.73	30.05	29.28	29.44	22.14	21.65	21.72	1,105	89.09
8	148.79	147.35	147.63	29.32	28.89	28.99	21.75	21.41	21.47	739	88.99
9	148.31	146.92	147.39	29.23	28.81	28.85	21.50	21.15	21.21	699	88.79
10	148.49	147.21	148.31	29.15	28.81	29.10	21.45	21.20	21.34	406	88.79
11	*	*	*	*	*	*	*	*	*	*	*
12	149.71	148.23	148.65	29.85	29.31	29.45	21.64	21.30	21.38	899	88.94
13	150.16	148.60	149.59	29.94	29.49	29.86	21.77	21.32	21.60	1,094	89.07
14	152.08	149.38	151.83	30.95	29.89	30.89	22.22	21.70	22.13	1,965	89.47
15	153.16	151.44	151.82	31.45	30.89	31.10	22.65	22.23	22.38	1,799	89.72
16	152.21	150.52	150.89	31.00	30.36	30.51	22.67	22.11	22.42	1,147	89.52
17	150.90	150.03	150.36	30.53	30.28	30.35	22.45	22.25	22.29	453	89.34
18	*	*	*	*	*	*	*	*	*	*	*
19	151.77	149.72	150.38	30.81	30.20	30.24	22.56	22.05	22.11	1,104	89.30
20	151.29	149.69	150.46	30.44	30.04	30.09	22.19	21.79	21.86	937	89.19
21	150.72	149.06	149.58	30.24	29.78	29.95	22.00	21.62	21.74	1,058	89.11
22	150.79	149.28	150.53	30.71	29.91	30.60	21.78	21.42	21.66	1,043	89.22
23	152.02	150.52	151.39	31.37	30.70	31.13	22.18	21.59	22.00	1,217	89.40
24	151.81	150.86	151.38	32.11	31.33	32.02	22.07	21.90	22.04	621	89.59
25	*	*	*	*	*	*	*	*	*	*	*
26	†	†	†	†	†	†	†	†	†	†	†
27	151.74	150.04	150.43	32.15	31.42	31.55	22.00	21.35	21.49	1,236	89.52
28	151.95	149.56	151.45	32.27	31.04	32.12	21.94	21.25	21.85	2,164	89.61
29	153.85	152.06	153.62	33.25	32.53	33.16	22.71	22.11	22.66	1,882	90.04
30	154.94	153.52	154.36	33.98	33.02	33.60	22.93	22.57	22.73	1,403	90.32
31	155.06	154.32	154.76	34.20	33.69	33.98	23.10	22.78	23.02	853	90.49
High			154.76			33.98			23.02	27,492	90.49
Low			147.39			28.85			21.21		88.79

*Sunday †Holiday

JANUARY, 1939

Date	Industrials			Railroads			Utilities			†Daily Sales	40 Bonds
	High	Low	Close	High	Low	Close	High	Low	Close		
1	*	*	*	*	*	*	*	*	*	*	*
2	†	†	†	†	†	†	†	†	†	†	†
3	154.99	153.16	153.64	34.43	33.60	33.78	23.20	22.72	22.85	1,153	90.62
4	155.19	153.14	154.85	34.65	33.56	34.33	23.30	22.70	23.20	1,500	91.00
5	155.47	153.02	153.18	34.30	33.21	33.26	23.78	22.89	22.96	1,572	90.97
6	153.55	152.42	152.87	33.48	33.03	33.25	23.77	22.94	23.64	951	91.03
7	152.64	151.31	151.54	33.40	32.88	32.93	23.92	23.39	23.49	632	90.96
8	*	*	*	*	*	*	*	*	*	*	*
9	151.07	149.23	150.19	32.83	32.18	32.50	23.45	22.85	23.07	1,100	90.76
10	151.32	150.04	150.48	32.86	32.35	32.46	23.44	23.10	23.21	713	90.89
11	150.18	148.45	148.65	31.93	31.29	31.39	23.15	22.67	22.78	916	90.80
12	149.43	146.17	147.33	31.85	30.63	31.08	23.15	22.38	22.65	1,363	90.46
13	147.84	146.03	146.52	31.40	30.75	30.94	22.80	22.26	22.50	845	90.32
14	148.49	147.01	148.26	32.00	31.46	31.95	23.55	22.80	23.49	470	90.43
15	*	*	*	*	*	*	*	*	*	*	*
16	148.71	147.70	148.26	31.88	31.56	31.68	23.89	23.31	23.50	667	90.51
17	149.23	147.49	148.93	31.94	31.52	31.88	24.16	23.34	24.13	824	90.58
18	149.56	148.55	148.99	32.27	31.86	32.01	24.40	23.95	24.18	631	90.72
19	149.88	148.35	149.47	32.29	31.73	32.11	24.65	23.86	24.65	887	91.02
20	149.75	148.77	149.11	32.23	31.85	31.97	24.97	24.42	24.68	740	90.95
21	148.69	146.53	146.76	31.68	30.96	31.10	24.58	23.74	23.97	657	90.76
22	*	*	*	*	*	*	*	*	*	*	*
23	144.13	141.00	141.32	29.94	28.96	29.13	23.32	22.58	22.70	1,874	89.95
24	142.83	139.62	141.35	29.61	28.60	29.25	23.11	22.26	22.89	1,699	89.79
25	141.68	139.37	140.72	29.28	28.48	28.84	23.15	22.53	22.89	903	89.70
26	139.58	136.10	136.42	28.68	27.70	27.93	22.81	21.98	22.30	1,536	89.28
27	139.27	136.84	138.90	28.69	28.01	28.56	23.15	22.42	23.03	1,055	89.39
28	139.90	138.32	138.79	28.96	28.44	28.49	23.36	22.83	22.99	583	89.35
29	*	*	*	*	*	*	*	*	*	*	*
30	141.80	139.32	141.56	29.38	28.68	29.37	23.54	22.67	23.28	790	89.41
31	144.74	142.52	143.76	30.04	29.60	29.74	23.76	23.29	23.40	1,122	89.87
High			154.85			34.33			24.68		91.03
Low			136.42			27.93			22.30		89.28
									Total	25,183	

*Sunday †Holiday ‡000 omitted

FEBRUARY, 1939

Date	Industrials			Railroads			Utilities			‡Daily Sales	40 Bonds
	High	Low	Close	High	Low	Close	High	Low	Close		
1	143.47	141.92	142.43	29.65	29.33	29.38	23.67	23.07	23.27	582	89.91
2	144.49	142.59	144.34	30.28	29.75	30.20	24.15	23.55	24.12	698	90.08
3	144.50	143.02	143.55	30.14	29.85	29.98	24.40	23.98	24.35	543	90.27
4	145.55	144.14	145.07	30.56	30.13	30.38	24.77	24.37	24.60	486	90.46
5	*	*	*						*		
6	146.43	144.78	145.03	30.65	30.18	30.25	25.99	25.23	25.52	1,041	90.53
7	145.11	143.50	144.10	30.20	29.86	29.94	25.55	24.83	24.92	570	90.39
8	145.55	144.45	145.43	30.39	30.01	30.36	25.35	24.93	25.29	612	90.37
9	145.56	143.83	143.99	30.31	29.85	30.00	25.24	24.60	24.67	547	90.26
10	144.01	142.70	143.68	29.98	29.62	29.93	24.82	24.41	24.78	445	90.19
11	145.04	144.07	144.61	30.23	29.98	30.18	25.07	24.85	24.93	322	90.22
12	*	*	*	*			*		*		
13	†	†	†	†	†	†	†	†	†	†	†
14	144.48	143.49	144.13	30.00	29.73	29.89	24.97	24.67	24.80	418	90.23
15	144.95	143.83	144.60	30.29	29.72	29.93	24.90	24.71	24.85	498	90.27
16	146.12	144.50	145.39	30.58	30.23	30.40	25.47	24.95	25.34	850	90.34
17	146.03	144.69	144.95	30.63	30.24	30.31	25.49	25.00	25.07	682	90.34
18	145.79	145.01	145.51	30.62	30.34	30.55	25.52	25.27	25.43	409	90.48
19	*		*	*			*		*		
20	144.54	142.48	142.74	30.08	29.52	29.55	25.20	24.67	24.73	693	90.21
21	143.13	142.05	142.64	29.73	29.40	29.61	24.94	24.70	24.82	466	90.08
22	†	†	†	†	†	†	†	†	†	†	†
23	143.63	142.45	142.93	30.03	29.76	29.83	24.95	24.61	24.76	455	90.24
24	145.69	143.46	145.44	30.91	30.31	30.90	25.49	24.85	25.45	967	90.42
25	147.30	146.10	146.82	31.43	31.10	31.25	25.84	25.43	25.60	784	90.54
26	*	*	*			*	*		*		
27	147.32	146.10	146.62	31.85	31.25	31.61	25.80	25.49	25.60	746	90.77
28	148.16	146.76	147.30	32.82	31.93	32.48	26.11	25.61	25.85	1,060	90.96
High			147.30			32.48			25.85		90.96
Low			142.43			29.38			23.27		89.91

*Sunday †Holiday ‡000 omitted Total 13,874

MARCH, 1939

Date	Industrials			Railroads			Utilities			‡Daily Sales	40 Bonds
	High	Low	Close	High	Low	Close	High	Low	Close		
1	147.88	146.62	147.15	32.68	32.20	32.45	26.06	25.71	25.85	635	90.94
2	147.19	146.34	146.96	32.55	32.13	32.47	25.85	25.55	25.76	599	91.04
3	148.89	147.31	148.76	33.11	32.70	33.00	26.11	25.79	26.05	1,016	91.42
4	149.99	148.94	149.49	33.21	32.91	32.98	26.24	26.01	26.09	585	91.47
5	*	*	*	*		*	*		*		*
6	150.23	148.37	148.84	33.11	32.42	32.53	26.19	25.70	25.78	842	91.51
7	149.88	148.86	149.37	33.08	32.71	32.80	26.10	25.82	25.97	568	91.52
8	151.56	149.17	151.42	33.68	32.93	33.66	26.35	25.93	26.24	1,049	92.00
9	152.42	150.52	151.33	33.79	33.21	33.33	26.51	26.07	26.28	1,358	92.14
10	152.71	151.22	152.28	33.68	33.21	33.37	26.66	26.19	26.52	1,210	92.22
11	152.57	151.53	151.77	33.33	33.03	33.07	26.59	26.21	26.28	533	92.13
12	*	*	*	*		*	*		*		*
13	151.58	150.20	150.79	32.73	32.41	32.45	26.31	25.99	26.05	648	91.83
14	151.39	149.91	151.10	32.83	32.40	32.75	26.15	25.76	26.00	685	91.81
15	150.28	147.16	147.66	32.21	31.38	31.55	25.88	25.13	25.30	1,113	91.36
16	148.17	146.45	147.54	31.56	31.20	31.42	25.41	25.02	25.21	669	91.40
17	146.13	142.99	143.89	30.85	29.78	30.19	24.92	24.14	24.35	1,470	90.69
18	142.40	140.60	141.68	29.69	29.25	29.58	24.10	23.74	23.92	1,007	90.22
19	*	*	*			*	*		*		*
20	143.14	140.57	141.28	29.96	29.36	29.46	24.22	23.55	23.69	947	90.15
21	144.31	142.67	143.41	30.23	29.96	30.01	24.35	23.94	24.17	689	90.53
22	141.97	138.42	139.51	29.33	28.58	28.96	23.83	23.12	23.26	1,440	89.90
23	142.17	139.42	140.33	29.84	29.23	29.36	23.89	23.45	23.65	834	90.05
24	142.80	141.13	141.82	30.10	29.71	29.87	24.39	23.94	24.14	646	90.43
25	142.53	140.97	141.55	30.05	29.61	29.73	24.26	23.87	24.05	439	90.36
26	*	*	*	*		*	*		*		*
27	143.14	140.91	141.14	30.39	29.69	29.74	24.33	23.81	23.88	566	90.39
28	139.98	138.46	139.33	29.51	29.06	29.34	23.66	23.35	23.50	677	90.29
29	140.55	138.84	139.75	29.78	29.31	29.75	23.95	23.60	23.87	465	90.43
30	140.55	136.41	136.69	29.92	28.58	28.61	24.07	22.98	23.08	985	90.15
31	138.01	131.35	131.84	28.82	26.21	26.38	23.27	21.58	21.70	2,888	89.27
High			152.28			33.66			26.52		92.22
Low			131.84			26.38			21.70		89.27

*Sunday. ‡000 omitted Total 24,563

Effective with 1:00 p. m. averages on March 14, American Telephone and United Aircraft were substituted in industrial average for International Business Machines and Nash Kelvinator.

APRIL, 1939

Date	Industrials High	Low	Close	Railroads High	Low	Close	Utilities High	Low	Close	‡Daily Sales	40 Bonds
1	133.75	130.04	132.83	27.35	26.52	27.24	22.60	21.70	22.50	1,558	89.05
2	*										
3	135.57	130.49	132.25	28.16	26.81	27.27	23.35	22.43	22.70	1,473	89.09
4	131.09	127.16	129.80	27.00	26.02	26.71	22.17	21.50	21.99	1,534	88.75
5	131.38	128.64	130.34	27.13	26.52	26.87	22.62	21.88	22.38	881	88.76
6	129.23	125.49	126.32	26.45	25.57	25.76	22.02	21.35	21.57	1,313	88.16
7	†	†	†	†	†	†	†	†	†		
8	124.21	121.01	121.44	24.97	23.98	24.14	21.23	20.54	20.71	1,640	87.42
9	*										
10	124.27	120.82	124.03	24.81	23.95	24.74	21.10	20.32	20.95	1,646	87.38
11	124.42	120.04	123.75	24.96	23.70	24.73	21.33	20.25	21.20	1,663	87.06
12	127.51	125.15	126.15	25.75	25.10	25.35	22.14	21.45	21.91	1,072	87.42
13	129.32	126.29	127.51	25.95	25.33	25.48	22.60	21.85	22.31	862	87.82
14	126.58	124.52	126.20	25.19	24.74	25.08	22.12	21.62	22.01	620	87.58
15	130.19	127.04	129.61	26.22	25.41	26.15	22.80	22.15	22.69	660	87.92
16	*	*	*	*			*				
17	128.01	126.15	127.34	25.76	25.36	25.68	22.31	21.95	22.18	524	87.87
18	127.02	124.81	125.38	25.51	25.16	25.30	22.13	21.87	21.94	442	87.77
19	127.61	125.63	127.01	25.75	25.43	25.63	22.12	21.85	22.06	437	87.82
20	129.59	127.87	128.41	26.05	25.76	25.86	22.40	22.19	22.25	516	87.89
21	129.62	127.97	128.71	26.01	25.69	25.75	22.55	22.25	22.37	392	88.03
22	129.01	128.32	128.55	25.81	25.72	25.73	22.37	22.26	22.29	155	88.13
23	*	*	*								
24	129.03	127.20	127.34	25.91	25.47	25.49	22.48	22.15	22.24	414	88.07
25	128.53	127.02	127.36	25.75	25.52	25.59	22.32	22.05	22.15	421	88.09
26	129.06	126.44	128.56	25.93	25.35	25.78	22.25	21.85	22.15	584	88.07
27	130.21	128.49	129.78	26.12	25.71	26.03	22.38	22.13	22.34	538	88.02
28	131.42	127.58	128.38	26.38	25.66	25.81	22.62	22.00	22.15	728	87.98
29	128.76	128.03	128.45	25.91	25.73	25.86	22.20	22.05	22.06	172	88.00
30	*	*	*	*			*				89.09
High			132.83			27.27			22.70		89.09
Low			121.44			24.14			20.71		87.06

*Sunday †Holiday ‡000 omitted

Total 20,245

MAY, 1939

Date	Industrials High	Low	Close	Railroads High	Low	Close	Utilities High	Low	Close	‡Daily Sales	40 Bonds
1	128.55	127.53	127.83	25.73	25.60	25.67	22.20	22.02	22.09	279	87.88
2	130.13	128.31	129.32	26.15	25.78	25.95	22.57	22.21	22.42	447	88.01
3	132.64	129.60	132.30	26.71	26.06	26.66	23.10	22.55	23.04	744	88.28
4	133.24	131.30	131.86	27.21	26.72	26.93	23.41	22.93	23.18	663	88.45
5	132.12	130.76	131.47	27.07	26.76	26.86	23.10	22.78	22.90	328	88.45
6	132.01	131.43	131.74	26.93	26.85	26.88	23.13	22.95	23.10	177	88.45
7	*	*	*	*			*			*	
8	132.22	130.70	131.67	26.87	26.43	26.68	23.08	22.88	22.98	350	88.49
9	134.02	132.11	133.67	27.50	26.82	27.43	23.50	23.05	23.49	710	88.80
10	134.66	132.63	132.82	27.82	27.30	27.38	23.75	23.31	23.40	692	88.88
11	133.26	131.85	132.92	27.36	27.07	27.31	23.44	23.16	23.31	400	88.77
12	132.79	131.74	132.16	27.23	27.02	27.13	23.34	23.10	23.17	344	88.81
13	132.78	132.21	132.40	27.36	27.28	27.32	23.25	23.19	23.23	159	88.74
14	*	*	*	*			*			*	
15	133.68	132.35	132.65	27.45	27.21	27.24	23.33	23.10	23.17	335	88.61
16	132.56	129.79	129.86	26.86	26.23	26.27	22.90	22.43	22.43	621	88.40
17	129.77	128.35	129.09	26.25	25.92	26.10	22.45	22.25	22.35	534	88.04
18	130.28	128.79	129.43	26.32	26.01	26.06	22.57	22.35	22.45	418	88.00
19	130.90	129.22	130.38	26.43	26.01	26.23	22.75	22.43	22.66	401	88.08
20	131.58	130.82	131.22	26.53	26.28	26.49	22.78	22.59	22.69	193	88.17
21	*	*	*	*			*			*	
22	132.54	130.50	132.45	27.08	26.45	27.05	22.92	22.59	22.89	417	88.18
23	132.88	131.49	131.77	27.10	26.82	26.90	22.95	22.75	22.82	423	88.29
24	135.14	132.09	135.04	27.70	26.98	27.66	23.57	22.99	23.54	1,014	88.63
25	137.16	135.11	135.53	28.08	27.63	27.68	23.77	23.41	23.44	1,010	88.83
26	136.76	135.22	136.09	27.91	27.67	27.78	23.68	23.35	23.54	624	88.95
27	137.16	136.10	136.80	28.29	27.85	28.18	23.72	23.58	23.65	383	89.10
28	*	*	*	*			*			*	
29	137.91	136.42	137.80	28.23	27.90	28.21	23.77	23.52	23.75	603	89.32
30	†	†	†	†	†	†	†	†	†	†	†
31	139.23	137.52	138.18	28.88	28.40	28.45	23.95	23.64	23.67	665	89.55
High			138.18			28.45			23.75		89.55
Low			127.83			25.67			22.09		87.88

*Sunday †Holiday ‡000 omitted

Total 12,934

JUNE, 1939

Date	Industrials High	Low	Close	Railroads High	Low	Close	Utilities High	Low	Close	‡Daily Sales	40 Bonds
1	137.36	135.52	136.20	28.13	27.79	27.95	23.55	23.28	23.40	599	89.51
2	137.42	136.29	136.74	28.18	27.85	28.00	23.59	23.45	23.47	397	89.57
3	137.41	136.82	137.12	28.01	27.91	27.94	23.55	23.48	23.52	176	89.62
4	*			*			*			*	*
5	137.36	136.34	137.06	27.97	27.78	27.90	23.61	23.40	23.46	349	89.52
6	138.84	136.98	138.36	28.53	28.16	28.43	23.88	23.47	23.81	599	89.68
7	139.79	138.17	138.71	28.63	28.27	28.34	24.16	23.84	24.04	531	89.74
8	138.84	137.53	138.49	28.23	27.91	28.11	23.95	23.65	23.80	411	89.83
9	140.75	138.61	140.09	28.54	28.15	28.38	24.13	23.85	24.05	786	89.85
10	140.59	139.90	140.14	28.47	28.30	28.33	23.99	23.88	23.91	255	89.95
11	*			*			*			*	*
12	139.95	138.34	139.13	28.10	27.86	27.93	24.00	23.68	23.82	424	89.71
13	139.09	137.38	138.20	27.93	27.60	27.81	24.10	23.56	23.93	532	89.67
14	138.02	136.44	137.50	27.74	27.49	27.73	23.92	23.58	23.77	399	89.56
15	137.03	134.26	134.41	27.68	27.15	27.15	23.82	23.40	23.45	584	89.29
16	135.36	133.79	134.67	27.13	26.82	26.98	23.51	23.25	23.35	400	89.16
17	135.55	134.71	135.31	27.33	27.04	27.25	23.45	23.35	23.40	171	89.17
18	*			*			*			*	*
19	137.02	135.72	136.40	27.53	27.30	27.33	23.68	23.46	23.55	345	89.21
20	137.97	136.72	137.57	27.73	27.48	27.68	24.18	23.74	24.12	485	89.39
21	138.04	136.87	137.61	27.81	27.57	27.66	24.25	23.92	24.08	466	89.44
22	137.63	136.34	136.88	27.66	27.48	27.56	24.09	23.79	24.00	451	89.39
23	137.95	136.48	137.42	27.81	27.61	27.75	24.21	23.88	24.10	478	89.35
24	137.57	137.18	137.36	27.82	27.75	27.76	24.07	24.02	24.05	188	89.42
25	*			*			*			*	*
26	136.77	134.83	135.09	27.53	27.25	27.27	23.87	23.38	23.45	502	89.22
27	135.77	134.01	135.42	27.53	27.18	27.44	23.70	23.27	23.63	476	89.13
28	135.06	132.76	132.83	27.14	26.81	26.82	23.65	23.22	23.24	541	88.86
29	131.81	129.71	130.05	26.49	25.91	25.99	23.02	22.57	22.69	823	88.43
30	131.16	128.97	130.63	25.90	25.57	25.85	23.08	22.55	22.97	599	88.34
High			140.14			28.43			24.12		89.95
Low			130.05			25.85			22.69		88.34

*Sunday ‡000 omitted   Total 11,967

JULY, 1939

Date	Industrials High	Low	Close	Railroads High	Low	Close	Utilities High	Low	Close	‡Daily Sales	40 Bonds
1	131.87	130.52	131.73	25.96	25.81	25.93	23.13	22.97	23.09	185	88.39
2	*			*			*			*	*
3	132.22	131.18	131.93	26.23	26.07	26.17	23.23	23.05	23.18	235	88.50
4	†	†	†	†	†	†	†	†	†	†	†
5	133.94	132.74	133.68	26.73	26.36	26.67	23.58	23.32	23.50	352	88.64
6	134.31	132.98	133.58	26.88	26.58	26.70	23.70	23.35	23.60	414	88.83
7	133.84	132.93	133.22	26.87	26.71	26.75	23.81	23.55	23.61	328	88.98
8	133.26	133.06	133.24	26.70	26.66	26.66	23.81	23.70	23.80	113	88.94
9	*			*			*			*	*
10	134.21	133.22	133.79	26.81	26.65	26.70	23.95	23.74	23.87	283	88.91
11	135.06	133.84	134.56	27.13	26.83	27.00	24.36	23.95	24.32	425	89.11
12	137.24	134.67	136.98	27.66	27.00	27.61	24.85	24.33	24.80	913	89.40
13	139.05	137.34	138.02	28.06	27.78	27.84	25.13	24.76	24.96	946	89.50
14	138.41	137.34	137.57	27.70	27.41	27.45	25.03	24.78	24.82	544	89.43
15	138.12	137.44	137.88	27.50	27.38	27.49	24.77	24.67	24.72	206	89.40
16	*			*			*			*	*
17	143.20	138.48	142.58	29.21	27.89	29.14	25.70	24.80	25.55	1,752	89.75
18	144.74	142.96	143.76	29.90	29.34	29.53	25.82	25.36	25.57	1,888	89.81
19	143.60	141.70	142.64	29.37	28.88	29.14	25.40	25.10	25.22	1,022	89.82
20	143.24	141.05	141.24	29.53	28.93	29.08	25.36	24.89	24.93	806	89.78
21	144.28	141.88	143.46	30.20	29.26	29.86	25.63	24.96	25.53	1,265	89.95
22	145.09	143.97	144.71	30.30	30.05	30.20	26.00	25.69	25.91	806	90.06
23	*			*			*			*	*
24	144.89	143.38	144.18	30.22	29.60	29.68	26.17	25.58	25.83	1,069	90.08
25	145.72	142.83	143.10	30.33	29.63	29.69	26.42	25.83	25.95	1,230	90.18
26	144.39	142.41	143.82	29.94	29.53	29.87	26.54	25.87	26.50	892	90.28
27	144.92	143.08	144.51	30.11	29.70	30.00	26.62	26.20	26.50	817	90.50
28	145.04	143.48	144.11	29.95	29.51	29.57	26.56	26.15	26.25	812	90.45
29	144.21	143.77	144.00	29.48	29.36	29.43	26.15	25.91	26.02	245	90.50
30	*			*			*			*	*
31	144.04	142.77	143.26	29.46	29.10	29.21	26.11	25.75	25.95	520	90.50
High			144.71			30.20			26.50		90.50
Low			131.73			25.93			23.09		88.39

*Sunday †Holiday ‡000 omitted   Total 18,068

AUGUST, 1939

Date	Industrials			Railroads			Utilities			‡Daily Sales	40 Bonds
	High	Low	Close	High	Low	Close	High	Low	Close		
1	143.89	142.45	143.36	29.42	29.15	29.26	26.40	25.89	26.24	575	90.32
2	144.90	142.69	144.26	29.63	29.21	29.49	27.13	26.01	27.10	1,027	90.34
3	145.75	143.79	144.24	30.17	29.50	29.64	27.51	26.98	27.07	1,008	90.53
4	144.06	141.26	141.73	29.56	28.82	28.97	27.18	26.35	26.50	901	90.13
5	142.41	141.57	142.11	29.27	29.03	29.20	26.81	26.43	26.74	237	90.13
6	*			*			*				
7	142.38	140.31	140.76	29.08	28.69	28.80	26.82	26.20	.45	519	89.97
8	141.93	140.55	141.10	29.05	28.70	28.76	26.88	26.37	26.55	449	90.09
9	140.58	139.14	139.75	28.77	28.50	28.56	26.56	25.14	26.33	468	89.97
10	138.83	136.62	137.25	28.31	27.89	28.00	26.21	25.63	25.88	700	89.86
11	138.93	136.38	137.29	28.31	27.83	27.97	26.25	25.77	26.05	701	89.60
12	138.55	137.45	138.42	28.36	28.07	28.35	26.37	26.12	26.36	258	89.65
13	*			*			*				
14	140.54	138.75	140.18	28.65	28.41	28.56	26.75	26.38	26.62	546	89.87
15	142.35	140.76	141.29	28.93	28.59	28.66	27.15	26.77	26.82	658	90.08
16	139.86	137.61	138.47	28.32	27.82	28.00	26.57	25.95	26.15	640	89.71
17	138.89	137.38	138.33	27.84	27.65	27.71	26.07	25.81	25.93	443	89.62
18	138.15	134.83	135.54	27.62	26.84	27.04	25.90	25.15	25.25	836	89.21
19	135.57	134.37	135.11	27.01	26.85	26.96	25.30	25.04	25.20	290	89.17
20	*			*			*				
21	133.93	132.11	132.81	26.73	26.19	26.36	24.91	24.14	24.45	848	88.78
22	135.84	133.07	135.07	26.98	26.18	26.74	25.18	24.28	24.84	862	88.97
23	134.80	131.49	131.82	26.39	25.68	25.71	24.74	23.95	24.00	793	88.61
24	132.42	128.60	131.33	25.98	24.96	25.80	24.29	23.27	24.12	1,294	88.15
25	134.53	130.58	133.73	26.41	25.68	26.26	24.70	23.92	24.50	693	88.02
26	136.93	135.16	136.39	26.98	26.58	26.88	25.23	24.78	25.13	521	88.21
27	*			*			*				
28	136.40	132.68	134.66	26.50	25.75	26.02	24.71	24.06	24.35	670	87.97
29	137.84	135.91	137.39	26.94	26.56	26.76	25.28	24.90	25.10	483	88.03
30	138.07	135.76	136.16	26.91	26.43	26.48	25.33	24.97	25.04	496	88.05
31	135.76	133.38	134.41	26.24	25.92	26.10	24.72	24.35	24.54	458	87.71
High			144.26			29.64			27.10		90.53
Low			131.33			25.71			24.00		87.71
									Total	17,374	

*Sunday ‡000 omitted

SEPTEMBER, 1939

Date	Industrials			Railroads			Utilities			‡Daily Sales	40 Bonds
	High	Low	Close	High	Low	Close	High	Low	Close		
1	136.03	127.51	135.25	25.99	24.90	25.93	23.79	22.90	23.59	1,970	86.51
2	139.80	136.39	138.09	26.60	25.89	26.18	23.76	23.05	23.41	1,791	86.52
3	*			*			*				
4	†			†			†			†	†
5	150.07	142.38	148.12	29.63	26.65	28.96	24.43	22.25	23.79	5,934	86.74
6	150.76	146.08	148.04	30.03	28.76	29.16	24.41	23.64	23.79	3,943	86.36
7	150.52	146.74	148.32	30.05	29.18	29.42	24.45	23.55	23.98	2,597	86.90
8	152.58	148.08	150.04	30.90	29.63	30.40	24.37	23.65	23.85	3,512	87.82
9	151.95	150.09	150.91	30.93	30.40	30.51	23.90	23.59	23.68	1,555	87.89
10	*			*			*				
11	156.34	150.85	155.12	31.78	30.86	31.30	23.89	23.35	23.49	4,684	88.14
12	157.30	151.78	155.92	33.05	30.78	32.85	24.25	23.15	24.08	4,169	88.26
13	157.77	152.74	154.10	33.61	32.40	32.57	24.75	23.92	24.30	3,762	88.25
14	155.54	151.96	153.71	32.93	32.10	32.40	24.62	24.18	24.31	2,009	88.30
15	155.57	152.56	154.03	32.77	32.15	32.48	24.69	24.15	24.54	1,594	88.32
16	153.55	151.08	152.15	32.34	31.76	32.07	25.10	24.48	25.01	1,084	88.19
17	*			*			*				
18	150.57	147.35	147.78	31.41	30.72	30.81	24.75	24.21	24.25	1,734	87.61
19	152.83	148.46	152.14	32.35	31.13	32.19	24.89	24.38	24.74	1,830	87.95
20	154.96	151.57	152.25	33.18	32.32	32.45	24.92	24.36	24.42	2,142	88.21
21	154.56	151.49	153.48	33.00	32.20	32.83	24.95	24.50	24.65	1,730	88.11
22	154.76	151.97	152.57	33.61	32.78	33.06	25.22	24.57	24.70	1,661	88.25
23	153.62	152.14	152.99	33.51	33.03	33.34	24.79	24.54	24.63	562	88.42
24	*			*			*				
25	153.91	152.05	152.64	34.20	33.37	33.81	24.95	24.58	24.70	1,226	88.70
26	154.27	151.77	153.54	35.76	33.65	35.73	24.94	24.50	24.86	1,712	89.41
27	154.92	152.01	153.08	36.70	35.67	35.90	25.58	24.91	25.28	2,342	89.69
28	153.13	150.41	151.12	35.69	34.66	35.02	25.35	24.93	25.09	1,574	89.48
29	150.89	148.92	150.16	34.52	33.93	34.31	25.03	24.63	24.83	1,129	89.21
30	152.84	150.82	152.54	35.75	34.68	35.61	25.17	24.91	25.13	843	89.49
High			155.92			35.90			25.28		89.69
Low			135.25			25.93			23.41		86.36
									Total	57,089	

*Sunday †Holiday ‡000 omitted

OCTOBER, 1939

Date	Industrials High	Low	Close	Railroads High	Low	Close	Utilities High	Low	Close	‡Daily Sales	40 Bonds
1	*	*	*	*	*	*	*	*	*	*	*
2	152.36	150.68	151.41	35.20	34.58	34.85	25.19	24.77	25.05	838	89.44
3	152.20	149.29	150.23	35.00	34.06	34.35	25.35	24.82	25.00	1,003	89.28
4	151.20	148.73	150.25	34.06	33.42	33.88	25.35	24.91	25.16	975	89.34
5	151.68	149.72	150.48	34.26	33.72	33.92	25.50	25.07	25.32	907	89.39
6	153.06	149.61	150.61	35.19	33.98	34.15	25.50	25.08	25.19	1,328	89.55
7	150.52	149.05	149.60	33.90	33.56	33.64	25.08	24.85	24.88	586	89.40
8	*	*	*	*	*	*	*	*	*	*	*
9	150.51	148.91	149.89	33.90	33.46	33.61	25.04	24.77	24.95	618	89.40
10	152.02	149.92	150.66	34.25	33.69	33.80	25.55	25.09	25.36	954	89.70
11	151.89	150.49	151.34	34.12	33.69	33.95	25.65	25.23	25.52	628	89.71
12	†	†	†	†	†	†	†	†	†	†	†
13	152.40	150.43	150.85	34.23	33.62	33.65	25.59	25.25	25.34	735	89.78
14	150.73	150.11	150.38	33.61	33.43	33.53	25.40	25.21	25.31	248	89.71
15	*	*	*	*	*	*	*	*	*	*	*
16	151.34	149.95	150.84	33.57	33.19	33.43	25.40	25.26	25.34	485	89.61
17	154.81	151.29	154.56	35.15	33.86	35.01	25.95	25.42	25.87	1,842	90.21
18	155.28	153.23	153.54	35.11	34.48	34.51	26.07	25.60	25.75	1,403	90.29
19	154.42	152.78	153.36	35.11	34.50	34.71	25.99	25.59	25.85	1,161	90.39
20	153.87	152.55	153.00	34.77	34.36	34.58	26.10	25.66	25.89	786	90.31
21	154.06	153.11	153.86	34.88	34.55	34.78	26.11	25.95	26.05	536	90.31
22	*	*	*	*	*	*	*	*	*	*	*
23	154.56	153.19	153.71	34.76	34.40	34.55	26.44	25.95	26.09	974	90.14
24	154.76	153.04	154.07	34.81	34.35	34.57	26.30	25.95	26.15	1,163	90.23
25	155.95	153.98	155.48	35.22	34.71	35.13	26.43	26.06	26.26	1,691	90.56
26	155.95	153.84	154.05	35.50	34.68	34.75	26.63	26.15	26.37	1,679	90.63
27	154.34	152.30	153.46	34.91	34.32	34.60	26.38	26.10	26.21	1,063	90.45
28	154.06	152.65	153.12	34.68	34.35	34.43	26.27	26.05	26.12	482	90.44
29	*	*	*	*	*	*	*	*	*	*	*
30	153.60	152.39	153.21	34.56	34.22	34.38	26.15	25.92	26.07	639	90.27
31	153.24	151.32	151.88	34.51	33.77	33.91	26.07	25.67	25.80	1,012	90.24
High			155.48			35.13			26.37		90.63
Low			149.60			33.43			24.88		89.28

*Sunday †Holiday ‡000 omitted

Total 23,736

NOVEMBER, 1939

Date	Industrials High	Low	Close	Railroads High	Low	Close	Utilities High	Low	Close	‡Daily Sales	40 Bonds
1	152.26	150.64	151.60	33.89	33.48	33.76	25.94	25.58	25.68	794	90.14
2	152.20	150.47	151.56	33.76	33.42	33.65	25.95	25.67	25.83	846	90.21
3	153.18	150.04	152.64	34.26	33.23	34.12	26.08	25.70	25.99	1,816	90.44
4	153.47	151.97	152.36	34.28	33.79	33.84	26.18	25.93	26.01	1,424	90.49
5	*	*	*	*	*	*	*	*	*	*	*
6	152.35	150.76	151.46	33.90	33.44	33.57	26.15	25.76	26.05	1,266	90.52
7	†	†	†	†	†	†	†	†	†	†	†
8	151.43	149.81	150.35	33.78	33.28	33.44	26.18	25.80	25.95	1,068	90.47
9	150.87	148.53	148.75	33.64	32.85	32.88	26.06	25.70	25.73	1,200	90.30
10	149.33	147.74	149.09	32.84	32.38	32.79	25.81	25.55	25.71	1,090	90.23
11	†	†	†	†	†	†	†	†	†	†	†
12	*	*	*	*	*	*	*	*	*	*	*
13	149.70	148.55	149.07	33.09	32.79	32.88	25.71	25.49	25.57	652	90.34
14	150.53	148.98	149.77	33.46	32.97	33.30	25.79	25.50	25.62	775	90.26
15	150.48	149.23	149.53	33.53	33.15	33.21	25.88	25.61	25.68	635	90.22
16	151.42	149.27	151.15	34.03	33.12	33.89	25.96	25.64	25.93	825	90.37
17	152.21	150.55	151.00	34.20	33.77	33.80	26.22	25.85	26.00	770	90.40
18	151.66	151.05	151.53	33.94	33.76	33.85	26.15	26.02	26.09	277	90.40
19	*	*	*	*	*	*	*	*	*	*	*
20	152.58	151.02	151.69	34.45	33.95	34.08	26.22	25.85	25.93	745	90.46
21	152.11	150.72	150.98	34.06	33.51	33.57	25.97	25.58	25.64	556	90.51
22	150.67	149.62	150.34	33.68	33.31	33.55	25.72	25.48	25.58	567	90.17
23	†	†	†	†	†	†	†	†	†	†	†
24	150.46	148.12	148.47	33.47	32.81	32.93	25.66	25.35	25.41	817	90.05
25	148.75	148.04	148.64	32.97	32.73	32.90	25.45	25.36	25.42	293	89.92
26	*	*	*	*	*	*	*	*	*	*	*
27	149.05	147.98	148.59	33.11	32.70	32.86	25.50	25.33	25.40	520	89.87
28	149.65	148.02	148.31	33.34	32.81	32.85	25.48	25.22	25.35	622	89.81
29	149.18	146.82	146.89	33.11	32.27	32.28	25.41	25.07	25.08	781	89.58
30	146.73	144.85	145.69	32.14	31.56	31.70	25.07	24.80	24.92	884	89.26
High			152.64			34.12			26.09		90.52
Low			145.69			31.70			24.92		89.26

*Sunday †Holiday ‡000 omitted

Total 19,223

DECEMBER, 1939

Date	Industrials			Railroads			Utilities			‡Daily Sales	40 Bonds
	High	Low	Close	High	Low	Close	High	Low	Close		
1	146.94	145.51	146.54	31.96	31.50	31.85	25.20	24.94	25.08	606	89.26
2	146.93	146.29	146.62	31.85	31.68	31.76	25.18	25.06	25.11	228	89.35
3	*			*			*			*	
4	146.79	145.74	146.34	31.69	31.33	31.53	25.20	24.92	25.09	428	89.28
5	147.29	146.05	146.49	31.80	31.47	31.63	25.25	25.01	25.09	590	89.31
6	148.99	146.83	148.78	32.30	31.63	32.14	25.30	25.04	25.21	991	89.57
7	149.59	147.98	148.70	32.45	32.07	32.23	25.41	25.07	25.14	1,005	89.52
8	148.57	147.50	147.86	32.24	31.82	31.91	25.20	24.93	25.03	575	89.39
9	148.08	147.54	147.93	31.93	31.80	31.86	25.07	24.96	25.02	262	89.37
10	*			*			*			*	
11	148.27	146.67	147.05	31.68	31.23	31.24	25.06	24.82	24.89	567	89.11
12	147.59	146.43	146.93	31.44	31.13	31.31	24.90	24.61	24.70	612	89.01
13	149.29	147.12	148.94	32.08	31.34	32.00	24.95	24.60	24.86	1,060	89.27
14	150.09	148.25	148.93	32.31	31.75	31.84	25.13	24.81	24.95	887	89.24
15	150.11	148.74	149.64	31.95	31.67	31.81	25.04	24.86	24.92	704	89.32
16	149.80	149.04	149.36	31.87	31.71	31.78	25.00	24.84	24.86	335	89.29
17	*			*			*			*	
18	149.80	148.69	149.22	31.80	31.43	31.53	24.99	24.79	24.86	725	89.29
19	149.59	148.35	148.93	31.40	31.06	31.13	24.96	24.75	24.82	752	89.19
20	149.86	148.41	149.13	31.68	31.05	31.42	25.00	24.75	24.87	909	89.15
21	149.90	148.59	149.10	31.62	31.17	31.20	25.10	24.81	24.92	743	89.20
22	149.97	148.87	149.59	31.55	31.22	31.44	25.09	24.78	24.95	720	89.21
23	150.04	149.40	149.85	31.62	31.48	31.58	25.00	24.84	24.91	332	89.19
24	*			*			*			*	
25	†	†	†	†	†	†	†	†	†	†	†
26	150.11	148.83	149.27	31.65	31.26	31.37	25.05	24.76	24.91	724	89.09
27	149.51	147.66	148.52	31.35	30.78	30.99	25.03	24.68	24.85	1,146	88.90
28	150.10	148.24	149.48	31.70	31.01	31.53	25.31	24.85	25.18	1,081	89.42
29	150.70	149.06	149.99	31.97	31.58	31.81	25.44	25.10	25.32	1,135	89.81
30	150.78	149.82	150.24	32.01	31.70	31.83	25.62	25.33	25.58	656	90.04
31	*			*			*			*	
High			150.24			32.23			25.58		90.04
Low			146.34			30.99			24.70		88.90

*Sunday †Holiday ‡000 omitted Total 17,773

JANUARY, 1940

Date	Industrials			Railroads			Utilities			‡Daily Sales	40 Bonds
	High	Low	Close	High	Low	Close	High	Low	Close		
1	†	†	†	†	†	†	†	†	†	†	†
2	151.79	150.45	151.43	32.35	32.11	32.28	25.97	25.67	25.90	579	90.24
3	153.29	151.86	152.80	32.95	32.40	32.66	26.52	26.04	26.45	1,021	90.61
4	153.26	152.06	152.43	33.00	32.59	32.67	26.55	26.22	26.35	855	90.51
5	152.89	151.27	151.54	32.68	32.18	32.20	26.44	26.03	26.07	758	90.39
6	151.49	150.71	151.19	32.31	32.15	32.25	26.31	26.04	26.25	342	90.42
7	*			*			*			*	
8	152.11	151.08	151.34	32.41	32.12	32.18	26.53	26.16	26.36	632	90.43
9	151.21	149.45	149.84	32.04	31.70	31.81	26.38	25.95	26.05	671	90.37
10	150.47	149.35	150.15	31.90	31.73	31.85	26.25	25.94	26.10	601	90.39
11	150.64	148.22	148.23	32.04	31.43	31.43	26.20	25.66	25.68	845	90.24
12	148.35	145.76	145.96	31.25	30.70	30.74	25.60	25.23	25.25	1,109	89.93
13	146.05	144.99	145.19	30.78	30.53	30.60	25.38	25.16	25.21	424	89.86
14	*			*			*			*	
15	145.95	143.06	144.65	30.56	30.05	30.33	25.25	24.83	25.03	861	89.58
16	146.11	144.37	145.67	30.45	30.15	30.33	25.32	25.00	25.20	526	89.65
17	146.71	145.30	145.81	30.58	30.30	30.41	25.25	25.05	25.14	474	89.65
18	146.44	144.77	145.61	30.41	30.09	30.21	25.35	25.04	25.12	605	89.53
19	146.75	145.52	145.86	30.41	30.16	30.24	25.27	25.00	25.10	639	89.46
20	146.07	145.38	145.64	30.30	30.19	30.25	25.30	25.14	25.25	271	89.31
21	*			*			*			*	
22	145.66	144.57	145.13	30.25	30.07	30.15	25.26	25.05	25.14	438	89.37
23	145.97	144.85	145.49	30.38	30.21	30.26	25.20	24.95	25.00	513	89.25
24	147.11	145.71	147.00	30.96	30.45	30.93	25.25	24.95	25.18	712	89.41
25	147.29	146.04	146.29	31.30	30.82	30.89	25.21	25.03	25.11	544	89.45
26	147.16	146.00	146.61	31.01	30.81	30.84	25.20	24.86	25.00	604	89.37
27	146.65	146.36	146.51	30.77	30.71	30.75	24.93	24.83	24.88	317	89.33
28	*			*			*			*	
29	147.05	145.86	146.26	30.86	30.63	30.69	25.09	24.87	24.95	490	89.28
30	146.37	145.19	145.63	30.78	30.60	30.72	25.01	24.83	24.93	548	89.30
31	145.91	145.12	145.33	30.73	30.53	30.56	24.90	24.65	24.70	610	89.28
High			152.80			32.67			26.45		90.61
Low			144.65			30.15			24.70		89.25

*Sunday †Holiday ‡000 omitted Total 15,989

FEBRUARY, 1940

Date	Industrials High	Low	Close	Railroads High	Low	Close	Utilities High	Low	Close	‡Daily Sales	40 Bonds
1	145.57	144.73	145.23	30.64	30.51	30.58	24.71	24.52	24.61	461	89.28
2	145.97	144.83	145.33	30.89	30.58	30.64	24.75	24.55	24.69	515	89.34
3	145.79	145.29	145.59	30.69	30.63	30.65	24.77	24.73	24.74	291	89.35
4	*	*	*	*	*	*	*	*	*	*	*
5	145.58	144.69	145.00	30.51	30.39	30.50	24.78	24.63	24.68	413	89.33
6	146.00	144.79	145.93	30.80	30.48	30.73	24.85	24.65	24.80	543	89.37
7	146.97	145.84	146.63	30.86	30.68	30.83	24.89	24.73	24.79	491	89.44
8	148.50	146.32	148.40	31.48	30.95	31.46	24.95	24.71	24.95	868	89.59
9	150.04	148.54	148.94	31.77	31.37	31.40	25.12	24.89	24.98	1,099	89.67
10	149.19	148.40	148.84	31.38	31.21	31.27	25.00	24.91	24.95	320	89.55
11	*	*	*	*	*	*	*	*	*	*	*
12	†	†	†	†	†	†	†	†	†	†	†
13	149.64	148.38	148.78	31.42	31.10	31.13	25.09	24.93	24.99	582	89.47
14	148.83	147.65	148.33	31.08	30.85	31.00	25.00	24.78	24.85	651	89.34
15	149.19	148.20	148.46	31.05	30.88	30.90	25.05	24.89	24.97	754	89.37
16	148.60	147.38	148.20	30.91	30.70	30.86	25.02	24.79	24.92	684	89.23
17	149.28	148.43	148.72	31.04	30.93	30.94	25.05	24.94	24.99	402	89.32
18	*	*	*	*	*	*	*	*	*	*	*
19	148.95	147.93	148.46	31.03	30.85	30.90	25.06	24.88	24.96	633	89.17
20	148.95	147.51	148.65	31.08	30.80	31.06	25.08	24.89	25.00	808	89.21
21	149.04	148.02	148.34	31.10	30.78	30.81	25.10	24.98	25.05	783	89.11
22	†	†	†	†	†	†	†	†	†	†	†
23	148.17	146.93	147.35	30.83	30.59	30.62	25.15	24.98	25.05	654	88.98
24	147.52	146.49	146.72	30.80	30.60	30.63	25.00	24.89	24.90	378	88.86
25	*	*	*	*	*	*	*	*	*	*	*
26	146.82	145.81	146.44	30.70	30.56	30.63	24.88	24.68	24.80	440	88.78
27	147.10	145.90	146.17	30.80	30.56	30.63	24.85	24.75	24.80	511	88.70
28	147.16	146.07	146.56	30.61	30.43	30.53	24.95	24.76	24.89	568	88.75
29	147.21	146.10	146.54	30.60	30.43	30.48	24.83	24.57	24.64	623	88.71
High			148.94			31.46			25.05		89.67
Low			145.00			30.48			24.61		88.70

*Sunday   †Holiday   ‡000 omitted   Total 13,472

MARCH, 1940

Date	Industrials High	Low	Close	Railroads High	Low	Close	Utilities High	Low	Close	‡Daily Sales	40 Bonds
1	146.79	145.85	146.23	30.53	30.37	30.41	24.61	24.06	24.17	601	88.62
2	146.52	146.07	146.33	30.44	30.40	30.41	24.21	24.01	24.11	275	88.60
3	*	*	*	*	*	*	*	*	*	*	*
4	146.77	146.00	146.43	30.51	30.38	30.46	24.26	23.95	24.19	458	88.63
5	147.15	146.41	146.89	30.71	30.47	30.68	24.29	24.09	24.15	573	88.77
6	148.37	147.08	147.97	31.18	30.77	31.01	24.40	24.17	24.30	855	88.78
7	148.67	147.83	148.32	31.11	30.90	30.94	24.35	24.14	24.27	691	88.84
8	148.80	147.76	148 07	31.01	30.84	30.87	24.36	24.12	24.24	745	88.90
9	148.46	147.85	148.14	30.90	30.82	30.84	24.32	24.19	24.24	331	88.90
10	*	*	*	*	*	*	*	*	*	*	*
11	148.65	147.57	148.15	30.90	30.71	30.80	24.23	24.07	24.12	588	88.85
12	149.45	147.93	148.37	31.01	30.73	30.75	24.20	24.05	24.09	884	88.96
13	148.92	147.69	148.32	30.82	30.65	30.67	24.22	24.02	24.15	626	88.93
14	148.57	147.63	148.11	30.66	30.48	30.52	24.27	24.04	24.14	662	88.90
15	148.21	146.34	146.53	30.45	29.95	30.01	24.25	24.05	24.10	882	88.74
16	146.43	145.38	145.76	29.86	29.68	29.78	24.07	24.00	24.02	479	88.60
17	*	*	*	*	*	*	*	*	*	*	*
18	146.18	145.08	145.59	29.89	29.66	29.86	24.11	23.94	24.04	513	88.72
19	146.85	145.61	146.43	30.03	29.76	29.95	24.13	23.97	24.07	654	88.69
20	147.30	146.34	146.91	30.23	30.05	30.13	24.19	24.01	24.10	645	88.78
21	147.20	146.38	146.73	30.26	30.03	30.19	24.36	24.13	24.29	579	88.78
22	†	†	†	†	†	†	†	†	†	†	†
23	147.01	146.49	146.73	30.16	30.03	30.10	24.31	24.18	24.24	392	88.63
24	*	*	*	*	*	*	*	*	*	*	*
25	146.96	146.15	146.25	30.16	29.96	30.04	24.25	24.06	24.09	595	88.83
26	146.56	145.49	145.86	30.11	29.93	29.98	24.19	24.05	24.15	623	88.65
27	147.83	146.24	147.47	30.85	30.24	30.79	24.34	24.15	24.28	1,192	88.73
28	148.16	146.92	147.25	30.89	30.53	30.55	24.68	24.35	24.55	1,020	88.78
29	148.04	146.82	147.54	30.74	30.48	30.66	25.23	24.50	25.15	837	88.81
30	148.19	147.57	147.95	30.86	30.66	30.86	25.30	25.10	25.22	572	88.97
31											
High			148.37			31.01			25.22		88.97
Low			145.59			29.78			24.02		88.60

*Sunday.   †Holiday   ‡000 omitted   Total 16,272

APRIL, 1940

Date	Industrials			Railroads			Utilities			‡Daily Sales	40 Bonds
	High	Low	Close	High	Low	Close	High	Low	Close		
1	148.44	147.49	147.72	30.92	30.71	30.73	25.35	25.02	25.10	750	89.07
2	148.37	147.48	147.92	30.71	30.53	30.59	25.25	24.95	25.17	835	89.16
3	149.74	147.56	149.65	31.35	30.68	31.32	25.73	25.07	25.68	1,725	89.57
4	151.15	149.56	150.41	32.14	31.49	31.86	26.04	25.47	25.78	1,994	89.77
5	151.32	149.94	150.36	32.07	31.71	31.82	25.90	25.57	25.68	1,256	89.82
6	151.34	150.27	151.10	32.11	31.89	32.08	25.97	25.78	25.92	710	89.91
7	*	*	*	*	*	*	*	*	*	*	
8	152.09	150.63	151.29	32.31	31.92	31.96	26.08	25.78	25.92	1,260	89.90
9	152.01	149.16	150.31	32.05	31.10	31.42	25.81	25.05	25.28	2,136	89.35
10	150.55	149.12	149.59	31.35	31.05	31.20	25.35	25.01	25.09	1,287	89.15
11	150.96	149.49	149.98	31.42	31.26	31.28	25.42	25.13	25.25	889	89.25
12	150.09	148.68	149.20	31.24	30.98	31.07	25.34	25.09	25.20	826	89.17
13	149.90	149.09	149.66	31.13	31.03	31.06	25.29	25.20	25.24	495	89.23
14	*	*	*	*	*	*	*	*	*	*	
15	150.67	149.20	149.72	31.20	30.90	30.98	25.30	25.07	25.13	1,260	89.29
16	150.24	147.43	148.18	31.00	30.51	30.64	25.14	24.70	24.81	1,506	88.90
17	149.12	147.77	148.35	30.74	30.50	30.59	25.00	24.63	24.83	902	89.01
18	148.64	146.76	147.15	30.59	30.26	30.30	24.89	24.50	24.60	1,205	88.92
19	147.31	145.86	146.80	30.50	30.12	30.37	24.60	24.36	24.43	1,155	88.89
20	148.00	146.91	147.67	30.68	30.48	30.60	24.70	24.50	24.63	721	88.90
21	*	*	*	*	*	*	*	*	*	*	
22	148.68	147.45	148.01	30.81	30.60	30.63	24.75	24.60	24.65	869	88.98
23	149.18	147.77	148.93	30.78	30.57	30.75	24.83	24.51	24.66	881	88.96
24	149.45	148.20	148.45	31.26	30.80	31.00	24.85	24.64	24.75	853	89.05
25	149.22	148.07	148.56	31.10	30.83	30.97	24.92	24.64	24.76	815	89.14
26	148.72	147.37	147.73	30.90	30.51	30.68	24.99	24.69	24.85	854	89.17
27	148.26	147.64	148.12	30.75	30.54	30.71	24.86	24.80	24.81	349	89.19
28	*	*	*	*	*	*	*	*	*	*	
29	148.88	148.02	148.41	30.91	30.66	30.74	25.04	24.82	24.98	568	89.29
30	149.06	147.98	148.43	30.78	30.63	30.69	25.28	24.95	25.10	592	89.40
High			151.29			32.08			25.92		89.91
Low			146.80			30.30			24.50		88.89

*Sunday.   †Holiday.   ‡000 omitted   Total 26,693

MAY, 1940

Date	Industrials			Railroads			Utilities			‡Daily Sales	40 Bonds
	High	Low	Close	High	Low	Close	High	Low	Close		
1	148.14	146.84	147.13	30.70	30.46	30.52	25.03	24.76	24.82	810	89.33
2	148.18	147.15	147.76	30.75	30.52	30.66	25.04	24.75	24.92	645	89.37
3	148.70	146.42	147.65	30.98	30.47	30.78	25.10	24.85	25.02	1,070	89.42
4	147.97	147.25	147.55	30.95	30.75	30.89	25.09	24.96	25.00	317	89.46
5	*	*	*	*	*	*	*	*	*	*	*
6	148.12	147.05	147.33	30.92	30.73	30.79	25.05	24.84	24.86	526	89.36
7	148.22	146.89	147.74	30.97	30.73	30.86	24.91	24.66	24.78	581	89.46
8	148.70	147.49	147.96	31.10	30.82	30.90	24.94	24.75	24.83	694	89.59
9	148.60	147.65	148.17	31.37	30.99	31.17	24.95	24.73	24.85	848	89.56
10	148.48	144.51	144.77	30.86	29.70	29.79	24.65	23.95	24.00	2,086	88.65
11	145.64	143.93	144.85	29.94	29.69	29.81	24.00	23.75	23.81	672	88.48
12	*	*	*	*	*	*	*	*	*	*	*
13	144.42	137.25	137.63	29.65	27.63	27.83	23.73	22.50	22.52	2,559	87.20
14	136.85	128.11	128.27	27.47	26.26	26.33	22.15	20.88	20.90	3,681	85.99
15	131.17	125.76	129.08	26.53	25.22	25.89	21.35	20.30	20.85	3,768	85.55
16	131.35	127.54	130.43	26.44	25.58	26.20	21.13	20.50	20.98	2,354	85.76
17	131.21	122.93	124.20	26.71	24.65	24.81	21.07	19.64	19.87	3,075	85.22
18	123.87	120.67	122.43	24.13	23.44	23.65	19.66	19.01	19.20	1,663	84.84
19	*	*	*	*	*	*	*	*	*	*	*
20	124.98	121.68	122.43	24.87	23.86	23.98	20.00	19.26	19.49	1,237	84.67
21	120.52	110.61	114.13	23.66	21.69	22.14	19.15	17.49	18.34	3,940	83.21
22	116.50	112.43	114.75	22.43	21.65	22.21	18.81	17.83	18.51	2,133	83.28
23	117.84	112.78	114.71	23.24	22.35	22.58	19.03	18.23	18.42	1,642	83.10
24	116.15	113.37	113.94	22.80	22.29	22.45	18.70	18.17	18.25	871	83.25
25	115.42	113.21	114.75	22.79	22.36	22.76	18.60	18.22	18.52	554	83.33
26	*	*	*	*	*	*	*	*	*	*	*
27	117.71	115.07	116.35	23.48	23.12	23.32	19.07	18.59	18.91	791	83.69
28	114.76	110.51	114.26	22.88	22.28	22.82	18.48	17.99	18.31	1,264	83.06
29	116.66	114.08	115.24	23.36	23.08	23.22	19.01	18.49	18.80	657	83.34
30	†	†	†	†	†	†	†	†	†	†	†
31	117.15	115.13	116.22	23.33	23.00	23.15	19.05	18.81	18.90	527	83.46
High			148.17			31.17			25.02		89.59
Low			113.94			22.14			18.25		83.06

*Sunday   †Holiday   ‡000 omitted.   Total 38,965

JUNE, 1940

Date	Industrials High	Low	Close	Railroads High	Low	Close	Utilities High	Low	Close	‡Daily Sales	40 Bonds
1	116.42	115.39	115.67	23.14	22.98	23.05	18.90	18.78	18.87	273	83.48
2	*										
3	116.44	114.35	114.73	23.26	23.10	23.15	18.89	18.60	18.62	446	83.48
4	116.25	114.75	115.79	23.45	23.19	23.35	18.75	18.55	18.66	410	83.77
5	115.12	112.30	113.25	23.24	22.79	22.94	18.45	17.95	18.10	669	83.64
6	114.80	113.05	114.48	23.13	22.95	23.09	18.33	18.13	18.24	427	83.62
7	116.58	114.60	115.67	23.92	23.56	23.91	18.62	18.39	18.50	469	83.89
8	116.05	115.20	115.36	23.87	23.78	23.79	18.63	18.45	18.57	199	83.87
9	*										
10	114.42	110.41	111.84	23.30	22.36	22.79	18.37	17.82	18.03	972	83.49
11	116.38	113.24	115.97	23.84	23.40	23.73	18.71	18.09	18.62	764	83.74
12	122.38	117.41	121.46	25.41	24.30	25.20	19.45	18.70	19.30	1,360	84.92
13	122.10	119.37	119.91	25.03	24.42	24.47	19.55	19.11	19.23	877	84.89
14	122.95	118.96	122.27	25.08	24.24	24.86	19.85	19.10	19.74	948	85.32
15	124.38	122.33	123.36	25.19	24.90	24.97	20.32	19.96	20.18	559	85.51
16	*										
17	123.73	119.18	122.80	25.16	24.24	25.04	20.84	19.57	20.60	1,208	85.25
18	125.31	122.35	123.21	26.16	25.41	25.63	21.08	20.65	20.79	719	85.63
19	124.51	122.50	123.86	25.86	25.31	25.73	21.11	20.68	21.02	564	86.14
20	123.79	121.96	122.35	25.91	25.36	25.51	21.47	20.99	21.10	586	86.40
21	123.07	121.89	122.61	25.61	25.42	25.53	21.20	21.04	21.13	333	86.59
22	123.08	122.23	122.83	25.63	25.48	25.56	21.51	21.16	21.50	204	86.63
23	*										
24	124.05	122.60	123.76	25.80	25.53	25.71	22.64	21.78	22.60	472	86.84
25	123.99	120.78	121.05	26.04	25.20	25.24	22.61	21.36	21.41	696	86.72
26	120.74	118.67	119.73	25.37	24.66	25.19	21.59	20.98	21.35	635	86.50
27	121.23	120.01	120.69	25.90	25.57	25.73	22.20	21.39	22.10	441	86.74
28	124.42	121.82	122.06	26.76	26.13	26.15	23.93	22.79	22.85	1,173	87.19
29	122.31	121.63	121.87	26.24	26.13	26.18	22.85	22.61	22.67	170	87.17
30	*										
High			123.86			26.18			22.85		87.19
Low			111.84			22.79			18.03		83.48

*Sunday. †Holiday. ‡000 omitted

Total 15,574

JULY, 1940

Date	Industrials High	Low	Close	Railroads High	Low	Close	Utilities High	Low	Close	‡Daily Sales	40 Bonds
1	121.77	120.79	121.12	25.88	25.60	25.70	22.57	22.15	22.30	273	87.08
2	122.01	120.71	120.96	25.91	25.66	25.79	22.45	22.22	22.28	320	87.19
3	121.68	120.14	120.96	25.94	25.76	25.84	22.42	22.18	22.34	377	87.45
4	†	†	†	†	†	†	†	†	†	†	†
5	121.96	121.02	121.51	26.15	25.91	25.99	22.55	22.40	22.47	283	87.85
6	121.57	121.17	121.59	26.10	26.03	26.06	22.60	22.51	22.57	132	87.97
7	*										
8	122.04	121.39	121.63	26.25	25.99	26.02	22.60	22.43	22.45	233	88.08
9	122.33	121.36	121.60	26.43	26.17	26.19	22.63	22.37	22.45	304	88.05
10	121.82	120.83	121.49	26.15	25.93	25.99	22.87	22.47	22.84	282	88.08
11	122.30	121.28	121.58	26.20	26.00	26.07	22.95	22.65	22.75	328	88.32
12	121.95	121.32	121.63	26.07	25.90	25.98	22.73	22.54	22.59	256	88.39
13	121.60	121.37	121.48	26.06	26.01	26.05	22.55	22.49	22.53	124	88.41
14	*										
15	122.13	121.29	121.72	26.15	26.08	26.10	22.62	22.47	22.52	227	88.37
16	123.73	121.82	123.12	26.42	26.12	26.33	22.77	22.40	22.64	437	88.58
17	123.91	122.34	122.82	26.56	26.32	26.35	22.68	22.45	22.51	382	88.61
18	123.22	122.52	123.00	26.51	26.25	26.49	22.64	22.46	22.57	222	88.64
19	122.93	122.01	122.18	26.53	26.38	26.40	22.59	22.42	22.44	255	88.44
20	122.16	121.80	121.87	26.34	26.24	26.26	22.35	22.26	22.30	111	88.38
21	*										
22	122.47	121.62	122.06	26.27	26.15	26.21	22.31	22.23	22.25	227	88.29
23	122.53	121.49	122.23	26.49	26.28	26.44	22.18	22.06	22.08	251	88.20
24	122.30	121.49	121.64	26.47	26.23	26.24	22.09	21.92	21.93	195	88.02
25	122.09	121.19	121.93	26.39	26.12	26.35	21.95	21.85	21.92	245	87.94
26	122.75	121.70	122.05	26.45	26.23	26.26	22.20	21.98	22.16	272	88.00
27	122.49	122.17	122.45	26.39	26.36	26.38	22.24	22.17	22.21	83	88.09
28	*										
29	123.38	122.16	123.15	26.64	26.34	26.58	22.43	22.25	22.37	256	88.19
30	126.18	123.58	125.97	27.10	26.64	27.09	22.80	22.48	22.75	674	88.41
31	127.18	125.47	126.14	27.21	26.89	26.92	22.85	22.63	22.70	556	88.38
High			126.14			27.09			22.84		88.64
Low			120.96			25.70			21.92		87.08

*Sunday †Holiday ‡000 omitted

Total 7,305

AUGUST, 1940

Date	Industrials			Railroads			Utilities			‡Daily Sales	40 Bonds
	High	Low	Close	High	Low	Close	High	Low	Close		
1	126.86	125.57	126.13	27.08	26.86	26.95	22.94	22.76	22.83	327	88.45
2	126.97	125.77	126.37	27.01	26.88	26.95	22.87	22.80	22.82	297	88.48
3	126.56	126.10	126.36	27.00	26.96	26.96	22.85	22.78	22.82	122	88.45
4	*	*	*	*	*	*	*	*	*	*	*
5	126.73	125.57	126.44	26.94	26.85	26.88	22.80	22.69	22.72	284	88.31
6	126.28	125.11	125.27	26.92	26.69	26.75	22.75	22.60	22.66	290	88.29
7	125.47	124.61	125.12	26.76	26.65	26.71	22.70	22.53	22.56	240	88.09
8	125.48	124.87	125.13	26.78	26.62	26.70	22.59	22.44	22.47	206	88.14
9	126.81	125.44	126.40	26.83	26.71	26.75	22.64	22.47	22.55	308	88.11
10	127.35	126.27	126.99	26.88	26.81	26.86	22.61	22.56	22.60	180	88.12
11	*	*	*	*	*	*	*	*	*	*	*
12	127.55	126.50	127.26	27.35	27.20	27.29	22.60	22.47	22.55	288	88.08
13	126.42	122.64	122.98	27.06	26.39	26.45	22.43	21.90	21.95	641	87.58
14	123.17	122.00	122.25	26.55	26.28	26.32	21.89	21.70	21.78	272	87.48
15	123.46	122.73	123.04	26.54	26.35	26.43	21.95	21.76	21.84	224	87.70
16	122.50	120.90	121.28	26.32	26.08	26.17	21.80	21.44	21.50	312	87.50
17	122.15	121.53	121.98	26.30	26.18	26.27	21.63	21.56	21.63	107	87.52
18	*	*	*	*	*	*	*	*	*	*	*
19	122.37	121.70	122.06	26.34	26.24	26.31	21.72	21.59	21.64	130	87.55
20	123.41	122.52	123.17	26.62	26.34	26.58	21.71	21.53	21.62	243	87.72
21	125.38	123.95	125.07	26.83	26.66	26.79	22.02	21.65	21.97	360	88.05
22	126.97	125.62	126.46	27.13	26.94	27.09	22.35	21.95	22.28	441	88.35
23	126.34	124.81	125.34	27.03	26.77	26.81	22.17	21.91	22.00	294	88.09
24	125.57	125.27	125.48	26.88	26.82	26.86	22.00	21.98	22.00	88	88.12
25	*	*	*	*	*	*	*	*	*	*	*
26	126.04	125.34	125.71	26.89	26.77	26.85	22.03	21.94	22.00	161	88.22
27	125.76	124.95	125.33	26.87	26.80	26.85	22.08	21.95	22.00	224	88.24
28	127.37	125.81	126.87	27.29	26.93	27.21	22.25	22.06	22.22	382	88.46
29	127.37	126.49	126.87	27.09	26.94	27.04	22.30	22.15	22.19	265	88.48
30	129.18	126.98	128.88	27.78	27.29	27.71	22.42	22.19	22.38	564	88.77
31	129.56	128.94	129.42	27.94	27.69	27.90	22.49	22.39	22.45	364	88.91
High			129.42			27.90			22.83		88.91
Low			121.28			26.17			21.50		87.48

*Sunday. †Holiday. ‡000 omitted.　　　　　　　　　　　　Total 7,615

SEPTEMBER, 1940

Date	Industrials			Railroads			Utilities			‡Daily Sales	40 Bonds
	High	Low	Close	High	Low	Close	High	Low	Close		
1	*	*	*	*	*	*	*	*	*	*	*
2	†	†	†	†	†	†	†	†	†	†	†
3	130.57	129.12	129.74	28.25	27.93	28.00	22.63	22.49	22.50	545	88.98
4	132.25	128.89	132.16	28.90	28.01	28.85	22.65	22.44	22.60	782	89.08
5	134.54	132.31	134.10	29.40	28.74	29.29	22.97	22.62	22.91	1,247	89.54
6	134.19	132.71	133.12	29.58	28.86	29.24	23.24	22.93	23.05	713	89.53
7	133.26	132.54	132.78	29.31	29.16	29.21	23.08	23.03	23.05	224	89.51
8	*	*	*	*	*	*	*	*	*	*	*
9	130.98	129.36	129.73	28.40	28.09	28.27	22.71	22.37	22.46	592	89.07
10	130.53	129.18	129.61	28.56	27.99	28.12	22.45	22.26	22.31	364	89.15
11	131.21	129.07	129.36	28.39	27.92	27.95	22.49	22.27	22.27	453	89.11
12	129.32	127.46	127.87	27.88	27.50	27.62	22.06	21.84	21.88	399	88.95
13	128.37	127.22	127.74	27.84	27.47	27.70	21.87	21.61	21.65	268	88.87
14	128.50	127.81	128.38	27.87	27.74	27.84	21.75	21.64	21.72	166	88.91
15	*	*	*	*	*	*	*	*	*	*	*
16	130.04	128.89	129.44	28.25	28.04	28.09	21.90	21.72	21.86	293	89.11
17	130.89	129.44	130.43	28.39	28.20	28.28	22.04	21.90	22.00	399	89.34
18	131.67	129.91	131.28	28.53	28.12	28.36	22.17	22.00	22.15	479	89.58
19	132.03	130.83	131.34	28.44	28.20	28.25	22.19	21.90	21.99	470	89.76
20	131.95	130.77	131.61	28.40	28.21	28.27	22.03	21.90	21.98	381	89.73
21	132.54	131.85	132.45	28.46	28.36	28.45	22.00	21.90	21.95	259	89.83
22	*	*	*	*	*	*	*	*	*	*	*
23	135.31	132.98	135.10	29.06	28.60	29.02	22.23	21.96	22.16	983	90.22
24	135.48	133.89	134.44	29.12	28.82	28.90	22.41	22.05	22.24	711	90.21
25	134.58	133.40	134.15	28.97	28.72	28.83	22.32	22.15	22.29	603	90.17
26	134.00	133.00	133.50	28.81	28.49	28.59	22.24	22.10	22.16	440	90.11
27	132.98	131.38	131.76	28.52	28.14	28.27	22.05	21.71	21.75	561	89.87
28	132.38	131.83	132.32	28.42	28.28	28.40	21.69	21.59	21.65	204	89.92
29	*	*	*	*	*	*	*	*	*	*	*
30	133.07	132.10	132.64	28.61	28.37	28.52	21.76	21.64	21.69	400	89.96
High			135.10			29.29			23.05		90.22
Low			127.74			27.62			21.65		88.87

*Sunday †Holiday ‡000 omitted　　　　　　　　　　　Total 11,940

OCTOBER, 1940

Date	Industrials			Railroads			Utilities			‡Daily Sales	40 Bonds
	High	Low	Close	High	Low	Close	High	Low	Close		
1	135.04	133.04	134.33	29.15	28.80	29.05	22.04	21.73	21.93	808	90.25
2	135.41	133.70	134.97	29.42	28.97	29.37	22.10	21.86	22.02	770	90.45
3	135.86	134.59	135.09	29.66	29.26	29.37	22.18	21.94	22.00	784	90.59
4	134.48	133.37	133.79	29.35	29.10	29.17	22.05	21.83	21.93	466	90.56
5	133.98	133.61	133.90	29.21	29.15	29.20	22.01	21.89	21.99	196	90.43
6	*	*	*	*	*	*	*	*	*	*	*
7	134.54	133.31	133.51	29.20	28.88	28.91	22.01	21.75	21.82	392	90.35
8	133.31	131.20	131.31	28.95	28.50	28.52	21.80	21.54	21.55	502	90.02
9	131.31	130.11	130.54	28.74	28.48	28.56	21.56	21.30	21.40	446	89.93
10	131.22	130.09	130.39	28.84	28.56	28.60	21.57	21.33	21.45	384	89.92
11	131.62	130.20	131.04	28.79	28.62	28.74	21.62	21.31	21.56	404	89.96
12	†	†	†	†	†	†	†	†	†	†	†
13	*										
14	131.49	130.32	130.73	28.67	28.52	28.57	21.68	21.44	21.52	404	89.98
15	131.63	129.47	131.48	28.72	28.33	28.64	21.95	21.40	21.92	547	89.94
16	132.69	131.05	131.97	28.83	28.61	28.71	22.27	21.89	22.19	663	90.13
17	132.84	131.20	132.49	28.82	28.64	28.80	22.37	21.93	22.32	649	90.13
18	132.90	131.92	132.45	28.99	28.70	28.96	22.47	22.17	22.33	590	90.21
19	132.58	131.99	132.18	28.93	28.85	28.89	22.25	22.15	22.20	216	90.17
20	*	*	*	*	*	*	*	*	*	*	*
21	132.28	131.13	131.37	28.83	28.61	28.68	22.22	21.88	21.94	373	90.22
22	132.44	131.04	131.98	28.85	28.64	28.77	22.28	21.91	22.07	536	90.16
23	132.79	131.26	132.40	29.04	28.70	28.92	22.34	22.03	22.29	807	90.15
24	132.29	131.06	131.36	28.90	28.63	28.65	22.31	22.06	22.13	540	89.97
25	131.71	130.38	131.16	28.62	28.44	28.57	22.31	22.02	22.27	519	89.88
26	132.47	131.48	132.26	28.73	28.60	28.65	22.59	22.38	22.52	418	89.96
27	*	*	*	*	*	*	*	*	*	*	*
28	132.27	130.96	131.77	28.55	28.37	28.46	22.45	22.20	22.33	471	89.82
29	132.80	131.66	132.19	28.60	28.42	28.52	22.60	22.30	22.49	586	89.76
30	133.43	131.90	132.98	29.01	28.65	28.90	22.81	22.50	22.74	674	89.87
31	135.10	133.06	134.61	29.48	29.00	29.30	23.09	22.71	23.00	1,344	90.13
High			135.09			29.37			23.00		90.59
Low			130.39			28.46			21.40		89.76

*Sunday. †Holiday. ‡(000) omitted.   Total 14,489

NOVEMBER, 1940

Date	Industrials			Railroads			Utilities			‡Daily Sales	40 Bonds
	High	Low	Close	High	Low	Close	High	Low	Close		
1	135.84	134.13	134.41	29.65	29.29	29.32	23.54	23.05	23.29	1,259	90.23
2	135.03	133.94	134.85	29.34	29.10	29.22	23.45	23.15	23.44	467	90.20
3	*	*	*	*	*	*	*	*	*	*	*
4	135.83	133.81	135.21	29.47	29.12	29.36	23.70	22.97	23.28	1,243	90.14
5	†	†	†	†	†	†	†	†	†	†	†
6	135.00	131.47	131.98	29.25	28.49	28.87	22.53	21.37	21.51	1,209	89.99
7	138.13	131.93	137.75	29.94	28.82	29.94	22.24	21.58	22.12	2,079	90.55
8	138.77	135.76	136.64	30.15	29.51	29.67	22.36	21.80	21.91	1,751	90.62
9	138.49	136.56	138.12	30.04	29.77	29.96	22.15	21.85	22.05	1,099	90.71
10	*	*	*	*	*	*	*	*	*	*	*
11	†	†	†	†	†	†	†	†	†	†	†
12	138.50	136.56	137.41	30.55	29.83	30.20	22.02	21.65	21.68	1,447	90.79
13	137.61	135.77	136.61	30.36	29.89	30.12	21.80	21.54	21.66	1,068	90.78
14	137.78	136.20	136.97	30.44	30.12	30.29	21.67	21.35	21.40	1,384	90.90
15	137.44	135.24	135.59	30.28	29.76	29.93	21.40	20.96	21.06	1,050	90.84
16	135.52	133.99	134.73	29.61	29.46	29.51	21.05	20.87	20.96	489	90.70
17	*	*	*	*	*	*	*	*	*	*	*
18	135.47	134.36	134.74	29.65	29.40	29.49	21.27	20.92	21.15	574	90.63
19	134.99	133.51	134.48	29.80	29.37	29.69	21.11	20.80	20.89	703	90.62
20	134.08	131.72	132.22	29.44	29.10	29.18	20.78	20.36	20.42	814	90.47
21	†	†	†	†	†	†	†	†	†	†	†
22	133.36	131.29	131.74	29.58	29.18	29.37	20.71	20.33	20.41	714	90.35
23	131.90	131.20	131.47	29.40	29.30	29.38	20.47	20.35	20.42	241	90.34
24	*	*	*	*	*	*	*	*	*	*	*
25	132.76	131.35	131.96	29.46	29.15	29.25	20.52	20.31	20.40	521	90.33
26	132.72	131.28	131.94	29.47	29.25	29.33	20.51	20.21	20.33	593	90.33
27	131.45	129.29	129.78	29.10	28.43	28.70	20.17	19.80	19.88	846	90.12
28	130.57	129.43	130.14	28.43	28.21	28.31	20.02	19.71	19.87	472	90.18
29	130.78	129.49	130.03	28.31	28.10	28.15	20.11	19.73	19.95	527	90.08
30	131.25	130.24	131.00	28.03	27.90	27.97	20.02	19.89	19.97	336	90.10
High			138.12			30.29			23.44		90.90
Low			129.78			27.97			19.87		89.99

*Sunday. †Holiday. ‡000 omitted.   Total 20,887

DECEMBER, 1940

Date	Industrials High	Low	Close	Railroads High	Low	Close	Utilities High	Low	Close	‡Daily Sales	40 Bonds
1 *											
2	131.96	130.54	130.93	28.20	27.95	28.03	20.24	19.94	20.11	479	90.14
3	131.23	130.25	130.78	28.10	27.85	28.00	20.37	20.02	20.25	451	90.14
4	131.21	129.99	130.75	27.89	27.75	27.78	20.40	20.10	20.27	651	90.16
5	130.81	129.54	129.96	27.81	27.61	27.67	20.36	20.17	20.25	598	90.14
6	130.86	129.62	130.33	27.75	27.46	27.57	20.39	20.05	20.15	536	90.18
7	131.43	130.48	131.29	27.81	27.57	27.80	20.19	20.05	20.14	404	90.22
8 *											
9	132.22	130.91	131.46	27.95	27.69	27.82	20.28	20.05	20.10	632	90.29
10	131.97	130.69	131.37	27.82	27.64	27.67	20.20	19.96	20.09	610	90.39
11	132.50	131.24	131.76	27.91	27.51	27.67	20.23	19.90	20.02	810	90.42
12	132.53	131.24	132.14	27.80	27.50	27.74	20.13	19.89	19.98	782	90.49
13	133.00	131.56	132.35	28.04	27.65	27.85	20.30	19.95	20.19	961	90.84
14	132.74	131.91	132.31	27.90	27.80	27.85	20.25	20.05	20.14	390	90.95
15 *											
16	132.28	130.74	131.07	27.85	27.59	27.62	20.19	19.84	19.93	660	91.01
17	131.34	130.09	130.53	27.66	27.39	27.48	19.99	19.75	19.81	702	90.95
18	130.92	129.31	129.42	27.55	27.24	27.25	19.89	19.65	19.68	781	90.83
19	129.43	128.19	128.84	27.30	27.04	27.09	19.65	19.41	19.51	792	90.59
20	129.66	128.19	128.87	27.35	27.00	27.14	19.70	19.39	19.56	832	90.60
21	129.32	128.45	128.89	27.27	27.05	27.17	19.63	19.50	19.59	421	90.57
22 *											
23	129.29	127.83	128.41	27.22	26.97	27.10	19.70	19.46	19.54	818	90.50
24	129.47	128.08	128.89	27.32	27.06	27.20	19.67	19.47	19.61	833	90.43
25 †	†	†	†	†	†	†	†	†	†	†	†
26	129.70	128.42	129.02	27.48	27.15	27.32	19.69	19.44	19.54	838	90.44
27	130.11	128.55	129.51	27.68	27.36	27.58	19.81	19.37	19.75	1,273	90.45
28	130.69	129.25	130.11	27.96	27.61	27.85	19.90	19.70	19.80	892	90.47
29 *											
30	131.85	130.18	131.04	28.15	27.88	27.99	20.00	19.60	19.79	1,178	90.73
31	131.86	130.40	131.13	28.25	27.88	28.13	19.94	19.63	19.85	1,073	90.90
High			132.35			28.13			20.27		91.01
Low			128.41			27.09			19.51		90.14

*Sunday. †Holiday. ‡000 omitted.

Total 18,397

JANUARY, 1941

Date	Industrials High	Low	Close	Railroads High	Low	Close	Utilities High	Low	Close	‡Daily Sales	40 Bonds
1	†	†	†	†	†	†	†	†	†	†	†
2	131.88	130.39	130.57	28.31	28.00	28.03	20.10	19.80	19.86	527	90.82
3	132.19	130.24	132.01	28.38	28.05	28.36	20.09	19.78	19.96	506	90.76
4	133.13	132.04	132.40	28.52	28.34	28.40	20.01	19.86	19.90	385	90.82
5 *											
6	133.68	132.42	132.83	28.60	28.33	28.40	20.12	19.89	20.05	721	90.93
7	133.50	132.19	133.02	28.49	28.24	28.39	20.11	20.00	20.07	526	91.04
8	133.74	132.35	133.02	28.96	28.38	28.78	20.16	20.01	20.08	644	91.26
9	133.94	132.79	133.39	29.68	28.91	29.65	20.29	20.04	20.21	860	91.78
10	134.27	133.14	133.59	29.95	29.60	29.73	20.60	20.32	20.55	752	91.87
11	133.81	133.27	133.49	29.80	29.59	29.65	20.60	20.50	20.53	361	91.95
12 *											
13	133.85	132.92	133.25	29.73	29.51	29.57	20.76	20.51	20.65	475	92.13
14	133.11	132.17	132.44	29.45	29.19	29.31	20.65	20.49	20.54	469	92.01
15	132.43	131.22	131.51	29.24	28.96	29.06	20.65	20.42	20.44	403	91.85
16	131.36	129.82	129.93	29.03	28.65	28.70	20.42	20.15	20.23	610	91.54
17	130.20	128.73	129.54	29.19	28.64	29.16	20.23	20.04	20.13	576	91.66
18	130.26	129.50	129.75	29.24	28.98	29.03	20.39	20.20	20.27	249	91.78
19 *											
20	129.99	128.78	129.24	29.04	28.78	28.85	20.25	20.08	20.15	379	91.65
21	129.51	127.83	128.20	29.25	28.75	28.90	20.19	19.96	20.04	578	91.68
22	129.03	127.98	128.65	29.35	28.96	29.28	20.32	20.00	20.18	523	91.98
23	129.15	127.74	128.34	29.70	29.41	29.48	20.43	20.15	20.27	466	91.95
24	128.92	127.68	128.52	29.58	29.33	29.48	20.44	20.18	20.35	413	91.92
25	129.08	128.73	128.96	29.72	29.50	29.65	20.51	20.35	20.48	219	92.02
26 *											
27	129.47	128.54	129.03	29.79	29.55	29.67	20.50	20.26	20.33	358	92.10
28	129.27	128.42	128.60	29.76	29.44	29.48	20.45	20.18	20.24	470	92.19
29	127.93	125.76	126.00	29.26	28.71	28.72	20.24	19.86	19.94	600	91.86
30	125.96	123.94	124.05	28.64	28.14	28.17	19.87	19.49	19.53	776	91.36
31	124.85	123.86	124.13	28.42	28.08	28.25	19.70	19.47	19.55	465	91.37
High			133.59			29.73			20.65		92.13
Low			124.05			28.03			19.53		90.76

*Sunday †Holiday ‡oco omitted

Total 13,313

FEBRUARY, 1941

Date	Industrials			Railroads			Utilities			‡Daily Sales	40 Bonds
1	124.02	122.99	123.28	28.26	28.04	28.10	19.70	19.53	19.56	308	91.07
2	*		*	*			*			*	
3	123.75	122.40	122.67	28.18	27.90	27.94	19.73	19.50	19.55	489	91.00
4	123.29	122.29	122.63	28.19	27.95	28.09	19.70	19.55	19.66	352	90.87
5	124.55	122.77	124.14	28.75	28.26	28.68	19.95	19.75	19.85	493	91.17
6	125.27	124.25	124.76	28.54	28.32	28.40	20.15	19.98	20.05	424	91.31
7	124.58	123.57	124.30	28.33	28.07	28.21	20.15	19.94	20.07	342	91.03
8	124.89	124.26	124.71	28.30	28.21	28.26	20.08	19.95	20.00	175	90.99
9	*		*	*			*			*	
10	125.13	123.93	124.19	28.40	28.23	28.28	20.00	19.80	19.89	295	91.00
11	123.80	122.51	122.61	28.21	27.91	27.92	19.85	19.60	19.61	416	90.69
12	†	†	†	†	†	†	†	†	†	†	†
13	122.06	120.57	121.10	27.79	27.45	27.56	19.61	19.19	19.28	644	90.33
14	120.74	117.57	117.66	27.47	26.53	26.54	19.25	18.84	18.85	925	89.82
15	118.89	117.88	118.55	26.78	26.50	26.65	19.00	18.79	18.95	404	89.81
16	*		*	*			*			*	
17	119.73	118.70	119.18	26.96	26.74	26.79	19.15	18.94	19.04	357	89.85
18	119.65	118.53	118.98	26.95	26.68	26.75	19.05	18.94	19.00	320	89.84
19	118.71	117.43	117.94	26.68	26.42	26.56	18.98	18.78	18.81	466	89.56
20	120.52	118.84	119.99	27.14	26.79	27.09	18.95	18.76	18.86	452	89.82
21	120.64	119.60	120.24	27.20	27.03	27.15	19.10	18.89	19.00	299	89.88
22	†	†	†	†	†	†	†	†	†	†	†
23	*		*	*			*			*	
24	121.74	120.44	121.49	27.42	27.07	27.35	19.12	18.90	19.05	350	90.00
25	122.77	121.60	122.40	27.50	27.29	27.43	19.24	19.07	19.15	360	90.11
26	122.90	121.99	122.39	27.64	27.41	27.52	19.25	19.08	19.16	380	90.17
27	122.22	121.22	121.87	27.34	27.13	27.28	19.18	18.99	19.02	310	90.10
28	122.69	121.60	121.97	27.51	27.33	27.43	19.70	18.97	19.62	410	90.19
High			124.76			28.68			20.07		91.31
Low			117.66			26.54			18.81		89.56

*Sunday †Holiday ‡000 omitted

Total 8,970

MARCH, 1941

Date	Industrials			Railroads			Utilities			‡Daily Sales	40 Bonds
1	122.06	121.73	121.86	27.62	27.57	27.58	19.65	19.44	19.53	141	90.28
2	*		*	*			*			*	
3	121.65	120.58	120.88	27.53	27.27	27.32	19.40	19.15	19.25	333	90.14
4	121.44	120.62	121.16	27.43	27.21	27.37	19.29	19.11	19.16	308	90.20
5	121.15	119.98	120.30	27.63	27.32	27.51	19.26	19.13	19.22	288	90.24
6	121.68	120.10	121.63	27.94	27.43	27.92	19.38	19.11	19.35	481	90.59
7	122.25	121.34	121.59	28.11	27.82	27.89	19.54	19.32	19.41	351	90.63
8	121.67	121.30	121.47	27.88	27.78	27.83	19.46	19.41	19.43	153	90.58
9	*		*	*			*			*	
10	123.71	121.48	123.64	28.20	27.81	28.18	19.67	19.42	19.57	621	90.75
11	124.20	123.03	123.27	28.28	27.98	28.00	19.78	19.55	19.58	509	90.79
12	124.04	122.73	123.19	28.14	27.94	27.96	19.70	19.50	19.59	462	90.76
13	123.27	122.35	122.56	28.07	27.90	27.92	19.65	19.41	19.46	340	90.70
14	123.12	122.42	122.75	28.09	27.94	28.01	19.74	19.43	19.65	321	90.83
15	123.54	122.63	123.40	28.10	28.02	28.09	19.80	19.65	19.74	265	90.95
16	*		*	*		*	*		*	*	
17	124.12	123.18	123.46	28.15	28.04	28.07	19.77	19.64	19.70	380	91.02
18	124.10	123.02	123.92	28.14	27.91	28.08	19.79	19.60	19.65	407	91.12
19	124.35	123.24	123.55	28.22	27.95	27.97	19.78	19.60	19.70	540	91.23
20	123.92	123.26	123.60	28.02	27.92	27.97	20.04	19.55	19.86	490	91.13
21	123.39	122.26	122.47	28.13	27.88	27.91	19.95	19.74	19.81	472	90.87
22	122.42	121.75	121.92	27.89	27.72	27.83	19.75	19.66	19.70	269	90.72
23	*		*	*			*			*	
24	122.62	121.82	122.39	28.07	27.85	28.02	19.70	19.55	19.62	370	90.74
25	123.00	121:98	122.78	28.40	28.05	28.37	19.76	19.52	19.70	448	90.90
26	123.21	122.55	122.70	28.82	28.51	28.62	19.80	19.45	19.59	534	91.00
27	123.75	122.84	123.33	28.84	28.56	28.66	19.74	19.48	19.59	551	91.22
28	123.70	122.47	122.68	28.69	28.40	28.45	19.62	19.37	19.46	443	91.22
29	122.67	122.22	122.37	28.62	28.46	28.55	19.53	19.39	19.49	209	91.35
30	*		*	*			*			*	
31	123.02	122.32	122.72	28.81	28.57	28.67	19.75	19.46	19.69	440	91.58
High			123.92			28.67			19.86		91.58
Low			120.30			27.32			19.16		90.14

*Sunday. †Holiday. ‡000 omitted.

Total 10,124

APRIL, 1941

Date	Industrials High	Low	Close	Railroads High	Low	Close	Utilities High	Low	Close	‡Daily Sales	40 Bonds
1	123.57	122.87	123.26	28.88	28.66	28.78	19.77	19.55	19.59	434	91.74
2	123.55	122.66	123.43	29.02	28.75	28.97	19.60	19.45	19.51	446	91.67
3	124.93	123.74	124.65	29.80	29.05	29.75	19.76	19.45	19.61	943	91.88
4	125.28	124.23	124.64	30.02	29.62	29.70	19.75	19.54	19.63	703	91.79
5	124.66	124.13	124.32	29.67	29.54	29.57	19.64	19.55	19.58	226	91.68
6	*			*			*			*	
7	124.11	123.36	123.64	29.43	29.17	29.32	19.62	19.46	19.50	362	91.44
8	122.94	121.00	121.21	29.05	28.36	28.40	19.46	19.19	19.23	736	90.86
9	120.72	119.56	119.85	28.45	28.12	28.33	19.13	18.87	18.98	585	90.69
10	120.45	119.40	119.66	28.40	28.03	28.11	19.00	18.84	18.89	357	90.73
11	†			†			†			†	
12	119.46	118.47	118.60	28.03	27.82	27.89	18.79	18.62	18.69	290	90.64
13	*			*			*			*	
14	119.05	118.01	118.89	28.12	27.82	28.06	18.74	18.56	18.62	459	90.61
15	119.61	118.24	118.59	28.27	27.91	27.95	18.71	18.51	18.56	453	90.51
16	119.01	117.65	118.60	28.22	27.94	28.22	18.57	18.44	18.49	437	90.53
17	118.75	117.78	118.16	28.50	28.14	28.27	18.55	18.37	18.45	401	90.69
18	117.74	116.11	116.28	28.16	27.73	27.75	18.42	18.10	18.12	485	90.60
19	116.44	115.80	116.15	27.79	27.58	27.72	18.21	18.15	18.17	230	90.57
20	*			*			*			*	
21	116.39	115.49	116.06	27.87	27.66	27.77	18.24	18.00	18.10	431	90.52
22	117.03	115.36	115.78	28.03	27.80	27.89	18.20	17.96	18.07	436	90.79
23	116.82	115.33	116.59	28.38	27.91	28.36	18.20	18.05	18.17	475	91.19
24	117.85	116.61	117.35	28.81	28.33	28.66	18.33	18.13	18.21	488	91.39
25	117.56	116.45	116.58	28.61	28.25	28.32	18.29	18.04	18.11	425	91.24
26	116.66	116.29	116.43	28.42	28.28	28.42	18.19	18.06	18.12	156	91.37
27	*			*			*			*	
28	116.86	115.96	116.63	28.61	28.45	28.57	18.23	18.03	18.07	311	91.47
29	117.48	116.45	116.73	28.95	28.59	28.76	18.27	17.99	18.15	512	91.65
30	116.78	115.36	115.54	28.70	28.37	28.40	18.14	17.87	17.90	406	91.36
High			124.65			29.75			19.63		91.88
Low			115.54			27.72			17.90		90.51

*Sunday. †Holiday.

Total 11,187

MAY, 1941

Date	Industrials High	Low	Close	Railroads High	Low	Close	Utilities High	Low	Close	‡Daily Sales	40 Bonds
1	115.64	114.78	115.30	28.45	28.24	28.33	17.91	17.76	17.84	310	91.45
2	116.34	115.41	115.72	28.70	28.40	28.51	17.90	17.74	17.80	401	91.64
3	115.76	115.33	115.55	28.71	28.51	28.68	17.88	17.75	17.85	198	91.74
4	*			*			*			*	
5	116.20	114.97	115.84	28.90	28.58	28.73	17.77	17.58	17.67	416	91.75
6	117.63	116.02	117.10	29.49	28.77	29.22	17.89	17.60	17.77	908	92.02
7	117.49	116.53	116.87	29.41	28.98	29.08	17.71	17.45	17.51	559	91.90
8	116.76	115.97	116.34	29.17	28.83	28.99	17.52	17.30	17.43	441	91.96
9	116.90	116.18	116.46	29.18	28.91	29.01	17.41	17.25	17.31	397	91.93
10	117.69	116.53	117.54	29.33	29.04	29.31	17.41	17.35	17.41	377	92.05
11	*			*			*			*	
12	117.83	115.85	117.14	29.27	28.83	28.88	17.56	17.36	17.46	436	91.99
13	117.93	116.88	117.21	29.07	28.71	28.73	17.56	17.30	17.38	432	91.83
14	117.36	116.67	117.01	28.64	28.17	28.27	17.50	17.40	17.44	322	91.61
15	117.37	115.54	115.73	28.39	27.74	27.77	17.47	17.29	17.32	496	91.31
16	116.38	115.36	115.86	27.99	27.79	27.94	17.41	17.29	17.35	287	91.36
17	116.26	115.96	116.11	27.87	27.75	27.82	17.34	17.20	17.22	141	91.35
18	*			*			*			*	
19	116.36	115.92	116.15	27.92	27.73	27.82	17.36	17.22	17.30	224	91.31
20	117.78	116.31	117.65	28.25	27.77	28.25	17.41	17.20	17.31	471	91.37
21	118.45	117.34	117.82	28.36	28.06	28.12	17.40	17.15	17.25	544	91.46
22	117.98	116.56	116.81	28.10	27.75	27.76	17.17	17.00	17.00	402	91.23
23	117.16	116.22	116.73	27.79	27.70	27.75	16.96	16.84	16.90	264	91.15
24	116.90	116.32	116.64	27.76	27.65	27.74	17.01	16.96	16.99	160	91.16
25	*			*			*			*	
26	116.28	115.51	115.73	27.67	27.47	27.54	16.90	16.75	16.85	301	91.01
27	116.31	115.33	115.95	27.69	27.51	27.65	16.89	16.75	16.82	386	91.06
28	116.50	115.56	116.16	27.75	27.41	27.65	16.93	16.71	16.85	344	91.04
29	116.80	115.84	116.23	27.66	27.45	27.57	17.01	16.86	16.95	345	91.12
30	†			†			†			†	
31	116.00	115.57	115.76	27.45	27.35	27.43	16.92	16.86	16.90	107	91.19
High			117.82			29.31			17.85		92.05
Low			115.30			27.43			16.82		91.01

*Sunday. †Holiday. ‡000 omitted

Total 9,669

JUNE, 1941

Date	Industrials			Railroads			Utilities			‡Daily Sales	40 Bonds
	High	Low	Close	High	Low	Close	High	Low	Close		
1	*	*	*	*	*	*	*	*	*	*	*
2	116.45	115.52	116.18	27.59	27.39	27.56	17.00	16.82	16.97	255	91.10
3	117.85	116.32	117.38	27.80	27.63	27.74	17.06	16.89	16.98	418	91.14
4	117.98	116.89	117.68	27.85	27.63	27.68	17.23	16.92	17.13	425	91.06
5	118.60	117.59	118.13	27.92	27.67	27.72	17.75	17.18	17.46	605	91.02
6	118.26	117.78	118.00	27.75	27.57	27.62	17.49	17.28	17.36	327	90.87
7	119.01	118.28	118.89	27.70	27.65	27.69	17.34	17.27	17.32	184	90.93
8	*	*	*	*	*	*	*	*	*	*	*
9	120.27	118.99	120.16	27.68	27.57	27.65	17.51	17.31	17.45	443	90.92
10	122.48	120.61	121.89	28.35	27.95	28.20	17.65	17.40	17.55	826	91.17
11	122.64	121.46	122.18	28.36	28.09	28.26	17.67	17.49	17.60	537	91.21
12	123.48	122.17	122.98	28.43	28.10	28.40	17.75	17.46	17.69	564	91.34
13	122.88	121.75	122.31	28.57	28.29	28.36	17.65	17.55	17.60	444	91.19
14	122.30	121.92	122.04	28.37	28.25	28.31	17.55	17.45	17.50	194	91.16
15	*	*	*	*	*	*	*	*	*	*	*
16	122.58	121.72	121.95	28.24	28.08	28.10	17.63	17.49	17.55	338	91.18
17	123.21	122.14	123.12	28.25	28.10	28.19	17.93	17.60	17.85	404	91.16
18	124.31	123.17	123.50	28.45	28.21	28.29	18.16	17.80	17.96	579	91.11
19	123.73	122.61	123.48	28.17	28.00	28.07	18.12	17.79	18.04	460	91.12
20	123.30	121.85	122.19	28.13	27.92	27.93	18.00	17.75	17.77	356	91.04
21	122.66	122.32	122.51	28.01	27.98	27.99	17.79	17.68	17.75	125	91.07
22	*	*	*	*	*	*	*	*	*	*	*
23	125.14	123.41	123.97	28.50	28.17	28.26	17.97	17.77	17.80	756	91.20
24	124.03	122.88	123.24	28.48	28.23	28.26	17.78	17.65	17.70	444	91.15
25	123.83	122.85	123.52	28.52	28.20	28.50	17.80	17.69	17.73	426	91.14
26	124.13	123.42	123.96	28.74	28.47	28.64	18.00	17.76	17.95	531	91.15
27	124.03	123.22	123.46	28.68	28.49	28.55	17.98	17.85	17.89	409	91.18
28	123.60	123.21	123.40	28.55	28.44	28.49	17.89	17.85	17.86	140	91.19
29	*	*	*	*	*	*	*	*	*	*	*
30	123.58	122.87	123.14	28.48	28.36	28.41	17.88	17.75	17.80	272	91.12
High			123.97			28.64			18.04		91.34
Low			116.18			27.56			16.97		90.87

*Sunday. †Holiday. ‡000 omitted.

Total 10,462

JULY, 1941

Date	Industrials			Railroads			Utilities			‡Daily Sales	40 Bonds
	High	Low	Close	High	Low	Close	High	Low	Close		
1	123.37	122.54	122.85	28.46	28.26	28.28	17.88	17.65	17.71	347	91.06
2	123.90	122.78	123.58	28.52	28.35	28.45	18.12	17.70	18.04	394	91.10
3	124.43	123.43	124.04	28.57	28.38	28.50	18.17	17.90	18.04	465	91.17
4	†	†	†	†	†	†	†	†	†	†	†
5	124.31	123.99	124.18	28.57	28.45	28.56	18.11	18.07	18.10	180	91.17
6	*	*	*	*	*	*	*	*	*	*	*
7	126.24	124.54	126.16	29.03	28.64	28.98	18.21	18.05	18.14	898	91.23
8	128.00	126.07	127.64	29.40	29.05	29.34	18.42	18.17	18.34	1,384	91.46
9	128.77	127.12	127.63	29.50	29.20	29.32	18.50	18.25	18.40	1,097	91.50
10	128.36	127.05	127.78	29.35	29.12	29.18	18.79	18.38	18.61	840	91.52
11	128.70	127.35	127.90	29.36	29.15	29.19	18.72	18.51	18.56	807	91.49
12	128.09	127.60	127.80	29.28	29.17	29.23	18.62	18.58	18.61	268	91.44
13	*	*	*	*	*	*	*	*	*	*	*
14	128.17	127.44	127.89	29.52	29.20	29.44	18.77	18.59	18.67	562	91.49
15	128.68	127.53	128.19	29.80	29.46	29.64	18.77	18.59	18.67	703	91.52
16	128.70	127.62	127.83	29.75	29.36	29.40	18.80	18.59	18.63	643	91.47
17	127.88	126.75	127.14	29.49	29.15	29.41	18.60	18.45	18.53	456	91.37
18	127.89	126.92	127.69	29.56	29.37	29.44	18.60	18.48	18.54	424	91.35
19	128.12	127.69	127.98	29.55	29.40	29.51	18.52	18.48	18.51	224	91.40
20	*	*	*	*	*	*	*	*	*	*	*
21	129.57	127.78	129.51	30.62	29.74	30.54	18.63	18.47	18.61	905	91.57
22	131.10	129.22	129.58	30.83	30.25	30.29	18.82	18.60	18.72	1,351	91.57
23	129.71	128.79	129.16	30.47	30.20	30.30	18.91	18.69	18.78	626	91.56
24	129.40	128.39	128.59	30.56	30.22	30.35	18.75	18.61	18.65	624	91.60
25	128.92	127.74	128.06	30.21	29.82	29.92	18.69	18.47	18.52	812	91.46
26	128.79	128.04	128.70	30.08	29.87	30.07	18.59	18.53	18.59	362	91.45
27	*	*	*	*	*	*	*	*	*	*	*
28	130.37	128.65	130.06	30.71	30.31	30.55	18.78	18.61	18.69	938	91.42
29	130.33	128.93	129.19	30.84	30.41	30.57	18.79	18.40	18.57	963	91.48
30	129.34	128.07	128.95	30.62	30.12	30.52	18.60	18.46	18.55	745	91.47
31	129.45	128.43	128.79	30.92	30.46	30.61	18.74	18.56	18.60	854	91.50
High			130.06			30.61			18.78		91.60
Low			122.85			28.28			17.71		91.06

*Sunday. †Holiday. ‡ 000 omitted

Total 17,872

AUGUST, 1941

Date	Industrials High	Low	Close	Railroads High	Low	Close	Utilities High	Low	Close	‡Daily Sales	40 Bonds
1	128.68	127.64	128.22	30.94	30.51	30.88	18.65	18.53	18.58	679	91.58
2	128.59	128.08	128.21	30.94	30.71	30.76	18.61	18.58	18.58	362	91.63
3	*	*	*	*	*	*	*	*	*	*	*
4	128.56	127.61	128.17	30.81	30.53	30.60	18.69	18.56	18.60	633	91.51
5	128.54	127.61	128.14	30.62	30.28	30.42	18.86	18.59	18.73	642	91.44
6	128.55	127.62	128.10	30.38	30.07	30.18	18.85	18.61	18.74	581	91.32
7	128.57	127.68	128.09	30.23	30.06	30.18	18.86	18.65	18.72	497	91.23
8	128.27	127.31	127.48	30.38	30.10	30.13	18.82	18.60	18.65	553	91.20
9	127.16	126.30	126.40	30.02	29.80	29.85	18.61	18.52	18.58	321	91.13
10	*	*	*	*	*	*	*	*	*	*	*
11	126.61	125.63	126.01	29.86	29.59	29.73	18.61	18.47	18.50	448	91.03
12	126.24	125.30	125.81	29.88	29.66	29.86	18.43	18.30	18.34	428	90.91
13	126.10	125.42	125.65	30.00	29.80	29.86	18.37	18.23	18.31	421	90.85
14	126.43	125.57	125.96	30.28	29.91	30.09	18.54	18.31	18.49	415	90.91
15	125.97	124.66	124.90	30.00	29.76	2.81	18.45	18.25	18.29	386	90.82
16	125.11	124.79	125.05	29.85	29.77	29.85	18.35	18.25	18.31	120	90.79
17	*	*	*	*	*	*	*	*	*	*	*
18	125.96	125.20	125.62	30.41	30.04	30.19	18.45	18.33	18.39	402	90.77
19	125.91	125.20	125.57	30.20	30.03	30.12	18.39	18.26	18.33	390	90.66
20	126.42	125.48	126.01	30.28	30.04	30.21	18.42	18.20	18.35	487	90.63
21	126.42	125.72	125.99	30.41	30.19	30.21	18.31	18.21	18.25	389	90.72
22	126.12	125.39	125.84	30.22	30.05	30.15	18.35	18.17	18.26	362	90.67
23	126.00	125.76	125.91	30.29	30.15	30.28	18.42	18.27	18.40	151	90.61
24	*	*	*	*	*	*	*	*	*	*	*
25	126.25	125.50	125.86	30.34	30.21	30.28	18.58	18.39	18.50	330	90.59
26	126.82	126.08	126.56	30.50	30.29	30.40	18.55	18.41	18.50	459	90.64
27	127.37	126.60	127.08	30.49	30.33	30.33	18.63	18.50	18.57	433	90.72
28	127.95	127.25	127.77	30.35	30.13	30.22	18.74	18.56	18.68	402	90.66
29	127.88	127.05	127.43	30.23	30.03	30.07	18.77	18.60	18.69	352	90.63
30	127.78	127.42	127.70	30.19	30.08	30.19	18.76	18.70	18.73	230	90.66
31	*	*	*	*	*	*	*	*	*	*	*
High			128.22			30.88			18.74		91.63
Low			124.90			29.73			18.25		90.59

*Sunday   †Holiday   ‡ 000 Omitted   Total 10,873

SEPTEMBER, 1941

Date	Industrials High	Low	Close	Railroads High	Low	Close	Utilities High	Low	Close	‡Daily Sales	40 Bonds
1	†	†	†	†	†	†	†	†	†	†	†
2	128.62	127.77	128.31	30.33	30.15	30.17	18.87	18.70	18.80	521	90.65
3	128.56	127.54	127.91	30.35	30.15	30.20	18.88	18.68	18.79	464	90.63
4	127.88	127.21	127.51	30.16	29.83	29.93	18.76	18.62	18.65	536	90.52
5	127.54	126.88	127.17	29.87	29.70	29.75	18.78	18.60	18.67	575	90.44
6	127.52	127.11	127.26	29.76	29.67	29.70	18.73	18.66	18.70	244	90.41
7	*	*	*	*	*	*	*	*	*	*	*
8	127.94	126.99	127.51	29.70	29.49	29.56	18.95	18.68	18.86	616	90.44
9	128.38	127.16	127.43	29.60	29.32	29.33	18.91	18.67	18.68	874	90.30
10	127.48	126.37	126.53	29.18	28.94	29.04	18.65	18.48	18.52	524	90.11
11	127.45	126.31	127.15	29.47	28.99	29.32	18.70	18.45	18.58	690	90.00
12	127.72	126.87	127.18	29.37	29.15	29.22	18.74	18.53	18.64	519	90.03
13	127.40	127.09	127.28	29.34	29.22	29.30	18.75	18.70	18.73	230	89.98
14	*	*	*	*	*	*	*	*	*	*	*
15	127.54	126.95	127.20	29.40	29.24	29.25	18.79	18.67	18.76	464	89.89
16	127.71	126.85	127.43	29.29	29.12	29.20	18.86	18.66	18.70	606	89.82
17	129.48	127.27	129.32	29.54	29.15	29.49	18.98	18.60	18.90	887	89.86
18	130.00	128.54	128.77	29.70	29.34	29.40	19.11	18.81	18.92	791	89.96
19	128.81	127.74	127.95	29.35	29.05	29.10	18.84	18.66	18.70	579	89.78
20	127.93	127.38	127.54	29.06	28.99	29.02	18.74	18.66	18.70	251	89.68
21	*	*	*	*	*	*	*	*	*	*	*
22	128.08	127.25	127.64	29.16	28.96	29.01	18.80	18.57	18.65	424	89.58
23	128.50	127.59	128.03	29.22	29.02	29.13	18.70	18.55	18.61	494	89.55
24	128.79	127.35	127.54	29.37	29.07	29.10	18.65	18.50	18.55	552	89.50
25	127.71	125.33	126.38	28.92	28.32	28.64	18.51	18.20	18.27	1,170	89.39
26	126.68	125.55	125.81	28.81	28.57	28.66	18.36	18.12	18.22	486	89.52
27	126.21	125.81	126.03	29.01	28.79	28.97	18.35	18.25	18.32	194	89.68
28	*	*	*	*	*	*	*	*	*	*	*
29	126.54	125.76	126.05	28.90	28.68	28.73	18.35	18.21	18.28	398	89.80
30	127.31	126.49	126.82	29.04	28.85	28.90	18.44	18.24	18.30	457	90.02
High			129.32			30.20			18.92		90.65
Low			125.81			28.64			18.22		89.39

*Sunday.   †Holiday.   ‡000 omitted   Total 13,546

OCTOBER, 1941

Date	Industrials High	Low	Close	Railroads High	Low	Close	Utilities High	Low	Close	‡Daily Sales	40 Bonds
1	127.20	126.39	126.85	28.95	28.79	28.83	18.41	18.22	18.27	369	90.14
2	127.06	126.08	126.15	28.95	28.80	28.90	18.35	18.24	18.28	465	90.34
3	126.44	125.57	126.06	29.03	28.85	29.02	18.37	18.25	18.33	424	90.42
4	126.46	125.95	126.10	29.20	29.00	29.16	18.46	18.39	18.45	214	90.63
5	*			*			*				
6	126.20	125.50	125.83	29.39	29.15	29.21	18.45	18.30	18.35	485	90.67
7	125.86	124.08	124.42	29.10	28.72	28.83	18.32	18.11	18.17	602	90.48
8	124.52	123.61	124.13	28.95	28.74	28.87	18.12	18.02	18.07	444	90.46
9	124.08	122.18	122.53	28.75	28.35	28.42	18.06	17.85	17.94	717	90.18
10	123.06	122.01	122.46	28.61	28.37	28.50	17.99	17.84	17.90	485	90.15
11	122.92	122.37	122.63	28.69	28.52	28.61	18.00	17.90	17.92	227	90.25
12	*			*			*			*	*
13	†	†	†	†	†	†	†	†	†	†	†
14	122.80	121.62	121.82	28.54	28.29	28.33	18.01	17.84	17.87	435	90.25
15	121.36	120.19	120.52	28.45	28.23	28.34	17.89	17.70	17.75	483	90.29
16	120.04	118.43	118.52	28.24	27.76	27.80	17.68	17.37	17.40	842	89.95
17	119.56	117.88	119.15	28.03	27.67	27.91	17.54	17.19	17.50	672	89.98
18	120.26	119.34	120.10	28.22	27.98	28.19	17.55	17.44	17.50	296	90.19
19	*			*			*			*	*
20	120.75	119.64	120.13	28.44	28.14	28.29	17.60	17.41	17.45	623	90.23
21	121.27	119.83	121.07	28.62	28.28	28.54	17.60	17.32	17.48	581	90.45
22	121.19	120.25	120.56	28.51	28.32	28.38	17.51	17.38	17.40	487	90.43
23	120.84	119.77	120.47	28.68	28.32	28.59	17.50	17.30	17.40	541	90.45
24	121.69	120.62	121.18	28.88	28.51	28.61	17.55	17.34	17.44	705	90.64
25	121.11	120.53	120.73	28.62	28.52	28.57	17.46	17.38	17.43	269	90.62
26	*			*			*			*	*
27	120.04	119.11	119.43	28.46	28.33	28.36	17.40	17.20	17.24	479	90.49
28	120.07	119.03	119.60	28.61	28.31	28.48	17.29	17.04	17.10	560	90.48
29	119.96	118.99	119.37	28.53	28.26	28.35	17.08	16.88	16.90	553	90.51
30	119.65	118.57	119.18	28.74	28.29	28.69	16.92	16.75	16.83	552	90.54
31	119.17	117.40	117.82	28.61	28.21	28.33	16.84	16.56	16.64	641	90.44
High			126.85			29.21			18.45		90.67
Low			117.82			27.80			16.64		89.95

*Sunday. †Holiday. ‡000 omitted.   Total 13,151

NOVEMBER, 1941

Date	Industrials High	Low	Close	Railroads High	Low	Close	Utilities High	Low	Close	‡Daily Sales	40 Bonds
1	118.36	117.71	118.11	28.35	28.22	28.32	16.67	16.51	16.58	240	90.45
2	*			*			*			*	*
3	119.32	118.11	118.87	28.62	28.34	28.58	16.73	16.50	16.65	597	90.56
4	†	†	†	†	†	†	†	†	†	†	†
5	120.34	118.84	119.85	29.38	28.58	29.14	16.75	16.48	16.60	919	90.87
6	119.80	118.41	118.84	28.81	28.25	28.51	16.63	16.34	16.40	668	90.67
7	118.84	117.64	118.33	28.68	28.21	28.48	16.45	16.14	16.22	701	90.66
8	118.50	117.87	118.26	28.38	28.20	28.27	16.24	16.15	16.21	289	90.52
9	*			*			*			†	†
10	118.41	117.24	117.45	28.24	27.90	27.94	16.22	15.95	16.02	627	90.35
11	†	†	†	†	†	†	†	†	†	†	†
12	117.16	115.03	115.44	27.67	27.15	27.36	15.86	15.47	15.52	1,018	90.13
13	116.34	114.91	115.67	27.38	27.12	27.24	15.75	15.45	15.52	831	90.04
14	117.30	115.75	116.81	27.66	27.31	27.46	15.81	15.50	15.70	840	90.19
15	117.15	116.43	116.72	27.58	27.44	27.51	15.85	15.74	15.76	354	90.24
16	*			*			*			*	*
17	117.03	115.69	116.20	27.70	27.43	27.59	15.94	15.67	15.79	628	90.16
18	116.62	115.20	115.87	27.67	27.44	27.61	15.85	15.59	15.71	679	90.11
19	116.90	115.47	116.68	27.96	27.53	27.92	15.90	15.58	15.81	802	90.12
20	†	†	†	†	†	†	†	†	†	†	†
21	117.50	116.07	117.05	28.54	27.95	28.42	15.93	15.66	15.82	854	90.38
22	117.43	116.76	117.04	28.41	28.22	28.29	15.96	15.76	15.87	364	90.45
23	*			*			*			*	*
24	118.19	116.89	117.30	28.57	28.27	28.35	16.05	15.80	15.84	820	90.52
25	117.60	116.38	116.96	28.35	28.04	28.10	16.03	15.75	15.80	835	90.43
26	116.98	115.61	115.93	28.15	27.84	27.89	15.91	15.65	15.74	851	90.40
27	116.49	115.00	115.64	27.45	27.22	27.33	15.76	15.52	15.69	811	90.25
28	115.68	114.10	114.66	27.23	26.81	26.94	15.80	15.48	15.56	868	90.04
29	114.78	113.98	114.23	27.04	26.87	26.96	15.65	15.50	15.63	451	90.10
30	*			*			*				
High			119.85			29.14			16.65		90.87
Low			114.23			26.94			15.52		90.04

*Sunday. †Holiday. ‡000 Omitted.   Total 15,047

DECEMBER, 1941

Date	Industrials			Railroads			Utilities			‡Daily Sales	40 Bonds
	High	Low	Close	High	Low	Close	High	Low	Close		
1	114.89	113.06	113.59	27.05	26.77	26.87	15.76	15.46	15.54	836	90.21
2	115.79	113.60	115.57	27.68	27.13	27.50	15.83	15.45	15.77	1,183	90.39
3	117.00	115.24	116.65	27.65	27.39	27.49	16.06	15.67	15.98	1,091	90.36
4	117.54	115.96	116.60	27.58	27.26	27.30	16.29	15.92	16.10	1,128	90.36
5	116.44	115.09	115.90	27.30	27.03	27.20	16.11	15.81	15.97	977	90.15
6	116.87	115.74	116.60	27.22	27.04	27.16	16.08	15.89	16.05	519	90.10
7	*	*	*	*	*	*	*	*	*		
8	115.46	111.53	112.52	26.75	25.49	25.65	15.73	15.07	15.16	2,028	88.76
9	112.73	107.56	109.27	25.48	23.81	24.45	15.14	14.15	14.37	2,555	87.43
10	109.76	106.87	109.01	24.48	23.64	24.25	14.35	13.88	14.12	2,088	87.28
11	111.73	108.38	110.91	24.79	24.16	24.73	14.53	14.05	14.36	1,401	87.70
12	111.76	109.53	110.58	24.99	24.48	24.61	14.45	14.08	14.17	1,119	87.78
13	111.81	110.18	110.73	24.97	24.58	24.71	14.18	13.99	14.06	629	87.91
14	*	*	*	*	*	*	*	*	*		
15	112.01	109.97	111.15	25.11	24.70	24.95	14.23	13.88	14.07	1,110	88.11
16	112.30	110.29	110.86	25.08	24.76	24.90	14.13	13.85	13.92	1,226	88.20
17	111.05	108.68	109.36	24.90	24.47	24.56	14.02	13.70	13.80	1,224	87.85
18	109.67	107.18	108.21	24.78	24.35	24.59	13.73	13.33	13.60	1,313	87.62
19	109.52	107.61	108.28	24.92	24.50	24.68	13.72	13.44	13.51	1,271	87.68
20	108.72	107.55	107.81	24.78	24.59	24.66	13.67	13.46	13.52	629	87.62
21	*	*	*	*	*	*	*	*	*		
22	108.83	106.23	106.59	24.78	24.35	24.38	13.82	13.45	13.55	1,460	87.59
23	107.21	105.57	106.34	24.59	24.28	24.46	13.75	13.39	13.66	1,420	87.39
24	107.56	105.52	106.67	24.71	24.32	24.56	13.90	13.48	13.79	1,375	87.31
25	†	†	†	†	†	†	†	†	†	†	†
26	107.86	105.92	106.95	24.71	24.29	24.38	13.85	13.50	13.56	1,411	87.21
27	108.23	106.19	107.54	24.66	24.31	24.61	13.75	13.40	13.57	1,162	87.13
28	*	*	*	*	*	*	*	*	*		
29	108.94	106.36	107.56	25.08	24.54	24.81	13.77	13.40	13.62	2,925	87.51
30	112.04	107.45	111.32	25.85	24.77	25.64	14.28	13.69	14.10	2,559	88.15
31	111.99	109.75	110.96	25.71	25.24	25.42	14.29	13.86	14.02	1,751	88.11
High			116.65			27.50			16.10		90.39
Low			106.34			24.25			13.51		87.13

*Sunday. †Holiday. ‡000 omitted   Total 36,390

JANUARY, 1942

Date	Industrials			Railroads			Utilities			‡Daily Sales	40 Bonds
	High	Low	Close	High	Low	Close	High	Low	Close		
1	†	†	†	†	†	†	†	†	†	†	†
2	113.00	110.07	112.77	26.70	25.58	26.66	14.34	14.05	14.32	582	88.36
3	114.03	113.07	113.75	27.28	26.97	27.15	14.75	14.60	14.70	517	88.80
4	*	*	*	*	*	*	*	*	*	*	*
5	114.76	113.20	114.22	27.64	27.27	27.44	14.96	14.70	14.92	721	89.11
6	114.96	113.22	113.99	27.63	27.14	27.27	15.10	14.82	14.94	802	89.20
7	113.93	112.62	113.10	27.63	27.05	27.54	14.94	14.80	14.84	630	89.49
8	112.91	111.20	111.55	27.59	27.22	27.34	14.86	14.46	14.51	533	89.64
9	111.97	110.45	111.02	27.98	27.43	27.74	14.70	14.45	14.60	655	89.80
10	111.25	110.31	110.54	27.76	27.59	27.66	14.60	14.47	14.50	293	89.78
11	*	*	*	*	*	*	*	*	*		
12	111.48	110.10	110.65	28.06	27.62	27.89	14.64	14.46	14.54	492	89.76
13	112.61	110.90	112.44	28.25	27.92	28.15	14.59	14.46	14.55	725	89.95
14	113.29	112.05	112.59	28.45	28.14	28.23	14.65	14.55	14.61	610	90.11
15	113.02	112.17	112.59	28.24	28.08	28.15	14.73	14.58	14.68	446	89.95
16	112.64	111.01	111.25	28.29	27.89	27.99	14.71	14.56	14.61	479	89.96
17	111.13	110.38	110.68	28.08	27.87	28.01	14.64	14.53	14.58	222	90.02
18	*	*	*	*	*	*	*	*	*		
19	111.34	109.98	110.81	28.30	27.88	28.24	14.59	14.45	14.50	429	90.15
20	111.21	110.24	110.45	28.67	28.27	28.42	14.49	14.35	14.39	487	90.32
21	110.12	108.71	109.06	28.43	27.81	28.04	14.36	14.05	14.10	584	90.03
22	109.16	108.30	108.94	28.48	28.14	28.23	14.15	14.01	14.05	430	90.22
23	109.44	108.39	109.12	28.40	28.06	28.35	14.17	14.00	14.07	432	90.31
24	109.55	109.10	109.42	28.79	28.48	28.71	14.12	14.03	14.05	292	90.41
25	*	*	*	*	*	*	*	*	*		
26	111.00	109.52	110.67	28.98	28.69	28.91	14.19	14.06	14.11	599	90.44
27	111.20	110.31	110.68	28.98	28.69	28.76	14.24	14.10	14.16	550	90.43
28	110.99	109.69	110.15	28.72	28.45	28.54	14.20	14.10	14.13	458	90.19
29	110.39	109.50	109.90	28.46	28.23	28.37	14.26	14.04	14.18	424	90.26
30	110.20	109.23	109.41	28.50	28.28	28.31	14.20	14.08	14.10	378	90.35
31	109.35	108.94	109.11	28.34	28.18	28.24	14.05	14.00	14.02	228	90.27
High			114.22			28.91			14.94		90.44
Low			108.94			26.66			14.02		88.36

*Sunday †Holiday ‡000 omitted   Total 12,998

FEBRUARY, 1942

Date	Industrials			Railroads			Utilities			‡Daily Sales	40 Bonds
	High	Low	Close	High	Low	Close	High	Low	Close		
1	*			*			*			*	*
2	109.68	109.08	109.47	29.34	28.16	28.29	14.17	14.03	14.09	330	90.25
3	110.29	109.38	109.99	28.36	28.20	28.30	14.31	14.16	14.26	374	90.29
4	111.04	109.91	110.80	28.73	28.41	28.68	14.33	14.22	14.27	502	90.45
5	110.97	110.09	110.44	29.05	28.71	29.01	14.30	14.22	14.25	440	90.52
6	110.53	109.30	109.47	28.95	28.50	28.56	14.21	14.05	14.09	432	90.44
7	109.61	109.23	109.56	28.79	28.48	28.73	14.14	14.06	14.10	223	90.54
8	*			*			*			*	*
9	108.92	107.92	108.12	28.49	28.14	28.20	14.15	14.04	14.08	404	90.36
10	107.81	106.21	106.75	28.02	27.34	27.56	13.97	13.80	13.84	640	89.97
11	107.19	106.00	106.51	27.40	27.04	27.19	13.95	13.75	13.82	416	89.87
12	†	†	†	†	†	†	†	†	†	†	†
13	107.01	106.12	106.73	27.35	27.03	27.30	13.85	13.75	13.80	319	89.98
14	107.40	106.94	107.30	27.70	27.53	27.69	13.89	13.81	13.85	167	90.07
15	*			*			*			*	*
16	107.96	106.70	107.31	27.86	27.43	27.60	13.95	13.83	13.90	376	89.92
17	107.05	105.20	105.40	27.68	27.26	27.28	13.82	13.66	13.67	389	89.81
18	105.70	104.67	105.35	27.55	27.20	27.50	13.60	13.48	13.53	344	89.78
19	106.03	104.93	105.57	27.67	27.52	27.58	13.63	13.55	13.59	345	89.98
20	105.57	104.78	105.10	27.66	27.40	27.56	13.62	13.51	13.54	326	90.08
21	105.55	104.74	105.38	27.72	27.59	27.69	13.59	13.55	13.58	214	90.15
22	*			*			*			*	*
23	†	†	†	†	†	†	†	†	†	†	†
24	106.73	105.54	106.00	27.90	27.62	27.72	13.68	13.59	13.63	394	90.18
25	106.30	105.41	105.64	27.75	27.53	27.58	13.70	13.53	13.57	339	90.07
26	106.24	105.40	105.88	27.60	27.19	27.58	13.64	13.50	13.59	353	90.06
27	106.93	106.16	106.58	27.65	27.43	27.49	13.68	13.46	13.56	363	90.15
28	106.95	106.52	106.79	27.55	27.42	27.52	13.61	13.54	13.60	234	90.24
High			110.80			29.01			14.27		90.54
Low			105.10			27.19			13.54		89.78

*Sunday †Holiday ‡000 omitted

MARCH, 1942

Date	Industrials			Railroads			Utilities			‡Daily Sales	40 Bonds
	High	Low	Close	High	Low	Close	High	Low	Close		
1	*			*			*			*	*
2	106.49	105.33	105.75	27.28	26.95	27.08	13.55	13.43	13.45	325	90.06
3	107.16	105.48	106.97	27.51	26.94	27.48	13.59	13.43	13.57	410	90.11
4	107.04	105.69	105.99	27.50	27.20	27.29	13.59	13.36	13.40	376	90.14
5	105.59	104.37	104.55	27.06	26.77	26.79	13.27	12.63	12.74	450	90.15
6	104.08	102.03	102.10	26.64	26.27	26.32	12.62	12.09	12.20	641	90.00
7	102.69	101.59	102.31	26.41	26.22	26.35	12.36	12.26	12.35	272	90.03
8	*			*			*			*	*
9	102.88	101.56	102.09	26.63	26.49	26.52	12.53	12.30	12.43	309	90.11
10	102.32	101.17	101.49	26.60	26.42	26.45	12.40	12.20	12.24	335	90.17
11	101.14	99.11	99.21	26.41	26.13	26.15	12.15	11.97	11.99	414	90.13
12	100.25	98.32	99.23	26.29	25.98	26.23	12.07	11.80	11.99	455	90.12
13	100.39	98.93	99.73	26.25	26.06	26.15	12.00	11.86	11.95	340	90.11
14	99.91	99.42	99.64	26.08	25.93	26.00	12.04	11.87	11.98	175	90.05
15	*			*			*			*	*
16	100.81	99.50	100.68	26.13	25.83	26.05	12.03	11.91	11.98	318	90.12
17	102.70	100.82	102.54	26.55	26.27	26.53	12.23	12.02	12.19	470	90.35
18	102.73	101.26	101.64	26.54	26.29	26.34	12.29	12.05	12.11	336	90.40
19	101.82	100.91	101.25	26.33	26.19	26.26	12.09	11.96	12.07	275	90.46
20	101.31	100.43	100.75	26.17	25.95	25.98	12.02	11.89	11.93	277	90.47
21	100.98	100.61	100.82	26.08	26.01	26.05	11.94	11.83	11.90	161	90.60
22	*			*			*			*	*
23	101.58	100.81	101.20	26.09	25.96	26.04	12.00	11.90	11.95	281	90.70
24	102.43	101.02	102.09	25.97	25.69	25.83	11.98	11.85	11.91	364	90.82
25	102.16	101.39	101.48	25.67	25.40	25.44	11.90	11.75	11.84	316	90.80
26	101.54	100.73	101.05	25.54	25.01	25.15	11.75	11.56	11.62	301	90.72
27	101.00	99.78	100.00	25.10	24.87	24.95	11.57	11.40	11.49	313	90.76
28	100.23	99.82	100.00	25.07	24.98	25.04	11.55	11.50	11.53	131	90.81
29	*			*			*			*	*
30	100.54	99.76	100.04	25.11	25.00	25.03	11.60	11.50	11.54	229	90.84
31	100.21	99.25	99.53	25.07	24.79	24.87	11.54	11.39	11.42	280	90.77
High			106.97			27.48			13.57		90.84
Low			99.21			24.87			11.42		90.00
									Total	8,554	

*Sunday. †Holiday. ‡000 omitted

APRIL, 1942

Date	Industrials			Railroads			Utilities			‡Daily Sales	40 Bonds
	High	Low	Close	High	Low	Close	High	Low	Close		
1	100.19	99.32	99.95	25.06	24.88	25.03	11.54	11.40	11.45	281	90.82
2	101.31	100.19	100.89	25.31	25.09	25.17	11.62	11.47	11.60	372	90.94
3	†	†	†	†	†	†	†	†	†	†	†
4	101.33	100.80	101.11	25.19	25.05	25.11	11.56	11.48	11.52	176	90.99
5	*										
6	102.69	101.05	102.50	25.58	25.34	25.50	11.62	11.53	11.58	335	91.00
7	102.75	101.73	101.89	25.69	25.52	25.60	11.63	11.55	11.60	308	91.01
8	101.97	100.89	101.23	25.62	25.41	25.43	11.64	11.54	11.58	295	91.03
9	100.56	99.51	99.69	25.26	25.04	25.06	11.50	11.39	11.39	349	90.68
10	100.15	99.31	99.74	25.11	24.94	25.07	11.38	11.20	11.21	295	90.68
11	99.66	99.37	99.45	25.15	25.07	25.11	11.25	11.18	11.20	143	90.67
12	*			*			*				*
13	99.78	99.25	99.44	25.11	25.01	25.06	11.20	11.08	11.16	238	90.63
14	99.21	97.77	97.89	24.91	24.31	24.34	11.10	10.95	10.95	557	90.21
15	98.75	97.50	98.06	24.49	24.25	24.41	11.00	10.87	10.97	348	90.33
16	98.46	97.61	97.87	24.33	24.12	24.23	11.00	10.90	10.95	263	90.40
17	97.61	95.80	96.05	24.21	23.75	23.92	10.90	10.81	10.82	418	90.36
18	97.29	96.44	96.92	24.18	24.02	24.11	10.91	10.80	10.87	185	90.40
19	*			*			*				*
20	97.47	96.63	97.25	24.20	24.05	24.17	10.95	10.80	10.89	240	90.41
21	98.02	97.16	97.51	24.58	24.38	24.52	10.96	10.80	10.87	270	90.49
22	97.64	96.79	97.20	24.51	24.38	24.45	10.94	10.83	10.87	257	90.46
23	96.91	94.84	94.98	24.32	24.00	24.03	10.82	10.67	10.70	429	90.37
24	94.80	93.59	94.13	23.83	23.62	23.72	10.76	10.62	10.65	390	90.28
25	94.47	93.82	94.31	23.77	23.68	23.76	10.68	10.62	10.66	156	90.34
26	*			*			*				†
27	94.89	93.66	93.89	24.10	23.79	23.86	10.74	10.57	10.60	281	90.36
28	93.69	92.69	92.92	23.96	23.80	23.85	10.77	10.56	10.58	313	90.36
29	95.18	92.74	94.65	24.28	23.85	24.25	10.89	10.62	10.83	412	90.47
30	95.76	94.71	95.35	24.36	24.22	24.30	11.05	10.84	10.97	279	90.48
High			102.50			25.60			11.60		91.03
Low			92.92			23.72			10.58		90.21

*Sunday.   †Holiday.   ‡000 Omitted

Total 7,588

MAY, 1942

Date	Industrials			Railroads			Utilities			†Daily Sales	40 Bonds
	High	Low	Close	High	Low	Close	High	Low	Close		
1	96.29	95.08	95.83	24.63	24.43	24.55	11.51	11.08	11.42	301	90.42
2	96.57	96.05	96.44	24.70	24.57	24.67	11.86	11.61	11.85	156	90.45
3	*			*			*				*
4	97.15	96.34	96.70	24.75	24.62	24.66	11.95	11.76	11.79	260	90.56
5	97.74	96.54	97.29	24.67	24.51	24.61	11.82	11.69	11.73	273	90.46
6	97.35	96.19	96.71	24.61	24.46	24.54	11.70	11.58	11.62	268	90.40
7	98.11	96.93	97.77	24.79	24.63	24.72	11.77	11.57	11.68	343	90.43
8	98.57	97.65	97.91	24.77	24.62	24.66	11.77	11.69	11.72	313	90.38
9	99.26	98.26	98.70	24.68	24.50	24.52	11.76	11.69	11.72	208	90.42
10	*			*			*				*
11	99.49	98.45	99.20	24.69	24.49	24.64	11.85	11.76	11.84	291	90.31
12	99.35	98.31	98.56	24.61	24.49	24.51	11.78	11.65	11.72	249	90.33
13	98.19	96.92	97.21	24.33	24.14	24.17	11.70	11.52	11.55	337	90.03
14	97.37	96.39	97.13	24.14	23.99	24.07	11.68	11.50	11.66	279	90.01
15	98.27	97.38	97.98	24.16	23.99	24.09	11.85	11.77	11.80	257	90.04
16	98.70	98.19	98.63	24.22	24.14	24.19	11.83	11.79	11.80	122	90.11
17	*			*			*				*
18	99.16	98.24	98.65	24.30	24.20	24.25	11.90	11.77	11.88	217	90.21
19	98.84	97.70	97.96	24.29	24.14	24.17	11.84	11.76	11.77	377	90.12
20	98.50	97.22	98.13	24.15	23.85	23.88	11.72	11.59	11.64	405	89.65
21	100.21	98.11	99.72	24.22	23.96	24.17	11.71	11.55	11.66	559	89.34
22	99.95	98.83	99.18	24.18	24.02	24.07	11.80	11.62	11.70	330	89.42
23	99.38	99.09	99.25	24.08	23.98	24.01	11.77	11.70	11.75	132	89.39
24	*			*			*				*
25	99.47	98.68	99.18	24.01	23.89	23.96	11.76	11.66	11.69	233	89.27
26	100.00	99.02	99.41	24.01	23.86	23.93	11.68	11.35	11.42	285	89.24
27	101.21	99.31	101.09	24.26	23.97	24.25	11.53	11.33	11.49	434	89.35
28	101.50	100.52	100.99	24.28	24.04	24.15	11.60	11.45	11.51	354	89.35
29	101.29	100.43	100.88	24.15	23.85	23.88	11.55	11.48	11.50	248	89.19
30	↓	↓	↓	↓	↓	↓	↓	↓	↓	↓	↓
31											
High			101.09			24.72			11.88		90.56
Low			95.83			23.88			11.42		89.19

*Sunday.   †Holiday.   ‡000 omitted

Total 7,231

JUNE, 1942

Date	Industrials High	Low	Close	Railroads High	Low	Close	Utilities High	Low	Close	‡Daily Sales	40 Bonds
1	101.84	100.96	101.37	23.80	23.57	23.59	11.55	11.41	11.49	309	88.71
2	101.67	100.93	101.30	23.43	23.21	23.31	11.58	11.40	11.48	316	88.36
3	102.33	101.01	102.15	23.39	23.17	23.37	11.54	11.37	11.48	334	88.45
4	103.87	102.25	103.61	23.46	23.25	23.35	11.85	11.52	11.80	524	88.63
5	105.26	103.60	104.41	23.66	23.42	23.54	12.15	11.85	12.06	486	88.73
6	104.82	104.08	104.52	23.56	23.45	23.48	12.28	12.13	12.25	193	88.80
7	*	*	*	*			*			*	*
8	105.86	104.71	105.55	23.87	23.54	23.85	12.49	12.26	12.39	356	88.86
9	106.34	104.83	105.09	23.97	23.68	23.70	12.45	12.24	12.35	398	88.76
10	104.90	103.70	104.19	23.67	23.54	23.57	12.28	12.15	12.21	313	88.54
11	104.69	103.94	104.49	23.50	23.34	23.41	12.26	12.15	12.23	282	88.40
12	104.32	103.27	103.77	23.48	23.35	23.40	12.15	12.06	12.10	220	88.43
13	104.23	103.71	104.08	23.45	23.41	23.45	12.15	12.10	12.15	109	88.40
14	*	*	*	*			*			*	*
15	104.54	103.99	104.41	23.49	23.38	23.45	12.21	12.09	12.14	263	88.32
16	104.94	104.18	104.51	23.56	23.42	23.47	12.17	12.09	12.10	279	88.30
17	106.38	104.68	106.29	23.64	23.44	23.63	12.18	12.06	12.11	388	88.33
18	106.63	105.49	105.70	23.71	23.55	23.56	12.19	12.06	12.13	352	88.36
19	105.52	104.55	104.77	23.72	23.53	23.59	12.05	11.95	12.00	288	88.28
20	104.71	104.32	104.42	23.60	23.53	23.57	12.00	11.97	11.99	127	88.21
21	*	*	*	*			*			*	*
22	103.52	102.11	102.77	23.48	23.32	23.43	11.87	11.75	11.79	313	88.12
23	103.44	102.73	103.03	23.66	23.51	23.59	11.83	11.73	11.78	208	88.33
24	103.24	102.43	102.67	23.58	23.48	23.51	11.75	11.63	11.65	244	88.25
25	103.06	101.94	102.71	23.57	23.39	23.50	11.65	11.56	11.60	245	88.39
26	103.09	102.27	102.54	23.87	23.59	23.78	11.71	11.56	11.67	289	88.55
27	102.76	102.33	102.67	23.91	23.78	23.89	11.72	11.70	11.71	113	88.60
28	*	*	*	*			*			*	*
29	103.57	102.68	103.17	24.32	23.85	24.17	11.76	11.68	11.74	262	88.84
30	103.61	102.93	103.34	24.32	24.01	24.17	11.75	11.69	11.73	248	88.82
High			106.29			24.17			12.39		88.86
Low			101.30			23.31			11.48		88.12

*Sunday. †Holiday. ‡000 omitted.   Total 7,466

JULY, 1942

Date	Industrials High	Low	Close	Railroads High	Low	Close	Utilities High	Low	Close	‡Daily Sales	40 Bonds
1	103 29	102.28	102.69	24.35	24.22	24.32	11.76	11.67	11.72	207	88.85
2	103.89	102.27	103.73	24.76	24.25	24.66	11.70	11.57	11.63	343	89.00
3	104.77	103.84	104.49	25.03	24.73	25.02	11.80	11.67	11.77	357	89.14
4	†	*	†	†	†	†	†	*	†	†	†
5	*			*			*			*	
6	106.30	104.92	106.10	25.32	25.03	25.24	11.86	11.75	11.80	420	89.25
7	106.34	105.32	105.76	25.39	25.12	25.22	11.85	11.77	11.81	332	89.23
8	108.01	105.48	107.94	25.50	25.11	25.46	11.95	11.80	11.95	577	89.33
9	109.26	107.60	108.75	25.91	25.50	25.80	12.26	12.00	12.18	844	89.46
10	108.99	107.68	108.66	25.77	25.57	25.70	12.20	12.03	12.12	435	89.35
11	109.03	108.55	108.70	25.77	25.67	25.70	12.11	12.05	12.09	154	89.34
12	*	*	*	*			*			*	
13	108.69	107.79	108.22	25.75	25.47	25.64	12.10	12.00	12.00	279	89.32
14	108.89	107.40	108.72	25.83	25.58	25.81	11.94	11.87	11.89	373	89.18
15	109.49	108.50	108.89	25.87	25.63	25.69	12.01	11.93	11.98	385	89.23
16	109.21	108.17	108.91	25.73	25.61	25.70	11.96	11.85	11.91	265	89.22
17	108.92	107.68	107.82	25.78	25.57	25.62	11.89	11.80	11.80	283	89.16
18	107.93	107.63	107.69	25.62	25.55	25.60	11.82	11.79	11.81	100	89.12
19	*			*			*			*	
20	108.26	107.50	107.98	25.83	25.62	25.79	11.89	11.81	11.86	214	89.14
21	108.68	107.94	108.36	25.97	25.80	25.87	11.85	11.75	11.79	284	89.17
22	108.94	107.69	108.03	26.35	25.97	26.08	11.80	11.74	11.77	436	89.24
23	107.88	106.45	106.65	26.06	25.80	25.87	11.74	11.56	11.59	333	89.19
24	106.65	105.84	106.37	26.04	25.83	26.01	11.55	11.47	11.51	262	89.19
25	106.69	106.36	106.53	26.19	26.08	26.19	11.47	11.47	11.47	116	89.19
26	*			*			*			*	
27	106.97	106.32	106.66	26.24	26.00	26.10	11.55	11.50	11.52	260	89.23
28	106.82	106.22	106.48	26.14	26.01	26.05	11.57	11.47	11.51	265	89.26
29	106.34	105.30	105.44	26.05	25.77	25.78	11.52	11.37	11.43	293	89.26
30	105.73	104.79	105.24	25.82	25.57	25.72	11.39	11.30	11.34	251	89.26
31	106.27	105.37	105.72	25.96	25.71	25.80	11.38	11.28	11.36	307	89.28
High			108.91			26.19			12.18		89.46
Low			102.69			24.32			11.34		88.85

*Sunday †Holiday ‡000 omitted   Total 8,375

AUGUST, 1942

Date	Industrials High	Low	Close	Railroads High	Low	Close	Utilities High	Low	Close	‡Daily Sales	40 Bonds
1	105.96	105.60	105.90	25.97	25.85	25.92	11.43	11.40	11.43	115	89.34
2*											
3	106.44	105.67	106.08	26.26	25.96	26.18	11.50	11.42	11.48	279	89.33
4	106.21	105.43	105.55	26.27	25.98	26.01	11.60	11.45	11.55	319	89.38
5	105.30	104.50	104.85	25.91	25.67	25.71	11.53	11.34	11.43	290	89.40
6	105.07	104.55	104.80	25.72	25.56	25.62	11.40	11.31	11.38	249	89.34
7	105.33	104.50	105.05	25.65	25.54	25.58	11.50	11.35	11.40	212	89.39
8	105.07	104.79	104.90	25.51	25.45	25.48	11.40	11.38	11.38	101	89.43
9*											
10	105.18	104.55	104.91	25.53	25.36	25.47	11.40	11.32	11.35	210	89.37
11	105.67	105.01	105.42	25.72	25.47	25.69	11.48	11.38	11.43	259	89.41
12	105.81	105.00	105.47	25.71	25.62	25.65	11.51	11.44	11.48	283	89.46
13	105.86	105.08	105.70	25.74	25.63	25.70	11.44	11.40	11.40	317	89.49
14	106.65	105.75	106.15	26.00	25.74	25.87	11.45	11.40	11.43	380	89.64
15	106.46	106.15	106.38	25.91	25.82	25.88	11.47	11.41	11.45	127	89.59
16*											
17	107.04	106.21	106.68	26.26	26.06	26.18	11.51	11.45	11.47	294	89.71
18	107.72	106.96	107.55	26.89	26.32	26.87	11.57	11.45	11.50	557	90.01
19	107.88	106.67	107.28	27.11	26.72	27.01	11.67	11.49	11.61	504	90.03
20	107.21	106.46	106.83	26.98	26.75	26.88	11.72	11.60	11.67	306	89.95
21	107.25	106.53	107.07	27.10	26.84	27.01	11.75	11.64	11.74	371	90.03
22	107.38	107.13	107.30	27.05	26.97	27.00	11.75	11.74	11.75	180	90.06
23*											
24	107.73	106.94	107.25	27.09	26.88	27.00	11.76	11.66	11.70	376	89.97
25	107.11	106.23	106.51	26.87	26.65	26.77	11.68	11.58	11.60	345	89.90
26	106.28	105.37	105.55	26.70	26.26	26.35	11.55	11.41	11.44	358	89.77
27	106.20	105.49	106.03	26.51	26.37	26.43	11.55	11.45	11.52	271	89.90
28	106.64	105.92	106.23	26.53	26.28	26.36	11.52	11.46	11.48	300	89.99
29	106.55	106.25	106.41	26.31	26.19	26.23	11.55	11.54	11.55	137	89.97
30*											
31	106.81	106.08	106.33	26.37	26.11	26.19	11.61	11.52	11.56	247	89.92
High			107.55			27.01			11.75		90.06
Low			104.80			25.47			11.35		89.33

*Sunday. †Holiday. ‡000 omitted. Total 7,387

SEPTEMBER, 1942

Date	Industrials High	Low	Close	Railroads High	Low	Close	Utilities High	Low	Close	‡Daily Sales	40 Bonds
1	106.52	105.76	106.28	26.25	26.01	26.19	11.60	11.50	11.56	291	89.89
2	106.68	106.05	106.49	26.16	25.93	26.00	11.71	11.54	11.66	270	89.96
3	106.50	106.07	106.34	26.19	26.01	26.09	11.75	11.59	11.71	283	90.06
4	106.70	106.09	106.39	26.33	26.09	26.25	11.67	11.54	11.57	309	90.06
5	106.82	106.54	106.68	26.53	26.32	26.51	11.57	11.56	11.57	145	90.07
6*											
7	†	†	†	†	†	†	†	†	†	†	†
8	107.88	106.76	107.62	26.83	26.48	26.73	11.59	11.47	11.52	399	90.14
9	107.80	106.97	107.26	26.76	26.61	26.67	11.60	11.44	11.56	362	90.19
10	107.17	106.30	106.38	26.70	26.47	26.62	11.64	11.48	11.51	345	90.17
11	106.36	105.58	106.03	26.59	26.41	26.51	11.50	11.35	11.39	376	90.11
12	106.25	106.06	106.20	26.54	26.44	26.44	11.40	11.37	11.37	116	90.12
13*											
14	106.32	105.92	106.15	26.64	26.45	26.52	11.42	11.35	11.38	313	90.09
15	106.82	106.17	106.49	26.58	26.47	26.48	11.83	11.57	11.75	386	90.16
16	106.93	106.19	106.66	26.55	26.29	26.47	11.83	11.67	11.77	378	90.20
17	106.96	106.44	106.66	26.87	26.61	26.79	11.81	11.67	11.73	408	90.24
18	107.59	106.72	107.47	26.88	26.73	26.83	11.82	11.62	11.75	417	90.23
19	107.41	107.16	107.22	26.84	26.73	26.81	11.79	11.73	11.77	178	90.27
20*											
21	107.45	107.01	107.27	26.85	26.68	26.75	11.80	11.62	11.70	320	90.25
22	107.83	107.16	107.59	26.99	26.72	26.96	11.90	11.68	11.82	522	90.27
23	108.40	107.45	108.27	27.23	26.82	27.08	11.92	11.72	11.82	701	90.33
24	109.42	108.18	109.11	27.45	27.14	27.41	12.15	11.88	12.07	851	90.38
25	109.72	108.89	109.37	27.68	27.31	27.52	12.24	12.06	12.18	680	90.33
26	109.54	109.07	109.32	27.42	27.24	27.28	12.15	12.08	12.12	227	90.25
27*											
28	109.98	109.29	109.56	27.49	27.16	27.30	12.18	12.01	12.15	402	90.28
29	109.75	109.01	109.24	27.72	27.20	27.52	12.37	12.17	12.30	427	90.38
30	109.37	108.70	109.11	27.49	27.20	27.34	12.30	12.23	12.27	342	90.35
High			109.56			27.52			12.30		90.38
Low			106.03			26.00			11.37		89.89

*Sunday. †Holiday. ‡000 omitted. Total 9,448

OCTOBER, 1942

Date	Industrials High	Low	Close	Railroads High	Low	Close	Utilities High	Low	Close	‡Daily Sales	40 Bonds
1	109.90	109.16	109.65	28.32	27.47	28.25	12.29	12.15	12.25	556	90.41
2	111.02	109.68	110.83	28.68	28.26	28.51	12.40	12.18	12.37	904	90.48
3	111.50	110.80	111.34	28.75	28.51	28.72	12.39	12.31	12.38	446	90.56
4	*			*			*			*	*
5	112.29	111.03	111.93	28.96	28.45	28.80	12.52	12.30	12.46	786	90.63
6	112.09	111.16	111.53	28.76	28.37	28.55	12.96	12.50	12.91	701	90.68
7	112.11	111.25	111.86	28.58	28.34	28.41	12.95	12.74	12.80	657	90.65
8	113.86	112.01	113.60	28.77	28.41	28.65	13.25	12.73	13.19	1,092	90.65
9	114.67	113.45	113.93	28.85	28.41	28.58	13.41	13.15	13.27	1,054	90.61
10	115.01	113.86	114.93	29.04	28.57	29.02	13.44	13.25	13.40	456	90.79
11	*			*			*			*	*
12	†	†	†	†	†	†	†	†	†	†	†
13	115.80	114.68	115.01	29.28	28.91	28.98	13.76	13.40	13.71	857	90.80
14	115.24	113.99	114.69	29.01	28.51	28.73	13.75	13.59	13.64	660	90.70
15	114.56	113.11	113.27	28.85	28.37	28.50	13.60	13.45	13.49	596	90.60
16	113.79	112.71	113.55	28.63	28.27	28.58	13.54	13.38	13.48	505	90.66
17	113.69	113.26	113.40	28.64	28.49	28.59	13.41	13.30	13.37	245	90.73
18	*			*			*			*	*
19	113.89	113.13	113.64	28.79	28.53	28.62	13.49	13.34	13.42	401	90.75
20	115.47	114.17	115.22	28.75	28.47	28.57	13.54	13.36	13.45	667	90.72
21	116.01	114.61	115.09	28.71	28.43	28.49	13.51	13.33	13.38	701	90.98
22	115.22	114.15	114.94	28.68	28.40	28.64	13.65	13.41	13.60	554	91.08
23	115.52	114.45	114.88	29.06	28.62	28.72	13.67	13.54	13.60	727	91.20
24	115.28	114.71	115.01	28.83	28.66	28.72	13.66	13.59	13.62	290	91.26
25	*			*			*			*	*
26	115.61	114.74	115.29	28.94	28.72	28.84	14.03	13.60	13.98	629	91.17
27	115.06	113.50	113.86	28.90	28.42	28.70	13.93	13.66	13.77	629	90.99
28	113.87	112.57	113.11	28.78	28.44	28.64	13.76	13.52	13.59	497	90.94
29	113.47	112.59	113.13	28.67	28.46	28.57	13.78	13.60	13.75	455	90.95
30	113.64	112.80	113.50	28.69	28.41	28.64	14.01	13.68	13.98	517	90.96
31	114.23	113.60	114.07	28.94	28.72	28.85	14.21	14.00	14.16	350	91.06
High			115.29			29.02			14.16		91.26
Low			109.65			28.25			12.25		90.41

*Sunday. †Holiday. ‡000 omitted. Total 15,932

NOVEMBER, 1942

Date	Industrials High	Low	Close	Railroads High	Low	Close	Utilities High	Low	Close	‡Daily Sales	40 Bonds
1	*			*			*			*	*
2	115.09	114.02	114.68	29.34	28.98	29.28	14.37	14.07	14.26	757	91.13
3	†	†	†	†	†	†	†	†	†	†	†
4	115.55	114.29	114.56	29.45	29.10	29.20	14.45	14.03	14.05	772	91.13
5	115.29	114.23	114.87	29.30	29.01	29.09	14.16	13.89	14.06	598	91.19
6	116.25	114.80	116.12	29.33	29.03	29.21	14.31	14.09	14.24	857	91.22
7	117.15	116.27	116.92	29.30	29.05	29.16	14.44	14.21	14.39	553	91.15
8	*			*			*			*	*
9	118.18	116.61	117.30	29.22	28.51	28.73	14.65	14.31	14.51	1,208	90.85
10	117.14	115.96	116.30	28.68	28.30	28.46	14.68	14.44	14.60	772	90.71
11	†	†	†	†	†	†	†	†	†	†	†
12	117.14	115.63	116.46	28.66	28.22	28.38	14.67	14.45	14.59	705	90.70
13	116.76	115.80	116.26	28.46	28.16	28.22	14.64	14.39	14.46	666	90.80
14	116.41	115.76	116.24	28.32	28.15	28.27	14.52	14.39	14.44	261	90.85
15	*			*			*			*	*
16	116.32	115.41	115.70	28.26	27.95	28.00	14.46	14.27	14.28	521	90.84
17	116.24	114.42	114.53	28.08	27.69	27.75	14.37	14.01	14.04	666	90.62
18	115.08	114.12	114.64	27.94	27.55	27.80	14.02	13.75	13.85	514	90.53
19	114.95	114.24	114.55	27.95	27.58	27.74	13.98	13.76	13.89	503	90.53
20	115.67	114.37	115.27	28.12	27.78	27.93	14.00	13.84	13.98	659	90.54
21	115.65	115.09	115.38	28.06	27.91	27.95	14.06	13.90	13.96	311	90.57
22	*			*			*			*	*
23	115.27	114.03	114.46	27.86	27.47	27.49	14.06	13.79	13.86	632	90.35
24	114.61	113.46	114.10	27.52	27.17	27.39	14.05	13.72	13.97	636	90.03
25	114.66	113.55	114.13	27.68	27.37	27.52	14.15	13.91	14.03	565	89.98
26	†	†	†	†	†	†	†	†	†	†	†
27	115.12	114.08	114.86	27.29	27.06	27.16	14.10	13.93	14.01	525	90.02
28	115.11	114.62	114.95	27.19	27.06	27.11	14.04	13.88	13.97	283	90.07
29	*			*			*			*	*
30	115.03	114.01	114.50	27.08	26.77	26.88	14.05	13.83	14.00	472	89.99
High			117.30			29.28			14.60		91.22
Low			114.10			26.88			13.85		89.98

*Sunday. †Holiday. (‡000 omitted.) Total 13,436

DECEMBER, 1942

Date	Industrials High	Low	Close	Railroads High	Low	Close	Utilities High	Low	Close	‡Daily Sales	40 Bonds
1	115.12	114.08	114.61	26.93	26.75	26.84	13.99	13.85	13.90	561	89.95
2	115.61	114.43	115.16	26.98	26.69	26.95	13.93	13.80	13.88	540	90.09
3	115.87	114.76	115.19	27.17	26.91	26.99	13.93	13.73	13.81	630	90.30
4	115.42	114.41	115.02	27.11	26.76	26.82	13.85	13.68	13.75	530	90.36
5	115.47	114.90	115.24	26.97	26.75	26.82	13.85	13.71	13.75	246	90.33
6 *											
7	115.57	114.71	115.00	26.66	26.35	26.43	13.79	13.58	13.66	495	89.94
8	116.05	115.03	115.76	26.58	26.27	26.41	13.77	13.56	13.69	618	89.96
9	116.38	115.35	115.93	26.50	26.22	26.38	13.80	13.61	13.71	616	89.87
10	116.38	115.41	116.00	26.37	26.15	26.20	13.79	13.61	13.70	574	89.83
11	116.55	115.16	115.70	26.32	26.11	26.20	13.85	13.62	13.74	641	89.80
12	116.01	115.38	115.82	26.25	26.12	26.16	13.82	13.70	13.78	341	89.84
13 *											
14	116.13	115.21	115.83	26.26	25.96	26.03	14.02	13.69	13.93	685	89.84
15	116.64	115.65	116.31	26.23	25.97	26.11	14.08	13.83	14.00	696	89.88
16	117.38	116.08	117.06	26.59	26.18	26.51	14.28	13.98	14.20	906	90.01
17	119.07	116.60	118.68	27.26	26.62	27.22	14.66	14.21	14.56	1,308	90.24
18	119.76	118.41	118.97	27.54	27.19	27.29	14.57	14.25	14.35	1,088	90.16
19	118.99	118.40	118.75	27.41	27.21	27.36	14.45	14.17	14.34	372	90.12
20 *											
21	119.35	118.12	118.66	27.59	27.28	27.43	14.38	14.10	14.17	771	90.07
22	119.23	118.09	118.49	27.49	27.14	27.27	14.28	14.00	14.09	780	90.05
23	119.58	118.24	119.07	27.33	27.00	27.18	14.17	13.93	14.02	924	90.13
24	119.67	118.56	119.27	27.28	27.01	27.13	14.15	13.90	14.08	804	90.14
25 †											
26	119.91	119.21	119.71	27.26	27.10	27.21	14.17	13.97	14.11	371	90.18
27 *											
28	119.96	118.22	118.50	27.25	26.81	26.92	14.45	14.03	14.18	1,202	90.06
29	118.95	117.30	118.40	27.02	26.62	26.88	14.35	14.02	14.22	1,441	90.00
30	119.83	118.28	119.56	27.45	26.86	27.33	14.45	14.09	14.35	1,122	90.27
31	120.19	119.08	119.40	27.58	27.27	27.39	14.58	14.26	14.54	1,051	90.55
High			119.71			27.39			14.56		90.55
Low			114.61			26.03			13.66		89.80

*Sundays. †Holidays. ‡000 omitted. Total 19,313

JANUARY, 1943

Date	Industrials High	Low	Close	Railroads High	Low	Close	Utilities High	Low	Close	‡Daily Sales	40 Bonds
1 †											
2	120.10	119.48	119.93	27.61	27.47	27.59	14.70	14.56	14.69	260	90.66
3 *											
4	120.82	119.75	120.25	28.26	27.90	28.22	14.93	14.71	14.80	620	90.68
5	120.62	119.50	119.70	28.32	27.92	28.03	14.88	14.66	14.74	674	90.81
6	120.31	119.40	119.66	28.19	27.90	28.14	14.87	14.72	14.81	554	90.79
7	119.95	118.84	119.37	28.16	27.88	28.04	15.10	14.78	15.10	711	91.01
8	119.71	118.92	119.26	28.18	27.96	28.08	15.51	15.15	15.48	801	91.11
9	119.58	119.12	119.47	28.17	28.00	28.06	15.54	15.43	15.50	438	91.19
10 *											
11	120.41	119.51	119.95	28.35	28.09	28.15	15.52	15.21	15.30	811	91.30
12	120.52	119.54	119.98	28.19	27.95	27.99	15.36	15.10	15.23	633	91.43
13	120.59	119.80	120.25	28.19	27.97	28.13	15.41	15.25	15.37	633	91.53
14	121.03	120.09	120.79	28.41	28.08	28.40	15.50	15.29	15.48	682	91.67
15	121.84	120.86	121.58	29.03	28.50	29.03	15.66	15.43	15.57	998	91.77
16	121.91	121.28	121.60	29.16	28.95	28.96	15.65	15.55	15.58	505	91.82
17 *											
18	121.93	121.24	121.56	29.22	28.89	29.08	15.75	15.55	15.65	708	91.79
19	121.59	120.25	120.48	29.16	28.63	28.70	15.68	15.43	15.48	771	91.71
20	120.86	119.71	120.55	28.79	28.47	28.75	15.53	15.34	15.46	518	91.81
21	122.00	120.63	121.79	28.97	28.71	28.93	15.77	15.53	15.70	810	92.13
22	122.92	121.50	121.99	29.11	28.76	28.87	15.88	15.68	15.77	883	92.27
23	122.49	121.94	122.38	29.08	28.89	29.08	15.80	15.71	15.79	322	92.39
24 *											
25	123.94	122.30	123.74	29.22	29.03	29.14	15.91	15.74	15.88	804	92.36
26	124.59	123.63	124.31	29.23	28.97	29.04	16.15	15.80	16.06	1,043	92.24
27	124.47	122.92	124.08	29.00	28.71	28.87	16.40	15.91	16.38	1,027	92.29
28	124.57	123.41	124.38	29.24	28.69	29.15	16.48	16.23	16.36	988	92.37
29	125.71	124.23	125.41	29.34	28.99	29.22	16.64	16.40	16.59	1,226	92.45
30	125.84	125.18	125.58	29.29	29.14	29.21	16.70	16.55	16.60	612	92.46
31 *											
High			125.58			29.22			16.60		92.46
Low			119.26			27.59			14.69		90.66

*Sundays. †Holiday. ‡000 omitted. Total 18,032

FEBRUARY, 1943

Date	Industrials High	Low	Close	Railroads High	Low	Close	Utilities High	Low	Close	‡Daily Sales	40 Bonds
1	126.15	124.87	125.86	29.57	29.11	29.55	16.70	16.51	16.64	1,087	92.52
2	126.38	125.51	125.88	29.68	29.40	29.51	16.76	16.57	16.62	1,053	92.55
3	126.10	124.84	125.56	29.45	29.14	29.24	16.65	16.40	16.49	826	92.46
4	125.57	124.69	125.07	29.37	29.00	29.20	16.51	16.31	16.40	795	92.35
5	126.00	124.71	125.75	29.25	29.03	29.18	16.53	16.26	16.42	875	92.39
6	126.17	125.39	125.81	29.24	29.07	29.08	16.44	16.36	16.40	500	92.37
7 *											
8	126.10	125.19	125.57	29.17	28.95	29.06	16.46	16.26	16.36	727	92.33
9	126.59	125.38	126.30	29.17	28.95	29.11	16.47	16.26	16.40	924	92.45
10	127.55	126.21	127.01	29.38	29.08	29.26	16.72	16.40	16.65	1,495	92.61
11	127.54	126.53	127.09	29.38	29.01	29.08	16.85	16.57	16.76	1,408	92.69
12 †	†	†	†	†	†	†	†	†	†	†	†
13	127.98	127.11	127.83	29.26	29.04	29.21	16.99	16.80	16.95	794	92.77
14 *											
15	129.15	128.00	128.60	29.55	29.14	29.30	17.37	17.02	17.27	1,836	92.87
16	128.88	127.70	128.31	29.36	29.12	29.27	17.35	16.99	17.23	1,182	92.84
17	128.88	127.86	128.41	29.64	29.22	29.53	17.34	17.10	17.19	1,097	93.00
18	128.29	126.82	127.06	29.52	29.10	29.23	17.17	16.87	16.95	1,040	93.00
19	127.25	125.82	126.67	29.54	28.99	29.51	16.94	16.71	16.89	897	92.96
20	127.89	126.62	127.80	29.94	29.51	29.92	17.05	16.90	17.02	620	93.02
21 *											
22 †	†	†	†	†	†	†	†	†	†	†	†
23	129.06	127.34	128.78	30.63	29.76	30.54	17.15	16.93	17.12	1,427	93.14
24	130.00	128.39	129.58	31.38	30.55	31.24	17.27	17.00	17.10	1,691	93.39
25	130.43	129.28	130.04	32.03	31.32	31.78	17.50	17.15	17.40	1,777	93.68
26	130.25	129.20	129.71	32.03	31.55	31.83	17.52	17.30	17.42	1,438	93.77
27	130.25	129.61	130.11	32.12	31.83	32.06	17.55	17.40	17.48	943	94.02
28 *											
High			130.11			32.06			17.48		94.02
Low			125.07			29.06			16.36		92.33

*Sundays. †Holidays. ‡000 omitted. Total 24,432

MARCH, 1943

Date	Industrials High	Low	Close	Railroads High	Low	Close	Utilities High	Low	Close	‡Daily Sales	40 Bonds
1	130.61	129.13	129.44	32.37	31.59	31.70	17.54	17.19	17.35	2,001	94.07
2	129.18	127.91	128.60	31.91	31.24	31.74	17.30	17.05	17.22	1,328	94.05
3	130.20	128.51	130.03	32.75	31.80	32.62	17.60	17.19	17.47	2,018	94.16
4	131.20	129.97	130.38	33.01	32.51	32.56	17.64	17.40	17.47	2,007	94.12
5	130.93	129.75	130.61	32.48	32.11	32.29	17.57	17.36	17.47	1,209	94.04
6	130.98	130.38	130.74	32.48	32.24	32.37	17.51	17.36	17.47	788	94.06
7 *											
8	131.23	130.14	130.56	32.53	32.14	32.29	17.66	17.39	17.50	1,246	94.16
9	130.52	128.68	129.80	32.27	31.53	32.06	17.53	17.25	17.41	1,420	94.21
10	129.76	128.49	129.16	32.08	31.69	31.89	17.40	17.20	17.31	929	94.16
11	130.74	128.95	130.48	32.37	31.64	32.15	17.66	17.22	17.61	1,430	94.23
12	131.39	130.07	130.73	32.96	32.30	32.78	17.92	17.56	17.85	1,972	94.28
13	131.11	130.55	130.73	32.93	32.59	32.69	17.99	17.79	17.90	830	94.29
14 *											
15	130.95	130.03	130.64	32.96	32.17	32.58	17.87	17.64	17.69	1,365	94.27
16	130.83	129.91	130.33	32.75	32.31	32.43	17.70	17.50	17.53	1,027	94.33
17	130.22	128.86	129.49	32.45	31.81	32.09	17.53	17.15	17.32	1,268	94.22
18	130.00	129.07	129.66	32.22	31.87	32.09	17.49	17.27	17.43	866	94.26
19	129.95	129.09	129.25	32.28	31.55	31.61	17.50	17.29	17.34	1,065	94.17
20	129.30	128.79	129.13	31.75	31.35	31.71	17.31	17.20	17.30	484	94.22
21 *											
22	129.65	128.67	129.44	32.20	31.66	32.14	17.41	17.22	17.32	851	94.30
23	130.47	129.46	129.98	32.43	32.11	32.19	17.52	17.20	17.31	1,192	94.39
24	131.00	129.74	130.62	32.30	31.97	32.12	17.41	17.19	17.32	1,161	94.53
25	133.30	130.91	133.22	32.75	32.15	32.70	17.66	17.35	17.62	2,121	94.75
26	134.51	133.21	133.96	33.26	32.75	33.06	18.00	17.66	17.90	2,143	95.10
27	134.83	133.89	134.56	33.18	32.88	33.00	17.98	17.85	17.91	798	95.12
28 *											
29	136.41	134.75	136.10	33.94	33.19	33.79	18.05	17.78	18.00	1,999	95.31
30	137.20	135.52	136.82	34.08	33.44	33.88	18.40	17.95	18.35	1,938	95.41
31	137.07	135.86	136.57	34.22	33.56	34.08	18.45	18.12	18.28	1,540	95.48
High			136.82			34.08			18.35		95.48
Low			128.60			31.61			17.22		94.04

*Sundays. †Holidays. ‡000 omitted. Total 36,996

APRIL, 1943

Date	Industrials High	Low	Close	Railroads High	Low	Close	Utilities High	Low	Close	‡Daily sales	40 Bonds
1	137.04	135.94	136.56	35.04	34.01	34.83	18.44	18.18	18.26	1,742	95.67
2	136.44	135.08	135.67	35.14	34.37	34.78	18.55	18.05	18.47	1,659	95.59
3	135.79	135.25	135.60	34.93	34.69	34.84	18.75	18.51	18.73	836	95.58
4 *											
5	137.10	135.62	136.44	36.08	34.99	35.91	19.16	18.74	19.01	2,648	95.70
6	137.45	136.09	136.93	36.19	35.58	35.87	19.15	18.81	18.90	2,464	95.75
7	136.73	135.14	136.00	35.90	35.87	35.49	19.20	18.65	19.09	2,100	95.57
8	136.68	135.18	135.52	35.75	35.20	35.30	19.24	18.80	18.98	1,810	95.60
9	134.02	131.01	131.22	31.92	33.50	33.59	18.79	18.14	18.21	2,521	95.13
10	131.95	130.70	131.63	33.82	33.20	33.70	18.14	17.78	17.90	1,057	95.04
11 *											
12	132.86	131.11	131.27	34.49	33.57	33.70	18.28	17.92	18.05	1,266	95.04
13	131.49	129.79	131.18	33.43	32.35	33.33	18.19	17.81	18.15	1,408	94.49
14	132.90	131.38	132.49	34.04	33.41	33.85	18.80	18.20	18.77	1,085	94.92
15	134.19	132.85	133.49	34.77	33.95	34.27	19.21	18.74	18.90	1,392	95.22
16	133.71	132.40	133.07	34.57	34.09	34.22	19.11	18.72	18.85	903	95.19
17	133.75	133.03	133.59	34.64	34.29	34.62	19.10	18.90	19.10	459	95.37
18 *											
19	134.23	133.20	133.46	34.88	34.39	34.41	19.43	19.09	19.25	907	95.35
20	133.64	132.68	133.09	34.62	34.30	34.46	19.37	19.07	19.21	732	95.31
21	134.31	133.17	134.00	35.11	34.53	35.01	19.78	19.30	19.71	1,141	95.41
22	134.75	133.70	134.20	35.25	34.88	35.00	19.93	19.63	19.76	1,249	95.41
23 †	†	†	†	†	†	†	†	†	†		
24	134.58	133.94	134.34	35.31	35.01	35.24	19.81	19.70	19.75	642	95.37
25 *											
26	134.89	133.91	134.34	35.50	35.06	35.30	19.86	19.55	19.64	1,125	95.33
27	134.75	133.75	134.39	35.31	34.83	34.95	19.68	19.40	19.56	828	95.27
28	134.61	133.46	134.14	35.12	34.54	35.04	19.59	19.25	19.46	880	95.22
29	135.49	134.11	135.24	35.64	34.97	35.58	19.79	19.40	19.67	1,341	95.40
30	136.17	135.01	135.48	35.89	35.36	35.56	19.83	19.54	19.61	1,359	95.64
High			136.93			35.91			19.76		95.75
Low			131.18			33.33			17.90		94.49

*Sunday. †Holiday. ‡000 omitted.   Total 33,554

MAY, 1943

Date	Industrials High	Low	Close	Railroads High	Low	Close	Utilities High	Low	Close	‡Daily Sales	40 Bonds
1	136.54	135.36	136.20	35.95	35.51	35.84	19.76	19.54	19.70	844	95.71
2 *											
3	137.69	136.08	137.43	36.33	35.80	36.25	20.14	19.72	20.06	2,349	95.71
4	138.71	137.27	138.18	36.64	36.01	36.12	20.33	19.95	20.18	2,805	96.01
5	138.79	137.54	138.34	37.00	35.94	36.81	20.34	20.04	20.24	2,470	96.19
6	139.13	137.97	138.85	37.12	36.56	36.89	20.21	19.94	20.04	2,078	96.29
7	139.04	136.99	137.27	37.00	35.83	35.97	20.28	19.76	19.90	2,150	96.18
8	138.55	137.25	138.36	36.57	36.03	36.47	20.16	19.76	20.11	1,063	96.27
9 *											
10	139.30	138.12	138.64	36.85	36.22	36.28	20.82	20.26	20.53	2,515	96.35
11	138.75	137.54	138.36	36.38	35.76	36.06	20.55	20.15	20.36	1,788	96.26
12	138.96	137.83	138.24	36.68	35.95	36.11	20.40	20.05	20.08	1,434	96.25
13	138.55	137.56	137.88	36.22	35.91	36.04	20.10	19.84	19.90	1,028	96.26
14	137.85	136.13	136.82	36.09	35.17	35.57	20.00	19.45	19.70	1,627	96.03
15	137.45	136.67	137.31	36.03	35.56	35.87	19.80	19.58	19.74	640	96.24
16 *											
17	137.43	136.30	136.98	36.22	35.59	36.06	19.92	19.60	19.78	848	96.08
18	138.39	136.92	138.05	36.46	35.89	36.22	20.15	19.72	20.02	930	96.25
19	139.39	138.04	139.15	36.90	36.23	36.69	20.52	20.03	20.45	1,493	96.41
20	140.09	138.60	138.84	37.08	36.37	36.44	20.67	20.23	20.26	1,299	96.40
21	139.25	138.10	138.90	36.75	35.96	36.52	20.35	20.05	20.27	922	96.34
22	139.07	138.55	138.78	36.56	36.35	36.45	20.38	20.20	20.25	433	96.43
23 *											
24	139.14	138.41	138.84	36.49	36.14	36.29	20.27	20.03	20.09	790	96.38
25	139.37	138.06	139.17	37.16	36.08	37.11	20.28	19.97	20.19	889	96.31
26	140.82	139.24	140.38	37.57	37.06	37.30	20.40	20.12	20.28	1,322	96.39
27	141.54	140.13	140.82	37.58	37.03	37.08	20.50	20.16	20.28	1,468	96.52
28	141.58	140.30	141.18	37.16	36.80	37.06	20.40	20.18	20.30	1,048	96.61
29	142.21	141.28	142.06	37.40	37.03	37.31	20.47	20.32	20.42	816	96.65
30 *											
31 †	†	†	†	†	†	†	†	†	†	†	†
High			142.06			37.31			20.53		96.65
Low			136.20			35.57			19.70		95.71

*Sunday. †Holiday. ‡000 omitted.   Total 35,049

JUNE, 1943

Date	Industrials High	Low	Close	Railroads High	Low	Close	Utilities High	Low	Close	‡Daily Sales	40 Bonds
1	142.90	141.72	142.43	37.37	36.95	37.04	20.52	20.20	20.45	1,260	96.57
2	143.17	141.85	142.39	37.01	36.56	36.66	20.55	20.22	20.30	1,310	96.55
3	143.05	141.51	142.75	37.01	36.47	36.91	20.39	20.11	20.28	1,179	96.52
4	143.04	141.82	142.28	37.01	36.54	36.62	20.39	20.02	20.23	1,255	96.40
5	143.19	142.49	143.08	36.79	36.58	36.69	20.35	20.23	20.33	733	96.42
6											
7	142.99	141.50	141.82	36.74	36.06	36.22	20.37	20.04	20.12	1,213	96.31
8	141.91	140.56	141.44	36.16	35.64	35.95	20.16	19.81	20.00	1,078	96.06
9	141.71	140.45	141.49	35.19	35.77	36.11	20.21	19.87	20 16	808	96.09
10	142.42	141.21	141.68	36.30	36.06	36.12	20.40	20.03	20.25	905	96.12
11	142.01	141.11	141.44	36.11	35.66	35.79	20.40	20.18	20.27	841	96.08
12	141.59	140.98	141.32	35.70	35.42	35.56	20.30	20.14	20.22	419	96.04
13											
14	140.91	138.86	139.09	35.50	34.51	34.77	20.43	19.76	19.98	1,352	95.75
15	139.58	138.21	139.39	35.16	34.62	35.10	20.15	19.76	20.10	1,010	95.80
16	140.55	139.26	139.78	35.56	35.10	35.19	20.36	20.05	20.23	877	95.99
17	140.41	139.49	139.85	35.65	35.22	35.38	20.46	20.14	20.24	741	96.02
18	140.22	139.27	139.68	35.41	35.18	35.19	20.32	20.13	20.27	683	96.06
19	139.90	139.25	139.73	35.25	35.14	35.21	20.33	20.18	20.26	303	96.05
20											
21	139.52	138.34	138.79	35.07	34.58	34.78	20.28	20.04	20.11	715	95.99
22	139.30	138.07	139.03	35.08	34.55	35.01	20.21	19.96	20.13	698	95.98
23	140.43	139.30	140.04	35.59	35.16	35.33	20.33	20.12	20.22	830	96.13
24	141.06	139.70	140.86	35.51	35.19	35.42	20.29	20.10	20.20	729	96.18
25	142.49	140.96	142.27	35.86	35.43	35.83	20.55	20.24	20.46	1,147	96.31
26	143.22	142.52	142.88	36.07	35.90	35.96	20.73	20.53	20.67	554	96.35
27											
28	143.70	142.44	143.00	36.41	36.03	36.23	21.23	20.80	21.17	1,029	96.33
29	143.30	142.06	142.62	36.34	35.90	36 19	21.20	20.85	21.00	808	96.40
30	143.57	142.50	143.38	36.57	36.16	36.48	21.44	20.99	21:34	942	96.39
High			143.38			37.04			21.34		96.57
Low			138.79			34.77			19.98		95.75

*Sunday. †Holiday. ‡000 omitted.　　　　Total 23,419

JULY, 1943

Date	Industrials High	Low	Close	Railroads High	Low	Close	Utilities High	Low	Close	‡Daily Sales	40 Bonds
1	144.02	142.98	143.58	36.91	36.44	36.72	21.55	21.22	21.35	1,153	96.50
2	144.05	143.17	143.68	36.76	36.44	36.51	21.50	21.22	21.27	893	96.54
3	143.97	143.33	143.70	36.50	36.34	36.50	21.55	21.29	21.54	452	96.59
4											
5	†	†	†	†	†	†	†	†	†	†	†
6	144.41	143.46	143.76	36.58	36.24	36.28	21.86	21.38	21.60	962	96.63
7	143.82	142.83	143.41	36.39	36.02	36.20	21.55	21.23	21.48	709	96.68
8	144.09	143.15	143.64	36.62	36.14	36.49	21.77	21.51	21.63	960	96.70
9	144.32	143.34	144.18	37.24	36.43	37.01	21.89	21.55	21.81	1,053	96.87
10	144.60	143.95	144.23	37.12	36.88	36.95	22.00	21.87	21.95	478	96.78
11											
12	144.79	143.94	144.62	37.37	36.78	37.29	22.03	21.75	21.84	1,054	96.78
13	145.54	144.37	145.30	37.95	37.31	37.88	21.99	21.71	21.84	1,394	96.95
14	146.26	145.08	145.82	38.51	37.87	38.11	22.42	21.94	22.30	1,679	96.99
15	146.41	144.76	144.87	38.29	37.55	37.72	22.38	21.99	22.05	1,223	96.99
16	145.67	144.41	144.75	38.13	37.58	37.80	22.29	21.91	22.08	1,041	96.98
17	145.00	144.47	144.72	37.95	37.78	37.85	22.28	22.10	22.20	397	96.94
18											
19	145.31	144.39	144.74	37.96	37.62	37.65	22.30	22.10	22.19	834	96.97
20	144.79	143.50	143.93	37.60	37.01	37.17	22.24	21.84	21.95	991	96.85
21	144.22	143.33	143.94	37.57	37.05	37.52	22.15	21.91	22.06	765	96.92
22	144.13	143.38	143.77	38.04	37.49	37.89	22.34	22.01	22.19	822	97.03
23	144.18	143.31	143.80	38.27	37.74	38.05	22.32	22.00	22.15	914	97.09
24	144.16	143.69	143.99	38.39	38.08	38.30	22.21	22.14	22.17	387	97.17
25											
26	143.65	141.73	142.07	37.72	36.53	36.90	22.10	21.48	21.70	1,456	96.70
27	142.07	138.65	138.75	37.03	35.54	35.67	21.85	21.02	21.05	1,786	96.41
28	139.08	136.72	137.64	36.11	34.98	35.70	21.35	20.85	21.10	1,848	96.12
29	139.90	138.28	139.41	36.56	35.85	36.09	21.60	21.25	21.48	1,024	96.42
30	139.66	136.87	137.25	36.04	34.76	35.14	21.53	20.86	21.05	1,225	96.21
31	136.87	135.47	135.95	34.87	34.33	34.51	20.98	20.59	20.69	823	96.03
High			145.82			38.30			22.30		97.17
Low			135.95			34.51			20.69		96.03

*Sunday. †Holiday. ‡000 omitted.　　　　Total 26,323

AUGUST, 1943

Date	Industrials			Railroads			Utilities			‡Daily Sales	40 Bonds
	High	Low	Close	High	Low	Close	High	Low	Close		
1											
2	136.50	133.87	134.00	34.69	33.66	33.73	20.86	20.21	20.26	1,345	95.97
3	136.00	134.04	135.64	34.55	33.74	34.37	20.73	20.19	20.67	1,204	96.09
4	137.54	136.20	136.87	34.79	34.32	34.49	20.95	20.63	20.73	734	96.24
5	137.17	136.33	136.76	34.59	34.22	34.45	20.76	20.55	20.60	542	96.19
6	136.80	135.36	135.58	34.45	34.00	34.05	20.75	20.41	20.50	615	96.13
7	135.58	135.13	135.38	34.17	34.04	34.13	20.59	20.50	20.51	291	96.13
8											
9	136.08	134.75	135.18	34.33	33.98	34.18	20.66	20.33	20.46	563	96.11
10	136.44	135.33	136.23	34.61	34.11	34.54	20.82	20.52	20.77	651	96.15
11	137.15	136.21	136.79	34.85	34.50	34.56	20.97	20.68	20.82	620	96.23
12	137.05	136.15	135.44	34.61	34.25	34.27	20.95	20.70	20.76	454	96.27
13	137.49	136.40	137.39	34.56	34.12	34.46	20.88	20.69	20.83	435	96.25
14	137.45	136.97	137.23	34.87	34.56	34.81	20.95	20.82	20.92	210	96.38
15											
16	137.74	136.78	137.08	35.24	34.72	34.77	21.00	20.83	20.91	489	96.35
17	137.93	136.96	137.54	35.16	34.85	35.04	21.04	20.86	20.99	553	96.34
18	138.83	137.59	138.45	35.30	34.95	35.11	21.09	20.88	21.00	560	96.28
19	138.83	137.93	138.34	35.02	34.74	34.85	21.09	20.91	20.97	469	96.23
20	138.31	136.80	136.93	34.70	34.34	34.44	21.03	20.75	20.83	544	96.13
21	136.53	135.97	136.16	34.20	33.97	34.01	20.83	20.62	20.65	326	96.06
22											
23	135.81	134.40	135.05	34.02	33.54	33.69	20.63	20.33	20.42	719	95.91
24	136.04	135.00	135.60	34.06	33.73	33.98	20.58	20.34	20.46	483	95.92
25	136.25	135.54	135.90	34.26	34.06	34.12	20.89	20.69	20.76	457	95.98
26	136.40	135.81	136.25	34.36	34.16	34.30	21.00	20.75	20.94	435	95.97
27	136.26	135.64	135.83	34.37	34.06	34.11	20.99	20.80	20.85	415	95.94
28	135.96	135.58	135.79	34.20	34.08	34.17	20.90	20.85	20.89	189	95.92
29											
30	136.10	135.30	135.73	34.20	34.06	34.13	20.97	20.78	20.87	335	95.91
31	137.01	135.95	136.62	34.62	34.24	34.55	21.30	20.95	21.17	614	96.04
High			138.45			35.11			21.17		96.38
Low			134.00			33.69			20.26		95.91

*Sunday. †Holiday. ‡000 omitted.   Total 14,252

SEPTEMBER, 1943

Date	Industrials			Railroads			Utilities			‡Daily Sales	40 Bonds
	High	Low	Close	High	Low	Close	High	Low	Close		
1	137.48	136.65	137.12	34.76	34.53	34.65	21.41	21.17	21.34	568	96.06
2	137.48	136.67	137.11	34.66	34.54	34.55	21.40	21.22	21.33	490	96.08
3	137.43	136.53	137.18	34.49	34.22	34.35	21.33	21.18	21.27	398	96.00
4	137.45	137.15	137.33	34.43	34.31	34.37	21.36	21.28	21.35	174	96.00
5											
6	†	†	†	†	†	†	†	†	†	†	†
7	137.75	137.17	137.59	34.37	34.20	34.32	21.37	21.23	21.29	346	95.99
8	137.72	136.37	136.91	34.15	33.46	33.71	21.29	21.04	21.19	798	95.77
9	138.12	136.92	137.75	34.06	33.59	33.85	21.70	21.17	21.48	1,092	95.70
10	138.26	137.50	137.96	34.12	33.80	34.01	21.73	21.48	21.58	760	95.64
11	138.24	137.86	138.04	34.25	34.08	34.22	21.60	21.50	21.54	296	95.61
12											
13	138.17	137.52	137.82	34.31	33.93	34.03	21.57	21.37	21.44	506	95.63
14	137.98	137.24	137.53	34.09	33.78	34.01	21.46	21.27	21.31	439	95.55
15	138.21	137.31	137.62	34.68	34.00	34.35	21.53	21.29	21.41	596	95.66
16	138.43	137.50	138.36	34.65	34.27	34.57	21.56	21.30	21.50	534	95.59
17	139.71	138.42	139.60	35.14	34.58	35.07	21.73	21.49	21.70	894	95.66
18	141.14	140.03	140.94	35.47	35.22	35.40	21.84	21.71	21.80	686	95.74
19											
20	142.50	141.42	141.75	35.74	35.27	35.43	21.85	21.57	21.71	1,098	95.80
21	141.87	141.03	141.49	35.46	35.17	35.35	21.81	21.64	21.76	743	95.82
22	141.68	140.61	141.09	35.33	34.87	35.20	21.76	21.60	21.68	661	95.86
23	141.18	139.75	140.30	35.15	34.83	34.93	21.75	21.50	21.56	667	95.79
24	140.61	139.79	140.21	35.14	34.93	35.09	21.75	21.50	21.65	642	95.78
25	140.34	140.00	140.18	35.24	35.04	35.17	21.80	21.64	21.74	331	95.80
26											
27	140.14	139.11	139.41	35.07	34.47	34.64	21.80	21.50	21.60	622	95.64
28	139.98	139.04	139.27	35.02	34.54	34.70	21.78	21.55	21.70	607	95.63
29	139.95	139.06	139.75	34.90	34.68	34.81	21.82	21.58	21.74	466	95.58
30	140.48	139.55	140.12	35.18	34.88	35.11	21.99	21.66	21.84	571	95.59
High			141.75			35.43			21.84		96.08
Low			136.91			33.71			21.19		95.55

*Sunday †Holiday ‡000 omitted   Total 14,985

OCTOBER, 1943

Date	Industrials			Railroads			Utilities			‡Daily Sales	40 Bonds
	High	Low	Close	High	Low	Close	High	Low	Close		
1	140.63	139.87	140.33	35.32	34.97	35.22	21.92	21.75	21.83	559	95.70
2	140.50	139.98	140.27	35.24	35.08	35.12	21.90	21.74	21.81	272	95.72
3	*										
4	140.17	139.36	139.63	35.11	34.76	35.00	21.90	21.51	21.73	497	95.64
5	139.76	138.87	139.27	34.99	34.77	34.87	21.90	21.70	21.79	490	95.63
6	139.15	137.71	137.84	35.04	34.52	34.58	21.92	21.57	21.60	716	95.62
7	137.43	136.01	136.39	34.52	34.20	34.35	21.54	21.16	21.29	854	95.58
8	137.17	136.21	136.74	34.67	34.33	34.54	21.45	21.15	21.23	559	95.67
9	137.20	136.72	137.10	34.85	34.54	34.84	21.42	21.30	21.38	226	95.66
10	*										
11	137.21	136.38	136.61	34.86	34.47	34.57	21.45	21.18	21.24	480	95.59
12	†	†	†	†	†	†	†	†	†		
13	136.91	135.92	136.48	34.65	34.27	34.60	21.27	21.05	21.19	592	95.53
14	137.30	136.34	137.01	34.91	34.53	34.76	21.41	21.20	21.36	474	95.59
15	138.30	137.30	137.90	35.16	34.79	35.01	21.54	21.27	21.41	556	95.76
16	138.46	137.88	138.40	35.08	34.87	35.05	21.60	21.37	21.53	267	95.81
17	*										
18	138.87	138.06	138.40	35.18	34.95	35.01	21.68	21.45	21.57	541	95.87
19	138.93	138.11	138.71	35.42	35.06	35.29	21.77	21.50	21.70	608	95.91
20	139.21	138.43	138.88	35.34	35.07	35.14	21.92	21.64	21.80	611	95.92
21	138.72	137.74	138.00	35.19	34.81	34.94	21.80	21.54	21.65	591	95.90
22	138.53	137.84	138.25	35.20	34.92	35.10	22.05	21.61	21.99	560	96.01
23	138.37	138.11	138.29	35.06	34.96	35.01	22.05	21.94	22.03	326	96.05
24	*										
25	138.66	137.88	138.22	35.07	34.86	34.93	22.10	21.82	21.98	651	96.09
26	139.08	138.19	138.69	35.25	34.91	35.20	22.09	21.88	21.95	896	96.17
27	139.65	138.55	139.35	35.65	35.17	35.53	22.04	21.86	21.95	877	96.21
28	139.74	138.84	138.97	35.58	35.20	35.25	22.15	21.90	22.01	715	96.25
29	139.06	138.02	138.29	35.24	34.93	35.04	22.05	21.85	21.93	668	96.29
30	138.46	138.11	138.27	35.30	34.95	35.24	21.98	21.88	21.95	338	96.34
31	*										
High			140.33			35.53			22.03		96.34
Low			136.39			34.35			21.19		95.53

*Sunday †Holiday ‡000 omitted

Total 13,924

NOVEMBER, 1943

Date	Industrials			Railroads			Utilities			‡Daily Sales	40 Bonds
	High	Low	Close	High	Low	Close	High	Low	Close		
1	138.79	137.85	138.50	35.25	34.85	35.06	21.97	21.70	21.81	649	96.23
2	†	†	†	†	†	†	†	†	†	†	†
3	138.96	137.19	137.35	35.12	34.38	34.54	22.01	21.39	21.50	1,072	96.12
4	137.94	136.10	136.30	34.56	33.74	33.86	21.61	21.15	21.22	1,154	95.96
5	136.49	135.23	135.47	34.06	33.56	33.67	21.40	21.01	21.11	795	96.02
6	135.57	135.07	135.24	33.71	33.50	33.55	21.17	21.08	21.12	337	95.99
7	*										
8	135.03	131.42	131.68	33.45	31.70	31.80	21.10	20.08	20.15	2,340	95.37
9	132.48	130.84	131.85	32.43	31.63	32.21	20.73	20.10	20.53	1,507	95.43
10	133.37	132.11	132.68	32.91	32.36	32.62	20.97	20.60	20.77	926	95.67
11	†	†	†	†	†	†	†	†	†		
12	133.07	131.63	132.15	32.88	32.41	32.57	21.21	20.60	20.91	796	95.56
13	132.09	131.68	131.76	32.64	32.47	32.53	21.08	20.95	21.01	314	95.63
14	*										
15	132.13	131.08	131.56	32.83	32.41	32.67	21.20	20.92	21.09	682	95.57
16	131.91	130.86	131.18	32.75	32.43	32.54	21.07	20.84	20.91	622	95.50
17	131.19	129.86	130.24	32.58	32.17	32.38	20.89	20.57	20.70	828	95.45
18	131.29	130.08	130.79	32.82	32.22	32.53	20.90	20.64	20.80	620	95.55
19	132.51	130.96	132.30	33.15	32.45	33.07	21.28	20.75	21.20	906	95.89
20	133.15	132.54	132.94	33.44	33.11	33.32	21.39	21.19	21.26	482	96.05
21	*										
22	133.10	132.30	132.65	33.50	33.02	33.40	21.30	21.03	21.15	610	96.00
23	132.93	132.26	132.45	33.65	33.16	33.29	21.29	20.99	21.10	540	96.13
24	132.86	131.76	132.10	33.21	32.74	32.82	21.15	20.85	20.93	707	95.83
25	†	†	†	†	†	†	†	†	†	†	†
26	132.25	131.06	131.33	32.46	32.00	32.08	21.01	20.68	20.78	601	95.63
27	131.57	131.04	131.25	32.08	31.82	31.88	20.85	20.68	20.70	341	95.59
28	*										
29	131.34	129.86	129.95	32.02	31.66	31.71	20.80	20.58	20.71	703	95.41
30	130.34	128.94	129.57	31.80	31.42	31.50	20.93	20.57	20.83	712	95.34
High			138.50			35.06			21.81		96.23
Low			129.57			31.50			20.15		95.34

*Sunday. †Holiday. ‡000 omitted.

Total 18,244

DECEMBER, 1943

Date	Industrials			Railroads			Utilities			‡Daily Sales	40 Bonds
	High	Low	Close	High	Low	Close	High	Low	Close		
1	131.16	129.76	130.68	32.05	31.57	31.91	21.20	20.80	21.10	711	95.52
2	132.06	130.75	131.67	32.30	31.97	32.16	21.26	21.00	21.12	715	95.77
3	132.32	131.42	131.91	32.42	32.13	32.24	21.30	21.00	21.26	558	95.79
4	132.07	131.51	131.87	32.24	32.11	32.17	21.43	21.21	21.40	302	95.87
5	*			*			*				
6	133.07	131.71	132.45	32.61	32.16	32.27	21.58	21.31	21.45	824	95.90
7	133.46	132.21	133.37	32.69	32.25	32.64	21.71	21.43	21.62	884	95.95
8	134.85	133.64	134.42	33.35	32.83	33.17	21.90	21.51	21.73	1,320	96.10
9	134.89	133.57	134.05	33.13	32.74	32.96	21.80	21.53	21.69	856	96.06
10	135.47	133.96	135.04	33.31	32.82	33.19	21.99	21.63	21.89	867	96.05
11	135.47	134.83	135.28	33.38	33.14	33.29	22.00	21.75	21.85	424	96.11
12	*			*			*				
13	135.81	134.37	134.80	33.38	33.05	33.09	21.94	21.66	21.78	731	96.10
14	134.74	133.72	134.19	33.05	32.73	32.85	21.85	21.60	21.76	683	96.11
15	134.53	133.69	134.18	33.15	32.82	33.03	21.80	21.60	21.70	664	96.24
16	135.47	133.96	135.19	32.89	32.54	32.76	21.70	21.52	21.63	761	96.21
17	135.90	134.92	135.44	33.36	32.64	33.21	21.84	21.56	21.78	875	96.35
18	136.09	135.31	135.89	33.37	33.18	33.30	22.00	21.80	21.97	483	96.46
19	*			*			*				
20	136.56	135.47	135.10	33.48	33.14	33.25	22.00	21.75	21.83	855	96.49
21	136.49	135.51	135.86	33.30	33.00	33.09	21.90	21.68	21.79	656	96.45
22	136.53	135.65	136.15	33.14	32.85	33.03	21.95	21.70	21.90	564	96.44
23	136.57	135.77	136.07	33.35	33.03	33.27	22.01	21.80	21.94	580	96.45
24	136.47	135.75	136.24	33.45	33.07	33.36	21.97	21.83	21.93	512	96.44
25	†			†			†			†	†
26	*			*			*				
27	136.60	135.67	136.14	33.34	33.06	33.12	21.95	21.75	21.79	651	96.44
28	136.08	134.81	135.04	33.24	32.71	32.79	21.75	21.46	21.52	922	96.47
29	135.51	134.08	134.61	33.18	32.51	32.93	21.60	21.36	21.50	997	96.48
30	135.37	135.00	136.20	33.58	33.07	33.53	21.85	21.48	21.80	1,143	96.66
31	136.73	135.54	135.89	33.88	33.41	33.56	21.96	21.70	21.87	990	96.77
High			136.24			33.56			21.97		96.77
Low			130.68			31.91			21.10		95.52

*Sunday. †Holiday. ‡000 omitted.   Total 19,528

JANUARY, 1944

Date	Industrials			Railroads			Utilities			‡Daily Sales	40 Bonds
	High	Low	Close	High	Low	Close	High	Low	Close		
1	†			†			†			†	†
2	*			*			*				
3	136.47	135.51	135.92	33.62	33.31	33.45	21.91	21.62	21.74	517	96.71
4	137.23	135.91	137.15	33.99	33.48	33.94	22.32	21.79	22.30	732	96.89
5	138.88	137.78	138.65	34.37	34.08	34.23	22.60	22.31	22.45	1,157	97.13
6	138.80	137.98	138.34	34.49	34.03	34.42	22.55	22.20	22.38	844	97.33
7	138.65	137.67	138.08	34.89	34.41	34.53	22.50	22.22	22.30	833	97.44
8	138.32	137.93	138.09	34.73	34.57	34.67	22.43	22.28	22.32	346	97.49
9	*			*			*				
10	138.21	137.40	137.80	34.89	34.53	34.82	22.50	22.20	22.33	722	97.54
11	138.89	137.97	138.47	35.35	34.80	35.12	22.64	22.35	22.55	996	97.72
12	138.71	137.74	137.94	35.19	34.80	34.86	22.55	22.30	22.35	705	97.68
13	137.86	136.99	137.36	34.98	34.54	34.91	22.32	22.15	22.25	678	97.75
14	138.31	137.21	138.15	35.45	34.96	35.37	22.44	22.17	22.36	935	97.86
15	138.57	137.96	138.40	35.88	35.51	35.77	22.43	22.26	22.37	662	97.98
16	*			*			*				
17	138.60	137.78	138.10	35.98	35.50	35.66	22.40	22.15	22.25	816	97.83
18	138.22	137.51	137.87	36.16	35.38	35.86	22.35	22.16	22.24	815	97.95
19	138.28	137.20	137.83	36.06	35.51	35.90	22.33	22.10	22.23	639	97.92
20	138.49	137.79	138.16	36.26	35.83	36.03	22.36	22.13	22.27	730	98.23
21	138.32	137.69	138.07	36.61	36.07	36.51	22.38	22.14	22.35	814	98.49
22	138.43	138.02	138.24	36.71	36.47	36.57	22.41	22.25	22.36	521	98.65
23	*			*			*				
24	138.50	137.70	137.97	36.75	36.37	36.45	22.51	22.27	22.37	690	98.72
25	138.21	137.59	137.97	36.58	36.27	36.32	22.52	22.31	22.41	688	98.63
26	137.77	136.59	136.71	36.29	35.70	35.75	22.37	22.14	22.18	778	98.57
27	137.10	136.38	136.59	35.80	35.37	35.63	22.30	22.10	22.19	595	98.67
28*	137.37	136.65	137.19	36.12	35.71	36.04	22.54	22.26	22.47	619	98.80
29	137.42	136.82	137.15	36.13	36.03	36.08	22.62	22.46	22.55	345	98.89
30	*			*			*				
31	137.85	136.83	137.40	36.43	36.00	36.36	22.66	22.42	22.57	632	98.99
High			138.65			36.57			22.57		98.99
Low			135.92			33.45			21.74		96.71

*Sunday. †Holiday. ‡000 omitted.   Total 17,809

FEBRUARY, 1944

Date	Industrials High	Low	Close	Railroads High	Low	Close	Utilities High	Low	Close	‡Daily sales	40 Bonds
1	137.69	137.09	137.45	36.51	36.21	36.34	22.75	22.52	22.63	855	99.16
2	137.45	136.79	137.08	36.83	36.23	36.80	22.74	22.49	22.57	903	99.24
3	137.16	135.76	136.24	36.82	35.98	36.16	22.61	22.28	22.40	963	99.08
4	135.89	134.75	135.04	36.10	35.56	35.80	22.41	22.15	22.27	600	98.90
5	135.34	134.85	135.12	36.16	35.90	36.10	22.38	22.24	22.32	310	98.95
6	*										
7	135.11	134.10	134.22	36.48	35.95	36.14	22.44	22.26	22.34	573	99.02
8	135.24	134.36	135.06	36.51	36.14	36.43	22.47	22.29	22.42	608	99.20
9	135.44	134.55	135.03	36.65	36.27	36.38	22.56	22.38	22.48	626	99.32
10	135.74	134.80	135.55	37.46	36.49	37.41	22.70	22.45	22.66	860	99.60
11	136.08	135.19	135.41	37.83	37.36	37.46	22.75	22.59	22.63	845	99.66
12	†	†	†	†	†	†	†	†	†	†	†
13	*										
14	135.71	135.00	135.39	37.68	37.34	37.55	22.71	22.58	22.65	548	99.74
15	136.36	135.28	136.19	38.37	37.74	38.26	22.82	22.56	22.72	1,026	99.83
16	136.73	135.64	136.04	38.40	37.86	37.92	22.86	22.68	22.74	872	99.92
17	136.77	135.74	136.58	38.88	37.93	38.82	22.99	22.78	22.90	902	100.02
18	136.74	135.81	136.08	38.84	38.11	38.35	22.96	22.77	22.85	670	100.01
19	136.10	135.75	135.91	38.39	38.14	38.22	22.92	22.79	22.89	346	99.97
20	*										
21	136.11	135.52	135.71	38.43	38.14	38.27	22.97	22.79	22.86	594	99.86
22	†	†	†	†	†	†	†	†	†	†	†
23	136.63	135.52	136.51	38.91	38.18	38.90	23.15	22.83	23.11	943	99.95
24	137.00	136.25	136.58	39.08	38.54	38.74	23.44	23.09	23.39	1,162	99.97
25	136.74	136.11	136.56	38.93	38.44	38.64	23.56	23.30	23.52	900	99.95
26	136.69	136.46	136.58	38.88	38.50	38.83	23.53	23.36	23.46	373	99.92
27	*										
28	137.01	136.36	136.79	39.03	38.75	38.88	23.56	23.26	23.40	754	99.88
29	136.91	136.02	136.30	39.00	38.08	38.23	23.50	23.18	23.26	866	99.81
High			137.45			38.90			23.52		100.02
Low			134.22			35.80			22.27		98.90
										Total 17,099	

*Sunday †Holiday ‡000 omitted.

MARCH, 1944

Date	Industrials High	Low	Close	Railroads High	Low	Close	Utilities High	Low	Close	‡Daily Sales	40 Bonds
1	136.75	135.86	136.44	38.51	38.09	38.47	23.45	23.18	23.42	633	99.77
2	136.91	136.33	136.69	38.74	38.40	38.48	23.48	23.30	23.37	706	99.83
3	136.97	136.38	136.59	38.51	38.16	38.17	23.65	23.37	23.61	757	99.82
4	136.89	136.47	136.79	38.20	38.04	38.12	23.64	23.51	23.59	332	99.75
5	*										
6	137.46	136.75	137.21	38.47	38.14	38.32	23.76	23.51	23.66	751	99.76
7	138.67	137.48	138.33	38.72	38.21	38.58	23.89	23.60	23.71	1,207	99.80
8	139.89	138.34	139.50	38.82	38.23	38.37	23.93	23.62	23.81	1,693	99.86
9	139.70	138.89	139.33	38.52	38.11	38.36	23.91	23.68	23.80	934	99.86
10	140.34	139.14	140.01	38.55	38.19	38.38	23.88	23.67	23.77	1,148	99.84
11	140.62	140.04	140.44	39.08	38.55	38.99	23.89	23.76	23.80	680	99.93
12	*										
13	141.37	140.33	141.00	39.52	38.95	39.35	23.95	23.76	23.88	1,619	99.95
14	140.75	139.90	140.37	39.46	38.97	39.19	23.95	23.70	23.90	1,007	99.92
15	141.00	140.08	140.71	39.32	39.05	39.23	24.04	23.80	23.95	1,185	100.00
16	141.43	140.44	140.91	40.06	39.36	39.87	24.10	23.87	23.93	1,594	100.03
17	141.10	140.24	140.80	40.46	39.80	40.32	24.03	23.81	23.91	1,353	100.07
18	140.82	140.14	140.30	40.37	40.12	40.21	24.00	23.87	23.93	727	100.15
19	*										
20	140.28	139.53	139.89	40.19	39.56	39.66	23.85	23.63	23.71	1,196	100.03
21	140.47	139.63	140.20	40.65	39.61	40.48	23.73	23.58	23.67	1,464	100.15
22	140.77	139.83	139.98	40.91	40.12	40.24	23.79	23.53	23.57	1,572	100.16
23	140.33	138.81	138.95	40.69	39.88	40.02	23.62	23.32	23.40	1,174	100.11
24	139.60	138.81	139.28	40.45	39.97	40.21	23.54	23.36	23.48	842	100.18
25	139.53	139.05	139.19	40.30	40.06	40.13	23.57	23.41	23.46	448	100.22
26	*										
27	139.67	138.99	139.12	40.37	39.93	39.99	23.45	23.29	23.35	693	100.21
28	139.36	137.64	137.88	40.20	38.93	39.21	23.32	23.03	23.08	1,344	100.07
29	138.17	136.98	137.45	39.45	38.70	39.14	23.14	22.91	23.02	1,107	99.94
30	138.89	137.74	138.60	39.66	39.18	39.50	23.27	23.05	23.20	682	100.14
31	139.29	138.50	138.84	39.84	39.43	39.54	23.22	23.07	23.11	797	100.30
High			141.00			40.48			23.95		100.30
Low			136.44			38.12			23.02		99.75
										Total 27,645	

*Sunday †Holiday ‡000 omitted

APRIL, 1944

Date	Industrials			Railroads			Utilities			‡Daily Sales	40 Bonds
	High	Low	Close	High	Low	Close	High	Low	Close		
1	138.95	138.73	138.84	39.70	39.48	39.61	23.15	23.04	23.08	323	100.37
2	*			*			*			*	*
3	138.66	137.70	138.01	39.59	39.09	39.29	23.13	22.90	23.01	693	100.40
4	138.39	137.67	138.06	39.42	39.14	39.33	23.13	22.92	23.05	572	100.35
5	138.63	137.95	138.17	39.69	39.23	39.38	23.15	22.81	22.98	772	100.59
6	139.24	138.31	138.91	39.55	39.21	39.40	23.00	22.80	22.91	758	100.69
7	†			†			†			†	†
8	139.29	138.86	139.10	39.70	39.39	39.56	23.07	22.95	23.05	365	100.76
9	*			*			*			*	*
10	139.45	138.80	139.11	39.87	39.58	39.72	23.10	22.92	23.02	566	100.85
11	139.16	138.50	138.74	40.32	39.68	40.17	23.18	23.01	23.10	732	101.04
12	138.86	137.88	137.98	40.43	39.72	39.84	23.13	22.93	22.99	718	101.10
13	137.93	137.33	137.65	39.83	39.38	39.68	22.96	22.74	22.90	660	100.97
14	137.95	137.52	137.69	39.73	39.49	39.54	23.00	22.82	22.90	477	101.13
15	138.13	137.74	138.06	39.62	39.46	39.60	23.06	22.93	23.02	242	101.30
16	*			*			*			*	*
17	138.25	137.64	137.77	39.61	39.22	39.32	23.02	22.87	22.89	538	101.35
18	137.76	135.99	136.07	39.24	38.09	38.20	22.90	22.44	22.47	1,193	100.92
19	136.15	135.09	135.48	38.13	37.50	37.75	22.51	22.25	22.37	904	100.79
20	136.59	135.74	136.20	38.38	37.96	38.26	22.56	22.35	22.50	534	100.94
21	136.61	135.96	136.17	38.63	38.29	38.53	22.60	22.45	22.55	481	101.19
22	136.41	136.10	136.19	38.61	38.40	38.48	22.65	22.43	22.52	258	101.13
23	*			*			*			*	*
24	136.22	134.91	135.00	38.48	37.79	37.83	22.51	22.25	22.26	688	100.95
25	135.41	134.75	135.11	38.16	37.78	37.96	22.25	22.08	22.15	553	100.96
26	135.93	135.18	135.67	38.37	38.01	38.22	22.33	22.15	22.29	491	101.04
27	136.53	135.69	136.07	38.69	38.35	38.57	22.39	22.22	22.33	520	101.16
28	136.50	135.77	136.21	38.96	38.53	38.88	22.53	22.35	22.48	561	101.21
29	136.36	136.13	136.23	38.90	38.77	38.81	22.52	22.38	22.45	246	101.21
30	*			*			*			*	*
High			139.11			40.17			23.10		101.35
Low			135.00			37.75			22.15		100.35

*Sunday †Holiday

Total 13,845

MAY, 1944

Date	Industrials			Railroads			Utilities			‡Daily Sales	40 Bonds
	High	Low	Close	High	Low	Close	High	Low	Close		
1	137.12	136.18	137.06	39.26	38.72	39.17	22.65	22.46	22.61	571	101.28
2	137.53	136.77	137.15	39.30	38.95	39.00	22.65	22.44	22.48	571	101.32
3	138.12	137.14	137.83	39.25	38.91	39.10	22.65	22.45	22.60	626	101.44
4	138.14	137.52	137.85	39.06	38.72	38.88	22.64	22.47	22.57	513	101.53
5	139.00	137.83	138.75	39.43	38.95	39.33	22.73	22.56	22.68	787	101.57
6	139.03	138.60	138.87	39.34	39.05	39.09	22.68	22.62	22.66	331	101.59
7	*			*			*			*	*
8	139.08	138.38	138.65	39.16	38.89	39.02	22.66	22.49	22.55	586	101.67
9	139.07	138.29	138.65	39.20	38.95	39.05	22.70	22.56	22.65	620	101.59
10	139.03	138.41	138.76	39.30	39.06	39.19	22.79	22.66	22.68	647	101.71
11	139.19	138.50	138.93	39.20	39.00	39.06	22.77	22.61	22.70	618	101.75
12	139.38	138.22	138.51	38.99	38.47	38.49	22.72	22.48	22.54	747	101.52
13	138.73	138.23	138.60	38.67	38.53	38.62	22.50	22.45	22.50	220	101.49
14	*			*			*			*	*
15	138.84	138.41	138.60	38.83	38.59	38.70	22.68	22.45	22.58	337	101.59
16	138.89	138.23	138.41	39.07	38.70	38.91	22.66	22.50	22.60	536	101.66
17	139.09	138.38	138.99	39.42	38.87	39.40	22.77	22.57	22.75	818	101.86
18	139.54	138.63	139.20	39.67	39.29	39.48	22.85	22.67	22.78	944	102.07
19	139.69	139.00	139.34	39.71	39.34	39.43	22.97	22.82	22.90	789	102.07
20	139.47	139.23	139.37	39.61	39.42	39.54	22.95	22.87	22.92	362	102.13
21	*			*			*			*	*
22	139.74	139.13	139.43	39.59	39.29	39.43	23.00	22.77	22.84	701	102.16
23	140.24	139.19	139.87	40.04	39.54	39.95	23.00	22.81	22.90	765	102.40
24	140.98	139.91	140.48	40.35	39.98	40.18	23.00	22.76	22.80	1,090	102.54
25	140.69	139.89	140.38	40.22	39.74	39.85	22.91	22.76	22.83	804	102.59
26	141.20	140.31	141.03	40.00	39.70	39.88	23.02	22.78	22.92	836	102.60
27	141.37	140.93	141.24	40.05	39.80	40.00	23.06	22.95	23.00	415	102.61
28	*			*			*			*	*
29	141.68	140.97	141.53	40.26	39.90	40.14	23.12	22.92	23.06	812	102.61
30	†	†	†	†	†	†	†	†	†	†	†
31	142.44	141.28	142.24	40.65	40.22	40.53	23.25	23.09	23.20	1,183	102.68
High			142.24			40.53			23.20		102.68
Low			137.06			38.49			22.48		101.28

*Sunday †Holiday ‡000 omitted

Total 17,229

JUNE, 1944

Date	Industrials High	Low	Close	Railroads High	Low	Close	Utilities High	Low	Close	‡Daily Sales	40 Bonds
1	142.92	141.95	142.14	40.72	40.24	40.35	23.31	23.10	23.15	1,193	102.66
2	142.52	141.80	142.07	40.41	40.08	40.19	23.25	23.00	23.12	819	102.65
3	142.50	142.02	142.34	40.30	40.16	40.19	23.17	23.09	23.10	386	102.64
4*											
5	142.53	141.49	141.62	40.33	39.79	39.85	23.15	22.92	22.98	858	102.53
6	143.01	140.90	142.21	40.19	39.41	39.80	23.14	22.81	23.01	1.789	102.18
7	142.77	141.76	142.12	39.68	39.12	39.33	23.08	22.87	22.97	857	101.76
8	142.60	141.61	141.93	39.23	38.78	38.85	22.99	22.77	22.80	862	101.25
9	142.37	141.58	142.06	39.22	38.75	39.00	22.98	22.76	22.92	849	101.50
10	142.68	142.10	142.53	39.40	39.10	39.31	23.01	22.89	22.95	727	101.67
11*											
12	144.31	142.90	144.08	39.72	39.28	39.62	23.52	23.01	23.48	2,237	101.75
13	145.55	144.13	145.05	40.27	39.74	40.09	23.61	23.28	23.38	2,331	101.86
14	145.60	144.26	145.03	40.30	39.87	40.12	23.51	23.25	23.41	1,443	101.93
15	146.38	144.73	145.86	40.43	39.92	40.32	23.60	23.37	23.49	1,851	101.98
16	147.57	145.94	146.96	41.04	40.38	40.82	23.60	23.40	23.52	2,517	102.02
17	147.61	146.92	147.28	41.30	40.81	41.23	23.59	23.45	23.52	1,064	102.04
18*											
19	149.07	147.46	148.42	41.72	41.23	41.44	23.77	23.43	23.65	2,371	101.98
20	149.15	147.79	148.63	41.50	40.90	41.34	23.95	23.65	23.83	1,619	101.78
21	148.95	147.30	147.90	41.42	40.83	41.03	23.96	23.70	23.85	1,516	101.73
22	148.32	147.18	147.65	41.45	40.82	41.24	23.91	23.70	23.81	1,279	101.66
23	147.94	147.15	147.50	41.71	41.21	41.63	23.92	23.69	23.79	1,301	101.68
24	147.63	147.12	147.48	41.67	41.47	41.56	23.90	23.78	23.86	558	101.70
25*											
26	148.46	147.40	148.12	41.98	41.48	41.73	24.07	23.85	23.99	1,720	101.71
27	149.00	147.76	148.48	42.02	41.59	41.70	24.22	23.93	24.09	2,179	101.69
28	148.52	147.40	147.93	41.71	41.19	41.56	24.08	23.78	23.87	1,746	101.67
29	148.54	147.25	148.07	41.50	41.14	41.31	23.93	23.65	23.80	1,890	101.65
30	148.82	147.93	148.38	41.81	41.13	41.54	24.18	23.77	24.00	1,751	101.73
High			148.63			41.73			24.09		102.66
Low			141.62			38.85			22.80		101.25
										Total 37,713	

*Sunday. †Holiday ‡000 omitted.

JULY, 1944

Date	Industrials High	Low	Close	Railroads High	Low	Close	Utilities High	Low	Close	‡Daily Sales	40 Bonds
1	148.65	148.22	148.46	41.56	41.43	41.49	24.09	23.98	24.05	647	101.78
2*											
3	149.50	148.42	149.32	41.85	41.53	41.82	24.26	23.98	24.21	1,562	101.96
4†											
5	150.42	149.17	149.66	42.04	41.64	41.71	24.34	24.11	24.23	2,436	102.21
6	150.12	148.69	149.07	42.29	41.54	41.82	24.28	24.05	24.12	1,713	102.25
7	149.61	148.61	149.36	42.09	41.66	42.02	24.34	24.08	24.28	1,277	102.28
8	150.16	149.48	150.03	42.54	42.17	42.48	24.45	24.30	24.43	855	102.37
9*											
10	150.88	149.97	150.50	42.71	42.36	42.51	24.52	24.32	24.38	1,837	102.39
11	150.80	149.53	150.18	42.49	42.03	42.27	24.42	24.17	24.25	1,347	102.34
12	150.84	149.69	150.42	42.73	42.27	42.53	24.38	24.11	24.20	1,417	102.33
13	150.80	149.66	150.08	42.61	42.11	42.41	24.30	24.05	24.15	1,377	102.32
14	150.86	149.86	150.34	42.52	42.19	42.43	24.30	24.10	24.15	1,088	102.32
15	150.6	150.27	150.49	42.56	42.37	42.46	24.24	24.11	24.21	421	102.37
16*											
17	150.49	148.71	149.28	42.74	41.77	42.09	24.28	23.87	23.92	1,482	102.32
18	149.01	147.74	148.10	42.09	41.48	41.79	24.00	23.77	23.83	1,279	102.25
19	149.46	147.98	149.01	42.48	41.83	42.38	24.00	23.80	23.97	1,139	102.25
20	149.57	148.11	148.27	42.95	41.97	42.04	24.10	23.79	23.80	1,343	102.31
21	148.01	146.42	146.77	42.10	41.32	41.53	23.80	23.49	23.55	1,431	102.08
22	146.65	145.38	145.58	41.46	40.73	40.93	23.54	23.30	23.32	837	101.80
23*											
24	146.37	145.26	145.77	41.38	40.79	41.03	23.51	23.31	23.40	1,005	101.74
25	146.87	145.91	146.74	41.81	41.15	41.68	23.72	23.48	23.63	831	101.91
26	147.59	146.40	146.64	41.75	41.32	41.41	23.88	23.59	23.70	829	101.94
27	147.08	146.07	146.74	41.62	41.23	41.51	23.84	23.59	23.81	694	101.84
28	146.68	145.88	146.14	41.52	41.14	41.27	23.84	23.68	23.75	563	101.87
29	146.25	146.00	146.14	41.35	41.24	41.32	23.75	23.70	23.73	231	101.76
30*											
31	146.59	145.86	146.11	41.48	41.19	41.29	24.01	23.72	23.90	579	101.78
High			150.50			42.53			24.43		102.39
Low			145.58			40.93			23.32		101.74
										Total 28,220	

*Sunday †Holiday ‡000 omitted

AUGUST, 1944

Date	Industrials High	Low	Close	Railroads High	Low	Close	Utilities High	Low	Close	‡Daily Sales	40 Bonds
1	146.92	145.92	146.39	41.74	41.30	41.51	24.20	23.91	24.14	746	101.80
2	147.07	146.50	146.77	41.81	41.43	41.62	24.31	24.12	24.25	797	101.83
3	146.99	146.08	146.29	41.75	41.18	41.25	24.33	24.02	24.09	804	101.81
4	146.49	145.20	145.30	41.30	40.73	40.80	24.20	23.96	23.98	1,115	101.76
5	145.38	144.78	145.07	40.88	40.61	40.86	24.03	23.90	23.98	463	101.76
6	*			*			*			*	
7	145.75	144.75	145.32	41.09	40.72	40.88	24.18	24.00	24.07	1,072	101.73
8	145.69	144.70	144.97	41.04	40.58	40.70	24.12	23.96	24.01	1,271	101.74
9	145.25	144.48	144.90	40.99	40.70	40.92	24.39	24.08	24.30	963	101.72
10	145.81	144.95	145.65	41.28	40.80	41.18	24.71	24.26	24.62	1,016	101.82
11	146.63	145.82	146.27	41.77	41.32	41.46	24.81	24.55	24.75	944	101.93
12	146.63	146.25	146.56	41.51	41.33	41.48	24.85	24.70	24.78	374	102.00
13	*			*			*			*	
14	146.99	146.45	146.77	41.59	41.20	41.27	24.91	24.70	24.82	688	101.97
15	146.83	146.06	146.45	41.27	40.99	41.08	24.88	24.65	24.77	784	101.98
16	147.42	146.40	147.30	41.51	41.02	41.45	24.99	24.68	24.97	860	102.03
17	148.58	147.62	148.46	41.86	41.62	41.81	25.10	24.87	24.98	1,238	102.14
18	149.28	148.42	148.96	42.11	41.71	41.93	25.08	24.85	24.96	1,152	102.06
19	↕	↕	↕	↕	↕	↕	↕	↕	↕	↕	↕
20											
21	149.27	148.31	148.52	41.75	41.33	41.40	25.19	24.96	25.15	828	101.96
22	148.44	147.59	147.81	41.14	40.81	40.97	25.17	24.90	25.00	803	101.91
23	148.18	147.49	147.87	41.12	40.89	41.02	25.40	25.03	25.35	788	101.86
24	147.88	146.81	147.11	40.96	40.48	40.70	25.32	25.02	25.19	774	101.64
25	147.38	146.42	147.02	40.75	40.46	40.65	25.28	25.06	25.20	599	101.69
26	↕	↕	↕	↕	↕	↕	↕	↕	↕	↕	↕
27											
28	147.17	146.53	146.87	40.81	40.46	40.54	25.33	25.15	25.25	554	101.70
29	147.40	146.70	147.12	40.79	40.50	40.72	25.31	25.15	25.22	620	101.61
30	147.69	146.93	147.28	41.06	40.67	40.95	25.38	25.23	25.31	895	101.65
31	147.42	146.77	146.99	41.01	40.81	40.89	25.35	25.22	25.29	605	101.68
High			148.96			41.93			25.35		102.14
Low			144.90			40.54			23.98		101.61

Sunday* Holiday† ooo omitted‡

Total 20,753

SEPTEMBER, 1944

Date	Industrials High	Low	Close	Railroads High	Low	Close	Utilities High	Low	Close	‡Daily Sales	40 Bonds
1	147.47	146.73	147.16	40.90	40.75	40.87	25.32	25.13	25.25	638	101.71
2	↕	↕	↕	↕	↕	↕	↕	↕	↕	↕	↕
3											
4	†	†	†	†	†	†	†	†	†	†	†
5	147.45	146.44	146.56	40.85	40.46	40.48	25.28	24.97	25.04	873	101.46
6	146.44	144.26	144.42	40.32	39.03	39.12	25.02	24.36	24.42	1,470	101.22
7	144.08	142.53	143.58	39.44	38.75	39.34	24.55	24.08	24.40	1,478	101.06
8	144.28	143.10	143.51	39.59	39.17	39.32	24.66	24.40	24.49	629	101.24
9	143.65	143.02	143.31	39.30	39.16	39.24	24.47	24.31	24.38	276	101.26
10	*			*			*			*	
11	144.56	143.64	144.30	39.61	39.17	39.47	24.62	24.39	24.56	572	101.19
12	145.09	144.40	144.88	39.55	39.32	39.50	24.71	24.48	24.64	547	101.12
13	145.05	143.87	143.94	39.50	38.94	39.00	24.69	24.28	24.30	880	100.95
14	143.44	142.65	142.96	38.88	38.58	38.71	24.45	24.18	24.26	728	100.90
15	144.24	143.36	144.08	39.18	38.82	39.09	24.47	24.23	24.40	642	101.06
16	144.61	144.17	144.36	39.28	39.04	39.19	24.56	24.45	24.53	275	101.08
17	*			*			*			*	
18	144.85	144.24	144.75	39.24	39.04	39.12	24.49	24.37	24.43	345	101.12
19	145.97	144.75	145.62	39.80	39.24	39.64	24.79	24.49	24.70	715	101.25
20	146.29	145.42	145.85	39.82	39.58	39.68	24.90	24.61	24.81	696	101.42
21	146.09	145.31	145.43	39.68	39.48	39.53	24.82	24.63	24.69	561	101.41
22	145.95	145.33	145.60	39.84	39.56	39.75	24.85	24.66	24.78	546	101.40
23	145.86	145.52	145.78	39.98	39.79	39.90	24.88	24.79	24.85	312	101.41
24	*			*			*			*	
25	147.06	146.07	146.77	40.59	40.12	40.40	25.00	24.83	24.91	793	101.49
26	147.08	146.32	146.52	40.52	40.22	40.34	24.97	24.81	24.88	602	101.44
27	146.76	146.03	146.28	40.52	40.28	40.42	24.95	24.80	24.92	484	101.47
28	146.49	145.67	146.11	40.55	40.20	40.32	24.95	24.74	24.79	637	101.52
29	146.47	145.70	146.31	40.81	40.34	40.72	24.88	24.69	24.80	747	101.68
30	146.85	146.31	146.73	40.97	40.72	40.93	24.92	24.75	24.88	502	101.78
High			147.16			40.93			25.25		101.78
Low			142.96			38.71			24.26		100.90

*Sunday. †Holiday. ‡ooo omitted.

Total 15,948

OCTOBER, 1944

Date	Industrials			Railroads			Utilities			‡Daily Sales	40 Bonds
1											
2	147.30	146.41	146.92	41.05	40.77	40.87	25.10	24.93	25.04	816	101.83
3	147.29	146.49	146.91	41.01	40.67	40.83	25.15	24.95	25.05	746	101.83
4	148.06	146.93	147.89	41.23	40.75	41.10	25.26	25.02	25.24	821	102.08
5	148.95	147.78	148.62	41.71	41.14	41.67	25.47	25.28	25.42	1,001	102.32
6	149.20	148.51	148.84	41.97	41.64	41.80	25.67	25.39	25.58	802	102.47
7	149.03	148.62	148.92	41.99	41.74	41.93	25.69	25.58	25.68	447	102.61
8											
9	148.86	147.98	148.06	41.91	41.43	41.45	25.70	25.47	25.52	611	102.59
10	148.56	147.68	148.25	41.54	41.24	41.46	25.69	25.45	25.60	598	102.61
11	149.00	148.19	148.79	41.66	41.43	41.59	25.76	25.59	25.73	717	102.39
12											
13	149.03	148.48	148.70	41.72	41.43	41.57	25.87	25.60	25.76	684	102.78
14	148.78	148.52	148.59	41.62	41.50	41.57	26.00	25.76	25.91	349	102.73
15											
16	148.67	147.97	148.09	41.65	41.36	41.40	26.06	25.76	25.85	583	102.75
17	148.58	147.85	148.39	41.71	41.40	41.64	26.00	25.78	25.95	671	102.87
18	149.18	148.47	148.87	42.21	41.72	42.01	26.22	25.91	26.16	908	102.96
19	149.18	148.21	148.55	42.27	41.91	42.11	26.10	25.85	25.99	829	103.14
20	148.70	147.96	148.21	42.16	41.81	41.91	26.09	25.83	25.93	745	103.18
21	148.49	148.19	148.35	42.02	41.94	42.00	25.99	25.90	25.94	357	103.18
22											
23	148.46	146.37	146.58	42.08	41.37	41.43	26.00	25.45	25.54	1,025	102.89
24	146.86	145.98	146.58	41.75	41.17	41.62	25.65	25.41	25.62	854	102.81
25	146.82	146.03	146.37	41.66	41.38	41.49	25.75	25.59	25.65	638	102.85
26	146.65	145.47	145.83	41.49	40.93	41.11	25.75	25.41	25.48	927	102.61
27	146.46	145.33	146.29	41.24	40.94	41.19	25.49	25.28	25.40	827	102.58
28	146.66	146.34	146.50	41.51	41.30	41.45	25.51	25.35	25.45	296	102.67
29											
30	146.68	145.80	146.28	41.47	41.17	41.30	25.54	25.30	25.37	605	102.69
31	147.01	146.12	146.53	41.67	41.27	41.59	25.52	25.31	25.40	676	102.79
High			148.92			42.11			26.16		103.18
Low			145.83			40.83			25.04		101.83

*Sunday. †Holiday. ‡000 omitted. Total 17,534

NOVEMBER, 1944

Date	Industrials			Railroads			Utilities			‡Daily Sales	40 Bonds
1	147.05	146.38	146.73	41.88	41.53	41.66	25.73	25.45	25.67	708	102.79
2	147.69	146.71	147.53	42.01	41.66	41.95	25.84	25.58	25.80	790	102.80
3	147.59	146.87	147.16	42.13	41.83	41.98	25.91	25.68	25.84	730	102.79
4	147.55	147.14	147.37	42.08	41.91	42.04	25.91	25.77	25.85	358	102.81
5											
6	148.19	147.06	147.92	42.13	41.71	41.93	25.93	25.65	25.79	866	102.73
7											
8	147.92	146.82	147.52	42.06	41.67	41.98	25.70	25.45	25.61	732	102.75
9	148.02	146.98	147.75	42.32	41.89	42.20	25.70	25.52	25.61	851	102.79
10	148.39	147.64	148.08	42.52	42.16	42.37	25.71	25.54	25.61	1,121	102.89
11											
12											
13	148.22	146.78	146.97	42.44	41.81	41.87	25.62	25.32	25.34	918	102.85
14	146.90	145.36	145.60	41.78	41.24	41.30	25.36	25.13	25.19	1,101	102.70
15	146.04	145.22	145.64	41.54	41.16	41.30	25.23	25.00	25.13	818	102.71
16	146.15	145.17	145.67	41.82	41.34	41.58	25.25	25.08	25.15	847	102.84
17	146.15	145.33	145.77	41.76	41.42	41.62	25.25	25.03	25.12	706	102.84
18	146.18	145.57	146.02	41.68	41.56	41.64	25.20	25.00	25.10	362	102.91
19											
20	146.56	145.71	146.33	42.06	41.60	42.03	25.28	25.08	25.21	692	103.17
21	147.27	146.34	147.03	42.59	42.11	42.43	25.48	25.22	25.35	864	103.21
22	147.59	146.74	146.92	42.71	42.44	42.56	25.44	25.30	25.40	767	103.39
23											
24	147.04	145.99	146.40	42.64	42.28	42.35	25.47	25.28	25.35	678	103.43
25	146.77	146.34	146.63	42.54	42.35	42.51	25.40	25.30	25.35	358	103.52
26											
27	147.21	146.30	146.92	42.67	42.30	42.62	25.50	25.32	25.43	738	103.50
28	147.40	146.62	147.14	42.81	42.48	42.64	25.55	25.31	25.45	868	103.53
29	148.07	146.89	147.81	43.21	42.64	43.08	25.61	25.40	25.57	1,161	103.60
30	148.06	147.06	147.33	43.14	42.77	42.88	25.60	25.35	25.45	985	103.79
High			148.08			43.08			25.85		103.79
Low			145.60			41.30			25.10		102.70

*Sunday. †Holiday. ‡000 omitted. Total 18,019

DECEMBER, 1944

Date	Industrials			Railroads			Utilities			‡Daily Sales	40 Bonds
	High	Low	Close	High	Low	Close	High	Low	Close		
1	147.65	146.76	147.30	42.96	42.67	42.87	25.52	25.35	25.40	925	103.87
2	147.70	147.09	147.50	43.45	42.88	43.37	25.47	25.35	25.40	706	103.90
3											
4	148.41	147.21	148.22	44.11	43.56	44.04	25.51	25.28	25.38	1,428	103.98
5	149.23	148.05	148.58	44.50	43.95	44.14	25.60	25.38	25.46	1,476	103.98
6	149.14	148.03	148.77	44.37	43.90	44.32	25.55	25.29	25.38	1,094	104.00
7	149.64	148.55	149.23	44.98	44.34	44.75	25.51	25.31	25.45	1,345	104.18
8	150.68	149.07	150.48	45.47	44.55	45.32	25.55	25.35	25.50	1,683	104.41
9	151.63	150.79	151.31	45.92	45.48	45.62	25.70	25.53	25.59	1,045	104.50
10											
11	152.14	150.65	151.62	46.17	45.40	45.90	25.77	25.55	25.65	1,502	104.57
12	151.75	150.69	151.20	46.06	45.33	45.78	25.80	25.57	25.71	1,155	104.60
13	151.34	150.43	150.64	46.03	45.57	45.70	25.89	25.67	25.77	1,128	104.67
14	151.02	150.11	150.80	46.98	45.68	46.90	26.06	25.77	25.99	1,386	104.75
15	152.75	150.93	152.28	47.63	46.89	47.34	26.21	25.92	26.10	2,136	104.87
16	153.00	152.15	152.53	47.41	46.93	46.98	26.36	26.12	26.25	1,021	104.92
17											
18	152.28	151.15	151.53	47.16	46.56	46.95	26.25	26.00	26.09	981	104.90
19	151.90	150.84	151.62	48.29	46.83	48.09	26.11	25.95	26.03	1,283	105.02
20	151.39	150.15	150.59	48.41	46.85	47.40	26.10	25.70	25.84	1,483	104.97
21	150.73	149.88	150.28	47.59	46.88	47.21	25.96	25.71	25.82	951	104.89
22	151.04	150.04	150.43	48.36	47.29	48.01	26.01	25.80	25.90	1,281	104.95
23	150.85	150.38	150.63	48.32	47.97	48.16	26.02	25.85	25.98	530	104.90
24											
25	†	†	†	†	†	†	†	†	†	†	†
26	150.36	149.41	149.66	48.54	47.79	48.04	26.03	25.81	25.90	997	104.88
27	149.46	147.93	148.71	47.85	46.58	47.32	25.86	25.58	25.70	1,583	104.73
28	150.73	148.62	150.47	47.95	47.22	47.62	26.01	25.65	25.96	1,232	104.86
29	152.53	150.48	151.93	48.56	47.87	48.30	26.36	26.00	26.26	1,894	104.98
30	152.88	152.10	152.32	48.62	48.24	48.40	26.48	26.30	26.37	1,016	105.12
31											
High			152.53			48.40			26.37		105.12
Low			147.30			42.87			25.38		103.87

Total 31,261

*Sunday †Holiday ‡000 omitted

JANUARY, 1945

Date	Industrials			Railroads			Utilities			‡Daily Sales	40 Bonds
	High	Low	Close	High	Low	Close	High	Low	Close		
1	†	†	†	†	†	†	†	†	†	†	†
2	152.83	151.63	152.58	48.54	48.08	48.43	26.52	26.17	26.41	1,341	105.03
3	154.61	153.02	154.31	49.29	48.47	49.04	26.52	26.20	26.39	2,164	105.36
4	155.00	153.72	154.42	49.59	48.84	49.43	26.49	26.20	26.31	1,827	105.47
5	155.02	153.79	154.00	50.21	49.32	49.83	26.43	26.20	26.26	1,798	105.59
6	153.83	153.19	153.58	49.92	49.36	49.76	26.33	26.19	26.25	743	105.59
7											
8	155.04	153.69	154.85	50.95	49.96	50.89	26.56	26.31	26.54	1,995	105.71
9	155.72	154.52	155.01	51.35	50.41	50.68	26.62	26.35	26.48	2,262	105.80
10	155.95	154.38	155.67	51.08	50.29	51.03	26.59	26.30	26.47	2,110	105.73
11	156.68	155.32	155.85	51.24	50.56	50.71	26.67	26.35	26.58	2,213	105.80
12	156.22	154.99	155.42	50.67	50.01	50.24	26.79	26.35	26.58	1,745	105.75
13	155.81	155.23	155.58	50.30	49.95	50.12	26.75	26.60	26.69	775	105.69
14											
15	155.72	154.30	154.76	50.00	48.86	48.98	26.75	26.48	26.55	2,013	105.45
16	155.04	153.96	154.60	49.24	48.53	48.95	26.73	26.47	26.63	1,209	105.38
17	155.99	154.53	155.33	49.96	49.04	49.69	26.86	26.62	26.78	1,833	105.54
18	155.50	153.95	154.61	49.66	48.70	49.01	26.89	26.66	26.81	1,631	105.27
19	154.58	153.37	153.84	48.60	47.85	48.22	26.80	26.53	26.62	1,609	105.17
20	153.37	152.49	152.71	48.06	47.53	47.70	26.63	26.32	26.38	829	105.00
21											
22	152.41	151.10	152.03	47.85	46.93	47.66	26.49	26.18	26.36	1,467	104.93
23	152.97	151.23	151.36	48.71	46.99	47.06	26.53	26.12	26.15	1,366	104.86
24	152.15	150.53	151.35	47.48	46.70	47.15	26.40	26.10	26.32	1,012	104.83
25	152.62	151.39	152.26	47.73	47.14	47.47	26.50	26.25	26.49	974	105.00
26	153.57	152.53	153.30	48.27	47.72	48.09	26.70	26.45	26.63	1,255	105.16
27	154.35	153.48	154.13	48.33	48.04	48.17	26.69	26.56	26.65	743	105.16
28											
29	154.25	153.30	154.06	48.22	47.73	48.07	26.82	26.50	26.76	1,374	105.09
30	154.58	153.31	153.45	48.10	47.10	47.17	27.01	26.73	26.77	1,529	104.99
31	153.93	152.62	153.67	47.17	46.62	47.03	26.95	26.65	26.91	1,178	104.90
High			155.85			51.03			26.91		105.80
Low			151.35			47.03			26.15		104.83

Total 38,995

*Sunday †Holiday ‡000 omitted

FEBRUARY, 1945

Date	Industrials High	Low	Close	Railroads High	Low	Close	Utilities High	Low	Close	‡Daily Sales	40 Bonds
1	154.15	153.22	153.79	47.61	47.11	47.45	27.39	26.91	27.35	1,559	104.96
2	154.71	153.30	154.45	48.62	47.55	48.39	27.65	27.33	27.50	1,871	105.06
3	154.92	154.27	154.76	48.79	48.24	48.72	27.55	27.37	27.49	1,035	105.18
4	*			*			*				*
5	155.76	154.56	155.35	49.09	48.72	48.89	27.61	27.45	27.54	1,800	105.43
6	156.00	155.18	155.50	49.82	48.95	49.61	27.63	27.44	27.55	1,598	105.58
7	156.07	155.13	155.71	50.15	49.38	49.96	27.66	27.40	27.58	1,499	105.66
8	156.17	155.19	155.54	50.22	49.61	49.85	27.69	27.45	27.52	1,528	105.78
9	155.48	154.25	154.75	49.64	48.86	49.35	27.60	27.30	27.47	1,180	105.64
10	155.11	154.61	154.85	49.53	49.12	49.38	27.52	27.38	27.49	506	105.67
11	†			†			†				†
12	†			†			†				†
13	156.49	154.90	156.34	50.41	49.59	50.32	27.85	27.50	27.78	1,797	105.81
14	157.81	156.37	157.08	50.86	50.25	50.49	27.97	27.75	27.90	2,057	105.94
15	158.37	157.06	158.24	51.36	50.20	51.22	28.23	27.84	28.15	1,869	106.01
16	158.82	157.57	158.23	51.65	50.91	51.22	28.29	28.07	28.19	1,895	106.05
17	158.48	158.01	158.23	51.37	51.06	51.31	28.22	28.10	28.20	701	105.98
18	*			*			*				*
19	159.54	157.92	159.01	52.16	51.32	51.94	28.44	28.21	28.40	1,876	106.06
20	159.86	158.69	159.57	52.34	51.74	52.07	28.53	28.28	28.44	1,773	106.16
21	160.17	158.04	159.66	52.16	51.31	51.95	28.40	28.00	28.28	1,720	106.29
22	†			†			†				†
23	159.80	158.55	158.99	51.98	51.32	51.49	28.39	27.95	28.07	1,319	106.32
24	159.20	158.50	158.69	51.43	51.14	51.25	28.09	27.92	28.01	624	106.30
25	*			*			*				*
26	158.91	157.45	158.41	51.16	50.47	50.90	28.14	27.80	28.06	1,257	106.30
27	159.47	158.23	159.30	51.31	50.66	51.22	28.36	28.08	28.29	1,190	106.38
28	160.85	159.51	160.40	51.86	51.29	51.56	28.60	28.33	28.47	1,957	106.61
High			160.40			52.07			28.47		106.61
Low			153.79			47.45			27.35		104.96

Total 32,611

*Sunday. †Holiday. ‡000 omitted.

MARCH, 1945

Date	Industrials High	Low	Close	Railroads High	Low	Close	Utilities High	Low	Close	‡Daily sales	40 Bonds
1	161.15	160.11	160.72	52.69	51.67	52.51	28.64	28.35	28.58	2,086	106.78
2	160.76	159.63	159.95	52.77	51.83	52.03	28.67	28.38	28.42	1,767	106.72
3	159.93	159.41	159.71	52.17	51.83	52.10	28.55	28.35	28.51	681	106.72
4	*			*			*				*
5	160.85	159.56	160.68	52.58	51.77	52.25	28.56	28.31	28.50	1,192	106.75
6	162.22	160.56	161.50	52.87	52.20	52.51	28.55	28.30	28.38	1,693	106.81
7	162.21	160.96	161.52	52.62	51.96	52.09	28.60	28.32	28.40	1,401	106.84
8	161.34	158.31	158.86	52.04	50.51	50.96	28.47	27.95	28.00	1,864	106.54
9	158.29	155.96	156.34	50.48	49.69	49.86	27.97	27.55	27.63	2,062	106.33
10	157.50	156.21	157.21	50.43	49.67	50.31	27.82	27.56	27.75	754	106.47
11	*			*			*				*
12	158.38	157.33	157.88	50.97	50.37	50.70	27.94	27.73	27.84	916	106.52
13	158.24	156.94	157.59	50.94	50.35	50.83	27.86	27.64	27.80	761	106.58
14	158.16	157.29	157.83	51.66	50.95	51.41	28.07	27.82	27.98	751	106.75
15	158.95	157.84	158.53	52.57	51.35	52.54	28.15	27.95	28.05	797	106.84
16	159.42	158.41	158.92	53.24	52.27	52.75	28.25	28.05	28.15	879	106.90
17	158.88	158.51	158.75	52.95	52.59	52.90	28.15	28.08	28.12	399	106.98
18	*			*			*				*
19	158.88	157.36	157.89	53.05	52.01	52.50	28.19	27.94	28.07	1,067	106.90
20	157.71	156.14	156.37	52.31	51.39	51.74	28.02	27.70	27.80	922	106.81
21	156.10	154.08	155.30	51.82	50.56	51.38	27.80	27.46	27.64	1,343	106.66
22	155.73	154.82	155.07	52.21	51.39	51.66	27.82	27.56	27.66	829	106.74
23	156.00	154.68	155.45	51.99	51.48	51.74	27.75	27.52	27.60	678	106.82
24	155.25	154.23	154.36	51.67	50.94	51.00	27.71	27.47	27.52	452	106.73
25	*			*			*				*
26	153.62	151.74	152.27	50.70	49.58	49.72	27.46	27.02	27.09	1,387	106.47
27	153.51	151.77	152.78	50.52	49.44	50.03	27.31	26.98	27.21	1,106	106.57
28	154.08	152.89	153.79	50.57	50.13	50.40	27.45	27.17	27.37	724	106.58
29	154.46	153.48	154.06	50.77	50.33	50.56	27.55	27.30	27.48	658	106.66
30	†			†			†				†
31	154.62	153.92	154.41	50.84	50.55	50.71	27.70	27.51	27.64	321	106.67
High			161.52			52.90			28.58		106.98
Low			152.27			49.72			27.09		106.33

Total 27,490

*Sunday †Holiday ‡000 omitted

APRIL, 1945

Date	Industrials High	Low	Close	Railroads High	Low	Close	Utilities High	Low	Close	‡Daily sales	40 Bonds
1	*			*			*			*	
2	156.05	154.51	155.86	51.42	50.67	51.27	27.85	27.50	27.75	647	106.66
3	156.97	155.94	156.20	51.86	51.20	51.31	28.02	27.70	27.86	730	106.69
4	156.41	155.69	155.96	51.57	51.09	51.24	27.98	27.71	27.87	516	106.77
5	156.26	154.77	154.99	51.43	50.41	50.64	27.90	27.52	27.54	684	106.77
6	155.95	154.70	155.85	51.19	50.53	51.06	27.82	27.50	27.74	612	106.76
7	156.57	156.06	156.33	51.51	51.15	51.35	27.97	27.77	27.92	372	106.77
8	*			*			*			*	
9	156.71	155.91	156.10	51.56	51.17	51.19	28.07	27.79	27.85	565	106.82
10	156.82	155.54	156.51	52.29	51.14	52.08	28.11	27.85	28.06	756	106.92
11	158.17	156.59	158.06	53.04	52.20	52.91	28.34	28.09	28.29	1,060	107.00
12	159.14	157.89	158.48	52.23	52.70	52.74	28.46	28.14	28.24	1,056	107.02
13	159.95	157.73	159.75	53.39	52.36	53.19	29.33	28.35	29.25	1,804	106.88
14	†	†	†	†	†	†	†	†	†	†	†
15											
16	162.76	160.57	162.43	54.58	53.49	54.22	29.86	29.40	29.78	2,504	107.11
17	163.72	162.15	162.60	55.11	54.21	54.54	29.99	29.63	29.77	2,072	....
18	164.17	162.35	163.83	55.74	54.21	55.62	29.94	29.59	29.87	1,710	107.13
19	164.45	162.72	163.18	55.82	54.58	54.86	30.07	29.60	29.76	1,680	107.12
20	163.67	162.46	162.83	55.54	54.83	54.96	30.04	29.68	29.80	1,127	107.21
21	163.27	162.62	163.20	55.25	54.79	55.19	29.89	29.70	29.84	590	107.21
22	*			*			*			*	
23	164.08	162.88	163.58	56.15	55.10	56.05	29.95	29.65	29.79	1,376	107.16
24	164.62	163.33	164.31	56.83	55.88	56.55	30.09	29.71	29.96	1,826	107.22
25	164.46	163.17	163.91	56.89	55.92	56.56	30.26	29.86	30.15	1,419	107.13
26	163.78	162.06	163.22	56.60	55.33	56.39	30.20	29.82	30.05	1,367	107.16
27	164.27	163.12	163.94	57.30	56.42	57.01	30.30	29.97	30.20	1,360	107.21
28	164.90	163.89	164.71	57.40	56.88	57.19	30.45	30.23	30.41	933	107.19
29	*			*			*			*	
30	165.71	164.10	165.44	57.48	56.61	57.08	30.55	30.25	30.46	1,504	107.26
High			165.44			57.19			30.46		
Low			154.99			50.64			27.54		107.26
Total										28,270	106.66

*Sunday. †Holiday. ‡000 omitted.

MAY, 1945

Date	Industrials High	Low	Close	Railroads High	Low	Close	Utilities High	Low	Close	‡Daily sales	40 Bonds
1	166.18	164.49	165.09	57.02	55.95	56.31	30.57	30.20	30.29	1,532	107.24
2	165.38	164.45	165.03	56.61	55.85	56.24	30.45	30.10	30.25	1,142	107.22
3	166.02	164.77	165.84	56.83	56.01	56.72	30.76	30.23	30.66	1,335	107.24
4	166.61	165.40	166.27	57.12	56.58	56.82	30.94	30.60	30.90	1,406	107.27
5	166.94	166.34	166.71	57.10	56.65	56.76	31.00	30.83	30.92	934	107.36
6	*			*			*			*	
7	167.25	165.76	166.53	57.03	55.84	56.31	31.06	30.71	30.88	1,951	107.34
8	167.25	165.62	166.42	56.84	55.92	56.42	31.05	30.68	30.85	1,578	107.32
9	166.72	165.06	165.24	56.64	55.48	55.51	31.06	30.64	30.73	1,491	107.26
10	164.56	162.68	163.09	55.54	54.42	54.70	30.73	30.32	30.45	1,509	107.10
11	163.82	162.60	163.21	55.39	54.81	55.18	30.66	30.37	30.48	1,067	107.16
12	164.11	163.20	163.96	55.88	55.26	55.84	30.75	30.53	30.73	562	107.20
13	*			*			*			*	
14	164.41	163.16	163.45	56.10	55.48	55.67	30.90	30.67	30.75	980	107.14
15	164.31	163.07	164.00	55.89	55.33	55.85	30.86	30.56	30.75	1,009	107.09
16	165.07	163.76	164.50	56.40	55.81	56.18	30.94	30.74	30.82	1,206	107.22
17	165.85	164.23	165.20	56.78	55.86	56.12	31.15	30.80	31.05	1,370	107.26
18	166.47	165.19	166.17	56.28	55.87	56.05	31.19	30.92	31.06	1,432	107.34
19	166.75	166.17	166.44	56.41	56.12	56.24	31.21	31.07	31.17	728	107.32
20	*			*			*			*	
21	166.93	165.61	165.99	56.27	55.84	55.95	31.23	31.03	31.10	1,082	107.36
22	166.61	165.47	165.91	56.18	55.62	55.74	31.21	31.04	31.11	1,049	107.31
23	165.72	163.80	164.50	55.90	54.86	55.49	31.15	30.80	30.90	1,313	107.34
24	164.81	163.73	164.41	56.02	55.09	55.97	31.01	30.76	30.92	962	107.35
25	165.55	164.38	165.12	57.15	56.11	57.02	31.06	30.84	30.94	1,304	107.38
26	166.58	165.39	166.40	57.68	57.24	57.49	31.05	30.90	30.96	697	107.40
27	*			*			*			*	
28	168.75	166.45	168.21	58.52	57.57	58.29	31.15	30.85	31.05	1,570	107.37
29	169.53	168.06	169.08	58.86	58.10	58.53	31.45	31.05	31.39	1,601	107.50
30	†	†	†	†	†	†	†	†	†	†	†
31	169.41	167.90	168.30	58.74	57.72	57.90	31.30	30.89	31.00	1,215	107.48
High			169.08			58.53			31.39		107.50
Low			163.09			54.70			30.25		107.09
Total										32,025	

*Sunday. †Holiday. ‡000 omitted.

JUNE, 1945

Date	Industrials High	Low	Close	Railroads High	Low	Close	Utilities High	Low	Close	†Daily sales	40 Bonds
1	168.51	167.47	168.08	59.06	57.57	58.89	31.54	31.15	31.45	1,430	107.46
2	168.42	167.71	167.96	59.37	58.81	58.90	31.95	31.46	31.82	980	107.56
3*											
4	168.49	167.36	168.08	58.91	58.07	58.50	31.99	31.65	31.86	1,540	107.47
5	168.80	167.54	168.13	58.88	58.15	58.48	32.00	31.68	31.85	1,510	107.48
6	168.16	166.58	167.29	58.83	57.89	58.33	32.08	31.67	31.87	1,520	107.42
7	167.63	166.58	167.16	59.04	58.22	58.89	32.00	31.71	31.90	1,300	107.58
8	167.67	166.54	166.83	60.16	58.91	59.46	32.05	31.74	31.85	1,710	107.63
9	166.98	166.59	166.85	59.60	59.29	59.48	31.95	31.80	31.85	660	107.75
10*											
11	167.20	166.09	166.25	59.59	58.68	58.74	32.01	31.72	31.85	1,490	107.68
12	166.78	165.89	166.39	59.30	58.37	58.95	32.11	31.70	32.05	1,320	107.72
13	167.10	166.07	166.75	59.47	58.83	59.17	32.35	31.94	32.19	1,590	107.84
14	167.47	166.51	167.08	60.11	59.21	59.87	32.65	32.30	32.57	1,850	107.85
15	168.10	166.92	167.64	60.88	59.93	60.60	32.73	32.40	32.52	1,900	107.82
16	167.76	167.26	167.54	61.40	60.69	61.14	32.65	32.38	32.52	1,100	107.85
17*											
18	167.72	166.67	166.94	62.44	60.97	61.72	32.72	32.42	32.61	1,930	107.85
19	167.80	166.50	167.23	61.95	61.10	61.41	32.78	32.47	32.58	1,560	107.88
20	168.01	166.81	167.74	62.48	61.27	62.10	32.80	32.49	32.72	1,680	107.96
21	168.84	167.53	168.14	63.14	62.21	62.84	33.04	32.70	33.02	2,100	108.00
22	168.69	167.48	167.90	63.23	62.19	62.36	33.23	32.87	33.06	1,850	107.96
23	168.46	167.96	168.24	62.56	62.14	62.29	33.15	33.00	33.08	960	107.95
24*											
25	168.90	167.97	168.59	63.35	62.25	63.06	33.26	33.00	33.15	1,890	108.00
26	169.55	168.40	168.92	63.62	62.73	63.06	33.44	33.10	33.35	2,140	107.94
27	169.27	168.36	168.78	63.14	62.51	62.87	33.55	33.18	33.43	1,690	107.80
28	168.80	165.70	166.22	62.80	59.92	60.56	33.68	32.86	33.03	2,940	107.53
29	166.24	163.78	164.57	60.92	59.49	60.18	33.05	32.51	32.72	2,020	107.53
30	165.59	164.66	165.29	60.74	60.20	60.62	33.22	32.74	33.13	660	107.54
High			168.92			63.06			33.43		108.00
Low			164.57			58.33			31.45		107.42

Total 41,320

*Sunday †Holiday ‡000 omitted.

JULY, 1945

Date	Industrials High	Low	Close	Railroads High	Low	Close	Utilities High	Low	Close	‡Daily sales	40 Bonds
1*											
2	166.75	165.39	165.91	61.42	60.59	60.73	33.67	33.15	33.35	1,380	107.68
3	166.39	165.35	165.73	61.14	60.47	60.69	33.55	33.26	33.49	861	107.69
4†											
5	165.36	164.02	164.26	60.24	59.21	59.23	33.32	32.89	32.95	915	107.63
6	165.07	163.47	164.67	59.84	58.79	59.71	33.22	32.65	33.15	959	107.60
7											
8											
9	166.76	164.64	166.55	60.54	59.58	60.52	33.40	33.11	33.34	797	107.65
10	167.79	166.60	167.09	61.32	60.58	60.86	33.60	33.25	33.35	939	107.64
11	167.49	166.16	166.59	60.84	60.16	60.33	33.59	33.33	33.45	814	107.66
12	167.24	165.51	166.85	60.92	60.05	60.80	33.57	33.23	33.50	968	107.64
13	167.41	166.29	166.67	60.89	60.24	60.40	33.64	33.29	33.43	961	107.61
14											
15											
16	167.08	165.46	165.82	60.45	59.56	59.71	33.47	33.07	33.21	787	107.51
17	165.22	162.29	162.43	59.28	57.40	57.63	33.25	32.63	32.68	1,556	107.25
18	162.87	160.62	161.69	58.21	56.70	57.60	33.02	32.28	32.67	1,452	107.14
19	163.39	161.95	162.81	58.12	57.45	57.72	33.22	32.76	32.91	782	107.10
20	163.22	162.04	162.50	57.96	57.48	57.63	33.10	32.79	32.92	651	107.16
21											
22											
23	162.82	161.49	161.65	57.76	56.76	56.99	32.99	32.55	32.64	755	107.02
24	162.00	160.98	161.73	57.16	56.52	56.95	32.71	32.46	32.66	638	107.00
25	162.63	162.10	163.44	57.74	57.04	57.64	32.88	32.60	32.81	617	106.98
26	162.91	160.71	160.91	57.19	55.54	55.71	32.73	32.10	32.22	1,441	106.86
27	161.34	159.95	160.92	56.50	55.43	56.35	32.42	31.94	32.30	924	106.75
28											
29											
30	162.51	160.88	162.09	57.23	56.50	57.12	32.50	32.24	32.40	909	106.77
31	163.36	162.21	162.88	57.45	57.05	57.12	32.79	32.45	32.66	871	106.84
High			167.09			60.86			33.50		107.69
Low			160.91			55.71			32.22		106.84

Total 19,977

*Sunday. †Holiday. ‡000 omitted.

AUGUST, 1945

Date	Industrials High	Low	Close	Railroads High	Low	Close	Utilities High	Low	Close	‡Daily sales	40 Bonds
1	163.21	162.27	162.72	57.43	56.87	57.22	32.70	32.40	32.55	650	106.82
2	163.08	161.82	162.49	57.27	56.67	56.89	32.50	32.20	32.35	600	106.72
3	163.23	162.27	163.06	57.59	56.98	57.41	32.51	32.36	32.42	510	106.59
4											
5											
6	163.69	162.66	163.19	57.84	57.24	57.36	32.59	32.39	32.45	490	106.60
7	162.87	161.16	161.55	57.11	55.97	56.29	32.48	31.90	32.11	980	106.51
8	162.74	161.17	161.83	56.89	56.05	56.46	32.32	31.87	32.05	700	106.54
9	164.82	161.14	164.55	57.95	55.84	57.80	32.68	31.85	32.56	1,460	106.57
10	166.54	164.07	165.14	58.11	56.08	56.24	32.85	32.35	32.51	1,690	106.41
11											
12											
13	165.02	162.81	164.11	55.56	54.24	54.66	32.67	32.25	32.42	970	106.02
14	165.22	164.04	164.79	55.05	54.10	54.53	32.66	31.41	32.53	910	105.95
15											
16											
17	166.08	164.01	164.38	54.64	52.52	53.05	32.80	32.23	32.34	1,210	105.61
18											
19											
20	164.82	162.68	163.11	53.25	51.00	51.48	32.38	31.80	31.90	1,320	105.31
21	163.88	162.28	163.38	52.38	50.76	52.18	32.14	31.67	32.05	1,160	105.02
22	164.94	163.35	164.54	53.34	52.23	52.79	32.10	31.75	31.92	760	105.12
23	167.94	164.99	167.64	54.39	52.89	54.06	32.25	31.82	32.15	1,190	105.44
24	170.04	167.54	169.89	54.73	53.98	54.61	32.41	32.13	32.36	1,320	105.66
25											
26											
27	172.26	170.11	171.96	55.58	54.65	55.36	32.82	32.50	32.70	1,570	105.78
28	172.93	171.43	172.32	55.56	54.92	55.08	32.81	32.44	32.60	1,260	105.79
29	172.51	171.34	172.09	55.14	54.31	54.72	32.75	32.50	32.63	920	105.82
30	172.58	171.46	172.37	55.08	54.37	54.99	32.72	32.51	32.65	890	105.90
31	174.54	172.73	174.29	55.37	54.86	55.28	33.06	32.77	33.01	1,110	106.04
High			174.29			57.80			33.01		106.82
Low			161.55			51.48			31.90		105.02

Total 21,670

*Sunday. †Holiday. ‡000 omitted.

SEPTEMBER, 1945

Date	Industrial High	Low	Close	Railroads High	Low	Close	Utilities High	Low	Close	‡Daily Sales	40 Bonds
1											
2											
3											
4	174.86	173.52	173.90	55.57	55.03	55.20	33.35	33.01	33.23	1,070	106.04
5	174.49	173.23	174.24	55.20	54.53	54.90	33.38	33.05	33.28	978	105.97
6	176.14	174.17	175.96	55.86	54.58	55.80	33.79	33.27	33.75	1,376	105.85
7	177.57	175.76	176.61	56.04	55.33	55.46	33.95	33.65	33.76	1,326	105.73
8	177.17	176.47	176.99	55.32	55.06	55.22	33.75	33.59	33.65	389	105.72
9											
10	177.78	176.62	177.03	56.12	55.16	55.86	33.85	33.56	33.70	1,111	105.77
11	178.04	176.33	177.77	56.30	55.53	56.16	33.83	33.49	33.74	1,126	105.69
12	179.33	177.55	178.99	56.73	55.93	56.41	33.95	33.60	33.81	1,341	105.68
13	179.33	178.21	178.59	57.39	56.35	57.27	33.97	33.63	33.86	1,168	105.73
14	178.59	177.20	177.74	57.44	56.63	57.17	33.94	33.58	33.78	1,024	105.70
15	176.84	175.48	175.65	56.67	55.83	56.02	33.70	33.45	33.50	655	105.62
16											
17	175.11	173.30	174.75	56.08	55.11	55.82	33.55	33.10	33.45	898	105.56
18	177.76	175.19	177.58	56.94	56.05	56.84	33.90	33.40	33.82	1,156	105.61
19	180.06	178.32	179.51	57.74	57.16	57.51	34.25	33.86	34.15	1,693	105.69
20	180.72	178.92	180.22	58.40	57.05	58.26	34.25	33.87	34.11	1,501	105.77
21	180.80	178.87	179.69	58.73	57.83	58.16	34.35	34.05	34.18	1,335	105.72
22	179.70	178.99	179.49	58.34	57.91	58.27	34.30	34.06	34.25	482	105.72
23											
24	179.79	178.71	179.51	58.73	58.04	58.53	34.31	34.09	34.21	892	105.78
25	180.42	178.89	179.42	59.57	58.71	59.09	34.39	34.01	34.18	1,186	105.86
26	179.41	178.12	178.95	59.34	58.59	58.92	34.55	34.07	34.40	1,038	105.82
27	179.36	177.82	178.57	58.93	58.20	58.69	34.50	34.13	34.39	1,060	105.82
28	180.31	178.83	180.11	59.13	58.45	58.98	34.90	34.30	34.80	1,377	105.83
29	181.85	180.85	181.71	59.22	58.91	59.06	34.96	34.75	34.90	953	105.86
30											
High			181.71			59.09			34.90		106.04
Low			173.90			54.90			33.23		105.56

Total 23,135

OCTOBER, 1945

Date	Industrials High	Low	Close	Railroads High	Low	Close	Utilities High	Low	Close	‡Daily Sales	40 Bonds
1	183.92	181.93	183.37	59.69	59.10	59.49	35.11	34.71	34.91	1,986	105.87
2	185.05	183.13	183.85	59.95	59.00	59.22	35.05	34.70	34.78	1,800	105.89
3	184.20	182.32	183.33	59.39	58.69	58.85	35.00	34.53	34.77	1,432	105.85
4	183.75	182.32	183.06	59.22	58.47	58.98	34.91	34.55	34.76	1,336	106.03
5	184.48	182.80	183.94	59.44	58.62	59.08	34.97	34.62	34.89	1,421	106.09
6	184.92	184.19	184.77	59.49	59.02	59.31	35.11	34.89	35.01	768	106.13
7	*			*			*				*
8	186.02	184.66	185.46	59.75	59.25	59.39	35.31	34.85	35.06	1,781	106.14
9	185.95	184.26	185.43	60.10	58.92	59.88	35.19	34.82	35.05	1,635	106.14
10	186.52	185.07	186.05	60.49	59.81	60.07	35.25	34.91	35.11	1,697	106.26
11	186.10	184.83	185.72	60.38	59.68	60.17	35.30	34.98	35.24	1,559	106.49
12	†			†			†			†	†
13	†			†			†			†	†
14											
15	186.32	185.00	185.51	60.73	60.00	60.10	35.39	35.04	35.18	1,626	106.39
16	185.98	184.42	185.49	60.33	59.73	59.89	35.45	34.94	35.34	1,629	106.37
17	186.72	184.92	186.10	60.32	59.71	60.10	35.60	35.24	35.51	1,796	106.31
18	187.55	185.68	186.78	60.77	59.94	60.40	35.82	35.37	35.72	1,674	106.41
19	187.50	185.12	185.34	60.81	59.56	59.64	35.96	35.46	35.57	1,734	106.45
20	185.73	184.72	185.60	60.03	59.30	59.79	35.87	35.56	35.81	709	106.42
21	*			*			*				*
22	187.26	185.29	187.06	60.36	59.68	60.24	35.99	35.69	35.85	1,136	106.44
23	187.52	184.76	186.15	60.22	59.26	59.56	35.96	35.50	35.70	1,370	106.47
24	185.52	183.02	183.72	59.53	58.81	59.19	35.70	35.21	35.42	1,369	106.36
25	185.13	183.43	184.54	59.64	58.89	59.32	35.63	35.29	35.54	1,232	106.50
26	186.01	184.09	185.39	60.01	59.22	59.76	36.24	35.63	36.15	1,295	106.55
27	†			†			†			†	†
28											
29	186.02	183.90	184.24	59.65	58.79	58.94	36.38	35.90	36.07	1,256	106.55
30	184.61	182.88	184.16	59.41	58.47	59.22	36.37	35.75	36.30	1,169	106.57
31	186.74	183.59	186.60	60.28	58.95	60.12	37.09	36.27	36.96	2,064	106.78
High			187.06			60.40			36.96		106.78
Low			183.06			58.85			34.76		105.85

*Sunday †Holiday ‡000 omitted

Total 35,474

NOVEMBER, 1945

Date	Industrials High	Low	Close	Railroads High	Low	Close	Utilities High	Low	Close	‡Daily Sales	40 Bonds
1	189.33	187.02	188.84	61.20	60.39	61.07	37.58	36.98	37.42	2,213	106.85
2	189.40	187.54	188.62	61.67	60.83	61.36	37.69	37.31	37.50	1,841	106.88
3	189.00	188.20	188.58	62.44	61.42	62.26	37.64	37.44	37.56	920	106.88
4	*			*			*				*
5	189.69	188.02	189.50	63.26	62.12	63.15	37.81	37.38	37.70	1,654	106.92
6	†			†			†			†	†
7	192.76	190.13	192.04	63.85	62.91	63.25	38.15	37.61	37.95	2,384	107.05
8	192.78	190.79	191.72	63.13	62.16	62.46	38.11	37.65	37.89	1,963	106.99
9	192.46	190.68	191.46	62.80	62.14	62.45	38.41	37.70	38.25	1,830	107.00
10	191.73	190.86	191.37	62.52	62.19	62.42	38.57	38.26	38.43	1,118	107.01
11	*			*			*				
12	†			†			†			†	†
13	192.46	190.23	190.56	62.96	61.74	61.84	38.82	38.00	38.13	2,497	107.08
14	190.61	188.82	189.77	62.27	61.22	62.00	38.40	37.77	38.06	1,607	107.14
15	191.60	189.58	191.13	64.02	61.89	63.70	38.40	37.83	38.14	2,010	107.19
16	192.95	191.02	192.13	64.62	63.72	64.06	38.55	38.00	38.39	2,336	107.18
17	192.66	191.84	192.27	64.16	63.76	63.97	38.55	38.22	38.36	1,087	107.24
18	*			*			*				
19	192.50	190.20	191.51	64.04	63.31	63.79	38.45	37.98	38.26	2,021	107.43
20	192.83	190.69	192.12	64.87	63.55	64.66	38.60	38.11	38.45	2,182	107.50
21	191.47	188.97	189.54	64.55	63.40	63.69	38.55	37.95	38.13	1,913	107.44
22	†			†			†			†	†
23	189.26	187.34	187.82	63.53	62.77	63.03	38.20	37.75	37.91	1,349	107.37
24	187.01	185.83	186.41	62.93	62.29	62.65	37.93	37.52	37.68	740	107.34
25	*			*			*				
26	188.55	186.44	188.16	63.95	62.57	63.72	38.19	37.62	38.08	1,533	107.47
27	190.90	188.79	190.45	64.79	63.83	64.26	38.63	38.07	38.41	1,834	107.44
28	191.47	189.58	189.99	64.40	63.34	63.43	38.68	38.24	38.39	1,804	107.39
29	190.22	188.80	189.58	63.73	62.85	63.19	38.71	38.22	38.51	1,751	107.44
30	191.84	189.77	191.46	64.13	63.08	63.90	38.87	38.45	38.77	1,817	107.57
High			192.27			64.66			38.77		107.57
Low			186.41			61.07			37.42		106.85

*Sunday. †Holiday. ‡000 omitted.

Total 40,404

DECEMBER, 1945

Date	Industrials			Railroads			Utilities			‡Daily Sales	40 Bonds
	High	Low	Close	High	Low	Close	High	Low	Close		
1	192.65	191.53	192.40	64.41	64.06	64.23	38.85	38.63	38.73	1,220	107.58
2	*			*			*			*	*
3	194.36	192.16	193.65	64.86	64.08	64.41	39.11	38.67	38.90	2,606	107.65
4	194.12	192.17	193.06	65.18	63.94	64.79	38.96	38.45	38.63	2,312	107.65
5	193.67	191.75	193.08	64.94	64.24	64.47	38.83	38.48	38.67	1,859	107.71
6	194.62	192.70	193.84	64.79	63.99	64.22	38.95	38.58	38.71	2,287	107.64
7	194.78	193.18	194.08	65.03	63.89	64.74	39.02	38.62	38.82	2,048	107.70
8	195.45	194.44	195.18	65.05	64.77	64.89	39.16	38.83	39.02	1,263	107.69
9	*			*			*			*	*
10	196.59	194.76	195.64	64.98	64.19	64.37	39.32	38.91	39.15	2,143	107.78
11	196.47	194.34	195.82	64.43	63.77	64.09	39.15	38.64	38.75	1,692	107.70
12	195.39	193.18	193.96	64.00	63.09	63.25	38.55	37.96	38.18	1,684	107.79
13	194.62	192.84	193.52	63.81	63.16	63.39	38.32	37.88	38.04	1,223	107.87
14	193.86	192.50	193.34	64.39	63.40	64.15	38.21	37.80	38.05	1,127	....
15	194.08	193.24	193.76	64.61	64.24	64.49	38.20	37.99	38.14	619	107.93
16	*			*			*			*	*
17	192.87	189.80	190.37	64.19	62.44	62.61	37.90	37.00	37.21	1,987	107.81
18	191.78	189.33	190.98	63.37	62.12	63.24	37.61	37.06	37.50	1,355	107.84
19	191.43	190.11	190.62	63.88	63.04	63.23	37.73	37.26	37.50	975	107.92
20	190.22	188.84	189.36	63.40	62.63	62.91	37.76	37.28	37.51	797	107.95
21	189.67	187.51	189.07	63.02	62.21	62.66	37.81	37.26	37.70	942	108.00
22	190.87	189.75	190.67	63.35	62.76	63.19	37.99	37.66	37.96	611	108.02
23	*			*			*			*	*
24	†	†	†	†	†	†	†	†	†	†	†
25	†	†	†	†	†	†	†	†	†	†	†
26	193.45	191.59	192.76	63.98	63.15	63.47	38.63	38.02	38.40	1,415	108.12
27	193.89	191.76	192.31	63.57	62.40	62.66	38.50	37.90	38.06	1,325	108.16
28	192.95	191.58	192.43	63.20	62.34	62.91	38.31	37.84	38.15	1,093	108.25
29	193.26	192.20	192.84	63.09	62.72	62.90	38.34	38.13	38.22	555	108.28
30	*			*			*			*	*
31	193.47	192.07	192.91	63.08	62.50	62.80	38.35	37.95	38.13	1,012	108.32
High			195.82			64.89			39.15		108.32
Low........			189.07			62.61			37.21		107.58

Total 34,150

*Sunday †Holiday ‡000 omitted

JANUARY, 1946

Date	Industrials			Railroads			Utilities			‡Daily Sales	40 Bonds
	High	Low	Close	High	Low	Close	High	Low	Close		
1	†	†	†	†	†	†	†	†	†	†	†
2	192.65	191.15	191.66	62.85	62.15	62.46	38.36	37.87	38.15	1,052	108.15
3	191.97	189.77	191.25	62.50	61.59	62.16	38.38	37.59	38.22	1,386	108.25
4	191.81	190.27	190.90	62.92	62.09	62.59	38.35	37.89	38.10	1,075	108.42
5	191.68	190.69	191.47	62.90	62.58	62.81	38.40	38.10	38.35	528	108.50
6	*			*			*			*	*
7	192.40	190.87	191.77	63.62	62.68	63.12	38.52	38.09	38.38	1,230	108.52
8	194.98	192.04	194.65	64.57	63.45	64.45	39.04	38.28	38.92	2,160	108.58
9	198.40	195.16	197.33	65.34	64.28	64.73	39.51	38.87	39.32	2,925	108.66
10	199.78	197.17	199.16	65.29	64.45	64.75	39.80	39.16	39.53	2,470	108.78
11	200.86	198.67	200.04	65.74	64.68	65.03	40.05	39.58	39.89	2,254	108.80
12	199.76	198.00	199.44	65.04	64.36	64.88	39.90	39.43	39.83	1,251	108.82
13	*			*			*			*	*
14	202.59	200.25	201.93	66.44	65.26	66.14	40.42	39.84	40.30	2,740	108.82
15	204.02	201.73	202.97	67.10	66.05	66.44	40.70	40.00	40.25	2,719	108.92
16	204.50	201.93	203.81	67.44	66.16	67.14	40.39	40.00	40.28	2,097	108.96
17	205.03	202.95	203.49	67.67	66.61	66.69	40.63	40.02	40.30	2,200	108.97
18	203.70	200.78	202.18	67.29	65.90	66.65	40.62	39.69	40.35	3,232	108.91
19	201.11	199.17	200.21	66.58	65.68	66.28	40.57	40.00	40.07	1,680	108.86
20	*			*			*			*	*
21	198.03	195.52	196.63	65.78	64.78	65.48	40.11	39.40	39.80	1,675	108.75
22	198.00	195.63	197.35	66.50	65.03	66.24	40.15	39.59	40.00	1,528	108.90
23	199.48	197.20	198.84	67.29	66.46	66.97	40.63	40.00	40.45	2,048	109.05
24	200.86	198.68	200.04	67.27	66.35	66.46	40.94	40.43	40.79	2,208	109.11
25	200.13	198.17	199.50	66.65	66.85	66.30	40.93	40.30	40.80	1,762	109.14
26	200.30	199.03	199.85	66.52	66.11	66.41	41.10	40.64	40.99	921	109.13
27	*			*			*			*	*
28	205.50	202.10	204.62	68.30	67.03	67.83	41.72	40.85	41.57	3,490	109.16
29	206.49	203.75	205.35	68.24	67.39	67.89	41.80	41.01	41.29	2,914	109.15
30	206.59	203.37	204.84	68.20	67.27	67.55	41.40	40.75	40.96	2,277	109.18
31	205.22	203.07	204.67	67.93	66.95	67.62	41.27	40.56	41.25	1,688	109.19
High			205.35			67.89			41.57		109.19
Low........			190.90			62.16			38.10		108.15

Total 51,510

*Sunday. †Holiday. ‡000 omitted.

FEBRUARY, 1946

Date	Industrials			Railroads			Utilities			‡Daily Sales	40 Bonds
	High	Low	Close	High	Low	Close	High	Low	Close		
1	206.06	203.69	205.79	68.21	67.35	67.85	41.82	41.23	41.74	1,556	109.20
2	207.16	205.88	206.97	68.34	67.80	68.18	41.81	41.50	41.71	997	109.20
3 *											
4	207.49	205.05	205.84	68.36	67.25	67.59	41.75	41.06	41.20	1,661	109.30
5	206.84	204.55	206.61	68.30	67.33	68.23	41.48	40.83	41.32	1,674	109.37
6	207.24	205.15	205.48	68.42	67.38	67.44	41.37	40.94	40.76	1,753	109.50
7	205.73	203.63	205.09	67.79	67.03	67.54	40.75	40.10	40.54	1,487	109.67
8	205.60	203.62	204.38	67.80	66.87	66.93	40.82	40.20	40.44	1,256	109.73
9	203.52	201.55	202.30	66.87	66.01	66.20	40.42	39.80	39.91	922	109.71
10 *											
11	202.72	200.59	201.14	65.98	65.00	65.11	40.40	39.80	40.00	1,444	109.60
12 †	†	†	†	†	†	†	†	†	†	†	†
13	200.81	197.65	198.74	65.24	64.24	64.81	40.07	39.24	39.72	1,691	109.59
14	201.18	198.45	199.75	65.62	64.79	65.11	40.40	39.64	40.14	1,290	109.58
15	203.56	201.06	203.09	66.42	65.46	66.35	40.82	40.17	40.72	1,777	109.58
16	205.35	203.72	204.41	67.33	66.57	66.95	41.15	40.81	40.90	1,379	109.63
17 *											
18	204.13	200.84	201.63	66.54	65.13	65.37	40.97	40.25	40.46	1,563	109.64
19	200.42	194.90	196.13	64.66	62.32	62.86	40.15	38.91	39.10	2,301	109.43
20	195.06	191.17	192.38	63.10	61.36	61.86	39.15	38.20	38.44	2,146	109.39
21	196.30	193.05	195.62	63.53	62.42	63.34	39.51	38.82	39.26	1,588	109.46
22 †	†	†	†	†	†	†	†	†	†	†	†
23 *											
24 *											
25	194.04	186.87	187.23	62.93	60.67	61.02	39.30	37.80	38.01	2,399	109.32
26	188.09	184.05	186.02	61.61	59.86	60.53	38.41	37.46	37.46	2,647	109.21
27	189.56	187.34	189.06	62.26	61.04	62.04	39.07	38.45	38.94	1,396	109.19
28	190.64	188.19	190.09	62.57	61.61	62.23	39.27	38.54	38.93	1,175	109.17
High			206.97			68.23			41.74		109.73
Low			186.02			60.53			37.97		109.17

*Sunday. †Holiday. ‡000 omitted.   Total 34,095

MARCH, 1946

Date	Industrials			Railroads			Utilities			‡Daily Sales	40 Bonds
	High	Low	Close	High	Low	Close	High	Low	Close		
1	190.58	188.90	189.42	62.55	61.71	62.22	39.20	38.70	39.01	822	109.16
2	189.03	188.07	188.73	62.14	61.65	61.86	38.95	38.61	38.80	519	109.21
3 *											
4	188.87	186.77	188.46	62.00	61.18	61.91	39.06	38.55	38.98	965	109.18
5	191.16	188.91	190.49	62.69	61.91	62.23	39.52	39.07	39.41	1,045	109.25
6	190.77	189.39	190.28	62.43	61.76	62.21	39.52	39.00	39.36	886	109.27
7	191.93	190.30	181.46	62.85	62.16	62.60	40.08	39.46	39.92	901	109.27
8	194.40	192.08	193.70	62.95	62.45	62.63	40.28	39.88	40.12	966	109.41
9	194.70	193.63	194.45	62.68	62.42	62.57	40.32	40.10	40.28	464	109.45
10 *											
11	194.73	192.34	192.89	62.70	61.71	61.81	40.44	39.85	40.08	877	109.44
12	193.86	192.39	193.52	62.33	61.60	62.26	40.20	39.86	40.12	721	109.50
13	192.87	188.86	190.36	62.08	60.87	61.39	39.79	38.98	39.30	1,622	109.41
14	191.76	189.32	189.98	61.92	61.14	61.44	39.77	39.22	39.39	1,090	109.36
15	192.14	189.71	191.66	62.27	61.11	62.19	40.19	39.45	40.05	1,061	109.43
16	194.11	192.61	193.94	62.87	62.26	62.80	40.40	40.15	40.40	552	109.34
17 *											
18	195.86	194.05	195.33	63.47	62.77	63.13	40.78	40.28	40.50	1,066	109.35
19	196.23	193.77	194.09	63.34	62.56	62.57	40.89	40.44	40.57	1,052	109.40
20	195.90	193.63	195.53	63.40	62.46	63.30	41.07	40.47	40.97	1,282	109.43
21	197.00	195.10	196.70	63.66	63.04	63.34	41.19	40.65	41.05	1,205	109.46
22	198.20	195.92	197.19	63.51	62.91	63.23	41.35	40.90	41.11	1,179	109.45
23	198.27	197.21	198.09	63.55	63.21	63.49	41.23	41.00	41.17	586	109.42
24 *											
25	200.80	198.27	200.55	65.15	63.71	64.73	41.78	41.31	41.59	1,636	109.46
26	201.85	200.04	200.56	65.22	64.48	64.58	41.91	41.41	41.61	1,438	109.51
27	199.81	197.83	198.73	64.24	63.46	64.04	41.61	41.17	41.32	1,003	109.55
28	198.92	197.27	198.18	64.27	63.55	64.10	41.63	41.18	41.45	895	109.56
29	200.36	198.23	199.56	64.65	64.01	64.32	41.72	41.27	41.60	1,225	109.57
30	200.02	199.32	199.75	64.39	64.16	64.26	41.88	41.60	41.81	608	109.55
31											
High			200.56			64.73			41.81		109.57
Low			188.46			61.39			38.80		109.16

*Sunday. †Holiday. ‡000 omitted.   Total 25,666

APRIL, 1946

| | —Industrials— | | | —Railroads— | | | —Utilities— | | | †Daily | 40 |
	High	Low	Close	High	Low	Close	High	Low	Close	Sales	Bonds
1	199.97	198.47	199.19	64.41	63.61	64.30	42.01	41.22	41.68	1,046	109.55
2	200.16	198.98	199.83	64.24	63.85	64.00	41.93	41.35	41.70	1,044	109.59
3	203.29	199.81	203.12	65.20	64.01	65.15	42.33	41.60	42.27	1,557	109.57
4	205.79	203.25	204.77	65.63	65.02	65.30	42.85	42.22	42.66	2,131	109.58
5	205.18	202.88	204.04	65.30	64.48	64.57	43.10	42.42	42.95	1,659	109.64
6	205.29	204.23	204.98	64.54	64.23	64.32	43.10	42.84	43.00	692	109.58
7	*	*	*								
8	206.00	204.31	205.43	64.28	63.49	63.74	43.32	42.81	43.05	1,246	109.53
9	208.54	205.43	208.03	64.37	63.21	64.27	43.28	42.77	43.13	1,706	109.53
10	208.93	207.20	208.02	64.64	63.96	64.19	43.24	42.65	42.75	1,578	109.49
11	207.90	206.05	206.93	64.28	63.54	64.06	42.92	42.52	42.73	1,209	109.40
12	207.89	206.16	206.96	64.16	63.55	63.63	42.93	42.50	42.70	1,235	109.33
13	206.57	205.72	206.02	63.63	63.26	63.43	42.77	42.37	42.54	616	109.33
14	*	*	*	*	*	*	*	*	*		
15	206.36	204.57	206.01	63.67	63.08	63.58	42.75	42.34	42.58	1,173	109.29
16	208.51	206.28	207.97	64.42	63.63	64.37	43.12	42.59	42.99	1,459	109.25
17	209.36	206.97	207.93	65.26	64.33	64.86	43.40	43.00	43.11	1,527	109.24
18	209.10	207.27	208.31	65.54	64.56	65.26	43.55	43.02	43.43	1,496	109.24
19	†	†	†	†	†	†	†	†	†	†	†
20	208.76	207.71	208.06	65.60	65.01	65.37	43.90	43.42	43.67	775	109.17
21	*	*	*	*							
22	208.94	207.33	207.99	65.55	64.91	65.04	44.19	43.46	43.68	1,213	109.13
23	208.19	206.01	207.31	65.18	64.42	64.87	43.80	43.09	43.52	1,376	108.90
24	208.12	205.81	206,13	64.77	63.77	63.79	43.59	42.74	42.86	1,502	108.55
25	205.60	203.09	204.60	63.94	63.17	63.49	43.06	42.44	42.85	1,385	108.24
26	205.21	203.13	204.59	63.88	62.91	63.77	43.47	42.61	43.27	1,211	108.23
27	206.36	204.88	206.13	63.99	63.59	63.94	43.44	43.19	43.39	595	108.32
28	*	*	*	*	*	*	*	*	*	*	*
29	206.97	205.07	206.09	64.19	63.52	64.04	43.60	43.20	43.37	999	108.21
30	207.23	205.53	206.77	64.36	63.87	64.17	43.57	43.10	43.34	996	108.03
High			208.31			65.37			43.68		109.64
Low			199.19			63.43			41.68		107.13

*Sunday. †Holiday. ‡000 omitted.

Total 31,426

MAY, 1946

| | ——Industrials— | | | ——Railroads— | | | ——Utilities— | | | ‡Daily | 40 |
	High	Low	Close	High	Low	Close	High	Low	Close	Sales	Bonds
1	206.59	205.07	205.67	64.84	64.05	64.75	43.51	43.07	43.19	978	108.02
2	206.25	204.47	204.98	64.66	64.09	64.20	43.40	42.96	43.14	1,001	107.97
3	204.31	202.53	203.25	63.89	63.26	63.39	43.15	42.65	42.88	1,015	107.84
4	202.84	202.14	202.52	63.35	63.05	63.15	42.87	42.65	42.75	457	107.83
5	*	*	*	*				*			*
6	202.00	199.26	200.65	63.23	62.47	63.06	42.74	42.29	42.55	1,078	107.84
7	203.97	199.94	203.51	64.06	62.75	63.96	42.96	42.23	42.80	1,345	107.86
8	205.05	202.35	204.17	63.95	63.32	63.57	43.04	42.50	42.72	1,213	107.85
9	204.68	202.37	204.07	63.53	62.73	63.25	43.09	42.50	42.98	1,072	107.86
10	207.84	204.09	207.10	64.64	63.00	64.41	43.40	42.77	43.25	1,820	107.88
11	208.66	207.49	208.06	64.57	64.27	64.37	43.44	43.06	43.24	898	107.98
12	*	*	*	*	*	*	*	*	*	*	*
13	208.40	206.63	207.34	64.46	63.83	64.04	43.35	42.92	43.06	1,251	107.96
14	207.47	205.88	206.69	64.04	63.45	63.85	42.94	42.52	42.70	1,142	107.91
15	206.82	204.23	205.07	64.02	63.32	63.78	42.94	42.50	42.73	1,020	107.89
16	206.53	204.38	206.17	64.32	63.37	63.96	42.99	42.51	42.86	1,141	107.83
17	207.04	205.50	206.56	63.89	63.42	63.60	42.94	42.54	42.67	979	107.90
18	206.30	205.49	205.80	63.60	63.36	63.52	42.80	42.60	42.69	415	107.84
19	*	*	*	*	*	*	*	*	*	*	*
20	207.42	205.05	207.13	64.54	63.68	64.36	42.90	42.55	42.75	914	107.78
21	208.53	206.58	207.25	65.24	64.45	64.98	43.01	42.57	42.75	1,247	107.92
22	208.38	207.00	208.00	66.25	64.79	66.14	43.25	42.65	43.02	1,614	107.92
23	209.15	207.21	208.05	66.61	65.79	66.09	43.51	42.81	43.30	1,350	107.81
24	208.26	205.96	207.69	66.87	65.08	66.39	43.59	42.80	43.32	1,213	107.75
25	†	†	†	†	†	†	†	†	†	†	†
26	*	*	*	*	*	*	*	*	*	*	*
27	210.34	208.41	209.42	67.18	66.35	66.65	43.57	43.05	43.28	1,726	107.75
28	212.18	209.29	211.70	68.22	66.51	68.06	43.84	43.22	43.71	2,215	107.91
29	213.36	210.34	212.50	68.42	67.61	67.87	43.95	43.45	43.74	1,997	107.93
30	†	†	†	†	†	†	†	†	†	†	†
31	213.29	210.97	212.28	68.11	67.09	67.87	43.79	43.22	43.55	1,308	107.97
High			212.50			68.06			43.74		108.02
Low			200.65			63.06			42.55		107.75

*Sunday. †Holiday. ‡000 omitted.

Total 30,409

JUNE, 1946

	Industrials			Railroads			Utilities			‡Daily Sales	40 Bonds
	High	Low	Close	High	Low	Close	High	Low	Close		
1											
2											
3	212.48	210.90	211.47	67.67	66.72	66.92	43.75	43.15	43.46	1,210	107.96
4	211.37	209.03	210.03	66.91	66.04	66.72	43.65	42.97	43.47	1,208	107.96
5	211.42	209.30	209.78	66.89	66.05	66.15	43.75	43.01	43.10	1,168	108.00
6	210.03	208.33	209.50	66.47	65.64	66.18	43.31	42.72	43.15	976	107.96
7	210.40	208.63	209.96	66.33	65.69	66.14	43.36	42.85	43.07	1,021	108.01
8											
9											
10	211.44	209.73	210.68	67.03	66.22	66.86	43.30	42.89	43.05	1,008	108.03
11	211.14	208.92	209.05	67.64	66.44	66.54	43.25	42.75	42.80	1,087	108.10
12	209.34	207.52	208.96	67.27	66.27	67.10	43.00	42.57	42.79	970	108.11
13	211.25	209.26	210.56	68.47	67.45	68.31	43.13	42.70	42.95	1,148	108.13
14	211.46	209.73	210.36	68.67	67.83	68.02	43.19	42.65	42.83	978	108.10
15											
16											
17	211.16	209.65	210.13	68.77	67.91	68.22	43.15	42.73	42.81	1,020	108.09
18	210.01	207.42	207.71	68.42	67.25	67.44	42.74	42.21	42.31	1,150	108.07
19	206.93	205.24	205.74	67.70	67.14	67.51	42.45	41.80	42.21	1,013	108.08
20	205.65	200.31	200.52	67.74	65.97	66.05	42.30	41.42	41.45	1,312	107.99
21	203.42	198.98	203.09	66.76	65.52	66.50	41.94	41.23	41.83	1,339	107.95
22											
23											
24	204.65	202.68	203.56	67.02	66.03	66.33	42.12	41.64	41.82	993	107.97
25	203.83	202.11	202.54	66.07	65.12	65.18	41.95	41.52	41.62	881	107.94
26	202.98	200.52	202.10	65.18	64.45	64.93	41.71	41.25	41.47	1,020	107.96
27	205.68	202.83	205.03	66.09	65.15	65.88	42.06	41.49	41.95	1,202	107.98
28	206.41	204.32	205.62	66.25	65.53	65.81	42.25	41.88	42.10	1,013	107.94
29											
30											
High			211.47			68.31			43.47		108.13
Low			200.52			64.93			41.45		107.94

Total 21,717

*Sunday. †Holiday. ‡000 omitted.

JULY, 1946

	Industrials			Railroads			Utilities			‡Daily Sales	40 Bonds
	High	Low	Close	High	Low	Close	High	Low	Close		
1	208.59	205.79	206.47	66.90	65.65	65.78	42.60	41.95	42.06	1,565	107.99
2	207.43	205.56	206.64	65.86	65.11	65.36	42.10	41.76	41.94	755	107.95
3	207.50	206.36	207.06	65.70	65.26	65.37	41.98	41.69	41.73	653	107.93
4											
5	207.40	206.47	206.72	65.37	65.06	65.24	41.91	41.63	41.76	487	108.01
6											
7											
8	207.40	206.37	206.62	65.45	64.91	65.05	41.88	41.55	41.61	678	108.00
9	207.91	206.16	207.43	65.18	64.36	64.81	41.85	41.48	41.67	787	108.06
10	208.17	206.84	207.56	65.02	64.40	64.72	41.90	41.50	41.71	908	108.12
11	207.52	205.96	206.30	64.90	64.42	64.59	41.70	41.40	41.46	993	108.08
12	205.49	202.85	204.20	64.50	63.36	63.87	41.55	41.06	41.33	1,134	108.00
13											
14											
15	204.42	200.31	200.86	64.00	62.87	63.04	41.41	40.29	40.45	1,174	107.80
16	201.44	199.48	200.71	63.09	62.38	62.78	40.67	40.00	40.52	1,181	107.78
17	202.79	200.85	202.25	63.05	62.45	62.95	40.92	40.32	40.85	921	107.73
18	203.46	201.47	201.86	63.48	62.84	63.19	41.14	40.73	40.83	729	107.71
19	202.06	200.68	201.13	63.23	62.78	62.98	41.01	40.54	40.72	654	107.69
20											
21											
22	201.60	199.89	200.54	63.09	62.64	62.78	41.02	40.45	40.58	692	107.62
23	199.83	194.79	195.22	62.37	60.28	60.41	40.46	39.49	39.63	1,685	107.59
24	196.30	194.33	195.37	61.05	60.26	60.65	40.05	39.38	39.67	1,173	107.57
25	197.58	195.28	196.25	61.40	60.63	60.95	40.22	39.65	39.86	899	107.62
26	198.53	196.47	197.63	61.62	60.95	61.17	40.45	39.85	40.24	978	107.58
27											
28											
29	199.11	197.46	198.22	61.67	61.13	61.40	40.69	40.25	40.53	719	107.48
30	200.13	198.15	199.40	62.11	61.27	61.85	40.79	40.40	40.67	807	107.52
31	202.15	198.78	201.56	62.13	61.34	61.86	41.41	40.79	41.32	1,023	107.46
High			207.56			65.78			42.06		108.12
Low			195.22			60.41			39.63		107.46

Total 20,595

*Sunday. †Holiday. ‡000 omitted.

AUGUST, 1946

August	Industrials High	Low	Close	Railroads High	Low	Close	Utilities High	Low	Close	‡Daily Sales	40 Bonds
1	202.97	201.32	202.26	62.55	61.94	62.30	41.63	41.22	41.54	831	107.49
2	203.38	201.70	202.82	62.82	62.18	63.63	41.68	41.26	41.50	747	107.49
3	†	†	†	†	†	†	†	†	†	†	
4	*										
5	203.03	201.39	201.93	62.87	62.36	62.53	41.67	41.30	41.50	703	107.36
6	202.05	200.47	201.35	62.50	62.08	62.31	41.52	41.16	41.32	730	107.37
7	203.08	201.18	202.96	62.74	61.93	62.57	41.45	41.06	41.36	875	107.36
8	204.56	203.13	204.10	63.09	62.61	62.74	41.74	41.35	41.62	885	107.44
9	204.46	203.16	203.57	62.83	62.48	62.68	41.77	41.36	41.64	909	107.46
10	†	†	†	†	†	†	†	†	†	†	†
11	*										
12	203.90	202.81	203.36	62.76	62.41	62.63	41.77	41.46	41.52	703	107.46
13	204.94	203.28	204.52	63.12	62.60	62.87	41.75	41.40	41.62	928	107.56
14	205.01	203.59	203.99	63.48	62.78	63.12	41.90	41.35	41.60	803	107.47
15	203.81	202.30	202.49	62.89	62.25	62.35	41.61	41.19	41.35	621	107.37
16	201.38	200.14	200.69	62.50	61.93	62.33	41.48	41.16	41.25	692	107.34
17	†	*		†	*		†	*		†	†
18											
19	201.18	198.90	200.19	62.51	61.81	62.26	41.46	41.09	41.35	661	107.24
20	201.54	200.22	201.27	62.60	62.22	62.39	41.55	41.28	41.45	696	107.20
21	202.49	199.70	200.00	62.76	62.04	62.16	41.60	41.20	41.23	837	107.23
22	198.05	194.53	196.66	61.77	60.50	61.22	41.05	40.50	40.76	1,540	106.96
23	198.69	196.91	197.75	61.61	61.22	61.35	41.00	40.58	40.75	772	107.10
24	†	*		†	*		†	*		†	†
25											
26	198.97	196.47	196.99	61.37	60.72	60.84	40.91	40.50	40.58	758	107.01
27	195.46	190.03	191.04	60.27	57.51	58.04	40.38	39.26	39.44	1,789	106.80
28	191.28	187.26	190.03	58.36	56.69	57.59	39.55	38.54	38.98	2,100	106.65
29	192.50	189.71	190.47	58.43	57.36	57.77	39.51	38.89	39.05	1,063	106.69
30	190.49	187.44	189.19	57.72	56.83	57.29	39.26	38.63	39.04	1,165	106.63
31	†	†	†	†	†	†	†	†	†	†	†
High			204.52			63.12			41.64	Total 20,808	107.56
Low			189.19			57.29			38.98		L106.63

*Sunday. †Holiday. ‡000 omitted

SEPTEMBER, 1946

	Industrials High	Low	Close	Railroads High	Low	Close	Utilities High	Low	Close	‡Daily Sales	40 Bonds
1	*	*	*	*	*	*	*	*	*	*	*
2	†	†	†	†	†	†	†	†	†	†	†
3	188.21	177.49	178.68	57.13	52.22	52.61	39.04	36.23	36.33	2,905	106.41
4	178.93	173.64	176.72	52.98	50.90	52.44	36.75	35.45	36.12	3,624	106.20
5	181.81	177.96	181.18	54.50	52.41	53.79	37.45	36.27	37.27	2,356	105.99
6	181.67	178.43	179.96	54.06	52.63	53.17	37.30	36.42	36.60	1,674	105.95
7	†	†	†	†	†	†	†	†	†	†	†
8	*										
9	177.52	170.53	172.03	52.61	50.08	50.45	36.34	34.77	35.00	2,835	105.53
10	172.89	166.56	167.30	50.92	48.39	48.59	34.80	33.60	33.80	3,299	105.05
11	173.20	167.80	172.13	50.83	48.98	50.36	34.92	33.83	34.78	2,869	104.73
12	173.34	170.00	171.70	51.01	49.43	50.36	35.48	34.54	35.02	2,007	104.71
13	173.99	170.87	173.39	51.31	50.24	51.03	35.72	34.98	35.66	1,715	104.76
14	†	†	†	†	*		†	†	†	†	†
15	*										
16	176.26	173.02	174.45	51.64	50.77	51.18	36.20	35.60	35.80	1,491	104.75
17	174.82	172.13	173.66	51.21	49.96	50.63	36.09	35.16	35.78	1,387	104.56
18	173.43	168.40	169.07	50.03	47.99	48.39	35.63	34.39	34.71	2,102	104.23
19	169.05	164.09	165.17	48.13	45.78	46.11	34.72	33.25	33.47	2,886	103.73
20	170.13	164.77	169.06	47.23	45.37	46.95	34.43	33.30	34.07	2,821	103.24
21	†	†	†	†	†	†	†	†	†	†	†
22	*										
23	172.15	166.09	166.56	48.09	45.45	45.69	34.90	33.58	33.69	2,115	103.13
24	169.75	164.21	168.89	47.29	44.76	47.14	34.45	33.29	34.29	2,225	102.67
25	173.44	169.43	172.95	48.77	47.07	48.00	34.80	34.13	34.59	1,803	102.47
26	175.45	171.59	174.96	48.89	47.33	48.68	35.01	34.31	34.87	1,304	102.79
27	175.18	173.35	174.09	49.03	47.87	48.42	34.98	34.50	34.78	975	103.08
28	*										
29											
30	173.56	170.44	172.42	48.31	47.14	47.72	34.65	33.98	34.45	1,058	103.02
High			181.18			53.79			37.27		106.41
Low			165.17			45.69			33.47	Total 43,451	102.47

*Sunday. †Holiday. ‡000 omitted.

OCTOBER, 1946

	Industrials			Railroads			Utilities			‡Daily Sales	40 Bonds
	High	Low	Close	High	Low	Close	High	Low	Close		
1	172.42	170.43	171.47	47.91	47.06	47.46	34.71	34.20	34.44	888	103.00
2	173.39	171.40	172.72	48.16	47.45	47.85	35.00	34.50	34.86	958	102.96
3	173.10	171.13	171.64	48.13	47.33	47.70	35.04	34.53	34.68	919	102.99
4	171.13	169.06	169.80	47.51	46.74	47.10	34.78	34.25	34.48	917	102.90
5	169.61	168.82	169.00	47.14	46.70	46.79	34.60	34.34	34.38	374	102.87
6	*	*	*	*	*	*	*	*	*	*	*
7	169.83	167.82	168.87	47.20	46.34	46.65	34.63	34.16	34.38	947	102.74
8	170.00	167.00	167.34	47.50	46.18	46.32	34.70	33.97	34.10	1,255	102.71
9	166.53	162.80	163.12	46.33	44.50	44.69	34.00	33.16	33.20	2,020	102.66
10	165.53	161.61	164.94	45.94	44.00	45.69	33.71	32.71	33.57	2,223	102.22
11	168.59	165.60	167.97	46.85	45.69	46.55	34.40	33.76	34.19	1,466	102.31
12	‡	‡	‡	‡	‡	‡	‡	‡	‡	‡	‡
13											
14	170.60	167.53	169.86	47.28	46.31	46.86	34.61	34.00	34.43	1,285	102.50
15	176.52	173.08	175.94	49.21	47.91	49.00	35.58	34.97	35.32	2,374	102.63
16	177.05	174.03	174.35	49.41	48.55	48.64	35.60	35.04	35.16	1,648	102.79
17	173.61	170.47	171.76	48.23	47.15	47.59	35.09	34.48	34.68	1,313	102.71
18	172.51	170.32	171.65	47.86	47.12	47.55	34.93	34.47	34.80	919	102.71
19	171.65	170.92	171.34	47.60	47.37	47.50	34.92	34.73	34.85	300	102.66
20	*	*	*	*	*	*	*	*	*	*	*
21	172.59	170.63	171.93	47.93	47.23	47.68	35.20	34.70	35.11	838	102.58
22	172.34	170.16	171.25	47.93	47.29	47.68	35.14	34.65	34.80	865	102.65
23	171.27	168.68	170.67	47.42	46.67	47.05	34.95	34.45	34.63	947	102.64
24	170.90	169.14	169.98	47.98	46.87	47.93	34.98	34.65	34.84	856	102.61
25	169.96	167.84	168.76	48.37	47.30	47.80	35.18	34.71	34.96	922	102.77
26	168.64	168.01	168.44	47.91	47.60	47.80	35.07	34.89	34.97	286	102.77
27	*	*	*	*	*	*	*	*	*	*	*
28	168.48	165.98	166.04	47.68	46.92	47.09	34.97	34.38	34.43	995	102.57
29	166.62	163.98	164.21	47.63	46.37	46.52	34.82	34.20	34.38	1,238	102.47
30	165.32	160.49	164.20	47.16	45.26	46.64	34.51	33.49	34.23	1,936	102.42
31	169.68	164.71	169.15	49.34	47.27	49.06	35.28	34.47	35.20	1,695	102.73
High			175.94			49.06			35.32		103.00
Low			163.12			44.69			33.20		102.22

*Sunday   †Holiday   ‡000 omitted

Total 30,384

NOVEMBER, 1946

	Industrials			Railroads			Utilities			‡Daily Sales	40 Bonds
	High	Low	Close	High	Low	Close	High	Low	Close		
1	172.33	169.50	171.76	50.92	49.36	50.63	35.75	35.15	35.67	1,667	103.02
2	172.79	171.56	172.53	51.23	50.58	51.22	36.15	35.70	36.10	694	103.11
3	*	*	*	*	*	*	*	*	*	*	*
4	175.78	173.03	174.40	51.84	50.85	51.10	36.70	36.12	36.41	1,828	103.31
5	†	†	†	†	†	†	†	†	†	†	†
6	175.00	168.38	168.88	51.33	48.41	48.62	36.60	35.09	35.23	1,997	103.14
7	170.59	167.50	169.60	49.96	48.36	49.49	35.87	35.05	35.56	1,144	103.18
8	171.78	169.75	170.79	50.89	49.60	50.18	36.08	35.50	35.69	998	103.28
9	172.15	170.88	171.80	50.99	50.37	50.73	35.98	35.71	35.95	593	103.29
10	*	*	*	*	*	*	*	*	*	*	*
11	†	†	†	†	†	†	†	†	†	†	†
12	173.48	170.41	170.87	51.14	50.00	50.12	36.29	35.49	35.60	1,365	103.32
13	170.52	168.02	169.84	49.90	49.05	49.68	35.64	34.91	35.34	1,045	103.37
14	171.45	169.16	170.88	50.30	49.52	50.08	35.60	35.13	35.40	955	103.27
15	171.48	168.89	169.67	50.40	49.15	49.64	35.70	35.00	35.12	932	103.26
16	169.37	168.64	169.03	49.77	49.24	49.54	35.31	35.09	35.26	317	103.19
17	*	*	*	*	*	*	*	*	*	*	*
18	169.11	167.23	167.91	49.27	48.23	48.50	35.21	34.84	35.03	770	103.13
19	168.35	166.28	167.88	48.32	47.72	48.16	35.07	34.53	34.83	914	103.11
20	167.99	166.20	166.91	48.25	47.70	47.95	35.08	34.55	34.87	969	102.98
21	165.98	163.50	164.12	47.79	46.67	46.96	34.92	34.33	34.43	1,382	102.76
22	164.49	162.29	163.55	47.36	46.62	47.08	34.50	34.14	34.30	1,203	102.63
23	165.55	163.75	165.10	48.43	47.42	48.19	34.65	34.26	34.55	624	102.61
24	*	*	*	*	*	*	*	*	*	*	*
25	165.99	164.37	165.23	48.26	47.59	47.89	34.51	34.16	34.39	787	102.52
26	167.81	165.31	166.94	48.67	47.87	48.51	34.90	34.26	34.77	1,082	102.46
27	169.18	167.35	168.34	49.19	48.34	48.90	35.30	34.83	35.10	1,072	102.54
28	†	†	†	†	†	†	†	†	†	†	†
29	170.25	168.23	169.78	49.95	48.81	49.68	35.55	35.07	35.45	1,013	102.70
30	170.66	169.52	169.80	49.84	49.45	49.58	35.55	35.26	35.35	469	102.71
High			174.40			51.22			36.41		103.37
Low			163.55			46.96			34.30		102.46

*Sunday   †Holiday   ‡000 omitted

Total 23,820

DECEMBER, 1946

	Industrials			Railroads			Utilities			‡Daily Sales	40 Bonds
	High	Low	Close	High	Low	Close	High	Low	Close		
1											
2	169.07	166.74	167.50	49.22	48.28	48.53	35.33	34.85	35.08	812	102.61
3	168.60	166.20	168.05	48.85	48.27	48.72	35.26	34.72	35.10	955	102.62
4	170.98	167.48	170.33	49.67	48.27	49.42	35.72	35.03	35.61	1,437	102.72
5	170.66	168.63	169.95	49.24	48.60	48.92	35.91	35.28	35.74	1,000	102.65
6	170.92	169.20	170.39	49.34	48.63	49.22	36.25	35.66	36.07	1,055	102.65
7	171.61	170.31	171.01	51.34	50.54	50.85	36.36	36.00	36.14	857	102.95
8											
9	176.48	173.43	175.76	52.96	51.68	52.67	36.90	36.40	36.73	2,841	103.44
10	177.21	174.84	175.92	52.95	52.12	52.37	37.02	36.65	36.75	1,728	103.49
11	176.67	174.80	176.07	52.50	51.96	52.27	37.21	36.59	37.10	1,226	103.51
12	175.75	173.17	173.91	52.22	51.35	51.46	37.30	36.72	36.96	1,057	103.44
13	174.41	172.57	173.90	51.74	51.14	51.54	37.36	36.86	37.10	999	103.48
14	174.96	173.56	174.73	52.07	51.61	51.99	37.36	36.95	37.30	549	103.52
15											
16	175.93	174.18	174.85	52.55	51.78	51.88	37.46	37.05	37.20	1,014	103.52
17	175.42	173.93	174.47	52.08	51.48	51.62	37.26	36.90	37.04	1,018	103.56
18	175.62	173.62	174.84	52.03	51.30	51.84	37.21	36.89	37.13	1,107	103.66
19	178.06	175.28	177.29	52.83	51.89	52.47	37.61	37.10	37.50	1,737	103.63
20	178.58	176.82	177.85	52.87	52.18	52.51	37.64	37.30	37.52	1,467	103.71
21	178.53	177.67	178.32	52.50	52.21	52.40	37.59	37.39	37.52	629	103.68
22											
23	178.54	176.85	177.36	52.27	51.71	51.84	37.50	37.18	37.33	1,166	103.59
24	177.51	176.25	176.95	51.90	51.44	51.69	37.34	37.04	37.22	948	103.55
25	†	†	†	†	†	†	†	†	†	†	†
26	176.79	174.54	175.21	51.66	50.90	50.93	37.18	36.70	36.84	1,152	103.60
27	176.17	173.88	175.66	51.25	50.26	51.02	37.05	36.59	36.86	1,287	103.61
28	176.06	175.23	175.77	51.32	50.88	51.17	37.07	36.84	36.95	566	103.70
29											
30	177.00	175.15	176.23	51.53	50.78	51.07	37.26	36.87	37.10	1,404	103.75
31	177.89	175.79	177.20	51.62	50.62	51.13	37.46	36.86	37.27	1,821	103.76
High			178.32			52.67			37.52		103.76
Low			167.50			48.53			35.08		102.61

*Sunday. †Holiday. ‡000 omitted.

Total 29,832

JANUARY, 1947

	Industrials			Railroads			Utilities			‡Daily Sales	40 Bonds
	High	Low	Close	High	Low	Close	High	Low	Close		
1	†	†	†	†	†	†	†	†	†	†	†
2	177.83	176.04	176.39	51.73	51.06	51.18	37.34	36.83	36.83	753	103.83
3	177.16	174.71	176.76	50.94	50.36	50.84	36.94	36.38	36.77	883	103.88
4	177.10	176.55	176.92	51.01	50.82	50.87	37.06	36.79	36.95	296	103.84
5											
6	179.04	176.99	178.43	51.89	50.92	51.33	37.30	36.88	37.07	977	103.85
7	179.25	177.12	177.49	51.40	50.56	50.57	37.47	36.81	36.96	983	103.99
8	178.43	176.54	178.06	50.71	50.24	50.46	37.30	36.73	37.04	786	104.09
9	179.06	177.94	178.43	50.79	50.33	50.48	37.34	36.95	37.06	715	104.21
10	178.84	176.59	177.43	50.35	49.45	49.58	37.03	36.42	36.60	1,057	104.31
11	177.03	175.15	175.25	49.27	48.55	48.59	36.48	36.05	36.15	628	104.28
12											
13	174.50	170.99	172.49	48.24	47.28	47.77	36.07	35.48	35.83	1,591	104.07
14	173.24	171.31	172.63	48.13	47.68	48.00	36.16	35.62	36.03	852	104.15
15	173.46	171.70	172.10	48.08	47.45	47.53	36.10	35.72	35.84	767	104.15
16	172.39	170.13	171.95	48.28	47.01	48.14	35.92	35.27	35.77	1,045	104.14
17	174.87	172.58	174.76	48.83	48.12	48.70	36.47	35.78	36.35	854	104.36
18	176.77	175.44	175.92	49.45	48.92	49.07	36.95	36.51	36.75	787	104.46
19											
20	175.46	173.69	174.06	49.19	48.42	48.76	36.68	36.23	36.39	807	104.40
21	173.95	172.64	173.51	48.69	48.12	48.31	36.40	36.09	36.28	696	104.45
22	174.19	172.81	173.77	48.72	48.18	48.51	36.47	36.16	36.39	666	104.44
23	175.35	173.59	175.13	49.22	48.63	49.16	36.74	36.21	36.66	875	104.52
24	175.94	174.49	175.49	49.73	49.00	49.39	36.84	36.49	36.68	954	104.58
25	175.78	175.06	175.35	49.44	49.04	49.22	36.58	36.34	36.42	429	104.55
26											
27	177.55	175.05	177.28	49.53	48.71	49.46	36.50	36.04	36.36	899	104.59
28	178.98	177.17	178.68	50.39	49.32	50.30	36.66	36.21	36.57	1,081	104.51
29	180.47	178.03	180.17	51.10	49.98	50.86	36.99	36.55	36.85	1,526	104.59
30	181.18	179.33	179.74	51.33	50.47	50.60	37.07	36.64	36.75	1,344	104.57
31	181.34	179.49	180.44	51.33	50.53	50.88	37.11	36.60	36.92	1,306	104.64
High			180.44			51.33			37.07		104.64
Low			171.95			47.53			35.77		103.83

*Sunday †Holiday ‡000 omitted.

Total 23,557

FEBRUARY, 1947

	Industrials High	Low	Close	Railroads High	Low	Close	Utilities High	Low	Close	‡Daily Sales	40 Bonds
1	181.23	180.01	180.88	51.82	50.93	51.67	37.15	36.95	37.06	877	104.66
2*											
3	182.37	180.57	181.92	52.47	51.62	52.06	37.16	36.80	37.01	1,362	104.79
4	183.15	181.44	182.28	52.26	51.50	51.80	37.16	36.83	36.92	1,345	104.79
5	183.12	181.45	182.52	51.98	51.33	51.72	37.10	36.82	36.97	1,176	104.83
6	182.27	180.72	181.57	52.33	51.29	52.16	37.17	36.90	37.07	1,119	104.84
7	184.18	181.33	183.74	53.65	52.29	53.34	37.55	37.05	37.51	1,975	104.89
8	184.83	183.71	184.49	53.60	53.25	53.42	37.68	37.40	37.55	933	104.89
9*											
10	184.96	183.12	183.57	53.02	52.28	52.55	37.76	37.23	37.32	1,304	104.88
11	184.43	131.81	184.06	52.84	51.98	52.67	37.52	37.09	37.45	1,300	104.90
12†											
13	184.25	181.64	182.18	'52.96	51.99	52.08	37.66	37.17	37.25	1,336	104.79
14	182.23	180.62	181.64	52.18	51.57	51.88	37.37	36.97	37.20	942	104.78
15	181.64	181.09	181.36	51.97	51.72	51.86	37.31	37.10	37.21	436	104.76
16*											
17	182.74	180.89	182.20	52.10	51.44	51.66	37.39	37.03	37.23	874	104.64
18	182.91	181.26	181.93	51.76	51.29	51.44	37.56	37.22	37.32	865	104.62
19	181.85	179.85	180.78	51.37	50.68	51.01	37.45	36.95	37.28	978	104.65
20	181.40	179.12	180.74	51.44	50.62	51.30	37.45	37.10	37.36	1,000	104.63
21	182.76	181.22	182.26	51.91	51.24	51.64	37.59	37.35	37.42	862	104.68
22											
23											
24	182.47	181.03	181.40	51.70	51.20	51.42	37.57	37.23	37.36	809	104.68
25	181.92	178.86	179.31	52.25	50.09	51.10	37.39	36.74	36.94	1,277	104.45
26	179.02	176.34	177.22	51.09	49.94	50.30	36.95	36.54	36.65	1,346	104.34
27	179.35	177.67	178.91	51.04	50.07	50.77	37.03	36.64	36.94	961	104.21
28	179.73	177.75	178.90	50.82	50.37	50.39	36.99	36.70	36.81	685	104.21
High			184.49			53.42			37.55		104.90
Low			177.22			50.30			36.65		104.21

Total 23,762

*Sunday †Holiday ‡000 omitted

MARCH, 1947

	Industrials High	Low	Close	Railroads High	Low	Close	Utilities High	Low	Close	‡Daily Sales	40 Bonds
1	179.60	178.63	179.29	50.65	50.46	50.54	36.91	36.78	36.84	301	104.31
2*											
3	179.84	178.29	179.43	50.56	50.04	50.28	36.94	36.60	36.70	687	104.31
4	180.31	178.46	179.77	50.63	50.01	50.41	36.70	36.39	36.52	679	104.27
5	181.56	179.32	181.16	51.17	50.40	51.00	36.85	36.50	36.72	987	104.28
6	182.48	180.60	181.88	51.82	50.92	51.50	37.01	36.65	36.85	1,017	104.26
7	181.19	176.87	177.05	51.10	49.66	49.77	36.89	36.04	36.07	1,212	104.25
8	176.89	175.48	175.84	49.64	49.15	49.32	36.26	35.95	36.10	741	104.18
9*											
10	176.36	174.73	175.18	49.33	48.83	48.90	36.26	35.90	36.04	834	104.14
11	175.20	173.09	173.83	48.96	48.19	48.41	36.05	35.55	35.74	1,194	104.09
12	175.62	173.43	174.68	49.13	48.24	48.88	36.21	35.78	36.10	945	104.17
13	175.32	173.95	174.35	49.25	48.66	48.82	36.28	35.95	36.02	650	104.20
14	173.95	171.94	172.58	48.70	47.95	48.17	36.00	35.62	35.84	818	104.13
15	172.63	171.90	172.37	48.14	47.89	48.01	35.85	35.63	35.80	368	104.14
16*											
17	174.15	172.53	173.35	48.68	47.98	48.25	35.75	35.45	35.65	640	104.19
18	175.22	173.26	174.95	48.88	48.23	48.70	35.90	35.61	35.78	658	104.20
19	176.90	175.11	175.78	49.24	48.70	48.83	35.87	35.61	35.70	756	104.19
20	176.06	174.76	175.37	48.72	48.24	48.42	35.83	35.57	35.71	632	104.20
21	177.12	175.37	176.90	49.06	48.42	48.87	35.80	35.47	35.75	712	104.26
22	177.51	177.01	177.27	49.16	48.88	49.00	35.88	35.68	35.74	341	104.27
23*											
24	177.61	176.18	176.40	48.97	48.53	48.55	35.90	35.61	35.70	581	104.29
25	176.66	175.05	175.29	48.68	48.16	48.28	35.74	35.45	35.50	660	104.23
26	177.31	174.61	177.10	48.73	48.13	48.70	35.78	35.43	35.67	944	104.32
27	179.51	177.67	179.19	49.39	48.77	49.24	36.10	35.74	36.00	1,143	104.30
28	179.68	178.18	178.63	49.49	49.07	49.24	36.20	35.95	36.05	827	104.37
29	178.59	178.09	178.36	49.22	49.01	49.15	36.07	35.92	35.99	292	104.47
30*											
31	178.58	177.01	177.20	49.17	48.60	48.64	36.05	35.78	35.88	720	104.50
High			181.88			51.50			36.85		104.50
Low			172.37			48.01			35.50		104.09

Total 19,339

*Sunday †Holiday ‡000 omitted

APRIL, 1947

	Industrials High	Industrials Low	Industrials Close	Railroads High	Railroads Low	Railroads Close	Utilities High	Utilities Low	Utilities Close	‡Daily Sales	40 Bonds
1	177.74	176.18	177.45	48.83	48.40	48.66	35.95	35.61	35.83	771	104.50
2	178.28	176.87	177.32	48.98	48.57	48.75	36.10	35.82	36.00	677	104.42
3	177.21	175.60	176.52	48.73	48.18	48.44	36.05	35.77	35.94	680	104.26
4	†	†	†	†	†	†	†	†	†	†	†
5	176.87	176.37	176.71	48.51	48.36	48.39	35.93	35.81	35.92	272	104.23
6	*										
7	176.16	174.82	175.39	48.25	47.82	47.90	35.86	35.63	35.74	633	104.23
8	175.52	172.68	173.29	47.94	47.06	47.25	35.82	35.15	35.25	1,020	104.20
9	173.72	172.39	173.40	47.40	46.83	47.12	35.25	34.94	35.08	849	104.21
10	174.78	173.44	173.98	47.63	47.13	47.27	35.30	34.93	35.03	676	104.27
11	174.76	172.90	173.43	47.35	46.63	46.72	35.11	34.70	34.76	855	104.26
12	172.92	171.35	171.76	46.58	46.03	46.14	34.68	34.35	34.38	631	104.22
13	*										
14	170.42	166.17	166.69	45.80	44.13	44.45	34.32	33.58	33.81	2,197	104.13
15	168.09	165.39	166.82	44.71	43.68	44.24	34.03	33.56	33.81	1,449	103.98
16	168.85	166.60	168.22	44.82	44.01	44.72	34.08	33.66	33.99	901	103.92
17	168.91	167.49	168.01	45.18	44.38	44.54	34.12	33.82	33.95	761	103.93
18	168.68	166.49	166.77	44.71	43.77	43.84	34.00	33.51	33.55	973	103.86
19	168.58	166.22	168.44	44.45	43.38	44.32	33.97	33.47	33.96	686	103.84
20	*										
21	171.47	169.32	169.50	45.39	44.54	44.71	34.41	33.95	34.10	1,158	103.85
22	171.25	169.24	170.94	45.30	44.58	45.26	34.33	33.95	34.21	891	103.77
23	171.71	169.92	170.87	45.62	44.97	45.26	34.47	34.16	34.29	696	103.80
24	171.20	169.81	170.19	45.41	44.94	45.09	34.28	34.00	34.13	624	103.78
25	170.38	168.60	168.93	45.20	44.56	44.84	34.28	33.71	33.86	776	103.61
26	169.23	168.73	169.13	44.74	44.51	44.68	33.95	33.78	33.90	294	103.63
27	*										
28	170.00	168.56	168.85	44.93	44.45	44.56	34.05	33.70	33.80	588	103.61
29	169.47	167.42	168.70	44.80	44.10	44.69	33.89	33.49	33.79	841	103.51
30	170.85	168.76	170.64	45.42	44.75	45.22	34.07	33.68	33.98	781	103.60
High			177.45			48.75			36.00		104.50
Low			166.69			43.84			33.55		103.51

*Sunday. †Holiday. ‡000 omitted.

Total 20,620

MAY, 1947

	Industrials High	Industrials Low	Industrials Close	Railroads High	Railroads Low	Railroads Close	Utilities High	Utilities Low	Utilities Close	‡Daily Sales	40 Bonds
1	172.65	170.62	171.91	45.73	45.11	45.52	34.26	33.93	34.19	916	103.59
2	174.45	171.85	173.45	45.79	45.21	45.52	34.34	34.01	34.25	954	103.63
3	174.17	173.44	174.00	45.73	45.54	45.69	34.25	34.15	34.22	250	103.60
4	*										
5	175.08	173.58	174.21	46.13	45.50	45.66	34.40	34.15	34.22	736	103.54
6	173.83	171.89	172.77	45.54	45.07	45.27	34.21	33.86	34.02	745	103.50
7	173.14	172.08	172.49	45.42	44.97	45.11	34.03	33.83	33.90	596	103.46
8	172.87	171.20	171.56	45.30	44.69	44.73	33.85	33.65	33.75	668	103.42
9	172.21	170.52	171.54	44.81	44.39	44.64	33.88	33.63	33.86	723	103.39
10	171.71	171.28	171.67	44.81	44.69	44.77	33.92	33.80	33.86	235	103.38
11	*										
12	171.69	169.76	169.80	44.75	44.19	44.32	34.00	33.77	33.83	699	103.29
13	169.17	167.07	167.34	44.01	43.03	43.16	33.72	33.31	33.38	1,211	103.04
14	167.34	165.93	166.68	43.32	42.76	43.07	33.56	33.20	33.34	1,051	102.86
15	168.42	166.96	167.88	43.50	42.98	43.24	33.35	33.13	33.29	771	102.69
16	168.02	164.46	164.96	43.25	42.02	42.18	33.37	32.89	32.93	1,429	102.51
17	164.61	162.98	163.21	41.76	41.15	41.20	32.85	32.65	32.68	978	102.28
18	*										
19	164.43	161.38	163.55	41.75	40.43	41.16	32.50	32.06	32.29	1,859	102.06
20	164.81	162.99	163.59	41.75	41.15	41.46	32.52	32.11	32.28	917	102.13
21	166.03	162.98	165.77	42.29	41.17	42.17	32.72	32.11	32.68	1,025	102.16
22	167.56	165.81	166.73	42.99	42.33	42.67	33.09	32.72	32.95	951	102.27
23	167.68	166.06	166.95	43.19	42.59	42.87	33.23	32.90	33.17	676	102.31
24	167.13	166.83	166.97	42.87	42.81	42.85	33.13	33.05	33.10	230	102.30
25	*										
26	167.22	165.86	166.29	42.82	42.29	42.33	33.20	32.99	33.07	543	102.24
27	166.53	164.59	166.17	42.61	41.89	42.46	33.06	32.73	32.89	663	102.15
28	168.90	166.64	168.06	43.77	42.61	43.64	33.41	32.95	33.35	889	102.30
29	169.78	168.06	169.25	44.41	43.72	44.24	33.55	33.21	33.37	902	102.36
30	†	†	†	†	†	†	†	†	†	†	†
31											
High			174.21			45.69			34.25		103.63
Low			163.21			41.16			32.28		102.06

*Sunday. †Holiday. ‡000 omitted.

Total 20,617

JUNE, 1947

	Industrials			Railroads			Utilities			‡Daily Sales	40 Bonds
	High	Low	Close	High	Low	Close	High	Low	Close		
1											
2	168.66	167.43	168.00	43.81	43.36	43.55	33.30	33.10	33.16	523	102.32
3	170.69	168.00	170.35	44.02	43.45	43.90	33.34	32.95	33.10	686	102.27
4	171.35	169.16	169.56	44.28	43.41	43.57	33.34	33.03	33.15	820	102.29
5	170.16	168.90	169.41	43.70	43.27	43.55	33.29	32.90	33.06	517	102.22
6	170.62	168.54	170.28	43.83	43.37	43.72	33.20	33.03	33.14	664	102.25
7											
8											
9	170.71	169.26	169.88	43.88	43.12	43.25	33.31	33.03	33.20	552	102.22
10	171.36	169.10	171.10	43.45	43.05	43.42	33.59	33.15	33.50	654	102.15
11	174.78	171.50	174.68	44.75	43.63	44.71	34.10	33.59	34.04	1,349	102.26
12	175.30	173.24	173.78	45.25	44.61	44.81	34.20	33.95	34.05	1,041	102.29
13	176.02	173.26	175.49	45.59	44.57	45.41	34.33	33.88	34.18	964	102.38
14											
15											
16	177.23	174.26	175.81	45.84	44.79	45.20	34.43	33.86	34.17	988	102.53
17	176.11	174.28	174.98	45.37	44.85	45.02	34.25	33.98	34.12	671	102.45
18	176.42	174.25	174.94	45.85	44.79	45.29	34.26	33.75	34.13	911	102.40
19	176.81	174.43	176.14	45.79	45.01	45.43	34.55	34.17	34.45	1,009	102.41
20	177.52	175.54	176.44	46.10	45.48	45.82	34.75	34.43	34.55	1,131	102.54
21											
22											
23	178.08	176.22	177.44	46.52	45.66	46.42	34.85	34.45	34.69	945	102.64
24	177.55	174.13	174.54	46.74	45.41	45.55	34.75	34.20	34.32	1,089	102.69
25	176.19	173.93	175.73	45.87	45.31	45.66	34.63	34.21	34.50	827	102.70
26	177.15	175.44	176.58	46.27	45.55	45.98	34.73	34.41	34.65	822	102.76
27	177.20	175.77	176.56	46.13	45.79	46.02	34.95	34.49	34.63	653	102.77
28											
29											
30	177.66	175.82	177.30	46.04	45.62	45.88	34.83	34.58	34.73	667	102.78
High			177.44			46.42			34.73		102.78
Low			168.00			43.25			33.06		102.15
										Total 17,483	

*Sunday. †Holiday. ‡000 omitted.

JULY, 1947

	Industrials			Railroads			Utilities			‡Daily Sales	40 Bonds
	High	Low	Close	High	Low	Close	High	Low	Close		
1	180.42	177.48	180.33	47.10	47.00	46.99	35.14	34.76	35.04	1,091	102.86
2	181.17	179.33	179.88	47.81	47.05	47.44	35.35	35.00	35.19	1,182	102.96
3	182.07	179.18	181.73	48.23	47.25	48.06	35.62	35.11	35.47	1,252	103.25
4											
5											
6											
7	182.61	180.62	182.04	48.70	47.77	48.25	35.80	35.46	35.63	1,052	103.35
8	183.74	181.53	182.66	49.10	48.13	48.57	35.86	35.46	35.66	1,394	103.65
9	183.29	181.12	181.72	48.59	47.77	47.92	35.79	35.50	35.57	1,036	103.54
10	183.24	180.82	182.80	48.55	47.76	48.45	35.80	35.37	35.68	1,024	103.54
11	185.52	183.14	184.77	49.39	48.45	49.21	36.12	35.76	35.95	1,591	103.65
12											
13											
14	187.15	184.64	185.60	50.18	49.34	49.83	36.15	35.76	35.88	1,662	103.68
15	186.24	184.23	185.38	50.03	49.54	49.80	35.91	35.55	35.68	1,178	103.63
16	186.23	184.05	185.46	49.81	49.26	49.69	35.75	35.51	35.65	1,069	103.70
17	185.92	183.43	183.83	49.90	49.20	49.26	35.68	35.48	35.52	1,108	103.68
18	184.87	182.51	184.60	49.48	48.78	49.33	35.61	35.36	35.51	922	103.66
19											
20											
21	184.86	183.02	183.52	50.64	49.40	50.24	35.53	35.35	35.44	845	103.80
22	184.41	182.73	183.78	50.64	50.15	50.37	35.55	35.40	35.49	783	103.80
23	185.59	183.86	184.95	51.09	50.33	50.83	35.80	35.47	35.64	1,072	103.85
24	187.36	185.08	186.85	51.89	50.94	51.63	35.92	35.64	35.84	1,570	103.82
25	187.66	185.59	186.38	51.92	51.35	51.52	36.10	35.72	35.95	1,154	103.87
26											
27											
28	187.51	184.76	184.95	51.75	50.69	50.72	36.22	35.80	35.85	1,089	103.91
29	185.28	181.47	182.05	50.56	49.19	49.53	36.00	35.50	35.59	1,391	103.74
30	182.33	179.77	180.91	49.67	48.53	49.04	35.65	35.35	35.44	1,171	103.64
31	183.56	181.17	183.18	50.03	49.34	49.96	35.80	35.53	35.65	837	103.63
High			186.85			51.63			35.95		103.91
Low			179.88			46.99			35.04		102.86
										Total 25,473	

*Sunday. †Holiday. ‡000 omitted.

AUGUST, 1947

	Industrials			Railroads			Utilities			‡Daily Sales	40 Bonds
	High	Low	Close	High	Low	Close	High	Low	Close		
1	184.38	182.35	183.81	50.03	49.62	49.83	35.90	35.59	35.78	767	103.68
2	↕	↕	↕	↕	↕	↕	↕	↕	↕	↕	↕
3											
4	183.69	182.01	182.51	49.59	49.05	49.15	35.89	35.58	35.70	731	103.67
5	184.05	182.27	183.08	49.79	48.93	49.15	35.85	35.57	35.72	748	103.68
6	183.48	181.85	182.35	49.14	48.70	48.82	35.90	35.62	35.75	660	103.67
7	182.57	181.03	182.11	49.32	48.88	49.13	35.85	35.59	35.70	662	103.58
8	181.99	179.77	180.13	48.93	48.15	48.21	35.75	35.52	35.55	791	103.49
9	↕	↕	↕	↕	↕	↕	↕	↕	↕	↕	↕
10											
11	180.16	178.22	178.98	48.10	47.55	47.91	35.54	35.31	35.35	715	103.48
12	180.76	179.14	179.94	48.62	47.94	48.32	35.63	35.28	35.44	687	103.54
13	180.71	179.17	179.80	48.42	48.13	48.30	35.57	35.35	35.47	694	103.51
14	180.43	178.64	179.87	48.87	48.12	48.79	35.56	35.37	35.50	685	103.48
15	181.58	179.44	181.04	49.51	48.89	49.41	35.72	35.51	35.66	880	103.45
16	↕	↕	↕	↕	↕	↕	↕	↕	↕	↕	↕
17											
18	181.43	179.98	180.44	49.62	49.09	49.30	35.77	35.58	35.62	713	103.41
19	180.64	179.23	179.75	49.45	48.90	49.15	35.72	35.50	35.61	602	103.35
20	180.10	178.76	179.01	49.05	48.62	48.69	35.74	35.55	35.60	599	103.25
21	179.77	178.50	179.42	49.01	48.64	48.93	35.76	35.50	35.68	577	103.28
22	180.29	179.34	179.74	49.18	48.84	48.94	35.87	35.73	35.78	581	103.22
23	↕	↕	↕	↕	↕	↕	↕	↕	↕	↕	↕
24											
25	179.78	177.33	177.57	48.77	48.04	48.09	35.62	35.29	35.42	812	103.13
26	178.05	176.54	177.73	48.13	47.66	48.04	35.56	35.32	35.47	619	102.97
27	178.24	177.14	177.88	48.49	48.10	48.28	35.47	35.28	35.39	476	102.99
28	178.64	177.22	177.70	48.56	47.94	48.19	35.55	35.36	35.47	577	102.98
29	179.15	177.63	178.85	48.94	48.15	48.77	35.64	35.39	35.58	577	102.98
30	↕	↕	↕	↕	↕	↕	↕	↕	↕	↕	↕
31											
High			183.81			49.83			35.78		103.68
Low			177.57			47.91			35.35		102.97

Total 14,153

*Sunday †Holiday ‡000 omitted.

SEPTEMBER, 1947

	Industrials			Railroads			Utilities			‡Daily Sales	40 Bonds
	High	Low	Close	High	Low	Close	High	Low	Close		
1	†	†	†	†	†	†	†	†	†	†	†
2	180.56	178.75	179.81	49.53	48.82	49.32	35.80	35.57	35.70	652	102.99
3	180.08	178.55	179.09	49.67	49.10	49.31	35.88	35.59	35.72	652	103.01
4	178.84	176.57	177.27	49.06	47.85	48.18	35.82	35.42	35.50	869	102.96
5	177.51	175.69	177.13	48.10	47.46	47.88	35.51	35.27	35.35	719	102.82
6	↕	↕	↕	↕	↕	↕	↕	↕	↕	↕	↕
7											
8	176.97	174.79	175.14	47.72	46.98	47.14	35.35	35.00	35.12	827	102.72
9	176.07	174.02	175.32	48.04	46.91	47.95	35.23	34.89	35.06	752	102.67
10	176.61	174.70	176.24	48.31	47.83	48.18	35.44	35.12	35.34	735	102.66
11	177.11	175.31	176.16	48.40	47.84	48.01	35.40	35.20	35.29	803	102.64
12	176.67	174.98	175.92	47.81	47.42	47.51	35.38	35.10	35.24	601	102.48
13	↕	↕	↕	↕	↕	↕	↕	↕	↕	↕	↕
14											
15	175.99	174.82	175.30	47.87	47.38	47.69	35.33	35.15	35.20	501	102.40
16	177.01	174.73	176.70	48.29	47.65	48.21	35.34	35.12	35.22	740	102.24
17	179.37	176.86	178.73	48.99	48.25	48.84	35.50	35.20	35.42	1,258	102.18
18	179.27	177.68	178.31	49.02	48.53	48.68	35.35	35.03	35.15	937	102.14
19	178.61	177.03	178.12	48.51	48.16	48.32	35.31	35.03	35.24	745	102.04
20	↕	↕	↕	↕	↕	↕	↕	↕	↕	↕	↕
21											
22	178.76	177.36	178.02	48.36	47.99	48.25	35.25	35.08	35.15	673	101.94
23	178.25	175.54	176.04	48.27	47.45	47.54	35.25	35.00	35.02	882	101.83
24	176.79	175.27	176.39	48.17	47.38	47.95	35.18	34.99	35.13	571	101.60
25	176.84	174.92	175.29	48.00	47.47	47.54	35.18	34.86	34.95	765	101.26
26	175.57	174.42	174.86	47.79	47.30	47.43	35.17	34.83	35.02	640	101.13
27	↕	↕	↕	↕	↕	↕	↕	↕	↕	↕	↕
28											
29	176.44	174.74	175.85	47.96	47.32	47.72	35.25	34.95	35.20	738	100.90
30	177.70	175.36	177.49	48.50	47.78	48.43	35.44	35.12	35.26	957	100.85
High			179.81			49.32			35.72		103.01
Low			174.86			47.14			34.95		100.85

Total 16,017

*Sunday †Holiday

OCTOBER, 1947

	Industrials			Railroads			Utilities			‡Daily sales	40 Bonds
	High	Low	Close	High	Low	Close	High	Low	Close		
1	178.87	176.89	178.10	48.96	48.22	48.59	35.49	35.23	35.36	1,155	100.68
2	178.96	177.50	178.47	48.67	48.29	48.51	35.55	35.23	35.45	854	100.68
3	180.31	178.26	179.53	49.19	48.58	49.11	35.60	35.29	35.50	1,266	100.67
4	180.10	179.19	179.44	49.55	49.28	49.39	35.54	35.42	35.51	435	100.68
5	*			*			*			*	
6	180.61	179.03	180.08	49.46	48.85	48.99	35.60	35.33	35.48	929	100.74
7	180.49	179.33	180.01	49.16	48.72	48.94	35.56	35.28	35.43	876	100.61
8	180.56	178.26	178.78	49.68	48.66	48.68	35.57	35.30	35.38	1,132	100.63
9	180.37	178.56	180.11	48.89	48.46	48.72	35.54	35.32	35.47	789	100.50
10	181.34	179.63	180.44	49.06	48.42	48.67	35.56	35.31	35.51	1,123	100.53
11	180.74	180.08	180.49	48.74	48.63	48.67	35.53	35.44	35.48	407	100.50
12	*			*			*			*	
13	†		†	†		†	†		†	†	
14	183.14	180.47	182.73	49.85	48.79	49.75	35.83	35.56	35.74	1,808	100.41
15	184.27	182.25	183.28	50.29	49.55	49.71	36.02	35.65	35.92	1,929	100.48
16	184.56	182.71	183.54	49.90	49.33	49.51	35.95	35.61	35.78	1,400	100.41
17	184.39	182.40	183.52	50.59	49.37	50.20	35.86	35.53	35.70	1,268	100.34
18	184.38	183.50	184.25	50.38	50.13	50.28	35.76	35.69	35.73	479	100.31
19	*			*			*			*	
20	186.24	184.27	185.29	51.67	50.40	51.19	35.85	35.50	35.71	1,774	100.24
21	186.01	184.05	185.09	51.26	50.44	50.88	35.87	35.58	35.62	1,395	100.33
22	185.89	184.00	184.36	51.19	50.24	50.55	35.80	35.55	35.62	1,264	100.36
23	185.30	183.71	184.50	50.97	50.36	50.53	35.70	35.45	35.62	1,189	100.35
24	184.47	181.55	182.53	50.26	49.36	49.46	35.58	35.13	35.25	1,654	100.24
25	183.07	182.36	182.73	49.77	49.54	49.66	35.39	35.32	35.32	402	100.17
26	*			*			*			*	
27	183.70	181.76	183.27	49.71	49.06	49.37	35.56	35.20	35.47	850	100.15
28	184.24	182.72	183.21	50.08	49.28	49.51	35.59	35.33	35.36	926	100.05
29	184.70	182.47	183.06	49.92	49.03	49.20	35.51	35.18	35.20	1,138	99.98
30	183.04	179.93	181.32	49.02	48.08	48.51	35.19	34.79	34.88	1,391	99.96
31	182.40	180.43	181.81	48.91	48.47	48.74	35.11	34.75	34.88	803	99.89
High			185.29			51.19			35.92		100.74
Low			178.10			48.51			34.88		99.89

*Sunday. †Holiday. ‡000 omitted.   Total 28,635

NOVEMBER, 1947

	Industrials			Railroads			Utilities			†Daily sales	40 Bonds
	High	Low	Close	High	Low	Close	High	Low	Close		
1	182.67	182.00	182.48	48.73	48.59	48.66	34.88	34.80	34.85	356	99.90
2	*			*			*			*	
3	183.51	181.85	182.65	48.81	48.33	48.58	35.06	34.75	34.89	757	99.85
4	†		†	†		†	†		†	†	
5	183.57	181.61	181.89	48.72	48.24	48.29	35.07	34.54	34.70	1,047	99.81
6	182.33	180.61	182.00	48.17	47.87	48.02	34.85	34.54	34.71	847	99.79
7	182.45	181.12	181.54	47.96	47.50	47.55	34.90	34.60	34.75	758	99.65
8	181.68	181.21	181.49	47.62	47.54	47.59	34.79	34.70	34.73	254	99.60
9	*			*			*			*	
10	182.70	181.17	182.21	47.95	47.36	47.59	34.80	34.51	34.65	723	99.44
11	†		†	†		†	†		†	†	
12	182.56	180.56	181.04	47.71	47.15	47.19	34.87	34.50	34.55	896	99.33
13	180.96	179.60	180.00	46.98	46.49	46.56	34.54	34.23	34.32	790	98.99
14	181.00	179.67	180.05	47.09	46.32	46.79	34.39	34.09	34.20	781	98.95
15	180.48	179.98	180.26	46.92	46.75	46.86	34.18	34.09	34.14	295	98.88
16	*			*			*			*	
17	180.95	179.57	180.40	47.23	46.71	47.08	34.21	33.90	34.01	751	98.65
18	181.99	180.12	181.71	48.05	47.11	47.78	34.15	33.85	34.00	930	98.61
19	182.98	181.69	182.71	48.46	47.83	48.04	34.17	33.85	34.00	1,047	98.48
20	183.68	181.15	183.17	49.01	47.82	48.76	34.09	33.81	33.90	962	98.51
21	183.97	182.23	182.61	49.28	48.54	48.72	34.10	33.80	33.92	976	98.67
22	182.62	182.16	182.33	48.80	48.51	48.66	34.01	33.81	33.95	324	98.65
23	*			*			*			*	
24	183.06	181.23	181.98	48.71	47.99	48.09	33.96	33.55	33.64	788	98.57
25	182.43	180.92	181.35	48.66	48.01	48.25	33.62	33.29	33.41	865	98.38
26	182.39	180.67	180.94	48.18	47.65	47.95	33.50	33.04	33.13	907	98.33
27	†		†	†		†	†		†	†	
28	181.15	179.30	179.51	47.91	47.17	47.29	33.15	32.79	32.88	928	98.24
29	179.60	178.87	179.40	47.21	46.99	47.12	32.97	32.81	32.94	387	98.19
30	*			*			*			*	
High			183.17			48.76			34.89		99.90
Low			179.40			46.56			32.88		98.19

*Sunday. †Holiday. ‡000 omitted.   Total 16,371

DECEMBER, 1947

	Industrials High	Low	Close	Railroads High	Low	Close	Utilities High	Low	Close	‡Daily sales	40 Bonds
1	181.09	179.09	180.61	47.88	47.17	47.65	33.10	32.78	32.96	798	98.04
2	181.77	180.20	180.76	48.20	47.61	47.84	33.15	32.75	33.06	894	98.05
3	180.57	179.18	179.63	47.91	47.31	47.49	33.10	32.81	32.94	928	98.05
4	179.83	178.16	178.79	47.40	46.76	46.94	32.99	32.74	32.83	971	97.86
5	178.57	175.46	176.10	47.06	46.00	46.28	32.95	32.55	32.62	1,292	97.74
6	175.99	175.44	175.74	46.33	46.05	46.28	32.68	32.60	32.65	420	97.72
7	*	*	*	*	*	*	*	*	*	*	*
8	177.35	175.19	176.71	47.03	46.30	46.88	33.12	32.70	32.95	956	97.65
9	177.98	176.00	177.47	47.62	46.70	47.39	33.05	32.75	32.86	1,100	97.56
10	178.22	176.89	177.58	48.21	47.41	47.81	33.03	32.73	32.86	1,120	97.59
11	177.98	176.44	177.37	48.07	47.38	47.65	33.11	32.70	32.88	935	97.51
12	178.92	176.82	178.37	48.49	47.56	48.19	33.15	32.76	32.97	1,224	97.58
13	179.45	178.58	179.34	49.02	48.33	49.02	33.13	33.00	33.06	565	97.60
14	*	*	*	*	*	*	*	*	*	*	*
15	180.56	178.74	179.69	50.15	49.05	49.51	33.41	33.05	33.22	1,434	97.80
16	180.25	178.91	179.44	49.73	49.08	49.32	33.30	32.81	33.01	1,086	97.83
17	180.23	178.69	179.81	50.63	49.12	50.50	33.18	32.81	33.04	1,250	97.92
18	180.53	179.03	179.44	50.98	50.08	50.24	33.08	32.73	32.93	1,128	97.94
19	180.64	178.62	180.09	50.72	49.92	50.58	33.18	32.79	32.98	1,247	97.91
20	181.34	179.86	181.06	51.78	50.77	51.70	33.25	33.06	33.25	797	97.88
21	*	*	*	*	*	*	*	*	*	*	*
22	181.78	179.98	180.21	52.05	51.07	51.39	33.49	33.07	33.20	1,446	97.84
23	181.25	179.61	180.71	52.69	51.41	52.48	33.53	32.95	33.35	1,358	97.60
24	181.49	179.72	180.84	52.88	51.90	52.45	33.51	33.25	33.37	1,191	97.13
25	†	†	†	†	†	†	†	†	†	†	†
26	180.71	178.90	179.28	52.22	51.46	51.62	33.42	33.04	33.21	933	96.82
27	179.51	178.85	179.23	51.62	51.25	51.47	33.21	33.12	33.17	409	96.74
28	*	*	*	*	*	*	*	*	*	*	*
29	179.81	177.93	178.58	51.47	50.75	51.01	33.25	32.96	33.10	1,194	96.57
30	180.93	178.43	180.56	51.84	50.70	51.69	33.35	32.85	33.23	1,379	96.54
31	181.82	180.29	181.16	53.17	52.21	52.48	33.55	33.25	33.40	1,540	96.74
High			181.16			52.48			33.40		98.05
Low			175.74			46.28			32.62		96.54

*Sunday. †Holiday. ‡000 omitted. Total 27,605

JANUARY, 1948

	Industrials High	Low	Close	Railroads High	Low	Close	Utilities High	Low	Close	‡Daily sales	40 Bonds
1	†	†	†	†	†	†	†	†	†	†	†
2	181.53	180.01	181.04	53.94	52.33	53.85	33.59	33.20	33.52	705	96.94
3	‡	‡	‡	‡	‡	‡	‡	‡	‡	‡	‡
4											
5	181.69	179.19	179.53	54.17	52.61	52.72	33.98	33.50	33.73	1,087	97.03
6	179.88	177.78	179.12	52.70	51.54	52.39	33.79	33.39	33.56	1,030	97.20
7	180.40	178.48	179.83	52.90	52.30	52.69	33.83	33.47	33.70	815	97.40
8	181.04	179.35	180.60	53.35	52.67	53.27	34.00	33.61	33.91	890	97.64
9	181.40	179.74	180.09	53.66	52.82	52.85	34.00	33.66	33.77	976	97.86
10	180.46	179.94	180.20	52.92	52.52	52.87	33.90	33.80	33.86	380	97.88
11	*	*	*	*	*	*	*	*	*	*	*
12	180.62	178.70	179.33	53.06	52.20	52.44	33.79	33.57	33.61	996	97.98
13	179.29	177.25	177.49	52.41	51.41	51.52	33.69	33.25	33.40	950	98.02
14	178.16	176.50	179.37	51.67	51.07	51.38	33.45	33.10	33.25	824	97.94
15	178.06	176.54	177.03	51.54	50.99	51.10	33.27	33.00	33.11	784	98.02
16	177.71	176.28	177.15	51.74	50.96	51.41	33.30	33.02	33.17	761	98.00
17	177.59	176.91	177.24	51.24	51.01	51.02	33.31	33.25	33.29	302	98.00
18	*	*	*	*	*	*	*	*	*	*	*
19	177.34	175.21	175.95	50.89	49.85	50.09	33.19	32.80	32.89	1,052	97.98
20	176.13	174.62	175.27	50.52	49.97	50.22	33.06	32.78	32.89	709	98.03
21	176.10	173.32	173.53	51.08	49.61	49.73	33.08	32.65	32.71	1,185	97.97
22	173.33	171.37	172.15	50.26	49.40	50.00	32.64	32.30	32.37	1,110	97.90
23	173.04	171.36	171.97	50.59	49.80	49.94	32.52	32.25	32.36	789	97.86
24	171.94	171.28	171.67	50.03	49.79	49.96	32.45	32.37	32.41	298	97.78
25	*	*	*	*	*	*	*	*	*	*	*
26	172.41	170.70	171.18	50.37	49.87	50.02	32.48	32.29	32.36	651	97.81
27	172.66	170.83	171.42	51.12	50.18	50.62	32.57	32.22	32.30	831	97.88
28	173.49	171.68	172.97	51.20	50.49	50.99	32.54	32.28	32.46	857	97.95
29	175.06	173.39	174.47	51.96	51.26	51.68	32.70	32.43	32.64	1,064	98.06
30	175.58	173.61	174.76	51.91	51.44	51.65	32.73	32.49	32.62	885	98.20
31	175.22	174.62	175.05	51.71	51.59	51.66	32.70	32.62	32.69	286	98.23
High			181.04			53.85			33.91		98.23
Low			171.18			49.73			32.30		96.94

*Sunday. †Holiday. ‡000 omitted. Total 20,217

FEBRUARY, 1948

	Industrials High	Low	Close	Railroads High	Low	Close	Utilities High	Low	Close	‡Daily sales	40 Bonds
1											
2	176.05	174.57	174.92	52.00	51.44	51.54	32.78	32.55	32.66	771	98.18
3	175.03	173.54	173.95	51.41	51.04	51.20	32.75	32.50	32.63	699	98.19
4	173.39	170.41	170.95	50.96	49.66	49.87	32.69	32.33	32.43	1,198	98.13
5	170.43	168.13	169.18	49.68	48.92	49.35	32.35	32.02	32.17	1,204	97.94
6	169.67	167.95	168.81	49.89	49.15	49.51	32.30	31.98	32.14	922	97.90
7	169.86	168.98	169.79	50.05	49.66	50.05	32.25	32.16	32.21	332	97.91
8											
9	170.83	169.33	169.82	50.42	49.97	50.13	32.34	32.15	32.25	655	97.97
10	168.92	165.26	165.65	49.62	48.04	48.13	32.08	31.62	31.65	1,458	97.88
11	166.41	164.07	165.69	48.62	47.48	48.35	31.81	31.45	31.68	1,487	97.79
12	†	†	†	†	†	†	†	†	†	†	
13	167.23	164.99	166.33	48.76	48.02	48.35	31.90	31.50	31.73	928	97.82
14	166.34	165.86	166.18	48.48	48.21	48.36	31.76	31.67	31.71	285	97.82
15											
16	168.96	166.86	168.30	49.42	48.62	49.11	32.04	31.73	31.95	831	97.83
17	169.23	167.47	167.89	49.37	48.89	49.02	32.13	31.69	31.91	719	97.93
18	168.36	167.23	168.04	48.96	48.62	48.80	32.09	31.76	31.95	606	97.96
19	168.98	167.34	167.86	49.29	48.62	48.68	32.05	31.80	31.94	680	98.05
20	167.96	166.38	167.44	48.47	48.13	48.40	31.86	31.69	31.74	701	98.04
21	167.79	167.25	167.60	48.58	48.47	48.52	31.78	31.71	31.75	233	98.07
22											
23	†	†	†	†	†	†	†	†	†	†	
24	168.24	166.81	167.80	48.95	48.40	48.91	31.80	31.65	31.75	641	98.14
25	169.01	167.72	168.39	49.38	48.84	48.96	31.83	31.57	31.66	710	98.18
26	168.71	167.17	167.56	49.08	48.59	48.75	31.76	31.59	31.69	623	98.24
27	167.56	165.92	166.80	48.93	48.25	48.83	31.70	31.50	31.65	766	98.19
28	167.42	166.74	167.30	49.28	48.89	49.27	31.77	31.66	31.70	352	98.20
29											
High			174.92			51.54			32.66		98.24
Low			165.65			48.13			31.65		97.79

*Sunday. †Holiday ‡000 omitted. Total 16,801

MARCH, 1948

	Industrials High	Low	Close	Railroads High	Low	Close	Utilities High	Low	Close	‡Daily sales	40 Bonds
1	168.62	167.46	168.14	50.08	49.58	49.81	31.87	31.69	31.73	767	98.19
2	169.18	167.78	168.75	50.25	49.67	50.03	31.88	31.70	31.78	775	98.17
3	169.28	168.04	168.61	50.37	49.86	50.17	31.87	31.63	31.79	757	98.20
4	168.92	167.69	168.13	49.79	49.39	49.46	31.93	31.72	31.82	582	98.13
5	168.64	167.20	168.35	49.62	49.31	49.53	31.97	31.75	31.90	625	98.11
6	169.05	168.49	168.94	49.72	49.57	49.68	31.96	31.85	31.95	321	98.10
7											
8	169.13	167.46	167.71	49.86	49.40	49.48	32.02	31.87	31.90	743	98.08
9	167.54	166.04	166.76	49.18	48.78	49.00	31.90	31.76	31.84	657	98.11
10	167.74	166.04	167.48	49.63	49.02	49.54	32.10	31.85	32.00	734	98.15
11	168.27	166.67	167.21	49.95	49.45	49.58	32.11	31.96	32.02	823	98.10
12	167.54	166.51	166.99	50.00	49.32	49.90	32.08	31.88	32.00	685	98.06
13	167.66	167.05	167.62	50.26	50.04	50.23	32.07	31.91	31.99	345	98.06
14											
15	168.16	167.09	167.62	50.39	49.86	50.11	32.26	32.03	32.12	691	98.05
16	167.21	165.03	165.39	49.72	48.83	48.90	32.20	31.80	31.86	941	97.97
17	166.60	165.03	166.24	49.73	48.99	49.46	31.97	31.73	31.88	933	97.93
18	168.02	166.07	166.92	50.12	49.38	49.56	32.04	31.76	31.90	885	98.04
19	169.75	166.50	169.67	50.46	49.56	50.40	32.33	31.91	32.29	1,161	98.09
20	173.28	170.76	173.12	51.86	50.82	51.78	32.65	32.45	32.62	1,264	98.10
21											
22	175.23	173.05	173.66	52.43	51.50	51.76	33.05	32.52	32.71	2,037	98.19
23	174.26	172.71	173.50	52.11	51.33	51.89	32.85	32.46	32.73	1,163	98.29
24	174.45	172.84	173.62	52.47	51.37	52.06	32.80	32.50	32.70	1,038	98.42
25	174.63	173.08	174.05	53.14	52.04	52.79	32.96	32.60	32.80	1,040	98.53
26	†	†	†	†	†	†	†	†	†	†	
27	174.47	173.48	173.95	52.90	52.43	52.51	32.85	32.76	32.80	428	98.54
28											
29	174.33	172.55	173.65	52.66	52.08	52.42	32.89	32.60	32.79	762	98.58
30	175.38	173.30	175.23	53.10	52.29	52.87	33.07	32.71	33.02	1,056	98.64
31	177.61	175.63	177.20	53.98	53.10	53.73	33.40	32.91	33.27	1,778	98.81
High			177.20			53.73			33.27		98.81
Low			165.39			48.90			31.73		97.93

*Sunday. †Holiday. ‡000 omitted. Total 22,993

APRIL, 1948

	Industrials			Railroads			Utilities			‡Daily sales	40 Bonds
	High	Low	Close	High	Low	Close	High	Low	Close		
1	178.14	176.08	177.61	54.06	53.16	53.76	33.46	33.20	33.35	1488	98.86
2	178.10	175.96	177.32	53.98	53.43	53.78	33.50	33.13	33.37	1080	98.89
3	177.75	176.91	177.45	54.00	53.59	53.93	33.45	33.34	33.41	486	98.94
4											
5	178.27	177.06	177.92	54.43	53.76	54.12	33.59	33.42	33.54	1037	99.06
6	179.31	177.62	178.77	54.80	53.85	54.52	33.64	33.36	33.56	1314	99.20
7	179.14	177.70	178.33	55.06	54.30	54.75	33.74	33.45	33.57	1160	99.37
8	179.38	177.91	178.80	55.12	54.33	54.90	33.80	33.47	33.75	1063	99.48
9	179.91	178.40	179.16	55.72	54.87	55.30	33.81	33.55	33.58	1379	99.53
10	179.63	178.87	179.48	55.32	54.97	55.27	33.76	33.66	33.71	520	99.56
11											
12	180.19	178.26	179.05	55.60	54.92	55.03	33.76	33.49	33.64	1025	99.53
13	179.89	178.58	179.45	55.18	54.65	54.98	33.63	33.36	33.54	946	99.62
14	179.91	178.59	179.13	55.23	54.53	54.76	33.72	33.45	33.60	1032	99.63
15	180.94	178.60	180.27	55.71	54.69	55.59	33.78	33.47	33.63	1654	99.66
16	181.69	179.90	180.63	56.54	55.52	55.86	33.87	33.52	33.75	2143	99.79
17	180.81	180.02	180.38	55.94	55.62	55.75	33.87	33.67	33.76	579	99.77
18											
19	181.42	179.90	181.05	56.60	55.72	56.46	33.90	33.64	33.77	1527	99.76
20	181.87	179.98	180.72	56.82	56.07	56.21	33.91	33.63	33.78	1695	99.77
21	181.79	179.49	181.37	57.20	55.84	57.03	33.92	33.52	33.80	1673	99.82
22	183.40	180.88	182.98	58.01	57.15	57.64	34.04	33.72	33.89	2325	99.86
23	184.48	182.67	183.78	58.68	57.65	58.47	34.11	33.76	34.05	2474	100.11
24	183.73	182.85	183.20	58.71	58.27	58.57	34.10	33.97	34.08	849	100.13
25											
26	183.09	180.93	181.32	58.62	57.29	57.49	34.08	33.73	33.87	1413	100.08
27	181.87	180.07	180.97	58.23	57.18	57.92	34.15	33.78	34.08	1424	100.03
28	182.01	180.16	181.01	58.50	57.65	58.21	34.28	33.92	34.15	1403	99.98
29	181.47	179.33	180.65	58.64	57.90	58.34	34.31	33.95	34.22	1477	99.93
30	181.64	179.69	180.51	59.00	57.90	58.15	34.23	33.94	34.08	1446	99.91
High			183.78			58.57			34.22		100.13
Low			177.32			53.76			33.35		98.86

*Sunday. †Holiday. ‡000 omitted.   Total 34,612

MAY, 1948

	Industrials			Railroads			Utilities			‡Daily sales	40 Bonds
	High	Low	Close	High	Low	Close	High	Low	Close		
1	180.58	179.96	180.28	58.29	57.94	58.05	34.13	33.99	34.02	477	99.96
2											
3	181.71	179.47	181.09	59.21	57.93	59.08	34.21	33.94	34.16	1,152	99.94
4	182.43	180.70	181.44	59.63	58.86	59.07	34.33	34.06	34.20	1,463	99.95
5	182.05	180.56	180.94	58.87	57.75	57.97	34.35	34.00	34.11	1,237	99.97
6	182.14	180.16	181.65	59.17	57.54	58.95	34.45	34.12	34.35	1,307	99.98
7	183.20	181.68	182.29	59.45	58.54	58.88	34.65	34.30	34.55	1,666	100.02
8	182.66	182.17	182.50	58.92	58.44	58.73	34.69	34.52	34.68	639	100.05
9											
10	183.46	181.68	182.94	59.10	58.16	58.96	34.78	34.46	34.65	1,442	100.03
11	184.25	182.21	183.75	59.70	58.84	59.12	34.84	34.55	34.76	1,750	100.04
12	184.39	182.49	183.95	59.66	58.81	59.45	35.19	34.72	35.00	1,526	100.17
13	185.40	183.32	184.82	60.16	59.32	59.91	35.21	34.82	35.09	2,027	100.28
14	188.93	185.01	188.60	62.49	59.94	62.24	35.66	35.16	35.54	3,837	100.48
15	191.39	189.58	190.25	63.07	61.99	62.18	35.94	35.60	35.79	2,592	100.52
16											
17	191.00	188.37	190.44	62.49	61.12	62.27	36.06	35.45	35.89	3,054	100.42
18	191.01	188.16	188.56	62.32	60.98	61.25	36.05	35.49	35.56	2,480	100.34
19	189.44	187.46	188.28	61.83	60.93	61.31	35.76	35.36	35.51	1,853	100.37
20	190.00	187.52	189.26	61.77	60.95	61.29	36.04	35.40	35.81	2,480	100.40
21	191.44	189.17	189.78	62.23	61.28	61.48	36.01	35.60	35.72	2,675	100.50
22	190.31	189.63	190.00	61.75	61.37	61.65	35.82	35.62	35.77	830	100.49
23											
24	190.67	188.98	189.82	62.04	61.31	61.61	35.93	35.58	35.77	1,559	100.53
25	190.77	188.55	189.71	61.66	60.67	61.04	35.78	35.46	35.68	1,810	100.46
26	191.57	189.06	191.06	61.67	60.79	61.48	35.80	35.47	35.68	1,841	100.54
27	192.31	190.39	190.97	61.75	60.72	60.87	35.85	35.48	35.73	1,832	100.54
28	191.48	189.49	190.74	60.99	60.37	60.81	35.93	35.61	35.83	1,242	100.57
29	‡	‡	‡	‡	‡	‡	‡	‡	‡	‡	‡
30	†	†	†	†	†	†	†	†	†	†	†
31	†	†	†	†	†	†	†	†	†	†	†
High			191.06			62.27			35.89		100.57
Low			180.28			57.97			34.02		99.94

*Sunday. †Holiday. ‡000 omitted.   Total 42,769

JUNE, 1948

| | —Industrials— | | | —Railroads— | | | —Utilities— | | | ‡Daily | 40 |
	High	Low	Close	High	Low	Close	High	Low	Close	Sales	Bonds
1	192.00	190.29	191.18	61.15	60.46	60.88	35.93	35.54	35.70	1,305	100.64
2	192.18	190.30	191.32	61.19	60.46	60.92	35.78	35.46	35.60	1,298	100.77
3	192.09	190.40	191.05	60.81	60.17	60.36	35.77	35.38	35.47	1,297	100.86
4	191.31	189.56	190.18	60.37	59.72	59.75	35.46	35.09	35.15	1,104	100.81
5											
6											
7	190.74	188.87	190.13	59.68	59.10	59.51	35.41	35.05	35.30	931	100.80
8	192.59	190.31	192.16	61.03	59.67	60.99	35.55	35.17	35.49	1,519	100.98
9	193.54	191.86	192.56	61.70	61.05	61.25	35.95	35.56	35.79	1,875	101.13
10	193.28	191.06	192.50	62.18	61.07	61.85	36.06	35.73	35.95	1,695	101.18
11	193.65	191.48	192.96	61.94	61.54	61.64	36.15	35.69	35.98	1,521	101.08
12											
13											
14	194.49	192.14	192.86	61.93	61.05	61.34	36.17	35.87	36.04	1,747	101.02
15	193.93	191.62	193.16	61.44	60.80	61.19	36.26	35.76	36.03	1,631	100.91
16	193.19	191.06	192.34	61.15	60.30	60.91	36.15	35.79	36.00	1,582	100.80
17	192.99	191.12	192.15	61.91	61.00	61.38	36.07	35.72	35.89	1,521	100.88
18	192.19	190.56	191 65	61.54	61.03	61.27	35.96	35.73	35.85	1,246	100.80
19											
20											
21	192.08	189.52	189.71	61.81	60.37	60.56	35.91	35.55	35.62	1,754	100.74
22	190.31	188.41	189.66	62.00	60.35	61.76	35.85	35.44	35.70	1,408	100.61
23	191.32	189.42	190.73	63.13	61.93	62.72	36.10	35.64	36.00	1,762	100.55
24	191.87	190.00	190.87	63.48	62.52	62.90	36.21	35.78	35.94	1,556	100.50
25	191.06	188.95	190.00	63.25	62.19	62.82	36.06	35.66	35.81	1,152	100.39
26											
27											
28	189.66	186.56	187.90	62.41	61.07	61.54	35.79	35.33	35.55	1,208	100.28
29	189.19	187.50	188.49	62.11	61.52	61.80	35.69	35.35	35.54	817	100.30
30	190.03	187.73	189.46	63.20	62.03	62.76	35.80	35.41	35.70	994	100.19
High			193.16			62.90			36.04		101.18
Low			187.90			59.51			35.15		100.19
										Total	30,922

*Sunday. †Holiday. ‡000 omitted.

JULY, 1948

| | —Industrials— | | | —Railroads— | | | —Utilities— | | | ‡Daily | 40 |
	High	Low	Close	High	Low	Close	High	Low	Close	Sales	Bonds
1	189.85	188.43	189.03	63.07	62.37	62.52	35.85	35.48	35.61	822	100.21
2	190.45	188.46	190.06	64.02	62.79	63.94	35.74	35.49	35.64	923	100.02
3											
4											
5											
6	191.37	189.54	190.55	64.46	63.38	63.89	35.70	35.48	35.61	945	100.03
7	191.04	189.31	190.06	64.03	63.37	63.70	35.74	35.34	35.58	916	99.97
8	191.16	189.73	190.58	64.32	63.43	64.04	35.79	35.56	35.69	999	100.00
9	192.09	189.98	191.62	65.08	64.14	64.76	35.85	35.58	35.75	1,372	100.01
10											
11											
12	192.38	190.95	191.47	65.23	64.59	64.82	36.10	35.75	36.01	1,296	100.06
13	191.65	190.08	190.36	65.21	64.42	64.67	36.00	35.73	35.92	1,198	100.12
14	191.13	189.41	190.66	65.17	64.08	64.95	36.01	35.76	35.90	1,337	100.12
15	190.69	187.62	187.70	64.89	63.01	63.15	36.01	35.63	35.67	1,619	100.05
16	188.34	184.98	185.90	63.46	61.71	62.06	35.62	35.15	35.21	1,760	99.87
17											
18											
19	184.76	179.58	181.20	61.13	58.39	59.48	35.13	34.45	34.63	2,567	99.65
20	184.41	181.27	183.57	60.67	59.51	60.40	35.20	34.60	35.11	1,470	99.55
21	185.96	183.39	184.44	61.28	60.15	60.25	35.41	35.02	35.19	1,203	99.63
22	185.90	184.19	185.29	61.37	60.30	60.96	35.26	35.00	35.09	848	99.66
23	186.36	184.74	185.31	61.53	60.80	61.15	35.43	35.12	35.30	819	99.56
24											
25											
26	185.83	183.81	184.17	61.30	60.42	60.50	35.46	35.13	35.20	719	99.56
27	186.37	183.81	186.09	61.45	60.50	61.33	35.45	35.00	35.39	867	99.52
28	187.00	184.92	185.15	62.07	61.03	61.45	35.49	35.12	35.19	843	99.50
29	185.28	183.19	183.57	61.57	60.83	60.89	35.14	34.85	34.90	750	99.47
30	182.56	180.04	181.33	60.91	59.52	60.15	34.91	34.45	34.70	1,312	99.36
31											
High			191.62			64.95			36.01		100.21
Low			181.20			59.48			34.63		99.36
										Total	24,585

*Sunday. †Holiday. ‡000 omitted.

	Industrials High	Low	Close	Railroads High	Low	Close	Utilities High	Low	Close	‡Daily Sales	40 Bonds
1											
2	182.61	180.61	181.13	60.38	59.73	59.83	34.85	34.54	34.64	714	99.36
3	181.72	180.24	180.98	60.39	59.71	60.28	34.73	34.33	34.62	717	99.31
4	183.29	180.82	183.06	61.48	60.60	61.44	35.00	34.55	34.85	873	99.11
5	184.54	182.45	182.92	62.14	61.15	61.19	35.03	34.78	34.83	883	99.12
6	183.44	181.89	183.01	61.50	60.97	61.44	35.01	34.66	34.96	676	99.00
7											
8											
9	183.75	182.02	182.26	61.29	60.40	60.45	35.02	34.72	34.82	667	98.98
10	182.26	179.91	180.02	60.40	59.63	59.68	34.77	34.45	34.55	836	98.71
11	179.88	177.40	179.27	59.49	58.24	59.06	34.49	34.09	34.32	1,307	98.61
12	180.17	178.51	179.63	59.42	58.77	59.16	34.43	34.20	34.30	630	98.55
13	180.44	178.99	179.63	59.13	58.73	58.79	34.34	34.05	34.15	509	98.47
14											
15											
16	180.62	179.46	180.30	58.76	58.46	58.66	34.27	34.08	34.20	465	98.36
17	182.63	180.75	182.15	59.81	58.70	59.54	34.85	34.47	34.75	681	98.41
18	183.21	181.76	182.12	59.82	59.35	59.37	34.85	34.59	34.69	637	98.58
19	182.78	181.45	182.57	59.70	59.23	59.60	34.80	34.60	34.76	580	98.59
20	183.92	182.50	183.60	60.83	59.88	60.72	34.94	34.75	34.86	714	98.70
21											
22											
23	183.52	181.45	181.75	60.81	59.95	60.10	34.88	34.61	34.67	634	98.78
24	182.99	181.67	182.58	61.08	60.12	60.90	34.74	34.56	34.66	617	98.77
25	183.01	181.89	182.41	61.50	60.62	61.00	34.70	34.49	34.56	523	98.74
26	182.99	181.93	182.52	61.53	60.47	60.75	34.71	34.45	34.63	544	98.77
27	183.55	182.38	183.21	61.49	60.84	61.44	34.90	34.56	34.82	540	98.76
28											
29											
30	183.95	181.89	182.09	62.21	61.13	61.34	34.95	34.61	34.75	688	98.68
31	182.47	181.18	181.71	61.66	61.07	61.53	34.92	34.73	34.85	605	98.66
High			183.60			61.53			34.96	Total 15,040	99.36
Low			179.27			58.66			34.15		98.36

*Sunday   †Holiday   ‡000 omitted

	Industrials High	Low	Close	Railroads High	Low	Close	Utilities High	Low	Close	‡Daily Sales	40 Bonds
1	183.99	181.44	183.60	62.93	61.85	62.67	35.16	34.94	35.11	923	98.76
2	184.88	183.16	184.39	63.36	62.62	62.90	35.45	35.10	35.38	897	98.93
3	184.90	183.49	184.35	63.04	62.52	62.77	35.46	35.28	35.39	662	98.93
4											
5											
6											
7	185.64	183.68	185.36	63.25	62.42	63.12	35.45	35.26	35.36	909	99.03
8	184.88	182.63	182.90	62.97	61.53	61.59	35.37	35.10	35.20	882	98.95
9	182.83	179.74	180.33	61.36	59.89	60.37	35.23	34.90	34.91	1,996	98.88
10	181.26	179.04	180.61	60.72	59.49	60.28	35.00	34.74	34.80	974	98.79
11											
12											
13	180.51	178.87	179.38	60.27	59.51	59.72	34.84	34.52	34.57	678	98.72
14	181.12	179.41	180.63	60.74	60.03	60.40	34.87	34.56	34.75	708	98.69
15	181.47	179.85	180.62	60.92	60.25	60.43	34.92	34.66	34.73	710	98.70
16	181.10	179.84	180.69	61.03	60.24	60.96	34.79	34.62	34.70	576	98.74
17	180.78	179.60	180.06	60.96	60.26	60.28	34.75	34.45	34.60	679	98.73
18											
19											
20	179.93	176.96	177.37	59.95	58.61	58.89	34.77	34.41	34.49	1,264	98.65
21	178.89	176.94	178.61	59.36	58.59	59.20	34.64	34.39	34.50	921	98.64
22	179.70	178.11	179.16	59.93	59.13	59.78	34.76	34.42	34.57	847	98.58
23	179.22	178.22	178.77	59.70	59.34	59.47	34.74	34.55	34.66	552	98.53
24	179.71	178.49	179.28	59.53	59.14	59.48	34.84	34.56	34.71	647	98.51
25											
26											
27	178.32	175.84	175.99	58.83	57.42	57.45	34.53	34.04	34.17	1,214	98.46
28	177.91	175.84	177.54	58.46	57.51	58.17	34.15	33.90	34.06	912	98.39
29	179.53	177.57	179.04	58.94	58.19	58.55	34.42	34.10	34.36	809	98.44
30	179.71	177.95	178.30	58.78	58.16	58.33	34.55	34.26	34.48	702	98.47
High			185.36			63.12			35.39		99.03
Low			175.99			57.45			34.06		98.39

Total 17,564

*Sunday.   †Holiday.   ‡000 omitted.

OCTOBER, 1948

	Industrials			Railroads			Utilities			‡Daily Sales	40 Bonds
	High	Low	Close	High	Low	Close	High	Low	Close		
1	180.08	178.22	179.87	59.02	58.31	58.94	34.50	34.32	34.46	675	98.45
2	180.91	180.35	180.78	59.45	59.10	59.20	34.65	34.54	34.62	322	98.46
3	*			*			*				
4	182.19	180.74	181.70	59.94	59.25	59.77	34.86	34.66	34.80	607	98.49
5	181.89	180.52	181.23	59.72	59.23	59.45	34.85	34.65	34.75	548	98.46
6	182.34	180.91	181.72	60.18	59.43	59.91	34.85	34.55	34.72	712	98.53
7	183.10	181.58	182.52	60.71	60.10	60.39	35.01	34.73	34.94	800	98.55
8	182.99	181.55	182.02	60.37	59.83	59.90	34.91	34.66	34.80	627	98.56
9	182.34	181.77	182.09	60.03	59.90	59.98	34.84	34.81	34.83	190	98.57
10	*			*			*				
11	182.76	181.71	182.41	60.00	59.44	59.57	35.12	34.70	35.06	508	98.52
12	†	†	†	†	†	†	†	†	†	†	†
13	184.25	182.30	183.84	60.55	59.78	60.46	35.22	34.86	35.15	834	98.52
14	185.46	183.65	184.52	60.93	60.29	60.42	35.31	35.07	35.21	976	98.56
15	185.26	183.76	184.62	60.09	60.09	60.23	35.32	35.03	35.22	914	98.49
16	185.12	184.48	184.93	60.22	60.10	60.17	35.24	35.20	35.23	393	98.50
17	*			*			*				
18	186.22	184.63	185.33	60.79	60.17	60.39	35.35	35.12	35.25	1,033	98.50
19	186.58	185.15	186.18	61.03	60.45	60.67	35.52	35.36	35.46	1,032	98.51
20	187.00	185.62	186.51	61.41	60.77	61.09	35.65	35.40	35.54	1,180	98.49
21	187.16	185.49	186.44	61.51	60.76	61.26	35.80	35.50	35.71	1,204	98.35
22	190.08	186.70	189.76	62.26	61.24	62.11	35.79	35.51	35.65	1,802	98.35
23	190.64	189.71	190.19	62.37	62.12	62.24	35.82	35.65	35.75	682	98.35
24	*			*			*				
25	190.53	188.54	189.52	62.17	61.30	61.73	35.75	35.45	35.60	1,104	98.32
26	190.88	188.97	189.76	62.35	61.67	62.00	35.82	35.51	35.69	1,137	98.19
27	190.06	188.11	189.28	62.06	61.16	61.84	35.51	35.23	35.40	970	98.22
28	189.59	187.29	187.73	61.99	61.09	61.23	35.52	35.22	35.31	973	98.26
29	188.60	186.99	188.28	61.46	60.81	61.29	35.50	35.25	35.42	863	98.18
30	188.72	188.19	188.62	61.45	61.23	61.34	35.44	35.38	35.40	348	98.21
31	*			*			*				
High			190.19			62.24			35.75		98.57
Low			179.87			58.94			34.46		98.18

Total 20,434

*Sunday. †Holiday. ‡000 omitted.

NOVEMBER, 1948

	Industrials			Railroads			Utilities			‡ Daily Sales	40 Bonds
	High	Low	Close	High	Low	Close	High	Low	Close		
1	190.45	188.39	189.76	62.11	61.52	61.97	35.82	35.44	35.74	1,222	98.28
2	†	†	†	†	†	†	†	†	†	†	†
3	183.08	179.65	182.46	58.83	57.50	58.52	34.64	34.00	34.28	3,237	98.07
4	185.79	182.92	184.54	59.75	58.83	59.30	34.85	34.39	34.60	1,527	98.14
5	184.42	178.11	178.38	58.97	55.94	56.22	34.65	33.55	33.71	2,531	98.07
6	180.09	178.43	178.94	57.16	56.30	56.59	33.90	33.68	33.78	875	98.10
7	*			*			*				
8	179.85	177.46	178.19	57.21	56.39	56.56	34.06	33.58	33.78	1,125	98.21
9	178.60	173.54	173.94	56.68	53.61	53.83	33.79	33.17	33.26	2,261	98.19
10	174.93	172.13	173.48	54.27	52.78	53.64	33.29	32.80	32.90	2,101	98.12
11	†	†	†	†	†	†	†	†	†	†	†
12	175.47	173.37	173.93	54.31	53.55	53.90	33.14	32.62	32.79	1,106	98.22
13	174.59	173.68	174.32	53.93	53.63	53.72	32.95	32.81	32.88	379	98.24
14	*			*			*				
15	176.56	174.37	176.01	54.74	53.66	54.34	33.34	32.89	33.10	1,027	98.31
16	177.42	175.44	176.20	55.23	54.43	54.85	33.36	33.07	33.16	1,062	98.44
17	176.92	175.14	176.07	54.90	54.18	54.46	33.18	32.83	33.00	975	98.43
18	176.89	175.52	176.07	54.64	54.15	54.39	33.25	32.90	33.10	780	98.57
19	177.96	175.99	176.98	55.38	54.48	54.93	33.18	32.98	33.11	993	98.56
20	177.63	177.14	177.42	55.22	55.00	55.15	33.20	33.08	33.15	340	98.54
21	*			*			*				
22	177.80	175.75	176.33	54.99	54.23	54.48	33.41	33.10	33.28	885	98.61
23	176.72	175.17	176.17	54.67	54.10	54.45	33.30	33.06	33.16	1,012	98.55
24	175.88	172.96	173.40	54.13	52.92	53.10	33.18	32.90	33.04	1,293	98.32
25	†	†	†	†	†	†	†	†	†	†	†
26	**174.14	172.38	173.16	53.57	52.76	53.08	33.12	32.82	32.95	1,037	98.25
27	173.18	172.71	172.90	53.14	52.92	53.06	33.01	32.93	32.96	343	98.24
28	*			*			*				
29	173.55	171.72	171.99	53.33	52.42	52.47	32.93	32.49	32.55	1,008	98.24
30	172.49	170.35	171.20	52.50	51.69	51.91	32.73	32.42	32.60	1,201	98.18
High			189.76			61.97			35.74		98.61
Low			171.20			51.91			32.55		98.07

Total 28,320

*Sunday. †Holiday. ‡000 omitted.

DECEMBER, 1948

	Industrials			Railroads			Utilities			‡Daily	40
	High	Low	Close	High	Low	Close	High	Low	Close	Sales	Bonds
1	174.02	171.67	173.22	53.59	52.18	53.38	32.98	32.66	32.91	1,315	98.17
2	174.88	173.15	173.61	53.94	53.09	53.19	33.00	32.68	32.76	1,213	98.20
3	175.34	173.20	175.00	53.48	52.82	53.38	32.96	32.66	32.85	1,103	98.33
4	176.30	175.20	176.22	53.82	53.46	53.76	32.95	32.83	32.95	512	98.33
5											
6	177.12	175.59	176.26	54.33	53.58	53.78	33.14	32.80	32.95	1,182	98.32
7	177.25	175.39	176.67	53.90	53.34	53.68	33.05	32.76	32.91	1,156	98.33
8	176.98	175.25	176.29	53.88	53.01	53.50	33.02	32.70	32.92	1,137	98.40
9	176.86	175.44	175.75	53.70	53.13	53.24	33.01	32.72	32.80	1,222	98.44
10	176.79	175.17	176.41	53.71	53.25	53.55	33.17	32.83	32.98	1,037	98.45
11	177.53	176.42	177.49	53.99	53.62	53.92	33.03	32.90	33.00	545	98.43
12											
13	178.43	176.67	177.34	54.41	53.82	54.00	33.22	32.93	33.02	1,183	98.36
14	177.73	175.86	176.59	54.03	53.32	53.55	33.19	32.97	33.13	1,002	98.42
15	177.26	175.78	176.20	53.73	53.14	53.31	33.38	32.99	33.20	921	98.45
16	176.59	175.20	175.83	53.51	52.97	53.06	33.29	33.02	33.17	1,006	98.52
17	176.78	175.17	175.92	53.38	52.59	52.97	33.32	32.97	33.17	1,006	98.57
18	176.01	175.36	175.69	53.12	52.82	52.89	33.29	33.17	33.20	360	98.57
19											
20	177.60	175.14	176.84	52.98	52.46	52.75	33.29	32.98	33.15	983	98.56
21	177.49	175.92	176.35	52.95	52.43	52.60	33.32	33.03	33.14	1,000	98.54
22	176.93	175.62	176.39	53.00	52.47	52.72	33.19	32.95	33.05	996	98.53
23	177.29	175.70	176.49	53.45	52.60	53.12	33.29	33.02	33.13	1,081	98.57
24	177.82	176.04	177.42	53.71	53.11	53.53	33.30	33.05	33.20	972	98.64
25											
26											
27	178.35	176.63	177.40	53.89	53.17	53.18	33.43	33.15	33.20	1,060	98.67
28	177.37	175.19	175.98	53.06	52.36	52.67	33.33	32.94	33.15	1,651	98.62
29	177.85	175.88	177.58	53.49	52.82	53.37	33.30	32.90	33.22	1,381	98.73
30	179.15	177.10	177.92	53.79	52.98	53.12	33.80	33.36	33.59	1,385	98.80
31	178.50	176.81	177.30	53.73	52.70	52.86	33.80	33.41	33.55	1,550	98.87
High			177.92			54.00			33.59		98.87
Low			173.22			52.60			32.76		98.17

Total 27,959

*Sunday. †Holiday.

JANUARY, 1949

	Industrials			Railroads			Utilities			‡Daily	40
	High	Low	Close	High	Low	Close	High	Low	Close	Sales	Bonds
1											
2											
3	176.99	174.37	175.03	52.83	51.63	51.87	33.67	33.30	33.36	980	98.90
4	175.97	174.56	175.49	52.36	51.92	52.22	33.55	33.30	33.45	640	98.90
5	177.76	175.50	177.08	52.97	52.27	52.56	33.65	33.27	33.58	804	99.07
6	180.59	177.16	180.22	53.70	52.50	53.62	34.19	33.62	34.05	1,149	99.24
7	182.50	180.47	181.31	54.93	53.94	54.29	34.40	33.98	34.22	1,396	99.36
8	181.69	181.13	181.41	54.33	54.02	54.12	34.40	34.28	34.39	370	99.41
9											
10	181.47	179.78	180.57	54.04	53.38	53.54	34.40	34.01	34.23	766	99.43
11	181.00	179.73	180.76	53.53	53.05	53.37	34.34	34.04	34.23	710	99.52
12	181.66	180.21	180.69	53.76	53.29	53.35	34.42	34.11	34.32	710	99.53
13	181.06	179.79	180.17	53.27	52.88	52.90	34.47	34.20	34.35	700	99.62
14	180.20	178.19	178.80	52.78	52.08	52.39	34.55	34.15	34.35	930	99.58
15	179.49	178.78	179.15	52.78	52.55	52.75	34.33	34.23	34.28	268	99.62
16											
17	180.48	177.99	180.14	53.17	52.52	53.13	34.46	34.09	34.38	719	99.75
18	181.55	180.09	180.55	53.48	52.96	53.09	34.69	34.30	34.58	766	99.80
19	181.47	179.75	181.12	53.66	53.01	53.63	34.80	34.50	34.72	755	99.95
20	181.85	180.44	181.43	54.09	53.57	53.99	34.96	34.71	34.90	818	100.00
21	181.89	180.69	181.00	54.42	53.77	53.91	35.06	34.81	34.94	770	100.12
22	181.68	181.22	181.54	54.04	53.88	53.95	35.03	34.85	35.00	280	100.13
23											
24	182.28	180.51	180.83	53.92	53.55	53.58	35.14	34.81	35.00	851	100.15
25	181.05	179.06	179.65	53.49	52.98	53.18	34.96	34.63	34.77	815	100.15
26	181.31	178.96	179.88	53.32	52.61	52.88	34.90	34.58	34.72	1,036	100.09
27	180.30	178.58	179.52	53.08	52.61	52.91	34.93	34.50	34.75	838	99.93
28	179.48	177.88	178.82	52.81	52.20	52.63	34.75	34.47	34.70	841	99.83
29	179.49	178.68	179.35	52.74	52.53	52.69	34.70	34.61	34.70	300	99.84
30											
31	179.73	178.46	179.12	52.92	52.43	52.57	34.76	34.59	34.68	613	99.83
High			181.54			54.29			35.00		100.15
Low			175.03			51.87			33.36		98.90

Total 18,825

*Sunday. †Holiday.

FEBRUARY, 1949

	Industrials			Railroads			Utilities			‡Daily Sales	40 Bonds
	High	Low	Close	High	Low	Close	High	Low	Close		
1	180.55	178.92	180.39	52.81	52.41	52.71	34.84	34.59	34.80	734	99.76
2	180.94	179.63	180.27	53.11	52.61	52.85	35.11	34.81	35.06	723	99.74
3	180.88	179.57	180.09	52.79	52.44	52.62	35.29	35.05	35.13	768	99.81
4	180.32	177.69	177.92	52.60	51.82	51.86	35.15	34.92	35.00	1,063	99.75
5	177.19	175.50	175.60	51.38	50.43	50.47	34.90	34.54	34.56	786	99.68
6	*										
7	176.76	173.79	174.43	50.73	49.38	49.59	34.60	34.16	34.24	1,328	99.59
8	174.37	172.91	173.71	50.17	49.43	49.90	34.45	34.13	34.30	960	99.55
9	175.20	173.57	174.61	50.47	49.86	50.08	34.30	33.97	34.20	881	99.47
10	174.80	172.23	172.41	50.08	48.71	48.94	34.30	34.00	34.05	983	99.42
11	172.69	171.03	171.93	48.98	48.43	48.70	34.26	33.92	34.11	881	99.48
12	†	†	†	†	†	†	†	†	†	†	†
13											
14	173.17	171.57	172.16	49.12	48.64	48.82	34.38	34.00	34.15	700	99.49
15	172.86	171.27	172.48	49.15	48.75	49.08	34.32	34.05	34.24	608	99.28
16	173.92	172.27	173.28	49.67	49.04	49.41	34.50	34.10	34.41	701	99.24
17	175.55	173.45	174.82	50.10	49.39	49.59	34.66	34.30	34.55	959	99.15
18	175.62	174.11	174.71	49.52	49.14	49.21	34.70	34.43	34.60	695	99.19
19	174.66	174.29	174.53	49.09	48.90	48.99	34.57	34.51	34.55	246	99.18
20	*										
21	174.67	173.63	174.19	48.90	48.46	48.67	34.81	34.54	34.75	556	99.00
22	†	†	†	†	†	†	†	†	†		
23	174.60	173.07	173.23	48.35	47.34	47.37	34.83	34.49	34.67	772	98.88
24	172.76	171.19	171.48	47.01	46.04	46.34	34.66	34.36	34.53	883	98.72
25	172.11	170.56	171.10	46.81	46.05	46.34	34.57	34.31	34.43	826	98.47
26	171.74	171.05	171.62	47.00	46.46	46.95	34.44	34.39	34.42	391	98.51
27	*										
28	173.38	171.63	173.06	47.97	47.12	47.71	34.65	34.40	34.56	738	98.50
High			180.39			52.85			35.13		99.81
Low			171.10			46.34			34.05		98.47

*Sunday. †Holiday. ‡000 omitted.

Total 17,182

MARCH, 1949

	Industrials			Railroads			Utilities			‡Daily Sales	40 Bonds
	High	Low	Close	High	Low	Close	High	Low	Close		
1	174.61	173.36	174.18	48.32	47.88	47.98	34.75	34.47	34.65	720	98.60
2	174.34	173.15	173.82	48.12	47.58	47.85	34.75	34.49	34.61	693	98.69
3	174.44	173.17	173.76	47.78	47.45	47.55	34.82	34.60	34.75	597	98.65
4	174.06	172.59	173.66	47.58	47.20	47.50	34.78	34.49	34.68	730	98.71
5	175.04	173.42	174.93	48.16	47.56	48.05	34.85	34.67	34.83	451	98.69
6	*										
7	175.82	174.30	175.55	48.77	48.10	48.55	34.94	34.66	34.81	841	98.75
8	176.62	175.30	176.09	48.63	48.07	48.24	35.11	34.71	35.02	940	98.79
9	176.29	175.22	175.76	48.11	47.72	47.90	35.01	34.85	34.97	642	98.74
10	176.20	175.03	175.64	48.04	47.62	47.84	35.07	34.84	35.01	628	98.86
11	176.87	175.41	176.52	49.29	47.90	49.13	35.16	34.98	35.10	1,071	98.90
12	177.14	176.55	176.96	49.40	49.13	49.28	35.23	35.10	35.19	394	98.96
13	*										
14	177.66	176.35	176.98	49.28	48.76	48.90	35.37	35.13	35.31	801	98.87
15	176.82	175.43	176.02	48.75	48.33	48.46	35.23	34.92	35.05	735	98.82
16	176.08	174.87	175.53	48.33	47.95	48.17	35.17	34.88	35.04	672	98.64
17	176.67	175.17	176.33	48.49	48.07	48.31	35.11	34.90	35.02	763	98.62
18	176.78	175.73	176.29	48.27	47.93	48.04	35.16	34.94	35.01	666	98.53
19	176.24	175.81	176.07	47.90	47.74	47.76	35.08	34.97	35.05	257	98.54
20	*										
21	176.47	175.27	175.61	47.80	47.47	47.54	35.19	34.90	35.00	619	98.54
22	175.85	174.34	174.83	47.66	46.83	46.92	35.10	34.87	34.98	843	98.50
23	176.54	174.32	176.20	47.85	46.98	47.80	35.22	34.80	35.14	960	98.55
24	177.37	176.13	176.41	48.50	47.98	48.15	35.46	35.11	35.32	918	98.57
25	176.49	175.29	175.83	48.10	47.66	47.78	35.37	35.18	35.30	628	98.52
26	176.02	175.49	175.82	47.94	47.80	47.88	35.33	35.25	35.30	236	98.52
27	*										
28	176.72	175.35	175.99	48.24	47.69	47.81	35.55	35.27	35.40	701	98.46
29	178.90	176.81	178.39	49.25	48.41	49.00	35.67	35.42	35.61	1,800	98.53
30	179.19	177.69	178.45	49.86	49.10	49.60	35.83	35.47	35.60	1,850	98.58
31	178.43	176.87	177.10	49.46	48.92	49.02	35.61	35.42	35.52	980	98.53
High			178.45			49.60			35.61		98.96
Low			173.66			46.92			34.61		98.46

*Sunday. †Holiday. ‡000 omitted.

Total 21,136

APRIL, 1949

	Industrials High	Low	Close	Railroads High	Low	Close	Utilities High	Low	Close	‡Daily Sales	40 Bonds
1	177.04	175.86	176.28	48.84	48.38	48.56	35.52	35.30	35.38	849	98.54
2	176.92	176.23	176.88	48.73	48.62	48.72	35.46	35.39	35.45	359	98.56
3	*										
4	177.78	176.15	176.59	49.01	48.51	48.69	35.65	35.35	35.44	922	98.53
5	177.67	175.94	177.04	48.94	48.44	48.80	35.80	35.46	35.75	902	98.49
6	177.53	176.19	176.71	48.83	48.43	48.54	36.02	35.70	35.88	930	98.61
7	176.94	175.43	176.04	48.67	48.29	48.49	36.00	35.75	35.90	845	98.58
8	176.62	175.34	176.44	49.46	48.42	49.44	35.91	35.74	35.90	850	98.55
9	176.87	176.41	176.75	49.70	49.42	49.56	35.81	35.73	35.74	385	98.62
10	*										
11	177.14	175.94	176.54	49.58	49.07	49.20	35.85	35.65	35.79	724	98.65
12	177.46	175.61	176.99	49.32	48.90	49.16	35.79	35.56	35.75	855	98.62
13	177.69	172.26	176.81	49.34	48.88	49.03	36.10	35.85	36.02	915	98.56
14	177.30	176.18	176.62	49.09	48.73	48.84	36.34	35.95	36.26	804	98.51
15	†	†	†	†	†	†	†	†	†	†	†
16	177.14	176.45	177.07	48.94	48.84	48.90	36.40	36.25	36.38	415	98.52
17	*										
18	177.71	176.47	177.16	48.89	48.41	48.46	36.46	36.16	36.30	892	98.56
19	177.50	176.39	176.73	48.39	48.07	48.17	36.25	36.07	36.15	830	98.53
20	176.79	175.38	175.69	48.42	48.08	48.24	36.19	35.94	36.02	969	98.52
21	175.49	173.08	173.24	48.04	47.28	47.33	35.88	35.58	35.64	1,305	98.46
22	173.77	172.64	173.42	47.41	46.83	47.15	35.64	35.45	35.55	893	98.48
23	174.00	173.37	173.76	47.49	47.27	47.45	35.64	35.50	35.55	339	98.51
24	*										
25	174.38	173.05	173.64	47.50	47.16	47.31	35.60	35.36	35.43	738	98.45
26	174.60	173.02	174.21	47.69	47.14	47.58	35.62	35.31	35.55	866	98.47
27	175.24	173.92	174.56	47.94	47.50	47.61	35.52	35.31	35.42	831	98.47
28	174.65	173.58	173.89	47.64	47.24	47.27	35.41	35.20	35.31	774	98.40
29	174.48	173.52	174.06	47.28	46.90	47.07	35.43	35.26	35.33	809	98.39
30	174.34	173.91	174.16	47.30	47.15	47.27	35.42	35.33	35.41	314	98.37
High			177.16			49.56			36.38		98.65
Low			173.24			47.07			35.31		98.37

*Sunday. †Holiday. ‡000 omitted. Total 19,315

MAY, 1949

	Industrials High	Low	Close	Railroads High	Low	Close	Utilities High	Low	Close	‡Daily Sales	40 Bonds
1	*										
2	175.06	173.93	174.53	47.45	47.00	47.13	35.55	35.25	35.40	744	98.41
3	175.32	173.86	175.00	47.27	46.79	47.10	35.60	35.29	35.50	829	98.44
4	177.04	175.09	176.63	47.79	47.26	47.72	36.08	35.58	35.95	1,182	98.52
5	177.18	175.91	176.33	47.89	47.41	47.52	36.04	35.80	35.89	919	98.57
6	176.24	174.74	175.50	47.51	47.25	47.38	35.97	35.75	35.90	779	98.49
7	175.61	175.20	175.39	47.49	47.34	47.43	35.92	35.87	35.89	240	98.46
8	*										
9	175.75	174.70	175.17	47.39	47.17	47.25	35.94	35.76	35.85	614	98.40
10	175.32	173.97	174.37	47.30	47.03	47.11	35.89	35.60	35.75	725	98.38
11	175.11	173.75	174.40	47.40	47.02	47.17	35.91	35.65	35.80	786	98.37
12	175.17	174.14	174.70	47.48	47.17	47.35	35.95	35.75	35.92	786	98.35
13	175.40	174.26	174.82	47.71	47.15	47.58	35.93	35.79	35.85	782	98.37
14	175.28	174.85	175.20	48.15	47.68	48.13	35.96	35.86	35.95	359	98.42
15	*										
16	176.26	175.17	175.76	48.28	47.83	48.10	36.29	35.96	36.14	1,030	98.44
17	176.07	174.86	175.32	48.18	47.75	47.87	36.32	36.12	36.19	781	98.45
18	175.61	174.39	174.92	48.28	47.70	48.02	36.23	35.86	35.99	751	98.49
19	175.12	173.76	174.14	47.99	47.30	47.35	35.90	35.63	35.74	837	98.46
20	174.18	172.86	173.49	47.25	46.82	46.96	35.82	35.60	35.73	735	98.47
21	173.60	173.31	173.49	47.11	47.04	47.10	35.75	35.70	35.72	226	98.46
22	*										
23	173.43	172.10	172.32	47.00	46.54	46.64	35.68	35.50	35.51	720	98.41
24	172.43	171.06	171.49	46.70	46.24	46.35	35.59	35.39	35.42	838	98.39
25	172.07	170.57	171.84	46.89	46.11	46.76	35.58	35.33	35.50	884	98.42
26	172.79	171.51	171.95	46.84	46.55	46.67	35.65	35.45	35.56	702	98.38
27	172.07	170.95	171.53	46.59	46.23	46.32	35.62	35.20	35.36	693	98.35
28	†	†	†	†	†	†	†	†	†	†	†
29	*										
30	†	†	†	†	†	†	†	†	†	†	†
31	171.60	168.14	168.36	46.10	44.49	44.49	35.37	34.98	35.05	1,237	98.22
High			176.63			48.13			36.19	Total 18,179	98.57
Low			168.36			44.49			35.05		98.22

*Sunday. †Holiday. ‡000 omitted.

JUNE, 1949

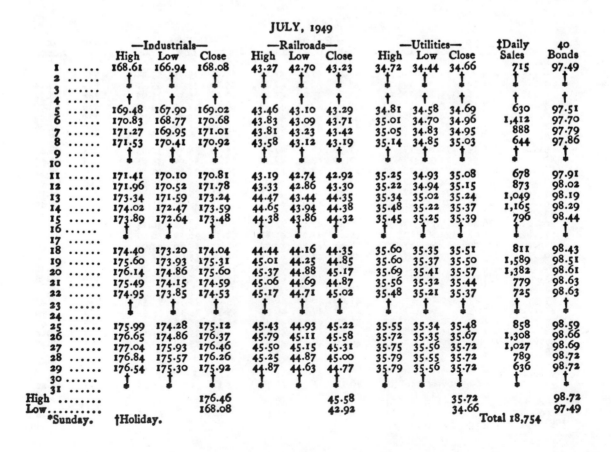

	Industrials High	Low	Close	Railroads High	Low	Close	Utilities High	Low	Close	‡Daily Sales	40 Bonds
1	168.54	166.53	167.98	44.75	44.12	44.60	35.03	34.77	34.96	1,137	98.16
2	168.98	167.59	168.15	44.81	44.23	44.39	35.05	34.85	34.90	665	98.11
3	168.31	166.77	167.24	44.20	43.61	43.76	34.96	34.76	34.87	703	98.09
4											
5											
6	167.35	164.27	165.15	43.73	42.13	42.58	34.84	34.45	34.51	1,379	97.86
7	165.96	164.32	165.29	43.08	42.29	42.86	34.52	34.25	34.39	1,043	97.67
8	166.39	164.96	165.76	43.67	42.90	43.43	34.54	34.31	34.42	791	97.71
9	166.28	165.19	165.73	43.61	43.07	43.40	34.60	34.35	34.51	595	97.71
10	165.53	164.14	164.61	43.27	42.58	42.70	34.45	34.14	34.21	797	97.72
11											
12											
13	163.90	160.95	161.60	42.40	40.90	41.03	34.26	33.83	34.00	1,345	97.56
14	162.51	160.62	161.86	41.81	40.88	41.41	34.05	33.78	33.89	1,123	97.42
15	164.81	162.10	164.58	42.56	41.62	42.43	34.13	33.86	34.08	945	97.46
16	165.03	163.50	163.94	42.60	41.98	42.11	34.18	33.98	34.06	681	97.48
17	164.30	162.95	163.78	42.40	41.73	42.22	33.97	33.73	33.82	541	97.45
18											
19											
20	165.68	163.46	165.49	43.41	42.25	43.28	34.17	33.65	34.05	783	97.47
21	166.65	165.09	165.71	43.61	43.09	43.27	34.22	33.95	34.06	772	97.42
22	165.97	165.09	165.64	43.08	42.68	42.90	34.33	33.88	34.25	548	97.40
23	167.30	165.74	166.77	43.42	42.94	43.26	34.45	34.12	34.29	731	97.37
24	167.49	166.39	166.99	43.50	43.18	43.25	34.45	34.25	34.37	571	97.39
25											
26											
27	167.82	166.29	166.79	43.39	43.12	43.23	34.60	34.31	34.48	666	97.37
28	166.52	164.65	165.75	42.80	42.11	42.45	34.32	34.03	34.13	787	97.33
29	167.05	165.24	166.76	42.57	42.29	42.45	34.31	34.09	34.22	585	97.26
30	167.96	166.72	167.42	42.82	42.49	42.57	34.47	34.27	34.41	580	97.43
High			168.15			44.60			34.96		98.16
Low			161.60			41.03			33.82		97.26

*Sunday. †Holiday.   Total 17,768

JULY, 1949

	Industrials High	Low	Close	Railroads High	Low	Close	Utilities High	Low	Close	‡Daily Sales	40 Bonds
1	168.61	166.94	168.08	43.27	42.70	43.23	34.72	34.44	34.66	715	97.49
2											
3											
4											
5	169.48	167.90	169.02	43.46	43.10	43.29	34.81	34.58	34.69	630	97.51
6	170.83	168.77	170.68	43.83	43.09	43.71	35.01	34.70	34.96	1,412	97.70
7	171.27	169.95	171.01	43.81	43.23	43.42	35.05	34.83	34.95	888	97.79
8	171.53	170.41	170.92	43.58	43.12	43.19	35.14	34.85	35.03	644	97.86
9											
10											
11	171.41	170.10	170.81	43.19	42.74	42.92	35.25	34.93	35.08	678	97.91
12	171.96	170.52	171.78	43.33	42.86	43.30	35.22	34.94	35.15	873	98.02
13	173.34	171.59	173.24	44.47	43.44	44.35	35.34	35.02	35.24	1,049	98.19
14	174.02	172.47	173.59	44.65	43.94	44.38	35.48	35.22	35.37	1,165	98.29
15	173.89	172.64	173.48	44.38	43.86	44.32	35.45	35.25	35.39	796	98.44
16											
17											
18	174.40	173.20	174.04	44.44	44.16	44.35	35.60	35.35	35.51	811	98.43
19	175.60	173.93	175.31	45.01	44.25	44.85	35.60	35.37	35.50	1,589	98.51
20	176.14	174.86	175.60	45.37	44.88	45.17	35.69	35.41	35.57	1,382	98.61
21	175.49	174.15	174.59	45.06	44.69	44.87	35.56	35.32	35.44	779	98.63
22	174.95	173.85	174.53	45.17	44.71	45.02	35.48	35.21	35.37	725	98.63
23											
24											
25	175.99	174.28	175.12	45.43	44.93	45.22	35.55	35.34	35.48	858	98.59
26	176.65	174.86	176.37	45.79	45.11	45.58	35.72	35.35	35.67	1,308	98.66
27	177.04	175.93	176.46	45.50	45.15	45.31	35.75	35.56	35.72	1,027	98.69
28	176.84	175.57	176.26	45.25	44.87	45.00	35.79	35.55	35.72	789	98.72
29	176.54	175.30	175.92	44.87	44.63	44.77	35.79	35.56	35.72	636	98.72
30											
31											
High			176.46			45.58			35.72		98.72
Low			168.08			42.92			34.66		97.49

*Sunday.   †Holiday.   Total 18,754

AUGUST, 1949

	Industrials High	Low	Close	Railroads High	Low	Close	Utilities High	Low	Close	‡Daily Sales	40 Bonds
1	177.17	175.68	176.84	45.07	44.73	44.95	35.88	35.70	35.85	862	98.70
2	177.78	176.35	177.56	45.19	44.83	45.07	36.03	35.85	36.00	799	98.81
3	177.91	176.72	177.19	45.23	44.85	44.99	36.22	35.95	36.12	1,272	98.80
4	177.44	176.51	177.06	45.07	44.73	44.84	36.32	36.15	36.29	911	98.82
5	179.38	176.77	179.07	45.98	44.91	45.92	36.74	36.35	36.69	1,437	99.02
6	↕	↕	↕	↕	↕	↕	↕	↕	↕	↕	↕
7	*	*	*	*	*	*	*	*	*	*	*
8	181.15	179.18	180.54	47.39	46.28	47.07	36.88	36.65	36.80	1,657	99.22
9	180.35	178.86	179.52	47.65	46.66	47.31	36.85	36.56	36.69	1,139	99.28
10	180.96	179.23	180.60	47.88	47.26	47.72	36.87	36.61	36.78	1,279	99.31
11	180.98	179.48	180.02	47.86	47.14	47.38	36.77	36.57	36.65	1,031	99.42
12	180.10	178.62	179.29	47.56	46.98	47.05	36.76	36.50	36.65	771	99.42
13	↕	↕	↕	↕	↕	↕	↕	↕	↕	↕	↕
14											
15	179.71	178.55	178.97	47.05	46.51	46.68	36.68	36.39	36.52	715	99.54
16	180.40	178.71	180.00	46.72	46.51	46.63	36.69	36.35	36.54	835	99.53
17	181.78	179.80	181.59	47.36	46.62	47.30	36.79	36.50	36.75	1,443	99.62
18	182.67	181.44	182.02	47.64	47.28	47.40	36.86	36.61	36.74	1,182	99.75
19	182.38	180.83	181.16	47.15	46.69	46.84	36.80	36.54	36.67	845	99.71
20	↕	↕	↕	↕	↕	↕	↕	↕	↕	↕	↕
21											
22	181.33	180.06	180.53	46.72	46.33	46.50	36.71	36.50	36.60	712	99.72
23	180.18	178.28	178.51	46.26	45.47	45.53	36.62	36.42	36.47	843	99.62
24	179.15	177.86	178.78	45.74	45.33	45.60	36.55	36.15	36.47	724	99.62
25	179.52	178.44	179.01	45.96	45.46	45.77	36.61	36.35	36.50	727	99.59
26	179.69	178.42	179.24	45.74	45.48	45.55	36.70	36.47	36.63	655	99.60
27	↕	↕	↕	↕	↕	↕	↕	↕	↕	↕	↕
28											
29	179.08	177.45	177.75	45.28	44.86	44.97	36.71	36.49	36.59	639	99.59
30	179.04	177.60	178.69	45.08	44.75	44.98	36.75	36.53	36.69	593	99.58
31	179.05	177.77	178.66	45.16	44.85	45.09	36.70	36.55	36.69	715	99.61
High			182.02			47.72			36.80		99.75
Low			176.84			44.84			35.85		98.70

*Sunday. †Holiday. Total 21,786

SEPTEMBER, 1949

	Industrials High	Low	Close	Railroads High	Low	Close	Utilities High	Low	Close	‡Daily Sales	40 Bonds
1	180.20	178.54	179.52	45.86	44.99	45.65	36.84	36.61	36.76	838	99.55
2	179.91	178.97	179.38	45.89	45.44	45.68	36.91	36.71	36.83	750	99.52
3	↕	↕	↕	↕	↕	↕	↕	↕	↕	↕	↕
4											
5	†			†			†			†	†
6	179.85	178.65	179.20	45.60	45.28	45.40	36.89	36.70	36.83	641	99.51
7	180.54	178.91	180.21	46.14	45.49	46.02	37.07	36.83	37.00	849	99.46
8	181.30	179.99	180.53	46.28	45.75	45.85	37.30	37.00	37.23	939	99.48
9	180.86	179.89	180.24	45.98	45.47	45.59	37.61	37.21	37.55	773	99.42
10	↕	↕	↕	↕	↕	↕	↕	↕	↕	↕	↕
11											
12	181.60	180.17	181.15	46.04	45.70	45.89	37.87	37.59	37.75	1,080	99.35
13	183.51	181.27	183.29	47.34	46.14	47.25	38.11	37.82	37.98	1,720	99.33
14	184.09	182.61	183.14	47.58	46.90	47.05	38.11	37.76	37.95	1,695	99.29
15	182.71	181.00	182.16	46.95	46.24	46.74	37.92	37.59	37.75	1,156	99.28
16	182.76	181.34	182.32	47.14	46.60	47.00	37.97	37.57	37.90	1,162	99.26
17	↕	↕	↕	↕	↕	↕	↕	↕	↕	↕	↕
18											
19	182.13	180.18	181.42	46.92	46.12	46.63	37.97	37.49	37.75	1,297	99.22
20	180.91	177.63	178.04	46.68	45.32	45.39	37.80	37.30	37.43	1,345	99.08
21	180.42	177.71	180.02	46.33	45.36	46.22	37.79	37.37	37.74	1,148	98.99
22	181.37	179.87	180.83	47.76	46.37	47.33	38.06	37.85	38.01	1,284	99.13
23	181.74	180.17	181.30	47.93	47.14	47.78	38.27	37.90	38.19	1,291	99.18
24	↕	↕	↕	↕	↕	↕	↕	↕	↕	↕	↕
25											
26	182.25	180.36	180.86	47.94	47.37	47.57	38.25	37.95	38.10	1,017	99.20
27	180.54	178.61	179.63	47.29	46.50	47.02	38.06	37.80	37.92	1,067	99.15
28	182.09	180.06	181.31	48.07	47.06	47.75	38.20	37.84	38.08	1,303	99.23
29	183.42	181.00	182.43	48.54	47.73	48.07	38.22	37.82	37.95	1,381	99.31
30	183.16	181.71	182.51	48.17	47.62	47.87	38.03	37.75	37.86	1,102	99.27
High			183.29			48.07			38.19		99.55
Low			178.04			45.39			36.76		98.99

*Sunday. †Holiday. ‡000 omitted. Total 23,838

OCTOBER, 1949

| | —Industrials— | | | —Railroads— | | | —Utilities— | | | ‡Daily | 40 |
	High	Low	Close	High	Low	Close	High	Low	Close	Sales	Bonds
1	182.17	181.74	181.98	47.69	47.50	47.63	37.76	37.67	37.75	309	99.31
2	*	*	*	*	*	*	*	*	*		
3	183.05	180.90	182.67	48.10	47.34	47.94	37.80	37.61	37.71	765	99.30
4	184.39	182.68	184.13	48.62	47.98	48.37	38.08	37.73	37.98	1,308	99.36
5	185.38	184.00	184.80	48.75	48.28	48.46	38.12	37.77	38.04	1,474	99.34
6	185.99	184.53	185.37	48.88	48.34	48.64	38.23	37.93	38.09	1,516	99.39
7	185.62	183.92	185.27	48.70	48.20	48.52	38.18	37.93	38.06	1,280	99.51
8	185.56	185.01	185.36	48.77	48.58	48.71	38.05	37.98	38.01	541	99.47
9	*	*	*	*	*	*	*	*	*		
10	185.55	184.49	185.15	48.94	48.47	48.75	38.05	37.83	37.93	1,124	99.53
11	187.04	184.75	186.74	49.89	48.53	49.77	38.10	37.77	38.02	1,656	99.45
12	†	†	†	†	†	†	†	†	†		
13	187.91	186.29	186.78	50.40	49.57	49.68	38.17	37.84	38.05	1,790	99.49
14	187.26	185.47	186.43	49.66	49.10	49.31	38.44	37.96	38.32	1,193	99.45
15	186.67	186.20	186.36	49.40	49.21	49.33	38.39	38.25	38.36	463	99.49
16	*	*	*	*	*	*	*	*	*		
17	186.06	183.94	184.72	48.96	48.25	48.54	38.38	38.07	38.20	1,132	99.36
18	186.56	184.72	186.12	49.34	48.39	49.21	38.35	38.04	38.25	1,215	99.44
19	187.34	185.81	187.04	49.53	48.83	49.11	38.39	38.10	38.22	1,369	99.45
20	187.65	185.87	186.64	49.09	48.36	48.54	38.41	38.10	38.30	1,268	99.38
21	186.97	185.62	186.20	48.81	48.37	48.51	38.47	38.16	38.35	1,289	99.44
22	186.46	186.03	186.*	48.57	48.43	48.49	38.37	38.30	38.34	355	99.43
23	*	*	*	*	*	*	*	*	*		
24	187.01	185.58	186.54	48.78	48.35	48.53	38.52	38.24	38.40	1,238	99.35
25	188.01	186.38	187.70	48.74	48.39	48.61	38.73	38.29	38.68	1,191	99.38
26	189.41	187.30	189.08	48.78	48.14	48.63	38.80	38.48	38.72	1,624	99.39
27	191.12	188.96	190.39	49.47	48.57	49.10	38.90	38.60	38.81	1,763	99.39
28	191.44	189.47	190.16	49.02	48.19	48.28	38.88	38.53	38.61	1,483	99.51
29	190.59	189.66	190.36	48.45	48.18	48.36	38.63	38.54	38.58	407	99.51
30	*	*	*	*	*	*	*	*	*		
31	191.08	189.15	189.54	48.42	47.74	47.86	38.65	38.45	38.53	1,141	99.45
High			190.36			49.77			38.81		99.53
Low			181.98			47.63			37.71		99.30

Total 28.894

*Sunday. †Holiday. ‡000 omitted.

NOVEMBER, 1949

| | —Industrials— | | | —Railroads— | | | —Utilities— | | | ‡Daily | 40 |
	High	Low	Close	High	Low	Close	High	Low	Close	Sales	Bonds
1	191.74	189.25	191.23	48.32	47.58	48.16	38.87	38.45	38.75	1,298	99.46
2	193.63	191.15	192.96	49.04	48.25	48.85	39.13	38.82	39.04	1,572	99.45
3	193.19	191.34	192.19	49.26	48.59	49.17	39.15	38.89	39.08	1,366	99.45
4	192.31	190.57	191.29	49.72	49.03	49.55	39.41	39.07	39.30	1,385	99.50
5	191.58	190.97	191.37	49.59	49.39	49.50	39.40	39.14	39.35	465	99.52
6	*	*	*	*	*	*	*	*	*		
7	192.05	190.41	190.89	49.63	49.13	49.24	39.47	39.09	39.16	1,171	99.49
8	†	†	†	†	†	†	†	†	†	†	†
9	192.43	190.06	190.60	49.22	48.50	48.65	39.49	39.10	39.19	1,508	99.56
10	191.07	189.65	190.42	48.55	48.15	48.30	39.25	38.99	39.12	1,173	99.64
11	†	†	†	†	†	†	†	†	†	†	†
12	190.88	190.09	190.46	48.39	48.20	48.23	39.22	39.12	39.15	465	99.69
13	*	*	*	*	*	*	*	*	*		
14	191.08	188.71	187.27	48.13	47.63	47.67	39.20	38.91	38.97	1,265	99.80
15	189.25	186.98	187.98	47.85	49.25	47.47	39.03	38.74	38.93	1,250	99.78
16	190.13	187.83	189.37	48.17	47.52	48.03	39.23	38.87	39.11	1,213	99.78
17	191.82	189.27	191.34	48.24	48.03	48.21	39.35	39.04	39.23	1,414	99.78
18	193.97	191.77	193.41	48.83	48.19	48.75	39.52	39.09	39.38	1,686	99.88
19	194.01	193.33	193.62	49.10	48.83	49.02	39.44	39.34	39.38	593	99.97
20	*	*	*	*	*	*	*	*	*		
21	193.84	191.72	192.35	48.97	48.43	48.48	39.47	39.25	39.36	1,176	99.98
22	193.65	191.69	193.23	49.06	48.24	48.88	39.45	39.20	39.34	1,395	99.95
23	194.35	192.48	193.52	48.98	48.37	48.54	39.59	39.37	39.50	1,457	99.99
24	†	†	†	†	†	†	†	†	†	†	†
25	194.34	192.27	192.78	48.55	47.91	47.97	39.71	39.28	39.51	1,265	99.99
26	193.52	192.63	193.23	48.17	47.93	48.09	39.53	39.42	39.46	412	99.98
27	*	*	*	*	*	*	*	*	*		
28	193.43	191.72	192.24	48.35	47.70	47.87	39.54	39.23	39.32	1,080	99.89
29	192.54	190.54	191.62	48.05	47.46	47.87	39.33	39.12	39.26	1,313	99.73
30	192.35	190.68	191.55	48.33	47.70	48.11	39.45	39.16	39.26	1,323	99.79
High			193.62			49.55			39.51		99.99
Low			187.98			47.47			38.75		99.45

Total 27,245

*Sunday †Holiday ooo Omitted.

DECEMBER, 1949

	Industrials			Railroads			Utilities			‡Daily Sales	40 Bonds
	High	Low	Close	High	Low	Close	High	Low	Close		
1	193.11	191.12	192.71	49.34	47.91	49.27	39.45	39.21	39.39	1,467	99.83
2	194.16	191.94	193.63	50.42	49.55	50.29	39.60	39.29	39.52	2,022	99.94
3	194.75	193.63	194.43	50.84	50.44	50.76	39.59	39.49	39.58	1,110	99.97
4	*	*	*	*	*	*	*	*	*	*	*
5	195.54	193.69	194.74	51.17	50.26	50.70	39.74	39.43	39.58	1,825	100.07
6	195.25	193.91	194.64	51.07	50.41	50.71	39.88	39.42	39.74	1,433	100.09
7	194.59	192.59	194.21	51.16	50.32	50.88	40.27	39.72	40.24	1,634	100.16
8	195.32	193.61	194.45	50.99	50.43	50.57	40.73	40.15	40.35	1,724	100.26
9	194.99	193.54	194.35	50.58	50.02	50.27	40.50	40.12	40.30	1,498	100.29
10	194.89	194.13	194.68	50.28	50.09	50.15	40.46	40.34	40.44	667	100.36
11	*	*	*	*	*	*	*	*	*	*	*
12	196.57	194.39	196.17	50.84	49.95	50.69	40.70	40.28	40.59	1,780	100.33
13	197.22	195.22	196.81	51.39	50.66	51.20	40.94	40.25	40.50	2,082	100.35
14	198.10	196.12	197.51	51.96	51.01	51.51	40.82	40.41	40.63	2,212	100.53
15	198.59	196.34	198.05	51.92	51.14	51.55	40.88	40.51	40.79	2,069	100.60
16	199.13	196.90	197.88	52.05	51.33	51.58	41.15	40.60	40.98	1,958	100.75
17	198.27	197.19	197.98	51.58	51.33	51.45	41.04	40.85	40.99	720	100.82
18	*	*	*	*	*	*	*	*	*	*	*
19	199.15	197.46	198.17	51.97	51.31	51.49	41.04	40.65	40.76	1,422	100.86
20	198.28	196.55	197.22	51.51	50.83	50.98	40.88	40.49	40.70	1,325	100.84
21	197.64	195.79	196.45	51.16	50.52	50.86	40.84	40.47	40.62	1,271	100.85
22	198.91	196.49	198.52	51.73	50.87	51.55	41.03	40.54	40.96	1,629	100.81
23	199.73	197.88	198.88	51.78	51.27	51.53	41.17	40.85	41.02	1,467	100.86
24	†	†	†	†	†	†	†	†	†	†	†
25	*	*	*	*	*	*	*	*	*	*	*
26	†	†	†	†	†	†	†	†	†	†	†
27	199.58	197.73	198.28	51.78	51.02	51.23	41.10	40.80	40.95	1,559	100.79
28	200.19	198.10	199.59	52.64	51.10	52.55	41.37	40.78	41.22	1,561	100.81
29	200.26	198.75	199.39	53.29	52.52	52.71	41.61	41.04	41.20	1,816	101.11
30	200.91	198.97	200.52	53.16	52.37	53.01	41.47	41.08	41.31	2,086	101.29
31	200.60	199.94	200.13	53.11	52.68	52.76	41.35	41.27	41.29	955	101.35
High			200.52			53.01			41.31		101.35
Low			192.71			49.27			39.39		99.83

*Sunday †Holiday. ‡000 Omitted.

Total 39,292

JANUARY, 1950

	Industrials			Railroads			Utilities			‡Daily Sales	40 Bonds
	High	Low	Close	High	Low	Close	High	Low	Close		
1	*	*	*	*	*	*	*	*	*	*	*
2	†	†	†	†	†	†	†	†	†	†	†
3	200.20	197.73	198.89	53.22	52.11	52.88	41.21	40.75	41.02	1,258	101.43
4	200.55	198.26	200.20	54.38	52.84	54.31	41.41	41.05	41.37	1,890	101.67
5	201.76	199.69	200.57	54.84	54.01	54.23	41.76	41.33	41.59	2,548	101.80
6	201.62	199.84	200.96	54.41	53.74	54.22	41.74	41.43	41.52	2,012	102.02
7	202.12	200.92	201.94	54.58	54.29	54.52	41.72	41.56	41.70	1,330	102.10
8	*	*	*	*	*	*	*	*	*	*	*
9	202.92	200.86	201.98	55.14	54.28	55.00	41.86	41.40	41.64	2,523	102.30
10	202.04	200.13	201.17	55.64	54.45	55.33	41.74	41.30	41.48	2,156	102.33
11	202.42	200.52	201.61	56.09	55.11	55.80	41.63	41.25	41.48	2,631	102.47
12	202.08	197.53	197.93	56.06	53.55	53.81	41.57	40.90	40.94	2,973	102.38
13	197.93	193.94	196.81	54.14	52.17	54.01	41.06	40.49	40.90	3,332	102.18
14	197.79	196.52	196.92	54.31	53.71	53.78	40.98	40.84	40.86	1,184	102.11
15	*	*	*	*	*	*	*	*	*	*	*
16	197.75	195.57	197.17	54.48	53.21	54.41	40.93	40.62	40.79	1,463	101.94
17	200.08	197.14	198.78	55.26	54.39	54.73	41.25	40.82	41.15	1,788	101.87
18	200.74	198.35	199.50	55.32	54.50	54.70	41.66	41.09	41.33	1,566	102.06
19	200.49	198.49	199.80	55.10	54.43	54.96	41.88	41.32	41.77	1,174	102.11
20	200.86	199.14	200.13	55.94	55.08	55.26	41.98	41.53	41.74	1,439	102.19
21	201.13	200.01	200.97	55.26	54.91	55.18	41.88	41.78	41.86	551	102.16
22	*	*	*	*	*	*	*	*	*	*	*
23	201.39	199.43	200.42	55.51	54.65	55.23	41.99	41.58	41.87	1,343	102.11
24	200.42	198.78	199.62	55.44	54.76	55.15	41.87	41.57	41.65	1,250	102.11
25	199.32	196.64	198.39	54.89	53.52	54.51	41.67	41.20	41.48	1,701	101.98
26	199.22	197.54	198.53	54.82	54.27	54.55	41.84	41.41	41.63	1,153	101.95
27	199.58	197.69	199.08	55.04	54.45	54.82	41.96	41.64	41.87	1,251	101.81
28	200.31	199.39	200.08	55.11	54.83	55.04	41.94	41.85	41.91	737	101.77
29	*	*	*	*	*	*	*	*	*	*	*
30	201.93	199.66	201.39	55.73	54.97	55.54	42.21	41.91	42.17	1,635	101.73
31	202.51	200.82	201.79	55.77	54.91	55.09	42.36	42.03	42.22	1,689	101.70
High			201.98			55.80			42.22		102.47
Low			196.81			52.88			40.79		101.43

*Sunday. †Holiday. ‡000 omitted.

Total 42,578

FEBRUARY, 1950

	Industrials			Railroads			Utilities			‡Daily Sales	40 Bonds
	High	Low	Close	High	Low	Close	High	Low	Close		
1	202.96	201.36	201.89	55.20	54.55	54.59	42.43	42.05	42.18	1,810	101.72
2	204.55	201.35	204.11	55.38	54.43	55.17	42.53	42.03	42.43	2,039	101.69
3	205.39	203.55	204.53	55.85	55.19	55.51	42.73	42.36	42.55	2,210	101.75
4	205.13	204.34	205.03	55.63	55.29	55.53	42.61	42.53	42.57	725	101.77
5	*	*	*	*	*	*	*	*	*	*	*
6	205.39	203.58	204.59	55.66	54.95	55.34	42.58	42.28	42.42	1,487	101.68
7	204.40	202.59	203.53	55.14	54.45	54.73	42.59	42.17	42.42	1,358	101.70
8	203.43	201.60	202.71	55.00	54.47	54.79	42.73	42.27	42.50	1,474	101.70
9	204.67	202.24	203.80	55.35	54.59	55.21	42.71	42.36	42.53	1,807	101.71
10	204.87	202.69	203.49	55.34	54.66	54.81	42.88	42.49	42.75	1,787	101.80
11	203.69	203.06	203.36	54.87	54.63	54.78	42.72	42.60	42.65	826	101.80
12	*	*	*	*	*	*	*	*	*	*	*
13	†	†	†	†	†	†	†	†	†	†	†
14	203.32	200.75	202.02	54.64	53.73	54.11	42.76	42.23	42.47	2,213	101.73
15	202.60	200.63	201.93	54.94	53.92	54.80	42.73	42.42	42.56	1,733	101.75
16	202.49	200.59	201.69	54.78	54.11	54.51	42.74	42.43	42.58	1,916	101.70
17	203.49	201.13	203.17	55.89	54.47	55.70	42.75	42.50	42.67	1,937	101.76
18	204.16	203.36	203.97	56.14	55.86	56.00	42.81	42.70	42.78	1,049	101.76
19	*	*	*	*	*	*	*	*	*	*	*
20	204.26	202.53	203.47	55.93	55.29	55.65	42.91	42.55	42.73	1,419	101.77
21	203.93	202.55	203.35	55.79	55.31	55.44	42.97	42.65	42.87	1,258	101.83
22	†	†	†	†	†	†	†	†	†	†	†
23	203.95	202.31	203.32	55.44	55.01	55.24	42.92	42.61	42.73	1,306	101.81
24	204.87	203.22	204.15	55.70	55.08	55.48	42.90	42.63	42.81	1,711	101.78
25	204.49	203.90	204.15	55.44	55.25	55.39	42.75	42.71	42.73	621	101.80
26	*	*	*	*	*	*	*	*	*	*	*
27	204.85	203.46	204.33	55.69	55.17	55.49	42.94	42.72	42.81	1,405	101.79
28	204.53	202.82	203.44	55.62	54.95	55.34	42.94	42.65	42.81	1,313	101.69
High			205.03			56.00			42.87		101.83
Low			201.69			54.11			42.18		101.68

Total 33,404

*Sunday. †Holiday. ‡000 Omitted.

MARCH, 1950

	Industrials			Railroads			Utilities			‡Daily Sales	40 Bonds
	High	Low	Close	High	Low	Close	High	Low	Close		
1	204.02	202.15	203.62	55.94	55.12	55.73	42.99	42.57	42.81	1,413	101.72
2	204.52	202.96	203.54	56.24	55.44	55.74	42.99	42.67	42.82	1,344	101.74
3	204.85	203.09	204.48	56.61	55.76	56.42	42.96	42.70	42.89	1,515	101.72
4	205.22	204.48	204.71	57.00	56.53	56.60	43.03	42.95	43.01	942	101.76
5	*	*	*	*	*	*	*	*	*	*	*
6	205.65	204.20	204.88	56.94	56.29	56.42	43.09	42.77	42.90	1,470	101.88
7	204.89	202.33	203.69	56.12	55.06	55.52	43.05	42.65	42.82	1,589	101.74
8	204.42	202.69	203.71	55.71	55.14	55.46	43.04	42.74	42.94	1,359	101.72
9	203.95	201.97	202.33	55.94	54.90	55.18	43.04	42.79	42.91	1,332	101.73
10	202.88	201.14	202.44	55.23	54.61	54.91	42.93	42.60	42.75	1,257	101.67
11	203.28	202.33	202.96	55.14	54.86	55.06	42.94	42.79	42.89	525	101.69
12	*	*	*	*	*	*	*	*	*	*	*
13	203.91	202.09	203.09	55.19	54.58	54.73	43.04	42.73	42.95	1,061	101.64
14	205.10	202.71	204.70	55.10	54.43	54.96	43.15	42.81	43.11	1,135	101.61
15	207.80	204.85	207.46	56.12	55.11	56.05	43.57	42.99	43.47	1,831	101.62
16	209.43	206.92	207.89	56.78	56.02	56.42	43.93	43.42	43.74	2,063	101.62
17	208.92	206.81	207.57	56.39	55.62	55.70	43.89	43.57	43.69	1,598	101.72
18	208.20	207.38	208.09	55.75	55.59	55.70	43.73	43.58	43.69	608	101.72
19	*	*	*	*	*	*	*	*	*	*	*
20	209.11	207.40	207.78	55.84	55.17	55.25	43.86	43.50	43.67	1,425	101.71
21	209.16	207.38	208.27	55.40	54.85	55.21	43.67	43.41	43.57	1,399	101.74
22	209.72	207.76	209.31	55.81	55.08	55.67	43.87	43.53	43.70	2,006	101.75
23	210.67	208.61	209.62	56.07	55.41	55.58	43.76	43.31	43.50	2,020	101.71
24	210.22	208.01	209.78	55.56	55.07	55.30	43.55	43.16	43.35	1,568	101.71
25	210.77	209.94	210.62	55.74	55.21	55.68	43.39	43.28	43.37	888	101.72
26	*	*	*	*	*	*	*	*	*	*	*
27	211.22	208.74	209.10	55.95	54.79	54.89	43.52	43.05	43.14	1,934	101.71
28	210.08	207.74	209.50	55.36	54.65	55.24	43.30	42.92	43.25	1,779	101.75
29	209.58	207.77	208.40	55.67	54.96	55.25	43.27	42.90	42.98	2,094	101.82
30	208.42	205.53	206.43	55.38	54.05	54.48	42.96	42.46	42.65	2,373	101.77
‡31	207.54	205.28	206.05	55.26	54.49	54.83	42.86	42.49	42.67	1,883	101.77
High			210.62			56.60			43.74		101.88
Low			202.33			54.48			42.65		101.61

Total 40,411

*Sunday. †Holiday. ‡000 Omitted.

APRIL, 1950

	Industrials High	Industrials Low	Industrials Close	Railroads High	Railroads Low	Railroads Close	Utilities High	Utilities Low	Utilities Close	‡Daily Sales	40 Bonds
1	206.54	205.67	206.37	55.56	54.82	55.43	42.74	42.64	42.69	683	101.78
2	*										
3	208.82	205.93	208.44	56.54	55.29	56.42	42.89	42.56	42.82	1,574	101.85
4	210.19	208.15	209.05	56.79	56.02	56.20	43.01	42.61	42.79	2,013	102.09
5	210.76	208.70	210.34	56.17	55.64	55.80	42.99	42.57	42.77	1,428	102.15
6	212.68	210.26	212.10	56.38	55.62	56.23	43.28	42.83	43.20	2,003	102.19
7	†										
8	212.85	211.69	212.55	56.55	56.23	56.36	43.32	43.15	43.25	1,093	102.19
9	*										
10	213.60	211.47	212.29	56.79	55.92	56.41	43.59	43.07	43.36	2,068	102.28
11	213.40	210.15	211.47	56.31	55.31	55.54	43.38	43.00	43.12	2,011	102.24
12	214.35	211.18	213.94	56.40	55.60	56.22	43.37	43.08	43.26	2,012	102.19
13	215.40	213.36	214.13	56.64	55.99	56.11	43.38	43.07	43.24	2,406	102.19
14	216.17	214.14	215.31	56.15	55.27	55.62	43.26	42.90	43.10	2,750	102.11
15	215.18	213.79	214.48	55.41	54.90	55.16	43.12	42.91	42.96	1,434	102.10
16	*										
17	215.27	213.18	214.41	55.69	54.82	55.31	43.05	42.67	42.89	2,517	101.99
18	216.04	213.59	215.05	56.38	54.87	56.04	43.05	42.69	42.87	3,322	101.93
19	216.32	214.22	215.21	57.03	55.92	56.61	43.01	42.67	42.74	2,945	101.97
20	215.65	212.67	213.72	56.64	55.20	55.53	42.89	42.33	42.44	2,585	101.96
21	215.09	212.85	214.14	55.96	55.42	55.54	42.74	42.37	42.57	2,711	101.95
22	214.61	213.52	213.90	55.71	55.41	55.53	42.75	42.61	42.67	1,256	101.96
23	*										
24	214.17	211.02	212.58	55.31	54.29	54.86	42.85	42.34	42.54	2,311	101.91
25	213.65	211.50	212.55	55.20	54.67	54.89	42.76	42.34	42.67	1,831	101.87
26	213.05	210.51	211.72	55.05	54.44	54.73	42.72	42.37	42.48	1,877	101.68
27	213.21	210.76	212.44	55.53	54.57	55.20	42.71	42.46	42.64	2,065	101.61
28	214.29	212.16	213.56	55.89	55.07	55.53	42.81	42.49	42.75	2,185	101.67
29	214.57	213.43	214.33	56.16	55.68	56.07	42.80	42.66	42.78	1,164	101.66
30	*										
High			215.31			56.61			43.36		102.28
Low			206.37			54.73			42.44		101.61

Total 48,245

*Sunday.   †Holiday.   ‡000 omitted.

MAY, 1950

	Industrials High	Industrials Low	Industrials Close	Railroads High	Railroads Low	Railroads Close	Utilities High	Utilities Low	Utilities Close	‡Daily Sales	40 Bonds
1	216.35	214.06	215.81	57.10	56.13	56.76	43.30	42.81	43.20	2,389	101.71
2	216.46	214.30	214.87	57.58	56.42	56.60	43.36	42.88	43.04	2,247	101.62
3	217.13	214.30	216.26	57.57	56.39	56.64	43.28	42.87	43.12	2,122	101.55
4	216.71	214.25	214.87	56.87	55.75	55.96	43.32	42.90	42.97	2,148	101.46
5	216.30	214.14	215.72	56.49	55.88	56.25	43.34	42.87	43.28	1,796	101.42
6	217.21	215.79	217.03	56.68	56.42	56.60	43.37	43.32	43.32	910	101.41
7	*										
8	217.76	215.72	216.71	56.79	56.28	56.42	43.52	43.25	43.45	1,684	101.45
9	217.86	216.00	217.40	56.58	56.12	56.36	43.46	43.18	43.28	1,722	101.40
10	219.64	217.41	218.64	56.48	55.98	56.11	43.60	43.16	43.44	1,877	101.38
11	219.32	217.26	218.72	56.29	55.54	56.10	43.54	43.20	43.46	1,752	101.30
12	218.96	216.37	217.61	55.88	55.32	55.45	43.56	43.23	43.45	1,787	101.30
13	217.99	217.35	217.78	55.56	55.30	55.44	43.52	43.46	43.50	574	101.28
14	*										
15	218.90	216.87	218.04	55.78	55.39	55.53	43.65	43.35	43.48	1,220	101.26
16	220.05	217.86	219.70	56.60	56.02	56.44	43.77	43.45	43.65	1,733	101.30
17	221.48	219.39	220.60	56.96	56.37	56.57	43.94	43.64	43.82	2,019	101.20
18	221.52	219.70	220.63	56.78	56.24	56.53	44.21	43.72	44.04	1,766	101.24
19	222.79	220.23	221.11	57.23	56.54	56.92	44.30	44.00	44.20	2,110	101.18
20	222.78	222.03	222.41	57.05	56.85	56.96	44.29	44.17	44.26	904	101.21
21	*										
22	223.14	220.95	221.55	56.96	56.35	56.45	44.39	43.96	44.14	1,616	101.21
23	222.82	220.85	222.47	57.06	56.46	56.85	44.28	43.86	44.13	1,459	101.20
24	224.24	221.83	222.57	57.29	56.45	56.60	44.20	43.82	43.96	1,848	101.22
25	223.10	220.74	222.44	56.69	56.25	56.54	43.86	43.53	43.72	1,478	101.26
26	223.11	221.22	221.93	56.74	56.11	56.35	43.82	43.55	43.71	1,333	101.19
27	222.00	221.41	221.71	56.43	56.23	56.29	43.68	43.65	43.67	467	101.17
28	*										
29	223.11	221.16	222.47	56.57	56.12	56.42	43.81	43.51	43.68	1,110	101.22
30	†										
31	224.18	222.40	223.42	56.49	56.07	56.28	43.97	43.54	43.80	1,533	101.16
High			223.42			56.96			44.26		101.71
Low			214.87			55.44			42.97		101.16

Total 41,604

*Sunday.   †Holiday.   ‡000 Omitted.

JUNE, 1950

	Industrials			Railroads			Utilities			‡Daily	40
	High	Low	Close	High	Low	Close	High	Low	Close	Sales	Bonds
1	224.06	222.40	223.23	56.25	55.64	55.70	43.64	43.32	43.50	1,578	101.04
2	224.34	222.53	223.71	55.76	55.19	55.33	43.65	43.35	43.50	1,453	100.95
3	†	†	†	†	†	†	†	†	†	†	†
4	*	*	*	*	*	*	*	*	*	*	*
5	224.12	221.13	221.76	55.17	54.16	54.37	43.59	43.14	43.31	1,631	100.94
6	224.32	218.66	223.46	54.84	53.62	54.72	43.51	42.99	43.28	2,250	100.87
7	225.17	221.82	223.68	55.53	54.59	55.13	43.80	43.21	43.71	1,748	100.82
8	226.21	223.57	225.52	55.93	54.97	55.74	43.84	43.51	43.73	1,782	100.73
9	227.82	225.16	226.86	56.91	55.67	56.65	44.03	43.67	43.84	2,131	100.80
10	†	†	†	†	†	†	†	†	†	†	†
11	*	*	*	*	*	*	*	*	*	*	*
12	229.20	226.40	228.38	57.18	56.52	56.87	43.99	43.56	43.69	1,791	100.83
13	228.09	225.58	226.44	57.55	55.88	56.87	43.82	43.37	43.63	1,785	100.77
14	226.02	222.76	223.32	57.23	56.18	56.34	43.67	43.31	43.46	1,652	100.65
15	224.97	221.79	222.46	56.81	56.05	56.15	43.56	43.24	43.36	1,526	100.71
16	223.67	221.89	222.71	56.35	55.82	55.95	43.52	43.12	43.34	1,175	100.73
17	†	†	†	†	†	†	†	†	†	†	†
18	*	*	*	*	*	*	*	*	*	*	*
19	223.94	221.49	222.09	55.98	55.46	55.53	43.59	43.20	43.35	1,291	100.68
20	222.19	218.99	220.72	55.54	54.67	55.30	43.35	42.99	43.26	1,472	100.65
21	223.07	220.81	222.53	55.92	55.36	55.62	43.54	43.20	43.45	1,749	100.62
22	225.00	222.47	224.51	56.14	55.61	55.89	43.82	43.44	43.68	1,830	100.66
23	225.55	223.57	224.35	56.24	55.61	55.85	44.06	43.66	43.95	1,704	100.60
24	†	†	†	†	†	†	†	†	†	†	†
25	*	*	*	*	*	*	*	*	*	*	*
26	220.75	213.03	213.91	54.56	52.36	52.39	43.49	42.17	42.31	3,949	100.37
27	217.13	206.33	212.22	53.70	50.66	52.05	42.50	41.04	41.60	4,859	100.02
28	216.99	212.39	214.68	53.84	52.50	53.10	42.15	41.44	41.90	2,597	100.05
29	214.74	206.33	206.72	52.94	51.10	51.24	41.71	40.33	40.37	3,035	99.79
30	211.96	206.03	209.11	52.52	51.33	52.24	41.09	40.12	40.64	2,658	99.73
High			228.38			56.87			43.95		101.04
Low			206.72			51.24			40.37		99.73
										Total	45,646

*Sunday. †Holiday. ‡ooo Omitted.

JULY, 1950

	Industrials			Railroads			Utilities			‡Daily	40
	High	Low	Close	High	Low	Close	High	Low	Close	Sales	Bonds
1	†	†	†	†	†	†	†	†	†	†	†
2	*	*	*	*	*	*	*	*	*	*	*
3	209.48	205.92	208.35	51.96	51.07	51.64	40.95	40.40	40.70	1,545	99.53
4	†	†	†	†	†	†	†	†	†	†	†
5	210.92	207.27	210.03	52.58	51.63	52.40	40.97	40.46	40.87	1,398	99.57
6	212.19	209.46	210.85	53.38	52.63	53.03	41.19	40.78	41.09	1,566	99.60
7	211.75	207.78	208.59	53.36	52.03	52.29	41.18	40.57	40.73	1,866	99.45
8	†	†	†	†	†	†	†	†	†	†	†
9	*	*	*	*	*	*	*	*	*	*	*
10	209.42	206.31	208.09	53.15	51.75	52.95	40.75	40.09	40.20	1,956	99.39
11	209.39	203.83	204.60	55.35	53.12	53.70	40.26	38.61	38.69	3,246	99.53
12	203.83	197.44	199.09	54.55	52.89	53.37	38.63	37.43	37.74	3,197	99.49
13	199.69	195.40	197.46	53.92	52.85	53.59	38.07	37.29	37.65	2,660	99.48
14	201.48	197.89	199.83	54.91	53.85	54.38	38.35	37.64	38.14	1,902	99.56
15	†	†	†	†	†	†	†	†	†	†	†
16	*	*	*	*	*	*	*	*	*	*	*
17	199.47	196.44	197.63	54.94	54.13	54.81	38.19	37.62	37.93	1,523	99.62
18	202.42	198.00	201.88	56.54	55.10	56.36	38.37	37.85	38.20	1,823	99.88
19	205.61	202.08	205.13	57.21	56.02	57.01	38.61	38.14	38.43	2,427	100.05
20	208.62	204.41	207.73	59.06	57.09	58.77	38.54	38.05	38.39	3,163	100.24
21	208.89	205.51	207.65	59.83	58.39	59.46	38.63	38.07	38.46	2,808	100.65
22	†	†	†	†	†	†	†	†	†	†	†
23	*	*	*	*	*	*	*	*	*	*	*
24	208.66	205.64	206.95	60.56	59.11	60.35	38.69	38.12	38.32	2,298	100.70
25	206.57	202.99	203.83	61.97	59.66	61.13	38.37	37.59	37.74	2,770	100.79
26	205.68	201.91	204.39	61.75	60.35	61.11	37.89	37.15	37.40	2,455	101.01
27	207.77	204.39	206.37	61.96	60.80	61.31	37.73	37.26	37.58	2,304	101.19
28	209.56	206.76	208.21	61.49	60.52	60.71	37.97	37.35	37.80	2,050	101.28
29	†	†	†	†	†	†	†	†	†	†	†
30	*	*	*	*	*	*	*	*	*	*	*
31	209.85	207.19	209.40	61.07	60.27	60.86	38.07	37.50	37.78	1,594	101.25
High			210.85			61.31			41.09		101.28
Low			197.46			51.64			37.40		99.39
										Total	44,551

*Sunday. †Holiday. ‡ooo omitted.

AUGUST, 1950

	Industrials High	Low	Close	Railroads High	Low	Close	Utilities High	Low	Close	‡Daily Sales	40 Bonds
1	212.98	209.56	211.87	61.60	60.89	61.27	38.20	37.70	38.04	1,973	101.33
2	213.71	209.78	211.26	61.59	60.32	60.76	38.35	37.83	38.09	1,982	101.43
3	212.28	209.55	211.26	61.43	60.57	61.20	38.28	37.88	38.02	1,655	101.65
4	213.14	210.41	212.66	61.94	61.25	61.78	38.30	37.88	38.14	1,599	101.76
5											
6											
7	216.21	212.48	215.82	63.23	61.76	62.85	38.49	38.04	38.33	1,851	101.88
8	217.53	214.76	215.44	63.21	62.15	62.24	38.67	38.26	38.51	2,179	101.92
9	217.45	214.16	216.97	62.59	61.62	62.41	38.66	38.17	38.53	1,759	101.99
10	217.48	215.56	216.64	62.71	61.98	62.24	38.90	38.28	38.71	1,867	102.04
11	216.89	214.41	215.03	62.35	61.57	62.00	39.02	38.50	38.67	1,678	102.07
12											
13											
14	216.10	213.98	215.31	62.34	61.64	62.08	38.89	38.62	38.77	1,277	102.09
15	216.24	214.11	215.31	62.36	61.92	62.10	39.13	38.76	38.98	1,331	102.13
16	216.58	214.65	215.78	62.92	62.04	62.61	39.31	38.88	39.14	1,772	102.21
17	218.94	215.82	217.76	63.87	62.66	63.18	39.81	39.16	39.70	2,166	102.38
18	219.88	217.26	219.23	63.81	63.12	63.39	39.82	39.40	39.62	1,777	102.44
19											
20											
21	222.12	218.87	220.21	63.59	62.96	63.09	39.76	39.34	39.49	1,842	102.37
22	220.81	218.91	219.79	63.60	62.67	63.00	39.67	39.33	39.56	1,547	102.27
23	221.93	219.48	221.51	63.58	63.01	63.40	39.76	39.46	39.60	1,574	102.31
24	222.17	220.34	221.13	63.48	62.48	63.12	39.72	39.44	39.51	1,624	102.32
25	219.45	217.10	218.10	62.90	62.04	62.43	39.29	39.06	39.19	1,610	102.21
26											
27											
28	219.29	216.81	218.55	62.85	62.21	62.52	39.23	38.91	39.03	1,297	102.16
29	220.20	217.86	218.29	63.74	62.57	63.32	39.19	38.92	39.03	1,485	102.28
30	218.83	216.43	217.05	64.18	63.04	63.21	38.95	38.64	38.77	1,490	102.25
31	217.79	216.21	216.87	63.44	62.68	62.90	38.86	38.60	38.79	1,136	102.15
High			221.51			63.40			39.70		102.44
Low			211.26			60.76			38.02		101.33

Total 38,471

*Sunday. †Holiday. ‡000 omitted.

SEPTEMBER, 1950

	Industrials High	Low	Close	Railroads High	Low	Close	Utilities High	Low	Close	‡Daily Sales	40 Bonds
1	219.00	217.12	218.42	63.45	62.90	63.38	38.82	38.58	38.67	1,290	102.16
2											
3											
4											
5	220.71	217.88	220.02	63.54	63.08	63.29	39.11	38.69	38.90	1,250	102.15
6	219.52	217.38	218.20	63.21	62.65	62.94	39.00	38.69	38.86	1,299	102.08
7	219.20	217.15	218.33	63.85	62.89	63.79	39.01	38.69	38.83	1,344	102.03
8	220.94	218.52	220.03	64.63	63.92	64.39	39.02	38.68	38.87	1,962	102.15
9											
10											
11	220.77	217.44	218.10	65.03	64.11	64.44	39.07	38.62	38.86	1,857	102.08
12	221.19	218.17	220.81	66.12	64.53	65.98	39.17	38.78	38.99	1,676	102.23
13	224.22	221.18	223.42	67.13	66.23	66.76	39.21	38.84	39.04	2,597	102.26
14	225.19	222.71	224.48	67.10	66.38	66.87	39.21	38.88	39.06	2,354	102.18
15	226.32	223.13	225.85	66.97	66.12	66.74	39.37	38.83	39.21	2,406	102.13
16											
17											
18	227.89	225.45	226.78	67.12	66.44	66.73	39.61	39.21	39.50	2,042	102.11
19	226.85	224.40	225.78	66.70	65.87	66.32	39.65	39.26	39.52	1,593	101.94
20	226.49	223.00	224.33	66.76	65.77	66.12	39.75	39.45	39.59	2,102	101.85
21	226.49	223.58	226.01	67.40	65.92	67.23	40.04	39.57	39.95	1,651	101.82
22	228.17	225.61	226.64	68.55	67.42	67.90	39.75	39.70	39.86	2,513	101.83
23											
24											
25	227.51	224.77	226.06	68.42	67.57	68.01	40.12	39.85	40.06	2,015	101.76
26	226.49	222.26	222.84	67.92	65.97	66.08	40.23	39.85	40.02	2,280	101.78
27	226.06	222.00	225.74	67.03	65.76	66.78	40.25	39.72	40.16	2,363	101.71
28	227.69	225.09	225.93	67.82	66.63	67.14	40.48	40.11	40.31	2,201	101.71
29	227.40	225.32	226.36	68.15	67.23	67.64	40.63	40.31	40.46	1,800	101.65
30											
High			226.78			68.01			40.46		102.26
Low			218.10			62.94			38.67		101.65

Total 38,595

*Sunday. †Holiday. ‡000 omitted.

OCTOBER, 1950

| | Industrials | | | Railroads | | | Utilities | | | ‡Daily | 40 |
	High	Low	Close	High	Low	Close	High	Low	Close	Sales	Bonds
1........	*										
2........	229.57	226.46	228.94	70.29	67.76	70.08	40.96	40.56	40.81	2,199	101.71
3........	230.86	228.01	228.89	70.74	68.76	69.02	40.93	40.57	40.69	2,479	101.76
4........	232.31	228.21	231.15	70.32	68.95	69.97	41.05	40.60	40.97	2,924	101.87
5........	232.17	229.16	229.85	69.94	68.95	69.13	40.89	40.51	40.62	2,489	101.86
6........	232.50	229.57	231.74	69.99	69.13	69.65	40.92	40.59	40.70	2,360	101.94
7........	232.26	231.29	231.81	69.96	69.57	69.72	40.80	40.73	40.78	974	101.95
8........	*										
9........	232.47	228.49	230.02	69.69	68.29	68.83	40.84	40.43	40.62	2,326	101.86
10........	230.33	226.79	227.60	68.99	68.03	68.54	40.70	40.39	40.46	1,874	101.73
11........	229.92	226.59	228.97	69.95	68.39	69.64	40.60	40.16	40.39	2,203	101.65
12........	†	†	†	†	†	†	†	†	†	†	†
13........	229.97	227.53	228.54	70.15	69.36	69.67	40.68	40.36	40.54	2,033	101.66
14........	228.21	227.00	227.63	69.55	69.07	69.36	40.54	40.46	40.52	823	101.63
15........	*										
16........	228.38	225.39	227.50	69.59	68.57	69.30	40.67	40.40	40.53	1,632	101.53
17........	229.74	227.42	229.22	70.30	69.49	70.10	40.78	40.50	40.73	2,011	101.58
18........	231.54	229.26	230.60	71.14	70.08	70.76	40.81	40.45	40.72	2,412	101.65
19........	232.01	229.62	230.83	71.31	70.06	70.59	41.05	40.61	40.88	2,252	101.67
20........	231.41	229.07	230.33	70.44	69.65	69.93	40.95	40.69	40.82	1,843	101.57
21........	231.15	230.00	230.88	69.96	69.65	69.86	40.95	40.83	40.89	733	101.62
22........	*										
23........	232.02	229.95	230.62	70.17	69.46	69.76	41.08	40.83	40.93	1,854	101.50
24........	231.87	229.55	231.39	69.67	69.19	69.45	41.16	40.76	41.03	1,789	101.48
25........	232.75	230.40	231.49	69.38	68.70	68.90	41.18	40.90	40.97	1,929	101.48
26........	230.85	225.44	226.65	68.74	66.49	66.79	40.88	40.07	40.26	2,999	101.33
27........	228.92	225.77	228.28	67.51	66.76	67.35	40.46	40.05	40.29	1,801	101.35
28........	228.87	227.95	228.56	67.95	67.67	67.82	40.42	40.31	40.38	646	101.36
29........	*										
30........	230.05	225.87	226.42	68.08	66.67	66.78	40.63	40.18	40.29	1,791	101.30
31........	227.32	223.59	225.01	67.03	65.78	66.28	40.27	39.87	40.02	2,014	101.31
High.........			231.81			70.76			41.03		101.95
Low..........			225.01			66.28			40.02		101.30

*Sunday. †Holiday. ‡000 omitted.   Total 48,390

NOVEMBER, 1950

| | Industrials | | | Railroads | | | Utilities | | | ‡Daily | 40 |
	High	Low	Close	High	Low	Close	High	Low	Close	Sales	Bonds
1........	226.75	223.07	225.69	66.72	65.67	66.51	40.33	39.85	40.13	1,783	101.40
2........	228.74	225.64	227.25	67.29	66.48	66.84	40.61	40.11	40.35	1,577	101.42
3........	229.44	226.21	228.10	67.27	66.48	66.67	40.54	40.31	40.44	1,555	101.49
4........	228.03	226.95	227.42	66.54	66.17	66.22	40.45	40.35	40.38	504	101.53
5........	*										
6........	224.91	220.59	222.52	64.97	64.00	64.48	40.06	39.62	39.70	2,581	101.44
7........	†	†	†	†	†	†	†	†	†	†	†
8........	226.55	222.86	224.25	66.47	65.26	65.62	40.26	39.84	40.00	1,845	101.50
9........	228.01	224.23	227.17	67.24	65.90	66.88	40.50	40.00	40.44	1,764	101.62
10........	229.90	226.74	229.29	67.41	66.61	67.30	40.78	40.43	40.73	1,637	101.77
11........	†	†	†	†	†	†	†	†	†	†	†
12........	*										
13........	230.83	227.98	229.44	67.88	67.08	67.48	40.91	40.69	40.79	1,631	101.99
14........	230.17	227.58	229.54	68.19	66.97	68.11	40.99	40.62	40.80	1,782	102.01
15........	230.45	227.98	229.52	68.93	68.03	68.65	40.91	40.62	40.79	1,621	102.16
16........	229.75	226.70	228.94	68.95	67.78	68.74	50.78	40.42	40.66	1,762	102.10
17........	231.01	228.29	230.27	70.39	68.58	70.11	40.71	40.47	40.59	2,126	102.16
18........	231.92	230.47	231.64	70.63	70.26	70.41	40.74	40.59	40.65	1,047	102.10
19........	*										
20........	233.55	230.48	231.53	70.92	70.03	70.32	40.90	40.50	40.64	2,252	102.25
21........	232.64	229.99	231.16	70.32	69.35	69.70	40.79	40.38	40.54	2,012	102.27
22........	234.26	230.37	233.81	70.97	69.65	70.76	40.74	40.42	40.54	2,731	102.31
23........	†	†	†	†	†	†	†	†	†	†	†
24........	236.63	233.81	235.47	71.54	70.77	71.06	40.93	40.50	40.70	2,620	102.36
25........	235.84	234.74	235.06	71.07	70.73	70.80	40.82	40.71	40.77	793	102.36
26........	*										
27........	236.09	232.75	234.96	70.92	69.79	70.52	40.85	40.63	40.69	1,743	102.24
28........	231.34	227.40	228.61	69.25	67.25	67.67	40.38	39.70	39.79	2,967	102.14
29........	227.78	223.82	226.42	68.01	66.46	67.90	39.79	39.30	39.62	2,768	102.00
30........	229.70	225.97	227.60	69.24	67.91	68.53	40.00	39.57	39.80	2,082	102.04
High..........			235.47			71.06			40.80		102.36
Low			222.52			64.48			39.62		101.40

*Sunday. †Holiday (000 omitted).   Total 43,083

DECEMBER, 1950

	Industrials High	Low	Close	Railroads High	Low	Close	Utilities High	Low	Close	‡Daily Sales	40 Bonds
1	230.42	227.05	228.89	70.02	68.67	69.82	40.12	39.65	40.01	1,874	102.00
2	229.09	227.20	227.55	70.12	69.46	69.57	39.96	39.83	39.87	777	102.01
3*											
4	225.23	221.31	222.33	67.92	66.69	66.92	39.58	38.97	39.19	2,511	101.90
5	225.97	222.01	225.44	68.89	67.43	68.82	39.55	39.06	39.33	1,938	101.87
6	228.10	224.78	226.16	71.02	69.29	70.49	39.48	39.19	39.31	2,013	102.00
7	227.35	224.41	225.94	70.74	69.64	70.35	39.46	39.05	39.25	1,814	102.04
8	227.33	224.23	226.74	72.67	69.93	72.50	39.33	38.89	39.07	2,308	102.20
9	227.73	226.47	227.30	73.83	72.68	73.57	39.14	39.01	39.12	1,230	102.26
10*											
11	230.78	227.05	229.19	75.32	73.69	74.42	39.68	39.11	39.37	2,597	102.28
12	231.13	228.13	229.27	74.55	73.30	73.48	39.36	39.05	39.26	2,137	102.21
13	230.35	227.42	228.82	74.30	73.17	73.80	39.55	39.14	39.31	2,027	102.24
14	229.47	224.98	225.89	74.23	72.02	72.78	39.27	38.79	38.95	2,656	102.16
15	226.57	223.19	224.70	73.77	72.07	73.38	38.90	38.62	38.75	2,419	102.22
16	228.89	225.79	228.34	75.69	74.17	75.61	38.97	38.69	38.89	2,020	102.29
17*											
18	233.27	228.58	231.01	76.69	75.30	76.01	39.19	38.68	39.03	4,500	102.33
19	233.05	229.77	231.54	77.64	75.71	77.30	39.17	38.77	38.99	3,649	102.52
20	232.27	229.10	231.20	78.01	76.55	77.74	39.18	38.75	38.97	3,507	102.65
21	232.02	229.06	230.43	78.01	76.93	77.35	40.12	38.89	39.93	2,994	102.87
22	232.94	229.65	231.54	77.25	76.36	76.84	40.27	39.74	40.07	2,722	102.93
23											
24	†	†	†	†	†	†	†	†	†	†	†
25											
26	232.41	228.44	229.65	76.90	75.46	75.62	40.40	39.82	40.12	2,657	102.76
27	234.64	230.30	234.21	77.42	75.88	77.32	40.61	40.10	40.51	2,936	102.86
28	236.25	233.02	235.34	78.20	77.13	77.89	40.98	40.45	40.88	3,562	102.88
29	236.52	233.63	235.42	77.94	77.27	77.64	41.15	40.76	41.04	3,442	102.88
30	236.24	234.69	235.41	77.83	77.35	77.64	41.10	40.95	40.98	1,530	102.89
31											
High			235.42			77.89			41.04		102.93
Low			222.33			66.92			38.75		101.87
									Total	59,820	

*Sunday. †Holiday. ‡000 omitted.

JANUARY, 1951

	Industrials High	Low	Close	Railroads High	Low	Close	Utilities High	Low	Close	Daily Sales	40 Bonds
1	†			†			†			†	†
2	240.46	234.93	239.92	79.17	77.41	79.00	41.54	40.98	41.47	3,034,725	102.85
3	241.29	237.43	238.99	79.37	78.13	78.36	41.79	41.32	41.48	3,366,552	102.85
4	241.71	237.64	240.86	79.24	78.18	79.03	41.99	41.40	41.75	3,390,240	102.87
5	242.60	240.15	240.96	80.00	78.67	79.12	42.05	41.54	41.90	3,394,950	102.88
6	241.24	239.90	240.68	79.16	78.47	78.91	41.99	41.82	41.91	1,164,380	102.81
7*											
8	243.05	239.62	242.29	79.35	78.36	79.17	41.98	41.62	41.77	2,783,715	102.80
9	245.10	242.02	243.50	80.40	79.11	79.75	42.25	41.72	42.04	3,804,730	102.94
10	244.61	239.12	240.40	80.16	78.04	78.50	42.12	41.55	41.63	3,266,600	102.96
11	245.20	240.35	244.72	80.80	78.56	80.67	42.26	41.68	42.09	3,486,205	103.02
12	245.87	242.77	243.81	83.01	80.01	81.63	42.32	41.98	42.15	2,954,098	103.09
13	244.11	242.52	243.61	82.27	81.40	82.08	42.10	41.93	42.08	1,066,550	103.07
14*											
15	245.75	241.47	245.02	82.58	80.91	82.40	42.27	41.83	42.11	2,833,880	103.10
16	247.64	244.76	246.65	84.49	82.53	83.93	42.50	42.05	42.25	3,738,400	103.12
17	248.95	243.76	248.01	84.82	82.32	84.53	42.49	41.79	42.35	3,877,470	103.12
18	249.07	245.60	247.39	84.64	83.38	83.78	42.50	42.17	42.32	3,488,050	103.09
19	248.62	245.45	246.76	84.84	82.99	83.81	42.55	42.15	42.40	3,166,535	103.15
20	247.48	246.00	246.91	84.31	83.68	84.02	42.49	42.42	42.48	1,143,860	103.13
21*											
22	247.48	242.70	244.33	84.71	82.86	83.30	42.54	42.10	42.21	2,569,180	103.14
23	245.87	242.40	245.30	83.53	82.14	82.83	42.48	42.13	42.36	2,077,090	103.25
24	246.28	243.45	244.36	83.12	82.14	82.28	42.42	41.96	42.04	1,989,440	103.25
25	244.08	240.11	242.22	82.32	80.34	81.80	42.17	41.72	41.99	2,522,110	103.21
26	245.42	241.86	244.51	83.18	81.89	82.86	42.20	41.80	41.99	2,234,020	103.26
27	247.96	245.24	247.36	84.21	83.30	83.91	42.30	42.05	42.22	1,387,100	103.31
28*											
29	249.48	246.50	248.64	85.40	83.96	84.90	42.42	41.98	42.18	2,627,130	103.35
30	250.46	247.49	249.58	86.75	84.33	86.19	42.34	42.09	42.21	2,477,980	103.49
31	250.56	247.43	248.83	86.99	85.62	86.58	42.34	42.03	42.23	2,335,740	103.43
High			249.58			86.58			42.48		103.49
Low			238.99			78.36			41.47		102.80
									Total	70,180,730	

*Sunday. †Holiday

FEBRUARY, 1951

	—Industrials—			—Railroads—			—Utilities—			Daily	40
	High	Low	Close	High	Low	Close	High	Low	Close	Sales	Bonds
1	251.17	247.04	250.76	88.67	85.94	88.52	42.34	41.97	42.17	2,384,940	103.44
2	253.71	250.66	252.78	89.64	88.62	89.12	42.54	42.16	42.42	3,029,950	103.41
3	254.42	252.70	253.92	89.44	88.85	89.27	42.49	42.36	42.44	1,391,310	103.39
4	*			*			*			*	
5	256.06	252.91	255.17	90.35	89.10	90.08	42.64	42.23	42.41	2,683,600	103.47
6	255.30	252.25	254.62	90.53	89.10	89.85	42.45	42.19	42.39	2,365,670	103.43
7	254.47	251.69	252.70	90.41	88.92	89.46	42.57	42.27	42.47	2,024,270	103.44
8	254.27	250.92	253.34	90.17	89.17	89.95	42.47	42.32	42.44	2,117,000	103.45
9	255.58	253.08	254.24	90.82	89.43	89.73	42.78	42.35	42.52	2,545,520	103.50
10	255.25	254.07	254.80	89.96	89.54	89.85	42.61	42.52	42.57	1,064,430	103.50
11	*			*			*			*	
12	†	†	†	†	*†	†	†	†	†	†	†
13	257.06	254.34	255.71	90.02	88.78	88.99	42.93	42.54	42.75	2,402,758	103.47
14	256.34	253.34	255.10	89.12	87.51	88.65	43.01	42.51	42.81	2,050,425	103.44
15	255.30	253.13	253.61	89.01	87.84	88.08	43.07	42.74	42.95	1,704,800	103.48
16	255.58	253.10	254.90	88.89	87.86	88.40	43.01	42.78	42.90	1,857,940	103.50
17	255.17	253.97	254.70	88.70	88.34	88.63	42.95	42.80	42.86	819,960	103.49
18	*			*			*			*	
19	255.08	251.29	251.67	88.19	86.58	86.64	42.90	42.66	42.72	1,908,814	103.39
20	252.15	248.78	251.12	86.86	85.58	86.68	42.89	42.34	42.81	2,007,450	103.31
21	253.53	250.77	252.28	87.50	86.23	86.69	43.09	42.71	42.99	1,674,500	103.24
22	†	†	†	†	†	†	†	†	†	†	†
23	253.59	251.21	252.18	86.88	86.27	86.51	43.66	43.03	43.52	1,541,690	103.10
24	253.19	251.97	252.93	86.70	86.42	86.58	43.95	43.60	43.91	684,110	103.04
25	*			*			*			*	
26	254.47	251.57	253.18	86.82	86.13	86.30	44.09	43.62	43.77	1,651,460	102.94
27	253.73	250.81	251.34	86.31	84.88	84.95	43.94	43.38	43.70	1,684,610	102.89
28	253.14	249.70	252.05	85.53	84.12	85.10	43.71	43.35	43.62	1,638,670	102.78
High			255.71			90.08			43.91		103.50
Low			250.76			84.95			42.17		102.78

*Sunday. †Holiday   Total 41,233,877

MARCH, 1951

	—Industrials—			—Railroads—			—Utilities—			Daily	40
	High	Low	Close	High	Low	Close	High	Low	Close	Sales	Bonds
1	253.73	250.96	252.80	86.22	84.63	85.77	43.74	43.40	43.67	1,610,100	102.65
2	254.42	252.22	253.61	86.52	85.78	86.26	43.89	43.59	43.80	1,570,870	102.64
3	253.86	253.21	253.43	86.43	86.12	86.35	43.87	43.75	43.84	617,300	102.64
4	*			*			*			*	
5	253.43	250.23	251.82	86.05	84.42	85.09	43.84	43.50	43.70	1,692,088	102.35
6	252.37	250.43	251.55	85.06	84.37	84.60	43.67	43.23	43.41	1,491,962	102.09
7	253.41	250.71	252.45	85.44	84.45	85.01	43.51	43.25	43.42	1,773,290	102.02
8	253.68	251.55	252.81	85.59	84.75	85.01	43.52	43.22	43.41	1,435,660	101.85
9	254.27	251.98	252.75	85.42	84.68	84.85	43.48	43.14	43.38	1,605,701	101.68
10	252.60	251.74	252.02	84.91	84.69	84.78	43.38	43.29	43.37	468,760	101.63
11	*	*	*				*			*	*
‡12	252.00	248.70	249.89	84.77	83.39	83.52	43.39	43.03	43.13	1,640,324	101.38
13	249.35	244.61	245.88	83.40	80.95	81.42	43.16	42.51	42.65	2,332,580	101.34
14	246.56	243.13	243.95	82.79	80.43	80.84	42.69	42.33	42.56	2,107,890	101.05
15	245.80	242.06	244.85	81.42	80.12	81.17	42.59	42.24	42.49	2,066,840	100.88
16	249.33	245.88	248.62	82.94	82.03	82.69	43.16	42.66	43.04	1,657,300	100.96
17	249.79	248.59	249.03	82.83	82.52	82.55	43.12	43.07	43.10	630,770	100.97
18	*			*			*			*	
19	249.45	246.45	248.08	82.50	81.57	82.04	43.11	42.77	42.88	1,122,540	100.89
20	248.64	246.53	247.87	81.91	81.10	81.50	42.93	42.61	42.78	1,015,900	100.82
21	250.39	247.45	249.37	82.50	81.59	82.30	43.01	42.73	42.90	1,313,020	100.71
22	251.57	249.04	250.52	82.48	81.91	81.99	43.23	42.70	43.06	1,293,750	100.71
23	†	†	†	†	†	†	†	†	†	†	†
24	250.74	248.09	248.14	81.46	80.18	80.26	43.07	42.85	42.91	899,420	100.70
25	*			*			*			*	
26	249.79	247.04	249.13	80.86	80.07	80.61	43.06	42.67	42.94	1,232,300	100.72
27	250.81	248.18	248.74	81.12	80.36	80.48	43.02	42.70	42.78	1,249,990	100.69
28	249.15	245.34	246.19	80.51	78.65	79.04	42.87	42.46	42.58	1,772,130	100.41
29	248.28	245.95	246.90	80.10	79.09	79.73	42.61	42.24	42.39	1,296,350	100.32
30	249.25	246.95	248.53	80.97	79.92	80.61	42.58	42.17	42.33	1,147,567	100.34
31	248.82	247.75	247.94	80.75	80.43	80.58	42.35	42.24	42.25	480,900	100.32
High			253.61			86.35			43.84		102.65
Low			243.95			79.04			42.25		100.32

*Sunday. †Holiday.   Total 35,625,302

APRIL, 1951

	Industrials High	Low	Close	Railroads High	Low	Close	Utilities High	Low	Close	Daily Sales	40 Bonds
1.......	*	*	*	*	*	*	*	*	*	*	
2.......	247.82	245.02	246.63	80.29	79.29	79.69	42.35	42.03	42.21	1,280,830	100.20
3.......	247.69	245.46	246.02	80.17	79.31	79.36	42.31	42.02	42.13	1,221,820	100.05
4.......	247.80	244.98	247.31	80.63	79.23	80.60	42.35	42.09	42.30	1,302,055	100.06
5.......	250.91	247.75	250.32	83.16	81.42	82.85	42.57	42.22	42.43	1,791,560	100.13
6.......	252.22	250.06	250.83	83.53	82.60	83.02	42.56	42.27	42.49	1,449,870	100.02
7.......	251.00	249.89	250.28	83.12	82.59	82.82	42.53	42.46	42.49	436,290	100.01
8.......	*	*	*	*	*	*	*	*	*	*	
9.......	251.46	249.62	250.57	83.28	82.55	82.84	42.65	42.40	42.48	1,114,543	100.01
10......	251.88	249.52	250.42	82.75	81.96	82.18	42.61	42.40	42.44	1,279,730	99.90
11......	250.57	247.70	249.76	81.86	80.99	81.59	42.63	42.40	42.57	1,419,855	99.92
12......	252.10	249.37	251.66	82.74	81.53	82.58	42.50	42.20	42.38	1,532,685	99.84
13......	255.31	251.76	254.75	83.63	82.72	83.44	42.55	42.30	42.42	2,122,470	99.78
14......	256.47	255.04	256.18	84.15	83.69	83.99	42.52	42.39	42.42	950,860	99.75
15......	*	*	*	*	*	*	*	*	*	*	
16......	257.03	254.05	254.85	84.83	83.56	83.90	42.48	42.21	42.32	1,729,120	99.44
17......	256.06	253.88	255.34	84.33	83.44	83.99	42.41	42.24	42.36	1,465,168	99.33
18......	257.30	254.53	256.01	84.63	83.60	83.92	42.50	42.13	42.33	1,783,320	99.28
19......	256.53	253.99	254.92	83.93	83.05	83.30	42.55	42.24	42.41	1,517,270	99.23
20......	255.51	253.44	254.82	83.07	82.40	82.67	42.46	42.25	42.35	935,370	99.25
21......	255.26	254.58	255.02	82.77	82.55	82.65	42.38	42.27	42.32	389,480	99.28
22......	*	*	*	*	*	*	*	*	*	*	
23......	255.92	253.94	255.12	82.94	82.46	82.65	‡42.49	42.21	42.38	1,164,300	99.25
24......	255.67	253.48	254.19	82.85	81.93	82.03	42.44	42.13	42.30	1,424,960	99.33
25......	255.38	252.53	254.75	82.12	81.05	81.92	42.33	42.04	42.24	1,524,840	99.35
26......	257.98	254.92	257.13	82.89	82.21	82.77	42.37	42.08	42.24	1,796,180	99.46
27......	259.95	257.33	258.96	84.07	83.04	83.60	42.42	42.13	42.23	2,120,760	99.48
28......	259.59	258.38	259.08	83.74	83.39	83.52	42.38	42.29	42.33	751,340	99.48
29......	*	*	*	*	*	*	*	*	*	*	
30......	260.83	257.99	259.13	83.95	82.73	82.92	42.56	42.22	42.36	1,785,058	99.55
High			259.13			83.99			42.57		100.20
Low			246.02			79.36			42.13		99.23

*Sunday. †Holiday.

Total 34,289,734

MAY, 1951

	Industrials High	Low	Close	Railroads High	Low	Close	Utilities High	Low	Close	Daily Sales	40 Bonds
1......	261.80	258.23	260.71	83.21	82.46	82.84	42.53	42.22	42.42	1,759,360	99.63
‡2......	262.41	259.70	261.27	84.13	82.90	83.84	42.66	42.22	42.50	1,901,360	99.60
3......	263.69	260.31	263.13	85.97	84.28	85.72	42.64	42.31	42.61	2,062,640	99.72
4......	264.44	261.74	262.77	86.51	84.97	85.06	42.78	42.41	42.60	2,047,130	99.74
5......	262.55	261.51	261.76	85.10	84.85	84.88	42.53	42.43	42.47	591,480	99.74
6......	*	*	*	*	*	*	*	*	*	*	*
7......	262.48	259.60	261.23	84.88	84.00	84.47	42.62	42.23	42.37	1,581,370	99.66
8......	262.05	259.31	261.10	85.44	84.46	85.03	42.70	42.43	42.52	1,598,480	99.70
9......	262.82	260.24	261.49	86.01	85.04	85.32	42.74	42.45	42.58	1,961,300	99.61
10.....	261.83	259.14	260.07	85.20	84.19	84.40	42.71	42.37	42.51	1,656,850	99.57
11.....	260.93	257.91	258.56	84.28	83.12	83.17	42.49	42.18	42.35	1,642,870	99.49
12.....	257.81	256.77	257.26	82.97	82.58	82.66	42.33	42.21	42.28	648,640	99.46
13.....	*	*	*	*	*	*	*	*	*	*	*
14.....	258.10	255.45	256.08	83.55	82.41	82.66	42.58	42.22	42.42	1,253,090	99.40
15.....	256.24	251.02	252.08	82.80	80.35	80.72	42.59	42.16	42.35	2,023,520	99.24
16.....	254.19	250.81	252.14	81.48	80.59	81.08	42.57	42.17	42.27	1,663,000	99.24
17.....	255.49	252.40	254.57	81.96	81.03	81.77	42.66	42.39	42.56	1,368,780	99.28
18.....	255.03	250.01	250.10	81.82	79.37	79.48	42.63	42.29	42.36	1,660,430	99.25
19.....	250.93	249.74	250.63	79.64	79.07	79.54	42.30	42.16	42.22	607,550	99.31
20.....	*	*	*	*	*	*	*	*	*	*	*
21.....	251.36	248.03	249.98	79.60	78.13	78.75	42.22	41.91	42.09	1,583,030	99.34
22.....	251.72	248.49	249.30	79.34	77.93	78.10	42.28	41.92	42.03	1,441,100	99.17
23.....	249.79	246.58	247.03	78.78	77.03	77.33	42.12	41.78	41.92	1,542,510	99.12
24.....	246.94	241.89	245.78	77.46	75.08	76.86	41.88	41.54	41.73	2,583,820	98.92
25.....	247.57	244.84	245.27	78.09	77.16	77.49	41.93	41.67	41.85	1,209,540	98.89
26.....	246.11	245.03	245.83	77.68	77.29	77.58	41.81	41.78	41.81	419,690	98.91
27.....	*	*	*	*	*	*	*	*	*	*	*
28.....	248.20	245.60	247.03	78.62	77.77	78.08	42.09	41.83	42.00	1,235,720	98.93
29.....	249.52	246.43	248.44	79.23	78.16	79.02	42.33	42.12	42.25	1,191,480	99.01
30.....	†	†	†	†	†	†	†	†	†	†	†
31.....	251.68	248.32	249.65	80.11	79.22	79.64	42.48	42.07	42.21	1,221,750	99.00
High			263.13			85.72			42.61		99.74
Low			245.27			76.86			41.73		98.89

*Sunday. †Holiday.

Total 38,456,890

JUNE, 1951

	Industrials			Railroads			Utilities			Daily Sales	40 Bonds
	High	Low	Close	High	Low	Close	High	Low	Close		
1	250.15	247.85	249.33	79.64	78.90	79.36	42.37	42.11	42.31	980,650	98.99
2	†	†	†	†	†	†	†	†	†	†	†
3	*										
4	249.14	246.11	246.79	78.87	77.78	78.11	42.41	42.16	42.32	1,104,730	98.89
5	248.15	244.91	247.59	78.42	77.31	78.32	42.52	42.16	42.45	1,182,620	98.83
6	250.73	247.66	249.64	79.33	78.45	79.10	42.76	42.30	42.65	1,199,090	98.74
7	251.73	249.24	250.81	80.72	79.64	80.28	43.00	42.66	42.92	1,339,869	98.70
8	251.27	249.19	250.39	80.35	79.67	80.03	42.95	42.62	42.69	1,002,450	98.65
9	†	†	†	†	†	†	†	†	†	†	†
10	*										
11	252.77	249.76	251.56	80.39	79.80	80.14	42.79	42.44	42.56	1,219,185	98.58
12	252.64	249.75	250.57	80.10	79.19	79.21	42.72	42.42	42.54	1,201,470	98.58
13	251.35	248.73	250.03	79.58	78.99	79.21	42.66	42.38	42.56	1,062,380	98.54
14	253.11	250.21	252.46	79.49	78.91	79.38	42.52	42.24	42.43	1,300,930	98.37
15	255.05	252.26	254.03	80.17	79.45	79.86	42.69	42.38	42.65	1,374,230	98.26
16	†	†	†	†	†	†	†	†	†	†	†
17	*										
18	255.23	252.55	253.80	79.85	79.25	79.64	42.88	42.62	42.71	1,054,511	98.13
19	254.54	251.70	253.53	79.97	79.24	79.78	42.89	42.54	42.82	1,098,260	97.93
20	254.47	251.41	251.86	79.95	79.02	79.12	42.95	42.67	42.81	1,118,245	97.84
21	251.57	249.20	250.43	78.90	78.27	78.55	42.83	42.54	42.68	1,101,420	97.62
22	250.21	246.66	247.86	78.38	77.62	77.87	42.76	42.46	42.64	1,338,100	97.46
23	†	†	†	†	†	†	†	†	†	†	†
24	*										
25	245.99	241.84	245.30	76.07	74.17	75.15	42.66	42.29	42.47	2,438,680	97.22
26	247.44	244.29	246.28	75.59	74.77	74.99	42.72	42.43	42.55	1,258,810	97.14
27	247.98	244.90	246.84	75.39	74.56	75.05	42.67	42.30	42.45	1,364,740	97.19
28	247.22	242.57	244.00	74.89	73.11	73.65	42.50	42.10	42.22	1,935,210	97.07
29	244.36	240.72	242.64	73.06	71.78	72.39	42.29	41.95	42.08	1,726,570	97.03
30	†	†	†	†	†	†	†	†	†	†	†
High			254.03			80.28			42.92		98.99
Low			242.64			72.39			42.08		97.03

*Sunday. †Holiday.   Total 27,402,150

JULY, 1951

	Industrials			Railroads			Utilities			Daily Sales	40 Bonds
	High	Low	Close	High	Low	Close	High	Low	Close		
1	*		*								†
2	244.92	241.06	243.98	73.36	72.33	73.16	42.41	42.01	42.34	1,353,240	97.00
3	246.77	244.07	245.92	74.11	73.38	73.92	42.62	42.35	42.50	1,249,940	97.10
4	†	†	†	†	†	†	†	†	†	†	†
5	250.90	247.01	250.27	76.25	74.51	76.05	42.80	42.48	42.70	1,409,870	97.35
6	251.30	248.78	250.01	76.27	75.72	75.21	42.98	42.71	42.82	1,170,021	97.41
7	†	†	†	†	†	†	†	†	†	†	†
8	*										
9	252.10	249.20	250.65	76.08	75.42	75.74	43.05	42.74	42.96	1,107,880	97.50
10	251.41	249.09	250.00	75.47	75.05	75.19	43.11	42.84	43.06	994,070	97.54
11	251.75	249.31	250.97	75.87	75.17	75.58	43.30	42.97	43.23	972,530	97.73
12	253.11	250.70	252.59	76.17	75.44	75.73	43.36	43.11	43.24	1,049,440	97.97
13	255.36	252.39	254.32	76.82	75.76	76.48	43.56	43.27	43.44	1,316,920	98.17
14	†	†	†	†	†	†	†	†	†	†	†
15	*										
16	254.98	251.72	252.31	76.54	75.53	75.60	43.59	43.38	43.50	1,196,420	98.08
17	254.18	251.05	253.89	76.30	75.22	75.98	43.74	43.41	43.67	1,281,950	98.20
18	255.18	252.84	253.67	76.56	75.80	76.11	43.83	43.56	43.69	1,363,880	98.26
19	254.56	252.24	253.75	76.36	75.72	76.20	43.99	43.58	43.88	1,115,710	98.26
20	255.48	252.78	253.73	77.53	76.56	76.83	44.49	44.11	44.37	1,391,190	98.28
21	†	†	†	†	†	†	†	†	†	†	†
22	*										
23	256.35	253.44	255.68	77.83	76.77	77.71	44.63	44.33	44.51	1,317,110	98.18
24	259.40	255.36	258.94	78.99	78.03	78.89	44.71	44.39	44.60	1,743,670	98.23
25	260.79	257.33	258.11	80.04	78.89	79.06	44.85	44.48	44.72	1,873,690	98.26
26	259.94	256.46	259.09	80.29	78.93	80.08	44.96	44.56	44.90	1,483,930	98.27
27	259.87	256.92	259.23	81.84	80.02	81.69	44.92	44.70	44.82	1,445,300	98.32
28	†	†	†	· †		†	†	†	†	†	†
29	*										
30	262.21	258.89	260.70	82.05	81.25	81.52	45.13	44.70	45.00	1,601,550	98.31
31	260.30	256.64	257.86	81.23	80.16	80.54	45.01	44.66	44.86	1,550,280	98.33
High			260.70			81.69			45.00		98.33
Low			243.98			73.16			42.34		97.00

*Sunday. †Holiday.   Total 27,988,591

AUGUST, 1951

	Industrials High	Industrials Low	Industrials Close	Railroads High	Railroads Low	Railroads Close	Utilities High	Utilities Low	Utilities Close	Daily Sales	40 Bonds
1	260.72	256.81	259.89	81.55	80.40	81.25	45.12	44.57	44.94	1,678,616	98.37
‡2	264.05	260.05	262.89	82.18	81.29	81.68	45.57	45.06	45.45	2,133,100	98.39
3	264.78	261.25	262.98	81.89	81.06	81.47	45.73	45.33	45.52	1,574,500	98.39
4											
5											
6	265.72	261.88	265.21	82.74	80.98	82.60	45.55	45.25	45.43	1,600,810	98.51
7	266.52	263.85	264.94	83.14	82.08	82.41	45.64	45.31	45.55	1,813,180	98.50
8	265.52	262.24	263.73	82.43	81.79	81.97	45.58	45.33	45.46	1,413,830	98.50
9	264.43	261.77	262.69	83.38	81.16	81.39	45.55	45.11	45.34	1,497,240	98.69
10	263.26	260.67	261.92	81.42	80.60	81.00	45.35	45.16	45.24	1,255,050	98.67
11											
12											
13	264.76	261.26	263.06	81.21	80.26	80.40	45.38	45.09	45.27	1,322,980	98.68
14	263.98	261.57	262.88	80.18	79.35	79.89	45.22	44.99	45.12	1,184,136	98.70
15	264.72	262.04	264.27	80.76	79.85	80.64	45.13	44.83	45.02	1,337,680	98.76
16	266.63	263.78	265.48	81.25	80.46	80.72	45.21	44.94	45.13	1,750,750	98.82
17	267.44	264.54	266.17	81.23	80.49	80.62	45.35	45.08	45.25	1,619,452	98.93
18											
19											
20	267.42	264.98	266.19	80.76	80.11	80.27	45.28	45.02	45.18	1,130,770	98.98
21	267.66	264.47	265.30	80.83	79.96	80.03	45.21	44.85	44.93	1,402,987	99.03
22	265.56	262.80	264.07	79.44	78.63	79.10	44.84	44.47	44.66	1,129,480	99.04
23	266.26	262.89	265.65	79.55	78.80	79.31	44.63	44.38	44.50	1,232,580	98.99
24	267.53	264.94	266.30	79.58	78.93	79.05	44.50	44.32	44.40	1,207,600	98.96
25											
26											
27	267.06	264.54	265.59	79.14	78.34	78.47	44.66	44.38	44.59	1,078,779	98.90
28	266.81	264.42	265.56	79.36	78.44	79.04	44.75	44.40	44.66	1,274,170	98.86
29	268.62	265.39	268.18	80.40	79.12	80.20	44.84	44.50	44.73	1,520,423	98.91
30	270.68	267.98	269.94	80.80	80.14	80.36	45.13	44.71	45.03	1,952,290	98.99
31	271.64	268.58	270.25	80.79	80.06	80.33	45.16	44.82	45.00	1,531,210	99.08
High			270.25			82.60			45.55		99.08
Low			259.89			78.47			44.40		98.37

*Sunday. †Holiday.

Total 33,641,623

SEPTEMBER, 1951

	Industrials High	Industrials Low	Industrials Close	Railroads High	Railroads Low	Railroads Close	Utilities High	Utilities Low	Utilities Close	Daily Sales	40 Bonds
1											
2											
3											
4	272.28	269.49	270.63	81.28	80.26	80.80	45.16	44.83	45.08	1,519,490	99.13
5	273.11	270.25	272.48	81.24	80.59	80.87	45.30	44.93	45.16	1,854,824	99.10
6	273.98	271.23	272.28	83.03	81.25	82.72	45.32	45.00	45.19	2,151,570	99.27
7	274.54	271.53	273.89	83.08	82.19	82.82	45.40	45.07	45.33	1,926,710	99.30
8											
9											
10	276.63	273.62	275.25	83.53	82.51	82.91	45.57	45.17	45.38	2,194,500	99.34
11	276.24	272.63	273.88	83.07	81.99	82.31	45.53	44.99	45.33	2,037,930	99.37
12	276.56	273.32	275.31	83.69	82.37	83.31	45.61	45.30	45.45	2,178,370	99.53
13	277.15	274.34	276.37	84.08	83.28	83.61	45.72	45.39	45.49	2,348,310	99.55
14	277.51	274.01	276.06	84.69	83.23	84.45	45.69	45.50	45.55	2,169,820	99.47
15											
16											
17	277.12	274.12	275.09	84.79	84.01	84.22	45.64	45.36	45.46	1,799,900	99.51
18	275.63	271.91	274.38	84.10	82.95	83.77	45.64	45.25	45.54	2,031,050	99.43
19	276.09	273.08	274.27	84.81	83.65	84.37	45.70	45.32	45.50	2,065,490	99.49
20	276.02	272.58	274.10	86.05	83.96	85.34	45.67	45.29	45.50	2,102,500	99.40
21	274.10	270.21	272.11	86.10	84.48	85.34	45.58	45.27	45.35	2,180,840	99.34
22											
23											
24	271.83	269.08	270.77	86.16	84.80	85.72	45.42	45.05	45.19	1,634,800	99.28
25	273.51	270.05	272.24	87.04	85.59	86.05	45.46	45.12	45.31	1,742,500	99.24
‡26	273.67	270.88	272.24	86.58	85.73	85.87	45.56	45.26	45.50	1,524,760	99.19
27	272.93	269.77	271.31	85.84	84.67	85.12	45.82	45.35	45.62	1,541,780	99.18
28	272.24	269.66	271.16	85.31	84.40	84.76	45.92	45.50	45.67	1,389,760	99.13
29											
30											
High			276.37			86.05			45.67		99.55
Low			270.63			80.80			45.08		99.10

*Sunday. †Holiday.

Total 36,394,904

OCTOBER, 1951

	—Industrials—			—Railroads—			—Utilities—			Daily Sales	40 Bonds
	High	Low	Close	High	Low	Close	High	Low	Close		
1	273.25	270.23	272.56	85.57	84.62	85.29	46.36	45.74	46.17	1,334,390	98.99
2	275.42	272.13	274.34	86.57	85.29	86.10	46.57	46.13	46.41	1,871,220	99.06
3	277.30	274.29	275.87	87.38	86.05	86.77	46.52	46.12	46.34	2,378,980	98.94
4	276.93	274.49	275.35	87.53	86.40	86.66	46.42	46.14	46.27	1,809,315	98.90
5	277.02	274.21	275.63	87.73	86.27	86.99	46.33	46.08	46.24	2,079,860	98.89
6	276.06	275.22	275.53	87.41	86.95	87.06	46.29	46.16	46.24	757,040	98.86
7	*	*	*	*	*	*	*	*	*		
8	276.59	274.23	275.14	87.80	86.68	87.06	46.56	46.19	46.34	1,860,950	98.84
9	275.26	272.65	273.38	87.22	86.29	86.77	46.48	46.23	46.36	1,752,470	98.90
10	274.47	271.46	272.76	86.79	86.11	86.51	46.59	46.17	46.41	1,321,165	98.85
11	274.68	271.80	274.10	87.24	86.36	86.88	46.43	46.17	46.35	1,764,650	98.80
12	†	†	†	†	†	†	†	†	†		†
13	275.37	274.03	275.13	87.25	86.67	87.00	46.48	46.42	46.48	745,950	98.82
14	*	*	*	*	*	*	*	*	*		*
15	276.93	274.25	275.74	87.60	86.74	86.92	46.66	46.32	46.50	1,715,280	98.77
16	276.02	272.50	274.40	86.83	85.41	86.06	46.51	46.16	46.38	1,727,190	98.60
17	275.24	272.86	273.53	86.15	85.01	85.13	46.67	46.26	46.49	1,460,580	98.47
18	274.75	272.22	273.51	85.49	84.67	85.09	46.60	46.29	46.45	1,447,390	98.29
19	274.10	269.23	269.68	85.71	83.63	83.79	46.68	46.18	46.23	1,992,900	98.25
20	268.93	267.00	267.42	83.57	82.62	82.80	46.09	45.94	46.01	1,025,580	98.24
21	*	*	*	*	*	*	*	*	*		*
22	265.90	259.46	262.29	82.61	80.53	81.67	46.60	45.44	45.55	2,692,830	97.99
23	264.80	259.76	263.50	82.81	80.98	82.04	45.70	45.31	45.52	2,114,480	97.92
24	266.79	263.22	264.95	83.15	82.06	82.58	45.81	45.53	45.69	1,668,350	97.90
25	266.20	262.66	264.17	82.54	81.55	81.72	45.73	45.43	45.61	1,361,990	97.93
26	264.26	260.08	262.27	81.53	80.29	80.83	45.62	45.33	45.49	1,707,675	97.86
27	261.34	257.73	258.53	80.36	78.52	78.93	45.51	45.09	45.13	1,137,370	97.84
28	*	*	*	*	*	*	*	*	*		*
29	261.12	256.39	260.43	80.24	78.49	79.93	45.29	44.82	45.16	1,780,820	97.58
30	263.46	259.69	260.52	80.78	79.42	79.59	45.50	45.18	45.41	1,531,367	97.58
31	263.15	258.44	262.35	80.55	78.83	80.26	45.81	45.39	45.75	1,494,750	97.56
High			275.87			87.06			46.50		99.06
Low			258.53			78.93			45.13		97.56
										Total 42,530,542	

*Sunday. †Holiday.

NOVEMBER, 1951

	—Industrials—			—Railroads—			—Utilities—			Daily Sales	40 Bonds
	High	Low	Close	High	Low	Close	High	Low	Close		
1	265.82	261.86	264.06	81.54	80.51	80.88	46.33	45.70	46.19	1,426,090	97.65
2	264.37	261.01	261.94	80.92	79.72	79.83	46.18	45.97	46.07	1,228,090	97.68
3	260.91	258.85	259.57	79.48	78.88	79.05	46.08	45.91	46.00	680,580	97.67
4	*	*	*	*	*	*	*	*	*		*
5	262.10	258.59	259.76	79.64	78.69	79.20	46.30	46.03	46.15	1,125,560	97.57
6	†	†	†	†	†	†	†	†	†		†
7	260.37	256.58	257.14	79.53	78.02	78.11	46.31	45.89	46.02	1,492,930	97.55
8	258.35	254.91	257.14	79.12	78.08	78.78	46.16	45.84	46.08	1,408,520	97.60
9	261.21	257.81	259.91	80.15	79.11	79.73	46.43	46.08	46.35	1,471,010	97.63
10	261.47	260.17	261.29	79.86	79.61	79.78	46.49	46.33	46.45	542,510	97.61
11	*	*	*	*	*	*	*	*	*		*
12	†	†	†	†	†	†	†	†	†		†
13	262.18	259.39	260.41	80.20	79.46	79.61	46.58	46.31	46.43	1,164,070	97.56
14	262.01	259.85	261.27	80.08	79.31	79.73	46.55	46.25	46.48	1,217,900	97.53
15	262.29	260.32	260.91	80.66	79.90	80.24	46.45	46.27	46.38	1,202,860	97.54
16	261.06	259.00	260.39	81.23	79.58	81.08	46.48	46.19	46.44	1,137,600	97.54
17	261.06	260.21	260.82	81.52	81.01	81.25	46.47	46.38	46.42	399,140	97.54
18	*	*	*	*	*	*	*	*	*		*
19	261.36	258.77	259.70	81.15	80.16	80.54	46.56	46.16	46.45	1,029,010	97.46
20	260.04	257.57	259.30	80.53	79.58	80.15	46.61	46.28	46.55	1,125,082	97.39
21	260.15	258.16	258.72	80.39	79.67	79.88	46.60	46.28	46.50	1,092,835	97.23
22	†	†	†	†	†	†	†	†	†		†
23	258.89	255.93	256.95	79.60	78.44	78.65	46.50	46.05	46.14	1,208,477	97.09
24	256.60	255.54	255.95	78.30	77.79	77.91	46.04	46.00	46.01	486,230	97.07
25	*	*	*	*	*	*	*	*	*		*
26	258.38	255.20	257.44	79.23	77.86	78.65	46.23	45.90	46.09	1,176,340	97.08
27	260.36	257.47	259.46	79.92	78.80	79.64	46.17	45.88	46.05	1,307,310	97.19
28	260.43	258.12	258.64	80.12	79.04	79.32	46.27	45.75	45.93	1,154,330	97.10
29	259.93	257.29	258.96	80.50	79.21	80.36	46.05	45.74	45.88	1,073,705	96.98
30	261.92	258.68	261.27	81.77	80.50	81.43	46.06	45.77	46.04	1,526,700	97.03
High			264.06			81.43			46.55		97.68
Low			255.95			77.91			45.88		96.98
										Total 25,676,879	

*Sunday. †Holiday.

DECEMBER, 1951

	Industrials High	Low	Close	Railroads High	Low	Close	Utilities High	Low	Close	Daily Sales	40 Bonds
1	262.72	261.62	262.29	81.93	81.60	81.75	46.10	46.02	46.08	504,333	97.04
2	*	*	*	*	*	*	*	*	*	*	*
‡3	264.77	261.73	263.24	82.23	81.25	81.47	46.33	46.04	46.18	1,221,580	97.04
4	265.19	262.48	264.29	82.09	81.30	81.88	46.37	46.03	46.29	1,282,345	97.08
5	265.21	262.71	263.72	82.25	81.22	81.81	46.56	46.25	46.39	1,331,931	97.14
6	266.90	263.85	266.23	83.84	81.67	83.58	46.50	46.20	46.41	1,835,408	97.21
7	268.95	265.96	266.99	84.94	83.24	83.47	46.72	46.42	46.64	1,990,302	97.14
8	267.24	266.30	266.90	84.02	83.46	83.94	46.59	46.50	46.55	582,766	97.11
9	*	*	*	*	*	*	*	*	*	*	*
10	268.45	266.07	267.38	84.24	83.20	83.60	46.66	46.42	46.58	1,342,480	97.12
11	267.68	265.14	265.77	83.78	82.54	82.74	46.73	46.36	46.53	1,363,810	97.08
12	267.24	264.33	266.09	82.97	82.20	82.59	46.75	46.44	46.64	1,280,530	96.99
13	266.92	264.56	265.81	82.99	82.22	82.70	46.82	46.51	46.65	1,382,800	97.02
14	267.07	264.60	265.71	82.87	82.11	82.25	47.00	46.60	46.81	1,355,775	96.99
15	265.96	265.10	265.48	82.28	82.09	82.11	46.91	46.81	46.86	418,490	97.00
16				*	*		*	*	*	*	*
17	266.71	264.50	265.79	82.57	81.76	82.10	47.05	46.76	46.87	1,218,638	97.00
18	267.45	265.14	266.61	82.60	81.77	82.02	46.94	46.65	46.75	1,292,982	96.92
19	268.93	265.92	267.61	82.89	81.93	82.52	46.99	46.65	46.88	1,505,180	96.93
20	268.91	266.42	267.45	83.09	82.25	82.40	46.99	46.73	46.92	1,340,530	96.90
21	267.78	265.37	266.34	82.59	81.85	82.11	47.00	46.76	46.90	1,253,110	96.91
22	266.63	265.54	265.94	82.14	81.95	82.05	47.00	46.88	46.97	450,530	96.90
23	*	*	*	*	*	*	*	*	*	*	*
24	266.69	264.91	265.79	82.08	81.69	81.89	46.96	46.76	46.86	680,110	96.82
25	†	†	†	†	†	†	†	†	†	†	†
26	266.67	263.26	264.06	82.30	80.74	80.86	47.00	46.64	46.81	1,516,415	96.70
27	267.26	263.85	266.74	82.20	80.83	81.99	47.10	46.81	46.99	1,455,990	96.71
28	269.02	266.30	268.18	82.73	81.80	82.11	47.25	46.97	47.11	1,472,560	96.76
29	268.91	267.95	268.52	82.15	81.77	81.89	47.24	47.12	47.16	564,030	96.74
30	*	*	*	*	*	*	*	*	*	*	*
31	270.00	267.84	269.23	82.27	81.34	82.70	47.38	47.12	47.22	1,440,229	96.84
High			269.23			83.94			47.22		97.21
Low			262.29			80.86			46.08		96.70

*Sunday.   †Holiday.

Total 30,802,854

JANUARY, 1952

	-30 Industrials-			-20 Railroads-			-15 Utilities-			Daily Sales -000-	40 Bonds
	High	Low	Close	High	Low	Close	High	Low	Close		
2	271.01	268.24	269.86	82.61	81.46	82.11	47.79	47.24	47.53	1,070	96.85
3	271.28	268.58	270.38	83.34	81.82	83.01	47.83	47.48	47.71	1,220	96.94
4	271.95	269.73	271.03	84.43	83.29	83.69	47.98	47.74	47.90	1,480	97.03
5	271.57	270.71	271.26	83.92	83.58	83.77	47.93	47.81	47.90	490	97.05
7	272.60	269.94	270.34	83.99	82.85	83.11	48.16	47.75	47.96	1,540	97.14
8	270.98	268.14	268.66	82.92	81.96	82.09	48.13	47.87	48.00	1,390	97.09
9	270.04	266.34	268.08	82.25	81.51	82.03	48.27	47.73	48.21	1,370	97.20
10	271.09	268.14	269.46	83.64	82.16	83.42	48.66	48.16	48.57	1,520	97.22
11	271.20	268.74	270.31	84.46	83.35	83.75	49.00	48.55	48.90	1,760	97.27
12	271.15	269.88	270.73	84.28	83.70	84.12	49.00	48.86	48.94	750	97.30
14	272.70	270.36	271.59	84.70	83.90	84.17	49.23	48.87	49.10	1,510	97.34
15	272.09	269.44	270.46	84.54	83.34	83.45	48.76	48.76	48.89	1,340	97.36
16	272.28	269.27	271.13	84.31	83.11	83.94	48.90	48.48	48.56	1,430	97.48
17	273.00	270.53	271.91	85.42	83.71	85.12	48.83	48.59	48.72	1,590	97.60
18	272.69	271.03	272.10	86.50	85.14	86.13	48.95	48.54	48.83	1,740	97.64
19	273.25	271.70	272.93	86.73	86.10	86.51	48.78	48.70	48.74	730	97.70
21	274.55	272.32	274.10	87.51	86.07	87.17	48.90	48.46	48.72	1,730	97.72
22	276.26	273.58	275.40	87.62	86.61	86.75	49.13	48.67	49.01	1,920	97.91
23	275.95	273.44	274.27	86.92	85.90	86.17	49.23	48.85	49.00	1,680	98.07
24	275.19	272.68	273.90	86.78	85.84	86.19	49.20	48.79	49.00	1,570	98.13
25	275.07	272.43	273.41	86.57	85.74	86.00	49.20	48.89	49.08	1,650	98.37
26	274.15	273.16	273.69	86.19	86.02	86.10	49.10	49.00	49.03	660	98.38
28	275.13	273.00	274.17	87.33	85.95	87.02	49.17	48.79	49.00	1,590	98.42
29	275.44	272.91	274.00	88.62	87.05	87.67	49.15	48.86	49.05	1,730	98.42
30	275.38	270.53	270.71	87.97	85.86	85.89	49.11	48.76	48.91	1,880	98.47
31	272.18	268.05	270.69	86.30	84.79	85.79	48.80	48.50	48.63	1,810	98.50
		High	275.40		High	87.67		High	49.10		High 98.50
		Low	268.08		Low	82.03		Low	47.53		Low 96.85

FEBRUARY, 1952

	-30 Industrials-			-20 Railroads-			-15 Utilities-			Daily Sales -000-	40 Bonds
	High	Low	Close	High	Low	Close	High	Low	Close		
1	272.91	269.94	271.68	86.49	85.71	86.06	49.20	48.64	49.00	1,350	98.59
2	272.83	271.76	272.51	86.67	86.20	86.56	49.18	49.05	49.18	610	98.59
4	272.64	268.79	269.79	86.73	84.86	85.21	49.32	48.99	49.08	1,640	98.62
5	270.17	266.80	269.04	85.35	84.07	84.86	49.16	48.77	49.03	1,590	98.51
6	270.27	267.38	268.77	85.76	84.86	85.04	49.28	49.02	49.19	1,310	98.61
7	269.50	267.05	268.35	86.03	84.90	85.55	49.19	48.81	49.07	1,170	98.67
8	270.48	267.61	269.85	86.73	85.61	86.21	49.29	48.98	49.24	1,350	98.75
9	270.17	269.52	269.83	86.30	85.99	86.09	49.21	49.15	49.17	480	98.78
11	269.88	267.57	268.45	86.46	85.74	86.15	49.32	49.00	49.24	1,140	98.74
13	268.37	265.52	266.21	86.08	85.09	85.16	49.27	48.96	49.16	1,300	98.65
14	266.67	264.54	265.88	85.45	84.42	84.96	49.29	48.88	49.00	1,340	98.57
15	267.57	265.29	266.27	86.28	84.97	85.26	49.43	49.03	49.22	1,200	98.52
16	266.55	265.92	266.30	85.51	85.09	85.35	49.22	49.15	49.21	390	98.52
18	266.94	264.35	265.35	85.70	84.61	85.20	49.27	48.92	49.03	1,140	98.46
19	265.14	260.93	261.37	85.39	83.70	83.82	48.96	48.54	48.61	1,630	98.36
20	261.46	257.46	258.49	84.24	82.51	83.00	48.65	48.09	48.12	1,970	98.23
21	261.63	258.49	259.60	84.14	83.19	83.60	48.57	48.08	48.30	1,360	98.27
23	261.65	259.83	261.40	84.83	84.03	84.76	48.50	48.34	48.43	530	98.30
25	262.86	259.89	260.58	85.44	84.18	84.32	48.73	48.45	48.68	1,200	98.29
26	260.98	258.69	259.30	84.37	83.32	83.84	48.73	48.39	48.59	1,080	98.24
27	260.49	257.44	259.68	85.37	83.28	85.02	48.64	48.31	48.45	1,260	98.31
28	261.79	259.28	260.49	85.88	84.92	85.32	48.63	48.39	48.53	1,150	98.35
29	261.46	259.36	260.08	85.54	84.73	84.87	48.64	48.30	48.43	1,000	98.27
		High	272.51		High	86.56		High	49.24		High 98.78
		Low	258.49		Low	83.00		Low	48.12		Low 98.23

MARCH, 1952

	—30 Industrials— High	Low	Close	—20 Railroads— High	Low	Close	—15 Utilities— High	Low	Close	Daily Sales -000-	40 Bonds
1	260.45	259.57	260.27	85.03	84.73	84.94	48.57	48.50	48.56	460	98.27
3	261.17	258.95	260.08	85.47	84.87	85.14	48.83	48.47	48.69	1,020	98.23
4	264.24	260.35	263.95	87.21	85.20	86.89	49.14	48.86	49.11	1,570	98.31
5	266.17	263.61	264.66	87.44	86.44	86.73	49.42	49.16	49.35	1,380	98.35
6	265.04	262.72	264.03	88.22	86.32	87.93	49.65	49.23	49.54	1,210	98.38
7	264.89	262.53	263.87	89.61	87.86	89.23	50.11	49.47	49.92	1,410	98.35
8	264.45	263.57	264.14	90.27	88.99	89.71	49.93	49.83	49.93	670	98.36
10	264.64	262.32	262.76	89.51	88.29	88.51	49.87	49.43	49.58	1,170	98.35
11	263.80	261.25	262.76	89.66	88.04	89.27	49.66	49.34	49.49	1,210	98.26
12	264.56	261.75	263.78	89.69	88.64	89.03	49.76	49.42	49.63	1,310	98.34
13	265.62	262.65	264.24	89.44	88.45	88.84	49.83	49.60	49.66	1,270	98.47
14	265.46	262.50	264.05	90.35	88.70	90.22	50.00	49.66	49.76	1,350	98.51
15	264.87	263.89	264.43	90.91	90.16	90.28	49.83	49.76	49.81	640	98.51
17	265.48	263.26	264.08	90.74	89.78	90.07	50.15	49.83	50.04	1,150	98.57
18	265.08	262.59	264.10	90.57	89.22	90.17	50.35	49.87	50.08	1,170	98.55
19	265.16	262.80	264.37	90.30	89.36	89.67	50.01	49.68	49.85	1,090	98.53
20	266.23	263.70	265.33	90.63	89.55	90.19	50.19	49.95	50.05	1,240	98.63
21	267.05	264.93	265.62	90.83	89.93	90.04	50.45	50.06	50.37	1,290	98.68
22	266.07	265.29	265.69	90.17	89.69	89.99	50.47	50.33	50.44	410	98.65
24	266.48	264.58	265.60	90.35	89.51	89.71	50.47	50.10	50.26	1,040	98.68
25	265.52	263.72	264.28	90.13	89.17	89.32	50.33	49.93	50.09	1,060	98.63
26	265.06	262.82	263.87	89.76	88.78	89.48	50.11	49.64	49.88	1,030	98.63
27	265.88	263.20	265.21	92.36	89.67	92.23	50.30	49.75	50.03	1,370	98.70
28	267.76	265.06	266.96	93.75	92.19	92.79	50.37	50.07	50.25	1,560	98.74
29	269.25	267.17	269.00	93.74	93.09	93.58	50.18	50.09	50.11	740	98.77
31	270.40	267.17	269.46	94.70	92.75	94.36	50.36	49.92	50.21	1,680	98.79
		High	269.46		High	94.36		High	50.44		High 98.79
		Low	260.08		Low	84.94		Low	48.56		Low 98.23

APRIL, 1952

	—30 Industrials— High	Low	Close	—20 Railroads— High	Low	Close	—15 Utilities— High	Low	Close	Daily Sales -000-	40 Bonds
1	269.81	266.42	267.22	94.78	92.28	93.29	50.07	49.69	49.75	1,720	98.91
2	268.08	265.79	267.03	93.63	92.44	93.03	49.90	49.60	49.66	1,260	98.90
3	267.87	265.81	266.80	93.81	92.86	93.28	49.94	49.53	49.73	1,280	98.89
4	266.86	264.45	265.62	92.93	92.24	92.46	49.84	49.56	49.66	1,190	98.89
5	265.73	265.04	265.44	92.48	92.24	92.38	49.75	49.64	49.71	430	98.88
7	265.31	262.44	263.38	92.13	90.69	91.21	49.74	49.46	49.60	1,230	98.81
8	265.88	262.57	265.29	92.14	91.15	92.00	49.83	49.47	49.69	1,090	98.79
9	266.09	263.89	265.04	92.27	91.40	91.58	49.72	49.47	49.61	980	98.80
10	266.96	264.31	265.75	93.49	91.90	93.12	49.69	49.43	49.57	1,130	98.79
12	266.55	265.44	266.29	93.66	93.24	93.40	49.58	49.44	49.53	500	98.78
14	267.11	263.24	264.10	94.46	91.58	92.18	49.71	49.20	49.34	1,790	98.76
15	264.29	260.33	261.29	92.15	89.56	90.28	49.40	48.99	49.15	1,720	98.74
16	263.05	260.03	261.48	91.57	89.79	90.10	49.25	49.02	49.09	1,400	98.28
17	261.60	258.40	259.85	90.34	88.65	89.87	48.87	48.40	48.68	1,620	98.71
18	261.88	258.84	260.52	91.47	90.12	90.69	48.93	48.60	48.80	1,240	98.83
19	260.54	259.66	260.14	91.28	90.65	91.25	48.85	48.80	48.85	340	98.82
21	262.50	259.60	261.63	92.64	91.60	92.29	49.01	48.66	48.88	1,110	98.86
22	263.03	260.64	261.10	92.87	91.46	91.63	49.18	48.73	48.82	1,240	98.89
23	261.56	259.41	259.97	91.81	90.83	91.23	48.98	48.65	48.71	1,090	98.77
24	260.26	257.04	258.86	92.04	89.86	91.58	48.65	48.21	48.39	1,580	98.70
25	260.08	257.88	259.80	93.55	91.62	93.25	48.67	48.16	48.63	1,240	98.74
26	260.56	259.49	260.27	94.49	93.35	94.22	48.72	48.63	48.69	550	98.72
28	260.96	258.65	259.95	94.40	93.33	93.78	48.77	48.52	48.69	980	98.72
29	260.52	258.19	259.34	94.32	92.31	93.88	48.78	48.42	48.60	1,170	98.72
30	259.39	257.06	257.63	93.74	92.47	92.81	48.60	48.22	48.43	1,000	98.63
		High	267.22		High	94.22		High	49.75		High 98.91
		Low	257.63		Low	89.87		Low	48.39		Low 98.28

MAY, 1952

	-30 Industrials-			-20 Railroads-			-15 Utilities-			Daily Sales -000-	40 Bonds
	High	Low	Close	High	Low	Close	High	Low	Close		
1	257.44	254.70	256.35	92.05	90.78	91.47	48.48	48.01	48.16	1,400	98.54
2	260.93	257.67	260.00	93.60	92.11	93.33	48.50	48.22	48.46	1,300	98.61
3	260.71	259.96	260.55	93.60	93.35	93.50	48.57	48.45	48.55	380	98.65
5	261.95	259.35	261.54	93.65	92.78	93.03	48.80	48.56	48.75	860	98.58
6	262.29	260.02	261.01	94.82	93.18	94.16	48.94	48.66	48.81	1,120	98.57
7	262.70	259.96	261.99	95.39	94.21	95.11	48.95	48.65	48.89	1,120	98.54
8	263.77	261.58	262.39	95.73	94.52	94.57	49.29	48.88	49.13	1,230	98.56
9	263.47	260.99	262.74	94.92	94.17	94.48	49.37	49.09	49.27	960	98.71
10	262.90	262.21	262.50	94.66	94.45	94.58	49.30	49.24	49.26	310	98.73
12	262.86	260.83	261.72	94.53	93.91	94.14	49.49	49.21	49.37	800	98.72
13	263.04	260.87	261.99	94.63	93.99	94.22	49.50	49.22	49.43	890	98.84
14	262.62	260.26	260.99	94.25	93.44	93.56	49.47	49.13	49.21	950	98.84
15	261.07	258.66	260.10	93.80	92.40	93.34	49.28	48.99	49.14	1,050	98.75
16	260.93	259.00	259.82	93.97	93.27	93.56	49.38	49.09	49.16	910	98.84
17	260.02	259.49	259.88	93.65	93.50	93.59	49.14	49.09	49.11	270	98.84
19	261.12	259.15	260.06	93.76	93.19	93.44	49.25	48.99	49.16	780	98.88
20	262.66	259.51	261.26	94.72	93.52	94.22	49.70	49.30	49.53	1,150	98.92
21	262.78	260.89	261.78	95.17	94.26	94.84	49.81	49.35	49.68	1,210	98.92
22	264.02	261.54	263.33	97.12	95.10	96.58	49.90	49.52	49.72	1,360	98.95
23	264.59	262.54	263.27	97.32	95.93	96.13	50.00	49.62	49.83	1,150	98.93
24	263.47	262.84	263.23	96.25	95.99	96.17	49.82	49.81	49.82	300	98.94
26	264.87	262.62	264.22	96.42	95.55	96.08	50.13	49.73	50.09	940	98.96
27	265.17	262.82	263.92	96.74	95.33	96.31	50.15	49.75	49.92	1,040	98.95
28	264.54	262.25	262.78	97.86	96.41	97.15	50.09	49.75	49.86	1,130	98.91
29	263.51	261.62	262.94	97.55	96.62	97.29	50.13	49.88	49.94	1,100	98.85
		High 264.22			High 97.29			High 50.09			High 98.96
		Low 256.35			Low 91.47			Low 48.16			Low 98.54

JUNE, 1952

	-30 Industrials-			-20 Railroads-			-15 Utilities-			Daily Sales -000-	40 Bonds
	High	Low	Close	High	Low	Close	High	Low	Close		
2	264.61	261.48	262.31	98.13	96.84	96.99	50.22	49.72	49.83	1,190	98.82
3	262.82	260.83	262.09	97.36	96.55	97.29	49.85	49.55	49.76	940	98.78
4	264.20	261.91	263.67	100.34	97.48	100.19	49.99	49.72	49.85	1,200	98.73
5	266.80	263.77	266.29	100.91	99.69	100.27	50.14	49.86	50.01	1,410	98.70
6	268.95	266.21	268.03	100.94	99.78	100.36	50.26	49.92	50.12	1,520	98.72
9	269.92	267.67	269.15	101.13	100.04	100.66	50.29	49.90	50.09	1,270	98.74
10	269.15	266.76	267.67	100.11	99.12	99.45	50.14	49.83	50.02	1,220	98.72
11	268.52	266.33	267.93	100.86	99.70	100.52	50.06	49.86	49.99	1,190	98.69
12	269.03	266.90	267.91	101.24	100.03	100.25	50.06	49.75	49.88	1,370	98.71
13	269.17	267.28	268.56	100.98	100.01	100.43	50.01	49.71	49.80	1,130	98.74
16	269.15	267.28	267.83	100.50	99.56	99.76	49.94	49.69	49.81	980	98.75
17	268.68	266.80	268.03	100.37	99.45	99.94	49.72	49.51	49.63	920	98.82
18	269.48	267.63	267.09	100.93	99.80	100.14	49.92	49.64	49.77	1,270	98.78
19	270.59	268.40	269.54	101.07	100.04	100.61	49.87	49.63	49.77	1,320	98.77
20	270.84	268.89	270.19	100.82	100.04	100.44	49.92	49.66	49.77	1,190	98.83
23	271.28	268.64	269.50	101.35	100.12	100.35	49.88	49.63	49.70	1,200	98.87
24	270.47	268.81	269.92	100.61	99.69	100.15	49.72	49.35	49.60	1,200	98.77
25	270.98	268.75	270.45	101.49	100.13	101.38	49.74	49.48	49.65	1,230	98.82
26	271.85	269.88	271.24	102.32	101.03	102.02	49.71	49.36	49.63	1,190	98.82
27	272.95	270.77	272.44	102.68	101.73	102.39	49.76	49.55	49.69	1,210	98.84
30	274.97	272.30	274.26	103.17	102.06	102.73	49.80	49.60	49.66	1,380	98.87
		High 274.26			High 102.73			High 50.12			High 98.87
		Low 262.09			Low 96.99			Low 49.60			Low 98.69

JULY, 1952

	—30 Industrials—			—20 Railroads—			—15 Utilities—			Daily Sales -000-	40 Bonds
	High	Low	Close	High	Low	Close	High	Low	Close		
1	276.25	273.94	275.46	103.42	102.38	102.91	49.95	49.65	49.78	1,450	98.92
2	276.09	273.86	274.87	103.20	101.90	102.47	49.83	49.49	49.58	1,320	98.94
3	275.64	273.59	274.95	102.73	101.98	102.36	49.82	49.56	49.72	1,150	98.98
7	275.58	273.27	274.20	102.26	101.31	101.44	49.83	49.61	49.72	1,080	98.97
8	275.10	273.51	274.43	101.59	100.93	101.42	49.81	49.54	49.71	850	98.95
9	275.62	272.93	273.25	101.76	100.63	100.77	49.73	49.43	49.52	1,120	98.94
10	273.80	271.73	272.58	101.09	100.42	100.65	49.56	49.34	49.41	1,010	98.93
11	274.89	272.28	274.22	101.80	100.73	101.55	49.61	49.26	49.54	1,040	98.92
14	276.07	274.06	275.08	102.03	101.09	101.22	49.67	49.50	49.62	1,090	98.84
15	277.35	274.81	276.76	101.94	101.02	101.57	49.76	49.48	49.67	1,220	98.85
16	278.02	275.83	276.76	102.10	101.35	101.55	49.87	49.64	49.75	1,120	98.77
17	277.17	274.95	275.62	101.82	100.91	101.23	49.83	49.63	49.68	1,010	98.73
18	275.85	273.11	273.90	101.26	100.23	100.60	49.66	49.35	49.56	1,020	98.77
21	275.54	273.17	274.91	101.10	100.34	100.73	49.84	49.54	49.77	780	98.78
22	276.54	274.14	275.95	101.41	100.36	101.19	50.10	49.83	50.00	910	98.75
23	278.28	275.64	277.63	101.91	101.07	101.59	50.17	49.96	50.05	1,020	98.78
24	280.05	277.63	279.26	103.19	101.81	102.57	50.30	50.01	50.23	1,270	98.82
25	279.76	277.02	277.71	103.01	101.94	102.29	50.43	50.16	50.20	1,130	98.77
28	278.95	276.92	277.94	102.88	101.78	102.39	50.34	50.06	50.24	1,030	98.68
29	279.40	277.17	278.57	103.27	102.12	102.95	50.33	50.00	50.25	1,010	98.69
30	280.07	277.78	279.24	103.81	102.80	103.52	50.46	50.17	50.37	1,240	98.77
31	280.25	278.34	279.56	104.38	103.29	103.82	50.65	50.39	50.55	1,230	98.83
			High 279.56			High 103.82			High 50.55		High 98.98
			Low 272.58			Low 100.60			Low 49.41		Low 98.68

AUGUST, 1952

	—30 Industrials—			—20 Railroads—			—15 Utilities—			Daily Sales -000-	40 Bonds
	High	Low	Close	High	Low	Close	High	Low	Close		
1	280.49	278.81	279.80	104.28	103.35	103.81	50.65	50.37	50.51	1,050	98.80
4	280.51	278.59	279.87	103.97	103.04	103.36	50.68	50.39	50.58	950	98.77
5	280.03	277.96	279.50	103.71	102.83	103.48	51.17	50.58	51.07	1,050	98.79
6	280.21	277.88	279.07	104.21	103.16	103.73	51.27	50.95	51.12	1,140	98.83
7	280.09	278.34	279.38	105.13	103.97	104.89	51.13	50.92	51.10	1,180	98.84
8	280.92	278.49	279.84	105.55	104.55	104.78	51.17	50.94	51.12	1,170	98.78
11	281.47	279.15	280.29	105.29	104.22	104.40	51.12	50.86	50.97	1,160	98.77
12	280.03	277.39	278.14	103.99	102.94	103.27	51.03	50.71	50.77	1,110	98.70
13	278.81	276.62	277.88	103.90	102.63	103.44	50.83	50.49	50.70	990	98.68
14	278.75	277.04	277.75	104.21	103.41	103.56	50.85	50.55	50.69	930	98.69
15	278.61	276.54	277.37	104.02	103.17	103.50	50.75	50.46	50.66	890	98.61
18	277.19	273.90	274.31	103.15	101.28	101.49	50.71	50.38	50.46	1,090	98.61
19	275.06	272.95	274.14	101.98	100.94	101.42	50.69	50.29	50.52	980	98.59
20	275.62	273.41	274.35	102.52	101.48	101.90	50.81	50.60	50.69	960	98.67
21	275.24	273.43	274.45	102.55	101.68	102.03	50.89	50.60	50.69	800	98.68
22	275.24	273.74	274.43	102.39	101.64	101.94	50.84	50.68	50.75	910	98.73
25	274.61	272.86	273.57	101.75	101.17	101.59	50.84	50.60	50.70	840	98.77
26	274.37	272.28	273.17	101.76	101.07	101.46	50.83	50.51	50.62	890	98.77
27	274.33	272.72	273.84	102.39	101.49	101.99	50.70	50.51	50.65	930	98.72
28	275.28	273.35	274.41	103.02	102.13	102.56	50.75	50.59	50.61	980	98.76
29	275.93	274.12	275.04	103.49	102.77	103.31	50.87	50.60	50.79	890	98.81
			High 280.29			High 104.89			High 51.12		High 98.84
			Low 273.17			Low 101.42			Low 50.46		Low 98.59

SEPTEMBER, 1952

	−30 Industrials−			−20 Railroads−			−15 Utilities−			Daily Sales -000-	40 Bonds
	High	Low	Close	High	Low	Close	High	Low	Close		
2	277.25	275.10	276.40	104.20	103.28	103.83	51.00	50.79	50.94	970	98.60
3	278.16	275.95	277.15	104.14	103.25	103.43	51.17	50.90	51.05	1,200	98.60
4	278.10	276.03	276.76	103.53	102.70	103.05	51.11	50.83	51.00	1,120	98.60
5	277.43	275.18	276.50	102.89	102.02	102.48	51.16	50.88	50.99	1,040	98.67
8	277.55	275.38	275.87	102.44	101.16	101.31	51.11	50.81	50.94	1,170	98.64
9	276.29	273.13	273.53	100.96	99.05	99.12	50.94	50.42	50.47	1,310	98.65
10	273.01	269.56	271.65	99.39	97.35	98.69	50.28	49.61	49.98	1,590	98.62
11	273.25	270.90	272.11	99.46	98.55	98.88	50.36	49.93	50.11	970	98.58
12	272.46	269.66	271.02	98.97	97.87	98.50	50.31	49.98	50.17	1,040	98.57
15	271.14	267.91	268.38	98.57	97.07	97.18	50.25	49.75	49.91	1,100	98.55
16	269.74	267.08	269.03	98.31	96.87	98.06	49.94	49.50	49.83	1,140	98.50
17	271.18	268.89	270.43	98.91	98.23	98.63	49.87	49.56	49.70	1,000	98.56
18	271.12	268.81	269.72	98.76	98.07	98.42	49.98	49.67	49.83	1,030	98.54
19	271.26	268.62	270.55	99.27	98.08	99.15	49.97	49.76	49.87	1,150	98.49
22	272.09	269.56	270.77	100.33	99.29	99.44	50.15	49.92	50.09	1,160	98.42
23	272.24	269.48	271.65	101.79	99.19	101.65	50.22	49.97	50.17	1,240	98.30
24	273.19	271.06	272.26	102.92	101.47	102.16	50.36	50.03	50.14	1,390	98.25
25	273.74	271.44	272.42	102.48	101.55	101.89	50.42	50.16	50.35	1,210	98.27
26	273.33	271.14	271.95	102.46	101.38	101.59	50.38	50.17	50.29	1,180	98.29
29	272.76	276.51	271.73	101.80	101.10	101.28	50.37	50.03	50.24	970	98.34
30	272.21	269.98	270.61	101.50	100.15	100.35	50.39	50.01	50.17	1,120	98.28
		High	277.15		High	103.83		High	51.05		High 98.67
		Low	268.38		Low	97.18		Low	49.70		Low 98.25

OCTOBER, 1952

	−30 Industrials−			−20 Railroads−			−15 Utilities−			Daily Sales -000-	40 Bonds
	High	Low	Close	High	Low	Close	High	Low	Close		
1	271.08	269.21	270.17	100.34	99.54	100.10	50.43	49.94	50.31	1,060	98.27
2	271.55	269.72	270.75	100.73	99.94	100.17	50.50	50.18	50.36	1,040	98.23
3	271.85	269.52	270.55	100.46	99.85	99.98	50.47	50.24	50.36	980	98.23
6	271.20	269.29	270.00	100.09	99.26	99.52	50.46	50.12	50.22	1,070	98.21
7	271.04	268.97	269.88	99.90	99.35	99.58	50.38	50.00	50.11	950	98.17
8	271.91	269.52	271.40	101.31	99.86	100.81	50.33	50.09	50.18	1,260	98.14
9	272.36	270.15	270.98	101.56	100.68	101.05	50.29	49.94	50.00	1,090	98.10
10	271.81	269.94	270.61	101.57	100.73	101.25	50.18	49.88	49.99	1,070	98.08
14	271.59	269.48	270.43	101.32	100.49	100.66	50.08	49.78	49.88	1,130	97.93
15	270.59	266.09	267.12	100.35	97.87	98.39	49.83	49.04	49.18	1,730	97.88
16	267.45	263.33	264.87	99.25	97.21	98.56	49.33	48.69	48.90	1,730	07.74
17	268.36	265.21	267.30	100.61	99.08	100.43	49.34	48.92	49.09	1,360	07.74
20	268.06	265.36	266.63	100.55	99.65	100.07	49.44	49.06	49.13	1,050	97.72
21	267.18	265.09	265.84	100.32	99.45	99.63	49.36	49.10	49.23	990	97.77
22	265.64	262.60	263.06	99.51	98.29	98.39	49.22	48.74	48.81	1,160	97.83
23	264.93	262.01	263.87	99.69	98.38	99.37	49.04	48.73	48.92	1,260	97.89
24	266.31	263.39	265.46	100.23	99.16	99.67	49.08	48.90	49.00	1,060	97.93
27	266.65	264.73	265.90	100.51	99.63	99.94	49.24	48.94	49.19	1,000	98.03
28	266.80	264.87	265.72	100.16	99.41	99.69	49.31	49.00	49.18	1,080	98.05
29	266.72	264.65	265.46	99.70	99.05	99.22	49.50	49.15	49.45	1,020	98.17
30	266.57	264.54	265.72	99.37	98.69	99.07	49.61	49.33	49.50	1,090	98.27
31	269.96	265.78	269.23	101.09	99.40	100.77	50.01	49.56	49.94	1,760	98.37
		High	271.40		High	101.25		High	50.36		High 98.37
		Low	263.06		Low	98.39		Low	48.81		Low 97.72

NOVEMBER, 1952

	–30 Industrials–			–20 Railroads–			–15 Utilities–			Daily Sales -000-	40 Bonds
	High	Low	Close	High	Low	Close	High	Low	Close		
3	271.53	268.79	270.23	101.38	100.01	100.59	50.35	49.91	50.03	1,670	98.35
5	274.77	270.65	271.30	102.24	100.01	100.16	50.98	50.29	50.36	2,030	98.38
6	273.82	268.89	272.58	100.96	99.15	100.86	50.61	50.15	50.32	1,390	98.52
7	274.77	271.89	273.47	102.49	101.04	101.89	50.64	50.18	50.45	1,540	98.64
10	274.39	272.11	273.47	102.45	101.06	102.32	50.88	50.48	50.76	1,360	98.74
12	274.28	271.30	271.97	102.58	101.40	101.62	51.02	50.72	50.90	1,490	98.78
13	273.68	271.16	272.54	102.06	101.16	101.62	51.07	50.65	50.97	1,330	98.78
14	274.10	271.22	273.27	102.05	100.97	101.51	50.91	50.50	50.86	1,700	98.78
17	275.16	272.44	274.45	102.06	101.09	101.68	51.23	50.76	51.01	1,490	98.75
18	279.03	274.20	278.04	103.40	101.76	103.14	51.66	50.94	51.57	2,250	98.76
19	281.16	277.78	280.05	104.16	103.16	103.86	51.87	51.38	51.66	2,350	98.89
20	280.80	278.02	279.50	104.29	103.13	103.95	51.67	51.29	51.47	1,740	98.89
21	280.31	278.16	279.32	104.89	103.71	104.36	51.70	51.24	51.48	1,760	99.00
24	281.59	278.67	281.08	106.01	104.48	105.79	51.53	51.17	51.38	2,100	99.04
25	282.32	279.99	280.90	106.48	105.15	105.66	51.61	51.23	51.37	1,930	99.13
26	283.13	279.93	282.44	107.56	105.35	107.03	51.61	51.29	51.49	1,920	99.27
28	284.65	281.59	283.66	108.65	107.11	108.16	51.71	51.40	51.60	2,160	99.29
		High 283.66			High 108.16			High 51.66			High 99.29
		Low 270.23			Low 100.16			Low 50.03			Low 98.35

DECEMBER, 1952

	–30 Industrials–			–20 Railroads–			–15 Utilities–			Daily Sales -000-	40 Bonds
	High	Low	Close	High	Low	Close	High	Low	Close		
1	285.20	282.58	283.70	108.90	107.63	108.02	51.83	51.46	51.66	2,100	99.33
2	284.65	281.89	283.78	108.11	107.09	107.87	51.81	51.41	51.64	1,610	99.26
3	284.69	282.00	282.89	108.02	107.02	107.27	51.73	51.38	51.50	1,610	99.15
4	283.82	281.10	281.63	107.97	106.62	106.95	51.71	51.39	51.64	1,570	99.13
5	283.03	280.68	282.06	108.33	106.61	107.94	51.73	51.38	51.51	1,510	99.14
8	284.37	281.45	283.62	108.82	107.65	108.30	51.92	51.35	51.73	1,790	99.15
9	286.32	283.25	285.12	109.62	108.28	108.86	52.08	51.70	51.90	2,120	99.21
10	286.03	282.77	284.55	109.24	107.94	108.73	52.03	51.72	51.90	1,880	99.21
11	285.69	283.48	284.57	108.96	108.10	108.52	52.05	51.75	51.91	1,790	99.16
12	286.18	283.76	285.20	109.87	108.38	109.37	52.21	51.81	52.11	2,030	99.11
15	287.13	284.45	285.99	110.93	109.30	110.29	52.29	51.98	52.10	1,940	99.13
16	287.58	285.00	286.16	111.07	109.81	110.32	52.38	51.96	52.20	1,980	99.18
17	286.95	284.55	285.67	110.63	109.67	110.04	52.31	51.99	52.20	1,700	99.11
18	286.68	284.41	285.36	111.03	109.68	110.60	52.45	52.14	52.27	1,860	99.09
19	287.15	284.55	286.52	111.79	110.50	111.46	52.42	52.10	52.33	2,050	99.04
22	288.85	285.55	288.02	112.79	111.30	112.53	52.50	52.19	52.37	2,100	98.99
23	289.18	286.22	286.99	113.94	112.26	112.50	52.46	52.13	52.20	2,100	98.96
24	288.59	285.69	287.37	112.57	111.62	111.93	52.31	52.04	52.19	1,510	98.95
26	289.10	285.67	288.23	111.83	110.80	111.28	52.42	52.05	52.33	1,290	98.85
29	290.74	287.66	289.65	112.03	110.87	111.18	52.70	52.18	52.44	1,820	98.88
30	292.83	289.46	292.00	112.06	111.01	111.40	52.75	52.34	52.64	2,070	98.80
31	293.50	290.86	291.90	111.84	110.82	111.27	52.79	52.47	52.60	2,050	98.88
		High 292.00			High 112.53			High 52.64			High 99.33
		Low 281.63			Low 106.95			Low 51.50			Low 98.80

JANUARY, 1953

	-30 Industrials-			-20 Railroads-			-15 Utilities-			Daily Sales -000-	40 Bonds
	High	Low	Close	High	Low	Close	High	Low	Close		
2	293.56	290.30	292.14	111.51	110.70	111.18	52.65	52.16	52.35	1,450	98.89
5	295.06	291.51	293.79	112.10	111.01	111.37	52.67	52.30	52.57	2,130	98.95
6	294.25	290.25	292.18	111.60	109.42	110.23	52.70	52.23	52.43	2,080	98.99
7	291.96	288.69	290.76	110.26	108.78	109.73	52.50	52.16	52.39	1,760	98.93
8	292.02	289.48	290.36	111.12	109.94	110.33	52.64	52.31	52.50	1,780	98.95
9	290.46	286.09	287.52	110.80	108.47	109.47	52.43	51.88	51.95	2,080	98.87
12	287.88	284.29	285.24	109.57	108.42	108.91	52.17	51.68	51.82	1,500	98.77
13	288.63	285.10	286.85	110.45	109.08	109.79	52.10	51.76	52.00	1,680	98.75
14	288.47	285.63	287.37	110.06	109.36	109.72	52.15	51.84	52.13	1,370	98.74
15	288.85	286.40	288.18	109.91	109.09	109.52	52.22	51.96	52.14	1,450	98.64
16	288.87	285.12	287.17	109.53	108.15	108.64	52.28	51.85	52.06	1,710	98.37
19	287.98	285.30	286.97	109.15	108.51	108.96	52.15	51.86	52.03	1,360	98.30
20	289.16	286.28	288.00	109.88	108.84	109.34	52.21	51.96	52.11	1,490	98.36
21	288.63	286.56	287.60	109.37	108.61	109.06	52.16	51.84	51.95	1,300	98.41
22	288.87	286.70	287.84	109.69	108.89	109.25	52.12	51.87	51.98	1,380	98.50
23	288.59	285.77	286.89	109.47	108.79	109.11	52.07	51.82	51.98	1,340	98.53
26	287.68	285.12	286.54	109.53	108.65	109.14	52.14	51.86	52.01	1,420	98.54
27	287.96	285.75	286.81	110.82	109.21	110.55	52.38	52.03	52.26	1,550	98.53
28	288.21	285.87	287.39	111.60	110.50	111.22	52.46	52.12	52.39	1,640	98.57
29	289.12	286.44	287.96	112.39	111.25	112.06	52.77	52.41	52.57	1,830	98.56
30	290.46	287.54	289.77	112.72	111.69	112.21	52.76	52.49	52.68	1,760	98.53
		High	293.79		High	112.21		High	52.68	High	98.99
		Low	285.24		Low	108.64		Low	51.82	Low	98.30

FEBRUARY, 1953

	-30 Industrials-			-20 Railroads-			-15 Utilities-			Daily Sales -000-	40 Bonds
	High	Low	Close	High	Low	Close	High	Low	Close		
2	290.94	288.00	290.03	112.27	110.94	111.18	53.22	52.74	53.08	1,890	98.49
3	290.88	287.90	290.19	111.47	110.36	110.90	53.32	52.89	53.07	1,560	98.48
4	290.84	288.33	289.08	111.30	110.41	110.70	53.30	52.94	53.11	1,660	98.49
5	289.04	285.16	286.20	111.00	108.89	109.63	53.19	52.64	52.69	1,900	98.39
6	286.42	282.14	282.85	109.40	107.58	107.85	52.85	52.33	52.45	1,870	98.23
9	283.31	279.93	281.96	107.66	106.25	107.26	52.37	52.00	52.25	1,780	98.18
10	283.50	280.84	281.67	108.00	106.68	106.90	52.60	52.20	52.40	1,350	98.19
11	283.05	280.53	281.57	108.33	107.01	108.06	52.61	52.20	52.50	1,240	98.18
13	283.86	281.10	283.11	109.15	108.21	108.79	52.81	52.49	52.61	1,350	98.22
16	284.25	281.71	282.18	109.08	107.89	108.11	52.90	52.60	52.70	1,330	98.17
17	282.73	280.23	281.51	108.09	106.73	107.32	52.69	52.33	52.42	1,290	98.15
18	281.96	279.72	281.14	108.25	107.15	107.85	52.47	52.17	52.32	1,220	98.11
19	283.01	280.51	281.55	109.27	107.90	108.89	52.44	52.11	52.26	1,390	98.23
20	283.29	280.74	281.89	110.07	108.72	109.22	52.51	52.19	52.34	1,400	98.14
24	285.04	282.04	282.99	111.00	109.36	109.92	52.70	52.35	52.51	2,300	98.09
25	285.22	281.93	284.45	110.47	109.40	110.07	52.68	52.33	52.56	2,360	97.95
26	285.95	283.27	284.35	110.80	109.53	109.79	52.72	52.47	52.57	2,290	97.87
27	285.40	282.32	284.27	110.14	109.09	110.05	52.70	52.33	52.50	1,990	97.82
		High	290.19		High	111.18		High	53.11	High	98.49
		Low	281.14		Low	106.90		Low	52.25	Low	97.82

MARCH, 1953

	-30 Industrials-			-20 Railroads-			-15 Utilities-			Daily Sales -000-	40 Bonds
	High	Low	Close	High	Low	Close	High	Low	Close		
2	285.67	283.09	284.71	110.56	109.68	109.90	52.55	52.30	52.48	1,760	97.78
3	286.40	283.84	285.99	110.25	109.44	109.87	52.70	52.39	52.63	1,850	97.80
4	286.09	282.52	283.70	109.93	108.09	108.64	52.77	52.32	52.50	2,010	97.80
5	284.84	282.46	283.86	109.22	108.22	109.05	52.63	52.27	52.45	1,540	97.91
6	285.28	283.01	284.82	109.27	108.57	108.93	52.74	52.39	52.57	1,690	97.97
9	285.99	283.88	284.90	109.57	108.74	109.14	52.78	52.40	52.64	1,600	97.96
10	285.97	283.17	285.22	109.92	108.82	109.67	52.92	52.55	52.86	1,530	97.95
11	288.75	284.94	288.02	110.86	109.75	110.52	53.21	52.82	53.10	1,890	97.96
12	289.14	286.70	288.00	111.13	110.00	110.19	53.46	53.10	53.36	1,780	97.88
13	289.59	286.76	289.04	110.70	109.81	110.45	53.93	53.19	53.88	1,760	97.86
16	290.52	288.08	289.52	111.40	110.11	111.36	54.14	53.65	53.77	1,770	97.86
17	291.78	289.10	290.64	112.80	111.53	112.03	53.96	53.57	53.77	2,110	97.91
18	291.96	289.26	290.32	112.25	111.41	111.62	53.93	53.60	53.73	2,110	97.92
19	291.09	288.49	289.97	112.01	111.03	111.58	53.83	53.60	53.74	1,840	97.86
20	291.01	288.63	289.69	111.76	111.17	111.40	53.76	53.53	53.65	1,730	97.89
23	289.69	286.74	287.39	111.58	110.54	110.79	53.73	53.27	53.36	1,750	97.80
24	289.18	286.72	288.83	111.98	110.50	111.77	53.76	53.33	53.64	1,970	97.68
25	290.78	287.47	287.98	112.87	111.30	111.40	54.01	53.71	53.81	2,320	97.69
26	289.08	285.63	286.60	111.79	110.35	110.81	53.84	53.34	53.43	2,000	97.55
27	288.63	285.97	287.33	111.43	110.64	110.94	53.58	53.25	53.50	1,640	97.39
30	286.16	281.59	283.07	110.11	107.71	108.22	53.41	52.86	53.06	2,740	97.29
31	282.73	277.57	279.87	108.44	105.50	107.02	52.95	51.97	52.25	3,120	97.26
		High	290.64		High	112.03		High	53.88		High 97.97
		Low	279.87		Low	107.02		Low	52.25		Low 97.26

APRIL, 1953

	-30 Industrials-			-20 Railroads-			-15 Utilities-			Daily Sales -000-	40 Bonds
	High	Low	Close	High	Low	Close	High	Low	Close		
1	281.47	277.53	280.09	107.60	106.10	107.32	52.49	51.87	52.27	2,240	97.21
2	281.81	279.26	280.03	107.60	106.00	106.11	52.71	52.27	52.42	1,720	97.20
6	279.42	272.40	274.10	105.75	102.29	103.11	52.26	51.37	51.46	3,050	97.19
7	276.33	271.99	275.16	104.85	102.93	104.55	51.66	51.08	51.41	2,500	97.17
8	278.85	275.38	276.84	106.05	104.57	105.14	52.25	51.57	52.09	1,860	97.15
9	278.08	274.83	276.23	105.34	104.34	104.43	52.17	51.89	52.00	1,520	96.95
10	276.52	274.28	275.50	104.65	103.57	104.27	52.07	51.68	51.95	1,360	96.94
13	276.46	274.10	274.73	104.51	103.86	104.04	52.14	51.82	51.97	1,280	96.92
14	276.76	273.86	275.85	105.09	104.02	104.91	52.14	51.77	52.03	1,480	96.91
15	278.79	276.01	277.35	106.30	105.33	105.84	52.20	51.91	52.10	1,580	96.89
16	278.51	275.97	276.74	106.13	105.06	105.22	52.23	51.87	51.87	1,310	96.85
17	276.86	273.70	274.41	104.83	103.28	103.47	52.14	51.58	51.73	1,430	96.48
20	276.62	272.80	275.99	104.21	102.62	104.13	51.75	51.37	51.65	1,520	96.40
21	277.88	274.67	275.48	104.66	103.64	103.88	52.01	51.68	51.77	1,250	96.28
22	275.93	272.86	273.55	104.04	102.62	102.69	51.69	51.35	51.43	1,390	96.12
23	273.51	270.15	270.73	103.22	101.42	101.63	51.58	50.81	50.88	1,920	95.96
24	272.30	269.25	271.26	102.27	101.02	101.88	50.95	50.35	50.74	1,780	95.85
27	274.14	271.30	272.70	103.45	102.29	102.67	51.02	50.62	50.71	1,400	95.69
28	274.59	271.32	273.96	103.37	102.17	103.19	50.79	50.43	50.64	1,330	95.55
29	276.37	273.31	275.38	104.00	103.12	103.40	51.12	50.64	50.89	1,310	95.52
30	276.07	273.31	274.75	103.44	102.58	103.07	51.12	50.69	51.07	1,140	95.43
		High	280.09		High	107.32		High	52.42		High 97.21
		Low	270.73		Low	101.63		Low	50.64		Low 95.43

MAY, 1953

	-30 Industrials-			-20 Railroads-			-15 Utilities-			Daily Sales -000-	40 Bonds
	High	Low	Close	High	Low	Close	High	Low	Close		
1	276.33	273.59	275.66	103.53	102.90	103.37	51.37	51.02	51.22	1,200	95.36
4	279.46	275.52	278.34	105.12	103.72	104.77	51.47	51.09	51.25	1,520	95.24
5	280.01	277.31	278.22	105.12	104.36	104.53	51.44	51.09	51.26	1,290	95.03
6	279.32	276.94	278.14	104.73	104.05	104.45	51.32	51.03	51.12	1,110	95.07
7	278.65	276.54	277.43	104.33	103.50	103.66	51.19	50.90	50.96	1,110	94.95
8	278.55	275.85	278.22	105.00	103.28	104.85	51.02	50.80	50.97	1,220	94.89
11	279.78	277.59	278.79	105.15	104.29	104.66	51.07	50.78	50.88	1,010	94.84
12	278.91	276.29	277.09	104.65	103.54	103.70	51.01	50.70	50.77	1,080	94.84
13	277.57	275.10	276.80	103.90	103.03	103.50	50.92	50.66	50.78	1,120	94.78
14	278.71	276.25	277.96	105.16	103.70	105.01	50.86	50.58	50.83	1,210	94.82
15	279.18	276.70	277.90	105.79	104.92	105.22	51.07	50.83	50.97	1,200	94.87
18	278.14	275.75	276.92	105.76	104.64	105.59	51.09	50.88	51.04	1,080	94.88
19	277.04	274.81	275.91	106.01	104.69	105.38	50.98	50.57	50.66	1,120	94.87
20	278.53	275.12	278.04	108.69	105.48	108.36	51.05	50.71	50.98	1,690	94.68
21	279.84	277.63	278.51	109.21	107.88	108.21	51.24	50.87	51.10	1,590	94.66
22	279.28	276.72	278.16	108.85	107.74	108.30	51.25	50.98	51.21	1,350	94.68
25	278.73	276.82	277.47	109.09	108.13	108.73	51.21	50.88	51.00	1,180	94.57
26	277.43	275.12	276.37	108.73	107.52	108.10	51.13	50.78	51.01	1,160	94.54
27	276.58	273.53	273.96	108.60	105.45	105.91	51.13	50.78	50.88	1,330	94.49
28	273.76	270.65	271.48	106.16	104.53	105.38	50.78	50.52	50.64	1,240	94.44
29	273.07	270.88	272.28	105.94	105.03	105.42	50.95	50.61	50.83	920	94.28
		High	278.79		High	108.73		High	51.26		High 95.36
		Low	271.48		Low	103.37		Low	50.64		Low 94.28

JUNE, 1953

	-30 Industrials-			-20 Railroads-			-15 Utilities-			Daily Sales -000-	40 Bonds
	High	Low	Close	High	Low	Close	High	Low	Close		
1	272.64	267.91	268.40	105.47	102.75	102.82	50.79	50.28	50.32	1,490	94.08
2	270.41	267.00	269.84	103.82	102.26	103.48	50.44	50.02	50.25	1,450	93.77
3	271.77	268.99	269.60	104.79	103.26	103.84	50.41	50.02	50.19	1,050	93.79
4	269.98	266.17	267.63	103.81	101.70	102.58	50.17	49.59	49.67	1,400	93.69
5	269.33	266.57	268.32	103.75	102.32	103.28	49.70	49.31	49.40	1,160	93.66
8	269.46	267.28	267.91	103.89	102.81	103.06	49.52	49.15	49.24	1,000	93.68
9	268.14	262.90	263.39	102.75	99.28	99.58	49.16	48.41	48.44	2,200	93.26
10	264.18	260.89	263.35	101.16	99.22	100.80	48.45	47.90	48.17	1,960	93.21
11	266.68	263.39	264.99	102.82	101.12	101.97	48.66	48.21	48.50	1,220	93.21
12	266.86	264.59	265.78	102.54	101.74	101.98	48.62	48.31	48.48	920	93.28
15	266.41	263.12	263.87	102.08	100.24	100.81	48.62	48.30	48.44	1,090	93.15
16	264.10	260.75	262.88	100.87	99.06	100.48	48.25	47.56	47.88	1,370	93.02
17	266.57	262.88	265.74	102.91	101.16	102.49	48.26	47.78	48.08	1,150	92.96
18	267.20	264.93	265.86	103.35	102.13	102.65	48.09	47.79	47.92	1,010	93.04
19	266.53	264.24	265.80	103.33	102.16	103.18	48.09	47.75	47.88	890	92.97
22	268.70	265.88	267.26	104.87	103.52	104.19	48.08	47.65	47.87	1,030	92.98
23	269.15	266.68	268.48	105.50	104.13	105.43	48.06	47.71	47.94	1,080	93.05
24	269.11	266.80	267.79	105.83	104.57	104.82	48.03	47.79	47.93	1,030	93.17
25	270.31	267.85	268.93	106.32	105.17	105.38	48.45	48.14	48.38	1,160	93.41
26	269.70	268.01	269.05	105.74	104.84	105.33	48.57	48.24	48.52	830	93.62
29	269.70	267.26	268.20	105.95	104.95	105.10	48.68	48.32	48.51	800	93.59
30	269.03	267.06	268.26	105.32	104.39	104.77	48.62	48.33	48.54	820	93.71
		High	269.84		High	105.43		High	50.32		High 94.08
		Low	262.88		Low	99.58		Low	47.87		Low 92.96

JULY, 1953

	-30 Industrials-			-20 Railroads-			-15 Utilities-			Daily Sales -000-	40 Bonds
	High	Low	Close	High	Low	Close	High	Low	Close		
1	269.90	267.51	269.39	107.01	104.98	106.57	48.76	48.48	48.69	910	93.77
2	271.20	269.15	270.23	107.76	106.61	106.84	49.02	48.66	48.88	1,030	93.94
3	271.44	269.41	270.53	107.27	106.61	107.15	49.18	48.91	49.15	830	93.97
6	271.71	269.94	270.88	107.54	106.77	107.03	49.41	49.14	49.24	820	94.04
7	272.60	270.17	272.13	107.70	106.45	107.47	49.50	49.18	49.36	1,030	94.13
8	272.82	271.06	272.19	108.34	107.48	107.95	49.57	49.26	49.44	950	94.24
9	272.38	270.98	271.32	108.00	107.02	107.38	49.55	49.34	49.50	910	94.33
10	271.93	270.31	271.06	107.20	106.45	106.81	49.51	49.26	49.39	860	94.47
13	271.16	268.08	268.52	106.55	104.71	105.03	49.38	49.09	49.25	1,120	94.43
14	269.19	266.96	268.06	105.13	103.69	104.75	49.36	49.02	49.16	1,030	94.57
15	270.02	267.73	268.75	105.84	104.61	105.01	49.26	48.98	49.06	840	94.74
16	270.17	268.48	269.41	105.48	104.84	105.19	49.19	48.79	48.90	790	94.65
17	271.59	268.95	270.96	106.26	105.26	106.03	49.20	48.98	49.08	840	94.73
20	270.94	268.85	269.74	106.00	104.82	105.48	49.17	48.87	49.01	830	94.77
21	269.90	268.28	268.99	105.53	104.57	104.86	48.98	48.73	48.82	850	94.84
22	270.23	267.95	269.39	105.26	104.45	105.04	48.71	48.45	48.60	900	94.82
23	271.14	268.89	269.94	106.10	105.10	105.69	48.85	48.59	48.70	1,000	94.92
24	270.92	268.79	269.76	105.81	105.03	105.22	48.95	48.65	48.85	890	94.96
27	270.71	267.83	268.46	105.22	103.51	103.70	48.81	48.56	48.66	1,210	94.99
28	269.52	267.30	269.13	103.53	102.22	103.09	48.78	48.51	48.65	1,080	95.06
29	271.16	268.83	270.43	103.80	102.90	103.55	49.04	48.72	48.89	1,000	95.12
30	273.41	270.49	272.82	105.19	103.77	104.98	49.22	48.94	49.05	1,200	95.12
31	275.85	272.58	275.38	106.23	105.16	105.86	49.60	49.02	49.45	1,320	95.34

High 275.38 High 107.95 High 49.50 High 95.34
Low 268.06 Low 103.09 Low 48.60 Low 93.77

AUGUST, 1953

	-30 Industrials-			-20 Railroads-			-15 Utilities-			Daily Sales -000-	40 Bonds
	High	Low	Close	High	Low	Close	High	Low	Close		
3	277.19	274.71	276.13	106.45	105.55	106.10	49.88	49.49	49.75	1,160	95.33
4	276.46	274.28	275.68	106.17	105.32	105.81	50.00	49.70	49.88	1,000	95.32
5	275.40	273.19	275.08	106.59	105.37	106.48	49.87	49.55	49.80	1,080	95.28
6	276.54	274.63	275.77	107.36	106.39	106.97	50.15	49.81	50.00	1,200	95.35
7	276.46	274.20	275.54	107.15	106.32	106.63	50.25	50.08	50.19	950	95.37
10	276.48	274.39	275.32	106.65	105.70	105.86	50.64	50.24	50.49	1,090	95.40
11	276.05	273.72	275.30	105.87	104.82	105.11	50.78	50.43	50.71	940	95.40
12	276.92	273.98	276.42	105.92	104.82	105.73	50.93	50.60	50.84	990	95.45
13	278.30	275.75	276.74	106.32	105.60	105.75	51.02	50.66	50.86	1,040	95.46
14	277.33	274.89	275.71	105.52	104.30	104.70	51.03	50.75	50.88	1,000	95.43
17	276.13	273.92	275.04	104.77	103.92	104.17	50.89	50.59	50.77	910	95.39
18	275.91	273.13	273.29	104.55	102.97	103.02	50.96	50.69	50.82	1,030	95.46
19	273.01	270.06	271.50	102.89	101.36	102.11	50.82	50.47	50.62	1,400	95.46
20	272.66	270.41	271.73	102.89	102.05	102.66	50.84	50.48	50.64	860	95.36
21	272.80	270.81	271.93	103.07	102.29	102.78	50.89	50.55	50.79	850	95.31
24	271.99	268.06	268.70	102.63	99.92	100.07	50.89	50.53	50.61	1,320	95.32
25	268.83	265.92	267.45	100.49	98.50	99.71	50.54	50.25	50.42	1,470	95.27
26	269.17	266.27	266.51	100.85	99.26	99.47	50.63	50.31	50.38	1,060	95.24
27	267.45	264.65	265.68	99.85	98.06	98.41	50.47	50.21	50.25	1,290	95.20
28	266.86	264.89	265.74	99.22	98.16	98.37	50.35	49.99	50.05	1,060	95.15
31	265.70	260.83	261.22	98.29	95.24	95.63	50.14	49.55	49.60	2,190	95.05

High 276.74 High 106.97 High 50.88 High 95.46
Low 261.22 Low 95.63 Low 49.60 Low 95.05

SEPTEMBER, 1953

	-30 Industrials-			-20 Railroads-			-15 Utilities-			Daily Sales -000-	40 Bonds
	High	Low	Close	High	Low	Close	High	Low	Close		
1	263.23	260.32	262.54	96.97	95.28	96.62	49.66	49.18	49.44	1,580	95.00
2	265.21	262.43	263.96	98.02	96.61	97.14	49.66	49.38	49.55	1,110	95.00
3	264.65	262.50	263.61	97.23	96.65	96.65	49.74	49.46	49.62	900	94.93
4	265.09	262.70	264.34	97.10	96.29	96.93	49.80	49.59	49.71	770	94.90
8	266.23	264.04	265.42	97.53	96.84	97.14	49.87	49.67	49.82	740	94.88
9	266.23	264.56	265.48	97.32	96.60	96.92	49.93	49.67	49.84	860	94.91
10	265.38	262.58	262.88	96.53	94.42	94.73	49.81	49.52	49.54	1,010	94.80
11	262.37	258.94	259.71	94.15	92.05	92.97	49.46	48.96	49.07	1,930	94.70
14	260.20	255.29	255.49	93.37	90.53	90.56	49.10	48.40	48.50	2,550	94.59
15	258.68	254.36	257.67	92.91	90.39	92.67	48.53	47.94	48.30	2,850	94.52
16	260.95	257.97	259.07	94.60	92.96	93.33	48.56	48.09	48.33	1,570	94.57
17	261.30	258.42	259.88	94.16	92.97	93.41	48.65	48.24	48.38	1,290	94.66
18	259.84	257.65	258.78	93.09	91.74	92.01	48.59	48.31	48.42	1,190	94.56
21	260.00	257.36	258.01	92.63	91.52	92.11	48.76	48.31	48.56	1,070	94.60
22	261.89	257.85	261.28	94.24	92.41	94.00	49.10	48.64	49.02	1,300	94.80
23	263.83	261.40	262.35	95.06	94.03	94.26	49.25	48.86	49.08	1,240	94.95
24	263.83	261.36	262.45	94.66	93.82	94.04	49.37	48.99	49.28	1,020	95.10
25	264.06	261.78	263.31	94.30	93.60	93.99	49.40	49.17	49.35	910	95.14
28	265.86	263.16	264.79	95.68	94.21	95.31	49.54	49.29	49.45	1,150	95.26
29	266.61	263.90	264.77	95.95	94.69	94.88	49.80	49.44	49.65	1,170	95.29
30	265.38	262.94	264.04	94.48	93.64	93.90	49.70	49.29	49.48	940	95.39
	High 265.48			High 97.14			High 49.84				High 95.39
	Low 255.49			Low 90.56			Low 48.30				Low 94.52

OCTOBER, 1953

	-30 Industrials-			-20 Railroads-			-15 Utilities-			Daily Sales -000-	40 Bonds
	High	Low	Close	High	Low	Close	High	Low	Close		
1	266.47	263.79	265.68	94.55	93.64	94.24	49.77	49.32	49.63	940	95.59
2	267.59	265.32	266.70	94.40	93.72	93.91	49.87	49.63	49.78	890	95.72
5	267.59	264.52	265.48	93.93	92.92	93.14	50.04	49.74	49.94	930	95.81
6	265.25	262.45	264.26	93.00	91.59	92.32	50.01	49.63	49.87	1,100	95.86
7	266.86	263.57	266.53	93.91	92.36	93.81	50.16	49.81	50.10	1,010	95.90
8	267.97	265.96	266.72	94.42	93.46	93.64	50.36	50.05	50.22	960	96.04
9	267.69	265.52	267.04	93.98	93.15	93.68	50.38	50.08	50.33	900	96.09
13	267.69	265.36	266.09	93.94	93.18	93.60	50.43	50.05	50.27	1,130	96.25
14	268.22	265.64	267.51	94.44	93.29	94.20	50.60	50.21	50.53	1,290	96.25
15	271.81	267.41	271.22	96.19	94.25	96.03	50.82	50.39	50.70	1,710	96.30
16	273.94	271.02	272.80	97.58	96.22	97.05	50.96	50.60	50.77	1,620	96.33
19	273.78	271.14	273.31	97.58	96.33	97.44	50.95	50.59	50.83	1,190	96.34
20	275.16	272.36	273.90	97.84	96.97	97.15	51.11	50.75	51.03	1,280	96.37
21	274.61	272.30	273.74	97.55	96.61	97.19	51.07	50.82	50.99	1,320	96.40
22	275.77	272.97	274.89	97.61	96.79	97.27	51.09	50.83	50.94	1,330	96.48
23	276.52	274.12	275.34	97.45	96.75	96.92	51.10	50.81	50.97	1,330	96.60
26	276.56	273.88	274.43	97.27	96.10	96.37	51.01	50.54	50.64	1,340	96.67
27	274.33	271.85	273.35	96.24	95.14	95.72	50.73	50.46	50.55	1,170	96.76
28	274.69	272.13	274.14	96.03	95.23	95.79	50.83	50.55	50.79	1,260	96.90
29	276.94	273.92	276.31	97.62	95.91	97.49	51.18	50.83	51.07	1,610	96.94
30	277.04	274.87	275.81	98.01	97.00	97.26	51.46	51.04	51.14	1,400	97.06
	High 276.31			High 97.49			High 51.14				High 97.06
	Low 264.26			Low 92.32			Low 49.63				Low 95.59

NOVEMBER, 1953

	−30 Industrials−			−20 Railroads−			−15 Utilities−			Daily Sales -000-	40 Bonds
	High	Low	Close	High	Low	Close	High	Low	Close		
2	278.18	274.83	276.72	97.52	96.66	97.02	51.52	51.05	51.39	1,340	97.08
4	277.72	274.83	276.82	97.19	96.26	96.72	51.54	51.19	51.44	1,480	97.18
5	280.33	276.80	279.09	97.76	96.55	97.43	51.73	51.34	51.49	1,720	97.21
6	280.25	277.57	278.83	99.18	97.50	98.25	51.65	51.29	51.50	1,700	97.26
9	279.93	276.80	278.26	98.82	97.89	98.21	51.56	51.30	51.45	1,440	97.26
10	277.86	275.06	275.89	97.85	97.05	97.41	51.59	51.31	51.39	1,340	97.29
12	277.65	274.63	276.23	98.10	97.18	97.50	51.54	51.11	51.33	1,390	97.14
13	278.08	275.16	277.53	97.81	97.01	97.37	51.65	51.30	51.57	1,540	97.20
16	278.57	275.48	275.93	97.77	96.60	96.77	51.74	51.44	51.57	1,490	97.16
17	275.58	273.01	273.88	97.12	96.07	96.61	51.43	51.20	51.32	1,250	96.99
18	275.52	273.05	274.51	97.21	96.34	96.96	51.34	50.98	51.31	1,250	97.00
19	277.02	274.16	276.09	98.08	96.87	97.52	51.55	51.20	51.39	1,420	97.02
20	277.47	274.79	276.05	97.52	96.72	97.00	51.67	51.34	51.52	1,300	96.98
23	276.58	273.80	275.42	96.82	95.76	96.22	51.82	51.46	51.70	1,410	96.97
24	277.61	274.26	277.13	96.57	95.54	96.30	51.91	51.58	51.86	1,470	96.92
25	278.87	276.40	277.78	96.77	95.67	96.37	51.96	51.66	51.80	1,540	96.86
27	280.78	277.19	280.23	97.75	96.28	97.68	52.06	51.75	51.94	1,600	96.90
30	282.46	279.80	281.37	99.07	97.83	98.86	52.42	51.94	52.33	1,960	96.77
		High	281.37		High	98.86		High	52.33		High 97.29
		Low	273.88		Low	96.22		Low	51.31		Low 96.77

DECEMBER, 1953

	−30 Industrials−			−20 Railroads−			−15 Utilities−			Daily Sales -000-	40 Bonds
	High	Low	Close	High	Low	Close	High	Low	Close		
1	282.08	279.46	281.10	99.39	98.26	98.91	52.61	52.28	52.52	1,580	96.75
2	283.74	280.33	282.81	98.39	98.33	98.88	52.84	52.46	52.78	1,850	96.84
3	285.20	282.10	283.25	99.49	98.34	98.52	53.07	52.68	52.97	1,740	97.00
4	284.11	281.55	282.71	98.69	97.97	98.33	53.10	52.83	53.01	1,390	97.03
7	283.50	281.20	282.00	98.55	97.57	97.75	52.93	52.61	52.72	1,410	97.03
8	282.48	279.34	281.45	97.44	96.55	96.92	52.70	52.47	52.63	1,390	96.98
9	282.54	279.78	281.12	97.21	96.59	96.88	52.80	52.54	52.71	1,410	96.99
10	281.53	278.93	279.89	97.24	96.43	96.72	53.01	52.63	52.88	1,420	96.99
11	280.76	278.38	279.91	96.60	95.89	96.22	53.12	52.67	52.86	1,440	97.06
14	280.98	278.18	279.26	96.66	95.73	95.97	53.01	52.65	52.81	1,540	97.11
15	280.27	277.49	279.52	96.04	95.13	95.73	52.80	52.46	52.62	1,450	97.10
16	283.88	279.36	282.87	97.15	95.89	96.95	52.76	52.37	52.61	1,880	97.18
17	284.55	281.57	282.67	97.75	96.70	96.97	52.68	52.44	52.57	1,600	97.12
18	284.35	281.71	283.54	97.32	96.61	97.02	52.68	52.40	52.58	1,550	97.06
21	284.69	282.38	282.99	97.18	96.25	96.38	52.79	52.47	52.70	1,690	97.01
22	282.85	278.95	279.99	96.12	94.82	94.97	52.60	52.19	52.31	1,720	96.99
23	281.08	278.14	279.84	95.60	94.49	95.10	52.27	51.92	52.18	1,570	97.01
24	281.69	279.15	280.92	95.57	94.86	95.22	52.25	51.93	52.18	1,270	97.10
28	281.25	278.81	279.91	95.38	94.36	94.60	52.27	51.89	52.12	1,570	97.13
29	279.74	275.91	278.30	94.43	92.69	93.58	52.14	51.80	51.97	2,140	97.19
30	281.08	277.92	280.43	94.66	93.59	94.38	52.18	51.85	52.03	2,050	97.32
31	282.18	279.52	280.90	94.89	93.86	94.03	52.22	51.87	52.04	2,490	97.34
		High	283.54		High	98.91		High	53.01		High 97.34
		Low	279.26		Low	93.58		Low	51.97		Low 96.75

JANUARY, 1954

	-30 Industrials-			-20 Railroads-			-15 Utilities-			Daily Sales -000-	40 Bonds
	High	Low	Close	High	Low	Close	High	Low	Close		
4	283.48	279.72	282.89	95.54	94.09	95.50	52.41	51.86	52.22	1,310	97.38
5	285.34	282.65	284.19	96.75	95.71	96.41	52.57	52.11	52.52	1,520	97.48
6	285.67	283.05	283.96	96.93	96.08	96.39	52.53	52.34	52.48	1,460	97.60
7	284.86	281.83	282.60	97.02	95.84	96.07	52.64	52.26	52.47	1,540	97.55
8	283.01	280.39	281.51	95.91	94.96	95.14	52.66	52.29	52.55	1,260	97.61
11	281.67	278.91	279.87	95.37	94.36	94.84	52.73	52.44	52.57	1,220	97.66
12	282.54	279.46	281.51	96.12	94.83	95.88	52.93	52.50	52.80	1,250	97.71
13	284.37	281.12	283.03	97.05	96.07	96.48	53.22	52.78	53.06	1,420	97.89
14	285.67	282.83	284.49	97.44	96.41	96.97	53.49	53.05	53.34	1,530	97.95
15	288.10	284.49	286.72	98.64	96.92	98.08	53.72	53.18	53.54	2,180	98.08
18	287.78	284.69	286.03	98.50	97.74	98.07	53.91	53.52	53.74	1,580	98.10
19	289.14	285.24	288.27	99.59	97.86	99.43	53.87	53.43	53.67	1,840	98.17
20	290.15	287.58	289.14	100.46	99.18	99.66	53.94	53.56	53.73	1,960	98.35
21	290.66	287.68	289.48	99.97	99.04	99.36	53.82	53.51	53.67	1,780	98.43
22	290.86	288.18	289.65	100.71	99.23	100.32	54.03	53.52	53.88	1,890	98.58
25	291.29	288.27	290.40	100.95	99.96	100.41	54.13	53.65	53.88	1,860	98.56
26	293.44	290.11	292.85	101.60	100.28	101.26	54.16	53.86	54.09	2,120	98.81
27	294.56	291.53	292.22	101.76	100.45	100.73	54.29	53.95	54.07	2,020	98.81
28	293.12	289.81	291.51	100.91	100.03	100.65	54.19	53.93	54.13	1,730	98.88
29	293.81	290.86	292.39	102.19	100.54	101.84	54.16	53.95	54.09	1,950	99.05
		High	292.85		High	101.84		High	54.13		High 99.05
		Low	279.87		Low	94.84		Low	52.22		Low 97.38

FEBRUARY, 1954

	-30 Industrials-			-20 Railroads-			-15 Utilities-			Daily Sales -000-	40 Bonds
	High	Low	Close	High	Low	Close	High	Low	Close		
1	293.50	290.46	291.84	102.50	101.23	101.53	54.21	53.90	54.11	1,740	99.09
2	291.88	289.75	291.17	101.69	100.54	100.96	54.33	53.94	54.21	1,420	99.12
3	292.99	289.20	292.32	102.38	100.98	102.10	54.42	53.98	54.24	1,690	99.19
4	295.10	292.06	294.03	103.39	102.36	103.04	54.56	54.15	54.38	2,040	99.42
5	295.43	292.53	293.97	104.02	102.86	103.35	54.67	54.28	54.49	2,030	99.64
8	294.92	292.20	293.58	103.60	102.69	103.13	54.64	54.32	54.42	2,180	99.66
9	294.84	291.94	293.79	103.24	102.15	102.62	54.70	54.21	54.41	1,880	99.79
10	294.50	292.00	292.95	103.62	102.28	103.09	54.59	54.25	54.47	1,790	99.86
11	294.84	291.27	292.45	104.08	102.86	103.21	54.66	54.32	54.52	1,860	99.85
12	294.78	291.90	293.99	104.13	102.90	103.49	54.67	54.47	54.58	1,730	99.89
15	294.92	291.93	292.55	104.50	103.07	103.31	54.71	54.34	54.55	2,080	99.91
16	292.95	288.61	289.61	102.87	101.61	101.89	54.58	54.22	54.36	1,870	99.88
17	290.92	287.37	290.11	102.95	101.11	102.51	54.35	53.91	54.23	1,740	99.83
18	292.67	289.08	291.51	103.26	102.25	102.63	54.40	54.12	54.32	1,500	99.82
19	292.59	289.87	291.07	102.87	101.87	102.38	54.53	54.18	54.39	1,510	99.87
23	291.98	289.00	290.03	102.50	101.36	101.69	54.47	54.12	54.33	1,470	99.94
24	290.42	287.84	289.54	101.67	100.85	101.34	54.43	54.13	54.30	1,350	99.99
25	292.04	289.06	291.41	102.24	101.22	101.89	54.59	54.14	54.46	1,470	100.10
26	295.19	290.78	294.54	102.68	101.67	102.20	54.82	54.36	54.67	1,910	100.24
		High	294.54		High	103.49		High	54.67		High 100.24
		Low	289.54		Low	100.96		Low	54.11		Low 99.09

MARCH, 1954

	—30 Industrials—			—20 Railroads—			—15 Utilities—			Daily Sales -000-	40 Bonds
	High	Low	Close	High	Low	Close	High	Low	Close		
1	297.80	294.23	296.55	102.51	101.61	102.02	54.95	54.44	54.70	2,040	100.41
2	298.66	294.78	297.48	102.46	101.40	102.14	54.81	54.43	54.71	1,980	100.50
3	299.65	295.79	297.03	102.64	100.91	101.63	55.00	54.70	54.81	2,240	100.57
4	298.80	295.37	297.48	103.07	101.22	102.47	54.83	54.55	54.74	1,830	100.59
5	300.68	296.50	299.45	103.57	102.20	102.99	55.09	54.54	54.92	2,030	100.63
8	300.66	297.44	298.64	103.38	102.07	102.44	55.25	54.83	55.18	1,650	100.55
9	300.50	297.09	299.45	102.54	101.66	102.25	55.32	54.92	55.26	1,630	100.64
10	300.95	298.01	299.59	102.54	101.63	102.07	55.61	55.22	55.53	1,870	100.71
11	301.68	298.76	300.83	102.87	101.71	102.10	55.98	55.57	55.83	2,050	100.75
12	302.17	298.76	299.71	102.44	101.20	101.52	56.08	55.74	55.91	1,980	100.73
15	300.12	296.81	298.88	101.57	100.51	101.12	56.02	55.64	55.84	1,680	100.81
16	300.50	297.34	298.09	101.92	100.65	101.03	55.94	55.56	55.68	1,540	100.84
17	299.22	296.14	298.31	101.91	100.45	101.65	55.92	55.49	55.87	1,740	100.88
18	301.44	297.99	300.10	102.60	101.56	102.14	56.16	55.80	55.98	2,020	100.91
19	302.65	300.12	301.44	102.87	101.96	102.28	56.53	55.99	56.35	1,930	101.02
22	302.80	299.49	301.60	102.51	101.57	102.06	56.61	56.15	56.48	1,800	100.99
23	302.49	298.39	299.02	102.20	100.45	100.81	56.65	56.21	56.29	2,180	100.96
24	299.73	295.59	296.89	100.81	99.52	100.05	56.22	55.82	55.98	1,900	100.89
25	297.68	294.76	296.40	99.98	98.76	99.36	56.07	55.64	55.87	1,720	100.87
26	300.10	296.67	299.08	99.97	98.18	99.47	56.19	55.71	55.95	1,550	100.93
29	301.46	297.66	300.06	99.66	98.66	99.22	56.18	55.84	56.01	1,870	100.99
30	302.57	299.47	300.89	99.96	99.07	99.59	56.07	55.69	55.85	2,130	101.00
31	305.15	301.01	303.51	102.44	99.49	101.42	56.18	55.82	55.99	2,690	100.92
		High	303.51		High	102.99		High	56.48	High	101.02
		Low	296.40		Low	99.22		Low	54.70	Low	100.41

APRIL, 1954

	—30 Industrials—			—20 Railroads—			—15 Utilities—			Daily Sales -000-	40 Bonds
	High	Low	Close	High	Low	Close	High	Low	Close		
1	307.30	303.18	306.27	102.58	101.52	102.07	56.23	55.92	56.19	2,270	100.98
2	307.95	304.52	306.67	102.06	101.12	101.49	56.39	56.11	56.26	1,830	100.98
5	308.46	305.27	307.04	101.51	100.50	100.58	56.41	56.04	56.20	1,710	100.96
6	308.50	302.78	304.26	101.03	98.97	99.47	56.39	55.92	56.05	2,120	101.00
7	306.45	301.70	305.41	100.38	98.76	100.12	56.33	55.92	56.12	1,830	101.06
8	309.57	305.82	307.79	102.33	100.45	101.53	56.66	56.21	56.43	2,300	101.02
9	310.32	307.20	309.39	102.20	101.09	101.84	56.61	56.29	56.45	2,360	101.12
12	310.77	307.44	309.19	102.50	101.33	102.02	56.65	56.40	56.49	1,790	101.11
13	310.93	307.58	308.98	103.69	102.31	102.94	56.75	56.41	56.54	2,020	101.00
14	312.96	308.38	311.76	103.91	102.68	103.11	56.95	56.45	56.79	2,330	101.01
15	314.44	310.71	313.77	103.55	102.73	103.09	57.04	56.50	56.78	2,200	100.94
19	316.15	310.65	311.78	103.38	101.80	101.98	57.22	56.53	56.73	2,430	100.93
20	314.38	310.02	311.89	102.33	101.17	101.54	56.89	56.30	56.57	1,860	100.92
21	313.94	309.92	310.91	101.87	101.07	101.27	56.83	56.34	56.62	1,870	100.91
22	312.54	309.05	311.48	101.51	100.80	101.27	56.66	56.13	56.39	1,750	100.88
23	314.34	311.16	313.37	102.69	101.47	102.09	56.77	55.95	56.34	1,990	100.90
26	316.23	312.35	314.54	102.69	101.76	102.05	56.47	55.87	56.32	2,150	100.89
27	315.74	310.91	313.49	102.07	101.05	101.62	56.43	55.89	55.97	1,970	100.86
28	315.01	309.37	313.75	103.84	100.85	103.12	56.12	55.63	55.93	2,120	100.80
29	319.76	314.02	318.22	105.12	103.16	104.63	56.83	56.12	56.58	2,150	100.79
30	321.71	317.24	319.33	105.50	103.95	104.31	56.79	56.31	56.49	2,450	100.72
		High	319.33		High	104.63		High	56.79	High	101.12
		Low	304.26		Low	99.47		Low	55.93	Low	100.72

MAY, 1954

	-30 Industrials-			-20 Railroads-			-15 Utilities-			Daily Sales -000-	40 Bonds
	High	Low	Close	High	Low	Close	High	Low	Close		
3	320.94	317.37	319.35	105.53	103.91	105.03	56.68	56.18	56.35	1,870	100.73
4	321.65	316.84	319.82	107.63	104.98	106.99	56.63	56.19	56.49	1,990	100.76
5	320.94	316.45	317.93	108.07	106.57	106.88	56.78	56.15	56.43	2,020	100.83
6	321.53	316.80	320.41	107.64	106.26	107.29	56.87	56.23	56.66	1,980	100.79
7	323.13	319.54	321.30	109.06	107.21	108.52	56.99	56.47	56.71	2,070	100.87
10	322.66	320.02	321.32	109.71	108.29	108.85	57.03	56.45	56.73	1,800	100.89
11	322.03	318.22	319.74	108.72	107.15	107.68	56.85	56.44	56.66	1,770	100.94
12	322.70	318.68	321.61	108.66	107.56	108.47	57.03	56.56	56.88	2,210	100.94
13	323.80	319.21	320.39	109.41	107.68	108.04	57.25	56.69	56.90	2,340	100.90
14	323.39	319.39	322.50	108.94	107.83	108.60	57.50	56.82	57.45	1,970	100.89
17	324.69	321.10	323.33	109.32	108.21	108.76	58.15	57.50	57.89	2,040	100.87
18	326.29	322.90	324.14	109.50	108.35	108.62	58.27	57.77	58.01	2,250	100.82
19	325.64	321.79	323.21	109.94	108.16	108.91	58.24	57.68	58.03	2,170	100.77
20	325.42	322.40	323.88	110.33	108.96	109.82	58.25	57.69	58.01	2,070	100.79
21	327.43	323.82	326.09	110.92	109.76	110.24	58.33	57.87	58.11	2,620	100.84
24	327.94	324.59	326.09	110.66	109.64	110.02	58.25	57.84	58.04	2,330	100.77
25	326.80	323.27	325.02	110.16	109.22	109.69	58.21	57.88	58.05	2,050	100.70
26	328.26	324.26	327.11	110.24	109.22	109.91	58.34	58.00	58.17	2,180	100.66
27	328.93	325.50	326.37	110.31	109.15	109.47	58.24	57.72	57.82	2,230	100.55
28	328.57	324.83	327.49	110.74	109.19	110.60	58.20	57.73	58.07	1,940	100.56
		High 327.49			High 110.60			High 58.17			High 100.94
		Low 317.93			Low 105.03			Low 56.35			Low 100.55

JUNE, 1954

	-30 Industrials-			-20 Railroads-			-15 Utilities-			Daily Sales -000-	40 Bonds
	High	Low	Close	High	Low	Close	High	Low	Close		
1	329.48	326.21	328.67	111.10	110.03	110.39	58.25	57.77	58.03	1,850	100.52
2	330.45	327.06	328.36	110.50	109.63	109.84	58.21	57.76	57.92	1,930	100.55
3	330.35	327.35	328.63	110.75	109.46	110.44	58.21	57.87	58.09	1,810	100.56
4	329.84	326.54	327.63	110.71	109.85	110.24	58.32	57.94	58.16	1,720	100.58
7	329.54	326.50	327.96	110.92	109.73	110.07	58.33	57.84	58.08	1,520	100.61
8	327.92	319.94	321.00	109.75	106.06	106.51	57.96	57.35	57.39	2,540	100.54
9	321.26	315.66	319.27	107.19	105.23	106.66	57.35	56.74	57.13	2,360	100.50
10	321.85	318.20	320.12	107.77	106.66	107.27	57.58	57.19	57.36	1,610	100.57
11	323.29	319.19	322.09	109.09	107.24	108.61	57.69	57.31	57.59	1,630	100.62
14	323.54	320.67	322.65	108.92	107.82	108.16	57.74	57.42	57.48	1,420	100.73
15	325.80	322.04	325.21	111.04	107.70	110.81	57.92	57.39	57.76	1,630	100.71
16	328.67	325.00	327.28	112.66	110.96	111.79	58.07	57.65	57.95	2,070	100.78
17	329.49	325.88	327.21	112.68	111.25	112.20	58.33	57.76	58.11	1,810	100.77
18	329.07	325.73	327.91	112.68	111.44	112.02	58.13	57.83	58.00	1,580	100.80
21	330.19	326.33	328.56	112.71	111.70	112.21	58.23	57.92	58.03	1,820	100.87
22	330.99	327.40	329.51	112.91	111.54	111.97	58.26	57.92	58.14	2,100	100.87
23	331.54	326.81	330.72	112.99	110.96	112.72	58.27	57.79	58.15	2,090	100.86
24	333.84	329.58	332.20	114.45	112.72	113.80	58.52	58.06	58.24	2,260	100.80
25	335.09	330.19	332.53	114.59	113.28	113.76	58.39	57.98	58.16	2,060	100.81
28	337.30	331.29	336.12	114.84	113.35	114.11	58.26	57.82	58.01	1,890	100.72
29	338.78	330.95	336.90	114.33	112.32	113.30	58.24	57.86	58.21	2,580	100.73
30	337.96	332.20	333.53	113.56	112.23	112.70	58.40	57.86	58.20	1,950	100.60
		High 336.90			High 114.11			High 58.24			High 100.87
		Low 319.27			Low 106.51			Low 57.13			Low 100.50

JULY, 1954

	-30 Industrials-			-20 Railroads-			-15 Utilities-			Daily Sales -000-	40 Bonds
	High	Low	Close	High	Low	Close	High	Low	Close		
1	335.44	330.68	334.12	112.94	111.91	112.54	58.49	58.00	58.41	1,860	100.63
2	338.64	333.00	337.66	113.22	112.14	112.87	58.68	58.26	58.60	1,980	100.64
6	342.10	337.71	341.12	114.58	112.48	114.00	59.03	58.51	58.90	2,560	100.66
7	343.20	338.15	340.34	115.26	113.45	114.43	59.17	58.76	59.06	2,380	100.67
8	341.63	337.64	339.81	114.90	113.76	114.41	59.68	58.77	59.06	2,080	100.69
9	342.91	337.62	341.25	115.37	113.69	115.22	59.28	58.87	59.19	2,240	100.71
12	343.59	339.43	340.91	116.43	115.15	115.80	59.29	58.92	59.15	2,330	100.84
13	342.82	338.53	340.04	117.79	115.93	116.50	59.43	58.99	59.22	2,430	100.87
14	341.25	337.37	340.44	117.76	115.75	117.43	59.67	59.29	59.61	2,520	100.87
15	343.01	339.17	341.06	118.56	117.26	117.80	59.97	59.35	59.69	3,000	100.91
16	342.12	338.03	339.96	118.05	116.52	117.16	59.79	59.26	59.57	2,540	100.90
19	340.87	336.96	338.64	117.79	116.25	116.80	59.97	59.49	59.78	2,370	100.90
20	339.09	334.80	337.62	116.95	115.30	116.05	59.85	59.37	59.64	2,580	100.94
21	341.06	336.46	339.98	117.06	115.72	116.88	59.86	59.39	59.64	2,510	100.90
22	344.54	338.94	342.97	118.20	116.63	117.69	59.79	59.42	59.67	2,890	100.92
23	344.92	341.51	343.48	118.38	117.40	117.95	59.74	59.37	59.54	2,520	100.94
26	345.05	341.42	343.39	118.54	117.51	118.04	59.70	59.32	59.52	2,110	100.95
27	346.41	342.06	344.69	119.91	118.25	119.58	59.82	59.45	59.66	2,690	101.08
28	346.83	342.72	345.11	120.59	118.88	119.55	60.03	59.58	59.91	2,740	100.98
29	347.77	344.01	346.15	120.18	119.08	119.48	60.15	59.77	60.01	2,710	101.04
30	349.21	345.22	347.92	120.15	119.04	119.56	60.41	59.89	60.10	2,800	101.01
		High 347.92			High 119.58			High 60.10			High 101.08
		Low 334.12			Low 112.54			Low 58.41			Low 100.63

AUGUST, 1954

	-30 Industrials-			-20 Railroads-			-15 Utilities-			Daily Sales -000-	40 Bonds
	High	Low	Close	High	Low	Close	High	Low	Close		
2	351.29	346.22	349.57	119.97	118.90	119.20	60.59	60.07	60.40	2,850	101.09
3	351.44	347.05	349.61	121.01	118.91	120.73	60.85	60.32	60.68	2,970	101.12
4	351.50	345.75	349.74	121.16	119.06	120.22	60.95	60.42	60.76	3,620	101.16
5	350.42	345.90	347.79	120.77	119.13	119.65	61.07	60.50	60.98	3,150	101.29
6	347.02	339.64	343.06	119.13	116.27	117.25	61.06	60.31	60.59	3,350	101.27
9	343.71	338.70	340.87	116.94	115.95	116.62	61.04	60.60	60.76	2,280	101.31
10	345.60	340.61	343.56	118.20	116.76	117.80	61.13	60.59	61.00	2,890	101.37
11	347.92	343.12	346.41	120.13	118.00	119.63	61.33	60.85	61.11	3,440	101.35
12	348.53	344.31	345.84	119.91	118.73	118.93	61.39	60.93	61.17	2,680	101.38
13	347.98	343.52	346.64	119.91	118.76	119.47	61.39	60.86	61.21	2,500	101.33
16	350.91	346.11	349.61	120.84	119.47	120.45	61.67	61.12	61.41	2,760	101.35
17	351.86	347.05	348.38	121.51	119.84	120.04	61.74	61.21	61.41	2,900	101.36
18	350.00	344.77	348.51	120.50	119.11	119.94	61.62	61.23	61.48	2,390	101.29
19	352.27	347.05	349.89	120.26	119.18	119.59	61.83	61.28	61.45	2,320	101.32
20	352.20	348.59	350.38	120.69	119.61	120.25	61.75	61.37	61.58	2,110	101.32
23	351.08	347.00	347.64	120.30	119.16	119.27	61.62	61.18	61.36	2,020	101.26
24	348.19	344.26	346.32	119.12	117.63	118.08	61.29	60.96	61.11	2,000	101.25
25	347.49	341.97	344.60	117.90	115.72	116.44	61.33	60.95	61.06	2,280	101.11
26	345.35	341.10	343.35	116.94	115.26	115.95	61.06	60.57	60.85	2,060	101.09
27	346.37	342.29	344.48	116.54	115.45	116.01	61.27	60.74	61.06	1,740	101.16
30	345.07	339.53	341.25	115.87	113.98	114.44	61.11	60.57	60.73	1,950	101.05
31	340.44	333.21	335.80	114.01	111.40	112.45	60.82	59.79	60.11	2,640	100.89
		High 350.38			High 120.73			High 61.58			High 101.38
		Low 335.80			Low 112.45			Low 60.11			Low 100.89

SEPTEMBER, 1954

	-30 Industrials-			-20 Railroads-			-15 Utilities-			Daily Sales -000-	40 Bonds
	High	Low	Close	High	Low	Close	High	Low	Close		
1	340.42	334.97	338.13	114.11	112.47	113.43	60.56	60.04	60.33	1,790	100.86
2	342.76	338.41	341.15	114.87	113.59	114.22	60.73	60.30	60.48	1,600	100.84
3	343.80	340.23	343.10	115.12	114.25	114.91	60.69	60.26	60.57	1,630	100.86
7	346.34	341.82	345.37	115.33	114.27	114.95	60.80	60.51	60.72	1,860	100.80
8	348.25	344.92	346.07	115.52	114.18	114.51	60.79	60.52	60.61	1,970	100.82
9	347.47	344.22	346.73	115.40	113.90	115.06	60.82	60.38	60.61	1,700	100.86
10	349.38	345.50	347.83	116.29	115.04	115.68	60.99	60.50	60.87	1,870	100.83
13	352.29	347.83	351.10	117.15	115.50	116.94	60.98	60.63	60.92	2,030	100.85
14	353.92	350.06	351.78	117.40	116.41	116.95	61.31	60.81	61.22	2,120	100.84
15	353.45	348.59	350.63	117.45	115.58	116.22	61.24	60.80	61.01	2,110	100.83
16	353.43	349.06	352.37	116.70	115.51	116.16	61.32	60.68	60.99	1,880	100.84
17	356.40	352.22	355.32	116.87	115.68	116.33	61.48	60.96	61.29	2,250	100.84
20	357.32	353.11	353.48	116.62	115.08	115.54	61.52	61.03	61.29	2,060	100.79
21	356.91	352.24	356.40	117.06	115.44	116.75	61.52	61.00	61.38	1,770	100.88
22	359.46	356.13	358.36	117.69	116.48	117.15	61.47	61.13	61.40	2,260	100.92
23	361.71	357.08	359.63	118.56	117.18	117.80	61.58	61.12	61.29	2,340	100.96
24	362.90	357.97	361.67	118.76	117.41	118.44	61.62	61.20	61.45	2,340	100.90
27	364.00	361.03	362.26	118.72	117.62	117.87	61.66	61.20	61.41	2,190	100.87
28	366.02	361.12	363.32	118.13	116.40	117.00	61.77	61.25	61.54	1,800	100.93
29	364.21	360.39	361.73	116.77	115.29	115.59	61.60	61.16	61.38	1,810	100.88
30	362.98	358.95	360.46	116.08	114.93	115.18	61.50	60.87	61.04	1,840	100.81
		High 363.32			High 118.44			High 61.54			High 100.96
		Low 338.13			Low 113.43			Low 60.33			Low 100.79

OCTOBER, 1954

	-30 Industrials-			-20 Railroads-			-15 Utilities-			Daily Sales -000-	40 Bonds
	High	Low	Close	High	Low	Close	High	Low	Close		
1	361.62	358.59	359.88	117.30	114.93	117.00	61.38	60.79	61.16	1,850	100.87
4	364.21	359.35	362.73	117.65	116.38	116.94	61.28	60.78	60.91	2,000	100.96
5	365.11	361.75	363.37	118.65	116.68	118.09	61.19	60.70	60.92	2,300	100.92
6	366.02	362.43	364.43	118.40	117.38	117.47	61.09	60.62	60.80	2,570	100.88
7	366.40	362.30	363.79	117.98	117.18	117.58	60.89	60.48	60.62	1,810	100.84
8	366.04	362.35	363.77	118.20	117.25	117.81	60.82	60.47	60.57	2,120	100.91
11	364.98	360.37	361.43	117.87	116.70	116.91	60.84	60.30	60.39	2,100	100.77
12	361.12	357.95	359.57	117.26	115.98	116.93	60.12	59.79	59.90	1,620	100.77
13	360.71	357.51	358.91	118.51	116.70	118.01	60.26	59.77	59.96	2,070	100.73
14	359.74	353.94	354.69	118.61	116.58	117.36	60.03	59.28	59.40	2,540	100.73
15	355.64	351.54	353.20	118.95	116.86	118.36	59.22	58.62	58.81	2,250	100.78
18	355.64	351.84	354.35	119.05	117.63	118.45	58.93	58.46	58.67	1,790	100.89
19	356.34	353.11	354.75	120.38	118.75	119.87	58.96	58.33	58.68	1,900	100.85
20	358.72	354.69	357.42	121.44	120.13	120.72	59.01	58.49	58.69	2,380	100.89
21	360.46	356.60	358.08	121.50	120.02	120.25	58.91	58.26	58.64	2,320	101.01
22	360.31	356.81	358.61	121.01	119.87	120.55	59.03	58.50	58.79	2,080	100.98
25	360.82	355.15	356.34	121.01	118.94	119.48	58.82	58.30	58.36	2,340	100.96
26	358.29	354.73	356.32	120.06	118.61	119.40	58.51	58.09	58.27	2,010	100.97
27	358.00	354.01	355.73	119.59	118.56	119.16	58.58	58.13	58.45	2,030	100.91
28	357.55	353.60	354.56	119.79	118.40	118.62	58.72	58.13	58.28	2,190	100.92
29	354.71	350.72	352.14	118.68	117.12	117.69	58.03	57.66	57.81	1,900	100.86
		High 364.43			High 120.72			High 61.16			High 101.01
		Low 352.14			Low 116.91			Low 57.81			Low 100.73

NOVEMBER, 1954

	-30 Industrials-			-20 Railroads-			-15 Utilities-			Daily Sales -000-	40 Bonds
	High	Low	Close	High	Low	Close	High	Low	Close		
1	354.90	350.16	353.96	118.59	117.23	118.33	58.19	57.38	57.78	1,790	100.82
3	363.30	355.45	361.50	120.69	118.81	119.93	59.17	58.04	58.94	2,700	100.82
4	368.50	361.99	366.95	121.94	119.81	121.65	59.38	58.82	59.16	3,140	100.84
5	368.31	363.90	366.00	122.33	120.72	121.59	59.57	59.02	59.35	2,950	100.87
8	371.60	365.28	369.46	124.55	121.70	124.15	60.01	59.42	59.76	3,180	100.87
9	372.83	368.52	371.07	124.70	123.33	124.01	60.00	59.63	59.86	3,240	100.87
10	374.00	368.88	371.88	125.75	123.68	124.95	60.41	59.84	60.31	2,070	100.89
11	375.89	371.47	374.91	128.12	124.79	127.40	60.79	60.18	60.62	2,960	100.91
12	379.73	374.19	377.10	128.05	126.30	127.65	60.90	60.34	60.60	3,720	100.94
15	379.20	374.04	376.74	127.77	126.33	126.88	60.62	59.99	60.24	3,080	100.95
16	380.77	373.85	379.39	127.52	125.69	127.09	60.49	59.96	60.33	3,260	100.91
17	382.06	377.46	379.69	130.23	127.15	129.31	60.64	60.08	60.22	3,830	100.92
18	381.32	376.29	377.44	130.05	127.76	128.22	60.60	60.12	60.36	3,530	100.90
19	380.34	375.29	378.01	130.23	127.73	129.72	60.76	60.04	60.57	3,130	100.97
22	381.21	376.82	379.47	130.65	129.43	129.97	60.83	60.33	60.60	3,000	101.01
23	384.29	378.65	382.74	131.04	129.70	130.36	60.78	60.26	60.68	3,690	101.00
24	387.05	382.47	384.63	131.83	130.01	131.08	60.94	60.38	60.69	3,990	101.04
26	388.96	384.06	387.79	132.68	130.84	132.27	60.87	60.33	60.75	3,010	101.09
29	390.72	385.90	388.51	133.87	131.80	133.04	61.03	60.45	60.87	3,300	101.11
30	391.21	385.67	386.77	133.58	131.26	131.47	61.09	60.58	60.75	3,440	101.13
		High 388.51			High 133.04			High 60.87			High 101.13
		Low 353.96			Low 118.33			Low 57.78			Low 100.82

DECEMBER, 1954

	-30 Industrials-			-20 Railroads-			-15 Utilities-			Daily Sales -000-	40 Bonds
	High	Low	Close	High	Low	Close	High	Low	Close		
1	388.68	381.81	384.04	131.98	129.18	129.80	61.13	60.60	60.73	3,100	101.14
2	388.05	382.80	385.63	131.94	129.94	131.66	61.07	60.55	60.87	3,190	101.08
3	391.74	385.58	389.60	133.72	132.02	133.30	61.37	60.72	61.20	3,790	101.18
6	394.01	389.77	392.48	136.41	133.58	135.58	61.66	60.99	61.53	3,960	101.29
7	395.67	390.32	393.88	137.18	134.75	136.87	61.78	61.21	61.41	3,820	101.34
8	395.43	390.85	393.08	137.90	135.38	136.77	61.90	61.12	61.43	4,150	101.40
9	393.56	388.75	391.53	136.43	134.36	135.20	61.50	60.93	61.06	3,300	101.41
10	393.54	388.41	390.08	136.87	135.16	135.87	61.57	61.00	61.32	3,250	101.37
13	391.87	387.73	389.79	137.58	135.47	136.45	61.67	61.20	61.38	2,750	101.22
14	390.98	386.56	387.03	137.98	135.94	136.58	61.72	61.11	61.37	2,650	101.25
15	389.96	385.03	388.92	137.36	135.33	137.16	61.47	60.82	61.26	2,740	101.18
16	394.54	389.28	393.14	140.79	138.02	140.20	61.94	61.37	61.65	3,390	101.20
17	396.34	391.85	394.94	143.38	140.00	142.47	61.89	61.35	61.62	3,730	101.09
20	399.59	393.31	397.32	144.82	142.62	144.06	61.87	61.44	61.61	3,770	101.10
21	400.04	395.35	398.11	145.05	143.31	144.12	61.76	61.19	61.38	3,630	100.98
22	399.97	395.73	397.07	144.86	143.47	144.11	61.55	61.12	61.25	3,460	100.96
23	398.85	395.28	397.15	145.45	143.20	144.76	61.62	61.02	61.51	3,310	100.97
27	397.77	392.33	393.88	145.58	142.75	143.84	61.75	61.11	61.37	2,970	100.90
28	399.61	392.06	398.51	146.00	143.22	145.36	61.71	61.09	61.43	3,660	101.00
29	404.20	398.17	401.97	147.44	145.23	146.23	62.04	61.56	61.78	4,430	100.99
30	404.41	399.42	401.97	146.69	144.79	145.73	62.13	61.63	61.85	3,590	101.04
31	407.17	401.48	404.39	147.04	145.20	145.86	62.71	61.89	62.47	3,840	101.00
		High 404.39			High 146.23			High 62.47			High 101.41
		Low 384.04			Low 129.80			Low 60.73			Low 100.90

JANUARY, 1955

	-30 Industrials-			-20 Railroads-			-15 Utilities-			Daily Sales -000-	40 Bonds
	High	Low	Close	High	Low	Close	High	Low	Close		
3	412.47	403.58	408.89	147.73	145.00	146.54	62.87	61.97	62.44	4,570	101.11
4	409.21	401.84	406.17	146.76	144.44	145.80	63.03	61.99	62.76	4,420	101.16
5	405.39	396.41	397.24	145.66	141.98	142.56	63.00	61.94	62.05	4,640	101.07
6	397.19	387.09	391.89	142.48	138.56	140.31	62.20	61.49	61.76	5,300	101.06
7	396.88	391.91	395.60	144.55	141.29	144.34	62.29	61.61	62.10	4,030	101.06
10	402.24	397.72	400.89	146.86	145.15	146.23	62.63	62.04	62.38	4,300	101.13
11	402.88	398.02	400.25	146.52	144.09	144.98	62.67	62.11	62.57	3,680	101.10
12	401.86	396.60	399.78	145.02	143.33	144.26	62.82	62.26	62.64	3,400	101.01
13	402.12	396.28	398.34	144.62	142.34	142.95	63.01	62.47	62.69	3,350	101.00
14	399.70	394.88	396.54	143.11	141.63	142.02	63.15	62.50	63.00	2,630	100.89
17	396.75	387.54	388.20	141.54	137.69	137.84	62.81	61.87	62.06	3,360	100.75
18	391.76	385.65	390.98	139.37	139.00	139.06	62.22	61.71	62.09	3,020	100.69
19	395.81	391.19	392.31	141.16	139.15	140.26	62.43	61.75	62.10	2,760	100.71
20	394.35	390.66	393.03	140.58	139.00	139.63	62.77	61.88	62.62	2,210	100.66
21	397.64	392.50	395.90	141.23	139.66	140.91	63.05	62.23	62.86	2,690	100.67
24	397.89	394.09	396.00	142.19	140.48	141.19	63.11	62.63	62.80	2,910	100.71
25	397.85	392.14	397.00	141.29	139.56	140.61	62.79	62.14	62.41	3,230	100.67
26	405.31	398.19	401.97	142.12	140.56	141.30	62.82	62.22	62.55	3,860	100.71
27	406.98	400.21	402.60	142.98	141.22	142.22	62.61	62.07	62.33	3,500	100.70
28	406.38	400.67	404.68	144.86	142.00	144.20	62.12	61.68	61.88	3,290	100.59
31	410.61	404.27	408.83	145.20	143.33	144.34	62.28	61.55	62.02	3,500	100.51
		High	408.89		High	146.54		High	63.00		High 101.16
		Low	388.20		Low	137.84		Low	61.76		Low 100.51

FEBRUARY, 1955

	-30 Industrials-			-20 Railroads-			-15 Utilities-			Daily Sales -000-	40 Bonds
	High	Low	Close	High	Low	Close	High	Low	Close		
1	411.63	406.72	409.70	144.56	143.00	143.66	62.32	61.87	62.09	3,320	100.49
2	410.17	405.42	407.11	143.81	142.63	142.97	62.57	61.96	62.23	3,210	100.37
3	408.20	403.51	405.85	143.56	142.34	143.02	62.57	62.11	62.43	2,890	100.36
4	411.17	405.09	409.76	143.91	142.52	143.37	62.97	62.20	62.81	3,370	100.43
7	412.93	407.20	409.59	143.84	142.45	142.95	63.25	62.77	62.99	3,610	100.45
8	410.78	403.73	405.70	143.06	141.31	141.72	62.95	62.08	62.32	3,400	100.46
9	411.34	405.20	410.32	144.95	141.19	144.19	63.02	62.36	62.95	3,360	100.49
10	414.90	410.41	412.89	146.79	144.54	146.02	63.58	62.95	63.30	3,460	100.47
11	416.55	410.74	413.99	146.66	145.09	145.52	63.84	63.28	63.66	3,260	100.32
14	415.42	410.26	411.39	146.44	144.66	145.69	64.00	63.34	63.62	2,950	100.23
15	414.69	409.54	411.95	147.59	145.23	146.52	64.09	63.31	63.77	3,510	100.26
16	414.27	408.91	409.98	147.48	145.62	146.12	64.14	63.52	63.79	3,660	100.24
17	412.78	408.55	410.41	146.94	145.29	145.65	63.94	63.43	63.60	3,030	100.28
18	414.62	409.07	411.63	147.44	145.06	146.61	63.85	63.34	63.65	3,660	100.34
21	414.21	409.57	411.28	148.48	146.41	148.11	64.14	63.54	63.93	3,010	100.29
23	413.04	409.72	411.48	150.31	147.55	149.58	64.06	63.65	63.80	3,030	100.26
24	412.65	407.63	410.30	149.64	146.88	148.33	64.01	63.38	63.69	2,920	100.19
25	411.17	406.35	409.50	148.60	146.55	147.75	63.98	63.52	63.78	2,540	100.20
28	413.62	408.18	411.87	149.79	147.69	149.47	64.25	63.74	64.05	2,620	100.16
		High	413.99		High	149.58		High	64.05		High 100.49
		Low	405.70		Low	141.72		Low	62.09		Low 100.16

MARCH, 1955

	—30 Industrials—			—20 Railroads—			—15 Utilities—			Daily Sales -000-	40 Bonds
	High	Low	Close	High	Low	Close	High	Low	Close		
1	416.10	411.24	413.71	151.91	149.68	150.85	64.59	64.06	64.41	2,830	100.11
2	418.33	413.95	417.18	153.77	151.33	153.32	64.88	64.34	64.68	3,370	100.12
3	420.61	416.25	418.33	154.69	152.89	153.36	65.55	64.69	65.36	3,330	100.10
4	421.83	416.53	419.68	154.16	152.83	153.52	65.75	65.23	65.52	2,770	100.13
7	420.85	415.69	416.84	154.25	152.42	153.08	65.65	65.01	65.25	2,630	100.10
8	416.27	408.52	409.13	153.02	148.87	149.47	65.12	64.39	64.53	3,160	100.09
9	409.22	400.84	404.90	149.59	146.02	148.27	64.18	63.49	63.57	3,590	100.07
10	410.06	404.90	406.83	150.91	149.14	149.82	64.09	63.50	63.67	2,760	100.02
11	406.66	398.56	401.08	149.64	145.09	146.79	63.78	63.09	63.23	3,040	99.83
14	400.06	387.50	391.36	145.39	141.17	142.52	63.18	61.83	62.17	4,220	99.75
15	399.67	391.18	399.28	146.02	142.71	145.90	62.69	61.76	62.50	3,160	99.84
16	405.94	399.60	403.14	148.02	145.84	146.44	63.30	62.24	63.02	2,900	99.85
17	406.14	401.41	405.23	146.95	145.74	146.58	63.46	62.85	63.26	2,200	99.88
18	408.09	402.88	404.75	147.06	145.65	146.44	64.01	63.12	63.69	2,050	99.89
21	406.16	401.64	402.40	147.19	145.03	145.38	63.87	63.08	63.38	2,020	99.79
22	405.68	401.28	404.47	146.86	145.15	146.34	63.83	63.28	63.77	1,910	99.82
23	411.32	405.68	410.87	148.78	146.64	148.39	64.09	63.50	63.88	2,730	99.96
24	416.42	411.39	414.49	150.32	148.62	149.68	64.39	63.82	64.27	3,170	99.97
25	416.64	412.06	414.77	151.18	148.96	150.26	64.53	63.87	64.21	2,540	99.99
28	416.16	411.87	412.91	151.97	149.92	150.79	64.30	63.74	63.94	2,540	100.02
29	415.10	411.39	413.73	152.14	150.10	151.36	63.94	63.59	63.85	2,770	99.97
30	414.82	409.07	410.13	152.09	148.71	149.22	63.87	63.29	63.38	3,410	99.92
31	413.21	407.96	409.70	151.39	149.25	150.32	63.74	63.27	63.57	2,680	99.92
	High 419.68			High 153.56			High 65.52				High 100.13
	Low 391.36			Low 142.52			Low 62.17				Low 99.75

APRIL, 1955

	—30 Industrials—			—20 Railroads—			—15 Utilities—			Daily Sales -000-	40 Bonds
	High	Low	Close	High	Low	Close	High	Low	Close		
1	414.80	409.78	413.84	151.96	150.32	151.07	64.09	63.60	63.91	2,660	99.95
4	416.71	412.10	412.97	151.88	150.58	150.82	64.25	63.79	63.97	2,500	99.95
5	416.84	411.84	415.90	152.33	150.25	151.99	64.18	63.66	64.00	2,100	99.92
6	419.33	414.75	416.42	153.80	151.90	152.50	64.07	63.52	63.73	2,500	99.97
7	419.79	415.84	418.20	155.12	152.80	154.42	63.93	63.51	63.78	2,330	100.05
11	420.89	416.27	418.77	155.56	154.19	155.03	64.41	63.81	64.13	2,680	99.96
12	422.85	418.12	420.94	157.43	154.88	157.08	64.82	64.16	64.60	2,770	99.97
13	424.19	419.87	421.57	158.57	156.45	157.55	65.09	64.51	64.86	2,820	99.97
14	424.52	419.05	422.46	157.52	156.01	156.87	64.91	64.42	64.68	2,890	99.92
15	427.23	421.71	425.45	159.06	156.86	158.30	65.02	64.44	64.72	3,180	99.93
18	430.03	425.02	428.42	160.56	158.27	159.77	65.37	64.68	65.22	3,080	99.86
19	429.25	425.30	427.88	161.51	159.23	161.18	65.42	64.90	65.15	2,700	99.87
20	430.85	426.04	428.62	162.05	160.49	161.31	65.35	64.94	65.14	3,090	99.91
21	431.18	425.54	428.45	162.47	160.37	161.03	65.18	64.49	64.63	2,810	99.88
22	430.27	423.24	425.52	161.03	158.22	159.11	64.93	64.33	64.62	2,800	99.88
25	428.34	420.52	426.86	160.53	156.74	160.20	65.13	64.18	64.89	2,720	98.85
26	432.76	427.62	430.64	162.60	160.22	161.54	65.36	64.80	64.99	2,720	99.92
27	432.07	425.41	428.10	161.85	159.33	160.35	65.20	64.60	64.85	2,660	99.87
28	428.92	421.96	423.19	161.13	158.76	159.65	64.87	64.32	64.56	2,550	99.83
29	426.99	422.82	425.65	161.03	159.30	160.52	64.88	64.41	64.79	2,230	99.82
	High 430.64			High 161.54			High 65.22				High 100.05
	Low 412.97			Low 150.82			Low 63.73				Low 99.82

MAY, 1955

	-30 Industrials-			-20 Railroads-			-15 Utilities-			Daily Sales -000-	40 Bonds
	High	Low	Close	High	Low	Close	High	Low	Close		
2	428.27	424.00	426.30	161.40	159.98	160.67	65.17	64.53	64.87	2,220	99.85
3	426.84	420.81	422.78	160.58	157.35	157.89	65.08	64.56	64.68	2,630	99.81
4	424.65	419.18	422.54	159.11	156.69	158.40	64.84	64.33	64.56	2,220	99.79
5	425.56	421.22	423.39	159.84	158.39	159.42	64.98	64.41	64.68	2,270	99.80
6	425.71	421.57	423.84	161.63	159.60	160.83	65.06	64.43	64.70	2,250	99.84
9	426.32	422.43	424.32	161.52	159.99	160.20	64.83	64.28	64.62	2,090	99.88
10	425.69	419.85	423.80	160.08	158.01	158.85	64.52	64.09	64.42	2,150	99.85
11	425.02	419.03	420.29	159.09	157.31	157.79	64.49	64.05	64.11	2,120	99.81
12	421.24	414.43	418.20	157.41	154.58	155.93	64.01	63.57	63.74	2,830	99.77
13	421.98	417.03	419.57	157.89	156.14	157.01	64.02	63.65	63.89	1,860	99.79
16	421.02	412.73	415.01	157.25	154.12	154.70	64.01	63.37	63.58	2,160	99.75
17	417.05	412.60	414.12	155.69	153.73	154.45	63.60	63.21	63.47	1,900	99.65
18	418.83	413.95	417.83	156.32	154.25	155.83	63.57	63.21	63.45	2,010	99.61
19	421.57	417.16	419.72	157.58	155.84	156.72	64.03	63.46	63.77	2,380	99.72
20	423.84	418.64	422.89	157.91	156.32	157.41	63.98	63.59	63.91	2,240	99.71
23	425.22	419.75	420.32	157.76	155.27	155.59	64.08	63.59	63.75	1,900	99.71
24	422.39	417.16	420.39	156.53	155.05	155.84	64.21	63.51	63.89	1,650	99.69
25	423.44	419.63	421.77	158.49	156.04	157.61	63.98	63.51	63.78	2,100	99.77
26	426.08	421.48	424.95	159.51	157.74	158.90	63.97	63.57	63.82	2,260	99.76
27	427.71	423.68	425.66	159.62	158.33	158.84	64.17	63.67	63.85	2,220	99.71
31	427.06	422.84	424.86	160.38	158.31	159.87	63.96	63.49	63.63	1,990	99.72
		High 426.30			High 160.83			High 64.87			High 99.88
		Low 414.12			Low 154.45			Low 63.45			Low 99.61

JUNE, 1955

	-30 Industrials-			-20 Railroads-			-15 Utilities-			Daily Sales -000-	40 Bonds
	High	Low	Close	High	Low	Close	High	Low	Close		
1	426.75	422.48	424.88	161.09	159.45	160.08	64.17	63.50	63.89	2,510	99.70
2	428.13	422.86	425.80	160.89	159.62	160.23	64.33	63.64	64.08	2,610	99.75
3	430.25	425.88	428.53	161.84	160.37	161.31	64.59	64.08	64.41	2,590	99.85
6	433.19	427.37	431.49	161.61	160.32	161.00	64.69	64.22	64.41	2,560	99.75
7	437.99	430.93	434.55	162.52	160.49	161.42	64.60	64.25	64.39	3,230	99.82
8	439.26	433.26	436.95	161.85	160.29	161.15	64.56	64.01	64.42	3,300	99.75
9	439.80	434.32	435.07	161.64	158.87	159.00	64.49	63.79	64.00	2,960	99.76
10	438.94	433.60	437.72	161.03	158.81	160.56	64.38	63.68	64.21	2,470	99.76
13	442.23	437.65	440.17	162.51	160.80	161.85	64.25	63.79	63.98	2,770	99.73
14	443.45	437.45	438.20	162.93	160.82	161.09	64.35	63.82	64.11	2,860	99.70
15	443.47	438.45	441.93	162.02	160.64	161.03	64.42	63.92	64.18	2,650	99.74
16	445.42	440.51	442.48	162.08	160.50	161.07	64.40	64.00	64.16	2,760	99.77
17	445.04	440.96	444.08	161.72	160.46	161.16	64.35	63.89	64.22	2,340	99.76
20	446.53	443.13	444.38	161.90	160.29	160.70	64.61	64.12	64.37	2,490	99.71
21	448.52	443.27	446.80	161.21	159.86	160.52	64.76	64.15	64.52	2,720	99.76
22	450.45	445.24	447.37	164.13	160.65	163.26	64.77	64.22	64.44	3,010	99.78
23	451.49	445.67	448.82	164.59	162.69	163.26	64.65	64.23	64.41	2,900	99.73
24	450.99	445.15	448.93	163.36	161.70	162.20	64.65	64.11	64.27	2,410	99.75
27	451.53	446.64	449.86	162.96	161.33	162.03	64.33	63.92	64.05	2,250	99.71
28	452.28	446.12	449.02	162.06	160.46	160.91	64.28	63.79	64.04	2,180	99.67
29	451.13	444.74	449.70	161.07	159.24	160.80	64.28	63.82	64.13	2,180	99.64
30	453.48	448.70	451.38	161.73	160.07	160.95	64.48	64.11	64.34	2,370	99.61
		High 451.38			High 163.26			High 64.52			High 99.85
		Low 424.08			Low 159.00			Low 63.89			Low 99.61

JULY, 1955

	—30 Industrials—			—20 Railroads—			—15 Utilities—			Daily Sales -000-	40 Bonds
	High	Low	Close	High	Low	Close	High	Low	Close		
1	456.11	449.50	453.82	161.94	160.43	161.42	64.69	64.11	64.48	2,540	99.61
5	462.22	454.80	459.42	162.79	161.31	161.75	64.75	64.23	64.62	2,680	99.63
6	471.15	460.89	467.41	162.36	159.78	160.56	64.91	64.48	64.67	3,140	99.61
7	469.06	458.28	460.23	160.43	157.58	158.21	64.96	64.30	64.51	3,300	99.68
8	465.08	456.68	461.18	158.57	156.45	157.65	64.91	64.42	64.76	2,450	99.70
11	466.10	460.32	464.24	160.04	157.82	159.21	65.12	64.68	64.92	2,420	99.74
12	468.99	460.62	462.97	160.58	158.58	159.05	65.25	64.65	65.00	2,630	99.80
13	464.96	456.06	457.40	159.12	156.95	157.53	65.31	64.70	64.98	2,360	99.82
14	460.71	454.82	458.49	158.34	157.22	158.03	65.15	64.70	64.98	1,980	99.79
15	463.15	457.94	460.23	159.75	157.88	159.17	65.40	64.82	65.15	2,230	99.79
18	463.45	458.08	460.07	159.68	157.59	158.06	65.50	64.94	65.27	2,160	99.77
19	460.86	453.39	456.72	158.34	155.92	156.93	65.68	65.11	65.47	2,300	99.66
20	459.89	454.34	458.10	158.28	156.29	157.98	65.96	65.25	65.80	2,080	99.68
21	462.86	457.65	461.07	159.15	157.46	158.24	66.32	65.72	66.10	2,530	99.66
22	466.28	460.73	464.69	160.74	158.18	159.98	66.63	65.89	66.45	2,500	99.67
25	470.53	464.35	468.02	161.09	159.45	159.95	66.84	66.33	66.59	2,500	99.68
26	471.73	465.14	468.41	160.52	158.88	159.47	66.86	66.39	66.68	2,340	99.61
27	471.35	465.71	468.45	160.65	158.90	159.71	66.89	66.41	66.65	2,170	99.55
28	470.74	463.26	466.46	159.95	158.46	158.60	66.81	66.33	66.60	2,090	99.58
29	468.75	463.45	465.85	158.88	157.55	158.19	66.91	66.32	66.59	2,070	99.54
		High 468.45			High 161.75			High 66.68			High 99.82
		Low 453.82			Low 156.93			Low 64.48			Low 99.54

AUGUST, 1955

	—30 Industrials—			—20 Railroads—			—15 Utilities—			Daily Sales -000-	40 Bonds
	High	Low	Close	High	Low	Close	High	Low	Close		
1	467.48	458.71	460.25	158.15	155.63	146.10	67.00	66.21	66.42	2,190	99.55
2	463.02	457.11	460.82	157.19	155.54	156.69	66.71	66.18	66.50	2,260	99.56
3	463.60	459.17	460.98	157.76	156.62	157.13	66.78	66.25	66.37	2,190	99.53
4	458.92	452.37	454.18	156.41	154.27	154.73	66.33	65.65	65.98	2,210	99.41
5	458.44	453.62	456.40	155.71	154.30	155.00	66.41	65.85	66.23	1,690	99.34
8	459.28	453.05	454.05	155.35	153.35	153.56	66.59	66.00	66.20	1,730	99.31
9	453.30	445.67	448.84	152.78	150.14	151.22	66.06	65.46	65.59	2,240	99.22
10	452.44	447.39	450.29	152.11	150.61	151.66	65.76	65.16	65.43	1,580	99.19
11	456.22	449.75	455.18	153.77	151.97	153.47	65.64	65.16	65.44	1,620	99.08
12	458.99	454.93	457.01	154.69	153.20	154.09	65.65	65.20	65.40	1,530	99.06
15	458.87	453.84	456.09	154.42	153.52	153.82	65.79	65.32	65.45	1,230	99.06
16	457.17	451.92	453.26	153.82	152.75	153.20	65.64	65.28	65.50	1,520	98.93
17	454.66	449.88	452.85	154.39	152.65	154.15	65.66	65.22	65.44	1,570	98.93
18	454.86	451.13	452.53	155.29	154.18	154.75	65.70	65.31	65.55	1,560	98.89
19	454.66	450.67	453.57	155.30	154.01	154.99	65.55	65.15	65.34	1,400	98.86
22	454.41	450.76	452.55	156.14	154.45	155.65	65.68	65.15	65.52	1,430	98.87
23	457.88	451.17	457.35	157.52	155.15	157.25	66.09	65.44	66.02	1,890	98.75
24	462.68	457.38	459.39	158.43	156.72	157.37	66.34	65.82	66.10	2,140	98.57
25	462.93	458.40	461.27	157.91	156.60	157.29	66.20	65.83	66.16	2,120	98.58
26	465.30	460.68	463.70	157.77	156.62	157.11	66.29	65.92	66.07	2,200	98.50
29	466.62	463.08	464.37	157.53	156.14	156.50	66.41	65.82	66.18	1,910	98.47
30	466.41	462.70	464.67	157.23	156.05	156.50	66.28	65.87	66.06	1,740	98.43
31	469.51	464.80	468.18	157.77	156.41	157.14	66.22	65.85	66.10	1,850	98.41
		High 468.18			High 157.37			High 66.50			High 99.56
		Low 448.84			Low 151.22			Low 65.34			Low 98.41

SEPTEMBER, 1955

	—30 Industrials—			—20 Railroads—			—15 Utilities—			Daily Sales -000-	40 Bonds
	High	Low	Close	High	Low	Close	High	Low	Close		
1	471.51	467.36	469.63	157.92	156.56	156.93	66.41	66.04	66.22	1,860	98.39
2	473.52	469.47	472.53	157.65	156.80	157.40	66.43	66.17	66.30	1,700	98.42
6	478.80	472.84	476.24	159.29	157.28	158.94	66.68	66.06	66.43	2,360	98.38
7	478.50	473.00	475.20	161.10	158.49	160.43	66.58	66.11	66.36	2,380	98.39
8	476.97	472.96	475.06	162.06	160.04	161.57	66.63	66.22	66.50	2,470	98.35
9	476.87	472.48	474.59	163.32	161.45	162.27	66.55	66.11	66.35	2,480	98.31
12	478.44	473.02	476.51	163.26	161.67	162.26	66.43	65.96	66.13	2,520	98.26
13	482.76	475.54	480.93	162.76	160.61	161.39	66.44	65.92	66.26	2,580	98.21
14	485.71	479.61	482.90	163.86	160.26	163.36	66.46	65.87	66.09	2,570	98.27
15	485.73	480.04	481.56	164.77	162.82	163.53	66.04	65.59	65.71	2,890	98.38
16	485.32	480.02	483.67	164.89	163.45	164.29	65.96	65.34	65.79	2,540	98.36
19	487.79	482.42	483.80	165.00	162.61	163.17	65.94	65.48	65.51	2,390	98.34
20	485.05	480.84	483.67	163.72	162.02	163.00	65.70	65.24	65.46	2,090	98.37
21	488.02	482.97	485.98	163.86	162.48	162.73	65.77	65.14	65.60	2,460	98.38
22	489.51	484.12	485.96	163.56	161.73	162.73	65.81	65.40	65.50	2,550	98.45
23	489.94	483.44	487.45	164.65	162.23	164.28	65.72	65.25	65.50	2,540	98.47
26	463.59	446.74	455.56	155.57	150.67	153.13	63.86	62.59	63.04	7,720	98.35
27	467.42	456.22	465.93	155.24	151.81	154.34	63.48	62.55	63.34	5,500	98.40
28	475.13	467.49	472.61	156.48	154.36	155.51	64.17	63.40	63.82	3,780	98.42
29	474.08	467.37	468.68	156.87	154.91	155.45	63.87	63.20	63.57	2,560	98.49
30	469.68	464.14	466.62	155.62	154.04	155.05	63.56	62.97	63.14	2,140	98.54
		High	487.45		High	164.29		High	66.50		High 98.54
		Low	455.56		Low	153.13		Low	63.04		Low 98.21

OCTOBER, 1955

	—30 Industrials—			—20 Railroads—			—15 Utilities—			Daily Sales -000-	40 Bonds
	High	Low	Close	High	Low	Close	High	Low	Close		
3	465.40	454.85	455.70	154.22	151.15	151.64	63.05	62.27	62.38	2,720	98.53
4	461.79	455.35	458.85	153.29	151.13	152.20	62.81	62.28	62.55	2,020	98.53
5	464.60	458.79	461.14	154.63	152.23	153.10	63.03	62.47	62.66	1,920	98.50
6	461.79	456.61	458.19	153.64	152.02	152.59	63.18	62.66	62.80	1,690	98.59
7	458.74	451.05	454.41	152.15	149.61	151.00	62.92	62.35	62.54	2,150	98.67
10	452.97	440.17	441.14	150.29	146.05	146.37	62.45	61.54	61.67	3,100	98.74
11	444.04	433.19	438.59	147.25	144.07	145.63	61.78	61.02	61.39	3,590	98.68
12	448.16	442.46	445.58	148.63	146.71	147.85	61.77	61.38	61.69	1,900	98.69
13	451.30	443.68	444.91	149.77	147.42	147.94	62.17	61.42	61.87	1,980	98.66
14	446.90	440.59	444.68	148.71	146.80	148.47	61.92	61.29	61.48	1,640	98.67
17	450.75	443.68	446.13	149.35	147.67	148.33	61.93	61.38	61.70	1,480	98.67
18	450.43	444.82	448.58	149.61	147.87	149.01	61.98	61.51	61.86	1,550	98.60
19	454.44	448.76	453.09	150.35	149.01	149.83	62.03	61.43	61.75	1,760	98.63
20	460.66	454.39	457.66	151.96	150.11	151.18	62.27	61.67	62.01	2,160	98.62
21	460.39	455.49	458.47	152.57	150.86	151.45	62.71	62.11	62.51	1,710	98.63
24	462.38	458.35	460.82	152.51	151.07	152.00	62.96	62.12	62.61	1,820	98.65
25	463.02	457.48	458.40	152.57	151.06	151.34	62.98	62.47	62.70	1,950	98.69
26	459.34	454.51	455.72	151.37	149.97	150.37	63.22	62.53	62.79	1,660	98.70
27	458.97	452.31	453.77	151.21	149.52	149.85	63.29	62.61	62.94	1,830	98.70
28	456.59	451.21	454.85	150.49	149.04	150.10	63.35	62.73	63.25	1,720	98.64
31	458.31	453.84	454.87	150.65	148.95	149.53	63.72	63.07	63.37	1,800	98.69
		High	461.14		High	153.10		High	63.37		High 98.74
		Low	438.59		Low	145.63		Low	61.39		Low 98.50

NOVEMBER, 1955

	—30 Industrials—			—20 Railroads—			—15 Utilities—			Daily Sales -000-	40 Bonds
	High	Low	Close	High	Low	Close	High	Low	Close		
1	456.84	452.86	454.89	150.11	148.95	149.58	63.89	63.31	63.73	1,590	98.77
2	456.18	452.12	454.92	150.34	149.11	149.98	64.07	63.57	63.88	1,610	98.80
3	463.09	455.99	461.97	151.60	150.04	151.30	64.49	63.90	64.24	2,260	98.96
4	468.70	461.03	467.35	152.95	151.15	152.42	64.47	63.79	64.17	2,430	99.16
7	472.45	466.73	470.58	154.19	152.33	153.37	64.56	63.91	64.29	2,230	99.10
9	476.68	469.29	473.90	156.45	153.85	156.19	64.50	63.90	64.27	2,580	99.05
10	478.70	471.48	472.52	157.89	154.96	156.08	64.62	64.08	64.31	2,550	99.05
11	478.01	472.21	476.54	160.19	156.19	159.60	64.77	64.51	64.68	2,000	99.09
14	486.69	479.20	484.88	163.20	160.55	161.81	65.06	64.35	64.83	2,760	99.15
15	490.35	480.84	487.07	162.21	159.99	161.09	65.00	64.54	64.75	2,560	99.13
16	490.75	483.60	487.38	162.11	160.19	161.30	65.14	64.55	64.96	2,460	99.05
17	488.99	484.17	485.26	161.94	159.87	161.04	65.09	64.66	65.00	2,310	99.07
18	485.74	478.89	482.91	160.76	159.00	160.05	65.05	64.44	64.89	2,320	98.98
21	483.48	476.42	477.30	160.85	158.85	159.50	65.21	64.46	64.73	1,960	98.82
22	483.38	477.25	481.91	162.23	158.78	161.67	65.11	64.39	64.89	2,270	98.81
23	485.97	480.72	482.62	164.71	161.66	163.42	65.54	64.83	65.19	2,550	98.72
25	485.40	480.98	482.88	168.69	163.95	167.83	65.58	65.03	65.31	2,190	98.70
28	485.81	479.87	480.96	168.79	165.45	166.05	65.72	65.06	65.43	2,460	98.72
29	484.03	479.13	482.60	167.47	165.73	166.78	65.82	65.35	65.71	2,370	98.75
30	485.95	481.53	483.26	168.39	165.76	166.65	66.10	65.47	65.92	2,900	98.70
		High 487.38			High 167.83			High 65.92			High 99.16
		Low 454.89			Low 149.58			Low 63.73			Low 98.70

DECEMBER, 1955

	—30 Industrials—			—20 Railroads—			—15 Utilities—			Daily Sales -000-	40 Bonds
	High	Low	Close	High	Low	Close	High	Low	Close		
1	485.48	480.01	481.39	166.92	164.94	165.28	66.06	65.61	65.84	2,370	98.64
2	483.88	478.87	482.72	165.87	164.49	165.45	66.00	65.63	65.87	2,400	98.60
5	488.71	483.15	487.16	166.54	165.06	165.70	66.11	65.77	65.94	2,440	98.66
6	490.56	485.55	486.73	167.08	165.48	166.38	66.26	65.83	66.10	2,540	98.59
7	489.11	484.81	486.35	166.36	164.08	164.94	66.12	65.72	65.93	2,480	98.53
8	489.68	484.83	487.80	165.57	163.80	165.00	66.13	65.72	65.99	2,970	98.49
9	490.37	486.14	487.64	165.42	163.93	164.74	66.11	65.67	65.82	2,660	98.38
12	487.42	482.41	483.72	164.61	163.21	163.74	65.71	65.29	65.45	2,510	98.35
13	487.04	482.41	484.29	163.78	162.38	162.78	65.57	65.15	65.35	2,430	98.25
14	485.48	479.70	480.84	162.78	161.06	161.42	65.48	64.88	65.04	2,670	98.14
15	483.38	478.32	480.72	161.45	160.34	161.00	65.16	64.36	64.62	2,260	98.14
16	484.17	479.87	482.08	162.05	160.70	161.36	64.76	64.23	64.37	2,310	98.04
19	485.22	480.69	481.80	162.58	160.92	161.42	64.57	64.01	64.21	2,380	98.04
20	483.87	478.59	481.84	161.69	160.44	161.06	64.59	63.91	64.31	2,280	98.11
21	487.37	481.87	485.49	163.00	161.01	162.57	64.85	64.15	64.52	2,540	98.11
22	489.45	484.56	486.08	163.96	162.39	162.78	64.80	64.22	64.40	2,650	98.15
23	489.31	484.83	486.59	163.74	162.12	162.50	64.65	64.08	64.33	2,090	98.18
27	488.91	484.00	485.81	164.35	162.36	163.39	64.31	63.87	64.12	2,010	98.00
28	487.13	483.41	484.22	163.78	162.66	163.09	64.39	63.77	64.13	1,990	98.06
29	487.18	482.77	484.56	163.63	161.88	162.15	64.34	63.85	64.00	2,190	98.11
30	490.33	484.71	488.40	164.11	162.02	163.29	64.36	63.85	64.16	2,820	98.16
		High 488.40			High 166.38			High 66.10			High 98.66
		Low 480.72			Low 161.00			Low 64.00			Low 98.00

JANUARY, 1956

	-30 Industrials-			-20 Railroads-			-15 Utilities-			Daily Sales	40 Bonds
	High	Low	Close	High	Low	Close	High	Low	Close	-000-	
3	490.92	484.27	485.78	164.10	161.94	162.21	64.26	63.55	63.73	2,390	98.13
4	487.79	481.01	484.00	162.32	160.08	160.91	63.78	63.38	63.52	2,290	98.23
5	487.25	482.31	484.02	161.72	160.04	160.55	63.90	63.45	63.64	2,110	98.30
6	488.18	483.78	485.68	161.47	160.08	161.13	64.21	63.57	64.04	2,570	98.40
9	487.91	478.62	479.74	161.31	158.28	158.69	64.15	63.56	63.61	2,700	98.49
10	479.69	472.65	476.12	158.52	156.89	157.68	63.69	63.09	63.45	2,640	98.56
11	481.33	475.85	478.42	160.10	157.94	159.71	63.91	63.32	63.58	2,310	98.58
12	483.70	478.71	481.80	160.91	159.27	160.11	64.25	63.44	63.91	2,330	98.66
13	484.41	479.96	481.80	161.69	160.02	160.68	64.24	63.72	64.01	2,120	98.70
16	481.50	475.19	476.24	160.17	158.06	158.37	64.09	63.62	63.75	2,260	98.78
17	480.55	475.12	477.73	159.54	157.79	158.69	63.95	63.47	63.68	2,050	98.76
18	479.69	472.40	472.89	158.67	156.62	156.84	64.01	63.50	63.71	2,110	98.74
19	473.43	466.60	468.49	156.96	154.61	155.53	63.70	63.13	63.22	2,500	98.88
20	472.11	463.16	464.40	156.74	154.19	154.52	63.58	62.92	63.07	2,430	98.86
23	465.85	458.21	462.35	155.47	152.49	153.97	63.46	62.78	63.03	2,720	98.85
24	469.78	463.91	467.88	156.69	154.50	156.01	63.77	63.04	63.60	2,160	98.82
25	472.57	467.93	470.71	157.54	155.90	156.59	63.97	63.47	63.72	1,950	98.86
26	471.62	465.38	466.82	156.54	155.41	155.80	64.01	63.27	63.35	1,840	98.87
27	468.73	463.33	466.56	155.55	154.22	155.19	63.68	63.10	63.44	1,950	98.94
30	470.10	465.23	467.56	155.94	154.57	155.15	63.86	63.38	63.76	1,830	99.04
31	471.99	466.78	470.74	158.70	155.13	158.36	64.00	63.47	63.88	1,900	99.04
		High 485.78			High 162.21			High 64.04			High 99.04
		Low 462.35			Low 153.97			Low 63.03			Low 98.13

FEBRUARY, 1956

	-30 Industrials-			-20 Railroads-			-15 Utilities-			Daily Sales	40 Bonds
	High	Low	Close	High	Low	Close	High	Low	Close	-000-	
1	475.41	470.69	473.28	159.49	157.53	158.70	64.31	63.78	64.08	2,010	99.07
2	475.51	470.54	473.43	159.01	157.62	158.47	64.41	63.99	64.35	1,900	99.08
3	479.10	472.26	477.44	159.68	158.36	159.22	64.80	64.22	64.68	2,110	99.08
6	481.80	475.88	478.57	159.69	158.40	158.74	65.92	64.92	65.69	2,230	99.09
7	479.18	474.16	476.56	159.14	157.48	158.27	66.28	65.39	65.59	2,060	99.08
8	478.52	470.08	471.23	158.27	156.38	156.51	65.76	65.12	65.26	2,170	99.06
9	471.45	465.50	467.22	156.09	154.37	154.81	65.30	64.70	64.92	2,080	99.09
10	470.25	465.14	467.66	156.01	154.54	155.38	65.20	64.81	65.09	1,770	99.12
13	469.56	465.60	467.17	155.69	154.71	155.27	65.50	64.91	65.05	1,420	99.13
14	468.24	463.89	465.72	155.39	154.22	154.51	65.09	64.29	64.44	1,590	99.15
15	476.02	469.25	470.64	157.71	155.75	156.28	65.07	64.36	64.56	3,000	99.18
16	471.79	467.80	469.61	156.42	154.98	155.94	64.93	64.46	64.86	1,750	99.23
17	477.91	469.12	477.05	159.15	156.29	158.83	65.46	64.40	64.90	2,840	99.33
20	480.21	473.28	476.46	159.74	157.81	159.28	65.26	64.67	64.93	2,530	99.43
21	478.20	474.19	476.93	159.90	158.47	159.17	65.34	64.82	65.24	2,240	99.42
23	482.75	477.03	481.50	160.44	158.92	159.88	65.70	65.16	65.44	2,900	99.44
24	487.30	481.55	485.66	161.21	159.69	160.36	65.58	65.01	65.27	2,890	99.36
27	488.06	482.50	485.00	160.89	159.52	159.97	65.60	65.06	65.32	2,440	99.26
28	487.03	482.48	485.71	160.70	159.18	160.07	65.51	65.03	65.32	2,540	99.27
29	491.09	482.77	483.65	161.13	158.91	159.62	65.69	64.94	65.09	3,900	99.24
		High 485.71			High 160.36			High 65.69			High 99.44
		Low 465.72			Low 154.51			Low 64.08			Low 99.06

MARCH, 1956

	30 Industrials			20 Railroads			15 Utilities			Daily Sales	40 Bonds
	High	Low	Close	High	Low	Close	High	Low	Close	-000-	
1	487.98	483.63	486.69	161.27	158.98	160.70	65.52	64.95	65.39	2,410	99.26
2	491.07	485.88	488.84	163.13	160.68	162.79	66.19	65.32	65.90	2,860	99.23
5	493.29	488.57	491.68	165.67	164.00	164.85	66.85	65.94	66.71	3,090	99.28
6	494.42	489.77	491.41	165.48	163.67	164.10	66.84	66.36	66.64	2,770	99.22
7	492.75	489.21	491.26	164.06	163.02	163.31	67.00	66.46	66.72	2,380	99.22
8	493.95	489.82	492.36	164.71	162.73	164.24	67.03	66.54	66.73	2,500	99.09
9	499.09	492.63	497.84	166.33	164.61	165.99	67.28	66.76	67.06	3,430	99.11
12	502.03	496.59	500.24	167.58	165.53	166.84	67.64	67.00	67.47	3,110	99.10
13	502.32	496.45	499.33	167.94	166.30	167.18	67.72	67.10	67.36	2,790	99.14
14	505.60	499.36	503.88	169.60	167.69	169.04	67.72	67.08	67.34	3,140	99.05
15	509.19	504.01	507.50	170.66	168.81	169.66	67.73	67.24	67.52	3,270	98.96
16	509.61	504.67	507.60	169.77	168.54	169.04	67.65	67.14	67.47	3,120	98.91
19	511.57	506.36	509.76	169.78	168.31	168.87	67.53	66.97	67.14	2,570	98.89
20	514.69	507.13	512.62	169.89	168.36	169.12	67.36	66.93	67.16	2,960	98.83
21	513.70	506.33	507.92	169.86	168.25	168.85	67.54	67.06	67.29	2,930	98.84
22	512.21	505.85	510.94	171.90	168.48	171.72	67.38	66.83	67.23	2,650	98.79
23	515.15	510.25	513.03	173.36	170.97	171.75	67.63	67.11	67.32	2,980	98.76
26	515.05	509.81	512.42	172.69	170.57	171.45	67.66	67.06	67.32	2,720	98.68
27	512.39	507.77	508.68	171.84	169.94	170.17	67.64	67.10	67.46	2,540	98.61
28	511.61	506.21	510.25	170.90	168.88	170.35	67.73	67.14	67.52	2,610	98.51
29	515.86	509.36	511.79	173.20	170.32	171.82	67.74	67.25	67.39	3,480	98.48
		High	513.03		High	171.82		High	67.52		High 99.28
		Low	486.69		Low	160.07		Low	65.39		Low 98.48

APRIL, 1956

	30 Industrials			20 Railroads			15 Utilities			Daily Sales	40 Bonds
	High	Low	Close	High	Low	Close	High	Low	Close	-000-	
2	519.10	510.67	515.10	173.43	171.44	172.37	67.72	67.14	67.41	3,120	98.30
3	519.85	513.33	515.91	173.01	171.05	171.41	67.72	67.06	67.17	2,760	98.20
4	519.88	513.54	518.65	172.47	170.34	171.64	67.41	66.84	67.14	2,760	98.15
5	522.86	514.90	516.57	172.97	171.31	171.44	67.35	66.86	67.08	2,950	98.04
6	522.12	516.28	521.05	172.21	171.08	171.58	67.36	66.84	67.14	2,600	97.92
9	524.37	517.40	518.52	172.29	170.59	170.90	67.47	66.96	67.07	2,760	97.92
10	516.72	508.24	510.04	170.46	168.16	168.54	67.07	66.61	66.68	2,590	97.99
11	514.61	508.89	512.70	170.49	168.30	169.78	66.76	66.35	66.54	2,440	97.98
12	515.03	508.27	509.15	171.90	169.67	170.48	66.86	66.30	66.57	2,700	97.84
13	511.61	506.73	509.99	172.47	169.74	171.96	66.62	66.07	66.29	2,450	97.51
16	512.83	506.99	509.15	174.07	172.15	172.89	66.57	65.99	66.33	2,310	97.31
17	511.11	505.81	507.95	173.73	171.96	172.57	66.48	66.09	66.23	2,330	97.23
18	511.03	504.61	506.55	173.85	171.72	172.61	66.37	65.92	66.17	2,470	97.02
19	507.95	502.45	504.33	173.03	171.48	171.92	66.19	65.65	65.78	2,210	96.91
20	508.66	503.91	507.20	174.78	171.76	174.24	66.18	65.59	65.76	2,320	96.86
23	510.77	506.00	507.28	176.39	174.35	175.80	66.04	65.29	65.43	2,440	96.88
24	508.95	501.77	503.36	176.54	174.24	174.89	65.68	64.89	65.14	2,500	96.75
25	505.48	500.99	503.02	176.31	174.05	175.51	65.38	64.90	65.08	2,270	96.61
26	508.92	503.86	507.12	177.41	175.21	176.22	65.27	64.67	64.98	2,630	96.57
27	513.98	507.95	512.03	178.03	176.00	176.96	65.34	64.70	65.01	2,760	96.50
30	518.42	511.19	516.12	177.92	175.99	176.63	65.70	64.95	65.24	2,730	96.54
		High	521.05		High	176.96		High	67.41		High 98.30
		Low	503.02		Low	168.54		Low	64.98		Low 96.50

MAY, 1956

	-30 Industrials-			-20 Railroads-			-15 Utilities-			Daily Sales -000-	40 Bonds
	High	Low	Close	High	Low	Close	High	Low	Close		
1	516.88	511.24	513.96	177.18	175.71	176.33	65.67	65.00	65.20	2,500	96.55
2	515.08	510.93	512.78	176.91	175.40	176.14	65.47	64.92	65.15	2,440	96.66
3	516.57	511.43	514.03	178.41	175.46	178.01	65.58	65.00	65.48	2,640	96.65
4	519.80	513.49	516.44	179.54	177.62	178.23	66.07	65.41	65.66	2,860	96.64
7	518.50	511.74	512.89	179.57	177.36	178.44	66.28	65.59	66.02	2,550	96.74
8	513.62	508.03	509.13	180.16	178.01	179.37	66.37	65.83	66.09	2,440	96.75
9	511.74	506.05	508.16	182.54	179.30	181.23	66.46	65.87	66.25	2,550	96.69
10	509.44	499.86	501.56	181.99	177.07	178.00	66.71	65.97	66.24	2,850	96.63
11	503.18	497.57	501.25	178.83	177.32	177.97	66.63	66.03	66.38	2,450	96.71
14	505.79	496.00	497.28	178.80	175.09	175.34	66.72	65.70	65.83	2,440	96.72
15	497.86	490.73	494.83	175.10	172.58	174.13	66.05	65.55	65.90	2,650	96.73
16	497.67	490.97	492.69	175.46	173.74	174.56	66.12	65.56	65.89	2,080	96.71
17	497.93	492.22	496.63	176.09	174.35	175.57	66.17	65.67	66.02	1,970	96.66
18	500.65	494.75	496.39	176.29	174.87	175.17	66.38	65.86	66.17	2,020	96.77
21	496.13	488.93	491.62	174.68	171.76	172.49	66.35	65.91	66.13	1,940	96.77
22	490.08	481.86	484.13	171.50	168.47	169.47	66.13	65.58	65.72	2,290	96.77
23	487.60	479.38	480.16	170.99	168.50	169.07	66.06	65.61	65.79	2,140	96.71
24	481.81	471.71	473.51	169.18	165.33	165.74	65.77	65.21	65.33	2,600	96.61
25	477.79	469.31	472.49	166.93	164.23	165.56	65.50	64.94	65.13	2,570	96.56
28	474.16	463.85	468.81	166.04	159.31	161.60	65.30	64.11	64.35	2,780	96.43
29	478.99	470.43	477.68	166.36	162.71	165.72	65.39	64.78	65.13	2,430	96.56
31	483.53	476.43	478.05	167.08	164.89	165.10	65.53	64.91	65.24	2,020	96.47
		High	516.44		High	181.23		High	66.38		High 96.77
		Low	468.81		Low	161.60		Low	64.35		Low 96.43

JUNE, 1956

	-30 Industrials-			-20 Railroads-			-15 Utilities-			Daily Sales -000-	40 Bonds
	High	Low	Close	High	Low	Close	High	Low	Close		
1	481.52	475.54	480.63	165.28	164.05	164.86	65.63	65.11	65.48	1,440	96.50
4	484.60	479.48	483.22	166.28	164.84	165.88	65.93	65.40	65.83	1,500	96.44
5	485.82	481.73	483.19	166.48	165.33	165.81	66.13	65.73	65.93	1,650	96.35
6	483.36	477.95	480.54	165.57	164.18	164.70	65.96	65.48	65.69	1,460	96.27
7	485.20	480.14	482.99	166.36	164.55	165.77	66.20	65.59	65.89	1,630	96.20
8	480.83	467.99	475.29	164.68	160.15	162.03	65.77	65.01	65.21	3,630	96.23
11	481.22	476.15	479.41	164.50	162.56	163.86	65.80	65.06	65.58	2,000	96.18
12	486.10	478.70	485.49	165.37	163.81	165.13	66.03	65.48	65.91	1,900	96.17
13	489.69	484.45	487.08	167.06	165.61	166.22	66.47	65.86	66.23	1,760	96.21
14	488.02	483.99	485.52	167.20	165.76	166.70	66.36	65.91	66.15	1,670	96.26
15	487.58	484.15	485.91	167.20	166.15	166.80	66.50	66.02	66.32	1,550	96.26
18	487.30	482.90	483.91	167.00	165.97	166.23	66.52	65.88	66.30	1,440	96.26
19	486.38	481.18	484.52	166.42	164.86	165.79	66.78	65.95	66.55	1,430	96.20
20	487.05	482.70	485.00	166.84	165.26	166.26	66.81	66.07	66.38	1,670	96.15
21	490.45	485.06	488.26	168.23	166.72	167.74	66.67	66.26	66.48	1,820	96.11
22	491.46	486.12	487.95	168.81	167.19	167.54	66.67	66.18	66.49	1,630	96.10
25	489.74	485.34	486.43	167.40	166.12	166.39	66.66	65.95	66.15	1,500	96.15
26	490.77	484.83	489.37	167.67	165.72	167.02	67.00	66.27	66.75	1,730	96.12
27	494.16	488.85	492.04	167.91	166.39	167.16	67.45	66.68	67.14	2,090	96.07
28	494.34	488.91	492.50	167.74	165.84	166.84	67.34	66.76	67.20	1,900	96.04
29	494.82	489.85	492.78	167.61	166.09	166.69	67.60	66.91	67.38	1,780	96.06
		High	492.78		High	167.74		High	67.38		High 96.50
		Low	475.29		Low	162.03		Low	65.21		Low 96.04

JULY, 1956

	-30 Industrials-			-20 Railroads-			-15 Utilities-			Daily Sales -000-	40 Bonds
	High	Low	Close	High	Low	Close	High	Low	Close		
2	493.65	488.36	491.92	166.58	165.14	165.90	68.16	67.19	67.98	1,610	96.16
3	496.97	491.02	495.74	166.33	164.42	165.19	68.69	67.85	68.56	1,840	96.14
5	502.51	494.67	500.54	166.83	164.74	166.21	68.96	68.28	68.65	2,240	96.18
6	506.24	500.08	504.14	167.46	165.74	167.16	69.02	68.43	68.71	2,180	96.17
9	509.08	503.24	506.52	167.60	165.88	166.30	69.32	68.57	68.94	2,180	96.12
10	510.72	504.85	508.34	168.16	165.70	167.39	69.13	68.71	68.98	2,450	96.04
11	511.92	507.20	509.65	168.61	167.04	167.61	69.48	68.63	69.34	2,520	96.03
12	511.05	505.26	507.44	168.30	166.58	167.12	69.47	68.94	69.21	2,180	96.03
13	512.36	506.46	511.10	168.58	167.02	168.02	69.51	69.03	69.38	2,020	96.06
16	515.19	510.17	512.98	169.05	167.77	168.30	70.12	69.51	69.91	2,260	96.02
17	516.78	510.91	514.43	169.31	167.42	168.81	70.34	69.71	70.04	2,520	95.98
18	517.59	511.73	513.39	170.05	168.12	168.70	70.23	69.58	69.77	2,530	95.79
19	515.96	511.65	513.86	169.33	167.75	168.25	70.02	69.38	69.71	1,950	95.76
20	516.37	512.36	514.57	168.61	167.44	167.96	70.03	69.43	69.83	2,020	95.75
23	516.01	511.65	513.61	170.65	167.53	170.44	70.34	69.76	70.25	1,970	95.74
24	516.78	511.26	513.17	171.86	170.24	171.09	70.82	69.92	70.34	2,040	95.68
25	516.80	511.67	514.13	172.91	170.59	171.37	70.78	70.13	70.51	2,220	95.62
26	517.62	513.20	515.85	171.75	170.26	170.86	71.03	70.37	70.79	2,060	95.56
27	516.50	507.85	512.30	170.79	168.26	169.07	71.12	70.51	70.85	2,240	95.56
30	515.22	508.59	513.42	169.67	168.00	169.03	71.24	70.31	70.90	2,100	95.54
31	519.97	512.85	517.81	171.87	168.49	170.65	71.29	70.88	71.15	2,520	95.46
		High	517.81		High	171.37		High	71.15		High 96.18
		Low	491.92		Low	165.19		Low	67.98		Low 95.46

AUGUST, 1956

	-30 Industrials-			-20 Railroads-			-15 Utilities-			Daily Sales -000-	40 Bonds
	High	Low	Close	High	Low	Close	High	Low	Close		
1	521.50	515.55	518.69	171.99	170.49	171.02	71.33	70.89	71.05	2,230	95.33
2	523.33	516.83	520.95	171.38	169.50	170.17	71.31	70.71	70.99	2,530	95.28
3	522.72	517.51	520.27	170.98	169.11	170.23	71.32	70.81	71.11	2,210	95.15
6	518.85	509.65	513.88	169.50	167.13	167.64	71.13	70.54	70.81	2,280	95.05
7	518.30	511.67	515.88	168.97	167.11	168.10	71.29	70.65	71.17	2,180	94.94
8	521.41	515.33	518.74	168.95	167.49	168.32	71.42	70.85	71.09	2,480	94.94
9	523.24	517.13	519.04	171.24	168.32	170.00	71.15	70.60	70.95	2,550	94.79
10	519.67	513.15	517.38	169.58	167.74	168.57	71.25	70.59	70.84	2,040	94.74
13	518.25	512.08	514.40	168.06	166.28	166.44	70.89	70.41	70.49	1,730	94.72
14	519.23	512.77	517.27	167.11	165.67	166.34	70.95	70.35	70.78	1,790	94.63
15	521.11	516.01	517.70	166.93	165.49	165.73	71.04	70.51	70.67	2,000	94.58
16	519.42	514.73	517.19	166.12	164.76	165.33	70.89	70.39	70.70	1,790	94.44
17	518.52	514.13	515.79	166.73	164.78	165.65	70.89	70.39	70.57	1,720	94.32
20	516.26	510.12	511.24	165.47	163.69	164.01	70.60	69.92	70.11	1,770	94.26
21	509.25	500.84	505.43	163.06	160.21	161.66	70.01	69.03	69.41	2,440	94.14
22	507.72	501.60	502.34	162.54	161.02	161.28	69.38	68.82	68.99	1,570	94.01
23	508.95	502.23	507.06	162.58	161.38	162.21	69.26	68.73	68.93	1,590	93.83
24	510.77	505.83	507.91	163.39	162.19	162.66	69.00	68.39	68.70	1,530	93.78
27	510.28	504.58	505.70	162.62	160.63	160.90	68.84	68.39	68.67	1,420	93.79
28	507.74	502.26	503.05	161.16	159.26	159.78	68.83	68.41	68.63	1,400	93.69
29	504.25	498.85	500.90	160.53	159.26	160.01	68.68	68.23	68.46	1,530	93.63
30	499.91	492.19	495.96	159.96	157.56	158.26	68.58	67.70	68.20	2,050	93.48
31	503.51	495.96	502.04	160.83	158.51	160.65	68.97	68.31	68.63	1,620	93.52
		High	520.95		High	171.02		High	71.17		High 95.33
		Low	495.96		Low	158.26		Low	68.20		Low 93.48

SEPTEMBER, 1956

	—30 Industrials—			—20 Railroads—			—15 Utilities—			Daily Sales -000-	40 Bonds
	High	Low	Close	High	Low	Close	High	Low	Close		
4	508.32	501.17	507.66	161.81	159.68	161.00	69.34	68.32	68.98	1,790	93.25
5	512.68	507.34	509.82	162.21	160.37	161.18	69.53	68.88	69.23	2,130	93.19
6	512.25	507.74	509.49	160.88	159.48	160.03	69.40	68.84	69.03	1,550	92.86
7	509.55	504.39	506.76	160.11	158.63	159.62	69.13	68.40	68.72	1,690	92.84
10	509.79	503.92	505.56	159.77	158.63	158.94	69.07	68.43	68.62	1,860	92.84
11	505.63	499.26	502.16	159.12	157.60	158.34	68.66	68.17	68.48	1,920	92.71
12	504.43	498.43	499.97	158.47	156.75	157.76	68.42	67.88	68.02	1,930	92.69
13	502.92	497.56	499.69	157.85	156.26	156.75	68.45	67.92	68.15	2,000	92.68
14	503.39	497.94	500.32	160.64	156.80	160.19	68.37	67.77	68.03	2,110	92.51
17	502.40	496.49	498.76	161.33	158.87	159.27	68.39	67.83	68.15	1,940	92.53
18	499.12	490.50	493.45	159.01	156.89	157.76	68.18	67.56	67.70	2,200	92.47
19	494.66	487.68	488.72	158.25	156.33	156.75	67.58	67.05	67.21	2,040	92.30
20	489.40	482.86	487.13	158.29	155.86	157.27	67.36	66.79	67.07	2,150	92.15
21	493.86	488.00	490.33	159.94	158.02	159.43	67.78	67.14	67.39	2,110	92.21
24	492.08	486.53	487.70	159.68	157.60	157.73	67.63	66.98	67.08	1,840	92.17
25	488.31	479.57	481.08	157.96	154.30	154.99	67.12	66.26	66.34	2,100	92.05
26	483.46	474.86	481.60	156.28	153.16	155.82	66.45	65.90	66.13	2,370	92.00
27	485.21	477.85	479.76	156.89	154.28	154.70	66.21	65.70	65.77	1,770	91.94
28	481.13	474.23	475.25	155.19	153.47	154.01	65.90	65.40	65.57	1,720	91.96
		High 509.82			High 161.18			High 69.23			High 93.25
		Low 475.25			Low 154.01			Low 65.57			Low 91.94

OCTOBER, 1956

	—30 Industrials—			—20 Railroads—			—15 Utilities—			Daily Sales -000-	40 Bonds
	High	Low	Close	High	Low	Close	High	Low	Close		
1	475.38	463.83	468.70	153.83	149.81	150.55	65.63	64.70	64.93	2,600	92.05
2	477.11	468.73	475.41	154.54	151.87	154.14	65.87	65.01	65.64	2,400	92.13
3	484.06	476.97	482.04	157.31	154.81	156.53	66.54	65.74	66.25	2,180	92.21
4	483.98	478.37	481.24	157.02	155.12	156.15	66.56	65.91	66.31	1,600	92.24
5	483.62	478.86	482.39	159.32	156.02	158.81	66.65	66.18	66.55	1,580	92.25
8	486.47	481.54	483.38	159.97	158.02	158.76	66.75	66.24	66.44	1,450	92.42
9	483.68	479.22	481.32	158.69	157.44	158.14	66.47	65.89	66.07	1,220	92.49
10	487.54	480.37	487.32	159.65	157.51	159.48	66.46	65.83	66.30	1,620	92.50
11	491.18	485.90	488.06	159.97	158.72	159.32	66.66	66.24	66.47	1,760	92.44
12	490.93	486.36	490.19	161.42	158.98	160.79	66.58	66.26	66.49	1,330	92.42
15	493.01	487.76	489.40	162.06	160.39	161.06	66.70	66.32	66.49	1,610	92.45
16	490.58	485.10	487.57	161.68	160.19	160.79	66.46	65.87	66.16	1,580	92.46
17	488.83	482.47	484.66	160.93	159.36	160.14	66.37	65.81	66.15	1,640	92.28
18	487.35	481.57	486.31	161.51	159.39	161.13	66.23	65.77	65.91	1,640	92.22
19	489.46	484.45	486.12	163.49	161.64	162.38	66.09	65.67	65.83	1,720	92.15
22	487.98	483.95	485.27	163.22	161.37	162.06	66.00	65.64	65.81	1,430	92.11
23	487.05	483.19	485.05	162.33	160.46	161.44	66.17	65.46	65.65	1,390	92.07
24	485.90	481.05	482.67	161.51	160.03	160.44	65.84	65.40	65.58	1,640	92.06
25	483.30	478.29	481.08	160.46	158.92	159.63	65.86	65.47	65.70	1,580	91.96
26	487.07	480.91	486.06	160.88	159.68	160.19	66.38	65.75	66.11	1,800	91.89
29	494.11	484.83	486.94	161.57	158.81	159.50	67.05	66.19	66.37	2,420	91.76
30	488.58	483.40	486.47	159.77	157.91	158.78	66.72	66.14	66.44	1,830	91.66
31	486.47	476.83	479.85	158.09	155.17	155.93	66.64	66.00	66.20	2,280	91.58
		High 490.19			High 162.38			High 66.55			High 92.50
		Low 468.70			Low 150.55			Low 64.93			Low 91.58

NOVEMBER, 1956

	—30 Industrials—			—20 Railroads—			—15 Utilities—			Daily Sales -000-	40 Bonds
	High	Low	Close	High	Low	Close	High	Low	Close		
1	488.72	480.23	487.62	159.07	156.57	158.78	67.01	66.29	66.84	1,890	91.61
2	493.40	486.42	490.47	160.68	158.49	159.54	67.25	66.68	67.08	2,180	91.67
5	497.70	488.72	495.37	162.18	159.16	161.46	67.47	66.68	67.24	2,830	91.63
7	500.52	490.22	491.15	162.31	159.83	159.92	67.89	67.31	67.56	2,650	91.53
8	491.32	483.21	488.72	159.39	157.62	158.67	67.45	66.72	67.11	1,970	91.47
9	490.50	483.57	485.35	158.85	156.91	157.22	67.31	66.87	67.08	1,690	91.48
12	488.91	483.60	487.05	158.38	157.04	157.89	67.28	66.55	67.01	1,600	91.60
13	490.71	484.99	486.69	159.16	157.44	158.11	67.44	66.81	67.17	2,140	91.49
14	487.27	479.96	482.36	157.94	155.79	157.00	67.40	66.84	67.12	2,290	91.28
15	486.28	479.11	480.20	157.91	156.40	156.73	67.10	66.38	66.57	2,210	91.20
16	483.51	478.15	480.67	157.76	156.02	156.51	66.96	66.41	66.81	1,820	91.07
19	481.05	472.54	474.56	157.00	153.41	154.21	67.20	66.48	66.78	2,560	90.97
20	475.66	468.16	470.07	154.95	152.71	153.38	66.80	66.18	66.42	2,240	90.67
21	472.37	466.16	467.91	154.39	152.67	153.11	66.75	66.04	66.26	2,310	90.47
23	473.69	466.73	472.56	154.39	152.27	154.16	66.52	66.08	66.35	1,880	90.46
26	476.89	468.73	470.29	155.06	152.76	153.23	66.68	66.17	66.37	2,230	90.36
27	472.18	467.25	470.18	153.81	151.71	152.98	66.32	65.86	66.08	2,130	90.34
28	472.81	465.20	466.10	153.38	150.97	151.15	66.32	65.84	65.93	2,190	90.23
29	468.10	460.41	466.62	151.08	148.47	150.44	66.16	65.56	65.97	2,440	90.22
30	474.59	467.09	472.78	152.69	150.48	151.69	66.58	66.00	66.42	2,300	90.27
		High	495.37		High	161.46		High	67.56		High 91.67
		Low	466.10		Low	150.44		Low	65.93		Low 90.22

DECEMBER, 1956

	—30 Industrials—			—20 Railroads—			—15 Utilities—			Daily Sales -000-	40 Bonds
	High	Low	Close	High	Low	Close	High	Low	Close		
3	482.80	474.26	480.61	154.45	151.60	153.67	67.34	66.40	67.17	2,570	90.31
4	483.82	479.08	481.38	153.94	151.71	152.45	67.47	66.91	67.30	2,180	90.38
5	490.71	480.61	488.55	154.14	151.51	153.32	67.70	67.00	67.51	2,360	90.44
6	495.18	487.32	492.74	157.67	152.78	157.36	67.87	67.32	67.59	2,470	90.44
7	497.09	491.21	494.79	159.41	156.80	158.38	68.19	67.46	67.95	2,400	90.54
10	498.95	492.14	493.18	158.49	155.99	156.24	67.97	67.40	67.58	2,600	90.41
11	494.44	487.68	490.36	156.28	154.52	155.10	67.82	67.38	67.67	2,210	90.43
12	491.75	486.06	487.51	154.88	152.42	152.91	67.99	67.18	67.26	2,180	90.42
13	492.77	486.03	490.47	156.37	152.96	155.97	67.72	67.09	67.50	2,370	90.34
14	493.75	488.69	492.08	156.84	154.83	155.24	67.87	67.32	67.59	2,450	90.24
17	497.26	490.82	493.75	156.15	154.32	154.65	67.86	67.42	67.58	2,500	89.98
18	497.70	491.97	495.09	156.78	154.45	154.88	67.79	67.15	67.39	2,370	89.92
19	497.15	492.19	493.81	155.44	153.41	153.83	67.52	67.00	67.27	1,900	89.84
20	494.57	489.29	490.44	153.81	151.82	152.20	67.66	66.92	67.26	2,060	89.86
21	496.22	489.10	494.38	154.21	151.98	153.70	67.95	67.27	67.66	2,380	89.77
26	500.32	494.00	496.74	154.01	152.47	152.74	68.13	67.41	67.69	2,440	89.76
27	499.39	494.79	496.38	154.48	152.56	153.34	68.01	67.53	67.71	2,420	89.70
28	498.68	493.89	496.41	154.32	152.87	153.56	68.55	67.65	68.33	2,790	89.74
31	501.56	494.96	499.47	154.34	152.38	153.23	68.66	68.23	68.54	3,680	89.59
		High	499.47		High	158.38		High	68.54		High 90.54
		Low	480.61		Low	152.20		Low	67.17		Low 89.59

JANUARY, 1957

	—30 Industrials—			—20 Railroads—			—15 Utilities—			Daily Sales -000-	40 Bonds
	High	Low	Close	High	Low	Close	High	Low	Close		
2	501.01	492.06	496.03	154.32	152.16	153.52	68.77	68.06	68.33	1,960	89.53
3	501.56	494.16	499.20	155.46	153.70	154.86	68.95	68.30	68.74	2,260	89.58
4	502.57	496.24	498.22	157.31	154.59	156.42	69.28	68.61	69.07	2,710	89.67
7	500.90	491.78	495.20	157.33	155.12	156.44	69.45	68.69	69.04	2,500	89.66
8	497.20	491.29	493.86	157.98	156.13	157.11	69.55	68.97	69.20	2,230	89.76
9	496.90	490.77	493.21	157.94	156.51	156.80	69.66	69.13	69.42	2,330	89.74
10	498.00	492.74	495.51	158.52	156.73	157.67	69.66	69.31	69.56	2,470	89.83
11	497.78	492.11	493.81	158.38	156.73	157.33	69.91	69.42	69.62	2,340	89.79
14	494.49	487.65	489.29	157.09	155.03	155.68	69.88	69.18	69.56	2,350	89.73
15	490.41	482.94	484.75	155.64	153.85	154.28	69.91	69.01	69.33	2,370	89.76
16	488.28	483.19	485.05	154.97	153.25	153.76	70.05	69.20	69.69	2,210	89.90
17	486.91	481.08	484.01	154.14	152.09	152.89	69.93	69.31	69.62	2,140	89.92
18	486.42	476.23	477.46	153.70	150.99	151.13	69.91	69.18	69.22	2,400	89.90
21	478.29	471.06	475.90	150.91	148.41	149.45	69.63	68.80	69.37	2,740	90.03
22	480.45	475.71	477.49	151.22	149.23	149.50	69.82	69.36	69.61	1,920	90.08
23	481.24	475.25	479.93	150.86	149.19	150.17	70.51	69.63	70.29	1,920	90.11
24	483.57	478.34	481.30	151.37	149.83	150.19	70.68	70.01	70.35	1,910	90.08
25	481.76	475.19	478.34	150.33	148.32	148.96	70.90	70.09	70.68	2,010	90.06
28	478.48	473.14	474.59	149.12	147.38	147.58	71.05	70.34	70.57	1,700	90.18
29	478.31	473.19	476.92	149.05	146.96	148.45	71.04	70.31	70.75	1,800	90.31
30	481.95	476.42	480.53	149.90	148.67	149.59	71.17	70.66	71.05	1,950	90.37
31	483.02	478.04	479.16	150.15	148.41	148.79	71.47	70.85	70.93	1,920	90.40
		High	499.20		High	157.67		High	71.05		High 90.40
		Low	474.59		Low	147.58		Low	68.33		Low 89.53

FEBRUARY, 1957

	—30 Industrials—			—20 Railroads—			—15 Utilities—			Daily Sales -000-	40 Bonds
	High	Low	Close	High	Low	Close	High	Low	Close		
1	479.76	474.43	477.22	148.99	147.87	148.47	71.46	70.96	71.31	1,680	90.40
4	479.54	475.49	477.19	148.94	147.27	148.29	71.58	71.15	71.42	1,750	90.40
5	476.18	466.65	469.96	148.05	145.44	146.26	71.47	70.74	70.87	2,610	90.49
6	472.02	466.40	470.81	146.93	145.19	146.38	71.13	70.55	70.90	2,110	90.63
7	473.93	467.42	468.71	146.62	144.92	145.10	71.61	70.65	71.23	1,840	90.80
8	468.88	463.19	466.29	145.10	142.83	144.10	71.49	70.85	71.16	2,120	90.73
11	465.50	456.01	457.44	143.74	138.99	139.28	71.19	70.07	70.25	2,740	90.82
12	459.87	453.07	454.82	140.97	138.43	139.23	70.47	69.23	69.39	2,550	90.92
13	462.70	454.87	462.14	142.05	139.52	141.69	69.92	69.22	69.74	2,380	90.89
14	467.04	459.69	461.56	143.38	141.18	141.49	70.12	69.50	69.62	2,220	91.00
15	468.83	459.37	468.07	143.30	140.48	143.09	69.94	69.45	69.89	2,060	90.94
18	471.22	465.21	467.40	143.61	141.96	142.40	70.15	69.61	70.04	1,800	90.99
19	469.23	463.63	466.84	142.85	141.67	142.40	70.19	69.68	70.06	1,670	91.01
20	471.10	465.99	469.00	143.50	142.07	142.74	70.31	69.76	70.12	1,790	90.99
21	470.08	465.15	466.93	143.12	141.78	142.22	70.50	69.82	70.34	1,680	90.94
25	469.00	463.40	466.90	142.29	140.91	141.26	70.78	70.19	70.53	1,710	90.87
26	470.34	465.76	467.72	141.91	140.42	140.93	70.88	70.31	70.48	1,580	90.79
27	469.00	463.95	466.26	141.62	140.35	141.04	70.78	70.17	70.53	1,620	90.82
28	468.50	463.51	464.62	141.98	140.64	141.04	70.81	70.03	70.40	1,620	90.81
		High	477.22		High	148.47		High	71.42		High 91.01
		Low	454.82		Low	139.23		Low	69.39		Low 90.40

MARCH, 1957

	—30 Industrials—			—20 Railroads—			—15 Utilities—			Daily Sales -000-	40 Bonds
	High	Low	Close	High	Low	Close	High	Low	Close		
1	469.76	463.66	468.91	142.60	140.93	142.42	70.97	70.32	70.79	1,700	90.83
4	472.97	468.15	471.48	143.59	142.02	143.05	71.17	70.74	70.97	1,890	90.82
5	475.13	471.04	472.88	144.68	142.96	144.14	71.41	70.88	71.28	1,860	90.87
6	475.77	470.43	474.87	143.99	142.63	143.32	71.52	70.96	71.41	1,840	90.94
7	477.58	472.62	474.17	144.12	142.78	143.27	71.49	71.13	71.30	1,830	90.90
8	474.40	470.40	471.63	143.52	142.16	142.72	71.11	70.63	70.74	1,630	90.89
11	472.06	467.37	469.50	142.72	141.55	141.96	70.94	70.50	70.69	1,650	90.84
12	471.45	466.69	470.31	142.25	141.09	141.80	71.21	70.66	70.98	1,600	90.87
13	474.37	469.88	472.53	143.54	141.82	142.92	71.34	70.97	71.19	1,840	90.90
14	475.45	471.39	473.93	143.70	142.76	143.21	71.67	70.99	71.41	1,580	90.98
15	476.12	471.19	474.28	143.59	142.51	142.87	71.80	71.32	71.58	1,600	90.84
18	474.66	470.17	472.30	142.89	141.71	141.89	71.56	71.11	71.34	1,450	90.85
19	475.22	471.01	473.93	142.94	141.60	142.67	71.49	70.90	71.30	1,540	90.77
20	476.38	472.85	473.93	143.56	142.13	142.65	71.36	70.80	70.93	1,830	90.79
21	475.98	471.36	474.02	143.94	142.51	143.59	70.97	70.47	70.63	1,630	90.77
22	475.57	471.04	472.94	144.32	142.87	143.52	70.99	70.42	70.78	1,610	90.76
25	474.05	469.70	471.51	144.25	142.89	143.47	70.92	70.43	70.69	1,590	90.65
26	474.02	468.91	472.24	143.96	142.72	143.34	70.86	70.35	70.63	1,660	90.69
27	475.10	471.01	473.12	144.70	143.38	144.17	71.40	70.50	71.25	1,710	90.64
28	476.88	472.27	475.01	145.42	143.76	144.43	71.84	71.19	71.58	1,930	90.66
29	477.32	473.14	474.81	144.86	143.56	144.05	71.62	71.30	71.47	1,650	90.66
		High 475.01			High 144.43			High 71.58			High 90.98
		Low 468.91			Low 141.80			Low 70.63			Low 90.64

APRIL, 1957

	—30 Industrials—			—20 Railroads—			—15 Utilities—			Daily Sales -000-	40 Bonds
	High	Low	Close	High	Low	Close	High	Low	Close		
1	476.82	473.09	474.98	144.28	143.43	143.76	71.75	71.22	71.53	1,620	90.73
2	478.40	473.70	477.55	144.86	143.74	144.43	71.68	71.23	71.42	2,300	90.68
3	481.08	476.73	478.31	145.73	144.59	145.21	71.92	71.37	71.61	2,160	90.67
4	479.62	475.45	477.43	145.84	144.79	145.21	71.91	71.42	71.66	1,820	90.72
5	479.45	475.68	477.61	145.88	144.79	145.44	72.05	71.09	71.61	1,830	90.71
8	480.44	475.86	479.04	146.06	144.43	145.17	71.66	71.07	71.29	1,950	90.69
9	484.32	478.40	482.66	145.88	144.68	145.46	71.54	71.00	71.27	2,400	90.85
10	486.98	482.02	485.17	148.09	145.30	147.38	71.66	71.18	71.36	2,920	90.92
11	486.86	481.75	484.70	148.00	146.55	147.11	71.80	71.16	71.50	2,350	90.78
12	488.76	482.78	486.72	147.22	145.88	146.51	71.88	71.11	71.61	2,370	90.73
15	488.53	483.62	485.84	146.87	145.82	146.20	71.86	71.19	71.55	2,010	90.76
16	487.15	482.69	484.32	146.17	145.30	145.59	71.98	71.41	71.69	1,890	90.75
17	487.47	482.22	485.02	146.42	144.95	145.57	72.23	71.58	71.98	2,290	90.70
18	489.43	483.51	488.03	146.29	144.75	145.26	72.40	71.84	72.22	2,480	90.67
22	491.59	485.90	488.79	145.91	144.41	144.97	72.71	71.81	72.40	2,560	90.60
23	494.10	487.12	491.88	146.53	144.66	145.91	73.21	72.37	72.99	2,840	90.40
24	497.22	489.87	493.66	147.58	145.79	146.55	73.42	72.44	72.73	2,990	90.25
25	496.03	490.19	492.29	148.50	145.82	147.49	73.22	72.53	72.95	2,640	90.08
26	493.92	488.41	491.50	147.78	146.24	146.98	73.22	72.62	72.99	2,380	90.11
29	496.67	490.77	493.95	147.31	146.04	146.38	73.27	72.62	72.96	2,290	90.10
30	496.49	491.62	494.36	146.87	145.55	145.84	73.28	72.79	73.01	2,200	90.01
		High 494.36			High 147.49			High 73.01			High 90.92
		Low 474.98			Low 143.76			Low 71.27			Low 90.01

MAY, 1957

	—30 Industrials—			—20 Railroads—			—15 Utilities—			Daily Sales -000-	40 Bonds
	High	Low	Close	High	Low	Close	High	Low	Close		
1	498.04	493.05	495.76	146.64	145.55	146.13	73.52	73.01	73.33	2,310	89.98
2	501.13	494.98	498.56	147.60	145.88	147.02	73.91	73.05	73.46	2,860	90.02
3	501.34	495.00	497.54	148.14	146.55	146.84	73.89	73.28	73.67	2,390	89.97
6	500.29	494.86	496.32	147.89	146.29	147.11	73.61	73.06	73.34	2,210	90.10
7	497.78	492.29	494.68	147.60	146.15	146.58	73.46	72.84	73.11	2,300	90.11
8	498.13	493.34	496.73	148.16	146.35	147.62	73.52	72.98	73.26	2,590	90.05
9	499.21	494.80	496.76	148.52	146.75	147.54	73.90	73.02	73.62	2,520	90.00
10	500.46	495.15	498.30	147.80	146.69	147.20	73.94	73.24	73.46	2,430	89.89
13	503.93	498.51	502.21	147.94	146.11	146.93	74.19	73.47	73.90	2,720	89.93
14	504.43	498.16	500.46	147.47	145.82	146.15	74.29	73.63	73.88	2,580	89.97
15	504.87	498.27	501.98	146.93	145.46	146.13	74.13	73.53	73.87	2,590	89.88
16	507.06	501.16	504.84	148.34	145.95	147.49	74.39	73.69	74.09	2,690	89.68
17	508.87	503.58	505.60	148.65	147.20	147.85	74.57	73.76	74.28	2,510	89.62
20	508.75	503.82	505.98	148.81	147.56	147.96	74.92	74.07	74.50	2,300	89.54
21	507.90	503.32	506.04	148.16	146.58	147.42	74.89	74.29	74.61	2,370	89.52
22	506.82	502.36	504.43	147.85	146.06	146.62	75.01	74.25	74.60	2,060	89.38
23	506.04	500.90	504.02	146.89	145.42	146.24	74.79	74.15	74.38	2,110	89.36
24	506.94	502.15	504.02	146.98	145.48	145.86	74.88	74.12	74.36	2,340	89.24
27	505.07	497.89	499.21	146.20	144.72	145.04	74.57	73.84	74.20	2,290	89.13
28	499.62	494.42	497.72	145.48	143.79	145.10	74.36	73.69	74.04	2,070	89.08
29	503.56	498.10	502.18	146.22	144.92	145.64	74.47	73.82	74.13	2,270	89.03
31	507.76	501.57	504.93	146.26	144.70	145.55	74.48	73.88	74.03	2,050	88.64
		High 506.04			High 147.96			High 74.61			High 90.11
		Low 494.68			Low 145.04			Low 73.11			Low 88.64

JUNE, 1957

	—30 Industrials—			—20 Railroads—			—15 Utilities—			Daily Sales -000-	40 Bonds
	High	Low	Close	High	Low	Close	High	Low	Close		
3	507.96	500.46	503.76	146.04	144.77	145.10	74.47	73.69	73.94	2,050	88.57
4	506.68	499.53	502.97	145.77	144.37	144.86	74.06	73.49	73.72	2,200	88.44
5	504.37	499.38	502.07	145.68	144.28	144.99	74.03	73.46	73.75	1,940	88.31
6	506.39	501.13	504.55	145.77	144.34	144.95	73.91	73.32	73.59	2,300	88.22
7	508.14	502.88	505.63	145.86	144.39	145.01	73.87	73.28	73.54	2,380	88.14
10	507.87	497.78	503.76	145.39	143.05	144.23	74.03	73.10	73.62	3,050	87.97
11	511.70	504.93	509.48	146.20	144.34	145.68	74.38	73.47	73.76	2,850	87.93
12	513.36	507.76	509.66	148.36	145.35	147.56	74.10	73.31	73.56	2,600	87.81
13	514.27	508.23	511.58	148.52	147.09	148.16	74.06	73.32	73.63	2,630	87.72
14	514.38	508.93	511.79	148.45	146.71	147.27	73.82	73.22	73.47	2,090	87.66
17	516.81	510.38	513.19	148.14	146.58	147.42	73.57	72.74	73.12	2,220	87.72
18	515.20	506.68	511.32	147.47	145.77	146.51	73.22	72.27	72.58	2,440	87.61
19	512.69	505.28	505.92	147.13	145.30	145.66	72.45	71.45	71.60	2,220	87.49
20	507.87	501.31	503.56	145.75	144.32	145.21	71.48	70.26	70.63	2,050	87.17
21	504.52	497.81	500.00	145.17	143.34	144.21	70.88	69.98	70.41	1,970	87.12
24	500.99	492.87	497.08	144.50	142.40	143.41	70.51	68.94	69.49	2,040	86.94
25	504.69	497.69	501.98	145.55	144.03	144.86	70.12	69.12	69.70	2,000	86.77
26	504.75	498.24	500.78	146.24	144.57	145.30	69.92	69.13	69.37	1,870	86.74
27	504.29	498.36	503.03	146.67	144.86	146.35	69.70	68.83	69.54	1,800	86.69
28	506.53	500.81	503.29	147.31	145.84	146.46	70.26	69.44	69.84	1,770	86.67
		High 513.19			High 148.16			High 73.94			High 88.57
		Low 497.08			Low 143.41			Low 69.37			Low 86.67

JULY, 1957

	-30 Industrials-			-20 Railroads-			-15 Utilities-			Daily Sales -000-	40 Bonds
	High	Low	Close	High	Low	Close	High	Low	Close		
1	506.18	500.75	503.29	147.00	145.68	146.49	70.44	69.66	70.28	1,840	86.74
2	509.36	502.86	507.55	147.71	146.33	147.00	70.97	70.28	70.76	2,450	86.84
3	515.23	507.99	513.25	148.29	146.69	147.47	71.42	70.53	70.95	2,720	86.90
5	518.70	513.42	516.89	148.90	147.62	148.36	71.51	70.72	71.32	2,240	86.98
8	521.71	515.32	518.41	149.88	148.32	149.30	71.98	71.11	71.71	2,840	87.00
9	520.22	513.51	516.37	150.70	148.56	149.92	72.12	71.26	71.45	2,450	86.95
10	521.68	515.11	519.81	152.78	150.26	152.42	71.68	70.92	71.30	2,880	86.96
11	522.20	515.00	517.97	153.27	151.24	151.95	71.68	71.02	71.18	2,830	86.89
12	521.94	514.88	520.77	153.03	151.26	152.51	72.12	70.92	71.70	2,240	87.04
15	522.91	516.60	520.16	153.70	152.27	152.89	71.95	71.20	71.64	2,480	86.89
16	523.11	516.28	517.42	154.48	152.53	153.45	71.71	71.01	71.23	2,510	86.86
17	518.64	513.13	515.11	153.61	151.93	152.16	71.43	70.70	70.95	2,060	86.84
18	519.34	513.33	515.64	152.65	150.39	151.64	71.26	70.61	70.94	2,130	86.73
19	517.94	512.08	515.73	152.31	150.68	151.84	71.17	70.55	70.67	1,930	86.67
22	518.24	513.62	515.32	152.38	151.42	151.55	70.86	70.36	70.53	1,950	86.64
23	517.65	513.33	515.61	152.56	151.40	152.22	70.82	70.04	70.57	1,840	86.50
24	518.24	512.46	515.78	153.67	152.07	152.91	70.67	70.22	70.51	1,730	86.53
25	518.26	514.15	516.69	154.70	152.69	153.81	70.88	70.17	70.47	1,800	86.38
26	517.97	512.89	514.59	153.83	152.00	152.33	70.55	69.85	70.03	1,710	86.42
29	515.64	507.00	508.25	151.66	148.87	149.32	70.35	69.51	69.91	1,990	86.33
30	510.44	504.90	508.93	149.77	147.98	149.23	70.17	69.47	69.73	1,780	86.25
31	512.69	507.26	508.52	150.73	149.08	149.79	70.29	69.69	69.88	1,830	86.13

High 520.77
Low 503.29

High 153.81
Low 146.49

High 71.71
Low 69.73

High 87.04
Low 86.13

AUGUST, 1957

	-30 Industrials-			-20 Railroads-			-15 Utilities-			Daily Sales -000-	40 Bonds
	High	Low	Close	High	Low	Close	High	Low	Close		
1	509.98	504.69	506.21	149.59	148.47	148.74	70.20	69.51	69.78	1,660	86.22
2	508.66	501.98	505.10	150.62	148.36	150.55	70.03	69.44	69.69	1,610	86.20
5	505.57	498.62	500.78	150.48	148.43	149.25	70.04	69.44	69.88	1,790	86.20
6	500.72	493.55	494.13	149.10	147.00	147.16	69.97	69.41	69.63	1,910	86.21
7	499.59	490.25	498.48	149.14	146.06	148.21	69.76	69.03	69.44	2,460	86.17
8	500.90	495.03	496.87	148.38	146.33	146.51	69.75	69.10	69.41	1,690	86.12
9	498.59	493.46	496.78	146.96	145.28	146.02	69.56	68.85	69.21	1,570	86.03
12	496.23	489.90	492.32	145.68	143.83	144.37	69.29	68.61	68.75	1,650	85.88
13	495.68	489.96	492.14	145.42	143.90	144.32	69.21	68.55	68.90	1,580	85.60
14	493.55	484.32	485.93	144.19	141.64	142.18	68.94	68.20	68.34	2,040	85.53
15	490.28	482.10	487.30	143.16	141.20	142.20	68.74	68.06	68.50	2,040	85.41
16	490.42	485.37	488.20	143.59	141.78	142.74	68.97	68.27	68.47	1,470	85.37
19	487.68	478.16	478.95	142.29	140.17	140.35	68.52	67.58	67.71	2,040	85.28
20	485.49	474.52	483.86	141.82	139.28	141.47	68.03	67.18	67.77	2,700	85.28
21	488.23	482.10	485.14	142.42	140.84	141.26	68.40	67.64	68.08	1,720	85.21
22	485.29	479.77	481.46	141.35	140.15	140.46	68.33	67.81	68.09	1,500	84.99
23	481.73	474.81	475.74	140.42	137.96	138.21	68.14	67.33	67.51	1,960	84.89
26	476.44	469.03	470.14	137.92	134.86	135.39	67.81	66.85	67.20	2,680	84.80
27	479.36	470.84	477.55	137.34	134.70	136.40	67.68	67.05	67.48	2,250	84.90
28	482.75	476.38	477.79	137.16	135.53	135.80	68.09	67.40	67.68	1,840	84.89
29	478.19	471.98	476.06	135.39	133.16	134.03	67.93	67.30	67.52	1,630	84.77
30	484.82	476.71	484.35	137.76	134.61	137.49	68.00	67.49	67.84	1,600	84.74

High 506.21
Low 470.14

High 150.55
Low 134.03

High 69.88
Low 67.20

High 86.22
Low 84.74

SEPTEMBER, 1957

	—30 Industrials—			—20 Railroads—			—15 Utilities—			Daily Sales -000-	40 Bonds
	High	Low	Close	High	Low	Close	High	Low	Close		
3	487.59	481.32	486.13	137.98	136.24	137.43	68.21	67.68	68.06	1,490	84.81
4	486.19	481.35	482.60	137.07	135.17	135.33	68.25	67.76	67.92	1,260	84.80
5	481.64	476.76	479.51	135.22	133.48	134.17	68.22	67.62	67.86	1,420	84.92
6	481.87	477.06	478.63	134.68	133.48	133.94	68.09	67.46	67.73	1,320	85.09
9	478.49	472.77	474.28	133.86	132.20	132.52	67.89	67.20	67.29	1,420	85.10
10	476.53	468.77	470.23	132.61	129.68	129.93	67.65	66.95	67.04	1,870	85.15
11	475.30	467.10	474.40	131.07	128.30	130.64	67.36	66.73	67.11	2,130	85.10
12	482.31	473.99	480.56	133.05	130.57	132.49	67.80	67.10	67.58	2,010	85.19
13	483.68	478.72	481.02	133.30	132.18	132.72	67.98	67.37	67.58	1,620	85.19
16	481.05	476.30	478.08	132.74	131.29	131.71	68.21	67.52	67.86	1,290	85.21
17	480.44	474.17	478.28	132.47	130.95	132.00	68.11	67.52	67.87	1,490	85.10
18	481.08	476.88	478.60	132.87	131.73	132.16	68.42	67.54	68.11	1,540	85.12
19	479.59	475.01	476.12	132.11	130.55	130.82	68.43	67.96	68.15	1,520	85.03
20	474.55	466.75	468.42	130.46	128.14	128.48	68.27	67.26	67.64	2,340	84.95
23	465.97	457.15	458.96	127.94	123.46	124.35	67.54	66.63	66.85	3,160	84.98
24	466.02	457.30	462.87	126.56	123.34	125.06	67.57	66.66	67.23	2,840	85.02
25	463.57	452.19	456.95	125.51	121.94	122.65	67.30	66.41	66.61	2,770	84.96
26	460.60	452.98	457.01	124.24	121.25	122.87	67.10	66.51	66.73	2,130	84.94
27	462.40	454.20	456.89	124.93	122.99	124.12	67.40	66.64	66.88	1,750	84.86
30	459.28	454.70	456.30	124.88	122.92	123.70	67.10	66.55	66.67	1,520	84.83
		High 486.13			High 137.43			High 68.15			High 85.21
		Low 456.30			Low 122.65			Low 66.61			Low 84.80

OCTOBER, 1957

	—30 Industrials—			—20 Railroads—			—15 Utilities—			Daily Sales -000-	40 Bonds
	High	Low	Close	High	Low	Close	High	Low	Close		
1	461.91	455.55	460.80	125.04	123.34	124.75	67.02	66.47	66.76	1,680	84.70
2	468.15	461.79	465.03	126.60	124.88	126.02	67.45	66.79	67.04	1,760	84.79
3	466.84	461.67	465.82	126.51	125.08	126.13	67.21	66.64	66.83	1,590	84.81
4	466.02	460.71	461.70	126.78	125.02	125.66	67.01	66.36	66.69	1,520	85.07
7	462.14	451.81	452.42	125.40	122.67	122.81	66.86	66.33	66.48	2,490	85.09
8	454.87	446.82	450.56	123.05	120.06	121.42	66.57	65.94	66.23	3,190	85.14
9	456.51	450.12	451.40	123.50	121.45	122.27	66.58	65.98	66.20	2,120	85.09
10	451.31	439.44	441.71	121.27	116.05	116.78	66.07	65.12	65.26	3,300	85.12
11	443.58	434.15	441.16	117.59	114.04	116.47	65.62	64.59	65.00	4,460	85.14
14	446.06	437.74	443.78	118.34	115.67	117.36	65.40	64.77	65.24	2,770	85.16
15	450.93	443.61	447.90	120.31	117.65	119.46	65.76	65.04	65.37	2,620	85.20
16	450.09	442.97	443.93	119.68	117.41	117.67	66.07	65.16	65.78	2,050	85.14
17	442.24	433.86	436.87	116.85	114.17	114.93	65.63	64.65	64.96	3,060	85.10
18	439.70	432.69	433.83	115.62	113.23	113.93	65.18	64.34	64.55	2,670	84.97
21	434.36	421.20	423.06	113.28	106.76	107.65	64.46	62.60	62.88	4,670	84.87
22	426.48	416.15	419.79	109.80	105.71	107.21	63.23	61.45	62.10	5,090	84.77
23	438.59	425.46	437.13	113.59	108.75	113.12	64.03	62.47	63.55	4,600	84.79
24	443.38	434.15	436.40	115.51	112.36	113.06	64.47	63.29	64.06	4,030	84.72
25	436.95	428.90	435.15	113.14	110.94	112.41	64.31	63.43	63.98	2,400	84.66
28	435.00	429.37	432.14	112.65	110.64	111.23	64.69	63.86	64.41	1,800	84.65
29	439.61	431.59	435.76	112.21	110.38	111.14	64.87	64.05	64.55	1,860	84.64
30	441.74	435.38	440.28	112.36	110.76	111.69	65.66	64.46	65.48	2,060	84.58
31	446.06	439.03	441.04	113.01	110.60	110.94	66.26	65.43	65.75	2,170	84.60
		High 465.82			High 126.13			High 67.04			High 85.20
		Low 419.79			Low 107.21			Low 62.10			Low 84.58

NOVEMBER, 1957

	—30 Industrials—			—20 Railroads—			—15 Utilities—			Daily Sales -000-	40 Bonds
	High	Low	Close	High	Low	Close	High	Low	Close		
1	438.76	431.50	434.71	109.95	107.34	108.03	65.97	65.13	65.54	2,060	84.49
4	435.20	425.46	434.04	108.39	105.11	107.34	65.28	64.49	64.94	2,380	84.28
6	440.60	434.01	435.82	109.60	107.07	107.57	65.48	64.59	64.96	2,550	84.34
7	440.49	432.14	438.91	108.81	106.67	108.55	65.26	64.46	64.97	2,580	84.37
8	438.65	432.11	434.12	108.52	106.38	107.19	65.38	64.47	64.85	2,140	84.33
11	437.16	432.37	434.94	107.97	106.40	107.48	65.10	64.68	64.84	1,540	84.32
12	435.96	428.70	429.75	107.94	105.76	106.03	65.10	64.62	64.83	2,050	84.24
13	432.61	426.51	430.07	105.96	104.37	105.33	65.09	64.47	64.91	2,120	83.85
14	434.94	426.89	427.94	106.69	103.57	103.77	65.32	64.69	64.84	2,450	83.69
15	442.82	434.50	439.35	108.03	105.40	106.67	66.39	65.59	65.89	3,510	84.02
18	439.48	432.49	434.96	106.78	102.01	102.92	66.04	65.32	65.48	2,110	84.08
19	435.84	427.23	431.73	102.37	97.92	98.77	65.89	65.15	65.41	2,240	84.08
20	435.22	427.32	433.37	101.63	98.39	100.83	66.19	65.50	65.92	2,400	84.09
21	443.21	434.51	439.80	103.77	101.38	102.70	67.08	65.95	66.83	2,900	84.12
22	445.64	437.74	442.68	104.20	102.03	103.46	67.33	66.26	67.10	2,850	84.20
25	446.11	439.01	444.38	104.98	102.45	104.35	67.52	66.61	67.42	2,600	84.23
26	448.49	434.43	435.34	104.13	99.78	99.93	67.65	66.55	66.69	3,650	84.39
27	448.02	439.51	446.03	103.59	100.71	103.01	67.80	66.77	67.58	3,330	84.38
29	452.49	445.76	449.87	104.66	102.77	103.97	68.24	67.37	67.73	2,740	84.41
		High	449.87		High	108.55		High	67.73		High 84.49
		Low	427.94		Low	98.77		Low	64.83		Low 83.69

DECEMBER, 1957

	—30 Industrials—			—20 Railroads—			—15 Utilities—			Daily Sales -000-	40 Bonds
	High	Low	Close	High	Low	Close	High	Low	Close		
2	452.16	444.18	446.91	103.91	101.61	102.23	68.02	67.21	67.46	2,430	84.47
3	448.99	444.00	446.55	102.52	101.05	101.65	67.87	67.16	67.52	2,060	84.49
4	451.55	446.03	448.87	101.96	100.42	101.23	67.98	67.14	67.76	2,220	84.66
5	451.81	446.52	449.55	101.72	100.38	100.71	68.25	67.52	67.96	2,020	84.74
6	450.69	445.29	447.20	100.76	98.37	99.20	68.25	67.27	67.80	2,350	85.03
9	447.49	441.21	443.76	99.13	96.74	97.21	68.12	67.45	67.76	2,230	85.18
10	443.03	436.34	439.24	97.39	95.49	95.98	67.99	67.30	67.65	2,360	85.22
11	441.53	435.87	439.36	96.72	94.91	96.05	68.03	67.26	67.76	2,240	85.48
12	441.94	436.31	438.48	101.05	96.58	100.89	68.12	67.48	67.87	2,330	85.61
13	443.00	437.27	440.48	102.21	100.29	101.12	68.58	67.77	68.39	2,310	85.90
16	440.30	432.05	433.40	101.23	97.23	98.88	68.52	67.90	68.17	2,350	86.01
17	433.22	424.85	425.65	97.70	95.69	96.05	68.08	67.23	67.30	2,820	86.31
18	431.93	424.15	426.18	98.01	95.36	95.96	68.02	67.16	67.55	2,750	86.54
19	432.90	424.62	431.26	98.17	95.58	97.37	68.25	67.30	67.92	2,740	86.64
20	434.13	425.94	427.20	98.86	96.58	96.92	68.28	67.67	67.95	2,500	87.09
23	430.40	423.86	428.08	97.34	95.31	96.00	68.24	67.68	67.93	2,790	87.24
24	432.22	426.67	429.11	96.76	95.40	95.67	68.22	67.74	67.99	2,220	87.31
26	436.13	429.58	434.16	98.73	95.92	98.17	68.33	67.83	68.06	2,280	87.40
27	437.39	431.52	432.90	99.24	96.90	97.39	68.80	68.14	68.65	2,620	87.43
30	434.04	428.35	431.78	97.19	94.98	96.05	68.88	68.18	68.66	3,750	87.54
31	438.54	432.43	435.69	98.12	95.76	96.96	69.06	68.33	68.58	5,070	87.63
		High	449.55		High	102.23		High	68.66		High 87.63
		Low	425.65		Low	95.67		Low	67.30		Low 84.47

JANUARY, 1958

	-30 Industrials-			-20 Railroads-			-15 Utilities-			Daily Sales -000-	40 Bonds
	High	Low	Close	High	Low	Close	High	Low	Close		
2	441.39	435.45	439.27	100.54	98.01	99.89	69.19	68.31	68.94	1,800	87.71
3	446.08	438.60	444.56	103.70	100.49	103.53	69.70	68.80	69.46	2,440	87.94
6	447.87	441.62	442.56	104.51	102.07	102.39	69.98	69.06	69.32	2,500	88.01
7	448.23	440.18	447.79	103.57	101.72	103.28	69.98	69.12	69.82	2,220	88.00
8	449.61	443.97	446.61	103.99	102.25	103.21	70.45	69.72	70.23	2,230	88.09
9	448.40	442.27	443.24	103.30	101.41	101.87	70.55	69.97	70.16	2,180	88.19
10	443.09	436.83	438.68	101.41	99.80	100.16	70.35	69.69	69.94	2,010	88.21
13	441.27	434.37	439.71	101.29	99.55	100.87	70.54	69.76	70.35	1,860	88.20
14	444.88	439.36	441.80	102.92	100.96	101.96	71.08	70.22	70.88	2,010	88.38
15	446.26	440.36	445.20	103.37	101.67	103.01	71.62	70.63	71.36	2,080	88.46
16	453.25	444.18	445.23	106.11	103.57	104.13	72.17	71.05	71.36	3,950	88.45
17	445.67	440.62	444.12	107.19	102.68	107.10	71.61	70.95	71.38	2,200	88.35
20	449.43	444.00	447.29	107.77	105.58	106.87	71.87	71.16	71.64	2,310	88.42
21	449.17	445.11	446.64	107.21	105.53	106.52	71.83	71.17	71.65	2,160	88.41
22	449.58	444.67	445.70	107.74	105.47	106.23	71.99	71.36	71.54	2,390	88.69
23	449.02	444.18	447.93	107.07	105.44	106.69	71.68	71.02	71.36	1,910	88.76
24	452.28	446.32	450.66	108.10	106.36	107.63	72.06	71.24	71.93	2,830	88.91
27	451.40	446.61	448.46	108.41	106.83	107.74	72.55	71.71	72.27	2,320	88.88
28	450.22	445.41	448.67	107.92	106.56	107.25	72.69	71.87	72.55	2,030	88.96
29	452.51	447.02	451.16	109.84	106.90	109.53	73.10	72.24	72.86	2,220	88.98
30	453.63	448.46	449.72	110.27	108.44	108.90	73.08	72.42	72.53	2,150	88.99
31	451.46	446.70	450.02	109.40	107.90	109.04	72.69	71.99	72.27	2,030	88.96
		High 451.16			High 109.53			High 72.86			High 88.99
		Low 438.68			Low 99.89			Low 68.94			Low 87.71

FEBRUARY, 1958

	-30 Industrials-			-20 Railroads-			-15 Utilities-			Daily Sales -000-	40 Bonds
	High	Low	Close	High	Low	Close	High	Low	Close		
3	455.10	449.52	453.98	110.62	109.04	110.00	72.77	72.02	72.49	2,490	88.88
4	459.77	451.63	458.65	111.36	109.37	111.16	72.78	72.09	72.49	2,970	88.93
5	458.39	453.34	454.89	111.92	110.18	110.85	72.77	72.06	72.56	2,480	88.72
6	455.30	450.14	453.13	110.85	109.51	110.22	73.02	72.30	72.80	2,210	88.73
7	453.07	446.73	448.76	109.91	108.06	108.70	72.90	72.36	72.53	2,220	88.87
10	448.52	443.68	445.94	108.41	106.78	107.77	72.66	71.98	72.40	1,900	88.82
11	447.61	440.97	442.35	108.28	106.11	106.43	72.59	71.92	72.12	2,110	88.81
12	443.29	438.13	441.21	106.74	104.13	105.38	71.93	71.30	71.64	2,030	88.78
13	445.29	439.27	440.24	107.39	105.51	106.05	72.14	71.51	71.74	1,880	88.86
14	445.76	439.54	444.44	108.15	105.71	107.70	72.28	71.58	72.05	2,070	88.82
17	445.47	441.03	442.27	108.21	106.83	107.01	72.37	71.80	72.12	1,700	88.82
18	444.32	439.89	442.71	107.68	106.11	106.98	72.27	71.67	71.96	1,680	88.81
19	446.47	441.44	443.06	107.43	106.38	106.54	72.36	71.68	71.92	2,070	88.75
20	445.53	438.89	439.74	107.05	105.40	105.80	72.40	71.84	72.08	2,060	88.80
21	441.42	437.33	439.62	105.87	104.66	105.31	72.18	71.76	71.93	1,700	88.99
24	440.80	436.16	437.19	105.18	103.93	104.15	72.27	71.84	72.08	1,570	88.93
25	438.13	434.04	436.89	104.40	103.17	103.70	72.20	71.67	72.06	1,920	88.84
26	442.24	437.42	440.42	104.26	102.74	103.44	72.46	71.87	72.27	1,880	88.92
27	441.18	436.13	437.80	103.68	102.37	102.70	72.43	71.79	72.01	1,670	88.89
28	441.15	436.66	439.92	103.48	102.16	102.95	72.53	71.80	72.49	1,580	88.85
		High 458.65			High 111.16			High 72.80			High 88.99
		Low 436.89			Low 102.70			Low 71.64			Low 88.72

MARCH, 1958

	—30 Industrials—			—20 Railroads—			—15 Utilities—			Daily Sales -000-	40 Bonds
	High	Low	Close	High	Low	Close	High	Low	Close		
3	444.56	439.24	443.38	103.46	102.16	102.52	72.66	72.17	72.42	1,810	88.97
4	447.11	443.03	445.06	103.21	101.90	102.32	72.61	72.03	72.34	2,010	88.84
5	448.14	442.56	446.58	103.10	101.76	102.74	72.75	72.09	72.52	2,020	88.80
6	452.43	446.05	450.96	105.40	102.77	104.89	73.00	72.45	72.90	2,470	88.76
7	452.81	448.58	451.49	105.58	104.20	104.69	73.24	72.68	73.05	2,130	88.89
10	453.45	448.96	451.90	105.07	103.99	104.31	73.24	72.72	73.06	1,980	88.93
11	457.27	450.58	455.92	106.03	104.13	105.65	73.40	72.75	73.18	2,640	88.97
12	456.83	452.72	454.60	106.11	104.93	105.51	73.66	72.91	73.37	2,420	88.93
13	456.80	451.87	454.10	107.94	105.49	106.83	73.59	72.97	73.24	2,830	88.88
14	454.75	450.52	453.04	106.87	105.58	106.27	73.44	72.74	73.12	2,150	88.86
17	453.25	447.08	448.23	106.23	104.55	104.73	73.41	72.72	73.15	2,130	88.87
18	448.84	443.41	447.38	104.93	103.50	104.15	73.18	72.52	73.05	2,070	88.89
19	452.37	446.91	449.96	105.58	103.95	104.82	73.21	72.61	73.02	2,410	88.90
20	452.57	447.76	449.46	105.15	103.97	104.33	73.46	72.69	73.18	2,280	88.87
21	453.57	447.79	452.49	105.96	104.46	105.69	73.57	72.77	73.44	2,430	88.89
24	455.36	450.25	453.75	106.90	105.22	106.56	73.71	73.13	73.44	2,580	88.79
25	454.31	449.52	450.96	106.78	105.36	105.58	73.85	73.35	73.75	2,210	88.79
26	451.46	447.61	449.70	105.74	104.49	105.04	73.97	73.47	73.76	1,990	88.78
27	451.81	447.02	448.64	105.42	104.28	104.69	74.15	73.69	73.88	2,140	88.72
28	450.17	446.64	448.61	105.20	104.13	104.60	74.25	73.68	74.03	1,930	88.56
31	450.05	445.56	446.76	104.80	103.57	103.88	74.26	73.63	74.00	2,050	88.47
		High 455.92			High 106.83			High 74.03			High 88.97
		Low 443.38			Low 102.32			Low 72.34			Low 88.47

APRIL, 1958

	—30 Industrials—			—20 Railroads—			—15 Utilities—			Daily Sales -000-	40 Bonds
	High	Low	Close	High	Low	Close	High	Low	Close		
1	447.82	443.29	445.47	103.95	102.95	103.26	74.32	73.73	74.16	2,070	88.55
2	447.29	440.06	441.21	103.57	101.99	102.19	74.42	73.84	74.04	2,390	88.75
3	442.97	437.98	440.50	102.37	100.80	101.43	74.16	73.60	74.06	2,130	88.72
7	441.97	437.25	440.09	101.16	100.00	100.67	74.38	73.57	74.12	2,090	88.76
8	444.79	439.59	442.59	102.01	100.69	101.61	74.63	73.91	74.32	2,190	88.77
9	445.20	440.97	441.88	102.70	101.45	102.07	74.83	74.35	74.70	2,040	88.87
10	442.94	438.77	441.06	103.30	101.47	102.99	75.00	74.36	74.83	2,000	88.78
11	442.65	438.83	441.24	105.62	102.99	104.95	75.27	74.73	75.13	2,060	88.73
14	444.88	440.06	443.76	106.16	104.51	105.56	75.71	75.01	75.52	2,180	88.79
15	448.96	442.62	447.58	106.83	105.07	106.67	76.01	75.20	75.77	2,590	88.82
16	447.85	442.53	444.35	106.74	105.40	105.98	76.14	75.36	75.76	2,240	88.82
17	446.14	442.35	445.09	110.29	105.80	109.55	76.23	75.60	76.01	2,500	89.08
18	450.75	445.03	449.31	111.05	109.53	110.18	76.56	75.96	76.36	2,700	89.41
21	452.49	448.34	450.72	112.01	110.06	111.60	76.84	76.17	76.53	2,550	89.32
22	452.34	448.37	449.55	111.72	110.20	110.76	76.87	76.17	76.43	2,440	89.56
23	451.87	445.88	450.11	110.09	108.46	109.66	76.84	76.27	76.59	2,720	89.68
24	455.51	449.34	453.42	111.43	109.53	111.00	77.31	76.45	77.13	2,870	89.85
25	457.10	451.13	454.92	111.94	110.33	111.52	77.74	76.86	77.38	3,020	89.89
28	458.33	452.66	454.51	111.47	110.00	110.58	77.87	76.86	77.35	2,400	89.89
29	454.42	449.78	451.78	110.80	109.66	110.02	77.52	76.84	77.19	2,190	89.89
30	457.39	451.19	455.86	112.65	109.31	111.87	77.69	76.93	77.37	2,900	89.97
		High 455.86			High 111.87			High 77.38			High 89.97
		Low 440.09			Low 100.67			Low 74.04			Low 88.55

MAY, 1958

	—30 Industrials—			—20 Railroads—			—15 Utilities—			Daily Sales -000-	40 Bonds
	High	Low	Close	High	Low	Close	High	Low	Close		
1	460.21	454.95	457.01	113.12	111.65	112.16	77.59	76.96	77.18	2,630	89.99
2	460.56	455.66	459.56	112.81	111.38	112.27	77.69	76.94	77.44	2,290	90.00
5	462.38	457.39	461.12	113.14	111.76	112.65	77.85	77.03	77.66	2,670	90.11
6	465.32	460.09	463.67	114.01	112.12	113.70	77.91	77.25	77.56	3,110	90.11
7	465.17	461.12	462.88	114.17	112.47	113.06	77.82	77.03	77.50	2,770	90.13
8	464.35	460.38	462.50	114.64	112.79	114.17	77.88	77.28	77.74	2,790	90.24
9	465.14	460.44	462.56	115.62	114.10	114.86	78.22	77.43	77.84	2,760	90.19
12	463.70	459.41	460.74	115.40	113.66	113.99	78.17	77.22	77.40	2,780	90.15
13	462.03	457.62	459.86	114.28	112.72	113.48	77.72	77.12	77.41	2,940	90.14
14	460.79	454.57	455.45	113.50	111.63	111.87	77.66	76.90	77.13	3,060	90.11
15	459.00	453.84	457.86	112.79	110.67	112.34	77.66	76.80	77.34	2,470	90.06
16	459.47	455.57	457.10	112.72	111.56	111.98	77.82	77.31	77.62	2,030	90.17
19	458.06	454.16	455.98	112.16	111.09	111.47	77.94	77.28	77.71	1,910	90.05
20	460.74	455.30	459.83	112.99	111.18	112.65	78.10	77.41	77.79	2,500	90.05
21	461.62	456.83	458.50	114.60	112.47	114.01	78.06	77.44	77.78	2,580	90.11
22	463.20	457.10	460.24	115.87	113.68	114.95	78.10	77.59	77.94	2,950	90.17
23	463.32	459.21	461.03	115.67	114.13	115.15	78.29	77.76	78.12	2,570	90.15
26	463.47	459.39	461.06	117.43	114.62	116.05	78.19	77.47	77.66	2,500	90.25
27	462.53	457.92	460.68	116.51	115.02	116.00	78.13	77.54	77.74	2,180	90.25
28	462.85	458.97	460.44	116.38	115.18	115.62	78.34	77.62	78.00	2,260	90.42
29	463.85	459.91	462.70	116.40	115.04	116.00	78.45	77.82	78.19	2,350	90.49
		High	463.67		High	116.05		High	78.19		High 90.49
		Low	455.45		Low	111.47		Low	77.13		Low 89.99

JUNE, 1958

	—30 Industrials—			—20 Railroads—			—15 Utilities—			Daily Sales -000-	40 Bonds
	High	Low	Close	High	Low	Close	High	Low	Close		
2	468.61	462.70	466.11	116.80	115.44	115.82	78.72	77.93	78.38	2,770	90.52
3	469.66	465.35	468.14	116.96	115.15	116.72	78.73	78.04	78.38	2,780	90.50
4	470.69	466.37	468.58	117.18	115.67	115.93	78.75	78.12	78.41	2,690	90.58
5	469.84	465.38	468.55	117.76	115.60	117.45	78.88	78.15	78.67	2,600	90.66
6	471.75	467.49	469.60	118.30	116.54	117.27	79.20	78.37	78.88	2,680	90.59
9	471.60	467.17	469.46	117.72	116.00	116.47	79.05	78.29	78.64	2,380	90.54
10	470.37	466.32	468.19	116.29	114.95	115.42	78.89	78.15	78.51	2,390	90.68
11	470.04	465.58	467.93	117.18	114.80	116.80	78.73	78.19	78.59	2,570	90.78
12	472.98	467.23	471.42	117.70	115.98	117.03	78.95	78.31	78.76	2,760	90.80
13	476.56	471.57	474.77	120.13	117.14	119.21	79.16	78.50	78.70	3,100	90.89
16	477.97	473.16	476.56	120.44	118.81	119.57	79.32	78.53	78.95	2,870	91.01
17	482.11	475.36	478.97	120.29	118.79	119.35	79.38	78.78	79.14	2,950	90.99
18	479.70	474.21	476.65	119.68	118.23	118.88	79.16	78.51	78.79	2,640	90.96
19	478.03	470.93	471.57	118.84	116.45	116.47	79.16	78.31	78.41	2,690	90.86
20	475.36	470.81	473.60	119.80	117.61	119.17	78.97	78.23	78.59	2,590	90.75
23	474.60	469.46	471.66	119.42	117.88	118.43	78.57	78.03	78.31	2,340	90.68
24	472.42	467.37	470.43	118.17	116.34	116.92	78.53	77.82	78.26	2,560	90.62
25	473.39	468.05	471.54	118.63	116.72	117.92	78.69	78.10	78.54	2,720	90.68
26	475.68	470.07	474.01	119.53	117.27	118.75	78.89	78.41	78.69	2,910	90.69
27	478.09	473.22	475.42	119.62	118.41	118.95	79.05	78.39	78.83	2,800	90.73
30	479.59	474.33	478.18	119.57	118.23	118.75	79.07	78.41	78.92	2,820	90.75
		High	478.97		High	119.57		High	79.14		High 91.01
		Low	466.11		Low	115.42		Low	78.26		Low 90.50

JULY, 1958

	—30 Industrials—			—20 Railroads—			—15 Utilities—			Daily Sales -000-	40 Bonds
	High	Low	Close	High	Low	Close	High	Low	Close		
1	480.64	476.83	478.82	119.86	118.66	119.35	79.38	78.82	79.22	2,600	90.73
2	481.61	476.86	480.15	119.77	118.46	118.92	79.66	78.88	79.48	2,370	90.69
3	482.26	478.03	480.17	119.91	118.84	119.42	79.82	79.27	79.57	2,630	90.74
7	483.76	478.88	481.85	120.09	118.84	119.53	79.89	79.30	79.70	2,510	90.67
8	482.99	478.12	480.00	120.78	119.19	119.75	80.02	79.30	79.57	2,430	90.57
9	482.79	476.92	477.59	121.33	119.33	119.64	79.95	79.33	79.66	2,630	90.54
10	480.35	475.01	478.97	120.91	119.15	120.51	80.20	79.16	79.99	2,510	90.54
11	484.23	478.94	482.85	122.74	120.84	122.34	80.71	79.92	80.55	2,400	90.54
14	482.55	475.74	476.89	122.54	120.33	120.82	80.74	79.86	80.15	2,540	90.59
15	479.82	472.07	478.82	122.94	119.73	122.58	80.18	79.44	79.92	3,090	90.50
16	485.87	478.88	481.00	124.84	122.50	122.96	80.26	79.66	79.86	3,240	90.34
17	487.60	478.00	485.70	125.53	122.43	124.93	79.98	79.05	79.55	3,180	90.17
18	489.89	483.43	486.55	126.40	124.57	125.31	79.79	79.08	79.36	3,350	90.01
21	494.36	487.10	493.36	127.92	125.37	127.25	79.74	79.01	79.35	3,440	89.99
22	496.74	490.01	494.89	127.78	126.16	127.54	79.77	78.83	79.26	3,420	90.03
23	497.21	490.86	494.06	129.01	127.25	127.81	79.70	78.94	79.44	3,550	90.05
24	498.50	492.42	497.12	129.90	127.56	129.55	79.76	79.23	79.54	3,740	90.03
25	502.64	496.71	501.76	131.51	129.30	130.84	80.02	79.29	79.74	4,430	90.08
28	504.43	498.67	502.81	132.32	130.22	131.80	79.99	79.35	79.64	3,940	90.07
29	504.52	498.73	501.38	132.34	130.15	130.64	79.87	79.29	79.58	3,310	89.85
30	505.10	497.38	504.37	132.27	129.99	132.02	79.71	78.98	79.46	3,680	89.80
31	508.39	501.49	502.99	133.25	131.24	131.67	79.82	79.19	79.58	4,440	89.75
		High	504.37		High	132.02		High	80.55		High 90.74
		Low	476.89		Low	118.92		Low	79.22		Low 89.75

AUGUST, 1958

	—30 Industrials—			—20 Railroads—			—15 Utilities—			Daily Sales -000-	40 Bonds
	High	Low	Close	High	Low	Close	High	Low	Close		
1	507.39	501.64	505.43	133.01	131.13	132.47	79.95	79.41	79.77	3,380	89.63
4	512.27	505.22	510.33	134.37	132.02	134.10	80.07	79.46	79.68	4,000	89.63
5	511.01	503.49	506.95	134.08	131.49	132.98	79.95	79.16	79.64	4,210	89.58
6	508.51	500.32	503.11	134.03	131.49	132.11	79.68	79.02	79.23	3,440	89.36
7	507.84	501.46	506.10	134.03	132.25	133.68	79.52	78.86	79.27	3,200	89.31
8	513.47	506.60	510.13	134.48	132.78	133.61	79.76	79.02	79.41	3,650	89.20
11	514.44	508.69	512.42	134.48	132.98	133.77	79.68	78.94	79.39	2,870	89.16
12	512.47	506.78	508.19	133.52	131.71	132.29	79.55	78.94	79.19	2,600	89.03
13	511.24	505.31	509.22	132.90	131.62	132.43	79.46	78.92	79.24	2,790	88.96
14	512.00	507.48	510.30	133.19	131.56	132.00	79.44	78.92	79.29	3,370	88.88
15	510.36	504.66	506.13	131.76	129.77	130.22	79.07	78.38	78.57	2,960	88.74
18	505.75	499.82	502.67	129.99	128.10	128.81	78.60	77.74	78.29	2,390	88.64
19	506.13	501.26	503.64	130.57	128.81	129.68	78.54	77.97	78.12	2,250	88.49
20	506.51	501.73	503.96	131.47	129.46	131.18	78.35	77.69	78.12	2,460	88.50
21	508.89	503.05	507.10	132.69	131.09	132.18	78.53	77.81	78.00	2,500	88.45
22	509.66	505.54	508.28	133.79	132.14	132.96	78.29	77.60	78.03	2,660	88.44
25	510.62	505.37	508.28	133.88	132.29	132.85	78.32	77.62	77.97	2,610	88.41
26	510.95	506.72	509.63	134.01	131.76	133.45	78.20	77.56	77.84	2,910	88.22
27	513.33	508.19	510.39	134.32	132.40	133.12	78.32	77.78	78.17	3,250	88.18
28	510.24	505.49	507.72	133.39	131.89	132.34	78.19	77.53	77.79	2,540	88.15
29	510.18	505.60	508.63	132.94	131.51	132.52	78.13	77.54	77.97	2,260	88.01
		High	512.42		High	134.10		High	79.77		High 89.63
		Low	502.67		Low	128.81		Low	77.79		Low 88.01

SEPTEMBER, 1958

	—30 Industrials—			—20 Railroads—			—15 Utilities—			Daily Sales -000-	40 Bonds
	High	Low	Close	High	Low	Close	High	Low	Close		
2	513.09	508.39	511.77	133.74	132.20	133.23	78.56	77.85	78.26	2,930	87.96
3	516.03	510.15	513.71	134.46	133.05	133.70	79.24	78.41	78.85	3,240	87.67
4	516.59	511.07	513.44	133.86	132.58	133.03	79.27	78.44	79.05	3,100	87.57
5	515.35	510.45	512.77	133.16	131.78	132.43	79.42	78.78	79.27	2,520	87.33
8	517.47	511.77	515.23	132.67	131.53	132.07	79.77	79.02	79.54	3,030	87.32
9	521.31	515.23	518.64	133.50	131.69	132.54	79.89	79.35	79.60	3,480	87.34
10	520.43	514.59	516.20	133.03	131.44	131.71	79.89	79.22	79.63	2,820	87.41
11	521.72	515.32	520.43	132.90	131.33	132.49	80.14	79.41	79.87	3,300	87.27
12	523.57	517.06	519.43	133.59	131.51	132.34	80.68	79.63	80.36	3,100	87.24
15	524.57	517.47	523.40	135.64	132.29	135.28	81.52	80.42	81.12	3,040	87.11
16	529.09	522.72	526.57	137.09	135.08	136.53	81.50	80.65	81.22	3,940	87.09
17	529.45	522.43	525.89	137.22	135.35	136.31	81.22	80.43	80.93	3,790	86.94
18	526.77	520.52	522.34	137.52	135.69	136.58	81.09	80.36	80.65	3,460	86.69
19	527.74	521.05	526.48	140.59	136.60	140.39	81.21	80.34	80.96	3,880	86.70
22	528.39	522.19	524.01	141.11	139.30	140.17	80.71	79.86	80.12	3,490	86.78
23	528.62	520.87	525.89	143.16	139.17	142.42	80.49	79.63	80.20	3,950	86.78
24	530.18	523.57	528.15	143.94	141.87	143.41	80.49	79.86	80.23	3,120	86.74
25	530.68	523.34	525.83	143.81	140.89	141.64	80.40	79.95	80.18	4,490	86.77
26	529.59	523.31	526.83	142.58	140.55	141.80	80.52	79.82	80.23	3,420	86.73
29	531.74	525.54	529.04	144.19	141.42	143.50	80.64	79.96	80.33	3,680	86.69
30	535.00	528.68	532.09	145.82	143.21	144.61	80.97	80.08	80.71	4,160	86.69
		High	532.09		High	144.61		High	81.22		High 87.96
		Low	511.77		Low	131.71		Low	78.26		Low 86.69

OCTOBER, 1958

	—30 Industrials—			—20 Railroads—			—15 Utilities—			Daily Sales -000-	40 Bonds
	High	Low	Close	High	Low	Close	High	Low	Close		
1	533.91	527.68	530.94	144.75	142.25	143.30	80.99	80.39	80.75	3,780	86.63
2	535.14	528.83	532.09	144.79	142.51	144.10	81.08	80.50	80.99	3,750	86.72
3	536.82	531.53	533.73	146.69	143.72	145.71	81.16	80.36	80.72	3,830	86.54
6	539.37	533.21	536.29	147.80	145.59	147.04	81.18	80.42	80.81	3,570	86.55
7	540.96	534.12	539.40	148.03	145.48	147.54	81.50	80.56	81.30	3,570	86.52
8	542.28	535.97	539.31	148.03	145.77	146.62	81.81	81.05	81.55	3,680	86.56
9	541.46	535.85	539.61	147.80	145.93	147.16	82.10	81.30	81.75	3,670	86.40
10	545.74	538.17	543.36	148.14	146.15	147.36	82.51	81.57	82.18	4,610	86.62
13	549.30	542.95	545.95	148.32	146.80	147.31	82.73	82.06	82.42	4,550	86.35
14	549.71	540.22	541.72	147.94	144.46	145.04	82.89	81.99	82.28	5,110	86.33
15	545.68	533.65	536.14	146.62	142.29	142.78	82.88	81.88	82.12	4,810	86.36
16	541.37	529.42	540.11	146.04	140.64	145.37	82.72	81.71	82.67	4,560	86.32
17	548.97	541.07	546.36	147.89	144.97	147.29	83.17	82.13	82.64	5,360	86.29
20	548.36	541.57	544.19	147.69	144.90	146.46	83.05	82.25	82.63	4,560	86.33
21	546.54	540.28	543.72	147.40	145.21	146.02	82.92	82.04	82.41	4,010	86.40
22	545.04	538.96	542.31	146.58	144.84	145.59	82.53	81.77	82.07	3,500	86.51
23	544.07	537.76	540.72	147.60	144.88	147.02	82.54	81.82	82.28	3,610	86.49
	543.16	536.43	539.52	148.74	146.33	147.76	82.64	81.88	82.28	3,770	86.31
	541.22	533.09	535.00	148.58	145.82	146.20	82.79	82.07	82.35	3,980	86.30
	538.26	530.94	536.88	148.25	145.66	147.89	82.59	81.87	82.38	3,670	86.39
	544.92	536.85	542.72	149.79	147.56	149.10	83.36	82.32	82.92	4,790	86.20
	6.83	540.69	543.31	150.24	147.69	148.83	83.67	82.63	82.97	4,360	86.26
	27	539.31	543.22	149.52	147.40	148.56	83.58	82.89	83.22	3,920	86.08
		High	546.36		High	149.10		High	83.22		High 86.72
		Low	530.94		Low	142.78		Low	80.72		Low 86.08

NOVEMBER, 1958

	—30 Industrials—			—20 Railroads—			—15 Utilities—			Daily Sales -000-	40 Bonds
	High	Low	Close	High	Low	Close	High	Low	Close		
3	547.15	540.28	545.16	149.72	147.96	149.01	83.61	82.76	83.13	3,240	86.14
5	552.35	543.34	550.68	151.44	149.03	150.91	84.18	83.14	83.96	4,080	86.24
6	559.43	550.76	554.85	153.83	151.26	152.51	84.74	83.79	84.36	4,890	86.32
7	558.22	550.85	554.26	153.16	150.84	151.80	84.53	83.85	84.05	3,700	86.23
10	560.10	552.64	557.72	153.45	151.22	152.71	84.86	84.08	84.70	3,730	86.42
11	563.60	556.93	561.13	156.24	152.60	155.61	85.34	84.71	85.27	4,040	86.42
12	565.53	558.19	562.39	156.66	154.03	154.99	85.97	84.97	85.77	4,440	86.46
13	564.42	557.43	560.75	155.68	153.41	154.48	86.21	85.31	85.90	4,200	86.58
14	566.91	559.07	564.68	155.64	153.36	154.70	87.30	85.97	86.88	4,390	86.67
17	572.05	561.54	567.44	157.44	154.57	156.46	87.64	86.63	87.33	4,540	86.62
18	569.06	560.48	564.89	157.13	155.12	156.11	87.83	86.79	87.35	3,820	86.59
19	568.68	562.10	565.97	158.45	155.68	157.91	87.77	86.94	87.25	4,090	86.59
20	569.70	563.21	566.24	158.31	155.26	156.19	87.64	86.95	87.44	4,320	86.61
21	566.50	558.16	559.57	156.78	154.34	154.99	87.54	86.56	86.81	3,950	86.56
24	554.88	543.07	544.89	153.72	149.30	150.41	86.69	85.27	85.56	4,770	86.73
25	546.95	538.43	540.52	151.69	148.87	150.19	85.28	83.90	84.30	3,940	86.71
26	551.50	542.40	549.15	154.28	151.28	153.74	85.14	84.14	84.83	4,090	86.69
28	559.04	550.41	557.46	156.33	153.58	155.68	85.49	84.51	85.25	4,120	86.73
		High	567.44		High	157.91		High	87.44		High 86.73
		Low	540.52		Low	149.01		Low	83.13		Low 86.14

DECEMBER, 1958

	—30 Industrials—			—20 Railroads—			—15 Utilities—			Daily Sales -000-	40 Bonds
	High	Low	Close	High	Low	Close	High	Low	Close		
1	563.30	555.52	560.07	157.38	155.01	156.02	85.96	84.96	85.66	3,800	86.71
2	562.98	555.37	558.57	156.04	153.92	154.32	86.26	85.34	85.91	3,320	86.61
3	560.95	554.55	558.81	154.90	152.74	154.05	86.29	85.46	86.06	3,460	86.73
4	563.19	556.40	559.10	155.03	153.23	154.01	86.54	85.62	86.16	3,630	86.82
5	560.37	554.85	556.75	154.86	153.29	154.07	86.86	85.84	86.47	3,360	86.86
8	559.54	553.70	556.08	154.90	153.23	153.78	87.96	86.34	87.20	3,590	86.88
9	561.51	555.58	558.13	154.88	152.76	153.94	87.80	86.92	87.45	3,790	86.87
10	566.50	558.05	564.98	156.17	153.34	155.64	88.37	87.22	87.95	4,340	86.91
11	569.50	561.57	563.07	157.04	154.79	155.30	88.54	87.51	87.86	4,250	86.80
12	565.01	559.43	562.27	155.50	153.90	154.70	88.33	87.41	87.95	3,140	86.79
15	566.24	559.96	563.98	155.24	153.36	154.12	88.46	87.69	88.04	3,340	86.80
16	568.29	562.25	565.18	155.19	153.47	154.36	88.33	87.54	87.89	3,970	86.72
17	573.29	561.51	569.38	154.77	153.27	154.03	88.84	87.64	88.48	3,900	86.69
18	575.52	568.24	572.38	155.70	153.92	154.79	89.46	88.27	88.89	3,900	86.71
19	577.90	570.38	573.17	155.99	154.16	154.68	89.66	88.48	89.00	3,540	86.72
22	574.84	568.12	571.23	155.37	153.47	154.34	89.46	88.52	88.95	3,030	86.73
23	573.26	564.15	566.39	155.64	153.16	154.28	89.49	88.48	89.02	2,870	86.51
24	573.64	564.27	572.73	157.04	154.45	157.00	89.49	88.42	89.22	3,050	86.32
29	580.63	572.73	577.31	158.07	156.31	156.86	90.53	89.12	90.26	3,790	86.22
30	584.59	577.13	581.80	157.89	155.90	156.98	90.85	89.84	90.50	3,900	86.21
31	587.44	579.25	583.65	158.34	156.53	157.65	91.33	90.25	91.00	3,970	86.29
		High	583.65		High	157.65		High	91.00		High 86.91
		Low	556.08		Low	153.78		Low	85.66		Low 86.21

JANUARY, 1959

	-30 Industrials-			-20 Railroads-			-15 Utilities-			Daily Sales -000-	40 Bonds
	High	Low	Close	High	Low	Close	High	Low	Close		
2	590.38	580.80	587.59	160.23	157.47	159.72	91.61	90.56	91.22	3,380	86.36
5	594.31	585.24	590.17	162.29	159.32	161.86	91.86	90.69	91.33	4,210	86.45
6	593.52	584.88	591.37	162.76	160.50	161.86	91.85	90.84	91.38	3,690	86.44
7	592.58	581.07	583.15	162.58	159.72	160.10	91.74	90.35	91.00	4,140	86.47
8	590.11	580.54	588.14	163.05	159.52	162.80	91.91	90.56	91.55	4,030	86.49
9	594.84	588.00	592.72	164.94	162.29	163.58	92.13	91.17	91.77	4,760	86.58
12	597.31	589.61	592.64	165.01	162.56	163.67	92.40	91.09	91.92	4,320	86.48
13	595.04	587.47	590.70	164.56	162.22	163.45	92.42	91.10	91.58	3,790	86.45
14	593.28	586.85	591.64	165.14	162.33	164.63	92.45	91.51	92.11	4,090	86.42
15	598.10	589.88	594.81	168.27	164.76	167.38	92.58	91.45	92.01	4,500	86.41
16	599.89	590.38	595.75	168.11	166.06	167.17	92.64	91.67	92.18	4,300	86.33
19	598.57	590.32	594.40	167.96	165.81	166.57	92.93	92.05	92.42	3,840	86.19
20	598.45	590.99	595.69	167.87	165.93	167.20	93.09	91.86	92.42	3,680	86.23
21	600.51	593.28	597.66	168.02	166.17	167.24	93.05	92.11	92.51	3,940	86.37
22	601.74	593.96	595.69	167.89	165.61	166.17	92.92	91.74	92.02	4,250	86.38
23	598.36	591.40	596.07	166.88	164.85	165.66	92.33	91.47	91.99	3,600	86.25
26	599.77	591.11	592.37	165.99	163.69	164.07	92.43	91.33	91.66	3,980	86.16
27	597.31	589.47	594.66	164.61	162.64	163.65	91.95	90.97	91.58	3,480	86.25
28	596.37	584.71	588.53	163.63	160.08	161.35	91.70	90.76	90.91	4,190	86.23
29	594.19	585.88	590.40	162.24	159.79	161.13	91.29	90.21	90.48	3,470	86.22
30	597.60	590.35	593.96	163.27	161.04	161.91	91.22	90.34	90.88	3,600	86.16
		High 597.66			High 167.38			High 92.51			High 86.58
		Low 583.15			Low 159.72			Low 90.48			Low 86.16

FEBRUARY, 1959

	-30 Industrials-			-20 Railroads-			-15 Utilities-			Daily Sales -000-	40 Bonds
	High	Low	Close	High	Low	Close	High	Low	Close		
2	597.66	589.14	592.23	162.80	160.95	161.57	91.36	90.35	90.72	3,610	86.28
3	595.60	589.35	592.34	162.80	160.95	162.33	91.39	90.35	91.20	3,220	86.26
4	594.16	587.50	589.38	162.62	161.17	161.60	91.66	90.51	90.97	3,170	86.21
5	591.14	584.06	586.12	162.13	160.46	160.84	91.22	90.32	90.65	3,140	86.27
6	587.56	580.54	582.33	161.35	159.54	160.35	90.98	90.04	90.40	3,010	86.27
9	581.36	571.73	574.46	160.12	157.20	157.94	90.43	89.33	89.78	3,130	86.31
10	583.89	574.72	582.65	160.61	157.76	160.03	91.09	89.81	90.87	2,960	86.31
11	588.17	581.63	584.03	162.27	159.88	160.95	91.33	90.57	90.79	3,000	86.36
12	586.73	579.98	581.89	161.71	159.61	160.12	90.92	90.06	90.38	2,630	86.45
13	589.91	580.01	587.97	161.55	159.52	160.77	90.94	89.91	90.81	3,070	86.37
16	593.14	584.39	587.91	162.93	160.68	161.35	91.38	90.25	90.88	3,480	86.34
17	591.58	583.83	586.71	162.02	160.12	160.90	91.35	90.40	90.94	3,190	86.36
18	590.76	583.62	588.82	162.64	160.57	162.18	91.32	90.41	90.92	3,480	86.33
19	597.48	589.58	595.04	165.03	162.33	164.21	91.52	90.82	91.28	4,160	86.43
20	603.91	594.93	602.21	165.32	163.27	164.39	92.07	91.00	91.74	4,190	86.58
24	607.61	599.57	602.91	165.59	163.67	164.52	92.29	91.31	91.92	4,340	86.52
25	605.35	597.86	601.18	164.25	162.58	163.09	92.04	91.22	91.57	3,780	86.41
26	604.44	596.84	602.00	163.94	161.68	162.73	92.17	91.17	91.76	3,930	86.40
27	606.53	599.77	603.50	163.56	161.53	162.20	92.54	91.47	92.05	4,300	86.39
		High 603.50			High 164.52			High 92.05			High 86.58
		Low 574.46			Low 157.94			Low 89.78			Low 86.21

MARCH, 1959

	30 Industrials High	Low	Close	20 Railroads High	Low	Close	15 Utilities High	Low	Close	Daily Sales -000-	40 Bonds
2	608.82	600.89	605.03	163.14	161.19	162.00	92.73	91.55	92.23	4,210	86.42
3	613.04	604.29	610.78	165.52	161.55	164.43	93.14	92.01	92.84	4,790	86.47
4	615.77	606.20	611.84	166.15	163.49	164.65	93.18	92.17	92.73	4,150	86.51
5	614.57	608.32	611.87	165.81	163.69	165.12	93.43	92.49	93.05	3,930	86.58
6	613.16	605.20	609.52	164.90	162.96	163.74	93.39	92.45	93.05	3,930	86.56
9	615.01	606.14	609.96	164.32	162.85	163.29	93.49	92.59	93.02	3,530	86.53
10	614.39	605.44	611.14	164.12	162.64	163.49	93.78	92.68	93.36	3,920	86.35
11	614.34	608.08	611.49	164.83	162.93	163.74	94.09	93.22	93.74	4,160	86.41
12	616.10	608.55	613.75	164.70	162.80	164.18	94.32	93.55	93.88	4,690	86.28
13	618.80	610.78	614.69	165.48	163.20	164.25	94.72	93.78	94.28	4,880	86.31
16	615.80	605.82	607.88	164.47	162.13	162.62	94.62	93.71	93.97	4,420	86.22
17	615.83	607.93	612.69	164.61	162.49	163.67	94.82	93.65	94.57	4,730	86.15
18	617.15	609.14	610.87	165.39	163.40	164.07	95.07	94.19	94.70	4,530	86.14
19	613.92	605.64	610.02	164.47	162.53	163.22	95.04	94.15	94.59	4,150	86.15
20	614.16	605.85	610.37	163.76	161.75	162.62	94.88	94.18	94.41	3,770	86.16
23	612.78	603.38	605.56	162.64	160.17	160.41	94.78	93.68	94.12	3,700	86.19
24	608.67	602.36	606.73	161.28	159.23	160.64	94.41	93.56	94.09	3,000	86.07
25	611.16	603.82	606.47	161.35	159.54	160.17	94.49	93.55	94.00	3,280	86.03
26	608.61	601.50	606.58	160.28	158.49	159.74	94.25	93.49	93.80	2,900	85.96
30	608.64	600.98	602.65	160.50	158.18	159.10	94.12	93.17	93.46	2,940	85.87
31	605.73	599.21	601.71	159.94	157.73	158.65	93.90	92.86	93.43	2,820	85.91
		High 614.69			High 165.12			High 94.70			High 86.58
		Low 601.71			Low 158.65			Low 92.23			Low 85.87

APRIL, 1959

	30 Industrials High	Low	Close	20 Railroads High	Low	Close	15 Utilities High	Low	Close	Daily Sales -000-	40 Bonds
1	606.97	599.65	602.94	159.77	158.00	158.81	93.87	92.81	93.30	2,980	85.88
2	610.25	602.97	607.52	161.62	158.78	161.08	93.62	92.81	93.24	3,220	85.89
3	614.39	607.52	611.93	163.18	161.24	162.22	94.24	93.14	93.88	3,680	85.90
6	616.42	608.26	611.16	163.96	161.68	162.82	94.54	93.42	93.93	3,510	85.94
7	612.66	606.08	610.34	163.51	161.39	162.62	94.19	93.33	93.69	3,020	85.84
8	612.28	605.15	606.44	163.72	161.80	162.53	94.19	93.33	93.64	3,260	85.84
9	609.11	602.12	605.50	163.31	161.39	162.11	93.78	92.62	92.95	2,830	85.88
10	609.52	603.56	605.97	163.85	161.80	163.11	93.24	92.51	92.59	3,000	85.94
13	610.81	603.47	607.76	164.70	162.58	164.21	92.87	91.74	92.18	3,140	85.88
14	611.98	605.44	609.53	166.57	164.25	165.90	92.70	91.91	92.49	3,320	85.92
15	615.07	608.65	612.50	167.78	165.59	166.55	93.14	92.05	92.70	3,680	85.72
16	620.58	611.41	617.58	169.03	166.37	168.38	93.33	92.21	92.71	3,790	85.65
17	626.66	618.34	624.06	170.14	168.07	168.92	93.64	92.59	93.22	3,870	85.74
20	630.69	622.54	627.08	169.92	167.96	168.87	93.44	92.55	92.84	3,610	85.61
21	632.17	623.42	629.23	169.76	167.87	168.36	93.18	92.04	92.48	3,650	85.57
22	631.62	622.69	625.15	168.76	166.71	167.55	92.77	91.82	92.20	3,430	85.53
23	627.39	618.94	623.27	168.60	166.51	167.42	92.37	91.44	91.85	3,310	85.44
24	630.26	622.60	627.39	169.12	167.06	168.00	92.23	91.36	91.66	3,790	85.37
27	635.29	624.60	629.87	169.23	166.68	167.22	91.95	91.07	91.52	3,850	85.38
28	633.95	625.24	628.87	167.35	165.39	166.08	91.74	90.89	91.22	3,920	85.28
29	629.75	622.60	625.87	167.60	165.34	167.06	91.55	90.70	91.14	3,470	85.21
30	628.69	620.91	623.75	167.64	166.01	166.82	91.83	90.87	91.33	3,510	85.08
		High 629.87			High 168.92			High 93.93			High 85.94
		Low 602.94			Low 158.81			Low 91.14			Low 85.08

MAY, 1959

	-30 Industrials-			-20 Railroads-			-15 Utilities-			Daily Sales -000-	40 Bonds
	High	Low	Close	High	Low	Close	High	Low	Close		
1	628.11	620.49	625.06	168.36	166.24	167.67	92.04	91.00	91.44	3,020	84.96
4	629.87	622.18	625.06	168.40	166.68	167.15	91.99	91.00	91.54	3,060	84.92
5	629.05	622.88	625.90	167.73	166.08	166.71	92.14	91.04	91.52	3,360	84.82
6	630.84	621.73	624.39	167.22	164.39	165.21	92.05	91.04	91.64	4,110	84.87
7	624.45	611.68	615.64	164.85	161.89	162.58	91.99	90.79	91.07	4,530	84.84
8	625.81	615.73	621.36	164.47	162.15	163.85	91.96	91.06	91.60	3,930	84.78
11	627.66	620.58	625.03	164.63	162.96	163.87	92.17	91.38	91.74	3,860	84.77
12	630.90	622.97	627.66	165.46	162.89	164.63	92.29	91.61	92.01	3,550	84.61
13	635.38	625.51	633.05	165.90	163.69	165.14	92.45	91.67	92.05	3,540	84.37
14	640.10	631.02	637.04	167.22	164.32	166.30	92.43	91.57	91.86	3,660	84.34
15	640.92	632.44	634.53	167.20	165.21	165.90	92.62	91.54	92.10	3,510	84.29
18	636.62	629.90	633.53	167.15	165.21	166.22	92.39	91.55	91.95	2,970	84.20
19	639.19	631.20	635.44	167.40	165.50	166.62	92.35	91.33	91.85	3,170	84.02
20	636.77	628.99	631.87	167.24	165.19	165.88	92.20	91.23	91.60	3,550	83.95
21	634.38	626.84	631.65	169.83	165.43	169.34	92.01	91.00	91.39	3,230	83.94
22	637.37	630.38	634.74	171.35	168.54	169.67	91.83	90.84	91.26	3,030	83.89
25	639.64	630.59	632.35	171.15	168.38	168.87	91.63	90.62	90.84	3,260	83.86
26	636.28	629.41	632.38	169.79	167.69	168.42	91.01	90.15	90.51	2,910	83.83
27	639.22	631.99	636.68	169.03	167.42	168.07	91.13	90.03	90.46	2,940	83.68
28	643.09	635.59	639.58	169.05	167.13	167.87	90.67	89.52	89.78	2,970	83.92
29	647.24	637.25	643.79	168.29	166.73	167.33	90.15	89.36	89.80	2,790	83.88
		High	643.79		High	169.67		High	92.10		High 84.96
		Low	615.64		Low	162.58		Low	89.78		Low 83.68

JUNE, 1959

	-30 Industrials-			-20 Railroads-			-15 Utilities-			Daily Sales -000-	40 Bonds
	High	Low	Close	High	Low	Close	High	Low	Close		
1	648.65	640.32	643.51	167.76	165.93	166.62	89.84	88.87	89.25	2,730	83.78
2	643.10	632.85	637.45	166.08	164.34	165.34	89.28	88.17	88.67	3,120	83.77
3	642.46	634.36	637.39	165.95	164.27	164.83	88.76	87.73	88.42	2,910	83.76
4	639.78	628.94	630.54	164.74	162.58	162.91	88.43	87.07	87.36	3,210	83.74
5	633.95	625.97	629.98	164.90	162.76	163.98	87.82	86.86	87.51	2,800	83.63
8	632.03	620.33	621.62	164.52	161.51	161.66	87.96	86.70	87.06	2,970	83.44
9	624.81	613.11	617.62	162.42	159.68	160.46	87.07	85.43	85.71	3,490	83.37
10	630.67	620.45	627.17	163.20	161.17	162.78	86.79	85.58	86.44	3,310	83.33
11	634.14	624.62	627.49	164.52	162.09	163.25	87.29	86.25	86.76	3,120	83.34
12	632.03	623.54	627.42	163.96	162.06	163.02	87.08	86.10	86.54	2,580	83.25
15	629.73	621.02	624.59	163.89	161.60	162.85	86.91	85.82	86.21	2,410	83.27
16	626.60	618.28	621.40	162.98	161.26	161.64	86.47	85.46	85.88	2,440	83.29
17	629.82	619.00	628.05	163.51	161.17	163.09	86.50	85.46	85.99	2,850	83.26
18	633.87	627.20	629.41	165.32	162.98	164.16	86.70	85.77	86.09	3,150	83.14
19	633.73	625.12	629.76	165.05	163.07	164.21	86.26	85.40	85.78	2,260	83.18
22	637.42	627.86	631.71	165.68	163.47	164.79	86.28	85.55	85.90	2,630	83.05
23	635.62	627.61	630.73	165.57	163.94	164.79	86.10	85.31	85.60	2,600	83.10
24	636.91	628.53	634.27	167.82	165.01	167.15	86.32	85.55	86.04	3,180	82.95
25	640.23	631.87	637.23	168.45	166.59	167.64	86.50	85.58	86.15	3,250	82.93
26	643.51	635.02	639.25	168.09	166.48	167.17	86.59	85.71	86.10	3,100	83.03
29	646.41	638.33	643.06	168.78	166.93	168.18	86.97	85.97	86.62	3,000	83.04
30	647.29	639.69	643.60	168.65	166.82	167.62	87.52	86.57	87.30	3,200	83.03
		High	643.60		High	168.18		High	89.25		High 83.78
		Low	617.62		Low	160.46		Low	85.60		Low 82.93

JULY, 1959

	-30 Industrials-			-20 Railroads-			-15 Utilities-			Daily Sales -000-	40 Bonds
	High	Low	Close	High	Low	Close	High	Low	Close		
1	654.01	643.60	650.88	169.12	167.15	168.40	88.17	86.89	87.71	3,150	83.03
2	659.18	650.22	654.76	169.79	168.11	168.92	88.59	87.67	88.10	3,610	83.05
6	663.31	653.79	660.09	169.88	167.73	169.12	89.11	87.79	88.74	3,720	83.00
7	665.89	656.31	663.21	171.77	168.85	171.21	89.27	88.29	88.83	3,840	82.97
8	668.26	658.23	663.81	174.20	171.42	173.56	89.40	88.33	88.84	4,010	83.04
9	667.12	658.89	663.09	174.41	172.22	172.98	89.36	88.45	88.80	3,560	83.00
10	667.34	659.24	663.56	173.83	171.50	172.22	89.24	88.32	88.78	3,600	83.00
13	665.45	655.05	657.35	172.78	169.94	170.46	89.05	88.20	88.58	3,360	83.01
14	661.13	653.53	657.70	172.11	169.67	171.55	89.15	88.34	88.84	3,230	82.98
15	663.91	655.90	660.57	171.95	169.90	170.34	89.44	88.45	88.93	3,280	83.01
16	662.93	655.46	658.29	170.39	167.53	168.49	89.47	88.81	89.19	3,170	83.11
17	659.81	653.69	657.13	168.22	166.30	166.95	89.33	88.49	88.95	2,510	83.19
20	659.87	651.83	654.54	166.80	165.10	165.75	89.40	88.73	88.95	2,500	83.10
21	663.78	652.62	661.48	167.58	165.30	167.00	89.72	88.83	89.41	2,950	83.10
22	667.69	660.06	664.38	168.60	166.91	167.89	90.26	88.96	89.58	3,310	83.18
23	668.23	661.26	664.63	168.94	167.31	168.09	90.04	89.30	89.63	3,310	83.28
24	668.10	661.29	663.72	168.76	166.84	167.69	90.00	89.18	89.63	2,720	83.26
27	671.92	663.34	669.08	168.60	166.75	167.71	90.31	89.06	89.68	2,910	83.30
28	675.76	666.62	672.04	168.29	166.59	167.51	90.09	89.19	89.62	3,190	83.29
29	677.12	668.48	673.18	169.32	166.59	168.49	90.04	89.28	89.71	3,460	83.28
30	678.67	668.29	673.37	168.98	167.24	167.82	90.13	89.41	89.71	3,240	83.31
31	677.28	670.50	674.88	168.42	167.11	167.80	90.34	89.49	89.99	2,270	83.37
		High	674.88		High	173.56		High	89.99		High 83.37
		Low	650.88		Low	165.75		Low	87.71		Low 82.97

AUGUST, 1959

	-30 Industrials-			-20 Railroads-			-15 Utilities-			Daily Sales -000-	40 Bonds
	High	Low	Close	High	Low	Close	High	Low	Close		
3	683.90	673.90	678.10	168.69	167.06	167.58	90.85	89.90	90.62	2,410	83.42
4	679.71	673.40	676.30	168.11	166.80	167.33	90.92	90.04	90.60	2,530	83.40
5	675.76	667.82	672.33	166.77	164.79	165.43	91.10	90.15	90.75	2,630	83.48
6	676.11	669.36	671.98	166.24	164.59	165.23	91.61	90.56	91.20	2,610	83.49
7	676.11	666.71	668.57	165.32	163.94	164.45	91.57	90.76	91.11	2,580	83.53
10	665.14	647.93	653.79	163.69	160.79	161.35	91.26	90.34	90.87	4,190	83.60
11	661.76	651.14	658.07	162.91	161.04	162.51	91.61	90.59	91.29	2,980	83.61
12	662.46	653.41	655.14	163.85	162.13	162.89	91.63	90.79	91.20	2,700	83.68
13	658.48	651.99	655.43	163.16	161.77	162.13	91.83	90.79	91.58	2,020	83.60
14	661.42	654.61	658.74	163.02	161.62	162.35	92.17	91.19	91.80	1,990	83.59
17	663.02	656.18	658.42	162.89	161.55	162.18	92.29	91.45	91.92	1,980	83.61
18	659.15	649.50	650.79	162.40	160.30	160.75	92.17	91.31	91.52	2,280	83.72
19	649.31	639.34	646.53	160.48	157.60	159.25	91.64	90.69	91.03	3,050	83.67
20	657.29	647.01	655.02	164.59	159.61	163.98	91.55	90.88	91.26	2,450	83.69
21	658.86	651.89	655.39	164.65	162.51	163.20	91.54	91.04	91.28	2,000	83.66
24	657.82	650.57	653.22	163.58	161.53	162.38	91.92	91.07	91.44	1,860	83.53
25	659.56	651.07	655.96	162.96	161.77	162.42	91.70	91.10	91.54	1,960	83.49
26	660.34	652.84	657.57	163.18	161.35	162.53	91.96	90.98	91.28	2,210	83.30
27	665.61	657.60	663.34	163.81	161.95	163.07	91.85	91.04	91.39	2,550	83.20
28	666.71	659.75	663.06	164.18	162.73	163.49	91.64	90.97	91.20	1,930	83.11
31	667.72	660.25	664.41	164.12	162.73	163.45	91.55	90.84	91.11	2,140	83.07
		High	678.10		High	167.58		High	91.92		High 83.72
		Low	646.53		Low	159.25		Low	90.60		Low 83.07

SEPTEMBER, 1959

	−30 Industrials−			−20 Railroads−			−15 Utilities−			Daily Sales -000-	40 Bonds
	High	Low	Close	High	Low	Close	High	Low	Close		
1	664.95	652.74	655.90	163.27	161.04	161.60	91.22	90.51	90.76	2,430	83.04
2	659.87	652.15	655.80	161.75	160.37	160.84	90.94	89.88	90.15	2,370	82.84
3	655.93	644.51	645.90	160.77	158.23	158.47	90.60	89.43	89.91	2,330	82.88
4	653.91	645.37	652.18	159.23	157.58	158.61	90.28	89.59	90.07	2,300	82.85
8	651.74	636.98	642.69	158.25	154.54	156.19	90.06	88.76	89.33	2,940	82.84
9	644.74	631.43	637.67	156.89	153.81	155.32	89.69	88.55	88.92	3,030	82.76
10	641.30	630.45	633.38	156.19	153.78	154.52	89.11	88.01	88.37	2,520	82.57
11	641.33	632.34	637.36	156.91	154.86	156.42	88.70	87.89	88.24	2,640	82.45
14	641.08	632.31	633.79	156.40	154.30	154.65	88.54	87.41	87.69	2,590	82.38
15	634.83	624.49	630.80	155.10	152.80	154.34	87.44	86.41	86.91	2,830	82.32
16	636.16	629.47	632.41	155.66	153.87	154.59	87.17	86.41	86.73	2,180	82.29
17	636.19	627.64	629.00	154.99	152.87	153.23	87.00	86.16	86.40	2,090	82.26
18	629.60	621.97	625.78	153.32	151.20	152.45	86.41	85.55	85.71	2,530	82.30
21	625.59	613.71	618.15	152.18	149.57	150.62	85.90	84.64	85.05	3,240	82.28
22	624.24	613.30	616.45	151.58	149.12	150.28	85.71	84.71	85.21	3,000	82.10
23	626.73	617.21	624.02	153.23	150.24	152.47	86.07	85.15	85.68	3,010	82.06
24	635.28	625.06	632.85	155.41	152.38	154.77	86.65	85.46	86.19	3,480	81.94
25	637.73	628.18	632.59	155.53	153.25	154.25	87.28	86.19	86.89	3,280	82.07
28	638.93	629.35	636.47	155.70	153.38	154.77	87.52	86.67	87.20	2,640	81.89
29	643.60	635.72	640.10	157.98	155.12	157.13	88.08	87.25	87.76	3,220	81.73
30	640.16	628.94	631.68	159.50	156.33	157.40	88.27	87.60	87.91	2,850	81.67
		High	655.90		High	161.60		High	90.76		High 83.04
		Low	616.45		Low	150.28		Low	85.05		Low 81.67

OCTOBER, 1959

	−30 Industrials−			−20 Railroads−			−15 Utilities−			Daily Sales -000-	40 Bonds
	High	Low	Close	High	Low	Close	High	Low	Close		
1	635.72	625.40	633.60	159.43	155.37	159.14	88.76	87.77	88.48	2,660	81.64
2	639.22	630.77	636.57	159.21	157.80	158.85	89.22	88.42	88.86	2,270	81.60
5	640.76	634.58	637.01	158.98	157.11	157.82	88.93	87.95	88.24	2,100	81.60
6	639.06	631.87	636.06	159.39	156.93	158.78	88.55	87.57	88.07	2,330	81.70
7	638.46	631.90	635.37	160.08	158.38	159.34	88.29	87.50	87.96	2,380	81.49
8	637.42	631.24	633.04	159.54	157.80	158.38	88.26	87.55	87.91	2,510	81.44
9	638.74	631.62	636.98	159.23	157.96	158.67	88.18	87.45	87.93	2,540	81.56
12	641.27	635.56	638.55	159.65	157.65	158.34	88.23	87.67	87.99	1,750	81.59
13	642.34	635.46	637.83	159.05	157.27	157.67	88.56	87.60	88.08	2,530	81.60
14	639.50	632.28	634.27	157.71	155.59	157.11	88.43	87.60	88.02	2,320	81.55
15	640.51	632.91	637.48	159.14	157.02	158.58	88.13	87.36	87.82	2,190	81.57
16	646.53	637.67	643.22	161.06	158.69	159.99	88.43	87.69	88.15	2,760	81.67
19	643.88	634.93	639.66	159.27	157.56	158.11	88.43	87.67	88.13	2,470	81.68
20	642.18	634.01	635.37	158.78	156.73	157.09	88.26	87.61	87.74	2,740	81.64
21	637.99	630.64	632.69	157.44	156.22	157.18	88.18	87.36	87.71	2,730	81.82
22	635.75	624.55	625.59	156.93	154.83	154.92	88.18	87.30	87.45	3,060	81.90
23	634.42	624.84	633.07	157.27	154.70	156.95	87.82	87.01	87.45	2,880	81.78
26	641.14	633.07	637.61	158.34	155.88	156.78	87.89	87.00	87.33	3,580	81.77
27	645.87	636.19	642.18	157.85	155.33	156.33	87.69	86.95	87.54	4,160	81.71
28	647.04	637.55	643.60	156.69	154.77	155.61	87.74	87.16	87.41	3,920	81.63
29	648.65	638.78	645.11	155.97	153.83	155.15	87.64	87.01	87.41	3,890	81.59
30	649.40	641.68	646.60	155.53	153.92	154.50	87.86	86.97	87.47	3,560	81.64
		High	646.60		High	159.99		High	88.86		High 81.90
		Low	625.59		Low	154.50		Low	87.33		Low 81.44

NOVEMBER, 1959

	—30 Industrials—			—20 Railroads—			—15 Utilities—			Daily Sales -000-	40 Bonds
	High	Low	Close	High	Low	Close	High	Low	Close		
2	650.85	642.24	645.46	154.92	152.67	153.74	87.82	86.88	87.29	3,320	81.48
4	651.96	641.01	645.74	153.74	151.80	152.51	87.48	86.47	86.79	3,940	81.45
5	651.61	641.99	647.57	152.71	150.77	151.58	87.26	86.43	86.97	3,170	81.51
6	654.38	644.92	650.92	154.36	151.35	154.10	87.28	86.45	87.06	3,450	81.51
9	658.86	648.27	650.92	157.31	153.83	154.14	87.52	86.79	87.11	3,700	81.58
10	652.08	644.86	648.14	154.54	152.38	152.96	87.54	86.84	87.14	3,020	81.51
11	649.94	644.96	647.32	153.54	152.13	152.45	87.42	86.95	87.22	2,820	81.57
12	650.88	642.78	644.26	153.18	150.88	151.44	87.70	86.84	86.97	3,600	81.61
13	647.38	640.01	641.71	151.83	149.24	149.45	87.26	86.37	86.67	3,050	81.64
16	644.48	632.72	634.46	149.76	145.97	146.81	86.85	85.84	85.93	3,710	81.64
17	639.60	630.99	635.62	147.95	145.45	146.65	86.40	85.66	86.09	3,570	81.63
18	644.96	634.77	641.99	150.07	146.60	149.41	86.75	85.88	86.28	3,660	81.63
19	648.36	639.63	643.32	150.94	148.46	149.34	86.57	85.93	86.22	3,230	81.67
20	649.97	641.42	645.46	150.65	148.25	149.36	86.48	85.77	86.04	2,960	81.48
23	651.51	641.77	646.75	149.81	147.36	148.25	86.34	85.66	85.90	3,400	81.56
24	653.66	644.86	649.69	148.58	146.20	147.21	86.34	85.59	85.91	3,650	81.63
25	655.55	646.69	651.10	147.73	145.19	146.91	86.51	85.66	86.10	3,550	81.59
27	655.58	647.92	652.52	149.03	146.27	148.60	86.63	85.94	86.40	3,030	81.59
30	661.23	651.55	659.18	150.98	148.56	150.11	86.88	86.19	86.56	3.670	81.58
		High	659.18		High	154.14		High	87.29		High 81.67
		Low	634.46		Low	146.65		Low	85.90		Low 81.45

DECEMBER, 1959

	—30 Industrials—			—20 Railroads—			—15 Utilities—			Daily Sales -000-	40 Bonds
	High	Low	Close	High	Low	Close	High	Low	Close		
1	668.70	659.97	664.38	151.95	149.38	150.94	87.03	86.37	86.70	3,990	81.51
2	668.48	658.64	661.29	152.82	150.30	151.31	87.13	86.35	86.67	3,490	81.47
3	666.05	658.48	662.96	153.11	150.68	152.49	87.17	86.45	86.81	3,280	81.43
4	668.04	659.87	664.00	153.88	151.67	152.73	87.23	86.50	86.75	3,590	81.41
7	670.44	661.83	665.67	153.69	151.90	153.01	87.38	86.53	87.13	3,620	81.22
8	679.36	665.07	675.39	155.27	152.04	154.90	87.61	86.82	87.13	3,870	81.13
9	678.03	668.76	671.26	156.03	153.39	154.38	87.60	86.69	87.10	3,430	81.13
10	676.96	668.80	672.74	155.51	153.55	154.40	87.45	86.84	87.22	3,170	81.08
11	674.72	667.28	670.50	154.57	153.18	153.65	87.29	86.84	87.08	2,910	81.15
14	678.26	669.02	675.07	155.08	153.03	154.09	87.55	86.86	87.30	3,100	81.17
15	681.00	671.63	673.78	156.26	153.55	154.85	87.89	86.97	87.17	3,450	81.24
16	679.20	671.41	675.20	155.89	154.09	154.99	87.45	86.69	87.04	3,270	81.16
17	678.54	671.54	673.90	155.91	153.65	154.33	87.42	86.70	87.01	3,040	81.06
18	679.52	671.35	676.65	155.58	153.77	154.78	87.35	86.65	87.00	3,230	81.02
21	681.54	673.05	675.92	155.81	153.84	154.61	87.50	86.62	87.04	3,290	81.02
22	677.34	669.90	671.82	155.49	153.60	154.40	87.54	86.72	87.29	2,930	80.97
23	675.73	667.75	670.18	155.30	153.13	154.05	87.44	86.72	86.98	2,890	80.87
24	674.69	666.93	670.69	154.68	153.11	154.28	87.32	86.65	87.01	2,320	80.85
28	674.41	665.96	669.77	154.92	152.87	153.32	87.51	86.82	87.14	2,830	80.83
29	675.01	667.13	672.23	154.64	152.52	153.72	87.60	86.92	87.29	3,020	80.78
30	679.49	672.00	676.97	154.75	152.96	154.02	87.86	86.94	87.35	3,680	80.82
31	682.72	676.32	679.36	155.44	153.36	154.05	88.13	87.26	87.83	3,810	80.85
		High	679.36		High	154.99		High	87.83		High 81.51
		Low	661.29		Low	150.94		Low	86.67		Low 80.78

JANUARY, 1960

	—30 Industrials—			—20 Railroads—			—15 Utilities—			Daily Sales -000-	40 Bonds
	High	Low	Close	High	Low	Close	High	Low	Close		
4	688.21	677.39	679.06	158.78	155.77	157.18	88.51	87.35	87.61	3,990	80.92
5	687.14	677.43	685.47	160.90	156.97	160.43	88.30	87.41	88.02	3,710	80.93
6	687.36	678.34	682.62	161.00	158.31	158.90	88.55	87.38	87.86	3,730	80.94
7	683.05	674.98	677.66	159.47	157.16	158.48	88.30	87.33	87.80	3,310	80.98
8	680.86	671.38	675.73	159.63	157.25	158.10	88.14	87.35	87.69	3,290	80.93
11	676.74	663.67	667.16	158.67	156.57	157.51	88.05	86.98	87.22	3,470	80.88
12	667.39	655.49	660.43	157.98	155.53	156.45	87.60	86.35	86.69	3,760	80.88
13	664.68	653.11	656.44	156.92	155.41	156.24	87.22	86.12	86.78	3,470	80.90
14	663.14	655.13	660.53	158.19	156.10	157.70	87.35	86.51	86.91	3,560	80.93
15	666.38	656.25	659.68	159.04	157.25	157.98	87.45	86.63	87.13	3,400	80.97
18	662.06	651.70	653.86	158.12	156.29	156.66	87.26	86.40	86.65	3,020	80.92
19	654.97	642.58	645.07	157.18	154.66	155.06	87.08	86.13	86.43	3,100	80.97
20	650.13	641.57	643.69	156.47	154.42	155.13	86.91	85.84	86.12	2,720	81.04
21	649.51	641.40	645.43	156.69	154.47	155.44	86.50	85.46	85.72	2,700	81.08
22	650.92	643.33	645.85	156.99	155.18	155.63	86.56	85.62	86.38	2,690	81.09
25	648.83	637.20	639.07	155.74	153.95	154.28	86.78	85.88	86.21	2,790	81.11
26	642.81	633.49	639.84	154.83	153.06	154.19	86.75	85.87	86.45	3,060	81.13
27	643.05	633.89	637.67	154.71	153.25	153.74	86.92	85.96	86.21	2,460	81.17
28	638.27	627.77	629.84	153.91	152.09	152.35	86.78	85.99	86.10	2,630	81.29
29	631.51	619.51	622.62	152.85	150.91	151.60	86.51	85.25	85.56	3,060	81.21
		High	685.47		High	160.43		High	88.02		High 81.29
		Low	622.62		Low	151.60		Low	85.56		Low 80.88

FEBRUARY, 1960

	—30 Industrials—			—20 Railroads—			—15 Utilities—			Daily Sales -000-	40 Bonds
	High	Low	Close	High	Low	Close	High	Low	Close		
1	630.75	619.68	626.20	152.35	150.80	151.27	86.41	85.55	85.99	2,820	81.38
2	638.86	628.04	636.92	153.62	151.36	153.15	86.50	85.82	86.22	3,080	81.43
3	640.30	629.03	630.97	153.51	151.13	151.34	86.51	85.50	85.82	3,020	81.41
4	634.53	627.11	631.14	152.68	150.87	151.74	86.04	85.49	85.87	2,600	81.39
5	632.10	623.63	626.77	152.63	150.80	151.50	86.15	85.49	85.75	2,530	81.49
8	626.50	610.17	619.43	151.39	148.70	149.74	86.06	84.97	85.49	3,350	81.59
9	630.53	617.72	628.45	151.57	149.38	150.80	86.29	85.43	85.94	2,860	81.70
10	631.79	620.25	623.36	151.81	150.00	150.77	86.41	85.71	86.06	2,440	81.71
11	626.09	617.34	618.57	151.57	149.67	150.16	86.19	85.46	85.72	2,610	81.90
12	623.70	617.38	622.23	151.88	149.88	151.20	85.87	85.19	85.47	2,230	81.93
15	624.31	615.94	617.58	151.57	149.88	150.25	85.90	85.14	85.34	2,780	82.00
16	619.29	608.94	611.33	150.11	147.99	148.37	85.49	84.86	85.02	3,270	82.02
17	615.33	603.34	613.55	148.98	146.06	148.42	85.71	84.74	85.36	4,210	81.97
18	625.95	615.29	622.19	150.63	148.42	149.69	85.96	85.21	85.58	3,800	82.03
19	630.26	621.31	628.45	152.66	149.43	151.90	86.21	85.38	85.99	3,230	82.08
23	633.50	624.04	626.19	152.33	150.75	151.10	86.47	85.63	85.97	2,960	82.08
24	627.90	620.79	623.73	151.57	149.74	150.87	86.34	85.58	86.01	2,740	82.10
25	630.22	621.65	628.51	152.48	150.21	151.48	86.62	85.82	86.41	3,600	82.10
26	636.30	627.76	632.00	152.27	150.38	150.86	86.98	86.28	86.57	3,380	82.16
29	635.31	627.56	630.12	151.00	149.02	149.95	87.06	86.37	86.76	2,990	82.18
		High	636.92		High	153.15		High	86.76		High 82.18
		Low	611.33		Low	148.37		Low	85.02		Low 81.38

MARCH, 1960

	High	Low	Close	High	Low	Close	High	Low	Close	Daily Sales -000-	40 Bonds
	−30 Industrials−			−20 Railroads−			−15 Utilities−				
1	632.65	623.77	626.87	149.40	148.35	148.61	87.54	86.60	87.33	2,920	82.18
2	628.34	618.95	621.37	148.66	146.99	146.90	87.80	86.98	87.32	3,110	82.15
3	622.64	610.03	612.05	146.44	142.41	142.98	87.45	86.65	87.04	3,160	82.11
4	613.55	600.36	609.79	143.07	139.61	141.83	87.14	86.19	86.53	4,060	82.15
7	614.61	601.59	604.02	142.64	138.82	138.97	86.76	85.82	86.04	2,900	82.14
8	607.88	596.64	599.10	140.30	137.63	138.18	86.45	85.46	85.80	3,370	82.22
9	608.29	596.20	607.16	141.38	138.01	140.57	86.50	85.52	86.21	3,580	82.27
10	609.72	600.40	602.31	143.26	140.73	141.66	86.51	85.71	85.97	3,350	82.28
11	608.70	599.61	605.83	143.89	141.69	143.17	86.70	85.74	86.28	2,770	82.35
14	610.17	602.96	606.79	144.98	142.33	144.22	87.08	86.18	86.84	2,530	82.51
15	614.68	605.52	612.18	145.75	143.96	144.94	87.54	86.84	87.26	2,690	82.60
16	620.90	611.74	616.73	147.32	144.79	146.51	88.02	87.28	87.71	2,960	82.58
17	618.61	610.85	615.09	146.49	144.67	145.61	87.91	87.23	87.42	2,140	82.58
18	620.69	613.52	616.42	146.63	144.79	145.44	87.82	87.11	87.44	2,620	82.59
21	620.52	613.99	617.00	145.56	143.55	143.98	88.01	87.06	87.57	2,500	82.59
22	622.09	614.20	618.09	145.49	143.24	144.55	88.26	87.33	87.76	2,490	82.71
23	624.35	616.25	622.06	146.32	144.22	145.34	88.70	87.58	88.33	3,020	82.72
24	627.86	621.51	624.00	147.37	144.91	146.56	88.83	88.07	88.48	2,940	82.80
25	625.95	619.29	622.47	147.37	145.84	146.44	88.74	87.92	88.15	2,640	82.87
28	625.68	618.81	621.78	147.04	144.77	145.56	88.80	87.85	88.55	2,500	82.86
29	623.97	617.68	620.35	145.77	144.44	145.20	88.74	88.02	88.37	2,320	82.87
30	623.56	616.28	619.94	146.11	144.39	144.87	88.84	87.98	88.52	2,450	82.90
31	622.74	614.75	616.59	145.15	143.43	143.74	88.86	87.92	88.30	2,690	82.99
			High 626.87			High 148.61			High 88.55		High 82.99
			Low 599.10			Low 138.18			Low 85.80		Low 82.11

APRIL, 1960

	High	Low	Close	High	Low	Close	High	Low	Close	Daily Sales -000-	40 Bonds
	−30 Industrials−			−20 Railroads−			−15 Utilities−				
1	619.94	612.94	615.98	144.29	142.98	143.43	88.68	88.01	88.42	2,260	82.98
4	621.68	613.35	618.54	144.12	142.45	143.41	88.70	87.98	88.46	2,450	83.02
5	624.69	616.56	622.19	144.63	143.12	143.91	88.80	87.93	88.52	2,840	82.98
6	631.35	622.64	628.31	145.34	143.79	144.89	88.99	88.21	88.61	3,450	83.11
7	634.08	626.91	629.03	146.06	144.03	144.91	89.44	88.64	89.18	3,070	83.08
8	632.07	624.14	628.10	145.68	143.72	144.96	89.56	88.49	89.12	2,820	83.04
11	631.28	622.40	624.89	145.80	143.86	144.75	89.72	88.80	89.33	2,520	83.13
12	628.62	621.41	626.50	145.53	143.98	145.01	89.56	88.87	89.41	2,470	83.07
13	630.15	623.39	626.50	145.68	143.60	144.41	89.77	89.14	89.47	2,730	83.06
14	632.54	624.62	630.12	144.72	143.15	143.91	89.78	88.93	89.36	2,730	83.05
18	637.16	626.33	630.77	144.65	142.88	143.55	90.07	88.86	89.72	3,200	83.02
19	634.97	624.86	626.40	144.27	142.57	142.98	90.15	89.06	89.62	3,080	82.97
20	625.68	615.94	618.71	143.15	141.45	142.05	89.61	88.67	89.06	3,150	82.87
21	621.92	615.19	619.15	142.84	141.31	142.31	89.71	88.93	89.43	2,700	82.83
22	622.64	614.47	616.32	143.26	141.57	142.38	89.99	89.12	89.65	2,850	82.86
25	617.00	607.71	611.13	142.67	140.21	141.09	89.78	88.87	89.05	2,980	82.87
26	613.76	606.65	610.92	141.74	139.83	141.00	89.53	88.80	89.19	2,940	82.91
27	616.76	606.89	609.96	141.90	140.14	140.83	89.58	88.80	89.08	3,020	82.94
28	612.22	599.27	604.33	140.83	139.23	139.85	89.25	88.32	88.56	3,190	82.91
29	607.85	598.35	601.70	140.85	138.87	139.83	89.15	88.30	88.71	2,850	82.91
			High 630.77			High 145.01			High 89.72		High 83.13
			Low 601.70			Low 139.83			Low 88.42		Low 82.83

MAY, 1960

	−30 Industrials−			−20 Railroads−			−15 Utilities−			Daily Sales -000-	40 Bonds
	High	Low	Close	High	Low	Close	High	Low	Close		
2	605.52	596.61	599.61	140.30	138.01	138.46	89.06	88.14	88.76	2,930	82.88
3	610.14	598.73	607.73	140.28	137.77	139.71	89.03	88.24	88.80	2,910	82.94
4	613.47	606.05	610.99	141.31	139.23	140.38	88.95	88.24	88.74	2,870	82.83
5	613.79	605.80	608.32	141.59	139.78	140.54	89.15	88.34	88.93	2,670	82.80
6	611.41	603.56	607.62	141.78	139.59	140.85	89.39	88.45	88.98	2,560	82.83
9	612.74	604.19	607.48	141.38	139.13	139.80	89.55	88.51	88.87	2,670	82.86
10	610.14	602.86	604.82	139.71	137.41	137.68	89.24	88.40	88.61	2,870	82.76
11	608.88	601.70	606.54	138.27	136.29	137.75	89.11	88.30	88.83	2,900	82.74
12	612.70	603.81	607.87	139.47	137.51	138.54	89.30	88.55	89.06	3,220	82.73
13	618.20	607.31	616.03	140.33	138.06	139.47	89.55	88.70	89.19	3,750	82.76
16	621.84	611.76	617.39	140.95	138.61	139.42	89.91	88.95	89.41	3,530	82.57
17	624.92	613.30	621.63	141.55	138.58	140.78	89.59	88.90	89.12	4,080	82.73
18	630.21	617.71	623.00	141.88	139.61	140.64	89.81	88.71	89.15	5,240	82.75
19	628.08	618.62	624.68	144.10	140.66	142.72	89.43	88.73	88.92	3,700	82.66
20	631.44	621.60	625.24	145.15	142.98	143.91	89.39	88.74	89.18	3,170	82.66
23	629.34	620.34	623.66	144.63	142.74	143.50	89.36	88.80	89.11	2,530	82.59
24	626.89	617.71	621.39	144.24	142.91	143.60	89.58	88.54	89.17	3,240	82.56
25	625.66	616.87	621.28	143.62	141.98	142.45	89.34	88.39	88.93	3,440	82.56
26	626.78	618.20	622.79	142.43	140.78	141.55	89.34	88.59	88.86	3,720	82.50
27	628.81	620.86	624.78	142.17	140.57	141.12	89.09	88.17	88.43	3,040	82.56
31	631.28	622.66	625.50	141.40	139.40	139.66	88.70	87.76	88.10	3,750	82.60
		High	625.50		High	143.91		High	89.41		High 82.94
		Low	599.61		Low	137.68		Low	88.10		Low 82.50

JUNE, 1960

	−30 Industrials−			−20 Railroads−			−15 Utilities−			Daily Sales -000-	40 Bonds
	High	Low	Close	High	Low	Close	High	Low	Close		
1	629.88	620.61	624.89	140.54	138.68	139.44	88.84	87.96	88.51	3,770	82.63
2	631.28	620.76	627.87	140.02	137.58	138.87	89.19	88.05	88.76	3,730	82.71
3	634.33	624.92	628.98	140.64	138.42	139.66	89.41	88.39	89.09	3,340	82.84
6	639.43	627.19	636.92	142.41	139.90	141.93	89.90	88.67	89.55	3,220	82.84
7	647.98	637.85	645.58	143.69	142.09	143.19	90.40	89.36	89.69	3,710	82.82
8	652.83	642.49	650.35	146.92	142.84	145.96	90.54	89.40	90.29	3,800	82.78
9	663.64	647.41	656.42	147.44	144.79	145.51	91.19	89.87	90.73	3,820	82.77
10	659.55	650.68	654.88	146.75	145.41	146.01	91.31	90.03	90.89	2,940	82.67
13	661.45	650.61	655.85	147.32	145.46	145.94	91.85	90.87	91.50	3,180	82.71
14	660.05	650.71	654.88	146.20	144.29	144.96	92.23	91.36	91.79	3,430	82.75
15	657.32	647.37	649.42	145.58	143.58	144.15	92.65	91.64	92.32	3,630	82.82
16	653.95	644.00	648.27	144.44	142.64	143.34	92.68	91.74	92.27	3,540	82.86
17	655.24	644.79	650.89	144.34	141.74	142.72	92.57	91.76	92.23	3,920	82.86
20	654.09	642.02	647.52	143.53	140.95	141.81	92.59	91.83	92.05	3,970	82.85
21	650.89	640.55	644.93	142.41	141.04	141.62	92.39	91.63	92.14	3,860	82.94
22	649.06	639.22	645.36	143.91	141.21	143.07	92.73	91.92	92.57	3,600	82.86
23	651.97	642.52	647.41	144.67	142.38	143.15	93.28	92.51	92.83	3,620	82.74
24	650.32	641.91	647.01	144.48	142.50	143.79	93.61	92.49	93.30	3,220	82.84
27	650.75	640.33	642.49	144.36	142.45	143.26	93.81	92.93	93.30	2,960	82.91
28	644.75	634.66	637.46	144.34	141.93	142.62	93.65	92.76	93.28	3,120	82.83
29	642.78	634.37	638.39	143.91	142.07	142.62	93.66	92.71	93.37	3,160	82.78
30	644.39	634.91	640.62	144.15	142.41	143.19	93.81	93.02	93.39	2,940	82.87
		High	656.42		High	146.01		High	93.39		High 82.94
		Low	624.89		Low	138.87		Low	88.51		Low 82.63

JULY, 1960

	—30 Industrials—			—20 Railroads—			—15 Utilities—			Daily Sales -000-	40 Bonds
	High	Low	Close	High	Low	Close	High	Low	Close		
1	644.71	636.60	641.30	143.58	142.12	142.76	93.83	93.11	93.49	2,620	82.84
5	645.11	636.27	640.91	143.53	141.81	142.21	93.90	93.18	93.56	2,780	82.86
6	645.22	636.45	640.37	142.52	140.88	141.35	94.07	93.21	93.69	2,970	83.03
7	646.83	638.21	644.89	142.41	141.02	141.70	94.72	93.36	94.50	3,050	83.13
8	650.10	641.52	646.91	143.10	141.40	142.29	95.16	94.27	94.87	3,010	83.30
11	649.17	637.60	640.44	142.67	140.40	140.64	95.12	94.12	94.62	2,920	83.27
12	642.24	631.64	634.12	140.85	139.23	139.71	94.84	93.87	94.09	2,860	83.27
13	638.18	629.16	632.11	140.40	138.80	139.44	94.56	93.69	94.34	2,590	83.29
14	637.14	629.34	631.32	139.85	138.13	138.44	94.68	93.59	94.10	2,480	83.30
15	635.16	627.47	630.24	139.40	138.13	138.89	94.63	93.42	93.99	2,140	83.36
18	632.93	623.85	626.00	140.11	138.23	138.66	94.73	93.74	94.49	2,350	83.41
19	629.52	621.22	624.78	139.44	138.18	138.94	94.84	93.94	94.43	2,490	83.48
20	629.23	620.72	624.13	139.73	138.32	138.85	94.92	93.99	94.27	2,370	83.50
21	626.76	614.22	616.63	139.63	137.34	137.60	94.60	93.53	93.81	2,510	83.51
22	617.60	605.45	609.87	137.77	135.10	135.84	93.78	92.84	93.12	2,850	83.68
25	612.17	597.30	601.68	136.32	133.64	134.02	92.98	91.66	91.86	2,840	83.72
26	612.78	600.50	606.75	135.65	133.59	134.40	92.57	91.31	92.02	2,720	83.77
27	611.96	600.35	601.76	134.93	131.85	132.37	92.62	91.26	91.63	2,560	83.80
28	610.88	599.53	605.67	134.79	132.52	133.86	92.54	91.22	92.17	3,020	83.90
29	618.35	605.24	616.73	135.86	134.29	135.26	93.06	92.23	92.83	2,730	83.94
		High 646.91			High 142.76			High 94.87			High 83.94
		Low 601.68			Low 132.37			Low 91.63			Low 82.84

AUGUST, 1960

	—30 Industrials—			—20 Railroads—			—15 Utilities—			Daily Sales -000-	40 Bonds
	High	Low	Close	High	Low	Close	High	Low	Close		
1	622.37	613.36	617.85	136.29	134.76	135.24	93.18	92.04	92.65	2,440	84.05
2	622.34	610.09	613.68	135.24	133.59	133.86	92.87	91.94	92.33	2,090	84.26
3	614.94	605.67	608.69	134.43	132.66	133.02	92.89	92.01	92.54	2,470	84.30
4	611.24	600.28	609.23	134.05	132.14	133.38	92.90	91.92	92.52	2,840	84.37
5	617.88	606.60	614.29	135.19	133.11	134.64	93.33	92.33	92.83	3,000	84.49
8	618.57	609.15	614.79	135.53	134.05	134.67	93.42	92.43	92.99	2,960	84.62
9	619.10	610.95	615.69	135.84	134.38	135.24	93.77	92.95	93.62	2,700	84.67
10	620.54	612.67	617.52	136.41	134.81	135.81	93.97	93.18	93.66	2,810	84.65
11	624.85	616.27	622.88	137.15	135.55	136.36	94.10	93.53	93.81	3,070	84.49
12	630.53	622.34	626.18	138.87	136.67	138.35	94.47	93.74	94.05	3,160	84.60
15	628.41	621.15	624.17	138.99	137.63	138.44	94.76	93.81	94.38	2,450	84.73
16	628.98	622.19	625.43	139.44	138.08	138.99	95.19	94.29	94.76	2,710	84.72
17	628.98	621.62	626.54	140.04	138.37	139.52	95.51	94.18	94.84	3,090	84.93
18	629.31	622.70	625.82	139.99	138.51	139.32	95.31	94.35	94.84	2,890	85.00
19	631.42	624.64	629.27	140.28	138.63	139.73	95.76	94.59	95.53	2,570	84.99
22	634.55	625.53	630.71	140.40	138.87	139.42	96.11	95.09	95.83	2,760	85.06
23	640.40	631.25	638.29	141.35	139.16	140.81	96.80	95.51	95.98	3,560	85.04
24	645.30	636.68	641.56	141.71	139.95	140.81	96.71	95.63	96.33	3,500	85.14
25	643.71	634.24	637.16	141.38	139.87	140.78	96.67	95.83	96.24	2,680	85.02
26	640.34	632.13	636.13	140.52	139.37	139.92	96.60	95.48	96.02	2,780	85.04
29	639.31	631.76	634.46	139.61	138.08	138.44	96.33	95.33	95.80	2,780	85.10
30	636.35	624.44	626.40	138.39	135.93	136.43	96.02	94.92	95.38	2,890	85.17
31	628.73	620.93	625.99	137.51	135.62	136.72	96.07	95.07	95.70	3,130	85.25
		High 641.56			High 140.81			High 96.33			High 85.25
		Low 608.69			Low 133.02			Low 92.33			Low 84.05

SEPTEMBER, 1960

	-30 Industrials-			-20 Railroads-			-15 Utilities-			Daily Sales -000-	40 Bonds
	High	Low	Close	High	Low	Close	High	Low	Close		
1	630.95	622.78	626.10	137.58	136.10	136.72	96.39	95.51	96.13	3,460	85.17
2	629.17	622.07	625.22	136.94	135.57	136.15	96.62	95.64	96.10	2,680	85.17
6	627.58	618.97	620.85	136.43	134.95	135.22	96.77	95.91	96.45	2,580	85.16
7	621.85	611.35	612.27	135.19	133.66	133.86	96.73	95.73	96.17	2,850	85.20
8	615.79	607.39	611.42	134.50	133.11	133.95	96.62	95.48	96.16	2,670	85.14
9	617.41	609.87	614.12	135.46	133.76	134.76	96.73	95.86	96.45	2,750	85.05
12	615.05	606.73	609.35	135.26	133.38	133.76	96.54	95.64	95.92	2,160	85.07
13	614.34	606.47	611.79	134.43	133.04	133.88	96.46	95.54	95.97	2,180	85.03
14	614.01	604.43	605.69	134.43	132.26	132.52	96.48	95.45	95.77	2,530	84.96
15	607.24	598.26	602.69	132.61	131.42	132.14	95.94	94.60	95.23	2,870	84.87
16	606.61	598.22	602.18	133.16	131.63	132.42	95.57	94.47	94.97	2,340	84.87
19	601.18	585.72	586.76	132.23	129.41	129.94	95.04	93.66	94.02	3,790	84.82
20	592.08	581.91	588.20	130.77	128.98	129.84	94.32	93.05	93.59	3,660	84.81
21	597.85	589.31	594.26	131.85	129.60	130.68	94.50	93.15	93.99	2,930	84.79
22	596.70	588.57	592.15	131.51	129.80	130.30	94.54	93.50	93.87	1,970	84.83
23	592.64	583.61	585.20	130.20	128.74	129.25	94.24	93.36	93.62	2,580	84.74
26	584.76	573.29	577.14	128.94	126.24	126.79	93.50	91.95	92.48	3,930	84.66
27	581.80	570.85	574.81	127.17	125.23	125.62	92.61	91.31	91.70	3,170	84.56
28	579.40	565.53	569.08	126.19	123.61	124.06	91.86	90.50	90.85	3,520	84.52
29	575.77	565.49	570.59	124.47	122.58	123.37	91.57	90.21	91.06	2,850	84.43
30	582.47	572.22	580.14	126.19	123.63	125.42	91.73	90.43	91.29	3,370	84.41
		High	626.10		High	136.72		High	96.45		High 85.20
		Low	569.08		Low	123.37		Low	90.85		Low 84.41

OCTOBER, 1960

	-30 Industrials-			-20 Railroads-			-15 Utilities-			Daily Sales -000-	40 Bonds
	High	Low	Close	High	Low	Close	High	Low	Close		
3	582.98	574.26	577.81	126.81	124.92	125.85	92.05	91.19	91.72	2,220	84.41
4	578.73	569.74	573.15	126.02	124.21	124.64	92.37	91.19	91.70	2,270	84.40
5	580.36	569.04	578.88	125.38	123.56	125.04	92.32	91.23	92.11	2,650	84.35
6	589.20	579.54	583.69	126.62	125.02	125.78	92.87	91.89	92.64	2,510	84.30
7	590.82	581.28	586.42	126.88	125.00	126.21	93.69	92.67	93.34	2,530	84.31
10	591.49	583.17	587.31	127.00	125.14	125.95	93.85	93.06	93.56	2,030	84.25
11	593.01	585.02	588.75	127.22	125.50	126.71	93.96	93.06	93.46	2,350	84.25
12	590.90	583.72	585.83	127.67	126.07	126.67	93.43	92.95	93.21	1,890	84.30
13	594.30	584.87	591.49	128.39	126.14	127.43	94.09	92.98	93.71	2,220	84.27
14	599.51	590.45	596.48	128.36	126.86	127.62	94.54	93.53	94.19	2,470	84.29
17	600.03	590.45	593.34	128.55	126.79	127.62	94.60	93.56	94.19	2,280	84.43
18	594.71	585.61	588.75	127.62	125.90	126.71	94.46	93.66	94.10	2,220	84.37
19	590.64	582.32	587.01	127.24	125.90	126.60	94.25	93.25	93.91	2,410	84.33
20	589.71	580.62	582.69	126.88	125.31	125.42	94.19	93.09	93.36	2,910	84.36
21	584.61	575.40	577.55	125.54	124.16	124.71	93.39	92.46	92.92	3,090	84.35
24	578.18	566.64	571.93	125.04	122.99	123.85	92.64	91.14	91.57	4,420	84.39
25	575.73	564.23	566.05	124.90	122.92	123.51	92.17	90.81	91.17	3,030	84.41
26	577.66	566.60	575.18	125.09	123.08	124.61	92.11	90.73	91.77	3,020	84.43
27	583.80	575.07	580.95	126.43	124.80	126.02	92.87	91.39	92.33	2,900	84.42
28	582.10	575.18	577.92	126.21	124.73	125.71	93.11	91.77	92.52	2,490	84.49
31	582.28	573.11	580.36	125.83	123.99	125.07	92.96	91.99	92.54	2,460	84.42
		High	596.48		High	127.62		High	94.19		High 84.49
		Low	566.05		Low	123.51		Low	91.17		Low 84.25

NOVEMBER, 1960

	—30 Industrials—			—20 Railroads—			—15 Utilities—			Daily Sales -000-	40 Bonds
	High	Low	Close	High	Low	Close	High	Low	Close		
1	589.42	579.43	585.24	125.76	124.33	125.11	93.25	92.11	92.64	2,600	84.41
2	592.97	584.35	588.23	127.07	124.90	126.60	93.30	92.07	93.02	2,780	84.42
3	592.60	584.65	590.82	128.46	126.17	127.88	93.49	92.49	93.28	2,580	84.42
4	599.40	589.71	596.07	128.79	126.69	128.22	94.02	93.12	93.75	3,050	84.39
7	604.32	593.52	597.63	128.89	126.98	128.03	93.93	92.76	93.17	3,540	84.51
9	603.62	587.35	602.25	128.48	125.90	127.79	93.66	92.45	93.09	3,450	84.49
10	614.09	600.48	612.01	129.99	127.79	129.75	93.88	92.65	93.61	4,030	84.55
11	611.79	604.43	608.61	130.03	128.70	129.46	93.91	93.00	93.58	2,730	84.55
14	610.09	600.66	604.80	129.58	127.93	128.65	94.03	93.05	93.75	2,660	84.60
15	608.83	598.66	606.87	129.22	127.53	128.70	94.00	93.15	93.71	2,990	84.57
16	611.61	602.29	604.77	129.44	127.65	128.39	94.34	93.39	94.10	3,110	84.53
17	606.58	598.89	602.18	128.94	127.65	128.39	94.16	93.40	93.84	2,450	84.53
18	608.02	599.96	603.62	129.58	127.77	128.98	94.49	93.61	94.13	2,760	84.58
21	607.87	600.44	604.54	130.08	128.46	129.34	95.00	94.07	94.81	3,090	84.55
22	608.02	598.55	601.10	130.03	128.03	128.79	95.61	94.38	95.07	3,430	84.50
23	605.10	597.00	602.47	130.20	128.51	129.80	95.64	94.81	95.32	3,000	84.51
25	608.57	600.18	606.47	130.80	128.96	130.13	95.83	94.84	95.45	3,190	84.54
28	611.31	602.25	605.43	130.82	129.13	129.58	95.97	94.94	95.64	3,860	84.54
29	606.98	599.03	602.40	130.27	128.60	129.37	95.92	95.03	95.57	3,630	84.41
30	602.99	595.15	597.22	130.15	128.63	129.34	95.94	94.94	95.19	3,080	84.50
		High 612.01			High 130.13			High 95.64			High 84.60
		Low 585.24			Low 125.11			Low 92.64			Low 84.39

DECEMBER, 1960

	—30 Industrials—			—20 Railroads—			—15 Utilities—			Daily Sales -000-	40 Bonds
	High	Low	Close	High	Low	Close	High	Low	Close		
1	598.18	589.82	594.56	128.91	127.14	127.88	95.70	94.78	95.48	3,090	84.41
2	600.14	592.12	596.00	128.89	127.41	128.12	95.95	94.91	95.38	3,140	84.31
5	597.52	590.79	593.49	128.74	126.71	127.34	96.24	94.97	95.66	3,290	84.29
6	599.44	591.34	597.11	127.65	126.26	126.86	96.64	95.38	96.35	3,360	84.28
7	606.84	595.93	604.62	127.88	126.05	126.83	97.03	96.07	96.76	3,660	84.24
8	608.61	601.14	605.17	127.50	126.02	126.74	97.12	96.26	96.65	3,540	84.19
9	612.86	601.88	610.90	128.08	126.05	127.77	97.25	96.46	97.02	4,460	84.25
12	615.31	606.87	611.94	128.58	126.81	127.86	97.59	96.80	97.28	3,020	84.15
13	615.49	606.80	611.72	128.46	125.74	126.74	97.97	96.87	97.65	3,500	84.22
14	618.34	608.24	612.68	128.39	125.95	127.10	97.90	97.12	97.49	3,880	84.21
15	616.42	607.21	610.76	128.48	125.78	126.88	97.91	97.08	97.64	3,660	84.39
16	620.37	609.06	617.78	128.36	126.52	127.86	98.54	97.24	98.22	3,770	84.39
19	621.07	612.50	615.56	128.94	127.17	128.36	98.75	97.56	98.19	3,630	84.54
20	619.82	610.94	614.82	128.94	127.02	127.96	98.85	97.77	98.38	3,340	84.61
21	621.33	610.42	615.42	128.94	127.05	128.08	98.85	97.99	98.47	4,060	84.69
22	619.67	610.65	613.31	130.01	127.79	129.10	99.13	98.00	98.75	3,820	84.66
23	617.52	608.28	613.23	130.37	128.43	129.65	99.13	98.35	98.71	3,580	84.69
27	617.78	609.65	613.38	130.54	128.86	129.84	99.56	98.38	99.06	3,270	84.69
28	618.60	610.76	615.75	132.21	129.37	131.01	99.82	98.79	99.38	3,620	84.78
29	620.37	612.42	616.19	132.16	130.15	131.16	100.38	99.34	100.07	4,340	84.81
30	620.80	612.76	615.89	132.06	129.58	130.85	100.43	99.39	100.02	5,300	84.79
		High 617.78			High 131.16			High 100.07			High 84.81
		Low 593.49			Low 126.74			Low 95.38			Low 84.15

JANUARY, 1961

	—30 Industrials—			—20 Railroads—			—15 Utilities—			Daily Sales -000-	40 Bonds
	High	Low	Close	High	Low	Close	High	Low	Close		
3	616.65	606.09	610.25	131.68	129.56	131.06	100.57	99.15	99.75	2,770	84.83
4	623.36	608.46	621.49	134.00	130.63	133.71	100.82	99.64	100.41	3,840	84.83
5	628.35	619.24	622.67	135.98	133.57	135.14	101.11	100.00	100.58	4,130	84.90
6	624.58	615.66	621.64	136.12	133.71	135.65	101.18	100.05	100.83	3,620	84.89
9	627.93	620.12	624.42	138.35	135.65	137.41	101.75	100.67	101.40	4,210	84.90
10	630.90	620.96	625.72	139.52	137.15	138.78	102.13	100.87	101.74	4,840	84.86
11	631.85	622.37	627.21	139.13	137.63	138.63	102.37	100.93	101.78	4,370	84.92
12	633.23	623.28	628.50	139.97	137.84	139.32	102.74	101.62	102.34	4,270	84.88
13	636.20	626.48	633.65	140.09	138.35	139.63	103.10	101.84	102.62	4,520	84.96
16	639.17	629.91	633.19	141.02	138.68	139.97	103.17	102.06	102.44	4,510	84.98
17	634.26	625.49	628.96	141.47	139.25	141.14	102.68	101.65	102.09	3,830	84.99
18	636.39	626.48	634.10	145.32	140.85	144.89	102.66	101.58	102.37	4,390	85.03
19	637.15	628.77	632.39	146.75	142.74	143.77	103.25	102.15	102.74	4,740	85.02
20	637.76	630.41	634.37	144.12	141.33	142.84	104.05	102.57	103.45	3,270	85.04
23	642.68	634.07	639.82	143.77	141.28	141.95	104.30	103.10	103.59	4,450	85.16
24	642.22	634.87	638.79	142.19	138.99	140.57	104.36	103.22	104.05	4,280	85.18
25	643.10	633.76	637.72	141.00	138.85	140.28	104.79	103.56	104.38	4,470	85.28
26	641.84	632.66	638.87	141.21	139.18	139.95	104.82	103.63	104.39	4,110	85.26
27	648.17	636.47	643.59	141.38	138.63	140.54	105.68	104.20	105.14	4,510	85.46
30	653.96	642.33	650.64	142.45	139.83	141.40	106.53	104.93	105.97	5,190	85.52
31	655.18	644.24	648.20	142.82	140.61	141.71	106.78	105.68	106.50	4,690	85.47
		High 650.64			High 144.89			High 106.50			High 85.52
		Low 610.25			Low 131.06			Low 99.75			Low 84.83

FEBRUARY, 1961

	—30 Industrials—			—20 Railroads—			—15 Utilities—			Daily Sales -000-	40 Bonds
	High	Low	Close	High	Low	Close	High	Low	Close		
1	652.82	643.67	649.39	142.95	140.95	142.45	107.64	106.18	107.19	4,380	85.42
2	655.56	646.41	653.62	143.46	141.69	142.91	108.29	107.00	107.91	4,900	85.44
3	657.20	647.37	652.97	143.91	142.05	143.10	108.55	107.37	107.79	5,210	85.48
6	653.65	642.07	645.65	143.29	141.52	142.09	108.47	107.28	107.75	3,890	85.50
7	647.48	637.99	643.94	142.52	141.14	141.66	108.08	106.94	107.56	4,020	85.45
8	651.41	641.04	648.85	143.15	141.31	142.41	108.49	107.01	107.72	4,940	85.44
9	651.56	641.57	645.12	143.03	141.23	141.76	108.45	107.40	107.94	5,590	85.46
10	645.99	635.55	639.67	141.93	139.80	140.64	108.39	107.19	107.72	4,840	85.52
13	640.89	632.81	637.04	140.90	139.16	139.68	107.89	106.81	107.29	3,560	85.60
14	646.37	635.44	642.91	140.97	139.30	140.45	107.53	106.71	107.18	4,490	85.64
15	651.94	641.46	648.89	143.79	140.11	143.31	107.94	106.87	107.44	5,200	85.69
16	656.36	646.64	651.86	146.15	142.88	144.29	108.05	106.81	107.37	5,070	85.77
17	656.21	647.90	651.67	145.01	143.10	144.32	107.94	106.78	107.56	4,640	85.87
20	657.27	649.04	653.65	145.22	142.95	144.05	108.16	107.09	107.67	4,680	85.94
21	657.54	649.00	652.40	144.82	143.19	143.86	108.19	106.99	107.53	5,070	86.00
23	657.46	648.55	654.42	145.53	143.46	144.91	108.32	106.87	107.79	5,620	86.00
24	659.56	650.99	655.60	146.44	143.81	145.49	108.32	107.12	107.89	5,330	86.02
27	662.11	652.59	660.44	146.90	144.72	145.82	108.85	107.66	108.48	5,470	86.05
28	667.03	657.16	662.08	147.16	145.15	146.01	109.05	107.92	108.49	5,830	85.99
		High 662.08			High 146.01			High 108.49			High 86.05
		Low 637.04			Low 139.68			Low 107.18			Low 85.42

MARCH, 1961

	—30 Industrials—			—20 Railroads—			—15 Utilities—			Daily Sales -000-	40 Bonds
	High	Low	Close	High	Low	Close	High	Low	Close		
1	666.27	657.12	663.03	146.08	144.01	145.25	108.95	107.70	108.33	4,970	86.17
2	671.53	661.01	669.39	146.25	144.55	145.65	108.89	107.89	108.42	5,300	86.07
3	676.14	666.61	671.57	146.47	144.48	144.84	109.32	107.83	108.74	5,530	86.23
6	678.23	668.78	674.46	145.94	144.05	144.77	109.55	108.17	108.70	5,650	86.21
7	674.84	662.76	667.14	145.25	142.84	143.62	109.01	107.72	107.98	5,540	86.17
8	670.54	660.70	666.15	143.60	141.98	142.24	108.83	107.40	108.26	5,910	86.19
9	670.08	660.40	663.33	143.31	141.09	142.69	108.73	107.25	107.98	6,010	86.25
10	667.91	658.57	663.56	144.05	142.09	143.00	108.83	107.79	108.38	5,950	86.27
13	668.52	659.48	664.44	143.72	142.00	142.67	109.08	108.00	108.64	5,080	86.34
14	667.11	657.85	661.08	143.48	141.76	142.33	109.27	108.32	109.01	4,900	86.34
15	665.96	656.36	662.88	143.10	141.43	142.09	109.56	108.58	109.21	4,900	86.34
16	674.19	660.36	670.38	144.10	141.83	143.55	110.24	108.58	109.65	5,610	86.32
17	681.63	670.80	676.48	145.75	143.43	144.67	110.94	109.61	110.40	5,960	86.37
20	684.07	674.12	678.84	146.66	144.22	146.20	111.59	110.03	110.82	5,780	86.31
21	682.92	672.44	678.73	150.12	146.18	149.81	112.07	110.65	111.79	5,800	86.39
22	685.32	675.19	679.38	152.72	149.55	150.81	112.41	111.15	112.07	5,840	86.34
23	680.48	671.79	675.45	150.60	147.78	148.59	112.52	111.12	111.67	5,170	86.33
24	677.28	668.59	672.48	149.16	147.25	148.18	112.36	111.22	111.75	4,390	86.36
27	675.30	667.22	671.03	149.43	147.16	147.61	112.30	111.09	111.98	4,190	86.35
28	674.96	665.73	669.58	148.83	146.94	148.07	112.47	111.23	112.04	4,630	86.28
29	679.19	667.64	676.41	148.59	146.80	147.42	112.88	111.37	112.16	5,330	86.29
30	682.01	673.13	676.63	147.95	145.72	146.20	112.58	111.43	111.91	5,610	86.25
		High	679.38		High	150.81		High	112.16		High 86.39
		Low	661.08		Low	142.09		Low	107.98		Low 86.07

APRIL, 1961

	—30 Industrials—			—20 Railroads—			—15 Utilities—			Daily Sales -000-	40 Bonds
	High	Low	Close	High	Low	Close	High	Low	Close		
3	684.29	672.98	677.59	146.70	144.15	145.03	112.80	111.72	112.41	6,470	86.17
4	683.11	673.81	678.73	145.80	143.81	144.44	113.10	111.60	112.26	7,080	86.12
5	680.98	671.79	677.32	144.72	142.84	143.69	112.71	111.44	112.13	5,430	86.15
6	682.58	673.39	679.34	145.20	143.29	144.12	112.66	111.09	111.84	4,910	86.16
7	687.76	676.52	683.68	145.08	143.48	144.41	113.02	111.16	112.23	5,100	86.25
10	695.77	684.16	692.06	145.49	143.67	144.58	113.10	111.81	112.63	5,550	86.18
11	700.31	687.87	694.11	145.20	143.22	143.50	113.27	111.85	112.29	5,230	86.13
12	697.39	686.96	690.16	144.27	142.62	142.93	113.08	111.54	112.11	4,870	86.14
13	696.12	685.54	692.02	143.86	142.07	143.17	112.77	111.34	112.13	4,770	86.14
14	698.45	688.07	693.72	143.72	141.76	142.31	112.70	111.31	111.97	5,240	86.08
17	700.75	689.29	696.72	143.36	141.23	142.36	113.02	111.56	112.44	5,860	86.11
18	697.43	687.63	690.60	143.00	141.38	141.88	113.14	111.56	111.95	4,830	85.88
19	690.67	679.58	686.21	141.95	140.35	141.19	112.41	111.32	111.94	4,870	85.79
20	689.02	679.77	684.24	142.05	139.95	140.76	112.66	111.34	111.89	4,810	85.68
21	689.41	678.79	685.26	141.74	139.87	140.88	112.58	111.44	112.16	4,340	85.67
24	684.16	671.64	672.66	141.43	139.06	140.04	112.30	110.96	111.22	4,590	85.54
25	686.72	672.59	683.09	141.74	139.52	141.04	111.89	110.47	111.40	4,670	85.49
26	688.98	678.94	682.18	142.26	140.59	141.55	112.51	111.12	111.89	4,980	85.45
27	686.76	675.78	679.54	142.62	141.19	141.74	112.45	111.21	111.73	4,450	85.58
28	683.96	673.34	678.71	142.07	140.47	141.07	112.42	111.10	111.72	3,710	85.59
		High	696.72		High	145.03		High	112.63		High 86.25
		Low	672.66		Low	140.04		Low	111.22		Low 85.45

MAY, 1961

	\-30 Industrials\-			\-20 Railroads\-			\-15 Utilities\-			Daily Sales -000-	40 Bonds
	High	Low	Close	High	Low	Close	High	Low	Close		
1	683.17	672.98	677.05	141.95	139.78	140.78	112.25	110.81	111.34	3,710	85.71
2	685.34	674.68	682.34	142.91	140.88	142.12	112.20	111.07	111.85	4,110	85.73
3	691.54	682.10	688.90	144.51	142.31	143.79	112.52	111.43	112.04	4,940	85.82
4	696.16	686.49	692.25	145.29	143.43	144.12	112.70	111.45	112.00	5,350	85.79
5	697.31	687.59	690.67	144.89	143.29	143.86	112.61	111.22	111.81	4,980	85.86
8	695.41	685.15	689.06	144.96	143.00	143.62	112.54	111.25	111.98	5,170	85.88
9	692.73	683.49	686.92	144.79	143.03	144.17	112.52	111.32	111.95	5,380	85.89
10	690.67	682.93	686.61	144.91	143.36	144.05	112.67	111.54	112.32	5,450	85.90
11	689.81	682.06	686.49	145.20	143.31	144.53	113.33	111.45	112.60	5,170	85.83
12	691.54	683.41	687.91	145.61	143.72	144.77	113.48	112.09	113.02	4,840	85.88
15	696.44	684.47	692.37	145.61	143.98	144.75	114.43	112.81	113.71	4,840	85.92
16	700.35	690.52	697.74	145.80	143.86	144.98	114.57	112.89	113.61	5,110	85.98
17	708.49	695.18	705.52	148.73	144.75	148.02	114.57	113.16	113.71	5,520	85.98
18	709.00	697.70	701.14	149.04	146.97	147.66	114.61	112.89	113.72	4,610	86.06
19	708.88	698.38	705.96	148.61	146.82	147.56	114.51	113.10	113.69	4,200	86.04
22	714.69	697.74	702.44	149.14	146.66	147.47	114.43	113.15	113.93	4,070	85.89
23	707.34	697.31	700.59	147.59	146.04	146.49	113.95	112.63	113.22	3,660	85.87
24	702.56	689.77	696.52	146.85	145.20	146.08	114.55	112.40	113.65	3,970	85.89
25	699.13	687.55	690.16	146.54	145.03	145.56	114.40	112.83	113.33	3,760	85.88
26	699.48	686.13	696.28	146.42	144.29	145.27	114.08	112.56	113.30	3,780	85.72
31	703.04	692.65	696.72	146.06	144.10	144.91	113.75	112.27	112.77	4,320	85.72
		High	705.96		High	148.02		High	113.93		High 86.06
		Low	677.05		Low	140.78		Low	111.34		Low 85.71

JUNE, 1961

	\-30 Industrials\-			\-20 Railroads\-			\-15 Utilities\-			Daily Sales -000-	40 Bonds
	High	Low	Close	High	Low	Close	High	Low	Close		
1	700.86	691.39	695.37	145.22	143.72	144.12	113.87	112.46	113.45	3,770	85.66
2	700.82	691.54	697.70	144.63	143.07	143.89	113.80	112.53	113.01	3,670	85.58
5	708.57	695.33	703.43	144.82	142.84	144.12	114.25	112.80	113.87	4,150	85.54
6	708.88	699.21	703.79	144.77	143.36	144.20	115.04	113.37	114.51	4,250	85.34
7	708.05	697.70	700.86	144.34	143.10	143.86	115.40	114.02	114.33	3,980	85.28
8	704.46	695.26	701.69	144.75	142.95	144.12	114.43	113.36	113.93	3,810	85.07
9	705.88	697.39	700.90	145.22	143.24	143.93	114.37	113.28	113.77	3,520	84.90
12	702.29	693.20	696.76	144.03	141.98	142.72	114.43	112.75	113.12	3,260	84.83
13	698.93	690.24	694.15	143.34	141.69	142.07	113.68	112.45	113.07	3,030	84.92
14	700.47	691.42	695.81	143.29	141.81	142.07	113.71	112.51	113.28	3,430	84.99
15	699.72	689.69	691.27	142.74	140.85	141.45	113.52	112.66	112.99	3,220	84.91
16	691.98	681.16	685.50	142.02	140.09	140.64	113.54	111.92	112.60	3,380	84.79
19	686.53	673.49	680.68	140.59	138.54	139.40	112.56	111.04	111.63	3,980	84.67
20	691.03	679.50	687.87	140.92	138.87	140.21	112.63	111.13	111.92	3,280	84.66
21	691.42	683.13	686.09	140.88	139.20	140.38	112.60	111.54	111.83	3,210	84.52
22	689.96	680.13	685.62	141.12	139.09	140.16	112.27	111.07	111.72	2,880	84.54
23	692.81	683.64	688.66	141.04	139.49	139.90	112.43	111.27	111.81	2,720	84.43
26	689.96	679.22	681.16	139.87	138.01	138.58	112.19	111.09	111.54	2,690	84.45
27	687.16	676.30	683.88	138.42	136.70	137.75	111.63	110.29	110.82	3,090	84.38
28	690.04	681.20	684.59	139.30	137.46	138.46	111.83	110.57	111.27	2,830	84.37
29	687.28	679.62	681.95	139.11	137.75	138.30	111.89	110.74	111.27	2,560	84.28
30	687.16	678.23	683.96	139.63	138.11	139.47	112.16	110.94	111.74	2,380	84.33
		High	703.79		High	144.20		High	114.51		High 85.66
		Low	680.68		Low	137.75		Low	110.82		Low 84.28

JULY, 1961

	High	Low	Close	High	Low	Close	High	Low	Close	Daily Sales -000-	40 Bonds
	—30 Industrials—			—20 Railroads—			—15 Utilities—				
3	691.50	681.91	689.81	140.69	138.89	140.11	112.72	111.59	112.39	2,180	84.25
5	696.76	688.34	692.77	141.38	139.90	140.97	114.10	112.22	113.66	3,270	84.25
6	698.97	690.36	694.27	143.26	140.09	142.48	114.58	112.96	113.86	3,470	84.16
7	697.90	689.61	692.73	142.76	140.84	141.36	114.48	113.28	113.93	3,030	84.12
10	698.49	689.33	693.16	141.59	139.86	140.56	114.80	113.69	114.30	3,180	84.02
11	698.18	690.95	694.47	140.75	139.23	139.91	114.76	113.68	114.17	3,160	84.02
12	696.28	687.28	690.79	139.72	138.24	138.85	114.61	113.49	113.99	3,070	83.98
13	690.83	683.17	685.90	138.81	136.72	137.50	114.14	113.24	113.78	2,670	83.95
14	693.68	682.58	690.95	137.96	135.93	137.05	114.90	113.36	114.37	2,760	84.02
17	693.48	683.49	684.59	137.40	135.13	135.65	114.63	113.51	113.81	2,690	83.83
18	687.95	677.44	679.30	135.95	133.77	134.57	114.22	113.01	113.58	3,010	83.63
19	685.22	674.80	682.74	134.29	132.84	133.49	113.95	112.57	113.21	2,940	83.66
20	686.21	678.31	682.97	135.01	133.40	134.24	114.02	113.07	113.72	2,530	83.73
21	686.84	679.10	682.81	135.39	133.56	134.69	114.40	113.07	113.99	2,360	83.75
24	687.16	678.27	682.14	135.76	134.24	135.20	114.58	113.72	114.16	2,490	83.70
25	688.89	679.66	686.37	136.51	134.90	136.04	115.01	113.81	114.60	3,010	83.94
26	697.98	687.63	694.19	138.81	136.28	137.82	115.61	114.19	114.89	4,070	83.89
27	705.96	693.40	702.80	139.70	137.33	138.90	115.88	114.60	115.26	4,170	83.85
28	709.75	700.00	705.13	139.77	138.15	139.06	115.84	114.73	115.39	3,610	83.94
31	709.75	700.51	705.37	139.39	137.50	137.89	116.55	115.13	115.85	3,170	83.88
		High	705.37		High	142.48		High	115.85		High 84.25
		Low	679.30		Low	133.49		Low	112.39		Low 83.63

AUGUST, 1961

	High	Low	Close	High	Low	Close	High	Low	Close	Daily Sales -000-	40 Bonds
	—30 Industrials—			—20 Railroads—			—15 Utilities—				
1	716.03	702.21	713.94	138.78	136.91	138.10	117.03	115.66	116.79	3,990	83.98
2	719.86	707.93	710.46	139.51	137.71	138.45	117.81	116.51	116.85	4,300	83.80
3	720.41	709.04	715.71	140.05	137.85	139.53	117.44	116.44	117.13	3,650	83.84
4	723.57	715.08	720.69	141.01	139.04	140.37	118.23	116.79	117.78	3,710	83.73
7	723.14	712.95	719.58	140.66	138.55	139.72	119.53	117.55	119.15	3,560	83.58
8	725.78	715.91	720.22	140.77	138.90	139.98	120.24	118.46	119.29	4,050	83.45
9	722.31	713.86	717.57	140.75	138.99	139.63	120.47	119.03	120.05	3,710	83.33
10	722.98	713.46	720.49	140.44	138.83	139.58	120.49	118.97	119.91	3,570	83.30
11	726.57	717.31	722.61	140.91	139.20	139.81	120.53	118.88	119.40	3,260	83.37
14	724.02	714.48	718.93	140.35	138.99	139.55	119.74	118.38	118.93	3,120	83.41
15	722.85	714.15	716.18	140.02	138.95	139.44	119.34	118.12	118.81	3,320	83.44
16	720.67	712.62	718.20	141.45	139.02	141.10	119.68	118.49	119.20	3,430	83.43
17	725.80	715.53	721.84	144.38	141.40	143.39	120.23	118.73	119.61	4,130	83.56
18	727.54	719.25	723.54	144.94	143.42	144.52	120.44	119.29	120.00	4,030	83.65
21	728.35	719.49	724.75	145.80	143.82	144.75	120.76	119.55	120.27	3,880	83.57
22	730.17	720.34	725.76	145.71	144.10	144.92	120.58	119.61	120.11	3,640	83.53
23	726.86	717.27	720.46	145.88	143.82	144.73	120.36	119.37	119.93	3,550	83.49
24	719.41	709.54	714.03	144.61	142.69	143.67	120.38	119.21	119.64	3,090	83.49
25	720.10	712.01	716.70	144.00	142.46	143.02	120.29	119.20	119.96	3,050	83.48
28	722.24	712.33	716.01	143.25	141.80	142.34	120.42	119.35	119.97	3,150	83.47
29	718.52	709.78	714.15	143.39	141.36	142.62	120.56	119.17	120.00	3,160	83.50
30	720.06	711.08	716.90	145.15	142.55	144.40	120.95	119.77	120.71	3,220	83.46
31	723.13	713.75	719.94	144.99	143.67	144.31	121.44	120.15	120.82	2,920	83.40
		High	725.76		High	144.92		High	120.82		High 83.98
		Low	710.46		Low	138.10		Low	116.79		Low 83.30

SEPTEMBER, 1961

	-30 Industrials-			-20 Railroads-			-15 Utilities-			Daily Sales -000-	40 Bonds
	High	Low	Close	High	Low	Close	High	Low	Close		
1	724.95	716.30	721.19	144.68	143.44	144.19	121.32	120.32	120.80	2,710	83.30
5	726.01	716.26	718.72	144.82	143.32	143.96	121.54	120.30	120.68	3,000	83.37
6	728.76	719.61	726.01	144.56	143.04	143.84	121.86	120.42	121.26	3,440	83.40
7	733.53	723.05	726.53	144.82	143.07	143.65	122.03	120.94	121.56	3,900	83.48
8	727.30	717.71	720.91	143.93	142.11	142.76	121.65	120.71	121.32	3,430	83.47
11	721.39	710.47	714.36	143.30	141.15	141.94	121.56	120.27	120.74	2,790	83.38
12	725.88	713.99	722.61	144.00	142.01	143.37	122.09	120.68	121.33	2,950	83.45
13	727.66	718.81	722.20	144.47	143.00	143.75	122.39	120.88	121.54	3,110	83.40
14	723.22	713.14	715.00	144.33	142.74	143.18	122.36	120.91	121.54	2,920	83.41
15	720.06	710.23	716.30	144.54	142.29	143.79	122.10	121.08	121.77	3,130	83.45
18	716.94	705.62	711.24	144.24	141.73	142.50	122.42	120.94	121.62	3,550	83.45
19	712.98	700.52	702.54	142.79	140.80	141.59	121.92	120.35	121.12	3,260	83.44
20	709.22	699.87	707.32	143.63	140.94	143.23	121.74	120.55	121.05	2,700	83.42
21	713.22	703.43	706.31	144.96	143.00	144.10	122.07	120.55	121.05	3,340	83.51
22	707.48	698.70	701.57	145.13	143.09	144.28	121.62	120.64	121.11	3,070	83.50
25	702.99	688.87	691.86	143.98	141.85	142.29	121.26	119.83	120.05	3,700	83.45
26	700.44	689.07	693.20	143.07	141.17	141.73	121.20	119.80	120.52	3,320	83.50
27	703.47	691.58	701.13	143.56	141.71	143.16	121.33	120.14	120.85	3,440	83.45
28	706.18	696.80	700.28	144.14	142.81	143.35	121.94	120.79	121.57	3,000	83.44
29	704.93	694.25	701.21	144.24	142.90	143.96	122.95	121.48	122.44	3,060	83.50
		High	726.53		High	144.28		High	122.44		High 83.51
		Low	691.86		Low	141.59		Low	120.05		Low 83.30

OCTOBER, 1961

	-30 Industrials-			-20 Railroads-			-15 Utilities-			Daily Sales -000-	40 Bonds
	High	Low	Close	High	Low	Close	High	Low	Close		
2	704.97	695.63	699.83	145.20	143.30	144.28	123.97	122.44	123.36	2,800	83.59
3	703.03	693.12	698.66	145.34	143.53	144.45	124.25	122.77	123.59	2,680	83.58
4	706.75	698.13	703.31	150.18	145.08	149.85	125.28	123.44	124.62	3,380	83.63
5	711.89	701.13	708.49	152.24	149.60	150.70	126.61	124.51	126.01	3,920	83.57
6	714.07	704.40	708.25	151.63	149.71	150.74	127.82	125.68	127.13	3,470	83.70
9	712.05	700.93	705.42	151.49	149.74	150.65	128.19	126.66	127.46	2,920	83.68
10	709.62	700.56	706.67	151.66	149.71	150.91	128.05	126.90	127.60	3,430	83.79
11	710.59	701.69	705.62	153.46	150.56	152.92	128.79	127.11	127.84	3,670	83.84
12	709.54	701.13	705.50	153.60	151.77	152.20	128.10	126.92	127.55	3,060	83.89
13	708.77	700.12	703.31	153.04	151.12	151.77	127.95	126.71	127.17	3,090	83.87
16	707.84	699.23	703.15	152.36	150.46	151.02	127.30	126.24	126.81	2,840	83.92
17	706.18	698.62	701.98	151.63	150.00	150.42	127.70	126.18	126.78	3,110	83.91
18	708.37	699.63	704.20	151.49	149.74	150.72	127.82	126.72	127.34	3,520	83.93
19	710.43	700.48	704.85	151.35	149.78	150.67	130.19	127.63	129.22	3,850	84.02
20	708.77	700.52	705.62	151.19	149.34	150.14	130.90	129.08	130.14	3,470	83.99
23	708.73	695.55	698.98	151.24	148.82	150.07	131.06	129.23	129.57	3,440	84.14
24	704.00	693.77	697.24	150.39	148.33	149.43	129.72	127.81	128.51	3,430	84.12
25	706.47	695.55	700.72	150.18	148.45	149.08	129.63	128.19	129.07	3,590	84.18
26	704.81	694.82	700.68	149.76	148.10	148.82	129.79	128.82	129.49	3,330	84.14
27	703.60	694.94	698.74	149.18	147.51	148.08	130.05	128.85	129.52	3,200	84.22
30	704.57	696.35	701.09	148.73	146.76	147.63	130.73	129.18	130.29	3,430	84.22
31	706.67	699.35	703.92	148.78	147.23	148.12	131.16	129.44	130.07	3,350	84.08
		High	708.49		High	152.92		High	130.29		High 84.22
		Low	697.24		Low	144.28		Low	123.36		Low 83.57

NOVEMBER, 1961

	—30 Industrials—			—20 Railroads—			—15 Utilities—			Daily Sales -000-	40 Bonds
	High	Low	Close	High	Low	Close	High	Low	Close		
1	708.09	700.12	703.84	148.45	147.23	147.77	130.91	129.51	130.21	3,210	84.16
2	710.35	701.29	706.83	148.87	147.26	148.33	131.16	129.66	130.57	3,890	84.16
3	712.62	702.62	709.26	150.18	147.96	149.46	131.74	129.88	130.84	4,070	84.22
6	717.47	707.11	714.60	151.00	148.54	149.69	132.22	130.64	131.51	4,340	84.21
8	726.73	714.68	723.74	151.59	148.73	150.60	132.99	131.22	132.23	6,090	84.22
9	726.82	717.75	722.28	151.94	149.90	150.65	133.13	131.55	132.30	4,680	84.31
10	727.46	718.28	724.83	150.77	149.20	149.85	133.69	132.03	133.10	4,180	84.37
13	732.48	721.27	728.43	151.14	149.36	150.28	134.76	132.99	134.21	4,540	84.37
14	736.65	724.35	732.56	151.96	149.25	151.19	135.25	133.72	134.76	4,750	84.46
15	741.30	730.86	734.34	152.38	149.97	150.51	135.85	134.27	135.05	4,660	84.52
16	737.54	725.84	733.33	151.31	149.71	150.23	135.71	133.92	134.79	3,980	84.46
17	736.00	724.83	729.53	151.61	149.41	151.02	136.52	134.62	135.79	3,960	84.57
20	735.59	725.32	730.09	151.82	149.69	150.49	136.57	134.84	135.90	4,190	84.55
21	737.58	724.06	729.32	150.58	148.15	148.66	136.50	133.99	134.79	4,890	84.52
22	734.18	724.95	730.42	149.15	146.98	148.19	135.79	134.24	134.97	4,500	84.54
24	735.92	726.61	732.60	148.87	147.07	147.75	135.82	134.47	135.39	4,020	84.54
27	738.38	726.94	731.99	148.38	146.46	147.05	136.13	134.11	134.76	4,700	84.47
28	735.19	724.23	728.07	147.63	145.99	146.95	135.72	134.11	134.54	4,360	84.39
29	732.11	722.57	727.18	147.72	146.02	146.83	135.65	133.99	134.84	4,550	84.41
30	727.50	717.88	721.60	146.93	145.13	145.80	135.17	133.56	134.22	4,210	84.34
		High	734.34		High	151.19		High	135.90		High 84.57
		Low	703.84		Low	145.80		Low	130.21		Low 84.16

DECEMBER, 1961

	—30 Industrials—			—20 Railroads—			—15 Utilities—			Daily Sales -000-	40 Bonds
	High	Low	Close	High	Low	Close	High	Low	Close		
1	731.99	719.74	728.80	147.09	145.13	146.39	135.42	133.53	134.77	4,420	84.49
4	737.62	725.16	731.22	147.40	145.92	146.60	136.00	134.24	135.00	4,560	84.44
5	734.91	726.82	731.31	147.02	145.34	145.85	135.88	133.96	134.67	4,330	84.37
6	735.80	725.04	730.09	146.55	144.92	145.41	135.22	133.69	134.37	4,200	84.22
7	732.96	723.42	726.45	145.97	144.42	144.77	134.71	132.70	133.59	3,900	84.20
8	732.92	722.24	728.23	146.25	144.19	145.71	134.64	132.96	133.84	4,010	84.19
11	736.40	725.84	732.56	146.76	144.33	145.48	135.54	133.96	134.94	4,360	84.18
12	739.36	728.23	734.02	145.83	144.31	144.87	135.98	133.93	134.97	4,680	84.09
13	739.88	730.58	734.91	145.38	143.91	144.45	135.59	133.53	133.98	4,890	83.96
14	737.82	727.34	730.94	144.99	143.21	143.63	134.37	132.42	133.20	4,350	83.87
15	734.58	725.72	729.40	144.77	143.21	143.91	133.84	132.38	132.93	3,710	83.76
18	734.91	724.43	727.71	144.59	142.79	143.11	133.30	131.73	132.03	3,810	83.79
19	727.66	719.25	722.41	143.18	141.15	141.57	132.27	130.34	130.92	3,440	83.81
20	728.19	718.32	722.57	141.94	140.02	140.66	131.07	138.83	129.16	3,640	83.76
21	725.64	717.27	720.10	141.87	139.74	141.10	129.78	127.80	128.35	3,440	83.76
22	725.08	714.60	720.87	142.76	140.33	141.61	129.28	127.25	128.12	3,390	83.84
26	727.42	717.92	723.09	143.07	141.08	141.64	128.73	126.79	127.52	3,180	83.76
27	734.54	723.34	731.43	143.86	141.85	143.04	128.70	126.69	128.07	4,170	83.79
28	738.79	728.88	731.51	144.54	142.62	143.63	128.83	127.55	128.33	4,530	83.77
29	734.99	726.41	731.14	144.28	142.60	143.84	129.61	128.13	129.16	5,370	83.85
		High	734.91		High	146.60		High	135.00		High 84.49
		Low	720.10		Low	140.66		Low	127.52		Low 83.76

JANUARY, 1962

	\-30 Industrials\-			\-20 Railroads\-			\-15 Utilities\-			Daily Sales -000-	40 Bonds
	High	Low	Close	High	Low	Close	High	Low	Close		
2	734.38	721.39	724.71	145.43	143.30	144.00	129.89	127.88	128.10	3,120	83.91
3	729.61	720.22	726.01	148.73	144.24	148.33	128.53	126.87	127.65	3,590	83.99
4	733.77	718.00	722.53	150.39	147.35	147.94	127.98	126.36	126.61	4,450	84.18
5	725.60	709.74	714.84	148.87	145.95	146.60	126.70	124.20	124.46	4,630	84.21
8	715.69	698.42	708.98	147.44	145.03	146.65	125.49	122.74	124.43	4,620	84.23
9	714.96	703.88	707.64	148.87	146.86	147.42	125.41	123.47	124.30	3,600	84.26
10	711.81	701.69	706.02	148.57	146.81	147.65	125.19	123.37	124.16	3,300	84.44
11	713.10	702.26	710.67	148.38	146.83	148.05	124.83	123.35	124.13	3,390	84.54
12	717.71	707.92	711.73	149.15	147.54	148.38	125.26	123.92	124.81	3,730	84.61
15	715.00	706.18	709.50	149.34	147.61	148.31	125.56	124.05	124.38	3,450	84.58
16	711.20	700.97	705.29	148.94	147.37	148.26	124.85	123.24	124.13	3,650	84.62
17	707.03	694.86	697.41	148.71	147.02	147.56	124.71	123.25	123.42	3,780	84.52
18	700.12	690.21	696.03	148.15	146.67	147.70	123.85	122.31	123.25	3,460	84.55
19	703.35	694.29	700.72	148.87	146.83	148.26	124.45	122.89	123.63	3,800	84.57
22	706.27	698.05	701.98	148.87	147.28	147.77	125.26	123.20	124.08	3,810	84.55
23	704.40	694.57	698.54	148.19	146.60	147.33	124.82	122.97	123.95	3,350	84.60
24	701.69	689.52	698.17	147.49	146.27	147.09	124.38	122.80	123.85	3,760	84.59
25	703.80	694.17	696.52	148.43	146.79	147.42	125.19	123.62	124.08	3,560	84.50
26	698.13	689.11	692.19	147.82	146.39	146.86	124.61	123.09	123.60	3,330	84.51
29	695.71	686.89	689.92	147.37	145.64	146.27	124.14	122.65	123.39	3,050	84.56
30	698.38	687.82	694.09	147.63	145.95	146.74	124.33	123.01	123.62	3,520	84.43
31	702.75	692.27	700.00	148.15	146.58	147.77	124.82	123.35	124.08	3,940	84.39
		High	726.01		High	148.38		High	128.10		High 84.62
		Low	689.92		Low	144.00		Low	123.25		Low 83.91

FEBRUARY, 1962

	\-30 Industrials\-			\-20 Railroads\-			\-15 Utilities\-			Daily Sales -000-	40 Bonds
	High	Low	Close	High	Low	Close	High	Low	Close		
1	707.36	696.07	702.54	149.74	147.54	149.04	125.20	124.00	124.80	4,260	84.49
2	709.34	699.11	706.55	150.30	148.78	149.83	125.30	124.10	124.94	3,950	84.51
5	710.84	702.34	706.14	150.77	149.04	149.67	125.99	124.48	125.51	3,890	84.53
6	713.22	702.06	710.39	150.02	148.71	149.60	126.39	124.92	125.76	3,650	84.57
7	717.35	708.94	715.73	150.42	148.71	149.74	127.09	125.38	126.10	4,140	84.62
8	719.86	712.45	716.82	150.21	148.75	149.53	127.13	125.80	126.50	3,810	84.67
9	718.40	709.34	714.27	149.90	147.96	148.64	127.13	126.10	126.73	3,370	84.65
12	718.52	711.81	714.92	149.41	148.54	149.08	127.67	126.58	127.08	2,620	84.75
13	718.72	711.32	714.32	149.71	148.43	149.13	128.51	126.71	127.74	3,400	84.76
14	716.90	709.14	713.67	149.97	148.64	149.34	129.16	127.42	128.47	3,630	84.72
15	720.79	711.77	717.27	149.76	148.78	149.36	129.71	127.97	129.17	3,470	84.70
16	721.39	713.22	716.46	149.71	148.66	149.04	129.96	128.12	128.77	3,700	84.66
19	720.14	711.28	714.36	149.32	148.12	148.54	129.65	128.22	128.56	3,350	84.65
20	719.61	711.24	717.55	148.99	147.84	148.33	129.56	128.01	129.14	3,300	84.67
21	720.14	710.43	713.02	148.75	147.40	147.75	129.71	128.26	128.47	3,310	84.68
23	713.71	705.09	709.54	148.10	146.46	147.14	129.56	127.95	128.75	3,230	84.67
26	711.77	702.91	706.22	147.47	145.62	146.69	129.40	127.65	128.41	2,910	84.70
27	712.98	704.16	709.22	147.47	145.92	146.81	129.17	127.86	128.37	3,110	84.70
28	713.75	704.93	708.05	147.47	145.57	146.30	129.25	127.70	128.32	3,030	84.74
		High	717.55		High	149.83		High	129.17		High 84.76
		Low	702.54		Low	146.30		Low	124.80		Low 84.49

MARCH, 1962

	−30 Industrials−			−20 Railroads−			−15 Utilities−			Daily Sales -000-	40 Bonds
	High	Low	Close	High	Low	Close	High	Low	Close		
1	715.89	706.67	711.81	147.30	145.80	146.44	128.96	127.76	128.26	2,960	84.82
2	715.61	707.64	711.00	147.28	145.71	146.25	129.16	127.80	128.54	2,980	84.97
5	714.15	706.02	709.99	147.05	145.31	146.04	129.25	127.59	128.33	3,020	84.96
6	712.94	704.81	708.17	146.44	144.92	145.55	128.47	127.32	127.82	2,870	84.89
7	710.63	703.88	706.63	146.09	144.82	145.34	128.35	127.44	127.70	2,890	85.12
8	715.25	704.57	713.75	146.11	144.75	145.52	129.44	127.55	129.10	3,210	85.14
9	718.28	710.96	714.44	146.27	144.87	145.71	130.55	128.87	129.90	3,340	85.04
12	718.44	709.62	714.68	146.25	144.70	145.20	130.78	129.29	130.36	3,280	85.04
13	719.66	711.56	716.58	145.99	144.61	145.64	131.12	129.90	130.49	3,200	85.10
14	724.67	715.89	720.95	146.06	144.87	145.29	131.43	129.79	130.40	3,670	85.12
15	726.65	718.08	723.54	146.09	144.61	145.22	130.99	129.84	130.38	3,250	85.22
16	727.14	719.29	722.27	146.32	144.77	145.83	131.08	129.88	130.51	3,060	85.31
19	725.28	717.39	720.38	146.27	144.94	145.31	131.66	129.92	130.85	3,220	85.25
20	723.17	716.78	719.66	146.41	144.66	145.55	131.37	130.17	130.68	3,060	85.16
21	722.49	713.59	716.62	145.90	144.40	144.87	131.33	130.09	130.74	3,360	85.14
22	720.18	713.38	716.70	145.03	143.72	144.38	131.18	130.09	130.53	3,130	85.27
23	720.18	713.02	716.46	145.03	143.86	144.40	131.14	129.88	130.55	3,050	85.25
26	717.88	708.69	710.67	144.96	143.56	143.91	131.18	130.00	130.51	3,040	85.26
27	713.34	704.12	707.28	144.66	143.56	144.24	131.12	130.03	130.53	3,090	85.26
28	714.64	705.70	712.25	145.80	144.26	145.34	130.91	129.80	130.32	2,940	85.32
29	716.94	709.58	711.28	145.78	144.75	144.96	130.89	129.86	130.01	2,870	85.34
30	712.17	703.27	706.95	145.27	143.79	144.28	130.76	129.25	130.01	2,950	85.40
		High	723.54		High	146.44		High	130.85		High 85.40
		Low	706.63		Low	143.91		Low	127.70		Low 84.82

APRIL, 1962

	−30 Industrials−			−20 Railroads−			−15 Utilities−			Daily Sales -000-	40 Bonds
	High	Low	Close	High	Low	Close	High	Low	Close		
2	709.74	702.91	705.42	144.52	143.09	143.37	130.40	129.19	129.71	2,790	85.38
3	707.52	697.61	700.60	143.84	141.92	142.69	130.15	128.66	129.04	3,350	85.41
4	705.05	695.26	696.88	143.35	141.80	142.01	129.69	128.62	129.04	3,290	85.48
5	703.35	693.32	700.88	143.00	140.96	142.64	130.01	128.51	129.79	3,130	85.55
6	705.42	697.73	699.63	143.77	141.99	142.86	130.72	129.10	130.15	2,730	85.76
9	701.17	691.30	692.96	143.56	141.43	141.80	130.57	129.14	129.35	3,020	85.81
10	697.85	688.75	695.46	143.51	141.69	143.04	130.43	129.12	129.90	2,880	85.72
11	703.68	693.40	694.90	144.33	142.76	143.37	130.74	129.10	129.48	3,240	85.78
12	694.37	683.49	685.67	143.37	141.45	142.39	129.65	127.86	128.24	3,320	85.84
13	691.86	679.08	687.90	143.32	141.17	142.18	129.00	127.67	128.22	3,470	85.94
16	690.65	681.18	684.06	143.32	141.52	142.43	129.27	127.82	128.49	3,070	86.00
17	690.93	681.31	688.43	144.19	142.20	143.39	129.75	128.03	129.04	2,940	86.00
18	696.03	686.77	691.01	145.10	143.23	144.31	130.07	128.49	129.98	3,350	86.08
19	696.80	688.63	694.25	144.94	143.25	143.86	130.20	129.02	129.56	3,100	86.09
23	700.04	690.37	694.61	144.63	142.79	143.70	130.85	129.40	130.26	3,240	86.13
24	698.42	690.29	693.00	144.24	142.88	143.18	131.06	130.01	130.53	3,040	86.17
25	694.13	681.55	683.69	143.35	140.91	140.98	131.08	129.67	130.15	3,340	86.21
26	687.82	676.29	678.68	141.78	139.77	140.28	130.36	129.04	129.33	3,650	86.21
27	685.84	668.40	672.20	140.87	138.52	138.76	129.88	128.24	128.77	4,140	86.19
30	678.64	661.48	665.33	140.66	137.26	138.48	129.46	126.33	126.96	4,150	86.10
		High	705.42		High	144.31		High	130.53		High 86.21
		Low	665.33		Low	138.48		Low	126.96		Low 85.38

MAY, 1962

	-30 Industrials-			-20 Railroads-			-15 Utilities-			Daily Sales -000-	40 Bonds
	High	Low	Close	High	Low	Close	High	Low	Close		
1	673.59	655.44	671.24	140.66	137.19	140.16	126.98	122.84	125.19	5,100	86.15
2	677.35	666.08	669.96	142.48	140.26	141.15	127.17	124.69	125.57	3,780	86.08
3	679.20	668.93	675.49	142.69	140.94	141.92	126.20	124.12	124.69	3,320	86.07
4	676.77	666.79	671.20	142.22	140.26	140.68	125.66	123.83	124.77	3,010	86.13
7	675.74	666.41	670.99	140.84	139.27	139.60	125.80	124.25	124.84	2,530	86.37
8	672.68	661.38	663.90	139.93	137.89	138.24	125.40	123.93	124.52	3,020	86.38
9	664.15	652.31	654.70	138.34	136.51	136.84	124.59	122.76	123.09	3,670	86.45
10	656.06	641.50	647.23	136.72	134.10	135.46	123.14	120.43	121.20	4,730	86.58
11	653.79	637.45	640.63	136.28	133.77	134.24	122.04	119.17	119.61	4,510	86.60
14	649.13	626.85	646.20	134.90	132.23	134.22	120.34	115.99	119.67	5,990	86.59
15	660.64	647.56	655.36	137.05	134.24	136.18	122.84	120.32	122.04	4,780	86.56
16	660.23	650.12	654.04	137.10	135.58	136.58	123.74	121.88	122.50	3,360	86.48
17	654.33	644.01	649.79	137.45	135.44	136.58	122.82	121.73	122.19	2,950	86.42
18	653.63	644.55	650.70	137.00	135.58	136.32	122.70	121.33	122.29	2,490	86.41
21	652.14	645.09	648.59	136.84	135.67	136.21	123.11	121.37	122.17	2,260	86.58
22	649.33	634.57	636.34	136.42	134.41	134.73	122.51	120.40	120.59	3,640	86.52
23	637.83	622.56	626.52	134.62	132.06	132.77	120.68	118.20	118.49	5,450	86.54
24	634.24	619.84	622.56	134.22	131.48	131.97	119.42	116.67	117.06	5,250	86.53
25	625.94	606.18	611.88	131.97	128.46	129.23	116.94	111.50	112.57	6,380	86.40
28	609.77	573.55	576.93	128.53	121.86	122.35	111.56	102.95	104.35	9,350	86.34
29	613.11	553.75	603.96	125.91	114.70	124.53	111.64	98.98	109.73	14,750	86.13
31	625.00	605.73	613.36	131.69	127.15	129.19	115.01	111.66	113.54	10,710	86.09
		High	675.49		High	141.92		High	125.57		High 86.60
		Low	576.93		Low	122.35		Low	104.35		Low 86.07

JUNE, 1962

	-30 Industrials-			-20 Railroads-			-15 Utilities-			Daily Sales -000-	40 Bonds
	High	Low	Close	High	Low	Close	High	Low	Close		
1	616.54	603.58	611.05	129.75	126.87	128.90	115.09	111.88	113.96	5,760	86.10
4	608.82	591.37	593.68	128.83	125.32	125.72	114.27	110.61	111.10	5,380	86.16
5	603.37	584.12	594.96	127.05	124.25	125.56	113.09	109.46	111.67	6,140	86.08
6	611.82	595.50	603.91	128.13	125.74	126.68	114.67	112.21	114.02	4,190	86.09
7	608.14	599.27	602.20	127.36	125.84	126.35	114.33	112.70	113.22	2,760	86.05
8	607.30	598.64	601.61	127.48	125.67	126.52	114.38	112.74	113.95	2,560	86.00
11	603.20	592.66	595.17	126.45	124.97	125.65	114.04	111.94	112.80	2,870	85.97
12	593.83	580.11	580.94	125.46	122.75	122.91	112.74	110.55	110.76	4,690	86.00
13	586.42	572.20	574.04	123.33	120.50	121.27	111.83	108.72	110.00	5,850	85.90
14	579.14	560.28	563.00	122.14	118.77	118.98	110.66	107.06	107.57	6,240	85.92
15	579.90	556.09	578.18	121.69	118.35	121.48	109.77	106.24	109.42	7,130	85.98
18	583.08	567.05	574.21	122.84	120.76	121.74	111.03	108.43	109.69	4,580	85.97
19	575.21	566.59	571.61	122.26	120.83	121.51	109.88	108.32	109.33	2,680	85.95
20	574.59	561.28	563.08	121.88	120.36	120.48	109.63	107.82	108.09	3,360	86.03
21	561.87	549.15	550.49	120.36	118.46	118.77	108.16	106.12	106.50	4,560	85.96
22	551.99	537.56	539.19	119.05	116.94	117.22	106.58	104.38	104.67	5,640	85.98
25	541.24	524.55	536.77	117.04	114.27	115.89	104.44	101.45	103.11	7,090	85.71
26	548.61	533.46	535.76	118.56	115.61	116.05	105.17	102.88	103.33	4,630	85.62
27	539.28	528.73	536.98	116.66	114.23	115.94	104.17	102.13	103.93	3,890	85.44
28	559.32	541.49	557.35	118.98	115.98	118.21	107.44	104.56	107.08	5,440	85.44
29	569.06	555.22	561.28	120.15	117.64	118.63	109.12	106.96	108.28	4,720	85.36
		High	611.05		High	128.90		High	114.02		High 86.16
		Low	535.76		Low	115.89		Low	103.11		Low 85.36

JULY, 1962

	High	Low	Close	High	Low	Close	High	Low	Close	Daily Sales -000-	40 Bonds
	—30 Industrials—			—20 Railroads—			—15 Utilities—				
2	576.63	557.31	573.75	120.62	118.30	120.29	110.19	107.84	109.92	3,450	85.30
3	582.99	570.53	579.48	122.49	119.73	122.12	111.73	109.82	111.35	3,920	85.28
5	586.30	577.39	583.87	122.91	121.02	122.05	112.88	111.25	112.48	3,350	85.31
6	582.58	571.28	576.17	122.42	120.52	121.46	113.14	111.27	112.36	3,110	85.18
9	582.28	569.65	580.82	122.40	120.97	121.83	113.30	111.43	112.72	2,950	85.33
10	599.02	583.50	586.01	125.51	122.94	123.24	115.66	113.05	113.60	7,120	85.32
11	590.94	580.36	589.06	124.83	122.94	124.34	115.05	113.11	114.56	4,250	85.36
12	596.59	586.68	590.27	126.19	124.06	125.49	115.85	114.48	115.05	5,370	85.36
13	592.99	583.87	590.19	125.86	124.04	125.28	115.32	113.96	114.69	3,380	85.38
16	591.23	582.41	588.10	126.05	124.43	125.49	115.83	114.37	115.09	3,130	85.45
17	588.77	576.59	577.85	125.65	123.73	124.13	115.32	113.51	113.79	3,500	85.45
18	577.39	568.02	571.24	123.68	121.79	122.58	114.10	112.17	112.84	3,620	85.34
19	578.68	568.98	573.16	123.31	121.86	122.51	114.00	111.75	113.12	3,090	85.30
20	579.86	570.78	577.18	123.54	122.35	123.05	114.31	112.72	113.56	2,610	85.22
23	582.24	574.50	577.47	123.64	122.14	122.56	114.29	113.11	113.75	2,770	85.33
24	579.31	572.03	574.12	122.77	121.32	121.74	114.46	113.07	113.91	2,560	85.23
25	576.55	568.10	574.67	122.14	120.73	121.60	114.75	112.99	113.93	2,910	85.26
26	582.87	574.08	579.61	122.42	121.06	121.86	115.82	114.12	115.17	2,790	85.30
27	586.80	577.14	585.00	122.37	120.97	121.83	116.08	114.52	115.61	2,890	85.25
30	593.03	583.87	591.44	122.72	121.23	122.09	117.67	115.93	117.19	3,200	85.26
31	601.15	591.78	597.93	122.94	121.23	122.12	118.45	116.54	117.32	4,190	85.24
		High	597.93		High	125.49		High	117.32		High 85.45
		Low	571.24		Low	120.29		Low	109.92		Low 85.18

AUGUST, 1962

	High	Low	Close	High	Low	Close	High	Low	Close	Daily Sales -000-	40 Bonds
	—30 Industrials—			—20 Railroads—			—15 Utilities—				
1	597.64	588.68	591.36	122.28	121.11	121.72	117.90	116.52	117.00	3,100	85.21
2	596.55	588.26	593.83	122.47	120.99	121.72	117.74	116.24	117.04	3,410	85.25
3	598.35	591.11	596.38	122.63	121.18	122.26	117.90	116.43	117.38	2,990	85.28
6	598.56	590.27	593.24	122.02	120.34	120.76	117.72	116.41	116.79	3,110	85.29
7	593.66	585.71	588.35	120.66	119.24	119.87	117.55	116.45	117.02	2,970	85.25
8	592.11	582.12	590.94	120.76	119.26	120.24	117.32	116.18	117.09	3,080	85.30
9	595.17	588.43	591.19	120.50	119.54	119.85	117.59	116.56	117.11	2,670	85.30
10	595.67	587.55	592.32	119.89	119.14	119.54	117.67	116.66	117.06	2,470	85.25
13	597.51	590.65	595.29	119.87	118.93	119.28	117.48	116.52	117.00	2,670	85.24
14	603.91	593.03	601.90	120.64	119.17	120.29	118.41	116.83	117.97	3,640	85.21
15	610.90	601.94	606.76	122.16	120.31	121.34	119.17	117.86	118.83	4,880	85.28
16	611.15	602.74	606.71	122.02	120.73	121.25	119.77	118.30	118.89	4,180	85.32
17	611.98	604.62	610.02	121.88	120.66	121.44	119.73	118.56	119.17	3,430	85.34
20	615.67	608.09	612.86	122.37	120.73	121.74	121.31	119.42	120.49	4,580	85.34
21	614.66	605.79	608.64	122.89	121.39	122.33	121.71	119.94	120.53	3,730	85.38
22	617.63	606.42	615.54	123.78	122.07	123.47	121.31	119.94	120.91	4,520	85.44
23	622.02	612.32	616.00	124.69	123.12	123.87	121.98	120.19	120.82	4,770	85.53
24	617.67	608.81	613.74	124.69	123.31	124.34	121.60	120.17	121.27	2,890	85.55
27	616.84	609.27	612.57	125.77	123.87	125.16	121.90	120.36	121.22	3,140	85.69
28	613.11	602.95	605.25	125.02	123.10	123.82	121.39	119.86	120.30	3,180	85.73
29	606.42	598.81	603.24	123.50	122.35	122.82	120.80	119.46	120.19	2,900	85.68
30	606.80	599.85	602.32	123.40	122.26	122.68	121.12	119.88	120.43	2,260	85.75
31	610.19	600.27	609.18	124.06	122.44	123.75	121.31	120.32	120.83	2,830	85.76
		High	616.00		High	125.16		High	121.27		High 85.76
		Low	588.35		Low	119.28		Low	116.79		Low 85.21

SEPTEMBER, 1962

	−30 Industrials−			−20 Railroads−			−15 Utilities−			Daily Sales -000-	40 Bonds
	High	Low	Close	High	Low	Close	High	Low	Close		
4	612.44	601.28	602.45	123.75	122.26	122.42	122.11	120.59	120.99	2,970	85.81
5	604.96	596.42	599.14	122.77	121.55	122.09	121.52	120.09	120.40	3,050	85.80
6	603.32	594.08	600.81	123.78	121.39	123.17	121.43	120.22	121.04	3,180	85.82
7	606.34	598.26	600.86	123.85	122.16	122.72	121.90 ·	120.95	121.39	2,890	85.87
10	603.66	595.38	602.03	122.75	121.65	122.35	121.77	120.55	121.33	2,520	85.95
11	607.88	599.23	603.99	122.77	120.78	121.44	121.96	120.74	121.31	3,040	85.99
12	608.97	601.28	606.34	121.81	120.48	121.20	121.96	120.85	121.48	3,100	85.97
13	609.77	601.94	603.99	121.72	120.36	120.69	122.06	120.91	121.48	3,100	85.97
14	607.93	601.28	605.84	121.65	120.50	121.23	122.08	120.41	121.48	2,880	86.05
17	611.57	603.45	607.63	121.83	120.50	121.04	122.53	120.87	121.77	3,330	86.06
18	612.44	604.83	607.09	121.44	119.66	120.20	123.35	121.56	122.21	3,690	86.03
19	609.89	603.66	607.09	120.29	118.53	119.24	122.90	121.58	122.48	2,950	86.07
20	608.93	600.31	601.65	119.52	118.28	118.70	122.84	121.35	121.73	3,350	86.09
21	601.32	589.52	591.78	119.00	117.34	117.79	122.13	120.34	120.80	4,280	86.15
24	589.06	578.73	582.91	118.30	116.47	117.01	120.66	118.30	118.96	5,000	86.11
25	590.52	578.73	588.22	117.83	115.89	117.18	119.12	117.51	118.45	3,620	86.17
26	591.28	576.30	578.48	117.62	115.73	115.94	119.23	117.29	117.65	3,550	86.21
27	581.99	572.16	574.12	116.38	115.07	115.44	118.51	116.88	117.46	3,540	86.31
28	582.70	573.20	578.98	116.24	115.05	115.68	118.37	116.90	117.61	2,850	86.34
		High	607.63		High	123.17		High	122.48		High 86.34
		Low	574.12		Low	115.44		Low	117.46		Low 85.80

OCTOBER, 1962

	−30 Industrials−			−20 Railroads−			−15 Utilities−			Daily Sales -000-	40 Bonds
	High	Low	Close	High	Low	Close	High	Low	Close		
1	579.90	569.23	571.95	116.03	114.32	114.86	117.88	116.31	116.69	3,090	86.27
2	582.66	570.78	578.73	115.96	114.32	115.35	118.30	116.33	118.09	3,000	86.36
3	584.37	576.09	578.52	116.15	115.00	115.61	118.41	117.00	117.59	2,610	86.36
4	583.37	575.38	582.41	116.29	115.02	115.96	118.68	117.21	118.14	2,530	86.32
5	588.47	581.11	586.59	116.90	115.77	116.36	119.63	118.30	118.91	2,730	86.36
8	589.90	583.24	586.09	116.85	115.82	116.38	120.47	119.08	119.92	1,950	86.37
9	589.35	582.70	587.18	117.25	116.05	116.73	120.72	119.61	120.30	2,340	86.36
10	594.00	586.26	588.14	118.56	116.97	118.00	121.92	120.30	121.33	3,040	86.43
11	590.69	584.08	586.47	118.42	117.32	117.90	121.64	120.40	120.97	2,460	86.47
12	589.02	582.83	586.47	118.37	117.50	118.04	120.95	120.09	120.59	2,020	86.47
15	592.28	584.08	589.69	119.17	117.86	118.89	121.03	119.80	120.30	2,640	86.43
16	594.12	587.01	589.35	119.28	117.74	118.23	121.03	119.35	120.13	2,860	86.42
17	590.52	581.91	587.68	118.49	117.04	117.60	120.53	119.04	119.84	3,240	86.64
18	588.01	579.44	581.15	117.79	116.69	116.90	120.38	118.91	119.48	3,280	86.68
19	582.78	570.44	573.29	117.32	115.91	116.17	119.69	117.55	117.80	4,650	86.68
22	573.41	563.16	568.60	117.93	114.74	116.87	117.78	115.91	116.58	5,690	86.74
23	573.96	556.18	558.06	119.38	116.31	117.20	116.22	112.32	112.69	6,110	86.64
24	578.52	549.65	576.68	119.87	116.29	119.17	114.56	110.28	114.17	6,720	86.45
25	575.84	562.79	570.86	119.70	117.97	119.05	114.16	111.88	113.07	3,950	86.44
26	573.54	564.88	569.02	119.42	118.42	118.93	113.62	112.15	113.12	2,580	86.44
29	586.59	576.13	579.35	120.50	118.84	119.28	116.88	114.37	115.45	4,280	86.46
30	591.49	578.94	588.98	120.78	118.91	120.17	117.21	115.36	116.69	3,830	86.54
31	594.79	586.13	589.77	121.16	120.01	120.71	117.73	116.40	116.89	3,090	86.54
		High	589.77		High	120.71		High	121.33		High 86.74
		Low	558.06		Low	114.86		Low	112.69		Low 86.27

NOVEMBER, 1962

	−30 Industrials−			−20 Railroads−			−15 Utilities−			Daily Sales -000-	40 Bonds
	High	Low	Close	High	Low	Close	High	Low	Close		
1	599.60	582.66	597.13	121.69	119.56	121.09	117.51	116.20	117.19	3,400	86.57
2	609.43	592.87	604.58	123.29	121.16	122.51	118.76	116.73	117.67	5,470	86.57
5	614.45	602.66	610.48	123.50	121.51	122.47	119.56	117.71	119.20	4,320	86.72
7	620.06	605.58	615.75	124.97	121.98	124.13	120.62	118.82	120.20	4,580	86.61
8	619.68	606.84	609.14	125.46	123.64	124.25	120.52	119.02	119.66	4,160	86.76
9	617.51	605.33	616.13	126.47	123.92	126.05	120.38	118.96	120.06	4,340	86.86
12	627.25	617.38	624.41	128.74	126.26	128.16	121.57	119.80	121.21	5,090	86.90
13	628.47	618.85	623.11	129.33	127.10	127.87	122.57	120.68	121.51	4,559	86.93
14	632.99	619.77	630.48	130.19	127.64	129.82	123.08	121.45	122.63	5,090	86.95
15	636.25	626.67	629.14	131.03	129.33	129.75	123.48	121.89	122.51	5,050	87.03
16	633.82	623.87	630.98	131.48	128.88	131.03	123.44	122.13	122.79	4,000	87.03
19	633.36	624.03	626.21	132.56	130.57	131.50	123.64	122.45	122.92	3,410	87.11
20	634.91	624.20	632.94	133.33	131.22	132.72	124.06	121.97	123.34	4,290	87.06
21	640.35	630.18	637.25	134.59	132.49	134.05	125.11	123.36	124.52	5,100	87.20
23	649.26	635.50	644.87	136.04	133.87	135.15	125.65	124.04	125.05	5,660	87.23
26	651.27	638.34	642.06	136.96	133.94	135.36	126.15	124.02	124.42	5,650	87.23
27	650.39	639.72	648.05	136.56	134.78	136.14	125.83	123.94	125.03	5,500	87.25
28	654.86	646.50	651.85	137.40	135.15	136.58	126.17	124.42	125.59	5,980	87.27
29	655.95	646.54	652.61	138.69	136.42	138.22	126.43	125.09	126.13	5,810	87.23
30	655.03	645.70	649.30	139.32	137.47	138.97	126.37	124.64	125.27	4,570	87.29
		High	652.61		High	138.97		High	126.13		High 87.29
		Low	597.13		Low	121.09		Low	117.19		Low 86.57

DECEMBER, 1962

	−30 Industrials−			−20 Railroads−			−15 Utilities−			Daily Sales -000-	40 Bonds
	High	Low	Close	High	Low	Close	High	Low	Close		
3	651.22	642.06	646.41	139.46	137.40	138.45	126.19	124.68	125.65	3,810	87.44
4	654.61	644.07	651.48	140.87	138.24	140.28	126.95	124.94	126.43	5,210	87.40
5	658.76	649.68	653.99	141.98	139.36	140.37	127.16	125.57	126.13	6,280	87.45
6	657.00	646.92	651.73	141.91	137.94	140.05	127.05	125.43	126.55	4,600	87.48
7	655.83	646.87	652.10	141.07	138.54	140.27	127.20	126.11	126.87	3,900	87.50
10	655.07	642.73	645.08	140.17	137.10	137.72	127.38	125.75	126.05	4,270	87.51
11	648.46	638.88	645.16	138.36	136.33	137.35	126.79	125.15	126.23	3,700	87.47
12	653.02	643.49	647.33	139.16	136.75	138.26	127.76	125.91	127.12	3,760	87.49
13	651.94	641.73	645.20	138.91	136.92	137.79	128.14	126.49	127.05	3,380	87.53
14	650.35	641.02	648.09	138.56	136.33	137.64	128.32	126.51	127.56	3,280	87.56
17	650.97	643.03	645.49	138.19	136.85	137.47	129.04	126.99	128.12	3,590	87.58
18	646.75	638.09	640.14	138.31	136.68	137.17	128.44	126.45	127.34	3,620	87.65
19	648.63	636.88	647.00	138.66	136.95	138.26	128.14	126.75	127.64	4,000	87.66
20	652.69	645.20	648.55	139.85	137.82	138.78	128.96	127.30	128.14	4,220	87.71
21	651.81	643.40	646.41	139.83	138.24	138.96	128.80	127.30	127.96	3,470	87.73
24	651.48	643.65	647.71	139.75	138.31	139.26	128.60	127.18	127.54	3,180	87.66
26	654.40	647.33	651.64	141.14	138.91	140.60	128.94	127.22	128.34	3,370	87.69
27	655.07	648.42	650.56	141.09	139.53	139.93	129.04	127.76	128.38	3,670	87.69
28	653.90	647.21	651.43	140.67	138.98	140.00	129.33	128.04	129.08	4,140	87.68
31	654.53	648.05	652.10	142.13	139.28	141.04	129.59	128.50	129.23	5,420	87.76
		High	653.99		High	141.04		High	129.23		High 87.76
		Low	640.14		Low	137.17		Low	125.65		Low 87.40

JANUARY, 1963

	\-30 Industrials\-			\-20 Railroads\-			\-15 Utilities\-			Daily Sales -000-	40 Bonds
	High	Low	Close	High	Low	Close	High	Low	Close		
2	654.53	643.57	646.79	142.88	140.52	142.03	129.87	128.74	129.19	2,540	87.83
3	659.17	646.62	657.42	146.40	142.28	146.05	130.55	129.10	130.27	4,570	87.90
4	665.66	656.25	662.23	148.71	145.75	147.51	131.56	130.05	131.01	5,400	87.91
7	666.70	657.83	662.14	149.62	147.42	148.43	132.20	130.75	131.74	4,440	87.90
8	672.18	661.10	669.88	151.38	148.11	150.52	133.35	131.46	132.76	5,410	87.99
9	674.23	665.95	668.00	151.38	148.53	149.65	133.87	132.24	133.00	5,110	88.16
10	673.73	666.54	669.51	150.74	148.80	149.50	134.05	132.58	133.30	4,520	88.23
11	673.61	665.91	671.60	149.65	147.54	148.68	134.01	132.62	133.39	4,410	88.28
14	678.46	669.38	675.74	149.65	147.54	148.31	134.39	132.88	133.63	5,000	88.24
15	680.80	672.14	675.36	149.37	146.80	147.49	134.23	132.84	133.31	4,540	88.45
16	676.03	666.66	669.00	148.11	145.88	147.17	133.91	132.42	133.05	4,260	88.49
17	676.07	665.07	672.98	147.81	145.70	147.02	134.04	132.65	133.65	5,230	88.50
18	679.09	669.55	672.52	147.44	145.75	146.25	134.47	133.09	133.85	4,760	88.47
21	676.74	668.42	675.24	146.94	144.79	146.30	134.74	133.15	134.16	4,090	88.37
22	679.13	671.81	675.53	148.58	146.10	147.64	135.01	133.52	134.25	4,810	88.25
23	680.38	674.02	677.58	149.62	147.49	148.93	135.32	133.91	134.74	4,820	88.29
24	681.09	673.94	676.99	150.02	148.36	149.33	135.78	134.27	135.16	4,810	88.32
25	683.81	673.31	679.71	150.47	148.68	149.97	135.74	134.35	135.12	4,770	88.25
28	686.53	678.50	682.89	151.14	149.20	150.14	136.65	134.66	135.94	4,720	88.26
29	686.91	678.29	683.73	151.21	149.52	150.62	136.21	135.18	135.80	4,360	88.34
30	684.48	675.82	678.58	150.96	149.03	149.87	136.32	134.93	135.36	3,740	88.32
31	685.24	675.28	682.85	150.94	148.83	150.07	136.09	134.80	135.67	4,270	88.38

High 683.73
Low 646.79

High 150.62
Low 142.03

High 135.94
Low 129.19

High 88.50
Low 87.83

FEBRUARY, 1963

	\-30 Industrials\-			\-20 Railroads\-			\-15 Utilities\-			Daily Sales -000-	40 Bonds
	High	Low	Close	High	Low	Close	High	Low	Close		
1	686.57	679.21	683.19	150.64	148.93	149.45	136.46	134.93	135.82	4,280	88.32
4	687.20	678.92	682.01	149.57	147.59	148.23	136.34	134.91	135.63	3,670	88.33
5	683.65	672.60	681.30	148.88	146.77	148.18	135.88	134.62	135.28	4,050	88.42
6	686.74	678.25	682.52	150.04	148.33	149.67	136.56	135.01	135.96	4,340	88.50
7	686.32	676.49	679.09	151.71	149.18	150.49	137.29	135.32	136.17	4,240	88.55
8	682.31	673.90	679.92	151.78	149.95	151.41	136.46	134.83	135.72	3,890	88.63
11	681.85	672.98	674.74	152.82	150.44	151.58	136.63	135.16	135.94	3,880	88.70
12	678.08	669.84	676.62	152.20	150.27	151.86	136.69	135.20	136.42	3,710	88.77
13	684.82	674.48	681.72	153.89	151.43	153.64	138.05	135.78	137.27	4,960	88.86
14	688.71	679.59	684.86	155.38	153.07	154.78	138.03	136.13	136.96	5,640	88.82
15	689.67	680.89	686.07	155.86	154.11	154.96	137.60	136.23	137.33	4,410	88.96
18	694.27	685.15	688.96	155.95	153.76	154.38	137.81	136.63	137.10	4,700	88.96
19	690.51	683.73	686.83	154.91	152.80	153.64	137.18	135.67	136.27	4,130	89.01
20	686.07	678.79	682.06	154.06	151.98	152.92	137.06	135.24	136.19	4,120	89.03
21	684.94	675.87	681.64	153.84	151.86	153.12	136.85	134.83	135.72	3,980	88.98
25	682.06	673.15	674.61	153.89	151.61	152.55	136.34	134.80	135.51	3,680	88.96
26	679.21	671.31	675.28	152.97	151.19	152.15	135.76	134.29	134.85	3,670	88.97
27	678.12	669.05	670.80	152.32	151.43	151.81	135.30	133.94	134.18	3,680	88.99
28	672.64	661.27	662.94	151.90	150.00	150.37	134.33	132.59	133.00	4,090	89.02

High 688.96
Low 662.94

High 154.96
Low 148.18

High 137.33
Low 133.00

High 89.03
Low 88.32

MARCH, 1963

	— 30 Industrials —			— 20 Railroads —			— 15 Utilities —			Daily Sales -000-	40 Bonds
	High	Low	Close	High	Low	Close	High	Low	Close		
1	667.63	656.66	659.72	150.84	149.10	149.67	133.46	131.93	132.28	3,920	88.97
4	670.30	659.22	667.04	155.28	149.70	153.91	133.60	131.80	133.13	3,650	88.93
5	672.85	663.02	667.16	154.76	152.62	153.05	133.87	132.36	133.19	3,280	88.92
6	669.80	662.02	668.08	152.77	151.19	152.15	133.73	132.34	133.09	3,100	88.91
7	675.03	667.12	671.43	152.67	151.01	151.61	134.29	133.05	133.73	3,350	88.89
8	675.57	668.38	672.43	152.23	150.54	151.04	134.85	133.38	133.85	3,360	88.88
11	677.83	670.01	674.02	151.48	149.90	150.66	134.76	133.23	134.45	3,180	88.90
12	678.17	671.31	675.20	151.46	149.80	150.91	134.78	133.62	134.25	3,350	88.92
13	680.93	673.56	677.66	152.33	150.57	151.58	135.34	133.81	134.97	4,120	88.87
14	680.09	671.97	673.73	152.30	150.89	151.58	136.23	134.25	135.55	3,540	88.93
15	679.30	671.72	676.33	152.18	150.71	151.71	136.05	134.74	135.65	3,400	88.94
18	678.92	671.14	673.56	152.55	150.86	151.28	136.27	135.07	135.72	3,250	88.95
19	675.95	669.17	672.06	151.76	150.14	150.79	135.96	134.64	135.26	3,180	88.93
20	679.34	671.10	677.12	151.83	150.02	151.46	136.46	134.72	135.90	3,690	88.97
21	680.01	673.15	675.57	152.13	150.74	151.28	136.48	135.16	135.61	3,220	89.02
22	680.68	673.19	677.83	152.10	150.89	151.58	136.23	135.09	135.67	3,820	88.98
25	682.31	674.94	678.17	152.75	151.19	151.90	136.46	135.12	135.82	3,700	88.99
26	684.23	676.79	680.38	152.55	151.28	151.90	136.32	135.38	135.80	4,100	88.96
27	686.95	679.17	684.73	152.90	151.19	152.50	136.29	135.01	136.00	4,270	88.92
28	687.37	680.80	682.47	153.99	151.78	152.75	136.71	135.53	136.15	3,890	88.90
29	685.74	678.92	682.52	153.57	152.05	152.92	136.85	135.55	136.19	3,390	88.88
		High	684.73		High	153.91		High	136.19		High 89.02
		Low	659.72		Low	149.67		Low	132.28		Low 88.87

APRIL, 1963

	— 30 Industrials —			— 20 Railroads —			— 15 Utilities —			Daily Sales -000-	40 Bonds
	High	Low	Close	High	Low	Close	High	Low	Close		
1	689.34	680.55	685.86	153.76	152.35	152.97	137.60	136.17	137.12	3,890	88.90
2	691.18	682.14	684.27	153.86	152.13	152.70	137.45	136.21	136.94	4,360	88.91
3	692.81	683.23	690.51	153.91	152.28	153.37	137.54	136.00	137.00	4,660	88.89
4	699.12	690.76	697.12	154.81	153.00	154.26	137.89	136.27	136.81	5,300	88.92
5	703.77	693.18	702.43	155.53	153.59	155.03	137.68	136.48	137.45	5,240	88.92
8	709.46	700.84	706.03	156.37	154.48	155.23	137.91	136.29	136.94	5,940	88.90
9	709.83	701.05	706.03	155.95	154.41	155.40	137.83	136.36	137.08	5,090	88.91
10	710.50	698.25	704.35	156.47	154.86	155.70	137.95	136.29	137.02	5,880	89.02
11	711.34	700.09	708.45	157.26	155.18	156.87	138.05	136.48	137.58	5,250	88.90
15	716.61	705.94	711.38	158.97	156.91	157.93	138.67	137.00	137.60	5,930	88.92
16	716.74	706.32	710.92	158.80	157.01	157.81	138.47	136.89	137.78	5,570	88.90
17	715.23	705.19	710.25	159.22	157.11	158.45	138.59	137.14	137.91	5,220	88.77
18	713.31	705.44	708.16	160.31	158.30	159.27	138.55	137.43	137.85	4,770	88.71
19	713.72	705.32	711.68	160.21	158.60	159.57	138.96	137.43	138.67	4,660	88.74
22	717.07	708.70	711.01	161.58	159.67	160.34	139.40	137.85	138.63	5,180	88.75
23	717.53	707.83	714.98	163.39	160.41	162.84	139.25	137.74	138.63	5,220	88.75
24	720.96	713.89	717.74	164.63	162.20	163.49	139.67	138.43	138.92	5,910	88.74
25	721.92	712.68	718.33	164.55	162.72	164.01	139.11	138.14	138.61	5,070	88.69
26	721.59	714.77	717.16	164.28	162.62	163.24	139.27	138.18	138.78	4,490	88.91
29	719.54	712.05	715.11	164.08	162.42	163.24	139.21	138.28	138.80	3,980	88.98
30	721.46	711.93	717.70	164.26	162.74	163.78	139.34	138.28	138.94	4,680	88.96
		High	718.33		High	164.01		High	138.94		High 89.02
		Low	684.27		Low	152.70		Low	136.81		Low 88.69

MAY, 1963

	—30 Industrials—			—20 Railroads—			—15 Utilities—			Daily Sales -000-	40 Bonds
	High	Low	Close	High	Low	Close	High	Low	Close		
1	723.89	716.40	719.67	165.25	163.31	164.28	139.44	138.28	138.67	5,060	88.99
2	724.69	717.32	721.09	165.69	163.54	164.78	139.67	138.24	139.09	4,480	89.06
3	723.77	716.53	718.08	165.67	163.69	164.33	140.08	138.92	139.61	4,760	89.08
6	721.84	711.68	713.77	164.13	162.17	162.52	140.00	138.70	139.25	4,090	89.14
7	716.78	708.16	712.55	163.81	161.78	162.82	140.04	138.49	138.99	4,140	89.13
8	720.96	710.96	718.54	164.48	162.54	163.71	139.67	138.34	138.74	5,140	89.12
9	726.48	717.20	721.97	164.15	163.39	164.40	140.04	138.41	139.63	5,600	89.29
10	726.02	718.62	723.30	165.22	163.59	164.60	140.37	138.96	139.90	5,260	89.29
13	727.13	720.53	723.01	165.60	163.88	164.65	141.14	139.46	140.45	4,920	89.14
14	724.94	717.95	719.84	167.16	164.60	166.31	141.37	139.79	140.85	4,740	89.14
15	727.69	717.22	724.34	168.62	166.46	167.90	141.70	140.31	141.41	5,650	.89.23
16	728.63	719.75	722.84	169.27	167.36	168.17	141.84	140.48	140.89	5,640	89.25
17	727.13	720.01	724.81	168.77	167.13	167.88	141.57	139.85	140.68	4,410	89.25
20	726.19	716.45	720.18	168.40	166.66	167.60	141.22	139.91	140.79	4,710	89.29
21	727.26	717.48	724.04	170.08	167.60	169.39	141.89	140.46	141.43	5,570	89.21
22	728.76	720.18	722.84	171.10	169.24	170.63	142.17	140.81	141.48	5,560	89.22
23	725.67	718.12	721.38	171.60	169.76	170.61	142.54	141.02	141.91	4,400	89.25
24	724.56	716.66	720.53	171.70	170.01	170.93	142.15	140.65	141.27	4,320	89.31
27	721.98	714.52	718.25	171.87	169.81	171.20	141.43	140.03	140.67	3,760	89.42
28	722.16	714.26	717.95	172.37	170.18	171.42	141.29	139.80	140.26	3,860	89.31
29	725.59	717.22	722.50	173.26	171.42	172.96	141.11	139.45	140.28	4,320	89.33
31	730.43	721.85	726.96	174.42	172.54	173.38	141.11	139.68	140.33	4,680	89.34
		High	726.96		High	173.38		High	141.91		High 89.42
		Low	712.55		Low	162.52		Low	138.67		Low 88.99

JUNE, 1963

	—30 Industrials—			—20 Railroads—			—15 Utilities—			Daily Sales -000-	40 Bonds
	High	Low	Close	High	Low	Close	High	Low	Close		
3	731.59	723.57	726.27	174.50	172.49	173.16	141.09	139.75	140.42	5,400	89.35
4	730.01	721.30	726.49	173.83	172.17	172.94	141.02	139.47	140.23	5,970	89.36
5	732.97	722.46	725.93	173.56	171.03	171.57	141.02	139.50	139.98	5,860	89.37
6	730.78	721.81	726.87	172.54	169.86	171.08	140.74	139.45	140.14	4,990	89.39
7	730.31	719.41	722.41	172.27	170.36	170.98	140.67	139.29	139.96	5,110	89.40
10	722.88	711.65	716.49	170.93	168.77	169.27	140.58	139.08	139.75	4,690	89.40
11	721.94	714.00	718.38	169.96	168.10	168.97	140.44	138.83	139.84	4,390	89.41
12	727.60	717.05	723.36	170.43	168.30	169.59	140.51	139.29	139.84	5,210	89.45
13	727.09	719.92	721.43	171.32	169.07	170.23	140.57	139.13	139.32	4,690	89.53
14	725.72	718.34	722.03	170.90	169.44	169.79	140.02	138.89	139.63	3,840	89.51
17	723.61	716.11	718.21	170.85	169.51	170.11	140.64	139.23	139.87	3,510	89.56
18	722.50	714.99	718.90	171.40	169.56	170.58	140.52	139.28	140.00	3,910	89.60
19	723.27	715.98	719.84	171.94	169.76	171.25	140.50	139.23	139.78	3,970	89.55
20	722.76	711.95	718.85	172.71	170.70	171.80	140.52	139.15	140.07	4,970	89.58
21	724.81	716.06	720.78	174.50	171.82	174.00	140.76	139.42	140.24	4,190	89.54
24	723.87	715.64	718.42	176.76	173.63	176.19	141.25	139.63	140.36	3,700	89.54
25	722.07	713.83	716.32	177.92	174.80	175.96	140.79	139.39	140.09	4,120	89.52
26	716.49	706.46	708.99	175.47	172.17	173.95	140.24	138.87	139.27	4,500	89.51
27	712.93	702.42	706.03	174.95	171.70	172.69	140.04	138.87	139.23	4,540	89.58
28	710.79	702.89	706.88	174.05	172.29	173.66	139.75	138.43	139.08	3,020	89.49
		High	726.87		High	176.19		High	140.42		High 89.60
		Low	706.03		Low	168.97		Low	139.08		Low 89.35

JULY, 1963

	-30 Industrials-			-20 Railroads-			-15 Utilities-			Daily Sales -000-	40 Bonds
	High	Low	Close	High	Low	Close	High	Low	Close		
1	709.11	698.86	701.35	174.85	172.32	173.04	139.54	138.14	138.60	3,360	89.45
2	711.35	699.93	708.94	175.17	172.86	174.47	139.68	138.00	139.11	3,540	89.47
3	716.19	708.51	713.36	176.46	174.13	175.59	139.95	138.17	139.15	4,030	89.50
5	719.02	712.20	716.45	175.89	174.45	174.75	139.68	138.91	139.35	2,910	89.53
8	717.22	708.64	710.66	174.05	171.35	172.07	139.85	138.75	139.23	3,290	89.45
9	717.22	709.07	714.09	174.95	172.07	174.25	140.02	138.67	139.49	3,830	89.39
10	716.28	708.90	712.12	176.46	173.09	175.00	139.90	138.41	139.11	3,730	89.40
11	715.98	707.87	709.76	176.48	174.30	174.87	139.92	138.75	139.39	4,100	89.35
12	712.55	705.21	707.70	175.24	173.41	174.00	140.07	138.94	139.61	3,660	89.44
15	708.86	700.58	703.28	174.10	172.39	172.99	139.92	138.19	138.67	3,290	89.35
16	706.28	699.76	702.12	173.26	172.02	172.66	139.39	137.69	138.14	3,000	89.37
17	705.73	697.10	699.72	172.96	171.00	171.37	138.70	137.04	137.88	3,940	89.25
18	703.20	693.93	695.90	172.42	169.74	170.28	138.41	136.99	137.76	3,710	89.21
19	697.53	689.21	693.89	170.48	168.60	169.29	138.46	137.11	137.95	3,340	89.23
22	696.16	684.41	688.74	169.49	166.34	167.06	138.60	136.85	137.16	3,700	89.27
23	694.83	685.74	687.84	167.46	164.23	164.88	138.31	136.92	137.47	3,500	89.19
24	693.41	685.99	690.88	165.84	163.88	165.07	138.26	136.53	137.25	2,810	89.17
25	696.20	685.95	687.71	167.75	165.17	165.92	138.94	137.23	138.24	3,710	89.14
26	691.44	684.58	689.38	166.69	165.25	165.79	139.39	137.88	138.87	2,510	89.10
29	693.20	686.68	690.71	166.96	165.50	166.17	140.12	138.75	139.42	2,840	89.10
30	698.30	697.07	696.42	167.46	165.89	167.21	140.64	139.11	140.12	3,550	89.14
31	701.99	693.03	695.43	168.47	166.71	166.96	140.81	139.39	140.00	3,960	89.14
		High 716.45			High 175.59			High 140.12			High 89.53
		Low 687.71			Low 164.88			Low 137.16			Low 89.10

AUGUST, 1963

	-30 Industrials-			-20 Railroads-			-15 Utilities-			Daily Sales -000-	40 Bonds
	High	Low	Close	High	Low	Close	High	Low	Close		
1	699.21	691.23	694.87	167.93	166.36	167.08	140.50	139.13	139.73	3,410	89.16
2	700.54	693.11	697.83	168.55	166.74	168.00	140.69	139.42	140.16	2,940	89.15
5	704.83	697.10	702.55	169.07	167.55	168.27	141.12	139.63	140.31	3,370	89.18
6	709.42	700.92	707.06	169.99	168.05	169.34	141.41	140.00	140.88	3,760	89.20
7	710.62	701.78	703.92	171.05	168.99	170.11	141.37	140.57	141.25	3,790	89.21
8	707.36	699.85	704.18	170.31	168.92	169.59	141.94	140.40	141.22	3,460	89.17
9	709.84	701.48	708.39	170.93	169.61	170.61	142.47	140.81	142.09	4,050	89.18
12	714.09	705.51	710.27	171.70	170.08	171.10	143.55	141.70	143.22	4,770	89.21
13	714.31	707.83	711.13	172.66	170.93	172.19	144.23	142.50	143.72	4,450	89.24
14	717.39	707.61	714.95	172.07	169.84	170.90	144.08	143.00	143.41	4,420	89.21
15	721.51	712.63	718.55	177.13	170.16	173.36	144.42	142.69	143.89	4,980	89.20
16	722.93	714.91	719.32	177.30	173.09	176.31	144.80	142.88	144.03	4,130	89.21
19	723.57	715.72	718.81	177.50	175.62	176.24	144.71	143.34	143.89	3,650	89.14
20	721.34	714.39	717.27	176.68	174.82	175.69	144.59	143.05	143.82	3,660	89.12
21	719.80	713.49	715.72	176.46	174.60	175.59	144.68	142.93	143.55	3,820	89.09
22	720.57	712.59	718.47	176.28	173.90	175.44	144.68	143.05	144.13	4,540	89.01
23	726.02	718.21	723.14	176.76	174.85	175.81	144.92	143.46	144.37	4,880	88.97
26	728.38	721.00	724.17	176.48	174.75	175.69	144.97	143.48	144.15	4,700	89.08
27	725.16	717.95	719.88	175.39	173.09	173.51	144.03	142.45	143.02	4,080	89.09
28	728.72	719.67	725.07	177.60	174.75	176.63	144.39	142.90	143.67	5,120	89.07
29	730.09	723.27	726.40	177.62	175.37	176.16	144.25	143.19	143.87	5,110	89.09
30	731.68	724.00	729.32	177.20	175.22	176.86	144.37	143.29	143.96	4,560	89.06
		High 729.32			High 176.86			High 144.37			High 89.24
		Low 694.87			Low 167.08			Low 139.73			Low 88.97

SEPTEMBER, 1963

	—30 Industrials—			—20 Railroads—			—15 Utilities—			Daily Sales -000-	40 Bonds
	High	Low	Close	High	Low	Close	High	Low	Close		
3	735.50	728.76	732.02	177.40	175.86	176.38	145.00	143.26	144.23	5,570	89.06
4	737.60	728.89	732.92	176.68	174.77	175.47	144.78	143.19	143.70	6,070	89.03
5	739.87	729.49	737.98	175.84	174.15	174.87	144.92	143.10	144.23	5,700	89.06
6	742.66	733.22	735.37	175.34	173.11	173.48	145.21	143.24	144.06	7,160	88.94
9	739.27	730.09	732.92	173.38	170.21	170.78	144.75	142.81	143.46	5,020	88.96
10	740.34	730.56	737.43	172.89	170.61	172.09	144.15	142.52	143.67	5,310	89.03
11	746.18	736.87	740.34	173.83	171.50	172.76	144.54	142.93	143.53	6,670	89.04
12	744.46	735.45	740.26	174.15	171.40	173.06	144.15	142.86	143.72	5,560	88.98
13	744.42	737.25	740.13	173.85	172.22	172.79	144.20	142.81	143.46	5,230	88.95
16	744.68	736.61	738.46	173.80	172.29	172.94	144.30	142.74	143.55	4,740	88.86
17	744.50	736.83	740.13	173.80	172.24	172.81	143.94	142.66	142.81	4,950	88.81
18	744.08	734.98	737.86	172.94	171.23	171.55	143.22	141.92	142.50	5,070	88.91
19	744.63	736.48	743.22	173.11	170.90	172.96	143.48	142.04	142.72	4,080	88.95
20	749.27	740.64	743.60	173.90	172.39	173.11	143.55	142.18	142.71	5,310	88.93
23	746.99	736.65	740.43	173.36	171.50	172.07	143.31	141.25	142.06	5,140	88.87
24	748.54	737.13	745.96	173.46	171.45	172.56	142.88	141.49	141.92	5,520	88.89
25	753.04	739.31	743.69	174.10	171.27	172.22	142.57	140.91	141.49	6,340	88.83
26	745.28	734.68	736.95	172.59	170.48	171.03	141.65	139.97	140.57	5,100	88.83
27	741.33	731.55	737.98	171.72	169.81	170.65	141.37	139.44	140.43	4,350	88.90
30	739.83	728.63	732.79	171.57	169.64	170.53	141.03	139.25	139.95	3,730	88.93
		High 745.96			High 176.38			High 144.23			High 89.06
		Low 732.02			Low 170.53			Low 139.95			Low 88.81

OCTOBER, 1963

	—30 Industrials—			—20 Railroads—			—15 Utilities—			Daily Sales -000-	40 Bonds
	High	Low	Close	High	Low	Close	High	Low	Close		
1	742.57	732.49	738.33	171.80	170.03	170.93	140.62	138.84	139.87	4,420	88.90
2	742.06	734.64	737.94	171.70	169.66	170.61	140.33	138.94	139.49	3,780	88.85
3	746.86	736.61	744.25	171.99	169.91	171.25	140.12	139.18	139.54	4,510	88.99
4	750.98	741.72	745.06	172.27	170.26	170.93	140.09	138.62	139.35	5,120	88.99
7	749.91	740.90	743.86	171.20	169.04	169.74	140.09	138.60	139.15	4,050	88.98
8	748.97	739.23	743.90	170.03	168.37	168.97	140.26	138.48	139.35	4,920	88.99
9	747.16	737.90	739.83	169.99	167.53	168.50	140.14	138.70	139.03	5,520	88.97
10	743.52	733.69	740.56	169.81	167.70	169.09	139.75	138.41	139.20	4,470	88.95
11	746.05	737.60	741.76	170.56	168.50	169.39	140.00	138.65	139.13	4,740	88.95
14	744.98	738.03	741.84	169.96	168.57	169.22	139.80	138.17	138.62	4,270	88.94
15	746.43	738.97	742.19	170.06	168.52	169.54	139.49	138.10	138.75	4,550	89.00
16	750.42	740.04	748.45	171.20	169.24	170.41	139.71	138.46	138.99	5,570	89.06
17	755.83	746.99	750.77	172.71	170.01	171.60	139.59	138.12	138.48	6,790	89.08
18	755.36	747.94	750.60	172.94	171.37	172.17	139.56	138.36	138.65	5,830	89.10
21	757.12	747.25	752.31	173.23	171.67	172.27	139.37	138.22	138.60	5,450	88.98
22	753.60	742.70	747.21	172.66	171.25	172.09	139.20	138.00	138.62	6,420	88.93
23	752.10	742.40	746.48	172.79	171.20	171.87	139.18	138.02	138.53	5,830	89.02
24	755.91	744.12	751.80	172.84	171.25	172.04	138.87	137.90	138.41	6,280	88.99
25	759.90	748.62	755.61	172.81	171.03	171.50	139.23	137.71	138.41	6,390	88.98
28	765.70	752.95	759.39	171.97	169.94	170.51	139.27	137.62	138.62	7,150	88.99
29	767.24	755.49	760.50	170.41	168.60	169.17	139.13	137.59	138.14	6,100	89.01
30	762.78	751.80	755.19	169.46	167.68	168.10	139.23	137.40	138.62	5,170	88.99
31	759.00	749.78	755.23	170.03	167.63	169.46	139.42	137.76	139.06	5,030	88.93
		High 760.50			High 172.27			High 139.87			High 89.10
		Low 737.94			Low 168.10			Low 138.14			Low 88.85

NOVEMBER, 1963

	—30 Industrials—			—20 Railroads—			—15 Utilities—			Daily Sales -000-	40 Bonds
	High	Low	Close	High	Low	Close	High	Low	Close		
1	759.56	750.30	753.73	171.27	169.46	170.56	139.66	138.00	138.99	5,240	88.93
4	757.12	746.09	749.22	171.15	169.17	169.84	139.49	137.74	138.34	5,440	88.93
6	749.82	738.41	744.03	170.03	167.93	169.07	138.77	137.01	137.45	5,600	88.90
7	750.21	740.99	745.66	170.95	168.70	170.16	138.65	137.16	137.88	4,320	88.83
8	753.47	744.63	750.81	172.32	170.51	171.80	138.72	137.42	138.12	4,570	88.75
11	756.56	749.95	753.77	174.15	172.02	173.78	138.53	137.62	138.10	3,970	88.79
12	756.82	748.36	750.21	175.17	173.16	173.98	138.70	137.23	137.59	4,610	88.78
13	753.77	745.88	751.11	174.55	172.96	173.71	138.41	137.04	138.00	4,710	88.84
14	753.30	744.42	747.04	174.40	172.81	173.41	138.58	137.25	138.05	4,610	88.80
15	749.22	737.90	740.00	173.48	171.52	172.34	138.96	137.52	138.36	4,790	88.75
18	743.09	731.08	734.85	172.22	170.16	170.73	138.72	137.40	137.98	4,730	88.78
19	743.13	731.64	736.65	172.02	170.48	171.18	139.42	137.47	138.67	4,430	88.80
20	747.51	733.44	742.06	172.44	170.13	171.30	138.99	137.62	138.07	5,330	88.83
21	744.69	730.57	732.65	171.42	169.12	169.69	138.62	136.63	136.92	5,670	88.87
22	739.00	710.83	711.49	170.73	166.41	166.41	137.47	134.95	134.97	6,630	88.89
26	746.60	732.96	743.52	171.52	167.88	170.80	137.50	135.14	136.49	9,320	88.90
27	746.91	735.87	741.00	171.67	169.49	170.36	136.99	135.60	136.15	5,210	88.96
29	752.39	738.56	750.52	172.27	170.31	171.85	137.11	135.62	136.44	4,810	88.90
		High 753.77			High 173.98			High 138.99			High 88.96
		Low 711.49			Low 166.41			Low 134.97			Low 88.75

DECEMBER, 1963

	—30 Industrials—			—20 Railroads—			—15 Utilities—			Daily Sales -000-	40 Bonds
	High	Low	Close	High	Low	Close	High	Low	Close		
2	757.95	746.78	751.91	173.46	171.23	172.79	137.64	136.27	137.01	4,770	88.90
3	756.82	747.26	751.82	173.46	171.92	172.56	137.64	136.29	136.99	4,520	88.86
4	758.51	747.17	755.51	173.56	171.60	172.49	137.21	136.15	136.75	4,790	88.89
5	766.21	753.69	763.86	173.63	171.70	172.79	137.59	136.34	137.16	5,190	88.88
6	767.21	757.12	760.25	174.30	172.19	173.43	137.71	136.17	136.80	4,830	88.82
9	764.29	755.43	759.08	174.67	172.81	173.66	137.86	136.49	137.04	4,430	88.82
10	764.25	754.95	759.25	175.42	173.18	174.77	137.88	136.49	137.45	4,560	88.83
11	762.03	754.04	757.21	178.22	174.70	177.10	138.10	137.01	137.59	4,400	88.71
12	761.60	754.30	757.43	178.86	176.43	177.65	138.38	137.09	137.69	4,220	88.74
13	762.82	756.25	760.17	179.24	177.15	178.19	138.65	137.09	137.83	4,290	88.74
16	765.03	756.12	761.64	178.51	177.43	178.42	138.87	137.52	138.31	4,280	88.66
17	769.51	758.99	766.38	179.91	177.80	178.79	138.94	137.42	138.22	5,140	88.61
18	773.07	762.43	767.21	180.50	178.44	179.46	139.06	137.45	138.10	6,000	88.71
19	769.81	760.73	763.86	179.63	177.67	178.22	139.03	137.62	138.12	4,410	88.69
20	767.29	757.91	762.08	178.76	176.76	177.35	139.11	137.64	138.60	4,600	88.65
23	765.03	754.43	758.30	177.77	175.34	176.01	139.23	137.28	138.14	4,540	88.57
24	763.16	752.82	756.86	176.81	174.72	175.49	138.82	137.50	137.95	3,970	88.49
26	764.47	754.91	760.21	177.38	175.59	177.08	138.70	137.50	138.19	3,700	88.55
27	767.77	758.51	762.95	178.42	176.76	177.28	138.84	137.59	138.36	4,360	88.48
30	764.12	756.64	759.90	178.34	176.36	177.23	138.91	137.33	137.90	4,930	88.53
31	767.55	758.64	762.95	179.24	177.03	178.54	139.37	137.74	138.99	6,730	88.53
		High 767.21			High 179.46			High 138.99			High 88.90
		Low 751.82			Low 172.49			Low 136.75			Low 88.48

JANUARY, 1964

	−30 Industrials−			−20 Railroads−			−15 Utilities−			Daily Sales -000-	40 Bonds
	High	Low	Close	High	Low	Close	High	Low	Close		
2	770.73	760.34	766.08	180.55	178.05	179.68	139.35	137.88	138.53	4,680	88.47
3	771.73	763.77	767.68	180.77	178.24	178.81	139.42	138.12	138.48	5,550	88.57
6	773.77	764.77	769.51	180.38	178.44	179.48	139.87	138.29	239.51	5,480	88.59
7	776.12	766.12	771.73	180.60	178.62	179.63	140.28	139.13	139.71	5,700	88.61
8	777.25	768.94	774.46	180.30	178.27	179.41	141.10	139.42	140.62	5,380	88.55
9	780.59	770.29	776.55	180.58	178.84	179.68	141.39	139.87	140.40	5,180	88.59
10	778.81	770.38	774.33	180.92	179.29	180.15	141.08	139.56	140.38	5,260	88.61
13	777.86	768.38	773.12	181.02	179.14	179.91	141.00	139.37	140.19	5,440	88.61
14	778.88	770.46	774.49	181.62	179.83	181.07	141.15	139.63	140.60	6,500	88.66
15	779.63	768.55	774.71	182.01	180.10	181.00	141.37	139.80	140.60	6,750	88.73
16	781.71	770.95	776.13	182.53	180.65	181.64	141.63	139.90	140.79	6,200	88.77
17	779.41	770.59	775.69	182.68	180.92	181.87	141.29	139.71	140.72	5,600	88.82
20	780.47	769.82	773.03	183.08	180.60	181.39	141.44	139.83	140.40	5,570	88.87
21	779.54	767.80	776.44	181.74	180.00	180.77	141.44	139.54	140.43	4,800	88.84
22	786.89	774.45	781.31	181.72	180.30	180.92	141.53	140.02	140.93	5,430	88.86
23	787.60	777.95	782.86	181.94	180.18	180.95	141.63	140.14	140.76	5,380	88.92
24	787.65	778.12	783.04	183.15	180.45	182.53	141.56	140.04	140.88	5,080	88.90
27	790.39	780.43	785.34	184.27	181.57	182.66	141.27	139.85	140.64	5,240	88.95
28	791.63	781.75	787.78	185.09	182.34	183.50	141.22	139.87	140.57	4,720	89.00
29	790.04	779.72	782.60	184.17	181.67	182.11	140.69	139.42	139.78	4,450	88.98
30	788.35	778.88	783.44	183.38	180.95	181.94	140.40	139.03	139.68	4,230	88.99
31	789.77	780.34	785.34	182.44	180.72	181.39	140.21	138.99	139.49	4,000	89.05
		High	787.78		High	183.50		High	140.93		High 89.05
		Low	766.08		Low	178.81		Low	138.48		Low 88.47

FEBRUARY, 1964

	−30 Industrials−			−20 Railroads−			−15 Utilities−			Daily Sales -000-	40 Bonds
	High	Low	Close	High	Low	Close	High	Low	Close		
3	789.90	780.25	784.72	182.11	180.18	180.65	140.40	139.06	139.83	4,140	89.05
4	787.78	778.96	783.30	181.05	179.16	179.66	140.50	139.20	139.75	4,320	89.14
5	789.82	777.99	783.04	181.29	178.81	180.75	140.60	139.15	139.75	4,010	89.14
6	789.42	780.69	786.41	181.91	179.96	180.97	140.84	139.44	140.07	4,110	89.20
7	795.40	784.37	791.59	183.40	180.62	182.06	140.84	139.49	140.14	4,710	89.20
10	797.17	786.76	788.71	183.65	181.29	182.04	141.34	139.61	140.38	4,150	89.23
11	795.04	786.58	792.16	183.80	181.34	183.11	141.03	139.51	140.16	4,040	89.22
12	798.14	790.39	794.82	184.20	181.87	183.03	140.88	139.71	140.43	4,650	89.22
13	799.07	789.99	794.42	184.05	182.09	183.13	140.84	139.59	140.31	4,820	89.23
14	798.85	789.95	794.56	184.35	182.61	183.75	140.74	139.27	140.07	4,360	89.24
17	800.40	791.45	796.19	185.41	183.43	184.52	140.72	139.03	139.54	4,780	89.23
18	800.67	791.32	795.40	185.54	183.38	184.47	140.28	138.75	139.20	4,660	89.29
19	800.27	791.32	794.91	185.71	183.82	184.94	140.07	138.96	139.66	4,280	89.35
20	800.93	791.41	796.99	187.40	184.74	186.83	140.36	139.20	139.80	4,690	89.41
24	802.93	793.32	797.12	188.98	186.21	187.94	140.98	139.30	140.40	5,630	89.33
25	800.54	792.96	796.59	190.42	186.87	189.13	140.91	139.54	140.48	5,010	89.30
26	802.00	793.80	799.38	190.12	188.04	189.36	141.44	139.68	140.84	5,350	89.35
27	803.46	795.44	797.04	191.02	188.59	189.40	141.34	139.95	140.36	5,420	89.32
28	802.35	793.80	800.14	191.34	188.66	190.74	141.15	139.78	140.50	4,980	89.30
		High	800.14		High	190.74		High	140.84		High 89.41
		Low	783.04		Low	179.66		Low	139.20		Low 89.05

MARCH, 1964

	—30 Industrials—			—20 Railroads—			—15 Utilities—			Daily Sales -000-	40 Bonds
	High	Low	Close	High	Low	Close	High	Low	Close		
2	807.22	798.05	802.75	192.85	190.67	192.03	141.68	139.92	140.84	5,690	89.15
3	809.75	801.33	805.72	192.95	190.47	191.69	141.17	139.44	140.14	5,350	89.23
4	810.19	800.80	804.70	192.33	190.12	191.04	141.27	139.59	140.21	5,250	89.19
5	807.93	799.78	803.77	191.71	190.12	191.29	141.10	139.73	140.55	4,680	89.16
6	809.13	801.16	806.03	192.70	190.77	191.98	141.08	139.90	140.45	4,790	89.16
9	812.14	803.41	807.18	192.88	191.12	191.79	141.17	139.59	140.21	5,510	89.12
10	811.96	803.37	809.39	192.93	190.79	192.13	140.57	139.18	139.61	5,500	89.09
11	817.01	807.84	813.87	193.94	191.86	193.08	140.48	139.13	139.75	6,180	89.11
12	818.08	809.22	814.22	194.27	192.50	193.22	140.40	138.82	139.73	5,290	89.17
13	819.85	810.94	816.22	193.82	192.23	192.60	140.36	139.08	139.75	5,660	89.16
16	821.35	813.25	816.48	192.11	189.75	190.52	140.43	138.91	139.47	5,140	89.04
17	821.80	812.58	818.16	192.36	189.70	191.39	139.95	138.72	139.39	5,480	89.09
18	824.23	814.67	820.25	193.42	190.94	192.08	140.19	138.60	139.27	5,890	89.11
19	824.72	815.91	819.36	194.02	191.76	192.85	139.87	138.36	139.01	5,670	89.08
20	820.47	810.81	814.93	194.44	192.08	193.47	139.44	138.05	138.43	5,020	89.06
23	817.72	809.93	813.60	193.60	191.34	191.88	139.03	137.45	138.26	4,940	88.89
24	816.92	808.95	811.43	192.75	190.32	191.17	138.75	137.13	138.12	5,210	88.88
25	816.35	808.60	813.16	192.11	190.17	191.19	138.75	137.57	138.02	5,420	88.78
26	819.45	811.39	815.91	193.17	190.77	192.16	138.77	137.28	137.76	5,760	88.66
30	819.98	812.18	815.29	193.37	191.31	192.01	138.70	137.23	137.88	6,060	88.51
31	817.94	810.37	813.29	192.80	190.87	191.88	138.36	136.99	137.30	5,270	88.54
		High 820.25			High 193.47			High 140.84			High 89.23
		Low 802.75			Low 190.52			Low 137.30			Low 88.51

APRIL, 1964

	—30 Industrials—			—20 Railroads—			—15 Utilities—			Daily Sales -000-	40 Bonds
	High	Low	Close	High	Low	Close	High	Low	Close		
1	819.23	809.79	816.08	193.27	190.92	192.73	138.29	137.04	137.64	5,510	88.58
2	825.12	815.20	820.87	195.16	192.53	194.51	138.36	136.87	137.40	6,840	88.70
3	828.49	818.43	822.99	196.50	194.29	195.46	138.36	137.11	137.71	5,990	88.77
6	828.88	820.51	824.76	197.47	195.01	196.42	138.53	136.85	137.81	5,840	88.75
7	829.42	819.18	822.77	198.01	195.85	196.87	138.60	137.35	137.81	5,900	88.76
8	828.09	818.87	824.19	197.22	193.47	194.59	138.55	137.57	138.07	5,380	88.83
9	827.51	819.54	821.35	194.99	192.68	193.47	139.01	137.59	138.26	5,300	88.83
10	825.34	819.14	821.75	196.15	193.94	195.28	139.11	137.71	138.58	4,990	88.70
13	826.71	818.21	821.31	196.72	194.91	196.23	139.59	137.88	138.60	5,330	88.78
14	826.63	818.12	822.95	198.06	195.38	197.02	139.73	138.14	139.03	5,120	88.84
15	828.62	820.38	825.43	197.99	195.78	196.47	139.90	138.53	139.42	5,270	88.87
16	830.12	821.22	825.65	197.54	195.95	196.70	140.07	138.67	139.51	5,240	88.87
17	831.63	822.51	827.33	198.23	195.78	197.07	140.38	139.11	140.00	6,030	88.88
20	829.81	821.49	824.54	198.66	196.15	197.69	140.72	139.25	140.09	5,560	88.84
21	830.70	820.47	826.45	199.13	196.85	197.84	140.74	139.18	139.63	5,750	88.75
22	828.09	820.25	823.57	199.35	197.27	198.04	140.86	139.37	140.16	5,390	88.70
23	830.04	819.32	821.66	202.05	198.73	199.45	141.05	139.68	140.12	6,690	88.75
24	823.79	813.51	814.89	199.37	195.63	196.18	140.69	139.56	139.95	5,610	88.81
27	817.68	807.71	811.87	196.45	193.62	194.94	140.40	138.99	139.54	5,070	88.81
28	820.11	809.04	816.70	197.49	195.36	197.12	140.67	138.96	140.31	4,790	88.82
29	821.97	810.32	812.81	198.04	194.79	196.18	140.64	139.32	139.56	6,200	88.88
30	816.88	807.18	810.77	196.55	194.09	195.13	140.04	138.75	139.23	5,690	88.86
		High 827.33			High 199.45			High 140.31			High 88.88
		Low 810.77			Low 192.73			Low 137.40			Low 88.58

MAY, 1964

	-30 Industrials-			-20 Railroads-			-15 Utilities-			Daily Sales -000-	40 Bonds
	High	Low	Close	High	Low	Close	High	Low	Close		
1	819.40	808.55	817.10	197.02	194.29	196.50	140.14	138.67	139.63	5,990	88.80
4	828.09	816.39	823.83	198.01	195.70	197.02	140.24	139.30	139.75	5,360	88.75
5	829.28	817.23	826.63	197.91	195.88	197.61	140.84	139.25	140.14	5,340	88.77
6	832.34	822.55	828.18	199.45	196.92	198.75	141.58	140.00	141.08	5,560	88.75
7	836.06	824.19	830.17	200.76	198.23	199.57	141.65	140.26	141.00	5,600	88.78
8	834.55	825.12	828.57	200.91	198.51	199.35	141.97	140.33	140.98	4,910	88.90
11	832.21	824.10	827.07	200.94	199.08	199.92	142.18	140.67	141.46	4,490	88.88
12	832.25	824.41	827.38	202.38	200.02	201.61	142.54	141.00	142.04	5,200	88.81
13	832.78	822.24	825.78	202.38	200.19	200.57	142.66	141.17	141.63	5,890	88.84
14	828.62	819.63	824.45	201.26	199.42	200.29	142.25	140.79	141.49	4,720	88.87
15	829.15	821.22	826.23	202.38	199.70	201.58	142.16	140.96	141.44	5,070	88.89
18	829.33	819.18	821.31	203.10	200.76	201.61	142.11	140.45	141.32	4,590	88.93
19	823.26	813.96	817.28	203.22	200.89	201.90	141.80	140.45	140.81	4,360	88.90
20	824.10	815.15	820.11	207.19	201.98	206.32	141.73	140.40	140.91	4,790	89.00
21	826.45	816.08	819.80	208.95	205.60	207.41	141.35	140.06	140.44	5,350	89.02
22	824.81	816.57	820.87	208.63	205.82	207.29	141.55	140.18	141.04	4,640	89.08
25	825.47	816.39	820.25	208.11	205.23	206.52	141.48	140.39	140.94	3,990	89.06
26	824.01	816.88	818.92	208.25	205.38	206.42	141.37	140.08	140.69	4,290	89.03
27	822.20	812.63	817.94	207.04	204.88	205.43	141.15	139.73	140.33	4,450	89.04
28	824.14	814.80	820.56	206.96	204.88	205.95	141.07	139.60	140.06	4,560	89.13
		High	830.17		High	207.41		High	142.04		High 89.13
		Low	817.10		Low	196.50		Low	139.63		Low 88.75

JUNE, 1964

	-30 Industrials-			-20 Railroads-			-15 Utilities-			Daily Sales -000-	40 Bonds
	High	Low	Close	High	Low	Close	High	Low	Close		
1	824.94	815.82	818.56	208.58	205.82	207.16	140.89	139.24	140.03	4,300	89.12
2	820.34	811.87	813.78	207.63	205.23	206.15	140.56	139.12	139.78	4,180	89.09
3	818.16	809.84	811.79	206.82	204.04	204.83	140.69	139.35	139.62	3,990	89.09
4	813.38	800.76	802.48	205.38	201.46	202.08	140.41	139.14	139.57	4,880	89.16
5	810.37	801.78	806.03	203.19	200.89	202.50	140.56	139.09	139.98	4,240	89.09
8	808.95	798.50	800.31	203.81	201.11	201.83	141.22	139.68	140.33	4,010	89.09
9	808.15	796.90	805.54	203.00	200.47	202.33	141.20	139.85	140.61	4,470	89.10
10	812.10	803.99	807.53	204.16	202.23	203.19	141.55	139.95	140.79	4,170	89.17
11	815.15	806.65	811.25	204.78	202.60	203.44	141.86	140.13	141.30	3,620	89.20
12	814.22	806.52	809.39	204.56	202.62	203.74	142.13	140.79	141.60	3,840	89.23
15	816.79	808.11	813.56	205.28	202.85	204.36	142.74	141.02	142.06	4,110	89.25
16	821.22	812.63	818.16	206.17	203.86	205.50	143.25	141.58	142.03	4,590	89.29
17	826.45	817.63	823.35	207.46	205.00	206.52	142.59	141.15	141.78	5,340	89.15
18	829.42	820.62	823.98	207.96	205.55	206.52	142.57	141.25	141.96	4,730	89.16
19	828.11	819.94	825.25	207.81	205.55	206.82	142.54	141.07	141.75	4,050	89.20
22	831.97	823.30	826.38	209.22	206.82	208.20	142.67	141.30	142.16	4,540	89.16
23	830.05	820.55	822.70	209.89	207.56	208.70	142.72	141.22	141.91	4,060	89.18
24	831.17	819.80	827.01	211.35	208.11	210.68	142.97	141.50	142.44	4,840	89.24
25	832.39	823.40	827.48	213.49	210.14	211.83	144.04	142.39	143.38	5,010	89.24
26	833.05	825.09	830.99	213.09	211.08	212.25	144.52	142.74	143.81	4,440	89.27
29	835.90	827.01	830.94	213.74	211.03	212.72	145.03	143.07	143.96	4,380	89.32
30	834.64	826.31	831.50	214.45	211.80	213.56	144.39	143.02	143.40	4,360	89.39
		High	831.50		High	213.56		High	143.96		High 89.39
		Low	800.31		Low	201.83		Low	139.57		Low 89.09

JULY, 1964

	—30 Industrials—			—20 Railroads—			—15 Utilities—			Daily Sales -000-	40 Bonds
	High	Low	Close	High	Low	Close	High	Low	Close		
1	839.88	829.30	838.06	216.29	213.04	215.79	144.70	142.92	144.09	5,320	89.31
2	844.75	836.04	841.47	218.57	215.72	217.80	144.62	143.10	143.83	5,230	89.35
6	848.64	838.01	844.24	220.08	216.66	218.65	145.10	143.50	144.44	5,080	89.40
7	849.15	841.66	844.94	219.66	217.33	218.05	145.86	144.01	145.03	5,240	89.44
8	849.34	839.98	845.45	219.02	216.49	217.95	146.27	144.39	145.66	4,760	89.55
9	849.85	841.01	845.13	218.87	216.88	217.41	146.62	144.97	145.81	5,040	89.47
10	852.52	841.99	847.51	219.22	217.06	218.20	147.26	145.56	146.57	5,420	89.47
13	851.54	841.90	845.55	219.99	217.43	218.17	147.43	146.09	146.70	4,800	89.47
14	849.53	839.60	843.63	219.94	217.23	218.20	147.66	146.27	146.88	4,760	89.50
15	849.06	839.27	844.80	219.79	217.85	218.72	147.28	146.19	146.77	4,610	89.50
16	850.04	842.04	847.47	219.81	218.10	218.99	148.04	146.80	147.46	4,640	89.50
17	854.11	845.45	851.35	221.37	218.70	220.98	148.70	147.05	148.25	4,640	89.58
20	855.19	847.00	849.39	221.97	220.03	220.85	149.13	147.56	148.32	4,390	89.64
21	851.49	841.85	846.95	221.08	218.94	220.06	148.73	147.48	148.32	4,570	89.73
22	851.45	841.71	847.65	221.00	219.09	219.86	149.18	147.81	148.47	4,570	89.71
23	851.54	842.93	846.48	221.35	219.39	220.38	149.54	148.09	148.96	4,560	89.68
24	850.32	842.88	845.64	221.40	219.46	220.48	149.94	148.55	149.36	4,210	89.67
27	849.53	838.95	841.05	221.05	218.94	219.64	150.10	148.37	148.80	4,090	89.68
28	842.27	833.47	837.35	219.91	217.85	218.75	149.67	148.19	149.06	3,860	89.71
29	842.93	834.31	838.67	219.27	217.63	218.47	149.89	148.89	149.41	4,050	89.67
30	843.86	836.14	839.37	219.04	217.16	217.85	150.25	148.90	150.00	4,530	89.69
31	844.80	836.89	841.10	218.57	217.13	217.80	150.53	149.11	149.89	4,220	89.73
		High 851.35			High 220.98			High 150.00		High 89.73	
		Low 837.35			Low 215.79			Low 143.83		Low 89.31	

AUGUST, 1964

	—30 Industrials—			—20 Railroads—			—15 Utilities—			Daily Sales -000-	40 Bonds
	High	Low	Close	High	Low	Close	High	Low	Close		
3	844.28	837.45	840.35	218.55	216.14	216.79	150.83	149.46	150.17	3,780	89.78
4	840.91	829.96	832.77	216.64	212.92	213.56	150.32	148.73	149.29	4,780	89.88
5	835.44	820.78	833.05	214.01	209.69	213.24	149.64	147.59	149.01	6,160	89.83
6	835.90	822.56	823.40	214.50	211.03	211.63	150.12	148.27	148.60	3,940	89.86
7	831.60	822.75	829.16	213.69	211.60	213.02	149.77	148.02	148.98	3,190	89.78
10	834.08	825.18	829.35	213.71	211.25	211.80	150.20	148.45	149.49	3,050	89.75
11	832.95	825.56	828.08	213.24	211.16	211.68	149.79	148.07	148.73	3,450	89.74
12	837.54	827.29	834.08	213.46	211.40	212.64	149.54	148.12	148.60	4,140	89.73
13	842.41	833.14	838.52	214.26	212.47	213.44	149.79	148.40	149.08	4,600	89.72
14	844.00	834.92	838.81	214.96	212.69	213.59	149.89	148.45	149.11	4,080	89.77
17	844.77	836.18	840.21	214.78	212.54	213.44	150.00	148.52	149.06	3,780	89.77
18	845.64	837.17	842.83	213.86	210.96	211.65	149.89	148.45	149.01	4,180	89.77
19	847.19	838.24	841.76	212.05	209.54	210.76	149.69	148.78	149.29	4,160	89.83
20	844.19	835.44	838.71	211.38	209.15	209.77	149.77	148.68	149.06	3,840	89.75
21	842.60	835.39	838.62	212.59	209.94	211.38	149.84	148.55	149.31	3,620	89.79
24	843.21	834.83	837.31	212.37	210.09	210.71	150.10	148.88	149.26	3,790	89.74
25	839.09	830.29	832.20	211.33	208.40	208.77	150.17	148.88	149.51	3,780	89.79
26	834.87	826.59	829.21	209.22	206.94	207.58	150.22	148.88	149.59	3,300	89.79
27	837.40	826.91	835.25	208.18	205.92	207.01	150.17	148.96	149.74	3,560	89.71
28	841.94	833.98	839.09	208.63	206.47	207.49	150.22	149.06	149.51	3,760	89.80
31	842.83	834.59	838.48	207.63	205.40	206.25	150.22	148.96	149.72	3,340	89.75
		High 842.83			High 216.79			High 150.17		High 89.88	
		Low 823.40			Low 206.25			Low 148.60		Low 89.71	

SEPTEMBER, 1964

	—30 Industrials—			—20 Railroads—			—15 Utilities—			Daily Sales -000-	40 Bonds
	High	Low	Close	High	Low	Close	High	Low	Close		
1	846.06	836.56	844.00	208.23	205.80	207.58	150.53	149.31	150.25	4,650	89.75
2	849.62	840.96	845.08	209.99	207.24	208.73	151.03	149.77	150.60	4,800	89.71
3	848.97	841.24	846.02	210.61	208.33	209.99	151.19	149.97	150.60	4,310	89.67
4	850.84	843.58	848.31	211.90	209.30	211.25	151.09	149.87	150.60	4,210	89.69
8	855.61	847.61	851.91	212.50	210.34	211.30	151.72	150.12	151.16	4,090	89.60
9	860.01	850.56	855.57	212.54	210.81	212.00	152.10	150.45	151.49	5,690	89.58
10	863.06	852.66	859.50	213.66	211.13	212.67	152.25	150.88	151.34	5,470	89.61
11	870.64	857.06	867.13	215.30	212.45	214.73	152.61	151.09	152.12	5,630	89.59
14	872.84	862.35	866.24	216.24	212.82	214.43	152.63	151.11	151.92	5,370	89.61
15	871.30	860.95	862.54	215.87	212.79	214.16	152.53	151.21	151.72	5,690	89.59
16	867.64	857.35	864.18	215.25	212.40	214.03	152.51	151.03	151.82	4,230	89.51
17	873.17	862.87	868.67	216.19	213.56	215.64	153.09	151.36	152.25	6,380	89.50
18	873.92	860.20	865.12	217.06	214.01	215.30	152.91	151.57	151.90	6,160	89.57
21	875.00	866.47	871.58	216.98	214.93	215.99	152.96	151.57	152.15	5,310	89.58
22	877.43	868.67	872.47	218.25	215.12	217.13	153.11	151.54	152.23	5,250	89.48
23	876.77	867.88	871.95	218.97	216.64	218.12	153.29	151.85	152.86	5,920	89.46
24	876.96	867.04	872.98	219.32	216.17	218.37	154.00	151.72	152.76	5,840	89.52
25	879.26	868.72	874.71	219.17	216.84	218.03	153.39	151.74	152.20	6,170	89.57
28	879.40	869.24	875.46	218.89	216.29	217.93	153.80	151.95	152.91	4,810	89.50
29	880.14	871.30	875.74	218.70	216.59	217.75	153.95	152.23	152.73	5,070	89.57
30	880.24	872.19	875.37	219.49	217.01	218.17	153.80	152.02	153.16	4,720	89.54
		High	875.74		High	218.37		High	153.16	High	89.75
		Low	844.00		Low	207.58		Low	150.25	Low	89.46

OCTOBER, 1964

	—30 Industrials—			—20 Railroads—			—15 Utilities—			Daily Sales -000-	40 Bonds
	High	Low	Close	High	Low	Close	High	Low	Close		
1	878.23	869.80	872.00	219.29	217.60	218.17	154.00	152.58	153.29	4,470	89.61
2	876.21	867.36	872.65	219.09	217.08	218.10	154.03	152.68	153.37	4,370	89.63
5	882.39	871.48	877.15	219.89	217.50	218.87	154.41	152.83	153.75	4,850	89.62
6	881.17	872.05	875.14	220.63	218.45	219.44	154.13	152.89	153.42	4,820	89.68
7	879.02	871.34	873.78	220.33	218.60	219.27	154.48	152.96	153.93	5,090	89.68
8	879.40	869.56	874.90	221.60	218.25	220.85	154.79	153.01	153.93	5,060	.89.76
9	881.78	872.65	878.08	222.81	220.13	222.12	154.79	153.34	154.20	5,290	89.79
12	881.50	874.76	877.57	223.18	220.90	222.24	154.89	153.62	154.13	4,110	89.76
13	881.88	871.95	876.21	223.98	221.75	222.64	154.81	153.77	154.46	5,400	89.72
14	880.00	872.00	875.18	223.33	221.37	222.02	155.60	153.72	154.84	4,530	89.74
15	876.40	861.42	868.44	222.22	217.98	219.76	155.12	153.04	153.65	6,500	89.71
16	877.71	866.80	873.54	222.73	219.68	221.84	155.42	153.29	154.71	5,140	89.67
19	879.82	870.41	876.21	224.20	221.59	223.11	155.73	153.95	154.79	5,010	89.68
20	884.87	873.97	881.50	224.69	222.35	223.82	155.75	154.10	154.56	5,140	89.68
21	886.28	876.49	879.72	225.57	223.37	224.18	155.60	153.82	154.66	5,170	89.64
22	883.33	872.51	877.01	225.55	223.04	224.36	155.24	153.65	154.05	4,670	89.74
23	879.91	872.14	877.62	225.19	222.55	224.28	154.53	152.83	153.93	3,830	89.68
26	883.33	873.45	877.01	226.39	223.42	224.91	154.81	153.32	154.05	5,230	89.79
27	880.33	872.75	875.98	225.29	223.26	224.13	154.58	152.94	153.44	4,470	89.77
28	879.58	867.79	871.16	225.19	221.97	223.04	154.36	152.94	153.39	4,890	89.82
29	876.87	867.83	871.86	224.69	222.12	223.34	153.90	152.48	152.89	4,390	89.85
30	876.91	868.91	873.08	224.91	222.50	223.54	153.75	152.10	152.96	4,120	89.87
		High	881.50		High	224.91		High	154.84	High	89.87
		Low	868.44		Low	218.10		Low	152.89	Low	89.61

NOVEMBER, 1964

	—30 Industrials—			—20 Railroads—			—15 Utilities—			Daily Sales -000-	40 Bonds
	High	Low	Close	High	Low	Close	High	Low	Close		
2	878.13	867.64	875.51	224.33	222.45	223.14	153.82	151.67	152.71	4,430	89.92
4	881.27	870.41	873.82	224.25	221.28	221.92	153.90	151.95	152.86	4,720	89.96
5	879.26	869.10	873.54	222.53	220.07	220.65	153.54	152.05	152.96	4,380	89.99
6	879.35	869.33	876.87	221.06	218.11	219.10	154.13	152.61	153.52	4,810	90.04
9	880.00	871.34	874.57	219.35	214.71	215.70	155.04	153.26	154.58	4,560	90.12
10	878.32	867.60	870.64	215.67	211.51	213.11	155.45	153.86	154.76	5,020	90.02
11	876.17	866.80	873.59	215.29	212.04	214.78	155.40	154.35	154.78	3,790	90.01
12	880.00	870.41	874.62	217.20	214.35	216.03	155.43	154.06	154.63	5,250	90.08
13	878.46	870.73	874.11	217.88	215.17	216.82	155.17	154.01	154.55	4,860	90.04
16	883.52	870.22	880.10	217.75	215.22	215.98	155.56	153.96	154.78	4,870	90.14
17	892.18	880.19	885.39	217.55	213.59	216.82	155.35	153.68	154.37	5,920	90.10
18	897.00	884.69	891.71	219.63	216.41	218.41	155.30	153.83	154.84	6,560	90.07
19	892.97	882.07	888.71	219.71	216.74	218.21	155.71	154.06	155.09	5,570	90.13
20	896.41	884.51	890.72	219.53	216.56	218.47	156.46	154.66	155.71	5,210	90.15
23	894.83	882.88	889.29	218.97	215.72	217.45	156.10	154.32	155.17	4,860	90.05
24	891.49	881.11	887.61	217.35	213.85	216.28	155.50	153.75	154.58	5,070	89.95
25	890.00	880.16	882.40	217.60	214.53	215.75	155.09	153.42	154.14	4,800	89.85
27	886.80	874.47	882.12	216.56	213.39	215.24	154.91	153.29	154.19	4,070	89.73
30	885.22	871.46	875.43	215.60	211.33	212.27	154.86	153.34	153.99	4,890	89.67
		High 891.71			High 223.14			High 155.71			High 90.15
		Low 870.64			Low 212.27			Low 152.71			Low 89.67

DECEMBER, 1964

	—30 Industrials—			—20 Railroads—			—15 Utilities—			Daily Sales -000-	40 Bonds
	High	Low	Close	High	Low	Close	High	Low	Close		
1	877.96	863.04	864.43	212.63	209.10	209.81	154.50	152.47	152.98	4,940	89.60
2	871.84	861.08	867.16	211.23	208.72	209.89	153.91	152.44	153.29	4,930	89.60
3	876.86	867.25	870.79	212.30	209.38	210.67	154.42	152.93	153.63	4,250	89.68
4	875.09	866.44	870.93	211.79	209.53	210.55	155.09	153.26	154.50	4,340	89.68
7	881.35	871.17	873.99	211.99	209.15	209.81	155.84	154.14	155.40	4,770	89.67
8	878.44	867.35	870.69	209.86	206.43	206.99	156.10	154.33	155.12	4,990	89.75
9	873.13	861.61	863.81	207.73	204.33	206.28	155.63	154.17	154.66	5,120	89.69
10	869.16	858.46	863.14	206.97	204.94	205.54	155.40	153.96	154.78	4,790	89.69
11	869.31	860.22	864.34	206.59	204.55	205.52	155.50	154.29	154.94	4,530	89.83
14	868.78	857.40	860.65	206.38	204.28	205.06	155.84	154.19	154.94	4,340	89.80
15	862.71	850.19	857.45	205.72	202.45	204.61	155.58	153.83	154.55	5,340	89.70
16	865.34	854.87	860.08	205.54	203.74	204.88	155.45	153.99	154.76	4,610	89.76
17	867.30	857.50	863.57	205.90	203.77	205.21	155.66	154.29	155.02	4,850	89.79
18	872.22	862.95	868.73	207.68	204.35	206.15	155.71	154.17	154.76	4,630	89.78
21	875.62	866.10	869.74	207.68	205.82	206.76	155.74	154.24	154.76	4,470	89.80
22	876.38	865.86	870.36	207.73	205.29	206.41	155.48	153.78	154.45	4,520	89.75
23	876.05	863.19	868.02	206.74	204.48	205.14	155.32	153.60	154.29	4,470	89.77
24	872.89	863.57	868.16	205.65	203.74	204.48	154.94	153.21	153.91	3,600	89.79
28	871.98	863.09	867.01	205.57	203.29	204.55	154.71	153.34	153.99	3,990	89.86
29	868.78	858.26	862.18	204.96	202.88	203.51	154.81	153.03	154.19	4,450	89.91
30	871.51	861.56	868.69	205.80	203.13	204.94	155.20	153.88	154.19	5,610	89.83
31	879.78	868.78	874.13	206.81	204.12	205.34	155.99	154.42	155.17	6,470	89.78
		High 874.13			High 210.67			High 155.40			High 89.91
		Low 857.45			Low 203.51			Low 152.98			Low 89.60

JANUARY, 1965

	—30 Industrials—			—20 Railroads—			—15 Utilities—			Daily Sales -000-	40 Bonds
	High	Low	Close	High	Low	Close	High	Low	Close		
4	877.19	865.10	869.78	206.76	203.18	205.14	155.48	153.96	154.66	3,930	89.82
5	879.87	868.69	875.86	206.94	204.63	206.15	155.50	154.35	154.89	4,110	89.86
6	885.08	875.04	879.68	208.41	206.15	207.30	155.94	154.66	155.43	4,850	89.96
7	887.52	876.95	884.36	208.69	206.43	207.78	156.25	154.86	155.56	5,080	89.95
8	888.62	878.87	882.60	208.77	206.89	208.06	156.51	155.04	155.97	5,340	89.91
11	887.42	877.43	883.22	209.28	206.76	208.13	156.92	155.56	156.10	5,440	89.94
12	889.34	880.97	885.89	209.63	207.32	209.02	157.26	155.76	156.84	5,400	89.94
13	891.77	883.22	886.85	210.77	208.34	209.58	157.85	156.56	157.38	6,160	89.98
14	892.30	881.59	887.18	211.33	209.00	210.24	158.41	156.97	157.74	5,810	90.04
15	895.12	884.65	891.15	213.85	209.78	212.93	158.52	157.00	158.05	5,340	90.06
18	898.90	889.86	895.21	214.30	211.31	212.55	159.37	157.72	158.70	5,550	90.03
19	902.10	891.10	896.27	214.05	211.59	212.91	159.83	158.41	159.55	5,550	90.10
20	901.43	891.92	895.31	214.30	211.79	212.70	160.73	159.24	160.27	5,550	90.14
21	897.46	887.81	893.26	212.91	211.13	211.84	160.96	159.32	160.11	4,780	90.13
22	898.70	888.43	893.59	213.67	211.31	212.09	160.60	159.34	159.91	5,430	90.10
25	900.71	890.82	896.46	213.34	210.82	211.97	160.60	158.98	159.75	5,370	90.10
26	901.86	892.30	897.84	213.13	210.29	211.28	160.35	158.54	159.29	5,760	90.13
27	904.44	894.26	899.52	213.03	210.19	211.89	160.78	158.80	160.27	6,010	90.15
28	906.26	895.79	900.95	213.95	211.26	212.47	161.38	159.75	160.68	6,730	90.16
29	907.79	898.32	902.86	214.18	211.46	212.78	161.56	160.06	160.68	6,940	90.21
		High	902.86		High	212.93		High	160.68		High 90.21
		Low	869.78		Low	205.14		Low	154.66		Low 89.82

FEBRUARY, 1965

	—30 Industrials—			—20 Railroads—			—15 Utilities—			Daily Sales -000-	40 Bonds
	High	Low	Close	High	Low	Close	High	Low	Close		
1	908.26	897.99	903.68	213.31	210.49	211.64	161.92	160.27	161.30	5,690	90.22
2	907.21	898.61	903.77	212.07	210.11	211.00	162.15	160.63	161.56	5,460	90.29
3	909.75	898.99	906.30	211.97	209.63	210.60	162.43	160.86	161.74	6,130	90.30
4	911.80	900.33	904.06	212.22	210.09	211.38	163.15	161.38	162.43	6,230	90.37
5	906.93	897.70	901.57	211.74	210.16	210.98	163.64	161.81	163.07	5,690	90.39
8	901.86	889.96	897.89	210.82	208.59	210.04	163.10	161.35	162.17	6,010	90.36
9	905.40	896.12	901.24	211.36	208.92	210.57	162.92	161.30	162.02	5,690	90.35
10	905.54	890.77	892.92	211.31	208.03	208.64	162.95	160.76	161.48	7,210	90.28
11	897.70	879.97	881.88	209.43	206.59	207.09	162.64	160.32	160.81	5,800	90.25
12	891.15	881.45	888.47	208.90	206.79	208.18	161.92	160.06	161.07	4,960	90.31
15	895.26	882.60	885.32	209.53	207.52	208.11	162.22	160.53	161.17	5,760	90.19
16	887.90	877.48	881.35	208.90	206.99	207.93	161.48	159.91	160.40	5,000	90.15
17	889.10	877.86	882.93	209.15	206.48	207.60	161.56	159.88	160.55	5,510	90.13
18	888.52	878.53	883.69	209.78	207.37	208.84	161.56	159.75	160.78	6,060	90.10
19	890.24	880.25	885.61	211.26	208.26	210.42	161.63	160.01	160.68	5,560	90.06
23	895.84	884.60	891.96	212.45	210.44	211.69	161.30	159.73	160.58	5,880	90.05
24	900.76	891.30	897.84	212.83	210.80	212.04	161.40	159.98	160.91	7,160	90.12
25	904.82	894.64	899.90	213.26	210.55	212.02	161.53	160.27	160.94	6,680	90.08
26	908.26	897.08	903.48	212.58	210.72	211.38	161.71	160.24	161.22	5,800	90.09
		High	906.30		High	212.04		High	163.07		High 90.39
		Low	881.35		Low	207.09		Low	160.40		Low 90.05

MARCH, 1965

	—30 Industrials—			—20 Railroads—			—15 Utilities—			Daily Sales -000-	40 Bonds
	High	Low	Close	High	Low	Close	High	Low	Close		
1	907.40	895.55	899.76	212.91	210.19	211.33	162.28	160.68	161.79	5,780	90.03
2	905.73	896.17	901.91	212.91	210.09	211.56	162.69	160.96	161.92	5,730	89.97
3	906.95	896.27	900.76	212.35	210.29	211.23	162.94	161.46	162.28	6,600	89.98
4	905.25	894.45	897.75	212.07	209.94	210.49	163.13	161.51	162.31	7,300	89.99
5	898.61	886.28	895.98	210.67	208.18	209.30	162.72	161.35	162.09	6,120	90.00
8	901.81	891.30	896.84	211.48	209.02	210.88	162.85	161.05	161.46	5,250	89.94
9	900.71	890.72	894.07	211.87	210.16	211.00	162.25	160.47	161.26	5,210	89.94
10	898.13	888.81	892.39	212.27	210.14	211.10	161.92	160.44	160.83	5,100	89.99
11	900.71	890.24	896.51	213.24	210.57	212.40	162.17	160.74	161.43	5,770	90.03
12	905.16	894.50	900.33	214.07	211.84	213.08	162.47	160.96	161.48	6,370	90.04
15	907.88	896.89	899.85	213.95	211.87	212.53	162.20	160.42	161.02	6,000	90.01
16	904.58	894.83	898.90	213.24	211.26	212.02	161.87	160.39	161.16	5,480	90.01
17	904.01	894.45	899.37	212.68	211.10	211.69	161.79	160.22	160.94	5,120	90.01
18	902.67	893.35	896.55	214.23	211.13	212.98	161.65	160.20	160.63	4,990	90.05
19	900.43	892.20	895.79	214.73	212.27	213.87	161.70	160.39	160.94	5,040	90.04
22	901.14	892.87	896.12	215.47	212.65	213.72	161.92	160.42	161.37	4,920	90.08
23	902.32	893.82	898.69	215.57	212.58	214.40	162.14	160.72	161.54	4,820	90.02
24	904.39	896.13	900.56	216.49	214.35	215.80	162.69	161.40	162.03	5,420	90.10
25	904.88	895.74	898.34	217.63	214.94	215.98	162.99	161.46	161.90	5,460	90.07
26	900.60	888.51	891.66	216.97	213.29	213.69	162.88	161.40	162.09	5,020	90.09
29	896.43	884.68	887.82	214.84	210.55	211.23	162.55	161.29	162.00	4,590	90.08
30	892.99	885.27	889.05	212.70	209.86	210.82	163.05	161.57	162.17	4,270	90.05
31	893.72	885.51	889.05	211.79	209.81	210.77	163.07	161.70	162.36	4,470	90.04

High 901.91
Low 887.82

High 215.98
Low 209.30

High 162.36
Low 160.63

High 90.10
Low 89.94

APRIL, 1965

	—30 Industrials—			—20 Railroads—			—15 Utilities—			Daily Sales -000-	40 Bonds
	High	Low	Close	High	Low	Close	High	Low	Close		
1	894.95	886.84	890.33	211.87	209.45	210.27	163.02	161.10	161.81	4,890	90.08
2	897.31	888.71	893.38	212.40	209.40	211.08	162.44	161.24	162.00	5,060	90.12
5	898.69	889.00	893.23	212.45	210.52	211.21	162.63	160.94	161.57	4,920	90.09
6	896.13	888.51	891.90	211.71	209.43	210.24	162.55	160.99	161.87	4,610	90.12
7	895.84	888.27	892.94	211.33	209.48	210.80	162.50	161.32	161.81	4,430	90.09
8	900.41	890.72	897.90	212.32	210.44	211.69	162.69	161.21	161.92	5,770	90.13
9	905.77	895.93	901.29	214.68	211.69	213.69	162.85	161.43	162.22	6,580	90.16
12	909.51	899.90	906.36	215.52	212.78	214.10	163.40	161.54	162.33	6,040	90.25
13	912.41	902.21	908.01	215.72	213.54	214.68	163.16	161.90	162.36	6,690	90.21
14	916.51	905.96	912.86	215.47	212.83	213.44	163.68	162.20	163.16	6,580	90.22
15	917.01	905.71	911.91	214.53	211.94	213.16	163.65	161.98	162.85	5,830	90.21
19	917.41	907.91	912.76	214.28	211.71	212.78	163.87	162.25	163.21	5,700	90.23
20	919.01	908.01	911.96	213.64	211.18	211.94	164.39	162.42	163.32	6,480	90.21
21	915.31	903.81	910.71	212.55	210.34	211.76	163.40	161.73	162.50	5,590	90.24
22	917.51	908.31	915.06	213.08	211.05	211.99	163.46	161.87	162.69	5,990	90.19
23	921.51	912.26	916.41	213.49	211.18	212.12	163.29	161.65	162.36	5,860	90.13
26	920.11	910.21	916.86	213.46	210.82	212.17	162.96	160.99	161.51	5,410	90.19
27	924.96	915.76	918.16	213.54	211.21	212.09	163.05	161.07	162.03	6,310	90.17
28	923.56	914.01	918.86	213.06	211.31	212.02	162.80	160.85	161.90	5,680	90.13
29	923.01	914.91	918.71	213.29	210.80	212.20	162.66	161.24	162.00	5,510	90.11
30	925.42	915.36	922.31	213.54	211.33	212.63	162.61	160.88	161.76	5,190	90.15

High 922.31
Low 890.33

High 214.68
Low 210.24

High 163.32
Low 161.51

High 90.25
Low 90.08

MAY, 1965

	−30 Industrials−			−20 Railroads−			−15 Utilities−			Daily Sales -000-	40 Bonds
	High	Low	Close	High	Low	Close	High	Low	Close		
3	926.97	916.66	922.11	214.07	211.84	212.65	162.69	161.13	161.79	5,340	90.15
4	931.07	919.71	928.22	214.66	211.87	213.77	162.99	161.32	162.22	5,720	90.25
5	936.37	924.91	932.22	215.65	212.55	214.18	163.13	161.48	162.14	6,350	90.21
6	938.12	928.02	933.52	215.57	212.25	213.54	163.13	161.59	162.11	6,340	90.19
7	937.07	927.07	932.52	214.20	211.71	213.39	162.42	160.80	161.26	5,820	90.19
10	937.22	926.62	931.47	213.34	211.13	211.81	162.17	160.55	161.21	5,600	90.14
11	934.87	925.62	930.92	212.22	210.16	211.10	162.14	160.74	161.57	5,150	90.13
12	938.12	928.72	934.17	212.53	210.47	211.36	162.39	161.13	161.65	6,310	90.16
13	942.37	933.52	938.87	212.55	209.83	210.72	162.55	161.05	161.81	6,460	90.17
14	944.82	933.82	939.62	211.41	208.62	209.50	162.55	161.21	161.87	5,860	90.19
17	941.52	928.07	930.67	210.06	206.97	207.40	162.82	161.16	161.89	4,980	90.14
18	932.82	924.36	930.62	208.41	205.67	207.42	162.53	160.81	161.51	5,130	90.12
19	936.87	926.97	932.12	209.38	207.19	208.44	162.73	160.90	161.95	5,860	90.12
20	934.17	922.41	927.27	208.77	206.38	207.45	162.82	161.10	161.89	5,750	90.13
21	928.02	918.66	922.01	207.83	205.90	206.26	162.67	161.05	161.60	4,660	90.09
24	924.27	910.89	914.21	206.86	204.45	205.29	162.00	159.62	160.00	4,790	90.06
25	924.58	912.55	921.00	207.35	205.06	206.43	161.16	159.30	160.26	4,950	90.01
26	927.48	915.09	917.16	206.51	204.58	204.76	161.13	159.59	160.44	5,330	89.98
27	918.20	904.82	913.22	204.55	202.02	203.16	160.64	158.75	159.71	5,520	89.86
28	920.69	910.89	918.04	205.57	202.93	205.04	160.93	158.81	160.17	4,270	89.79
		High	939.62		High	214.18		High	162.22		High 90.25
		Low	913.22		Low	203.16		Low	159.71		Low 89.79

JUNE, 1965

	−30 Industrials−			−20 Railroads−			−15 Utilities−			Daily Sales -000-	40 Bonds
	High	Low	Close	High	Low	Close	High	Low	Close		
1	921.85	907.04	908.53	205.44	202.27	203.16	161.42	159.21	160.09	4,830	89.86
2	910.08	894.75	904.06	203.06	198.56	200.87	160.15	157.90	158.36	6,790	89.80
3	913.11	896.40	899.22	203.31	199.35	200.42	159.63	157.42	157.81	5,720	89.84
4	905.02	894.69	900.87	201.48	198.61	200.47	159.03	157.18	158.12	4,530	89.84
7	907.47	889.90	902.15	201.80	197.50	199.10	158.93	156.81	158.00	4,680	89.83
8	903.16	886.71	889.05	200.24	196.91	197.67	158.27	156.30	156.75	4,660	89.82
9	893.79	875.90	879.84	198.72	195.24	196.35	156.96	154.48	155.00	7,070	89.70
10	887.56	869.35	876.49	197.73	193.71	194.53	155.66	153.03	154.00	7,470	89.67
11	886.55	874.52	881.70	197.12	194.27	195.80	155.42	153.39	154.33	5,350	89.66
14	885.43	863.87	868.71	197.50	192.27	193.11	155.45	152.87	153.27	5,920	89.65
15	876.75	859.13	874.57	196.15	190.36	195.62	154.42	151.60	153.33	8,450	89.63
16	886.13	873.40	878.07	198.92	195.42	197.19	156.27	153.69	155.12	6,290	89.64
17	888.44	876.20	883.06	198.61	195.95	197.62	156.63	154.48	155.45	5,220	89.59
18	888.22	875.10	879.17	198.69	196.00	196.56	156.33	154.33	154.81	4,330	89.68
21	881.47	868.79	874.12	196.91	194.78	195.82	155.54	153.84	154.66	3,280	89.62
22	882.18	871.48	875.43	197.19	194.91	196.18	155.48	153.84	154.72	3,330	89.57
23	879.38	868.25	870.22	196.86	194.45	194.70	155.48	153.81	154.39	3,580	89.59
24	870.93	854.64	857.76	194.53	191.46	191.79	154.93	152.60	153.09	5,840	89.68
25	861.99	849.75	854.36	192.37	189.78	190.74	153.45	151.45	152.00	5,790	89.63
28	858.86	838.78	840.59	191.28	187.01	187.29	152.39	149.66	150.12	7,640	89.68
29	856.45	832.74	851.40	190.41	184.63	188.74	152.00	149.15	150.93	10,450	89.51
30	873.35	856.94	868.03	194.53	189.91	193.69	154.60	151.42	154.15	6,930	89.50
		High	908.53		High	203.16		High	160.09		High 89.86
		Low	840.59		Low	187.29		Low	150.12		Low 89.50

JULY, 1965

	—30 Industrials—			—20 Railroads—			—15 Utilities—			Daily Sales -000-	40 Bonds
	High	Low	Close	High	Low	Close	High	Low	Close		
1	873.84	861.88	871.59	196.18	192.70	195.80	155.06	153.36	154.30	4,520	89.44
2	878.40	866.76	875.16	198.13	194.83	197.70	156.18	153.90	155.18	4,260	89.33
6	879.60	870.00	873.18	198.87	195.72	196.61	156.57	154.72	155.60	3,400	89.35
7	874.61	866.71	870.77	197.45	195.11	196.51	156.24	154.78	155.45	3,020	89.33
8	880.59	867.20	877.85	198.77	195.44	198.54	156.63	155.06	156.30	4,380	89.33
9	885.04	874.72	879.49	201.66	198.36	200.24	158.09	155.93	157.48	4,800	89.37
12	883.99	874.39	877.96	201.74	198.61	200.29	158.42	156.66	157.60	3,690	89.36
13	881.03	872.47	876.97	201.00	198.97	199.88	157.81	156.21	156.78	3,260	89.38
14	886.24	874.23	883.23	202.75	199.78	201.74	157.75	155.90	156.66	4,100	89.40
15	889.98	878.62	880.98	204.33	201.36	202.24	158.21	156.15	157.24	4,420	89.45
16	885.91	875.98	880.43	203.01	200.54	201.79	157.63	156.03	156.78	3,520	89.42
19	884.54	876.09	880.26	202.68	200.57	201.56	157.54	155.93	156.87	3,220	89.40
20	882.02	866.82	868.79	201.61	197.73	198.03	157.51	155.21	155.63	4,670	89.31
21	872.58	860.95	865.01	198.49	196.18	196.99	156.39	154.54	155.03	4,350	89.34
22	868.08	857.71	861.77	197.90	196.02	196.63	156.09	154.54	155.36	3,310	89.33
23	869.40	859.58	863.97	198.21	195.92	197.12	156.09	154.63	155.30	3,600	89.28
26	870.66	858.75	867.26	197.88	196.02	196.71	155.69	153.90	154.57	3,790	89.22
27	872.09	860.78	863.53	199.73	196.96	198.54	155.42	153.24	153.78	4,190	89.19
28	873.18	858.42	867.92	201.63	197.75	200.31	154.72	153.12	153.96	4,760	89.18
29	877.85	864.62	874.23	205.16	200.87	204.66	155.36	153.57	154.66	4,690	89.26
30	885.31	875.49	881.74	209.35	205.60	207.73	156.09	154.15	155.36	5,200	89.25
		High 883.23			High 207.73			High 157.60			High 89.45
		Low 861.77			Low 195.80			Low 153.78			Low 89.18

AUGUST, 1965

	—30 Industrials—			—20 Railroads—			—15 Utilities—			Daily Sales -000-	40 Bonds
	High	Low	Close	High	Low	Close	High	Low	Close		
2	888.11	876.48	881.85	209.99	206.92	208.49	156.36	154.36	155.21	4,220	89.28
3	885.04	874.78	881.20	209.56	207.17	208.69	155.72	154.33	154.93	4,640	89.29
4	888.11	878.40	883.88	211.08	208.59	210.65	156.36	154.87	155.87	4,830	89.24
5	886.96	878.34	881.63	211.56	209.56	210.47	156.30	154.84	155.60	4,920	89.31
6	886.57	875.38	882.51	210.95	209.02	210.14	156.24	154.75	155.69	4,200	89.25
9	887.40	876.31	879.77	210.88	208.46	209.48	156.60	154.63	155.54	4,540	89.31
10	883.39	875.43	878.89	210.62	208.29	209.78	156.36	154.69	155.51	4,690	89.23
11	885.42	876.48	881.47	211.31	209.23	210.65	155.93	154.54	154.96	5,030	89.21
12	886.90	876.86	881.96	213.41	210.77	212.73	156.21	154.72	155.48	5,160	89.12
13	891.95	880.48	888.82	216.49	212.73	215.32	156.21	154.54	155.24	5,430	89.12
16	896.89	886.41	891.13	217.32	214.40	215.60	156.06	154.48	155.33	5,270	89.02
17	898.37	888.11	894.26	216.38	213.69	215.39	156.39	154.81	155.96	4,520	89.09
18	901.39	890.30	894.37	218.59	214.91	217.12	156.69	154.84	155.60	5,850	89.08
19	900.13	889.43	891.79	218.47	214.99	215.37	156.96	155.27	156.21	5,000	89.05
20	894.97	884.71	889.92	216.92	213.62	215.67	156.48	155.12	155.51	4,170	89.07
23	893.65	883.94	887.07	217.73	214.89	216.31	156.24	154.81	155.24	4,470	89.03
24	893.05	883.50	887.12	218.16	215.17	217.37	156.33	154.90	155.36	4,740	89.01
25	895.79	884.38	890.85	220.01	216.69	218.29	156.15	154.72	155.24	6,240	88.95
26	899.25	886.74	896.18	219.66	216.89	218.44	155.75	154.36	154.96	6,010	88.96
27	901.88	891.95	895.96	220.24	218.36	219.18	156.24	154.81	155.30	5,570	88.94
30	899.69	890.52	895.63	219.94	217.91	218.77	156.30	155.12	155.60	4,400	88.87
31	900.84	888.22	893.10	220.01	217.60	218.67	156.12	154.66	155.24	5,170	88.86
		High 896.18			High 219.18			High 156.21			High 89.31
		Low 878.89			Low 208.49			Low 154.93			Low 88.86

SEPTEMBER, 1965

	—30 Industrials—			—20 Railroads—			—15 Utilities—			Daily Sales -000-	40 Bonds
	High	Low	Close	High	Low	Close	High	Low	Close		
1	897.93	886.96	893.60	220.24	215.52	217.07	155.81	154.48	155.27	5,890	88.91
2	903.03	892.17	900.40	219.84	216.03	218.34	156.54	154.63	155.87	6,470	88.92
3	910.28	900.46	907.97	219.15	216.54	217.75	157.18	155.57	156.66	6,010	88.98
7	915.22	904.30	910.11	218.62	216.21	217.25	158.00	156.06	157.24	5,750	88.94
8	918.45	905.67	913.68	217.91	215.55	216.33	157.93	156.36	157.12	6,240	88.93
9	923.12	911.81	917.47	218.26	215.22	217.07	158.81	156.56	157.75	7,360	88.86
10	924.00	911.65	918.95	217.55	215.39	216.21	158.81	157.00	157.78	6,650	88.80
13	927.62	913.41	920.92	217.37	214.89	215.77	159.42	157.18	158.33	7,020	88.83
14	928.22	913.57	916.59	217.45	214.38	214.99	159.18	157.48	158.15	7,830	88.90
15	927.89	913.41	922.95	216.21	213.67	214.96	159.12	157.51	158.18	6,220	88.88
16	935.46	922.73	931.18	217.25	214.20	216.00	159.45	157.60	158.66	7,410	88.87
17	934.59	922.57	928.99	217.86	214.51	216.79	159.09	156.90	157.84	6,610	88.84
20	937.00	924.27	931.18	219.81	216.74	219.10	159.12	156.87	158.15	7,040	88.83
21	936.73	923.45	926.52	221.18	218.41	219.99	159.00	157.48	157.93	7,750	88.70
22	936.62	922.35	931.62	222.38	219.13	221.21	158.66	157.06	157.87	8,290	88.71
23	938.37	922.95	927.45	222.53	219.10	219.89	158.45	156.72	157.69	9,990	88.68
24	933.65	918.89	929.54	223.75	218.57	222.38	158.51	156.66	157.33	7,810	88.72
27	944.74	927.89	937.88	225.75	222.02	224.51	158.21	156.90	157.48	6,820	88.65
28	943.42	928.66	935.85	226.61	222.96	224.23	158.45	156.81	157.42	8,750	88.69
29	944.96	927.89	932.39	226.13	222.30	223.37	158.45	156.63	157.33	10,600	88.69
30	939.20	927.40	930.58	225.04	221.94	222.91	158.24	156.69	157.60	8,670	88.68
		High	937.88		High	224.51		High	158.66		High 88.98
		Low	893.60		Low	214.96		Low	155.27		Low 88.65

OCTOBER, 1965

	—30 Industrials—			—20 Railroads—			—15 Utilities—			Daily Sales -000-	40 Bonds
	High	Low	Close	High	Low	Close	High	Low	Close		
1	936.07	923.23	929.65	223.92	221.84	222.93	158.57	156.84	157.60	7,470	88.58
4	935.57	924.05	930.86	224.05	222.12	223.52	158.72	156.63	157.39	5,590	88.70
5	942.49	930.14	938.70	225.70	222.71	224.63	158.60	156.90	157.78	6,980	88.65
6	942.49	927.29	936.84	225.37	222.65	224.51	158.42	156.84	157.69	6,010	88.70
7	941.83	930.75	934.42	227.76	223.75	226.56	158.33	156.75	157.36	6,670	88.61
8	944.08	932.50	938.32	230.22	225.95	228.87	158.09	156.45	157.09	7,670	88.61
11	948.30	936.40	942.65	231.18	228.34	229.58	158.12	156.39	157.12	9,600	88.51
12	947.92	936.73	941.12	231.18	228.19	229.71	157.39	156.00	156.96	9,470	88.52
13	945.84	935.74	941.01	230.52	228.14	229.13	157.48	155.93	156.87	9,470	88.52
14	946.22	933.87	937.50	231.14	228.10	230.17	157.90	156.42	157.42	8,580	88.54
15	945.07	934.15	940.68	233.95	230.04	232.95	158.21	156.48	157.15	7,470	88.55
18	952.31	939.31	945.84	235.44	232.58	233.97	157.96	156.12	156.81	8,180	88.55
19	955.49	943.15	947.76	235.39	230.39	232.40	157.78	156.12	156.81	8,620	88.61
20	953.57	941.72	948.47	234.27	231.11	233.70	157.48	155.87	156.48	8,200	88.69
21	957.36	944.90	950.28	238.40	232.75	236.93	157.72	156.30	157.03	9,170	88.66
22	959.39	946.71	952.42	238.70	234.37	235.61	157.69	155.69	156.66	8,960	88.55
25	958.95	944.30	948.14	236.58	232.78	233.82	157.69	155.90	156.81	7,090	88.56
26	959.44	945.95	956.32	237.21	233.72	235.61	157.63	155.84	156.63	6,750	88.55
27	967.46	954.83	959.50	237.41	234.72	236.06	158.39	156.57	157.72	7,670	88.55
28	965.21	952.75	959.11	238.05	234.87	236.29	158.48	156.75	157.57	7,230	88.53
29	966.47	955.38	960.82	236.88	234.74	235.86	158.69	157.06	157.96	7,240	88.52
		High	960.82		High	236.93		High	157.96		High 88.70
		Low	929.65		Low	222.93		Low	156.48		Low 88.51

NOVEMBER, 1965

	−30 Industrials−			−20 Railroads−			−15 Utilities−			Daily Sales -000-	40 Bonds
	High	Low	Close	High	Low	Close	High	Low	Close		
1	964.36	953.61	958.96	236.91	233.77	234.67	158.90	156.93	157.96	6,340	88.48
3	965.97	953.06	961.13	236.71	233.35	235.84	159.18	157.21	158.24	7,520	88.38
4	969.98	956.23	961.85	238.90	235.94	237.85	159.45	157.78	158.42	8,380	88.39
5	967.42	953.89	959.46	239.69	236.83	238.53	159.33	157.81	158.72	7,310	88.37
8	961.74	948.60	953.95	238.35	235.61	236.56	159.84	157.75	158.90	7,000	88.30
9	959.13	945.76	951.72	237.95	235.66	236.71	159.75	158.15	158.84	6,680	88.29
10	957.34	946.60	951.22	237.55	235.81	236.56	159.45	157.60	158.33	4,860	88.26
11	955.84	946.15	953.28	236.86	234.67	235.99	158.93	157.39	158.12	5,430	88.25
12	961.80	949.44	956.29	239.55	236.26	238.55	158.93	156.87	157.78	7,780	88.22
15	963.91	951.39	955.90	240.22	237.33	238.77	158.42	156.48	157.36	8,310	88.20
16	962.08	950.27	956.51	239.74	237.46	238.53	157.93	156.06	156.87	8,380	88.11
17	963.14	950.66	956.57	239.32	236.53	237.65	158.00	156.36	157.30	9,120	88.12
18	958.24	945.26	950.50	238.75	236.04	237.26	158.15	156.45	157.24	7,040	88.12
19	958.51	946.88	952.72	238.23	236.14	237.08	157.78	156.18	156.81	6,850	88.13
22	954.95	941.48	946.38	238.38	235.12	236.21	157.27	155.42	156.18	6,370	88.03
23	953.28	941.87	948.94	238.38	235.46	237.78	156.81	154.72	156.06	7,150	87.96
24	956.06	942.98	948.94	242.06	237.75	240.89	156.63	155.03	155.69	7,870	87.99
26	953.56	943.76	948.16	243.40	240.62	242.33	156.12	154.69	155.24	6,970	87.96
29	954.84	942.48	946.93	243.87	241.21	241.96	155.66	153.69	154.21	8,760	88.02
30	950.89	937.24	946.71	244.15	240.39	242.53	154.87	152.81	153.90	8,990	88.01
		High 961.85			High 242.53			High 158.90			High 88.48
		Low 946.38			Low 234.67			Low 153.90			Low 87.96

DECEMBER, 1965

	−30 Industrials−			−20 Railroads−			−15 Utilities−			Daily Sales -000-	40 Bonds
	High	Low	Close	High	Low	Close	High	Low	Close		
1	953.00	941.81	947.60	245.14	241.49	243.15	154.60	152.54	153.24	10,140	87.89
2	951.11	938.80	944.59	244.94	242.06	243.43	153.81	152.00	152.96	9,070	87.93
3	950.94	939.36	946.10	245.12	242.28	243.70	154.09	152.42	153.51	8,160	87.88
6	946.15	924.44	939.53	241.83	237.80	240.89	153.60	150.69	152.33	11,440	87.83
7	958.63	938.80	951.33	244.37	240.34	243.55	154.06	152.00	153.09	9,340	87.67
8	959.63	943.42	946.60	245.82	242.08	243.53	153.69	152.24	152.57	10,120	87.63
9	955.67	942.59	949.55	245.82	242.33	244.22	153.78	151.75	152.63	9,150	87.59
10	957.51	945.71	952.72	246.34	242.61	244.72	153.69	151.42	152.57	8,740	87.35
13	959.52	946.54	951.55	246.84	242.63	243.85	153.72	151.81	152.54	8,660	87.42
14	959.85	948.05	954.06	246.31	242.95	245.02	153.51	151.36	152.00	9,920	87.32
15	964.81	947.99	958.74	246.88	243.33	245.27	152.78	150.45	151.48	9,560	87.17
16	967.14	953.78	959.13	249.35	244.77	248.13	152.57	150.21	151.39	9,950	87.23
17	966.09	952.61	957.85	251.41	247.93	249.55	152.15	149.78	150.57	9,490	87.21
20	960.69	947.16	952.22	250.04	246.64	247.38	151.15	149.03	149.84	7,350	87.31
21	964.86	950.05	959.46	249.00	246.19	247.43	151.84	149.33	151.03	8,230	87.23
22	974.16	956.34	965.86	249.85	245.79	247.46	153.03	150.66	151.93	9,720	87.26
23	972.93	959.35	966.36	248.80	244.97	246.84	152.72	151.03	151.78	6,870	87.14
27	972.49	958.29	959.79	247.95	244.79	245.47	152.78	150.57	151.57	5,950	87.15
28	966.09	950.05	957.96	245.62	243.00	244.60	152.66	150.21	151.30	7,280	87.09
29	969.15	953.67	960.30	247.76	244.07	245.84	152.51	150.57	151.15	7,610	86.98
30	969.76	957.62	963.69	247.18	244.84	245.72	152.51	150.78	151.96	7,060	86.96
31	976.61	962.58	969.26	248.20	245.24	247.48	153.59	151.36	152.63	7,240	87.08
		High 969.26			High 249.55			High 153.51			High 87.93
		Low 939.53			Low 240.89			Low 149.84			Low 86.96

JANUARY, 1966

	\-30 Industrials\-			\-20 Railroads\-			\-15 Utilities\-			Daily Sales -000-	40 Bonds
	High	Low	Close	High	Low	Close	High	Low	Close		
3	974.55	961.91	968.54	249.10	245.91	247.38	152.78	150.75	151.87	5,950	87.01
4	978.50	963.02	969.26	250.29	245.47	247.98	152.72	150.87	151.60	7,540	87.12
5	984.85	968.76	981.62	250.09	246.88	248.40	152.66	150.87	151.72	9,650	87.12
6	992.26	979.00	985.46	249.80	247.11	248.60	152.84	151.21	151.96	7,880	87.12
7	991.59	978.61	986.13	249.77	246.88	248.20	152.93	151.30	152.30	7,600	87.12
10	991.92	980.56	985.41	251.34	247.46	250.04	153.18	151.51	152.36	7,720	87.07
11	993.04	980.34	986.85	254.17	250.02	252.73	153.30	151.54	152.27	8,910	87.10
12	992.59	980.45	983.96	255.00	252.06	253.58	153.54	151.51	152.39	8,530	86.97
13	992.65	980.23	985.69	256.99	253.11	255.67	152.96	151.06	151.90	8,860	87.00
14	994.09	982.07	987.30	259.80	255.17	257.73	153.06	151.18	151.60	9,210	87.08
17	996.60	984.02	989.75	260.97	256.86	258.58	152.96	150.57	151.84	9,430	86.96
18	1,000.50	984.68	994.20	260.97	257.24	258.40	153.12	150.90	152.03	9,790	86.95
19	1,000.55	985.30	991.14	259.33	255.07	257.19	153.45	150.66	151.84	10,230	86.92
20	997.77	983.90	987.80	259.55	255.54	258.28	152.66	150.66	151.15	8,670	86.93
21	993.20	980.62	988.14	259.35	255.42	257.29	152.30	150.51	151.45	9,180	87.01
24	999.22	984.63	991.42	259.05	256.02	257.36	152.12	149.87	150.60	8,780	86.98
25	998.21	986.52	991.64	260.10	256.74	259.23	151.54	149.51	150.69	9,300	87.06
26	999.16	984.13	990.92	262.78	258.70	261.46	151.21	149.18	149.57	9,910	87.02
27	997.49	985.02	990.36	263.90	259.95	262.71	150.42	148.66	149.54	8,970	87.06
28	994.59	979.95	985.35	265.00	261.61	263.46	150.24	148.33	149.12	9,000	86.94
31	992.53	979.67	983.51	264.15	260.37	261.69	150.51	148.09	148.75	7,800	86.93
		High 994.20			High 263.46			High 152.39			High 87.12
		Low 968.54			Low 247.38			Low 148.75			Low 86.92

FEBRUARY, 1966

	\-30 Industrials\-			\-20 Railroads\-			\-15 Utilities\-			Daily Sales -000-	40 Bonds
	High	Low	Close	High	Low	Close	High	Low	Close		
1	987.47	969.43	975.89	262.39	256.07	258.06	149.36	147.15	148.39	9,090	86.90
2	985.35	967.81	982.29	258.95	255.67	257.91	149.12	146.57	147.39	8,130	86.81
3	991.59	976.33	981.23	260.57	256.64	258.01	149.18	146.96	148.00	8,160	86.77
4	991.53	976.00	986.35	260.42	257.83	259.70	149.42	147.24	148.48	7,560	86.78
7	996.71	981.84	989.69	262.93	259.72	261.99	149.39	147.12	148.24	8,000	86.66
8	998.71	979.28	991.03	265.52	260.47	262.96	149.66	147.88	148.54	10,560	86.70
9	1,001.11	987.63	995.15	266.44	262.53	264.82	149.66	147.36	148.30	9,760	86.67
10	1,000.27	986.74	990.81	267.59	263.98	265.87	149.00	146.81	147.84	9,790	86.53
11	997.99	984.96	989.03	270.32	266.02	269.40	148.42	146.84	147.63	8,150	86.59
14	995.60	983.24	987.69	273.56	269.40	271.64	148.09	145.66	146.36	8,360	86.37
15	990.81	977.61	981.57	274.33	269.48	271.72	147.00	144.87	145.54	8,750	86.32
16	987.80	976.22	982.40	273.48	269.50	271.59	146.18	144.15	145.21	9,180	86.06
17	985.85	969.93	975.27	273.06	267.59	269.75	145.93	143.69	144.57	9,330	86.02
18	982.07	966.31	975.22	270.94	266.12	267.73	145.63	143.66	144.51	8,470	86.04
21	977.11	962.80	966.48	270.20	264.87	266.39	145.21	142.96	143.60	8,510	85.95
23	967.87	955.12	960.13	265.84	262.14	263.88	144.33	142.48	142.78	8,080	85.80
24	962.19	946.60	950.66	264.08	260.20	262.36	143.66	141.60	142.60	7,860	85.74
25	962.30	946.10	953.00	266.44	261.56	264.23	143.15	141.24	141.78	8,140	85.71
28	960.41	948.21	951.89	268.23	264.05	266.76	143.21	141.18	141.75	9,910	85.77
		High 995.15			High 271.72			High 148.54			High 86.90
		Low 950.66			Low 257.91			Low 141.75			Low 85.71

MARCH, 1966

	—30 Industrials—			—20 Railroads—			—15 Utilities—			Daily Sales -000-	40 Bonds
	High	Low	Close	High	Low	Close	High	Low	Close		
1	955.17	935.52	938.19	268.58	261.51	262.81	142.81	139.66	140.33	11,030	85.61
2	943.09	927.78	932.01	262.96	258.26	259.35	140.81	138.12	139.03	10,470	85.60
3	941.25	922.27	936.35	262.06	256.07	261.14	140.54	137.15	139.21	9,900	85.46
4	943.31	928.89	932.34	264.05	258.68	259.90	140.78	138.66	139.93	9,000	85.35
7	932.46	914.81	917.76	258.85	254.27	255.57	141.03	138.78	139.63	9,370	85.26
8	928.95	909.57	919.98	252.46	251.66	253.75	141.09	138.69	140.03	10,120	85.23
9	933.51	918.98	929.84	256.91	253.85	255.82	141.72	139.54	141.03	7,980	85.13
10	941.42	924.10	929.23	258.16	253.48	254.55	143.69	140.60	141.93	10,310	84.99
11	937.30	924.72	927.95	256.19	252.63	254.40	143.30	141.27	142.21	7,000	84.76
14	930.01	914.36	917.09	254.32	248.28	248.78	143.03	140.96	141.66	7,400	84.63
15	919.15	905.40	911.08	248.63	239.92	243.60	142.69	140.51	141.51	9,440	84.53
16	922.27	909.13	916.03	246.41	242.31	244.32	143.27	140.84	142.39	7,330	84.44
17	922.99	912.58	919.32	248.33	244.82	246.88	143.51	141.21	142.63	5,460	84.44
18	928.95	914.58	922.88	251.29	246.93	249.62	144.00	142.09	142.93	6,450	84.47
21	935.52	921.65	929.17	253.58	250.44	252.13	144.00	142.15	143.09	7,230	84.54
22	942.92	929.28	934.52	255.07	251.89	253.01	144.18	141.75	142.27	8,910	84.54
23	935.91	924.88	929.00	253.50	251.64	252.28	143.21	141.18	142.06	6,720	84.53
24	933.35	923.37	928.61	252.81	250.62	252.04	143.15	141.09	142.54	7,880	84.46
25	936.52	925.38	929.95	253.65	250.89	252.28	143.93	141.93	142.90	7,750	84.41
28	940.36	928.61	932.62	254.37	250.62	252.46	144.06	141.81	142.27	8,640	84.37
29	937.19	922.88	929.39	253.83	250.24	251.69	142.93	141.18	142.12	8,300	84.40
30	928.00	915.31	919.76	251.54	248.30	248.85	142.27	140.60	141.36	7,980	84.52
31	929.12	916.31	924.77	250.34	247.31	249.17	142.00	140.36	141.24	6,690	84.50

High 938.19   High 262.81   High 143.09   High 85.61
Low 911.08   Low 243.60   Low 139.03   Low 84.37

APRIL, 1966

	—30 Industrials—			—20 Railroads—			—15 Utilities—			Daily Sales -000-	40 Bonds
	High	Low	Close	High	Low	Close	High	Low	Close		
1	936.30	921.77	931.29	252.38	249.22	251.66	141.93	140.39	141.21	9,050	84.34
4	945.48	930.51	937.86	256.54	252.63	255.27	142.48	140.42	141.09	9,360	84.32
5	951.44	935.91	944.71	260.00	255.22	258.33	142.12	140.36	141.15	10,560	84.43
6	951.22	937.58	945.26	260.64	257.19	259.42	142.12	140.45	141.09	9,040	84.48
7	952.39	939.53	945.76	263.78	258.40	262.56	141.93	140.36	140.96	9,650	84.42
11	950.77	937.69	942.42	265.25	261.09	263.11	142.24	140.33	141.00	9,310	84.56
12	947.10	932.51	937.24	265.30	261.66	263.18	142.36	140.03	140.72	10,500	84.59
13	945.32	930.01	938.36	264.25	261.17	262.49	141.48	139.96	140.75	10,440	84.58
14	953.67	936.52	945.48	264.62	261.02	262.34	141.72	139.57	140.48	12,980	84.63
15	957.40	941.70	947.77	264.25	260.62	263.16	141.84	139.75	140.54	10,270	84.54
18	953.22	936.91	941.98	265.22	260.99	262.46	141.42	139.45	140.30	9,150	84.51
19	946.99	934.02	941.64	264.70	261.49	263.51	140.54	138.69	139.66	8,820	84.45
20	957.01	941.75	951.28	266.96	263.33	265.97	140.63	138.42	139.45	10,530	84.49
21	961.91	946.82	954.73	267.66	264.23	265.92	140.36	138.48	139.45	9,560	84.67
22	957.23	944.09	949.83	266.37	262.24	263.98	139.84	138.30	139.06	8,650	84.65
25	957.51	942.09	950.55	265.22	261.59	264.00	140.12	138.39	139.27	7,270	84.57
26	955.56	943.20	947.21	265.05	260.84	261.61	140.30	138.24	139.15	7,540	84.51
27	951.28	937.58	944.54	262.06	256.34	257.46	140.27	138.15	139.69	7,950	84.34
28	945.54	927.22	937.41	256.49	249.73	252.78	140.72	138.78	140.00	8,310	84.45
29	942.09	930.23	933.68	255.29	251.56	253.68	141.06	139.00	140.21	7,220	84.50

High 954.73   High 265.97   High 141.21   High 84.67
Low 931.29   Low 251.66   Low 139.06   Low 84.32

MAY, 1966

	-30 Industrials-			-20 Railroads-			-15 Utilities-			Daily Sales -000-	40 Bonds
	High	Low	Close	High	Low	Close	High	Low	Close		
2	939.64	926.61	931.95	254.82	250.00	250.62	141.30	139.33	140.39	7,070	84.44
3	932.12	919.20	921.77	250.92	245.07	247.31	140.96	138.78	139.42	8,020	84.34
4	923.38	906.23	914.86	247.95	243.40	246.21	140.12	137.87	138.90	9,740	84.28
5	919.65	897.55	899.77	247.36	239.67	240.96	139.51	137.30	138.15	10,100	84.27
6	909.18	882.90	902.83	242.33	235.81	240.54	138.84	136.81	138.09	13,110	84.33
9	903.39	883.18	886.80	240.17	234.35	235.51	138.75	136.75	137.78	9,290	84.35
10	904.39	886.35	895.48	238.82	234.12	235.96	139.09	137.00	138.09	9,050	84.46
11	908.40	892.70	895.43	238.97	235.07	236.14	139.15	137.27	137.81	7,470	84.50
12	900.00	878.84	885.57	235.19	230.17	231.91	138.27	136.48	137.12	8,210	84.41
13	884.85	868.65	876.11	230.91	226.68	228.50	137.36	135.72	136.63	8,970	84.37
16	881.73	862.86	867.53	229.69	222.23	223.15	137.18	135.21	136.03	9,260	84.38
17	876.83	859.13	864.14	225.31	219.57	220.54	137.09	134.54	135.78	9,870	84.32
18	883.96	864.42	878.50	226.61	221.23	225.94	137.30	135.30	136.36	9,310	84.05
19	887.86	869.65	872.99	229.62	223.90	225.14	137.60	135.60	136.60	8,640	83.95
20	880.06	863.53	876.89	226.73	222.43	226.08	137.69	135.75	137.03	6,430	84.00
23	889.86	873.49	882.46	230.69	226.23	228.62	138.12	135.78	136.66	7,080	83.97
24	898.38	882.12	888.41	232.98	228.77	230.89	138.06	136.12	136.84	7,210	83.93
25	894.98	881.29	890.42	232.08	228.77	231.06	137.75	136.06	137.18	5,820	83.91
26	900.33	886.80	891.75	233.23	229.94	231.16	138.03	135.79	136.66	6,080	83.98
27	899.77	885.85	897.04	231.91	227.07	230.89	137.27	135.57	136.60	4,790	83.94
31	899.61	881.73	884.07	231.11	226.46	227.28	137.03	135.03	135.60	5,770	83.95
		High	931.95		High	250.62		High	140.39		High 84.50
		Low	864.14		Low	220.54		Low	135.60		Low 83.91

JUNE, 1966

	-30 Industrials-			-20 Railroads-			-15 Utilities-			Daily Sales -000-	40 Bonds
	High	Low	Close	High	Low	Close	High	Low	Close		
1	888.53	877.33	883.63	227.70	225.14	226.68	136.45	134.33	135.24	5,290	83.84
2	890.64	878.34	882.73	228.67	225.74	227.15	136.57	134.51	135.51	5,080	83.76
3	890.86	879.73	887.86	228.67	225.94	228.00	136.63	134.42	135.66	4,430	83.77
6	888.95	876.22	881.68	228.32	225.14	225.79	137.03	134.93	136.09	4,260	83.73
7	882.62	870.32	877.33	225.59	222.23	223.75	136.42	134.90	135.60	5,040	83.70
8	883.68	872.16	879.34	225.09	222.95	224.24	136.24	134.87	135.54	4,580	83.57
9	887.30	874.05	882.62	228.45	224.87	227.70	136.15	134.63	135.48	5,810	83.48
10	896.77	880.84	891.75	232.43	227.10	231.24	136.51	134.30	135.27	8,240	83.41
13	904.67	891.64	897.60	233.25	229.34	230.91	136.37	133.84	135.33	7,600	83.29
14	907.18	891.53	903.17	232.63	228.97	231.43	135.69	133.63	134.84	7,600	83.27
15	910.35	897.82	901.11	234.00	230.69	232.01	135.84	134.30	134.84	8,520	83.24
16	903.61	890.92	897.16	233.80	230.54	232.33	135.24	133.36	134.12	6,870	83.21
17	900.55	889.75	894.26	233.85	230.81	231.96	135.21	132.87	134.03	6,580	83.23
20	898.21	887.24	892.76	233.23	230.79	232.03	134.63	132.54	133.18	5,940	83.18
21	900.44	889.36	894.98	233.97	230.84	232.06	133.84	131.90	132.96	6,860	83.23
22	904.62	892.59	901.00	233.23	229.59	231.41	133.54	131.84	132.75	7,800	83.28
23	908.51	893.48	896.43	233.80	230.86	231.88	133.84	131.84	132.63	7,930	83.23
24	904.17	888.41	897.16	232.58	229.97	231.56	133.75	131.57	132.48	7,140	83.20
27	904.06	887.47	888.97	232.23	229.37	229.87	133.81	131.72	132.27	5,330	83.23
28	890.81	874.83	880.90	230.02	227.23	228.27	132.84	131.33	132.24	6,280	83.24
29	884.29	869.15	871.60	228.97	225.96	227.03	132.72	131.12	131.84	6,020	83.32
30	876.33	858.90	870.10	227.85	223.00	226.06	132.57	130.48	131.60	7,250	83.25
		High	903.17		High	232.33		High	136.09		High 83.84
		Low	870.10		Low	223.75		Low	131.60		Low 83.18

JULY, 1966

	-30 Industrials-			-20 Railroads-			-15 Utilities-			Daily Sales -000-	40 Bonds
	High	Low	Close	High	Low	Close	High	Low	Close		
1	884.02	869.93	877.06	228.40	225.49	227.25	132.54	130.66	131.66	5,200	83.18
5	884.13	869.09	875.27	228.62	225.74	226.91	132.57	130.72	132.06	4,610	83.14
6	893.20	872.43	888.86	231.63	226.98	231.26	133.57	131.48	133.15	6,860	83.07
7	898.21	883.90	891.64	234.54	230.69	233.25	134.87	132.57	133.96	7,200	83.09
8	898.44	885.57	894.04	234.27	231.98	233.30	135.39	133.51	134.63	6,100	83.10
11	901.16	888.64	893.09	234.67	231.91	232.90	135.81	133.69	134.93	6,200	82.99
12	896.65	882.46	886.19	233.42	230.26	231.46	135.75	133.90	134.93	5,180	82.88
13	887.58	875.33	881.40	231.63	228.50	229.77	135.39	133.84	134.54	5,580	82.80
14	892.48	878.17	887.80	231.06	228.37	230.04	136.00	133.84	135.24	5,950	82.82
15	896.65	883.74	889.36	232.26	229.37	231.24	135.84	134.09	135.03	6,090	82.80
18	892.98	882.18	888.41	232.16	229.69	230.41	136.03	134.12	135.24	5,110	82.74
19	889.81	876.55	884.07	230.49	227.08	227.35	135.87	133.84	134.69	5,960	82.60
20	887.08	872.60	874.49	228.55	225.04	225.89	135.09	133.21	133.81	5,470	82.53
21	880.34	866.98	873.99	226.58	223.62	224.89	134.84	132.84	133.72	6,200	82.59
22	877.50	864.97	869.15	226.48	223.62	224.77	134.87	132.78	133.96	6,540	82.51
25	870.43	850.50	852.83	225.26	220.16	220.81	134.54	132.42	133.36	7,050	82.48
26	861.19	846.88	852.17	222.97	218.84	220.26	133.63	131.48	132.15	7,610	82.44
27	863.30	850.55	856.23	223.27	219.24	221.68	133.21	131.72	132.54	6,070	82.38
28	862.75	850.50	854.06	223.55	219.62	220.09	133.39	131.81	132.36	5,680	82.45
29	857.46	843.76	847.38	221.18	219.32	220.19	133.27	131.51	132.42	5,150	82.45
		High	894.04		High	233.30		High	135.24		High 83.18
		Low	847.38		Low	220.09		Low	131.66		Low 82.38

AUGUST, 1966

	-30 Industrials-			-20 Railroads-			-15 Utilities-			Daily Sales -000-	40 Bonds
	High	Low	Close	High	Low	Close	High	Low	Close		
1	846.60	830.84	835.18	219.32	216.61	217.28	132.60	130.72	131.15	5,880	82.43
2	840.97	827.28	832.57	218.40	215.81	216.56	131.84	130.06	130.69	5,710	82.36
3	847.99	832.90	841.70	219.77	216.38	218.20	131.84	130.12	130.69	6,220	82.24
4	858.57	841.20	851.50	220.98	218.12	219.39	132.39	129.93	131.45	6,880	82.24
5	860.57	845.71	852.39	220.41	218.40	219.62	132.54	130.48	131.33	5,500	82.14
8	854.78	842.42	849.05	220.14	217.25	218.72	131.96	130.21	130.87	4,900	82.13
9	853.11	841.09	844.82	219.44	217.38	217.97	131.93	130.27	130.75	6,270	82.13
10	846.71	835.02	838.53	217.43	215.34	215.88	131.57	129.87	130.48	5,290	82.06
11	843.65	830.56	837.91	216.41	213.79	214.64	131.24	129.48	129.96	5,700	82.10
12	847.66	834.68	840.53	215.76	213.52	214.54	130.81	128.57	129.57	6,230	82.07
15	845.65	831.79	834.85	215.26	212.80	212.95	130.03	127.90	128.57	5,680	82.03
16	834.79	820.04	823.83	212.97	209.46	210.01	128.96	127.09	127.75	6,130	81.88
17	827.28	813.69	819.59	210.56	207.00	208.00	128.33	126.45	127.09	6,630	81.68
18	821.15	804.73	810.74	207.87	203.14	204.84	127.27	125.18	125.78	7,000	81.55
19	816.75	801.50	804.62	205.71	201.93	202.55	126.93	124.84	125.57	7,070	81.44
22	807.79	786.85	792.03	203.27	197.35	198.94	126.06	122.66	123.03	8,690	81.27
23	801.78	781.90	790.14	201.01	195.51	197.99	124.60	121.33	122.78	9,830	81.20
24	805.45	790.20	799.55	202.50	198.19	200.88	124.06	121.66	122.72	7,050	81.00
25	806.23	789.08	792.37	202.62	197.92	198.62	124.18	121.96	122.72	6,760	80.87
26	792.53	776.22	780.56	198.37	193.69	195.03	123.03	120.18	120.90	8,190	80.74
29	781.06	763.97	767.03	194.71	189.16	190.48	121.33	118.48	118.96	10,900	80.55
30	781.62	759.52	775.72	194.36	188.66	193.04	121.00	117.57	119.57	11,230	80.26
31	796.49	777.44	788.41	197.87	192.77	195.76	122.15	119.30	121.33	8,690	80.32
		High	852.39		High	219.62		High	131.45		High 82.43
		Low	767.03		Low	190.48		Low	118.96		Low 80.26

SEPTEMBER, 1966

	-30 Industrials-			-20 Railroads-			-15 Utilities-			Daily Sales -000-	40 Bonds
	High	Low	Close	High	Low	Close	High	Low	Close		
1	798.94	782.12	792.09	197.85	194.24	195.73	124.30	121.27	123.45	6,250	80.29
2	796.26	776.72	787.69	196.80	193.57	195.18	125.12	122.72	124.36	6,080	80.19
6	795.15	778.84	782.34	196.75	193.37	194.11	125.87	123.69	124.72	4,350	80.37
7	787.30	771.77	777.39	194.74	190.95	192.50	125.30	123.30	124.15	5,530	80.49
8	782.46	763.36	774.88	195.06	190.53	194.04	124.96	122.63	123.51	6,660	80.29
9	781.01	767.92	775.55	195.43	192.55	194.46	125.63	122.63	124.30	5,280	80.40
12	795.32	775.61	790.59	199.36	194.21	198.39	127.00	124.27	125.93	6,780	80.19
13	803.11	789.25	795.48	200.76	197.27	198.44	127.81	125.51	126.48	6,870	80.33
14	809.02	789.58	806.23	201.50	197.27	201.23	129.15	125.96	128.60	6,250	80.47
15	821.26	804.62	814.30	203.74	200.86	202.52	130.45	128.09	129.72	6,140	80.44
16	822.93	808.35	814.30	203.22	200.18	201.68	130.42	128.27	129.33	5,150	80.46
19	818.54	804.00	810.85	202.37	199.79	200.36	130.00	128.03	128.78	4,920	80.57
20	813.08	801.22	806.01	200.93	198.94	199.61	129.00	127.36	127.93	4,560	80.26
21	806.73	792.53	793.59	200.43	195.63	196.55	128.90	126.87	127.75	5,360	80.11
22	801.83	785.69	797.77	198.00	194.19	196.80	128.30	126.27	127.48	5,760	80.19
23	800.11	787.36	790.97	199.19	194.66	196.78	128.48	125.93	126.60	4,560	80.20
26	797.32	784.46	792.70	198.69	195.28	197.67	127.42	125.45	126.57	4,960	80.14
27	805.45	789.53	794.09	200.76	196.97	198.19	127.45	125.24	126.21	6,300	80.21
28	795.60	777.33	780.95	198.54	195.38	196.03	126.78	124.72	125.33	5,990	80.38
29	783.18	768.26	772.66	196.30	193.47	194.19	126.06	123.39	124.21	6,110	80.36
30	779.34	763.91	774.22	195.58	191.82	193.49	125.36	123.09	124.72	6,170	80.38
		High	814.30		High	202.52		High	129.72	High	80.57
		Low	772.66		Low	192.50		Low	123.45	Low	80.11

OCTOBER, 1966

	-30 Industrials-			-20 Railroads-			-15 Utilities-			Daily Sales -000-	40 Bonds
	High	Low	Close	High	Low	Close	High	Low	Close		
3	778.11	756.79	757.96	194.46	189.29	189.88	125.39	122.84	123.15	6,490	80.40
4	767.53	750.33	763.19	190.41	187.22	189.54	124.84	122.45	123.69	8,910	80.53
5	768.04	751.72	755.45	191.80	188.17	188.81	125.39	123.21	124.27	5,880	80.43
6	759.52	744.09	749.61	189.14	186.45	187.47	124.87	122.78	123.84	8,110	80.54
7	756.84	739.64	744.32	187.87	183.81	184.34	124.27	122.39	122.72	8,140	80.63
10	758.07	735.74	754.51	187.00	181.97	185.85	124.15	121.66	123.81	9,630	80.77
11	771.43	752.44	758.63	189.51	185.60	186.82	125.45	123.09	124.24	8,430	80.82
12	780.12	752.89	778.17	192.17	186.13	192.17	125.87	123.54	125.66	6,910	80.69
13	791.09	768.81	772.93	195.31	191.20	192.47	128.15	125.78	127.15	8,680	80.75
14	782.90	765.14	771.71	193.27	190.63	191.92	129.42	126.81	128.48	5,610	80.76
17	789.14	770.82	778.89	195.01	191.50	193.86	131.60	127.78	130.33	5,570	80.82
18	795.65	777.44	791.87	196.18	192.35	195.23	133.30	130.12	132.87	7,180	80.85
19	799.22	779.84	785.35	195.66	192.40	193.12	134.72	131.84	132.69	6,460	80.89
20	796.04	778.11	783.68	194.83	191.15	192.35	134.63	132.15	133.75	6,840	80.97
21	791.36	777.17	787.30	194.16	190.85	193.07	134.51	131.96	133.03	5,690	80.88
24	796.10	781.73	787.75	195.18	191.85	193.32	134.96	132.27	133.21	5,780	80.89
25	796.60	780.34	793.09	193.84	190.06	192.80	134.75	132.39	133.90	6,190	80.87
26	809.29	792.31	801.11	195.51	192.00	194.49	136.87	133.75	136.00	6,760	80.81
27	814.97	800.77	809.57	197.20	193.29	196.38	137.69	135.27	137.33	6,670	80.98
28	816.64	801.44	807.96	201.03	195.53	199.51	138.12	135.42	136.87	6,420	80.97
31	812.91	797.04	807.07	201.95	198.17	200.88	137.81	135.57	136.72	5,860	81.12
		High	809.57		High	200.88		High	137.33	High	81.12
		Low	744.32		Low	184.34		Low	122.72	Low	80.40

NOVEMBER, 1966

	-30 Industrials-			-20 Railroads-			-15 Utilities-			Daily Sales -000-	40 Bonds
	High	Low	Close	High	Low	Close	High	Low	Close		
1	814.30	800.33	809.63	203.42	199.84	202.12	137.72	135.84	137.03	6,480	81.22
2	815.92	801.61	807.29	203.34	200.16	201.23	138.21	136.39	137.48	6,740	81.01
3	812.24	798.32	804.34	201.73	199.24	199.94	137.96	136.24	137.09	5,860	81.03
4	809.57	793.54	805.06	200.76	197.22	199.66	138.75	136.24	137.54	6,530	80.89
7	809.85	796.38	802.22	200.86	197.60	198.74	139.03	136.45	137.24	6,120	81.01
9	815.64	799.72	809.91	201.25	198.09	199.86	138.69	136.45	137.15	8,390	80.87
10	822.38	807.18	816.87	201.80	198.82	199.96	138.63	136.54	137.27	8,870	80.80
11	822.32	810.46	819.09	202.03	199.19	200.53	138.39	136.63	137.54	6,690	80.89
14	823.10	808.29	813.75	201.95	199.41	200.56	138.63	136.39	137.33	6,540	80.84
15	819.48	808.12	815.31	204.64	199.89	204.14	137.96	136.24	137.09	7,190	80.75
16	827.33	812.69	820.87	209.51	204.81	208.79	138.78	136.54	137.66	10,350	80.68
17	825.61	808.90	816.03	209.09	204.21	205.73	138.27	136.42	137.33	8,900	80.50
18	817.81	804.95	809.40	206.01	202.95	203.77	138.06	136.06	136.84	6,900	80.48
21	807.73	791.09	798.16	202.87	199.04	200.76	137.39	134.12	135.33	7,450	80.35
22	799.55	785.46	794.98	201.08	198.57	199.54	135.75	133.90	134.66	6,430	80.34
23	804.78	789.36	796.82	202.50	199.21	201.68	136.21	134.21	135.24	7,350	80.16
25	807.68	793.87	803.34	204.44	201.08	203.44	135.87	133.84	134.81	6,810	80.10
28	808.24	793.59	801.16	204.69	201.43	203.49	135.75	134.00	135.06	7,630	80.06
29	803.28	791.59	795.26	204.46	201.50	202.50	135.87	133.87	134.66	7,320	80.17
30	796.21	784.79	791.59	203.29	200.68	202.27	135.36	133.18	134.18	7,230	80.13
		High 820.87			High 208.79			High 137.66			High 81.22
		Low 791.59			Low 198.74			Low 134.18			Low 80.06

DECEMBER, 1966

	-30 Industrials-			-20 Railroads-			-15 Utilities-			Daily Sales -000-	40 Bonds
	High	Low	Close	High	Low	Close	High	Low	Close		
1	797.93	785.63	789.75	203.49	200.31	201.23	135.03	132.96	133.54	8,480	80.18
2	794.82	783.51	789.47	202.77	200.58	201.50	135.00	132.69	134.12	6,230	80.19
5	795.54	784.35	791.59	202.92	200.33	201.13	135.09	133.09	134.09	6,470	79.98
6	800.94	788.25	797.43	204.02	200.93	203.32	135.18	133.45	134.36	7,670	79.99
7	812.41	795.43	808.01	206.80	202.45	205.41	135.18	133.48	134.27	8,980	80.04
8	818.81	805.95	812.80	207.87	204.84	206.28	135.42	133.72	134.33	8,370	80.06
9	818.20	804.95	813.02	208.05	205.11	206.68	135.45	133.42	135.03	7,650	80.07
12	826.67	810.52	820.54	209.61	206.03	208.49	136.45	133.93	135.42	9,530	80.02
13	827.22	812.08	816.70	210.86	207.28	208.82	137.00	134.75	136.03	9,650	80.16
14	823.66	810.63	817.98	209.71	206.98	208.42	137.39	135.60	136.72	7,470	80.26
15	820.82	804.45	809.18	209.12	206.33	206.73	137.45	135.78	136.78	7,150	80.32
16	813.02	802.22	807.18	207.82	205.66	206.80	137.87	135.75	136.75	6,980	80.53
19	807.46	792.70	798.99	208.37	205.81	207.25	137.84	135.51	136.08	7,340	80.60
20	800.66	789.42	794.59	207.70	205.21	205.61	136.98	135.06	136.15	6,830	80.66
21	802.00	789.69	797.43	208.30	205.01	207.62	137.42	135.12	136.15	7,690	80.60
22	807.18	793.87	801.67	210.21	207.03	209.07	137.65	135.19	136.34	8,560	80.57
23	806.51	793.09	799.10	209.91	207.10	207.92	137.78	135.80	136.72	7,350	80.60
27	802.61	788.25	792.20	208.59	206.33	207.18	137.87	135.57	136.82	6,280	80.60
28	799.38	785.96	788.58	208.10	205.36	205.76	137.84	135.76	136.82	7,160	80.74
29	792.70	781.51	786.35	205.71	202.82	203.29	137.42	135.86	136.63	7,900	80.76
30	794.59	779.34	785.69	205.04	201.73	202.97	137.62	135.48	136.18	11,330	80.89
		High 820.54			High 209.07			High 136.82			High 80.89
		Low 785.69			Low 201.13			Low 133.54			Low 79.98

JANUARY, 1967

	—30 Industrials—			—20 Railroads—			—15 Utilities—			Daily Sales -000-	40 Bonds
	High	Low	Close	High	Low	Close	High	Low	Close		
3	800.55	782.34	786.41	206.68	203.77	205.16	138.03	135.38	136.24	6,100	80.93
4	795.54	776.16	791.14	205.86	202.52	205.31	137.30	135.44	136.56	6,150	81.04
5	807.90	791.64	805.51	210.09	205.76	209.39	138.58	136.24	137.36	7,320	81.18
6	816.53	801.67	808.74	211.98	209.19	210.98	139.66	137.11	138.61	7,830	81.43
9	818.87	803.34	813.47	214.49	210.71	213.67	139.44	137.42	138.42	9,180	81.66
10	820.93	808.18	814.14	215.04	211.95	213.15	139.25	137.33	138.32	8,120	81.83
11	827.11	798.71	822.49	215.56	209.02	214.91	139.05	136.59	138.22	13,230	82.10
12	839.25	819.76	829.95	218.82	214.84	217.90	139.41	137.36	138.19	12,830	82.29
13	838.47	821.15	835.13	221.43	217.18	220.41	139.57	137.17	138.93	10,000	82.44
16	842.48	828.12	833.24	223.03	219.70	220.82	139.67	137.24	138.42	10,280	82.70
17	848.72	830.57	843.65	224.77	220.14	223.68	139.95	137.59	139.31	11,590	83.01
18	853.34	839.14	847.49	225.44	222.16	224.02	140.56	138.71	139.79	11,390	83.20
19	853.73	840.81	846.44	226.89	223.45	225.69	140.88	138.90	139.99	10,230	83.22
20	851.39	838.59	847.16	227.93	223.90	226.84	140.66	138.80	139.79	9,530	83.40
23	856.68	841.43	847.72	229.60	226.19	227.76	140.88	138.45	139.70	10,830	83.45
24	853.12	836.30	847.72	229.15	225.52	227.91	140.18	138.13	139.19	10,430	83.42
25	852.67	837.69	840.59	229.67	224.77	226.09	139.99	137.94	138.48	10,260	83.33
26	848.27	830.18	838.70	227.61	223.68	225.84	139.63	137.40	138.64	10,630	83.39
27	850.17	836.14	844.04	227.73	224.40	226.71	139.83	137.56	138.80	9,690	83.46
30	854.57	840.48	848.11	229.22	225.72	228.01	140.24	138.04	139.38	10,250	83.56
31	857.02	844.82	849.89	229.65	226.91	228.01	140.18	138.16	139.19	11,540	83.52
		High	849.89		High	228.01		High	139.99		High 83.56
		Low	786.41		Low	205.16		Low	136.24		Low 80.93

FEBRUARY, 1967

	—30 Industrials—			—20 Railroads—			—15 Utilities—			Daily Sales -000-	40 Bonds
	High	Low	Close	High	Low	Close	High	Low	Close		
1	854.51	842.54	848.39	228.78	226.64	227.46	139.60	137.56	138.45	9,580	83.53
2	857.68	842.20	853.12	228.85	225.44	227.01	139.83	137.81	138.84	10,720	83.53
3	864.09	849.78	857.46	229.05	225.94	228.03	139.83	138.13	138.90	12,010	83.50
6	862.53	849.72	855.12	230.37	227.46	228.90	139.89	137.97	139.35	10,680	83.52
7	857.68	847.27	852.51	229.32	226.84	227.38	139.63	137.97	138.58	6,400	83.44
8	865.37	850.11	860.97	229.47	226.74	228.63	140.08	138.04	139.25	11,220	83.47
9	871.71	854.06	857.52	230.54	227.63	228.33	140.27	138.20	138.74	10,970	83.49
10	861.36	847.72	855.73	229.30	227.23	227.93	139.73	137.85	138.55	8,850	83.37
13	860.52	848.72	853.34	229.92	227.71	229.03	139.92	137.85	138.74	7,570	83.47
14	862.64	848.39	856.90	231.84	228.93	230.97	140.08	137.72	138.68	9,760	83.39
15	863.47	850.22	855.79	232.93	229.97	230.99	139.79	137.81	138.84	10,480	83.39
16	863.42	846.60	851.56	232.09	229.82	230.54	139.79	137.69	138.64	8,490	83.32
17	856.35	845.88	850.84	231.89	229.22	230.34	139.38	137.53	138.13	8,530	83.27
20	853.90	839.81	847.88	230.72	228.33	229.03	138.55	136.47	136.73	8,640	83.23
21	851.39	840.03	844.10	230.05	228.30	229.08	137.75	135.93	136.98	9,030	83.14
23	851.67	837.31	846.77	230.74	227.73	229.17	137.65	135.80	136.69	10,010	83.16
24	854.79	839.64	847.33	230.17	228.13	229.15	137.65	135.58	136.79	9,830	83.11
27	849.44	830.46	836.64	228.98	225.47	226.46	137.27	134.75	135.70	10,210	83.05
28	844.27	827.95	839.37	227.56	224.85	226.64	136.85	134.62	135.99	9,970	82.95
		High	860.97		High	230.99		High	139.35		High 83.53
		Low	836.64		Low	226.46		Low	135.70		Low 82.95

MARCH, 1967

	—30 Industrials—			—20 Railroads—			—15 Utilities—			Daily Sales -000-	40 Bonds
	High	Low	Close	High	Low	Close	High	Low	Close		
1	852.12	836.47	843.49	229.85	226.71	228.63	137.14	134.87	135.93	11,510	83.02
2	852.62	840.87	846.71	230.32	228.20	229.22	137.46	135.03	136.34	11,900	82.92
3	853.51	841.04	846.60	230.54	227.63	229.08	137.53	135.42	136.28	11,100	83.01
6	851.45	837.86	842.20	231.44	228.73	230.20	137.49	135.38	135.99	10,400	82.88
7	847.10	835.30	841.76	231.24	229.15	230.29	137.21	134.94	136.09	9,810	82.94
8	851.00	836.36	843.32	231.76	229.37	230.62	136.79	134.97	135.54	11,070	82.91
9	850.72	836.53	844.15	232.51	229.60	231.69	136.50	134.27	135.61	10,480	82.93
10	864.25	845.43	848.50	237.31	233.38	234.18	137.40	134.71	135.22	14,900	82.91
13	853.56	840.59	844.82	234.67	231.84	232.29	136.28	134.20	134.75	9,910	82.98
14	850.33	836.86	844.27	233.21	230.87	231.99	135.54	133.44	134.49	10,260	82.93
15	856.90	842.65	854.06	233.88	230.92	232.78	135.83	133.28	134.52	10,830	82.93
16	872.33	854.51	868.49	235.77	232.61	234.80	136.83	133.53	134.65	12,170	83.04
17	876.50	861.80	869.77	236.61	233.78	235.17	136.15	133.69	135.19	10,020	83.06
20	877.28	862.36	870.43	236.34	232.86	234.82	136.44	134.01	135.29	9,040	83.13
21	879.18	861.25	866.59	236.44	232.73	233.63	136.57	134.36	135.16	9,820	83.12
22	875.11	857.68	870.55	234.23	230.74	233.33	136.15	134.14	135.16	8,820	83.18
23	882.29	868.82	876.67	235.35	232.26	233.33	136.82	134.52	136.18	9,500	83.25
27	883.41	869.15	873.72	233.75	228.70	231.09	138.04	135.07	137.27	9,260	83.32
28	882.13	868.37	875.28	232.78	229.77	231.79	138.36	136.18	137.08	8,940	83.29
29	880.40	866.31	871.10	233.58	230.84	232.29	138.42	136.66	137.78	8,430	83.40
30	875.39	863.92	869.99	233.61	230.87	231.81	138.87	137.01	138.04	8,340	83.34
31	874.28	861.19	865.98	232.61	229.72	230.59	139.44	137.33	138.55	8,130	83.26
	High 876.67			High 235.17			High 138.55				High 83.40
	Low 841.76			Low 228.63			Low 134.49				Low 82.88

APRIL, 1967

	—30 Industrials—			—20 Railroads—			—15 Utilities—			Daily Sales -000-	40 Bonds
	High	Low	Close	High	Low	Close	High	Low	Close		
3	868.43	854.45	859.97	230.22	226.04	226.89	139.28	137.37	138.45	8,530	83.16
4	865.65	852.17	859.19	227.98	224.92	226.26	139.25	137.11	138.23	8,750	83.22
5	867.26	855.23	861.19	228.03	225.39	227.26	139.16	137.53	138.20	8,810	83.21
6	867.59	856.51	861.25	229.72	226.44	228.25	139.06	137.69	138.36	9,470	83.14
7	866.59	850.22	853.34	229.82	225.97	227.48	139.67	138.04	138.90	9,090	83.30
10	852.84	839.76	842.43	228.98	223.83	225.77	139.95	138.07	139.19	8,110	83.36
11	852.39	838.98	847.66	227.98	224.97	227.26	139.73	137.49	138.64	7,710	83.38
12	852.67	841.48	844.65	229.13	226.59	227.43	139.63	137.81	138.61	7,750	83.32
13	852.84	840.81	848.83	228.35	225.87	227.36	139.79	138.00	138.87	7,610	83.43
14	865.03	847.05	859.74	229.77	226.46	228.85	140.43	139.00	139.70	8,810	83.45
17	874.83	857.91	866.59	230.62	227.38	228.70	140.27	138.80	139.57	9,070	83.49
18	876.73	861.92	873.00	230.22	227.21	229.15	140.75	139.00	139.95	10,500	83.40
19	882.07	868.76	873.94	230.17	227.78	229.30	140.82	139.41	140.24	10,860	83.34
20	882.18	869.04	878.62	230.12	227.58	229.03	141.17	139.25	140.43	9,690	83.22
21	888.30	873.61	883.18	231.84	228.63	230.52	141.01	139.16	139.95	10,210	83.36
24	894.82	877.84	887.53	232.04	228.86	230.31	141.17	139.31	140.15	10,250	83.28
25	894.93	880.73	891.20	232.17	229.17	231.03	140.98	139.16	139.89	10,420	83.23
26	898.50	883.96	889.03	232.35	229.38	230.46	140.75	138.87	139.89	10,560	83.09
27	898.33	882.74	894.82	232.90	229.53	232.15	140.24	138.00	139.16	10,250	83.03
28	903.73	891.20	897.05	233.91	230.59	231.91	140.63	138.48	139.35	11,200	82.83
	High 897.05			High 232.15			High 140.43				High 83.49
	Low 842.43			Low 225.77			Low 138.20				Low 82.83

MAY, 1967

	\-30 Industrials\-			\-20 Railroads\-			\-15 Utilities\-			Daily Sales -000-	40 Bonds
	High	Low	Close	High	Low	Close	High	Low	Close		
1	900.50	887.81	892.93	233.67	230.75	231.89	140.18	138.07	139.09	9,410	82.77
2	898.39	886.19	891.65	232.66	230.34	231.81	139.95	137.85	138.84	10,260	82.60
3	900.95	886.41	896.77	233.23	230.05	231.58	139.31	137.56	138.42	11,550	82.64
4	906.57	892.65	901.95	234.14	229.90	232.15	139.19	137.33	138.29	12,850	82.57
5	910.91	898.05	905.96	236.78	231.29	235.87	139.51	137.56	138.61	10,630	82.67
8	915.31	899.44	909.63	239.26	234.40	237.53	139.76	137.65	138.80	10,330	82.66
9	915.87	897.05	899.89	239.68	234.37	235.69	139.63	137.72	138.45	10,830	82.62
10	902.23	888.47	894.10	237.84	234.22	236.44	138.90	136.63	137.78	10,410	82.23
11	901.56	888.25	896.21	238.85	235.36	237.45	138.64	136.44	137.81	10,320	82.23
12	900.67	885.86	890.03	239.49	235.64	237.68	139.03	136.79	137.91	10,470	82.19
15	892.26	878.67	882.41	238.85	236.00	236.80	138.71	136.73	137.72	8,320	82.16
16	891.76	877.90	885.80	239.93	236.29	238.49	139.41	137.11	138.23	10,700	81.97
17	891.37	878.40	882.24	240.30	237.35	238.15	139.41	137.11	138.00	9,560	81.87
18	885.13	873.27	877.34	240.61	236.75	239.39	138.71	136.76	137.49	10,290	81.65
19	881.24	867.59	874.55	241.18	237.79	239.81	138.23	136.50	137.33	10,560	81.59
22	876.61	863.75	871.05	241.46	237.50	239.88	137.88	135.96	136.28	9,600	81.49
23	875.72	862.03	868.71	241.67	238.64	240.09	137.08	135.13	136.06	9,810	81.21
24	870.49	857.18	862.42	240.81	237.61	239.44	136.76	134.49	134.94	10,290	81.24
25	876.50	860.36	870.71	243.45	238.43	242.34	136.12	134.07	134.91	8,960	81.29
26	875.22	863.31	870.32	248.86	241.05	247.33	135.48	133.82	135.03	7,810	81.21
29	871.60	860.24	864.98	252.28	245.99	248.58	135.48	133.63	134.30	6,590	81.20
31	864.64	850.39	852.56	249.84	243.09	243.61	134.81	132.67	132.99	8,870	81.15
		High	909.63		High	248.58		High	139.09	High	82.77
		Low	852.56		Low	231.58		Low	132.99	Low	81.15

JUNE, 1967

	\-30 Industrials\-			\-20 Railroads\-			\-15 Utilities\-			Daily Sales -000-	40 Bonds
	High	Low	Close	High	Low	Close	High	Low	Close		
1	869.60	850.56	864.98	249.92	243.58	248.97	134.33	132.45	133.37	9,040	81.21
2	870.82	857.46	863.31	251.40	246.38	247.46	134.43	132.39	133.05	8,070	81.15
5	858.41	836.92	847.77	247.39	241.90	244.46	133.47	130.91	131.71	11,110	81.09
6	868.46	848.33	862.71	250.54	245.39	249.46	133.56	131.17	132.67	9,230	80.98
7	877.14	860.57	869.19	253.47	248.94	251.24	133.50	131.55	132.83	10,170	80.84
8	875.17	861.64	873.20	252.59	249.22	251.37	134.20	131.90	132.96	8,300	80.85
9	881.94	865.08	874.89	255.56	250.52	254.55	133.98	131.45	132.76	9,650	80.92
12	884.77	870.49	878.93	258.85	254.35	257.19	133.66	131.84	133.08	10,230	80.85
13	892.68	875.75	886.15	259.34	255.30	257.58	133.85	132.06	132.76	11,570	80.83
14	890.78	876.39	880.61	259.13	255.43	256.83	133.44	131.58	132.41	10,960	80.81
15	891.24	873.32	883.26	258.64	254.79	256.65	133.24	130.85	131.90	11,240	80.79
16	892.80	879.68	885.00	258.36	255.15	256.47	133.24	130.98	131.65	10,740	80.62
19	890.03	877.43	884.54	258.54	255.36	257.84	132.51	130.40	131.58	8,570	80.65
20	890.72	876.44	880.61	259.34	254.61	256.70	132.41	130.37	131.20	10,350	80.61
21	886.90	872.52	877.66	258.44	253.08	254.45	132.38	130.02	131.45	9,760	80.46
22	881.13	868.82	875.69	256.57	252.95	254.66	132.25	130.34	131.33	9,550	80.51
23	883.32	870.95	877.37	256.62	253.31	255.05	132.48	130.85	131.87	9,130	80.29
26	884.30	866.91	872.11	256.11	252.77	253.52	132.67	129.95	130.75	9,040	80.39
27	875.87	864.14	869.39	255.67	251.84	254.50	131.55	129.60	130.27	8,780	80.39
28	875.17	864.14	868.87	257.61	253.83	256.47	131.61	129.35	130.59	9,310	80.30
29	873.67	859.45	861.94	257.92	254.32	255.51	131.71	129.60	130.75	9,940	80.43
30	867.83	855.58	860.26	256.49	253.47	254.84	132.06	129.95	131.39	7,850	80.29
		High	886.15		High	257.84		High	133.37	High	81.21
		Low	847.77		Low	244.46		Low	130.27	Low	80.29

JULY, 1967

	–30 Industrials–			–20 Railroads–			–15 Utilities–			Daily Sales -000-	40 Bonds
	High	Low	Close	High	Low	Close	High	Low	Close		
3	864.60	853.21	859.69	255.98	253.48	254.61	132.38	130.56	131.65	6,040	80.26
5	871.01	857.43	864.94	257.84	254.95	256.75	132.83	130.78	132.00	9,170	80.10
6	871.24	858.70	864.02	259.00	255.72	257.24	132.96	131.23	132.22	10,170	80.04
7	874.42	860.32	869.05	261.91	256.81	260.75	133.28	131.49	132.25	11,540	80.12
10	880.37	866.04	875.52	266.19	260.70	265.29	133.34	131.42	132.54	12,130	80.22
11	886.15	870.90	879.45	269.88	265.72	267.53	133.76	131.71	132.57	12,400	80.27
12	885.40	870.55	878.70	268.33	265.05	267.07	133.60	131.39	132.35	11,240	80.22
13	885.81	873.04	878.53	268.74	265.62	267.30	133.53	131.39	132.29	10,730	80.23
14	889.62	872.52	882.05	269.00	265.78	267.27	133.05	131.49	132.51	10,880	80.12
17	891.30	875.35	882.74	270.16	265.39	268.51	133.44	131.42	132.45	10,390	80.15
18	899.79	879.39	896.09	272.07	268.51	270.55	134.17	131.65	133.05	12,060	80.13
19	908.75	892.63	903.32	273.79	269.49	272.17	134.46	132.22	133.21	12,850	80.18
20	913.83	896.79	908.69	273.74	269.93	272.66	134.20	131.93	133.08	11,160	80.07
21	918.69	903.03	909.56	274.67	270.96	272.99	133.95	131.84	132.57	11,710	80.03
24	912.68	897.48	904.53	273.79	270.24	271.89	133.40	131.49	132.57	9,580	80.05
25	909.56	895.52	901.29	272.87	270.11	271.45	133.88	131.77	132.92	9,890	79.90
26	908.17	895.75	903.14	274.21	269.05	272.32	134.27	132.16	133.47	11,160	80.08
27	912.79	896.96	903.14	274.18	269.46	272.32	134.46	132.73	133.66	12,400	79.94
28	910.31	896.15	901.53	275.21	269.64	272.38	134.68	132.70	133.79	10,900	79.92
31	912.85	896.67	904.24	273.82	270.91	271.94	134.59	132.70	133.34	10,330	79.93

High 909.56 High 272.99 High 133.79 High 80.27
Low 859.69 Low 254.61 Low 131.65 Low 79.90

AUGUST, 1967

	–30 Industrials–			–20 Railroads–			–15 Utilities–			Daily Sales -000-	40 Bonds
	High	Low	Close	High	Low	Close	High	Low	Close		
1	917.19	900.25	912.97	275.78	271.89	274.03	134.78	133.05	134.04	12,290	80.04
2	931.29	913.55	922.27	276.24	272.48	274.05	135.32	133.44	134.59	13,510	80.08
3	929.67	908.11	921.98	274.64	269.31	273.25	135.48	133.18	134.27	13,440	80.11
4	931.06	917.65	923.77	275.80	271.94	274.49	135.19	133.18	134.23	11,130	80.22
7	930.65	915.34	920.37	277.02	271.89	273.56	135.64	132.89	134.49	10,160	80.02
8	927.88	916.67	922.45	266.03	263.84	264.77	135.48	133.40	134.30	8,970	79.77
9	931.75	919.09	926.72	266.45	262.53	265.39	135.45	133.53	134.78	10,100	79.78
10	933.14	920.77	925.22	266.37	262.61	263.64	135.42	133.31	134.01	9,040	79.74
11	928.11	915.57	920.65	264.28	261.24	262.04	134.71	132.51	133.79	8,250	79.81
14	922.16	909.96	916.32	263.07	260.00	261.08	134.62	132.35	133.15	7,990	79.79
15	924.93	912.85	919.15	262.35	259.33	260.44	134.01	132.25	132.83	8,710	79.74
16	921.64	910.83	915.68	261.57	258.89	259.87	133.69	132.35	133.05	8,220	79.69
17	923.89	912.85	918.23	260.70	258.56	259.25	133.60	131.77	132.54	8,790	79.61
18	925.51	912.79	919.04	260.13	257.53	258.07	133.18	131.17	132.09	8,250	79.30
21	921.64	907.48	912.27	258.97	256.08	257.06	133.28	131.04	131.65	8,600	79.34
22	916.15	903.61	907.48	258.51	255.18	256.06	132.41	130.59	131.33	7,940	79.32
23	910.14	896.44	905.11	257.97	254.79	256.08	131.84	129.95	130.69	8,760	79.19
24	910.54	896.09	898.46	258.30	254.82	256.19	131.61	129.67	130.56	7,740	79.22
25	900.49	888.81	894.07	257.91	255.13	256.96	131.04	129.31	130.21	7,250	79.22
28	902.16	887.83	894.71	259.59	255.52	258.27	131.20	129.31	129.98	6,270	79.26
29	900.20	887.94	894.76	260.03	257.73	258.53	130.94	129.15	129.73	6,350	79.29
30	900.72	888.64	893.72	261.81	257.06	260.52	130.78	129.12	129.63	7,200	79.28
31	906.38	893.09	901.29	263.33	260.03	261.94	130.94	128.96	129.92	8,840	79.31

High 926.72 High 274.49 High 134.78 High 80.22
Low 893.72 Low 256.06 Low 129.63 Low 79.19

SEPTEMBER, 1967

	—30 Industrials—			—20 Railroads—			—15 Utilities—			Daily Sales -000-	40 Bonds
	High	Low	Close	High	Low	Close	High	Low	Close		
1	906.84	894.19	901.18	263.48	260.80	262.37	131.23	129.19	130.34	7,460	79.41
5	909.91	895.69	904.13	264.69	261.55	263.33	131.71	129.73	130.66	8,320	79.23
6	913.55	899.27	906.96	264.13	261.29	262.35	131.74	129.92	130.98	9,550	79.23
7	913.49	901.64	908.17	263.66	260.80	262.06	131.84	130.34	131.01	8,910	79.23
8	914.41	901.24	907.54	262.79	259.74	260.88	131.77	130.21	131.04	9,300	79.32
11	916.20	902.68	909.62	261.86	258.58	259.28	132.32	130.62	131.42	9,170	79.28
12	916.84	905.05	911.75	262.12	258.04	260.39	132.80	131.13	131.87	9,930	79.24
13	928.40	911.64	923.77	262.89	259.07	260.78	133.40	131.45	132.38	12,400	79.18
14	939.38	923.72	929.44	262.86	259.69	261.14	133.72	131.58	132.41	12,220	79.30
15	938.51	923.25	933.48	262.40	260.08	261.42	133.21	131.29	132.03	10,270	79.32
18	944.58	929.73	938.74	267.68	261.88	265.11	133.34	131.26	132.51	11,620	79.26
19	944.64	926.95	930.07	266.76	262.37	263.61	133.21	131.29	131.87	11,540	79.10
20	936.89	922.50	929.79	265.78	262.45	264.31	132.60	130.88	131.71	10,980	79.08
21	938.22	924.12	930.48	265.34	261.55	262.37	132.80	131.10	131.84	11,290	79.12
22	940.48	923.95	934.35	264.08	261.24	262.37	132.64	131.04	131.49	11,160	79.14
25	949.66	931.75	943.08	263.71	259.85	261.34	132.29	130.37	130.94	10,910	78.95
26	951.57	934.12	937.18	262.35	259.59	260.31	131.77	129.82	130.62	10,940	78.95
27	942.61	927.88	933.14	261.57	259.07	259.80	131.42	129.76	130.69	8,810	78.79
28	937.30	925.05	929.38	261.68	258.74	260.72	131.58	129.79	130.37	10,470	78.74
29	933.77	919.85	926.66	263.55	259.98	261.83	131.33	129.60	130.34	9,710	78.68
		High	943.08		High	265.11		High	132.51		High 79.41
		Low	901.18		Low	259.28		Low	130.34		Low 78.68

OCTOBER, 1967

	—30 Industrials—			—20 Railroads—			—15 Utilities—			Daily Sales -000-	40 Bonds
	High	Low	Close	High	Low	Close	High	Low	Close		
2	930.42	915.92	921.00	264.95	260.31	263.02	131.36	129.35	130.02	9,240	78.64
3	930.77	916.49	924.47	264.18	259.69	261.03	130.72	128.90	129.54	10,320	78.42
4	932.33	916.32	921.29	262.58	258.58	260.08	130.56	128.48	129.12	11,520	78.40
5	931.46	917.88	927.13	261.14	257.99	259.25	130.21	128.36	129.03	8,490	78.37
6	935.74	921.58	928.74	260.80	257.97	258.74	129.82	128.23	128.99	9,830	78.34
9	940.36	924.47	933.31	259.54	255.72	256.73	129.98	127.94	128.45	11,180	78.33
10	940.07	921.35	926.61	257.66	253.53	254.59	129.12	127.27	127.84	12,000	78.15
11	929.73	916.61	920.25	255.26	252.17	253.35	128.42	126.47	127.17	11,230	78.03
12	922.56	909.79	913.20	254.02	251.13	251.93	127.46	125.89	126.31	7,770	78.15
13	924.41	908.58	918.17	252.94	250.46	251.55	127.65	125.03	125.96	9,040	78.11
16	922.97	905.46	908.52	252.14	247.91	248.40	126.37	124.58	125.38	9,080	78.08
17	912.97	896.73	904.36	249.48	245.21	248.14	126.02	124.33	125.32	10,290	77.87
18	910.48	896.15	903.49	249.43	246.67	247.91	125.89	124.27	124.94	10,500	77.71
19	914.41	899.68	903.72	251.65	247.42	248.74	126.31	124.20	124.87	11,620	77.67
20	906.96	891.35	896.73	250.80	246.70	247.50	125.77	123.88	124.65	9,510	77.59
23	900.43	883.03	894.65	248.09	244.61	246.18	125.54	123.50	124.36	9,680	77.49
24	903.84	885.52	888.18	248.30	244.38	245.08	125.26	123.15	123.98	11,110	77.52
25	893.44	877.31	886.73	246.55	242.96	244.97	124.87	123.15	123.85	10,300	77.30
26	896.04	881.99	890.89	246.31	242.09	244.53	124.90	123.15	123.63	9,920	77.33
27	896.15	882.98	888.18	244.69	241.80	243.07	124.90	122.96	124.04	9,880	77.16
30	894.07	880.37	886.62	243.19	239.02	239.87	124.49	122.70	123.15	10,250	77.08
31	890.72	876.21	879.74	240.18	236.70	237.45	124.46	122.35	123.11	12,020	76.88
		High	933.31		High	263.02		High	130.02		High 78.64
		Low	879.74		Low	237.45		Low	123.11		Low 76.88

NOVEMBER, 1967

	—30 Industrials—			—20 Railroads—			—15 Utilities—			Daily Sales -000-	40 Bonds
	High	Low	Close	High	Low	Close	High	Low	Close		
1	880.95	863.44	867.08	237.21	231.49	232.96	123.82	122.00	123.08	10,930	76.75
2	878.87	860.55	864.83	235.07	230.25	231.80	124.17	122.09	122.92	10,760	76.70
3	867.95	853.10	856.62	232.73	228.89	229.74	124.07	122.00	122.70	8,800	76.68
6	860.61	844.89	855.29	230.41	226.10	228.19	123.18	120.85	121.77	10,320	76.59
8	870.67	847.61	849.57	233.09	227.34	228.81	122.89	120.69	120.97	12,630	76.43
9	862.86	846.28	856.97	230.41	226.98	228.99	122.28	120.05	121.26	8,890	76.19
10	868.93	854.83	862.81	233.09	228.60	231.70	122.44	120.33	121.42	9,960	76.18
13	872.98	855.06	859.74	233.81	229.38	230.41	122.57	120.72	121.68	10,130	76.09
14	864.60	849.23	852.40	230.77	227.03	227.88	123.08	120.88	122.19	10,350	76.15
15	860.44	845.01	855.18	229.61	226.34	228.19	123.85	121.17	122.83	10,000	76.26
16	867.49	852.12	859.74	231.49	227.42	230.51	124.46	122.19	123.50	10,570	76.22
17	869.28	853.96	862.11	232.88	229.43	230.92	124.62	122.41	123.82	10,050	76.10
20	862.58	839.40	857.78	229.27	225.28	227.73	123.27	119.95	122.25	12,750	76.07
21	876.68	857.49	870.95	232.65	227.86	230.95	124.04	121.71	123.21	12,300	75.93
22	884.54	865.87	874.02	233.58	231.41	231.41	124.71	123.50	123.50	12,180	75.85
24	882.80	867.26	877.60	232.60	229.69	231.31	124.84	122.92	123.98	9,470	75.46
27	887.77	873.21	882.11	232.93	229.66	230.98	125.32	123.24	124.55	10,040	75.36
28	890.43	876.62	884.88	234.71	230.31	233.19	126.28	123.98	125.51	11,040	75.33
29	894.88	878.24	883.15	236.41	233.04	235.18	126.50	124.36	125.35	11,400	75.42
30	887.48	872.63	875.81	235.46	232.81	233.86	126.15	123.88	124.52	8,860	75.42
		High 884.88			High 235.18			High 125.51			High 76.75
		Low 849.57			Low 227.73			Low 120.97			Low 75.33

DECEMBER, 1967

	—30 Industrials—			—20 Railroads—			—15 Utilities—			Daily Sales -000-	40 Bonds
	High	Low	Close	High	Low	Close	High	Low	Close		
1	882.69	868.76	879.16	236.65	233.55	235.38	125.54	123.66	124.74	9,740	75.45
4	888.35	876.33	883.50	237.63	234.97	236.67	126.18	123.79	124.58	11,740	75.30
5	895.80	881.24	888.12	237.70	235.20	236.21	126.34	124.17	125.13	12,940	75.16
6	896.50	884.19	892.28	236.65	233.66	234.71	125.70	123.66	124.52	11,940	75.14
7	901.76	887.94	892.22	236.52	233.40	235.10	125.73	123.85	124.39	12,490	75.15
8	895.92	883.55	887.25	236.49	233.30	234.51	125.61	123.91	124.90	10,710	75.08
11	892.16	876.96	882.05	236.11	232.75	234.22	125.58	123.37	124.27	10,500	75.10
12	887.54	873.32	881.30	235.38	231.98	233.42	125.19	123.27	123.95	10,860	75.13
13	887.77	887.14	882.34	234.43	232.11	233.45	125.26	122.96	124.23	12,480	74.83
14	891.47	878.53	883.44	234.64	232.01	233.58	125.42	123.59	124.39	12,310	74.78
15	890.43	875.87	880.61	235.80	233.19	234.35	125.42	123.69	124.36	11,530	74.79
18	889.91	874.94	881.65	235.25	231.26	232.26	125.77	123.37	124.49	10,320	74.85
19	886.96	875.69	881.36	232.44	229.38	230.43	125.70	123.34	124.39	10,610	74.79
20	892.86	876.33	886.90	231.28	228.89	230.20	126.77	123.50	125.16	11,390	74.67
21	897.71	883.78	888.35	232.32	229.48	231.00	126.73	124.30	125.73	11,010	74.69
22	894.94	880.95	887.37	232.03	229.27	230.54	127.20	125.00	125.61	9,570	74.62
26	893.96	881.93	888.12	232.26	229.27	231.05	126.85	124.97	126.18	9,150	74.66
27	900.14	884.59	894.94	232.93	229.82	231.93	127.65	125.32	127.04	12,690	74.78
28	902.97	886.73	897.83	232.81	229.66	231.65	128.51	126.02	127.84	12,530	74.84
29	910.37	893.44	905.11	234.82	231.00	233.24	128.83	126.60	127.91	14,950	74.64
		High 905.11			High 236.67			High 127.91			High 75.45
		Low 879.16			Low 230.20			Low 123.95			Low 74.62

JANUARY, 1968

	−30 Industrials−			−20 Railroads−			−15 Utilities−			Daily Sales -000-	40 Bonds
	High	Low	Close	High	Low	Close	High	Low	Close		
2	914.30	897.54	906.84	238.12	233.14	236.44	130.08	127.24	129.31	11,080	74.70
3	916.15	899.56	904.13	238.76	234.43	235.46	130.62	128.61	129.63	12,650	74.78
4	908.23	889.51	899.39	237.01	232.91	235.56	131.39	128.83	130.75	13,440	75.05
5	908.06	893.55	901.24	236.80	234.38	235.62	134.17	130.43	133.37	11,880	75.37
8	915.63	896.27	908.92	238.19	234.66	236.80	136.41	133.37	135.42	14,260	75.63
9	921.87	903.26	908.29	238.55	235.28	236.80	137.05	134.55	135.93	13,720	75.91
10	911.87	897.94	903.95	237.99	235.00	236.52	136.54	133.91	134.87	11,670	76.13
11	911.35	895.28	899.79	239.15	235.82	237.55	136.25	133.95	135.22	13,220	76.45
12	906.58	891.07	898.98	238.81	235.49	237.06	136.15	134.11	134.84	13,080	76.59
15	903.03	888.93	892.74	239.66	234.28	235.64	135.83	133.72	134.65	12,640	76.67
16	896.56	882.34	887.14	236.44	232.68	233.37	135.42	133.21	134.33	12,340	76.64
17	890.89	877.48	883.78	234.48	230.82	233.24	135.19	133.05	134.04	12,910	76.63
18	893.49	879.33	882.80	235.23	232.19	233.84	135.00	132.92	133.82	13,840	76.58
19	889.27	876.21	880.32	235.10	232.06	233.09	134.52	132.76	133.53	11,950	76.56
22	881.24	866.68	871.71	234.02	231.05	231.80	133.66	131.65	132.35	10,630	76.40
23	875.06	860.15	864.77	232.42	229.58	230.87	133.12	131.36	132.19	11,030	76.39
24	870.20	854.83	862.23	231.36	228.86	230.15	132.99	130.08	131.04	10,570	76.37
25	871.24	853.44	864.25	232.57	228.71	230.56	131.68	129.28	130.34	12,410	76.44
26	873.79	859.51	865.06	233.45	230.43	231.75	131.71	129.28	130.24	9,980	76.44
29	873.04	858.53	863.67	233.12	230.49	231.31	131.55	128.99	129.92	9,950	76.42
30	867.95	852.92	859.57	231.83	229.22	230.20	130.88	128.48	129.73	10,110	76.43
31	863.90	850.50	855.47	231.03	228.04	229.02	130.34	128.32	129.06	9,410	76.34
		High 908.92			High 237.55			High 135.93			High 76.67
		Low 855.47			Low 229.02			Low 129.06			Low 74.70

FEBRUARY, 1968

	−30 Industrials−			−20 Railroads−			−15 Utilities−			Daily Sales -000-	40 Bonds
	High	Low	Close	High	Low	Close	High	Low	Close		
1	864.89	850.55	861.36	230.63	226.72	229.81	130.59	128.90	129.76	10,590	76.26
2	871.30	856.22	863.56	231.61	227.31	228.31	130.69	128.87	129.54	10,120	76.28
5	867.66	854.77	861.13	228.85	225.72	226.54	130.53	128.55	129.70	8,980	76.23
6	867.31	854.83	861.25	228.29	226.02	227.59	130.37	128.58	129.25	8,560	76.24
7	867.78	855.93	859.92	228.85	226.18	227.54	130.56	128.48	129.76	8,380	76.27
8	863.27	847.84	850.32	227.41	224.48	224.87	131.01	128.83	129.41	9,660	76.19
9	851.65	834.84	840.04	224.97	222.11	223.63	130.24	128.26	128.90	11,850	76.18
13	843.68	828.36	831.77	225.17	221.03	221.68	129.92	127.30	127.88	10,830	76.26
14	841.94	826.46	837.38	224.02	221.06	222.91	128.99	126.82	128.23	11,390	76.26
15	846.16	833.62	839.23	226.00	223.19	224.69	129.86	127.20	128.96	9,770	76.22
16	841.66	830.85	836.34	225.56	223.48	224.66	129.73	127.27	128.04	9,070	76.13
19	843.97	830.50	838.65	225.92	223.84	225.17	130.18	127.46	129.22	7,270	76.22
20	847.67	836.05	843.10	226.49	224.15	225.07	130.18	128.04	128.61	8,800	76.16
21	855.06	840.50	849.23	227.52	224.66	226.64	130.11	128.20	128.96	9,170	76.13
23	857.78	844.43	849.80	227.72	224.81	225.84	129.70	127.46	128.48	8,810	76.20
26	850.79	836.40	841.77	225.97	222.47	223.12	129.28	127.30	128.45	7,810	76.23
27	848.59	835.93	846.68	223.37	220.54	221.11	129.41	127.56	128.87	7,600	76.09
28	853.33	841.71	844.72	221.96	219.52	220.08	129.47	128.10	128.58	8,020	76.20
29	847.03	835.76	840.50	220.13	218.23	218.69	129.38	127.17	127.84	7,700	76.23
		High 863.56			High 229.81			High 129.76			High 76.28
		Low 831.77			Low 218.69			Low 127.84			Low 76.09

MARCH, 1968

	—30 Industrials—			—20 Railroads—			—15 Utilities—			Daily Sales -000-	40 Bonds
	High	Low	Close	High	Low	Close	High	Low	Close		
1	845.24	836.05	840.44	219.46	216.45	217.41	129.38	126.92	128.36	8,610	76.19
4	842.75	828.02	830.56	218.10	215.22	216.35	129.25	126.66	127.33	10,590	76.22
5	837.44	821.72	827.03	217.46	213.68	214.58	127.97	125.58	126.31	11,440	76.24
6	841.37	826.46	837.21	217.59	214.60	216.74	127.59	125.67	126.89	9,900	76.09
7	843.62	830.33	836.22	217.66	215.32	215.86	127.56	125.61	126.44	8,630	76.10
8	840.38	828.59	835.24	216.51	214.06	215.14	127.04	125.26	126.02	7,410	76.14
11	846.63	833.56	843.04	219.46	214.29	218.59	126.92	125.03	126.12	9,520	76.04
12	847.55	834.72	843.22	220.31	217.20	218.85	126.85	125.06	125.77	9,250	76.07
13	847.72	836.22	842.23	221.32	217.92	219.75	126.21	124.17	124.81	8,990	75.93
14	841.54	824.26	830.91	219.26	215.71	217.10	124.68	121.90	122.80	11,640	75.71
15	843.39	825.01	837.55	218.92	215.48	217.95	123.69	121.42	123.11	11,210	75.57
18	854.25	836.28	840.09	221.75	217.69	219.59	124.30	121.49	122.41	10,800	75.46
19	842.35	829.63	832.99	221.11	218.15	219.34	123.43	121.23	122.32	7,410	75.49
20	836.63	826.34	830.85	220.70	218.43	219.90	122.96	121.01	121.68	7,390	75.48
21	836.40	822.58	825.13	221.21	218.98	219.52	122.64	120.53	121.26	8,580	75.42
22	831.48	817.61	826.05	219.90	217.05	218.54	121.87	120.14	120.91	9,900	75.37
25	831.25	819.87	827.27	219.10	216.69	217.87	121.71	119.38	119.79	6,700	75.42
26	836.17	823.62	831.54	218.61	216.66	217.71	121.45	119.44	120.46	8,670	75.41
27	841.42	830.33	836.57	219.05	217.35	218.38	122.16	120.11	121.39	8,970	75.27
28	841.08	830.67	835.12	219.47	217.43	218.53	122.54	120.21	121.13	8,000	75.23
29	845.87	831.48	840.67	220.24	217.86	218.99	122.19	120.33	121.58	9,000	75.07
		High 843.22			High 219.90			High 128.36			High 76.24
		Low 825.13			Low 214.58			Low 119.79			Low 75.07

APRIL, 1968

	—30 Industrials—			—20 Railroads—			—15 Utilities—			Daily Sales -000-	40 Bonds
	High	Low	Close	High	Low	Close	High	Low	Close		
1	870.90	849.23	861.25	222.62	219.22	220.70	124.84	121.87	123.15	17,730	75.09
2	869.63	852.12	863.96	222.57	219.19	221.29	124.04	121.93	122.92	14,520	75.05
3	883.38	859.45	869.11	224.64	220.39	223.11	125.58	122.16	123.75	19,290	75.27
4	879.68	862.46	872.52	225.54	221.95	224.10	124.94	122.32	123.53	14,340	75.26
5	877.31	862.11	865.81	226.20	222.70	223.90	124.68	122.28	123.56	12,570	75.28
8	888.35	865.18	884.42	227.79	223.18	226.79	125.10	122.64	123.72	13,010	75.23
10	905.74	884.07	892.63	230.60	225.59	227.53	125.19	122.32	123.75	20,410	75.23
11	908.29	886.56	905.69	230.45	225.61	229.40	125.32	122.96	124.27	14,230	75.21
15	916.03	893.61	910.19	231.17	227.66	229.99	125.29	123.05	124.62	14,220	75.19
16	917.36	899.33	906.78	233.62	229.91	231.83	125.70	123.79	124.68	15,680	75.13
17	912.74	896.84	908.17	234.95	230.78	233.65	126.31	123.91	125.58	14,090	75.10
18	916.78	901.24	909.21	238.92	233.83	237.21	126.53	124.74	125.83	15,890	75.06
19	908.40	890.72	897.65	238.72	233.67	236.31	125.70	123.37	124.36	14,560	75.02
22	897.88	881.24	891.99	237.26	231.58	234.21	124.52	122.32	123.02	11,720	74.95
23	904.47	890.43	897.48	236.51	232.14	234.44	124.07	122.06	123.15	14,010	74.68
24	904.65	889.68	898.46	236.85	233.78	235.41	124.23	122.22	122.80	14,810	74.86
25	912.56	895.98	905.57	237.36	233.78	234.83	123.56	121.71	122.60	14,430	74.89
26	912.27	898.00	906.03	236.11	233.19	234.67	123.40	121.58	122.41	13,500	75.06
29	914.01	900.72	908.34	237.28	233.70	236.28	123.40	121.33	122.09	12,030	75.13
30	918.11	901.70	912.22	238.59	234.67	237.00	123.05	121.23	121.96	14,380	75.26
		High 912.22			High 237.21			High 125.83			High 75.28
		Low 861.25			Low 220.70			Low 121.96			Low 74.68

MAY, 1968

	\-30 Industrials\- High	Low	Close	\-20 Railroads\- High	Low	Close	\-15 Utilities\- High	Low	Close	Daily Sales -000-	40 Bonds
1	919.85	902.51	913.20	240.20	236.03	238.97	123.21	120.97	122.12	14,440	75.26
2	923.43	906.90	918.05	241.73	237.87	239.97	123.24	120.91	122.03	14,260	75.27
3	935.68	913.49	919.21	243.22	238.82	240.35	124.52	121.29	122.48	17,990	75.33
6	922.79	903.61	914.53	240.71	237.46	239.43	123.88	121.13	122.60	12,160	75.32
7	926.78	910.54	919.90	243.45	238.56	242.04	124.07	121.90	123.02	13,920	75.37
8	927.42	911.52	918.86	244.06	240.79	242.91	124.30	121.84	123.53	13,120	75.38
9	921.81	904.82	911.35	244.85	240.07	241.79	124.55	122.28	123.21	12,890	75.44
10	920.48	906.38	912.91	243.73	240.02	241.71	124.68	122.48	123.31	11,700	75.36
13	918.34	903.90	909.96	244.75	241.10	243.86	124.65	122.35	123.27	11,860	75.22
14	915.28	900.89	908.06	245.34	241.79	244.34	124.42	122.48	123.15	13,160	75.17
15	914.64	900.08	907.82	246.11	242.07	245.14	124.17	122.25	123.05	13,180	75.15
16	913.08	898.17	903.72	247.44	242.30	244.37	123.91	121.80	122.70	13,030	75.04
17	905.92	891.18	898.98	247.13	242.55	246.42	123.91	121.68	122.51	11,830	74.94
20	902.10	887.54	894.19	249.51	244.73	247.72	123.53	121.49	122.32	11,180	74.97
21	902.39	886.33	896.32	251.94	247.65	250.84	123.50	121.52	122.70	13,160	74.82
22	906.73	891.82	896.79	256.22	250.46	253.33	123.59	121.74	122.28	14,200	74.82
23	901.47	888.23	893.15	255.58	250.87	252.84	123.56	121.42	122.57	12,840	74.77
24	900.49	886.67	895.28	255.37	251.51	253.71	123.53	121.39	123.02	13,300	74.66
27	898.76	885.53	891.60	255.32	251.61	253.22	123.66	121.42	122.64	12,720	74.55
28	901.95	886.97	896.78	257.34	252.61	256.45	123.40	121.33	122.28	13,850	74.67
29	903.69	889.44	895.21	258.34	253.28	255.60	123.21	121.58	122.09	14,100	74.76
31	907.96	891.72	899.00	257.86	253.97	255.66	123.98	121.77	123.02	13,090	74.88

High 919.90
Low 891.60

High 256.45
Low 238.97

High 123.53
Low 122.03

High 75.44
Low 74.55

JUNE, 1968

	\-30 Industrials\- High	Low	Close	\-20 Railroads\- High	Low	Close	\-15 Utilities\- High	Low	Close	Daily Sales -000-	40 Bonds
3	912.12	896.23	905.38	258.60	255.22	256.63	124.84	122.32	123.79	14,970	74.88
4	923.00	902.43	916.63	260.41	256.37	258.60	124.97	122.86	123.95	18,030	74.87
5	922.10	904.05	907.42	259.29	255.99	257.14	124.94	123.02	123.91	15,590	74.91
6	918.01	901.71	910.13	261.36	256.01	260.64	124.97	122.92	124.14	16,130	74.91
7	920.84	906.28	914.88	267.81	260.77	266.17	125.13	123.11	124.04	17,320	74.95
10	922.94	907.54	913.38	267.76	263.69	265.43	125.10	122.73	123.98	14,640	74.92
11	924.81	909.41	917.95	267.73	264.00	266.45	124.78	122.96	124.04	15,700	74.94
13	924.93	908.93	913.86	269.75	264.66	266.35	125.32	123.34	124.49	21,350	75.00
14	918.91	904.48	913.62	267.48	263.77	265.58	125.80	123.79	125.35	14,690	75.05
17	917.35	898.40	903.45	267.81	262.56	264.43	126.69	124.49	125.54	12,570	75.08
18	909.17	895.09	900.20	266.84	262.08	263.95	129.12	125.45	128.51	13,630	75.09
20	909.29	892.63	898.28	265.81	261.51	263.23	133.15	129.57	131.77	16,290	75.18
21	907.96	891.48	900.93	265.81	262.67	264.15	134.14	131.20	133.44	13,450	75.42
24	908.14	895.09	901.83	266.35	262.54	264.79	134.81	132.64	134.27	12,320	75.43
25	908.08	895.09	901.41	266.48	261.64	262.67	134.71	132.09	133.50	13,200	75.48
27	909.23	891.78	898.76	265.23	259.93	262.23	134.65	132.16	132.89	15,370	75.53
28	905.14	892.26	897.80	264.69	260.64	261.77	134.11	131.74	132.60	12,040	75.43

High 917.95
Low 897.80

High 266.45
Low 256.63

High 134.27
Low 123.79

High 75.53
Low 74.87

JULY, 1968

	−30 Industrials−			−20 Railroads−			−15 Utilities−			Daily Sales -000-	40 Bonds
	High	Low	Close	High	Low	Close	High	Low	Close		
1	904.05	889.68	896.35	263.46	260.24	261.77	133.63	131.36	132.54	11,280	75.34
2	902.97	889.62	896.84	264.97	260.88	263.63	133.66	131.29	132.60	13,350	75.54
3	907.18	893.29	903.51	268.63	264.26	266.88	134.78	132.00	133.82	14,390	75.56
8	920.00	901.89	912.60	271.55	266.68	269.61	135.64	133.05	134.39	16,860	75.71
9	924.87	908.63	920.42	271.07	266.58	268.42	135.67	133.53	134.49	16,540	75.93
11	933.83	915.78	922.82	270.42	265.90	267.67	135.45	133.05	134.27	20,290	75.84
12	929.92	914.88	922.46	268.20	264.31	265.82	135.19	133.50	134.71	14,810	75.81
15	929.32	915.24	923.72	266.86	262.87	264.28	135.38	133.15	134.43	13,390	75.86
16	928.84	913.56	921.20	264.56	259.56	261.66	135.16	133.34	134.17	13,380	75.98
18	926.55	911.93	917.95	263.75	257.07	259.41	135.16	132.64	133.95	17,420	76.01
19	924.21	907.60	913.92	260.30	256.31	257.80	134.62	132.51	133.28	14,620	76.05
22	914.52	894.31	900.32	257.90	253.38	254.21	133.66	131.10	132.06	13,530	76.15
23	904.48	889.68	898.10	255.20	251.49	254.44	133.18	131.17	132.19	13,570	76.16
25	901.29	880.41	885.47	257.07	251.41	252.04	133.12	130.59	131.55	16,140	76.24
26	895.21	878.55	888.47	253.18	249.02	250.86	132.80	130.40	131.81	11,690	76.46
29	893.59	877.23	883.36	252.30	248.03	249.60	132.60	130.59	131.29	10,940	76.55
30	890.64	876.99	883.00	252.47	249.12	251.11	132.29	130.05	131.29	10,250	76.47
		High 923.72			High 269.61			High 134.71			High 76.55
		Low 883.00			Low 249.60			Low 131.29			Low 75.34

AUGUST, 1968

	−30 Industrials−			−20 Railroads−			−15 Utilities−			Daily Sales -000-	40 Bonds
	High	Low	Close	High	Low	Close	High	Low	Close		
1	892.02	874.94	878.07	252.07	248.49	249.55	132.96	130.11	131.23	14,380	76.67
2	879.27	865.19	871.27	248.94	244.70	246.42	132.32	130.14	130.85	9,860	76.82
5	879.33	865.86	872.53	248.81	244.78	247.20	131.87	129.89	130.87	8,850	76.83
6	881.38	868.86	876.92	249.42	246.32	247.70	132.06	129.89	131.04	9,620	76.86
8	882.82	866.58	870.37	248.64	245.13	245.81	132.96	130.62	131.45	12,920	77.00
9	876.26	863.33	869.65	246.67	244.20	245.76	132.35	130.21	131.52	8,390	76.95
12	884.20	867.66	881.02	249.17	245.46	248.33	132.19	130.21	131.13	10,420	76.99
13	890.82	877.71	884.68	251.14	247.85	250.05	131.93	130.27	131.04	12,730	77.20
15	892.32	874.76	879.51	253.13	248.81	250.10	132.54	129.76	131.01	12,710	77.19
16	889.44	877.17	885.89	252.50	249.14	250.45	132.38	130.34	131.52	9,940	77.13
19	893.15	880.66	887.68	253.94	250.00	252.62	132.70	130.94	132.09	9,900	77.20
20	894.64	879.97	888.67	253.43	250.91	251.94	132.86	131.04	132.13	10,640	77.17
22	894.95	878.85	888.30	253.68	249.70	251.56	132.54	130.21	131.10	15,140	77.13
23	899.37	883.83	892.34	252.60	249.87	251.11	132.25	130.43	131.55	9,890	77.07
26	902.23	890.04	896.13	252.04	249.47	250.38	132.03	130.21	131.07	9,740	77.07
27	901.48	888.18	893.65	252.75	248.76	251.11	131.90	129.95	130.62	9,710	76.93
29	900.73	886.69	894.33	251.69	248.16	250.25	131.26	129.31	130.02	10,940	76.87
30	902.35	891.29	896.01	252.35	249.44	251.11	131.20	129.89	130.53	8,190	76.89
		High 896.13			High 252.62			High 132.13			High 77.20
		Low 869.65			Low 245.76			Low 130.02			Low 76.67

SEPTEMBER, 1968

	−30 Industrials−			−20 Railroads−			−15 Utilities−			Daily Sales -000-	40 Bonds
	High	Low	Close	High	Low	Close	High	Low	Close		
3	904.96	892.59	900.36	252.68	249.29	251.03	131.20	129.60	130.56	8,620	76.86
4	911.18	896.26	906.95	252.55	250.03	251.36	131.81	129.92	130.66	10,040	76.94
5	921.87	904.03	917.52	254.42	251.54	253.15	132.38	130.37	131.45	12,980	76.97
6	928.27	912.54	921.25	256.64	252.35	255.65	132.64	130.85	131.93	13,180	76.97
9	932.31	916.89	924.98	258.43	255.25	257.09	132.80	130.78	131.65	11,890	76.95
10	931.32	914.41	919.38	257.72	254.95	255.75	132.67	130.75	131.42	11,430	76.99
12	923.26	908.07	915.65	257.87	254.80	256.49	132.32	130.24	131.26	14,630	77.01
13	923.36	909.12	917.21	257.72	254.62	256.08	131.93	130.43	131.23	13,070	76.82
16	927.46	912.98	921.37	257.92	255.20	256.11	131.90	130.40	131.23	13,260	76.88
17	929.08	916.77	923.05	259.39	255.75	258.45	132.00	130.08	130.94	13,920	76.66
19	933.43	916.27	923.98	262.16	258.10	260.12	131.55	129.38	129.98	17,910	76.76
20	930.01	917.14	924.42	262.39	258.98	261.13	131.01	129.03	129.95	14,190	76.59
23	934.05	920.93	930.45	261.96	258.61	260.65	130.98	129.03	129.89	11,550	76.64
24	942.69	926.22	938.28	263.55	259.77	262.21	131.07	129.31	130.21	15,210	76.71
26	945.86	928.08	933.24	267.51	262.49	266.05	131.61	129.70	130.56	18,950	76.62
27	938.40	926.09	933.80	267.84	264.28	266.08	131.07	129.57	130.24	13,860	76.71
30	941.45	926.59	935.79	269.99	265.80	267.69	131.20	129.47	130.37	13,610	76.69
		High	938.28		High	267.69		High	131.93		High 77.01
		Low	900.36		Low	251.03		Low	129.89		Low 76.59

OCTOBER, 1968

	−30 Industrials−			−20 Railroads−			−15 Utilities−			Daily Sales -000-	40 Bonds
	High	Low	Close	High	Low	Close	High	Low	Close		
1	948.66	932.93	942.32	271.68	267.51	270.24	131.04	129.28	130.14	15,560	76.69
3	954.81	940.39	949.47	273.98	269.00	272.33	131.33	129.15	130.08	21,110	76.64
4	957.30	943.93	952.95	275.14	270.37	273.04	130.62	128.71	129.86	15,350	76.68
7	961.03	946.98	956.68	275.01	270.75	272.92	130.72	128.83	129.89	12,420	76.56
8	963.33	950.58	956.24	273.55	270.22	271.58	130.56	128.71	129.38	14,000	76.62
10	958.66	944.24	949.78	272.71	268.32	269.63	131.17	128.71	130.02	17,000	76.50
11	955.18	942.96	949.59	270.72	267.79	269.46	130.94	129.09	130.18	12,650	76.48
14	955.37	942.50	949.96	272.69	269.31	271.55	131.10	129.12	130.30	11,980	76.32
15	960.47	946.05	955.31	273.27	270.06	271.05	131.20	129.09	130.14	13,410	76.19
17	969.29	952.51	958.91	273.27	269.63	271.33	131.65	129.54	130.02	21,060	76.23
18	971.72	955.06	967.49	273.52	270.63	272.46	131.20	129.38	130.85	15,130	76.30
21	974.27	959.54	967.49	274.20	270.64	272.41	131.84	129.98	131.04	14,380	76.33
22	970.41	957.92	963.14	273.24	269.96	271.33	131.90	129.89	130.75	13,670	76.21
24	967.37	949.34	956.68	271.73	267.34	268.63	131.58	129.15	130.46	18,300	76.13
25	966.81	950.96	961.28	269.74	266.71	268.40	131.74	129.76	130.62	14,150	76.09
28	966.50	951.45	957.73	269.26	265.67	267.64	131.93	130.18	131.39	11,740	76.01
29	961.96	945.67	951.08	268.95	265.62	267.06	131.97	130.14	130.82	12,340	76.07
31	965.00	944.06	952.39	269.46	265.09	266.40	132.41	130.02	131.26	17,650	76.13
		High	967.49		High	273.04		High	131.39		High 76.69
		Low	942.32		Low	266.40		Low	129.38		Low 76.01

NOVEMBER, 1968

	—30 Industrials—			—20 Railroads—			—15 Utilities—			Daily Sales -000-	40 Bonds
	High	Low	Close	High	Low	Close	High	Low	Close		
1	961.15	941.88	948.41	268.22	264.28	265.37	132.67	130.46	131.33	14,480	76.17
4	952.01	936.54	946.23	266.63	262.69	265.09	132.76	130.66	131.71	10,930	76.21
6	959.97	941.01	949.47	267.21	263.07	264.96	133.15	131.04	131.84	12,640	76.11
7	957.55	938.59	950.65	265.92	262.37	264.41	133.24	131.07	132.51	11,660	76.23
8	965.07	947.41	958.98	268.07	263.05	266.76	134.46	132.16	133.56	14,250	76.13
12	972.15	953.75	964.20	269.31	265.65	267.24	136.22	133.28	135.54	17,250	76.02
13	973.83	958.98	967.43	271.48	266.71	270.37	138.61	135.51	138.00	15,660	75.99
14	972.90	957.86	963.89	272.59	268.88	271.25	139.86	137.24	138.87	14,900	75.85
15	972.59	956.24	965.88	273.32	269.43	271.83	140.47	137.91	139.86	15,040	75.92
18	970.85	957.11	963.70	274.25	269.76	271.35	141.71	139.16	140.31	14,390	76.02
19	972.40	957.48	966.75	274.40	269.21	272.46	142.03	139.63	141.30	15,120	75.82
21	971.35	953.69	965.13	273.87	270.34	272.16	142.48	139.60	140.37	18,320	75.73
22	973.89	958.23	967.06	273.95	270.64	272.46	141.65	139.54	140.34	15,420	75.86
25	977.13	961.46	971.35	274.45	270.06	273.27	141.42	139.57	140.66	14,480	75.87
26	986.20	969.11	979.49	275.99	272.01	274.33	142.03	140.05	141.17	16,360	75.81
27	984.96	969.17	976.32	277.58	273.27	276.04	142.09	140.34	140.94	16,550	75.68
29	989.56	971.59	985.08	280.56	276.52	279.28	141.97	139.70	140.34	14,390	75.56
		High	985.08		High	279.28		High	141.30		High 76.23
		Low	946.23		Low	264.41		Low	131.33		Low 75.56

DECEMBER, 1968

	—30 Industrials—			—20 Railroads—			—15 Utilities—			Daily Sales -000-	40 Bonds
	High	Low	Close	High	Low	Close	High	Low	Close		
2	994.65	974.76	983.34	281.75	277.71	279.48	141.36	138.68	139.95	15,390	75.55
3	990.99	973.83	985.21	281.55	276.52	278.19	140.27	137.72	138.84	15,460	75.48
5	989.31	969.67	977.69	280.84	275.72	277.84	139.70	136.76	138.39	19,330	75.32
6	986.39	970.10	978.24	279.50	275.64	278.06	139.95	137.46	139.06	15,320	75.05
9	987.01	971.41	979.36	279.60	276.20	277.81	139.92	138.04	138.87	15,800	75.02
10	986.01	971.06	977.69	279.75	276.65	278.32	139.79	137.78	138.55	14,500	74.90
12	987.20	969.05	977.13	279.55	275.74	277.43	139.44	137.43	138.36	18,160	74.66
13	990.99	972.03	981.29	280.34	276.04	278.64	139.51	137.17	138.52	16,740	74.72
16	989.12	970.60	976.32	279.40	275.87	276.88	139.86	137.62	138.48	15,950	74.73
17	978.80	962.46	970.91	276.95	273.77	274.93	139.41	136.82	137.65	14,700	74.70
19	980.11	954.62	975.14	277.13	270.77	274.43	138.90	135.96	137.75	19,630	74.40
20	983.90	962.83	966.99	276.42	272.26	273.62	139.70	136.63	138.20	15,910	74.15
23	969.05	949.47	953.75	274.33	271.15	272.66	139.38	136.85	137.91	12,970	73.92
24	961.28	945.11	952.32	274.10	271.20	272.31	139.12	136.57	137.88	11,540	73.91
26	961.52	948.47	954.25	274.03	271.30	272.59	139.28	137.24	138.04	9,670	73.92
27	961.96	947.54	952.51	274.08	270.37	272.36	139.09	136.98	137.59	11,200	74.01
30	955.87	938.90	945.11	272.89	268.90	269.31	138.52	136.66	137.46	12,080	74.05
31	950.46	936.66	943.75	272.44	268.85	271.60	138.55	136.31	137.17	13,130	73.98
		High	985.21		High	279.48		High	139.95		High 75.55
		Low	943.75		Low	269.31		Low	137.17		Low 73.91

JANUARY, 1969

	-30 Industrials-			-20 Railroads-			-15 Utilities-			Daily Sales -000-	40 Bonds
	High	Low	Close	High	Low	Close	High	Low	Close		
2	956.36	940.39	947.73	273.52	270.14	271.63	138.04	135.99	137.14	9,800	74.16
3	960.16	942.94	951.89	274.61	270.19	272.61	138.07	136.12	136.98	12,750	74.40
6	956.05	932.93	936.66	273.62	269.00	270.67	137.78	135.48	136.44	12,720	74.50
7	939.33	915.84	925.72	271.10	264.74	266.53	136.92	134.23	135.03	15,740	74.44
8	932.19	915.53	921.25	268.60	264.01	264.89	136.18	133.79	134.39	13,840	74.34
9	935.67	918.64	927.46	267.41	264.13	265.12	135.35	133.15	134.33	12,100	74.27
10	937.22	921.31	925.53	266.20	262.47	263.10	135.29	133.34	134.07	12,680	74.43
13	930.63	917.14	923.11	262.82	258.86	260.04	134.97	133.02	133.69	11,160	74.35
14	931.56	918.32	928.33	262.14	259.26	261.10	134.84	132.80	133.98	10,700	74.39
15	940.51	924.23	931.75	265.09	261.68	263.55	134.87	133.15	133.63	11,810	74.57
16	945.55	930.07	938.59	267.54	263.88	265.92	135.77	133.66	134.52	13,120	74.62
17	944.06	930.20	935.54	268.80	265.37	267.82	135.45	133.69	134.39	11,590	74.80
20	939.40	927.09	931.25	270.22	266.83	269.08	135.45	133.08	134.27	10,950	74.91
21	936.29	923.92	929.82	270.90	267.01	268.75	135.10	133.31	134.30	10,910	74.87
22	938.46	925.16	934.17	270.19	267.29	269.16	135.83	133.40	134.75	11,480	74.86
23	945.98	932.56	940.20	272.66	269.03	271.48	136.28	134.30	135.45	13,140	74.92
24	946.85	932.93	938.59	273.80	270.42	272.36	137.14	134.71	135.77	12,520	74.96
27	944.37	932.00	937.47	275.31	272.03	274.13	137.49	135.10	136.31	11,020	74.94
28	944.49	930.88	938.40	275.54	271.86	273.29	138.23	135.83	137.24	12,070	74.94
29	943.62	931.94	938.09	275.57	271.53	273.17	139.12	136.89	138.07	11,470	74.90
30	947.23	934.36	942.13	275.67	272.18	273.87	139.70	137.91	138.87	13,010	74.99
31	950.71	937.28	946.05	276.98	272.81	274.88	140.56	138.42	139.95	12,020	74.96
		High 951.89			High 274.88			High 139.95			High 74.99
		Low 921.25			Low 260.04			Low 133.63			Low 74.16

FEBRUARY, 1969

	-30 Industrials-			-20 Railroads-			-15 Utilities-			Daily Sales -000-	40 Bonds
	High	Low	Close	High	Low	Close	High	Low	Close		
3	953.01	936.41	946.85	277.86	273.87	276.27	141.10	138.55	139.63	12,510	74.92
4	951.27	938.59	945.11	279.68	274.66	278.39	140.75	138.48	139.38	12,550	74.99
5	952.32	938.53	945.98	280.81	276.98	279.02	140.69	138.71	139.44	13,750	74.90
6	954.07	939.46	946.67	281.98	277.84	279.40	140.56	138.45	139.57	12,570	74.87
7	954.00	940.39	947.85	281.72	278.01	279.88	140.78	138.68	139.28	12,780	74.91
11	954.00	941.94	948.97	280.87	272.43	278.77	140.53	138.42	139.54	12,320	74.82
12	954.00	942.81	949.09	280.87	277.69	279.10	140.02	138.20	138.93	11,530	74.92
13	957.73	942.57	952.70	279.40	275.67	277.58	139.76	137.65	138.55	12,010	75.01
14	959.16	945.67	951.95	278.27	274.58	275.72	139.35	137.40	138.10	11,460	74.98
17	954.87	935.11	937.72	276.12	270.52	271.55	139.22	136.98	137.56	11,670	74.89
18	937.53	923.11	930.82	270.77	265.22	267.24	137.49	135.58	136.34	12,490	74.81
19	936.91	923.23	925.10	268.27	264.92	265.55	137.21	135.26	136.12	10,390	74.85
20	928.46	913.04	916.65	265.75	262.80	263.55	136.54	134.43	135.32	10,990	74.80
24	918.95	900.17	903.97	263.83	260.20	260.65	136.02	133.40	134.23	12,730	74.61
25	914.41	896.32	899.80	260.80	256.33	257.07	135.10	132.67	133.60	12,320	74.54
26	912.11	895.39	905.77	258.68	255.12	256.84	134.43	131.97	133.12	9,540	74.55
27	908.88	897.07	903.03	258.28	253.58	255.20	133.63	131.71	132.70	9,670	74.42
28	911.74	900.17	905.21	256.59	252.80	253.68	133.55	131.45	132.57	8,990	74.36
		High 952.70			High 279.88			High 139.63			High 75.01
		Low 899.80			Low 253.68			Low 132.57			Low 74.36

MARCH, 1969

	—30 Industrials—			—20 Railroads—			—15 Utilities—			Daily Sales -000-	40 Bonds
	High	Low	Close	High	Low	Close	High	Low	Close		
3	914.04	902.04	908.63	254.16	251.29	251.97	133.31	131.39	132.35	8,260	74.24
4	922.55	908.50	919.51	254.04	250.88	252.65	133.56	132.00	132.89	9,320	74.24
5	929.89	916.65	923.11	254.24	250.71	252.50	134.11	132.19	133.02	11,370	74.23
6	923.79	908.94	913.54	252.83	248.11	249.17	133.31	131.33	132.19	9,670	74.14
7	914.59	900.67	911.18	248.97	243.94	246.26	132.38	130.50	131.45	10,830	74.03
10	920.87	906.51	917.14	246.79	243.34	245.03	132.80	130.53	131.90	8,920	73.88
11	928.77	914.53	920.93	247.63	243.82	245.31	132.57	130.85	131.42	9,870	73.84
12	926.22	912.67	917.52	245.91	243.67	244.22	132.35	130.69	131.58	8,720	73.68
13	916.77	903.97	907.14	245.08	242.38	243.19	132.41	130.46	130.91	10,030	73.65
14	911.36	899.55	904.28	244.04	240.56	241.92	131.93	129.95	130.72	8,640	73.69
17	909.00	895.76	904.03	242.68	239.73	241.87	131.84	129.51	130.24	9,150	73.53
18	913.97	902.16	907.38	244.09	240.76	242.91	131.61	129.67	130.11	11,210	73.44
19	917.52	903.53	912.11	245.91	242.83	244.70	131.23	129.41	130.21	9,740	73.44
20	924.79	911.24	920.13	247.32	244.25	245.71	131.10	129.09	129.76	10,260	73.39
21	926.16	913.35	920.00	246.82	242.30	243.97	130.85	129.15	130.34	9,830	73.20
24	924.04	912.48	917.08	244.55	241.60	242.73	131.04	128.96	129.76	8,110	73.13
25	923.05	911.30	917.08	243.44	240.13	241.44	130.59	128.64	129.38	9,820	73.07
26	926.84	914.72	923.30	244.02	240.69	242.83	130.85	128.96	130.08	11,030	73.03
27	936.16	921.74	930.88	245.10	241.34	243.14	130.91	129.12	130.02	11,900	73.09
28	941.38	928.02	935.48	244.65	242.33	243.69	130.75	128.77	129.67	12,430	73.00
		High	935.48		High	252.65		High	133.02		High 74.24
		Low	904.03		Low	241.44		Low	129.38		Low 73.00

APRIL, 1969

	—30 Industrials—			—20 Railroads—			—15 Utilities—			Daily Sales -000-	40 Bonds
	High	Low	Close	High	Low	Close	High	Low	Close		
1	942.23	928.38	933.08	244.73	241.67	242.58	130.72	128.96	129.82	12,360	73.00
2	936.90	924.57	930.92	243.99	240.99	241.82	130.40	128.99	129.41	10,110	73.07
3	933.66	921.39	927.30	242.98	240.11	241.52	130.14	128.39	129.06	10,300	73.23
7	926.09	911.03	918.78	241.82	238.87	240.23	129.60	127.78	128.64	9,430	73.21
8	927.81	913.89	923.17	241.52	238.77	240.36	129.25	127.72	128.29	9,360	73.23
9	933.59	920.63	929.97	242.23	239.12	240.91	129.06	127.46	128.32	12,530	73.24
10	941.28	927.87	932.89	241.72	239.05	240.26	129.35	127.62	128.48	12,200	73.31
11	939.12	927.17	933.46	240.84	238.49	239.48	129.41	127.72	128.32	10,650	73.38
14	938.36	926.73	932.64	241.17	238.59	239.70	129.15	127.40	128.13	8,990	73.55
15	937.28	924.63	931.94	239.78	237.33	238.47	128.99	127.59	128.55	9,610	73.69
16	932.89	920.69	923.49	239.12	236.07	237.18	129.47	128.10	128.93	9,680	73.58
17	930.80	917.90	924.12	238.90	235.41	236.90	130.11	128.36	129.19	9,360	73.62
18	932.26	916.94	924.82	238.84	234.93	236.40	129.92	128.26	129.35	10,850	73.44
21	928.19	913.76	917.51	237.13	233.97	234.58	130.24	128.71	129.28	10,010	73.64
22	922.09	908.81	918.59	234.78	231.90	233.32	130.18	128.39	129.54	10,250	73.72
23	927.43	913.13	917.64	235.08	232.13	233.72	130.56	128.64	129.63	12,220	73.71
24	925.65	911.60	921.20	235.59	232.54	234.38	130.62	128.93	130.14	11,340	73.89
25	929.65	916.24	924.00	237.05	233.92	236.02	130.72	129.06	129.82	12,480	74.04
28	930.73	917.13	925.08	237.38	234.58	235.99	130.37	128.16	129.57	11,120	73.95
29	937.60	922.28	934.10	237.46	234.33	235.99	130.66	128.58	129.35	14,730	73.87
30	956.28	933.97	950.18	239.83	236.07	238.34	131.13	128.93	130.05	19,350	73.83
		High	950.18		High	242.58		High	130.14		High 74.04
		Low	917.51		Low	233.32		Low	128.13		Low 73.00

MAY, 1969

	–30 Industrials–			–20 Railroads–			–15 Utilities–			Daily Sales -000-	40 Bonds
	High	Low	Close	High	Low	Close	High	Low	Close		
1	958.69	942.74	949.22	240.04	236.86	238.02	131.07	128.99	130.27	14,380	73.82
2	961.68	945.41	957.17	239.06	236.28	237.36	131.36	129.35	130.08	13,070	73.85
5	965.43	951.07	958.95	239.79	236.76	238.63	131.55	129.38	130.50	13,300	73.90
6	968.23	954.05	962.06	239.84	236.30	237.97	131.26	129.25	129.86	14,700	73.89
7	967.36	953.08	959.60	239.99	236.76	238.45	131.20	129.06	129.98	14,030	73.84
8	970.14	954.76	963.68	239.59	237.21	238.55	131.68	129.38	130.98	13,050	73.96
9	971.11	955.86	961.61	239.69	237.41	238.85	132.38	130.24	131.42	12,530	74.01
12	964.97	951.14	957.86	240.62	238.15	239.79	132.16	129.92	130.91	10,550	74.08
13	967.62	954.37	962.97	241.23	237.26	239.79	132.45	130.24	131.77	12,910	73.94
14	974.92	959.86	968.85	243.28	239.69	241.58	133.31	131.29	132.45	14,360	73.93
15	973.18	958.51	965.16	242.32	239.74	241.48	133.79	131.68	132.76	11,930	73.91
16	971.56	959.80	967.30	242.57	240.09	241.41	133.40	131.58	132.54	12,280	73.81
19	968.98	954.56	959.02	242.34	239.23	239.79	133.28	131.20	131.97	9,790	73.82
20	959.86	944.35	949.26	239.97	237.29	237.89	132.57	130.66	131.26	10,280	73.73
21	956.18	941.31	951.78	238.98	236.30	237.26	132.03	130.14	131.26	12,100	73.56
22	963.09	946.10	950.04	239.33	236.63	237.97	132.09	130.11	130.98	13,710	73.55
23	953.92	942.48	947.45	239.39	236.61	238.30	131.68	129.86	130.56	10,900	73.34
26	954.05	942.22	946.94	238.02	235.04	235.97	131.04	128.93	129.86	9,030	73.36
27	950.23	934.33	938.66	236.61	234.03	234.79	130.88	129.25	129.92	10,580	73.21
28	941.96	928.58	936.92	234.89	232.81	233.98	130.02	128.16	128.87	11,330	73.20
29	944.29	931.62	937.56	235.54	232.18	233.40	130.08	128.42	129.15	11,770	73.23
		High	968.85		High	241.58		High	132.76		High 74.08
		Low	936.92		Low	233.40		Low	128.87		Low 73.20

JUNE, 1969

	–30 Industrials–			–20 Railroads–			–15 Utilities–			Daily Sales -000-	40 Bonds
	High	Low	Close	High	Low	Close	High	Low	Close		
2	938.73	927.68	933.17	234.43	232.16	232.81	129.82	128.13	129.06	9,180	73.16
3	937.56	925.74	930.78	233.88	231.47	232.71	129.98	128.42	128.99	11,190	73.18
4	936.47	925.87	928.84	234.18	231.30	232.06	129.82	128.32	128.74	10,840	72.97
5	937.24	925.35	930.71	233.45	230.82	232.11	129.70	127.91	128.77	12,350	73.04
6	936.14	921.41	924.77	232.46	229.68	230.39	129.63	127.78	128.42	12,520	73.02
9	925.48	911.91	918.05	230.12	227.04	227.86	128.64	126.95	127.56	10,650	72.85
10	922.83	909.32	912.49	228.70	226.33	227.30	127.78	125.89	126.18	10,660	72.75
11	913.39	899.24	904.60	227.33	223.72	225.12	126.73	124.55	125.42	13,640	72.74
12	906.22	890.71	892.58	225.80	222.93	223.64	125.96	123.88	124.20	11,790	72.65
13	902.28	886.89	894.84	224.40	221.40	222.69	125.32	123.27	124.27	13,070	72.88
16	902.79	888.83	891.16	223.90	220.63	221.29	125.83	123.66	124.42	10,400	72.87
17	893.29	876.55	885.73	220.85	217.87	218.89	124.71	123.05	123.59	12,210	72.88
18	897.10	882.30	887.09	221.53	217.66	219.08	124.30	122.70	122.99	11,290	72.73
19	889.54	877.46	882.37	219.74	216.94	217.81	123.79	121.80	122.64	11,160	72.70
20	888.77	873.32	876.16	218.97	215.44	216.13	123.27	121.07	121.61	11,360	72.60
23	880.75	862.46	870.86	216.89	212.44	213.97	122.16	120.11	120.85	12,900	72.55
24	883.73	869.25	877.20	216.68	213.49	215.68	122.60	120.49	121.17	11,460	72.61
25	884.69	870.41	874.10	216.63	213.49	214.44	122.06	120.49	121.20	10,490	72.74
26	876.16	862.78	870.28	214.41	211.65	213.12	121.93	120.21	120.88	10,310	72.71
27	876.49	863.56	869.76	214.07	211.30	212.62	121.68	120.11	120.94	9,020	72.69
30	880.69	867.18	873.19	213.60	210.93	211.99	122.64	120.56	122.09	8,640	72.60
		High	933.17		High	232.81		High	129.06		High 73.18
		Low	869.76		Low	211.99		Low	120.85		Low 72.55

JULY, 1969

	—30 Industrials—			—20 Railroads—			—15 Utilities—			Daily Sales -000-	40 Bonds
	High	Low	Close	High	Low	Close	High	Low	Close		
1	881.27	867.83	875.90	213.54	210.22	211.99	123.37	121.23	122.54	9,890	72.55
2	884.69	872.87	880.69	213.89	211.07	212.65	123.66	121.68	122.96	11,350	72.60
3	891.55	877.71	886.12	214.02	210.91	212.30	124.42	122.38	123.79	10,110	72.62
7	893.87	879.27	883.21	213.28	210.70	211.57	124.81	121.93	122.67	9,970	72.67
8	880.82	866.47	870.35	211.57	209.33	210.06	123.27	120.85	121.74	9,320	72.64
9	871.06	857.94	861.62	210.57	208.38	209.17	122.80	120.97	122.03	9,320	72.54
10	861.04	844.30	847.79	209.25	205.53	206.90	122.70	120.69	121.36	11,450	72.45
11	858.91	844.49	852.25	207.61	204.77	205.58	122.76	120.69	121.80	11,730	72.35
14	855.93	841.07	843.14	205.71	202.18	202.53	122.67	120.81	121.55	8,310	72.29
15	847.60	832.79	841.13	202.76	199.89	201.29	121.87	120.11	120.94	11,110	72.46
16	854.64	840.29	849.34	203.47	200.47	202.24	122.51	120.40	121.58	10,470	72.49
17	863.04	845.79	853.09	204.08	201.63	202.95	122.44	120.59	121.68	10,450	72.42
18	853.54	839.06	845.92	203.16	200.31	201.52	122.09	120.21	120.97	8,590	72.47
22	851.54	831.76	834.02	202.05	198.83	199.57	121.58	118.74	119.28	9,780	72.41
23	836.48	821.35	827.95	200.02	196.73	198.41	120.27	118.07	119.34	11,680	72.60
24	834.22	821.10	826.53	200.28	197.02	198.23	120.14	118.32	119.09	9,750	72.61
25	830.08	814.83	818.06	199.02	195.86	196.86	119.82	118.07	118.58	9,800	72.58
28	819.48	803.26	806.23	196.41	193.33	194.06	118.51	116.47	117.17	11,800	72.39
29	817.86	798.41	801.96	195.70	191.88	193.62	117.87	115.35	116.24	13,630	72.31
30	809.40	788.07	803.58	194.80	190.53	193.19	117.01	114.84	116.05	15,580	72.32
31	819.87	800.67	815.47	196.88	192.90	195.88	117.81	115.38	117.04	14,160	72.20

High 886.12
Low 801.96

High 212.65
Low 193.19

High 123.79
Low 116.05

High 72.67
Low 72.20

AUGUST, 1969

	—30 Industrials—			—20 Railroads—			—15 Utilities—			Daily Sales -000-	40 Bonds
	High	Low	Close	High	Low	Close	High	Low	Close		
1	833.63	815.60	826.59	200.13	196.25	199.31	118.39	116.34	117.62	15,070	72.23
4	835.06	817.61	822.58	200.13	198.78	200.10	119.28	116.79	117.97	10,700	72.14
5	827.30	813.40	821.23	200.15	197.04	198.33	118.39	116.56	117.01	8,940	72.17
6	831.63	817.67	825.88	200.21	197.81	198.78	117.71	116.05	116.79	11,100	72.25
7	832.02	820.26	826.27	199.60	196.46	197.86	117.62	115.93	116.63	9,450	72.07
8	830.27	819.87	824.46	198.89	196.65	197.81	117.24	115.48	116.09	8,760	72.08
11	826.76	816.33	819.83	199.34	196.17	198.44	116.69	114.65	115.32	6,680	72.11
12	821.54	810.39	812.96	198.99	195.72	196.73	115.83	113.62	113.91	7,870	72.07
13	815.07	800.62	809.13	196.96	194.22	195.99	115.32	112.54	113.98	9,910	72.02
14	818.11	805.37	813.23	197.41	195.09	196.23	114.90	112.70	113.56	9,690	71.92
15	825.17	810.52	820.88	199.26	196.20	198.12	114.84	112.83	114.04	10,210	71.87
18	830.39	816.46	827.68	200.71	197.75	199.47	115.99	113.91	115.32	9,420	71.96
19	841.28	824.97	833.69	202.58	198.91	201.02	117.14	114.68	116.09	12,640	72.07
20	837.91	827.55	833.22	202.21	198.65	200.26	116.63	115.00	115.64	9,680	72.05
21	839.69	828.60	834.87	202.18	199.60	201.42	116.79	115.16	115.83	8,420	72.07
22	843.72	829.33	837.25	203.26	200.26	202.02	116.98	115.32	116.28	10,140	72.01
25	841.54	828.01	831.44	203.40	200.73	201.89	116.72	115.29	115.99	8,410	72.00
26	830.39	818.84	823.52	201.23	198.89	199.73	116.37	114.81	115.51	8,910	71.92
27	830.39	819.43	824.78	200.92	198.36	199.73	116.18	114.62	115.48	9,100	71.85
28	832.23	822.14	828.41	200.97	198.14	199.65	116.09	114.68	115.57	7,730	71.80
29	839.96	825.37	836.72	202.07	199.05	201.18	117.08	115.45	116.31	8,850	71.90

High 837.25
Low 809.13

High 202.02
Low 195.99

High 117.97
Low 113.56

High 72.25
Low 71.80

SEPTEMBER, 1969

	-30 Industrials-			-20 Railroads-			-15 Utilities-			Daily Sales -000-	40 Bonds
	High	Low	Close	High	Low	Close	High	Low	Close		
2	845.96	831.31	837.78	202.95	199.88	201.10	117.43	115.77	116.72	8,560	71.76
3	841.61	829.86	835.67	201.81	198.50	199.93	117.08	115.51	115.99	8,760	71.70
4	835.67	822.20	825.30	200.69	197.95	199.52	116.31	114.62	115.06	9,380	71.55
5	826.82	816.46	819.50	199.05	196.18	197.88	115.61	113.72	114.30	8,890	71.54
8	820.55	808.67	811.84	198.47	195.77	196.60	114.93	113.24	113.59	8,310	71.56
9	822.20	804.45	815.67	198.47	194.67	196.99	114.07	111.93	113.11	10,980	71.34
10	831.71	813.69	828.01	198.84	196.50	198.24	114.52	112.47	113.75	11,490	71.39
11	838.50	821.94	825.77	199.96	196.24	197.72	115.35	112.92	114.33	12,370	71.38
12	830.65	818.37	824.25	199.52	196.60	198.45	115.25	113.27	113.91	10,800	71.45
15	835.73	821.28	830.45	200.40	197.59	199.52	114.87	113.15	114.26	10,680	71.38
16	836.85	824.84	831.64	201.57	198.24	199.62	114.84	112.76	113.62	11,160	71.36
17	835.47	821.61	826.56	200.58	197.35	198.89	114.49	112.54	113.31	10,980	71.39
18	836.66	822.80	831.57	200.45	198.47	199.62	113.98	112.06	112.76	11,170	71.48
19	837.32	825.30	830.39	201.94	198.29	200.35	113.94	111.93	112.92	12,270	71.50
22	835.80	823.79	831.77	200.92	198.89	200.11	113.85	112.19	112.86	9,280	71.58
23	841.80	827.28	834.81	202.15	199.39	200.97	113.56	111.80	112.67	13,030	71.45
24	840.48	829.53	834.68	202.28	199.57	200.66	113.05	111.04	111.64	11,320	71.40
25	838.50	826.49	829.92	201.18	198.68	199.59	112.57	110.91	111.74	10,690	71.20
26	832.83	820.09	824.18	200.92	198.42	199.54	112.41	110.88	111.39	9,680	71.17
29	826.03	811.05	818.04	200.40	197.62	198.45	112.12	110.40	111.26	10,170	71.19
30	821.67	808.54	813.09	198.45	196.00	196.60	112.19	110.33	111.16	9,180	70.86
		High	837.78		High	201.10		High	116.72		High 71.76
		Low	811.84		Low	196.60		Low	111.16		Low 70.86

OCTOBER, 1969

	-30 Industrials-			-20 Railroads-			-15 Utilities-			Daily Sales -000-	40 Bonds
	High	Low	Close	High	Low	Close	High	Low	Close		
1	814.48	803.39	806.89	197.12	194.75	195.64	112.47	109.82	110.24	9,090	70.71
2	815.87	797.78	811.84	196.91	193.68	195.64	111.26	109.25	110.49	11,430	70.82
3	819.76	803.59	808.41	197.52	194.66	196.07	112.06	109.89	111.36	12,410	70.61
6	814.94	802.73	809.40	197.20	194.24	195.48	112.06	110.17	111.07	9,180	70.74
7	813.23	803.13	806.23	197.31	194.42	195.72	112.00	110.08	111.20	10,050	70.61
8	809.79	797.65	802.20	196.57	193.50	194.85	111.23	109.47	110.37	10,370	70.52
9	808.94	793.95	803.79	196.04	193.10	194.72	111.04	109.31	109.98	10,420	70.31
10	813.23	799.89	806.96	197.20	193.87	196.09	111.52	109.66	110.78	12,210	70.36
13	820.88	804.51	819.30	198.74	195.32	197.23	112.70	110.59	112.03	13,620	70.47
14	839.49	821.21	832.43	200.17	195.88	198.02	115.19	111.68	114.52	19,950	70.35
15	837.12	823.13	830.06	199.53	196.78	197.89	115.70	113.53	114.90	15,740	70.41
16	848.14	825.50	838.77	200.96	197.02	199.51	116.92	114.10	115.64	19,500	70.38
17	845.23	829.73	836.06	200.91	197.95	199.56	117.46	115.00	116.72	13,740	70.64
20	844.18	829.59	839.23	201.23	197.50	199.03	118.80	116.24	117.87	13,540	70.65
21	850.78	834.94	846.88	200.62	197.60	199.53	119.44	117.24	118.39	16,460	70.81
22	864.37	844.90	860.35	201.36	198.66	200.04	120.08	117.97	119.28	19,320	71.05
23	863.38	845.23	855.73	201.33	198.85	200.25	120.37	117.68	118.93	14,780	70.98
24	868.00	851.31	862.26	202.45	199.45	201.23	119.86	118.00	119.15	15,430	70.95
27	866.95	852.56	860.28	203.93	200.41	202.37	120.30	118.13	119.28	12,160	71.05
28	865.23	851.90	855.86	204.11	200.91	202.45	120.27	118.13	118.93	12,410	70.99
29	858.83	845.37	848.34	203.51	199.85	200.96	119.82	118.13	118.80	12,380	71.18
30	854.28	839.82	850.51	201.65	198.61	200.41	119.76	117.55	118.77	12,820	71.30
31	860.61	845.04	855.99	201.84	198.90	200.20	119.76	117.75	119.02	13,100	71.35
		High	862.26		High	202.45		High	119.28		High 71.35
		Low	802.20		Low	194.72		Low	109.98		Low 70.31

NOVEMBER, 1969

	-30 Industrials-			-20 Railroads-			-15 Utilities-			Daily Sales -000-	40 Bonds
	High	Low	Close	High	Low	Close	High	Low	Close		
3	860.68	847.41	854.54	201.18	198.95	200.41	119.47	117.75	118.87	11,140	71.30
4	859.82	841.67	853.48	201.28	199.19	200.65	119.60	117.36	118.23	12,340	71.30
5	862.59	847.54	854.08	202.00	199.16	200.70	119.79	117.91	118.93	12,110	71.14
6	859.82	846.49	855.20	201.04	198.58	199.64	119.54	117.94	118.93	11,110	70.83
7	867.28	850.38	860.48	200.83	197.89	199.16	119.86	118.32	119.09	13,280	70.84
10	871.77	856.65	863.05	200.22	197.10	198.45	120.14	118.23	119.18	12,490	70.67
11	866.62	853.62	859.75	199.88	197.44	199.22	120.18	118.45	119.31	10,080	70.67
12	863.98	851.70	855.99	199.93	196.97	198.26	120.24	118.19	119.02	12,480	70.58
13	858.90	844.64	849.85	199.08	196.01	197.07	119.66	117.43	118.29	12,090	70.53
14	854.74	842.00	849.26	197.84	195.35	196.22	118.48	116.69	117.36	10,580	70.53
17	851.04	837.45	842.53	197.20	194.05	195.01	117.84	115.25	115.73	10,120	70.57
18	848.67	836.99	845.17	198.08	194.72	197.26	116.56	114.33	115.22	11,010	70.36
19	848.60	835.93	839.96	198.21	195.56	196.22	116.56	113.94	115.06	11,240	70.12
20	840.28	823.98	831.18	196.01	193.39	194.50	115.77	113.15	114.10	12,010	69.93
21	832.43	820.35	823.13	194.42	192.23	192.91	114.23	112.38	112.99	9,840	69.83
24	825.96	808.01	812.90	191.75	187.33	188.41	113.31	110.88	111.36	10,940	69.75
25	818.37	803.92	807.29	189.58	186.16	187.01	112.38	110.40	111.07	11,560	69.62
26	814.15	800.36	810.52	187.75	184.39	186.24	111.90	109.76	110.69	10,630	69.64
28	818.57	805.37	812.30	187.54	185.08	186.64	112.35	110.37	111.39	8,550	69.55
		High 863.05			High 200.70			High 119.31			High 71.30
		Low 807.29			Low 186.24			Low 110.69			Low 69.55

DECEMBER, 1969

	-30 Industrials-			-20 Railroads-			-15 Utilities-			Daily Sales -000-	40 Bonds
	High	Low	Close	High	Low	Close	High	Low	Close		
1	816.39	802.20	805.04	187.62	184.44	185.69	112.41	110.49	111.04	9,950	69.67
2	808.34	794.94	801.35	185.24	182.83	184.18	111.52	109.69	110.27	9,940	69.52
3	804.78	789.93	793.36	183.75	179.52	180.44	110.24	108.19	108.77	11,300	69.40
4	801.15	783.86	796.53	181.40	176.74	180.58	109.73	107.65	108.48	13,230	69.45
5	804.05	788.94	793.03	182.80	178.86	179.76	110.05	107.87	108.74	11,150	69.43
8	797.32	781.48	785.04	179.65	174.80	175.65	109.28	106.63	107.43	9,990	69.41
9	794.42	778.18	783.79	176.90	173.08	173.96	108.00	105.41	106.31	12,290	69.10
10	791.51	773.76	783.99	175.02	171.49	173.90	107.04	105.00	106.31	12,590	69.10
11	791.25	778.38	783.53	175.02	171.79	173.35	108.19	105.76	107.17	10,430	69.05
12	794.61	780.23	786.69	174.70	171.63	173.06	108.77	106.66	107.75	11,630	68.95
15	791.97	779.63	784.05	174.01	170.83	172.47	108.38	106.15	106.66	11,100	68.89
16	787.42	770.46	773.83	172.77	168.34	169.43	107.78	105.60	106.56	11,880	68.66
17	780.16	765.71	769.93	170.83	167.47	169.03	107.55	105.73	106.69	12,840	68.63
18	788.87	764.45	783.79	172.00	167.79	171.04	108.26	105.73	107.43	15,950	68.38
19	798.18	780.76	789.86	174.20	170.20	172.50	109.98	106.98	108.77	15,420	68.32
22	796.13	781.48	785.97	173.61	170.14	171.20	110.14	107.62	108.74	12,680	68.21
23	789.66	776.27	783.79	172.74	168.87	170.94	110.79	107.62	108.80	13,890	68.33
24	799.63	782.67	794.15	175.97	171.12	175.10	110.11	107.97	109.31	11,670	68.13
26	802.47	790.85	797.65	177.29	174.38	176.90	110.46	108.86	109.82	6,750	68.16
29	803.19	787.62	792.37	178.35	174.20	175.55	110.56	108.54	109.28	12,500	68.21
30	799.63	786.30	794.68	177.11	173.59	176.07	110.49	108.32	109.53	15,790	68.07
31	806.69	792.24	800.36	178.27	173.90	176.34	111.52	108.96	110.08	19,380	68.11
		High 805.04			High 185.69			High 111.04			High 69.67
		Low 769.93			Low 169.03			Low 106.31			Low 68.07

JANUARY, 1970

	—30 Industrials—			—20 Transportations—			—15 Utilities—			Daily Sales -000-	40 Bonds
	High	Low	Close	High	Low	Close	High	Low	Close		
2	813.56	797.32	809.20	181.87	176.91	181.07	112.73	110.27	112.25	8,050	68.43
5	819.23	804.84	811.31	184.04	181.19	183.31	114.52	111.64	113.56	11,490	68.65
6	814.08	798.71	803.66	184.01	180.09	181.19	114.14	111.07	112.00	11,460	68.85
7	808.47	796.20	801.81	181.90	178.53	180.03	112.31	110.11	111.04	10,010	68.90
8	809.33	796.92	802.07	180.95	177.77	179.14	112.47	110.81	112.00	10,670	69.05
9	805.70	794.35	798.11	179.82	176.79	177.77	112.31	110.81	111.58	9,380	69.16
12	799.23	786.30	790.52	178.26	174.40	175.81	112.57	110.88	111.87	8,900	69.24
13	796.79	782.47	788.01	176.54	172.04	173.73	112.25	110.27	111.16	9,870	69.26
14	796.73	780.36	787.16	175.20	171.95	173.73	111.36	109.63	110.37	10,380	69.28
15	791.25	777.98	785.04	175.50	171.89	173.91	110.94	109.18	109.82	11,120	69.42
16	791.97	778.25	782.60	176.02	172.20	173.39	110.49	108.74	109.53	11,940	69.38
19	784.52	772.18	776.07	174.37	170.82	172.10	110.40	108.19	109.18	9,500	69.33
20	783.13	770.72	777.85	173.48	170.27	172.23	109.79	107.68	108.64	11,050	69.43
21	788.61	773.96	782.27	174.03	170.91	172.41	109.53	107.55	108.35	9,880	69.06
22	793.16	777.39	786.10	174.03	171.00	172.07	109.09	107.30	108.22	11,050	69.18
23	789.40	774.35	775.54	172.99	169.44	170.24	109.09	106.98	107.71	11,000	69.10
26	777.52	762.54	768.88	170.85	167.51	168.98	108.58	106.44	107.07	10,670	68.94
27	773.03	757.92	763.99	169.81	166.96	168.13	107.62	105.89	106.50	9,630	68.90
28	769.87	755.74	758.84	170.57	166.53	167.76	107.46	105.41	105.92	10,510	68.65
29	760.69	743.73	748.35	168.37	164.48	165.77	106.82	104.77	105.89	12,210	68.57
30	756.20	739.11	744.06	166.81	162.71	163.72	106.91	104.87	105.19	12,320	68.64
		High	811.31		High	183.31		High	113.56		High 69.43
		Low	744.06		Low	163.72		Low	105.19		Low 68.43

FEBRUARY, 1970

	—30 Industrials—			—20 Transportations—			—15 Utilities—			Daily Sales -000-	40 Bonds
	High	Low	Close	High	Low	Close	High	Low	Close		
2	756.47	739.37	746.44	167.30	163.20	165.55	106.91	104.74	105.96	13,440	68.64
3	764.45	738.78	757.46	167.48	162.46	165.52	108.26	105.32	107.27	16,050	68.79
4	765.97	748.09	754.49	167.70	164.15	165.46	108.64	106.47	107.30	11,040	69.03
5	756.73	743.33	750.26	166.04	162.59	164.36	108.03	105.89	106.88	9,430	68.94
6	758.71	744.98	752.77	167.54	163.29	166.96	107.62	105.86	106.63	10,150	68.96
9	764.92	750.40	755.68	170.27	166.60	169.41	108.42	106.12	106.98	10,830	69.01
10	758.51	743.20	746.63	169.75	166.84	167.67	107.55	106.05	106.75	10,110	68.93
11	760.69	739.90	757.33	170.85	166.14	170.15	107.81	105.76	107.55	12,260	68.87
12	762.28	748.88	755.61	172.07	168.77	170.85	108.38	106.66	107.84	10,010	68.92
13	758.65	745.97	753.30	171.71	169.04	170.82	108.35	106.60	107.49	11,060	69.17
16	761.09	748.02	753.70	172.23	169.11	170.33	108.67	106.56	107.52	9,780	69.13
17	757.13	741.09	747.43	170.79	167.39	168.62	108.70	107.07	107.78	10,140	69.15
18	762.61	745.45	756.80	171.55	168.13	170.30	109.69	107.59	109.22	11,950	69.02
19	766.90	751.58	757.92	172.53	169.35	171.00	110.59	108.38	109.38	12,890	69.04
20	764.45	749.34	757.46	172.10	169.23	170.76	110.88	108.77	110.17	10,790	69.12
24	761.68	748.88	754.42	172.53	169.32	170.94	112.41	109.41	110.97	10,810	69.01
25	772.70	749.47	768.28	175.35	170.64	174.43	114.26	110.69	113.62	13,210	69.13
26	770.53	755.48	764.45	177.12	172.78	176.11	114.68	112.19	113.88	11,540	69.22
27	784.19	762.61	777.59	179.02	174.74	177.58	116.15	113.25	115.25	12,890	69.33
		High	777.59		High	177.58		High	115.25		High 69.33
		Low	746.44		Low	164.36		Low	105.96		Low 68.64

MARCH, 1970

	—30 Industrials—			—20 Transportations—			—15 Utilities—			Daily Sales -000-	40 Bonds
	High	Low	Close	High	Low	Close	High	Low	Close		
2	790.52	774.49	780.23	180.43	175.84	178.10	117.43	115.03	116.66	12,270	69.53
3	790.52	775.08	787.42	179.73	176.30	178.65	118.61	115.93	117.94	11,700	69.57
4	795.54	782.27	788.15	179.77	176.51	178.08	119.47	116.79	118.29	11,850	69.69
5	795.54	783.13	787.55	180.39	177.46	178.85	119.89	117.65	118.71	11,370	69.57
6	789.93	779.37	784.12	179.59	176.54	177.86	119.63	117.78	118.51	10,980	69.67
9	785.57	773.56	778.31	178.23	174.69	176.32	118.90	117.01	117.71	9,760	69.70
10	785.37	772.18	779.70	177.99	175.25	176.48	118.55	116.60	117.24	9,450	69.73
11	785.84	774.29	778.12	177.80	175.18	176.08	117.91	115.93	116.82	9,180	69.65
12	781.55	771.77	776.47	176.88	173.65	174.26	117.27	115.48	116.09	9,140	69.46
13	779.30	768.02	772.11	175.46	172.04	173.21	116.76	114.90	115.73	9,560	69.42
16	772.84	760.16	765.05	174.32	171.18	172.29	116.28	113.88	114.39	8,910	69.40
17	773.36	759.17	767.42	173.52	171.00	172.41	114.81	112.99	113.66	9,090	69.46
18	775.67	763.93	767.95	173.86	171.31	172.51	115.22	113.40	114.33	9,790	69.31
19	773.76	761.55	764.98	173.89	170.75	171.71	115.29	113.72	114.39	8,930	69.41
20	768.55	758.91	763.66	172.44	169.49	170.78	115.13	113.43	113.98	7,910	69.48
23	768.41	757.99	763.60	171.37	167.89	169.86	115.00	113.02	114.23	7,330	69.50
24	776.99	764.52	773.76	171.83	168.29	170.41	116.02	113.75	115.29	8,840	69.48
25	803.26	775.67	790.13	176.11	170.29	173.74	119.44	115.57	118.16	17,500	69.49
26	797.45	785.24	791.05	174.82	171.43	173.28	119.02	117.01	117.94	11,350	69.60
30	792.37	779.17	784.65	174.45	172.01	172.84	118.74	116.82	117.71	9,600	69.51
31	789.20	778.38	785.57	174.14	171.15	173.06	118.48	116.69	117.75	8,370	69.58
		High 791.05			High 178.85			High 118.71			High 69.73
		Low 763.60			Low 169.86			Low 113.66			Low 69.31

APRIL, 1970

	—30 Industrials—			—20 Transportations—			—15 Utilities—			Daily Sales -000-	40 Bonds
	High	Low	Close	High	Low	Close	High	Low	Close		
1	795.67	784.05	792.04	175.09	171.49	173.52	118.74	116.92	118.00	9,810	69.51
2	797.91	787.02	792.37	175.09	172.01	173.43	119.12	117.14	118.00	10,520	69.58
3	796.40	787.02	791.84	175.18	172.66	174.35	119.09	117.20	118.26	9,920	69.33
6	796.07	786.30	791.18	175.06	172.63	173.71	118.83	116.72	117.97	8,380	69.27
7	797.12	785.70	791.64	173.74	171.46	172.14	119.02	117.24	118.23	8,490	69.40
8	796.00	787.42	791.64	174.11	171.34	173.00	119.28	117.49	118.23	9,070	69.20
9	798.84	786.96	792.50	174.35	171.74	173.25	118.90	117.33	118.10	9,060	69.20
10	797.25	785.04	790.46	173.95	171.52	172.38	118.87	117.08	117.65	10,020	69.16
13	793.82	782.07	785.90	172.63	169.80	170.54	118.16	116.40	116.76	8,810	69.18
14	787.35	772.90	780.56	171.09	168.01	169.18	117.59	115.64	116.34	10,840	69.09
15	788.87	777.06	782.60	171.03	168.47	169.27	117.27	115.51	116.28	9,410	69.12
16	787.22	773.03	775.87	170.17	167.24	167.95	116.79	114.62	115.09	10,250	69.01
17	781.22	766.96	775.94	168.93	165.98	167.40	115.45	113.40	114.33	10,990	69.05
20	780.56	769.67	775.87	168.87	166.41	168.29	115.06	112.83	113.72	8,280	68.96
21	783.00	769.87	772.51	169.67	166.87	167.40	114.87	112.19	112.95	8,490	68.93
22	774.35	758.51	762.61	167.64	164.81	165.46	113.08	111.16	112.03	10,780	68.83
23	760.63	745.45	750.59	165.79	162.96	163.61	112.19	109.60	110.11	11,050	68.68
24	754.42	742.21	747.29	164.10	160.87	161.82	111.10	108.61	110.05	10,410	68.69
27	750.46	731.72	735.15	162.04	157.39	157.94	110.65	108.80	109.34	10,240	68.72
28	740.76	720.70	724.33	160.13	154.40	155.39	110.05	108.06	108.80	12,620	68.78
29	740.03	716.74	737.39	158.81	153.97	157.74	109.57	106.91	108.67	15,800	68.66
30	745.58	728.48	736.07	159.21	155.11	156.37	109.73	107.62	108.67	9,880	68.70
		High 792.50			High 174.35			High 118.26			High 69.58
		Low 724.33			Low 155.39			Low 108.67			Low 68.66

MAY, 1970

	—30 Industrials—			—20 Transportations—			—15 Utilities—			Daily Sales -000-	40 Bonds
	High	Low	Close	High	Low	Close	High	Low	Close		
1	740.76	723.60	733.63	157.91	154.83	156.53	109.50	106.91	108.29	8,290	68.74
4	732.38	710.40	714.56	156.71	152.19	153.14	108.22	105.80	106.40	11,450	68.63
5	720.63	704.46	709.74	153.88	150.40	151.66	106.72	104.97	105.67	10,580	68.43
6	731.19	707.76	718.39	156.07	151.54	153.76	107.59	105.13	106.08	14,380	68.44
7	730.33	713.37	723.07	156.31	153.20	154.90	107.39	105.19	106.31	9,530	68.50
8	725.51	713.04	717.73	155.88	153.26	154.34	107.07	105.32	106.08	6,930	68.56
11	721.03	707.04	710.07	153.73	150.25	150.65	106.47	104.58	104.97	6,650	68.61
12	715.15	699.31	704.59	151.45	146.92	148.52	105.73	103.85	104.74	10,850	68.52
13	703.80	686.64	693.84	148.49	145.17	146.67	104.84	102.82	103.24	10,720	68.41
14	693.57	673.51	684.79	146.92	142.64	144.46	103.78	101.58	102.76	13,920	68.18
15	705.58	680.37	702.22	148.49	143.78	147.66	104.29	101.99	103.18	14,570	68.10
18	709.74	695.35	702.81	150.06	147.11	148.52	104.87	102.86	103.78	8,280	68.09
19	704.20	689.62	691.40	148.80	145.44	146.03	104.42	102.51	103.11	9,480	68.11
20	690.72	674.56	676.55	145.91	141.53	142.30	103.27	101.10	101.51	13,020	68.09
21	676.62	654.37	665.25	142.80	138.49	140.67	102.22	99.21	100.36	16,710	68.05
22	675.11	653.27	662.17	142.46	137.47	139.25	102.15	99.31	100.52	12,170	67.96
25	660.80	639.10	641.36	138.70	133.10	133.87	100.43	98.00	98.73	12,660	67.81
26	649.64	627.46	631.16	136.21	130.08	131.53	99.44	96.69	97.84	17,030	67.71
27	668.81	631.98	663.20	140.39	131.53	139.75	100.52	97.17	100.04	17,460	67.63
28	690.92	666.96	684.15	144.83	139.25	143.50	102.28	99.44	101.16	18,910	67.64
29	703.86	673.06	700.44	145.47	140.46	144.46	103.11	100.36	102.25	14,630	67.70
		High 733.63			High 156.53			High 108.29			High 68.74
		Low 631.16			Low 131.53			Low 97.84			Low 67.63

JUNE, 1970

	—30 Industrials—			—20 Transportations—			—15 Utilities—			Daily Sales -000-	40 Bonds
	High	Low	Close	High	Low	Close	High	Low	Close		
1	715.64	694.14	710.36	147.88	143.50	146.80	103.82	101.45	103.02	15,020	67.73
2	719.13	698.32	709.61	148.86	144.21	146.83	104.04	101.93	103.02	13,480	67.55
3	721.73	702.22	713.86	148.61	144.24	146.98	104.55	101.99	103.85	16,600	67.71
4	723.92	704.41	706.53	148.98	144.30	145.29	104.71	101.99	102.57	14,380	67.64
5	707.56	687.91	695.03	145.04	140.98	142.21	102.66	100.20	101.61	12,450	67.66
8	709.75	689.83	700.23	144.98	141.35	143.53	102.38	100.65	101.32	8,040	67.86
9	705.64	695.17	700.16	145.04	142.33	143.84	101.71	99.98	100.62	7,050	67.66
10	703.24	690.03	694.35	144.12	140.76	141.44	101.00	99.57	100.27	7,240	67.34
11	695.44	677.85	684.42	141.87	138.82	139.87	100.04	98.03	98.83	7,770	67.08
12	688.66	674.90	684.21	139.93	136.33	138.27	99.37	97.30	98.13	8,890	67.02
15	694.82	679.83	687.36	139.22	135.90	137.41	99.15	96.91	98.29	6,920	67.15
16	711.80	686.88	706.26	140.52	136.42	138.95	99.53	97.52	98.32	11,330	67.04
17	715.36	699.55	704.68	140.79	137.04	138.39	99.28	97.14	98.13	9,870	67.06
18	718.92	696.95	712.69	139.84	137.01	139.01	99.18	97.33	98.26	8,870	67.03
19	728.23	713.65	720.43	141.35	138.39	139.87	99.47	97.65	98.54	10,980	67.00
22	723.17	707.15	716.11	138.24	134.51	136.30	98.99	97.04	97.74	8,700	66.94
23	716.66	696.40	698.11	136.21	132.05	132.48	98.16	96.43	96.72	10,790	66.64
24	705.37	685.31	692.29	133.41	129.28	130.70	97.71	95.73	96.59	12,630	66.52
25	701.60	686.40	693.59	131.16	127.71	128.73	97.90	96.11	97.11	8,200	66.52
26	700.51	686.06	687.84	129.53	125.86	126.75	97.81	95.89	96.59	9,160	66.34
29	691.13	679.15	682.91	126.66	120.38	121.46	97.14	95.41	95.99	8,770	65.09
30	692.36	679.08	683.53	123.43	118.53	120.57	96.88	95.09	95.86	9,280	65.06
		High 720.43			High 146.98			High 103.85			High 67.86
		Low 682.91			Low 120.57			Low 95.86			Low 65.06

JULY, 1970

	-30 Industrials-			-20 Transportations-			-15 Utilities-			Daily Sales -000-	40 Bonds
	High	Low	Close	High	Low	Close	High	Low	Close		
1	692.02	678.26	687.64	122.23	118.87	120.63	96.88	95.25	96.37	8,610	64.85
2	697.02	684.76	689.14	122.38	119.03	120.47	97.46	95.70	96.88	8,440	64.86
6	689.90	671.69	675.66	121.24	117.55	118.57	97.52	95.95	96.72	9,340	65.11
7	679.90	665.32	669.36	118.84	115.76	116.69	97.94	95.86	97.39	10,470	65.31
8	684.08	666.00	682.09	119.77	116.32	119.06	100.75	97.52	100.20	10,970	65.41
9	697.63	681.48	692.77	123.12	119.18	121.92	103.18	100.27	102.51	12,820	65.54
10	704.41	689.69	700.10	124.54	121.40	123.80	104.52	102.22	103.53	10,160	65.48
13	709.34	696.19	702.22	125.22	122.14	124.05	104.74	102.35	103.21	7,450	65.54
14	707.69	696.40	703.04	124.88	122.63	123.65	104.01	102.35	103.08	7,360	65.25
15	716.32	699.48	711.66	124.45	121.89	123.46	104.52	102.44	103.88	8,860	65.07
16	730.76	712.14	723.44	126.20	122.75	125.15	105.38	103.27	104.61	12,200	65.39
17	739.46	725.49	735.08	129.77	124.69	128.73	105.96	103.62	104.93	13,870	65.58
20	743.36	728.64	733.91	132.02	128.39	129.80	107.33	104.93	106.24	11,660	65.56
21	734.12	717.96	722.07	130.73	128.23	129.50	106.50	104.23	105.32	9,940	65.46
22	735.01	716.25	724.67	131.80	128.36	130.02	106.02	103.94	104.55	12,460	65.49
23	737.88	718.44	732.68	131.59	128.85	130.73	106.02	103.91	105.32	12,460	65.49
24	736.58	722.96	730.22	131.53	129.50	130.60	106.21	104.23	104.93	9,520	65.60
27	735.01	724.53	730.08	131.87	129.53	130.73	105.76	104.01	104.65	7,460	65.49
28	735.49	724.40	731.45	131.43	127.65	128.82	105.44	103.46	104.20	9,040	65.56
29	742.40	729.39	735.56	131.03	127.74	129.50	105.38	103.05	104.23	12,580	65.77
30	740.07	728.78	734.73	130.88	127.92	129.90	105.38	103.50	104.49	10,430	65.56
31	743.36	728.23	734.12	133.25	129.03	130.73	105.64	103.78	104.93	11,640	65.56
		High	735.56		High	130.73		High	106.24		High 65.77
		Low	669.36		Low	116.69		Low	96.37		Low 64.85

AUGUST, 1970

	-30 Industrials-			-20 Transportations-			-15 Utilities-			Daily Sales -000-	40 Bonds
	High	Low	Close	High	Low	Close	High	Low	Close		
3	734.67	718.65	722.96	131.74	127.96	128.85	105.51	103.75	104.39	7,650	65.61
4	728.85	714.88	725.90	130.76	127.74	130.26	104.65	102.76	103.66	8,310	65.69
5	732.06	719.67	724.81	131.53	128.63	129.74	104.58	102.92	103.82	7,660	65.57
6	728.92	716.86	722.82	130.26	127.74	128.73	104.45	102.98	103.59	7,560	65.60
7	731.93	718.03	725.70	131.22	127.52	129.83	104.77	102.98	104.36	9,370	65.74
10	725.01	709.95	713.92	130.45	127.34	128.29	104.84	103.11	103.85	7,580	65.60
11	716.73	706.39	712.55	128.69	126.60	127.83	104.10	102.31	103.08	7,330	65.49
12	716.87	707.83	710.64	130.14	127.25	128.60	103.69	102.41	102.92	7,440	65.11
13	713.51	702.83	707.35	129.74	127.37	128.66	103.72	102.03	102.98	8,640	65.12
14	715.84	704.75	710.84	130.57	128.02	129.59	104.04	102.41	103.24	7,850	64.99
17	713.92	704.41	709.06	129.50	126.26	127.25	104.36	102.82	103.53	6,940	64.92
18	721.11	709.47	716.66	129.56	126.57	127.92	104.84	102.98	104.10	9,500	64.85
19	728.92	715.09	723.99	130.05	127.68	128.97	105.57	103.91	104.97	9,870	64.61
20	732.82	717.76	729.60	129.93	127.12	128.54	106.02	104.17	105.22	10,170	64.36
21	748.84	728.78	745.41	131.77	127.22	130.60	107.43	104.87	106.82	13,420	64.44
24	765.68	747.19	759.58	134.05	130.05	132.60	109.41	106.98	108.61	18,910	64.49
25	764.17	747.47	758.97	135.19	131.10	134.30	109.50	107.23	108.22	17,520	64.52
26	769.78	755.34	760.47	137.78	133.16	135.90	109.50	107.43	108.45	15,970	64.67
27	766.84	752.53	759.79	137.84	134.05	136.64	110.01	107.91	109.44	12,440	64.69
28	772.04	756.37	765.81	139.01	135.62	138.12	110.84	108.96	110.30	13,820	64.83
31	770.67	759.86	764.58	139.16	136.21	137.81	111.07	109.06	110.08	10,740	64.90
		High	765.81		High	138.12		High	110.30		High 65.74
		Low	707.35		Low	127.25		Low	102.92		Low 64.36

SEPTEMBER, 1970

	-30 Industrials-			-20 Transportations-			-15 Utilities-			Daily Sales -000-	40 Bonds
	High	Low	Close	High	Low	Close	High	Low	Close		
1	766.16	754.93	758.15	138.21	135.41	136.51	110.65	108.83	109.66	10,440	64.80
2	760.13	748.43	756.64	137.22	134.30	136.36	110.30	108.61	110.21	9,710	64.81
3	770.33	755.89	765.27	138.08	135.38	137.04	110.94	109.22	109.79	14,110	64.94
4	775.12	761.91	771.15	139.04	135.59	137.65	111.00	109.02	110.27	15,360	64.64
8	778.27	759.99	773.14	139.66	134.58	138.15	110.97	108.99	110.24	17,110	64.79
9	776.97	759.31	766.43	139.75	135.59	138.05	110.94	108.93	109.82	16,250	65.01
10	768.69	754.65	760.75	138.89	135.65	137.50	110.14	108.32	108.99	11,900	64.98
11	767.32	755.48	761.84	140.92	136.88	140.02	109.73	107.94	108.70	12,140	65.00
14	766.84	751.37	757.12	140.98	138.08	139.56	109.95	107.52	108.42	11,900	65.11
15	757.05	745.14	750.55	139.32	136.11	137.13	108.93	107.04	107.43	9,830	65.15
16	759.45	744.18	754.31	138.95	135.62	137.81	108.51	106.56	108.06	12,090	65.27
17	766.29	751.57	757.67	141.38	137.07	139.44	108.74	107.14	107.62	15,530	65.30
18	766.29	751.92	758.49	143.41	139.01	142.55	108.80	107.23	107.97	15,900	65.38
21	763.96	748.22	751.92	143.13	140.58	141.29	108.86	107.36	107.71	12,540	65.36
22	753.15	741.51	747.47	141.93	138.95	140.36	108.48	106.79	107.91	12,110	65.31
23	762.32	744.25	754.38	142.55	139.53	141.50	109.18	107.59	108.51	16,940	65.54
24	764.99	749.04	759.31	146.71	141.69	145.38	109.76	107.84	109.02	21,340	65.72
25	767.39	754.65	761.77	146.86	143.69	145.23	109.60	108.16	108.86	20,470	65.69
28	764.65	750.68	758.97	149.32	144.80	148.21	109.34	108.00	108.77	14,390	65.58
29	766.09	749.66	760.88	154.40	146.55	153.14	109.34	107.39	108.51	17,880	65.61
30	766.91	754.79	760.68	155.54	151.35	153.45	109.31	107.75	108.19	14,830	65.75
		High	773.14		High	153.45		High	110.27		High 65.75
		Low	747.47		Low	136.36		Low	107.43		Low 64.64

OCTOBER, 1970

	-30 Industrials-			-20 Transportations-			-15 Utilities-			Daily Sales -000-	40 Bonds
	High	Low	Close	High	Low	Close	High	Low	Close		
1	764.79	754.38	760.68	155.42	152.09	154.50	108.83	107.39	107.84	9,700	65.73
2	769.72	756.43	766.16	159.51	154.43	158.71	108.51	106.88	107.84	15,420	65.77
5	780.53	763.76	776.70	162.44	157.70	161.15	108.70	107.14	107.87	19,760	65.80
6	791.07	773.62	782.45	162.81	158.28	159.88	108.42	106.98	107.43	20,240	65.82
7	788.47	771.22	783.68	159.73	155.05	157.45	108.10	106.08	107.14	15,610	65.81
8	789.29	773.48	777.04	158.99	154.62	155.73	108.00	106.12	106.72	14,500	65.81
9	780.46	764.72	768.69	157.08	153.54	154.83	107.65	106.02	106.47	13,980	65.88
12	770.47	758.42	764.24	155.05	151.94	152.89	107.14	105.83	106.34	8,570	65.83
13	767.11	754.38	760.06	153.11	150.65	151.29	107.01	105.83	106.37	9,500	65.85
14	767.25	754.72	762.73	153.69	150.15	152.46	107.07	105.70	106.44	9,920	65.67
15	773.27	760.88	767.87	157.05	153.42	155.67	107.04	105.64	106.47	11,250	65.68
16	771.70	759.10	763.35	156.50	153.33	154.06	107.07	105.86	106.60	11,300	65.75
19	766.09	753.29	756.50	153.91	150.58	150.99	107.07	105.44	106.15	9,890	65.67
20	764.03	750.82	758.83	152.19	149.54	151.14	107.14	105.29	106.72	10,630	65.62
21	769.24	756.64	759.65	153.51	149.91	151.05	107.52	106.02	106.88	11,330	65.48
22	763.28	753.22	757.87	152.03	149.01	150.00	107.27	105.60	106.34	9,000	65.39
23	764.03	753.90	759.38	151.42	148.86	150.25	107.49	105.96	106.56	10,270	65.45
26	764.24	753.42	756.43	150.71	147.84	148.49	107.23	105.70	106.24	9,200	65.53
27	759.38	750.21	754.45	148.86	146.24	147.35	106.72	105.32	106.28	9,680	65.54
28	759.31	746.71	755.96	148.83	146.06	148.09	106.91	105.25	106.18	10,660	65.52
29	760.34	749.45	753.56	148.92	145.84	146.95	106.98	105.25	105.80	10,440	65.51
30	759.38	748.36	755.61	147.63	144.21	145.72	106.91	105.35	106.37	10,520	65.40
		High	783.68		High	161.15		High	107.87		High 65.88
		Low	753.56		Low	145.72		Low	105.80		Low 65.39

NOVEMBER, 1970

	—30 Industrials—			—20 Transportations—			—15 Utilities—			Daily Sales -000-	40 Bonds
	High	Low	Close	High	Low	Close	High	Low	Close		
2	762.25	750.68	758.01	146.80	144.09	146.21	107.39	106.02	106.82	9,470	65.50
3	771.50	756.02	768.07	148.92	146.12	147.94	108.61	106.66	107.87	11,760	65.48
4	777.25	764.92	770.81	150.43	147.60	148.83	109.12	107.55	108.22	12,180	65.48
5	775.94	765.68	771.56	150.06	147.54	148.12	109.25	107.71	108.86	10,800	65.60
6	777.38	765.81	771.97	150.31	147.51	148.92	109.89	108.32	109.41	9,970	65.66
9	782.38	769.85	777.66	150.43	147.71	149.05	110.78	108.90	110.24	10,890	65.67
10	783.00	773.34	777.38	151.48	148.18	150.58	111.93	109.92	111.20	12,030	65.74
11	788.75	776.29	779.50	153.11	149.45	150.80	112.95	111.23	111.93	13,520	65.85
12	781.76	765.88	768.00	151.54	148.61	149.32	112.67	111.10	111.71	12,520	65.89
13	767.94	755.61	759.79	149.60	146.71	147.51	111.77	110.21	110.88	11,890	65.83
16	764.99	752.46	760.13	147.72	145.35	146.55	111.39	110.14	110.75	9,160	66.02
17	768.48	756.37	760.47	148.09	145.97	146.92	112.00	110.37	111.13	9,450	65.88
18	761.77	751.78	754.24	147.08	144.80	145.66	111.29	109.50	110.21	9,850	66.02
19	760.47	749.52	755.82	146.64	144.21	145.44	111.45	109.38	110.27	9,280	66.07
20	764.10	752.19	761.57	147.41	144.98	146.74	111.52	109.73	110.75	10,920	66.08
23	773.41	759.79	767.52	149.35	146.49	148.00	112.83	111.07	112.22	12,720	66.32
24	775.60	762.60	772.73	149.42	146.18	148.58	113.53	111.55	113.11	12,560	66.50
25	780.94	768.48	774.71	150.31	147.81	149.23	114.58	112.60	113.59	13,490	66.62
27	783.61	771.15	781.35	150.43	148.00	149.60	115.13	113.08	114.68	10,130	66.84
30	797.51	780.26	794.09	154.19	149.35	153.36	116.28	114.42	115.77	17,700	67.11
		High 794.09			High 153.36			High 115.77			High 67.11
		Low 754.24			Low 145.44			Low 106.82			Low 65.48

DECEMBER, 1970

	—30 Industrials—			—20 Transportations—			—15 Utilities—			Daily Sales -000-	40 Bonds
	High	Low	Close	High	Low	Close	High	Low	Close		
1	805.65	787.45	794.29	156.28	152.74	154.31	117.40	114.97	116.53	20,170	67.44
2	805.72	787.86	802.64	156.93	152.37	155.97	117.87	115.32	117.01	17,960	67.82
3	816.88	801.48	808.53	158.50	154.96	156.93	119.22	117.04	118.19	20,480	67.78
4	819.07	801.34	816.06	159.30	155.36	158.59	119.06	117.20	118.48	15,980	67.79
7	823.59	810.24	818.66	159.94	156.13	158.10	119.86	117.97	118.99	15,530	67.89
8	822.49	809.69	815.10	159.45	156.99	157.94	119.41	117.33	118.39	14,370	67.96
9	819.96	806.27	815.24	158.50	155.82	157.51	119.02	117.27	118.16	13,550	67.84
10	824.75	811.68	821.06	158.90	156.25	157.82	119.22	117.30	118.51	14,610	68.10
11	831.67	818.18	825.92	159.51	156.65	158.16	119.66	117.68	118.99	15,790	68.25
14	832.28	818.66	823.18	158.90	156.10	157.08	119.47	117.30	118.00	13,810	68.16
15	826.12	813.25	819.62	158.19	155.45	157.36	119.06	117.43	118.23	13,420	68.14
16	823.52	810.17	819.07	158.22	155.94	157.05	118.83	117.14	118.13	14,240	68.09
17	826.94	815.85	822.15	159.70	156.19	158.87	119.25	117.33	118.32	13,660	68.09
18	828.79	815.51	822.77	160.01	157.79	159.02	119.54	117.68	118.71	14,360	68.07
21	828.45	815.31	821.54	160.68	158.00	159.58	119.76	117.78	118.71	12,690	68.01
22	828.93	815.65	822.77	161.85	158.68	160.62	120.14	118.10	119.09	14,510	68.29
23	830.16	816.54	823.11	162.62	159.30	161.55	120.21	118.16	119.06	15,400	68.29
24	831.67	820.65	828.38	163.73	160.93	162.59	120.75	118.55	119.92	12,140	68.42
28	834.75	824.07	830.91	165.49	162.68	164.75	121.39	119.31	120.27	12,290	68.60
29	844.19	828.04	842.00	170.35	164.96	169.92	121.61	119.47	121.04	17,750	68.70
30	848.23	836.05	841.32	174.01	169.24	172.08	122.48	120.49	121.29	19,140	68.75
31	844.95	832.56	838.92	172.94	169.40	171.52	122.32	120.24	121.84	13,390	68.77
		High 842.00			High 172.08			High 121.84			High 68.77
		Low 794.29			Low 154.31			Low 116.53			Low 67.44

JANUARY, 1971

	—30 Industrials—			—20 Transportations—			—15 Utilities—			Daily Sales —000—	40 Bonds
	High	Low	Close	High	Low	Close	High	Low	Close		
4	839.06	826.53	830.57	171.74	168.53	169.70	122.22	120.14	121.10	10,010	68.62
5	840.09	827.35	835.77	172.57	169.09	171.71	122.12	120.24	121.36	12,600	68.62
6	843.92	831.67	837.97	176.51	172.51	175.46	122.83	120.69	121.77	16,960	68.77
7	843.78	832.42	837.83	177.99	174.91	176.14	123.27	121.36	122.19	16,460	69.01
8	843.31	831.94	837.01	177.96	174.91	176.75	123.69	121.55	122.48	14,100	69.32
11	841.46	828.31	837.21	177.62	174.38	175.52	123.56	121.74	123.08	14,720	69.34
12	849.19	834.68	844.19	178.76	175.06	177.59	125.19	122.70	124.62	17,820	69.52
13	853.44	835.57	841.11	180.42	176.94	178.57	126.21	124.27	125.58	19,070	69.57
14	849.26	832.97	843.31	179.68	176.39	178.45	126.50	124.04	125.51	17,600	69.72
15	853.37	838.72	845.70	181.00	177.96	179.53	127.88	124.71	126.69	18,010	70.13
18	854.39	841.25	847.82	181.53	178.45	179.99	128.58	126.34	127.84	15,400	70.20
19	853.78	841.87	849.47	182.20	178.85	180.70	129.12	127.01	128.39	15,800	70.37
20	856.24	842.96	849.95	182.70	179.62	181.43	129.03	127.01	127.75	18,330	70.38
21	859.60	845.08	854.74	185.07	180.82	184.45	128.67	126.28	127.43	19,060	70.65
22	866.58	854.46	861.31	188.39	183.74	186.95	128.48	125.77	126.95	21,680	70.78
25	870.48	855.28	865.62	188.24	185.01	186.51	127.75	125.10	126.02	19,050	70.84
26	873.84	859.19	866.79	189.32	185.41	187.53	126.98	124.84	125.54	21,380	71.09
27	867.47	853.85	860.83	190.27	184.54	187.75	125.83	123.47	124.36	20,640	71.14
28	869.11	853.92	865.14	191.35	187.07	190.15	125.00	123.21	124.23	18,840	71.10
29	873.49	860.15	868.50	193.17	188.85	192.06	125.35	123.18	124.30	20,960	71.09
		High	868.50			192.06			128.39		71.14
		Low	830.57			169.70			121.10		68.62

FEBRUARY, 1971

	—30 Industrials—			—20 Transportations—			—15 Utilities—			Daily Sales —000—	40 Bonds
	High	Low	Close	High	Low	Close	High	Low	Close		
1	882.19	866.03	877.81	194.27	190.76	192.40	125.38	122.99	124.33	20,650	71.31
2	882.39	868.09	874.59	193.47	189.19	191.19	125.48	123.56	124.81	22,030	71.25
3	880.61	866.51	876.23	192.95	188.85	191.47	125.16	123.21	123.95	21,680	71.44
4	880.07	868.29	874.79	193.63	189.66	192.06	124.65	122.83	123.91	20,860	71.43
5	882.67	868.22	876.57	193.75	189.69	192.58	124.62	123.02	123.79	20,480	71.52
8	885.47	870.41	882.12	195.75	191.72	194.70	124.46	122.86	123.88	25,590	71.53
9	889.17	874.79	879.79	196.74	192.52	193.20	124.78	122.73	132.59	28,250	71.55
10	884.99	869.04	881.09	193.81	190.12	192.15	124.33	122.44	123.53	19,040	71.75
11	891.02	878.77	885.34	194.58	191.47	193.57	125.19	123.08	124.23	19,260	71.71
12	894.03	881.30	888.83	196.09	193.04	195.01	126.05	123.88	125.32	18,470	71.93
16	898.14	882.26	890.06	197.44	194.03	195.38	126.47	124.46	125.48	21,350	71.70
17	894.78	879.38	887.87	196.43	193.33	194.98	126.31	124.58	125.45	18,720	71.53
18	891.16	877.67	885.06	196.55	193.23	194.80	126.50	124.23	125.10	16,650	71.43
19	886.50	875.00	878.56	195.44	192.80	193.69	125.80	123.66	124.20	17,860	71.08
22	877.05	863.29	868.98	193.81	190.55	192.24	124.27	122.09	122.76	15,840	71.10
23	875.62	861.99	870.00	194.86	191.10	193.75	123.47	121.17	122.06	15,080	71.08
24	881.37	868.29	875.62	197.57	193.44	195.75	122.89	121.39	121.90	15,930	71.24
25	887.53	871.92	881.98	199.23	195.01	196.98	122.86	121.04	121.90	16,200	71.33
26	886.36	870.55	878.83	198.25	195.38	196.40	122.44	120.46	121.42	17,250	71.29
		High	890.06			196.98			125.48		71.93
		Low	868.98			191.19			121.42		71.08

MARCH, 1971

	—30 Industrials—			—60 Transportations—			—15 Utilities—			Daily Sales —000—	40 Bonds
	High	Low	Close	High	Low	Close	High	Low	Close		
1	887.46	873.22	882.53	197.32	195.17	196.49	122.06	120.49	121.29	13,020	71.18
2	887.94	875.27	883.01	198.21	195.63	196.98	122.25	120.11	121.01	14,870	70.92
3	888.55	876.85	882.39	199.01	195.81	197.48	122.16	120.24	121.58	14,680	70.96
4	894.92	878.01	891.36	200.92	196.34	200.00	122.99	120.78	122.03	17,350	70.86
5	903.61	889.24	898.00	204.03	199.85	203.23	123.08	121.29	122.12	22,430	70.72
8	905.19	891.43	898.62	204.80	201.51	202.86	123.47	121.49	122.67	19,340	70.78
9	906.15	892.25	899.10	203.91	200.37	201.48	123.66	121.77	122.32	20,490	70.80
10	902.59	891.50	895.88	202.62	199.42	200.74	123.31	121.49	122.12	17,220	70.91
11	906.76	890.81	899.44	203.02	199.85	201.29	123.66	121.64	122.89	19,830	71.10
12	903.14	892.25	898.34	203.08	199.45	202.03	123.98	122.16	123.05	14,680	71.10
15	911.21	895.33	908.20	204.34	200.92	203.69	124.62	122.44	124.27	18,920	71.29
16	920.93	908.06	914.64	206.43	202.34	204.25	125.38	123.34	124.17	22,270	71.29
17	918.06	904.16	914.02	204.90	201.23	202.99	124.81	122.99	123.82	17,070	71.30
18	922.30	910.46	916.83	204.37	201.42	202.31	125.70	123.79	125.00	17,910	71.46
19	921.69	908.61	912.92	203.79	201.08	202.28	126.21	124.42	125.42	15,150	71.57
22	917.78	905.53	910.60	203.20	199.85	200.74	125.89	124.30	124.74	14,290	71.63
23	915.32	902.31	908.89	201.39	198.34	199.66	125.42	123.79	124.20	16,470	71.60
24	910.05	896.77	899.37	200.65	197.88	198.55	124.84	123.34	124.01	15,770	71.78
25	903.96	889.03	900.81	199.20	195.60	197.84	124.62	122.57	123.69	15,870	71.72
26	910.32	895.95	903.48	200.09	197.11	198.77	124.65	122.89	123.69	15,560	71.70
29	909.78	896.29	903.48	200.80	197.91	199.35	124.62	122.86	123.66	13,650	71.79
30	909.99	896.78	903.39	200.99	197.81	199.75	124.58	122.57	123.56	15,430	71.75
31	910.98	898.33	904.37	201.45	198.68	200.00	123.95	122.32	122.83	17,610	71.76
	High 916.83					204.25			125.42		71.79
	Low 882.39					196.49			121.01		70.72

APRIL, 1971

	—30 Industrials—			—20 Transportations—			—15 Utilities—			Daily Sales —000—	40 Bonds
	High	Low	Close	High	Low	Close	High	Low	Close		
1	910.06	898.75	903.88	202.92	199.69	201.54	123.66	122.22	123.02	13,470	71.73
2	910.06	898.96	903.04	203.63	200.06	201.72	123.82	122.06	122.92	14,520	71.81
5	909.99	897.48	905.07	203.36	200.86	202.31	123.72	121.84	123.05	16,040	71.94
6	917.79	901.77	912.73	205.67	202.03	204.59	124.27	122.38	123.21	19,990	71.98
7	925.59	908.94	918.49	208.62	204.25	207.48	125.03	122.76	124.14	22,270	71.92
8	925.94	911.68	920.39	209.82	206.50	208.87	124.81	123.08	123.69	17,590	71.82
12	932.83	917.02	926.64	212.90	207.91	212.01	124.62	122.83	123.72	19,410	71.85
13	935.99	921.51	927.28	217.30	212.68	215.33	124.55	122.73	123.66	23,200	71.78
14	937.96	921.51	932.55	219.33	214.16	218.01	124.90	122.89	124.01	19,440	71.78
15	945.69	930.44	938.17	221.71	216.78	219.24	125.06	123.05	124.20	22,540	71.85
16	945.55	932.55	940.21	220.78	216.23	218.23	124.90	123.08	124.01	18,280	71.72
19	953.49	939.01	948.85	219.52	216.59	218.01	125.16	123.56	124.27	17,730	71.68
20	952.43	940.49	944.42	219.64	216.10	217.58	125.10	123.31	124.04	17,880	71.74
21	949.20	933.39	941.33	220.32	215.98	218.84	124.46	122.73	123.08	17,040	71.59
22	947.65	932.97	940.63	226.91	217.70	224.29	123.75	122.06	122.64	19,270	71.41
23	952.92	934.87	947.79	227.03	222.26	225.40	123.27	121.17	122.28	20,150	71.38
26	953.20	937.46	944.00	228.82	223.95	227.46	122.67	120.65	121.77	18,860	71.31
27	953.63	935.22	947.09	231.83	225.34	230.48	122.76	120.94	121.77	21,250	71.36
28	958.12	941.82	950.82	235.01	227.83	232.79	122.76	120.85	121.71	24,820	71.33
29	957.35	941.75	948.15	234.70	228.39	230.30	122.06	120.02	120.43	20,340	71.13
30	951.31	936.20	941.75	229.83	224.48	225.89	121.13	118.96	119.79	17,490	71.12
	High 950.82					232.79			124.27		71.98
	Low 903.04					201.54			119.79		71.12

MAY, 1971

	30 Industrials			20 Transportations			15 Utilities			Daily Sales —000—	40 Bonds
	High	Low	Close	High	Low	Close	High	Low	Close		
3	942.17	923.83	932.41	227.52	222.08	225.80	120.24	118.19	119.22	16,120	71.24
4	942.38	927.42	938.45	230.08	224.51	228.08	120.81	118.45	120.27	17,310	71.29
5	943.02	929.45	939.92	230.85	226.23	229.83	120.78	118.53	119.66	17,270	71.09
6	948.85	933.53	937.39	231.13	226.32	227.03	119.82	118.16	118.77	19,300	71.11
7	941.96	927.35	936.97	227.31	223.15	225.34	119.54	117.75	118.39	16,490	70.96
10	938.87	925.24	932.55	225.46	222.29	223.61	119.34	117.68	118.35	12,810	71.01
11	943.79	927.63	937.25	226.14	222.81	225.22	119.73	117.59	118.74	17,730	71.02
12	943.86	930.65	937.46	226.82	223.95	225.18	120.40	118.19	119.82	15,140	70.86
13	944.63	928.12	936.34	225.77	222.97	223.71	120.33	118.71	119.18	17,640	70.76
14	942.03	930.37	936.06	224.38	221.61	222.60	119.70	117.87	118.80	16,430	70.69
17	935.15	916.60	921.30	222.23	216.59	216.93	118.99	116.92	117.30	15,980	70.60
18	926.64	909.99	918.56	220.69	215.21	218.17	118.00	116.24	117.14	17,640	70.74
19	926.64	913.93	920.04	219.77	216.59	217.89	117.87	116.18	117.04	11,740	70.84
20	931.42	917.93	923.41	220.35	217.06	218.75	118.10	116.28	117.49	13,340	70.84
21	927.84	917.30	921.87	219.43	216.01	216.56	118.45	116.79	117.40	12,090	70.85
24	923.69	911.05	913.15	216.59	213.89	214.50	118.61	116.31	117.43	12,060	70.75
25	913.86	898.61	906.69	214.87	211.02	213.08	117.27	114.90	115.70	16,050	70.69
26	914.91	901.07	906.41	216.29	212.65	214.50	116.56	114.39	115.32	13,550	70.58
27	911.96	899.94	905.78	218.29	214.07	217.73	115.57	113.66	114.62	12,610	70.48
28	912.24	900.58	907.81	219.00	216.10	217.40	115.35	113.59	114.42	11,760	70.38
		High	939.92			229.83			120.27		71.29
		Low	905.78			213.08			114.42		70.38

JUNE, 1971

	30 Industrials			20 Transportations			15 Utilities			Daily Sales —000—	40 Bonds
	High	Low	Close	High	Low	Close	High	Low	Close		
1	918.49	903.74	913.65	219.12	216.29	218.29	115.13	113.05	113.69	11,930	70.41
2	925.31	911.96	919.62	224.78	218.17	223.65	114.81	112.89	113.88	17,740	70.49
3	929.60	914.63	921.30	227.36	222.98	225.42	114.87	112.95	113.82	18,790	70.61
4	926.78	915.40	922.15	227.26	223.65	225.69	114.93	113.34	114.33	14,400	70.67
7	928.54	917.44	923.06	227.26	224.02	224.95	114.84	113.11	113.62	13,800	70.65
8	925.89	911.95	915.01	225.25	222.35	223.18	114.20	112.63	113.11	13,610	70.68
9	919.54	905.74	912.46	223.82	220.44	222.28	113.85	112.15	113.15	14,250	70.71
10	921.00	907.78	915.96	223.35	220.95	221.71	114.26	112.60	113.50	12,450	70.71
11	923.70	909.68	916.47	224.25	221.11	223.08	114.42	112.92	113.94	12,270	70.63
14	917.79	904.13	907.71	223.18	219.64	220.55	114.52	113.08	113.88	11,530	70.66
15	915.23	899.39	907.20	222.01	219.04	220.58	114.84	112.99	113.78	13,550	70.59
16	915.52	901.29	908.59	221.81	218.41	219.94	114.71	112.92	113.98	14,300	70.57
17	915.08	902.16	906.25	221.21	217.77	219.21	116.18	113.56	115.13	13,980	70.49
18	906.47	887.63	889.16	219.24	212.46	213.77	115.80	114.10	114.39	15,040	70.49
21	890.48	872.74	876.53	214.43	209.79	211.36	115.13	113.11	113.37	16,490	70.50
22	884.56	866.31	874.42	213.13	208.99	210.69	114.93	113.05	113.88	15,200	70.36
23	886.61	870.04	879.45	213.33	210.63	212.53	114.84	112.92	114.26	12,640	70.21
24	885.44	872.01	877.26	213.30	210.29	210.99	115.19	113.53	114.46	11,360	70.17
25	882.45	870.04	876.68	212.03	208.26	210.33	115.61	114.01	114.78	10,580	70.22
28	879.53	866.82	873.10	210.49	207.52	208.89	115.83	114.17	115.25	9,810	70.27
29	887.63	871.20	882.30	213.83	209.26	212.83	117.59	115.03	117.17	14,460	70.15
30	895.66	881.28	891.14	217.31	212.73	215.60	119.18	117.04	118.45	15,410	69.94
		High	923.06			225.69			118.45		70.71
		Low	873.10			208.89			113.11		69.94

JULY, 1971

	—30 Industrials—			—20 Transportations—			—15 Utilities—			Daily Sales —000—	40 Bonds
	High	Low	Close	High	Low	Close	High	Low	Close		
1	899.39	886.24	893.03	217.17	214.07	215.13	119.82	117.65	118.55	13,090	69.99
2	895.52	885.73	890.19	216.54	213.90	215.70	119.57	117.49	118.32	9,960	70.02
6	896.83	885.29	892.30	217.11	214.37	215.50	119.70	117.65	118.71	10,440	70.07
7	903.18	888.87	895.88	219.31	215.00	217.94	120.21	118.00	119.41	14,520	70.01
8	906.10	894.20	900.99	220.58	216.74	219.21	120.21	118.74	119.63	13,920	69.96
9	908.73	896.69	901.80	221.38	218.27	219.98	120.59	118.74	119.92	12,640	69.92
12	908.81	896.47	903.40	221.71	219.18	220.21	120.69	118.83	119.66	12,020	70.10
13	906.47	888.80	892.38	220.31	216.50	217.04	120.46	118.58	119.09	13,540	70.13
14	895.88	882.52	891.21	217.57	215.24	217.01	119.34	117.49	118.48	14,360	70.12
15	901.43	885.00	888.87	219.51	215.64	217.37	119.57	117.87	118.45	13,080	70.13
16	898.73	884.71	888.51	219.84	216.34	217.17	119.50	117.81	118.45	13,870	70.17
19	893.47	879.23	886.39	217.41	213.87	214.83	119.12	117.59	118.13	11,430	70.26
20	896.90	885.15	892.30	217.57	213.43	216.17	118.87	117.20	118.13	12,540	70.40
21	896.54	886.61	890.84	217.34	214.30	215.10	119.22	117.59	118.19	11,920	70.36
22	893.55	882.74	886.68	216.80	212.70	214.43	118.77	117.17	117.84	12,570	70.46
23	893.03	880.33	887.78	216.14	213.53	214.83	118.58	116.98	117.46	12,370	70.34
26	895.15	882.96	888.87	216.00	212.86	213.93	118.45	116.95	117.65	9,930	70.40
27	891.28	877.04	880.70	213.93	209.99	210.33	118.51	116.95	117.36	11,560	70.31
28	882.16	868.36	872.01	211.13	206.72	208.06	117.94	116.12	116.63	13,940	70.16
29	873.03	856.97	861.42	209.72	205.58	207.49	116.72	114.71	115.35	14,570	70.22
30	868.50	854.41	858.43	208.89	205.58	206.39	116.40	114.46	115.09	12,970	70.22
		High	903.40			220.21			119.92		70.46
		Low	858.43			206.39			115.09		69.92

AUGUST, 1971

	—30 Industrials—			—20 Transportations—			—15 Utilities—			Daily Sales —000—	40 Bonds
	High	Low	Close	High	Low	Close	High	Low	Close		
2	871.86	857.70	864.92	210.83	206.35	209.66	116.34	114.78	115.32	11,870	70.28
3	865.87	845.94	850.03	210.03	205.15	205.55	115.83	114.01	114.74	13,490	70.24
4	857.70	840.10	844.92	207.52	202.41	203.61	114.84	112.79	113.24	15,410	70.19
5	855.72	841.19	849.45	206.29	203.01	205.45	114.07	112.38	112.73	12,100	70.15
6	855.94	844.70	850.61	207.15	204.88	205.98	113.59	112.15	112.83	9,490	70.27
9	853.46	839.52	842.65	206.65	204.45	205.12	113.34	111.74	111.93	8,110	70.13
10	846.82	834.92	839.59	206.15	203.95	205.05	112.70	111.36	112.15	9,460	69.97
11	851.12	836.96	846.38	209.96	204.41	209.26	113.24	111.45	112.38	11,370	69.86
12	863.46	848.57	859.01	214.80	210.16	213.83	113.78	111.96	113.15	15,910	69.95
13	864.41	851.64	856.02	216.10	212.63	214.23	113.69	112.35	113.02	9,960	69.92
16	906.32	882.59	888.95	229.43	221.95	225.22	117.30	114.42	115.16	31,730	70.02
17	908.66	885.29	899.90	228.99	222.38	226.82	115.99	113.85	114.42	26,790	70.33
18	901.36	882.08	886.17	229.53	224.15	227.02	114.84	113.27	113.69	20,680	70.35
19	889.68	873.90	880.77	232.03	225.52	230.53	114.68	112.79	113.53	14,190	70.48
20	887.27	874.93	880.91	234.40	230.13	232.60	114.07	112.44	113.31	11,890	70.59
23	897.20	880.99	892.38	238.08	232.03	237.04	114.39	112.63	113.53	13,040	70.61
24	909.02	892.09	904.13	244.29	236.61	241.18	114.49	113.02	113.75	18,700	70.52
25	917.79	901.80	908.37	244.89	239.48	242.32	114.42	112.89	113.50	18,280	70.61
26	914.06	898.88	906.10	244.56	239.31	241.55	114.23	112.09	112.89	13,990	70.67
27	915.45	902.02	908.15	243.49	239.75	241.82	113.62	111.96	113.05	12,490	70.85
30	912.53	898.51	901.43	243.59	238.98	240.22	113.40	111.87	112.28	11,140	70.74
31	903.84	892.01	898.07	241.08	237.88	239.51	112.51	111.00	111.68	10,430	70.73
		High	908.37			242.32			115.32		70.85
		Low	839.59			203.61			111.68		69.86

SEPTEMBER, 1971

	—30 Industrials—			—20 Transportations—			—15 Utilities—			Daily Sales —000—	40 Bonds
	High	Low	Close	High	Low	Close	High	Low	Close		
1	906.25	894.20	899.02	242.79	238.41	240.82	112.47	110.91	111.52	10,770	70.80
2	905.37	893.84	900.63	243.22	240.01	241.58	112.28	111.00	111.71	10,690	70.97
3	914.06	899.53	912.75	246.56	241.48	245.99	113.02	111.00	112.70	14,040	71.06
7	925.67	909.75	916.47	250.67	245.16	248.33	114.55	112.44	113.50	17,080	71.17
8	925.67	911.87	920.93	249.33	244.96	246.83	114.23	112.83	113.62	14,230	71.24
9	925.23	912.38	915.89	248.83	244.96	246.43	114.04	112.09	112.63	15,790	71.36
10	916.84	904.42	911.00	247.06	243.69	245.52	113.40	111.96	112.73	11,380	71.35
13	915.67	903.91	909.39	246.13	242.59	243.89	113.37	111.68	112.38	10,000	71.49
14	911.73	898.58	901.65	244.62	241.12	241.88	113.02	111.36	111.96	11,410	71.44
15	907.71	896.25	904.86	243.19	239.81	241.92	112.63	111.13	112.22	11,080	71.27
16	908.81	898.66	903.11	243.05	240.42	241.58	112.35	110.59	111.00	10,550	71.21
17	912.16	901.07	908.22	244.16	240.92	242.62	111.87	110.40	111.32	11,020	71.23
20	911.29	900.19	905.15	243.32	240.75	241.65	111.90	110.49	110.94	9,540	71.28
21	907.78	897.78	903.40	242.82	239.91	241.12	111.45	110.05	110.78	10,640	71.02
22	904.94	891.72	893.55	241.99	238.95	239.91	111.16	109.60	109.89	14,250	70.99
23	899.39	884.64	891.28	240.82	237.04	239.71	110.69	108.86	109.69	13,250	70.99
24	900.26	886.24	889.31	240.35	236.34	237.01	110.59	108.86	109.50	13,460	70.95
27	891.72	877.48	883.47	237.21	234.00	234.77	109.98	108.58	109.18	10,220	70.99
28	891.50	877.77	884.42	236.61	233.07	235.01	110.05	108.61	109.38	11,250	71.06
29	890.41	877.70	883.83	236.68	233.90	235.67	110.01	108.74	109.28	8,580	71.06
30	894.13	878.14	887.19	238.41	234.60	237.18	110.05	108.74	109.31	13,490	71.10
		High	920.93			248.33			113.62		71.49
		Low	883.47			234.77			109.18		70.80

OCTOBER, 1971

	—30 Industrials—			—20 Transportations—			—15 Utilities—			Daily Sales —000—	40 Bonds
	High	Low	Close	High	Low	Close	High	Low	Close		
1	898.44	884.49	893.98	239.54	236.11	237.86	111.45	109.28	110.91	13,400	71.07
4	904.42	892.01	895.66	240.68	237.00	239.36	112.44	110.84	111.87	14,570	71.11
5	898.66	885.81	891.14	241.11	237.86	239.68	112.67	111.32	111.96	12,360	71.23
6	902.38	886.90	900.55	242.68	237.93	241.79	113.46	111.68	113.18	15,630	71.22
7	910.56	896.10	901.80	245.00	240.64	242.82	114.81	112.95	114.14	17,780	71.30
8	902.82	890.55	893.91	244.46	240.00	241.89	115.25	113.37	114.39	13,870	71.48
11	896.39	886.32	891.94	242.79	239.96	241.86	115.54	114.20	115.19	7,800	71.52
12	899.61	888.29	893.55	245.82	240.93	244.21	116.88	114.97	116.09	14,340	71.59
13	897.12	885.22	888.80	245.75	241.21	242.64	117.30	115.38	116.40	13,540	71.70
14	889.16	875.22	878.36	242.39	238.68	239.54	117.08	115.38	115.96	12,870	71.78
15	881.64	868.50	874.58	239.82	235.57	237.54	116.60	115.09	115.86	13,120	71.75
18	880.40	868.87	872.44	238.86	235.79	236.68	116.28	114.55	114.78	10,420	71.78
19	874.34	860.11	868.43	237.21	232.50	234.82	115.45	113.88	114.65	13,040	71.82
20	873.39	851.20	855.65	236.29	230.75	232.54	115.48	113.78	114.04	16,340	71.93
21	861.05	846.45	854.85	235.11	229.79	233.36	114.71	113.11	114.07	14,990	71.87
22	863.90	848.57	852.37	237.21	231.54	232.64	114.87	113.21	113.78	14,560	72.01
25	854.63	843.38	848.50	233.29	230.21	231.86	114.30	112.76	113.56	7,340	72.12
26	857.26	842.95	845.36	235.32	230.43	231.32	114.01	111.93	112.54	13,390	72.30
27	846.31	832.29	836.38	231.86	226.79	227.50	113.02	111.52	112.06	13,480	72.37
28	844.63	827.83	837.62	230.04	224.25	227.86	112.67	111.00	111.55	15,530	72.31
29	843.03	831.85	839.00	230.43	226.07	229.21	112.70	110.62	111.90	11,710	72.23
		High	901.80			244.21			116.40		72.37
		Low	836.38			227.50			110.91		71.07

NOVEMBER, 1971

	—30 Industrials—			—20 Transportations—			—15 Utilities—			Daily Sales —000—	40 Bonds
	High	Low	Close	High	Low	Close	High	Low	Close		
1	840.25	823.21	825.86	229.75	222.86	223.32	112.51	110.84	111.29	10,960	72.24
2	833.53	814.69	827.98	225.04	220.39	223.39	112.12	110.62	111.32	13,330	72.24
3	845.87	828.34	842.58	228.96	223.04	228.57	113.08	111.20	112.38	14,590	72.43
4	855.21	838.49	843.17	232.07	227.54	229.14	113.85	111.96	112.86	15,750	72.45
5	845.94	832.94	840.39	230.11	226.86	229.32	113.53	112.03	112.76	10,780	72.59
8	843.60	832.51	837.54	230.71	227.93	229.57	113.40	112.15	112.54	8,520	72.58
9	845.72	832.21	837.91	232.21	228.39	229.64	113.72	112.31	113.15	12,080	72.65
10	842.22	821.85	826.15	230.43	225.96	226.79	113.34	111.48	111.93	13,410	72.56
11	827.91	810.82	814.91	226.57	221.71	222.93	112.51	110.75	111.61	13,310	72.61
12	821.12	802.21	812.94	224.39	220.21	223.04	112.44	110.46	111.42	14,540	72.62
15	820.68	806.66	810.53	224.64	220.71	221.68	112.06	110.24	110.91	9,370	72.68
16	823.89	806.59	818.71	222.29	216.43	221.25	112.00	109.69	111.29	13,300	72.52
17	825.79	812.13	822.14	223.11	218.57	221.50	112.12	110.40	111.29	12,840	72.57
18	829.66	813.81	815.35	222.71	217.96	218.75	112.15	110.56	111.07	13,010	72.47
19	817.98	804.83	810.67	219.54	214.61	215.82	111.58	110.08	110.91	12,420	72.46
22	817.03	800.89	803.15	217.29	211.25	211.82	111.23	109.41	109.85	11,390	72.59
23	807.10	790.67	797.97	212.07	206.00	208.43	109.57	107.62	108.42	16,840	72.57
24	807.90	793.88	798.63	210.86	206.79	208.96	109.18	107.55	108.03	11,870	72.55
26	818.12	799.87	816.59	214.82	208.50	214.18	109.44	107.59	108.86	10,870	72.52
29	838.57	815.79	829.73	222.71	215.68	220.61	110.14	108.70	109.44	18,910	72.56
30	837.03	819.22	831.34	223.54	217.54	222.32	110.75	108.86	110.37	18,320	72.75
		High	843.17			229.64			113.15		72.75
		Low	797.97			208.43			108.03		72.24

DECEMBER, 1971

	—30 Industrials—			—20 Transportations—			—15 Utilities—			Daily Sales —000—	40 Bonds
	High	Low	Close	High	Low	Close	High	Low	Close		
1	851.85	831.12	846.01	229.50	222.96	228.11	111.36	109.47	110.46	21,040	72.67
2	854.70	837.47	848.79	231.50	226.28	228.94	111.71	109.98	110.91	17,780	72.54
3	864.05	845.58	859.59	233.07	227.96	231.71	112.54	110.59	111.80	16,760	72.55
6	872.59	852.58	855.72	236.08	231.20	232.46	112.60	110.43	110.78	17,480	72.55
7	862.44	845.28	857.40	236.52	230.48	235.70	111.16	109.63	110.27	15,250	72.55
8	861.71	847.91	854.85	238.60	234.71	236.69	111.36	109.79	110.56	16,650	72.73
9	858.43	844.55	852.15	238.94	234.68	238.02	111.55	109.73	110.10	14,710	72.70
10	861.86	847.69	856.75	240.96	236.55	238.81	112.54	110.53	111.74	17,510	72.76
13	868.28	852.22	858.79	241.23	236.83	238.81	112.63	110.97	111.71	17,020	72.86
14	864.92	851.12	855.14	240.24	236.21	237.27	112.31	110.78	111.48	16,070	73.09
15	867.84	849.81	863.76	239.32	235.02	238.33	111.80	110.33	111.10	16,890	72.93
16	878.69	863.26	871.39	241.33	238.16	239.22	112.44	110.40	111.55	21,070	72.89
17	879.29	865.29	873.80	241.37	237.34	239.39	112.28	110.49	111.48	18,270	72.89
20	895.17	876.28	885.01	244.20	239.18	241.33	113.02	111.26	112.25	23,810	72.98
21	896.22	875.30	888.32	242.97	238.60	241.13	112.92	111.55	112.41	20,460	73.03
22	893.81	878.54	884.86	242.94	238.64	239.80	113.05	111.61	112.15	18,930	72.96
23	889.98	873.34	881.17	240.62	236.86	238.88	113.18	111.59	112.38	16,000	73.03
27	889.83	875.68	881.47	240.58	237.34	238.53	113.94	112.38	113.50	11,890	73.12
28	892.84	877.18	889.98	241.37	237.78	240.68	115.29	113.15	114.81	15,090	73.14
29	902.47	886.59	893.66	243.58	239.59	241.47	116.98	114.87	116.53	17,150	73.23
30	898.78	883.05	889.07	244.13	240.17	242.83	117.43	115.70	116.79	13,810	73.29
31	895.77	884.48	890.20	245.12	241.43	243.72	118.23	116.05	117.75	14,040	73.29
		High	893.66			243.72			117.75		73.29
		Low	846.01			228.11			110.27		72.54

JANUARY, 1972

	—30 Industrials—			—20 Transportations—			—15 Utilities—			Daily Sales —000—	40 Bonds
	High	Low	Close	High	Low	Close	High	Low	Close		
3	898.71	884.63	889.30	245.97	241.64	243.14	118.51	117.08	117.62	12,570	73.43
4	897.73	882.75	892.23	245.43	241.64	244.51	118.61	116.88	118.26	15,190	73.41
5	910.07	893.06	904.43	248.29	243.89	246.49	119.44	117.62	118.61	21,350	73.53
6	913.83	901.87	908.49	248.64	244.37	245.73	119.89	117.84	119.12	21,100	73.84
7	916.47	903.37	910.37	247.24	244.10	245.63	120.30	118.61	119.34	17,140	73.77
10	914.43	898.48	907.96	247.17	243.52	245.80	120.59	119.22	120.24	15,320	73.80
11	919.02	903.67	912.10	248.60	244.71	247.47	121.39	119.79	120.85	17,970	73.91
12	922.03	906.01	910.82	251.40	246.69	249.08	122.16	120.21	121.13	20,970	74.06
13	912.93	899.98	905.18	249.04	244.92	246.45	121.52	119.66	120.21	16,410	74.11
14	901.82	899.16	906.68	249.52	245.29	248.50	121.55	119.73	120.69	14,960	74.12
17	914.51	902.77	911.12	252.53	248.46	251.60	121.52	119.76	120.62	15,860	74.07
18	923.99	908.94	917.22	257.34	251.88	254.50	121.29	119.31	119.98	21,070	74.17
19	922.34	904.58	914.96	255.94	250.89	254.47	120.62	118.64	119.76	18,800	74.26
20	922.19	906.76	910.30	256.18	251.64	252.97	120.56	118.55	118.90	20,210	74.18
21	913.91	898.93	907.44	253.72	249.42	251.71	119.06	117.11	118.03	18,810	74.15
24	911.20	893.81	896.82	252.32	248.26	249.42	118.61	116.79	117.30	15,640	74.24
25	902.17	887.49	894.72	252.12	246.28	250.44	117.87	116.12	116.85	17,570	74.13
26	897.65	883.43	889.15	252.59	248.87	251.06	117.65	116.02	117.04	14,940	74.25
27	902.92	887.87	899.83	255.53	249.97	254.40	118.00	116.15	117.30	20,360	74.31
28	913.23	896.60	906.38	258.53	253.72	256.76	118.23	116.21	117.17	25,000	74.22
31	911.20	897.05	902.17	259.08	254.16	256.76	117.78	115.93	116.72	18,250	74.06
		High	917.22			256.76			121.13		74.31
		Low	889.15			243.14			116.72		73.41

FEBRUARY, 1972

	—30 Industrials—			—20 Transportations—			—15 Utilities—			Daily Sales —000—	20 Bonds
	High	Low	Close	High	Low	Close	High	Low	Close		
1	906.23	894.34	901.79	257.99	254.57	256.18	117.30	115.41	115.80	19,600	74.12
2	913.76	896.15	905.85	259.01	253.14	255.36	116.47	114.81	115.57	24,070	74.04
3	910.97	896.30	903.15	257.23	251.95	254.71	116.50	114.42	115.19	19,880	74.12
4	912.10	897.50	906.68	257.30	252.59	256.01	115.73	114.33	114.87	17,890	73.96
7	913.61	898.93	903.97	257.51	253.79	254.78	115.38	113.72	114.52	16,930	73.90
8	910.97	898.18	907.13	255.53	251.84	253.96	115.03	113.59	114.23	17,390	73.90
9	921.81	905.18	918.72	255.94	252.56	254.98	114.81	113.37	114.17	19,850	73.89
10	931.89	914.89	921.28	258.80	253.86	256.48	114.97	113.21	113.66	23,460	73.92
11	924.82	910.52	917.59	257.81	254.06	255.70	113.78	111.77	112.57	17,850	73.92
14	921.96	906.01	910.90	256.58	252.77	253.91	113.05	111.52	112.22	15,840	73.98
15	920.98	906.46	914.51	254.48	250.85	252.49	112.86	111.13	111.71	17,770	73.90
16	928.58	911.65	922.94	255.90	251.17	254.59	112.47	110.65	111.42	20,670	73.88
17	933.25	916.84	922.03	257.72	253.88	255.09	112.92	111.00	111.87	22,330	74.04
18	925.35	911.12	917.52	256.79	253.31	254.73	112.70	111.20	112.25	16,590	74.10
22	922.86	909.17	913.46	258.11	253.52	255.58	113.56	111.55	112.79	16,670	74.13
23	919.85	906.98	911.88	257.61	253.34	254.98	113.37	111.93	112.47	16,770	74.03
24	919.25	906.61	912.70	257.01	253.02	255.09	113.53	112.00	112.95	16,000	74.01
25	927.75	909.39	922.79	258.04	253.77	256.05	114.01	112.47	113.59	18,180	74.07
28	930.31	917.14	924.29	258.39	254.16	255.69	114.17	112.51	112.99	18,200	74.03
29	932.34	916.24	928.13	257.29	253.73	255.62	113.98	112.35	113.34	20,320	74.22
		High	928.13			256.48			115.80		74.22
		Low	901.79			252.49			111.42		73.88

MARCH, 1972

	—30 Industrials—			—20 Transportations—			—15 Utilities—			Daily Sales —000—	20 Bonds
	High	Low	Close	High	Low	Close	High	Low	Close		
1	943.03	924.14	935.43	258.75	254.52	256.65	114.20	112.51	113.21	23,670	74.26
2	943.78	927.90	933.77	259.85	255.33	257.25	114.01	112.57	113.15	22,200	74.27
3	948.00	930.69	942.43	260.42	255.90	258.71	114.81	112.73	114.23	20,420	74.24
6	957.03	940.47	950.18	263.44	257.86	262.06	115.83	113.94	115.29	21,000	74.13
7	956.20	940.40	946.87	256.15	259.67	262.09	116.60	114.93	115.83	22,640	74.16
8	953.57	937.09	945.59	264.65	259.99	262.34	116.50	115.06	115.80	21,290	74.23
9	950.78	937.61	942.81	264.58	260.78	262.62	116.40	114.68	115.48	21,460	74.38
10	948.60	932.95	939.87	263.34	259.46	260.63	116.12	114.58	115.41	19,690	74.35
13	941.23	924.22	928.66	263.23	258.57	261.20	115.96	114.20	115.06	16,730	74.35
14	938.82	925.35	934.00	262.94	259.28	261.24	115.67	114.20	115.09	22,370	74.22
15	945.44	929.18	937.31	263.83	260.03	261.42	115.83	114.46	115.19	19,460	74.27
16	942.88	927.68	936.71	262.87	258.07	259.46	115.83	114.36	115.06	16,700	74.29
17	949.88	931.52	942.88	261.52	257.50	259.82	116.24	114.71	115.70	16,040	74.20
20	951.84	937.31	941.15	261.59	257.54	258.68	116.53	114.84	115.54	16,420	74.25
21	940.32	925.95	934.00	258.39	253.13	254.98	115.73	113.94	114.36	18,610	74.14
22	938.59	926.78	933.93	258.50	254.45	256.79	114.84	113.24	114.17	15,400	74.22
23	949.20	932.34	944.69	261.02	256.65	259.28	114.84	113.50	114.36	18,380	74.19
24	950.03	937.91	942.28	262.41	258.53	259.92	114.55	112.63	113.24	15,390	74.13
27	946.57	933.77	939.72	260.60	257.47	258.96	114.14	111.96	112.67	12,180	74.21
28	947.02	932.65	937.01	260.63	257.33	258.96	113.53	111.84	112.09	15,380	74.08
29	940.17	925.87	933.02	259.53	256.15	256.58	112.99	111.58	112.15	13,860	74.09
30	943.78	929.79	940.70	259.89	256.40	258.93	113.05	111.55	112.47	14,360	74.09
		High	950.18			262.62			115.83		74.38
		Low	928.66			254.98			112.09		74.08

APRIL, 1972

	—30 Industrials—			—20 Transportations—			—15 Utilities—			Daily Sales —000—	20 Bonds
	High	Low	Close	High	Low	Close	High	Low	Close		
3	948.75	935.66	940.92	261.91	258.25	260.74	113.05	111.16	112.00	14,990	74.20
4	948.52	933.62	943.41	267.46	259.71	266.82	112.83	111.32	112.00	18,110	74.21
5	958.99	943.33	954.55	272.19	267.12	270.59	112.79	111.00	111.71	22,960	74.10
6	968.24	951.76	959.44	275.60	270.16	274.43	112.57	110.97	111.68	22,830	74.04
7	965.91	950.26	962.60	276.60	272.80	275.71	112.86	111.20	112.19	19,900	74.15
10	970.57	953.42	958.08	277.70	274.18	275.07	112.86	111.16	111.90	19,470	74.17
11	967.79	951.23	962.60	276.78	274.04	275.57	112.79	111.39	112.19	19,930	74.00
12	976.44	960.64	966.96	278.27	274.22	275.68	112.63	111.13	111.45	24,690	73.93
13	973.28	960.42	965.53	276.85	273.51	274.22	112.12	110.59	111.20	17,990	74.06
14	973.06	959.59	967.72	275.85	272.83	274.08	111.68	110.17	111.00	17,460	73.93
17	972.16	959.36	966.59	275.78	272.83	275.04	111.45	109.82	110.37	15,390	73.86
18	977.72	961.62	968.92	277.20	273.29	275.36	111.00	109.44	110.27	19,410	73.77
19	975.92	959.36	964.78	276.96	273.29	274.08	110.56	109.12	109.66	19,180	73.76
20	971.33	954.17	966.29	274.32	270.23	272.19	110.30	108.74	109.50	18,190	73.60
21	974.64	959.21	963.80	274.00	270.55	271.66	110.08	108.80	109.38	18,200	73.65
24	966.59	950.93	957.48	271.59	267.60	268.88	109.85	108.42	108.80	14,650	73.56
25	959.14	943.63	946.49	267.50	262.55	263.09	109.31	107.97	108.48	17,030	73.56
26	954.39	938.29	946.94	263.73	259.39	260.78	109.41	107.97	108.64	17,710	73.64
27	954.92	940.70	945.97	261.95	257.57	258.85	109.66	108.32	109.28	15,740	73.71
28	959.74	944.46	954.17	260.99	257.01	258.78	110.37	108.83	109.76	14,160	73.70
		High	968.92			275.71			112.19		74.21
		Low	940.92			258.78			108.48		73.56

MAY, 1972

	—30 Industrials—			—20 Transportations—			—15 Utilities—			Daily Sales —000—	40 Bonds
	High	Low	Close	High	Low	Close	High	Low	Close		
1	956.95	938.59	942.28	259.46	255.87	256.86	110.42	108.99	109.69	12,880	73.59
2	947.32	930.61	935.20	258.43	253.49	254.52	110.65	109.22	109.85	15,370	73.56
3	947.32	927.90	933.47	256.58	251.99	253.20	110.33	109.09	109.50	15,900	73.63
4	942.43	927.60	937.31	225.48	250.78	253.52	110.49	109.12	109.73	14,790	73.56
5	948.30	932.57	941.23	256.29	251.99	254.30	110.59	109.15	109.79	13,210	73.70
8	943.18	930.01	937.84	254.87	251.92	253.56	110.37	109.09	109.63	11,250	73.67
9	937.54	917.37	925.12	252.60	247.23	249.40	109.63	108.19	108.83	19,910	73.60
10	938.06	922.03	931.07	253.20	248.86	252.06	109.50	108.38	108.93	13,870	73.71
11	941.15	925.87	934.83	255.69	251.21	254.20	109.47	108.32	108.86	12,900	73.76
12	947.40	934.23	941.83	258.14	253.73	256.58	109.47	108.29	108.86	13,990	73.73
15	948.45	936.63	942.20	260.60	256.15	259.10	109.69	108.54	108.93	13,600	73.71
16	947.17	934.83	939.27	261.45	257.50	258.61	109.60	108.22	108.77	14,070	73.72
17	944.61	932.95	941.15	260.74	257.97	259.57	109.34	108.19	108.74	13,600	73.75
18	955.67	939.95	951.23	261.59	258.46	260.21	109.25	108.03	108.38	17,370	73.71
19	957.56	950.11	961.54	263.80	259.14	261.06	109.09	107.81	108.03	19,580	73.81
22	972.00	958.76	965.31	263.55	259.64	261.56	109.06	107.65	108.35	16,030	73.84
23	970.05	956.20	962.30	263.41	259.67	261.84	109.15	107.78	108.48	16,410	73.85
24	973.06	958.76	965.46	264.33	260.46	261.98	108.74	107.33	107.97	17,870	74.00
25	975.54	960.57	969.07	263.83	260.03	261.88	108.67	107.49	108.06	16,480	74.22
26	977.42	963.80	971.25	262.70	259.64	261.06	108.86	107.23	108.16	15,730	74.29
30	979.46	966.51	971.18	263.04	257.42	258.70	108.90	107.71	108.16	15,810	74.18
31	970.88	955.52	960.72	259.06	254.82	257.71	108.64	107.46	108.00	15,230	74.15
		High	971.25			261.98			109.85		74.29
		Low	925.12			249.40			107.97		73.56

JUNE, 1972

	—30 Industrials—			—20 Transportations—			—15 Utilities—			Daily Sales —000—	40 Bonds
	High	Low	Close	High	Low	Close	High	Low	Close		
1	966.36	954.85	960.72	258.81	255.81	257.02	108.51	107.43	107.84	14,910	74.17
2	967.72	954.24	961.39	258.26	252.45	253.84	108.54	107.17	107.87	15,400	74.22
5	964.48	948.52	954.39	253.69	247.73	249.89	108.38	107.01	107.59	13,450	74.15
6	961.02	946.87	951.46	250.91	244.63	246.02	108.10	106.91	107.52	15,980	74.18
7	952.51	938.52	944.08	247.62	242.29	244.96	107.91	106.50	107.11	15,220	74.35
8	953.19	938.82	941.30	248.90	243.53	245.07	107.68	106.63	107.01	13,820	74.44
9	942.88	930.01	934.45	246.27	243.06	244.77	107.36	106.18	106.63	12,790	74.37
12	943.63	930.39	936.71	247.66	244.30	245.83	107.11	105.70	106.21	13,390	74.34
13	943.33	928.88	938.29	247.62	243.86	245.43	106.40	105.16	105.51	15,710	74.29
14	954.24	936.11	946.79	249.05	243.17	244.74	106.37	104.87	105.48	18,320	74.33
15	956.05	940.25	945.97	247.70	243.53	244.45	106.37	104.93	105.64	16,940	74.35
16	949.88	936.94	945.06	245.72	241.08	243.35	106.18	104.71	105.38	13,010	74.33
19	947.62	935.43	941.83	244.63	241.08	242.84	105.86	104.65	105.06	11,660	74.38
20	952.14	940.10	948.22	247.55	242.22	246.05	106.15	104.58	105.51	14,970	74.55
21	959.96	943.63	951.61	248.14	243.82	245.03	106.12	104.81	105.32	15,510	74.45
22	956.58	940.02	950.71	246.35	241.96	244.26	106.15	104.77	105.67	13,410	74.46
23	957.25	939.27	944.69	245.14	241.27	241.85	106.47	105.13	105.67	13,940	74.38
26	942.50	928.13	936.41	241.78	237.69	239.81	106.47	105.00	105.92	12,720	74.40
27	943.33	928.96	935.28	241.12	236.81	237.91	106.79	104.97	105.80	13,750	74.44
28	938.14	925.80	930.84	238.53	234.47	235.46	106.72	105.32	106.24	12,140	74.28
29	932.95	917.75	926.25	235.27	230.42	232.61	107.04	105.41	106.34	14,610	74.22
30	935.81	921.21	929.03	235.02	231.18	233.30	107.46	105.89	106.63	12,860	74.19
		High	961.39			257.02			107.87		74.55
		Low	926.25			232.61			105.06		74.15

JULY, 1972

	—30 Industrials—			—20 Transportations—			—15 Utilities—			Daily Sales —000—	40 Bonds
	High	Low	Close	High	Low	Close	High	Low	Close		
3	935.05	922.71	928.66	235.79	232.61	235.02	107.75	106.08	107.36	8,140	74.25
5	939.64	926.25	933.47	238.09	234.11	236.37	108.22	107.04	107.68	14,710	74.24
6	955.45	934.90	942.13	240.50	235.06	236.22	109.15	107.52	108.45	19,520	74.23
7	948.15	932.34	938.06	237.10	233.89	235.17	108.99	107.87	108.45	12,900	74.12
10	943.03	928.73	932.27	237.50	233.09	234.06	108.99	107.62	108.13	11,700	74.20
11	934.90	921.81	925.87	233.64	229.38	230.11	108.42	107.07	107.71	12,830	74.22
12	934.15	919.33	923.69	231.58	224.16	225.47	108.26	106.82	107.27	16,150	74.17
13	926.02	912.93	916.99	228.92	222.69	226.21	107.65	106.24	107.07	14,740	74.10
14	927.83	911.88	922.26	230.27	225.20	228.26	107.43	106.12	106.82	13,910	74.10
17	928.43	912.70	914.96	230.15	225.74	226.48	107.55	106.31	106.85	13,170	74.01
18	917.97	900.06	911.72	228.26	223.46	226.94	107.23	105.89	106.50	16,820	74.03
19	927.00	909.69	916.69	230.46	225.24	226.83	107.36	105.92	106.56	17,880	74.03
20	919.40	905.55	910.45	228.37	224.58	226.32	107.23	105.60	106.44	15,050	74.06
21	923.24	903.90	920.45	230.00	224.89	229.30	107.04	105.76	106.56	14,010	74.04
24	941.98	922.19	935.36	235.11	229.88	233.44	107.23	105.86	106.69	18,020	74.13
25	946.79	930.24	934.45	235.49	230.00	231.20	107.23	105.80	106.56	17,180	74.04
26	940.92	927.60	932.57	232.44	227.87	229.34	107.36	105.92	106.82	14,130	74.06
27	938.37	923.62	926.85	230.58	225.97	227.60	107.23	105.99	106.75	13,870	74.12
28	933.93	920.15	926.70	229.81	225.67	227.56	107.11	106.08	106.66	13,050	73.86
31	932.72	917.37	924.74	228.92	225.67	227.17	107.04	105.76	106.50	11,120	73.88
		High 942.13				236.37			108.45		74.25
		Low 910.45				225.47			106.44		73.86

AUGUST, 1972

	—30 Industrials—			—20 Transportations—			—15 Utilities—			Daily Sales —000—	40 Bonds
	High	Low	Close	High	Low	Close	High	Low	Close		
1	935.36	922.03	930.46	231.43	227.10	230.46	106.88	105.67	106.56	15,540	73.87
2	944.61	931.07	941.15	234.52	230.11	233.13	107.11	106.02	106.47	17,920	73.94
3	953.19	939.12	947.70	236.23	231.86	233.48	107.46	106.18	106.88	19,970	73.95
4	957.10	942.28	951.76	234.68	231.16	233.94	107.52	106.28	106.95	15,700	74.01
7	959.36	945.67	953.12	236.38	231.74	234.68	107.62	106.18	106.75	13,220	73.88
8	958.01	944.31	952.44	236.27	232.16	234.29	107.46	106.24	106.88	14,550	73.91
9	958.99	943.86	951.16	239.44	233.94	236.65	107.39	106.24	106.82	15,730	73.97
10	958.84	945.29	952.89	238.78	234.56	237.35	107.87	106.40	107.46	15,260	74.03
11	966.59	948.75	964.18	239.83	235.65	237.62	108.16	107.14	107.78	16,570	73.93
14	980.21	964.18	973.51	240.25	234.22	236.03	108.67	107.27	108.19	18,870	74.06
15	978.33	962.30	969.97	237.35	232.16	234.45	109.18	107.59	108.58	16,670	73.99
16	974.94	958.46	964.25	235.76	230.69	232.51	109.50	108.10	109.15	14,950	73.96
17	971.25	955.60	961.39	233.79	228.99	231.24	110.05	108.48	109.41	14,360	73.97
18	972.23	957.48	965.83	233.36	230.23	232.09	110.81	109.25	110.24	16,150	74.01
21	974.19	958.16	967.19	234.10	230.35	232.47	111.74	109.60	110.81	14,290	74.04
22	979.76	963.88	973.51	235.65	231.08	234.06	112.09	110.53	111.64	18,560	74.06
23	980.36	962.60	970.35	236.85	231.82	234.72	112.70	111.86	112.06	18,670	73.98
24	974.56	955.98	958.38	235.92	231.78	232.98	112.95	111.23	111.87	18,280	73.99
25	964.86	949.80	959.36	234.60	231.35	232.78	112.35	110.88	111.42	13,840	74.19
28	964.33	952.59	956.95	234.06	230.08	231.04	112.00	110.43	110.94	10,720	74.13
29	961.62	945.29	954.70	232.36	229.07	231.20	111.48	109.92	110.69	12,300	74.15
30	964.03	951.16	957.86	233.48	230.04	231.70	111.39	109.95	110.43	12,470	74.20
31	966.89	953.57	963.73	233.36	230.04	232.40	111.23	109.89	110.56	12,340	74.15
		High 973.51				237.62			112.06		74.20
		Low 930.46				230.46			106.47		73.87

SEPTEMBER, 1972

	—30 Industrials—			—20 Transportations—			—15 Utilities—			Daily Sales —000—	40 Bonds
	High	Low	Close	High	Low	Close	High	Low	Close		
1	975.62	962.30	970.05	234.91	231.51	233.91	111.23	110.14	110.75	11,600	74.24
5	977.35	964.63	969.37	234.76	230.62	231.70	111.32	110.11	110.84	10,630	74.27
6	970.35	958.91	963.43	232.01	228.53	229.96	111.16	109.98	110.46	12,010	74.19
7	968.02	957.41	962.45	231.00	227.79	229.07	111.04	110.01	110.56	11,090	74.21
8	968.24	957.33	961.24	230.77	226.59	227.87	111.00	109.85	110.46	10,980	74.15
11	964.55	951.08	955.00	229.11	223.77	225.20	110.65	109.53	110.05	10,710	74.19
12	957.86	940.62	946.04	225.86	221.53	223.07	110.46	109.09	109.60	13,560	74.20
13	954.09	941.30	949.88	224.35	220.67	222.96	110.11	108.83	109.31	13,070	74.13
14	955.30	942.05	947.55	224.85	220.60	222.03	109.85	108.80	109.31	12,500	73.97
15	952.29	940.62	947.32	222.76	219.55	221.22	109.76	108.74	109.25	11,690	74.00
18	951.16	938.67	945.36	222.80	219.32	221.26	109.50	108.67	109.02	8,880	73.93
19	952.44	939.12	943.18	224.23	220.33	221.84	109.57	108.16	108.54	13,330	74.04
20	946.12	934.75	940.25	222.88	219.05	220.64	109.53	108.16	108.77	11,980	73.89
21	945.44	932.72	939.49	221.99	218.47	219.86	109.69	108.22	109.02	11,940	73.93
22	948.98	934.38	943.03	221.60	217.70	219.05	109.92	108.77	109.44	12,570	73.86
25	947.47	933.10	935.73	219.75	215.34	216.23	110.21	108.80	109.38	10,920	73.83
26	942.13	927.15	936.56	218.51	214.25	216.15	110.14	108.80	109.53	13,150	73.79
27	949.05	932.95	947.25	220.21	215.03	219.55	110.49	109.02	109.89	14,620	73.84
28	956.88	939.87	955.15	219.75	215.03	217.85	111.00	109.73	110.56	14,710	73.89
29	965.08	949.05	953.27	220.79	216.26	217.70	111.10	109.85	110.56	16,250	73.87
		High	970.05			233.91			110.84		74.27
		Low	935.73			216.15			108.54		73.79

OCTOBER, 1972

	—30 Industrials—			—20 Transportations—			—15 Utilities—			Daily Sales —000—	20 Bonds
	High	Low	Close	High	Low	Close	High	Low	Close		
2	959.59	945.44	953.27	219.98	215.14	217.62	111.45	109.85	110.72	12,440	73.89
3	959.96	948.22	954.47	218.39	214.72	215.92	111.55	110.24	111.23	13,090	74.01
4	964.10	947.85	951.31	218.59	213.67	215.57	112.09	110.65	111.48	16,640	73.96
5	955.67	937.54	941.30	217.23	213.32	214.14	112.31	111.10	111.58	17,730	73.98
6	954.39	930.39	945.36	217.93	212.36	215.84	112.38	110.94	111.90	16,630	74.03
9	952.21	941.00	948.75	217.77	215.30	216.77	112.41	111.42	112.19	7,940	74.04
10	960.49	946.34	951.84	220.17	216.26	217.70	112.60	111.20	112.06	13,310	74.10
11	956.05	941.60	946.42	218.62	215.26	215.88	112.63	111.42	111.96	11,900	74.19
12	947.10	932.42	937.46	216.73	213.13	214.37	112.35	111.23	111.68	13,130	74.29
13	940.17	923.77	930.46	215.92	212.94	214.83	111.96	111.10	111.36	12,870	74.29
16	934.53	919.25	921.66	216.23	213.32	213.90	111.96	110.81	111.42	10,940	74.24
17	931.29	917.07	926.48	215.88	212.82	214.45	112.31	111.20	112.00	13,410	74.13
18	940.85	925.80	932.34	218.24	214.33	215.80	112.89	111.52	112.22	17,290	74.16
19	939.27	926.70	932.12	216.96	212.12	213.48	113.15	112.12	112.70	13,850	74.28
20	946.72	927.98	942.81	215.61	210.19	212.24	113.78	112.44	113.15	15,740	74.31
23	958.31	945.21	951.31	215.99	211.89	213.79	114.74	113.24	114.36	14,190	74.26
24	957.10	941.30	952.51	216.61	211.27	214.76	115.09	113.72	144.65	15,240	74.33
25	958.46	944.99	951.38	219.09	212.51	216.19	115.64	114.10	115.06	17,430	74.33
26	962.45	946.27	950.56	222.14	215.88	219.13	116.47	114.78	115.86	20,790	74.34
27	956.20	941.07	946.42	220.48	217.19	218.55	117.17	115.48	116.40	15,470	74.32
30	950.71	936.56	946.42	219.67	216.23	218.16	117.24	115.70	116.44	11,820	74.27
31	958.53	944.39	955.52	221.87	217.00	220.29	117.52	115.93	116.88	15,450	74.27
		High	955.52			220.29			116.88		74.34
		Low	921.66			212.24			110.72		73.89

NOVEMBER, 1972

	—30 Industrials—			—20 Transportations—			—15 Utilities—			Daily Sales —000—	40 Bonds
	High	Low	Close	High	Low	Close	High	Low	Close		
1	975.24	955.30	968.54	224.70	218.74	222.18	118.55	116.76	118.07	21,360	74.29
2	977.80	961.77	973.06	224.12	219.86	223.07	119.06	117.62	118.51	20,690	74.16
3	988.94	969.22	984.12	226.25	220.91	224.43	120.14	117.75	119.28	22,510	74.17
6	993.38	977.05	984.80	226.90	221.29	223.11	120.59	118.64	119.79	21,330	74.32
8	998.42	978.63	983.74	227.06	221.14	223.00	121.04	119.06	119.70	24,620	74.38
9	992.32	973.89	988.26	224.89	220.21	223.89	120.08	118.10	119.28	17,040	74.38
10	1007.15	986.08	995.26	227.06	221.99	224.35	120.53	118.29	119.73	24,360	74.42
13	1004.89	988.49	997.07	227.17	222.57	224.74	120.72	118.90	120.14	17,210	74.39
14	1006.92	991.12	1003.16	227.52	222.88	226.48	121.29	119.60	120.97	20,200	74.49
15	1013.55	993.08	998.42	229.19	224.35	225.47	122.03	120.53	121.13	23,270	74.36
16	1008.13	991.57	1003.69	228.45	224.31	227.06	122.12	120.69	121.55	19,580	74.41
17	1012.34	998.57	1005.57	229.50	225.47	227.60	122.48	120.94	121.96	20,220	74.56
20	1011.14	997.14	1005.04	229.50	226.32	228.06	122.76	121.36	122.22	16,680	74.69
21	1017.61	1002.86	1013.25	232.94	226.94	231.24	124.30	122.09	123.79	22,110	74.73
22	1026.87	1009.93	1020.54	233.79	230.08	232.01	125.32	123.37	124.11	24,510	74.81
24	1029.73	1014.15	1025.21	233.52	230.23	232.63	125.00	123.27	124.14	15,760	74.81
27	1026.87	1008.65	1017.76	233.09	229.38	231.47	124.30	122.35	123.37	18,190	74.80
28	1026.79	1012.57	1019.34	235.57	229.65	233.94	123.82	122.38	123.02	19,210	74.88
29	1023.63	1011.89	1018.81	237.04	233.05	235.88	123.66	122.03	122.86	17,380	74.89
30	1025.81	1010.54	1018.21	239.09	233.33	237.12	123.82	122.06	123.02	19,340	74.97
		High	1025.21			237.12			124.14		74.97
		Low	968.54			222.18			118.07		74.16

DECEMBER, 1972

	—30 Industrials—			—20 Transportations—			—15 Utilities—			Daily Sales —000—	40 Bonds
	High	Low	Close	High	Low	Close	High	Low	Close		
1	1031.53	1016.56	1023.93	239.90	235.11	237.19	123.98	122.32	123.11	22,570	74.87
4	1033.19	1021.45	1027.02	241.30	236.54	238.74	124.04	122.41	123.05	19,730	74.89
5	1030.85	1017.46	1022.95	241.37	236.65	238.86	123.82	122.38	123.05	17,800	75.00
6	1031.16	1018.29	1027.54	241.64	236.61	239.44	123.63	121.93	122.83	18,610	74.99
7	1037.85	1025.36	1033.26	241.95	237.93	239.32	123.75	122.12	123.18	19,320	74.94
8	1039.21	1027.17	1033.19	241.22	237.00	238.66	123.66	122.32	122.67	18,030	74.96
11	1041.32	1029.80	1036.27	242.22	237.27	240.41	123.40	121.93	122.73	17,230	74.88
12	1042.44	1029.65	1033.19	241.41	237.85	239.55	123.66	122.00	122.86	17,040	74.71
13	1036.65	1025.14	1030.48	240.17	236.03	237.58	123.66	122.32	122.67	16,540	74.82
14	1035.45	1020.09	1025.06	237.58	230.66	232.59	122.99	121.52	122.09	17,930	74.88
15	1034.69	1018.59	1027.24	235.65	230.23	232.71	122.70	121.26	122.00	18,300	74.91
18	1022.05	1004.29	1013.25	232.01	226.94	229.92	122.41	120.65	121.23	17,540	74.87
19	1017.99	1004.06	1009.18	230.93	226.59	227.68	122.03	120.27	120.85	17,000	74.97
20	1014.98	1001.88	1004.82	227.92	223.15	224.27	121.55	119.60	120.21	18,490	74.89
21	1010.91	996.09	1000.00	225.70	220.60	223.15	120.53	118.87	119.28	18,290	75.07
22	1010.01	996.84	1004.21	226.09	222.07	224.81	119.73	118.26	118.93	12,540	74.94
26	1010.91	999.85	1006.70	226.86	223.61	225.32	119.41	117.97	118.80	11,120	74.92
27	1014.22	1001.13	1007.68	226.63	223.00	224.70	119.70	117.94	118.87	19,100	74.94
29	1027.39	1008.58	1020.02	228.72	223.38	227.17	120.11	118.55	119.50	27,550	75.01
		High	1036.27			240.41			123.18		75.07
		Low	1000.00			223.15			118.80		74.71

JANUARY, 1973

	-30 Industrials-			-20 Transportations-			-15 Utilities-			Daily Sales —000—	40 Bonds
	High	Low	Close	High	Low	Close	High	Low	Close		
2	1038.98	1022.88	1031.68	231.66	225.90	228.10	121.45	119.63	120.72	17,090	75.10
3	1049.59	1032.21	1043.80	231.20	225.82	227.21	121.36	119.60	120.40	20,620	75.08
4	1047.86	1027.62	1039.81	228.33	222.34	225.47	121.23	119.63	120.65	20,230	75.17
5	1053.43	1037.40	1047.49	226.98	222.65	225.20	121.39	119.54	120.49	19,330	75.25
8	1053.58	1040.86	1047.86	226.17	222.88	224.66	121.26	119.57	120.40	16,840	75.27
9	1053.21	1040.49	1047.11	225.01	222.03	223.58	120.69	119.15	119.82	16,830	75.32
10	1053.28	1040.94	1046.06	223.58	218.86	220.44	120.53	119.38	119.86	20,880	75.26
11	1067.20	1039.28	1051.70	223.42	218.82	220.67	120.72	119.38	120.14	25,050	75.32
12	1059.90	1033.41	1039.36	221.64	216.03	217.35	120.97	119.50	120.05	22,230	75.33
15	1053.28	1022.88	1025.59	220.95	214.37	214.64	120.91	118.83	119.38	21,520	75.21
16	1033.34	1014.37	1024.31	217.77	212.09	215.68	119.98	117.94	118.87	19,170	75.22
17	1036.35	1020.32	1029.12	220.13	215.30	218.35	119.70	118.23	118.96	17,680	75.25
18	1039.96	1024.01	1029.12	219.98	215.14	216.42	119.44	117.78	118.16	17,810	75.34
19	1031.68	1014.00	1026.19	217.15	212.05	214.06	118.42	116.53	117.33	17,020	75.23
22	1034.69	1014.52	1018.81	215.14	209.57	211.39	118.10	116.37	116.72	15,570	75.11
23	1024.68	1007.22	1018.66	211.82	206.67	209.96	116.98	115.00	115.67	19,060	75.16
24	1025.74	998.57	1004.59	211.82	205.47	207.02	116.44	114.68	115.00	20,870	75.15
26	1008.50	989.46	1003.54	209.49	204.35	207.71	115.57	113.56	114.58	21,130	75.08
29	1008.80	988.18	996.46	208.76	204.39	206.67	115.38	113.72	114.42	14,680	74.94
30	1005.34	989.09	992.93	208.53	205.01	206.52	114.93	113.27	113.88	15,270	74.83
31	1004.06	988.11	999.02	208.72	205.32	207.13	114.68	113.02	113.82	14,870	74.83
		High	1051.70			228.10			120.72		75.34
		Low	992.93			206.52			113.82		74.83

FEBRUARY, 1973

	-30 Industrials-			-20 Transportations-			-15 Utilities-			Daily Sales —000—	40 Bonds
	High	Low	Close	High	Low	Close	High	Low	Close		
1	1008.58	983.14	985.78	209.15	204.54	205.43	114.93	113.27	114.10	20,670	74.77
2	992.32	975.02	980.81	205.51	201.72	203.38	114.71	113.11	113.75	17,470	74.69
5	987.06	974.11	978.40	205.01	202.10	203.38	114.46	112.86	113.56	14,580	74.71
6	986.00	972.23	979.91	205.43	202.07	203.88	114.30	112.79	113.46	15,720	74.72
7	989.16	965.53	968.32	205.55	201.52	202.41	114.93	113.02	113.27	17,960	74.74
8	973.81	954.17	967.19	203.69	199.78	202.10	113.78	112.38	113.15	18,440	74.63
9	983.14	964.93	979.46	207.06	202.30	206.17	113.98	112.70	113.34	19,260	74.57
12	996.24	980.81	991.57	208.64	205.39	207.13	114.71	113.21	114.04	16,130	74.57
13	1019.94	991.65	996.76	211.62	205.74	206.94	115.51	113.15	113.75	25,320	74.57
14	997.97	974.11	979.91	207.44	203.11	204.16	114.42	112.73	113.46	16,520	74.53
15	984.12	966.29	973.13	205.28	201.80	202.99	114.10	112.83	113.34	13,940	74.66
16	981.86	965.76	979.23	204.43	200.60	203.30	114.17	112.54	113.15	13,320	74.64
20	991.04	975.69	983.59	206.09	201.64	203.77	114.23	112.83	113.56	14,020	74.76
21	988.79	970.27	974.34	204.39	200.21	201.21	114.30	112.63	113.27	14,880	74.65
22	978.63	963.05	971.78	201.76	198.51	200.36	113.75	112.22	112.95	14,570	74.67
23	973.81	957.10	959.89	201.06	197.23	198.20	113.66	111.96	112.44	15,450	74.63
26	962.90	943.78	953.79	197.73	193.86	196.15	112.47	111.13	111.68	15,860	74.62
27	963.12	943.26	947.92	196.96	192.47	193.44	112.31	110.59	111.04	16,130	74.61
28	958.31	938.82	955.07	195.61	190.92	194.37	111.74	110.33	111.13	17,950	74.62
		High	996.76			207.13			114.10		74.77
		Low	947.92			193.44			111.04		74.53

MARCH, 1973

	—30 Industrials—			—20 Transportations—			—15 Utilities—			Daily Sales —000—	40 Bonds
	High	Low	Close	High	Low	Close	High	Low	Close		
1	967.04	947.17	949.65	195.84	190.89	191.74	112.00	110.81	111.48	18,210	74.60
2	962.97	937.69	961.32	192.74	188.68	191.62	111.96	110.75	111.48	17,710	74.58
5	972.00	955.67	966.89	193.32	189.34	191.58	112.19	110.78	111.58	13,720	74.60
6	982.39	966.44	979.00	195.64	191.16	194.83	112.15	110.65	111.16	17,710	74.46
7	984.80	966.74	979.98	199.05	193.90	198.35	111.90	110.43	111.36	19,310	74.60
8	985.25	973.59	976.44	199.78	195.88	197.04	111.80	109.98	110.53	15,100	74.53
9	978.03	963.58	972.23	198.39	193.25	195.61	111.39	109.95	110.88	14,070	74.62
12	979.00	965.68	969.75	197.27	192.86	194.13	111.23	109.85	110.46	13,810	74.66
13	980.13	966.29	976.07	195.64	191.93	194.10	111.48	110.11	110.69	14,210	74.67
14	982.31	972.00	978.85	196.80	192.70	195.30	111.52	110.21	110.94	14,460	74.69
15	982.47	966.21	969.82	196.80	193.86	194.72	111.26	109.76	110.21	14,450	74.69
16	973.21	957.41	963.05	196.19	192.59	193.83	110.84	109.66	110.14	15,130	74.71
19	962.45	946.79	952.06	195.06	191.74	193.28	110.49	103.83	109.28	12,460	74.70
20	956.80	941.15	949.43	195.80	192.01	194.60	109.82	108.45	108.83	13,250	74.67
21	958.84	934.90	938.37	196.30	191.89	192.08	109.69	108.13	108.38	16,080	74.59
22	937.46	919.25	925.20	193.13	187.71	189.22	108.32	106.66	107.11	17,130	74.53
23	934.53	911.12	922.71	191.23	187.36	189.22	107.65	105.86	106.60	18,470	74.43
26	931.74	914.28	927.90	193.09	188.60	192.36	107.75	106.28	107.01	14,980	74.46
27	948.52	930.16	944.91	198.35	193.01	197.46	108.22	106.75	107.91	17,500	74.48
28	955.82	936.94	948.00	199.98	195.33	198.58	108.58	107.04	107.62	15,850	74.47
29	962.82	941.75	959.14	202.18	197.66	201.41	108.35	106.91	107.78	16,050	74.53
30	961.69	944.84	951.01	202.38	198.55	200.13	108.51	107.23	108.00	13,740	74.45
		High	979.98			201.41			111.58		74.71
		Low	922.71			189.22			106.60		74.43

APRIL, 1973

	—30 Industrials—			—20 Transportations—			—15 Utilities—			Daily Sales —000—	40 Bonds
	High	Low	Close	High	Low	Close	High	Low	Close		
2	951.84	932.72	936.18	201.21	196.57	197.69	108.51	107.23	107.97	10,640	74.45
3	936.71	920.45	927.75	198.39	194.06	195.45	108.10	106.82	107.23	12,910	74.39
4	935.66	919.55	925.05	196.77	193.21	194.33	107.75	106.18	106.66	11,890	74.38
5	929.03	914.81	923.46	195.18	191.70	193.83	106.95	105.60	106.28	12,750	74.29
6	937.31	921.43	931.07	196.73	193.36	195.30	106.98	105.73	106.50	13,890	74.30
9	950.63	927.45	947.55	200.13	194.48	199.28	107.71	106.18	107.14	13,740	74.39
10	966.74	950.71	960.49	202.07	198.89	200.44	108.77	106.98	108.32	16,770	74.54
11	970.50	953.94	967.41	202.14	197.35	200.91	109.47	107.78	108.86	14,890	74.52
12	975.32	956.73	964.03	202.10	198.70	199.59	110.08	108.54	109.50	16,360	74.56
13	967.56	950.71	959.36	201.60	197.58	199.82	109.95	108.77	109.15	14,390	74.62
16	965.53	950.03	956.73	200.48	196.77	197.77	109.82	108.58	108.96	11,350	74.76
17	959.29	947.62	953.42	198.00	194.72	195.95	109.73	108.51	109.28	12,830	74.80
18	961.47	944.39	958.31	197.77	193.98	196.69	109.63	108.70	109.22	13,890	74.76
19	970.95	953.79	963.20	198.35	194.99	196.61	109.89	108.54	109.25	14,560	74.69
23	966.51	951.23	955.37	197.58	193.55	194.75	109.79	108.61	108.99	12,580	74.62
24	958.68	938.37	940.77	194.98	187.44	188.68	109.57	107.97	108.35	13,830	74.59
25	941.60	925.42	930.54	188.33	182.49	183.65	108.86	107.43	108.00	15,960	74.60
26	944.24	919.78	937.76	187.40	181.56	186.20	108.29	107.07	107.62	16,210	74.58
27	941.38	918.05	922.19	187.71	182.18	183.23	108.03	106.63	106.85	13,730	74.49
30	929.18	907.51	921.43	185.47	180.52	184.19	108.10	105.99	107.20	14,820	74.54
		High	967.41			200.91			109.50		74.80
		Low	921.43			183.23			106.28		74.29

MAY, 1973

	—30 Industrials—			—20 Transportations—			—15 Utilities—			Daily Sales —000—	40 Bonds
	High	Low	Close	High	Low	Close	High	Low	Close		
1	929.03	905.40	921.21	185.93	180.32	183.30	108.06	106.60	107.27	15,380	74.62
2	938.37	920.23	932.34	186.51	182.45	185.20	108.54	107.01	107.91	14,380	74.69
3	950.03	915.04	945.67	188.91	182.84	188.29	108.83	106.85	108.38	17,760	74.80
4	962.67	944.31	953.87	190.42	186.55	188.06	109.44	107.97	108.61	19,510	74.68
7	956.80	941.98	950.71	188.10	184.11	185.24	109.09	107.71	108.45	12,500	74.71
8	961.24	940.92	956.58	187.40	183.61	186.90	109.12	107.94	108.80	13,730	74.70
9	965.16	945.29	949.05	188.18	183.96	185.47	109.41	108.19	108.48	16,050	74.59
10	950.63	934.75	939.34	185.86	181.83	183.23	109.09	107.91	108.29	13,520	74.64
11	939.12	924.14	927.98	182.95	178.93	179.51	108.83	107.87	108.29	12,980	74.69
14	925.27	906.31	909.69	179.47	175.49	176.57	108.51	107.33	107.78	13,520	74.62
15	920.83	894.49	917.44	179.05	173.71	177.42	108.19	106.50	107.39	18,530	74.66
16	927.83	907.66	917.14	179.39	175.29	176.69	108.10	106.91	107.27	13,800	74.59
17	919.93	907.59	911.72	177.46	168.37	169.37	107.65	106.37	106.72	13,060	74.56
18	908.79	889.00	895.17	170.07	164.04	165.43	107.17	105.70	105.96	17,080	74.55
21	894.79	875.45	886.51	165.78	160.32	162.33	106.21	104.65	105.22	20,690	74.39
22	905.93	884.86	892.46	167.63	161.95	165.43	106.50	104.90	105.76	18,020	74.50
23	904.80	884.18	895.02	167.36	163.88	166.09	106.88	105.29	106.31	14,950	74.47
24	926.48	890.35	924.44	170.46	164.50	169.80	107.49	105.86	107.14	17,310	74.41
25	938.82	915.64	930.84	172.20	167.13	170.30	108.26	106.50	107.52	19,270	74.47
29	934.08	921.36	925.57	171.54	168.41	169.49	108.06	106.75	107.33	11,300	74.26
30	924.37	906.01	908.87	169.26	163.84	164.38	107.68	106.24	106.82	11,730	74.38
31	912.03	895.62	901.41	165.16	161.68	163.11	107.46	106.02	106.69	12,190	74.38
		High	956.58			188.29			108.80		74.80
		Low	886.51			162.33			105.22		74.26

JUNE, 1973

	—30 Industrials—			—20 Transportations—			—15 Utilities—			Daily Sales —000—	40 Bonds
	High	Low	Close	High	Low	Close	High	Low	Close		
1	902.32	887.27	893.96	163.30	160.01	161.52	107.36	106.12	106.85	10,410	74.26
4	894.42	880.72	885.91	162.33	157.54	159.35	107.14	105.86	106.47	11,230	74.17
5	905.63	883.43	900.81	162.22	157.96	160.63	107.14	105.67	106.40	14,089	74.14
6	908.87	891.71	898.18	163.46	158.54	159.47	107.11	105.86	106.53	13,080	74.19
7	913.68	896.37	909.62	162.33	157.85	160.48	107.55	106.18	107.01	14,160	74.20
8	926.85	908.19	920.00	163.92	160.13	162.41	105.81	106.56	107.33	14,050	74.22
11	924.67	911.05	915.11	163.34	160.40	161.56	108.06	106.79	107.59	9,940	74.22
12	930.01	912.85	927.00	166.13	161.13	165.85	108.90	106.79	107.75	13,840	74.25
13	935.58	912.48	915.49	170.03	165.24	167.75	108.45	107.11	107.55	15,700	74.26
14	922.49	899.61	902.92	168.02	164.69	165.39	108.06	106.50	107.04	13,210	74.27
15	899.68	882.60	888.55	164.73	161.44	162.88	107.17	105.48	106.12	11,970	74.28
18	887.34	869.36	875.08	163.03	158.50	158.85	106.37	104.81	105.25	11,460	74.22
19	889.52	868.08	881.55	161.71	156.88	159.05	105.92	104.42	105.22	12,970	74.21
20	890.65	876.28	884.71	160.44	157.42	159.08	105.86	104.39	104.65	10,600	74.24
21	887.49	871.84	873.65	159.78	155.25	155.99	104.84	103.53	103.78	11,630	74.27
22	897.58	875.23	879.82	159.86	154.71	155.91	105.25	103.14	103.82	18,470	74.31
25	880.72	865.67	869.13	156.92	153.16	154.36	103.94	102.35	102.70	11,670	74.28
26	881.85	864.46	879.44	157.77	153.24	156.72	103.34	102.19	102.73	14,040	74.25
27	888.09	872.44	884.63	157.42	153.82	155.64	103.53	102.06	102.86	12,660	74.20
28	897.88	880.87	894.64	157.88	154.71	156.53	103.46	101.64	102.47	12,760	74.16
29	900.59	886.59	891.71	157.69	155.14	156.18	103.05	101.42	102.12	10,770	74.19
		High	927.00			167.75			107.75		74.31
		Low	869.13			154.36			102.12		74.14

JULY, 1973

	—30 Industrials—			—20 Transportations—			—15 Utilities—			Daily Sales	40
	High	Low	Close	High	Low	Close	High	Low	Close	—000—	Bonds
2	890.20	876.66	880.57	156.88	153.74	155.33	101.96	100.43	100.94	9,830	74.05
3	882.53	868.75	874.17	156.45	153.90	155.60	101.45	100.01	100.56	10,560	74.09
5	879.74	867.10	874.32	157.96	154.67	156.99	101.20	99.88	100.56	10,500	73.95
6	878.09	865.82	870.11	157.77	154.75	155.83	101.23	100.04	100.62	9,980	73.84
9	879.74	863.94	877.26	159.66	154.56	158.74	101.61	99.98	101.04	11,560	73.67
10	894.64	879.06	888.32	162.68	158.85	161.33	101.99	100.65	101.42	15,090	73.68
11	911.80	889.90	908.19	165.35	160.98	164.11	102.66	101.35	102.28	18,730	73.73
12	910.82	895.39	901.94	165.97	162.06	164.00	102.82	101.51	102.15	16,400	73.87
13	902.77	883.05	885.99	164.23	160.79	161.75	102.60	101.13	101.55	11,390	73.82
16	900.44	881.32	897.58	164.04	159.43	163.26	102.06	100.62	101.39	12,920	73.73
17	911.80	892.84	898.03	165.35	161.21	162.88	102.03	100.59	100.94	18,750	73.57
18	911.20	889.90	905.40	166.13	161.79	164.81	101.64	100.24	101.20	17,020	73.37
19	916.47	893.66	906.68	166.78	160.86	164.46	101.87	100.46	101.23	18,650	73.34
20	918.05	902.54	910.90	166.20	161.99	164.19	102.22	100.59	101.39	16,300	72.93
23	921.88	907.36	913.15	166.71	163.03	164.69	102.31	100.62	101.64	15,580	72.89
24	922.19	903.67	918.72	167.83	162.29	166.51	102.44	100.81	101.51	16,280	72.75
25	942.58	917.22	933.02	169.14	164.73	166.74	103.24	101.29	102.19	22,220	72.85
26	944.08	924.74	934.53	168.87	164.85	167.29	102.57	100.91	101.20	18,410	72.72
27	942.28	925.65	936.71	167.90	165.24	166.74	101.71	100.17	100.56	12,910	72.60
30	942.35	926.32	933.77	167.90	164.23	166.16	101.04	99.76	100.30	11,170	72.55
31	941.15	923.39	926.40	167.83	164.23	165.20	100.65	99.15	99.31	13,530	72.43
		High	936.71			167.29			102.28		74.09
		Low	870.11			155.33			99.31		72.43

AUGUST, 1973

	—30 Industrials—			—20 Transportations—			—15 Utilities—			Daily Sales	40
	High	Low	Close	High	Low	Close	High	Low	Close	—000—	Bonds
1	924.37	907.28	912.18	165.82	162.80	164.15	99.47	97.97	98.29	13,530	72.38
2	917.37	899.46	910.14	165.89	162.26	164.27	98.51	96.88	97.58	16,080	72.22
3	913.91	900.36	908.87	164.35	161.41	162.29	98.19	96.91	97.39	9,940	72.20
6	918.50	900.96	912.78	164.00	160.63	162.76	98.00	96.34	96.95	12,320	71.88
7	920.38	905.25	911.95	163.73	160.52	161.64	97.74	96.15	96.98	13,510	71.76
8	913.23	897.43	902.02	161.64	158.58	159.51	97.36	95.70	96.24	12,440	71.67
9	910.60	893.96	901.49	161.64	157.92	159.74	97.01	95.64	96.02	12,880	71.76
10	903.52	887.12	892.38	160.52	157.23	158.35	96.72	95.35	96.08	10,870	71.57
13	892.91	878.09	883.20	159.08	156.61	157.81	96.18	94.58	95.06	11,330	71.46
14	887.42	867.70	870.71	158.62	155.41	156.41	95.54	94.33	94.64	11,740	71.40
15	879.82	863.71	874.17	158.35	154.91	157.03	95.64	94.17	94.64	12,040	71.33
16	886.44	867.62	872.74	158.50	154.98	156.07	95.70	94.13	94.55	12,990	71.38
17	877.18	864.69	871.84	156.96	154.02	155.37	95.54	94.20	95.12	11,110	71.46
20	875.08	862.73	867.40	156.41	153.20	154.48	95.99	94.45	95.16	8,970	71.38
21	869.96	855.51	857.84	155.29	151.85	152.86	95.64	94.42	95.03	11,480	71.44
22	860.55	845.50	851.90	153.59	150.38	151.97	95.48	94.26	94.55	10,770	71.33
23	869.81	853.48	864.46	154.60	151.46	153.67	95.48	94.13	95.00	11,390	71.47
24	873.12	856.56	863.49	156.07	152.97	154.44	95.89	94.52	95.16	11,200	71.49
27	874.32	860.02	870.71	156.53	153.94	155.64	95.60	94.36	94.84	9,740	71.60
28	877.63	865.37	872.07	156.34	153.32	155.25	95.95	94.55	95.28	11,810	71.64
29	890.35	870.56	883.43	158.39	154.48	157.50	96.08	94.61	95.22	15,690	71.61
30	892.31	877.48	882.53	158.89	155.76	156.96	96.24	94.80	95.83	12,100	71.63
31	890.95	876.51	887.57	160.13	156.61	159.35	96.53	95.32	96.02	10,530	71.71
		High	912.78			164.27			98.29		72.38
		Low	851.90			151.97			94.55		71.33

SEPTEMBER, 1973

	—30 Industrials—			—20 Transportations—			—15 Utilities—			Daily Sales —000—	40 Bonds
	High	Low	Close	High	Low	Close	High	Low	Close		
4	900.25	885.69	895.39	162.72	158.77	161.33	96.88	95.38	96.11	14,210	71.73
5	903.52	887.94	899.08	163.46	159.97	162.33	97.52	95.73	97.04	14,580	71.74
6	908.04	894.04	901.04	164.15	160.75	162.49	100.24	97.01	99.66	15,670	71.91
7	905.70	892.61	898.63	164.35	161.06	162.88	101.48	98.96	100.84	14,930	72.07
10	903.45	888.62	891.33	164.11	160.98	162.18	101.51	99.47	100.08	11,620	72.00
11	892.46	878.61	885.76	162.22	158.58	160.32	100.24	98.61	99.15	12,690	72.15
12	889.75	874.77	881.32	161.68	159.01	160.05	99.92	98.06	98.96	12,040	72.06
13	888.09	874.17	880.57	161.64	159.12	160.32	99.41	98.03	98.70	11,670	71.99
14	889.15	873.34	886.36	163.34	159.59	162.57	99.18	97.78	98.45	13,760	71.97
17	900.29	884.86	892.99	164.81	161.10	162.57	99.57	97.87	98.80	15,100	71.96
18	900.14	882.38	891.26	164.65	160.79	163.07	99.63	97.94	98.83	16,400	71.98
19	915.41	891.26	910.37	169.34	162.99	168.37	100.24	98.38	99.57	24,570	71.96
20	925.42	909.54	920.53	172.04	167.17	170.07	100.46	98.83	99.73	25,960	72.02
21	934.38	911.72	927.90	174.09	168.79	172.47	101.23	99.28	100.65	23,760	72.18
24	940.70	924.37	936.71	175.26	170.46	173.75	101.83	100.11	101.13	19,490	72.24
25	947.02	927.53	940.55	176.42	171.62	174.68	102.38	100.43	101.42	21,530	72.38
26	954.55	935.43	949.50	177.65	172.90	176.49	103.21	101.07	102.82	21,130	72.54
27	964.55	942.50	953.27	179.82	174.09	176.65	104.68	102.19	103.97	23,660	72.67
28	954.92	937.54	947.10	178.00	174.25	176.96	104.61	102.60	103.40	16,300	72.93
		High	953.27			176.96			103.97		72.93
		Low	880.57			160.05			96.11		71.73

OCTOBER, 1973

	—30 Industrials—			—20 Transportations—			—15 Utilities—			Daily Sales —000—	40 Bonds
	High	Low	Close	High	Low	Close	High	Low	Close		
1	954.09	937.69	948.83	180.40	175.26	179.55	104.10	102.41	103.72	15,830	72.98
2	961.54	943.93	956.80	183.30	178.97	182.45	104.39	102.70	103.69	20,770	72.87
3	971.78	952.14	964.55	184.50	179.32	181.95	104.07	102.54	103.27	22,040	72.81
4	969.30	949.50	955.90	183.23	179.51	181.10	104.01	102.38	103.18	19,730	72.99
5	975.92	950.78	971.25	184.35	179.36	183.34	103.82	102.12	103.02	18,820	72.99
8	983.22	955.82	977.65	184.73	180.17	183.57	104.29	102.25	103.82	18,990	73.06
9	984.65	964.63	974.19	184.50	180.01	182.30	104.52	103.05	103.85	19,440	73.01
10	980.28	953.79	960.57	183.19	178.89	180.21	104.42	102.73	103.05	19,010	73.15
11	981.19	957.71	976.07	184.23	179.59	183.19	103.94	102.22	102.98	20,740	73.22
12	991.80	972.00	978.63	185.82	181.45	183.11	103.94	102.28	103.08	22,730	73.20
15	977.80	960.19	967.04	184.62	180.09	182.99	103.34	101.64	101.90	16,160	73.12
16	971.63	951.76	967.41	185.04	179.86	183.46	102.12	100.46	101.04	18,780	73.20
17	976.67	956.35	962.52	187.13	182.45	184.00	101.80	99.66	100.52	18,600	73.16
18	974.34	950.11	959.74	187.17	181.25	183.88	100.91	99.12	99.63	19,210	73.06
19	974.04	954.55	963.73	185.66	181.33	183.38	100.46	98.86	99.37	17,880	73.20
22	970.42	951.08	960.57	184.04	179.94	182.26	99.82	98.45	99.15	14,290	73.23
23	976.44	944.46	966.51	184.42	178.66	181.83	100.01	98.26	99.50	17,230	73.02
24	977.50	960.79	971.85	184.70	180.44	182.84	100.84	99.21	100.20	15,840	73.08
25	981.26	957.10	974.49	185.04	180.40	183.42	100.94	99.37	100.59	15,580	73.06
26	992.62	972.61	987.06	186.05	182.06	184.85	101.77	100.11	101.16	17,800	73.07
29	997.59	979.98	984.80	187.21	183.30	185.20	102.12	100.75	101.55	17,960	73.11
30	985.93	963.65	968.54	185.70	181.02	182.10	102.09	100.27	100.75	17,580	73.06
31	973.13	951.31	956.58	184.62	180.40	182.26	101.16	99.09	99.37	17,890	73.09
		High	987.06			185.20			103.85		73.23
		Low	948.83			179.55			99.15		72.81

NOVEMBER, 1973

	—30 Industrials—			—20 Transportations—			—15 Utilities—			Daily Sales —000—	40 Bonds
	High	Low	Close	High	Low	Close	High	Low	Close		
1	963.80	941.83	948.83	184.08	178.89	180.79	99.92	98.22	98.80	16,920	72.99
2	951.31	929.11	935.28	183.84	178.54	180.01	99.28	97.81	98.38	16,340	73.02
5	932.87	912.55	919.40	180.52	175.56	176.73	98.86	97.14	97.78	17,150	72.92
6	933.77	909.69	913.08	178.70	172.39	173.71	98.35	96.75	96.95	16,430	72.93
7	929.64	909.69	920.08	182.92	173.44	180.83	97.90	96.27	97.20	16,570	72.94
8	946.79	923.92	932.65	189.69	182.99	186.13	97.78	95.83	96.47	19,650	72.96
9	932.95	902.92	908.41	189.57	183.57	185.39	97.20	95.19	96.11	17,320	73.08
12	910.82	885.54	897.65	186.90	179.24	181.37	96.47	94.04	94.64	19,250	73.03
13	902.47	876.88	891.03	182.45	176.53	179.09	94.96	92.86	93.91	20,310	73.03
14	899.53	865.37	869.88	180.79	173.32	174.25	94.64	91.90	92.44	22,710	72.88
15	886.82	859.27	874.55	176.80	169.68	174.25	93.59	91.61	92.89	24,530	72.87
16	905.10	869.21	891.33	178.04	171.93	175.68	94.55	91.71	93.27	22,510	72.80
19	889.75	860.78	862.66	176.42	170.19	171.50	94.04	91.13	91.55	16,700	72.90
20	862.43	836.17	844.90	171.81	166.20	167.60	92.02	89.44	90.01	23,960	72.96
21	869.21	839.78	854.98	173.51	165.93	171.19	91.71	89.63	90.81	24,260	72.95
23	861.45	847.46	854.00	174.79	170.50	172.90	92.06	90.01	91.13	11,470	72.90
26	844.15	816.60	824.95	173.51	167.48	169.72	91.39	89.08	89.63	19,830	73.04
27	833.16	810.36	817.73	172.35	166.82	168.91	90.65	88.70	89.28	19,750	72.98
28	843.47	814.80	839.78	174.02	167.01	172.97	90.20	87.84	89.12	19,990	72.96
29	846.93	824.28	835.11	178.93	171.50	176.38	89.53	87.68	88.38	18,870	72.97
30	836.02	819.39	822.25	178.47	173.63	175.18	89.34	87.42	87.93	15,380	73.20
		High	948.83			186.13			98.80		73.20
		Low	817.73			167.60			87.93		72.80

DECEMBER, 1973

	—30 Industrials—			—20 Transportations—			—15 Utilities—			Daily Sales —000—	40 Bonds
	High	Low	Close	High	Low	Close	High	Low	Close		
3	820.51	798.31	806.52	176.42	169.53	172.12	88.51	85.89	86.40	17,900	73.13
4	817.73	795.68	803.21	173.71	168.18	171.23	87.07	85.06	86.05	19,030	73.27
5	806.82	783.56	788.31	172.12	165.70	166.86	86.43	83.97	84.42	19,180	73.36
6	816.68	786.50	814.12	171.81	165.04	170.07	86.30	83.81	85.28	23,260	73.27
7	846.63	815.47	838.05	176.65	169.45	174.60	87.68	85.15	86.98	23,230	73.18
10	857.31	829.17	851.14	179.28	174.06	178.31	89.50	86.46	88.86	18,590	73.15
11	861.09	830.80	834.18	181.52	175.87	177.42	90.27	87.46	88.09	20,100	73.09
12	828.64	805.27	810.73	176.76	170.81	172.20	88.51	86.72	87.84	18,190	73.04
13	821.57	794.43	800.43	173.48	168.79	169.92	88.25	85.99	86.62	18,130	72.91
14	823.57	793.51	815.65	174.75	168.02	172.39	88.09	85.95	87.17	20,000	72.89
17	821.42	804.20	811.12	175.02	171.04	172.78	88.22	86.11	86.94	12,930	72.85
18	834.72	807.12	829.49	177.50	172.55	176.42	88.13	86.37	87.20	19,490	72.94
19	847.86	820.96	829.57	180.44	174.48	176.45	88.93	86.82	87.23	20,670	72.91
20	841.64	820.50	828.11	180.21	175.29	177.65	88.45	86.50	87.33	17,340	72.93
21	830.72	809.81	818.73	179.82	175.64	177.46	88.25	86.18	87.39	18,680	72.82
24	820.73	805.73	814.81	181.41	176.30	180.63	88.00	86.53	87.42	11,540	72.74
26	844.10	820.19	837.56	190.27	182.64	189.03	89.21	86.98	88.61	18,620	72.74
27	858.93	839.02	851.01	195.57	189.57	193.13	90.84	88.80	89.92	22,720	72.94
28	857.63	839.94	848.02	195.84	190.85	194.33	90.62	88.48	89.21	21,310	72.93
31	857.09	836.18	850.86	197.73	192.59	196.19	90.27	88.32	89.37	23,470	72.75
		High	851.14			196.19			89.92		73.36
		Low	788.31			166.86			84.42		72.74

JANUARY, 1974

	—30 Industrials—			—20 Transportations—			—15 Utilities—			Daily Sales —000—	40 Bonds
	High	Low	Close	High	Low	Close	High	Low	Close		
2	859.16	841.41	855.32	199.94	194.60	198.20	91.45	89.02	91.23	12,060	72.73
3	886.69	858.86	880.69	204.85	199.28	202.45	94.39	91.96	93.85	24,850	72.73
4	890.38	868.08	880.23	204.89	197.46	201.06	95.22	93.05	94.52	21,700	72.81
7	883.99	866.31	876.85	202.26	193.90	197.54	95.83	93.65	95.09	19,070	72.92
8	880.77	857.70	861.78	197.69	190.46	191.58	95.41	93.33	94.07	18,080	73.29
9	853.01	831.41	834.79	191.04	183.65	186.75	94.17	92.06	92.79	18,070	73.05
10	845.17	816.57	823.11	188.18	181.52	182.61	93.69	91.74	92.54	16,120	73.09
11	847.63	819.88	841.48	189.18	182.49	188.10	92.79	91.13	91.86	15,140	73.03
14	855.63	833.26	840.18	192.70	187.17	190.23	93.11	91.07	91.83	14,610	73.02
15	855.78	834.64	846.40	193.40	189.30	191.16	93.05	91.55	92.41	13,250	73.15
16	861.16	842.48	856.09	194.06	189.84	192.59	93.49	91.77	92.89	14,930	73.23
17	878.54	856.32	872.16	196.96	191.23	193.98	93.88	92.38	92.98	21,040	73.22
18	873.15	850.86	855.47	194.37	188.10	189.61	93.97	92.28	92.98	16,470	73.10
21	858.86	835.79	854.63	190.65	184.97	189.34	93.75	92.28	92.95	15,630	73.11
22	871.62	850.71	863.47	193.40	187.21	190.19	94.07	92.63	93.30	17,330	73.11
23	878.69	859.01	871.00	193.44	187.98	190.50	94.23	92.79	93.53	16,890	73.21
24	875.85	853.47	863.08	191.23	187.60	189.72	94.01	92.50	93.40	15,980	73.08
25	869.16	850.71	859.39	190.92	186.86	188.95	93.97	92.70	93.46	14,860	73.02
28	862.16	847.32	853.01	190.50	186.13	187.48	93.94	92.44	93.14	13,410	73.05
29	858.86	844.48	852.32	188.37	184.42	186.05	93.97	92.70	93.49	12,850	73.13
30	869.77	853.09	862.32	189.38	185.04	187.56	94.45	93.14	94.07	16,790	73.17
31	868.85	852.01	855.55	190.65	185.93	187.52	94.26	92.79	93.21	14,020	73.25
		High 880.69				202.45			95.09		73.29
		Low 823.11				182.61			91.23		72.73

FEBRUARY, 1974

	—30 Industrials—			—20 Transportations—			—15 Utilities—			Daily Sales —000—	40 Bonds
	High	Low	Close	High	Low	Close	High	Low	Close		
1	856.55	838.02	843.94	187.71	182.92	184.15	94.01	92.66	93.27	12,480	73.22
4	838.63	816.49	821.50	183.88	178.97	181.02	93.43	91.71	92.38	14,380	73.29
5	829.87	811.95	820.64	183.38	179.67	181.72	92.98	91.64	92.15	12,820	73.21
6	831.35	817.51	824.62	184.42	180.75	182.64	93.05	91.83	92.41	11,610	73.24
7	833.93	819.38	828.46	185.82	181.72	185.00	93.81	92.44	93.53	11,750	73.29
8	831.90	817.82	820.40	185.55	181.56	182.68	94.20	92.82	93.49	12,990	73.25
11	821.26	802.24	803.90	183.42	179.39	180.01	94.07	92.73	93.37	12,930	73.35
12	811.72	795.68	806.63	182.34	176.73	180.87	93.62	92.38	93.33	12,920	73.37
13	816.18	803.04	806.87	182.72	179.24	180.71	93.88	92.47	93.02	10,990	73.36
14	816.57	802.17	809.92	183.84	179.94	182.57	93.85	92.28	92.79	12,230	73.32
15	825.72	808.12	820.32	185.58	181.52	184.77	93.65	92.22	93.24	12,640	73.44
19	840.50	816.65	819.54	189.11	182.95	183.69	93.78	92.18	92.70	15,940	73.50
20	834.87	814.22	831.04	187.67	182.57	186.59	93.21	91.77	92.50	11,670	73.31
21	849.66	830.18	846.84	189.69	185.43	188.87	93.97	92.31	93.37	13,930	73.30
22	862.41	843.01	855.99	192.51	187.48	190.96	94.45	93.05	94.10	16,360	73.31
25	859.20	843.79	851.38	193.25	189.57	191.74	94.23	92.92	93.37	12,900	73.22
26	861.78	843.09	859.51	195.57	190.92	195.06	94.45	92.95	93.97	15,860	73.24
27	871.40	855.76	863.42	199.51	193.28	196.53	94.71	93.40	94.20	18,730	73.23
28	868.19	851.85	860.53	198.97	194.06	197.31	94.52	92.92	93.40	13,680	73.28
		High 863.42				197.31			94.20		73.50
		Low 803.90				180.01			92.15		73.21

MARCH, 1974

	—30 Industrials—			—20 Transportations—			—15 Utilities—			Daily Sales —000—	40 Bonds
	High	Low	Close	High	Low	Close	High	Low	Close		
1	861.62	845.90	851.92	198.12	193.48	195.68	94.01	92.34	93.24	12,880	73.10
4	854.97	841.76	853.18	196.92	192.24	195.10	93.69	92.34	93.17	12,270	73.13
5	880.40	860.40	872.42	200.25	195.10	197.62	94.20	92.60	93.53	21,980	73.14
6	885.25	866.47	879.85	199.32	195.06	197.46	94.42	92.50	93.85	19,140	73.00
7	880.24	865.07	869.06	197.66	193.86	194.83	94.10	92.89	93.56	14,500	72.99
8	880.94	858.81	878.05	197.00	192.20	195.45	94.13	92.73	93.69	16,210	72.85
11	893.30	865.93	888.45	198.16	192.66	197.08	94.13	92.76	93.72	18,470	72.82
12	895.57	877.50	887.12	198.93	194.87	196.46	94.45	93.24	93.91	17,250	72.78
13	900.81	881.88	891.66	198.74	194.91	196.84	94.58	93.17	94.10	16,820	72.79
14	904.02	885.17	889.78	198.93	195.14	196.49	94.80	93.53	93.91	19,770	72.60
15	893.38	878.68	887.83	196.84	193.17	195.41	94.07	92.98	93.33	14,500	72.58
18	889.86	870.38	874.22	196.07	191.70	192.86	93.65	92.22	92.76	14,010	72.46
19	875.70	861.86	867.57	194.13	190.77	191.77	93.08	91.83	92.34	12,800	72.26
20	878.60	863.03	872.34	194.44	190.77	193.13	93.05	91.64	92.34	12,960	72.31
21	887.12	870.23	875.47	195.64	191.85	193.59	92.89	91.80	92.22	12,950	72.12
22	884.31	868.43	878.13	194.48	191.35	193.17	92.76	91.48	91.90	11,930	72.14
25	884.78	866.79	881.02	193.79	190.65	192.12	92.50	91.32	91.64	10,540	71.95
26	890.18	875.16	883.68	194.99	191.81	193.48	92.57	91.10	91.86	11,840	71.88
27	887.83	869.76	871.17	193.83	189.92	190.65	92.34	91.07	91.67	11,690	71.90
28	867.18	850.59	854.35	189.34	184.97	186.17	91.93	90.59	91.03	14,940	71.74
29	858.57	842.38	846.68	186.86	183.65	185.08	91.42	89.92	90.75	12,150	71.65
		High 891.66				197.62			94.10		73.14
		Low 846.68				185.08			90.75		71.65

APRIL, 1974

	—30 Industrials—			—20 Transportations—			—15 Utilities—			Daily Sales —000—	40 Bonds
	High	Low	Close	High	Low	Close	High	Low	Close		
1	856.38	839.72	843.48	187.09	183.65	184.66	90.84	89.66	90.08	11,470	71.56
2	853.18	839.17	846.61	186.17	183.19	184.27	90.52	89.21	89.85	12,010	71.44
3	860.45	844.65	858.03	187.09	184.00	186.55	90.59	89.21	89.95	11,500	71.30
4	865.46	852.32	858.89	187.94	184.93	186.05	90.46	89.50	89.92	11,650	71.28
5	858.57	842.46	847.54	186.44	182.14	183.50	90.11	88.93	89.24	11,670	71.18
8	847.23	834.25	839.96	183.92	180.56	181.83	89.05	87.74	88.09	10,740	70.95
9	852.55	836.12	846.84	183.96	180.52	182.37	88.80	87.49	88.09	11,330	70.88
10	855.52	840.27	843.71	184.00	181.14	181.99	88.99	87.65	88.09	11,160	70.89
11	849.97	837.77	844.81	182.80	180.21	181.21	88.54	87.23	87.36	9,970	70.88
15	852.00	839.33	843.79	182.61	179.86	181.06	87.84	86.34	87.10	10,130	70.86
16	863.58	845.74	861.23	184.81	181.14	183.73	87.90	86.59	87.39	14,530	70.75
17	874.45	856.38	867.41	186.82	183.53	185.31	88.09	86.75	87.23	14,020	70.71
18	875.94	862.64	869.92	187.67	184.62	186.59	88.03	86.72	87.23	12,470	70.79
19	868.90	856.15	859.90	186.24	182.24	183.92	87.62	86.05	86.69	10,710	70.77
22	864.28	852.39	858.57	184.58	181.48	183.19	86.85	85.67	85.99	10,520	70.64
23	859.51	843.55	845.98	183.88	179.36	180.01	84.71	80.97	81.83	14,110	70.45
24	847.23	828.22	832.37	180.25	176.07	176.49	81.70	79.91	80.49	16,010	70.12
25	835.11	818.68	827.68	175.80	171.89	173.17	80.27	77.84	78.80	15,870	69.99
26	841.29	823.22	834.64	175.26	171.00	172.51	79.75	77.90	78.51	13,250	69.76
29	839.80	824.70	835.42	174.17	170.57	172.08	79.02	76.53	77.04	10,170	69.62
30	844.49	829.63	836.75	174.33	170.84	173.20	77.68	75.41	76.30	10,980	69.64
		High 869.92				186.59			90.08		71.56
		Low 827.68				172.08			76.30		69.62

MAY, 1974

| | —30 Industrials— | | | —20 Transportations— | | | —15 Utilities— | | | Daily Sales | 40 |
	High	Low	Close	High	Low	Close	High	Low	Close	—000—	Bonds
1	861.08	832.77	853.88	177.46	171.77	176.45	78.00	75.41	77.29	15,120	69.67
2	865.85	845.90	851.06	178.27	174.79	175.84	79.12	77.01	78.22	13,620	69.63
3	852.78	839.88	845.90	176.22	173.24	174.48	78.89	77.20	78.28	11,080	69.49
6	847.47	834.32	844.88	174.64	171.39	173.13	79.34	77.65	78.32	9,450	69.43
7	855.84	840.50	847.15	174.37	171.12	172.70	79.31	77.29	78.00	10,710	69.53
8	856.93	843.01	850.99	174.17	171.50	172.93	79.24	77.33	78.44	11,850	69.58
9	870.07	849.19	865.77	175.49	172.08	174.33	79.53	77.71	78.89	14,710	69.50
10	870.38	846.84	850.44	175.41	170.38	171.12	79.56	77.36	78.03	15,270	69.19
13	854.82	838.70	845.59	171.23	167.32	168.87	78.19	76.46	77.04	11,290	69.20
14	856.07	842.30	847.86	171.23	167.87	169.57	77.39	74.77	75.22	10,880	69.05
15	853.02	839.25	846.06	171.12	167.90	169.61	75.57	73.36	73.88	11,240	69.07
16	853.41	833.15	835.34	171.35	168.06	168.76	76.75	73.94	75.63	12,090	69.27
17	833.31	813.75	818.84	169.10	165.00	166.36	76.50	74.61	75.57	13,870	69.25
20	826.19	807.49	812.42	167.67	163.07	163.96	76.91	75.15	75.89	10,550	69.13
21	822.67	803.04	809.53	165.66	162.99	163.77	76.43	74.48	74.93	12,190	69.11
22	818.84	800.14	802.57	165.27	160.48	161.10	75.76	73.72	73.91	15,450	69.15
23	811.33	796.15	805.23	162.10	158.58	160.40	75.09	73.56	74.45	14,770	68.96
24	824.31	806.24	816.65	163.18	159.39	162.14	75.50	73.65	74.39	13,740	68.88
28	824.55	809.14	814.30	163.65	160.52	161.68	75.35	73.49	74.04	10,580	68.87
29	817.27	793.02	795.37	162.29	158.74	159.39	74.64	72.92	73.33	12,300	68.77
30	808.28	788.80	803.58	161.13	157.65	159.86	74.26	72.47	73.59	13,580	68.73
31	808.04	792.32	802.17	161.33	158.43	160.09	74.00	72.41	73.36	10,810	68.72
		High	865.77			176.45			78.89		69.67
		Low	795.37			159.39			73.33		68.72

JUNE, 1974

| | —30 Industrials— | | | —20 Transportations— | | | —15 Utilities— | | | Daily Sales | 40 |
	High	Low	Close	High	Low	Close	High	Low	Close	—000—	Bonds
3	822.36	799.83	821.26	164.96	159.82	164.46	75.03	73.01	74.39	12,490	68.78
4	837.06	821.81	828.69	169.84	165.24	167.87	75.89	74.00	74.77	16,040	68.70
5	839.41	819.23	830.18	171.89	166.94	170.19	75.63	73.84	74.77	13,680	68.68
6	847.54	824.08	845.35	173.86	169.49	172.97	75.66	74.04	75.35	13,360	68.75
7	863.27	845.59	853.72	177.27	173.44	175.68	76.37	74.35	75.12	19,020	68.92
10	864.60	846.14	859.67	178.39	173.67	177.54	76.05	74.07	74.99	13,540	68.95
11	865.54	848.09	852.08	178.97	175.33	176.42	75.54	73.91	74.51	12,380	68.84
12	853.80	837.92	848.56	175.80	172.90	173.94	74.80	73.11	74.10	11,150	68.78
13	861.00	843.79	852.08	176.57	173.17	175.33	74.42	73.01	73.72	11,540	68.72
14	850.67	837.84	843.09	175.02	172.86	173.63	73.68	72.28	72.47	10,030	68.67
17	843.24	829.47	833.23	174.13	170.65	171.31	72.92	70.71	71.29	9,680	68.69
18	838.55	826.50	830.26	172.70	169.26	170.11	71.73	70.07	70.62	10,110	68.63
19	833.54	821.26	826.11	171.54	168.18	169.03	71.06	69.37	70.14	10,550	68.54
20	831.20	818.13	820.79	170.03	167.01	168.10	70.55	68.38	68.89	11,990	68.42
21	822.59	810.15	815.39	168.60	165.00	165.89	69.21	67.52	68.16	11,830	68.16
24	822.43	808.90	816.33	167.48	164.27	165.66	69.05	67.48	68.44	9,960	68.02
25	832.53	817.66	828.85	168.41	165.08	167.29	69.98	68.09	69.21	11,920	67.82
26	830.41	815.47	816.96	168.18	164.62	164.96	69.95	68.22	68.86	11,410	67.90
27	817.27	800.77	803.66	165.31	161.64	162.80	69.21	67.58	68.19	12,650	67.78
28	808.20	796.46	802.41	163.77	160.05	162.18	68.79	67.07	68.22	12,010	67.66
		High	859.67			177.54			75.35		68.95
		Low	802.41			162.18			68.16		67.66

JULY, 1974

	30 Industrials			20 Transportations			15 Utilities			Daily Sales	40
	High	Low	Close	High	Low	Close	High	Low	Close	—000—	Bonds
1	811.95	797.48	806.24	163.15	160.24	161.60	69.91	67.80	68.99	10,270	67.56
2	808.75	788.25	790.68	162.22	157.27	157.69	69.95	68.19	68.60	13,460	67.54
3	798.58	785.12	792.87	158.89	154.94	156.96	69.82	68.06	68.76	13,430	67.35
5	796.31	786.22	791.77	158.12	155.33	156.76	69.66	68.09	69.15	7,400	67.24
8	788.41	765.33	770.57	155.95	150.77	152.12	69.27	66.94	67.48	15,510	67.14
9	782.85	764.63	772.29	154.79	150.65	152.86	68.32	66.46	67.01	15,580	67.04
10	779.18	759.54	762.12	154.21	149.06	149.99	67.48	65.79	65.98	13,490	66.92
11	769.76	753.13	759.62	151.08	147.94	148.72	66.65	65.31	66.08	14,640	66.93
12	790.68	770.03	787.23	156.10	150.92	155.33	68.09	65.79	67.23	17,770	66.99
15	800.92	777.85	786.61	158.97	154.98	157.27	68.54	66.78	67.71	13,560	66.74
16	785.20	771.82	775.97	158.27	155.18	156.49	68.06	66.75	67.58	9,920	66.72
17	788.56	765.80	784.97	158.66	154.48	158.16	68.32	66.81	67.74	11,320	66.40
18	803.04	781.45	789.19	163.69	157.58	160.82	69.15	67.10	68.06	13,980	66.54
19	796.62	780.43	787.94	163.49	160.32	161.99	69.08	67.55	68.51	11,080	66.67
22	795.53	779.49	790.36	163.18	160.17	161.83	68.99	67.32	68.16	9,290	66.63
23	805.62	789.82	797.72	165.39	161.60	163.92	70.62	68.54	69.85	12,910	66.77
24	809.76	791.54	805.77	166.13	163.18	165.24	71.38	69.27	70.90	12,870	66.82
25	807.65	790.05	795.68	168.06	163.69	165.35	71.89	70.26	71.03	13,310	66.86
26	798.03	781.52	784.57	166.01	162.33	163.30	71.64	70.20	70.62	10,420	66.84
29	780.74	764.55	770.89	163.03	159.66	160.86	70.94	69.11	69.50	11,560	66.85
30	775.03	758.84	765.57	161.44	157.61	158.77	69.98	68.51	69.08	11,360	66.60
31	767.44	754.38	757.43	159.78	156.72	157.96	69.37	68.16	68.41	10,960	66.54
		High	806.24			165.35			71.03		67.56
		Low	757.43			148.72			65.98		66.40

AUGUST, 1974

	30 Industrials			20 Transportations			15 Utilities			Daily Sales	40
	High	Low	Close	High	Low	Close	High	Low	Close	—000—	Bonds
1	764.16	745.62	751.10	160.21	156.84	158.31	68.79	67.32	68.00	11,470	66.47
2	758.45	745.31	752.58	158.85	156.34	157.77	68.73	66.75	67.68	10,110	66.31
5	768.46	747.97	760.40	159.39	156.30	157.85	69.05	67.04	68.06	11,230	66.14
6	790.99	766.97	773.78	163.46	158.12	159.63	70.30	68.12	68.92	15,770	65.99
7	798.89	770.81	797.56	163.96	158.54	163.03	70.23	68.48	69.79	13,380	65.90
8	803.43	779.02	784.89	165.35	160.63	162.33	70.74	69.02	69.66	16,060	66.10
9	787.47	771.90	777.30	162.76	160.63	161.52	70.55	69.05	69.72	10,160	66.00
12	780.04	762.83	767.29	162.22	159.59	160.05	70.04	68.67	69.34	7,780	65.92
13	768.54	750.55	756.44	160.79	157.11	157.96	69.66	67.96	68.32	10,140	66.01
14	755.01	735.37	740.54	158.27	153.16	154.13	68.99	67.10	67.58	11,750	65.89
15	749.14	732.24	737.88	155.33	152.16	153.86	68.09	66.40	67.01	11,130	65.94
16	744.45	728.65	731.54	155.14	151.39	152.12	67.87	66.43	66.97	10,510	65.95
19	731.15	715.35	721.84	152.47	148.91	149.88	67.58	65.89	66.21	11,670	65.90
20	736.31	717.46	726.85	152.74	148.68	150.34	67.29	65.60	66.14	13,820	65.88
21	730.05	709.25	711.59	151.62	148.52	149.22	66.81	64.45	64.90	11,650	65.88
22	713.94	694.15	704.63	149.03	145.16	146.74	65.89	63.91	64.93	15,690	65.86
23	710.73	683.90	686.80	147.75	142.72	143.07	65.47	63.71	64.16	13,590	65.72
26	697.12	671.46	688.13	144.46	140.13	142.95	64.67	62.66	63.59	14,630	65.56
27	690.86	668.02	671.54	143.76	139.62	140.13	64.26	62.69	62.95	12,970	65.48
28	681.79	663.56	666.61	141.40	138.08	139.20	63.46	61.57	61.96	16,670	65.31
29	669.51	651.60	656.84	139.12	135.21	135.87	62.24	60.01	60.49	13,690	65.31
30	681.71	661.14	678.58	141.60	136.26	140.94	61.89	59.30	60.71	16,230	65.37
		High	797.56			163.03			69.79		66.47
		Low	656.84			135.87			60.49		65.31

SEPTEMBER, 1974

	—30 Industrials—			—20 Transportations—			—15 Utilities—			Daily Sales —000—	40 Bonds
	High	Low	Close	High	Low	Close	High	Low	Close		
3	686.48	662.23	663.33	142.68	137.38	138.04	62.12	60.26	60.97	12,750	65.33
4	657.46	638.38	648.00	138.04	132.12	134.25	61.38	59.46	60.10	16,930	65.14
5	673.50	649.95	670.76	138.58	133.82	137.42	61.13	59.53	60.30	14,210	65.14
6	685.00	663.56	677.88	142.33	136.99	140.24	61.57	59.98	61.19	15,130	65.10
9	676.71	660.59	662.94	140.84	136.41	137.11	61.61	60.04	60.20	11,160	64.98
10	669.51	652.22	658.17	138.70	135.37	137.76	61.03	59.40	60.07	11,980	64.96
11	665.60	650.58	654.72	137.53	135.29	136.03	60.65	59.05	59.69	11,820	65.00
12	655.04	637.44	641.74	136.03	130.49	131.42	59.94	57.87	58.60	16,920	65.02
13	643.77	624.37	627.19	132.12	126.28	127.21	58.99	57.36	57.93	16,070	65.07
16	645.89	617.73	639.79	130.42	125.46	128.44	59.21	57.10	58.60	18,370	64.96
17	662.16	642.76	648.78	134.13	129.10	132.62	60.30	58.44	59.30	13,730	64.76
18	654.57	635.09	651.91	133.70	130.22	132.58	60.26	58.41	59.59	11,760	64.70
19	679.83	659.34	674.05	137.96	133.67	136.99	61.73	59.46	61.51	17,000	64.55
20	680.54	659.34	670.76	138.77	134.64	137.61	63.91	61.13	63.52	16,250	64.59
23	678.19	657.78	663.72	140.78	136.61	137.92	65.02	63.04	63.62	12,130	64.59
24	662.08	648.78	654.10	138.31	135.14	135.91	63.59	61.92	62.44	9,840	64.68
25	671.46	643.77	649.95	140.63	134.59	137.07	64.45	61.83	62.66	17,620	64.90
26	648.39	633.60	637.98	136.76	132.66	133.78	63.01	61.51	62.56	9,060	64.85
27	643.62	619.37	621.95	134.67	131.54	132.20	62.98	61.45	61.92	12,320	64.87
30	619.37	598.80	607.87	132.20	127.24	128.48	62.37	60.39	61.16	15,000	64.44
		High	677.88			140.24			63.62		65.33
		Low	607.87			127.21			57.93		64.44

OCTOBER, 1974

	—30 Industrials—			—20 Transportations—			—15 Utilities—			Daily Sales —000—	40 Bonds
	High	Low	Close	High	Low	Close	High	Low	Close		
1	613.27	589.57	604.82	129.72	125.31	127.48	61.19	59.56	60.49	16,890	64.29
2	613.89	596.84	601.53	131.00	126.93	128.52	61.80	60.17	61.25	12,230	64.23
3	600.75	582.21	587.61	128.71	124.73	125.93	61.67	60.30	60.90	13,150	64.18
4	593.71	573.22	584.56	128.79	124.30	127.71	61.99	60.26	61.54	15,910	64.13
7	610.45	587.77	607.56	134.71	128.10	133.90	63.49	61.51	62.92	15,000	64.13
8	615.93	596.21	602.63	137.34	133.55	135.06	64.26	62.40	63.20	15,460	64.14
9	633.37	591.91	631.02	142.56	134.29	141.91	65.73	62.69	65.25	18,820	64.20
10	664.03	634.00	648.08	147.48	142.60	144.92	68.92	65.76	67.68	26,360	64.34
11	665.91	638.14	658.17	149.99	143.07	148.14	69.66	66.81	68.92	20,090	64.44
14	689.30	659.73	673.50	153.05	147.71	150.65	71.26	68.70	70.30	19,770	64.64
15	679.21	652.38	658.40	151.27	145.81	147.40	70.81	68.70	69.75	17,390	64.79
16	660.51	636.97	642.29	148.25	144.00	145.00	70.10	68.35	69.08	14,790	64.92
17	657.31	635.48	651.44	148.29	143.38	146.82	70.20	67.77	69.63	14,470	65.01
18	669.51	646.04	654.88	151.15	146.90	149.03	70.71	69.02	70.20	16,460	65.03
21	674.12	645.65	669.82	153.09	147.98	152.43	70.42	68.35	68.99	14,500	65.26
22	680.07	658.56	662.86	156.23	151.39	152.74	70.04	68.12	68.48	18,930	65.39
23	660.51	637.83	645.03	151.97	147.71	148.72	68.83	67.39	67.84	14,200	65.26
24	643.85	624.30	636.26	148.60	143.80	145.62	67.80	66.30	66.88	14,910	65.39
25	648.00	629.93	636.19	148.06	144.31	146.28	68.22	66.65	67.29	12,650	65.32
28	639.63	624.06	633.84	147.01	143.34	145.78	67.64	66.08	67.04	10,540	65.50
29	661.53	638.77	659.34	149.80	146.16	148.56	68.25	66.56	67.77	15,610	65.61
30	681.40	655.19	673.03	154.56	149.45	153.28	68.89	67.17	68.09	20,130	65.93
31	685.62	659.18	665.52	156.61	151.50	153.01	69.11	67.36	67.96	18,840	66.18
		High	673.50			153.28			70.30		65.93
		Low	584.56			125.93			60.49		64.13

NOVEMBER, 1974

	—30 Industrials—			—20 Transportations—			—15 Utilities—			Daily Sales —000—	40 Bonds
	High	Low	Close	High	Low	Close	High	Low	Close		
1	673.03	655.74	665.28	155.06	151.50	153.55	69.08	67.36	68.60	13,470	66.39
4	664.19	647.37	657.23	152.70	148.79	150.88	69.27	67.90	68.73	12,740	66.47
5	676.63	651.83	674.75	153.71	148.52	153.05	70.33	68.44	69.82	15,960	66.31
6	692.82	666.07	669.12	158.23	151.85	153.55	71.16	68.99	69.69	23,930	66.44
7	681.79	660.75	671.93	157.65	153.16	156.61	71.29	69.15	70.68	17,150	66.55
8	676.55	661.53	667.16	157.65	153.51	154.91	71.54	70.10	71.19	15,890	66.50
11	675.69	660.51	672.64	156.03	152.92	155.18	71.86	70.36	71.22	13,220	66.61
12	675.06	656.45	659.18	155.91	151.27	151.77	72.12	70.07	70.62	15,040	66.65
13	666.22	647.29	659.18	153.16	149.68	151.23	71.03	69.24	70.20	16,040	66.85
14	671.31	635.55	658.40	155.22	151.54	152.62	71.19	69.40	69.85	13,540	66.83
15	660.04	642.60	647.61	153.67	150.96	151.66	70.46	68.54	69.24	12,480	66.93
18	641.11	621.71	624.92	150.57	146.05	146.63	69.24	67.29	67.55	15,230	67.31
19	627.42	609.75	614.05	146.74	143.57	144.03	67.84	66.14	66.69	15,720	67.08
20	622.81	605.76	609.59	145.39	142.37	143.42	67.36	65.38	65.98	12,430	67.06
21	616.55	599.81	608.57	145.70	142.25	144.23	66.85	65.02	66.30	13,820	67.04
22	625.31	609.59	615.30	148.02	144.42	146.78	67.52	66.08	66.49	13,020	67.07
25	620.70	604.43	611.94	148.48	144.73	145.97	67.36	65.60	66.24	11,300	67.12
26	625.08	606.85	617.26	148.48	145.08	146.82	67.77	65.76	66.94	13,600	67.09
27	633.45	612.64	619.29	149.61	146.32	147.17	68.35	66.56	67.29	14,810	67.09
29	623.90	610.92	618.66	149.30	146.05	148.25	67.96	66.49	67.39	7,400	67.10
		High 674.75				156.61			71.22		67.31
		Low 608.57				143.42			65.98		66.31

DECEMBER, 1974

	—30 Industrials—			—20 Transportations—			—15 Utilities—			Daily Sales —000—	40 Bonds
	High	Low	Close	High	Low	Close	High	Low	Close		
2	616.08	599.58	603.02	148.64	145.74	146.36	67.77	66.01	66.46	11,140	67.02
3	603.33	590.82	596.61	145.85	142.56	143.57	66.94	65.38	66.11	13,620	66.87
4	606.77	592.07	598.64	145.43	142.06	144.50	67.29	65.63	66.59	12,580	66.79
5	604.11	585.11	587.06	145.23	140.75	141.29	67.74	65.92	66.40	12,890	66.60
6	588.00	572.12	577.60	141.40	137.81	138.70	66.94	65.38	65.89	15,500	66.62
9	587.14	570.01	579.94	140.28	136.57	138.39	67.20	65.09	65.86	14,660	66.87
10	602.08	582.21	593.87	142.33	138.35	140.67	68.22	66.21	67.55	15,690	66.74
11	606.15	589.17	595.35	143.88	140.28	141.64	68.92	67.10	68.16	15,700	66.63
12	604.27	586.67	596.37	142.72	139.62	140.48	69.05	67.52	68.44	15,390	66.52
13	602.00	586.67	592.77	141.02	137.96	139.20	69.02	67.07	67.90	14,000	66.48
16	598.09	584.25	586.83	140.36	136.99	138.31	68.51	66.37	67.13	15,370	66.42
17	599.42	582.45	597.54	140.82	136.95	139.93	68.51	66.46	68.12	16,880	66.49
18	610.84	597.62	603.49	143.03	139.39	140.98	68.92	67.29	68.00	18,050	66.60
19	611.00	596.21	604.43	143.11	139.74	141.44	68.83	66.94	67.87	15,900	66.40
20	607.01	594.49	598.48	142.76	139.66	140.94	68.09	65.98	66.43	15,840	66.43
23	598.95	583.70	589.64	141.48	138.35	139.28	67.10	65.22	66.05	18,040	66.37
24	602.16	589.57	598.40	141.44	138.89	140.24	67.39	65.63	66.69	9,540	66.32
26	610.37	597.07	604.74	142.76	139.74	141.52	67.42	65.82	66.49	11,810	66.26
27	608.26	597.47	602.16	143.03	139.89	140.90	67.23	65.86	66.53	13,060	66.25
30	607.24	595.04	603.25	142.90	139.79	141.27	67.36	65.66	66.69	18,520	66.26
31	619.84	602.86	616.24	144.58	141.14	143.44	69.15	66.40	68.76	20,970	66.14
		High 616.24				146.36			68.76		67.02
		Low 577.60				138.31			65.86		66.14

JANUARY, 1975

	—30 Industrials—			—20 Transportations—			—15 Utilities—			Daily Sales —000—	40 Bonds
	High	Low	Close	High	Low	Close	High	Low	Close		
2	637.12	619.13	632.04	147.98	143.23	146.47	72.69	69.53	72.02	14,800	66.19
3	642.60	623.67	634.54	149.17	144.58	146.84	74.90	71.16	74.39	15,270	66.16
6	646.43	631.88	637.20	150.98	147.25	149.34	76.53	74.45	75.66	17,550	66.23
7	645.42	630.24	641.19	150.98	146.88	149.21	76.30	74.71	75.60	14,890	66.33
8	646.28	632.12	635.40	149.50	145.57	146.63	76.24	74.19	74.93	15,600	66.36
9	646.90	627.58	645.26	150.98	145.98	150.65	76.24	73.94	75.92	16,340	66.53
10	666.69	650.11	658.79	154.95	150.69	153.19	78.86	76.56	77.90	25,890	66.70
13	669.27	651.36	654.18	155.15	151.02	152.45	79.02	77.07	77.84	19,780	66.89
14	657.93	644.01	648.70	153.72	149.42	151.38	78.25	76.40	77.20	16,610	67.03
15	657.15	640.25	653.39	154.66	149.95	153.23	78.13	76.40	77.55	16,580	67.17
16	660.12	648.08	655.74	157.16	153.35	156.01	78.54	76.91	77.97	17,110	67.22
17	657.70	641.90	644.63	157.53	153.80	154.62	78.73	76.85	77.55	14,260	67.18
20	650.19	635.09	647.45	155.28	151.26	153.31	78.06	76.34	77.23	13,450	67.29
21	656.60	637.91	641.90	155.20	151.59	152.57	78.09	76.62	77.10	14,780	67.32
22	654.02	634.39	652.61	153.88	149.99	152.70	77.97	76.24	77.26	15,330	67.31
23	666.61	647.45	656.76	154.29	151.10	152.45	78.22	76.50	77.45	17,960	67.43
24	671.46	652.69	666.61	154.42	150.93	153.19	79.50	77.17	78.96	20,670	67.59
27	698.69	678.43	692.66	158.60	153.35	156.79	81.54	78.83	80.75	32,130	67.62
28	705.10	689.69	694.77	160.73	156.30	157.86	82.09	79.85	80.59	31,760	67.69
29	712.22	686.95	705.96	162.08	155.60	161.05	81.13	79.53	80.39	27,410	67.82
30	717.30	693.13	696.42	164.82	157.16	157.65	81.22	79.08	79.56	29,740	68.01
31	709.56	690.16	703.69	162.24	155.52	159.62	81.19	78.83	80.27	24,640	68.28
		High	705.96			161.05			80.75		68.28
		Low	632.04			146.47			72.02		66.16

FEBRUARY, 1975

	—30 Industrials—			—20 Transportations—			—15 Utilities—			Daily Sales —000—	40 Bonds
	High	Low	Close	High	Low	Close	High	Low	Close		
3	717.62	696.50	711.44	162.20	158.43	160.28	81.70	79.53	81.06	25,400	68.60
4	713.47	695.24	708.07	159.70	155.77	157.33	81.70	79.85	81.06	25,040	68.59
5	721.45	699.78	717.85	159.95	155.40	158.64	81.90	80.30	81.54	25,830	68.76
6	731.54	710.81	714.17	161.26	156.67	157.86	83.11	80.81	81.80	32,020	68.76
7	715.97	697.51	711.91	159.09	155.11	157.90	82.12	80.11	81.64	19,060	68.98
10	717.85	702.75	708.39	158.96	156.42	157.78	82.25	80.65	81.38	16,120	69.02
11	711.67	697.83	707.60	159.41	156.26	158.31	81.54	80.07	80.62	16,470	69.89
12	716.83	700.64	715.03	160.73	157.16	160.07	81.58	80.11	81.10	19,790	68.99
13	738.27	718.48	726.92	164.41	159.95	161.55	82.15	80.65	81.42	35,160	69.07
14	739.52	719.81	734.20	163.51	159.74	161.18	82.34	80.75	81.70	23,290	69.22
18	742.10	722.39	731.30	162.82	159.09	160.44	82.60	80.62	81.64	23,990	69.24
19	740.61	721.92	736.39	162.24	158.31	160.93	82.41	80.65	81.61	21,930	69.29
20	749.53	731.38	745.38	163.31	159.37	162.00	82.47	81.10	81.90	22,260	69.34
21	757.35	742.49	749.77	163.96	160.77	162.53	82.73	81.38	81.96	24,440	69.36
24	750.16	733.49	736.94	163.14	159.70	161.14	82.28	80.52	81.03	19,150	69.55
25	732.79	714.57	719.18	161.59	156.87	157.41	80.94	79.12	79.56	20,910	69.59
26	731.77	713.70	728.10	160.56	156.34	159.66	80.11	78.70	79.50	18,790	69.70
27	738.50	725.13	731.15	162.00	159.05	160.44	80.23	79.02	79.50	16,430	69.66
28	741.94	724.50	739.05	164.70	159.70	163.80	80.23	78.51	79.34	17,560	69.56
		High	749.77			163.80			81.96		69.89
		Low	707.60			157.33			79.34		68.59

MARCH, 1975

	30 Industrials			20 Transportations			15 Utilities			Daily Sales —000—	40 Bonds
	High	Low	Close	High	Low	Close	High	Low	Close		
3	756.49	737.64	753.13	167.69	163.47	166.54	80.43	78.76	80.01	24,100	69.64
4	773.23	753.82	757.74	171.50	165.93	168.02	81.29	79.59	80.30	34,140	69.61
5	766.97	745.54	752.82	169.00	163.31	164.54	81.03	79.28	80.07	24,120	69.61
6	764.71	761.81	761.81	166.91	162.90	165.72	81.00	79.28	80.55	21,780	69.60
7	755.66	759.62	770.10	167.94	164.78	166.46	81.10	79.69	80.39	25,930	69.55
10	779.41	761.58	776.13	168.43	164.33	166.83	81.22	79.05	80.20	25,890	69.64
11	784.73	765.64	770.89	169.33	164.45	166.18	80.75	79.31	79.47	31,280	69.74
12	774.33	756.73	763.69	167.57	163.72	165.52	79.95	78.41	78.96	21,560	69.68
13	766.97	752.58	762.98	166.50	163.39	165.52	79.85	78.16	79.18	18,620	69.46
14	779.57	761.81	773.47	167.36	164.62	166.13	79.88	78.51	79.37	24,840	69.31
17	789.42	771.35	786.53	169.25	165.36	167.28	79.98	78.70	79.56	26,780	69.30
18	796.93	776.60	779.41	168.55	164.45	166.01	80.07	78.54	78.92	29,180	69.26
19	776.83	761.19	769.48	166.71	163.59	165.44	79.15	77.77	78.09	19,030	69.13
20	779.65	758.29	764.00	166.46	162.98	163.76	78.28	76.46	77.26	20,960	69.17
21	768.93	753.13	763.06	165.36	161.42	162.98	77.65	76.11	76.97	15,940	69.21
24	752.50	737.48	743.43	162.20	158.43	160.56	76.59	74.71	75.41	17,810	69.14
25	753.29	731.46	747.89	161.67	156.83	160.44	76.34	74.77	75.79	18,500	68.95
26	769.97	750.94	766.19	165.48	160.97	163.93	77.17	75.47	76.40	18,580	68.91
27	778.63	763.45	770.26	167.94	163.68	166.13	77.55	76.37	76.94	18,300	68.90
31	779.72	764.39	768.15	167.94	164.33	165.48	78.22	76.50	77.20	16,270	68.75
	High 786.53					168.02			80.55		69.74
	Low 743.43					160.44			75.41		68.75

APRIL, 1975

	30 Industrials			20 Transportations			15 Utilities			Daily Sales —000—	40 Bonds
	High	Low	Close	High	Low	Close	High	Low	Close		
1	771.12	756.49	761.58	165.56	162.16	163.39	77.36	75.76	76.24	14,480	68.60
2	770.96	754.77	760.56	165.85	162.57	163.84	77.23	75.79	76.59	15,600	68.60
3	763.22	749.06	752.19	165.52	162.28	163.14	77.20	75.95	76.27	13,920	68.21
4	755.40	740.69	747.26	164.04	160.81	161.63	76.94	75.76	76.18	14,170	67.92
7	749.84	736.62	742.88	161.87	158.84	159.58	76.59	75.19	75.50	13,860	67.72
8	755.38	741.00	749.22	161.50	158.72	160.36	76.14	74.80	75.41	14,320	67.75
9	771.04	748.44	767.99	163.76	160.11	163.10	76.18	74.99	75.60	18,120	67.90
10	788.25	769.40	781.29	167.08	163.47	165.48	76.69	74.83	75.54	24,990	68.04
11	792.94	775.81	789.50	166.50	162.90	164.50	76.56	75.09	75.98	20,160	67.78
14	811.48	790.83	806.95	167.12	163.39	165.48	76.91	75.44	76.37	26,800	67.95
15	822.43	801.31	815.08	168.80	164.90	166.71	77.07	75.73	76.34	29,620	67.88
16	819.77	800.30	815.71	169.00	164.64	168.43	77.17	75.76	76.72	22,970	67.93
17	835.18	813.75	819.46	172.85	167.73	170.60	77.81	76.30	76.72	32,650	67.86
18	822.12	802.25	808.43	171.34	167.28	169.37	77.20	76.02	76.56	26,610	67.66
21	821.57	803.74	815.86	172.69	167.90	171.13	77.42	75.79	76.50	23,960	67.58
22	828.93	811.17	814.14	176.63	168.84	169.86	77.07	75.35	75.82	26,120	67.74
23	815.94	798.97	802.49	170.15	165.81	166.95	76.21	74.87	75.50	20,040	67.71
24	810.15	792.32	803.66	168.80	164.90	167.57	75.98	74.77	75.19	19,050	67.63
25	819.77	800.77	811.80	170.52	166.67	169.45	75.82	74.48	75.03	20,260	67.47
28	820.56	803.50	810.00	171.62	167.69	169.66	75.57	74.26	74.77	17,850	67.33
29	817.04	797.79	803.04	170.48	166.54	168.02	75.06	73.81	74.16	17,740	67.37
30	823.22	796.93	821.34	172.12	166.99	171.38	74.61	73.40	74.04	18,060	67.24
	High 821.34					171.38			76.72		68.60
	Low 742.88					159.58			74.04		67.24

MAY, 1975

| | 30 Industrials | | | 20 Transportations | | | 15 Utilities | | | Daily Sales | 40 |
	High	Low	Close	High	Low	Close	High	Low	Close	—000—	Bonds
1	837.22	817.82	830.96	174.29	168.92	170.76	75.03	73.72	74.29	20,660	67.23
2	853.25	832.21	848.48	174.25	169.29	171.99	75.19	73.97	74.64	25,210	67.32
5	860.06	839.72	855.60	175.35	170.48	174.12	75.60	74.32	75.19	22,370	67.54
6	860.06	832.68	834.72	175.60	170.52	171.30	76.18	74.64	75.25	25,410	67.63
7	842.69	822.67	836.44	172.57	168.96	170.85	75.98	74.64	75.47	22,250	67.58
8	845.20	828.07	840.50	172.36	168.96	170.72	76.75	75.19	76.37	22,980	67.69
9	856.77	839.41	850.13	173.18	169.70	171.91	78.44	76.24	77.90	28,440	67.64
12	857.32	841.99	847.47	173.14	169.90	171.38	79.05	77.49	78.48	22,410	67.61
13	857.87	840.19	850.13	174.08	169.78	172.36	79.18	77.87	78.64	24,950	67.65
14	866.00	846.84	858.73	175.35	171.38	173.47	79.56	78.19	78.80	29,050	67.61
15	868.58	847.15	848.80	174.49	169.33	170.39	79.66	78.22	78.86	27,690	67.64
16	849.03	831.35	837.61	170.89	167.40	168.80	79.05	77.58	78.16	16,630	67.95
19	843.71	823.22	837.69	170.80	166.50	169.66	78.76	77.42	78.16	17,870	67.96
20	843.79	827.52	830.49	171.09	167.57	168.22	78.86	77.39	78.03	18,310	67.85
21	830.26	815.24	818.68	168.55	165.44	166.42	78.16	76.66	77.17	17,640	67.94
22	828.54	807.96	818.91	168.59	165.52	166.87	77.61	76.37	77.23	17,610	67.90
23	835.50	818.28	831.90	169.25	166.30	167.98	77.55	76.43	77.17	17,870	67.89
27	837.53	820.09	826.11	168.84	165.56	166.99	78.00	76.56	77.45	17,050	67.85
28	832.84	812.81	817.04	168.22	163.80	165.64	78.51	76.81	77.45	21,850	67.85
29	823.53	808.12	815.00	167.04	164.13	165.72	78.96	77.23	78.64	18,570	67.81
30	836.20	817.43	832.29	168.67	165.52	167.85	80.30	78.64	79.82	22,670	67.82
		High 858.73				174.12			79.82		67.96
		Low 815.00				165.64			74.29		67.23

JUNE, 1975

| | 30 Industrials | | | 20 Transportations | | | 15 Utilities | | | Daily Sales | 40 |
	High	Low	Close	High	Low	Close	High	Low	Close	—000—	Bonds
2	853.49	835.73	846.61	171.21	167.08	169.04	81.42	79.63	80.71	28,240	67.85
3	855.44	839.57	846.14	171.01	167.40	168.88	82.95	80.78	82.37	26,560	67.79
4	850.83	834.17	839.96	170.31	167.13	168.92	83.68	82.25	83.01	24,900	67.89
5	845.04	829.94	842.15	169.74	167.16	168.72	83.27	81.93	82.82	21,610	67.78
6	849.73	833.15	839.64	171.95	168.59	170.52	83.78	82.34	82.82	22,230	67.91
9	844.49	827.99	830.10	172.40	169.08	170.07	83.40	81.74	82.21	20,670	68.04
10	829.08	813.75	822.12	171.01	167.28	168.88	82.47	81.13	81.80	21,130	68.27
11	833.54	819.85	824.55	171.30	168.31	169.21	82.50	80.87	81.51	18,230	68.46
12	831.43	815.39	819.31	170.64	166.75	167.69	82.02	80.97	81.61	15,970	68.58
13	829.01	811.23	824.47	168.84	166.01	167.53	82.21	81.00	81.90	16,300	68.76
16	837.77	821.34	834.56	168.96	164.90	167.16	83.05	81.77	82.60	16,660	68.96
17	843.09	824.00	828.61	168.47	164.41	165.19	83.62	82.25	82.82	19,440	68.93
18	834.01	818.99	827.83	166.46	162.65	164.58	83.97	82.60	83.40	15,590	68.72
19	848.64	826.11	845.35	166.99	163.18	166.38	86.62	83.56	86.37	21,450	69.06
20	864.67	847.86	855.44	169.08	165.52	166.75	88.19	85.86	86.24	26,260	69.26
23	867.10	846.92	864.83	169.12	165.27	167.81	87.20	85.31	86.50	20,720	69.35
24	878.44	861.00	869.06	170.80	166.50	168.10	87.87	86.27	87.07	26,620	69.62
25	878.05	861.94	872.73	169.94	166.34	168.59	87.62	86.18	86.69	21,610	69.57
26	883.37	866.55	874.14	171.21	167.45	169.90	87.14	85.79	86.34	24,560	69.51
27	880.48	867.18	873.12	172.69	169.12	171.34	86.98	85.28	86.02	18,820	69.42
30	884.62	867.96	878.99	172.73	169.12	171.13	86.88	85.35	85.99	19,430	69.32
		High 878.99				171.34			87.07		69.62
		Low 819.31				164.58			80.71		67.78

JULY, 1975

	30 Industrials			20 Transportations			15 Utilities			Daily Sales —000—	40 Bonds
	High	Low	Close	High	Low	Close	High	Low	Close		
1	884.86	869.60	877.42	172.98	169.74	171.71	86.66	84.77	85.44	20,390	69.28
2	876.25	861.62	870.38	172.28	168.59	170.07	85.57	83.75	84.74	18,530	68.96
3	877.42	863.50	871.79	171.46	168.22	169.78	85.31	83.56	84.45	19,000	68.89
7	873.36	859.04	861.08	171.26	168.14	169.21	84.90	83.11	83.59	15,850	68.69
8	863.97	850.52	857.79	171.34	167.12	169.86	84.10	82.57	83.24	18,990	68.85
9	875.00	858.65	871.87	173.06	169.41	172.03	84.29	82.25	83.81	26,350	68.85
10	884.46	868.19	871.87	175.84	171.58	172.48	84.84	83.43	84.20	28,880	68.93
11	881.49	862.80	871.09	174.41	171.09	172.69	84.80	83.72	84.48	22,210	68.79
14	880.71	865.22	875.86	174.12	171.05	172.89	85.12	83.84	84.71	21,900	68.80
15	888.85	874.14	881.81	176.25	171.26	173.88	85.54	84.13	84.74	28,340	68.91
16	888.53	868.59	872.11	175.11	171.83	172.61	85.09	83.30	83.81	25,250	68.93
17	877.35	858.73	864.28	174.25	170.48	172.16	84.58	82.89	83.65	21,420	68.88
18	867.02	854.27	862.41	173.26	169.66	170.80	84.20	82.63	83.30	16,870	68.83
21	867.88	852.00	854.74	172.53	169.25	170.15	84.16	82.66	83.14	16,690	68.81
22	854.97	838.70	846.76	169.70	165.15	167.12	83.24	81.64	82.37	20,660	68.93
23	853.41	834.64	836.67	168.10	162.24	162.69	82.89	80.94	81.13	20,150	68.97
24	847.78	829.24	840.27	163.84	159.70	161.55	81.61	79.66	80.01	20,550	68.88
25	846.92	829.40	834.09	163.43	159.50	161.22	80.87	79.53	80.11	15,110	68.81
28	836.91	821.96	827.83	162.08	158.92	160.23	80.81	78.89	79.50	14,850	68.83
29	840.74	820.32	824.86	162.86	158.35	159.29	80.39	78.83	79.34	19,000	68.86
30	837.69	819.15	831.66	162.16	158.06	161.26	80.30	78.76	79.50	16,150	68.82
31	843.09	828.77	831.51	163.55	160.64	161.83	80.43	78.96	79.63	14,540	68.61
	High 881.81					173.88			85.44		69.28
	Low 824.86					159.29			79.34		68.61

AUGUST, 1975

	30 Industrials			20 Transportations			15 Utilities			Daily Sales —000—	40 Bonds
	High	Low	Close	High	Low	Close	High	Low	Close		
1	833.78	822.20	826.50	162.82	159.25	160.40	80.23	79.02	79.66	13,320	68.64
4	826.81	813.52	818.05	160.03	157.45	157.98	80.04	78.57	79.05	12,620	68.57
5	824.94	806.95	810.15	159.58	156.26	156.79	79.69	78.19	78.57	15,470	68.31
6	820.40	804.60	813.67	158.14	155.36	156.71	79.12	77.74	78.48	16,280	68.24
7	824.86	809.84	815.79	158.31	155.69	156.63	79.40	77.97	78.64	12,390	68.28
8	826.19	812.66	817.74	157.98	156.01	156.63	79.24	77.97	78.67	11,660	68.25
11	825.33	809.92	823.76	157.65	154.74	156.59	79.08	77.77	78.22	12,350	68.25
12	838.63	823.29	828.54	159.29	156.06	157.45	79.50	77.93	78.38	14,510	68.28
13	831.20	817.43	820.56	158.76	156.14	156.87	79.18	77.45	77.84	12,000	68.26
14	824.08	812.73	817.04	157.94	155.77	156.67	78.03	76.91	77.26	12,460	68.27
15	830.73	814.06	825.64	159.01	156.55	158.23	78.16	76.94	77.68	10,610	68.18
18	833.31	819.38	822.75	160.44	157.45	158.60	78.76	77.33	78.09	10,810	68.07
19	824.23	806.56	808.51	159.17	155.97	156.47	78.67	76.91	77.45	14,990	67.75
20	805.46	789.58	793.26	156.96	153.76	154.58	77.58	75.89	76.40	18,630	67.80
21	801.31	785.75	791.69	155.48	152.25	153.39	76.85	75.28	76.18	16,610	67.73
22	806.95	789.97	804.76	155.52	152.74	154.58	76.91	75.66	76.43	13,050	67.68
25	817.43	803.19	812.34	156.51	153.88	155.24	77.49	76.08	77.23	11,250	67.65
26	815.55	799.98	803.11	156.22	152.16	153.19	77.81	76.56	76.94	11,350	67.61
27	809.61	797.09	807.20	154.01	151.26	152.82	77.58	76.40	77.29	11,100	67.61
28	831.59	809.92	829.47	156.47	153.35	155.60	79.02	77.23	78.70	14,530	67.58
29	844.02	828.69	835.34	158.64	155.40	157.24	79.98	78.60	79.24	15,480	67.76
	High 835.34					160.40			79.66		68.64
	Low 791.69					152.82			76.18		67.58

SEPTEMBER, 1975

	—30 Industrials—			—20 Transportations—			—15 Utilities—			Daily Sales	40
	High	Low	Close	High	Low	Close	High	Low	Close	—000—	Bonds
2	840.19	821.26	823.69	158.43	155.03	156.34	79.82	78.13	78.25	11,460	67.80
3	834.64	815.94	832.29	157.78	154.87	157.00	78.80	77.68	78.44	12,260	67.93
4	843.55	827.21	838.31	157.90	155.28	156.34	78.92	77.61	78.19	12,810	67.84
5	843.63	830.26	835.97	156.71	154.58	155.32	78.38	77.36	77.74	11,680	67.70
8	843.95	830.18	840.11	156.38	153.88	155.52	78.70	77.26	78.22	11,500	67.62
9	849.03	826.58	827.75	157.04	153.88	154.74	79.18	77.84	78.44	15,790	67.63
10	825.33	809.53	817.66	154.46	151.30	152.29	78.67	77.42	77.87	14,780	67.64
11	820.32	808.12	812.66	153.11	150.85	151.55	78.09	76.85	77.20	11,100	67.40
12	823.69	806.63	809.23	153.39	150.57	151.43	77.93	76.72	77.23	12,230	67.47
15	811.25	799.05	803.19	152.04	149.91	150.73	77.49	76.24	76.69	8,670	67.49
16	809.76	792.79	795.13	151.30	148.76	149.38	77.26	75.54	75.95	13,090	67.25
17	804.52	792.01	799.05	151.22	148.27	150.07	76.69	75.25	75.98	12,190	67.27
18	817.19	797.64	814.61	153.43	149.75	152.86	76.81	75.54	76.37	14,560	67.17
19	834.72	816.72	829.79	158.19	152.74	156.83	77.61	76.05	76.97	20,830	67.19
22	835.65	817.58	820.40	159.33	155.20	156.55	77.77	76.59	77.01	14,750	67.35
23	824.31	807.96	819.85	158.64	155.44	157.74	77.20	75.79	76.40	12,800	67.23
24	836.83	820.24	826.19	161.59	158.23	159.74	77.87	76.50	77.26	16,060	67.25
25	828.85	812.89	820.24	160.48	157.16	158.88	78.03	76.94	77.45	12,890	67.36
26	827.28	811.33	818.60	161.05	157.90	159.58	78.35	77.04	78.00	12,570	67.34
29	820.56	803.43	805.23	160.23	157.24	158.14	78.16	76.94	77.17	10,580	67.30
30	804.44	789.66	793.88	158.35	155.28	155.97	77.71	76.62	76.97	12,520	67.21
		High 840.11				159.74			78.44		67.93
		Low 793.88				149.38			75.95		67.17

OCTOBER, 1975

	—30 Industrials—			—20 Transportations—			—15 Utilities—			Daily Sales	40
	High	Low	Close	High	Low	Close	High	Low	Close	—000—	Bonds
1	799.35	780.54	784.16	157.16	153.92	154.79	77.77	76.46	76.85	14,070	67.22
2	799.28	781.72	794.55	157.20	154.05	155.93	77.68	76.69	77.29	14,290	67.05
3	816.12	794.71	813.21	159.41	155.73	158.39	78.73	77.39	78.18	16,360	67.05
6	826.83	811.32	819.66	161.01	158.60	159.87	79.40	78.00	78.80	15,470	67.21
7	821.79	806.12	816.51	161.55	158.72	160.11	79.34	78.28	78.70	13,530	67.36
8	829.35	809.82	823.91	164.09	169.91	165.15	79.31	78.03	78.83	17,800	67.57
9	834.93	817.30	824.54	165.19	161.83	162.73	79.95	78.57	79.56	17,770	67.75
10	832.57	817.14	823.91	164.62	161.83	163.01	80.75	79.24	80.39	14,880	67.72
13	838.95	818.48	837.77	165.95	162.49	165.15	81.54	80.11	81.19	12,020	67.95
14	852.41	830.13	835.25	169.49	165.56	167.28	82.31	80.68	81.51	19,960	67.94
15	843.91	828.01	837.22	168.18	165.44	166.38	82.34	80.78	81.86	14,440	68.03
16	851.46	833.60	837.85	168.14	164.99	165.52	82.95	81.80	82.31	18,910	68.09
17	841.23	824.46	832.18	166.67	163.39	164.86	82.92	81.42	82.31	15,650	67.98
20	844.14	828.24	842.25	167.85	164.41	166.71	82.85	81.42	82.12	13,250	68.14
21	855.71	841.23	846.82	169.66	166.26	168.02	83.49	82.12	82.89	20,800	68.16
22	855.09	840.37	849.57	169.41	166.63	167.81	83.43	82.25	82.79	16,060	68.34
23	859.57	844.46	855.16	169.37	166.83	168.18	83.59	82.06	82.89	17,900	68.37
24	857.76	837.22	840.52	169.08	165.85	166.58	83.33	82.15	82.47	18,120	68.34
27	845.17	831.31	838.48	168.22	165.19	166.75	83.17	81.96	82.44	13,100	68.35
28	853.67	837.53	851.46	168.47	165.19	166.54	83.43	81.67	82.66	17,060	68.51
29	850.83	834.86	838.63	167.40	164.04	165.23	82.95	81.58	82.02	16,110	68.58
30	847.29	832.97	839.42	168.31	163.84	167.67	82.66	81.35	81.96	15,080	68.53
31	842.49	829.97	836.04	167.69	164.50	166.38	83.01	81.77	82.63	12,910	68.58
		High 855.16				168.18			82.89		68.58
		Low 784.16				154.79			76.85		67.05

NOVEMBER, 1975

	—30 Industrials—			—20 Transportations—			—15 Utilities—			Daily Sales —000—	40 Bonds
	High	Low	Close	High	Low	Close	High	Low	Close		
3	836.82	822.26	825.72	168.10	164.74	166.26	83.17	81.77	82.31	11,400	68.67
4	834.07	821.08	830.13	168.26	165.44	167.61	83.08	81.83	82.44	11,570	68.55
5	843.91	829.50	836.27	170.35	166.30	168.18	83.27	81.90	82.66	17,390	68.60
6	845.40	827.93	840.92	170.48	166.50	169.58	83.43	81.96	82.89	18,600	68.57
7	843.83	830.29	835.80	171.01	168.22	169.99	83.33	82.02	82.73	15,930	68.58
10	840.99	824.62	835.48	170.60	167.81	169.62	83.17	82.12	82.57	14,910	68.60
11	843.28	831.63	838.55	170.85	168.59	170.03	83.05	82.06	82.57	14,640	68.51
12	855.64	838.40	852.25	174.00	169.58	173.22	83.78	82.21	83.08	23,960	68.53
13	863.11	848.47	851.23	176.75	172.81	173.88	84.13	82.79	83.40	25,070	68.73
14	857.92	845.32	853.67	174.94	172.57	173.43	84.10	82.76	83.56	16,460	68.75
17	862.56	847.61	856.66	176.21	172.89	174.57	84.39	83.17	83.88	17,660	68.83
18	865.79	851.78	855.24	177.07	173.55	174.45	84.42	83.05	83.37	20,760	68.83
19	857.53	842.25	848.24	175.35	171.13	172.03	83.65	82.34	82.69	16,820	68.70
20	853.35	838.87	843.51	173.14	170.15	171.13	83.40	82.15	82.66	16,460	68.86
21	848.39	834.62	840.76	172.03	169.08	170.60	83.17	82.02	82.66	14,110	68.79
24	849.10	833.83	845.64	171.05	167.85	169.53	83.33	81.96	82.89	13,930	68.67
25	859.10	845.56	855.40	170.39	167.81	168.84	83.43	82.21	83.05	17,490	68.70
26	863.90	851.07	858.55	170.27	167.65	169.00	83.68	82.50	83.17	18,780	68.63
28	865.24	854.06	860.67	170.27	167.77	169.29	83.75	82.66	83.27	12,870	68.64
		High	860.67			174.57			83.88		68.86
		Low	825.72			166.26			82.31		68.51

DECEMBER, 1975

	—30 Industrials—			—20 Transportations—			—15 Utilities—			Daily Sales —000—	40 Bonds
	High	Low	Close	High	Low	Close	High	Low	Close		
1	865.95	853.04	856.34	171.62	168.39	169.49	83.84	82.57	82.89	16,050	68.51
2	856.66	841.70	843.20	169.90	166.91	167.85	83.43	82.18	82.63	17,930	68.46
3	836.67	822.10	825.49	167.45	164.21	165.23	82.53	80.71	81.06	21,320	68.32
4	833.67	818.17	829.11	166.26	163.43	164.90	81.45	80.04	80.71	16,380	68.37
5	833.60	816.99	818.80	166.05	163.35	163.84	81.38	80.30	80.81	14,050	68.42
8	826.43	812.81	821.63	164.70	161.96	163.14	81.67	80.14	80.65	14,150	68.39
9	827.53	814.47	824.15	164.00	161.42	162.53	81.19	79.88	80.65	16,040	68.30
10	835.72	820.92	833.99	165.81	162.73	165.07	81.29	80.04	81.03	15,680	68.27
11	840.13	828.87	832.73	167.08	163.96	165.11	81.58	80.33	80.94	15,300	68.15
12	836.74	825.53	832.81	166.01	163.43	164.78	81.58	80.36	81.00	13,100	68.09
15	841.23	828.72	836.59	165.72	163.31	164.54	81.90	80.39	81.13	13,960	68.16
16	849.73	833.91	844.30	166.54	163.76	165.52	82.09	80.62	81.35	18,350	68.21
17	852.17	840.37	846.27	167.16	164.74	166.09	81.99	80.65	81.32	16,560	68.34
18	857.13	843.12	852.09	168.22	165.64	167.81	82.06	80.75	81.42	18,040	68.38
19	854.30	841.39	844.38	168.76	165.93	166.95	82.12	80.75	81.16	17,720	68.41
22	847.29	835.33	838.63	167.77	165.03	165.85	81.83	80.55	81.35	15,340	68.56
23	847.84	833.36	843.75	168.67	164.37	167.20	81.80	80.65	81.19	17,750	68.65
24	854.93	845.01	851.94	170.15	167.24	169.12	82.34	81.16	82.12	11,150	68.58
26	860.91	850.20	859.81	171.17	168.88	170.68	83.01	81.74	82.73	10,020	68.72
29	866.11	853.59	856.66	172.61	169.82	170.85	83.62	82.06	82.79	17,070	68.87
30	860.75	847.13	852.41	172.28	169.78	171.21	83.37	81.96	82.69	16,040	69.06
31	859.65	848.71	852.41	173.26	170.48	172.65	83.91	82.50	83.65	16,970	69.02
		High	859.81			172.65			83.65		69.06
		Low	818.80			162.53			80.65		68.09

JANUARY, 1976

	—30 Industrials—			—20 Transportations—			—15 Utilities—			Daily Sales —000—	40 Bonds
	High	Low	Close	High	Low	Close	High	Low	Close		
2	860.44	848.63	858.71	176.24	172.07	175.69	85.09	83.53	84.84	10,300	69.11
5	879.80	858.63	877.83	179.86	175.18	178.57	86.75	84.80	86.43	21,960	69.28
6	894.99	878.70	890.82	182.38	178.17	181.32	87.87	86.27	87.36	31,270	69.57
7	908.69	886.41	898.69	184.35	179.83	182.50	88.41	86.50	87.39	33,170	69.52
8	916.64	893.89	907.98	186.63	181.83	185.06	88.51	86.78	87.71	29,030	69.77
9	916.88	903.73	911.13	186.95	184.00	185.81	88.67	87.04	87.97	26,510	69.92
12	925.93	905.38	922.39	189.19	184.19	188.41	89.18	87.39	88.70	30,440	70.06
13	930.26	909.40	912.94	190.26	186.24	187.11	89.47	87.81	88.29	34,530	70.27
14	932.62	908.22	929.63	191.36	186.04	190.69	89.47	87.62	89.24	30,340	70.35
15	940.26	921.21	924.51	192.93	188.76	190.33	90.30	88.64	89.34	38,450	70.54
16	935.22	917.98	929.63	192.30	188.41	191.32	90.55	89.02	89.95	25,940	70.58
19	946.08	923.80	943.72	196.79	190.49	196.08	90.75	89.08	90.30	29,450	70.67
20	954.03	935.77	949.86	199.27	194.51	197.42	90.97	89.34	90.39	36,690	70.73
21	954.97	934.35	946.24	197.73	192.50	195.77	91.00	89.34	90.24	34,470	70.83
22	949.62	933.96	943.48	196.83	193.13	195.57	91.00	89.15	89.98	27,420	70.85
23	958.38	940.57	953.95	198.56	194.58	197.38	91.00	89.47	90.62	33,640	70.90
26	969.22	953.87	961.51	200.33	195.57	197.26	91.55	89.85	90.65	34,470	70.94
27	973.16	950.80	957.81	199.58	194.35	197.26	91.26	90.01	90.75	32,070	70.92
28	963.08	942.38	951.35	198.72	194.23	195.84	91.42	90.01	90.55	27,370	71.13
29	970.80	948.13	968.75	199.23	195.10	198.05	91.61	90.30	91.07	29,800	71.20
30	985.99	966.07	975.28	201.63	196.87	199.35	91.99	90.17	90.87	38,510	71.26
		High	975.28			199.35			91.07		71.26
		Low	858.71			175.69			84.84		69.11

FEBRUARY, 1976

	—30 Industrials—			—20 Transportations—			—15 Utilities—			Daily Sales —000—	40 Bonds
	High	Low	Close	High	Low	Close	High	Low	Close		
2	976.54	962.06	971.35	200.49	197.30	199.03	91.67	90.17	91.00	24,000	71.21
3	979.69	960.80	972.61	201.55	197.85	199.43	91.96	90.36	91.29	34,080	71.16
4	981.66	966.94	976.62	203.32	198.72	201.94	92.50	90.81	91.90	38,270	71.04
5	980.71	961.98	964.81	203.20	199.23	199.82	92.57	90.43	91.13	33,780	71.23
6	965.60	948.84	954.90	200.09	196.83	198.36	90.65	89.34	89.82	27,360	71.16
9	967.18	948.44	957.18	201.05	197.30	199.94	90.49	88.96	89.47	25,340	71.22
10	971.74	953.09	968.75	201.87	198.44	200.41	90.20	88.83	89.60	27,660	71.21
11	980.24	965.76	971.90	203.79	200.06	202.73	90.17	88.96	89.31	32,300	71.28
12	978.12	963.00	966.78	203.60	200.45	201.31	89.85	88.57	89.15	28,610	71.32
13	968.99	953.56	958.36	202.53	199.15	200.96	89.24	87.65	88.03	23,870	71.36
17	963.48	946.63	950.57	203.72	199.98	202.61	88.61	86.82	87.52	25,460	71.43
18	965.68	946.16	960.09	204.82	201.35	203.64	88.99	87.36	88.48	29,900	71.60
19	979.85	961.74	975.76	207.30	203.56	205.64	89.82	88.38	89.34	39,210	71.66
20	996.93	977.80	987.80	209.03	204.74	206.94	90.08	88.77	89.37	44,510	71.72
23	993.39	977.25	985.28	208.60	204.82	207.22	89.72	88.38	88.89	31,460	71.64
24	1001.65	983.00	993.55	210.17	205.80	208.79	89.50	88.16	88.67	34,380	71.84
25	1002.83	983.39	994.57	210.96	207.14	208.99	89.12	87.39	87.97	34,680	72.09
26	1000.94	975.99	978.83	210.45	205.84	206.98	88.61	87.23	87.58	34,320	72.10
27	980.71	962.30	972.61	207.53	203.60	205.57	88.19	86.72	87.58	26,940	72.09
		High	994.57			208.99			91.90		72.10
		Low	950.57			198.36			87.52		71.04

MARCH, 1976

	30 Industrials High	Low	Close	20 Transportations High	Low	Close	15 Utilities High	Low	Close	Daily Sales —000—	40 Bonds
1	981.19	964.18	975.36	206.79	202.97	205.29	87.97	86.66	87.39	22,070	72.27
2	991.11	974.26	985.12	208.44	204.19	206.79	88.13	87.01	87.62	25,590	72.13
3	988.98	973.00	978.83	208.52	204.11	205.96	87.68	86.50	86.82	25,450	72.11
4	984.26	967.18	970.64	207.45	203.24	204.82	87.23	85.47	86.08	24,410	72.13
5	981.03	965.37	972.92	206.75	203.36	205.21	86.56	85.25	85.79	23,030	72.18
8	991.73	973.08	988.74	208.36	204.11	207.38	86.82	85.57	86.15	25,060	72.20
9	1005.67	987.88	993.70	211.59	207.14	208.95	87.14	85.83	86.53	31,770	72.09
10	1003.15	987.17	995.28	212.26	207.89	209.93	87.55	86.21	87.04	24,900	71.97
11	1008.42	992.76	1003.31	212.93	209.26	211.51	87.65	86.43	87.26	27.300	72.06
12	1006.61	984.49	987.64	213.48	208.95	209.62	87.77	86.43	86.88	26,020	72.29
15	986.85	969.69	974.50	209.62	205.37	206.67	87.04	85.86	86.37	19,570	72.21
16	986.62	970.09	983.47	209.30	205.72	208.48	86.66	85.60	86.21	22,780	72.18
17	995.59	981.03	985.99	210.45	206.51	207.77	86.78	85.67	86.30	26,190	72.31
18	988.98	971.35	979.85	208.71	205.33	206.71	87.26	86.08	86.78	20,330	72.29
19	985.36	970.80	979.85	208.16	204.74	206.35	87.46	86.08	86.85	18,090	72.23
22	988.27	977.64	982.29	208.75	204.94	206.67	87.65	86.21	86.98	19,410	72.18
23	997.01	978.12	995.43	210.01	205.21	208.24	87.62	86.27	87.14	22,450	72.37
24	1018.03	1001.65	1009.21	212.93	207.57	209.78	88.13	86.72	87.20	32,610	72.49
25	1014.72	997.72	1002.13	211.47	207.81	209.38	88.00	86.50	87.36	22,510	72.55
26	1009.68	997.64	1003.46	211.04	207.65	209.62	87.97	86.69	87.30	18,510	72.58
29	1007.40	993.78	997.40	210.60	208.04	208.87	88.03	86.72	87.46	16,100	72.67
30	1000.31	985.04	992.13	208.99	205.49	207.34	87.68	86.46	87.14	17,930	72.64
31	1000.79	988.35	999.45	209.42	205.92	207.97	87.90	86.43	87.55	17,520	72.86
	High 1009.21					211.51			87.62		72.86
	Low 970.64					204.82			85.79		71.97

APRIL, 1976

	30 Industrials High	Low	Close	20 Transportations High	Low	Close	15 Utilities High	Low	Close	Daily Sales —000—	40 Bonds
1	1003.31	987.72	994.10	208.48	205.33	206.90	87.90	86.72	87.26	17,910	72.82
2	996.54	982.13	991.58	208.44	205.01	206.98	87.68	86.66	87.10	17,420	72.82
5	1008.74	992.99	1004.09	211.47	207.41	210.29	88.06	86.91	87.62	21,940	72.88
6	1015.35	998.90	1001.65	213.20	209.66	210.64	88.03	86.72	87.14	24,170	73.01
7	1004.80	983.08	986.22	211.39	207.10	207.97	88.19	86.21	86.98	20,190	73.20
8	987.80	968.99	977.09	208.44	204.70	205.96	87.39	85.86	86.62	20,860	73.19
9	981.58	964.34	968.28	206.19	201.12	202.34	86.82	85.41	85.79	19,050	73.27
12	978.90	963.00	971.27	203.32	199.27	200.88	86.37	85.15	85.76	16,030	73.25
13	985.99	969.54	984.26	202.77	199.15	201.94	86.46	85.38	86.11	15,990	73.34
14	990.24	972.76	974.65	203.79	200.41	201.51	86.82	85.63	86.18	18,440	73.37
15	984.81	969.30	980.48	205.33	200.84	204.23	87.36	86.02	87.17	15,100	73.53
19	991.18	979.16	988.11	207.85	203.80	206.51	87.55	86.43	87.07	16,500	73.50
20	1008.19	998.51	1003.46	212.26	206.90	211.51	88.16	86.91	87.84	23,500	73.51
21	1016.85	1000.31	1011.02	214.93	210.37	212.89	88.80	87.23	87.77	26,600	73.56
22	1017.71	1003.70	1007.71	215.25	211.86	213.48	88.61	87.14	87.62	20,220	73.60
23	1008.89	995.36	1000.71	214.42	210.76	212.14	88.38	87.01	87.87	17,000	73.52
26	1005.20	991.03	1002.76	213.71	209.50	212.45	88.51	87.20	87.87	15,520	73.47
27	1008.42	993.15	995.51	214.11	209.78	210.52	88.38	87.07	87.33	17,760	73.34
28	1002.36	987.09	1000.70	212.37	208.48	211.59	87.87	86.69	87.55	15,790	73.35
29	1010.39	996.62	1002.13	214.26	210.37	212.65	88.13	87.01	87.68	17,740	73.15
30	1007.01	993.31	996.85	213.99	211.27	212.77	88.25	87.17	87.74	14,530	73.06
	High 1011.02					213.48			87.87		73.60
	Low 968.28					200.88			85.76		72.82

MAY, 1976

	—30 Industrials—			—20 Transportations—			—15 Utilities—			Daily Sales —000—	40 Bonds
	High	Low	Close	High	Low	Close	High	Low	Close		
3	995.83	981.74	990.32	212.33	208.75	210.45	88.09	87.01	87.62	15,180	72.88
4	998.03	982.21	993.70	212.93	208.79	212.02	87.93	86.91	87.58	17,240	72.74
5	997.09	982.53	986.46	213.28	210.01	211.63	87.90	86.94	87.42	14,970	72.82
6	995.43	981.50	989.53	213.24	210.92	212.41	87.90	86.72	87.65	16,200	72.86
7	999.53	984.97	996.22	214.70	211.86	214.15	88.22	87.30	87.87	17,810	72.78
10	1010.39	994.10	1007.48	220.40	214.66	219.58	88.25	87.01	87.33	22,760	72.67
11	1015.82	1001.42	1006.61	222.49	218.75	220.91	88.19	86.88	87.46	23,590	72.57
12	1012.52	999.53	1005.67	222.02	218.91	220.28	88.09	87.14	87.58	18,510	72.48
13	1008.66	997.48	1001.10	221.15	218.00	219.22	88.00	86.85	87.30	16,730	72.52
14	1000.24	988.74	992.60	220.99	216.90	219.54	87.74	86.43	86.98	16,800	72.56
17	993.47	982.05	987.64	220.44	216.19	217.77	87.46	86.46	86.88	14,720	72.56
18	994.80	984.41	989.45	219.89	215.40	216.94	87.33	86.15	86.56	17,410	72.37
19	996.14	983.99	988.90	219.38	216.31	217.73	87.17	85.95	86.85	18,450	72.37
20	1001.05	985.76	997.27	220.36	217.02	219.77	87.14	85.76	86.62	22,560	72.37
21	999.03	986.41	990.75	220.60	217.69	218.75	86.94	85.86	86.34	18,730	72.21
24	988.82	969.03	971.53	218.95	214.03	214.70	86.50	85.09	85.54	16,560	72.33
25	976.99	961.95	971.69	214.38	210.72	211.98	85.44	84.26	84.52	18,770	72.33
26	976.43	963.48	968.63	213.55	210.76	212.02	85.19	84.04	84.80	16,750	72.33
27	970.48	955.84	965.57	212.41	209.30	211.35	85.31	84.20	84.93	15,310	72.35
28	978.60	962.92	975.23	214.42	210.76	212.96	85.73	84.55	85.28	16,860	72.20
		High	1007.48			220.91			87.87		72.88
		Low	965.57			210.45			84.52		72.20

JUNE, 1976

	—30 Industrials—			—20 Transportations—			—15 Utilities—			Daily Sales —000—	40 Bonds
	High	Low	Close	High	Low	Close	High	Low	Close		
1	981.26	969.27	973.13	214.77	212.14	213.44	86.05	84.90	85.28	13,880	72.28
2	979.37	968.57	975.93	215.05	211.90	213.99	85.92	85.03	85.60	16,120	72.16
3	983.14	971.02	973.80	216.78	213.20	215.29	86.24	84.90	85.70	18,900	72.24
4	973.97	961.28	963.90	215.99	213.55	214.38	86.27	85.12	85.63	15,960	72.36
7	965.62	951.70	958.09	214.50	210.72	212.22	86.30	85.12	85.86	14,510	72.31
8	968.48	956.45	959.97	214.22	210.64	211.74	86.30	85.28	85.89	16,660	72.44
9	965.54	954.98	958.09	212.41	209.78	210.84	86.43	85.28	85.92	14,560	72.37
10	967.99	956.12	964.39	213.36	209.50	211.86	86.56	85.47	86.02	16,100	72.28
11	980.52	963.98	978.80	215.76	211.78	214.74	86.56	85.19	85.89	19,470	72.40
14	995.17	979.78	991.24	218.32	214.70	217.45	86.62	85.38	86.02	21,250	72.37
15	994.19	981.42	985.92	218.24	214.66	215.68	86.37	85.38	85.70	18,440	72.40
16	995.66	979.94	988.62	219.34	215.17	217.37	86.18	85.22	85.57	21,620	72.44
17	1007.86	988.38	1003.19	221.03	216.55	218.95	86.37	85.22	85.95	27,810	72.68
18	1012.93	996.97	1001.88	222.25	218.08	220.48	86.85	85.63	86.15	25,720	72.71
21	1010.97	997.54	1007.45	222.80	219.03	221.62	86.59	85.54	86.05	18,930	72.68
22	1011.87	995.74	997.63	223.08	220.09	221.07	86.43	85.35	85.70	21,150	72.75
23	1002.05	987.23	996.56	222.45	218.83	220.64	86.30	85.19	85.95	17,530	72.75
24	1009.09	994.52	1003.77	223.08	219.81	221.78	86.94	85.73	86.59	19,850	72.81
25	1008.35	995.58	999.84	224.02	220.48	222.21	87.84	86.43	87.52	17,830	72.78
28	1006.30	993.45	997.38	223.43	220.44	221.43	88.09	86.75	87.39	17,490	72.69
29	1004.50	992.47	1000.65	223.51	220.40	222.45	88.00	86.85	87.55	19,620	72.59
30	1011.79	995.99	1002.78	225.95	222.13	224.77	88.16	87.10	87.55	23,830	72.69
		High	1007.45			224.77			87.55		72.81
		Low	958.09			210.84			85.28		72.16

JULY, 1976

	—30 Industrials—			—20 Transportations—			—15 Utilities—			Daily Sales —000—	40 Bonds
	High	Low	Close	High	Low	Close	High	Low	Close		
1	1009.00	990.26	994.84	226.27	222.69	223.79	88.25	87.10	87.74	21,130	85.70
2	1003.85	991.00	999.84	225.64	222.41	224.26	88.73	87.49	88.54	16,730	85.80
6	1003.85	989.19	991.81	225.48	222.65	223.28	89.21	87.97	88.57	16,130	86.27
7	994.43	982.56	991.16	224.93	222.21	224.14	89.56	88.32	89.24	18,470	86.33
8	998.85	987.15	991.98	226.78	223.87	225.56	89.92	88.67	89.18	21,710	86.44
9	1007.53	989.60	1003.11	229.30	224.97	228.35	89.82	88.64	89.53	23,500	86.58
12	1015.72	998.94	1011.21	230.75	227.49	229.53	90.39	89.12	90.04	23,750	86.64
13	1017.93	1001.64	1006.06	231.82	228.47	229.65	90.97	89.85	90.36	27,550	86.71
14	1012.20	997.95	1005.16	232.56	228.79	231.27	91.23	89.92	90.91	23,840	86.76
15	1006.79	993.21	997.46	231.93	228.94	229.69	91.42	90.46	90.97	20,400	86.99
16	997.30	985.43	993.21	229.97	227.25	228.67	91.13	90.01	90.55	20,450	86.77
19	999.10	986.08	990.83	229.89	226.11	227.33	91.10	90.11	90.71	18,200	86.78
20	994.43	983.06	988.29	228.20	224.34	225.60	91.26	90.36	90.97	18,810	86.76
21	996.77	984.20	989.44	228.31	224.54	226.42	91.23	90.08	90.78	18,350	86.90
22	995.99	982.97	991.08	227.96	224.65	226.66	91.10	90.27	90.68	15,600	86.77
23	997.71	985.43	990.91	228.20	225.64	226.70	91.42	90.20	91.10	15,870	86.88
26	997.20	985.91	991.51	227.76	224.89	226.03	91.32	90.27	90.75	13,530	86.95
27	994.99	981.92	984.13	226.46	222.37	222.96	91.67	90.24	91.00	15,580	86.98
28	984.89	974.71	981.33	224.02	220.68	222.17	91.67	90.39	91.07	16,000	87.01
29	985.74	974.20	979.29	222.84	219.38	220.68	91.67	90.71	91.26	13,330	87.13
30	987.95	974.71	984.64	222.57	219.62	221.54	92.09	90.94	91.55	14,830	87.13
		High	1011.21			231.27			91.55		87.13
		Low	979.29			220.68			87.74		85.70

AUGUST, 1976

	—30 Industrials—			—20 Transportations—			—15 Utilities—			Daily Sales —000—	40 Bonds
	High	Low	Close	High	Low	Close	High	Low	Close		
2	988.97	977.43	982.26	222.36	219.55	220.69	92.44	91.39	92.18	13,870	87.10
3	992.96	978.70	990.33	223.58	219.79	222.68	93.17	91.71	92.89	18,500	87.16
4	998.73	986.42	992.28	225.50	221.99	223.62	93.72	92.63	93.40	20,650	87.33
5	995.76	983.28	986.68	224.72	221.42	222.85	93.81	92.63	93.08	15,530	87.39
6	989.90	978.70	986.00	223.79	221.67	222.52	93.91	92.86	93.56	13,930	87.45
9	987.53	979.06	983.46	223.09	221.05	221.79	93.81	92.68	93.27	11,700	87.51
10	995.68	981.13	993.43	223.54	220.69	222.93	93.94	92.89	93.40	16,690	87.63
11	1000.00	984.46	986.79	225.13	222.11	222.97	94.01	92.63	93.17	18,710	87.73
12	992.10	979.22	987.12	224.48	222.20	223.38	93.56	92.34	93.08	15,560	87.77
13	994.35	983.05	990.19	224.27	221.58	222.28	93.59	92.60	92.98	13,930	87.98
16	997.51	986.95	992.77	223.38	220.81	221.91	93.53	92.57	93.27	16,210	87.94
17	1002.41	990.44	999.34	223.83	220.03	222.24	93.85	92.89	93.56	18,500	87.95
18	1004.74	992.60	995.01	223.91	220.69	222.64	93.97	92.82	93.37	17,150	88.01
19	995.84	979.31	983.88	223.30	219.22	219.99	93.78	92.57	93.02	17,230	88.06
20	982.63	970.99	974.07	219.95	216.65	217.51	93.40	92.31	92.66	14,920	88.09
23	975.73	962.18	971.49	217.67	214.12	215.55	92.86	91.61	92.34	15,450	88.02
24	977.14	960.77	962.93	216.89	213.59	214.53	93.17	91.64	92.41	16,740	88.19
25	973.82	956.37	970.83	216.41	212.65	215.75	92.95	91.61	92.47	17,400	88.23
26	975.90	958.28	960.44	217.22	213.76	214.73	92.98	91.77	92.34	15,270	88.36
27	967.50	954.12	963.93	216.73	213.02	216.08	92.54	91.48	92.22	12,120	88.32
30	972.91	961.44	968.92	217.91	215.79	216.73	92.89	91.74	92.41	11,140	88.34
31	979.97	966.84	973.74	219.14	216.24	218.04	93.24	92.06	92.95	15,480	88.34
		High	999.34			223.62			93.56		88.36
		Low	960.44			214.53			92.18		87.10

SEPTEMBER, 1976

	30 Industrials			20 Transportations			15 Utilities			Daily Sales —000—	40 Bonds
	High	Low	Close	High	Low	Close	High	Low	Close		
1	987.95	971.24	985.95	221.26	217.37	220.40	93.78	92.57	93.43	18,640	88.34
2	993.10	980.14	984.79	222.28	218.85	219.91	94.55	93.21	93.59	18,920	88.39
3	991.19	979.22	989.11	221.67	218.93	220.40	94.64	93.40	94.52	13,280	88.44
7	998.67	985.12	996.59	221.67	217.95	220.28	95.67	94.23	95.35	16,310	88.71
8	1001.41	987.87	992.94	221.71	218.81	220.03	95.86	94.68	95.28	19,750	88.75
9	993.43	983.05	986.87	220.65	217.67	219.06	95.89	94.74	95.38	16,540	88.77
10	991.86	981.05	988.36	219.87	217.10	218.73	96.47	95.19	96.15	16,930	88.84
13	994.02	980.30	983.29	220.08	216.81	218.12	96.72	95.51	96.02	16,100	88.90
14	983.96	973.57	978.64	218.77	215.59	217.18	96.40	95.22	95.99	15,550	89.07
15	983.96	971.24	979.31	218.44	215.51	217.42	96.59	95.48	95.95	17,570	89.15
16	989.44	974.82	987.95	218.53	215.88	217.71	97.11	95.86	96.82	19,620	89.06
17	1000.50	986.62	995.10	220.44	217.10	218.77	98.03	96.53	97.36	28,270	89.21
20	1002.74	990.69	994.51	220.61	218.20	219.34	98.38	97.30	97.81	21,730	89.56
21	1016.54	993.60	1014.79	223.30	219.22	222.73	99.21	97.52	99.02	30,300	89.85
22	1026.26	1009.56	1014.05	224.76	221.67	222.60	99.73	98.32	98.61	32,970	89.85
23	1019.78	1005.32	1010.80	223.46	220.48	221.34	99.09	97.78	98.16	24,210	89.86
24	1014.13	1001.75	1009.31	222.68	219.67	221.34	98.48	97.07	97.81	17,400	89.44
27	1016.54	1004.40	1013.13	222.56	219.91	221.46	98.93	97.65	98.26	17,430	89.50
28	1014.38	992.11	994.93	222.28	218.85	219.26	98.89	97.87	98.19	20,440	89.28
29	1001.25	985.54	991.19	219.75	216.53	217.22	98.45	97.33	97.84	18,090	89.18
30	995.84	983.79	990.19	218.36	215.71	217.34	98.26	97.39	97.78	14,700	89.26
		High 1014.79				222.73			99.02		89.86
		Low 978.64				217.18			93.43		88.34

OCTOBER, 1976

	30 Industrials			20 Transportations			15 Utilities			Daily Sales —000—	40 Bonds
	High	Low	Close	High	Low	Close	High	Low	Close		
1	995.60	974.40	979.89	218.40	214.00	215.10	98.48	97.49	97.74	20,620	89.39
4	983.21	971.83	977.98	215.88	213.43	214.86	98.48	97.49	98.00	12,630	89.45
5	979.97	960.69	966.76	215.26	210.86	212.12	98.32	97.55	97.90	19,200	89.59
6	968.33	949.88	959.69	213.10	209.23	210.25	98.51	97.42	97.97	20,870	89.47
7	968.50	951.71	965.09	212.29	208.29	211.02	98.67	97.58	97.42	19,830	89.63
8	969.25	949.72	952.38	213.06	208.58	209.56	98.99	97.74	98.16	16,740	89.65
11	948.88	934.26	940.82	208.58	204.09	205.32	98.26	97.23	97.58	14,620	89.64
12	946.31	928.27	932.35	206.25	202.99	203.85	97.94	96.63	97.17	18,210	89.68
13	950.38	932.01	948.30	207.56	204.01	206.99	97.97	96.66	97.71	21,690	89.80
14	947.56	931.02	935.92	207.88	204.26	204.87	97.97	96.79	97.39	18,610	89.56
15	942.74	928.27	937.00	205.64	203.03	204.70	97.55	96.50	96.69	16,210	89.60
18	950.13	936.59	946.56	208.21	204.05	206.91	97.42	96.27	96.85	15,710	89.82
19	953.87	938.66	949.97	207.88	204.87	206.87	97.26	96.24	96.88	16,200	89.67
20	958.86	944.40	954.87	208.90	205.72	208.46	97.52	96.34	97.01	15,860	89.70
21	960.77	942.74	944.90	210.33	206.82	207.93	97.39	96.34	96.69	17,980	89.66
22	946.56	932.26	938.75	208.41	203.52	205.23	96.91	95.89	96.18	17,870	89.71
25	942.65	932.51	938.00	206.58	203.07	205.23	96.63	95.60	96.24	13,310	89.53
26	951.63	937.17	948.14	207.56	204.17	206.58	97.11	95.99	96.63	15,490	89.58
27	959.77	944.56	956.12	208.98	205.97	207.68	97.26	96.08	96.82	15,790	89.62
28	962.35	948.72	952.63	209.34	206.55	207.81	97.94	96.56	97.42	16,920	89.61
29	966.26	947.47	964.93	210.59	206.91	210.37	98.26	97.01	98.03	17,030	89.69
		High 979.89				215.10			98.42		89.82
		Low 932.35				203.85			96.18		89.39

NOVEMBER, 1976

	—30 Industrials—			—20 Transportations—			—15 Utilities—			Daily Sales —000—	40 Bonds
	High	Low	Close	High	Low	Close	High	Low	Close		
1	971.99	957.61	966.09	213.11	209.38	211.85	99.02	97.42	98.54	18,390	89.71
3	960.44	944.73	956.53	211.27	207.72	209.92	98.42	97.01	97.97	19,350	89.77
4	967.75	951.30	960.44	216.79	209.92	215.75	98.83	97.20	98.42	21,700	89.67
5	962.93	940.24	943.07	217.68	213.11	214.23	98.77	97.74	98.00	20,780	89.53
8	941.41	928.94	933.68	213.96	210.46	211.76	98.35	97.17	97.58	16,520	89.60
9	939.33	924.45	930.77	213.46	209.20	211.76	98.61	97.39	98.22	19,210	89.70
10	936.92	917.89	924.04	213.33	209.16	210.50	98.73	97.58	98.13	18,890	89.53
11	932.85	917.97	931.43	212.66	209.11	211.76	98.67	97.90	98.45	13,230	89.69
12	933.93	920.21	927.69	213.15	209.87	211.31	98.99	97.87	98.67	15,550	89.69
15	937.25	921.63	935.42	213.96	209.16	212.93	99.12	98.03	98.86	16,710	89.79
16	946.73	931.77	935.34	216.88	212.84	215.44	99.44	98.10	98.45	21,020	89.90
17	943.90	930.44	938.08	220.11	215.04	218.40	99.50	98.19	99.05	19,900	89.97
18	953.46	935.51	950.13	222.76	218.04	211.99	100.65	98.86	100.40	24,000	90.08
19	957.86	942.49	948.80	223.65	219.79	221.90	101.07	99.76	100.24	24,550	90.29
22	959.94	945.81	955.87	225.45	220.96	223.74	101.58	100.01	101.10	20,930	90.25
23	958.94	945.98	949.30	225.76	222.35	223.97	101.87	100.56	101.26	19,090	90.34
24	956.20	941.74	950.96	225.31	222.40	224.37	102.54	101.00	101.99	20,420	90.37
26	959.28	947.97	956.62	226.89	223.47	226.26	103.02	101.77	102.76	15,000	90.35
29	959.86	947.14	950.05	228.19	225.00	226.57	103.05	101.55	101.99	18,750	90.39
30	952.13	941.41	947.22	227.56	224.33	226.12	102.57	101.16	101.77	17,030	90.57
		High	966.09			226.57			102.76		90.57
		Low	924.04			209.92			97.58		89.53

DECEMBER, 1976

	—30 Industrials—			—20 Transportations—			—15 Utilities—			Daily Sales —000—	20 Bonds
	High	Low	Close	High	Low	Close	High	Low	Close		
1	954.12	942.24	949.38	228.41	225.40	227.20	102.15	100.94	101.71	21,960	90.89
2	956.62	944.07	946.64	228.68	225.49	226.26	102.57	101.39	101.96	23,300	91.09
3	956.28	943.07	950.55	229.26	225.58	228.59	103.50	101.96	103.14	22,640	91.32
6	966.59	948.72	961.77	232.14	227.24	231.01	104.68	103.02	104.20	24,830	91.46
7	968.67	957.03	960.69	232.68	229.22	230.16	105.54	103.82	104.77	26,140	91.64
8	966.01	953.54	963.26	231.33	228.68	230.79	105.57	104.17	105.16	24,560	91.59
9	976.31	962.35	970.74	233.26	229.22	231.10	106.02	104.81	105.57	31,800	91.82
10	978.31	965.59	973.15	232.23	228.90	230.88	106.31	104.87	105.70	25,960	91.76
13	980.14	967.50	974.24	231.91	228.90	230.30	105.89	104.58	105.44	24,830	91.81
14	983.13	966.92	980.63	233.53	229.08	232.85	106.05	104.52	105.54	25,130	91.82
15	989.11	974.82	983.79	235.82	231.82	234.43	106.40	105.19	105.86	28,300	91.81
16	988.20	973.90	981.30	235.86	231.78	234.38	106.15	104.81	105.19	23,920	92.02
17	990.53	976.23	979.06	237.07	233.44	234.87	105.99	104.71	105.13	23,870	91.96
20	981.96	969.00	972.41	235.91	232.09	233.62	105.89	104.33	105.13	20,690	91.86
21	981.05	966.17	978.39	235.91	231.82	234.87	105.76	104.33	104.97	24,390	91.89
22	993.35	977.73	984.54	237.48	234.29	235.73	106.18	104.10	104.93	26,970	92.00
23	991.61	978.47	985.62	235.77	230.25	231.87	105.60	103.97	104.39	24,560	92.27
27	997.92	982.71	996.09	234.25	230.57	233.35	105.54	104.01	105.25	20,130	92.17
28	1006.82	992.77	1000.08	235.73	232.63	234.34	106.56	104.97	106.24	25,790	92.49
29	1003.49	990.94	994.93	235.73	233.03	234.29	106.82	105.60	106.24	21,910	92.59
30	1005.49	991.69	999.09	236.67	233.35	235.55	107.81	105.92	107.43	23,700	93.07
31	1006.32	997.34	1004.65	238.06	234.65	237.03	108.64	107.27	108.38	19,170	93.20
		High	1004.65			237.03			108.38		93.20
		Low	946.64			226.26			101.71		90.89

JANUARY, 1977

	—30 Industrials—			—20 Transportations—			—15 Utilities—			Daily Sales —000—	20 Bonds
	High	Low	Close	High	Low	Close	High	Low	Close		
3	1007.81	994.18	999.75	238.91	234.78	237.52	109.22	107.91	108.64	21,280	93.16
4	1001.99	985.70	987.87	238.24	234.96	235.46	109.09	107.55	108.03	22,740	93.19
5	990.69	974.07	978.06	236.09	232.36	233.21	108.38	106.98	107.59	25,010	93.36
6	989.03	974.07	979.89	235.95	232.18	234.61	108.35	107.07	107.75	23,920	93.37
7	987.03	975.40	983.13	236.80	233.48	236.13	108.54	107.20	107.81	21,720	93.36
10	990.69	979.31	986.87	237.75	234.25	236.80	108.48	107.07	108.10	20,860	92.98
11	991.11	972.16	976.65	237.88	233.39	234.34	108.80	107.11	107.46	24,100	92.76
12	976.23	962.52	968.25	234.96	231.19	233.12	107.68	106.18	106.56	22,670	92.48
13	979.55	966.51	976.15	235.95	232.36	234.74	107.59	106.12	107.33	24,780	92.50
14	979.22	967.00	972.16	235.77	232.50	233.66	108.99	107.04	108.22	24,480	92.57
17	972.99	961.10	967.25	234.74	231.55	232.81	108.86	107.49	108.45	21,060	92.43
18	970.08	958.53	962.43	233.84	230.30	231.82	109.15	107.68	108.61	24,380	92.01
19	972.16	959.69	968.67	234.20	230.61	233.30	109.41	108.10	108.77	27,120	91.81
20	973.82	954.70	959.03	234.69	230.16	231.28	110.27	108.51	109.38	26,520	91.95
21	967.42	953.87	962.43	232.00	228.46	230.61	110.11	108.70	109.57	23,930	91.93
24	968.83	956.87	963.60	232.59	229.44	231.64	111.00	109.38	110.78	22,890	91.78
25	973.57	959.36	965.92	233.84	230.30	232.41	112.51	110.62	111.87	26,340	91.52
26	968.33	953.13	958.53	233.30	229.53	230.34	112.22	110.75	111.13	27,840	91.60
27	963.93	950.47	954.54	231.60	227.87	228.73	111.64	110.21	110.94	24,360	91.52
28	961.85	949.38	957.53	229.62	225.63	226.97	111.07	109.53	110.08	22,700	91.53
31	958.03	944.90	954.37	227.96	224.28	226.62	110.30	108.80	109.31	22,920	91.55
		High	999.75			237.52			111.87		93.37
		Low	954.37			226.62			106.56		91.52

FEBRUARY, 1977

	—30 Industrials—			—20 Transportations—			—15 Utilities—			Daily Sales —000—	20 Bonds
	High	Low	Close	High	Low	Close	High	Low	Close		
1	962.02	950.05	958.36	228.46	224.73	226.89	110.27	108.77	109.57	23,700	91.51
2	963.76	949.97	952.79	230.21	225.90	227.78	110.17	108.74	109.31	25,700	91.40
3	954.95	941.99	947.14	228.59	225.18	226.66	109.82	108.29	108.90	23,790	91.26
4	955.70	941.90	947.89	229.49	225.45	227.78	109.76	108.42	109.18	23,130	91.15
7	954.70	941.82	946.31	229.98	226.35	228.19	109.79	108.61	109.47	20,700	91.36
8	952.79	938.66	942.24	229.89	225.81	227.74	110.01	108.93	109.53	24,040	91.39
9	944.98	928.27	933.84	228.28	225.00	225.94	109.66	107.65	107.94	23,640	91.47
10	943.57	930.60	937.92	228.23	225.18	226.97	108.16	106.75	107.17	22,340	91.39
11	940.91	926.03	931.52	227.24	222.76	224.24	107.52	105.32	106.08	20,510	91.33
14	939.91	926.11	938.33	225.81	221.14	223.74	106.53	105.13	105.89	19,230	91.29
15	948.39	937.08	944.32	225.72	222.35	224.33	106.56	104.84	105.83	21,620	91.40
16	957.28	941.24	948.30	227.60	223.66	225.90	107.23	105.54	106.95	23,430	91.35
17	950.71	939.58	943.73	226.53	223.51	225.21	107.30	106.28	106.82	19,040	91.34
18	944.73	935.09	940.24	226.38	223.36	224.92	107.11	106.15	106.69	18,040	91.33
22	946.06	933.84	939.91	226.48	222.49	223.66	106.82	105.64	106.21	17,730	91.05
23	943.82	934.59	938.25	224.44	222.00	222.88	106.56	105.25	105.86	18,240	91.08
24	940.24	927.69	932.60	224.34	220.00	221.90	106.28	104.84	105.60	19,730	90.94
25	938.75	926.20	933.43	223.02	219.96	221.81	105.73	104.49	104.97	17,610	90.98
28	938.50	928.61	936.42	222.93	219.91	221.90	105.38	104.23	105.29	16,220	90.84
		High	958.36			228.19			109.57		91.51
		Low	931.52			221.81			104.97		90.84

MARCH, 1977

	—30 Industrials—			—20 Transportations—			—15 Utilities—			Daily Sales —000—	20 Bonds
	High	Low	Close	High	Low	Close	High	Low	Close		
1	948.47	936.25	944.73	224.48	220.59	223.75	106.05	104.71	105.67	19,480	90.81
2	949.97	938.50	942.07	225.26	222.00	223.41	106.47	105.19	106.12	18,010	90.84
3	951.88	940.16	948.64	225.02	222.20	224.00	107.01	105.73	106.53	17,560	90.81
4	956.28	947.39	953.46	225.80	222.54	224.14	107.39	105.99	107.23	18,950	90.83
7	958.61	949.22	955.12	225.07	224.34	223.56	108.26	107.01	107.75	17,410	90.69
8	960.36	949.47	952.04	225.07	222.93	273.61	108.42	107.07	107.46	19,520	90.45
9	950.96	938.66	942.90	223.85	221.61	222.63	107.87	106.60	107.04	19,680	90.87
10	948.89	938.00	946.73	224.39	222.20	223.56	107.55	105.99	106.88	18,620	90.92
11	952.96	942.90	947.72	225.90	223.22	224.48	107.36	106.24	106.69	18,230	90.81
14	960.19	944.73	958.36	226.87	223.22	225.36	107.14	105.73	106.56	19,290	90.90
15	970.33	958.19	965.01	228.14	225.26	227.36	107.27	105.89	106.44	23,940	90.94
16	971.58	961.44	968.00	229.35	226.19	228.38	107.30	106.05	106.82	22,140	91.06
17	970.08	958.78	964.84	231.06	226.48	229.89	107.65	106.31	107.36	20,700	91.10
18	967.50	956.95	961.02	232.96	229.60	231.35	107.94	107.52	107.52	19,840	91.09
21	961.44	949.47	953.54	232.28	229.30	230.18	107.68	106.47	106.88	18,040	91.20
22	955.95	944.65	950.96	231.01	228.28	229.55	107.14	105.80	106.40	18,660	91.22
23	954.37	940.16	942.32	230.18	227.55	228.72	106.91	105.60	106.12	19,360	91.44
24	944.48	931.93	935.67	229.89	227.06	228.23	106.40	105.00	105.60	19,650	91.10
25	937.50	925.12	928.86	228.87	225.75	226.29	105.99	104.71	105.22	16,550	91.13
28	931.27	920.71	926.11	227.11	224.19	225.31	106.12	104.36	105.32	16,710	91.05
29	936.67	925.78	932.01	227.55	224.63	226.24	106.18	105.06	105.83	17,030	90.89
30	935.84	917.64	921.21	227.06	222.73	223.61	106.31	105.13	105.57	18,810	90.75
31	926.86	914.15	919.13	224.58	221.56	222.97	106.50	105.32	106.02	16,510	90.78
High			968.00			231.35			107.75		91.44
Low			919.13			222.63			105.22		90.45

APRIL, 1977

	—30 Industrials—			—20 Transportations—			—15 Utilities—			Daily Sales —000—	20 Bonds
	High	Low	Close	High	Low	Close	High	Low	Close		
1	930.27	919.55	927.36	225.36	221.51	223.61	107.23	105.80	106.88	17,050	90.84
4	929.36	913.48	915.56	226.09	222.15	223.46	107.65	106.47	107.20	16,250	90.94
5	920.88	909.74	916.14	224.58	220.83	223.17	107.52	106.34	106.98	18,330	90.91
6	922.12	910.07	914.73	224.39	221.46	222.78	107.62	106.63	107.14	16,600	90.84
7	921.21	910.57	918.88	225.12	221.61	224.00	107.59	106.37	107.07	17,260	90.83
11	928.85	916.47	924.10	227.31	223.90	225.70	107.62	106.47	107.11	17,650	90.83
12	940.98	924.69	937.16	230.81	226.24	229.69	108.42	106.98	108.06	23,760	91.03
13	942.76	927.49	938.18	232.08	227.70	230.86	108.64	107.46	108.19	21,800	91.07
14	956.07	943.69	947.00	236.85	232.37	234.17	109.92	108.03	108.93	30,490	91.35
15	953.10	941.74	947.76	236.22	232.62	234.42	109.47	108.06	108.83	20,230	91.26
18	951.32	939.28	942.76	236.46	233.15	235.10	109.22	108.06	108.64	17,830	91.45
19	944.28	934.79	938.77	239.29	234.13	237.63	108.96	107.65	108.32	19,510	91.33
20	948.69	933.43	942.59	241.48	236.85	240.36	108.83	107.71	108.26	25,090	91.39
21	949.37	933.43	935.80	242.16	236.22	237.58	109.02	107.68	108.16	22,740	91.37
22	935.13	923.59	927.07	237.58	232.28	233.59	108.48	107.49	107.97	20,700	91.23
25	924.02	910.45	914.60	234.51	230.28	232.08	108.10	106.60	107.39	20,440	91.09
26	922.74	910.36	915.62	233.05	229.60	230.77	107.87	106.66	107.11	20,040	91.10
27	928.34	913.08	923.76	234.42	229.94	233.25	108.29	106.95	107.87	20,590	91.23
28	931.14	919.78	927.32	235.10	231.59	233.35	108.86	107.30	108.35	18,370	91.27
29	931.99	922.32	926.90	235.78	231.69	234.51	108.99	108.30	108.67	18,330	91.19
High			947.76			240.36			108.93		91.45
Low			914.60			222.78			106.88		90.83

MAY, 1977

	—30 Industrials—			—20 Transportations—			—15 Utilities—			Daily Sales —000—	20 Bonds
	High	Low	Close	High	Low	Close	High	Low	Close		
2	934.02	923.00	931.22	236.22	233.05	235.34	109.79	108.42	109.34	17,970	91.07
3	939.70	929.27	934.19	238.80	234.61	237.10	110.53	109.02	110.21	21,950	91.06
4	944.96	929.44	940.72	242.35	236.66	240.36	110.75	109.47	110.21	23,330	91.13
5	949.46	934.53	943.44	241.77	238.07	239.58	110.69	109.44	109.92	23,450	91.12
6	943.27	932.24	936.74	240.02	237.10	238.36	110.59	109.25	110.11	19,370	91.26
9	938.52	928.77	933.09	240.50	237.05	238.70	110.49	109.25	109.69	15,230	91.25
10	941.40	930.55	936.14	241.33	238.07	240.31	110.43	109.41	109.92	21,090	91.16
11	937.84	923.85	926.90	241.87	238.75	240.02	110.40	109.44	109.92	18,980	91.23
12	930.04	917.74	925.54	241.28	238.22	240.11	110.62	109.34	110.24	21,980	91.29
13	932.58	923.17	928.34	241.67	238.56	240.26	111.00	109.89	110.46	19,780	91.31
16	938.43	926.73	932.50	243.86	240.26	243.04	111.32	110.05	111.07	21,170	91.29
17	939.45	925.20	936.48	244.94	241.48	243.72	111.80	110.65	111.39	22,290	91.31
18	947.34	935.46	941.91	247.91	243.72	246.64	112.28	111.16	111.93	27,800	91.46
19	945.13	933.34	936.48	247.66	243.91	245.18	112.41	111.29	111.84	21,280	91.43
20	937.16	925.71	930.46	246.40	243.13	245.03	112.47	111.00	111.74	18,950	91.37
23	928.17	915.03	917.06	246.35	242.35	244.01	112.03	110.62	110.94	18,290	91.39
24	917.83	906.55	912.40	244.25	241.28	242.55	111.20	110.05	110.56	20,050	91.32
25	916.72	901.46	903.24	244.40	239.97	240.89	111.26	110.14	110.40	20,710	91.40
26	910.45	899.17	908.07	242.94	238.65	240.60	110.62	109.66	110.11	18,620	91.47
27	909.60	896.29	898.83	241.53	237.68	238.02	110.84	109.69	110.17	15,730	91.41
31	904.77	892.55	898.66	238.66	234.56	235.83	110.65	109.63	110.11	17,800	91.44
			High 943.44			246.64			111.93		91.47
			Low 898.66			235.34			109.34		91.06

JUNE, 1977

	—30 Industrials—			—20 Transportations—			—15 Utilities—			Daily Sales —000—	20 Bonds
	High	Low	Close	High	Low	Close	High	Low	Close		
1	909.35	896.46	906.55	238.17	234.56	236.75	111.07	109.60	110.56	18,320	91.63
2	912.91	899.42	903.15	237.87	234.95	235.98	111.52	110.24	111.00	18,620	91.81
3	915.88	901.03	912.23	238.36	234.61	237.14	112.15	110.75	111.77	20,330	91.90
6	916.13	901.03	903.04	238.75	234.86	235.73	112.57	111.32	111.93	18,930	92.09
7	910.79	896.79	908.67	236.32	233.54	235.05	112.76	111.15	112.38	21,110	92.19
8	918.25	906.21	912.99	238.07	234.51	236.90	113.27	112.00	112.73	22,200	92.15
9	914.69	904.34	909.85	237.29	234.08	235.63	113.15	112.19	112.89	19,940	92.21
10	915.20	904.77	910.79	238.22	234.71	237.29	113.24	112.19	112.79	20,630	92.40
13	917.15	906.21	912.40	238.56	235.10	236.61	112.95	111.93	112.41	20,250	92.43
14	924.27	912.14	922.57	238.95	236.37	238.36	113.88	112.63	113.62	25,390	92.47
15	925.03	914.43	917.57	239.87	237.05	237.78	114.17	112.89	113.43	22,640	92.37
16	924.53	910.53	920.45	239.63	236.51	238.41	114.17	112.83	113.56	24,310	92.48
17	924.78	915.79	920.45	239.92	236.75	238.80	114.39	113.18	113.88	21,960	92.39
20	926.98	916.89	924.27	240.16	237.29	239.48	114.78	113.40	114.26	22,950	92.53
21	934.36	923.51	928.60	241.09	237.78	239.19	115.96	114.20	115.64	29,730	92.60
22	930.89	921.13	926.31	240.55	236.66	238.61	116.15	114.68	115.57	25,070	92.54
23	930.46	922.45	925.37	239.34	236.41	237.97	115.99	114.81	115.45	24,330	92.49
24	933.77	924.02	929.70	239.97	236.80	238.41	116.05	115.16	115.73	27,490	92.39
27	931.73	920.12	924.10	239.68	237.05	238.12	116.37	115.06	115.77	19,870	92.41
28	926.98	914.01	915.62	238.99	236.02	236.90	115.80	114.42	115.03	22,670	92.55
29	917.73	906.63	913.33	238.12	235.20	236.61	115.16	113.94	114.74	19,000	92.46
30	920.88	909.09	916.30	239.14	235.83	238.80	115.22	114.07	114.68	19,410	92.55
			High 929.70			239.48			115.77		92.60
			Low 903.04			235.05			110.56		91.63

JULY, 1977

	30 Industrials			20 Transportations			15 Utilities			Daily Sales —000—	20 Bonds
	High	Low	Close	High	Low	Close	High	Low	Close		
1	918.25	907.48	912.65	239.73	236.56	237.83	115.45	114.20	115.06	18,160	92.49
5	919.01	907.90	913.59	239.68	236.32	238.02	115.77	114.71	115.29	16,850	92.66
6	915.37	904.94	907.73	239.04	236.02	237.29	115.96	114.55	115.48	21,230	92.68
7	913.42	903.49	909.51	239.19	235.10	237.10	116.31	115.03	115.86	21,740	92.69
8	914.94	904.17	907.99	239.09	236.17	237.29	116.69	115.41	116.07	23,820	92.55
11	910.96	900.27	905.53	238.07	235.49	237.05	116.69	115.45	116.53	19,790	92.56
12	906.26	898.58	903.41	237.87	234.22	236.41	117.52	116.15	117.43	22,470	92.66
13	906.80	896.29	902.99	237.99	234.61	236.07	118.03	116.56	117.65	23,160	92.74
15	910.62	899.68	905.95	238.07	234.86	235.93	118.23	116.72	117.84	29,120	92.69
18	915.02	901.25	910.60	238.61	234.13	236.46	118.42	116.60	117.62	29,890	92.72
19	921.86	908.26	919.27	240.07	236.32	238.51	118.61	117.20	118.29	31,930	92.65
20	927.75	915.45	920.48	240.89	237.73	239.53	119.09	117.84	118.58	29,380	92.70
21	926.20	914.67	921.78	240.89	237.29	239.38	118.96	117.97	118.48	26,880	92.79
22	927.84	916.75	923.42	240.70	237.63	239.34	119.02	117.87	118.67	23,110	92.65
25	923.94	911.73	914.24	239.97	236.66	237.58	118.99	117.68	118.10	20,430	92.64
26	914.33	902.98	908.18	237.34	234.03	235.39	118.42	117.49	117.87	21,390	92.70
27	907.31	884.27	888.43	236.12	231.45	232.42	118.26	116.76	116.98	26,440	92.74
28	893.71	879.76	889.99	233.05	228.82	230.47	117.49	116.37	116.95	26,340	92.50
29	892.24	878.81	890.07	230.91	226.87	229.30	116.92	115.86	116.37	20,350	92.51
		High 923.42				239.53			118.67		92.79
		Low 888.43				229.30			115.06		92.50

AUGUST, 1977

	30 Industrials			20 Transportations			15 Utilities			Daily Sales —000—	20 Bonds
	High	Low	Close	High	Low	Close	High	Low	Close		
1	900.03	886.17	891.81	231.45	228.53	229.40	117.36	116.02	116.95	17,920	92.49
2	893.97	884.27	887.39	229.99	226.38	227.11	117.14	116.05	116.44	17,910	92.67
3	888.95	877.25	886.00	227.50	223.32	225.26	117.01	115.77	116.12	21,710	92.59
4	891.89	880.11	888.17	226.48	223.46	225.46	116.37	115.29	115.77	18,870	92.57
5	894.84	884.36	888.69	227.02	224.05	225.51	116.34	115.09	115.64	19,940	92.62
8	888.17	877.43	879.42	225.46	220.98	221.95	116.02	114.90	115.38	15,870	92.49
9	884.53	873.70	879.42	222.93	219.52	220.88	115.93	114.78	115.19	19,900	92.43
10	887.65	875.69	887.04	222.93	219.42	222.20	115.80	114.65	115.61	18,280	92.38
11	891.46	876.04	877.43	223.51	219.52	220.15	116.02	114.87	115.25	21,740	92.41
12	879.24	866.86	871.10	220.88	217.23	218.88	115.38	114.26	114.68	16,870	92.36
15	877.60	864.09	874.13	219.52	215.91	218.10	114.65	113.50	114.23	15,750	92.53
16	877.17	865.99	869.28	218.69	215.77	216.60	114.55	113.37	113.66	19,340	92.41
17	872.75	859.58	864.69	217.86	214.65	216.40	114.04	112.38	112.76	20,920	92.45
18	873.96	860.36	864.26	217.81	214.06	215.33	113.15	111.64	111.87	21,040	92.43
19	870.06	856.64	863.48	216.64	213.24	214.70	112.03	110.01	110.81	20,800	92.39
22	871.45	856.55	867.29	217.03	213.19	216.01	111.39	110.40	110.91	17,870	92.39
23	875.61	862.70	865.56	218.98	215.09	217.33	112.06	110.81	111.52	20,290	92.36
24	869.63	858.80	862.87	219.81	215.67	217.91	111.90	110.88	111.26	18,170	93.41
25	863.13	851.18	854.12	218.64	215.04	215.77	111.36	109.92	110.43	19,400	93.50
26	857.76	844.42	855.42	216.06	212.60	214.55	110.62	109.41	109.95	18,480	93.45
29	866.77	855.77	864.09	217.62	214.40	217.03	111.07	109.73	110.59	15,280	93.51
30	867.55	855.51	858.89	218.45	214.60	215.91	111.55	110.11	110.84	18,220	93.55
31	862.87	850.92	861.49	216.89	213.53	215.23	111.55	110.21	110.88	19,080	93.68
		High 891.81				229.40			116.95		93.68
		Low 854.12				214.55			109.95		92.36

SEPTEMBER, 1977

	—30 Industrials—			—20 Transportations—			—15 Utilities—			Daily Sales —000—	20 Bonds
	High	Low	Close	High	Low	Close	High	Low	Close		
1	869.80	858.71	864.86	217.91	214.70	216.55	112.03	110.78	111.48	18,820	93.63
2	873.79	862.44	872.31	218.98	216.06	218.06	112.70	111.36	112.28	15,620	93.84
6	877.43	866.77	873.27	220.20	217.62	219.37	113.29	112.07	112.96	16,130	93.75
7	878.98	869.80	876.39	220.69	217.76	219.32	113.71	112.53	113.45	18,070	93.87
8	879.76	866.25	869.16	220.73	217.81	218.69	113.88	112.69	113.25	18,290	93.82
9	865.47	853.17	857.04	219.66	214.50	216.64	113.32	112.10	112.50	18,100	93.82
12	860.71	847.71	854.38	217.18	213.87	214.99	112.86	111.44	112.33	18,700	93.73
13	859.58	848.49	854.56	215.72	213.14	214.21	112.53	111.58	112.04	14,900	93.74
14	861.49	850.49	858.71	216.01	212.94	215.09	112.53	111.51	112.23	17,330	93.71
15	866.16	855.51	860.79	217.03	214.06	215.86	112.66	111.51	112.23	18,230	93.70
16	865.38	853.52	856.81	217.42	214.01	215.18	112.96	111.87	112.63	18,340	93.75
19	857.42	848.23	851.52	215.86	212.02	213.33	113.09	112.04	112.37	16,890	93.69
20	855.16	846.67	851.78	215.23	212.36	214.16	112.89	111.71	112.13	19,030	93.53
21	856.29	838.79	840.96	215.82	212.07	212.75	112.86	111.44	111.94	22,200	93.46
22	844.25	833.16	839.41	214.55	211.87	213.19	112.53	111.11	111.84	16,660	93.55
23	844.77	834.81	839.14	215.52	212.31	213.48	113.12	111.64	112.50	18,760	93.65
26	844.16	831.51	841.65	215.43	211.53	214.01	112.92	111.51	111.87	18,230	93.39
27	845.55	831.95	835.85	215.82	211.82	213.19	112.79	111.25	111.90	19,080	93.44
28	841.56	830.30	834.72	214.79	212.07	213.38	112.63	111.48	112.13	17,960	93.49
29	843.56	832.55	840.09	216.30	212.60	215.13	112.79	111.67	112.37	21,160	93.40
30	848.84	839.14	847.11	216.84	213.43	215.48	113.48	112.10	113.25	21,170	93.43
		High	876.39			219.37			113.45		93.87
		Low	834.72			212.75			111.48		93.39

OCTOBER, 1977

	—30 Industrials—			—20 Transportations—			—15 Utilities—			Daily Sales —000—	20 Bonds
	High	Low	Close	High	Low	Close	High	Low	Close		
3	853.60	842.08	851.96	217.42	214.11	216.01	114.08	112.73	113.62	19,460	93.42
4	855.57	839.57	842.00	218.15	214.84	215.77	114.11	113.06	113.58	20,850	93.22
5	843.73	832.38	837.32	216.79	214.16	214.99	114.04	113.06	113.55	18,300	93.12
6	845.20	834.98	842.08	217.91	214.26	216.94	114.49	113.39	114.21	18,490	93.09
7	845.98	836.11	840.35	218.45	215.67	216.89	114.50	113.58	114.04	16,250	93.06
10	844.33	834.46	840.26	217.23	215.18	216.30	114.50	113.81	114.11	10,580	93.02
11	841.39	830.47	832.29	216.94	214.01	214.89	114.44	113.65	113.88	17,870	92.80
12	830.65	818.60	823.98	214.74	210.51	212.21	114.17	113.06	113.78	22,440	92.50
13	824.67	811.42	818.17	212.36	208.27	209.58	113.81	112.04	112.37	23,870	92.47
14	826.66	814.02	821.64	211.68	208.07	210.61	112.76	111.48	112.17	20,410	92.59
17	824.93	813.76	820.34	211.87	207.39	208.37	112.23	111.21	111.67	17,340	92.38
18	826.84	815.84	820.51	209.53	206.47	207.59	112.46	111.21	111.74	20,130	92.44
19	823.20	809.08	812.20	208.80	204.13	205.20	112.20	111.05	111.41	22,030	92.09
20	819.65	804.66	814.80	206.71	202.57	205.15	111.74	110.19	111.05	20,520	92.19
21	815.75	804.57	808.30	206.76	202.77	204.81	111.31	109.93	110.52	20,230	92.06
24	810.90	800.85	802.32	205.59	200.92	201.74	100.72	109.44	109.86	19,210	92.00
25	805.35	792.79	801.54	202.28	197.46	199.60	109.93	108.22	108.71	23,590	91.94
26	816.01	795.56	813.41	203.45	198.29	202.57	109.50	108.05	109.17	24,860	91.98
27	825.71	809.42	818.61	205.69	202.28	204.28	110.16	108.52	109.17	21,920	91.86
28	826.49	814.54	822.68	207.54	203.20	205.78	110.00	108.88	109.40	18,050	91.85
31	824.93	813.93	818.35	207.68	204.23	206.08	110.13	108.78	109.04	17,070	91.78
		High	851.96			216.94			114.21		93.42
		Low	801.54			199.60			108.71		91.78

NOVEMBER, 1977

	—30 Industrials—			—20 Transportations—			—15 Utilities—			Daily Sales —000—	20 Bonds
	High	Low	Close	High	Low	Close	High	Low	Close		
1	816.01	804.40	806.91	206.17	203.01	203.64	109.24	108.02	108.38	17,170	91.87
2	809.51	797.73	800.85	205.05	201.26	202.52	108.58	106.87	107.46	20,760	91.73
3	805.87	794.53	802.67	203.25	200.67	201.99	107.79	106.54	107.23	18,090	91.47
4	814.02	802.41	809.94	205.30	202.18	204.37	108.12	106.84	107.79	21,700	91.36
7	820.17	808.56	816.44	206.90	203.30	206.08	108.91	107.66	108.38	21,270	91.44
8	821.29	810.81	816.27	208.27	204.86	206.52	109.34	108.19	108.71	19,210	91.50
9	821.29	810.20	818.43	207.78	204.96	206.56	109.73	108.45	109.57	21,330	91.44
10	836.11	814.10	832.55	212.31	206.56	210.95	111.58	109.31	111.28	31,980	91.48
11	850.05	837.66	845.89	217.13	212.26	215.96	112.92	111.54	112.50	35,260	91.55
14	849.01	834.46	838.36	218.54	214.36	215.62	113.06	111.48	112.04	23,220	91.53
15	846.85	831.86	842.78	218.20	213.53	216.98	112.43	111.25	111.84	27,740	91.55
16	846.24	834.03	837.06	218.49	214.55	216.06	112.60	111.31	111.74	24,950	91.71
17	838.88	827.53	831.86	216.74	213.67	215.72	112.73	111.01	111.97	25,110	91.84
18	840.26	829.18	835.76	216.79	213.77	215.18	112.63	111.28	112.10	23,930	91.89
21	840.18	829.18	836.11	217.23	213.97	215.57	112.56	111.31	111.74	20,110	91.88
22	846.15	834.63	842.52	218.59	214.70	217.33	112.53	111.35	112.33	28,600	91.93
23	847.11	836.28	843.30	220.54	217.08	219.66	112.96	111.71	112.56	29,150	91.96
25	847.63	838.70	844.42	220.98	217.96	219.76	113.39	112.23	113.06	17,910	92.11
28	846.67	836.71	839.57	220.98	216.60	217.52	113.65	112.46	113.09	21,570	92.15
29	839.48	824.24	827.27	218.15	213.67	214.16	113.39	111.74	112.04	22,950	92.04
30	831.77	821.29	829.70	215.82	211.53	214.50	112.40	111.48	112.00	22,670	92.02
		High	845.89			219.76			113.09		92.15
		Low	800.85			201.99			107.23		91.36

DECEMBER, 1977

	—30 Industrials—			—20 Transportations—			—15 Utilities—			Daily Sales —000—	20 Bonds
	High	Low	Close	High	Low	Close	High	Low	Close		
1	832.81	823.02	825.71	217.03	213.82	215.62	113.12	111.97	112.69	24,220	92.01
2	830.56	819.30	823.98	217.08	214.06	215.57	113.32	112.23	112.92	21,160	91.91
5	826.84	818.78	821.03	216.74	213.62	214.74	113.42	112.37	112.89	19,160	91.91
6	819.91	804.23	806.91	214.45	209.39	210.22	113.32	111.90	112.40	23,770	91.95
7	812.54	802.06	807.43	211.34	208.02	210.07	112.92	111.84	112.37	21,050	91.82
8	815.49	804.14	806.91	212.21	209.63	210.80	112.99	111.90	112.27	20,400	92.01
9	819.04	806.65	815.23	212.85	209.83	212.12	112.92	111.81	112.37	19,210	92.03
12	820.51	811.76	815.75	213.72	210.85	212.26	112.46	111.25	111.64	18,180	91.99
13	818.61	809.94	815.23	214.50	211.09	212.99	111.84	110.36	110.92	19,190	91.62
14	823.63	811.42	822.68	214.45	211.77	213.53	111.44	110.06	111.02	22,110	91.60
15	825.10	815.23	817.91	214.84	211.92	213.04	111.74	110.36	111.28	21,610	91.47
16	821.55	812.37	815.32	215.62	211.87	214.26	111.90	110.65	111.28	20,270	91.41
19	817.31	806.13	807.95	215.18	211.97	212.80	111.81	110.59	110.88	21,150	91.26
20	810.46	800.42	806.22	212.99	209.78	211.77	111.15	109.86	110.49	23,250	91.27
21	817.83	805.35	813.93	214.11	210.07	213.19	111.05	109.73	110.23	24,510	91.09
22	825.62	815.32	821.81	216.74	212.70	215.82	111.11	109.90	110.19	28,100	91.26
23	832.64	822.16	829.87	217.96	214.94	217.13	111.21	110.16	110.69	20,080	91.16
27	833.77	823.46	829.70	218.01	215.62	216.79	111.44	110.33	110.59	16,750	91.14
28	833.33	822.77	829.70	218.06	215.38	216.74	111.41	110.23	110.85	19,630	90.96
29	834.37	823.63	830.39	218.64	215.18	217.81	111.58	110.19	111.28	23,610	90.94
30	835.15	825.80	831.17	219.03	215.86	217.18	111.94	110.82	111.28	23,560	90.95
		High	831.17			217.81			112.92		92.03
		Low	806.22			210.07			110.19		90.94

JANUARY, 1978

| | —30 Industrials— | | | —20 Transportations— | | | —15 Utilities— | | | Daily Sales | 20 |
	High	Low	Close	High	Low	Close	High	Low	Close	—000—	Bonds
3	830.47	815.06	817.74	217.86	214.94	215.77	111.84	110.49	110.98	17,720	90.78
4	817.48	804.92	813.58	216.74	213.14	215.43	111.41.	110.06	110.75	24,090	90.86
5	822.77	820.58	804.92	218.06	213.53	213.97	111.51	110.16	110.52	23,570	90.78
6	803.36	788.29	793.49	214.11	209.49	210.17	110.69	108.91	109.24	26,150	90.52
9	790.89	778.41	784.56	209.73	205.10	206.61	108.84	107.00	107.50	27,990	90.15
10	790.89	777.55	781.53	208.12	204.71	205.74	108.25	106.33	107.04	25,180	90.16
11	785.95	771.74	775.90	207.54	204.37	205.69	107.68	105.89	106.60	22,880	89.89
12	785.00	772.78	778.15	208.85	204.91	207.64	107.54	105.62	106.46	22,730	89.70
13	784.04	773.65	775.73	209.78	206.86	208.17	107.41	106.09	106.63	18,010	89.69
16	777.81	767.41	771.74	209.24	206.17	207.68	107.44	105.92	106.36	18,760	89.75
17	781.26	770.62	779.02	209.38	206.71	209.19	107.41	106.06	106.73	19,360	89.62
18	788.20	776.25	786.30	212.60	208.80	212.07	107.41	106.22	106.80	21,390	89.76
19	790.02	777.03	778.67	213.33	209.73	211.24	107.31	106.22	106.73	21,500	89.60
20	780.15	772.52	776.94	211.77	209.73	210.85	107.00	106.33	106.77	7,580	89.68
23	777.98	766.55	770.70	212.26	208.95	210.51	107.17	105.95	106.26	19,380	89.56
24	776.42	765.68	771.57	212.21	208.76	210.26	106.66	105.35	105.75	18,690	89.54
25	777.72	768.02	772.44.	213.28	209.34	211.43	106.43	105.24	105.58	18,690	89.53
26	775.81	761.00	763.34	212.60	208.76	209.58	106.29	104.94	105.14	19,600	89.33
27	768.54	759.44	764.12	210.61	207.64	208.71	105.58	104.33	104.84	17,600	89.37
30	774.95	761.09	772.44	210.31	207.20	208.71	105.48	104.16	104.91	17,400	89.40
31	778.59	762.91	769.92	210.61	207.54	208.56	105.65	104.26	104.77	19,870	89.64
		High 817.74				215.77			110.98		90.86
		Low 763.34				205.69			104.77		89.33

FEBRUARY, 1978

| | —30 Industrials— | | | —20 Transportations— | | | —15 Utilities— | | | Daily Sales | 20 |
	High	Low	Close	High	Low	Close	High	Low	Close	—000—	Bonds
1	777.89	764.81	774.34	221.38	207.29	210.31	105.55	104.23	105.24	22,240	89.57
2	781.88	770.88	775.38	214.06	210.22	212.65	105.85	104.77	105.48	23,050	89.72
3	776.59	766.98	770.96	214.55	211.53	212.99	105.99	105.04	105.51	19,400	89.74
6	772.96	764.21	768.62	213.28	211.34	212.16	105.55	104.53	105.21	11,630	89.79
7	780.23	768.62	778.85	214.26	211.63	213.48	105.85	104.97	105.51	14,730	89.70
8	787.42	776.68	782.66	215.48	212.65	214.55	106.29	105.11	106.12	21,300	89.54
9	783.00	774.43	777.81	214.99	212.26	213.38	106.26	105.18	105.62	17,940	89.66
10	781.01	772.61	775.99	214.36	211.00	212.65	106.22	104.80	105.65	19,480	89.79
13	777.37	770.44	774.43	212.31	208.80	209.88	105.92	104.60	104.97	16,810	89.77
14	773.91	762.65	765.16	210.70	207.00	207.98	105.21	103.76	104.33	20,470	89.64
15	767.07	758.32	761.69	208.61	204.81	205.59	104.80	103.59	103.96	20,170	89.61
16	760.14	749.65	753.29	205.74	201.84	203.50	104.36	102.88	103.55	21,570	89.34
17	759.96	748.18	752.69	205.25	201.99	203.84	104.36	102.88	103.52	18,500	89.35
21	753.90	745.24	749.31	204.76	201.74	203.01	104.09	102.27	102.84	21,890	89.59
22	753.55	746.71	749.05	205.35	202.13	203.84	103.32	102.06	102.54	18,450	89.44
23	752.51	742.98	750.95	204.71	202.33	203.79	102.98	102.20	102.64	18,720	89.36
24	760.40	750.78	756.24	206.61	204.03	205.83	103.72	102.23	103.21	22,510	89.51
27	761.26	746.62	748.35	206.90	203.40	203.89	103.79	102.47	102.94	19,990	89.62
28	748.61	739.17	742.12	204.18	201.06	201.40	103.79	102.33	103.25	19,750	89.49
		High 782.66				214.55			106.12		89.79
		Low 742.12				201.40			102.54		89.34

MARCH, 1978

	—30 Industrials—			—20 Transportations—			—15 Utilities—			Daily Sales	20
	High	Low	Close	High	Low	Close	High	Low	Close	—000—	Bonds
1	747.92	736.75	743.33	202.77	199.41	201.11	103.82	103.01	103.55	21,010	89.48
2	749.13	739.78	746.45	202.77	200.09	201.84	103.99	102.98	103.45	20,280	89.46
3	751.30	742.72	747.31	203.01	200.43	201.65	104.06	103.01	103.65	20,120	89.50
6	746.97	740.12	742.72	201.60	198.92	199.75	104.19	103.18	103.72	17,230	89.58
7	748.70	739.78	746.79	201.01	198.33	199.60	104.70	103.48	104.36	19,900	89.52
8	752.86	743.76	750.87	200.87	198.48	200.14	105.58	104.36	105.41	22,030	89.54
9	755.46	746.45	750.00	201.06	198.19	199.31	106.09	104.97	105.62	21,820	89.58
10	760.91	750.09	758.58	202.28	199.07	201.69	106.26	105.11	105.82	27,090	89.72
13	766.63	756.41	759.96	203.30	200.67	201.40	106.73	105.51	106.43	24,070	89.85
14	764.99	752.86	762.56	205.59	200.72	205.10	106.63	105.78	106.19	24,300	89.87
15	763.60	754.24	758.58	206.71	203.50	205.20	106.87	105.95	106.50	23,340	89.80
16	764.03	754.42	762.82	206.22	203.69	205.54	107.07	105.82	106.46	25,400	89.75
17	770.79	760.31	768.71	208.12	204.76	207.29	106.90	105.65	106.19	28,470	89.72
20	777.81	768.88	773.82	210.90	207.20	209.78	107.07	105.85	106.60	28,360	89.92
21	774.69	760.91	762.82	211.24	207.54	207.83	106.73	105.75	106.06	24,410	89.88
22	764.38	754.50	757.54	208.76	206.03	207.34	106.53	105.35	105.72	21,950	89.88
23	760.91	752.69	756.50	208.66	206.03	207.88	106.16	105.24	105.65	21,290	90.04
27	758.14	750.52	753.21	208.95	205.59	206.81	106.29	105.21	105.72	18,870	89.77
28	760.22	749.91	758.84	208.76	205.35	207.68	106.29	105.35	105.95	21,600	89.83
29	765.42	755.80	761.78	209.10	206.42	207.73	106.39	105.55	106.06	25,450	89.89
30	764.03	756.15	759.62	208.76	206.13	207.20	106.29	105.35	105.72	20,460	89.76
31	761.78	753.12	757.36	208.41	205.15	207.15	106.16	105.14	105.68	20,130	89.54
		High	773.82			209.78			106.60		90.04
		Low	742.72			199.31			103.45		89.46

APRIL, 1978

	—30 Industrials—			—20 Transportations—			—15 Utilities—			Daily Sales	20
	High	Low	Close	High	Low	Close	High	Low	Close	—000—	Bonds
3	756.67	747.05	751.04	207.59	204.42	205.40	105.82	104.47	104.74	20,230	89.46
4	757.19	748.79	755.37	206.66	203.74	205.49	105.48	104.47	105.04	20,130	89.49
5	764.47	753.21	763.08	206.95	204.13	206.27	105.68	104.67	105.31	27,260	89.50
6	768.10	759.62	763.95	208.22	205.49	206.86	106.09	104.87	105.55	27,360	89.40
7	772.00	760.83	769.58	209.19	206.08	208.02	106.33	105.07	105.95	25,160	89.35
10	776.16	766.11	773.65	209.88	207.00	208.80	106.60	105.31	105.92	25,740	89.35
11	775.38	766.20	770.18	209.49	206.37	207.78	106.36	105.55	105.99	24,300	89.30
12	772.96	764.30	766.29	209.05	206.52	207.44	106.77	105.45	105.82	26,210	89.20
13	777.29	764.47	775.21	210.02	206.61	209.58	106.56	105.38	105.99	31,580	89.21
14	797.73	780.41	795.13	214.65	209.88	213.77	107.87	105.45	106.09	52,280	89.34
17	824.24	803.45	810.12	221.42	214.70	218.30	106.90	104.87	105.72	63,510	89.36
18	814.97	798.15	803.27	219.37	214.65	216.16	106.02	104.40	104.97	38,950	89.35
19	812.72	797.56	808.04	218.69	214.79	217.72	105.75	104.36	105.35	35,060	89.42
20	825.10	810.38	814.54	222.97	218.01	220.49	106.56	105.01	105.75	43,230	89.29
21	818.95	807.17	812.80	222.54	218.54	220.59	107.17	105.45	105.77	31,540	89.20
24	827.36	810.38	826.06	224.09	220.00	222.39	107.61	106.19	106.97	34,510	89.13
25	845.81	828.83	833.59	226.58	221.90	223.66	108.02	106.19	106.70	55,800	89.03
26	846.15	828.48	836.97	226.09	221.76	224.34	107.00	105.55	106.12	44,430	89.12
27	836.37	822.77	826.92	224.97	221.27	222.34	106.53	105.14	105.89	35,470	89.01
28	838.79	822.16	837.32	225.46	220.69	224.58	107.07	105.45	106.36	32,850	89.01
		High	837.32			224.58			106.97		89.50
		Low	751.04			205.40			104.74		89.01

MAY, 1978

	30 Industrials			20 Transportations			15 Utilities			Daily Sales —000—	20 Bonds
	High	Low	Close	High	Low	Close	High	Low	Close		
1	849.45	832.81	844.33	227.45	222.97	225.51	107.10	105.82	106.43	37,020	88.95
2	847.54	833.42	840.18	226.87	223.02	224.78	106.90	105.72	106.33	41,400	88.85
3	841.82	826.58	828.83	226.97	222.83	224.29	106.94	105.75	106.12	37,560	89.04
4	829.09	813.84	824.41	225.46	220.93	223.90	105.95	104.47	105.01	37,520	89.06
5	837.32	820.86	829.09	227.02	222.54	224.78	106.29	105.24	105.85	42,680	88.90
8	837.14	822.77	824.58	226.33	221.90	223.41	106.60	105.21	105.48	34,680	88.89
9	829.44	817.65	822.07	223.75	220.15	221.51	105.89	104.47	104.84	30,860	88.80
10	829.61	817.22	822.16	224.00	219.96	222.00	105.51	104.23	104.63	33,330	88.74
11	835.33	821.12	834.20	225.36	221.42	224.68	105.11	103.76	104.47	36,630	88.80
12	847.54	834.11	840.70	228.82	224.68	227.75	105.28	103.82	104.60	46,600	88.81
15	848.84	834.72	846.76	229.30	225.70	227.94	105.24	103.55	104.43	33,890	88.64
16	861.05	848.15	854.30	232.13	227.50	229.65	104.91	103.42	104.09	48,170	88.59
17	865.64	847.89	858.37	233.15	227.60	231.25	104.70	103.45	104.06	45,490	88.55
18	863.57	848.67	850.92	234.03	228.53	230.91	105.04	103.72	104.09	42,270	88.59
19	855.16	840.87	846.85	231.35	227.60	229.16	104.80	103.48	104.26	34,360	88.47
22	857.76	842.34	855.42	232.37	228.57	231.30	105.04	103.92	104.67	28,680	88.31
23	856.12	842.17	845.29	232.62	226.77	227.80	105.07	103.72	104.36	33,230	88.41
24	842.86	829.87	837.92	226.82	222.54	224.68	104.94	103.42	104.03	31,450	88.19
25	843.04	830.99	835.41	226.92	222.97	224.14	105.14	103.76	104.33	28,410	88.23
26	836.37	827.79	831.69	225.02	221.85	223.70	104.87	103.82	104.47	21,410	88.19
30	837.32	826.40	834.20	225.21	221.85	224.09	105.35	104.09	104.87	21,040	88.14
31	846.85	832.99	840.61	225.94	222.58	223.95	105.78	104.57	105.31	29,070	88.01
		High 858.37				231.30			106.43		89.06
		Low 822.07				221.51			104.03		88.01

JUNE, 1978

	30 Industrials			20 Transportations			15 Utilities			Daily Sales —000—	20 Bonds
	High	Low	Close	High	Low	Close	High	Low	Close		
1	845.81	835.24	840.70	225.70	222.68	224.58	106.19	104.97	105.75	28,750	87.96
2	849.79	838.62	847.54	227.50	222.97	226.04	106.83	105.45	106.09	31,860	87.96
5	865.47	848.41	863.83	230.81	225.60	229.55	107.04	105.82	106.39	39,580	88.05
6	879.33	863.22	866.51	235.10	229.84	231.35	107.44	106.12	106.66	51,970	87.81
7	868.94	855.51	861.92	232.96	228.92	231.30	107.27	106.19	106.94	33,060	87.83
8	871.88	856.46	862.09	233.59	229.99	231.30	107.58	106.36	107.10	39,380	87.79
9	867.20	854.30	859.23	232.13	229.06	230.72	107.61	106.33	106.83	32,470	87.50
12	866.94	853.34	856.72	232.96	228.72	230.18	107.10	105.89	106.36	24,440	87.60
13	859.75	848.15	856.98	230.72	226.77	229.74	106.53	105.58	106.02	30,760	87.66
14	865.82	850.57	854.56	231.79	227.21	229.21	106.60	105.51	106.16	37,290	87.89
15	854.21	842.17	844.25	228.82	224.78	225.46	106.43	105.24	105.51	29,280	87.96
16	846.85	834.98	836.97	225.80	221.71	222.34	105.85	104.77	105.18	27,690	87.90
19	841.04	829.87	838.62	223.80	219.66	222.24	105.82	104.43	104.97	25,500	88.15
20	804.44	828.40	830.04	223.27	219.66	221.17	105.51	103.92	104.26	27,920	88.02
21	830.82	820.34	824.93	220.83	217.23	218.88	104.91	103.89	104.26	29,100	87.81
22	831.77	822.16	827.70	220.98	217.67	220.05	105.01	103.96	104.60	27,160	87.83
23	832.55	821.12	823.02	222.49	218.40	219.61	105.18	104.23	104.63	28,530	87.59
26	824.15	810.03	812.28	220.05	215.57	216.40	105.18	103.79	104.19	29,250	87.52
27	820.95	807.95	817.31	218.35	214.50	217.33	104.80	103.65	104.30	29,280	87.46
28	824.24	811.59	819.91	219.61	216.06	218.69	105.21	103.86	104.63	23,260	87.53
29	827.88	816.79	821.64	220.73	217.23	219.32	105.48	104.33	104.80	21,660	87.60
30	823.20	815.06	818.95	221.08	217.57	219.86	105.31	104.33	104.94	18,100	87.34
		High 866.51				231.35			107.10		88.15
		Low 812.28				216.40			104.19		87.34

JULY, 1978

	—30 Industrials—			—20 Transportations—			—15 Utilities—			Daily Sales —000—	20 Bonds
	High	Low	Close	High	Low	Close	High	Low	Close		
3	818.95	809.71	812.89	220.34	217.72	219.32	105.68	104.74	105.38	11,560	87.22
5	812.63	802.15	805.79	219.22	215.62	216.50	105.62	104.63	105.28	23,730	87.20
6	810.72	800.94	807.17	217.67	214.36	216.30	105.62	104.63	105.07	24,990	87.20
7	816.18	805.79	812.46	219.08	215.48	218.25	105.65	104.70	105.35	23,480	87.19
10	819.56	808.13	816.79	221.37	216.84	220.30	105.72	104.70	105.01	22,470	86.91
11	826.32	814.62	821.29	224.00	219.96	222.54	105.75	104.57	105.24	27,470	86,73
12	829.18	819.39	824.93	225.26	221.76	223.56	105.95	104.77	105.72	26,640	87.05
13	827.88	818.09	824.76	225.17	221.51	223.07	105.89	104.94	104.45	23,620	89.95
14	841.22	823.02	839.83	226.38	222.44	225.36	105.92	104.97	105.65	28,370	86.94
17	848.58	835.59	839.05	229.60	224.73	227.60	106.16	104.80	105.28	29,180	87.00
18	840.00	826.75	829.00	228.92	224.73	226.82	105.78	104.74	105.18	22,860	87.13
19	842.52	828.05	840.70	230.62	227.16	229.69	105.78	104.77	105.28	30,850	87.20
20	849.45	835.24	838.62	231.93	227.65	229.30	106.06	104.87	105.28	33,350	87.10
21	842.00	828.83	833.42	230.77	227.02	228.96	105.78	104.77	105.07	26,060	87.20
24	835.07	823.46	831.60	230.86	226.63	229.99	105.85	104.67	105.38	23,280	87.20
25	841.65	827.18	839.57	233.69	229.79	233.05	106.16	104.91	105.95	25,400	87.15
26	852.48	839.05	847.19	237.53	232.66	235.00	106.50	105.35	105.95	36,830	87.29
27	857.16	843.04	850.57	237.58	233.59	236.17	106.53	105.41	106.09	33,970	87.48
28	860.27	844.77	856.29	239.92	235.25	238.31	107.10	105.75	106.46	33,390	87.68
31	866.34	852.56	862.27	242.65	237.44	241.14	107.24	105.82	106.66	33,990	87.73
		High	862.27			241.14			106.66		87.73
		Low	805.79			216.30			104.45		86.73

AUGUST, 1978

	—30 Industrials—			—20 Transportations—			—15 Utilities—			Daily Sales —000—	20 Bonds
	High	Low	Close	High	Low	Close	High	Low	Close		
1	868.16	855.34	860.71	243.96	239.09	241.48	107.41	106.09	106.94	34,810	87.80
2	884.88	857.50	883.49	247.91	240.21	246.79	107.81	106.43	107.24	47,470	87.87
3	905.15	881.84	886.87	253.26	246.98	248.73	108.56	106.94	107.85	66,370	88.14
4	895.79	879.33	888.43	250.88	246.74	248.83	108.69	107.21	108.19	37,910	88.26
7	896.22	881.41	885.05	251.51	246.64	248.78	108.93	107.54	108.09	33,350	88.38
8	891.55	877.51	889.21	250.68	246.74	249.61	108.59	107.44	107.98	34,290	88.69
9	903.67	886.61	891.63	253.26	246.83	249.90	108.56	107.07	107.48	48,800	88.96
10	898.39	880.20	885.48	250.78	244.94	246.45	108.12	106.63	107.41	39,760	88.95
11	895.70	880.20	890.85	249.51	243.43	247.57	107.85	106.80	107.27	33,550	88.95
14	899.17	884.27	888.17	249.85	246.54	247.76	107.58	106.43	106.87	32,320	88.95
15	891.37	879.16	887.13	249.17	244.98	247.81	107.31	106.12	106.73	29,760	88.98
16	898.30	884.88	894.58	251.51	246.83	250.68	107.27	106.19	106.77	36,120	88.81
17	911.21	894.66	900.12	254.82	250.00	251.80	107.68	106.46	106.87	45,270	88.90
18	909.22	892.93	896.83	253.55	249.27	251.07	107.41	106.22	106.66	34,650	88.85
21	900.38	884.88	888.95	252.14	246.64	248.05	107.14	105.92	106.19	29,440	88.91
22	896.05	881.15	892.41	250.78	245.91	249.76	106.73	105.51	106.33	29,620	89.02
23	904.28	890.94	897.00	253.80	249.81	251.66	107.04	105.78	106.56	39,630	88.97
24	904.80	890.94	897.35	255.31	250.54	253.41	107.17	105.78	106.46	38,500	88.91
25	902.55	890.59	895.53	255.21	251.17	252.09	106.97	105.78	106.39	36,190	89.06
28	895.70	882.62	884.88	252.05	247.27	248.78	106.80	105.72	106.09	31,760	89.21
29	887.13	875.95	880.20	251.02	245.52	247.76	106.90	105.68	106.16	33,780	89.15
30	888.17	873.61	880.72	251.85	246.54	249.27	106.87	105.92	106.46	37,750	89.02
31	883.66	871.36	876.82	250.15	245.96	247.95	107.07	106.06	106.66	33,850	89.08
		High	900.12			253.41			108.19		89.21
		Low	860.71			241.48			106.09		87.80

SEPTEMBER, 1978

	—30 Industrials—			—20 Transportations—			—15 Utilities—			Daily Sales —000—	20 Bonds
	High	Low	Close	High	Low	Close	High	Low	Close		
1	884.88	871.36	879.33	252.73	246.79	251.61	107.65	106.12	107.21	35,070	89.09
5	889.73	876.91	886.61	255.75	250.73	254.67	107.95	106.80	107.44	32,170	89.27
6	902.03	887.91	895.79	260.52	255.41	258.62	108.09	106.83	107.41	42,600	89.19
7	903.15	889.55	893.71	262.95	257.21	259.25	107.85	106.60	107.21	40,310	89.31
8	909.91	895.62	907.74	263.78	258.86	261.49	108.32	106.94	107.92	42,170	89.41
11	917.24	904.80	907.74	264.95	259.20	260.62	108.42	107.10	107.75	39,670	89.43
12	910.26	899.43	906.44	261.88	257.40	260.08	108.02	106.87	107.58	34,400	89.55
13	913.29	896.83	899.60	261.54	256.48	257.21	108.15	106.94	107.48	43,340	89.43
14	900.21	885.48	887.04	257.55	252.48	253.51	107.92	106.53	106.70	37,400	89.47
15	886.17	874.05	878.55	253.26	249.22	250.73	106.97	105.85	106.43	37,290	89.54
18	884.88	866.86	870.15	252.87	245.13	247.03	107.14	105.82	106.39	35,860	89.50
19	873.87	859.06	861.57	248.88	244.16	245.96	106.56	105.51	105.92	31,660	89.56
20	870.50	853.95	857.16	247.57	242.31	243.13	106.66	105.24	105.85	35,080	89.35
21	865.38	850.92	861.14	244.55	239.04	242.01	106.60	105.14	105.99	33,640	89.13
22	868.16	855.42	862.44	243.82	239.09	241.58	106.56	105.31	105.72	27,960	89.06
25	865.47	856.20	862.35	243.77	329.04	242.35	106.33	105.41	105.78	20,970	88.90
26	872.66	859.67	868.16	247.27	241.38	245.42	106.60	105.45	106.09	26,330	88.94
27	875.43	858.45	860.19	247.71	241.77	242.65	107.10	105.89	106.26	28,370	88.93
28	864.43	854.90	861.31	244.35	239.97	242.94	106.94	105.85	106.12	24,390	88.92
29	870.84	858.89	865.82	245.62	242.01	244.11	106.77	105.62	106.12	23,610	88.84
		High	907.74			261.49			107.92		89.56
		Low	857.16			241.58			105.72		88.84

OCTOBER, 1978

	—30 Industrials—			—20 Transportations—			—15 Utilities—			Daily Sales —000—	20 Bonds
	High	Low	Close	High	Low	Close	High	Low	Close		
2	874.48	863.13	871.36	246.30	242.70	244.74	106.53	105.45	105.92	18,700	88.75
3	876.30	865.56	867.90	246.98	243.09	244.40	106.39	105.45	105.95	22,540	88.52
4	875.52	860.10	873.96	247.08	241.38	245.86	106.39	105.28	106.06	25,090	88.47
5	883.32	869.63	876.47	248.20	243.96	246.35	106.60	105.51	106.12	27,820	88.31
6	885.14	873.79	880.02	248.78	244.69	246.88	106.80	105.55	106.29	27,380	88.32
9	894.92	877.86	893.19	249.37	245.71	248.30	107.04	106.02	106.63	19,720	88.30
10	899.26	887.56	891.63	250.83	246.69	248.59	107.34	106.12	106.73	25,470	88.28
11	902.29	885.14	901.42	250.34	246.74	249.85	107.48	106.39	106.97	21,740	88.21
12	909.39	892.84	896.74	252.97	248.10	250.15	107.75	106.39	106.70	30,170	88.33
13	902.20	891.55	897.09	251.27	248.10	249.81	107.41	106.33	106.77	21,920	88.30
16	894.84	874.39	875.17	250.34	243.33	243.96	107.04	105.38	105.89	24,600	88.08
17	872.49	858.11	866.34	241.33	234.56	237.44	105.82	104.50	104.84	37,870	88.02
18	871.19	853.60	859.67	238.31	230.67	232.71	105.15	103.89	104.23	32,940	87.86
19	862.87	844.42	846.41	234.76	227.89	228.67	104.67	103.08	103.38	31,810	87.72
20	847.37	830.47	838.01	228.38	220.54	223.85	103.28	101.86	102.30	43,670	87.71
23	845.89	825.80	839.66	226.72	220.20	224.73	102.98	101.45	102.17	36,090	87.54
24	846.93	830.35	832.55	226.29	220.88	222.34	102.77	101.35	101.79	28,880	87.51
25	842.86	822.85	830.21	225.02	218.88	221.81	102.44	101.18	101.93	31,380	87.41
26	835.41	816.61	821.12	222.93	216.35	217.52	101.76	100.24	100.47	31,990	87.24
27	825.54	804.49	806.05	218.59	211.34	212.26	100.85	98.71	98.92	40,360	87.24
30	814.36	782.05	811.85	214.45	203.50	213.04	99.19	96.35	98.07	59,480	86.89
31	818.26	789.67	792.45	215.72	207.83	208.71	98.61	96.79	97.33	42,720	86.70
		High	901.42			250.15			106.97		88.75
		Low	792.45			208.71			97.33		86.70

NOVEMBER, 1978

	—30 Industrials—			—20 Transportations—			—15 Utilities—			Daily Sales —000—	20 Bonds
	High	Low	Close	High	Low	Close	High	Low	Close		
1	831.69	805.53	827.79	220.10	212.07	219.03	99.49	97.19	98.58	50,450	86.67
2	831.34	811.07	816.96	220.54	213.77	215.04	99.66	97.94	98.48	41,030	86.62
3	829.00	809.51	823.11	219.08	214.01	216.84	98.92	97.83	98.31	25,990	86.33
6	825.88	812.63	814.88	218.69	213.62	215.04	98.95	97.73	98.31	20,450	86.44
7	808.13	793.92	800.07	214.36	209.24	211.14	98.44	97.02	97.67	25,320	86.36
8	809.60	790.97	807.61	212.65	208.12	211.53	98.34	97.09	98.04	23,560	86.41
9	815.75	798.86	803.97	213.53	209.68	210.90	98.58	97.50	98.00	23,320	86.34
10	812.02	799.55	807.09	215.04	210.70	213.62	98.55	97.56	98.24	16,750	86.24
13	806.83	790.71	792.01	214.16	206.81	207.64	98.27	96.85	97.09	20,960	86.12
14	795.22	779.11	785.26	208.51	203.74	205.49	97.53	96.04	96.35	30,610	86.26
15	798.08	782.66	785.60	209.92	205.05	206.76	97.16	96.04	96.55	26,280	86.54
16	797.38	785.26	794.18	211.04	206.86	209.49	97.80	96.35	97.36	21,340	86.65
17	804.49	792.19	797.73	212.70	208.61	210.41	98.61	97.19	98.04	25,170	86.91
20	811.24	797.47	805.61	213.48	209.19	211.63	99.29	97.80	99.02	24,440	86.93
21	810.55	799.98	804.05	213.19	209.14	211.04	99.90	98.38	99.15	20,750	87.02
22	810.98	799.46	807.00	213.19	209.92	212.36	100.00	98.75	99.46	20,010	86.96
24	812.98	803.36	810.12	215.48	211.77	214.60	100.00	98.85	99.32	14,590	86.98
27	817.22	806.31	813.84	216.79	212.80	215.04	100.30	99.12	99.73	19,790	86.71
28	817.91	802.67	804.14	216.40	210.65	211.87	100.54	99.39	99.90	22,740	86.50
29	801.89	788.63	790.11	211.48	207.78	208.71	100.20	98.99	99.26	21,160	86.44
30	800.94	786.64	799.03	212.75	208.02	212.36	100.00	98.65	99.56	19,900	86.41
		High	827.79			219.03			99.90		87.02
		Low	785.26			205.49			96.35		86.12

DECEMBER, 1978

	—30 Industrials—			—20 Transportations—			—15 Utilities—			Daily Sales —000—	20 Bonds
	High	Low	Close	High	Low	Close	High	Low	Close		
1	815.06	801.98	811.50	218.10	212.55	216.60	100.54	99.29	99.97	26,830	86.26
4	814.80	802.23	806.83	217.72	214.26	215.33	100.78	99.53	100.27	22,020	86.28
5	821.81	805.01	820.51	218.88	214.16	218.20	101.49	99.97	100.78	25,670	86.31
6	829.87	815.23	821.90	221.66	216.01	218.20	101.83	100.74	101.32	29,680	86.49
7	826.49	812.98	816.09	219.22	215.62	216.60	102.06	100.68	101.29	21,170	86.56
8	819.56	807.95	811.85	217.52	214.55	215.43	101.73	100.47	101.08	18,560	86.47
11	821.29	808.73	817.65	218.01	213.92	216.64	101.56	100.37	101.12	21,000	86.56
12	821.90	811.50	814.97	218.01	212.60	214.16	101.49	100.14	100.68	22,210	86.40
13	819.21	806.48	809.86	214.99	210.85	212.36	100.78	99.49	100.14	22,480	85.97
14	814.97	804.40	812.54	212.80	209.73	211.14	100.20	99.05	99.73	20,840	85.91
15	813.76	801.80	805.35	212.02	208.41	209.34	100.14	98.88	99.19	23,620	85.88
18	794.87	781.01	787.51	206.81	201.74	204.03	98.71	97.23	97.77	32,900	85.64
19	795.30	782.92	789.85	206.61	202.52	204.62	98.48	97.12	97.77	25,960	85.24
20	797.90	785.69	793.66	205.49	201.65	203.45	98.34	96.96	97.73	26,520	85.03
21	801.63	790.11	794.79	206.08	202.43	204.42	98.51	97.16	97.77	28,670	84.92
22	811.16	795.05	808.47	209.44	204.42	208.46	98.48	97.33	98.21	23,790	84.91
26	819.13	804.66	816.01	212.21	208.07	211.19	98.92	97.67	98.31	21,470	84.83
27	815.32	804.57	808.56	211.63	207.68	208.76	98.71	97.63	98.00	23,580	84.69
28	813.06	802.75	805.96	209.63	205.44	206.95	98.71	97.50	98.14	25,440	84.71
29	812.20	800.50	805.01	208.76	204.37	206.56	98.75	97.63	98.24	30,030	84.54
		High	821.90			218.20			101.32		86.56
		Low	787.51			203.45			97.73		84.54

JANUARY, 1979

	—30 Industrials—			—20 Transportations—			—15 Utilities—			Daily Sales —000—	20 Bonds
	High	Low	Close	High	Low	Close	High	Low	Close		
2	813.06	798.51	811.42	210.51	205.40	210.17	99.22	97.83	99.19	18,340	84.62
3	822.68	811.42	817.39	216.01	210.90	214.55	100.54	99.12	100.37	29,180	84.35
4	832.55	815.92	826.14	219.22	213.67	217.23	101.56	100.07	101.08	33,290	84.53
5	837.23	823.89	830.73	219.22	215.13	217.37	101.86	100.68	101.39	28,890	84.49
8	832.12	821.38	828.14	217.57	214.36	216.01	101.89	100.47	101.45	21,440	84.50
9	836.80	825.80	831.43	217.81	214.89	216.60	101.73	100.74	101.29	27,340	84.49
10	833.68	821.47	824.93	217.33	213.09	214.50	101.59	100.54	101.22	24,990	84.27
11	829.44	817.31	828.05	216.11	211.97	215.48	101.62	100.51	101.25	24,580	84.36
12	843.38	830.04	836.28	220.30	215.96	217.67	102.98	101.35	102.00	37,120	84.11
15	851.00	831.69	848.67	220.20	216.11	218.79	102.81	101.56	102.10	27,520	84.09
16	848.06	833.25	835.59	219.91	215.33	216.89	102.71	101.39	101.96	30,340	84.15
17	839.05	825.80	834.20	217.96	213.72	216.50	102.54	101.52	102.20	25,310	84.16
18	843.73	829.35	839.14	221.03	216.01	219.32	102.98	101.76	102.37	27,260	84.45
19	846.67	833.94	837.49	221.90	218.01	219.86	102.94	101.89	102.40	26,800	84.20
22	841.74	829.95	838.53	220.88	215.62	217.57	102.64	101.52	102.00	24,390	84.39
23	851.35	835.67	846.85	220.00	214.26	217.86	103.11	101.79	102.77	30,130	84.43
24	856.81	840.61	846.41	220.25	215.28	217.23	103.45	102.17	102.67	31,730	84.50
25	858.11	843.90	854.64	220.54	216.30	218.93	104.06	102.67	103.52	31,440	84.88
26	865.04	853.26	859.75	221.27	216.74	218.74	104.53	103.32	104.06	34,230	85.04
29	862.96	851.61	855.77	219.81	216.01	217.91	104.94	103.76	104.50	24,170	85.24
30	861.83	848.75	851.78	218.74	215.48	216.89	105.07	104.03	104.67	26,910	85.19
31	853.52	835.67	839.22	217.81	213.58	214.55	105.31	104.30	104.91	30,330	85.41
		High	859.75			219.86			104.91		85.41
		Low	811.42			210.17			99.19		84.09

FEBRUARY, 1979

	—30 Industrials—			—20 Transportations—			—15 Utilities—			Daily Sales —000—	20 Bonds
	High	Low	Close	High	Low	Close	High	Low	Close		
1	843.99	832.55	840.87	215.72	211.97	214.31	104.94	103.96	104.53	27,930	85.51
2	843.38	832.47	834.63	215.82	212.50	213.43	105.01	103.96	104.26	25,350	85.90
5	830.65	819.13	823.98	212.94	208.46	209.53	104.67	103.28	103.96	26,490	85.87
6	828.48	819.21	822.85	210.65	207.05	209.29	104.13	103.01	103.32	23,570	85.51
7	823.46	810.81	816.01	209.58	205.64	206.56	103.82	102.91	103.42	28,450	85.32
8	823.02	812.89	818.87	208.17	204.91	206.71	103.65	102.88	103.25	23,360	85.47
9	826.49	817.05	822.23	209.44	205.88	207.73	103.72	102.74	103.21	24,320	85.56
12	827.62	816.61	824.84	209.83	206.22	209.29	103.92	102.71	103.38	20,610	85.59
13	836.19	826.14	830.21	213.67	209.39	212.50	104.13	103.18	103.72	28,470	85.20
14	836.88	825.71	829.78	215.91	211.09	213.62	104.30	103.38	104.06	27,220	85.21
15	831.25	822.68	829.09	213.58	210.07	212.02	104.36	103.35	104.09	22,550	85.28
16	831.69	823.54	827.01	213.19	210.26	211.77	104.84	103.86	104.36	21,110	85.10
20	836.19	824.15	834.55	213.87	210.31	213.19	104.84	103.62	104.57	22,010	85.04
21	841.56	830.91	834.55	214.70	211.53	212.50	105.07	104.03	104.53	26,050	84.80
22	834.98	825.10	828.57	213.62	201.56	211.82	104.94	103.79	104.43	26,290	84.81
23	828.83	819.99	823.28	212.55	209.58	211.19	104.70	103.76	104.16	22,750	84.80
26	826.40	818.35	821.12	211.77	209.49	210.65	104.47	103.15	103.45	22,620	84.62
27	821.12	803.53	807.00	210.36	204.96	205.78	103.62	102.00	102.23	31,470	84.57
28	811.76	802.23	808.82	207.15	203.84	205.83	102.77	101.69	102.30	25,090	84.50
		High	840.87			214.31			104.57		85.90
		Low	807.00			205.78			102.23		84.50

MARCH, 1979

	—30 Industrials—			—20 Transportations—			—15 Utilities—			Daily Sales —000—	20 Bonds
	High	Low	Close	High	Low	Close	High	Low	Close		
1	818.17	807.26	815.84	208.71	205.25	207.98	103.55	101.96	103.11	23,830	84.42
2	820.69	811.50	815.75	209.68	207.25	208.56	103.65	102.60	103.11	23,130	84.43
5	832.55	818.00	827.36	212.65	208.32	211.04	103.86	102.84	103.38	25,690	84.47
6	831.34	821.55	826.58	212.12	209.05	207.97	104.03	102.71	103.48	24,490	84.60
7	841.04	825.28	834.29	213.72	209.63	211.73	104.06	102.91	103.59	28,930	84.75
8	846.41	831.69	844.85	214.45	211.14	213.82	104.33	103.04	104.06	32,000	84.76
9	851.44	840.00	842.86	216.06	212.36	214.01	104.63	103.59	104.16	33,410	84.64
12	846.33	833.85	844.68	214.74	211.92	213.97	103.96	102.88	103.55	25,740	84.46
13	855.60	840.78	846.93	216.79	213.04	215.28	103.72	102.71	103.35	31,170	84.43
14	852.56	841.74	845.37	216.64	213.53	214.55	103.59	102.37	102.88	24,630	84.32
15	853.17	841.39	847.02	217.52	213.58	216.35	103.28	102.37	102.88	29,370	84.32
16	856.72	843.21	852.82	218.79	215.04	217.28	103.62	102.44	103.25	31,770	84.35
19	864.95	852.65	857.59	219.96	216.40	218.01	104.23	102.91	103.89	34,620	84.46
20	858.89	847.45	850.31	219.37	215.77	216.98	104.77	103.32	103.72	27,180	84.40
21	859.23	844.68	857.76	218.25	214.84	217.42	104.50	103.42	104.23	31,120	84.45
22	867.46	856.03	861.31	220.34	216.21	218.20	104.87	103.82	104.53	34,380	84.42
23	867.20	855.08	859.75	221.90	217.18	219.76	104.91	103.99	104.70	33,570	84.25
26	860.01	851.52	854.82	221.51	218.30	219.91	105.07	103.96	104.47	23,430	84.47
27	872.49	852.91	871.36	224.14	219.57	223.70	105.24	104.13	104.80	32,940	84.39
28	876.99	863.83	866.25	227.02	222.83	223.80	105.55	104.36	104.77	39,920	84.68
29	873.53	860.19	866.77	226.19	221.85	224.19	105.31	104.33	104.63	28,510	84.62
30	870.58	858.11	862.18	227.06	222.44	225.17	104.97	103.79	104.19	29,970	84.59
		High	871.36			225.17			104.80		84.76
		Low	815.95			207.98			102.88		84.25

APRIL, 1979

	—30 Industrials—			—20 Transportations—			—15 Utilities—			Daily Sales —000—	20 Bonds
	High	Low	Close	High	Low	Close	High	Low	Close		
2	859.93	849.27	855.25	227.11	222.93	225.36	104.03	102.57	103.32	28,990	84.61
3	870.67	854.21	868.33	231.16	225.36	230.18	104.67	103.32	104.13	33,530	84.59
4	878.38	867.12	869.80	234.32	229.69	231.35	105.41	104.16	104.84	41,940	84.62
5	880.02	866.68	877.60	233.49	229.79	232.62	105.28	104.13	104.87	34,520	84.63
6	884.01	871.88	875.69	235.78	232.03	234.08	105.62	104.23	104.94	34,710	84.56
9	879.07	869.46	873.70	236.66	232.71	234.22	105.21	103.92	104.47	27,230	84.54
10	882.54	869.80	878.72	236.02	232.96	235.25	105.01	103.55	104.26	31,900	84.45
11	884.62	868.68	871.71	236.61	232.13	233.69	104.87	103.32	103.96	32,900	84.35
12	875.78	865.21	870.50	234.76	232.23	233.35	104.40	103.35	103.72	26,780	84.35
16	868.42	856.81	860.45	233.49	230.33	231.25	103.89	102.57	103.18	28,050	84.21
17	865.64	853.95	857.93	232.91	229.89	230.96	103.59	102.33	103.04	29,260	84.27
18	865.90	856.38	860.27	233.83	229.94	232.62	103.52	102.37	103.04	29,510	84.08
19	865.73	852.91	855.25	234.71	230.72	231.89	103.76	102.64	103.35	31,150	84.14
20	861.57	848.93	856.98	232.86	229.65	231.01	103.38	102.40	102.74	28,830	84.12
23	863.31	852.39	860.10	232.33	229.21	231.11	103.21	102.00	102.33	25,610	84.15
24	873.35	858.54	866.86	234.51	229.84	232.62	103.01	101.83	102.27	35,540	84.24
25	872.31	863.22	867.46	233.88	231.59	232.81	102.91	101.56	102.20	31,750	84.14
26	869.02	858.71	860.97	234.17	230.28	231.84	102.67	101.42	101.73	32,400	84.01
27	860.79	852.39	856.64	232.13	229.16	230.86	102.13	100.61	101.18	29,610	83.69
30	859.49	847.28	854.90	231.16	226.63	229.06	101.79	100.30	100.98	26,440	83.59
		High	878.72			235.25			104.94		84.63
		Low	854.90			225.36			100.98		83.59

MAY, 1979

	—30 Industrials—			—20 Transportations—			—15 Utilities—			Daily Sales —000—	20 Bonds
	High	Low	Close	High	Low	Close	High	Low	Close		
1	861.40	850.83	855.51	230.67	226.92	228.38	101.69	100.54	100.91	31,040	83.62
2	860.27	849.97	855.51	229.40	226.29	227.89	101.39	100.30	100.85	30,510	83.58
3	863.22	852.74	857.59	229.50	226.72	228.38	101.56	100.44	100.81	30,870	83.58
4	859.23	845.89	847.54	228.92	225.21	226.24	101.29	99.86	100.44	30,630	83.16
7	846.07	832.03	833.42	235.36	220.59	221.08	100.41	98.95	99.39	30,480	83.08
8	838.10	823.63	834.89	222.05	218.49	220.88	99.66	98.51	98.99	32,720	82.92
9	842.26	829.09	838.62	222.93	219.66	221.90	99.80	98.65	99.56	27,670	83.06
10	839.92	827.53	828.92	223.56	220.44	221.56	99.90	98.88	99.26	25,230	82.99
11	834.11	824.76	830.56	223.41	220.05	222.49	99.76	98.75	99.32	24,010	83.17
14	834.03	823.02	825.02	224.68	221.12	222.15	99.46	98.21	98.61	22,450	83.21
15	832.12	821.55	825.88	225.31	221.42	223.75	99.05	98.07	98.51	26,190	83.19
16	832.47	821.03	828.48	225.56	222.39	224.09	99.22	98.21	98.95	28,350	83.49
17	845.03	827.44	842.95	229.06	224.58	228.38	100.64	98.61	100.44	30,550	83.83
18	848.32	837.40	841.91	231.64	227.94	230.38	101.15	100.00	100.61	26,590	83.91
21	847.80	836.28	842.43	232.76	229.26	231.54	101.69	100.20	101.05	25,550	83.79
22	848.41	837.23	845.37	234.17	230.28	233.49	101.01	99.97	100.41	30,400	83.55
23	851.26	836.19	837.40	237.00	231.89	233.44	101.01	99.90	100.20	30,390	83.81
24	842.69	832.38	837.66	234.76	231.25	233.44	101.29	99.80	100.85	25,710	83.94
25	840.26	831.86	836.28	236.17	231.69	234.71	101.89	100.58	101.45	27,810	84.11
29	837.75	829.26	832.55	236.85	232.71	234.27	102.17	100.71	101.59	27,040	84.39
30	832.47	820.17	822.16	235.73	231.54	232.62	102.23	101.08	101.79	29,250	84.47
31	827.01	815.14	822.33	234.61	230.52	233.15	102.17	101.22	101.69	30,300	84.45
		High	857.59			234.17			101.79		84.47
		Low	822.16			220.88			98.51		82.92

JUNE, 1979

	—30 Industrials—			—20 Transportations—			—15 Utilities—			Daily Sales —000—	20 Bonds
	High	Low	Close	High	Low	Close	High	Low	Close		
1	826.14	817.74	821.21	234.71	231.30	233.10	102.17	101.18	101.83	24,560	84.39
2	825.36	817.83	821.90	235.68	232.03	234.51	102.47	101.39	102.20	24,040	84.21
5	834.46	820.25	831.34	237.63	234.08	236.61	102.84	101.79	102.47	35,050	84.38
6	841.04	829.26	835.50	240.16	235.00	238.12	103.83	102.13	103.08	39,830	84.73
7	842.78	833.16	836.97	241.87	236.80	239.24	104.40	103.01	103.79	43,380	84.82
8	839.48	831.25	835.15	240.26	236.75	238.46	104.47	103.35	103.82	31,470	84.93
11	839.66	830.73	837.58	240.50	236.71	239.29	104.30	103.32	103.99	28,270	84.77
12	851.61	837.14	845.29	243.33	239.09	241.87	105.51	103.89	105.18	45,450	85.00
13	850.31	840.00	842.17	244.40	240.11	241.72	106.50	104.70	105.75	40,740	85.32
14	844.07	834.29	842.34	242.11	238.41	241.09	105.82	104.53	105.07	37,850	85.26
15	847.11	837.40	843.30	242.70	239.04	240.80	105.78	104.53	105.28	40,740	85.51
18	845.20	836.28	839.40	241.97	238.12	239.73	105.99	104.67	105.35	30,970	85.36
19	843.99	835.85	839.40	241.72	237.63	240.11	105.99	104.60	105.58	30,780	85.25
20	843.56	836.11	839.83	240.94	237.78	239.48	105.92	104.84	105.38	33,790	85.47
21	847.80	837.40	843.64	241.72	237.92	240.02	106.06	104.70	105.31	36,490	85.49
22	853.06	842.34	849.10	242.55	239.38	241.38	105.92	104.91	105.51	36,410	85.45
25	850.83	839.66	844.25	243.18	238.99	240.85	105.72	104.50	105.11	31,330	85.35
26	849.19	834.46	837.66	242.50	238.26	239.82	105.89	104.47	105.28	34,680	85.52
27	846.15	834.20	840.52	242.79	238.56	241.92	106.09	104.94	105.48	36,720	85.70
28	848.84	836.97	843.04	244.89	240.36	242.89	106.26	104.63	105.55	38,470	85.75
29	848.12	837.20	841.98	244.74	240.31	242.26	105.99	104.77	105.45	34,690	85.70
		High	849.10			242.89			105.75		85.75
		Low	821.21			233.10			101.83		84.21

JULY, 1979

	—30 Industrials—			—20 Transportations—			—15 Utilities—			Daily Sales —000—	20 Bonds
	High	Low	Close	High	Low	Close	High	Low	Close		
2	840.61	830.46	834.04	243.77	239.82	241.33	105.92	104.53	105.21	32,060	85.78
3	838.99	829.27	835.58	243.18	239.09	242.01	105.82	104.70	105.45	31,670	85.97
5	840.02	830.97	835.75	244.55	240.11	243.57	105.99	104.97	105.62	30,290	85.94
6	847.27	834.22	846.16	249.22	242.70	248.64	107.00	105.48	106.70	38,570	85.92
9	856.57	844.28	852.99	253.17	247.91	251.56	107.95	106.16	107.75	42,460	85.83
10	857.00	845.73	850.34	253.70	248.05	250.34	108.86	107.54	108.29	39,730	85.83
11	849.40	839.16	843.86	251.17	246.30	248.64	108.76	107.44	108.09	36,650	85.70
12	844.62	834.22	836.86	249.22	245.23	246.54	108.46	107.17	107.61	31,780	85.59
13	837.88	827.47	833.53	247.66	242.50	246.06	108.42	106.83	107.95	33,080	85.76
16	838.57	828.92	834.90	251.36	245.81	250.54	108.36	107.17	107.75	26,620	85.57
17	836.35	824.66	828.50	252.19	246.20	247.32	108.22	106.94	107.65	34,270	85.61
18	830.97	818.00	828.58	248.93	243.09	248.25	107.61	106.56	107.24	35,950	85.77
19	834.04	822.78	827.30	250.10	246.15	248.25	107.85	106.73	107.21	26,780	85.68
20	832.08	822.70	828.07	249.90	246.06	248.64	108.32	106.73	107.85	26,360	85.74
23	829.69	819.97	825.51	249.46	245.71	247.52	108.12	106.83	107.31	26,860	85.59
24	833.28	822.61	829.78	249.37	245.71	247.86	107.92	106.83	107.34	29,690	85.62
25	840.78	829.18	839.51	251.95	247.27	250.73	108.49	107.07	107.98	34,890	85.70
26	843.17	833.96	839.76	251.90	248.44	250.68	108.76	107.44	108.15	32,270	85.73
27	842.66	833.28	839.76	252.78	249.22	251.70	108.73	107.44	108.15	27,760	85.59
30	842.49	833.45	838.74	253.31	249.71	252.09	108.63	107.48	108.02	28,640	85.51
31	849.06	837.80	846.42	255.41	251.36	254.53	109.03	107.61	108.80	34,360	85.78
		High 852.99				254.53			108.80		85.97
		Low 825.51				241.33			105.21		85.51

AUGUST, 1979

	—30 Industrials—			—20 Transportations—			—15 Utilities—			Daily Sales —000—	20 Bonds
	High	Low	Close	High	Low	Close	High	Low	Close		
1	852.30	841.38	850.34	257.99	252.73	256.72	109.00	107.98	108.49	36,570	85.90
2	855.03	844.28	847.95	258.77	254.92	256.33	108.93	107.27	108.15	37,720	85.99
3	850.51	843.32	846.16	257.06	253.75	254.97	108.63	107.10	108.02	28,160	85.86
6	850.77	839.08	848.55	256.77	253.36	255.45	108.66	107.37	108.36	27,190	85.86
7	863.99	848.04	859.81	261.30	255.26	259.50	109.00	107.95	108.59	45,410	85.90
8	870.14	857.42	863.14	265.34	259.11	262.86	109.10	107.95	108.63	44,970	85.86
9	864.51	855.12	858.28	263.88	260.42	262.22	108.90	107.57	108.29	34,630	85.87
10	869.54	852.30	867.06	265.34	260.81	264.46	108.80	107.71	108.15	36,740	85.85
13	878.58	867.15	875.26	269.28	264.32	268.11	109.03	107.61	108.49	41,980	85.74
14	880.72	868.69	876.71	271.67	265.68	269.58	109.27	108.12	108.86	40,910	85.80
15	888.23	871.50	885.84	273.42	268.11	271.77	109.34	108.15	108.93	46,130	86.10
16	893.60	878.75	884.04	273.24	268.21	269.96	109.54	108.49	109.00	47,000	85.86
17	888.31	877.05	883.36	270.99	266.07	268.70	109.64	108.49	109.13	31,630	86.01
20	890.27	878.07	886.52	271.57	265.73	270.31	109.78	108.46	109.24	32,300	85.83
21	892.32	880.63	886.01	272.35	268.36	270.35	109.91	108.86	109.51	38,860	86.02
22	890.02	879.44	885.84	272.01	267.68	270.65	109.98	109.00	109.27	38,450	86.05
23	888.40	877.22	880.38	272.89	268.31	270.35	110.18	108.86	109.61	35,710	85.92
24	883.87	872.18	880.20	270.21	266.56	268.60	110.42	108.93	109.44	32,730	85.76
27	891.81	877.47	885.41	271.82	267.14	270.11	109.54	108.53	108.86	32,050	85.51
28	889.68	881.40	884.64	271.91	267.72	269.38	109.47	108.15	108.69	29,430	85.47
29	888.23	879.52	884.90	269.87	266.80	268.46	109.71	108.19	108.93	30,810	85.44
30	887.63	879.52	883.70	269.19	265.97	267.04	109.78	108.15	109.00	29,300	85.22
31	890.10	881.14	887.63	268.55	264.85	266.41	109.44	108.15	108.76	26,370	85.14
		High 887.63				271.77			109.61		86.10
		Low 846.16				254.97			108.02		85.14

SEPTEMBER, 1979

	—30 Industrials—			—20 Transportations—			—15 Utilities—			Daily Sales —000—	20 Bonds
	High	Low	Close	High	Low	Close	High	Low	Close		
4	887.63	871.16	872.61	267.24	261.15	261.78	109.03	107.71	107.98	33,350	84.76
5	871.08	857.85	866.13	261.25	256.18	258.62	108.12	106.63	107.04	41,650	84.78
6	874.74	862.63	867.32	260.66	255.99	257.40	108.36	106.46	107.54	30,330	84.55
7	877.39	863.32	874.15	259.79	256.04	258.57	108.93	107.10	108.42	34,360	84.16
10	881.06	870.14	876.88	262.27	257.69	260.62	108.86	107.54	108.09	32,980	83.96
11	880.80	864.93	869.71	262.90	257.84	258.81	108.66	107.31	107.71	42,530	83.82
12	874.91	862.97	870.90	262.76	256.91	260.86	108.49	107.00	108.19	39,350	83.83
13	876.37	864.93	870.73	265.68	260.96	263.93	108.19	106.94	107.48	35,240	83.53
14	884.56	868.60	879.10	267.53	262.32	265.00	107.78	106.46	107.00	41,980	83.60
17	890.02	877.39	881.31	268.80	264.12	265.87	108.02	106.26	107.17	37,610	83.51
18	882.00	869.45	874.15	266.70	261.69	263.68	107.41	105.75	106.26	38,750	83.40
19	883.36	870.39	876.45	265.39	261.54	263.15	106.53	104.80	105.51	35,370	83.37
20	894.62	870.99	893.69	265.10	260.37	264.37	107.41	104.84	107.00	45,100	83.40
21	902.13	886.52	893.94	266.99	262.95	265.24	107.21	105.35	106.29	52,380	83.47
24	896.59	882.85	885.84	265.97	262.51	263.15	106.77	105.14	105.75	33,790	83.24
25	889.68	875.00	886.18	263.63	260.03	262.66	106.29	104.80	105.68	32,410	83.12
26	898.63	883.02	886.35	265.29	261.49	262.47	107.31	105.58	106.36	37,700	83.05
27	892.32	880.55	887.46	264.12	259.79	262.17	107.54	106.16	107.17	33,110	82.84
28	889.93	875.00	878.58	264.07	258.57	260.47	107.44	106.22	106.90	35,950	82.78
		High	893.94			265.87			108.42		84.78
		Low	866.13			257.40			105.51		82.78

OCTOBER, 1979

	—30 Industrials—			—20 Transportations—			—15 Utilities—			Daily Sales —000—	20 Bonds
	High	Low	Close	High	Low	Close	High	Low	Close		
1	877.73	866.55	872.95	260.23	256.67	258.03	106.60	105.38	105.92	24,980	82.56
2	889.16	868.77	885.32	260.91	256.67	259.89	107.34	105.62	106.80	38,310	81.98
3	891.98	879.35	885.15	262.27	258.33	260.13	107.81	106.46	107.37	36,470	81.65
4	895.82	882.25	890.10	263.49	259.15	262.37	108.12	106.80	107.58	38,800	81.17
5	904.86	889.59	897.61	267.14	262.22	264.80	108.90	107.31	108.12	48,250	81.04
8	900.26	882.59	884.04	265.63	261.74	262.61	108.53	107.00	107.41	32,610	80.95
9	879.35	854.10	857.59	260.52	251.31	252.24	107.04	104.57	104.84	55,560	80.56
10	855.03	826.54	849.32	249.03	238.95	245.23	103.79	100.51	101.62	81,620	80.04
11	854.69	834.98	844.62	247.95	241.23	243.86	103.11	101.32	102.64	47,530	79.33
12	852.90	835.67	838.99	247.22	242.01	242.89	104.06	102.47	103.42	36,390	79.19
15	840.36	823.89	831.06	243.67	236.32	238.46	103.48	101.93	102.50	34,850	78.85
16	838.51	825.68	829.52	240.26	235.63	236.85	103.04	101.66	102.37	33,770	78.83
17	840.53	827.39	830.72	240.26	235.88	237.53	103.38	101.96	102.64	29,650	79.05
18	838.74	826.71	830.12	239.87	235.00	237.49	103.48	102.13	102.64	29,590	79.10
19	829.18	812.46	814.68	236.95	229.89	231.20	102.57	100.81	101.15	42,430	78.44
22	813.91	795.99	809.13	229.21	223.32	227.02	100.81	98.92	99.59	45,240	78.26
23	816.38	801.96	806.83	229.30	224.29	226.43	99.93	97.80	98.27	32,910	77.68
24	816.64	803.24	808.36	228.96	225.17	226.92	99.26	97.77	98.24	31,480	77.24
25	816.38	803.07	808.46	229.60	225.99	226.87	99.26	97.70	98.38	28,440	77.32
26	814.68	801.62	809.30	230.33	226.19	228.53	100.10	98.41	99.59	29,660	77.29
29	815.53	804.86	808.62	231.40	227.75	229.69	100.51	99.22	99.83	22,720	77.53
30	824.66	805.80	823.81	233.54	228.77	232.86	100.71	99.39	100.58	28,890	76.32
31	826.88	812.88	815.70	234.76	230.42	231.93	100.91	99.76	100.03	27,780	76.55
		High	897.61			264.80			108.12		82.56
		Low	805.46			226.43			98.24		76.32

NOVEMBER, 1979

	—30 Industrials—			—20 Transportations—			—15 Utilities—			Daily Sales —000—	20 Bonds
	High	Low	Close	High	Low	Close	High	Low	Close		
1	823.63	809.73	820.14	234.95	230.38	234.51	101.32	99.70	100.81	25,880	76.30
2	824.74	814.42	818.94	235.20	231.93	232.81	101.15	100.10	100.54	23,670	75.88
5	819.37	808.45	812.63	233.49	229.74	231.01	100.74	99.53	99.76	20,470	75.75
6	813.40	804.61	806.48	232.13	228.67	230.33	100.07	98.85	99.49	21,960	75.93
7	805.20	793.43	796.67	230.96	227.60	228.96	99.42	98.07	98.51	30,830	75.76
8	804.27	792.24	797.61	231.54	227.89	230.23	99.15	98.11	98.61	26,270	75.54
9	812.29	799.91	806.48	235.05	230.72	232.86	99.80	98.38	99.19	30,060	75.53
12	823.72	805.63	821.93	236.90	232.23	235.93	100.41	98,78	100.10	26,640	76.03
13	825.85	811.52	814.08	239.04	235.25	236.75	101.56	100.24	100.85	29,240	75.99
14	823.04	805.03	816.55	238.70	235.00	237.73	101.93	100.00	101.45	30,970	75.93
15	827.56	813.57	821.33	243.04	236.75	241.33	102.71	101.12	102.17	32,380	75.91
16	822.61	812.54	815.70	243.67	238.56	241.33	102.91	101.42	102.33	30,060	75.98
19	822.95	810.07	815.27	244.19	239.43	241.72	103.55	101.66	102.60	33,090	75.92
20	820.14	805.12	809.22	243.91	238.70	240.46	103.79	102.13	103.21	35,010	75.76
21	810.49	793.60	807.42	242.35	236.90	241.97	104.26	101.86	104.06	37,020	75.64
23	815.96	804.86	811.77	245.18	241.09	243.67	105.62	103.52	104.94	23,300	75.66
26	833.11	813.82	828.75	250.78	245.08	248.88	107.51	104.91	106.73	47,940	75.98
27	837.29	820.73	825.85	252.48	247.81	249.42	108.66	106.22	107.54	45,140	76.91
28	835.92	818.09	830.46	251.90	246.76	250.58	108.42	106.43	108.02	39,690	76.82
29	838.57	826.45	831.74	252.92	248.69	250.39	108.59	107.31	108.02	33,550	77.07
30	830.80	819.88	822.35	251.51	247.27	248.49	108.42	107.14	107.61	30,480	76.64
		High 831.74				250.58			108.02		77.07
		Low 796.67				228.96			98.51		75.53

DECEMBER, 1979

	—30 Industrials—			—20 Transportations—			—15 Utilities—			Daily Sales —000—	20 Bonds
	High	Low	Close	High	Low	Close	High	Low	Close		
3	825.51	814.76	819.62	249.51	245.47	247.47	108.05	106.70	107.24	29,030	76.66
4	828.33	818.09	824.91	251.41	246.69	250.29	107.81	106.50	107.10	33,510	76.47
5	837.37	824.15	828.41	254.14	250.10	251.51	108.49	106.90	107.68	39,300	76.63
6	837.46	826.19	835.07	255.55	250.49	255.02	109.13	107.24	108.46	37,510	76.62
7	844.71	829.35	833.19	259.20	252.58	254.29	109.68	107.95	108.19	42,370	76.45
10	837.29	826.62	833.87	256.53	252.29	254.87	108.93	107.54	108.46	32,270	76.59
11	841.47	828.41	833.70	256.67	252.73	254.58	109.24	107.27	108.49	36,160	76.33
12	840.87	830.20	835.67	255.89	252.53	253.94	109.57	107.51	108.53	34,630	76.15
13	840.53	830.03	836.09	254.38	250.63	252.78	109.27	107.61	108.73	36,690	75.43
14	846.93	833.28	842.75	256.04	251.22	254.24	110.18	107.98	109.47	41,800	75.37
17	851.54	838.05	844.62	257.50	252.39	254.38	110.76	109.00	109.74	43,830	75.28
18	849.15	835.32	838.65	255.16	251.66	252.48	110.86	109.13	109.51	43,310	75.22
19	842.75	830.46	838.91	255.26	250.58	253.60	109.84	108.53	109.17	41,780	75.00
20	848.55	835.32	843.34	258.23	252.48	256.04	109.64	107.85	108.56	40,380	75.14
21	847.35	834.56	838.91	257.84	253.21	254.53	108.63	106.87	107.34	36,160	74.81
24	842.32	833.19	839.16	254.97	252.24	253.94	107.98	106.80	107.61	19,150	74.44
26	843.09	833.74	838.14	254.58	251.12	252.87	108.29	107.10	107.85	24,960	73.78
27	842.83	834.47	840.10	255.06	251.12	252.97	108.39	107.21	107.61	31,410	73.99
28	843.43	834.64	838.91	255.06	251.66	253.26	107.92	106.73	107.04	34,430	73.85
31	843.17	834.39	838.74	254.04	251.12	252.39	107.37	105.92	106.60	31,530	73.35
		High 844.62				256.04			109.74		76.66
		Low 819.62				247.47			106.60		73.35

JANUARY, 1980

	—30 Industrials—			—20 Transportations—			—15 Utilities—			Daily Sales	20
	High	Low	Close	High	Low	Close	High	Low	Close	—000—	Bonds
2	841.21	822.35	824.57	253.99	248.83	249.71	107.24	105.55	105.89	40,610	73.47
3	827.73	809.04	820.31	249.27	243.72	247.22	106.63	104.36	106.16	50,480	73.76
4	833.53	819.03	828.84	252.34	247.18	251.31	107.34	105.75	106.94	39,130	73.76
7	839.85	824.74	832.00	252.63	248.05	250.15	108.09	106.50	107.51	44,500	73.62
8	853.67	828.84	851.71	255.60	247.47	253.17	108.86	107.17	108.59	53,390	73.84
9	865.70	846.76	850.09	257.26	251.36	253.85	110.01	108.05	109.10	65,260	74.01
10	866.72	848.89	858.96	257.21	252.24	255.94	110.05	108.56	109.27	55,980	74.00
11	868.17	848.89	858.53	260.08	254.67	257.01	110.22	108.69	109.17	52,890	73.92
14	870.65	854.95	863.57	260.86	255.60	258.23	110.05	108.39	109.30	52,930	73.81
15	873.81	855.89	868.60	260.91	255.75	259.74	109.88	108.36	109.03	52,320	73.81
16	881.14	862.12	865.19	265.39	259.30	261.69	110.08	108.12	108.56	67,700	73.86
17	872.95	857.00	863.57	265.78	259.50	264.41	109.00	107.68	108.12	54,170	73.86
18	873.21	855.29	867.15	265.78	261.35	263.68	108.56	106.73	107.95	47,150	73.64
21	880.03	863.65	872.78	270.60	262.90	268.99	108.29	106.83	107.65	48,040	73.14
22	879.95	861.95	866.21	272.69	266.60	268.84	108.46	106.70	107.51	50,620	73.27
23	883.02	859.39	877.56	273.76	267.09	272.84	108.63	106.94	107.71	50,730	72.77
24	891.38	874.15	879.95	278.49	272.79	275.18	108.69	107.10	107.92	59,070	72.66
25	882.25	869.03	876.11	277.85	272.01	275.66	108.49	107.17	107.58	47,100	71.89
28	884.56	866.64	878.50	278.54	273.71	277.07	108.53	107.14	107.75	53,620	71.44
29	885.67	864.59	874.40	280.78	275.13	277.17	108.59	107.07	107.75	55,480	71.36
30	886.09	870.14	881.91	281.99	275.52	280.82	109.95	107.48	109.27	51,170	71.24
31	897.87	873.04	875.85	287.11	280.19	281.60	111.84	108.76	110.15	65,900	71.25
		High 881.91				281.60			110.15		74.01
		Low 820.31				247.22			105.89		71.24

FEBRUARY, 1980

	—30 Industrials—			—20 Transportations—			—15 Utilities—			Daily Sales	20
	High	Low	Close	High	Low	Close	High	Low	Close	—000—	Bonds
1	886.64	866.30	881.48	284.67	279.02	283.50	110.99	109.30	110.32	46,610	71.01
4	887.37	870.48	875.09	286.62	280.00	282.58	111.03	109.44	110.12	43,070	70.91
5	880.89	868.17	876.62	286.23	280.19	284.18	110.72	109.30	110.15	41,880	70.71
6	888.05	867.92	881.83	297.67	283.55	294.51	111.57	109.47	110.89	51,950	70.41
7	897.27	878.24	885.49	305.85	293.92	299.08	112.45	110.55	111.23	57,690	69.79
8	901.11	879.86	895.73	308.29	296.46	305.80	112.14	109.98	111.33	57,860	69.30
11	902.39	884.04	889.59	309.70	298.11	300.64	113.23	111.64	112.28	58,660	69.04
12	901.37	880.97	898.98	299.72	292.27	297.33	113.63	111.23	112.92	48,090	68.54
13	918.17	896.59	903.84	302.30	296.09	297.72	114.68	112.31	113.46	65,230	68.16
14	912.03	886.86	893.77	298.35	289.25	290.86	114.01	112.04	112.65	50,540	68.57
15	892.92	875.09	884.98	290.66	284.67	287.20	112.72	110.76	111.20	46,680	68.18
19	883.96	869.37	876.02	288.13	281.36	284.96	111.27	109.00	109.64	39,480	67.40
20	891.30	872.44	886.86	291.63	284.38	290.08	111.50	108.22	110.32	44,340	66.61
21	891.13	863.99	868.52	295.04	286.42	289.15	112.35	109.44	110.93	51,530	66.63
22	877.47	855.80	868.77	293.44	283.89	289.00	111.77	109.30	110.93	48,210	66.02
25	868.94	854.61	859.81	288.37	280.82	282.58	111.06	108.93	109.61	39,140	65.72
26	869.45	853.24	864.25	287.40	279.51	286.13	109.98	108.49	109.07	40,000	65.54
27	875.26	850.09	855.12	293.19	284.52	286.28	110.12	107.85	108.42	46,430	65.40
28	865.10	847.27	854.44	290.56	283.60	287.15	108.63	107.10	107.61	40,330	65.45
29	866.55	850.85	863.14	292.07	285.16	289.44	110.01	107.37	109.68	38,810	65.80
		High 903.84				305.80			113.46		71.01
		Low 854.44				282.58			107.61		65.40

MARCH, 1980

	—30 Industrials—			—20 Transportations—			—15 Utilities—			Daily Sales —000—	20 Bonds
	High	Low	Close	High	Low	Close	High	Low	Close		
3	868.26	851.37	854.35	292.22	286.13	287.54	110.22	107.98	108.73	38,690	65.69
4	859.90	842.75	856.48	289.05	283.31	286.81	108.83	106.39	107.85	44,310	65.60
5	868.69	840.78	844.88	288.76	282.72	283.45	108.96	106.46	106.94	49,240	65.13
6	848.12	822.44	828.07	283.84	275.61	277.07	107.14	104.50	104.80	49,610	64.06
7	832.51	813.23	820.56	277.32	271.43	272.84	105.48	102.57	103.42	50,950	64.24
10	828.84	807.25	818.94	274.01	267.82	271.13	105.01	102.57	104.13	43,750	64.16
11	831.91	817.58	826.45	275.18	268.60	271.33	105.18	102.98	104.57	41,350	64.49
12	829.86	808.70	819.54	271.28	261.93	265.58	105.68	102.30	103.38	37,990	64.52
13	825.26	806.57	809.56	267.34	260.57	263.15	104.47	102.57	103.21	33,070	64.41
14	819.11	800.68	811.69	263.88	258.47	261.78	103.79	101.12	102.81	35,180	64.39
17	811.26	784.98	788.65	261.30	252.39	253.31	103.25	100.10	100.54	37,020	64.20
18	806.66	780.97	801.62	257.26	249.66	254.97	101.83	100.10	101.29	47,340	64.62
19	812.12	794.97	800.94	260.57	253.94	256.38	102.47	101.01	101.79	36,520	64.70
20	804.61	785.92	789.08	257.50	250.68	252.92	102.74	101.01	101.79	32,580	65.16
21	794.71	779.52	785.15	253.99	249.12	250.10	102.37	100.47	100.88	32,220	64.82
24	784.98	761.69	765.44	249.71	241.67	242.50	100.81	97.94	98.27	39,230	64.52
25	777.47	758.36	767.83	244.35	238.56	240.94	98.44	96.35	97.36	43,790	64.23
26	781.66	758.79	762.12	245.57	240.31	241.04	98.31	97.12	97.36	37,370	64.28
27	767.41	729.95	759.98	239.82	229.79	233.69	97.33	95.23	96.04	63,680	64.17
28	784.39	756.57	777.65	243.62	235.68	242.21	98.55	95.70	97.73	46,720	63.87
31	790.87	772.18	785.75	247.47	241.48	246.30	99.86	97.63	99.70	35,840	64.11
		High	856.48			287.54			108.73		65.69
		Low	759.98			233.69			96.04		63.87

APRIL, 1980

	—30 Industrials—			—20 Transportations—			—15 Utilities—			Daily Sales —000—	20 Bonds
	High	Low	Close	High	Low	Close	High	Low	Close		
1	792.15	776.28	784.47	249.95	244.01	247.47	101.69	99.70	101.45	32,230	64.11
2	796.40	779.95	787.80	251.27	246.30	248.98	102.88	100.58	102.00	35,210	64.12
3	791.98	778.24	784.13	252.05	246.25	249.17	103.25	101.08	102.03	27,970	64.19
7	784.39	765.44	768.34	249.17	242.40	243.38	102.77	101.18	101.83	29,130	64.53
8	779.61	759.81	775.00	246.79	239.87	246.06	102.81	101.39	102.27	31,700	65.22
9	790.02	772.44	785.92	252.05	245.62	250.58	104.36	101.93	103.99	33,020	65.60
10	796.42	783.02	791.47	256.18	250.34	253.46	106.63	104.40	106.06	33,940	65.78
11	800.85	786.52	791.55	254.97	250.19	250.68	107.34	105.92	106.43	29,960	66.64
14	791.81	779.52	784.90	251.27	246.45	248.00	106.70	105.01	105.68	23,060	66.66
15	792.41	778.84	783.36	249.61	245.62	246.35	106.63	104.97	105.65	26,670	66.93
16	794.88	769.80	771.25	249.90	242.16	242.94	108.19	106.02	106.77	39,730	68.52
17	776.37	762.12	768.86	244.69	237.05	240.85	108.12	105.65	106.97	32,770	68.71
18	775.94	760.32	763.40	242.70	236.66	238.17	107.75	106.02	106.60	26,880	68.87
21	769.62	751.37	759.13	240.55	233.74	235.20	107.31	104.91	105.24	27,560	69.89
22	793.43	771.33	789.85	244.94	237.87	243.43	107.78	104.63	107.07	47,920	69.97
23	801.11	784.13	789.25	246.98	241.72	243.72	108.90	107.17	108.15	42,620	70.34
24	804.95	785.24	797.10	244.06	239.19	240.99	109.81	107.65	109.07	35,790	70.29
25	806.74	786.35	803.58	242.21	236.90	241.19	109.13	107.68	108.56	28,590	70.70
28	814.68	798.72	805.46	243.52	237.87	239.29	109.57	108.09	108.63	30,600	71.14
29	816.21	802.65	811.09	242.45	237.68	240.55	109.34	108.02	108.66	27,940	70.67
30	818.52	801.02	817.06	242.89	238.46	241.92	109.17	107.65	108.76	30,850	70.95
		High	817.06			253.46			109.07		71.14
		Low	759.13			235.20			101.45		64.11

MAY, 1980

	—30 Industrials—			—20 Transportations—			—15 Utilities—			Daily Sales —000—	20 Bonds
	High	Low	Close	High	Low	Close	High	Low	Close		
1	820.22	803.24	808.79	244.79	239.87	242.11	109.44	107.65	108.53	32,480	71.52
2	815.70	802.99	810.92	248.44	241.14	247.52	108.86	107.68	108.32	28,040	71.71
5	819.20	803.58	816.30	252.00	245.52	250.29	109.20	107.65	108.66	34,090	72.22
6	827.65	808.28	816.04	252.43	247.76	249.76	110.32	108.25	109.03	40,160	72.29
7	828.67	810.49	821.25	252.82	248.10	251.36	110.89	108.93	110.32	42,600	72.69
8	827.47	811.01	815.19	255.41	249.76	251.31	111.03	108.56	109.27	39,280	72.59
9	815.10	802.47	805.80	251.75	247.66	249.66	109.24	107.68	108.42	30,280	72.39
12	810.32	795.82	805.20	250.98	245.85	249.79	108.66	107.54	108.22	28,220	72.31
13	820.39	803.07	816.89	255.75	249.12	253.83	109.34	107.51	108.59	35,460	72.34
14	827.73	813.74	819.62	262.75	254.46	260.11	109.64	107.98	108.66	40,840	72.18
15	829.35	816.04	822.53	262.49	256.79	259.17	109.37	108.05	109.07	41,120	72.45
16	829.52	819.11	826.88	260.73	255.03	258.76	109.91	108.39	109.17	31,710	72.32
19	835.75	820.65	830.89	259.95	255.70	257.98	109.74	108.02	108.73	30,970	72.01
20	837.12	825.60	832.51	260.31	255,80	257.83	109.17	107.51	108.25	31,800	72.01
21	836.43	821.50	831.06	260.73	253.52	258.29	108.56	107.00	107.88	34,830	71.91
22	848.63	828.84	842.92	264.77	257.46	263.01	108.96	107.41	108.19	41,040	72.27
23	858.62	843.34	854.10	267.52	261.71	265.34	109.54	107.75	109.13	45,790	72.28
27	864.42	851.28	857.76	272.39	265.65	269.69	110.39	108.42	109.88	40,810	72.02
28	866.13	850.09	860.32	273.37	267.46	271.20	110.99	109.30	110.49	38,580	72.38
29	863.65	844.71	846.25	272.96	266.79	268.14	111.27	109.47	109.91	42,000	72.58
30	853.24	835.07	850.85	271.56	263.68	269.23	110.72	108.46	110.28	34,820	72.55
		High	860.32			271.20			110.49		72.69
		Low	805.20			242.11			107.88		71.52

JUNE, 1980

	—30 Industrials—			—20 Transportations—			—15 Utilities—			Daily Sales —000—	20 Bonds
	High	Low	Close	High	Low	Close	High	Low	Close		
2	857.94	842.92	847.35	273.17	266.22	269.59	110.41	108.73	109.28	32,710	72.46
3	851.96	840.70	843.77	272.75	267.52	270.37	109.97	108.04	108.77	33,150	72.56
4	860.49	842.75	858.02	275.70	269.49	273.48	110.05	108.22	109.28	44,180	72.86
5	868.60	853.50	858.70	280.01	274.10	277.36	110.70	108.73	109.53	49,070	73.04
6	867.06	853.07	861.52	279.80	274.93	278.09	110.74	109.06	110.08	37,230	73.22
9	867.66	855.72	860.67	279.80	275.50	277.73	111.58	109.83	110.92	36,820	73.67
10	870.73	855.20	863.99	280.52	275.29	278.09	112.71	110.48	111.91	42,030	73.91
11	876.88	860.24	872.70	280.32	275.76	278.24	113.77	111.69	112.96	43,800	73.97
12	881.40	863.05	872.61	280.58	275.03	277.10	113.66	112.01	113.00	47,300	74.15
13	883.96	866.81	876.37	279.95	275.08	277.73	114.64	112.93	113.77	41,880	74.81
16	883.19	868.77	877.73	279.44	275.60	277.62	115.15	112.89	114.46	36,190	75.68
17	887.63	872.35	879.27	279.90	273.48	277.31	115.74	113.91	115.33	41,990	76.22
18	885.32	870.14	881.91	278.09	273.58	275.39	115.95	113.98	115.37	41,960	76.48
19	886.01	869.62	870.90	276.02	269.59	270.32	115.88	114.20	114.50	38,280	76.58
20	875.09	863.31	869.71	271.66	266.27	269.02	115.04	113.55	114.20	36,530	76.60
23	879.61	864.85	873.81	271.30	266.01	269.75	114.79	113.44	113.98	34,180	76.61
24	881.31	867.15	877.30	272.91	268.24	271.82	115.08	113.51	114.28	37,730	76.15
25	892.49	874.91	887.54	277.21	272.03	275.39	115.55	113.84	114.82	46,500	75.89
26	896.33	880.03	883.45	279.33	273.99	276.12	115.74	114.06	114.64	45,110	75.84
27	889.08	874.49	881.83	277.88	273.99	275.96	115.15	113.47	114.60	33,110	75.35
30	880.89	864.33	867.92	276.35	271.97	273.50	114.64	112.78	113.33	29,910	74.97
		High	887.54			278.24			115.37		76.61
		Low	843.77			269.02			108.77		72.46

JULY, 1980

	—30 Industrials—			—20 Transportations—			—15 Utilities—			Daily Sales —000—	20 Bonds
	High	Low	Close	High	Low	Close	High	Low	Close		
1	876.02	862.63	872.27	276.62	271.80	275.25	113.73	112.45	113.22	34,340	74.87
2	880.46	867.06	876.02	282.21	275.31	280.46	114.20	112.38	113.51	42,950	74.26
3	890.78	874.83	888.91	287.41	280.40	285.77	115.81	113.11	115.59	47,230	74.32
7	900.77	886.86	898.21	291.90	285.17	290.64	116.83	114.90	115.74	42,540	74.25
8	904.86	891.38	897.35	293.82	287.19	290.32	116.72	115.22	115.88	45,830	73.89
9	908.87	892.58	897.27	294.86	288.34	291.68	116.17	114.53	115.08	52,010	73.57
10	900.34	883.28	885.92	293.16	288.45	290.04	115.52	114.24	114.90	43,730	73.58
11	895.22	880.80	897.13	292.67	287.91	291.52	115.41	113.98	114.68	38,310	73.13
14	908.28	887.20	905.55	298.15	290.64	297.87	115.37	113.80	114.68	45,500	73.01
15	916.04	899.23	901.54	302.59	295.90	298.59	115.48	113.73	114.06	60,920	73.03
16	912.97	898.21	904.44	301.93	295.25	298.37	115.15	113.73	114.57	49,140	73.01
17	916.64	902.05	915.10	305.76	298.09	305.05	115.52	113.80	114.68	48,850	73.06
18	930.80	914.42	923.98	312.61	305.76	309.60	115.08	113.44	114.28	58.040	73.25
21	933.28	916.38	928.67	314.53	308.17	313.43	114.71	113.29	114.17	42,750	73.34
22	940.78	922.18	927.30	318.14	311.29	312.55	114.79	113.62	114.28	52,230	73.35
23	937.71	920.99	928.58	314.36	307.95	309.71	114.53	112.89	113.47	45,890	73.18
24	933.79	919.97	926.11	312.23	306.31	308.50	114.20	112.63	113.36	42,420	72.93
25	925.34	913.23	918.09	308.28	301.65	303.90	113.73	111.98	112.93	36,250	72.69
28	927.73	911.69	925.43	306.75	300.18	304.45	113.33	111.32	111.65	35,330	72.84
29	935.15	921.33	931.91	312.28	303.90	310.91	112.60	111.10	111.94	44,840	72.68
30	946.93	926.54	936.18	317.87	310.58	314.47	112.71	111.29	112.01	58,060	72.69
31	939.51	918.77	935.32	314.42	307.24	312.01	111.94	110.26	111.39	54,610	72.12
		High 936.18				314.47			115.88		74.87
		Low 872.27				275.25			111.39		72.12

AUGUST, 1980

	—30 Industrials—			—20 Transportations—			—15 Utilities—			Daily Sales —000—	20 Bonds
	High	Low	Close	High	Low	Close	High	Low	Close		
1	940.02	924.83	931.48	314.25	307.30	311.08	111.50	109.94	110.45	46,440	71.84
4	935.24	918.52	931.06	312.55	306.80	310.31	110.70	108.62	109.46	41,550	71.50
5	938.82	924.23	929.78	313.81	307.79	310.47	109.90	108.29	108.91	45,510	71.08
6	941.04	923.63	938.23	313.49	308.06	311.51	109.72	108.15	108.99	45,050	71.07
7	953.75	935.84	950.94	316.88	310.36	314.31	110.23	108.40	109.68	61,820	70.94
8	965.87	949.74	954.69	320.94	314.03	316.17	111.14	109.46	110.41	58,860	70.93
11	966.89	950.43	964.08	319.35	313.43	317.05	111.10	109.50	110.26	44,690	70.77
12	969.97	948.72	952.39	319.84	313.98	316.12	110.99	109.50	110.45	52,050	70.59
13	958.79	944.45	949.23	316.83	312.34	313.76	111.25	109.79	110.19	44,350	70.54
14	965.36	943.69	962.63	321.15	312.34	320.28	111.03	109.75	110.56	47,700	70.44
15	972.35	956.31	966.72	324.11	317.92	321.37	111.65	109.97	111.03	47,780	70.24
18	961.95	944.97	948.63	321.87	315.62	317.38	111.32	109.79	110.30	41,890	70.14
19	952.13	937.37	939.85	319.84	314.47	317.05	110.99	109.32	110.23	41,930	69.43
20	948.98	934.47	945.31	321.65	315.18	320.39	111.14	109.21	110.70	42,560	69.21
21	958.53	943.94	955.03	326.25	320.88	324.93	112.12	110.23	111.61	50.770	69.43
22	969.45	952.73	958.19	331.73	324.44	327.73	112.56	110.58	111.29	58,210	69.27
25	961.35	947.70	956.23	328.44	321.87	324.61	111.69	110.52	110.03	35,400	69.31
26	964.59	949.91	953.41	327.13	321.05	323.35	111.65	110.19	110.77	41,700	69.10
27	953.24	939.68	943.09	324.00	318.20	320.17	111.36	109.97	110.45	44,000	68.87
28	944.03	927.22	930.38	322.63	315.84	317.98	111.25	109.90	110.26	39,890	68.82
29	936.43	923.04	932.59	321.54	315.18	320.11	111.58	109.94	110.96	33,510	68.09
		High 966.72				327.73			111.61		71.84
		Low 929.78				310.31			108.91		68.82

SEPTEMBER, 1980

	—30 Industrials—			—20 Transportations—			—15 Utilities—			Daily Sales —000—	20 Bonds
	High	Low	Close	High	Low	Close	High	Low	Close		
2	944.80	928.16	940.78	327.40	319.68	324.82	112.12	110.48	111.50	35,290	68.99
3	955.20	939.85	953.16	331.73	323.51	329.15	113.66	111.10	113.36	52,370	69.15
4	964.85	942.92	948.81	333.64	325.54	327.78	114.31	112.56	112.96	59,030	69.40
5	950.68	937.03	940.96	328.93	323.40	325.43	113.55	112.12	112.78	37,990	69.50
8	945.48	925.34	928.58	326.41	319.95	321.05	113.22	111.54	111.72	42,050	69.24
9	936.09	919.03	934.73	322.80	316.72	320.77	112.49	110.96	111.76	44,460	69.51
10	946.16	930.63	938.48	323.73	319.07	320.66	113.07	111.50	112.38	51,430	69.48
11	947.78	934.39	941.30	323.67	318.74	321.21	112.96	111.80	112.42	44,770	69.32
12	945.48	932.51	936.52	324.00	319.62	321.26	113.11	111.83	112.16	47,180	69.15
15	942.58	926.96	937.63	330.36	320.11	329.48	112.63	111.07	111.80	44,630	68.98
16	953.07	935.32	945.90	341.53	330.30	339.01	113.33	111.50	112.71	57,290	68.14
17	966.98	943.69	961.26	347.83	338.79	345.91	113.69	112.23	112.60	63,990	68.22
18	972.01	950.26	956.48	350.57	343.56	345.09	113.51	111.61	112.38	63,390	68.26
19	972.70	950.77	963.74	349.15	342.63	346.52	113.11	111.72	112.34	53,780	68.21
22	977.05	955.29	974.57	351.12	342.63	350.02	112.89	110.96	112.05	53,140	68.01
23	980.72	957.94	962.03	355.77	346.02	349.20	112.34	110.52	110.85	64,390	68.01
24	972.78	952.73	964.76	353.20	344.38	348.98	111.10	109.75	110.59	56,860	67.80
25	972.61	953.07	955.97	351.94	344.22	345.59	111.14	109.43	109.86	49.510	67.34
26	952.65	934.98	940.10	344.33	335.89	337.53	110.12	108.40	108.81	49,460	66.81
29	934.81	918.00	921.93	332.93	326.14	328.77	108.59	107.09	107.38	46,410	66.30
30	937.20	921.59	932.42	335.34	328.49	333.86	108.33	106.94	107.82	40,290	66.07
	High 974.57					350.02			113.36		69.51
	Low 921.93					320.66			107.38		66.07

OCTOBER, 1980

	—30 Industrials—			—20 Transportations—			—15 Utilities—			Daily Sales —000—	20 Bonds
	High	Low	Close	High	Low	Close	High	Low	Close		
1	945.14	923.04	939.42	339.50	331.40	337.59	109.32	107.35	108.70	48,720	65.87
2	948.21	931.31	942.24	344.22	336.99	341.04	110.45	108.40	109.43	46,160	66.55
3	957.85	938.40	950.68	347.50	340.87	345.42	111.58	109.13	111.21	47,510	66.94
6	969.62	950.85	965.70	350.95	344.65	348.60	114.93	111.07	113.84	50,130	67.03
7	973.04	955.55	960.67	352.49	346.52	348.05	115.12	112.85	113.73	50,310	66.92
8	971.42	955.29	963.99	351.99	344.93	348.32	114.53	112.74	113.95	46,580	66.86
9	971.08	953.07	958.96	352.05	345.59	349.20	114.57	112.67	113.40	43,980	67.05
10	965.70	946.25	950.68	354.35	346.84	350.08	114.20	112.27	113.11	44,040	67.30
13	963.65	946.50	959.90	352.98	347.34	352.10	113.77	112.34	113.00	31,360	67.34
14	971.67	957.08	962.20	357.14	350.79	353.03	114.31	112.05	113.04	48,830	67.42
15	975.94	959.73	972.44	357.09	350.02	354.79	114.42	112.45	113.80	48,260	67.46
16	987.29	956.57	958.70	363.28	354.13	356.21	115.70	112.56	112.96	65,450	67.46
17	966.04	946.42	956.14	358.79	353.31	356.32	113.62	112.20	112.93	43,920	67.37
20	964.42	946.59	960.84	364.37	355.39	362.89	113.77	112.20	112.74	40,910	67.27
21	968.69	949.91	954.44	373.58	363.66	369.41	113.77	112.34	112.93	51,220	67.28
22	961.77	947.87	955.12	382.45	368.26	381.08	113.77	112.27	113.07	43,060	66.94
23	958.28	936.69	939.51	385.79	371.49	373.85	113.84	112.53	112.93	49,200	66.59
24	947.35	931.06	943.60	375.93	367.66	373.47	113.36	112.20	112.74	41,050	66.61
27	944.62	930.12	931.74	372.81	362.95	365.14	113.18	111.32	112.01	34,430	66.21
28	937.54	922.78	932.59	367.06	360.16	363.94	112.71	110.96	111.83	40,300	66.09
29	941.64	925.68	929.18	369.25	362.18	365.74	112.78	110.48	111.43	37,200	66.08
30	932.51	915.02	917.75	366.45	359.50	360.87	111.65	109.64	110.15	39.060	65.80
31	929.35	911.60	924.49	363.88	357.42	361.31	111.39	109.57	110.99	40,110	65.86
	High 972.44					381.08			113.95		67.46
	Low 917.75					337.59			108.70		65.80

NOVEMBER, 1980

	—30 Industrials—			—20 Transportations—			—15 Utilities—			Daily Sales —000—	20 Bonds
	High	Low	Close	High	Low	Close	High	Low	Close		
3	941.30	924.49	937.20	366.35	359.88	363.88	111.76	110.26	110.96	35,820	65.63
5	982.59	950.34	953.16	379.35	367.51	369.49	114.02	111.10	111.43	84,080	65.88
6	950.43	932.08	935.41	367.46	360.68	363.05	111.54	109.50	110.23	48,890	65.61
7	940.53	926.11	932.42	365.58	360.02	363.22	110.52	108.55	109.94	40,070	65.14
10	940.44	926.71	933.79	369.55	361.34	366.35	111.07	109.17	109.86	35,720	64.99
11	951.19	933.02	944.03	378.85	366.91	376.10	112.82	109.79	112.12	41,520	64.96
12	968.86	943.77	964.93	386.29	375.17	385.13	114.42	111.94	114.09	58,500	65.10
13	984.64	962.20	982.42	392.51	382.76	388.60	116.17	113.44	115.30	69,340	65.50
14	997.35	973.21	986.35	396.70	385.85	391.96	117.56	114.13	116.76	71,630	65.14
17	990.78	968.94	986.26	395.81	384.80	394.11	117.67	114.82	116.36	50,260	64.04
18	1005.20	985.92	997.95	410.08	395.98	407.76	118.69	116.72	117.34	70,380	63.99
19	1009.39	983.36	991.04	415.14	403.19	407.32	118.14	116.14	116.98	69,230	64.41
20	1004.61	984.90	1000.17	417.35	402.31	414.43	117.49	115.74	116.50	60,180	64.53
21	1004.69	984.30	989.93	418.72	410.57	413.60	116.98	115.63	116.21	55,950	64.15
24	988.14	967.66	978.75	414.15	407.49	412.56	116.72	114.57	115.22	51,120	64.07
25	993.52	973.04	982.68	416.80	410.79	414.37	117.49	114.28	116.54	55,840	63.98
26	1000.77	979.86	989.68	430.18	416.63	421.59	118.51	115.92	117.01	55,340	63.72
28	998.72	980.38	993.34	428.89	418.83	425.68	118.11	116.46	116.94	34,240	63.83
		High	1000.17			425.68			117.34		65.88
		Low	932.42			363.05			109.86		63.72

DECEMBER, 1980

	—30 Industrials—			—20 Transportations—			—15 Utilities—			Daily Sales —000—	20 Bonds
	High	Low	Close	High	Low	Close	High	Low	Close		
1	991.13	966.38	969.45	424.83	413.01	414.16	117.45	115.52	116.14	48,180	63.53
2	979.69	954.95	974.40	415.37	401.67	409.74	116.76	114.93	115.70	52,340	63.52
3	981.57	963.57	972.27	412.83	403.79	407.86	116.46	114.50	115.55	43,430	63.26
4	984.22	963.31	970.48	414.22	405.37	409.31	116.76	115.12	115.88	51,170	63.42
5	972.61	951.45	956.23	408.83	396.16	398.40	115.63	113.88	114.24	51,990	63.01
8	951.19	928.33	933.70	396.16	383.18	385.55	114.17	111.98	112.34	53,390	62.96
9	944.28	921.59	934.04	387.55	379.49	385.79	113.51	111.58	112.67	53,220	62.98
10	943.52	914.16	916.21	390.70	381.30	382.03	113.95	111.94	112.60	49,860	62.14
11	918.52	894.45	908.45	383.12	373.00	376.64	112.78	110.08	110.85	60,220	61.70
12	923.12	906.48	917.15	384.03	374.88	381.24	112.27	109.72	111.47	39,530	61.83
15	927.65	907.85	911.60	385.61	379.00	381.67	112.20	110.67	111.14	39,700	61.49
16	922.35	902.47	918.09	384.82	377.67	382.82	111.61	109.57	110.63	41,630	61.26
17	933.96	913.05	928.50	391.43	382.58	389.73	112.12	110.34	111.65	50,800	61.49
18	948.38	925.00	930.20	399.49	388.94	393.37	116.46	111.91	115.01	69,570	60.96
19	945.31	924.57	937.20	396.82	387.79	392.03	117.01	114.60	115.70	50,770	61.67
22	962.17	934.64	958.79	400.64	391.19	398.52	117.78	115.08	117.30	51,950	63.47
23	971.25	949.49	958.28	404.58	392.28	395.55	118.62	116.06	117.30	55,260	63.62
24	968.17	950.85	963.05	398.70	391.19	396.76	117.67	116.04	116.87	29,490	64.04
26	969.37	958.45	966.38	401.98	395.37	399.92	117.41	116.10	116.79	16,130	63.99
29	974.57	956.40	960.58	402.10	391.91	393.67	116.76	114.46	114.68	36,060	63.15
30	969.54	952.99	962.03	398.76	391.25	396.22	115.37	113.51	114.20	39,750	63.41
31	971.50	955.55	963.99	400.40	393.85	398.10	115.30	113.51	114.42	41,210	63.68
		High	974.40			414.16			117.30		64.04
		Low	908.45			376.64			110.63		60.96